A History of Christendom
Vol. 3

Warren H. Carroll

A History of Christendom (in seven volumes)

ISBN: 931888-54-9 PAPER
ISBN: 931888-55-7 CLOTH

The Glory
of Christendom

Warren H. Carroll

Christendom Press
Front Royal, Virginia

Contents

DEDICATED
to my beloved wife,
ANNE
whose bright example and unceasing prayer
brought to me the grace of faith
and membership in the Church of Christ

1

The Coming of the White Monks
(1100-1122)
(Popes Paschal II 1099-1118, Gelasius II 1118-19, Calixtus II 1119-24)

"Besides the bond of apostolical paternity which links us together, and besides the bond between us of the imperial dignity, which the German kings receive solely through the Roman pontiffs, we are bound to hear and to love one another by our close blood relationship. . . . [The Church] desires not any of your rights for herself, but, like a mother, gives freely of her own to all. . . . You have soldiers on your side, but the Church has to defend her the King of Kings . . . and her lords and patrons are the Apostles Peter and Paul. Give up, then, what does not belong to your province, that you may the better administer what does."—Pope Calixtus II to Holy Roman Emperor Henry V, February 1122[1]

Christendom at the beginning of the twelfth century after the Incarnation of Our Lord and Savior Jesus Christ was almost entirely islanded on the continent of Europe. From the Caucasus to the Atlantic ran the battlefront with Islam, Christendom's enemy for more than 450 years, a bristling barrier challenged by the First Crusade just victoriously completed, but still cutting off Christian Europe from all direct access to the rest of the world. North of the Caucasus a wasteland of pagan barbarism swept from the steppes of the Don through the forests of the upper Volga and the Ural Mountains to the Arctic Ocean, and no man knew how far eastward. Beyond the great arc of the North Atlantic Ocean was only the handful of Norsemen huddled on the barren coast of Greenland under the loom of a mile-thick ice-cap. Lost in mists of legend and half-understood third-hand traveller's tales were the only two surviving outposts of Christendom east of Europe—the Thomas Christians of India and the black Christians of Ethiopia—with whom, because of the interposing barrier of Islam, no direct communication had been possible for nearly five hundred years.

Christendom was the creation of the Church, the new civilization it had built on the ruins of the old Roman empire. Its head, Christendom's central

---

[1]Horace K. Mann, *The Lives of the Popes in the Middle Ages*, Volume IX (London, 1925), p. 171.

figure, was as ever the Pope, the Vicar of Christ, in direct line of succession
from St. Peter as Bishop of Rome.[2] In 1100 a gentle and kindly monk from the
Apennines south of Bologna, Rainerius who had taken the name Paschal II, had
sat in the Chair of Peter less than a year.[3] From his immediate predecessors,
especially the great Hildebrand who had been Pope St. Gregory VII from 1073
to 1085, Paschal II had inherited a struggle which had divided Christendom
almost as deeply as the First Crusade had unified it: the defiance of the Pope
by the Holy Roman Emperor. For a long time Christendom had been free of
major heresy, but schism stalked it.

In Rome and in the West the Roman empire had fallen, but its memory
lived on, still shaping political structures and ideas even in the new universe
Christianity had created. Centuries of feudal anarchy, during which only the
Church had preserved civilized life, had created a longing for the order and
unity which the memory of the empire represented. Most Christians
understood that such order and unity could no longer be autocratic, because the
Church could neither be subject to it nor provide it. A supreme but not
totalitarian temporal authority was needed, a final court of appeal for disputes
in the public order, a leader against the infidel without and the heretic within.
In the year 800 Pope St. Leo III designated the mighty and faithful King of the
Franks, Charlemagne, to be the first Emperor of this new kind. Because of the
new conception of his office, he came to be called the Holy Roman Emperor.[4]

But Charlemagne's successors, especially after his last grandson was dead,
had let the office of Holy Roman Emperor be so degraded that it was virtually
abandoned for three quarters of a century. Meanwhile the Popes were
dangerously weakened, victimized by feudal anarchy in Italy, often almost cut
off by poor transportation and communications and the constant turmoil from
the Church they led. Many of the Popes in the tenth and early eleventh
centuries were not free agents. But in 962 the German Otto the Great had
revived the Holy Roman Empire, and in 1046 his descendant Henry III had
marched to Rome and once and for all broke the power of the fractious, self-
seeking nobles who had been largely if not entirely controlling that city.
Christendom welcomed his action, as did the Popes; the reigning Pope at the
time, Gregory VI, had resigned to help make it possible.[5]

The liberated Popes had quickly regained the fullness of their powers, and
under Hildebrand's guidance had fearlessly proclaimed their God-given right

---

[2]See the earlier volumes of this history, *passim*, for the extensive historical evidence
and analysis showing that the primacy in the Church of St. Peter and his successors as
Bishops of Rome had always been accepted by all Christians except those directly
involved in defiance of his authority, or their heirs.

[3]Mann, *Popes in the Middle Ages*, IX, 7-11.

[4]See Volume II, Chapter 12 of this history.

[5]See Volume II, Chapter 17 of this history.

and duty to act as the moral judge of all men's acts, including the acts of kings and emperors. If the moral judgment of the Popes were defied, if any temporal authority tried to take control of the Church, the reigning Pope could dispense the subjects of the offending monarch from their normal duty of allegiance to their earthly sovereign, and authorize or even recommend (though never require) rebellion. Hildebrand as Pope Gregory VII had done exactly that with Holy Roman Emperor Henry IV, son of Henry III. Despite the resulting internal resistance Henry IV still ruled in 1100, though excommunicated for twenty years. During all that time he had maintained Archbishop Wibert of Ravenna as antipope.

The flashpoint of this confrontation between Pope and Holy Roman Emperor was the issue of lay investiture. Pope St. Gregory VII had insisted that the Church retained sole right and authority to invest bishops and abbots with the insignia of their office, to consecrate them and to grant them their powers within the Church. But bishops and abbots were also great landowners, which gave them important places in the feudal system which formed the legal, social, and political structure of most of Europe. Consequently it had long been the practice, especially in Germany, for laymen to invest many bishops and abbots. Pope St. Gregory VII absolutely prohibited this practice; Holy Roman Emperor Henry IV defiantly continued it.

No doctrinal issue was involved in this confrontation. Not even Papal primacy was challenged; otherwise Henry IV would not have bothered to maintain an antipope. But the divisions it created ran deep, and no solution was in sight.

To the east, in Greece and adjoining areas in the Balkan peninsula and along some of the coastal fringes of Asia Minor, the ghost of the old Roman empire still walked as the Byzantine Empire, ruled in 1100 by Alexius Comnenus. Alexius insisted that he was the direct heir of Caesar Augustus; the Byzantine Empire still called itself Rome, though it had not actually ruled in the Eternal City for more than four hundred years. Its domain steadily whittled down by incessant Muslim attack, it now lived mainly on pride and tradition, though its capital of Constantinople remained the largest and richest Christian city in the world. Forty-six years before, the Church in the Byzantine Empire had broken away from the Catholic Church on the issue of obedience to the Pope. The schism remained, a raw unhealed wound splitting off the Byzantine Empire—and its cultural satellite, the Kievan state in Ukraine (later to be extended to Russia)—from the rest of Christendom, its leaders regarded as excommunicated like Henry IV.

So there were two Christian Emperors in the year 1100, but neither of them would speak to the Pope.

The nucleus of Christian Europe comprised Germany, Italy, and France. France was untroubled by the controversies that rocked Germany and

Italy. France—the "eldest daughter of the Church"—was orthodox, loyal to the Pope, and hostile to emperors who defied him. From France had come the majority of the fighting men who against all odds had brought the Cross to Jerusalem in arms and won the First Crusade. From France had come the two greatest leaders of that crusade: Godfrey of Bouillon, Defender of the Holy Sepulcher, who died in Jerusalem in that year 1100; and Raymond of Toulouse, the man most responsible for its reconquest. France's weak and self-willed king, Philip I, was in bad standing with the Church because he would not live with his wife and claimed to be married to another woman; but the great nobles of France lived and ruled their feudal domains almost as though there were no king. The greatest of them all, Duke William of Normandy, had conquered England in 1066 and died in 1087. His eldest son Robert had been another leader of the First Crusade; his second son William Rufus had been King of England after him, but died mysteriously in 1100, to be succeeded by his third son Henry I. England's ruling class was totally French, many of them nobles with extensive holdings in both countries.

In France, where the great monastic reform had been launched from Cluny nearly two hundred years before and was still largely maintained, men took their faith very seriously indeed. The quest for the way of perfection never ceased. A Benedictine abbot named Robert, noted for his advocacy of extraordinary austerity, had been directed by Pope Alexander II to take charge of a group of hermits in the forest of Collan in French Burgundy who wished to live strictly and completely by the Benedictine rule. In extreme poverty, Robert and his new community built wooden cells and a chapel in the nearby forest of Molesme. Their holiness attracted local attention, and soon their poverty was at an end; they received great benefactions, and their discipline and austerity were mitigated. Twenty-one of the monks objected to the lessened rigor. They persuaded Abbot Robert, though he was past seventy, to lead them in a new community. They obtained land in a wild wood about fourteen miles from Dijon, full of swamps covered with thorny undergrowth; the area was called Cîteaux. On Palm Sunday of 1098 the monks arrived there, setting to work at once to build a temporary residence and to begin clearing the land with their own hands. The Molesme community vigorously protested the departure of its abbot, and the next year a council of bishops ordered St. Robert to return to Molesme. But he left the younger and even more zealous St. Alberic to lead the new community at Cîteaux, and before he left it had already completed a church in stone—like all Cistercian churches in times to come, unadorned save by the light from God's sky that poured in through the clear glass windows. Under St. Alberic the monks of Cîteaux adopted a white habit, though the usual garb for monks was black; the tradition is that the Blessed Virgin Mary appeared to Alberic to give him the white habit.[6]

Around France and Germany and England to the north swung an arc of countries poor or newly formed, not yet able to exert much historical influence, bit players only on the historical stage: Ireland; Scotland; Iceland; Norway; Sweden; Denmark; Poland; Hungary. All were Catholic now, and loyal to the Pope.

To the south, in Spain, the longest war in the history of the world still pursued its relentless course, at almost exactly the mid-point of its 770-year span. In the year 711 Muslims (the Spanish called them Moors) from Arabia and North Africa had landed near Gibraltar and conquered the whole Iberian peninsula in just three years. In a hidden eyrie in the Cantabrian Mountains on the northern edge of Spain, their backs to the Bay of Biscay, without help from anywhere, Pelayo with a small band had risen against them and won the Battle of Covadonga in 722 that launched the war. In the 378 ensuing years the Christians had fought their way acre by acre, mile by mile back to the center of their country, so that Spain and Portugal were now almost evenly divided between Christian and Moor. The legendary hero Rodrigo Diaz de Vivar, El Cid, had died in 1099, holding the key port city of Valencia against the ancient foe to his last hour. Alfonso VI, king of Castile—the principal Christian state in Spain—was hard pressed. Most men did not like or altogether trust Alfonso VI. He was harsh, designing, uncharitable. His political and military judgment had never been good. But the Reconquest was in his blood, and there was iron in his soul. He persevered; he never accepted defeat. He was 63 years old;[7] he had been 35 years on the firing line, and the end was not yet.

In the east, in the Levant beyond the Byzantine Empire, the crusaders had carried to victory the first great Christian counterattack against the Muslim realms which had so long assaulted Christendom, particularly in Spain and Asia Minor. In 1099 they had, against all odds, stormed Jerusalem. But then most of the crusaders had gone home, their vows fulfilled. Baldwin I, brother and successor of Godfrey of Bouillon, who had taken the title King of Jerusalem

---

[6]Bede K. Lackner, *The Eleventh-Century Background of Cîteaux* (Washington, 1972), pp. 217-274; Archdale A. King, *Cîteaux and Her Elder Daughters* (London, 1954), pp. 1-10; *Butler's Lives of the Saints*, edited, revised and supplemented by Herbert Thurston and Donald Attwater (New York, 1956), I, 173; II, 189-190. Though the early use of the white habit by the Cistercians is well attested (Abbot Peter the Venerable of Cluny mentioned it specifically in a letter to St. Bernard of Clairvaux in 1123), King makes the puzzling remark that "there is no evidence for the tradition which would connect St. Alberic with the change in the color of the habit, beyond providing for the wool to be of a natural color" (*op. cit.*, p. 10). The natural color of most wool is gray or white, since most sheep are white not black; the use of this color obviously was a change from the customary black. The refusal to use dye was in keeping with Cistercian austerity.

[7]Bernard F. Reilly, *The Kingdom of León-Castilla under King Alfonso VI, 1065-1109* (Princeton, 1988), p. 20.

that Godfrey had rejected, commanded only a few hundred knights and at most two thousand infantry.[8] With these he had to try to hold the hill country of Palestine from the Sea of Galilee past Jerusalem to Hebron, where almost all of the action reported in the New Testament took place, along with two stretches of the coast which included no protected harbors.

There were two other crusader kingdoms in the Middle East—the principality of Antioch and the county of Edessa—with no more if as many men as King Baldwin of Jerusalem had. Antioch remained a large city, though not nearly as populous as it had been before the original Muslim conquest, and it had huge and easily defensible walls. Not far away was the Mediterranean across which the Christians could receive help from Western Europe. Antioch had been seized by the south Italian Norman leader Bohemond in defiance of his promises to Emperor Alexius of Constantinople; but Bohemond had recently been captured by the Turks, and his nephew Tancred ruled as regent in his stead. The county of Edessa, well inland east of the Euphrates near the ancient city of Harran that dated back to Abraham, had been established by Baldwin himself before he became King of Jerusalem. Edessa itself was the oldest Christian city in the world, to which the Apostle Jude had brought the Holy Face soon after the Resurrection of Christ. It was now ruled by another Baldwin, of Le Bourg.[9]

The three small and vulnerable crusader kingdoms, surrounded by a seething sea of hostile Muslims kept from overwhelming the Christians only by their disunity, required substantial reinforcement in order to survive. Almost every communication from them emphasized the gravity and magnitude of this need. In 1100 Western Europe was ready to respond to their need, almost as vigorously as it had responded to Pope Urban II's original call for a crusade. The returning crusaders were telling marvelous tales of what they had done, of what others like them could do, of opportunities still to be seized and victories for Christ's people against the infidel still to be won. Many who had missed the First Crusade were now eager to undertake another one, and they did. Consisting of many components and contingents, it is known collectively as the crusade of 1101.[10]

Its first component was a large force assembled in Lombardy (northern Italy). Pope Paschal II had persuaded Archbishop Anselm of Milan, the principal Lombard city, to preach the crusade. Fired by his words and by the

---

[8]Kenneth M. Setton, ed., *A History of the Crusades*, Volume I: "The First Hundred Years," ed. Marshall W. Baldwin (Madison WI, 1969), p. 344.

[9]Steven Runciman, *A History of the Crusades*, Volume II: "The Kingdom of Jerusalem and the Frankish East, 1100-1187," (Cambridge, England, 1952), pp. 9-10. See Volume I, Chapter 17 of this history for the evidence for the early conversion of Edessa.

[10]Setton, *Crusades*, I, 344-346.

stories of returning crusaders who had followed the Italian Norman leader Bohemond—now a prisoner of the Danishmend Turks—perhaps as many as 20,000 answered the call. However, few of them had military experience. They were commanded by Archbishop Anselm and Count Albert of Biandrate. Encamped outside Constantinople in March 1101, they clashed with Byzantine Emperor Alexius. But Raymond of Toulouse was in the great Christian imperial city. He was the only crusading leader Alexius really trusted, and had been more responsible than any other man for the liberation of Jerusalem. He made peace between Alexius and the Lombard crusaders, and they moved across the Bosporus to await other crusading armies coming up behind them.[11]

In France the new crusade was widely and vigorously preached following the issuance of an encyclical letter from Pope Paschal II to all the French clergy urging it. Three separate crusading armies were assembled, from northern, eastern, and southern France. The northern French army had no single commander; its best known leaders were Stephen of Blois and Hugh of Vermandois, who had been on the First Crusade but had never reached Jerusalem and had been much criticized and even mocked because of it. They were resolved to redeem themselves. The eastern and southern French armies were commanded by Count William of Nevers and Duke William of Aquitaine, respectively. The southern French army was the largest of the three, about the size of the Lombard army. But the northern French army arrived in the East first, and along with a small group of Germans under Constable Conrad, joining the Lombards at Nicomedia fifty miles east of the Bosporus in May. From there, early in June, they set out against the infidel.[12]

But they did not, as Raymond and Stephen urged them, march directly for Antioch and Jerusalem along the route followed by the First Crusade. Instead, the Lombard majority demanded that the host first go into northern Turkey to try to rescue Bohemond. The newcomers who urged this course knew nothing of this region—mountainous, poor in supplies, easily defensible—but they would not listen to Raymond and Stephen who knew it well. Raymond was known to be a foe of Bohemond and Stephen was believed to have been a coward in the First Crusade, so they were thought to have ulterior motives for their advice against this diversion. Therefore, after capturing Ankara late in June, the ill-prepared and now essentially leaderless army plunged into the Danishmend country. The local emir had called for help from other Turkish states; vividly aware now of the danger of the crusaders, they sent it. Early in August a large Turkish force surrounded the crusaders near Mersivan, their horse archers peppering the Christians with arrows but refusing to come to close grips with them. Ill provisioned, far from any source of help, with many of

---

[11]*Ibid.*, I, 346-347, 352-354; Runciman, *Crusades*, II, 18-20.
[12]Setton, *Crusades*, I, 345-351, 354; Runciman, *Crusades*, II, 20-21.

its infantry untrained in war, the crusading host broke up. Most of its leading noblemen and knights—including Raymond, who defended himself splendidly for hours on a rocky height—escaped in the night. Almost all the foot soldiers were slain. The numerous civilian camp followers (including many women of both high and low estate) were either killed, or captured and sold into slavery.[13]

Within the next thirty days the two remaining armies from France, along with a large contingent from Germany under Duke Welf of Bavaria, met identical fates on the route of the First Crusade through Asia Minor toward Antioch. First the smaller army of Duke William of Nevers, and then the combined force of Count William of Aquitaine and Duke Welf of Bavaria, were ambushed at Heraclea, where the Turks had stopped up all the wells and only a single river remained in a very dry and hot country as a source of water. Broken by Turkish attacks at or near the river, the armies disintegrated as their predecessor had disintegrated at Marsivan. A number of the knights escaped on their horses. The infantry were slain and the surviving noncombatants enslaved.[14]

The crusade of 1101 had met with total disaster. Only a few hundred knights out of the tens of thousands of crusaders reached gravely threatened Jerusalem, and many of these did not stay.[15] The overland route through Asia Minor to Antioch and Edessa and Jerusalem had been effectively closed, and was to remain closed for fifty years. Any further help for the crusading kingdoms must come by sea. And the Muslims had learned that these seemingly invincible "Franks" could not only be beaten in battle, but wiped out. All that had been won just two years before was now in deadly peril.

But on the very day after the destruction of the army of William of Aquitaine and Welf of Bavaria at Heraclea, King Baldwin I had saved Jerusalem. At Ramleh on September 6, 1101 he faced an Egyptian army of 32,000 men with just 260 knights and 900 infantry. Knowing that no army in the open field can stand on the defensive against odds of thirty to one, he divided his meager force into four companies and ordered an attack at dawn. On the eve of the battle he made a public confession before the True Cross, and addressed his men in a magnificent fighting speech. Dawn came. The knight Bervold led the assault of the first company; he died with almost all his men. Geldemar Carpenel led the assault of the second company; he died with almost all his men. Hugh of St. Omer led the assault of the third company; after heavy losses the survivors fled toward the coast. Then, under a clear blue summer sky over the ancient battleground of peoples, nations, civilizations, and faiths, of God and man, of Christ and Satan, King Baldwin I of Jerusalem, mounted on his Arab steed Gazelle, lance gleaming in the sunlight and pennons flying in the

---

[13]Setton, *Crusades*, I, 354-358; Runciman, *Crusades*, II, 21-24.

[14]Setton, *Crusades*, I, 358-362; Runciman, *Crusades*, II, 25-29.

[15]Setton, *Crusades*, I, 365.

wind, charged the infidel center with his last company. The enemy dissolved before his eyes, fleeing to their coastal fortress of Ascalon. Jerusalem was saved.[16]

The Egyptian camp fell into the hands of Baldwin and his heroic men. He gave one-tenth of all the spoils to the Hospital of St. John in Jerusalem, which was to become the nucleus of the first of the crusading military orders whose members took religious vows to live as monks and fight the enemies of Christendom so long as they could lift a sword.[17]

In the spring of 1102 Raymond of Toulouse—the relentless, steel-true crusader who had taken a vow when he departed on the First Crusade never to return to his native land, but to devote the rest of his life to the struggle against the infidel—approached Tripoli on the coast of Lebanon with just three hundred men. Twenty times that number of Muslims assembled to stop him, but he defeated them, and laid siege to the city. The siege continued for years; during its course Raymond built a mighty castle on a ridge three miles from Tripoli, which he called Mount Pilgrim. In the summer of 1104 he was severely burned when a blazing roof fell on him during a Muslim attack on Mount Pilgrim. On February 25, 1105 the grim, grizzled old warrior died. He had never made many friends; but he had never broken his word, and he above all had brought the Cross back to Jerusalem. The exact site of his grave is not known, but is probably there at Mount Pilgrim; surely that was where he would have wanted his battered bones to rest. Four years later the heroic King Baldwin finally took Tripoli for Raymond's son Bertrand.[18]

During the intervening years Baldwin had continued to be the heart and soul of the defense of Jerusalem. In May 1102, after a defeat by the Egyptians, he escaped from a crumbling tower with just three companions, while Stephen of Blois and Hugh of Lusignan (who had come east with Count William of Aquitaine and was to leave illustrious descendants in the Holy Land) were killed. With the aid of a fleet opportunely arrived at Jaffa from England, he drove off the Egyptians once again. Recovering from a severe battle wound received on Mount Carmel, he besieged and took Acre, the only good seaport along the Palestinian coast south of Lebanon, in May 1104. A year later he inflicted another defeat on the Egyptians against heavy odds at Ramleh, site of his extraordinary triumph in 1101.[19]

Meanwhile Bohemond had finally been ransomed, but suffered a major defeat at Harran in May 1104, at which Baldwin of Le Bourg, Count of Edessa,

[16]Runciman, *Crusades*, II, 74-75.

[17]Jonathan Riley-Smith, *The Knights of St. John in Jerusalem and Cyprus* (New York, 1967), p. 39.

[18]Runciman, *Crusades*, II, 58-61, 68-69; John H. and Laurita L. Hill, *Raymond IV, Count of Toulouse* (Syracuse NY, 1962), pp. 153-157.

[19]Runciman, *Crusades*, II, 77-80, 87-90; Setton, *Crusades*, I, 364-365.

was captured and Edessa barely saved. Bohemond then returned to Europe to try to pick up reinforcements; but when he returned it was not to fight with the crusaders, but against the Byzantine Empire, falsely accusing Emperor Alexius of betraying the crusades. Repulsed from Dyrrachium, Bohemond was forced to surrender to Alexius, and retired to his Italian homeland, to fight no more. His nephew Tancred continued to hold Antioch, while Baldwin of Le Bourg regained his freedom and was restored as Count of Edessa.[20]

From the beginning of his pontificate, Paschal II had firmly maintained the position of his great predecessor St. Gregory VII regarding Holy Roman Emperor Henry IV. In 1102, at a council at the Lateran palace in Rome, the Pope solemnly renewed his excommunication. When approached by Henry IV's 23-year-old son and namesake, the Pope told him that it would be no sin for him to overthrow his father if as Emperor he redressed the grievances the Church had suffered under his father's rule. Prince Henry at once rebelled, in December 1104.[21]

Though the old Emperor was strongly supported in the Rhineland, he had little support elsewhere, while there was clearly a widespread desire for reconciliation with the Church. At long last Henry IV now shared it, and asked his son to help. But the son had learned and refined the treachery of his father. Pretending to be willing to help him gain absolution from Pope Paschal II as he had gained absolution from Pope St. Gregory VII at winter-bound Canossa thirty years before, Prince Henry persuaded his father to dismiss his guard, and then—claiming that his father was still trying to undermine him—seized and held him prisoner in the castle of Böckelheim. Several sources declare that the old Emperor announced his abdication before the imperial Diet at Ingelheim on the last day of the year 1105 and pleaded with the Pope's legates for absolution, but they replied that only the Pope could give it. The Pope was invited to come to Germany, while his son continued to hold Henry IV in confinement.[22]

On February 1, 1106 Henry V was formally crowned Emperor at Mainz by

---

[20]Runciman, *Crusades*, II, 39, 42-43, 46-51; Setton, *Crusades*, I, 388-389, 393-394; John J. Norwich, *The Other Conquest* (New York, 1967), p. 285.

[21]Mann, *Popes of the Middle Ages*, IX, 18-20, 85-86; Uta-Renate Blumenthal, *The Early Councils of Pope Paschal II, 1100-1110* (Toronto, 1978), pp. 20-21; Alfred Haverkamp, *Medieval Germany, 1056-1273* (New York, 1988), pp. 124-125.

[22]*The Cambridge Medieval History*, ed. J. R. Tanner, C. W. Previté-Orton and Z. N. Brooke, Volume V (Cambridge, England, 1926), pp. 150-151; Mann, *Popes in the Middle Ages*, IX, 24-27. There is disagreement among historians as to whether father or son was the more deceitful. In view of Henry V's later record it hardly appears likely that he was acting in good faith, and his father's attitude immediately before and during his captivity strongly suggests genuine repentance at least at that time, as he may well have felt at Canossa. As that experience had shown, however, Henry IV's repentances tended to be brief. See Volume II, Chapter 19 of this history.

its Archbishop Ruothard. As he placed the imperial crown on the young man's head, he offered the rather grim prayer that "what had befallen his father might happen to him if he did not prove a just ruler of his kingdom, and a defender of the churches of God."[23] But the old Emperor could not endure the loss of his power. Later that month he escaped and gathered a new army. He appealed to St. Hugh, the venerable Abbot of Cluny, promising to do whatever he recommended to be reconciled with the Pope, but was careful to qualify this promise by the convenient phrase "saving my honor."[24] He appealed to the people, insisting that his son had deceived him, and that he now fully intended to be a loyal son of the Church. But his long record of infidelity and broken promises was against him. Some answered his call, but many did not. A major battle and possibly a prolonged civil war was averted only by the death of the old Emperor on August 7. Though his fatal illness came on suddenly, there was time for him to make what the contemporary chronicler Ekkehard called a good confession, to receive viaticum, and to send messages of forgiveness to his son and of respect and good will to the Pope. Nevertheless, since he had died excommunicate, his body was refused burial in consecrated ground.[25]

Pope Paschal II set out from Rome to come to Germany, in response to the Diet's invitation issued at Ingelheim at the end of the previous year. On his way north he held councils at Florence and at Guastalla in the territory of Countess Matilda of Tuscany, who had been the ever-faithful supporter of Pope St. Gregory VII. He declared that all priests and abbots and bishops ordained and consecrated in Germany during the many years of its schism over investiture could retain their church offices, but that henceforth lay investiture would be strictly prohibited. King Coloman (Kálmán) the Learned of Hungary declared to the council at Guastalla that henceforth he would renounce all lay investiture in his kingdom; Pope Paschal II responded by granting him the right to nominate bishops and abbots, already exercised by the recognized Catholic kings in Europe. But the representatives of the new Emperor showed no signs of yielding on this fundamental issue, and information reaching the Pope soon confirmed him that Henry V had no more intention of respecting the ban on lay investiture than had his father. With deep regret, and believing that his personal liberty would be in danger in Germany, Pope Paschal went to France instead, to spend Christmas 1106 at Cluny, and to appeal for help against the new Emperor to King Philip I (who had been reconciled with the Church in 1104 after his long period of defiant adultery) and his son, soon to succeed him as Louis VI. Philip had conformed to Papal directives on lay investiture since 1098; he and Louis made a pact with the Pope in the spring of 1107 to support

---

[23]Mann, *Popes of the Middle Ages*, IX, 27.
[24]*Ibid.*, IX, 28.
[25]*Ibid.*, IX, 28-32; Haverkamp, *Medieval Germany*, p. 126.

him against Henry V on this issue.[26]

That summer the Pope won another signal victory in the long-drawn-out investiture contest, when he and Archbishop St. Anselm of Canterbury prevailed over the prolonged resistance of King Henry I and induced him to bring an end once and for all to lay investiture in England. Following the mysterious slaying of Henry's brother William II Rufus, who died without issue in 1100,[27] Henry had taken over the country in defiance of the rights of his older brother Robert "Curthose," Duke of Normandy, who had not yet returned from the First Crusade. Anselm, universally revered, had supported Henry I, and Henry greatly needed to maintain that support in view of his own dubious position and the peculiar circumstances surrounding the death of his predecessor. He pledged Anselm that he would obey the Pope, but made repeated efforts to persuade Paschal to let him continue lay investiture, despite the fact that it was over this very issue that Anselm had left England during William's reign.[28]   All Henry I's efforts failed; when his envoy William of Veraval said to the Pope in 1103: "I would have you know that my lord the king of England will rather suffer the loss of his kingdom than lose the investiture of the churches," Paschal uncompromisingly replied, "If your king will not give up the investiture of the churches even at the cost of the loss of his kingdom, know that not even for the loss of his life will Paschal ever allow him to retain it with impunity."[29]   Anselm remained in Rome while Henry I maintained this defiant mood, and popular demand for his return to England grew. When Pope Paschal II made the same offer to England that he had made to Germany at the council of Guastalla, to recognize all clerics in the offices they now held so long as no more were invested by laymen, Henry accepted and Anselm returned in August 1106. The next month Henry I defeated and captured his brother Robert at Tinchebrai in Normandy. But he wished no further conflict with Anselm, and at a council of the English church in London in August 1107 lay investiture in England was formally prohibited with the king's consent, though it was still required that bishops and abbots do homage to him for their lands.[30]

In January 1110, without prior consultation with the Pope, Emperor

---

[26]Mann, *Popes of the Middle Ages*, Volume VIII, 2nd ed. (London, 1925), p. 315, and Volume IX, pp. 35-39; Zoltan J. Kosztolynik, *From Coloman the Learned to Bela III (1095-1196); Hungarian Domestic Policies and Their Impact upon Foreign Affairs* (New York, 1987), pp. 62-64; Haverkamp, *Medieval Germany*, p. 128.

[27]See Volume II, Chapter 20 of this history.

[28]Mann, *Popes in the Middle Ages*, IX, 83-86.

[29]*Ibid.*, IX, 86.

[30]*Ibid.*, IX, 86-88; Austin Lane Poole, *From Domesday Book to Magna Carta, 1087-1216* (Oxford History of England), 2d ed. (Oxford, 1955), pp. 120, 179. Anselm, who was 74, lived less than two more years, working hard until his last hours to rebuild the church in England in full harmony with both king and pope (Mann, *Popes in the Middle Ages*, IX, 89).

Henry V announced his intention of leading an army to Rome, establishing order in northern Italy on the way and culminating in his coronation as Holy Roman Emperor by Paschal II. A dowry of 10,000 silver marks for eight-year-old Princess Matilda of England, whom Henry V was to marry when she was old enough, helped greatly to finance the expedition. Since no one, including the Pope, was sure of the Emperor's intentions, Countess Matilda of Tuscany did not oppose his advance. By the end of December he had taken up temporary residence at Arezzo just south of Florence. From there he sent Archbishop Albert of Mainz as head of a party to negotiate with representatives of the Pope headed by Pierleoni at a small church called Santa Maria in Turri, near St. Peter's. By February 4 they had made an astonishing agreement: the Emperor would renounce lay investiture, but in return would be granted all the lands, properties and revenues held by bishops and abbots in Germany, excepting only tithes. During the following week, both Emperor and Pope signed the agreement.[31]

In Germany, where bishops and abbots ruled whole principalities and administered more property than anywhere else in Christendom—where hundreds of nobles held land from them in feudal tenure—such a change would almost have amounted to a revolution. Henry V would have profited immensely if it could have been achieved; but it seems most unlikely that he thought it actually possible. Most contemporary chroniclers insist he must have known that the bishops, abbots, and feudal lords of Germany would never agree to such a transfer, and that consequently he was acting in bad faith. But Pope Paschal II must have thought it possible, or he would not have made the agreement. He is often described as a rather unworldly monk, and this would seem to be strong evidence of it.[32]

On February 12, 1111, a Sunday, Henry V and his army entered Rome, after the Emperor had again sworn to respect the life, liberty, and property of the Pope and to give up his claim to lay investiture as a right. Paschal II received him at St. Peter's. Upon its steps he kissed the Pope's feet, swearing loyalty to him and protection to the Church. Pope and Emperor sat in great chairs set up on discs of porphyry in the nave of St. Peter's. Paschal now called for formal ratification of the agreement drafted February 4, which provided for the renunciation of lay investiture by the Emperor in return for his receiving all the temporalities of the bishops and abbots of Germany except the tithe. Henry descended from his ornate chair and took the document into a corner of the church where he showed it to the bishops and nobles, many of whom were probably unaware of its contents until that moment. They vehemently denounced it, even presuming to call it heresy. The entire day passed in

---

[31]Mann, *Popes in the Middle Ages*, IX, 42-47; Haverkamp, *Medieval Germany*, pp. 129-130.

[32]Mann, *Popes in the Middle Ages*, IX, 47-48; Haverkamp, *Medieval Germany*, p. 130.

argument. Some of the German nobles demanded the immediate coronation of the Emperor without regard to the agreement. Pope Paschal refused to do that, and announced a Mass that would bring the day's proceedings to an end.[33]

During Mass the German soldiers present began to push toward the altar, so that the servers could hardly make their way through them. The moment Mass was over they seized the Pope, along with several cardinals and other Papal officials. Pandemonium struck the premier church in Christendom. Some of the Romans in St. Peter's tried to flee, others to fight. Weapons were brandished. A number of people were killed, including some children. Sacred vessels were stolen; priests had ornate vestments ripped off their backs. Archbishop Conrad of Salzburg heroically protested his willingness to offer his life in defense of the Pope, but no one paid heed to him or responded to his call. It might have been the "robber council" of Ephesus all over again.[34]

When the Romans heard the news, they killed every German they could catch in the city that night, and the next morning launched a vigorous but disorganized attack on Henry and his army, trying to rescue the Pope. They failed, but not before forcing Henry V personally into the action. During the night of the 15th the Emperor and his army withdrew from the city, taking the Pope with them, stripped of his pontifical insignia. German horsemen dragged cardinals through the mud with ropes. Eventually the Pope and six cardinals were put in a castle at Trebicum south of Rome. It was probably there that a young man of thirty-one named Norbert, a canon of the cathedral of Cologne attached to the party of the Emperor's chaplain, horrified by what had happened, went to see the Pope, threw himself at his feet, and begged his pardon. But no other help or comfort that we know came to Pope Paschal II.[35]

Past Popes had often been able to look for help against German aggression to the Normans of south Italy, who were not always themselves dutiful sons of the Church, but emphatically did not wish to see German power solidly established in the Italian peninsula. On the day the Pope was seized in St. Peter's, two mighty and famous Norman leaders lived and ruled in south Italy: Roger of Apulia and Bohemond the crusader. It would have been an unforgettable moment in the history of Christendom if Bohemond, that splendid soldier who had yet so often misused crusading for personal gain, had come thundering out of the shadows that had fallen about him in one last magnificent charge to save the Pope. But it was not to be. Bohemond died March 6, while Roger died February 22. The three reigning Normans in south Italy were, for the first time in Italian Norman history, all women: Adelaide in Sicily, Alaine in Salerno, and Constance in Taranto. Time was when Countess

---

[33]Mann, *Popes of the Middle Ages*, IX, 48-52; Haverkamp, *Medieval Germany*, p. 130. Mann is incorrect in stating that Sunday that year fell on the preceding day, the 11th.

[34]Mann, *Popes in the Middle Ages*, IX, 53-55.

[35]*Ibid.*, IX, 55-57; Cornelius Kirkfleet, *History of St. Norbert* (St. Louis, 1916), p. 11.

Matilda of Tuscany, despite her sex, would have taken the field to save the Pope; but she was 65 now, no longer able to do so. No rescue was at hand. The Emperor's army was ravaging Italy. He threatened to kill or mutilate all his prisoners from Rome if the Pope did not yield to him on lay investiture.[36]

In a moment of weakness for which he never forgave himself, Pope Paschal II gave way, overwhelmed by the thought of the sufferings those for whom he was reponsible would endure if he held out. On April 11 he agreed to all of Henry V's demands. He promised to concede to him the right of lay investiture, not to excommunicate him, and to crown him emperor. All Henry promised in return was to release his prisoners and leave Rome in peace. The next day he said Mass for Henry and gave him communion; the day afterward Henry returned to Rome and the Pope crowned him Holy Roman Emperor in St. Peter's, and then was once again given his liberty. By the end of May Henry V was back in Germany.[37]

No issue of doctrine had been involved in the Pope's surrender, and most of his critics at the time realized it. But there were very many critics, and they were very angry. Some were even to be found in Germany. Paschal's surrender had broken faith with the whole line of Popes since St. Leo IX who had reformed the Church and insisted on the Church's independence of temporal power. Some hot-headed objectors lost sight of the Pope's authority to make such an agreement, however weak and misguided he had been, and declared it null and void. Others, wiser and more loyal, confined themselves properly to sad but measured condemnation. It was more than enough to move Paschal, who knew he had failed and broken trust. In September 1111 he put off his Papal insignia and fled to the island of Ponza. But he made no formal declaration of resignation, and was soon informed that what the critics were demanding was not his resignation, but his recovery of courage and resolution. In October he returned to Rome, and in March 1112 he convened a council at the Lateran palace, attended by 126 bishops and cardinals and many other clergy. To the council Pope Paschal expressed his profound regret for what he had done, also pointing out the obvious fact that he had acted under duress. He formally withdrew the privilege of lay investiture which Henry V had extorted from him, and though he did not personally excommunicate him, made no objection when the bishops of France did so on their own authority.[38]

In Spain in 1107, when in the spring a council assembled at the ancient city of León, King Alfonso VI of Castile and León was seventy years old. None of his four successive wives had borne him a son, though the Muslim princess Zaida—to whom he was not married—had done so. This illegitimate son was

---

[36]Mann, *Popes in the Middle Ages*, IX, 57-58; Runciman, *Crusades*, II, 51n.
[37]Mann, *Popes in the Middle Ages*, IX, 58-62.
[38]*Ibid.*, IX, 62-68.

named Sancho. Alfonso VI also had an illegitimate daughter Teresa, married to Count Henry of Portugal. The king's one legitimate child was another daughter, Urraca, married to Count Raymond of Galicia. Both Henry and Raymond were Frenchmen, cousins who had grown up in Burgundy and were related to its duke—ambitious, designing men who cared only about expanding their dominions. Alfonso VI trusted neither them nor his daughters. Warm feelings for family had never characterized Alfonso VI; men still whispered that decades ago he had killed his own brother to gain the throne of Castile. But he knew what was at stake in the long, long war of the Reconquest, that its imperatives must in a crisis override every other political and personal consideration. He saw no sign that his sons-in-law knew that. The dangerous Almoravids from Morocco were still on the attack. Five years before they had finally driven El Cid's heroic widow Jimena out of Valencia. Just the year before they had made the Muslim ruler of Zaragoza their vassal, after securing the strategic stronghold of Fraga north of the Ebro River near the border of Catalonia and the small Spanish Christian kingdom of Aragon. Early that year the new Almoravid king Ali, son of the redoubtable Yusuf ibn-Tashfin who had been Christian Spain's deadliest foe for a generation, had arrived in Spain; there was good reason to believe that he was planning a new war. Alfonso VI was resolved that his successor should be a Spanish warrior king like himself, not a foreigner or a woman. He demanded that the council meeting at León recognize his illegitimate son Sancho as his heir, though Sancho was just fourteen years old; and they did so.[39]

In September 1107 Urraca's husband, Count Raymond of Galicia, died leaving their two-year-old son Alfonso as heir. Another council was held at León in December to determine Urraca's status in the realm as a widow; the old king allowed her to rule Galicia, but only so long as she did not remarry. If she remarried, the title to Galicia would pass immediately to her son. This surprising and unusual provision clearly indicates that Alfonso VI wanted no new husband of Urraca to become a rival to his designated heir Sancho. About this time Alfonso VI's fourth wife died; he promptly took a fifth, perhaps still hoping for a legitimate son even at his advanced age. As the snow melted on the high slopes of the Guadarramas in the early spring of 1108, news came that the ancient enemy was on the march. A Muslim army commanded by King Ali ben Yusuf's brother Tamin came surging north out of the plains of La Mancha and laid siege to the fortress of Uclés fifty miles east of Toledo. Alfonso VI, recently stricken by severe illness, sent his young son and heir with an army and

---

[39]Bernard F. Reilly, *Alfonso VI*, pp. 327-328, 332-335, 338-340, and *The Kingdom of León-Castilla under Queen Urraca, 1109-1126* (Princeton, 1982), pp. 25-42, 50; R. A. Fletcher, *Saint James's Catapult; the Life and Times of Diego Gelmírez of Santiago de Compostela* (Oxford, 1984), p. 120; Derek W. Lomax, *The Reconquest of Spain* (London, 1978), p. 83. Reilly (*Alfonso VI*, p. 328) dates Prince Sancho's birth to 1093.

eight of the greatest captains of Christian Spain to relieve Uclés. On May 29 the armies met. The battle was a smashing victory for the infidel. Seven of the great lords fell on the field—all but Alvar Fáñez —and so did Prince Sancho.[40]

Surely the old king's memories flashed back then to his worst defeat at the hands of the Moors, the Battle of Sagrajas twenty-two years before. Then he had fled the field with a bleeding wound and ridden alone for sixty miles before reaching temporary safety; the cause of Christian Spain seemed lost. But he had rallied, and saved his country.[41]   Age and illness had not dimmed the dauntless courage of King Alfonso VI in adversity. While Almoravid columns reached out to Huete and Cuenca east of Uclés and to Ocaña to the west of it, halfway to Toledo, he headed south with a strong force. He probably had to be carried; we may picture a gaunt form with burning eyes upon a litter, hoarsely urging his men onward. His son was dead; the enemy was at the gates; he was 71 years old and at death's door; but he was counterattacking. Legend tells of El Cid, dead, propped in his armor upon a horse and riding out for a last sally against the Moors besieging Valencia. That may or may not have happened; but Alfonso VI did almost the like in his southward march in the summer of 1108.[42]

The great white castle of Segovia rose at last before him, the red and gold banners of Castile flying from its battlements. Toledo—which he had captured 23 years ago, if only by trickery—was holding fast, impregnable as ever when stoutly defended. Alfonso VI wanted to go on to it, but apparently his malady made it impossible for him to cross the lofty Guadarramas which rise between Segovia and Toledo. So he summoned his daughter Urraca to join him in Segovia. We would give much to know what they said to each other, but the records of the early twelfth century rarely provide such personal details. However, the information we do have suggests that it was at this time and place that the old king gave his daughter orders with such firmness and finality that despite her own willful and inconstant character (which her later history was clearly to show) and what she later describes as her personal dislike for what he demanded, she could not disobey: she would marry the greatest warrior in

---

[40]Reilly, *Alfonso VI*, pp. 341-350, and *Queen Urraca*, pp. 43-44, 49-51; Fletcher, *St. James's Catapult*, pp. 124-126.

[41]See Volume II, Chapter 20 of this history.

[42]Reilly, *Alfonso VI*, pp. 351-352, and *Queen Urraca*, pp. 51-52; José Maria Lacarra, *Alfonso el Batallador* (Zaragoza, 1978), p. 33. Fletcher (*St. James's Catapult*, p. 126) suggests that Alfonso VI was totally incapacitated by his illness, physically and possibly even mentally; he appears unaware of his extraordinary journey to Segovia, described by Reilly, and its significance. A contemporary source does state that Alfonso VI was ill for 19 months before his death, that is from December 1107, but as Reilly well says: "One may be permitted to wonder if his fatal illness did not look more continuous in retrospect than it in fact was" (*Queen Urraca*, p. 52n). In his biography of Alfonso VI Reilly describes the king during this period as "partially active" (*Alfonso VI*, p. 346).

Spain, Alfonso I the Battler, King of Aragon, just as soon as her father was dead.[43]

Alfonso the Battler was then thirty-five years old. He had never married. Campaigning almost ceaselessly during the four years of his reign thus far, he had led two major counteroffensives against the Muslims of Zaragoza, reconquering strips of territory pointing toward the Ebro River on both sides of that city. War was his life; he had little or no interest in political maneuvering or financial gain. It did not even seem to matter to him that he was unmarried and had no heirs; indeed, he is reputed to have scorned the company of women.[44] But the man could fight, and in that critical hour nothing else mattered to old Alfonso VI. Alfonso the Battler could effectively command the united forces of Aragon and Castile against the victorious infidel foe. His daughter would marry him, with no questions asked. The two were second cousins, which meant that by canon law their marriage required a Papal dispensation; but Alfonso VI, never known for piety, would not hear of waiting for it. The revered Archbishop Bernard of Toledo protested in vain. And so, when the old king died on July 1 of the next year—again, we long for but do not have any account of his last days—Urraca did as her father had commanded, about four months later. Included in the marriage agreement was a pledge by Alfonso and Urraca that they would not separate because of consanguinity or even in the face of excommunication by the Pope.[45]

The uncanonical marriage was a disaster; Alfonso VI's single-minded concentration on the military crisis had eclipsed his awareness—never keen—of the religious and human factors involved. By the spring of 1110 Pope Paschal II had annulled the marriage.[46] Crusading Spain could not afford to defy the Pope, for it was only the Catholic Church and Faith that gave real meaning to their struggle. Alfonso the Battler and Urraca were profoundly unsuited to each other, as they soon realized. For as long as it lasted, this misconceived marriage greatly distracted Alfonso the Battler from his military responsibilities as leader of the War of the Reconquest.

Fortunately for him and for Catholic Spain, others took up the burden of

---

[43]Reilly, *Queen Urraca*, pp. 51-55, 57; Fletcher, *St. James's Catapult*, pp. 126-127. When he came to write his biography of Alfonso VI, Reilly had concluded that when the old king saw his daughter at Segovia he told her only that she would be his heir, and that he did not decide upon the marriage with Alfonso the Battler until consulting with his nobles in the fall (*Alfonso VI*, p. 356). But since the nobles generally objected to the marriage and Alfonso VI probably expected that they would, it seems more likely that he first confronted them with his intentions with his mind already made up, and that he did the same with his daughter.

[44]Reilly, *Queen Urraca*, pp. 40, 59-60; Lacarra, *Alfonso el Batallador*, pp. 17, 27-32.

[45]Reilly, *Alfonso VI*, p. 363, and *Queen Urraca*, pp. 55-59; Anselm G. Biggs, *Diego Gelmírez, First Archbishop of Compostela* (Washington, 1949), pp. 67-68; Lacarra, *Alfonso el Batallador*, pp. 37-38.

[46]Reilly, *Queen Urraca*, p. 67.

the struggle while for five years (1109-1114) he journeyed fruitlessly to and fro through Castile trying to garner support, impose his authority, and settle his burgeoning difficulties with his new queen and her fractious nobility.[47] Ali ben Yusuf marched north in person in 1109; he stormed and sacked Talavera down the Tagus from Toledo, thereby threatening it simultaneously from Uclés on the east and Talavera on the west, ravaged the countryside around Toledo, and finally attacked it directly. Castile's champion Alvar Fáñez commanded the garrison; he and his men fought while the aged Archbishop Bernard and the clergy, the old men, and the women prayed continuously in the cathedral. Ali brought battering rams, siege engines and ladders up the long slope to Toledo's Almohada gate; Fáñez led a magnificent sally and put them to the torch. The Moors withdrew, but took Madrid (except for the citadel) and other towns in the region.[48] In 1111 Alfonso the Battler arrived in Toledo, expelled Archbishop Bernard, and had himself proclaimed king there,[49] but it was an empty gesture; the great warrior was effectively handcuffed by his domestic troubles in Castile, and the defense of Toledo remained in the hands of its garrison. The Moors kept pressure on it for all the five years of Alfonso the Battler's preoccupation with his illicit and unworkable marriage. Defeated by the Moors at Oreja just twenty miles from Toledo in 1113, Alvar Fáñez was killed the next year in a quarrel with his fellow Christians of Segovia (probably generated by the ongoing hostilities between Urraca and Alfonso the Battler); but when Governor al-Mazdali of Córdoba tried to take advantage of his removal from the scene by another assault on Toledo, it was beaten off as its predecessors had been. Then in March 1115 a column from Toledo marched all the way to Córdoba and killed al-Mazdali trying to defend his own city.[50]

Meanwhile in Portugal, Lisbon, Santarem, and Porto had fallen to the advancing infidel; almost the whole country except for a northern strip on the Galician border was under Moorish control. Count Henry of Portugal went to his native France to seek help and died there in 1112, leaving a three-year- old son—Afonso Henriques, later the first King of Portugal—to succeed him under the regency of Alfonso VI's daughter Teresa. Muslim warships made repeated raids on the coasts of Galicia, until by 1115 they had become almost deserted.[51] In 1114, the last year that Alfonso the Battler was preoccupied in Castile, while

---

[47]For extended discussions of this unedifying and extremely complex story, which brought little credit to anyone concerned, see Reilly, *Queen Urraca*, pp. 66-102; Lacarra, *Alfonso el Batallador*, pp. 41-61; Biggs, *Gelmírez*, pp. 70-100; Joseph F. O'Callaghan, *A History of Medieval Spain*, (Ithaca NY, 1975), p. 217.

[48]Lomax, *Reconquest of Spain*, pp. 76-77.

[49]Lacarra, *Alfonso el Batallador*, p. 49; Biggs, *Gelmírez*, p. 79.

[50]Lomax, *Reconquest of Spain*, p. 77; Reilly, *Queen Urraca*, pp. 97, 105; Fletcher, *St. James's Catapult*, p. 131.

[51]Lomax, *Reconquest of Spain*, pp. 64-65; Lacarra, *Alfonso el Batallador*, p. 59; Reilly, *Queen Urraca*, pp. 82-83, 88, 96; Biggs, *Gelmírez*, p. 105.

Count Ramón Berenguer of Barcelona was absent beginning the reconquest of the Balearic Islands, the Moors of Zaragoza attacked the Catalan capital of Barcelona, but were defeated in a battle near Martorell in which their commander was killed. Alfonso the Battler called for help from the knights of France, and many of them responded; with their aid he began to press toward Zaragoza from the south, attempting to cut off its communications with Muslim Spain.[52] Finally deciding to cut his losses in Castile and abandon his illicit marriage as the Church was calling upon him to do, he began to plan a mighty offensive against Zaragoza, with the French to take the place of the Castilians as allies. As for Queen Urraca, she barely escaped with her life from an uprising in Santiago de Compostela in 1117. Emerging from a burning bell tower, she was seized, partially stripped, rolled in the mud, and bashed in the face with a rock.[53] Old Alfonso VI had chosen the wrong remedy, but he had been only too right about her incapacity to rule.

In the fall of the year of the great humiliation of Pope Paschal II, 1111, a young man of 21 named Bernard was riding to overtake his father Tescelin and his uncle Gaudry, members of the lesser nobility of Burgundy in France, on a march with their Duke to besiege Grancey-le-Chateau near the upper course of the Seine River. Bernard was slender, handsome, very fair, kind and charming of manner, but passionate, full of inner fire. His mother Aleth had raised him in total devotion to the Catholic Faith, with a particular emphasis on the Blessed Virgin Mary. She had died four years before, but her memory was constantly with him, and he felt that she was calling him to a religious vocation. The new and uniquely rigorous monastery of Cîteaux was located nearby, and undoubtedly much discussed by the people of this region. Bernard felt drawn to it, as did his uncle Gaudry, but his brothers were strongly opposed in view of Cîteaux's reputation for extreme severity. Now, as he was passing a church by the road to Grancey-le-Chateau, he went inside to pray, and emerged with a firmly fixed resolution to join the monastic community at Cîteaux and to take his brothers with him. So persuasive was he in his enthusiasm for his new commitment that his uncle Gaudry and his brothers Bartholomew, Andrew, and Guy agreed immediately to join the Cistercian community with him. Soon afterward his friend Hugh of Vitry said he would join too. A fourth brother, Gerard, who had initially resisted the call, decided the following March—after he had been wounded, taken prisoner, and escaped—to come with them also. By the time Bernard actually set out for Cîteaux in April 1112, he brought with him no less than thirty postulants—as many, or more than the membership of the entire existing community at Cîteaux.[54]

---

[52]Lomax, *Reconquest of Spain*, p. 83.
[53]Biggs, *Gelmírez*, pp. 125-130.
[54]Watkin Williams, *Saint Bernard of Clairvaux* (Manchester, 1935), pp. 3-12; King,

St. Stephen Harding was then abbot of Cîteaux, having succeeded St. Alberic in 1108. He soon learned that these young men had come not out of some temporary surge of emotion, but as the fruit of deep and carefully considered decisions. Here was proof that God had indeed blessed their new way of life, with its uncompromising austerity, its unadorned simplicity, the limpid purity of its dedication to God symbolized by its white habit. Now the new monastic house could multiply like those earlier mother-houses of imperishable spiritual fame: Monte Cassino of St. Benedict and Cluny of St. Berno and St. Odo. The very next year St. Stephen established a Cistercian house at La Ferté, south of Dijon on the Grône River near its confluence with the Saone; Bertrand, probably one of the original Cistercian community, was named its abbot with twelve monks accompanying him. In 1114 a second Cistercian foundation was made at Pontigny, near Auxerre to the northwest of Cîteaux; Bernard's friend Hugh of Vitry (now known as Hugh of Mâcon), though only a year past his notivitate, was named its abbot.[55]

Meanwhile St. Bernard had been quietly studying Scripture, for which he was to manifest a lifelong passion which ultimately caused him to be called "the last of the fathers of the Church." He wished only to live out his life humbly and obscurely, in total devotion to Christ. But his extraordinary qualities of leadership became increasingly evident to Abbot St. Stephen, and in 1115 he was chosen as abbot of the third Cistercian monastery to be founded after the mother-house, at Clairvaux in the valley of the Aube in Champagne, the River of Dawn. Among Bernard's founding community of twelve were three of his brothers—Gerard, Guy, and Andrew—his uncle Gaudry, and two other relatives of his from the original thirty he had brought to Cîteaux. Two years later his 70-year-old father Tescelin joined the community as well.[56]

The site of the new monastery was in a deep, thickly wooded hollow between two hills, known as the Valley of Absinthe. The first building at Clairvaux was the residence of the monks, with a kitchen and eating area on the dirt floor below and a story above, reached by a ladder, where the monks slept on a wooden floor with wooden blocks for pillows. There was a small separate room for the abbot and a guest room. The chapel had three altars: the high altar dedicated to the Blessed Virgin Mary, and two others to St. Benedict and St. Lawrence. At the beginning the monks had nothing to eat but beechnuts, berries, roots, wild greens, and a lumpy bread made from the poorest grains.

Cîteaux and Her Elder Daughters, pp. 18-19; Bruno S. James, *Saint Bernard of Clairvaux* (New York, 1957), pp. 19-27; Jean Marillier, "Les premières années; les études de Châtillon" and "La vocation" in Commission d'histoire de l'ordre de Cîteaux, *Bernard de Clairvaux* (Paris, 1953), pp. 17-37.

[55]King, *Cîteaux and Her Elder Daughters*, pp. 106-108, 148-150; Williams, *St. Bernard*, pp. 12-13.

[56]Williams, *St. Bernard*, pp. 14-19, 29.

They had no shoes, and did all their work by hand except for the help of a single donkey.[57]

Well might St. Bernard say to the postulants who entered: "Leave your body at the door; here is the kingdom of souls; the flesh has nothing more to do with it."[58] Yet in his second year at Clairvaux, in 1116, he saw a vision of a throng of men "of all ages and all conditions," filling his valley to overflowing; for Clairvaux was to have no less than 68 daughter houses in St. Bernard's lifetime, and 263 by the end of his century; its own community was to grow from the original twelve to more than 700 at St. Bernard's death, and to give to the Church a Pope, five cardinals, and 11 bishops.[59]

Just two months before St. Bernard founded Clairvaux Norbert, the young canon of Cologne cathedral whom we last saw horrified at his Emperor's violent treatment of the Pope in Rome, underwent a conversion experience like that of St. Paul, which changed his life forever. Caught in a thunderstorm, he was thrown from his horse, and heard a voice calling him to "turn from evil and do good." He spent days in prayer before a crucifix, put on a hair shirt, and took up residence at the Benedictine monastery of Siburg near Cologne, putting himself under the spiritual direction of its Abbot Conon. He was ordained a priest in Cologne cathedral, and began to preach to increasing numbers of people despite the opposition of the other canons of Xanten, his former associates. Like St. Bernard earlier, St. Norbert too was in search of his true and complete vocation.[60]

In March 1117 Emperor Henry V, after invading Italy with an army to seize the lands of the faithfully Catholic Countess Matilda of Tuscany who had just died, entered Rome as the Pope fled. Henry had himself crowned Emperor by Archbishop Maurice Bourdin of Braga in St. Peter's (though not at the traditional place of coronation before the high altar, but in the chapel of St. Gregory). Henry stayed only a few days; Archbishop Bourdin was promptly excommunicated; early the next year Pope Paschal II returned to Rome, only to die there January 21, 1118.[61]

Three days later four of the seven cardinal bishops, 27 of the 28 cardinal priests, and all 18 cardinal deacons met in conclave to select his successor. There seems never to have been any doubt about their choice: John of Gaeta, chancellor to both Paschal II and his immediate predecessor Urban II, who was unanimously elected despite his advanced age and ill health. He took the name Gelasius, only the second Pope to do so. The monastery where the election was

---

[57]*Ibid.*, pp. 22-26; King, *Cîteaux and Her Elder Daughters*, pp. 208-215.
[58]King, *Cîteaux and Her Elder Daughters*, p. 215.
[59]*Ibid.*, pp. 215, 222, 226.
[60]Kirkfleet, *St. Norbert*, pp. 13-30.
[61]Mann, *Popes in the Middle Ages*, IX, 72-81.

held was promptly stormed by the turbulent Roman noble Cencius Frangipane and his men, who captured and beat the new Pope. But the militia of the city rallied to rescue him, and Frangipane and his adherents begged the Pope's forgiveness and received it.[62]

As soon as he heard the news, Emperor Henry V turned about at Verona in northern Italy, made a surprise forced march south, and entered Rome on the night of March 1. The next night the Pope attempted to flee by sea despite a severe storm. The Germans pursued, actually firing poisoned arrows at his galley. It escaped them, but had to be beached because of the storm. Cardinal Hugh of Alatri carried the aged and infirm Pope on his back through the darkness and the tempest to the castle of Ardea thirty miles from Rome. Before the Germans could find him there, the next night the Pope was put on another boat and taken to his native city of Gaeta in south Italy, where the Norman nobility welcomed him and pledged to defend him. He was consecrated Pope there on March 10, while Emperor Henry V had Archbishop Bourdin of Braga proclaimed Pope "Gregory VIII"—another imperial antipope. Pope Gelasius II promptly renewed the excommunication of both the Emperor and the Antipope on Palm Sunday, April 7. The Normans then marched on Rome. Henry, after having himself again crowned Emperor, returned to Germany, which allowed Gelasius to return to Rome early in July. But no sooner had he come back than he was again ferociously attacked by the Frangipani. Concluding that the city was at least for the time being ungovernable, he went to Pisa, then to Genoa, and then to France, where he remained for the short span of life left to him. At the shrine of St. Giles in Languedoc he received St. Norbert in audience and granted him permission to preach in any diocese he chose.[63]

Meanwhile on May 22, 1118 Alfonso the Battler with the aid of a large number of French knights had laid siege to Zaragoza, the northernmost outpost of Islam in Europe, since the days of the original Muslim conquest of Spain their principal base in the northern part of the Iberian peninsula. The most distinguished figure among the French at the siege was Viscount Gaston V of Béarn, who had assembled the siege engines for the taking of Jerusalem in the First Crusade. Later in the year Pope Gelasius II, after his arrival in France, blessed their enterprise as a crusade. Ali ben Yusuf, after failing to take Coimbra in Portugal the year before, had returned to Morocco, and the Muslim commanders remaining in Spain did not coordinate their efforts effectively. Only when the defenders of Zaragoza were at their last extremity did a relieving force arrive, on December 8, but it was routed by the crusaders, whose numbers now exceeded those of the Moors. Ten days later Zaragoza capitulated. It was

---

[62]*Ibid.*, IX, 120-125.
[63]*Ibid.*, IX, 127-135; Kirkfleet, *St. Norbert,* pp. 37-40.

the greatest offensive victory of the Reconquest since the recapture of Toledo by Alfonso VI in 1085. Over the next two years Alfonso the Battler secured effective control of much of the Ebro River valley, the heartland of northeastern Spain; restored the city and archbishopric of Tarragona on the coast; and won a notable victory at Calatayud forty miles southwest of Zaragoza, defeating a relieving force under Ibrahim, a younger son of Yusuf ibn-Tashfin, with the aid of the Duke of Aquitaine and six hundred crusading French knights. Aragon was established as a powerful Spanish kingdom, and the Moors had received a major reverse.[64]

The brief and troubled pontificate of Gelasius II included another event of substantial importance in the history of Christendom: the death of the great King Baldwin I of Jerusalem and his succession by Baldwin of Le Boùrg, now Baldwin II, who was crowned King of Jerusalem by Patriarch Arnulf on Easter Sunday 1118 (April 14). Earlier in the year Baldwin I had launched an incredible invasion of Egypt, which had a population of millions, with just 216 horsemen and 400 infantry. Despite the enormous odds against him, he reached the Nile with his force intact, only to fall mortally ill with barely enough time to return to the holy city to die. His last legacy to the crusading cause was one of his greatest: another new military order, the Knights of the Temple, warriors vowed to celibacy, poverty, and obedience as soldiers, following the Benedictine rule, with the red cross their symbol, soon to be known through all of Christendom as the Templars.[65]

Baldwin II, a noble figure and worthy successor of his namesake, had close ties to the Christian Armenians of the Middle East, whose help the crusaders much needed but had often scorned; his wife Morphia, to whom he was devoted, was of their race. Within a year he had to rush north to save Antioch after the Muslims had destroyed its army at what was known as the Battle of the Field of Blood. Bringing the True Cross with him, he prevailed at the Battle of Tel-Danith in August 1119, installed his trusted friend Joscelin as Count of Edessa (where he had ruled before becoming King of Jerusalem), and brought his Queen Morphia from Edessa to Jerusalem.[66]

---

[64]Lomax, *Reconquest of Spain*, pp. 83-84; O'Callaghan, *History of Medieval Spain*, pp. 219-220; Lacarra, *Alfonso el Batallador*, pp. 67-71; Reilly, *Queen Urraca*, pp. 125, 128; Fletcher, *St. James's Catapult*, p. 131. Lomax and O'Callaghan (*op. cit.*), the standard English histories covering the Reconquest, both strongly imply that Pope Gelasius II gave his blessing to the campaign in Aragon as a crusade before it began, at a council at Toulouse in southern France. The Pope could not have been at Toulouse before September 1118, by which time the siege was four months old; nor in view of the tumultuous events involving him in March and April is it likely that he had much time to deal with affairs in Spain then. His blessing on the enterprise must therefore have come while it was in progress, probably in the fall.

[65]Runciman, *Crusades*, II, 99-106, 144; Setton, *Crusades*, I, 410-411; Riley-Smith, *Knights*, p. 157.

[66]Runciman, *Crusades*, II, 143-155.

Weakened by his infirmities and exhausted by his ordeals since becoming Pope, at Christmastide 1118 Gelasius II asked to be taken to the famous monastery of Cluny to die. He wanted Cardinal Conon of Palestrina to be his successor, but the Cardinal told him that what the Church needed now was a wealthy, influential bishop experienced in politics who could still be trusted; such a man, he said, was Archbishop Guy of Vienne in France. Pope Gelasius II made this recommendation his own. He died on January 29, 1119; three days later Archbishop Guy was elected by the cardinals who had accompanied Gelasius II to France. On March 1 the cardinals remaining in Rome confirmed his election. He took the name Calixtus II. He was 59 years old, in excellent health and full of energy—a man of determination and perseverance. His father had been Count of Burgundy and a strong supporter of Pope St. Gregory VII, and his numerous brothers and sisters had married into many of the royal families of Europe. He was cousin of Emperor Henry V and King Henry I of England; the Queen of France was his niece, and Alfonso Raimúndez, the only child of Queen Urraca of Castile, was his nephew. His sister was married to the Count of Flanders. Three of his brothers had died fighting for Christendom in Palestine and Syria. He had been a legate in Spain under Pope Paschal II. His record as Archbishop of Vienne was stained by a totally unjustified seizure of the churches of the district of Sermorens which belonged to the diocese of Grenoble, but as Pope it was to be unblemished; Calixtus II was one of the great Vicars of Christ.[67]

The new Pope remained in France for the first year of his pontificate. In October 1119 he presided over a large and important council at Reims, attended by no less than 427 bishops and abbots from France and Germany. After meeting Emperor Henry V at Mouzon near Sedan and finding him armed, intransigent and threatening, Calixtus II proclaimed his excommunication anew at the council and absolved his subjects once again from their duty of allegiance to him. Nor did he fear to challenge another powerful ruler, Henry I of England, youngest son of William the Conqueror. At the council the Pope consecrated Thurstan Archbishop of York despite the King's strong opposition. He also received an appeal from Bishop Urban of Llandaff in Wales against the oppression of Wales and its ancient church by the conquering Normans, and responded by placing the see of Llandaff under his special protection. On the strong recommendation of Bishop Bartholomew of Laon in France, he renewed the universal permission to preach which Gelasius II had given to St. Norbert. He heard reports of the steady growth of the new Cistercian order, which now had no less than twelve monasteries, one of which was established at Fontenay by monks from St. Bernard's Clairvaux during the council itself. Soon after the council ended, on December 23, the Pope

---

[67]Mann, *Popes of the Middle Ages*, IX, 136-149.

confirmed the Cistercian rule, the Charter of Charity. Interestingly enough, the confirmation was signed at Cluny. The old order and the new were flourishing side by side, each with its own charism, each making its own contribution.[68]

During the next three years this great Pope followed up his firm assertion of authority at the Council of Reims with triumphs over both the monarchs he had denounced and a settlement in badly disordered Castile, while seeing the Cistercians and St. Norbert move onward to more spiritual victories.

In March 1120 Calixtus II ordered Henry I of England to admit to England Archbishop Thurstan of York, whom the Pope had consecrated, or face excommunication. At first the King defied the Pope; but in November 1120 he suffered a shattering personal disaster when his only son William was drowned in the English Channel in the wreck of the "White Ship" with almost everyone else on board. Whether due to simple depression or a genuine awakening to his duties as a Catholic as a result of this tragedy, Henry relented in the winter of 1121 and admitted Archbishop Thurstan.[69]

Then he stepped boldly into the midst of the turmoil in Spain, which he had experienced first-hand when sent there as Paschal II's legate. He was aware that Queen Urraca was very inconstant and unable to keep order in her kingdom. Her first husband, Raymond of Burgundy, had been his brother; he was determined to safeguard the interests of his nephew Alfonso, now at 15 almost old enough to rule, and at the same time to strengthen the church in Spain to check the disintegration that had been apparent since the death of Alfonso VI. Archbishop Bernard of Toledo was a national hero and a holy man, but very old; Bishop Diego Gelmírez of Santiago de Compostela, if excessively ambitious, had at least shown himself to be vigorous and persistent in defense of the Church. Therefore in March 1120 Pope Calixtus II wrote to the bishops and counts of Spain condemning Urraca's hostile behavior toward her son and deprivation of his rights; and on July 25 the Pope made Gelmírez an archbishop, with the bishops of Salamanca in Castile and Coimbra in Portugal dependent on him, and also designated him Papal legate for the archdiocese of Braga, whose former archbishop had gone into rebellion as the antipope, and for the whole of Galicia in northwestern Spain.[70]

---

[68]*Ibid.*, IX, 95, 152-159, 200; Kirkfleet, *St. Norbert*, pp. 58-62; King, *Cîteaux and Her Elder Daughters*, pp. 13-15; Williams, *St. Bernard*, pp. 28-29, 39-42.

[69]Mann, *Popes of the Middle Ages*, IX, 95-96; Lane Poole, *Domesday Book to Magna Carta*, pp. 125-126.

[70]Reilly, *Queen Urraca*, pp. 143, 151-152; Biggs, *Gelmírez*, pp. 158-160, 163-164; Fletcher, *St. James's Catapult*, pp. 144-147, 199. Gelmírez had first asked the Pope to make Santiago de Compostela an archdiocese soon after his election, in the spring of 1119, on the grounds that all other cities where apostles were buried had metropolitan status. (The Spanish were convinced that the body of the Apostle James was preserved at Compostela.) He could only make his request through envoys, since Queen Urraca had forbidden him to leave Castile and Alfonso the Battler, an old enemy, had

The Pope had acted none too soon; just five days before he issued his bull making Gelmírez an archbishop, Queen Urraca had thrown him in jail in Santiago de Compostela and deprived him of his temporal authority there. Her son promptly left the city, its people rioted, and Urraca had to release Gelmírez. The news of Gelmírez's imprisonment and deprivation reached Rome before the news of his release; on October 7 Calixtus II fired off a demand that Urraca release him and restore his authority at once on pain of excommunication and an interdict. The next summer a national council of Spanish bishops and abbots met at Sahagún, but both archbishops were absent; the council imposed an interdict on Castile to take effect November 11, in an attempt to depose the Queen. The Pope was wiser; he met with Archbishop Bernard of Toledo in Rome, confirmed him as metropolitan of Spain (except for the northwestern dioceses where Gelmírez was metropolitan), and accepted him as guarantor of an agreement whereby Urraca would be allowed to rule (insofar as she could) for the rest of her life, but to do nothing to prejudice the rights of her son Alfonso as her successor. This settlement insured the peaceful succession of Alfonso VII when his mother died in 1126, after a reign during which from start to finish she was never really in control.[71]

Following his renewed approval by Pope Calixtus II at the Council of Reims, in the winter of 1120 St. Norbert's patron Bishop Bartholomew of Laon showed him the site of a hermitage in the valley of Prémontré about 25 miles northwest of Reims. St. Norbert was convinced at once that this was the place God wanted for the mother-house of the new order he now intended to establish. The monastery of Clairvaux had acquired rights to the hermitage, but St. Bernard gladly gave them up to St. Norbert on Bishop Bartholomew's request. At about this time St. Norbert—like St. Alberic of Cîteaux before him—had a vision of the Blessed Virgin Mary giving him a white habit. On Easter 1121 Bishop Bartholomew invested him and thirteen of his first disciples with that white habit, and made them an unconditional grant of the valley of Prémontré. On Christmas day that year St. Norbert and his monks, now numbering thirty, made their solemn profession; the Premonstratensian or Norbertine order had been established. Before the next year was over it had two more houses, one in Belgium (at Floreffe near Namur) and the other in Germany, where the Count of Cappenberg had donated his castle in the mountains near Münster and joined the new order himself.[72]

---

forbidden him to cross Aragon; but eventually Bishop Hugh of Porto managed to get through disguised as a beggar, went to the Pope at Cluny in January 1120, and obtained his agreement to the action finally taken in July (Biggs, *op. cit.*, pp. 149-154).

[71]Reilly, *Queen Urraca*, pp. 146-147, 151-152, 158-162, 181-204, 243.

[72]Kirkfleet, *St. Norbert*, pp. 67-69, 77-81, 101-110, 132, 143-144; Leopold Grill, "Morimond, soeur jumelle de Clairvaux," in Commission d'histoire de l'ordre de Cîteaux, *Bernard de Clairvaux*, pp. 126-127; François Petit, "Bernard et l'Ordre de Prémontré," *ibid.*, pp. 288-291.

Meanwhile the Cistercian order was growing apace. St. Bernard, after a year (1118-19) when he was almost completely incapacitated due to his own excessive austerities and the enormous strain of establishing a monastic community with almost no resources, had returned to his post now aware of the dangers of excess, with a spreading fame which brought a steady flow of gifts to his community and its daughters.[73]   The Cistercians held firmly to their principles regarding plain living and lack of church adornment, but they no longer faced poverty so desperate as to threaten their physical survival; and the surge of new vocations—by no means all with such strong characters as the founders—had tempered their enthusiasm with wisdom. To the founding abbot of the monastery of Foigny near the Belgian border, his third daughter house founded in July 1121,[74] St. Bernard wrote:

> You must understand that you are especially the abbot of the sad, faint-hearted, and discontented among your flock. You were given to them as abbot not to be comforted but to comfort, because you were the strongest of them all and, by God's grace, able to comfort them all without needing to be comforted by any.[75]

On June 3, 1121 Pope Calixtus II finally arrived in Rome, for the first time since his election more than two years before. He was welcomed with the greatest honor. He then made a tour of southern Italy to secure his support from the Normans there. By the next spring he felt strong enough to challenge Antipope Bourdin in his stronghold at Sutri. The city was besieged and taken and the Antipope made captive, to spend the remaining sixteen years of his life in prison.[76]

Emperor Henry V had done nothing to save his creature, and the Pope had established so formidable a reputation for decisive action that he believed the stubborn monarch might now be willing to negotiate with him on the investiture controversy which had so deeply divided Pope and Holy Roman Emperor, against all the purposes and intentions of Pope St. Leo III and Charlemagne who had established the office. Many of the bishops and high nobility of Germany thought so too; at the Diet of Würzburg in September 1121 they urged the Emperor toward reconciliation with the Pope. In January 1122 Henry V sent an embassy to Rome; it was well received, and returned by three Cardinal-Legates.[77] In February Calixtus II wrote Henry V the letter whose

---

[73]Williams, *St. Bernard*, pp. 27-28; Robert Fossier, "L'installation et les premières années de Clairvaux," in Commission d'histoire de l'ordre de Cîteaux, *Bernard de Clairvaux*, pp. 91-93.

[74]King, *Cîteaux and Her Elder Daughters*, p. 228.

[75]St. Bernard of Clairvaux, *Letters*, ed. Bruno S. James (London, 1953) p. 107.

[76]Mann, *Popes of the Middle Ages*, IX, 160-165.

[77]*Ibid.*, IX, 169-170; *Cambridge Medieval History*, V, 162.

excerpts stand at the head of this chapter.

That summer the imperial court was held at Worms in Germany. St. Norbert—fresh from the dedication of the third Premonstratensian community at Cappenberg—was there. Though we have no proof of any specific intervention by him in the investiture controversy, it is at least an interesting coincidence that this great apostle was at hand on the very eve of the final settlement of this dispute which had so damaged Christendom. He may well have played a part at least in creating a propitious climate for its acceptance.[78]

Cardinal Lambert, representing the Pope, called for a council to meet at Mainz in September 1122 for the specific purpose of discussing such a settlement. Its purpose, he announced, was "by the authority of our lord the Pope and the whole Roman Church to make peace between that Church and the empire."[79] Henry V agreed to the meeting, so long as the site was changed to Worms where he was. At first the old positions were maintained immovably; but then, after about a week of debate, an agreement was hammered out on September 23[80]—the Concordat of Worms, one of the finest and most just compromises in history:

> I, Calixtus, servant of the servants of God, do grant to thee, beloved son Henry, by the grace of God august emperor of the Romans, that the elections of the bishops and abbots of the German kingdom, who belong to the kingdom [that is, not in Italy or Burgundy, where the Empire claimed some jurisdiction], shall take place in thy presence, without simony and without any violence; so that if any discord shall arise between the parties concerned, you, by the counsel or judgment of the metropolitan and the co-provincials, may give consent and aid to the part which has more right. The one elected, morever, without any exaction, may receive the regalia from you. . . .
>
> I, Henry, by the grace of God august emperor of the Romans, for the love of God, and of the Holy Roman Church, and of our lord Pope Calixtus, and for the healing of my soul, do remit to God, and to the holy apostles of God, Peter and Paul, and to the Holy Catholic Church, all investiture through ring and staff, and do grant that in all the churches that are in my kingdom or empire there may be canonical election and free consecration. All the possessions and regalia of St. Peter, which from the beginning of this discord unto this day, whether in the time of my father or else in mine, have been abstracted and which I hold, I restore to that same Holy Roman Church.[81]

The concept of separating the investiture of bishops with spiritual authority from their investiture with temporal authority had been developed by the extraordinarily able Abbot Suger of St. Denis in France as a compromise

---

[78]Kirkfleet, *St. Norbert*, pp. 148-149.
[79]Mann, *Popes in the Middle Ages*, IX, 234.
[80]*Ibid.*, IX, 172-173; Haverkamp, *Medieval Germany*, p. 134.
[81]Mann, *Popes of the Middle Ages*, IX, 173-174.

formula at the Council of Reims in 1119, and there accepted by both Pope Calixtus and King Louis VI of France.[82] Now it was accepted in Germany as well. The Concordat of Worms was promptly ratified by the Pope, and on November 11 by a diet at Bamberg composed mostly of the great noblemen of Germany who had not been at Worms. The investiture controversy was resolved, once and for all.[83]

Pope Calixtus II had justified the faith placed in him by the dying Pope Gelasius II and by his Cardinal Conon; Cardinal Lambert, the future Pope Honorius II, had justified the faith placed in him by Pope Calixtus. Emperor Henry V had wearied of the struggle, which he had learned that he could not win against the indestructible Church. He had preserved his right to supervise episcopal elections and the bestowal of the temporal authority (symbolized by the "regalia") upon German bishops. But their ultimate spiritual authority, and the right to confer its symbols of ring and staff—symbols which bishops still bear today, though only a dwindling number of the faithful know their meaning and history—remained where God had placed it, with the Church His Son had established and the successor of Peter the fisherman who ruled it.

---

[82]Williams, *St. Bernard*, p. 223.
[83]Mann, *Popes of the Middle Ages*, IX, 176; *Cambridge Medieval History*, V, 163.

2
The Age of St. Bernard of Clairvaux
(1122-1153)
(Popes Calixtus II 1119-24, Honorius II 1124-30, Innocent II 1130-43, Celestine II 1143-44, Lucius II 1144-45, Bd. Eugenius III 1145-53)

> "I brought to you words of peace and, finding you the sons of peace, I left
> my peace with you. I went forth to sow seed, God's seed, not mine, and the
> good seed I sowed fell on good ground yielding a hundredfold with
> wonderful speed, because the necessity was great. I experienced no
> difficulty or delay, but almost on one and the same day I both sowed and
> reaped, 'returning with joy as I carried with me the sheaves' of peace. And
> this was the harvest I reaped: a joyous hope of release and home for men
> in captivity, chains, and prison; and fear for our enemies, disgrace for the
> schismatics, glory for the Church, and great joy for everyone."—St.
> Bernard of Clairvaux to the clergy and people of Genoa, winter 1134[1]

The second quarter of the twelfth century of the Christian era was
dominated throughout most of Christendom by a single extraordinary, indeed
unique figure: St. Bernard of Clairvaux. No man before or since who held no
office of power throughout his life bestrode his age as did this monk of genius
and of leashed but flaming passion, juridically only one of the many hundreds of
abbots in the Church, yet the terror and inspiration of emperors and kings, the
shield and sword—and where necessary the goad—of Popes. No historical
determinist theory, no calculations of material or institutional power and
influence can begin to account for St. Bernard of Clairvaux and what he did.
He soars above such petty analyses like an eagle. And in addition to his
immense ecclesiastical and political accomplishments on which we must
primarily focus in these pages, he continued throughout to live the humble and
ascetic life he had promised to God; to maintain his studies and write his books
on Scripture and theology and devotion; to compose prayers (such as the
"Memorare" to the Blessed Virgin Mary) and hymns (such as "O Sacred Head
Surrounded") that are still prayed and sung, part of the living faith of living
Catholics, though now separated from him by more than eight hundred years.

---

[1]*The Letters of St. Bernard of Clairvaux*, tr. Bruno Scott James (London, 1953), p.
200; for the date of the letter see Watkin Williams, *Saint Bernard of Clairvaux*
(Manchester, England, 1935), p. 121.

During these years St. Bernard of Clairvaux reformed and transformed the religious life of Europe, from Spain to Scandinavia; saved the Papacy from a devastating schism that might otherwise have been even more destructive in effects than the Great Western Schism of 1378; destroyed a developing heresy and converted its leader; and launched a crusade on a far grander scale than the First Crusade which had stormed Jerusalem, whose success might have changed the world forever, and for whose failure he can in no way justly be blamed. All this was in addition to intervening, time and again, in disputes where clashing personal and institutional interests had obscured justice, casting beams of his relentless light into their darkest corners.

He did not emerge clearly into view as the voice and heart and conscience of Christendom until the Papal schism burst upon an unsuspecting Europe in the winter of 1130. Until that time his influence was exerted very much behind the scenes, yet still significantly: for example, upon Cardinal Haimeric, chancellor of Pope Honorius II (elected in December 1124), the former Cardinal Lambert who had negotiated the Concordat of Worms settling the great dispute on lay investiture;[2] upon Abbot Suger of St. Denis, the royal abbey of Paris dear to the heart of the kings of France;[3] upon Count Theobald of Champagne, grandson of William the Conqueror and brother of the future King of England, one of the greatest noblemen in France.[4] All three he counselled; all three felt Christ speaking to them through him; all three were to play central roles in the dramas to come, exercising the power St. Bernard never had nor wanted, trying to use it by the standards he had set for them.

St. Bernard made one other visible mark upon Christendom before 1130, when in January 1128 a delegation of six members of the newly established military order of the Knights of the Temple (Templars) in Jerualem, led by their first Master, Hugh of Payens, appeared before Papal legate Matthew and St. Bernard at the Council of Troyes in France. They had been sent by King Baldwin II of Jerusalem to regularize their order and to obtain support for it. The Papal legate and the Council approved the new order and asked St. Bernard to draw up a rule for it to submit to the Pope. St. Bernard's draft rule strongly endorsed the new concept of a monastic life dedicated to physical warfare against evil, recalling Christ cleansing the Temple, but prescribed a strict ascetic mode of life. It provided for the wearing of a white garment, in imitation of the white monks.[5]

---

[2] Williams, *St. Bernard*, p. 203.

[3] St. Bernard of Clairvaux to Abbot Suger (c. 1127), *Letters of St. Bernard*, tr. James, pp. 110-118.

[4] St. Bernard of Clairvaux to Count Theobald of Champagne (c. 1127), *Letters of St. Bernard*, tr. James, pp. 73-74.

[5] Williams, *St. Bernard*, pp. 234-240; Horace K. Mann, *The Lives of the Popes in the Middle Ages*, Volume IX (London, 1925), pp. 297-299.

Like all the Kings of Jerusalem during the twelfth century, Baldwin II was in constant need of help from home. Five years before Hugh of Payens met St. Bernard at Troyes, Baldwin had been captured and his army destroyed on the Euphrates River; his kingdom was saved only by the opportune arrival of a Venetian fleet which defeated the Egyptians and captured the great fortress of Tyre in July 1124.[6] Finally ransomed, Baldwin carried on the endless struggle, ranging throughout the four crusader kingdoms (the Kingdom of Jerusalem, the Principality of Antioch, the County of Tripoli and the County of Edessa) to fight the Muslims attacking their borders and to try to keep peace among them. He was helped by the native Christian Armenians who were more reliable allies for him than his Latin Christian brethren, being devoted to him because of his devotion to his Armenian wife Morphia. However, she gave him only daughters—romantic, willful and wayward princesses who trail incongruously (all but the youngest) through the blood and iron of those battling decades in the Holy Land: Melisende, Alice, Hodierna, and Joveta. Along with obtaining a rule for his new order, Master Hugh Payens of the Templars had been directed by Baldwin II to find a good solid husband for Melisende, his heir. Master Hugh's choice was Count Fulk of Anjou, who married Princess Melisende in May 1129, though she made it quite clear that he would not have been her choice. Meanwhile her sister Alice had already been married to Bohemond II of Antioch, son and heir of the mighty Bohemond of the First Crusade.[7]

The election of Pope Honorius II to succeed Calixtus II in December 1124 had been tumultuous, foreshadowing the disastrous division that was to follow Honorius' death in 1130. The rival Roman parties of Pierleoni and Frangipani clashed, the former nominating Cardinal Theobald Buccapecu and the latter Cardinal Lambert, in circumstances so confused that Cardinal Lambert, proclaimed Honorius II, declared his own election invalid, resigned, and demanded another one, in which he was acclaimed unanimously by the Cardinals. But this was still only eight days after Calixtus' death, and Pope Honorius was not further challenged.[8]

Only a few months later, in May 1125, came the sudden, unexpected, and generally unlamented death of Emperor Henry V, only 44 years old, without issue. On his deathbed he nominated his nephew Duke Frederick of Swabia as his successor; but Henry V's dynasty was no longer popular in Germany, and Church leaders no longer trusted it despite the Concordat of Worms. Under

---

[6]Steven Runciman, *A History of the Crusades*, Volume II: "The Kingdom of Jerusalem and the Frankish East, 1100-1187" (Cambridge, England, 1952), pp. 162, 166-171; Kenneth M. Setton, ed., *A History of the Crusades*, Volume I: "The First Hundred Years," ed. Marshall W. Baldwin (Madison WI, 1969), pp. 419, 421-422.

[7]Runciman, *Crusades*, II, 163-164, 177-178; Setton, *Crusades*, I, 428.

[8]Mann, *Popes in the Middle Ages*, IX, 232-233.

the skillful guidance of Archbishop Adalbert of Mainz the electoral assembly of forty—ten each from the principal German states of Bavaria, Swabia, Franconia, and Saxony—rejected Duke Frederick and elected Duke Lothair of Saxony, fifty years old and without a male heir, thus being unlikely to establish a dynasty of his own. On September 13 he was crowned at Aachen as Emperor Lothair II. He was known as a friend of the Church who would do his duty as Holy Roman Emperor, and so by and large he proved to be. The Church gave him full support when Duke Frederick's brother Conrad revolted against him in December 1127; Pope Honorius promptly excommunicated the rebel.[9]

Moving to strengthen further the Church in Germany, Pope Honorius—after formally confirming the Premonstratensian foundations and order in February 1126[10]—ordered the reluctant St. Norbert to abandon his beloved monastery of Prémontré and accept election as Archbishop of Magdeburg in July of that year. The Archbishop of Magdeburg had jurisdiction not only over a turbulent area of central Germany but also over the missionary lands to the east where the ferociously anti-Christian Wends dwelt. Clearly the Pope wanted a man in that critical position upon whom he could absolutely rely, whose holiness would help revive a truly Catholic spirit in Germany. In St. Norbert he saw just such a man.[11]

Pope Honorius II never lost the delicate diplomatic touch he had displayed when negotiating the Concordat of Worms as Cardinal Lambert. When Duke William of Apulia in southern Italy died without issue in July 1127 and the powerful Roger II of Sicily moved to take possession not only of Apulia but also of Salerno, the Pope excommunicated him and formed a league against him; for he knew that Sicily, with its large native population containing more Muslims and persons of Greek blood and speech than Latins, was not reliably Catholic. It represented a growing potential threat in the south at the very moment when the threat in the north, from hostile German emperors, had receded. But when it was clear that Roger was going to prevail, the Pope was reconciled with him, investing him as Duke of Apulia along with recognizing his rule over Sicily and Calabria in August 1128. Still he would not recognize him as king—Roger's great desire.[12]

---

[9]*The Cambridge Medieval History*, ed. J. R. Tanner, C. W. Previté-Orton and Z. N. Brooke, Volume V (Cambridge, England, 1926), pp. 165-166, 334-336, 338; Alfred Haverkamp, *Medieval Germany, 1056-1273* (New York, 1988), pp. 137-138; Mann, *Popes in the Middle Ages*, IX, 240-241.

[10]Mann, *Popes in the Middle Ages*, IX, 243-244; Cornelius Kirkfleet, *History of St. Norbert* (St. Louis, 1916), pp. 212-216.

[11]Mann, *Popes in the Middle Ages*, IX, 208-209, and Volume X (London, 1925), p. 21n; Kirkfleet, *St. Norbert*, pp. 234-237, 241-244, 253.

[12]John J. Norwich, *The Other Conquest* (New York, 1967), pp. 307-322; John J. Norwich, *The Kingdom in the Sun, 1130-1194* (New York, 1970), pp. 3-5; Mann, *Popes in the Middle Ages*, IX, 252-256.

During the last half of the year 1129 we hear of almost no activity by Pope Honorius II; it appears that his health was rapidly failing. His chancellor Haimeric—the friend and confidant of St. Bernard—and his other trusted advisors had ample warning that another Papal election would soon be required, and knew that the severe disturbances that had accompanied Honorius' own election were likely to be even worse the next time.[13] The Pierleoni and the Frangipani hated each other more than ever; neither would accept a candidate supported by the other. And Cardinal Peter Pierleoni—head of an extensive family descended from a Roman Jew converted to Christianity eighty years before by Pope St. Leo IX—had decided that now was the time to strike for the Papacy and would settle for nothing less than his own election, regardless of the consequences. Pierleoni had been a monk at Cluny before being recalled to Rome to be made a Cardinal by Pope Paschal II. Peter the Venerable, the Abbot of Cluny, though universally known for gentleness and charity, declared that he was marked by "ambition, cupidity, sacrilege, simony, perjury . . . and yet worse."[14]

The battle over this fateful Papal succession was fought essentially by two men: Pierleoni and Haimeric. Pierleoni was resolved to make himself Pope; Haimeric was resolved he should not be Pope. Each marshalled his resources and planned his political tactics. Each held what was in essence his own Papal election—Pierleoni for himself, Haimeric for Cardinal Gregory of St. Angelo. Which was valid?

Like so many Papal succession controversies, this one was bedevilled then and has been ever since by the failure of contemporary commentators and later historians fully to grasp the unique characteristics of Papal power—the only power on earth not subject to *any* check, control, or veto from *any* source. Since that power belongs equally to every Pope, and applies to arrangements for Papal succession as well as to any other matter lying within the Pope's jurisdiction as head of the Church, canon law *does not bind* a Pope arranging for his succession. If he makes no changes in the existing procedures for choosing his successor, then those existing procedures govern; but he can change them in any way he wishes, up to the very moment of his death, and any changes he makes are just as authoritative as the procedures previously in effect. The electors, on the other hand—since 1061, the College of Cardinals—*cannot* change the procedures, for they have no authority to do so; they are bound by the will of the preceding Pope, or the last Pope to prescribe rules for a Papal election.[15]

---

[13]Mann, *Popes in the Middle Ages*, IX, 303.

[14]Williams, *St. Bernard*, pp. 98-99.

[15]To take a modern example, Pope Paul VI changed the procedures for eligibility to vote in conclave so as to deprive all cardinals over 80 years of age of the vote. That limitation will stand unless and until some future Pope changes it; but any future Pope

In determining the validity of the hotly disputed Papal election of a successor to Honorius II in February 1130, therefore, the most critical question was one that few then or since have asked: what did Pope Honorius know about the changes in the election procedures that Chancellor Haimeric worked out, and did he approve them? It is on that question we must focus to conclude who was the valid Pope.

We have several accounts of this disputed election, and despite varying biases and the inevitable confusion created by such fast-moving and turbulent events, the story that emerges is reasonably clear as far as it goes. On Tuesday, February 11, when it was clear that Pope Honorius was dying, Chancellor Haimeric assembled the cardinals at the monastery of St. Andrew the Apostle. Most of the cardinals appear to have participated in this meeting, which was not difficult for them despite the short notice because all cardinals then resided in Rome. Haimeric proposed that to avoid a disputed election and to act quickly when the Pope should die, a commission of eight cardinals should be selected to choose the next Pope. The eight chosen were two Cardinal Bishops—William of Palestrina and Conrad of Sabina; three Cardinal Priests, all named Peter—Peter Pierleoni, Peter of Pisa, and Peter the Red; and three Cardinal Deacons—Gregory of St. Angelo, Jonathan, and Haimeric himself. All agreed that anyone opposing the choice of this commission would be anathematized; Pierleoni specifically agreed to this, saying "he would rather be drowned than that scandal should arise on his account."[16]

But Pope Honorius was still alive; did this new electoral procedure have his assent? For the cardinals probably had no authority to make a procedural change of this importance in any case, and certainly no authority to make it while the Pope was still alive, unless he approved. There is every reason to believe he did approve it, though we do not have positive proof. Haimeric was, and had long been, his closest advisor. We know that the dying Pope was still conscious, for two days later he was induced to show himself at a window to disprove rumors that he was already dead.[17] Furthermore, two contemporary accounts refer to a designation of Cardinal Gregory as Pope by Honorius while

---

has the authority to make such a change, and no one can override his decision—any more than Pope Paul VI's removal of the vote from cardinals past 80 could be "appealed" or overridden.

[16]Williams, *St. Bernard*, pp. 100-101; Bruno Scott James, *St. Bernard of Clairvaux* (New York, 1957), p. 100. The presence of Cardinal Priests and Cardinal Deacons making up a majority of the special electoral commission is fully sufficient evidence to prove that the question of whether cardinals of all three classes—bishops, priests, and deacons—had a vote in the election of a Pope, previously debated on the basis of varying interpretations and manuscript versions of Pope Nicholas II's decree *In Nomine Domini* which had created the College of Cardinals in 1061, played no significant part in this otherwise much disputed election. Clearly everyone assumed that all cardinals' votes were equal.

[17]Mann, *Popes in the Middle Ages*, X, 8.

he was still alive, one referring to it as a "dispensation," the other as a "right conferred upon him by Pope Honorius."[18] A Pope does have the power to designate his successor specifically and individually, without any sort of electoral procedure; precisely this had been done at least once in Papal history, by Pope Felix III in 530.[19] However, subsequent events suggest that these two sources have confused the desire of Pope Honorius II for Gregory to be his successor and his plans to bring that about, with his actual investiture as Pope which came so quickly after Honorius' death. The important fact here is not so much when Gregory was invested as the testimony of these sources to Honorius' desire to have him elected—strong evidence that the Pope endorsed what Haimeric was doing, including the establishment of the electoral commission.

Pope Honorius II died during the night of February 13-14.[20] Early in the morning of Friday the 14th Haimeric again summoned the cardinals to St. Andrew's, but without telling them of the Pope's death until they had arrived. Though a total of 19 cardinals were present, only members of the previously designated electoral commission voted on the next Pope. Pierleoni and Cardinal Jonathan, a supporter of his, did not come. Cardinals William of Palestrina, Conrad of Sabina, Peter the Red, and Haimeric all voted for Cardinal Gregory of St. Angelo (also a member of the commission)—in all probability Pope Honorius' choice, as we have seen—who reluctantly accepted, this consequently counting as a vote for himself. Peter of Pisa voted against the entire proceeding. Five of the eight members of the electoral commission—a bare majority—had therefore agreed to the election of Gregory, who took the name of Innocent II. He went, with the body of Honorius, to the Lateran basilica, and was then invested with the Papal insignia at the Palladium monastery on the Palatine hill.[21]

Pierleoni then gathered his supporters at noon that same day in the Church of St. Mark, where conflicting evidence states that at some point the cardinals had agreed to meet for the Papal election. (The location of the election, however, clearly did not affect its validity.) A letter written, possibly by a Pierleoni partisan, to Bishop Diego Gelmírez of Santiago de Compostela declares that 24 cardinals were present at St. Mark's, and that they unanimously elected Pierleoni, who took the name Anacletus II.[22] Other evidence, however,

---

[18]Williams, *St. Bernard*, p. 99. The two sources are the Chronicle of Maurigny and Anselm of Gembloux.

[19]See Volume II, Chapter 6 of this history.

[20]Williams, *St. Bernard*, p. 96.

[21]*Ibid.*, pp. 101-102; Mann, *Popes in the Middle Ages*, X, 8-10; James, *St. Bernard*, pp. 101-102.

[22]In accordance with the uniform practice in these volumes regarding Antipopes, Pierleoni will be identified only by his own name. Though a surprising number of histories do not do this, or at least not consistently, it is the only way to avoid complete confusion regarding Papal numbers, since the list of true Popes (with a very few

shows that these cardinals were only part of a large crowd which included many clergymen who were not cardinals, and also numerous laymen. No enclosure was attempted; there was no meaningful discussion; the accounts we have imply that the cardinals voted *viva voce*. In light of these facts, the alleged presence of a larger number of cardinals at St. Mark's than at St. Andrew's signifies little, even if the establishment of the electoral commission and the priority of the vote for Innocent II are disregarded.[23]

Pierleoni proceeded at once to rally his armed forces. Though repulsed by the Frangipani from their quarter of Rome, where they were defending Pope Innocent II, he took possession of St. Peter's, seizing some of its treasures—including a golden crucifix—and plundering other churches as well. On February 23 Pope and Antipope were consecrated on the same day. Both wrote letters to Emperor Lothair II asking for his support. In March they excommunicated each other. But Pierleoni had so much strength in Rome that Innocent did not dare remain there. He left Rome in May, going first to Pisa, then to France.[24]

Now Christendom had to choose between the two Papal contenders. At the Council of Étampes in France, convened by request of King Louis VI probably late that summer to consider the two claimants, St. Bernard of Clairvaux announced his choice, which he later explained in his incandescent, inimitable style in a letter to the bishops of Aquitaine:

> Who else can he be but that man of sin who, notwithstanding that a Catholic had been canonically elected [Pope] by Catholics, invaded the holy place, not because it was a holy place but because it was the highest place. He invaded it, I say, and he invaded it with arms, with fire, and with bribes, not by the merits and virtues of his life. And he has arrived there, and he stands there, by the same means that brought him there. The election of his supporters of which he makes so much was not an election but a faction, a mere shadow and excuse, a cover for his malice. It could be called an election of a sort, but to do so were an impudent lie. The authentic decree of the Church still holds: after one election there cannot be a second. When the first election has taken place, a second one is no election at all, it is completely null. Even if the first election did take place with less solemnity and order than the second, as the enemies of unity contend, how can anyone have presumed to hold a second without first discussing the manner of the former and suppressing it by judgement?[25]

To the formidable advocacy of St. Bernard the gentler but almost equally

---

exceptions due to clerical errors) does not reflect the numbers of Antipopes, so that an antipapal name and number can be—and in several cases is—identical with a true papal name and number.

[23]Mann, *Popes of the Middle Ages*, X, 9-12; Williams, *St. Bernard*, pp. 99-100, 102.
[24]Mann, *Popes in the Middle Ages*, X, 15-17; Williams, *St. Bernard*, pp. 102-104.
[25]St. Bernard to the bishops of Aquitaine, *Letters of St. Bernard*, tr. James, p. 195.

respected Peter the Venerable, Abbot of Cluny, added his unqualified endorsement and support for Innocent II, inviting him to come to his world-famous monastery, where on October 25 he dedicated the splendid new abbey church to replace the structure destroyed five years previously when the nave collapsed. Shortly before the dedication, news arrived of the first major political victory for the Antipope. On September 27, Roger II of Sicily had agreed to recognize Pierleoni as Pope in return for his recognition as King rather than merely Duke of Sicily; on Christmas day the Antipope crowned him. But in Germany, during October, a synod of bishops in Würzburg, guided by St. Norbert, declared for Innocent in the presence of Emperor Lothair, who at once endorsed their recommendation.[26]

Of the heartland of Europe, there remained England—with its extensive dominions in France inherited from William the Conqueror—to gain for Pope Innocent II. King Henry I, youngest son of the Conqueror, was 63 years old, still desolated by the loss of his only son in the White Ship disaster ten years before, disinclined to take sides. Pierleoni had been a Papal legate to England and was popular among the English bishops, who knew little or nothing of what had happened in Rome in February and urged Henry to endorse him. While Pope Innocent was at Chartres, probably about the end of the year, St. Bernard went into the Norman territories of Henry I to meet with him personally. The King pleaded conscientious scruple; he was not sure who the rightful Pope was, and feared he would sin if he committed himself without being sure. The answer he received was one only St. Bernard of Clairvaux could have given:

> Are you afraid of sinning by obeying Innocent? Just consider for how many other sins you have to answer to God! Leave this one to me; I will answer for it.[27]

There was nothing in Henry I of England that could hold out against this. In the only bold and striking action of the last fifteen years of his reign, he overrode the recommendation of his bishops, went to Chartres, and on January 13, 1131 prostrated himself at the feet of Pope Innocent II, pledging that he and his kingdom would be unfailingly loyal to him.[28]

In March St. Bernard made his way to Liège in Belgium, where a synod of the empire was meeting, attended by 25 archbishops and bishops, 53 abbots, numerous nobles, and Emperor Lothair himself. The blazing spirit of St. Bernard dominated this august assembly like a tournament champion. The Pope arrived on March 22, the third Sunday in Lent; the Emperor met him with

---

[26]Mann, *Popes in the Middle Ages*, X, 19, 21-22, 32-33; Norwich, *Other Conquest*, pp. 328-331; Williams, *St. Bernard*, pp. 108-109; *Cambridge Medieval History* V, 342.
[27]Williams, *St. Bernard*, p. 109.
[28]Mann, *Popes in the Middle Ages*, X, 20-21.

the traditional act of homage and offer of protection going back to Charlemagne, taking the bridle of the Pope's horse and walking before it at the head of the welcoming procession, while carrying the imperial staff in his free hand. The assembly committed the forces of the Empire to a major campaign into Italy the next year to install the true Pope in Rome.[29] But when Lothair let it be known that he intended to restore the practice of lay investiture of German bishops with ring and staff, St. Bernard, in the words of his contemporary biographer, "opposed himself like a wall. Boldly resisting the king, with surprising freedom he rebuked him for his spiteful suggestion and by his amazing authority restrained him from his purpose."[30] As even secular historians admit, no more was heard of any defiance of the Church on this or other ecclesiastical issues during the remainder of Emperor Lothair's reign.[31] On March 29 the Pope crowned him Emperor, and returned to France to be magnificently honored by Abbot Suger at Easter Mass in the royal abbey of St. Denis. That summer Pope Innocent visited St. Bernard at Clairvaux.[32]

The Pope called an international council to meet at Reims in October, summoning bishops from Germany and the Empire, Normandy, England, and Spain as well as France. About fifty bishops responded to his call, along with more than 300 abbots. Both St. Norbert and St. Bernard were present, with St. Bernard acting as the Pope's closest advisor, conferring with him in private as well as at meetings of the cardinals. (Again we see St. Bernard dominating a great assembly full of persons holding far more exalted offices than he, by the sheer force of his holiness and character.) In documents issued during and after the council which the two saints had requested, the Pope made a special point of thanking them for all they had done for him and for the Church, and he made a visit to Prémontré. The council of Reims reaffirmed Church laws requiring priestly celibacy and condemning simony and violence by clerics. The council also confirmed and reiterated the excommunications of both the Antipope and Conrad, the imperial rebel against Lothair. Letters of fealty to Pope Innocent II were received and read from Kings Henry I of England, Alfonso I "the Battler" of Aragon, and Alfonso VII of Castile (the two Spanish kings, characteristically, did not fail to add a request for Papal help in their perpetual crusade against the Moors). At this council Louis VI of France asked the Pope to crown his son and namesake as his heir, since his elder son Philip had just died tragically in a riding accident. It is the first apperance in history of the future Louis VII, then only nine years old, who was to reign over "the eldest daughter of the Church" for 43 eventful years.[33]

[29] *Ibid.*, X, 22-23.
[30] Williams, *St. Bernard*, p. 110.
[31] *Cambridge Medieval History*, V, 342-343.
[32] Mann, *Popes in the Middle Ages*, X, 23-24; Williams, *St. Bernard*, pp. 110-111..
[33] Mann, *Popes in the Middle Ages*, X, 25-28; Williams, *St. Bernard*, pp. 111-112;

Passing Christmas of 1131 again at Cluny, the Pope received a letter of fealty from William of Messines, installed the previous year as Patriarch of Jerusalem.[34] That humble and saintly bishop was seeing plenty of trouble near at hand: the heroic King Baldwin II of Jerusalem had died in August, his daughter Melisende succeeding him with her husband Fulk of Anjou as king, but within a year she was involved head over heels in a scandalous affair with her young, handsome married cousin Hugh of Le Puiset, who eventually ducked a challenge to a duel and fled to Muslim Egypt. The result was to draw the army of Jerusalem in the direction of Egypt while on their other flank the Muslims of Damascas secured the important fortress of Banyas on high ground overlooking the Sea of Galilee. Meanwhile Melisende's recently widowed sister Alice in Antioch had asked the dangerous Muslim leader Zengi for help against her enemies within that city; her treasonable correspondence was intercepted, and her father Baldwin II had to remove her as regent in Antioch for her two-year-old daughter Constance and take over the regency himself. When he died she demanded it back, and King Fulk was forced to march to Antioch with an army and fight a battle to establish his rights there.[35] When that stout-hearted Angevin came to the Holy Land in 1129 to defend the Holy Sepulcher, he had undoubtedly not expected to have to spend so much time and effort reining in Melisende and Alice; nor did these antics augur well for the future of the Crusader kingdoms. They were to bear bitter fruit in the failure of the Second Crusade.

In the course of the year 1132 reports came to the Pope and St. Bernard that Duke William of Aquitaine, the richest and most powerful nobleman in France outside the family of William the Conqueror, was leaning away from Pope Innocent II and toward the Antipope due to the pressure and persuasion of Bishop Gerard of Angoulême. Gerard had hoped to be named Papal legate for Aquitaine; when Innocent did not appoint him, he adhered to the Antipope and got his nomination as legate. In his letter to the bishops of Aquitaine, quoted earlier, St. Bernard shredded Gerard in one of his masterpieces of denunciation:

> Where does he get this privilege? Who gave him this prerogative?
> Does he possess the sanctuary of God by inheritance? Why does he accuse
> Pope Innocent of being in schism? He was his "Holy Father" so long as
> there was the slightest chance of securing from him the favour he had the
> effrontery to ask for. His papal dignity and holiness vanished at the same
> time as his vain hope for the legateship. How wonderful that in so short a

---

Kirkfleet, *St. Norbert*, pp. 304-307.

[34]He mentions receipt of this letter, along with a similar letter from the Bishop of Bethlehem, in a letter to Louis VI of France dated February 2, 1132 (Williams, *St. Bernard*, p. 113).

[35]Runciman, *Crusades*, II, 177, 183-192.

time sweet and bitter waters could flow from the same source! Yesterday Pope Innocent was holy and Catholic and the supreme Pontiff, but today he is a wicked and schismatic disturber of the peace! Yesterday he was Holy Father Pope Innocent, but today he is simply Gregory, Cardinal Deacon of Sant' Angelo! So from a double heart out of one mouth come two contradictory statements.[36]

Yet Gerard, though rejected by the majority in southern France and excommunicated, clung to power in Bordeaux whose see he had usurped, and continued to exercise substantial influence on Duke William of Aquitaine—never noted for constancy in thought or action, traits which were also to be manifested by his famous daughter Eleanor. Eventually the Duke too was excommunicated. In the fall of 1134 St. Bernard went to Aquitaine. At first Duke William refused to meet with him, not even at the gates of his own castle at Parthenay. St. Bernard proceeded to say Mass in the Church of Notre Dame de la Couldre outside these gates, which served as the castle chapel. An enormous crowd assembled. The Duke could not stay away. He followed the crowd to the door of the church, which as an excommunicate he was not allowed to enter.[37] Inside, St. Bernard proceeded through the liturgy and the consecration to the kiss of peace. He then placed the Host upon the paten and carried it from the sanctuary down the center aisle and out to the door, presenting it to the Duke, and saying:

> We have petitioned you and you have spurned us; in the recent council the servants of God at your footstool you have treated with contempt. Lo, here has come forth to you the Virgin's Son, the head and lord of that Church which you persecute. Your Judge is present, in Whose name every knee in heaven, on earth, and below the earth is bowed. Do you spurn Him? Do you treat Him with the contempt with which you treat His servants?[38]

William fell to the ground, foaming at the mouth. St. Bernard came nearer, touched him, and called upon him to rise.

> The Bishop of Poitiers, whom you drove from his church, is here. Go and be reconciled to him. Pledge yourself to him in the kiss of peace and restore him to his see. Then, making satisfaction to God, render to him glory for contempt. Throughout your dominions recall the divided and discordant to the unity of love. Submit to Innocent as Pope; and even as every church obeys him, so do you obey so great a pontiff, God's elect.[39]

---

[36]*Letters of St. Bernard*, tr. James, pp. 192-193.
[37]Williams, *St. Bernard*, pp. 131-132.
[38]*Ibid.*, pp. 132-133.
[39]*Ibid.*, p. 133.

No whisper of support for the Antipope was heard again in southern France, and Duke William's conversion was permanent. The next year he endowed a Cistercian monastery, a daughter of Clairvaux, in the diocese of Saintes in Aquitaine; on Good Friday 1137 he died on pilgrimage to Santiago de Compostela.[40]

Assembling armies in Germany for service in Italy was always a long slow process. Despite the confident plans made at Liège in March 1131, by September 1132 when Emperor Lothair finally arrived in Italy he had only 2,000 men with him. Antipope Pierleoni still held firm possession of Rome and continued to be strongly supported by Roger of Sicily, though Roger was hampered by a revolt of many of the feudal nobles of south Italy. A larger imperial army would be required to risk a campaign south of the Apennines, and strong naval support from some of the Italian cities. In the winter of 1133 St. Bernard went to Genoa and Pisa, made peace between them, and gained their commitment to the cause of Pope Innocent; this was the occasion to which he referred in his letter to the people of Genoa quoted at the head of this chapter. With their help, and some reinforcements from Germany, Emperor Lothair marched to Rome in the spring of 1133, but Pierleoni held out in a fortified quarter of the city strongly defended by his partisans, and the still inadequate imperial army was unable to dislodge him. When the Emperor left for Germany, in that hot and pestilential month of August which had been the graveyard for so many German soldiers in Rome, Pope Innocent could not maintain himself there and had to retire to Pisa, where he remained for the next three and a half years.[41]

In November 1134 Pope Innocent II called for a council to meet at Pisa the next May,[42] seeking once again to rouse enough support, particularly in Italy, to make possible the expulsion of the Antipope from Rome; for as the true Pope Innocent could never believe it right that he should remain outside the city of Peter. Louis VI of France at first demurred on the frivolous ground that Pisa was too hot, to which St. Bernard shot back: "You say the heat will be too great. We are not made of ice! Or is it that our hearts are frozen within us, so that, in the words of the Prophet, 'there is none who care for the ruin of Joseph?'"[43]

The council was held as scheduled, with St. Bernard attending. Its main

---

[40]*Ibid.*

[41]Mann, *Popes in the Middle Ages*, X, 34-35, 38, 42; William, *St. Bernard*, pp. 119-124; Norwich, *Kingdom in the Sun*, pp. 24-27. It should be noted that Norwich, though he gives a brilliantly written account of this period in Italian history based on excellent research, is strongly biased against St. Bernard and to a considerable degree against the Catholic Church as a whole. Nevertheless, at points his masterly narrative remains valuable for the Catholic historian.

[42]Williams, *St. Bernard*, pp. 137, 139.

[43]*Letters of St. Bernard*, tr. James, p. 203.

achievement was to detach Milan, the last substantial Italian state north of Roger's domain to uphold the Antipope, from the Pierleoni cause. Archbishop Anselm of Milan, a supporter of Pierleoni, fled. After the council at Pisa St. Bernard went to Milan with two cardinals and the Bishop of Chartres, to explain to its people what they must do and why. They received him rapturously. "All alike were delighted to gaze upon him," his contemporary biographer tells us; "they who could hear his voice accounted themselves most fortunate."[44] Miracles happened in his presence and at his touch; but, the biographer goes on: "He never exalted himself, he never strutted proudly in the midst of his wonders but, thinking humbly of himself, he believed himself to be not the author but the agent of the venerable works which he wrought; and although he stood supreme in the judgement of all men, in his own judgement he stood very low indeed."[45] The Church and people in Milan reaffirmed their loyalty to the true Pope and the true Emperor, rejecting Pierleoni and Conrad whom they had previously acclaimed. They even stripped their churches of some of their costly ornamentation to show their determination to reform in the spirit of St. Bernard. Robald of Alba was made their new archbishop, and St. Bernard kept closely in touch with the leaders and people of the great north Italian city until he was sure its loyalty to the true Pope was secure.[46]

In that year of 1135 the two great rebels against Emperor Lothair II in Germany—the brothers Frederick and Conrad Hohenstaufen of Swabia—made their submission to him on very favorable terms. They were freed from excommunication, receiving back all the possessions of which they had been deprived as rebels, and were required only to accompany the Emperor on a new campaign in Italy on behalf of Pope Innocent which he had pledged to undertake the following year. St. Bernard came to Germany to help arrange this settlement, and is primarily to be credited with its attainment.[47]

Even Byzantine Emperor John II Comnenus promised help to Lothair for his upcoming campaign in Italy, since the only remaining military supporter of the Antipope, Roger of Sicily, was also a great enemy of the Byzantine Empire. The German imperial army arrived in Italy in September 1136. At Bologna in February 1137, Lothair sent a column under his son-in-law Duke Henry of Bavaria toward Rome while leading the rest of the army along the Adriatic coast. The campaign was prolonged and Roger fought hard in southern Italy, but Pope Innocent II was at last established permanently in Rome. In December the hard-pressed Roger agreed to hear formal arguments on who was the true Pope, with St. Bernard the advocate for Innocent, and Cardinal Peter of Pisa, one of the three members of the original electoral commission of

---

[44]Williams, *St. Bernard*, p. 140.
[45]*Ibid.*, p. 141.
[46]*Ibid.*, pp. 141-145; James, *St. Bernard*, p. 121.
[47]*Cambridge Medieval History*, V, 340-341.

cardinals who had voted for Pierleoni nearly eight years before, speaking for the Antipope.[48]

St. Bernard rose. It is hard to say what was this holy man's finest hour—he had so many which were so fine—but it may well have been here:

> There is one Lord, one baptism, and one faith; we know nothing of two lords, a double baptism, or two faiths. Everyone agrees that the ark which Noah built at the time of the flood to save the lives of eight people is a type of the Church. Lately another ark has been built and of these two arks one must be fraudulent and destined to sink. If the ark of which Peter Leon is captain is the true ark of God, then it follows that the ark of Innocent is doomed and with it the whole Church, all the people of France, Germany, Spain, and England; all the monks of Camaldoli, the Chartreuse, Grandmont, Cluny, and Cîteaux and the canons of Prémontré together with countless other religious orders of men and women; all these are sitting and, as it were with millstones round their necks, doomed to be swallowed up in the depths. Can we believe that Count Roger here of all the princes of the earth is the only one who will be saved, all the others being in the ark of Innocent? God forbid that the world should perish so that Peter Leon, with whose life and manners we are all too familiar, should alone be saved.
>
> Towards the end of this discourse Peter of Pisa rose slowly to his feet and came over to Bernard, who clasped him by the hand with the words, "Welcome, Peter, to the safer ark." All those present were profoundly moved with the exception of Roger, who declared that the matter was beyond him and that he could not understand it.[49]

No one else had Roger's problem. St. Bernard's spectacular conversion of Cardinal Peter, one of the original promoters of the schism, for all practical purposes marked its end. The next month Pierleoni died. From March to May 1138 Cardinal Gregory tried feebly to carry on his cause as Pope "Victor IV," but then he gave it up, coming by night to St. Bernard to ask what he should do. The great Cistercian led him by the hand to the Pope for submission and forgiveness. The long schism was over.[50]

Roger of Sicily remained recalcitrant, and in 1139 fought another war with the Pope in which Innocent was captured; but the Pope made peace with him by confirming Roger's royal title in return for his recognition of Innocent's Papal authority.[51] Meanwhile Emperor Lothair II, worn out by his hard campaigning in Italy, had died crossing the Alps on his way home, and had been succeeded by his erstwhile foe Conrad of Hohenstaufen, as

---

[48]Norwich, *Kingdom in the Sun*, pp. 39-51, 57-60; Williams, *St. Bernard*, pp. 148, 152-153; Mann, *Popes in the Middle Ages*, X, 8-9, 53-54.

[49]James, *St. Bernard*, pp. 124-125.

[50]Mann, *Popes in the Middle Ages*, X, 55-56; Williams, *St. Bernard*, pp. 153-155; Norwich, *Kingdom in the Sun*, pp. 64-65.

[51]Mann, *Popes in the Middle Ages*, X, 63-66; Norwich, *Kingdom in the Sun*, pp. 67-69.

Emperor Conrad III.[52]

Pope Innocent II did not prove altogether merciful in victory. At the Lateran Council in April 1139 he deprived of their offices many who had supported the Antipope but had later been reconciled with the true Pope, including Cardinal Peter of Pisa.[53] On his behalf in particular, St. Bernard delivered to his leader a measured rebuke. No man, no hero or saint could have been more loyal to a Pope than St. Bernard had been to Innocent. He did not forget, and in his words clearly avowed, the supreme and sovereign power of the Vicar of Christ. But St. Bernard knew that even Popes may sin, that they may judge wrongly in individual cases, that at need Peter may justly be rebuked by Paul:

> If I had a judge before whom I could bring you, I would soon show you (I speak as one in travail) what you deserve. There is the tribunal of Christ, but God forbid that I should summon you before that; far sooner would I stand up and defend you there, should such a thing be necessary for you or possible for me. And so I hasten to him whose duty it is in the present time to judge all things, and that is yourself. I arraign you against yourself, to judge between yourself and myself. . . . Were you not pleased to appoint me as your representative for the reconciliation of Peter of Pisa, should God deign through me to call him from the foul condition of schism? . . . And after this was not the man received back to his position and honours according to your plighted word?[54]

The growth of daughter monasteries of Clairvaux reflected the rapidly spreading fame of Clairvaux's abbot. Before the Pierleoni schism there were only six, all in France; by the time the schism ended there were 22 more, in England, Germany, Italy, Spain, and Portugal in addition to France.[55]

The first daughter monastery of Clairvaux in Spain was established in 1132 at Moreruela near León by young King Alfonso VII of Castile and León, who had supported Pope Innocent II almost from the beginning, apparently without needing strong persuasion by St. Bernard.[56] Equally firm in Pope Innocent's support had been young Alfonso's redoubtable cousin and erstwhile unwilling father-in-law (because of a marriage with Queen Urraca of Castile never approved by the Church), Alfonso I "the Battler" of Aragon. It will be recalled that in his letter pledging support to Pope Innocent, the Battler included a request for help in his unending combat against the Moors. That combat was the lodestar of his life, from which he always turned reluctantly, and

---

[52]*Cambridge Medieval History*, V, 345-346; Haverkamp, *Medieval Germany*, p. 141.
[53]Mann, *Popes in the Middle Ages*, X, 59-60.
[54]*Letters of St. Bernard*, tr. James, p. 354.
[55]Williams, *St. Bernard*, pp. 94-95. The foundations from Clairvaux in England, Ireland and Scandinavia will be further discussed later in this chapter.
[56]*Ibid.*, p. 90.

never for long. In all the history of its 770-year war of liberation, since Pelayo and Alfonso II the Chaste in its early years of almost superhuman heroism, Spain never knew a king so totally dedicated to the Reconquest as Alfonso the Battler.

His father had died in battle against the Moors under the walls of Huesca; when he succeeded his brother as king of Aragon in 1104 that kingdom was little more than a pocket state in the foothills of the central Pyrenees. He had built it into a power in Spain, reconquering from the Moors the great city of Zaragoza on the Ebro River.[57] But the ancient enemy still held the river's mouth and much of its lower course, and the green banners with the Prophet's crescent still flew up the rich valley of the Segre northward to Lérida and Fraga. It was Islam's northernmost extension in Europe, the counterweight to all that Castile had accomplished in the reconquest of central Spain south to Toledo. In the year 1126, when the feckless Queen Urraca died and her untried 21-year-old son Alfonso VII took the throne of Castile and León,[58] Alfonso the Battler was 53 years old, veteran of a hundred engagements, the greatest warrior in Spain and probably in all Christendom. And in that year he launched an enterprise unique in the history of the Reconquest between Pelayo and Isabel.

Responding to an appeal of the Christians of Granada far to the southward to come and liberate them, Alfonso the Battler set out with 4,000 horse and 15,000 foot to do just that, though it required a march through the greater part of Muslim-occupied Spain, penetrating regions where no Christian soldier had set foot for more than four hundred years. He marched through Moor-held Valencia, calling on local Christians to join him, and many did; there all the men of his army took oath with him never to abandon one another. He had previously secured Peña Cadiella Pass south of Valencia; through that they pushed to Murcia, then on past Baza to lay siege to Guadix, where he passed Christmas, and more Christians joined him. He could not take Guadix; 363 years later Fernando and Isabel, the Catholic kings, at the height of their power were to need a full punishing year to take it with the aid of cannon and gunpowder, of which no one in Alfonso the Battler's time had yet dreamed. But his army had now grown to 50,000, and with it he swept down on mountain-crowned Granada and on January 7, 1127 camped beneath its ochre walls.[59] The red-gold banners of Christian Spain were not to fly there again until Fernando and Isabel brought them to their camp of the Holy Faith in 1490.

Heavy rains came; Alfonso the Battler found it almost impossible to supply so large an army so far into enemy country, and he had no siege

---

[57]See Chapter One, above.

[58]Bernard F. Reilly, *The Kingdom of León-Castilla under Queen Urraca, 1109-1126* (Princeton, 1982), pp. 200-201; Manuel Recuero Astray, *Alfonso VII, Emperador* (León, 1979), p. 73.

[59]José María Lacarra, *Alfonso el Batallador* (Zaragoza, 1978), pp. 87-89.

machines. But the Moors were divided, and in any case had no force to match his in the open field. During the winter of 1127 he marched back and forth across Andalusia, winning a great battle March 10 at a bridge over the Genil River near Lucena, reaching the coast at Vélez-Málaga, and finding allies both Christian and Muslim at Córdoba, once the capital of all Moorish Spain, and Sevilla. When he finally had to retreat in May, he took no less than ten thousand Christian civilians from the Granada region with him—men, women, and children—and brought them all back under his protection to Aragon.[60]

Alfonso the Battler had rescued his people, and let the Moors know that henceforth no corner of Spain would be safe from him and those who would follow him. Just six years later, supported as the Battler had been by local Christians and Muslim dissidents, Alfonso VII of Castile made a raid all the way to Cádiz almost at the southern tip of Spain.[61]

The next month a formal peace agreement, the Pact of Támara, was made between the namesake monarchs of Aragon and Castile, Alfonso the Battler and Alfonso VII, ending the sporadic but ugly conflict that had begun with the resistance to the Battler's attempt to rule Castile when he was married to Urraca. In 1128 the Battler reconquered Molina on the Ebro; the next year he laid seige to Valencia and, though unable to take it, defeated a Muslim army at Cullera nearby, inflicting no less than 12,000 casualties (killed, wounded, and prisoners) according to Moorish sources, despite strong numerical odds in their favor.[62]

Except for his illicit and ill-fated union with Urraca, Alfonso the Battler had never been married; he had no children, by her or so far as is known by any other woman. Now 58, he had no intention of changing his way of life again. His one surviving brother was a monk. In September 1131 he announced his will: he would leave his kingdom of Aragon (most of which he had conquered himself from the infidel) to the three new crusading military orders recently formed in the Holy Land: the Templars, the Knights of St. John of the Hospital, and the Knights of the Holy Sepulcher. His horse and arms he left specifically to the Templars. The leaders of his army were required to swear a solemn oath to uphold this unprecedented bequest.[63]

At the end of the next year he laid siege to Fraga, the enemy's farthest advanced salient, pointed like an arrow at the original mountain home of Aragon. Several noblemen came with their knights from southern France to his aid. The leaders of the army, French and Spanish alike, swore on holy relics to maintain the siege until the city was taken, no matter how long it might be. All through 1133 the great siege went on. But Fraga was strongly defended; the

---

[60]*Ibid.*, pp. 89-91; Derek W. Lomax, *The Reconquest of Spain* (London, 1978), p. 85.
[61]Recuero Astray, *Alfonso VII*, pp. 120-121; Lomax, *Reconquest of Spain*, p. 88.
[62]Lacarra, *Alfonso el Batallador*, pp. 95-102; Recuero Astray, *Alfonso VII*, pp. 92-94.
[63]Lacarra, *Alfonso el Batallador*, pp. 107-108.

Battler still lacked siege engines; and his besieging forces made a stationary target. During the winter of 1134 two attempts at relief by the vigorous Moorish governor of Valencia, Ibn Ghaniya, were beaten off. But in the heat of summer, always preferred fighting weather for Moors, Ibn Ghaniya brought up a much larger army. On June 17 he struck, catching the Christians by surprise. All day long a titanic struggle raged. The French Counts of Béarn and Narbonne fell, and the Spanish Bishops of Huesca and Roda; Bishop Guido of Lescar was captured (he was taken to Valencia and tortured to force him to renounce his faith, but he would not) along with a piece of the True Cross; at the end the Battler was penned by flashing scimitars in a turbanned ring with the Prince of Navarra and sixty knights. He and the Prince fought their way out sword in hand, only ten of the knights surviving with them.

The day was lost, and for a brief time the old warrior gave way to an almost berserk fury, wildly attacking Moors loading ships on the Ebro with the heads of his dead soldiers; this apparently gave rise to the later reports in Muslim sources that he became insane. He may well have been wounded and he was very angry, but he certainly had not lost his mind; a few weeks later we find him confirming the Knights of St. John of the Hospital in the possession of gifts he had given then, and nominating new bishops for Huesca and Roda. Then he solemnly confirmed his will, leaving as his last command that the Reconquest should continue until it was completed, however long and hard the road might be. On September 9, 1134 he died at the village of Poleñino a little southeast of Huesca, and was buried in the monastery-castle of Montearagon which he had earlier ordered built "for the honor of all Christendom."[64]

The lay of Rodrigo Diaz de Vivar, El Cid, is the national epic of Spain; but one wonders why there was never a lay of Alfonso the Battler.

There was deep confusion and trouble in Aragon following his heroic death; it did not seem practicable that three military orders based in Jerusalem could really govern the kingdom, though large money payments were eventually made to them in partial honoring of the Battler's bequest. A peculiar sequence of events unfolded, which perhaps it is not fair for anyone at a great distance from that consuming war to judge. While Alfonso VII of Castile protected and kept order in Zaragoza, the Battler's brother Ramiro, a monk, left his monastery with the consent of his abbot and at least the tacit acquiescence of Aragon's bishops, though not with the approval of Pope Innocent. Designated king, Ramiro held the office just long enough to marry Agnes of Poitiers, sister of Duke William of Aquitaine (whom we have already met) and "a widow of proven fecundity." In precisely nine months they had a daughter, Petronilla. Within a year Agnes had entered a convent, Ramiro had returned to his monastery, and Count Ramón Berenguer of Barcelona had "married" the

---

[64]*Ibid.*, pp. 125, 134-137.

infant Petronilla and assumed the guardianship of Aragon and Catalonia, which were thereby united and remained united in the Kingdom of Aragon until the time of Fernando and Isabel the Catholic.[65]

Meanwhile in May 1135 Alfonso VII of Castile and León was proclaimed "emperor" in Spain, apparently as a way of claiming overall responsibility for its defense and the pursuance of the Reconquest in the absence of anyone else to fill the shoes of Alfonso the Battler. The title was never used again, but in this crisis it strengthened the hand of Alfonso VII, especially when he later became the leader of the Second Crusade on the Spanish front.[66]

In 1139, the year after the great Papal schism had at last been ended largely by his efforts, St. Bernard had an unexpected visitor at Clairvaux from a far country: Bishop Malachy O'More of Ireland, on his way to Rome. For fifteen years Malachy had been engaged in tireless efforts to bring the Church in Ireland into conformity with the practices of the Church in the rest of Europe. For two centuries Catholic Ireland had been torn apart by marauding pagan Vikings. Then, because of the tragic death of Brian Boru, his son, his grandson, and his nephew at the Battle of Clontarf in 1014 when the Irish at last inflicted a decisive defeat on the Vikings on their soil, civil war had raged for another century and more after the invasions, doing almost as much damage as they had done. All this conflict and devastation had driven the Irish Church in upon itself, making the great lords the Irish called "kings," the equivalent of the feudal nobility elsewhere, laws unto themselves. They had taken over what remained of the churches and their revenues, installing their own choices as bishops and abbots. Bishops were often subject to abbots. The sacraments of baptism, confirmation, marriage, and ordination were improperly administered—partly due to ignorance, and partly to simple usurpation on the part of the "kings." (They certainly knew, for example, that married laymen had no right to be bishops and abbots, yet eight generations of them had acted as St. Patrick's successors in the see of Armagh.) Bishop Celsus (1105-29) finally gained control of Armagh with a view to reform, and demanded Malachy as his successor; but only after years of struggle was Malachy able to exercise his episcopal office. The Church in Ireland had now reorganized itself and established true dioceses for the first time in centuries, along with archdioceses at Armagh and Cashel; but for these arrangements the Pope's approval was

[65]Recuero Astray, Alfonso VII, pp. 125-126, 152, 154-155; Joseph J. O'Callaghan, A History of Medieval Spain (Ithaca NY, 1975), pp. 222-225; R. A. Fletcher, Saint James's Catapult; the Life and Times of Diego Gelmírez of Santiago de Compostela (Oxford, 1984), pp. 272-273.
[66]Recuero Astray, Alfonso VII, pp. 118, 130-133; O'Callaghan, Medieval Spain, pp. 223-224; Anselm G. Biggs, Diego Gelmírez, First Archbishop of Compostela (Washington, 1949), pp. 315-317.

needed, and that was what St. Malachy was going to Rome to seek.[67]

St. Bernard was so impressed with Bishop Malachy that he took time in the midst of his fantastically busy life to write his biography, full of praise for his holiness and zeal, which later became a prime authority for his canonization. He trained monks at Clairvaux to establish Cistercian monasteries in Ireland to reform monastic life there; in 1142 the first Cistercian abbey in Ireland was founded at Mellifont, and six others soon followed. Pope Innocent II greatly approved of Bishop Malachy, sending him back to Ireland as his legate. In 1148, when much progress had been made in Irish Church reform, a national synod was held at Inispatrick Island near Dublin, which formally requested the *pallium* for the archbishops of Armagh and Cashel. Malachy insisted on going again to Rome to deliver the request. Stopping again at Clairvaux in October 1148, he died there in the odor of sanctity November 2. A little over three years later, a synod of the Irish Church was convened at Kells by the new Papal legate, Cardinal Paparo, which reorganized the Irish church under four archdioceses—Armagh, Cashel, Dublin (formerly Norse), and Tuam—and subjected all Irish abbots to them.[68]

Tragically, a new invader was soon to undo much of what St. Malachy had done, once again setting Irishman against Irishman and using the difficulties of their Church as an excuse for foreign conquest: the English under Henry II, beginning in 1171.[69]

It was probably also in the year 1139 that St. Bernard was drawn into a controversy lasting a little over a year[70] which was to make a great though rather confused impression on posterity, but seems to have made a lesser impression on him; for though at its peak in the spring and summer of 1140 it threw off many of the sparks typical of Bernard in spiritual combat, it was very quickly and satisfactorily resolved, and he makes only occasional and passing references to it afterward. The centerpiece of this controversy was St. Bernard's great debate with Peter Abelard that never was.

Peter Abelard was an intellectual with inclinations alien to his time, indeed to the whole tenor of Christian faith in the Age of Faith. He was a rationalist, a skeptic, something of an empiricist and also something of a subjectivist. He liked to play with words and ideas, even those with the most

---

[67]Williams, *St. Bernard*, pp. 176-181; Mann, *Popes in the Middle Ages*, X, 91-94; E. A. D'Alton, *History of Ireland from the Earliest Times to the Year 1547* (Dublin, 1903), I, 120-152; Ailbe J. Luddy, *Life of St. Malachy* (Dublin, 1930), pp. 8-60.

[68]Williams, *St. Bernard*, pp. 181-183; Luddy, *St. Malachy*, pp. 81-109; Mann, *Popes in the Middle Ages*, X, 217. The *pallium* was a consecrated cloth bestowed upon archbishops by the Pope as a sign of his approval and blessing, and a confirmation of their office.

[69]See Chapter Three, below.

[70]For the chronology of these events followed here, see Regine Pernoud, *Héloïse and Abelard* (New York, 1973), pp. 188-195.

profound doctrinal content—to put them together in new combinations which shook up traditional thinking. Even in that age there were some, particularly among students, who enjoyed this, finding in it the thrill of the forbidden fruit. There are always those who relish watching the "gadfly" biting the stolid old horse—until the gadflies kill the horse, and no substitute for him can be found. To the vision of St. Bernard, spanning the ages, this kind of undisciplined criticism for its own sake was both irresponsible and dangerous. If it was making a real impact it would have to be stopped. Otherwise faith would be trivialized, reduced to a merely human level; wordsmiths would rule the world in place of the Word. St. Bernard would not have been surprised to see how this happened in the twentieth century of our era.

But though St. Bernard has often been condemned for his public denunciation of Abelard, he was in fact profoundly charitable toward him, seeing in him the capacity to reject his errors. From the beginning of the controversy he prayed that Abelard might repent;[71] and his prayers were answered. It may well be that St. Bernard not only destroyed Abelard's errors but achieved the salvation of his soul. That is what he would have wanted to accomplish.

The monk William of St. Thierry denounced Abelard's rationalistic definitions of the mysteries of the Most Holy Trinity in a letter to St. Bernard that first brought him into the controversy. Bernard met with Abelard and read his works, admonishing him to correct his errors. Abelard responded by challenging him to a debate at the council at Sens in the octave of Pentecost, in June 1140. Bernard at first demurred; he was not a theological debater; the bishops should decide whether Abelard's teachings were orthodox or heretical. But Abelard pressed him, and he decided he must not refuse the challenge. The arguments St. Bernard presented to the council were in all probability much the same as those he later sent to Rome, in his "Tract on the Errors of Abelard."[72] Its most timeless passage was this:

> He [Abelard] defines faith as opinion; as if, indeed, a man were at liberty to think and talk about it as he liked! As if the sacred things of our faith depended on vague surmise and were not founded on the solid basis of certain truth. If our faith were thus unsure, would not our hope also be uncertain? How foolish our martyrs would have been to suffer so much for so long for something so doubtful! How can anyone dare to describe our faith as a mere opinion unless he has not yet received the Holy Spirit or is ignorant of the Gospels or thinks them no better than fables! "I know in whom I have believed and I am sure of him," cries the Apostle [Paul], and does this man mutter to me that it is only a matter of opinion?[73]

---

[71]James, *St. Bernard*, pp. 137-138.
[72]Williams, *St. Bernard*, pp. 300-307.
[73]James, *St. Bernard*, pp. 139-140.

Present at Sens that June day was an extraordinary galaxy of distinguished men of both Church and state: Bishops Geoffrey of Chartres and Hugh of Auxerre and Archbishop Samson of Reims, along with others from the episcopate; the King and Queen of France, young Louis VII and the coldly beautiful Queen Eleanor of Aquitaine; Count Theobald of Champagne, the pious grandson of William the Conqueror, and Count William of Nevers, who ended his days in a Carthusian monastery. St. Bernard presented his case against the brilliant and popular teacher. All awaited Abelard's response.[74]

None came. To the utter astonishment of the entire assembly and of all subsequent historians and commentators, Abelard refused to reply. Though he himself had requested the debate, he withdrew from it without ever engaging in it, and appealed to Rome.[75]

Explanations of why he did so range from the politically oversophisticated (he is said to have known that his condemnation was already decided upon regardless of what he said)[76] to the medically fanciful (he had Hodgkin's disease which gave him a sudden fainting fit).[77] No solid evidence supports any such conjectures. We are left with the simple, hard fact: the greatest academic debater of his time found himself utterly silent in the face of St. Bernard of Clairvaux. He was not the first, nor would he be the last of those whom Christ's spiritual athlete had silenced by his very presence, and by the passionate totality of his faith.

St. Bernard did not appear to be as surprised as everyone else by his victory; he had seen such victories before, and firmly believed that the Victor was Christ, not he. Abelard had transferred the venue of the case to Rome; St. Bernard's arguments would follow him there. "We have escaped Peter the lion," he wrote to Pope Innocent II, recalling Antipope Pierleoni, "only to fall victims to Peter the dragon."[78] Pope Innocent wasted no time; before the end of July he convicted Abelard of heresy on the basis of his writings without waiting for his personal appearance in Rome, silenced him, and ordered his objectionable works burned.[79]

But Peter Abelard had already made his choice even before the Papal sentence arrived. He had shut himself up in the monastery of Cluny, where Abbot Peter the Venerable invited him to stay; he had imposed silence upon himself; and he had written his recantation and simple profession of faith to the person he loved most, with whom a stormy, star-crossed, once mortally sinful relationship that has become romantic legend ended in final surrender to the

---

[74]Pernoud, *Héloise and Abelard*, pp. 197-199.
[75]Mann, *Popes in the Middle Ages*, IX, 282.
[76]George W. Greenaway, *Arnold of Brescia* (Cambridge, England, 1931), p. 72.
[77]Pernoud, *Héloise and Abelard*, p. 199.
[78]James, *St. Bernard*, p. 139.
[79]Williams, *St. Bernard*, p. 310.

ultimate Source of Love in this, the last of Abelard's world-famous letters to Héloise:[80]

> I have no wish to be a philosopher if it means rebelling against Paul.
> I have no wish to be Aristotle if it means severing myself from Christ, for it
> is in His Name, and none other under Heaven, that I must find my
> salvation. . . . So that any concern or uncertainty may be banished from the
> heart that beats within your breast, I want to assure you personally that I
> have founded my conscience upon the rock whereon Christ has built his
> Church. Here, in brief, is the inscription it bears.
>   I believe in Father, Son and Holy Spirit, God by nature One, true
> God in whom Unity of Substance is unimpaired by Trinity of Persons. I
> believe that the Son is equal to the Father in all things, in eternity, in
> might, in will and in the exercise of power . . . I attest that the Holy Spirit is
> in every respect equal to, and consubstantial with, the Father and the Son .
> . . I further believe that the Son of God became the Son of Man in such a
> way that one Person consists and subsists in two natures. Having met all
> the demands of the human condition which He had assumed, even unto
> death itself, He rose again and ascended into Heaven, whence he shall
> come to judge the quick and the dead. . . . Let the storm break, it will not
> disturb me. Let the winds blow, they will not budge me. I am founded on
> firm rock.[81]

This—not any self-conscious paean to "free thought"—was Peter Abelard's true last testament. On April 21, 1142, as he sat in his cell reading and praying, in the beautiful words of Peter the Venerable, "the Visitor foretold by the Gospel found him." He was 63 years old, dying the humblest monk at Cluny.[82]

In the year 1137, as has been mentioned, the repentant Duke William X of Aquitaine, the largest landowner in France, died on Good Friday, on pilgrimage to Santiago de Compostela. He left a fifteen-year-old daughter, Eleanor, as his sole heiress. As Duke William lay dying on the pilgrim road, he offered his daughter in marriage to the son and heir of King Louis VI of France, just her age, though he seemed younger as she seemed older. In July they were married; in October the King died, and Louis VII, known ever afterward as "the Young," was monarch of France.[83]

Eleanor of Aquitaine—"Alianora, the swan maiden" of troubadour legend—was all her long life (she lived to be 82, rarer in that age than a

---

[80]Pernoud, *Héloise and Abelard*, pp. 203-204 and *passim*. With regard to the romance between Abelard and Héloise, one point at least should be made clear: at the time it started, Abelard was not a priest or a monk, but only in minor orders; he was not only free to marry, but (though it would have been unusual) he could have continued his teaching as a married man. On this point see Étienne Gilson, *Héloise and Abelard* (Ann Arbor MI, 1960), pp. 8-36.
[81]Pernoud, *Héloise and Abelard*, pp. 204-205.
[82]*Ibid.*, pp. 213, 216.
[83]Regine Pernoud, *Eleanor of Aquitaine* (New York, 1968), pp. 13-27.

centenarian today) in love with wealth and power, which her striking personality and surpassing beauty gave her unique opportunities to capture. Her royal husband was innocent, guileless, and devout. He was overwhelmed by this lovely creature so suddenly become his wife. He could refuse her nothing. When in 1141 her younger sister Peronelle, whose goals in life seem to have been similar to Eleanor's, demanded marriage to one of the richest nobles and most powerful officials at court, the Seneschal Raoul of Vermandois, though he was old enough to be her father, Eleanor made her royal husband promise that Peronelle would get her wish. But Seneschal Raoul was already married to another Eleanor, the niece of Count Theobald of Champagne, who had St. Bernard as his spiritual director. A three-man episcopal commission, doubtless with encouragement from the King, pronounced Raoul's marriage invalid on grounds of consanguinity, whereupon he promptly married Peronelle.[84]

St. Bernard denounced the three bishops as "shameless men . . . who, despite the law of God, have not scrupled to separate what God has joined together. Nor is this all. They have gone further and added one sin to another by uniting what should not be united. The sacred rites of the Church have been violated and the robes of Christ have been torn, and to make matters worse this has been done by those very persons whose business it ought to be to mend them."[85] He did not hesitate to point out that Louis' own marriage to Eleanor was within the prohibited degrees of consanguinity, yet had received no Papal dispensation. Pope Innocent II responded in 1142 by excommunicating Raoul of Vermandois and imposing an interdict on his lands, and suspending the three bishops.[86]

In that same year 1142 another dispute, initially unrelated, also brought down the Papal wrath on Louis VII's head. Louis had taken a hasty oath, for reasons unknown, that he would never permit Peter de la Châtre, a nephew of Pope Innocent II's chancellor Cardinal Haimeric, to be Archbishop of Bourges. When Peter was nevertheless elected to that see by the cathedral chapter of Bourges,[87] Louis refused to permit him to accept it. Theobald of Champagne gave Peter refuge, and Pope Innocent imposed an interdict on much of France in punishment for the King's treatment of Peter. St. Bernard agreed that the King had acted wrongly, but sought to excuse him by his youth, and to work out a compromise. The Pope would have none of it. Louis VII led an army into

---

[84]*Ibid.*, p. 35; Williams, *St. Bernard*, pp. 208-209. Peronelle is more commonly known as Petronilla, the Spanish form of her name, but since her family was French it is virtually certain they used the French form.

[85]St. Bernard to Pope Innocent II (1142), *Letters of St. Bernard*, tr. James, pp. 361-362.

[86]Williams, *St. Bernard*, p. 209.

[87]The cathedral chapter consisted of the priests and other designated clerics resident at or near a cathedral. The chapter had the sole canonical responsibility for episcopal elections—though pressure was often brought from outside, as in this case.

Champagne, and in January 1143 stormed the little town of Vitry, held for Theobald, with such ferocity that the whole town was reduced to ashes and about a thousand people burned to death inside their church in which they had taken refuge.[88]

This was enough. The frail abbot of Clairvaux now loosed upon Louis VII the thunderbolts that no man in Christendom, be he king or nobleman or bishop, could withstand:

> From whom but the devil could the advice come under which you are acting, advice which causes burnings upon burnings, and slaughter upon slaughter, and the voice of the poor and the groans of captives and the blood of the slain to echo in the ears of the Father of orphans and the Judge of widows? ...
>
> Whatever you may be pleased to do with your own kingdom, crown, and soul, we, the sons of the Church, cannot overlook the injuries, contempt and ignominy to which you have subjected our mother. . . . We shall make a stand and, if necessary, fight even to the death for our mother with the weapons that are permitted to us, that is with prayers and lamentations to God. . . .
>
> I shall not withhold the fact that you are again trying to make common cause with excommunicated persons, that I hear you are associating with robbers and thieves in the slaughter of men, the burning of homesteads, the destruction of churches, and the scattering of the poor. . . . I tell you, you will not remain long unpunished if you continue in this way.[89]

At approximately this juncture Pope Innocent II died, to be succeeded on September 25, 1143 by Cardinal Guido of Castelli, who had been a student of Peter Abelard without imbibing his errors, and had faithfully supported Innocent throughout the Pierleoni schism. The new Pope took the name Celestine II. The one major achievement of his short pontificate of six months was to lift the interdict from France in return for Louis VII's acceptance of Peter de la Châtre as Archbishop of Bourges; the marital status of Raoul of Vermandois was left for the time being unsettled.[90] Louis had been profoundly chastened by St. Bernard's searing denunciation. In June 1144 he came to the dedication of the new building of the royal abbey of St. Denis at Paris in the gray robe and sandals of a penitent, in startling contrast to the brocade and pearls Queen Eleanor wore for the occasion; he gave to Abbot Suger of St. Denis a luxuriantly decorated vase Eleanor had given him; he banished her favorite troubadour from court, and spent hours daily at his prayers.

---

[88]Williams, *St. Bernard*, pp. 207-208; Mann, *Popes in the Middle Ages*, X, 109-110; Pernoud, *Eleanor of Aquitaine*, pp. 31-32.

[89]*Letters of St. Bernard*, tr. James, pp. 364-366.

[90]Mann, *Popes in the Middle Ages*, X, 102-111; Williams, *St. Bernard*, pp. 214-215.

"Sometimes I feel I've married a monk," Eleanor told her friends.[91]

St. Bernard was present at the dedication of St. Denis. His unerring spiritual instinct showed him now, if it had not done so before, where the real trouble in the royal household lay. He told Eleanor openly that she was abusing her influence with the King in the matter of Raoul and Peronelle, to the detriment of justice, the sacrament of marriage, the Church, and the peace of France. The fire and beauty of Eleanor of Aquitaine could overwhelm almost anyone who came in direct contact with her. But she did not even try to argue with St. Bernard; she submitted at once, and begged him to pray that she might have a child, for she was haunted by her failure to conceive in seven years of marriage.[92]

"Strive for peace within the realm," St. Bernard responded, "and I promise you that God in His infinite mercy will grant what you request."[93]

The next year a daughter was born to Louis VII and Eleanor, whom they named for the Blessed Virgin Mary.[94] But, tragically, even this signal favor did not bring in Eleanor the permanent change that St. Bernard's stern words and loving prayers had wrought in the soul of her husband King Louis VII.

During these same years (1141-1144) a controversy over the appointment of the Archbishop of York, the only other metropolitan see in Great Britain besides Canterbury, had also deeply involved St. Bernard, setting him against King Stephen of England and his brother Henry, Bishop of Winchester. Though our knowledge of the origins of this controversy is sketchy, it evidently grew out of the extraordinary turmoil in England during the year 1141. When William the Conqueror's last grandson, Henry I, died after a 35-year reign in 1135, he left only a daughter to succeed him: Matilda, widow of Holy Roman Emperor Henry V and consequently known as "the Empress."[95] Though her father had required his nobles to take oaths to support her, many of them, preferring a male ruler, disregarded their oaths after his death and supported Stephen of Blois, William the Conqueror's grandson through his daughter Adela. Stephen was able to secure the succession promptly in England, but unable to maintain it in Normandy. By 1138 Robert of Gloucester, an illegitimate son of Henry I, had taken up arms against Stephen in the name of "Empress" Matilda. Pope Innocent II supported Stephen's claim over

---

[91]Pernoud, *Eleanor of Aquitaine*, pp. 38-42.

[92]*Ibid.*, pp. 42-45; Williams, *St. Bernard*, p. 215. Pernoud thinks Eleanor sought the interview with St. Bernard, Williams that Bernard sought it. Either supposition could be true, or both could in fact have desired the meeting for different reasons.

[93]Pernoud, *Eleanor of Aquitaine*, p. 46.

[94]*Ibid.*

[95]Austin Lane Poole, *From Domesday Book to Magna Carta, 1087-1216* (Oxford History of England), 2nd ed. (Oxford, 1955), pp. 129-130. Henry I's only legitimate son had been drowned in the disaster of the "White Ship" in 1120 (see Chapter One, above).

Matilda's. When in 1138 Henry of Winchester was denied the appointment he expected as Archbishop of Canterbury, he was named Papal legate to England as a kind of consolation prize, but was increasingly hostile to his brother, King Stephen. He seized the occasion of Stephen's arrests the next year of the Bishops of Salisbury and Lincoln to denounce Stephen for interfering with the liberties of the Church, which he had solemnly promised to maintain in a document called the Oxford Charter of Liberties signed in the first year of his reign. Matilda then landed in England, Bishop Henry gave her his support, King Stephen was captured, and on March 3, 1141 Matilda was formally proclaimed Queen of England at Winchester in Bishop Henry's own cathedral.[96]

At this dramatic and inconvenient moment Archbishop Thurstan of York died.[97] Bishop Henry's intent to control the Church in England, insofar as he possibly could, was clear. That purpose of his was in no way changed, but rather reinforced by the tumultuous sequence of events which followed. Matilda went to London, but after just a few weeks there was driven out by its people, having antagonized during that brief period most of the leading churchmen and noblemen of the nation along with the people of London. Those antagonized included Bishop Henry, who promptly changed sides again. Robert of Gloucester was then captured and exchanged for Stephen, again proclaimed king with Bishop Henry's support.[98]

At some time during or shortly after these upheavals, which all occurred during 1141, pressure was evidently brought to bear by Bishop Henry on the cathedral chapter of York to elect his nephew William Fitzherbert Archbishop. The pressure seems to have been applied in the name of King Stephen, though it is by no means sure that Stephen actually knew much about it at the time. (Going into and out of captivity, he had many other matters on his mind.) In January 1142 the chapter did elect Fitzherbert. The Cistercian abbots of Fountains and Rievaulx near York vehemently objected, and the case was appealed to Rome, with strong interventions by St. Bernard in opposition to William and in denunciation of Bishop Henry as the author of the evil.[99]

The case was heard in March 1143. Fitzherbert was present to argue in his own defense, but the weight of the evidence indicated that his election by the cathedral chapter of York had not been free. Pope Innocent II decided that

---

[96]*Ibid.*, pp. 133-137, 141-143, 193; R. H. C. Davis, *King Stephen, 1135-1154* (Berkeley CA, 1967), pp. 17-20, 27-35, 37, 39-40, 52, 54, 56-57; W. L. Warren, *Henry II* (Berkeley CA, 1973), pp. 23, 26, 31; Mann, *Popes in the Middle Ages*, X, 77-78, 80-81.

[97]Williams, *St. Bernard*, p. 167, gives the date as February 1141.

[98]Lane Poole, *Domesday Book to Magna Carta*, pp. 143-145; Davis, *Stephen*, pp. 59-67; Mann, *Popes in the Middle Ages*, X, 87-88.

[99]Williams, *St. Bernard*, pp. 167-168; James, *St. Bernard*, pp. 144-145. Williams' more circumstancial and precise account must be used to correct James' lively narrative on points of chronology.

William of St. Barbe, Dean of York, should settle the case by swearing (or refusing to swear) that no pressure had been brought on the cathedral chapter to elect Fitzherbert. Most unhappy to be thus put "on the spot," William of St. Barbe had someone else take the required oath in his place. This naturally settled nothing, though Fitzherbert went ahead with his formal consecration in September 1143. As Abbot Richard of the Cistercian monastery of Fountains near York had just died, St. Bernard appointed as his successor Henry Murdach, abbot of the Cistercian monastery of Vauclair in France but himself a Yorkshireman, to carry on the struggle against the uncanonically elected Archbishop, and called upon just-elected Pope Celestine II to undertake a new investigation of the case. Celestine II died before he could do so, though he did cancel the designation of Bishop Henry of Winchester as Papal legate. The responsibility for the York case therefore fell upon Celestine's successor Lucius II, the former Cardinal Caccianemici of Bologna, elected Pope in March 1144, who promptly despatched the ever-reliable Cardinal Hincmar to York.[100]

Pope Lucius II soon had a crisis much nearer home to deal with. In June 1144 the people of Rome, led by Jordan Pierleoni, a nephew of the late Antipope, rose against his authority and proclaimed a republic. The Pope and St. Bernard both urged Emperor Conrad to intervene to restore Rome to its proper obedience. Conrad was slow to respond, so the Pope collected supporters as best he could from Rome and neighboring Italy, and in February 1145 attempted to put down the rebellion by force of arms. Jordan Pierleoni repulsed the Papal force from the Capitoline Hill in a day of fierce fighting in which, according to one unconfirmed report, the Pope himself was wounded by stones. Whether because of this or from strictly natural causes, he died February 15.[101]

In this critical situation obviously not a moment was to be lost in electing a new Pope, and he must be a man around whom all men of good will could immediately unite. Totally unexpected by all, the choice of the cardinals two days later fell upon Bernard Paganelli, who had been a monk under St. Bernard at Clairvaux, sent back by him to his native Italy to be abbot of the Cistercian monastery of St. Anastasius of the Three Fountains in 1140.[102] No one was more surprised than St. Bernard. He had always rejected all thought or suggestion of his own elevation to the highest office in the Church, and had never looked for it to go to one of his own monks.[103] Now his beloved

---

[100]Williams, *St. Bernard*, pp. 168-173; James, *St. Bernard*, pp. 145-149; Mann, *Popes in the Middle Ages*, X, 114-115, 119; David Knowles, *The Monastic Order in England* (Cambridge, England, 1950), p. 255.

[101]Mann, *Popes in the Middle Ages*, X, 117-119; Greenaway, *Arnold of Brescia*, pp. 104-107; St. Bernard to Emperor Conrad, *Letters of St. Bernard* tr. James, pp. 394-395.

[102]Mann, *Popes in the Middle Ages*, X, 131-134; Williams, *St. Bernard*, pp. 67-69.

[103]St. Bernard to the Cardinals and bishops of the Roman Curia, on the occasion of the election of Pope Eugenius III (1145), *Letters of St. Bernard* tr. James, pp. 385-386.

namesake was Pope Eugenius III; he had exchanged his cowl for the tiara. In many ways it was the supreme moment of St. Bernard's life, as is shown by the saint's incomparable letter to the new Pope on the occasion of his election:

> I will speak to my lord. I do not dare to call you a son any longer. You were my son, but now you have become my father. I was your father, but now I have become your son. You who came after me have been preferred before me. But I am not jealous, for I am sure that you who not only came after me but also, in a manner, through me, will make up in your person for what is lacking to me. For, if you will pardon my saying so, it was I who, as it were, begot you in the Gospel. What is it that I hope will be my joy and a glorious crown for me? It is you before God. . . .
>
> You have been called to hold a high position, but not a safe one; a sublime position, but not a secure one. How terrible, how very terrible is the place you hold! The place where you stand is holy ground. It is the place of Peter, the place of the Prince of the Apostles, the very place where his feet have stood. It is the place of him whom the Lord made master of his household and chief over all his possessions. He is buried there in that very place to watch over you and bear witness against you if your feet should ever stray from the path of righteousness.[104]

The Roman rebels demanded that the new Pope recognize their republic, and when he refused they drove him out of the city before he could be consecrated. From Viterbo he excommunicated Jordan Pierleoni, whose followers now disgraced themselves and their political cause in the eyes of all devout and reasonable men by indiscriminate pillage of the homes of cardinals and nobles, the robbery of pilgrims, and the plundering and defilement of churches. The consequence was that by the end of the year most of Jordan's support had dwindled away, and the Pope was able to return to Rome in triumph just before Christmas. Despite all his other concerns during this busy and angry year, Pope Eugenius reviewed the problem of the archdiocese of York, suspending William Fitzherbert unless and until his Dean should personally swear the required oath that undue pressure had not been exerted on the cathedral chapter of York to obtain his election as Archbishop.[105]

The new Pope's triumph in Rome was short-lived. Though Jordan Pierleoni had been discredited, Arnold of Brescia—student of Peter Abelard turned firebrand revolutionary, a caustic critic of bishops and even of St. Bernard himself—was available to take his place. In September 1145 he had come to the Pope at Viterbo confessing his sins and promising obedience in the future. He was given a penance and reconciled to the Church. But his repentance, if ever sincere, was short-lived, and he probably bore substantial responsibility for the new upsurge of hostility to Papal government which forced

---

[104]St. Bernard to Pope Eugenius III, *Letters of St. Bernard* tr. James, pp. 277-279.

[105]Mann, *Popes in the Middle Ages*, X, 137-138, 147-153; Greenaway, *Arnold of Brescia*, pp. 111-112; James, *St. Bernard*, p. 150.

Pope Eugenius III out of Rome again in March 1146—to the deep distress of St. Bernard, who wrote a vehement letter to the people of Rome condemning them for raising their hands against the Vicar of Christ.[106]

Meanwhile the Cistercian Pope—and Christendom—had received profoundly disturbing news. In November 1144 Zengi, Atabeg of Mosul, had laid siege to Edessa in the absence of its Count Joscelin and his army. Edessa was the oldest Christian city in the world, regained from the infidel on the First Crusade, the eastern outpost of Christendom and of the Crusader kingdoms. Count Joscelin was unable to raise Zengi's siege, and Prince Raymond of Antioch sent no help. On Christmas Eve 1144 Edessa fell; Zengi massacred its French defenders. The Caliph at Baghdad made him a king to honor his victory, which threatened the whole Christian position in the east, from Antioch to Jerusalem.[107]

Prince Raymond, who did not help Edessa, was Eleanor of Aquitaine's uncle. He had come to Antioch in 1136 from France to marry its nine-year-old heiress Constance before Byzantine Prince Manuel Comnenus could wed her. The marriage was done in secret, so that it would not become known ahead of time either to the Byzantines or to the bride's mother, the irrepressible Princess Alice, who had been told the handsome, dashing Raymond had come to marry her. Full of the fury of a woman scorned, Alice had to be exiled from the city. In November 1143 King Fulk of Jerusalem was thrown from his horse and killed, leaving as his heir 13-year-old Baldwin III under the regency of Alice's sister, Queen Melisende, who had never distinguished herself for leadership or statesmanship. Military resources in the crusader kingdoms were at a low ebb. It was time for another crusade, and on December 1 Pope Eugenius III sent a bull to France urging that it be undertaken.[108]

Louis VII of France responded instantly; a substantial part of his motive

---

[106]Mann, *Popes in the Middle Ages*, X, 153-157; Greenaway, *Arnold of Brescia*, pp. 119-121; St. Bernard "to the nobles, chief citizens, and all the people of Rome," *Letters of St. Bernard* tr. James, pp. 391-394. Greenaway does not think that Arnold of Brescia became a leader of the republican movement in Rome until several months, or even a year or more, after his return; but he does recognize that in all probability Arnold returned to Rome very soon after his reconciliation with the Church in September 1145. It is hard to imagine a man of Arnold's dynamism, charisma and proven leadership ability staying out of the events surrounding and following Pope Eugenius' return to Rome in December 1145; later reports on his activities imply that he was involved then, and the absence of explicit attestation of his role in the tumults of the winter of 1146 seems an insufficient basis to assume that he had none.

[107]Runciman, *Crusades*, II, 235-238, 247; Setton, *Crusades*, I, 446-447.

[108]Runciman, *Crusades*, II, 198-200, 202-205, 232-234; Setton, *Crusades*, I, 436-438, 444; Williams, *St. Bernard*, p. 264. For a detailed analysis of this important Papal bull, *Quantum predecessores*, and the theory of crusade which it expressed, see Giles Constable, "The Second Crusade as Seen by Contemporaries," *Traditio* IX (1953), 248-254.

may well have been the desire to atone for his sins in warring against the
Church earlier in the decade, which St. Bernard had so forcefully called to his
attention. On Christmas day 1145, significantly at Bourges—the place of his
earlier defiance of the Church—he told his court he intended to take the Cross.
Caught wholly by surprise, almost all his noblemen, bishops and abbots pleaded
with him not to leave the kingdom, and persuaded him to delay a public call for
participation in the crusade for three months. But his resolve remained fixed,
and St. Bernard gave it full support. On Easter (March 31) 1146, at the shrine
of St. Mary Magdalen at Vézélay, St. Bernard called upon the knights of France
and Europe to march again to Jerusalem, as they had done so gloriously fifty
years before. King Louis VII personally took the cross from him.[109]

Before the year was over St. Bernard had extended his preaching of the
new crusade to Flanders, Switzerland and the Rhineland, while reproving in the
strongest terms the earlier and concurrent preaching of a Cistercian monk
named Raoul who incited the crusaders to begin their mission by slaughtering
Jews:[110]

> Is it not a far better triumph for the Church to convince and convert
> the Jews than to put them all to the sword? Has that prayer which the
> Church offers for the Jews, from the rising up of the sun to the going down
> thereof, that the veil may be taken from their hearts so that they may be
> led from the darkness of error into the light of truth, been instituted in
> vain? If she did not hope that they would believe and be converted, it
> would seem useless and vain for her to pray for them. But with the eye of
> mercy she considers how the Lord regards with favour him who renders
> good for evil and love for hatred. . . . Who is this man [Raoul] that he
> should make out the Prophet to be a liar and render void the treasures of
> Christ's love and pity?[111]

At Frankfurt at the end of November, St. Bernard urged Emperor Conrad
III to join and lead the Second Crusade, as indeed was his duty as Holy Roman

---

[109]Runciman, *Crusades*, II, 252-253; Setton, *Crusades*, I, 467-469; Pernoud, *Eleanor
of Aquitaine*, pp. 47-49; Williams, *St. Bernard*, pp. 263-265; Mann, *Popes in the Middle
Ages*, X, 183-185. Williams believes that St. Bernard was the prime mover of the
Crusade from the beginning, but as he himself recognizes, no contemporary evidence
supports this conclusion, while the chronicler Otto of Friesing specifically states that
Louis VII "had a secret wish to go to Jerusalem because his brother Philip, bound by a
vow to do so, had been prevented by death from fulfilling it" and also to atone for the
burning of the church at Vitry. Williams is incorrect in stating that St. Bernard's
proclamation of the crusade occurred on Palm Sunday; Easter fell on March 31 in 1146
(see C. R. Cheney, *Handbook of Dates for Students of English History* [London, 1955],
p. 158).

[110]Williams, *St. Bernard*, pp. 269-272; Setton, *Crusades*, I, 471-474.

[111]St. Bernard to Archbishop Henry of Mainz, 1146, *Letters of St. Bernard*, tr. James,
p. 466.

Emperor.[112] At first Conrad flatly refused, saying "I have no intention of taking part in the expedition."[113] But the passionate abbot of Clairvaux was nothing if not persistent, and as he had already amply demonstrated, essentially impossible to withstand. On December 27, at the Diet of Speier, he preached before the Emperor on the theme (from the reproaches of Christ on Good Friday): "Man, what ought I to have done for you that I have not done?" The next day the Emperor took the cross, saying with tears, to an assembly which included St. Bernard: "I do indeed acknowledge the benefactions of His divine grace; henceforth with His aid I will not be found ungrateful; seeing that you call upon me, I am ready to serve Him."[114]

Duke Welf of Bavaria, King Ladislas of Bohemia, the Marquis of Styria and the Count of Carinthia all took the cross with the Emperor, and King Boleslav IV of Poland soon afterward. In the winter and spring of 1147 all Christendom united in support of the crusade. The central European crusading army under Emperor Conrad III—some 20,000 Germans, Czechs and Poles—departed from Regensburg in May. The French crusading army under King Louis VII (accompanied by his wife Eleanor of Aquitaine), only a little less numerous than the central European host, departed from Paris June 8 in the presence of the Pope.[115] King Stephen of England faced too many troubles at home to go, but he encouraged his noblemen to participate, and a substantial contingent prepared to make their crusade to the Holy Land by sea. In Spain Alfonso VII secured the great Moorish fortress of Calatrava in La Mancha in January, garrisoning it with members of the crusading order of the Templars. In May he gathered a crusading army at Toledo, while in March Afonso Henriques of Portugal took Santarem on the Tagus, a major step toward the encirclement of Moor-held Lisbon. The crusading fleet from England, carrying 13,000 fighting men including Germans, Flemings and French Normans as well as Englishmen, arrived in Portugal June 28 and agreed to join with Afonso Henriques to take Lisbon.[116] "You have held our cities and lands already for

---

[112]The Emperor had not led the First Crusade or the crusade of 1101 because the Emperor at that time was Henry IV, excommunicated and defying the Church on the issue of lay investiture (see Volume II of this history, Chapters 19 and 20, and Chapter One, above).

[113]Williams, *St. Bernard*, p. 272; indirect discourse in original changed to direct.

[114]*Ibid.*, pp. 273-274.

[115]*Ibid.*, pp. 274, 281-282; Runciman, *Crusades*, II, 259, 261-262; Mann, *Popes in the Middle Ages*, X, 189.

[116]Lomax, *Reconquest of Spain*, pp. 90-92, 108; Setton, *Crusades*, I, 481-482; O'Callaghan, *Medieval Spain*, p. 230; Recuero Astray, *Alfonso VII*, p. 180. Contemporaries clearly regarded the operations in Spain as part of the crusade, seen therefore not only as a means of strengthening the kingdom of Jerusalem, but of carrying on a general war of Christendom against Islam, as the First Crusade had also been seen. See Constable, "The Second Crusade as Seen by Contemporaries," *Traditio* IX, 220-224, and Volume II, Chapter 20 of this history.

358 years," thundered the Archbishop of Braga, primate of Portugal. "Return to the homeland of the Moors whence you came, leaving to us what is ours!"[117] In April Pope Eugenius III called upon German and Danish knights who were not going to Jerusalem to join in a crusade against the pagan Wends, who had ravaged eastern Germany for many years. By July some 40,000 Germans had marched against them.[118]

In striking contrast to this almost universal crusading commitment in the West, Byzantine Emperor Manuel Comnenus, though offering fair words of praise and promises of help to the crusaders, at this critical moment in the spring of 1147 treacherously made a truce with the Danishmend Turks, the principal Muslim force in Asia Minor, across which the crusading armies had already (at a council of war held at Étampes in France in February) decided to march.[119] Consequently when the German crusading army, after stopping at Constantinople for about a month, pushed on into Asia Minor it was attacked and badly defeated October 25 at Dorylaeum (where Bohemond had triumphed in the First Crusade); Emperor Conrad was wounded. Much of the army scattered on the ensuing retreat to the coast, and it could not be reconstituted as a striking force. Conrad, discouraged and ill even after recovering from his wound, retired to Constantinople and urged Louis VII to do likewise. Byzantine Emperor Manuel Comnenus added a blunt warning that in view of previous clashes between his people and the "Latins" he could not be responsible for any damage the crusaders might henceforth suffer in his territory. But the young French king dauntlessly pressed on along the south coast of Asia Minor as the new year 1148 began.[120]

The crusade against the Wends accomplished little; Nyklot, the Wendish chief, easily drove off the Danes, who were distracted by conflict and civil war among four claimants to the Danish throne, and held his own against two German forces, one commanded by Duke Henry the Lion of Saxony and the

---

[117]O'Callaghan, *Medieval Spain*, p. 231.

[118]Setton, *Crusades*, I, 479, 483; *Cambridge Medieval History*, V, 354.

[119]Setton, *Crusades*, I, 477-478, 490; Runciman, *Crusades*, II, 266. Attempts then and since (e.g. Runciman, *loc. cit.*), to justify or palliate this act of treachery are thoroughly unconvincing (see Setton, *op. cit.*, I, 502). While there very likely were some in the crusading army who had designs against the Byzantine Empire, to make a truce with the infidel at the beginning of so mighty a crusade could only magnify existing distrust and hostility. Loyal service to Christendom and alliance with the crusaders was the best and, indeed, the only way for the Byzantine Emperor to win or deserve their trust. But it seems that very few Byzantines ever really believed in the sincerity of the Crusades or the crusaders. (Too many modern historians have followed their cynical example.) Many examples of insincerity, self-seeking and deliberate aggression on the part of crusaders may certainly be found. But the crusading movement as a whole, at least up to this time, meant far more than that. Certainly St. Bernard never doubted that this was so.

[120]Runciman, *Crusades*, II, 261, 267-271; Setton, *Crusades* I, 486, 496-498.

other by Duke Albert the Bear of Brandenburg. Eventually Duke Henry and his attendant bishops accepted a token submission from the Wends accompanied by a ceremony of baptism for them which they obviously did not take seriously. The first page had been turned of the dismal and disreputable history of crusading along the Baltic Sea, for which little justification or palliation can be provided even by the historian strongly in sympathy with crusading in the Holy Land and in Spain and Portugal.[121]

In Spain, by contrast, two remarkable victories were won by the crusaders in October 1147. Alfonso VII of Castile and León took Almería in the far south of Spain, facing Africa, with the aid of the Count of Barcelona, the King of Navarra, and Italian and French crusaders, together with fleets from Barcelona, Genoa and Pisa. The crusading army of English, Norman French, Flemings and Germans which had come by sea to Portugal took Lisbon after a 17-week siege, forcing a capitulation after breaching the walls. Shortly afterward, as if to emphasize the international character of this triumph, the Englishman Gilbert of Hastings was made Bishop of Lisbon.[122]

In the east, on the march to the Holy Land, all responsibility had now fallen upon the shoulders of Louis VII, just 26 years old. He had feudal commanders to advise him, but few if any of them had ever fought Muslims in their own territory. The Danishmend Turks were not only wholly unhampered by the Byzantines, thanks to Manuel Comnenus' truce, but by means unexplained were able periodically to make use of Byzantine strongholds as refuges and bases. Manuel Comnenus might not have personally arranged for this, but he was certainly doing nothing to prevent it. The army felt treason all around them. The country was wild and forbidding—all jagged mountains, barren hills and deep gorges, supplying little food; the Greeks knew it as Lycia and Caria, whose hinterland had remained barbarian despite two thousand years of Greek presence here and there along its rock-bound coast. Eleanor of Aquitaine longed, probably openly, for the luxurious comforts and gorgeous ceremony of Constantinople. Nothing would have been easier than for Louis VII to have found an excuse to turn back. Most historians to this day seem to think he should have.[123]

But Louis "the Young" had a vow to keep in Jerusalem, and St. Bernard of Clairvaux had pinned the Cross upon his shoulder. He marched on eastward.

Six days into the Carian maze, near Mount Cadmus on the feast of

---

[121]Setton, *Crusades*, I, 493-494; *Cambridge Medieval History*, V, 355-356; Eric Christiansen, *The Northern Crusades; the Baltic and the Catholic Frontier, 1100-1525* (Minneapolis MN, 1980), pp. 52-53; J. H. S. Birch, *Denmark in History* (London, 1938), pp. 52-53.
[122]Lomax, *Reconquest of Spain*, pp. 91-92; Recuero Astray, *Alfonso VII*, pp. 181-182; Setton, *Crusades*, I, 482-483.
[123]Runciman, *Crusades*, II, 271-272; Setton, *Crusades*, I, 498-499; Pernoud, *Eleanor of Aquitaine*, pp. 56-63.

Epiphany, with the crusading army divided by the formidable terrain, the Turks attacked in force. Louis galloped to the sounds of battle. He found disorder and the beginnings of panic. Again and again he charged with the horsemen of his guard to check the momentum of the enemy attack. One after another his guardsmen fell. The king was pressed back toward the base of a cliff. Seizing the branches of a tree growing out of a pocket of soil on a ledge above the ground, he swung himself to the top of a huge boulder resting against the cliff. For more than an hour at sunset he stood alone with flashing sword, literally with his back to the wall. Fortunately he wore no royal insignia; the Turks did not know who he was, or they would have surely concentrated to capture or kill him. But they knew his valor, and as twilight deepened they pulled away and he survived.[124]

That night there must have been fierce recriminations and anguished counsels in the French camp. The crusaders had many dead to find and bury. But before the next day ended, they formed up in response to the king's order—and marched on again eastward.[125]

Twelve days later Louis came out of the maze to the Byzantine port of Adalia on the south coast of Asia Minor, located in a small poor plain under the savage mountains. There was not enough food in Adalia for his army, which had already begun killing its horses for food. Conditions on the road ahead were reported even worse. Louis was finally, very reluctantly persuaded to agree to transport his army the rest of the way by sea. Manuel Comnenus promised him the necessary ships. But Manuel's promises were worthless. Less than half the needed number of ships ever came to Adalia. Louis took the pick of the army with him on what ships there were; the greater part of those he had to leave behind perished. An intrepid and fortunate minority struggled through to Tarsus and Antioch.[126]

It must have been a grim Louis VII who arrived in Antioch that March, in the midst of Lent, battle-worn and agonized by the necessity of leaving so many of his men at Adalia, no great general, but already a hero to match any the Crusades had produced—a man to whom Raymond of Toulouse, Godfrey of Bouillon, Alfonso the Battler and El Cid would all have been proud to lift a glass. The history of Christendom shows us many women, faithful unto death, who would have felt honored to stand at the side of Louis VII at this moment:

---

[124]Setton, *Crusades*, I, 499; Pernoud, *Eleanor of Aquitaine*, pp. 63-64.

[125]Setton, *Crusades*, I, 499-500.

[126]*Ibid.*, I, 500-503; Runciman, *Crusades*, II, 273-274. Louis has been blamed for deserting his army, and he may have trusted Manuel Comnenus too readily in view of his record; but in his situation he had little choice. The Byzantine Emperor and his representatives had originally advised him to take the coastal route, and had not fully explained its difficulties to him. A substantial part, though not a majority, of the troops he left behind did eventually attain their objective, and he saved most of his best men and commanders as a nucleus for a new army assembled after his arrival in Palestine.

Isabel the Catholic of Spain, Countess Matilda of Tuscany, Clovis' St. Clotilda, St. Hermenegild's Ingunthis, Queen Margaret of Scotland, El Cid's Jimena . . . but Eleanor of Aquitaine was not of their kind. Within a few days of their landing at Antioch she had plunged into a passionate love affair with its prince, her own uncle, Raymond of Poitiers, who was demanding that Louis launch an immediate attack with his depleted forces on Aleppo in Syria. Eleanor vigorously seconded his arguments. Louis replied only that he had a vow to keep in Jerusalem. Eleanor then asked him for an annulment of their marriage on grounds of consanguinity. Louis placed her under arrest and marched south toward Tripoli. Perhaps at that point Eleanor was not quite so sure that she had "married a monk."[127]

At Tripoli Louis learned that Emperor Conrad had reappeared on the scene, landing at Acre just after Easter with his chief princes and richly welcomed by Queen Melisende at Jerusalem. He also learned that a substantial contingent of crusaders from southern France arrived at Acre, led by Alfonso-Jordan, son of the famous Raymond of Toulouse of the First Crusade, who had taken the Cross from St. Bernard with Louis VII at Easter at Vézélay. However, Tripoli had for some time been ruled by Raymond II, grand-nephew of the original Raymond of Toulouse and the husband of Hodierna, third of the imperious daughters of Baldwin II of Jerusalem, sister of Melisende and Alice. Clearly Alfonso-Jordan's title to the county of Tripoli that Raymond of Toulouse had personally wrested from the infidel was better than Raymond II's, and Alfonso-Jordan announced that he intended to make use of it. Marching to Jerusalem, Alfonso-Jordan died in agony on the way, from some affliction of the stomach. No foul play was ever proved, but Melisende and Hodierna were both suspected of having poisoned him.[128]

Louis VII seems to have arrived at Jerusalem in early June. After performing all the devotions prescribed for a pilgrim to Jerusalem, he joined with the Emperor and the Papal legate, Cardinal Guido of Florence, Queen Melisende, and a galaxy of noblemen and bishops, including the masters of the new crusading orders—Robert of Craon of the Templars and Raymond of Le Puy of the Knights of St. John, also known as the Hospitallers—for a general

---

[127]Setton, *Crusades*, I, 503-504; Runciman, *Crusades*, II, 278-279; Pernoud, *Eleanor of Aquitaine*, pp. 66-74. Odo of Deuil, an assiduous chronicler who wrote a detailed history of the entire French crusading expedition from its beginning to the arrival of Louis and Eleanor in Antioch, brings it to an abrupt and unexplained halt on the very day of their arrival. William of Tyre, the principal historian of the kingdom of Jerusalem, vouches for the incestuous affair of Eleanor and Raymond.

[128]Runciman, *Crusades*, II, 279-280; Setton, *Crusades*, I, 504-506. It is pleasant to record that at least no scandal ever attached to the youngest of the four daughters of Baldwin II and Morphia, Joveta (Yvette), who spent most of her long life as abbess of a convent near Bethany where Jesus had stayed with Martha and Mary (see Runciman, *op. cit.*, pp. 231-232).

council of war to discuss how best to carry forward the Second Crusade. Despite all reverses and disasters along the way, the Emperor and the King now commanded a combined army of about 50,000, which should have been adequate to challenge any force the Muslims could muster on their frontiers. After prolonged discussion, the decision was made to attack Damascus.[129]

The chorus of scornful condemnation with which almost all modern historians dealing with the Second Crusade have assailed this decision is vastly exaggerated if not totally unjustified. Most historians, like middle echelon State Department bureaucrats, love *realpolitik*. They delight in diplomatic fencing, in describing political leaders and generals playing off their opposite numbers against one another. They tend to dismiss grand strategy as naive and mortal blows delivered to a sworn enemy as ungentlemanly or impossible. And in formulating their arguments they have the inestimable advantage of "20-20 hindsight."

Their case against the decision to attack Damascus is based on the belief that the only chance of the crusading states to survive in the Middle East was to keep their Muslim opponents divided by helping the weaker against the stronger. Since Damascus was historically one of the weaker Muslim Middle Eastern states, so the argument goes, the Crusaders should have left it alone or even made alliance with it. The real danger came from the new ruler in Syria, Nureddin, who had succeeded Zengi there when he was assassinated in September 1146.[130]

Indeed Nureddin did eventually do great harm to the crusader kingdoms and his son Saladin almost destroyed them. But in 1148 no one could have known this was going to happen, nor was an attack on Nureddin in Syria then the only way to have prevented it from happening. As Hilaire Belloc pointed out repeatedly in his writings on the crusades, Damascus was the strategic key to the Levant:

> Had the Crusaders permanently occupied the *whole* maritime belt of Syria between the Mediterranean and the desert they would have cut Islam in two. That is the central strategic truth of the Crusades—but they never occupied the whole. They held the western side of it; they failed to hold the eastern side, and along that eastern side of the "Bridge" which the Christians never mastered, the Moslems could communicate at will, pass from their eastern to their western half and bring armies down behind the western invaders of the seacoast. . . .
>
> But though they failed to hold the eastern road, might they not have cut it and so destroyed its usefulness as an avenue of approach for hostile armies? Yes, they could have cut it at Damascus and to have cut it there would have been permanently effective; for just at the point of Damascus the desert approaches the inhabitable belt, so that, with Damascus held

---

[129]Setton, *Crusades*, I, 506-507.
[130]*Ibid.*, I, 513-514.

against them, Moslem armies could not have marched round it on their way south. . . .

It would be an exaggeration to say that the capital strategic importance of Damascus decided the objective of the Second Crusade; a dozen cross motives came in—including the quarrel of Louis VII with his wife and his reluctance to help the Lord of Antioch (his wife's relative and perhaps more) by attacking Aleppo. But it would be a worse exaggeration to say that the march on Damascus was a mere blunder. Had it succeeded and had Damascus been held—a thing perhaps impossible with the effectives available—not only this campaign would have been decided at a blow but the future of Palestine might have been decided in favor of Christendom.[131]

Belloc's brilliant strategic argument has never been answered or even seriously addressed by any of the standard authorities on the history of the Crusades. The army led by Louis VII and Emperor Conrad was the only crusading army that ever attempted to take Damascus. Their victory could have permanently secured the triumph of the Crusades, very possibly reconquering Syria and eastern Asia Minor for Christendom as Palestine had been reconquered, and saving Eastern Europe from centuries of subjection to the Turks. If we take a hard look at the position of Damascus on the map instead of seeing only the foreign policy of the man then ruling it, the stakes and the opportunities of this climactic operation of the Second Crusade become clear. The game was worth the candle.

The crusading host arrived in the vicinity of Damascus July 23, led by the knights of the crusader kingdoms in the east, followed by Louis VII and his French, with Emperor Conrad (rather appropriately, in view of his record in the Crusade so far) bringing up the rear. The Crusaders pushed through the orchards southwest of the city and drove the defenders back from the Barada River that flows beside it. Inside the city there was much fear; but Unur, their governor, held firm, appearing before the people holding the Koran of Caliph Othman, successor of the mighty conqueror Omar. He also got in touch with knights of Antioch whom he knew would listen to him, warning of a massive attack on them by Nureddin and his brother Saif-ad-din if they did not retire quickly from Damascus. Furthermore, Emperor Conrad and King Louis had agreed to grant Damascus when conquered to Count Thierry of Flanders, but Queen Melisende and the Jerusalem nobles wanted Guy of Beirut to have it, and were resentful in consequence.[132]

For reasons never satisfactorily explained, but probably involving deliberate misdirection by some who no longer wanted to see Damascus taken,[133] the besiegers were now persuaded to move to the eastern or desert

---

[131]Hilaire Belloc, *The Crusades* (Milwaukee WI, 1937), pp. 229-230, 260-261.

[132]Setton, *Crusades*, I, 507-509; Runciman, *Crusades*, II, 281-283.

[133]Emperor Conrad III himself later declared that this was the true explanation for

side of Damascus, despite its lack of water. The defenders promptly reoccupied and fortified the orchard and river area which the crusaders had first penetrated, which had plenty of water. Nureddin was reported to be on the march south, though he was still more than a hundred miles away, at Homs. On July 28, just four days after beginning the siege, the crusaders gave it up.[134] Groping through the fog of confusion surrounding these events at the time and ever since, we can come to no better conclusion than that both Conrad and Louis decided that they could no longer effectively command an army which had so many among its officers and in its ranks whom—with good reason—they did not trust.

Suddenly, the Second Crusade was over—with the exception of a final and very important victory in Spain, where on the last day of 1148 Count Ramon Berenguer IV of Barcelona, aided by the Genoese and the Templars, took Tortosa at the mouth of the Ebro River after a six months' siege, thereby delivering a death-blow to Moorish power in the north of Spain.[135] Emperor Conrad left for Constantinople almost immediately; Louis tarried until the next Easter, hoping for a change of fortune and some new opportunity. But none came. His return was long and painful. He and Eleanor sailed separately. Reaching Sicily, they were feted by its King Roger, but Eleanor fell suddenly ill on learning that her paramour and uncle Raymond of Poitiers had been slain in battle by Nureddin. Stopping in Rome to see the Pope, they found him almost embarrassingly solicitous for their reconciliation; he pointed out that the impediment of consanguinity Eleanor was now citing could easily be dispensed and that he would be happy to do it, and even led them personally to their bed. But Eleanor had made up her mind to reject Louis, and not even the Pope could change her mind. She and Louis completed their voyage home from Rome again in separate ships.[136]

But the Crusader cause still burned in men's hearts. No one could understand or explain the defeat that had been suffered, but the cause could not be abandoned. St. Bernard urged the reluctant Pope Eugenius to try again:

> Because God does what he wishes, it is no reason why we should not do our duty. But I as a faithful Christian hope for better things and think it

---

this fatal move (Setton, *Crusades*, I, 510).

[134]Runciman, *Crusades*, II, 283-285; Setton, *Crusades*, I, 509-510, 514-515.

[135]Lomax, *Reconquest of Spain*, p. 93; O'Callaghan, *Medieval Spain*, pp. 231-232. Lérida and Fraga (where Alfonso the Battler had been fatally ambushed) were reconquered in October 1149. Two years later Alfonso VII and Ramon Berenguer made a treaty at Tudejar dividing between them all of Spain not yet reconquered from the Moors, thereby demonstrating their commitment to the completion of the reconquest and their expectation that it would come soon. See Recuero Astray, *Alfonso VII*, pp. 188-189, in addition to the abovementioned authorities.

[136]Setton, *Crusades*, I, 510-511; Runciman, *Crusades*, II, 326; Pernoud, *Eleanor of Aquitaine*, pp. 76-79; Norwich, *Kingdom in the Sun*, pp. 139-141.

great joy that we have fallen on divers trials. Truly we have eaten the
bread of grief and drunk the wine of sorrow. Why are you, the friend of
the Bridegroom, fearful, as though the kind and wise Bridegroom had not,
according to His custom, saved the good wine until now? "Who knows but
he will relent and be appeased, and leave behind a blessing." Certainly the
Divine Goodness is wont to act in this way, as you know better than I do.
When has not great good been preceded by great evils? To mention
nothing else, was not that unique and unparalleled gift of our salvation
preceded by the death of Our Savior?[137]

The only result of St. Bernard's impassioned pleas then was a desperate
proposal to place him in command of another crusade, which he rightly rejected
as totally inappropriate.[138] But in Jerusalem a new figure had appeared, the
young King Baldwin III, now 19, showing much of the spirit of his two
magnificent namesakes who had reigned there before him. After Nureddin had
killed Raymond of Poitiers and sent his skull to the Caliph of Baghdad in a
silver case, Baldwin with the Templars rode to the rescue of Antioch, and it was
held. In 1152 he secured the crown of Jerusalem for himself alone, removing
(not without difficulty) his mother Melisende at last from all power. Whatever
the mistakes and even the treason before Damascus, most of the knights of the
crusader kingdoms still knew what was at stake; Joscelin II, former Count of
Edessa, was captured by Nureddin in April 1150, blinded, and held prisoner in
Aleppo for the rest of his life, but despite great pressure he held true to his
Christian faith to the end.[139]

As St. Bernard's life drew toward its close, like a blazing meteor dipping at
last toward the horizon, he could observe the rise of a family in his own France
that would have a mighty impact in years to come, though even he probably did
not imagine through how many years that impact was to be felt: the
Plantagenets of Anjou.[140] After the death of Emperor Henry V many years
before, Count Geoffrey of Anjou had married the Emperor's widow Matilda,
the claimant to the throne of England who was the only surviving child of the
English King Henry I. In 1133 they had a son, also named Henry, now vigorous
and ambitious and unusually mature for his age. In 1148 Matilda had left
England, essentially abandoning her claim to rule it in favor of her son.
Stephen was still holding out as King of England, but his power was dwindling.

---

[137]St. Bernard to Pope Eugenius III, *Letters of St. Bernard*, tr. James, p. 471.
[138]Williams, *St. Bernard*, pp. 286-287.
[139]Runciman, *Crusades*, II, 327-328, 334-335; Robert L. Nicholson, *Joscelyn III and the Fall of the Crusader States, 1134-1199* (Leiden, 1973), pp. 16, 21.
[140]Count Geoffrey of Anjou received that name from his practice of planting broom-plants (*genestas*) for hunting cover. The Plantagenet dynasty ruled England for more than 300 years, from Henry II in 1154 to Richard III in 1485—one of the most vigorous ruling families in all of history, with most of its members distinguished by remarkable physical strength as well as mental ability.

He had bowed to the will of Pope Eugenius and St. Bernard by removing William Fitzherbert as Archbishop of York and recognizing the Cistercian Henry Murdach, hoping thereby to gain Papal recognition of his son Eustace as heir to the English throne; but the Pope still would not grant that recognition.[141]

Young Henry's was the rising star, and in August 1151 he appeared in Paris with his father at court to do homage to Louis VII for Normandy and Anjou. Count Geoffrey was in his prime, not yet forty, strong, handsome, self-willed. While Louis VII was away on crusade, Count Geoffrey had arrested the King's seneschal in Poitou, Gerard Berlai. Such acts of defiance of a monarch absent on crusade incurred excommunication, and this penalty had been levied on Geoffrey. Yet he still brought Gerard to court in chains. St. Bernard urged Geoffrey to release his prisoner, saying that he would absolve him of his excommunication if he did so. Geoffrey refused, with a blasphemous cry that if holding a prisoner was a sin, he would refuse to be absolved of it.

St. Bernard was now sixty years old, pale, drawn, emaciated; Count Geoffrey could probably have picked him up with one hand. But the eyes that had cowed emperors and kings, cardinals and antipopes still burned with a fire from beyond this world, and his voice came like the trump of the Archangel Gabriel.

"Beware, Count of Anjou," St. Bernard said, "for with what measure ye mete, it shall be meted unto you."

Gerard, in his chains, went down on his knees to ask the saint's blessing.

"It is not for myself I grieve," he said, "but for my family."

"Fear not," St. Bernard said. "Rest assured that God will help you, and sooner than you would have dared to hope."

Within a few days Count Geoffrey had set Girard free, and his son had done homage to King Louis for Normandy. The next month the Count of Anjou suddenly died.[142]

But young Henry does not seem to have been abashed; and there is reason to believe that it was on this occasion that he decided to marry the Queen of France. Her estrangement from her husband and desire for an annulment was hardly a secret, in view of the sensational events at Antioch during the Second Crusade; because of Eleanor's stubborn rejection of Louis, a reconciliation was clearly impossible, though Louis had long desired it. Two daughters had been born to them, but no son. Louis was evidently tired of battling her adamantine will. There is a tradition that St. Bernard recommended the annulment; it may be true, though one hesitates to believe that Bernard would urge the break-up of any marriage on such flimsy grounds, so easily dispensed from. But he may have seen that this woman could only

---

[141]Lane Poole, *Domesday Book to Magna Carta*, pp. 128-129, 148; Davis, *Stephen*, p. 117.

[142]Williams, *St. Bernard*, pp. 216-217; Pernoud, *Eleanor of Aquitaine*, pp. 81-83.

bring grief and sin to everyone associated with her. Louis had already suffered much from her. St. Bernard had led Louis along the road to spiritual more than worldly glory, and could have wished to guard him from the spiritual perils to which she exposed him. But no more than anyone at Louis' court did St. Bernard guess that Eleanor would take instant advantage of the annulment to marry Henry, now heir to Anjou and Normandy and arguably to England, joining thereby to all that he had and claimed her own extensive lands of Aquitaine, creating a domain exceeding that of France itself in area, population, and wealth. It all happened in the spring of 1152, sowing the seeds of centuries of war between France and England.[143]

During these years Pope Eugenius III continued to have trouble with the people of Rome. Though he had excommunicated Arnold of Brescia, he was unable to expel him from the city, and finally in June 1150 was compelled to leave it again himself. He urged Emperor Conrad to come south to be crowned in Rome and to restore it to order. Conrad agreed to come, but died before he could do so, in February 1152; he was the first Holy Roman Emperor since Otto the Great never to be crowned at Rome. The new Emperor, the vigorous and able 26-year-old Frederick "Barbarossa" (so called for his red beard), promised the Pope full support, and in December 1152 Rome submitted once more to Pope Eugenius, who remained in it for the remaining seven months of his life.[144]

During his period of enforced absence from Rome, Pope Eugenius performed a major service for the Church through the mission to Scandinavia of his legate Cardinal Nicholas Breakspear, an Englishman (the future Pope Adrian IV). Scandinavia was still not far removed from Viking savagery. Bloody civil wars among claimants to the thrones of the Scandinavian countries were the rule rather than the exception. Christianity was well established in Denmark, somewhat less solidly in Norway; in Sweden there was still much popular paganism, but two Cistercian monasteries, daughters of Clairvaux, had been founded in 1143 at Alfwastra and Nydala on the central waterways of the country through which the Göta Canal now runs, in the diocese of Linköping. The Archbishop of Lund in the area of far southern Sweden called Scania, then part of Denmark, was metropolitan of the whole of Scandinavia, which Norway and Sweden saw as insulting to their status as independent nations. Going first to Norway in the summer of 1152, Cardinal Breakspear obtained recognition of the authority of young, deformed King Ingi from his two hostile half-brothers; Ingi's widespread popular support despite his handicap indicated a growing political maturity and sense of Christian charity in Norway. The Cardinal then

---

[143]Pernoud, *Eleanor of Aquitaine*, pp. 87-91; Williams, *St. Bernard*, pp. 217-218; Lane Poole, *Domesday Book to Magna Carta*, pp. 162-163.

[144]Mann, *Popes in the Middle Ages*, X, 158, 164-167, 173; Greenaway, *Arnold of Brescia*, pp. 126, 143-144; Haverkamp, *Medieval Germany*, p. 147; Marcel Pacaut, *Frederick Barbarossa* (New York, 1970), pp. 62-64.

created Nidaros (Trondheim) an archdiocese, using as justification the presence of the grave of St. Olaf there. He brought under it four dioceses in Norway, two in Iceland, and one each in Greenland, the Faeroe Islands, the Shetlands and Orkneys, and the Hebrides and the Isle of Man. He then prepared the first codification of canon law for Norway, introduced the tithe and Peter's Pence, and attempted with limited success to enforce clerical celibacy.[145]

Cardinal Breakspear was considerably less successful in Sweden, whose internal divisions were such that he could not establish a native archbishopric; but he did consecrate the Englishman St. Henry as Bishop of Uppsala, later to be Sweden's primatial see. St. Henry later became the apostle of Finland. Cardinal Breakspear completed his Scandinavian journey with a visit to Denmark and its Archbishop Eskil of Lund, who seems to have accepted the loss of his jurisdiction over Norway with equanimity, as we would expect from a known admirer of St. Bernard who had corresponded warmly with him, welcomed a daughter of Clairvaux established in Danish territory in 1151, and ended his days (long after St. Bernard's death) as himself a monk at Clairvaux.[146]

In the winter of 1153 St. Bernard came close to death; it may have been at this time that he wrote Pope Eugenius: "As for myself, your child, I am more feeble than usual. My life ebbs slowly away, drop by drop, probably because I do not deserve a quick death and prompt entry into life."[147] In the spring he found the strength for a last peacemaking mission, to stop a war between Metz and Lorraine on the eastern border of France. On July 8 Pope Eugenius III, once his monk at Clairvaux, died at Tivoli just outside Rome. On August 13 the new Cistercian monastery of La Peyrouse was founded near Thiviers in the Dordogne, the last daughter of Clairvaux to be established in St. Bernard's lifetime—altogether there had been 68 of them, or 159 if monasteries founded by daughter monasteries of Clairvaux are also counted. The 68 direct daughters of Clairvaux were founded in France, Italy, Sicily, Sardinia, Spain, Portugal, Belgium, England, Ireland, Denmark and Sweden.[148] On August 17 the succession of Henry Plantagenet to the throne of England became assured when on the same day King Stephen's son Eustace died and a son was born to Eleanor and Henry.[149] But by this time St. Bernard had passed beyond all

---

[145]Edith M. Almedingen, *The English Pope (Adrian IV)* (London, 1925), pp. 55-56, 81, 90-92, 106-110, 115-122; Williams, *St. Bernard*, pp. 77-78; Karen Larsen, *A History of Norway* (New York, 1948), pp. 130-135.

[146]Almedingen, *English Pope*, pp. 123, 127-133; Eino Jutikkala and Kauko Pirinen, *A History of Finland* (New York, 1988), pp. 22-24; Williams, *St. Bernard*, pp. 88-89; St. Bernard to Archbishop Eskil, *Letters of St. Bernard*, tr. James, pp. 493-494.

[147]*Letters of St. Bernard*, tr. James, p. 419.

[148]Williams, *St. Bernard*, pp. 92, 358-359; Mann, *Popes in the Middle Ages*, X, 174.

[149]Lane Poole, *Domesday Book to Magna Carta*, pp. 164-165; Warren, *Henry II*, pp. 51, 78.

political concerns. On August 20 he died, aged 62. This Son of Thunder left the world gently, almost silently; all Christendom acclaimed him in death, as in life, a saint. Within 21 years he was canonized.[150]

Indeed, for 23 years, since the outbreak of the Pierleoni schism, he had almost *been* Christendom, in his own person. Christendom in those years lived under St. Bernard's white mantle. Sword and scepter were vanquished by the spirit. The world was still, as it must always be until the Judgment, full of sin and evil; but the world of Christendom was also full of the radiance of St. Bernard. The Church has had great saints since, perhaps even greater, but none ever again whose life and universal impact quite matched that of Bernard of Clairvaux.

---

[150]Williams, *St. Bernard*, pp. 360-362.

3
The Church Checks Royal Power
(1153-1181)
(Popes Anastasius IV 1153-54, Adrian IV 1154-59, Alexander III 1159-81)

"You know how loyal I have been to you, from whom I expect only a temporal reward. How much more ought we both to do faithful and honest service to Almighty God, from Whom we receive temporal and hope for eternal goods! You are indeed my lord, but He is my lord and yours. It would be useful neither to you nor to me if I were to neglect His will in order to obey yours. For on His fearful Day of Judgment you and I will both be judged as servants of one Lord."—Archbishop of Canterbury Thomas Becket to King Henry II of England, November 1163[1]

"For the name of Jesus and the defense of the Church, I embrace death."—last words of Archbishop Thomas Becket as he was slain by the sword in Canterbury cathedral, December 29, 1170[2]

In Catholic Christendom in the second half of the twelfth century there were three monarchs whose power was of a higher order of magnitude than any others: Holy Roman Emperor Frederick Barbarossa, ruling Germany and northern Italy; Henry II ruling England and half France; Louis VII ruling the remainder of France. The first two, in the arrogance of their power, directly challenged the Church and sought to make it, at least in their own domains, subordinate to them. Frederick Barbarossa aspired to conquer Italy and choose the Popes; Henry II aspired to bring the whole Church in England—beginning with its primate, the Archbishop of Canterbury—under his jurisdiction and control. Both sought to restore the absolutist government which, in memory and in law, was Rome's darkest legacy. Both were stopped and defeated by the Church. Their defeats provide the clearest object lesson in the years of the glory of Christendom of how and why totalitarian government is *impossible* in a truly Catholic political and social order.

The third of these leading monarchs of Catholic Christendom, Louis VII, the hero of the Second Crusade (even if not properly appreciated as such, in his own time or later) alone remained faithful to the Catholic vision of limited

---

[1]Richard Winston, *Thomas Becket* (New York, 1967), p. 153.
[2]*Ibid.*, p. 366.

government. To the envoys of Henry II he said, with pride rather than shame, just after Archbishop of Canterbury Thomas Becket had fled to his dominions for refuge: "I am as much a king as the King of the English, but I do not have the power to depose the least of the clerks in my realm."[3] The embattled Popes of this time of absolutist challenge found Louis VII of France the only one of the great kings upon whom they could always rely.

Blessed Pope Eugenius III had died only six weeks before his incomparable mentor, St. Bernard of Clairvaux. His successor—chosen without demur—was Conrad, Cardinal Bishop of Sabina, the Pope's governor of Rome, a highly respected prelate famous for his unswerving loyalty to Pope Innocent II during the Pierleoni schism. But this election was made with a surprising lack of foresight; for the new Pope, who took the name Anastasius IV, was nearly ninety years old, quite possibly the oldest of all the Popes in the Church's history at the time of his consecration. The assumption of the greatest responsibility that can be borne by any human being on earth descends with a crushing weight on the stoutest mind and heart; more than twenty Popes have died within six months of their consecration. In view of this, it is perhaps surprising that the aged Anastasius IV lived as long as he did—nearly a year and a half, until December 3, 1154. But, crippled by age and weakness, he made almost no mark on history during that time.[4]

His successor was Nicholas Breakspear, the only English Pope, born in Hertfordshire, near the famous Benedictine abbey of St. Albans. His father had left the world to join that abbey, but for whatever reason the community would not admit the son, who therefore left England for France, where eventually he gained admission to the monastery of St. Rufus near Avignon and was elected their abbot. When hostility developed against him later because he was a foreigner, and the dispute came to the attention of Pope Eugenius III, that former Cistercian monk recognized in Nicholas Breakspear a kindred spirit, removed him from his abbey, made him Cardinal Bishop of Albano near Rome, and several years later sent him on the very important mission to Scandinavia reviewed in the preceding chapter. Highly regarded for his success on that mission, energetic, resolute, and young for a Pope (probably no more than fifty), he was elected Vicar of Christ the day after Anastasius IV died, taking the name of Adrian (Hadrian) IV—a name which ran in his English family.[5]

The next day, December 5, 1154, was a Sunday, and on that day Pope Adrian IV was consecrated. On the same day the new Holy Roman Emperor

---

[3]*Ibid.*, p. 214.

[4]Horace K. Mann, *The Lives of the Popes in the Middle Ages*, Volume X (London, 1925), pp. 222-230; George W. Greenaway, *Arnold of Brescia* (Cambridge, England, 1931), p. 147.

[5]Mann, *Popes in the Middle Ages*, X, 235-246; Greenaway, *Arnold of Brescia*, pp. 147-150.

Frederick, known as "Barbarossa" for his red beard, not yet thirty years old, was holding court at Roncaglia on the Po River near Piacenza in northern Italy. He had come south from Germany across the Brenner Pass in October, his first departure from his native land where he had been chosen emperor to succeed his uncle Conrad III in March of 1152. Frederick Barbarossa was the great-grandson of Emperor Henry IV, the unyielding foe of the Pope St. Gregory VII, through his daughter Agnes. Frederick's father being dead, the nobles and bishops gathered in electoral assembly chose him in preference to Conrad III's seven-year-old son to avoid a long royal minority, and in preference to the rival Welf family of Bavaria because Frederick's family, the Hohenstaufens, had furnished four of the last five Holy Roman Emperors.

A man of striking intelligence, vitality, and willpower, Frederick Barbarossa had a very exalted concept of the office to which he had been elected. The scholars of his century had rediscovered Roman law; and although Frederick himself never became at ease with the Latin language in which virtually all writing in Catholic Christendom was then done, he was well aware of their finding that the power of the Roman Emperor had been unlimited. Charlemagne, the first Holy Roman Emperor, had known little of the original Roman Emperors except their legendary, 300-year-old memory. He saw them through Christian eyes, from the Christian world-view. Frederick Barbarossa was a practicing Catholic who recognized his obligation to rule justly. But his head was turned by what he had heard of the absolute power of the ancient emperors. He bore their title, thought of himself as their equal, and wanted to wield the same power they had. In his first letter to Pope Eugenius III he declared his aim to be restoration of "the grandeur of the empire in all its former glory."[6]

Frederick Barbarossa had a sharp, perceptive, quick but not reflective mind. For at least the first two decades of his long reign it does not seem to have occurred to him seriously to examine the merits of the question on which Pope St. Gregory VII and his great-grandfather had differed so fundamentally: the Pope's authority as moral judge of kings and emperors. He neither denied it nor recognized it; he simply ignored it. He did not expect the Pope to challenge him directly; when that happened, he reacted with anger and an even greater determination to have his way.

He was not initially hostile to the papacy. On March 23, 1153 he had signed a solemn treaty with Pope Eugenius in which he called himself "Advocate and Defender of the Holy Roman Church" and pledged himself to "maintain and defend the honor of the papacy," while the Pope in turn promised to crown him Holy Roman Emperor and to honor him and his office. The two parties agreed not to give any support to Byzantine imperial ambitions

---

[6]Marcel Pacaut, *Frederick Barbarossa* (New York, 1970), pp. 46-57.

in Italy and that the Emperor would help the Pope suppress rebellion in the city of Rome.[7]

Frederick, however, was determined to treat at least northern Italy (the plain of Lombardy) as part of his own domain, just as much as Germany was. He came there in the fall of 1154 with a small army. He heard complaints and grievances from all sides, freely gave judgment, and was acclaimed by nearly everyone present. He seemed to forget the difficult history of his four predecessors as Holy Roman Emperors in Italy, assuming it was his already.[8]

Meanwhile the new Pope faced a severe challenge in Rome, where the pugnacious rebel Arnold of Brescia claimed to have revived the ancient Roman senate, which had refused to recognize the validity of Adrian IV's election, at least until he recognized the Roman "republic" for which the senate claimed to speak. Arnold, a disciple of Peter Abelard who never repented as his master had done, had long been seeking political power in Rome. But in Pope Adrian IV he found his match. The Pope would not negotiate with him, and flatly demanded his expulsion from the city before he would negotiate with the senate. The greater part of Rome was under rebel control, and when Cardinal Guido was attacked in its streets during Lent 1155 while on his way to an audience with the Pope and badly wounded, Adrian took unprecedented action: he imposed an interdict on the Eternal City until Arnold was removed. It was the first interdict on Rome in the history of the Church. With Holy Week impending and all their famous and historic churches closed, the Roman people forced the senate to make peace with the Pope, and Arnold was driven out.[9]

He sought aid from the Emperor as a last resort, but Frederick Barbarossa had no use whatsoever for demagogic rebels, and turned Arnold over to Adrian, who had him executed. It was rare for Popes to inflict capital punishment, but Arnold of Brescia had kept Rome in a turmoil, rendering it constantly dangerous for four successive Popes, and nearly fatal for Cardinal Guido; he had never shown signs of seeking reconciliation, nor being willing to accept reconciliation. He had many sympathizers; there could be no assurance that any prison would hold him. Execution was probably the only practical solution.[10]

On June 9, 1155 Pope Adrian IV and Emperor Frederick Barbarossa met at the Emperor's camp near Sutri. Though Frederick had been told of the famous incident of King Pepin of the Franks personally leading Pope Stephen III's horse when he met him in France, with the twelve-year-old Charlemagne in

---

[7]*Ibid.*, pp. 62-63.
[8]*Ibid.*, pp. 65-66; W. F. Butler, *The Lombard Communes; a History of the Republics of North Italy* (London, 1906; Westport CT, 1969), pp. 101-102.
[9]Greenaway, *Arnold of Brescia*, pp. 150-151.
[10]*Ibid.*, pp. 152-153; Mann, *Popes in the Middle Ages*, X, 256-259.

attendance,[11] and of later similar marks of respect to Popes by the now almost legendary Charlemagne, he balked at making a comparable gesture—holding Pope Adrian's stirrup as he dismounted. Seeing this as an important test of the new Emperor's attitude toward him, Adrian thereupon withheld from Frederick the kiss of peace. The next day the Emperor thought better of it. When the Pope appeared he led his horse for a few steps and then held his stirrup, following which Pope and Emperor exchanged the kiss of peace.[12]

All was now harmonious (at least for the time being) between the two men. Frederick scornfully dismissed a deputation from the now collapsing Roman "senate" and quickly made arrangements for his formal coronation in St. Peter's as Holy Roman Emperor, on a Saturday rather than the Sunday which was usual for such ceremonies, and without notifying the people of Rome.[13] The Pope crowned Frederick June 18 with the most solemn ceremony, invoking the Most Holy Trinity and praying that Frederick would "so wear it [the crown] in justice and mercy that you may receive from our Lord the crown of eternal life."[14] A distressing battle followed in the city with the remaining adherents of the republic, but the German soldiers defeated them with heavy losses. Pope Adrian personally intervened with Frederick to secure the release of all the prisoners. As the unfamiliar Italian summer heat began to take its toll on the health of his men, the Emperor marched back to Germany.[15]

For the moment Pope Adrian had excellent relations with Emperor Frederick Barbarossa, and at the same time he encouraged the able young Byzantine Emperor Manuel Comnenus, who was known to be pro-western though still schismatic, to send troops to southern Italy to fight the Sicilians. Their notoriously intransigent King Roger had died in 1154, succeeded by his only surviving son, William I. Victorious in southern Italy but facing a potential threat from no less than two emperors, William made his peace with the Pope in June 1156. By the Treaty of Benevento Adrian recognized William as King of Sicily and received his homage. William was conceded substantial influence in the church in Sicily, much less in the church in southern Italy.[16]

In the summer of 1157 Emperor Frederick marched into Poland to punish its harsh and oppressive King Boleslav IV for failing to pay him promised

---

[11]See Volume II, Chapter 11 of this history.

[12]Mann, *Popes in the Middle Ages*, X, 260-262; Peter Munz, *Frederick Barbarossa, a Study in Medieval Politics* (Ithaca NY, 1969), pp. 80-83.

[13]Munz, *Frederick Barbarossa*, pp. 85-86; Greenaway, *Arnold of Brescia*, pp. 154-155.

[14]Mann, *Popes in the Middle Ages*, X, 266.

[15]*Ibid.*, X, 266-270; Munz, *Frederick Barbarossa*, pp. 86-91; Greenaway, *Arnold of Brescia*, pp. 155-156; *The Cambridge Medieval History*, ed. J. R. Tanner, C. W. Previté-Orton, and Z. N. Brooke, Volume V (Cambridge, England, 1926), pp. 421-422.

[16]Mann, *Popes in the Middle Ages*, X, 255, 274-278; John J. Norwich, *The Kingdom in the Sun, 1130-1194* (New York, 1970), pp. 187-199; *Cambridge Medieval History*, V, 423-424.

tribute. Frederick captured Breslau and Poznán and compelled the reluctant king to agree to the Peace of Krzyszkowo which admitted imperial authority in Poland and promised payment of an even larger tribute.[17] He then went to Burgundy, the ancient state in southeastern France which was the third and least important of the great realms in his domain (the others being Germany and Italy). His purpose in Burgundy was to take formal possession of the great estates in that country of his wife Beatrice, whom he had married the previous year, to receive the homage and regulate the authority of the Burgundian nobility, and to provide for more efficient government there. A congress (or "diet," as the Germans called it) was held at Burgundy's capital of Besançon in October.[18] And there occurred a sudden, unexpected, and serious clash between the Emperor and the Pope.

It will be recalled that shortly before becoming Pope, Adrian IV had conducted a highly successful visit to the Scandinavian countries in which he established a full Norwegian hierarchy for the first time, giving Norway its own metropolitan and removing that entire country from the jurisdiction of the metropolitan of Denmark, Archbishop Eskil of Lund. Rather untypically, Eskil had not objected.[19] Pope Adrian clearly had great love and respect for Archbishop Eskil, and was distressed and angry to learn that the aged prelate had been waylaid in Burgundy by a rogue nobleman who mistreated him and held him for ransom despite his ecclesiastical status. Emperor Frederick had been requested to act in Eskil's behalf, but had not done so. Pope Adrian IV therefore sent a sharp letter of reproof to be read at the diet of Besançon by his chancellor, Cardinal Rolando Bandinelli.[20] After reviewing the treatment of Archbishop Eskil and the failure of the Emperor to aid him, the letter continued:

> You ought, most noble son, to keep constantly before your mind's eye with
> how much joy and pleasure your holy mother, the sacred church, received

---

[17]Ibid., p. 77; Cambridge Medieval History, V, 388-389; Tadeusz Manteuffel, The Formation of the Polish State; the Period of Ducal Rule, 963-1194 (Detroit, 1982), pp. 132-133. This campaign of Frederick Barbarossa in Poland is almost sufficient by itself to dispose of the extraordinary theory propounded by Barbarossa's recent biographer, P. E. Munz, that by 1156 he had developed a "Great Design" for establishing a unitary state in the valleys of the upper Rhine, the Rhone, and the Ticino while permitting the rest of Germany to remain in feudal anarchy. Frederick undoubtedly wanted to exercise strong rule in the areas Munz focusses on, but he had the same ambitions everywhere else, as Munz's own data on his pressure northeast to Chemnitz and the Erzegebirge show (Frederick Barbarossa, p. 113). Munz does not even mention the Polish campaign of 1157 and the Peace of Krzyskowo.
[18]Pacaut, Frederick Barbarossa, pp. 77-78. Pacaut states that Frederick came to Burgundy in February 1157 and "stayed for several months." If so, he must have then left to campaign in Poland and returned for the October diet.
[19]See Chapter Two, above.
[20]Mann, Popes in the Middle Ages, X, 286-287.

you some years back; the cordial affection she has always borne you; the great dignity and honor she showed you when she so liberally conferred [*conferre*] the imperial crown upon you; the manner in which she watched with benevolent attention over your elevation to the sublime honors, careful never to oppose your royal will in any way. Nor do we regret having in all ways satisfied your wishes, and had Your Excellency received still greater benefits [*beneficia*] at our hands—if this were possible—we should have been overjoyed at the great advantages and profits that might, thanks to you, have accrued to the church and ourselves.[21]

Inoffensive and complimentary as this passage appeared, it was the occasion of an explosion. For *beneficium*, in addition to its normal and general meaning still expressed by the English word "benefits," was also a technical term in feudal law, there meaning "fief"—a grant of land or income which required homage and service ("fealty") in return. And the word *conferre*, in addition to its normal and general meaning still expressed by the English word "confer," was also the verb used in feudal law for the granting of a fief.[22]

It is very important to recall here that Emperor Frederick Barbarossa knew almost no Latin and that, so far as we know, Cardinal Bandinelli knew no German. The document was translated as he read it by the imperial chancellor, Rainald of Dassel, one of the chief architects of Frederick Barbarossa's empire-building strategy. In German, the word "benefit" in its general sense is *Wohltat*, and in its feudal legal sense is *Lehen*. No such distinction exists in Latin. Rainald translated *beneficia* in the Pope's letter as *Lehen*.[23]

The resulting tumult could have been wholly spontaneous—angry nobles thinking their emperor had been slighted by a claim that he was the Pope's liege man—or it could have been stirred up by Chancellor Rainald and other persons who wanted to see the worst interpretation placed on the Pope's words.[24] In the excitement, either Cardinal Bandinelli or the other Papal legate was believed to have said: "From whom did he [Frederick] receive the empire, if not from the Pope?" Though there is some doubt that these words were

---

[21]Pacaut, *Frederick Barbarossa*, p. 80.

[22]*Cambridge Medieval History*, V, 390-391.

[23]Mann, *Popes in the Middle Ages*, X, 287; Karl Breul, *Cassell's New German and English Dictionary* (New York, 1936-1939), I, 369, 734; II, 48. For Rainald see Munz, *Frederick Barbarossa*, pp. 93-95, 125-126.

[24]Marshall W. Baldwin, *Alexander III and the Twelfth Century* (New York, 1968), p. 35, mentions this as a distinct possibility, as does Mann, *Popes in the Middle Ages*, X, 287. The possibility of deliberate misinterpretation by Rainald and others is at least as credible as the suggestion made by generally anti-papal historians that Pope Adrian IV was laying a semantic trap for Frederick, hoping to provoke the Emperor and arouse him to anger (e.g., Pacaut, *Frederick Barbarossa*, pp. 79-80, and Munz, *Frederick Barbarossa*, pp. 142-145) or that Machiavellian wordsmiths in the Papal curia had intended the Emperor to accept the word *beneficia* in the normal general sense and then tax him with having accepted it in the technical feudal sense (*Cambridge Medieval History*, V, 392).

actually spoken, or who spoke them if they were said,[25] the statement itself makes sense (if undiplomatic, and imprudent in the circumstances) in light of the concept of the Holy Roman Empire and the fact that Frederick Barbarossa had indeed been crowned by Pope Adrian IV at his own request. Why was coronation by the Pope necessary, if the Pope did not have unique authority to confer the fullness of imperial authority as leader of Christendom? This was more than the specific and immediate political authority the Emperor had as ruler of Germany and Burgundy, which he no more held directly from the Pope than the kings of England or France held their political authority directly from the Pope. The Emperor's authority over Italy did depend substantially on his status as Holy Roman Emperor, and was called into question, as we shall see, by his insistence that the papal coronation was a ceremony of little real meaning.

During the outburst the Papal legates had been physically threatened. Frederick intervened to protect them from harm, but ordered their baggage searched and their documents seized, and curtly dismissed them, telling them to return directly to Rome, "turning neither to the right nor to the left, nor stopping on the way."[26] Very soon afterward he sent a circular letter to his kingdom denouncing the Pope in terms that recalled the language of his great-grandfather Henry IV, when he demanded that Pope St. Gregory VII resign (before coming to Canossa). Pope Adrian IV, Frederick Barbarossa declared, was "the cause of dissension, the seed of evil, the poison of pestiferous disease."[27]

The Pope responded with a letter to the German bishops urging them to help persuade Frederick to act more calmly and rationally in this matter, and to counteract the influence upon him of Chancellor Rainald. Their reply, though often misrepresented as cold or timid, quite clearly indicates that they were attempting to do just what the Pope asked them. Fortunately for all concerned, Chancellor Rainald went to Italy the following spring. Separated from his negative influence, Frederick became more reasonable. Pope Adrian wrote to him directly, this time taking the precaution of sending the letter by the distinguished German bishop and historian Otto of Friesing, who could be trusted to translate it correctly. The Pope explained that he had never intended the word *beneficia* to indicate anything like a feudal fief nor to claim temporal sovereignty anywhere by it. Receiving the Pope's letter at Augsburg in June,

---

[25]Mann, *Popes in the Middle Ages*, X, 287-288.

[26]*Ibid.*, X, 288. Munz's argument of a Machiavellian plot by Cardinal Bandinelli to provoke a hostile reaction by the Emperor in Besançon reaches a *reductio ad absurdum* when he argues (*Frederick Barbarossa*, pp. 186-190) that Bandinelli had intended to provoke Frederick, but not enough to be kept out of Germany!

[27]Mann, *Popes in the Middle Ages*, X, 289.

Frederick accepted it graciously and harmony was apparently restored.[28]

The whole episode was a warning of trouble to come. Even if it was no more than an honest misunderstanding by Frederick and his advisors, it showed an alarming suspicion and hostility toward the papacy.

Within a few days of this apparent concord between Pope and Emperor, Frederick Barbarossa left Augsburg for another march into Italy. The cities of the Lombard plain continued to war against one another and denounce one another to him; and the largest of them, Milan, had directly defied him, conquering cities, capturing castles, strengthening its defenses, and destroying the rival city of Lodi when its government would only take an oath of obedience to Milan "saving the fidelity due to the Emperor." In August he laid siege to Milan and took it in a month. The surrender terms provided that Milan should rebuild Lodi, pay a large indemnity, build a castle for the Emperor in the heart of the city, and submit their nominations for each year's consuls (Milan, like other Italian cities at this period, had adopted the old Roman system, at least in theory) to the Emperor for approval.[29]

Another diet was called to meet at Roncaglia, where the diet had met four years before at the beginning of Adrian's pontificate, this one to spell out still more clearly Frederick's imperial powers in Italy. They were nothing if not sweeping. The city representatives, cowed by the quick defeat of powerful Milan, made almost no objection. Doctors of jurisprudence from the nearby University of Bologna, carried away by their recent rediscovery of Roman law and the heady wine of imperial consultation and approval, proclaimed that the Emperor's will alone made law. According to "constitutions" published by the Emperor at Roncaglia November 11, 1157, all activities of municipal and feudal governments were under his ultimate authority, to direct as he saw fit. Local self-government could exist only and to the extent that he granted it. While Frederick did recognize some long-standing traditional local authority where documents could be adduced to prove its existence, the authority of city governments was a new phenomenon in Italy as in the rest of Europe, not antedating the twelfth century, and there was often little or no documentary basis for it. The Emperor cut at the heart of city self-government by

---

[28]*Ibid.*, X, 290-295; Pacaut, *Frederick Barbarossa*, pp. 82-83; Baldwin, *Alexander III*, pp. 36-38; *Cambridge Medieval History*, V, 391-392, 425-426. It is absurd to call this "a resounding victory for Barbarossa" (Pacaut, *op. cit.*, p. 83). Since neither Pope Adrian IV nor any other Pope had ever claimed temporal sovereignty over Germany, it was hardly a "victory" to cause the Pope to say so. Much more nearly correct is the statement of Baldwin (*op. cit.*, p. 38) that by maintaining that "the symbol of government, the crown, was properly bestowed [upon the Emperor] by the earthly representative of God, the Pope, and the bestowal was a great benefit or favor," Adrian IV had made "not a retreat, but a reaffirmation."

[29]Butler, *Lombard Communes*, pp. 105-109; Pacaut, *Frederick Barbarossa*, p. 84; Munz, *Frederick Barbarossa*, pp. 160-165.

proclaiming his sole right to appoint their consuls and judges. War among the cities was forbidden, and all male Italians between 18 and 70 were to take a public oath to keep the peace.[30]

Neither the Italian cities nor the Church could accept such a view of the Emperor's authority. Frederick Barbarossa was the legitimate ruler of Germany and Burgundy by hereditary succession and local law, but he ruled in Italy only as Holy Roman Emperor, and the Holy Roman Emperor's authority outside Germany had been intended, ever since Charlemagne, to be the authority of an ultimate arbiter and military commander against infidels and heretics, not a man who appointed magistrates in every city. Even in feudal Germany or France or England, the assertion of power for such direct rule, bypassing the feudal system and city charters, would have been strongly resisted. Roman absolutism (except to a considerable extent in the Byzantine empire) was dead. Just because the law professors at Bologna had rediscovered it did not mean that it should be revived in practice. It was not the Christian and Catholic way.[31]

By the winter and spring of 1159 the resistance was taking form. First Genoa, then Milan, then the little city of Crema defied the Emperor's claims of direct governmental authority in them. Pope Adrian IV challenged the Emperor's right to seize, control, or bestow Papal lands in Tuscany, part of the donation of the pious Countess Matilda at the beginning of the century. The Emperor's response was to call into question even the Pope's right to rule Rome itself. If he was King of the Romans, he declared, then he should rule temporally in Rome.[32]

Under these circumstances, the Pope and the Lombard cities had a broad and obvious common interest, which they quickly moved to express in practical terms. While the little city of Crema fought heroically against the imperial armies in August 1159, Milan, Brescia, and Piacenza leagued with the Pope against the Emperor, and Adrian IV pledged to excommunicate Frederick Barbarossa in forty days if he did not significantly change his course.[33]

---

[30]Butler, *Lombard Communes*, pp. 109-113; Pacaut, *Frederick Barbarossa*, pp. 85-86; Munz, *Frederick Barbarossa*, pp. 119-121, 165-170.

[31]Munz, *Frederick Barbarossa*, p. 168n, argues that Roman law was the basis for the Pope's authority over the universal Church. In this argument he misses the fundamental distinction between canon and civil law and also the fact, amply documented in the preceding volumes of this history, that the Popes exercised such authority, beginning as early as the first century, whenever and to the extent that they were strong enough to do so; they certainly did not need to wait and did not wait for the scholarly rediscovery of Roman law in the twelfth century.

[32]*Cambridge Medieval History*, V, 429-430; Mann, *Popes in the Middle Ages*, X, 303-306; Butler, *Lombard Communes*, p. 115; Pacaut, *Frederick Barbarossa*, p. 90-92.

[33]Mann, *Popes in the Middle Ages*, X, 307-309; *Cambridge Medieval History*, V, 430. The alliance—sometimes called the First Lombard League—is poorly documented. Several chroniclers allude to it, but we have nothing in writing stating the specific

But Pope Adrian IV did not live out those forty days. On September 1 he died suddenly, apparently of a heart attack.[34]

On September 5 thirty-one cardinals assembled in conclave at a closed chamber in St. Peter's cathedral to elect the next Pope. The majority favored Cardinal Bandinelli, the Papal chancellor who had stood his ground so well at the tumultuous diet in Burgundy, who was committed to maintaining Adrian IV's policies and was especially highly regarded for his knowledge of canon law. Two days later a large majority—no vote was taken, but it appears from the best account we have that there were only three dissenters—chose Bandinelli. His opponent was Cardinal Octavian, a favorite of Emperor Frederick Barbarossa, who came of the line of Tusculan counts that had produced the sinister Marozia and Alberic who so dominated the papacy in the tenth and early eleventh centuries. There is substantial evidence indicating that Frederick had promised Octavian to make him Pope regardless of all opposition and the votes of the cardinals.[35]

Once Cardinal Bandinelli had been elected, the distinctive scarlet mantle then worn by the Popes was brought out to be put over his shoulders. He hesitated, pleading that the honor of the election was greater than he deserved. Then Octavian stepped forward and forbade him, in the name of the Emperor, to don the mantle. This only made the other cardinals more determined that Bandinelli should take it, and he bent his head in a gesture of acceptance. To the utter astonishment of everyone present, the distinguished Cardinal Octavian now sprang at the mantle. A struggle ensued for possession of the ceremonial cloth, and it was finally torn out of Octavian's grasp. But Octavian had been prepared for this; his chaplain stood by with another scarlet mantle, which he quickly popped over his master's head. In his hurry and excitement, however, he put it on backwards; the hood was in front, and had it been drawn up in the usual manner would have entirely covered Octavian's face.[36]

Yanking wildly at the misplaced hood, Octavian rushed out into the nave

---

pledges that were made, nor the reasons or conditions for Pope Adrian IV's promised excommunication of Emperor Frederick Barbarossa.

[34]*Cambridge Medieval History*, V, 430.

[35]Mann, *Popes in the Middle Ages*, Volume XI (London, 1925), pp. 15-18; Paul J. Knapke, *Frederick Barbarossa's Conflict with the Papacy* (Washington, 1939), pp. 56-62; Munz, *Frederick Barbarossa*, pp. 205-210. Knapke quotes the account of Gerhoh of Reichersberg which states that there were only three votes for the Antipope, and gives an excellent summary of the evidence that Frederick planned and orchestrated these events. Munz's tendentious account, which says that only a "slight majority" favored Bandinelli, despite abundant footnoting does not cite Gerhoh and strongly denies Frederick's personal involvement, though he admits that Frederick's representative in Rome, Otto von Wittelsbach, was deeply involved.

[36]Mann, *Popes in the Middle Ages*, XI, 18-19. The description of this extraordinary scene, both outrageous and hilarious, comes from Cardinal Boso, who was present; it is quoted at length by Baldwin, *Alexander III*, pp. 46-47.

of the cathedral, where a group of clergymen were eagerly awaiting the result of the conclave. Seeing him in the scarlet mantle, not noticing that it was put on backwards, they acclaimed him Pope; and at almost that moment a group of armed men burst into the cathedral, shouting the Papal name that Octavian had obviously already told them he was going to assume, "Victor IV." The unarmed cardinals, including the truly elected Pope, fled at once, and the Antipope, now able to turn his mantle around, was enthroned and then escorted to the Vatican palace, while Cardinal Bandinelli took refuge in the fortress attached to St. Peter's, controlled by his supporter Cardinal Boso, where he announced that his Papal name would be Alexander III. After a ten-day siege Octavian left by night. The next day Pope Alexander III was taken through Rome in procession. But Rome was not safe for either Pope or Antipope; the following day Alexander departed as well. Two days later he was consecrated and crowned in the little town of Nympha, beginning a pontificate of 22 years—the longest since Adrian I during the reign of Charlemagne—and a schism of 18 years, marked by the mutual excommunications of Pope and Antipope within the next two weeks.[37]

Frederick now called for a council to meet at Pavia in northern Italy to decide between the two Papal claimants, whom he pretended to place on a footing of complete equality in his mind. Alexander III naturally refused to attend a council called without his approval by the sovereign whose support for the Antipope was widely known or suspected.[38] Writing to Frederick, he reminded him forcibly of the duties of his office:

> Our wish is to honor you as the special defender and patron of the Roman Church, and as far as in us lies we desire the increase of your glory. Therefore we supplicate you to love and honor the Holy Roman Church your mother; to watch over her peace as becomes your imperial excellence, and not to favor in any way the great iniquity of the invading schismatic.[39]

The synod at Pavia was held in February 1160, attended mostly by bishops supporting the Emperor and entirely controlled by his men. No one dared vote against his wishes, though the few bishops who could not accept his antipope tried to slip away before the vote was taken. Even historians sharply critical of most of the medieval Popes admit that the synod of Pavia was packed and its arguments and proceedings farcical. Octavian was proclaimed Pope as "Victor IV"; we hear of no dissenting votes. Later that month, upon hearing the news, Pope Alexander excommunicated the Emperor and, following the course first mapped out by Pope St. Gregory VII, declared his subjects absolved from their

---

[37]Mann, *Popes in the Middle Ages*, XI, 19-24; *Cambridge Medieval History*, V, 431; Baldwin, *Alexander III*, p. 47.
[38]Baldwin, *Alexander III*, pp. 48-50; Knapke, *Barbarossa's Conflict*, pp. 62-64.
[39]*Cambridge Medieval History*, V, 432.

duty of allegiance to Frederick.[40]

The battle lines were now clearly drawn, and it was to be many long years before Frederick Barbarossa—proud, angry, confident, in his prime and at the peak of his powers, sure of the support of his people as his great-grandfather Henry IV had not been—would come to Canossa. During the latter part of the year 1160 Frederick attempted to cut off communications to and from Alexander III in central Italy, imprisoning, hanging, and mutilating the messengers. His antipope had no significant support outside the lands he ruled directly, except for Scandinavia, where the kings of Denmark and Norway favored him. Fernando II of León in Spain, who also had a strong influence in the affairs of Castile where his five-year-old nephew was titular king, supported Alexander III, along with the Count of Barcelona, Ramón Berenguer. Duke Vladislav I of Bohemia and King Geza II of Hungary proclaimed Alexander, as did a church council in Nazareth in the kingdom of Jerusalem. But the decisive choice would be made by the kings of France and England. They were so much stronger than any of the other kings in Christendom except for the Emperor that the adhesion of even one of them to Frederick's cause might make it impossible for Alexander to prevail. Ever-faithful Louis VII of France stood firm for Alexander III. The primate of England, Archbishop Theobald of Canterbury, meeting with the English bishops in June 1160, took his stand with them for Alexander.[41]

But Henry II Plantagenet, king of England and half of France, whose father had been cursed by St. Bernard of Clairvaux, who was aggressively ambitious and already had three sons by Eleanor of Aquitaine, exacted a price for his support. Meeting with the legates of Pope Alexander III and Norman bishops at Neufmarché in Normandy, Henry insisted that before he would proclaim Alexander as Pope, the legates must agree to the "marriage" of his five-year-old son Henry with two-year-old Princess Margaret of France.[42]

Arranged marriages among royalty were a staple of medieval and Renaissance diplomacy, and marriage agreements often involved very young children; but very young children were rarely if ever compelled actually to take part in a marriage ceremony, at their age an obvious mockery of that holy sacrament. But such a mockery Henry II demanded and got. Louis VII

---

[40]For the admissions of historians critical of the Papacy, see Pacaut, *Frederick Barbarossa*, pp. 95-97; Munz, *Frederick Barbarossa*, pp. 216-220; *Cambridge Medieval History*, V, 433-434; Norwich, *Kingdom in the Sun*, p. 267. For accounts more sympathetic with Pope Alexander III, see Mann, *Popes in the Middle Ages*, XI, 30-37; Baldwin, *Alexander III*, pp. 50-51; Knapke, *Barbarossa's Conflict*, pp. 64-67.

[41]Mann, *Popes in the Middle Ages*, XI, 39-40, 45-47; Baldwin, *Alexander III*, pp. 52-55; Pacaut, *Frederick Barbarossa*, p. 103.

[42]Baldwin, *Alexander III*, p. 53; Knapke, *Barbarossa's Conflict*, p. 69; W. L. Warren, *Henry II* (Berkeley CA, 1973), pp. 72, 90; Régine Pernoud, *Éleanor of Aquitaine* (New York, 1968), pp. 133-134.

protested vehemently when he heard of it; Pope Alexander assured him that the legates had made this agreement without his consent or knowledge, but admitted that he did not dare countermand their action in view of the damage to the Church that would be done by Henry II's adherence to Emperor Frederick's schism. On November 2, 1160 the little boy was scandalously married to the infant girl. The marriage and dowry agreements were drafted and their execution supervised by Henry II's brilliant and worldly chancellor, Thomas Becket of London.[43]

Though Rome was still unsafe, Pope Alexander III was able to remain in Italy even after Emperor Frederick Barbarossa appeared in the spring of 1161 with another huge army (said to number 100,000) and laid siege to Milan, demanding the destruction of its walls and its total submission to his appointed governors. The increasingly desperate defenders held out for nearly a year, to no avail. On March 1, 1162 starvation forced them to surrender unconditionally. Frederick ordered their great city razed to the ground, and this was done in just six days. On April 1 he actually celebrated Palm Sunday on its ruins. He moved quickly to impose his full and direct rule on the cities of the Lombard plain. Most were forced to accept his appointed governor, the podestà, usually a German nobleman who knew little and cared less of Italian traditions and customs and was concerned only with extorting as much money as possible from the city he ruled.[44]

The Pope had been staying in Genoa, but the fall of Milan made it imperative that he leave Italy. He and his party embarked on Genoese ships March 25. It was too early for safe sailing in the Mediterranean, infamous for its winter storms; the Pope's vessel could make no headway against the winds and seas, yet dared not turn back. At some time during Holy Week they disembarked on a small rocky island off the coast, and there spent the high holy days. Only the Pope's staff and the ship's crew were with him to kiss the cross on Good Friday and hear the Easter proclamation read during the night-watch of the Resurrection. Once again, for the Vicar of Christ as for his Master, it was "foxes have holes, and birds of the air have nests, but the Son of Man has nowhere to lay his head."[45]

Pope Alexander III arrived in France on Wednesday of Easter week. The next month, at a synod of bishops meeting at Montpellier, he resolutely renewed his excommunication of the Emperor and his antipope. His presence did much to encourage Louis VII to stand firm against the Emperor's blandishments and to refuse a meeting with the Emperor and Antipope in

---

[43]Mann, *Popes in the Middle Ages*, XI, 44-45; Winston, *Becket*, pp. 93-95.

[44]Butler, *Lombard Communes*, pp. 120-122; Pacaut, *Frederick Barbarossa*, pp. 99-100; Munz, *Frederick Barbarossa*, pp. 179-185, 273-275; *Cambridge Medieval History*, V, 434-435.

[45]Matthew 8:20; Baldwin, *Alexander III*, p. 60.

August 1162. On September 23 Louis and Henry II both met with Alexander III at Coucy on the Loire and formally recognized him as Pope, while making peace with each other.[46]

The following May the Pope presided at a council meeting at Tours, attended by no less than 17 cardinals, 124 bishops and more than 400 abbots. The council proclaimed Alexander III, condemned the Antipope, and denounced Manichaean heretics. One of the most eminent of its participants was the former chancellor of England, Thomas Becket, who had arranged the scandalous marriage of the royal children and helped insist on its approval as a condition for support of Pope Alexander III by King Henry II of England. Becket had been made Archbishop of Canterbury, primate of England, following the death of staunch old Theobald, who had held that office and unwaveringly supported the true Pope. Already, Thomas Becket's way of life had strikingly changed, for he had embraced his new duties and responsibilities with a total commitment, making it clear even to his erstwhile friend and lord, the king, that he knew what it meant now to be in the service of the King of kings. He was greeted with enthusiasm by the people and with great honor by the Pope, who rose to greet him when he arrived. It was the first time the Pope had met Thomas Becket.[47]

Our sources tell us nothing specific about the impression each of these two men made upon the other; but, in the words of Becket's best modern biographer:

> It is surely not speculating too far to assume that both men were struck by their similarities. Alexander, like Thomas, was a former chancellor (of the papacy), an experienced canon lawyer, a theologian who had been influenced by Abelard, a man of diplomatic skill and high executive capacity who dispatched his cardinal-legates unceasingly throughout the Christian world. The most important feature of this council was the meeting of the two men, though neither could know this at the time. Nevertheless, Pope and archbishop had an opportunity to exchange views and to take the measure of each other; and it must have surprised and pleased the Pope to learn that this English archbishop held an even more stiffly high-Gregorian position on the privileges and immunities of the Church than he himself.[48]

---

[46]Baldwin, *Alexander III*, pp. 60-62; *Cambridge Medieval History*, V, 436-437; Pacaut, *Frederick Barbarossa*, pp. 104-105.

[47]Mann, *Popes in the Middle Ages*, XI, 65-66; Knapke, *Barbarossa's Conflict*, p. 72; Winston, *Becket*, pp. 136-138; David Knowles, *Thomas Becket* (Stanford CA, 1970), p. 79; Frank Barlow, *Thomas Becket* (Berkeley CA, 1986), pp. 84-86. For the great change in Thomas Becket following his consecration as archbishop, see Winston, *op. cit.*, pp. 125-130, and Barlow, *op. cit.*, pp. 74-82. Barlow's review of the evidence on Becket's transformation is particularly significant in light of Barlow's general tone of hostility to Becket and doubt of his sanctity.

[48]Winston, *Becket*, p. 138.

Indeed we may be sure that Pope Alexander III, with all his diplomatic experience, marked this man, by virtue of his office one of the chief prelates of Christendom, by virtue of his close friendship with the King of England a figure of great political influence as well. The Pope already had unforgettable proof of Henry II's duplicity and ambition. Louis VII of France was single-hearted and straightforward, needing only to be reminded of his duty. Henry II, on the other hand, could never be trusted; yet for the Church's sake he must be prevented at all costs from ever joining Frederick Barbarossa and the schism. Could Thomas Becket help the Pope accomplish this? After all, he was Henry's closest friend; when he returned from the Council of Tours, the mighty monarch of England and half France greeted him "with the affection of a son."[49]

Neither the Pope nor the Archbishop could then have imagined the road to Calvary they would walk together during the next seven years.

Parallelling the rediscovery of Roman civil law in the twelfth century was the codification and spreading application and enforcement of canon law, the law of the Church. The central figure in this important development was Gratian, a monk of Bologna, who about 1140 published his compilation of canon law, the *Concordia discordantium canonum*, generally known as the Decretals of Gratian. Rolando Bandinelli, the future Pope Alexander III, was one of the first masters of the study of canon law based on Gratian's Decretals. The future archbishop Thomas Becket had also studied canon law at Bologna. One of the major elements of canon law was its provision for jurisdiction over the clergy and their discipline. The bishop had this jurisdiction, with appeal to the Pope provided for under specified conditions. A bishop could deprive a cleric of his clerical status and privileges as part of his punishment for a major offense; after this deprivation he fell under civil rather than ecclesiastical jurisdiction. But could he be punished twice for the same offense, first by degradation by the Church court, then by civil penalties in the civil court? This point had remained unclear. But it was very clear that initial jurisdiction over a cleric accused of violation of civil or canon law belonged to the bishop, not to the king. In England this had been specified both by the laws of Canute the Great in Anglo-Saxon times and by the laws of William the Conqueror after the Norman conquest. It rendered fraudulent at the outset all the later claims of Henry II that in demanding double jeopardy for clerical offenders in both ecclesiastical and civil court he was only maintaining "the ancient customs of England."[50]

---

[49]Mann, *Popes in the Middle Ages*, XI, 161.
[50]See the masterful review of this thorny and oft-disputed topic by the great English medieval scholar and Church historian David Knowles in his *Becket*, pp. 26-27, 80-85.

But Henry II had little knowledge of, and less concern for canon law. He was determined to restore and maintain order and suppress crime in an England ruled by mighty feudal nobles lording it over a conquered people whose language they disdained to speak—nobles whose predatory instincts had been sharpened by twenty years of license during the chaotic reign of Stephen. It was reported to Henry that more than a hundred murders had been committed in England by clerics since the beginning of his reign nine years before.[51] Henry did not believe these murderers and other clerics guilty of violent crime were receiving sufficiently harsh sentences in the Church courts, which by canon law could not order execution or mutilation.[52] Therefore, at a meeting of his bishops and barons convened at Northampton October 1, 1163, Henry demanded that "clerks who are caught committing crimes, or have confessed them, be degraded, deprived of all protection of the Church, and handed over to my court for corporal punishment."[53]

After consulting with his bishops, surprised and confused by the sudden crisis, Archbishop Becket replied:

> The customs of Holy Church are fully set forth in the canons and decrees of the Fathers. It is not fitting for you, my lord king, to demand, nor for us to grant, anything that goes beyond these, nor ought we consent to any innovation.[54]

Denying (contrary to historical truth) that he was proposing an innovation, Henry II insisted on submission to his authority. Becket replied that he and his fellow bishops would always obey the King's rightful authority, "saving our order."

Henry's famous Angevin temper exploded. "By the eyes of God!" he roared, "let me hear no word of your order! I demand absolute and express

---

See also Austin Lane Poole, *From Domesday Book to Magna Carta, 1087-1216* (Oxford History of England), 2nd ed. (Oxford, England, 1955), p. 196.

[51]Winston, *Becket*, pp. 143-144.

[52]Barlow, *Becket*, p. 91. The term "clerics" as then used included all those in minor orders; it was by no means limited to priests or those who would now be called "religious." "Benefit of clergy" was claimed with some frequency by criminals who only pretended to be clerics (Winston, *Becket*, p. 142).

[53]Winston, *Becket*, p. 149. Historians discussing the dispute between Archbishop Becket and King Henry II customarily refer to these clerics accused or convicted of crime as "criminous clerks." There is no such word as "criminous" in modern English, and historians use it in no other context. It must derive from some old English translation of the contemporary documents on this dispute, all of which were in Latin. There is no apparent reason for its use but self-conscious archaism or sophomoric mockery of the "quaint." Furthermore, the use of the word "clerks" in modern English, when clerics are meant, is archaic and confusing.

[54]Winston, *Becket*, p. 150.

agreement to my customs!"[55]

Then he polled the bishops. All but one repeated Becket's statement, firmly reiterating its essential qualification "saving my order." (The one exception, Hilary of Chichester, omitted this clause but substituted "in good faith.") Speechless with anger at this defiance, Henry II abruptly left the hall. The next day he ordered his son Henry removed from Becket's tutelage and deprived Becket of all the material holdings and rewards he had received while royal chancellor.[56]

The next month the two men met again, on horseback in a field. The King reproached Becket for ingratitude.

> Have I not raised you from poverty and lowliness to the summit of honor and rank? Even that seemed little to me unless I also made you the father of the kingdom, placing you above myself. How is it then that after so many benefits, so many proofs of my love for you, which everyone is aware of, you have so soon been able to blot them from your mind, so that you are not only ungrateful but oppose me in everything?[57]

The primate of England answered the King with the words that stand at the head of this chapter—words which define once and for all why a faithful Christendom can never tolerate an absolute monarchy.

The split was now complete; nothing remained but to appeal to the Pope. Henry's envoys—two French clerics, Bishop Arnulf of nearby Lisieux and Archdeacon Richard of Poitiers—reached him first, residing as he was at Sens in northern France near the frontier of Normandy. Pope Alexander did not realize how deep the dispute had already gone; he saw it as more of a semantic disagreement, and could not consider it apart from the overriding danger of the schism promoted by Emperor Frederick Barbarossa and how much it would be strengthened if Henry II joined it. The Pope urged compromise, and sent Abbot Philip of l'Aumône, a daughter house of Clairvaux—Abbot Philip had been trained by St. Bernard—to try to make peace. Philip devised a formula which he persuaded both Henry II and Becket to accept: the King would swear that he would not introduce any new customs or make any demand upon the English bishops contrary to their ecclesiastical responsibilities; Becket would drop the reservation "saving my order" in pledging loyalty to Henry II. The precise language to which Becket ultimately and reluctantly agreed in December was to say to the King: "Know that I shall observe the customs of your kingdom in good faith, and as is only proper, shall be obedient to you in

---

[55]*Ibid.* Note the significance of the expression *my* customs. A custom is not created by royal decree. Henry II was in effect admitting that he had in fact introduced an innovation, just as Becket had said.

[56]*Ibid.*, pp. 151-152.

[57]*Ibid.*, p. 153.

everything that is right."[58]

Henry did not regard this statement as a full capitulation. He demanded a public submission and apology from Becket at another assembly of barons and bishops called to meet at the royal hunting lodge of Clarendon in January 1164. When Becket resisted this, Henry flew into a terrifying rage, threatening to inflict death or mutilation on the bishops. Some of them pleaded with Becket to change his position; others—notably Bishop Foliot of London—later claimed to have stood firm. Leading nobles also begged Becket to promise publicly to observe "the customs." Two Templars went so far as to pledge on the surety of their immortal souls that if Becket made public avowal to observe the customs, Henry would never demand anything of him "contrary to your will or your order."[59]

It is fortunate that God does not accept such wagers, or the Templars would have ended in Hell. When after three days Becket (followed by all the other bishops) announced in the King's hall: "I declare that I will observe the customs of the kingdom in good faith," Henry at once raised the question of what these customs actually were, and ordered them formally defined by two of his officials. In short order they returned with a document that was to become the legal heart of the great controversy: the 16-point Constitutions of Clarendon, demanding that Becket and his fellow bishops sign and seal it.[60]

The articles in the Constitutions of Clarendon to which Becket (and, later Pope Alexander III) most strongly objected were: (1) royal courts rather than Church courts to decide cases involving land and income granted to local churches, called "advowsons" (Article I); (2) royal courts to issue summonses to clerics accused of crimes and, if they are convicted in Church court, to punish them like lay offenders (Article III); (3) no clergy to leave England without the King's permission (Article IV); (4) no royal official nor feudal nobleman holding land directly from the King to be excommunicated, or his lands placed

---

[58]*Ibid.*, pp. 156-157.

[59]*Ibid.*, pp. 158-160. Bishop Foliot's later self-serving but eloquent declaration contrasting his allegedly unbreakable firmness with what he calls Becket's shameful surrender at Clarendon is quoted or cited with glee by every critic of Becket (e.g. Warren, *Henry II*, pp. 474-475). But the simple truth is that if Foliot indeed stood firm in support of Becket's position and in defiance of the King at Clarendon, he never did it again; while though Becket seemed to give way at Clarendon, he never gave way again. The later record of both men casts grave doubt on the credibility of Foliot's account of his own constancy at Clarendon.

[60]Winston, *Becket*, pp. 160-165; Barlow, *Becket*, p. 99. Barlow's curious conclusion that "the procedure would have surprised no one" because "sworn recognitions were a familiar part of Anglo-Norman judicial and administrative proceedings" stands in direct contradiction to the later statement of Henry II's own mother, the former Empress Matilda, that reducing to writing these "customs" regarding relations between Church and state in England "was without precedent" (Winston, *op. cit.*, p. 165). Clearly the demand did surprise Becket.

under interdict, without the King's permission (Article VII); (5) appeals in Church courts to proceed from archdeacon to bishop to archbishop, but no higher (that is, not to the Pope) without the King's consent (Article VIII); (6) the King to hold vacant archdioceses or dioceses with their revenue, until the vacancy is filled by an election in his chapel with his assent (Article XII).[61]

Historians may discuss and argue endlessly to what extent any or all of these six provisions had actually ever been "customs of the kingdom" (at times strong kings had demanded or even enforced some of them, while weaker kings or those more respectful of papal authority had not), but it should be obvious at a glance that they authorized large-scale lay intervention in the working of the Church and the sanctions the Church could impose on recalcitrants.

Becket had no doubt of the threat posed by the Constitutions of Clarendon. He had been trapped by Henry's deceit. Assured that he needed only to make a general promise to abide by unspecified "customs" in the King's dealings with the Church, he was now confronted with these unprecedented written demands, alleged to be a codification of the "customs," which he knew that he must not and would not accept. The Constitutions included a declaration that he and the bishops had orally endorsed the "customs" they claimed to specify; but to make his assent final and unequivocal the Archbishop of Canterbury must place his seal upon it. This Thomas Becket resolutely refused to do. But he had made the oral agreement, even though never assenting to this document; he had opened the way for it, abandoned his strongest position. On the road back to Canterbury his Welsh cross-bearer, Alexander Llewellyn, reproached him for this to his face: "When the shepherd has fled, the sheep lie scattered before the wolf."[62]

> Whereupon Thomas groaned and said, sighing: "I repent, and am so horrified by my sin that I judge myself unworthy to approach as a priest Him whose Church I have vilely bartered. I will sit silent in grief until the 'day-spring from on high hath visited me,' so that I merit absolution by God and the lord pope."[63]

It was not the first time in the history of Christendom, nor the last, when the repentance of a contrite and resolute soul proved a mightier weapon for justice and the Faith than any that could have been forged if he had not first fallen grom grace.[64] St. Peter had first marked out that road, when he denied

---

[61]Knowles, *Becket*, pp. 89-90; Baldwin, *Alexander III*, pp. 90-91.

[62]Winston, *Becket*, p. 167.

[63]*Ibid.*, pp. 167-168.

[64]The spiteful attempts of some historians to cast doubt on the sincerity of Becket's repentance for his actions at Clarendon are not worthy of refutation—especially when we are dealing with a man later hewed down by the swords of armored soldiers in his own cathedral for his fidelity.

his Lord three times before the cock crowed twice, but came back to be the first Vicar of Christ.

Pope Alexander III, apprised of the Constitutions of Clarendon by both Becket and Henry II, promptly rejected ten of the 16 articles (including the most seriously objectionable six reviewed above) and absolved Becket from any sin he had incurred by agreeing to them. In a diplomatic gesture, the Pope agreed to Henry's request to name Becket's rival Archbishop Roger of York Papal legate, but without giving Roger jurisdiction over Canterbury.[65]

In April 1164 Pope Alexander's position was strengthened when Antipope Octavian died after becoming insane. Though Archbishop Rainald of Cologne, the real head of the antipapal party, secured the immediate unanonical election of a successor, Guy of Crema, who called himself Paschal III, the change of antipopes and the obviously uncanonical election and consecration of Guy substantially weakened the schism; resistance to it began mounting even in Germany itself.[66]

But nothing could now divert King Henry II from his fatal course. He saw Becket's repentance as betrayal, and set his face against him once and for all. In November he summoned Becket to another meeting of the royal council at Northampton, where he began by convicting him on trumped-up charges and fining him 800 pounds, then demanded a general accounting of his finances and a bond of 20,000 pounds—a sum far beyond Becket's ability to raise without a great deal of advance notice. His bishops were divided (Bishop Foliot of London, who had claimed to be staunch at Clarendon at the beginning of the year, now called for his resignation). Becket had a kidney stone attack which confined him to bed, unable to stand. In that condition he was told that the King was planning to imprison him for life or mutilate him.[67]

The next day, November 13, 1164, Becket forbade his bishops to sit in judgment on him, their superior, and said that if the laity raised their hands against him, the other bishops should excommunicate those responsible and appeal to the Pope. Bishop Foliot openly defied him and announced that he would appeal to the Pope against him. Becket said the Mass of St. Stephen the martyr and went to Northampton castle, where the council was being held, taking his archepiscopal cross from the hands of faithful Alexander Llewellyn and bearing it himself into the castle. Bishop Foliot was at the door with Archdeacon Hugh of Lisieux. "My lord Bishop of London," Hugh said, "can you as his dean allow the Archbishop to carry his own cross?" "He always was a fool and always will be," Foliot viciously replied, and actually attempted to

---

[65]Winston, *Becket*, pp. 168-169; Baldwin, *Alexander III*, p. 92.

[66]Baldwin, *Alexander III*, pp. 68-70; Mann, *Popes in the Middle Ages*, XI, 69; Munz, *Frederick Barbarossa*, pp. 236-238.

[67]Winston, *Becket*, pp. 174-182; Barlow, *Becket*, pp. 109-111; Knowles, *Becket*, pp. 94-96; Warren, *Henry II*, pp. 485-487.

wrestle the cross away from Thomas; not until the time of another Henry who did so much to cleave Christendom in two did an English bishop fall so low.[68]

In the great hall of the castle, Bishop Bartholomew of Exeter fell to his knees before Becket, pleading: "Father, spare yourself and us, your brother bishops. The king has let it be known that he will treat all who oppose him as traitors."[69] He, too, was to be echoed by bishops of equally faint heart in the time of Henry VIII.

Thomas, who had fallen himself at Clarendon, was not to be tempted again. "Go," he said to Bishop Bartholomew. "You do not understand the will of God."[70]

When other bishops came to him to plead that they had all promised at Clarendon to observe the customs, Thomas told them:

> The lord king sent these same articles which you call royal dignities to the Pope for confirmation, and they have been returned with disapproval rather than approval. Thus the Pope has given us a lesson. We should be ready to accept what the Roman Church accepts, reject what it rejects. Moreover, if we fell at Clarendon—for the flesh is weak—we ought to regain our courage and with the strength of the Holy Spirit strive against the ancient enemy who forever seeks to make one who stands fall, and to keep the fallen from rising again. If we yielded or swore unjustly, you know that an illegal oath is not binding.[71]

Strengthened or shamed by Thomas' courage, the other bishops now all refused to take any part in the proceedings against him, leaving Henry no recourse but to obtain the Archbishop's condemnation for treason by the noblemen of his council alone. Under the hammering of his domineering and frightening personality, they gave the verdict he demanded in an upstairs room, but for a long time none of them dared announce it to Thomas. When at length they attempted to do so, Becket refused to listen, denying the King's authority to try or judge him, and got up to leave the castle. A wild tumult ensued, with shouts of "Traitor!" and hurling of missiles, before Becket and his attendants could get out of the great hall. (We may imagine the faithful Alexander Llewellyn in the thick of the fray, protecting his holy master.) The castle gate was locked, but the keys were hanging beside it, and the first key tried opened the gate. Someone found the horses of the Archbishop's party. The animals were as upset as the men by the confusion—neighing, stamping, side-stepping. Becket's attendant and later biographer Herbert of Bosham could not mount his skittish horse; the Archbishop, an accomplished horseman, told Herbert to

---

[68]Winston, *Becket*, pp. 182-184; Barlow, *Becket*, pp. 112-113; Knowles, *Becket*, pp. 96-97; Warren, *Henry II*, pp. 486-487.

[69]Winston, *Becket*, p. 188.

[70]*Ibid.*

[71]*Ibid.*, p. 190.

mount behind him on his. Holding the reins in one hand and his archepiscopal cross in the other, Becket on his horse with its double burden cantered away into the town of Northampton, where the townspeople crowded round him with delight, having heard that he had been killed. Their cheers further excited the much-tried horse, so that Thomas had the greatest difficulty controlling it with his one free hand.[72]

Dusk of the short autumn day was coming on in a gale of wind and rain as Thomas arrived at the monastery of St. Andrew's, where he brought all of his attendants into the refectory and ordered supper. Many in his household came to him then to tell him they were leaving him, fearing the King's anger. Thomas, remembering his Lord, called for their places at the table to be filled by beggars and some of the loyal townsmen gathered outside. "This has been a bitter day," he told William FitzStephen. "The Last Day will be more bitter." There was a reading from the history of Cassiodorus. When he heard Christ's words quoted by Cassiodorus, "if they persecute you in one city, flee to another," the Archbishop looked up and met the eyes of Herbert of Bosham. Within an hour Herbert was riding hard for Canterbury.[73]

Becket called for a bed to be made up and brought into the chapel. When the monks came in to sing compline they saw him in it, apparently asleep. But at midnight he tiptoed out of the chapel and, with just three attendants, left the monastery, mounted four now calm horses, and rode out through an unguarded northern gate into the storm. Through the rest of that night they galloped fifty miles into a driving rain, the Archbishop's woollen cloak so soaked that he twice had to cut part of it off to lighten its weight. Continuing for twenty miles after the sun rose, they came to Lincoln, where they found lodging; the Archbishop wore a monk's cowl and called himself Brother Christian.[74]

For the next two weeks Becket carefully made his way from the fen country south to Kent. No king's official found him; as later with Charles II after Worcester and the Royal Oak and Bonnie Prince Charlie after Culloden, not one of the many who knew who he was and where he was betrayed him. On November 2, in the first gray light of dawn, he set sail from Sandwich on the Channel in a small boat, and landed near Gravelines before nightfall. He was given shelter by Abbot Godescalc of St. Bertin, the same abbey that had sheltered a previous Archbishop of Canterbury, St. Anselm, fleeing 67 years ago from another ruthless and self-willed King of England, William II Rufus.[75]

Henry wrote at once to Louis VII of France asking him to give no refuge to Thomas Becket, "who was Archbishop of Canterbury." Louis pounced on

---

[72]*Ibid.*, pp. 190-194; Barlow, *Becket*, pp. 113-114; Knowles, *Becket*, pp. 97-99; Warren, *Henry II*, pp. 487-488.

[73]Winston, *Becket*, p. 194; Barlow, *Becket*, p. 115.

[74]Winston, *Becket*, pp. 195, 199; Knowles, *Becket*, pp. 99-100.

[75]Winston, *Becket*, pp. 200-202.

that past tense. "Who *was* Archbishop of Canterbury?" he demanded of Henry's envoy. "Who has deposed him? Tell me that now, my lords, who has deposed him? Who has deposed him?" It was now that Louis firmly declared (as mentioned earlier in this chapter) that he had no power "to depose the least of the clerks in my realm." He added: "Tell my lord Pope Alexander from me . . . that I hope he will receive the Archbishop of Canterbury with kindness, and not heed any unjust accusation against him."[76]

With Louis VII of France, faithful Catholic and crusader, the fugitive Archbishop of Canterbury was safe.

He was equally safe with Pope Alexander III, who was not going to give up Becket and his cause for any temporary political advantage in the struggle against the Emperor's schism. Herbert of Bosham went first to Sens, where the Pope received him and was moved to tears by his account of Becket's sufferings, flight, and exile. "Your lord still lives in the flesh as you say," Alexander declared, "but while still living he can claim the privilege of martyrdom." The next day Henry II's envoys arrived, including the spiteful Bishop Foliot, who actually said to the Pope—in the course of a long speech—what he had said at the Northampton castle gate, that Becket was a fool.[77]

The Vicar of Christ measured him.

"*Parce, frater,*" he said. "Gently, brother!"

"*Domine, parcam ei,*" Foliot replied. "My lord, I shall not be unkind to him."

"*Non dico, frater, quod parcas ei, sed tibi,*" the Pope said, in one of the memorable rebukes of papal history. "I do not say you are unkind to him, brother, but to yourself."[78]

A few days later Becket himself arrived at Sens, warmly greeted and highly honored by the Pope. The Constitutions of Clarendon were presented, studied, debated, and condemned. Becket may have offered to resign his office, though our sources conflict on this point; if such an offer was made, the Pope refused it. But he did not immediately demand Becket's restoration to Canterbury, hoping that Henry II would eventually think better of the Archbishop. He recommended that Becket take up residence in the Cistercian abbey of Pontigny pending an improvement of the situation in England.[79]

The four and a half years that followed were highly frustrating for both the Archbishop of Canterbury and the Pope. Becket, who knew Henry II much better than the Pope did, never had much hope that he would relent; but the Pope kept expecting Henry finally to see reason, and feared that to press him too hard would drive him into the arms of Frederick Barbarossa and his schism.

---

[76] *Ibid.,* pp. 203-204.
[77] *Ibid.,* p. 205.
[78] *Ibid.,* p. 206; Knowles, *Becket,* p. 105.
[79] Winston, *Becket,* pp. 208-214.

Frederick's chief counsellor Archbishop Rainald of Cologne expected exactly that; in May 1165 he induced a reluctant Emperor Frederick to demand an oath of loyalty to Antipope Guy from nearly all the bishops and great nobles present in council at Würzburg, Germany, mainly on the strength of reports from English clergy accompanying Archbishop Rainald that Henry II was about to join their cause (though most of those taking the oath attached various conditions to it).[80]

In June 1165 Pope Alexander declared the sentence against Archbishop Becket delivered at Northampton the previous November null and void, and ordered Bishop Foliot to go to Henry, then campaigning in Wales, and protest formally against the restrictions on appeals and visits to the Pope in the Constitutions of Clarendon, his expulsion of Becket and ill treatment of the Church, and his negotiations and intercourse with supporters of the Antipope. Foliot later wrote back that Henry had received the Papal reproofs "modestly," that he would not limit visits to the Pope but would limit appeals to Rome by "the ancient customs of England," that Becket was free to return to England but would have to stand trial if he did. Foliot went on to warn that if the Pope put too much pressure on Henry he would go over to the Antipope.[81]

Henry II had other troubles than the Becket controversy during 1165. His campaign in Wales was a complete failure; Owen the Great, King of Gwynedd in north Wales, drove the invading English army to distraction in the tangled Berwyn Mountains. Finally, when floods filled the narrow valleys where his army was encamped, Henry had to withdraw, taking out his fury on the Welsh hostages—mostly children; he blinded the boys and mutilated the girls.[82] When he returned to England, he found his Queen Eleanor of Aquitaine gone to France and having an affair with the nobleman Ralph de Faye, whereupon Henry may have began his famous liaison with "Fair Rosamond" Clifford, for whom he built a legendary "bower" at Woodstock. (However, the next year Henry and Eleanor were temporarily reconciled, and their last child—John, later the infamous king of that name—was born.)[83] Meanwhile, late in November 1165, Pope Alexander III was at last restored to Rome with the help of a Norman army from Sicily.[84]

On Easter 1166 Pope Alexander III confirmed Becket as Papal legate for England, and on May 3 he formally demanded that his property and retainers

---

[80]*Ibid*, pp. 226-227; Baldwin, *Alexander III*, pp. 72-73; Pacaut, *Frederick Barbarossa*, pp. 116-117; Munz, *Frederick Barbarossa*, pp. 239-242.

[81]Winston, *Becket*, pp. 228-231; Barlow, *Becket*, pp. 137-138.

[82]Winston, *Becket*, pp. 231-233; John E. Lloyd, *A History of Wales*, 3rd ed. (London, 1939), II, 516-518; R. R. Davies, *Conquest, Coexistence, and Change; Wales 1063-1415* (Oxford, 1987), p. 53.

[83]Winston, *Becket*, pp. 234-235; Warren, *Henry II*, pp. 17, 100; Pernoud, *Eleanor of Aquitaine*, pp. 117-118.

[84]Baldwin, *Alexander III*, p. 66; Norwich, *Kingdom in the Sun*, p. 269.

be restored to him by Henry II. On Pentecost Sunday at the great shrine of St. Mary Magdalene in Vézélay, France, Becket announced the solemn condemnation and annulment of the Constitutions of Clarendon and the excommunication of the two laymen who had drafted them and the two English clerics who had gone to Würzburg with the schismatic Archbishop of Cologne and encouraged support for the Antipope. He did not condemn the King, but urged him to repent; however, he threatened him with excommunication if he did not. Henry struck back by threatening to seize all Cistercian monasteries in England because the Cistercian monastery of Pontigny in France gave refuge to Becket; consequently Becket left Pontigny, but Louis VII offered him sanctuary anywhere in his dominions, and he chose the Benedictine abbey of St. Columba at Sens. Hard pressed financially and threatened politically by a new German invasion of Italy, Pope Alexander at the end of 1166 forbade Becket to take any further direct action against England, and appointed two cardinals (William of Pavia, a critic of Becket, and Otto of St. Nicholas, a supporter) to negotiate with Henry II, with Louis VII as arbiter.[85]

In March 1167 Pope Alexander III unsheathed the mighty papal weapon forged by Pope St. Gregory VII by declaring the subjects of the schismatic Emperor Frederick Barbarossa absolved from allegiance to him. Several of the cities of northern Italy—notably revived Milan, whose fortifications were rebuilt that spring—thereupon joined the Lombard League against Frederick. That spring Byzantine ambassadors came to Rome to propose the reunion of the Greek Orthodox Church with the Catholic Church in return for the Pope's acceptance of Manuel Comnenus as Emperor in place of the condemned Frederick. But the prudent Pope was in no hurry to take what might prove to be a jump from the frying pan into the fire; the Byzantine Empire and its prelates and rulers had given the Popes and the lay leaders of Western Christendom very little reason to trust them during the past century and a quarter. The Byzantines, fighting hard against the Hungarians in Dalmatia, were in no position to offer immediate military help even if their dangerous offer were to be accepted. Late in July Frederick Barbarossa appeared before Rome and undertook to storm St. Peter's. After several days of fierce fighting he set fire to the oratory of Santa Maria in Turri, adjoining the basilica, and the defenders surrendered so that the whole church might not go up in flames. On July 30 Frederick enthroned Antipope Guy there, who two days later crowned Frederick and his wife Emperor and Empress, while Pope Alexander III escaped in disguise to Benevento.[86]

---

[85]Winston, *Becket*, pp. 237-238, 243-246, 261-266; Barlow, *Becket*, pp. 145-149, 157-158, 162-163; Knowles, *Becket*, pp. 76, 113, 117-118; Warren, *Henry II*, pp. 104, 494-496.
[86]Mann, *Popes in the Middle Ages*, XI, 83-85, 88-90; Norwich, *Kingdom in the Sun*, pp. 270-274; Pacaut, *Frederick Barbarossa*, pp. 122-124; Munz, *Frederick Barbarossa*,

The very next night a torrential rainstorm struck Rome, flooding the sewers and depositing their germ-laden contents upon the city. Plague broke out, spreading with astonishing rapidity throughout the German army in the oppressive summer heat. By the end of the month Frederick Barbarossa had lost 25,000 men and his evil genius, Archbishop Rainald of Cologne. He had to leave the city; but he did not return to Germany, resolving to hold his position in northern Italy, where 16 cities were now joined in the Lombard League against him.[87]

Under these threatening and bloody circumstances, it is hardly surprising that Pope Alexander III somewhat relaxed his pressure against Henry II of England and kept urging Becket and the two cardinal mediators to look harder for some formula to settle the dispute. But Henry's pride had become so deeply involved that successful mediation seemed impossible; Becket, who knew him best, had little hope for it, at least unless accompanied by major ecclesiastical penalties. But these the Pope did not allow him to impose during 1167 or 1168.[88]

Meanwhile the struggle in Italy continued, with Pope Alexander III now directly allied with the Lombard League against Emperor Frederick, championing the cause of local independence upheld by the north Italian cities. Byzantine Emperor Manuel Comnenus renewed his offer to support the allies against Frederick Barbarossa and end the Eastern schism if the Pope would recognize him alone as Emperor; but Alexander now formally rejected this proposal, increasingly confident that the Lombard cities would prevail in any case. Emperor Frederick had to return to Germany in March 1168 by crossing the Alps disguised as a servant. In September the second Antipope died in Rome, which he still controlled; Abbot John of Struma was elected as his antipapal successor, taking the name of Calixtus III. Though each time a new Antipope was chosen—clearly uncanonically—there was a further erosion of support for the imperial schism, the strong will and determination of Frederick Barbarossa continued to keep the schism alive.[89]

In May 1168 Pope Alexander III had written to Becket that the restraints he had placed on the Archbishop's authority to excommunicate persons in England would definitely be lifted the following Holy Week, in 1169. Under the

---

pp. 278-279; Baldwin, *Alexander III*, pp. 77-78; Zoltan J. Kosztolynik, *From Coloman the Learned to Bela III (1095-1196); Hungarian Domestic Policies and Their Impact upon Foreign Affairs* (New York, 1987), pp. 190-192.

[87]Pacaut, *Frederick Barbarossa*, pp. 124-129; Munz, *Frederick Barbarossa*, pp. 283-285; Mann, *Popes in the Middle Ages*, XI, 91-93; Butler, *Lombard Communes*, pp. 133-136; Norwich, *Kingdom in the Sun*, pp. 273-274.

[88]Winston, *Becket*, pp. 270-280; Barlow, *Becket*, pp. 170-179; Knowles, *Becket*, pp. 119-120; Baldwin, *Alexander III*, pp. 107-108.

[89]Pacaut, *Frederick Barbarossa*, pp. 137-140; Mann, *Popes in the Middle Ages*, XI, 93-97.

pressure of this deadline, Henry II was almost prevailed upon to be reasonable. He met with Louis VII of France in a peace conference at Montmirail, agreeing to seal the peace by the marriage of Henry's son Richard (later known as the Lion-hearted) to Louis' daughter Alice (a marriage which never took place) and to meet Becket. But at the meeting Henry demanded that Becket throw himself unconditionally on his mercy, and Becket would not do so without the essential qualifying phrase "saving the honor of God." Henry exploded into another of his famous rages, and even Louis at first condemned Thomas for intransigence, but (once again displaying the true character of this most Christian king) was soon on his knees begging Thomas' pardon for having temporarily abandoned his cause. Pope Alexander appointed two new legates to make a last attempt to mediate the dispute, Cardinal Vivian and Subdeacon Gratian. They had no better success than their predecessors, and on Palm Sunday Becket renewed the excommunications he had pronounced at Vézélay in 1166 and added excommunications of Bishop Foliot of London, the Bishop of Salisbury, and five other laymen for disobedience to his authority and disturbing the peace of the Church.[90]

In July 1169 Pope Alexander III wrote to Henry II telling him in no uncertain terms that he must restore Becket to his see of Canterbury, together with all its possessions, and that in return Becket would do for his king everything an archbishop should do, "saving the honor of God and his order." When Henry met the Papal legates at Domfront in Normandy late in August, he raged and stormed about this until Gratian coldly reminded him: "Don't threaten us, lord. We are the emissaries of a court which is accustomed to giving orders to emperors and kings, and we fear no man's threats." Temporarily abashed, Henry now decided that two could use the "saving" phraseology. He would pledge to comply with the Pope's demands only "saving the dignity of his kingdom." The legates refused to accept this reservation, the negotiations broke up, and Gratian went back to Rome in disgust.[91]

In November Cardinal Vivian decided to try again. He worked out a compromise whereby Henry II would restore Becket and his property, permit appeals to Rome, and abandon the Constitutions of Clarendon, in return for Becket's dropping all "saving" clauses. Since the Archbishop was not now being asked to assent to any "customs" in church-state relations or to throw himself on the King's mercy, he no longer had need of "saving" clauses; Henry's insistence on this as the sole condition for his many concessions shows how irrationally fixated on this semantic point he had become. But the crisis remained unresolved, for when the King and the Archbishop met at Montmartre, Henry refused Becket the kiss of peace which was regarded as the

---

[90]Winston, *Becket*, pp. 280-288; Barlow, *Becket*, pp. 180-184; Knowles, *Becket*, pp. 120-121; Baldwin, *Alexander III*, pp. 109-110.
[91]Barlow, *Becket*, pp. 187-191.

seal of the agreement, saying he had earlier sworn never to give a kiss of peace to Thomas Becket.[92]

Henry's stubbornness regarding Becket had gone beyond reason; with the threat of the imperial schism gradually fading, Pope Alexander III was ready at last to exert his full authority. On January 19, 1170 the Pope condemned Henry II for refusing Becket the kiss of peace and threatened both his English and French domains with an interdict if he did not accept the previously announced terms of settlement of the dispute. Partly to try to divert attention from the Becket controversy, partly because of growing problems within his own family (to be described shortly), Henry now unexpectedly declared his intention to crown his eldest son and namesake King of England that spring. Traditionally, coronation of a king was the sole prerogative of the Archbishop of Canterbury. In February the Pope explicitly prohibited any bishop in England but Becket from crowning Prince Henry. But King Henry simply ignored the prohibition and had the Prince crowned by Archbishop Roger of York on June 14.[93]

This barefaced defiance was the last straw for Pope Alexander. He ordered the prompt restoration of Becket of England on pain of immediate interdict—closing every church in England. Henry gave way with the worst possible grace, still refusing Becket the kiss of peace.[94] On July 21, the day before his "reconciliation" with Thomas was to be officially announced, Henry had the following conversation with Louis VII of France:

> Henry quipped in public to Louis, "Tomorrow your thief shall have his peace, and have it good."
> "What thief, for Heaven's sake?" Louis asked.
> "Your archbishop of Canterbury," Henry replied.
> To which Louis answered, "I only wish he was ours. And if you really are going to grant him a good peace, I thank you."[95]

Louis' doubts about Henry's intentions were to prove only too well justified.

The long unfolding drama now rushes to the curtain scene. On November 3 Becket left his long-time refuge at Sens. On November 30, as he boarded ship to cross the English Channel, he sent the Papal documents suspending Archbishop Roger of York and renewing the excomunication of Bishop Foliot of London on into England by messenger. On December 2 he was given a splendid welcome at Canterbury, and preached a sermon in the cathedral on the text: "Here we have no abiding city, but we seek one to come." On

---

[92]*Ibid.*, pp. 193-195; Winston, *Becket*, pp. 291-295; Warren, *Henry II*, pp. 499-500.
[93]Winston, *Becket*, pp. 296-297, 299, 302-304; Barlow, *Becket*, pp. 200-203, 206-207; Knowles, *Becket*, pp. 125-126, 129-130; Warren, *Henry II*, pp. 501-505.
[94]Barlow, *Becket*, pp. 208-209.
[95]*Ibid.*, p. 208.

Christmas Eve Henry, at Bures in Normandy, hearing reports of Thomas' activities and widespread popular support, told (probably by Archbishop Roger of York) that "while Thomas lives you will have no good days, nor quiet times, nor a tranquil kingdom," flew into another of his wild rages, crying out: "What disloyal cowards do I have in my court, that not one will free me of this lowborn priest!"[96]

Now comes that climactic moment on December 29, 1170, seared into the history of Christendom as by a branding iron. Books, poems, sagas, plays, and the tales of millions of pilgrims over eight centuries have lovingly traced and enshrined every detail of that unforgettable murder in the cathedral. The four muscular, bellowing killers bursting into the presence of the Archbishop; Thomas refusing to flee, for a bishop does not leave his church and his people under attack; Thomas paraphrasing his Lord in Gethsemane: "They have the force and the power of darkness;" the four killers putting on their armor with a mighty clanging and clattering, so that no man in or around the cathedral was capable of resisting them, and rushing through the Archbishop's residence shouting "King's men, King's men!"; their axes upon the door of the Archbishop's bedroom; Thomas proceeding into the cathedral, with his cross carried before him, to claim the ancient right of sanctuary; Thomas opening the bolts of the cathedral doors, saying "Christ's Church is not a fortress"; many of his most faithful companions deserting him, until only three were left, including Edward Grim, a visiting monk from Cambridge of the old Anglo-Saxon stock, who had never been to Canterbury nor seen Thomas Becket before this day; the killers entering, overtaking Thomas at the great pillar between the Lady chapel and the chapel of St. Benedict; Reginald FitzUrse swinging his sword just above the Archbishop's head as Thomas said: "I commend myself and my church to God and the Blessed Virgin Mary, to St. Denis and St. Alphege," the last being the Archbishop of Canterbury martyred by the pagan Danes, whose martyrdom began the series of conversions that brought Scandinavia to the Faith; William de Tracy, screaming "Strike! Strike," finally swinging his sword downward, the heroic Englishman Grim throwing up his arm to ward off the blow and almost losing it as the sword sliced into Thomas' skull; Thomas sinking to his knees, murmuring, "Into thy hands, O Lord, I commend my spirit; for the name of Jesus and the defense of the Church, I embrace death"; Richard de Brito's final blow with the strength of Hell behind it that cut off Thomas' head and broke his sword in two on the bloody pavement; Hugh Mauclerc looking down upon the ravaged hummocks of flesh that had been the primate of England and saying: "Let us go, knights; this fellow will not rise again"—even as the Sanhedrin had said when Jesus Christ was taken down from the Cross.[97]

---

[96]Winston, *Becket*, pp. 318-320, 346-350; Barlow, *Becket*, pp. 224-226; Knowles, *Becket*, pp. 136, 139-140; Warren, *Henry II*, pp. 507-508.

[97]Winston, *Becket*, pp. 355-356; Barlow, *Becket*, pp. 240-247; Knowles, *Becket*, pp.

Hugh Mauclerc was wrong—as wrong as the Sanhedrin had been. For though the body of St. Thomas Becket will not be seen whole again until the Resurrection, his memory swept like an avenging angel over all who had compassed his death.   Bloodless historians may still present Henry II Plantagenet as the great wise lawgiver and administrator of England, but for the nineteen years of life that remained to him Henry was a haunted man, betrayed by his wife and children, restless, groping, twisting, turning, never at rest. Every year he had to watch the growing stream of pilgrims to the shrine of the man for whose murder he knew himself to be ultimately responsible; every year he had to listen to the growing list of miracles wrought by Thomas Becket's intercession, which led to his canonization just three years after his martyrdom.[98] When the news of the murder in the cathedral came to Henry II, on New Year's day of 1171, he "burst into loud lamentations and exchanged his royal robes for sackcloth and ashes.... At times he fell into a stupor, after which he would again utter groans and cries more bitter than before. For three whole days he remained shut up in his chamber, and would neither take food nor admit anyone to comfort him, until it seemed from the excess of his grief that he had determined to contrive his own death."[99]

That was only the beginning. Condemned by all Christendom,[100] ordered by the Pope on Holy Thursday 1171 not to enter any church,[101] fleeing vainly to Ireland to try to escape the loathing he felt all around him,[102] reconciled with the Church more than a year later at the price of giving up all he had taken from and contended for against Becket,[103] compelled finally (not by the Pope,

---

140-148.

[98]Winston, *Becket*, pp. 375-376.

[99]letter of Bishop Arnulf of Lisieux to Pope Alexander III, quoted in Warren, *Henry II*, p. 520.

[100]Louis VII of France, that gentlest and most forgiving of kings, declared: "Such unprecedented cruelty demands unprecedented retribution. Let the sword of St. Peter be unleashed to avenge the martyr of Christianity." (Warren, *Henry II*, p. 112)

[101]Warren, *Henry II*, pp. 519-520.

[102]See below for a brief account of his actions in Ireland.

[103]The reconciliation agreement was proclaimed at Avranches in Normandy May 22, 1172. Henry was required to restore to the see of Canterbury all its lands and churches as they had been at the time of Becket's exile; to restore what they had lost to all persons—clerics and laymen—who had been dispossessed for kinship with or support of Becket; to allow all appeals to Rome; and to "utterly abolish customs prejudicial to the Church which had been introduced in his reign." This last point obviously meant the revocation of the Constitutions of Clarendon, a fact driven home by Henry's public statement a week later that the bishops were released from their oath to observe the Constitutions, though historians partial to Henry II still perversely try to deny it because the Constitutions were not specifically mentioned in the reconciliation agreement (Winston, *Becket*, pp. 374-375; Knowles, *Becket*, p. 153; Warren, *Henry II*, pp. 531-534.

but by the sheer force of public opinion) to walk to Canterbury in the summer of 1174, barefoot in the rain, wearing a hair shirt such as was found on Becket's body after his murder, kissing the pillar where Thomas was struck down, kneeling at his tomb and giving money so that lamps might forever burn there, having himself publicly whipped by several bishops, an abbot, and eighty monks[104]—still he found no balm for his soul. One shrinks from saying that the repentance of Henry II was not sincere; but he did not live and reign as though it was. Georges-Jacques Danton, one-time leader of the French Revolution, made a good confession, sought to destroy the monster he had created, and went to the guillotine at peace with God.[105] But Henry Plantagenet, by all indications, never knew peace again.

The four knights who killed Becket were simpler men; perhaps they found it easier to believe in forgiveness. Before the end of the year 1171 they went to Rome and threw themselves on the mercy of the Pope. He heard their confessions and gave them the crusade as penance. They took vows of poverty, chastity, and obedience, joined the celibate military order of the Templars, and went to Jerusalem. Within three years all four of them had given their lives in the struggle against the infidel.[106] We would give much to know how they died, but we may dare to imagine them in the forefront of the battle, the swords that had taken a martyr's blood turned in expiation to the defense of the holy places. Danton would have understood them; they would have understood him. We cannot say as much for Henry Plantagenet.

In May 1173 his sons—Henry, 18; Richard, 15; and Geoffrey, 14—revolted against him, supported by their mother, the faithless Eleanor of Aquitaine. Henry was still an excellent campaigner, and his sons were too young to have much experience of war. By the end of the year he had captured his wife, whom he kept imprisoned for the next eleven years. After his public penance for the murder of Becket in July 1174 public opinion shifted significantly in his favor, and with the help of a Papal legate he made peace with his sons in September of that year. But his sons lost nothing and suffered no penalty; they kept all the lands they had possessed before the war started, and gained some additional revenues as well.[107]

During the remainder of his reign Henry II regarded all his sons with suspicion (except John, the youngest, who had been only six at the time of the rebellion of his three older brothers), as they regarded him. In the end all of them, including John, revolted against him once more, and were about to

---

[104]Winston, *Becket*, p. 377.

[105]See my *The Guillotine and the Cross* (Manassas VA, 1986), pp. 111-164, *passim*.

[106]Baldwin, *Alexander III*, p. 122.

[107]Warren, *Henry II*, pp. 117-138; Régine Pernoud, *Eleanor of Aquitaine* (New York, 1968), pp. 161-172; Mann, *Popes in the Middle Ages*, XI, 214.

overthrow him when he died in 1189.[108]

Henry II's visit to Ireland, begun less than a year after the murder of Becket (in October 1171) and continued for a full seven months, was obviously an attempt to escape the impact of his almost universal condemnation in England and the rest of Europe, while building his reputation in an entirely different area.[109] It was not politically necessary at that particular time, for there is no evidence whatsoever that any of his noblemen who had been fighting successfully against various Irish chieftains had the slightest intention of abandoning their normal liege loyalty to their King.[110] More difficult to explain, at first sight, is the strong support Pope Alexander III gave to this expedition of a man who, by his own order, was still not allowed to enter a church.[111]

But it must always be remembered that the Pope is the spiritual head of *all* Christendom, and the nature of his office requires that he not focus on one nation or ruler or problem at the expense of other peoples and rulers and problems. The problem in Ireland in 1171 was large, simple, and ugly. In the wake of the centuries of warfare with the Vikings, the island had become ungovernable and the church was almost entirely under lay control. The constant warfare made political unity and the enforcement of the most fundamental laws impossible. Warfare in Ireland was almost untouched by moral considerations. A pagan ideal of personal bravery required the local chieftains—usually called "kings" in Ireland—always to expose themselves at the forefront of the battle, with the result that most of their "reigns" came to a quick and bloody end. Men became so hardened by the constant conflict, and the church was so lacking in moral influence, that frightful atrocities—rapes, blindings—were not the exception, but the rule. The ancient right of sanctuary in church, whose violation at Canterbury had so shocked Christendom, was

---

[108]Warren, *Henry II*, pp. 584-626. Warren, a meticulous historian with an almost unbounded admiration for Henry II, has to admit the magnitude and viciousness of the two rebellions of Henry's sons, but believes there was a period of harmony and fulfillment for Henry from 1174 to 1182. Since Henry kept his wife imprisoned for that whole period, and it is known that Richard in particular was devoted to her and deeply resented his father's treatment of her (however justified), we can hardly see in this period either a picture of family harmony.

[109]*A New History of Ireland*, Volume II: "Medieval Ireland, 1169-1534," ed. Art Cosgrove (Oxford, 1987), p. 81; Goddard H. Orpen, *Ireland under the Normans, 1169-1216* (Oxford, 1911), I, 249-250.

[110]Richard de Clare, known as "Strongbow," the principal leader of the Anglo-Normans in Ireland, had never been in high favor with Henry II. However, Henry had initially permitted him to go to Ireland, though later ordering him not to sail from Wales on the eve of his planned departure. Strongbow went anyway, but returned to England before Henry's departure to offer to him all his conquests in Ireland. Several of the most important nobles who had fought with Strongbow in Ireland testified to Henry that he sought no independent kingdoms there (*New History of Ireland*, Volume II [ed. Cosgrove], pp. 86-88).

[111]Warren, *Henry II*, p. 197.

rarely respected in Ireland. The Pope had no voice in the selection of bishops and abbots, nor even in establishing the procedures for their selection. Irish marriage law was substantially out of conformity with Catholic practice elsewhere. The attempt to reform the Irish church which St. Malachy O'More had undertaken in St. Bernard's time had essentially failed. In practice if not by deliberate decision, the Irish church was schismatic; the Pope's writ did not run in Ireland.[112]

There was then no heresy, no doctrinal difference like that which developed when England under Henry VIII became Protestant while Ireland remained Catholic. It was that difference which ultimately raised the struggle between England and Ireland to a far higher plane, on which by and large it has ever since remained. But in 1171 it was reasonable to see even Henry II as a bearer of order to a brutalized Ireland sunk nearly to anarchy, a monarch whose strength of will and arms could protect the Church as the necessary thoroughgoing reform was undertaken and went forward. Most of the Irish church leaders did in fact see Henry in this light, surprising as it seems given his character and history. In the winter of 1172 the Council of Cashel confirmed the existing degradation of Catholic religious practice in Ireland, demanded reforms, and upheld Henry as overlord and patron of reform. St. Laurence O'Toole, the holy Bishop of Dublin, played an active role in this council. Every Irish bishop was present there except 85-year-old Gelasius of Armagh, the see of St. Patrick, whose great age prevented him from attending; all, including Gelasius, assented freely to the acts of the council.[113]

The unpleasant truth about the state of Ireland when the Anglo-Normans arrived is very difficult for those who love Ireland to accept—particularly in view of the fact that the man who called in Henry II and his barons, Dermot Macmurrough[114] of Leinster, was one of the worst of the chieftains, a man who loved nothing but power, who had raped the wife of Tiernan O'Rourke, supported High King Murtaugh McLochlan after he blinded the king of Ulidia and dragged several of the king's loyal retainers from sanctuary to their deaths, and eagerly took part in the ravaging of his own country alongside the Anglo-

---

[112]See F. J. Byrne's grim account of the condition of Ireland in 1169, extensively documented from native Irish sources and entitled "The Trembling Sod," in *New History of Ireland*, Volume II [ed. Cosgrove], pp. 1-42, and Orpen's chapter, "Social and Physical Aspects of Ireland," in *Ireland under the Normans*, I, 101-140. Papal support for intervention in Ireland by Henry II had already been given by Adrian IV in 1155 or 1156 in the bull *Laudabiliter*, whose authenticity there is no longer any reasonable basis to doubt (*New History of Ireland*, II, 57-58; Warren, *Henry II*, pp. 195-196).

[113]*New History of Ireland*, Volume II (ed. Cosgrove), pp. 91-94; Orpen, *Ireland under the Normans*, II, 274-278.

[114]The spelling of Irish names is anglicized throughout this history, due to the great differences between what Gaelic spelling signifies to the modern reader and its actual pronunciation.

Norman lords.[115] But Dermot Macmurrough differed from hundreds like him only in his eagerness to deal with foreigners. Somehow, Ireland had to be united and brought under law and order. As it turned out, Irish national feeling was too strong to permit Henry II and his men—or any Englishmen ever—to fully accomplish that; instead, gradually over the centuries, the Irish themselves developed their own unity and loyalty out of the struggle with the invader. Perhaps that was the only way it could have been done—once again, Christ whom the Irish like the English worshipped, bringing good out of evil, as He has done so often.

In May 1169, at Dermot Macmurrough's invitation, 100 Anglo-Norman knights and 500 Welsh archers landed near Wexford in southeast Ireland and promptly took it, the Irish never having used armor in battle and (more surprisingly) being quite unfamiliar with military archery. Within a few months the invaders from England had secured the whole of the kingdom of Leinster (essentially the southeastern quarter of Ireland) and were gradually reinforced, until in August 1170 Richard de Clare, Earl of Pembroke (known as "Strongbow") arrived with 200 knights and a thousand light-armed men. He married Dermot Macmurrough's daughter and succeeded Dermot as King of Leinster when he died the following year, though Strongbow held Leinster only under Henry II as overlord.[116]

The Irish High King, Rory O'Connor, came to Leinster to challenge Strongbow and besieged him in Dublin in the summer of 1171, but Strongbow sallied and prevailed against heavy odds because of his armor and archery. On October 17 Henry II landed near Waterford. The Irish chieftains, impressed that he was the son of an Empress and knowing little if anything of Frederick Barbarossa as Emperor, hastened to swear fealty to him, High King Rory O'Connor among them, though it does not appear that most of them paid formal feudal homage to Henry. (Indeed, the feudal system was still little understood in Ireland.) Only the kings of Tyrone and Tyrconnell in the north held aloof. The previously mentioned Council of Cashel met that winter, and in April 1172 Henry II returned to England to make his peace with the Pope for Becket's murder.[117]

Despite Pope Alexander III's support for Henry's presence in Ireland, at no time did the Pope recognize the incorporation of Ireland into the kingdom of England nor bring the Irish church under the control of the church in England

---

[115]For Macmurrough's personal history and character see *New History of Ireland*, Volume II (ed. Cosgrove), pp. 43-66, 69-70; Orpen, *Ireland under the Normans*, II, 39-100, 155-161.

[116]*New History of Ireland*, Volume II (ed. Cosgrove), pp. 69-79; Orpen, *Ireland under the Normans*, I, 145-203, 217-218.

[117]*New History of Ireland*, Volume II (ed. Cosgrove), pp. 81-97; Orpen, *Ireland under the Normans*, I, 222-239, 248-284.

(except for a long-standing link between Dublin, which for centuries had been a Norse rather than an Irish center, and Canterbury).[118] In October 1175, by the Treaty of Windsor, Henry II recognized Rory O'Connor as High King of Ireland, but tributary to him, in the parts of Ireland (still the majority of the island) not conquered by the English.[119] Two years later John de Courcy made an amazing march through Ulster, the hostile north of Ireland, defeating two great Irish armies, the second commanded by High King Rory O'Connor in person, at Downpatrick.[120] Anglo-Norman lordships began to be established in many parts of the island, but as early as 1180 there was increasing intermingling and intermarriage between these lords and the Irish chiefs; the island could not yet be rightly described as conquered.[121]

Henry II of England, despite his energy and ambition, did not exercise unlimited power anywhere—neither in England nor Wales nor Ireland nor his portions of France. The Church was his check; in his better moments his guide, in his worse moments his foe. In northern Italy and in central Europe the Church was exercising exactly the same function. In northern Serbia the frontier of the schismatic Byzantine empire under Manuel Comnenus marched with that of Catholic Hungary. With the skillful intrigue for which they were famous (or infamous), the Byzantines sought to exclude young Stephen III from the throne of his illustrious namesake the founder of the Hungarian monarchy, but without success; by the fall of 1164 Manuel agreed to recognize him in return for the abandonment of Hungarian claims to Dalmatia. When Stephen III tried to pay off his debts for the wars against the Byzantine empire by plundering churches, the primate of Hungary, Archbishop Lukacs of Esztergom, excommunicated him. In a response strikingly different from that of Henry II, Stephen III went as a pilgrim to Ezstergom to seek forgiveness; Archbishop Lukacs met him on the road and absolved him. Shortly afterward he issued an Ecclesiastical Constitution, which contrasts vividly with Henry II's Constitutions of Clarendon. Stephen III agreed not to depose any Hungarian bishop or abbot without the Pope's approval, not to turn over Church property to laymen except in time of enemy invasion and even then only with the bishop's consent, and not to use the income of vacant sees and abbeys for secular purposes.[122]

---

[118]*New History of Ireland*, Volume II (ed. Cosgrove), p. 93; Orpen, *Ireland under the Normans*, I, 301-308; Warren, *Henry II*, p. 534; Mann, *Popes in the Middle Ages*, X, 331-334.

[119]*New History of Ireland*, Volume II (ed. Cosgrove), pp. 107-108; Orpen, *Ireland under the Normans*, I, 349-352.

[120]*New History of Ireland*, Volume II (ed. Cosgrove), pp. 114-116; Orpen, *Ireland under the Normans*, II, 10-15.

[121]*New History of Ireland*, Volume II (ed. Cosgrove), p. 117; Lane Poole, *Domesday Book to Magna Carta*, p. 312.

[122]Kosztolynik, *Coloman the Learned to Bela III*, pp. 183-186, 192-193, 198.

It was a much longer road to bring Emperor Frederick Barbarossa into his right relation to the Church. When Becket was murdered in his cathedral the Emperor's struggle against the Church was already eleven years old, with no end in sight. The Lombard League, founded in 1167, was strong enough to defy Frederick from 1168 to 1174; but his extraordinary persistence and strength of will caused him still to reject reconciliation with Pope Alexander III when that meant—as he knew it must—giving up his pretensions for direct rule of the cities of northern Italy. In October 1174 he laid siege to the newly constructed city of Alessandria, named by the Lombard League for the Pope; it strongly resisted him. The siege reached its climax in Holy Week 1175, when Frederick, in violation of the universally observed Truce of God from Good Friday to Easter Sunday, dug tunnels under its walls during those days, but the defenders rallied when the Emperor's soldiers first emerged from the tunnels on Holy Saturday and destroyed them.[123]

On April 17, at the little town of Montebello, the League proposed peace terms: the cities would recognize Frederick's overall imperial authority, in return for his restoration of property confiscated during the war; his permission for the cities (including Alessandria) to keep their self-government, their fortifications, and their right to ally with one another; and above all his recognition of Alexander III as Pope, which in fifteen years he had never tendered. After first seeming to agree, Frederick refused these very reasonable terms, and the war went on.[124]

On May 29, 1176 came the decisive battle, in the dead-flat Lombard plain near the town of Legnano. This was not far from Milan, the leading city of the Lombard League; the Milanese army constituted the bulk of the Lombard host and included 1,200 young men of Milan who had sworn themselves to victory or death. They formed a square around the *carroccio*, the carriage that was the symbol of their city. When the initially successful German cavalry approached, they fell to their knees together for a moment to pray for the protection and help of St. Peter and St. Ambrose, patron of Milan; then they rose, stood like a wall, fended off the cavalry charge, and counter-attacked with an irresistible impetus. The Emperor himself plunged into the fray, was unhorsed, and

---

[123]*Cambridge Medieval History*, V, 445; Munz, *Frederick Barbarossa*, pp. 298-302; Pacaut, *Frederick Barbarossa*, pp. 147-148.

[124]Pacaut, *Frederick Barbarossa*, pp. 147-153; Munz, *Frederick Barbarossa*, pp. 303-307. These two learned authorities on Frederick Barbarossa disagree almost completely on why Frederick rejected the "Peace of Montebello." Pacaut attributes the rejection primarily to Frederick's continued reluctance to accept Alexander III as Pope; Munz says he was quite ready to do accept Alexander, but could not bring himself to accept the right of the city of Alessandria to exist. Pacaut's argument seems stronger, while Munz's seems to a substantial extent vitiated by his wholly unsupported theories about a "Great Design" of Frederick—to set up a personal empire in Switzerland, Burgundy and northern Italy alone—allegedly abandoned at this time.

disappeared in the melee. There were cries that he was dead, and on hearing this his army disintegrated. Not until several days later did Frederick reappear, almost alone, to gain safety behind the walls of Pavia.[125]

But he knew that the war was lost; to his great credit, he did not prolong the agony. On November 4, 1176, by the Treaty of Anagni, he recognized Alexander III as Pope and made peace with him, ending the schism in return for the Pope's recognition of him as emperor and his son Henry as his heir, the revocation of his excommunication, and the validity of ordinations by the bishops he and his antipopes had appointed during the schism.[126] On July 24, 1177, at Venice's world-famous St. Mark's cathedral, this treaty was solemnly confirmed in a splendid ceremony, and extended to include peace with the Lombards and Sicily as well, on essentially the same terms for the Lombards that Frederick had rejected after the preliminary agreement at Montebello in April 1175. With his hand on the Gospels Frederick declared: "That all may know that I am Christian in name and in fact, I abjure Octavian of Crema and John of Struma and their supporters, and I acknowledge Alexander and his successors as true Popes." When Alexander III arrived, Frederick took off the purple mantle of the Emperor and threw himself at the Pope's feet. Like Henry IV before him, he had come to Canossa at last.[127]

It was nine years before Frederick Barbarossa troubled a Pope again. For most of that period he was absorbed in the problems of Germany, particularly the long-drawn-out feudal punishment of his mightiest subject, Henry the Lion, Duke of Bavaria and Saxony, who was charged with having "sorely oppressed the liberty of the Church and of the princes of the Empire by seizing their possessions and by threatening their rights." By September 1480 Henry the Lion had been deprived of both his duchies and defeated militarily in the field.[128]

---

[125]Butler, *Lombard Communes*, pp. 147-148; Pacaut, *Frederick Barbarossa*, pp. 154-155; Munz, *Frederick Barbarossa*, pp. 310-313; *Cambridge Medieval History*, V, 446-447. Munz denies that Legnano was a decisive battle, claiming that "most historians nowadays" agree with him; but his contemporary Pacaut does not seem to (of Frederick after Legnano Pacaut says "he had fought and lost once again, but he was enough of a statesman to accept the inevitable, and to cut his suit according to his cloth" [*op. cit.*, p. 155]). The simple and determinative fact is that Frederick refused to make peace with the Lombards and the Pope before the battle, but did make peace with them afterwards.

[126]*Cambridge Medieval History*, V, 447-448; Baldwin, *Alexander III*, pp. 139-140; Knapke, *Barbarossa's Conflict*, pp. 79-82.

[127]Mann, *Popes in the Middle Ages*, XI, 123-124; Munz, *Frederick Barbarossa*, pp. 329-332.

[128]*Cambridge Medieval History*, V, 404-405; Munz, *Frederick Barbarossa*, pp. 338-354. Munz regards Frederick as having only at this time accepted feudal law, having previously been unconcerned with the rise of Henry's power. It would seem more reasonable to assume that he became concerned only once Henry had accumulated the power, while his attention had been focussed on Italy and his struggle with the Pope.

With the whole Church west of the Byzantine empire reunited, in his last years Pope Alexander III was finally able to legislate for it effectively, thorugh the Third Lateran Council held in March 1179, attended by more than 300 bishops representing most of Christendom. The Pope and Council required a two-thirds vote of cardinals present in conclave to elect a Pope; required bishops to be at least thirty years old—a regulation which, if duly observed, would have prevented one of the great grievances that later led to the Protestant revolt; provided for free education to be given by cathedral schools to poor young men seeking it; and condemned the neo-Manichaean heretics called Albigensians or Catharists (the "perfect") who were beginning to appear in southern France, and who were to mount a devastating challenge to the Church a generation in the future. Pope Alexander made Archbishop St. Laurence O'Toole of Dublin his legate in Ireland and metropolitan of five nearby Irish dioceses in addition to his own.[129]

That same year, in September, the lifelong enemies Louis VII of France and Henry II of England together made the now famous pilgrimage to the shrine of St. Thomas Becket at Canterbury.[130] For Louis this was an act of simple duty; he had known, loved, honored and protected St. Thomas, he felt death approaching, and he was determined to make the pilgrimage while yet he lived. In Henry there was still no sign of fundamental change; but it seems he did not feel he could refrain from the pilgrimage when the King of France was making it, though already having made it once before. Shortly after Louis' return to France he suffered a stroke. In November 1179 he crowned his young son Philip II co-regent; a year later he died and Philip at fifteen was sole king.[131] Insufficiently appreciated in his own time and still less appreciated by historians since, Louis VII had ruled France for forty-three years, accepting correction for his earlier errors from St. Bernard of Clairvaux, commanding bravely and with constancy in the Second Crusade, faithfully upholding the greatest saint of his time after St. Bernard, not even embittered by betrayal and abandonment by his wife Eleanor of Aquitaine. All contemporary testimony agrees in portraying Louis VII's genuine charity, piety, love of goodness, and readiness to forgive. He was a worthy progenitor and foreshadowing of his great-grandson and namesake St. Louis IX.

On August 31, 1181 Pope Alexander III followed him to the Judgment.[132] He was 71 years old, a great age in those days; his pontificate had been the

---

Despite Munz's lengthy and learned discussion, it is hard to believe that feudal law in some form was not followed in Germany long before this.

[129]Mann, *Popes in the Middle Ages*, XI, 139-147; Baldwin, *Alexander III*, pp. 186-202; *New History of Ireland*, Volume II (ed. Cosgrove), p. 119.

[130]Pernoud, *Eleanor of Aquitaine*, p. 174.

[131]Warren, *Henry II*, pp. 147-148.

[132]Mann, *Popes in the Middle Ages*, XI, 147-148.

longest in nearly four hundred years, and one of the most troubled. He had stood firm whenever he could, yielding only when unavoidably necessary, and never on any essential element of his duty as Vicar of Christ. No Pope in all the history of the Church has displayed more prudence and wisdom through so long a time of travail. He had endured and triumphed despite the opposition throughout most of his long pontificate of two of the three most powerful monarchs in Christendom: Emperor Frederick Barbarossa and Henry II of England and half France. Only the third of these kings, Louis VII, never departed from his side. Under Pope Alexander III, the Church had decisively checked the aggrandizement of royal power. There would be no absolute monarchy in Latin Christendom while it remained all Catholic.

It remains to speak of the progress of the crusade. On the perennial battlefront in Spain, the Muslims there had received another strong reinforcement from the other side of the Straits of Gibraltar as a new Islamic sect called the Almohads inspired a renewal of their fanatical zeal for conquest which Spain knew so well. Swarming into Andalusia, in 1157 the Almohads drove out the first Spanish garrisons established beyond the gloomy defile that cut through Andalusia's northern mountains to make a gateway from the high plains to the north, which the Christians had grimly named Despeñaperros, the Pass of the Overthrow of the Infidel Dogs. Marching to the rescue, Alfonso VII of Castile, who had claimed the title of Spanish Emperor, faced mutiny among his disheartened men. Retreating in bitter anger, he sickened and died in the pass itself after dividing his kingdom between his two sons, Sancho III whom he named king of Castile and Fernando II whom he named king of León.[133]

North of the pass, the mighty fortress of Calatrava stood on the banks of the upper Guadiana River. Its defense had been entrusted to the Templars. Regarding their chief responsibility as the defense of the Holy Land, seeing the new Muslim wave rolling upon Spain and the division of the principal Christian kingdom in the path of their onslaught, the Templars announced they could no longer be responsible for Calatrava, and turned it back to the new King Sancho III.[134]

The war for the reconquest of Spain was 435 years old that dark summer of 1157; its cardinal law for the Christians had always been "never despair!" When even the greatest and bravest dropped the torch, others were always ready to pick it up. This time rescue came in an even more surprising manner than usual. At the Cistercian monastery of Fitero humbly dwelt a monk named

---

[133]Manuel Recuero Astray, *Alfonso VII, Emperador* (León, 1979), pp. 198-199; Derek W. Lomax, *The Reconquest of Spain* (London, 1978), p. 93; Joseph J. O'Callaghan, *A History of Medieval Spain* (Ithaca NY, 1975), pp. 232, 235; Julio González, *Regesta de Fernando II* (Madrid, 1943), p. 21.

[134]Lomax, *Reconquest of Spain*, p. 108.

Diego Velázquez, who had been a knight. On hearing of the prospective abandonment of Calatrava, Diego went to his abbot, Raimundo, to ask him to ask Sancho III for the fortress. It was an astonishing request, for Abbot Raimundo knew nothing of war; still more astonishingly, it was granted by the King. Diego took command of the fortress; Archbishop Juan of Toledo granted a plenary indulgence for remission of sins to all who would help in the defense of Calatrava. Hundreds of the young men of Toledo committed themselves to its defense, while many others in the city offered horses, arms, or money. Abbot Raimundo made the volunteers a religious confraternity under the Cistercian rule, the nucleus of the military order of Calatrava which was formally established six years later. Diego and Raimundo and their consecrated soldiers raised the shield, while in Avila to the north an even stranger figure took up the sword: hunchbacked Sancho Jiménez, whose squat misshapen figure obviously had no place in an infantry battle line, but who could ride like the wind. He was made commander of the Avila militia; before the year 1158 was out he had led a raid all the way to Sevilla in the heart of Andalusia, the first of 26 far-flung raids the bold hunchback was to lead before he fell at last in battle. Faced with enemies like these, the Almohads stayed south of the Pass of the Overthrow of the Infidel Dogs.[135]

Later in 1158 Sancho III of Castile, not yet thirty, suddenly died, leaving his kingdom to his two-year-old son Alfonso VIII, whose mother had died at his birth. Fernando II of León was unsuccessful in his attempt to gain control of the child's person, so León and Castile remained politically divided; but until the little boy reached maturity, Fernando would clearly be the military leader of the two kingdoms.[136]

Fernando's principal rival was Afonso Henriques of Portugal, though at first the two cooperated effectively in the face of the Almohad advance. In 1158 Afonso Henriques secured the fortress of Alcácer do Sal, a position of great military importance in the southern Portuguese province of Alentejo, which resembled Calatrava in Spain. It gave the Portuguese a base for operations against the Moors in Extremadura province, which both Spain and Portugal claimed. In 1165 yet another extraordinary and unforgettable warrior appeared, matching Diego Velázquez the Cistercian monk and Sancho Jiménez the hunchbacked raider from Avila: Gerald called Sempavor, the Fearless, of Portugal, who took towns by placing a ladder at a hidden corner of their walls at night, climbing it, descending into the town, and opening the gates to his men waiting outside. The Moors must have been very poor sentries to permit this to keep happening, but it did: first Gerald took Trujillo in Extremadura, then Évora in Portugal, then Montánchez and Serpa in Extremadura, all in the years

---

[135]Lomax, *Reconquest of Spain*, pp. 108, 112.
[136]O'Callaghan, *Medieval Spain*, pp. 235-236; González, *Fernando II*, pp. 35-36.

1165 and 1166. A military order of Portuguese was founded to defend Évora, first named for that city and later called the Order of Aviz. Then in the spring of 1169 Gerald the Fearless took the fortified city of Badajoz, the capital of Extremadura, except for the citadel, and called on his lord Afonso Henriques for help in holding it and eliminating the resistance of the citadel. Afonso came himself in response to Gerald's appeal.[137]

But the Reconquest of Spain and Portugal, though one of the greatest heroic stories of all time, is not all a tale of selfless devotion to the centuries-old cause. The warriors of the Reconquest too were fallen men, cursed at times by pride and jealousy; and never in all the centuries of the Reconquest was there a worse example of this than what now ensued at Badajoz, and its consequences. Fernando II of León claimed Extremadura as his territory; he was quite willing for Gerald to take its cities for him by his unique tactics, but not willing for him to bring in his Portuguese lord. Fernando led an army to Badajoz and captured Afonso when he broke his leg trying to flee; he expelled Gerald and gave Badajoz back to its Muslim inhabitants on their promise to hold it as his vassals. As soon as he left they broke their oath and returned it to the Almohads.[138]

In March 1170 Gerald returned, but his trademark attack technique could not easily be used in the same city twice; he was forced to besiege Badajoz, without help from other Christians, and an Almohad army came up and drove him away. In November Fernando II made a treaty with the Almohad caliph which recognized Christian possession of the Extremaduran cities they currently held (including several taken by Gerald and now defended by the new military Order of Santiago) but guaranteed Muslim possession of Badajoz. This despicable betrayal gnawed at Gerald's own honor; in the summer of 1172, after quarreling with Afonso Henriques, he abandoned his allegiance and joined the Muslims, who executed him two years later.[139]

Caliph Yusuf of the Almohads moved quickly to take advantage of the division among the Christians. In that same summer of 1172 he struck north almost to Madrid, barely repulsed by the heroic defenders of Huete under Nuño Manrique. On April 6, 1173 the Almohad army defeated the Christians at the Battle of Caracuel. A few days later came Sancho Jiménez's last ride; the hunchbacked raider of Avila was caught deep in Andalusia and went down fighting. Caliph Yusuf marched north again, going as far as Talavera on the Tagus, not far from Toledo.[140]

---

[137]O'Callaghan, *Medieval Spain*, p. 237; Lomax, *Reconquest of Spain*, pp. 110, 113-114; Julio González, *El reino de Castilla en la época de Alfonso VIII* (Madrid, 1960), I, 686, 900, 903-904.

[138]González, *Fernando II*, pp. 80-82.

[139]*Ibid.*, pp. 86-93; Lomax, *Reconquest of Spain*, pp. 109, 114-115.

[140]Lomax, *Reconquest of Spain*, p. 115; González, *Fernando II*, p. 107; González, *Alfonso VIII*, pp. 910-921.

But, along with all his other concerns, Pope Alexander III was keeping a close watch on the situation in Spain. In this hour of incipient disintegration of the Christian position, in the summer of 1173 he sent Cardinal Jacinto to Spain as his legate, who brought together at Soria in north Castile Kings Fernando II of León, young Alfonso VIII of Castile, and Alfonso II of Aragon to pledge peace with one another and support for the new Order of Santiago which was holding some of the most critically important fortresses. In September 1174 the Moors took Cáceres and Alcántara on the Tagus, giving them control of most of Extremadura, and pressed on into León itself, assaulting Ciudad Rodrigo whose defenses were still under construction. Its garrison defended itself magnificently behind makeshift walls of carts, boxes and furniture until Fernando II came up to relieve them. Like Alfonso VI before him, Fernando II of León was no moral paragon and could not stand prosperity, but with his back to the wall in his own country he knew how to fight to the finish. Ciudad Rodrigo held out successfully. With the Pope's approval, it was made a diocese.[141]

As ever, as the struggle went on, the Christians soon began to counterattack. In the summer of 1177 Fernando II, in the tradition of Sancho Jiménez, personally led a raid to Sevilla, while Alfonso VIII of Castile, now 21 and becoming a famous warrior in his own right, besieged and took Cuenca in the center of Spain, while Afonso Henriques led his Portuguese in raids into the Algarve at the southern extremity of Portugal. To avoid a repetition of what had happened in Extremadura after Gerald the Fearless took Badajoz, the Kings of Castile and Aragon carefully delimited the areas of the southeast coast of Spain that each of their kingdoms would rule when they were fully reconquered from the Moors. Still none of the Spanish kings wanted to recognize Afonso Henriques of Portugal, but Pope Alexander III took the matter out of their hands. Following precedents established in eastern Europe with Hungary and Poland, in 1179 the Pope formally acknowledged Afonso as Portugal's first king, calling him "the intrepid destroyer of the enemies of the Christian name and the energetic defender of the Christian faith."[142]

In 1174 King Amaury of Jerusalem, the younger son of Fulk of Anjou and Queen Melisende, died at the age of 38. His heir was his son, only thirteen and still considered too young to rule; but in the fast-maturing east he could expect to assume full authority soon. The boy, named Baldwin for his uncle and great-grandfather, was of striking intelligence, quick-witted, well-spoken, handsome, personable, and extraordinarily brave.[143]

---

[141]González, *Fernando II*, pp. 105, 108-111; Lomax, *Reconquest of Spain*, pp. 115-116.
[142]O'Callaghan, *Medieval Spain*, pp. 240-241; Lomax, *Reconquest of Spain*, pp. 116-117; Baldwin, *Alexander III*, p. 158; González, *Alfonso VIII*, pp. 812, 928-930.
[143]Kenneth M. Setton, *A History of the Crusades*, Volume I (Madison WI, 1969), p.

He was also a leper. The most dreaded disease of the Middle Ages had been found upon his body four years before, when he was only nine years old. William of Tyre, the greatest historian of the kingdom of Jerusalem, tells the terrible story of that discovery:

> One day when he [Prince Baldwin] was playing with the young nobles of his entourage, it happened that they began to scratch one another in the hands and arms. The other boys cried when they were hurt, but Baldwin made no sound. This was repeated many times, until his teacher, Archdeacon William, became disturbed. He thought at first that the boy was simply bearing himself with courage, that he would not cry out when he was hurt. He spoke to him about it and asked him why he endured what was done to him and gave it no importance. Baldwin replied that they did not hurt him and he felt no pain from the scratches. Then his teacher examined his arm and hand and saw that they had no feeling. Even when bitten, he felt nothing. Then he went to the king his father and told him everything. The king gave him oils and drugs and other remedies, but they had no effect.... When he had attained the age of puberty, we could not speak of him without weeping, knowing that the young man had leprosy.[144]

The first regent appointed for young Baldwin IV after his father's death was Milo of Plancy, seneschal of the kingdom but unpopular among the other noblemen, who was soon assassinated. His successor as regent was Count Raymond III of Tripoli, a direct descendant of the great crusader Raymond of Toulouse, just emerged from ten years in Muslim captivity. Raymond was strongly supported by Humphrey of Toron, Constable of the Kingdom of Jerusalem for thirty years, famous among Muslims as well as Christians for his bravery and loyalty. In the same year as Amaury (1174) the Muslim King Nureddin died, who had ruled from Mosul in Iraq to Egypt. Nureddin's nominal successor was his eleven-year-old son, but his actual successor soon proved to be Saladin, the Syrian governor of Egypt, a devout, resolute and highly capable leader who was to devote the rest of his life to driving the Christians out of the Middle East and uniting the Muslims of the area sufficiently to make this possible. Within a year Saladin had secured control of all of Muslim Syria except the major city of Aleppo, which an expedition by Raymond III prevented him from taking from Muslims who would not accept his rule. The Caliph at Baghdad recognized Saladin as king of both Syria and Egypt.[145]

The increasingly crippled young leper king and his advisors looked about

---

591; John B. Glubb, *The Lost Centuries; from the Muslim Empires to the Renaissance of Europe, 1145-1453* (London, 1967), p. 83.

[144]William of Tyre's history, quoted by Pierre Aubé, *Baudouin IV de Jérusalem, le roi lépreux* (Paris, 1981), p. 62.

[145]Marshall W. Baldwin, *Raymond III of Tripolis and the Fall of Jerusalem (1140-1187)* (Princeton, 1936), pp. 7, 10-16, 24-30; Setton, *Crusades*, I, 513-527, 563-570.

desperately for help. Any hope of obtaining it from the often faithless Byzantine empire had to be abandoned when Emperor Manuel Comnenus suffered a devastating defeat by the Turks at Myriocephalon in Asia Minor in 1176, a blow from which the once vigorous and moderately pro-Western emperor never recovered (he died four years later, never having regained his position in Asia Minor).[146] William Longsword, eldest son and heir to the Marquis of Montferrat, specially recommended by Louis VII, came from France to marry Baldwin IV's sister Sibyl, but died the next year; a posthumous son, also named Baldwin, was born to Sibyl. Count Philip of Flanders, son of the crusader Thierry of Anjou, arrived in Jerusalem in August 1177. Baldwin offered him the regency of the kingdom of Jerusalem if he would lead a joint attack on Egypt in conjunction with the still operational Byzantine fleet, which was ready to go. But Philip refused; he said his main purpose in coming to Jerusalem had been to marry two of his cousins to two sons of one of his vassals who was in Jerusalem.[147] "We thought you had come to fight for the Cross and you merely talk of marriages,"[148] one of the nobles of Jerusalem reproached him, and Philip left in anger to join Raymond III of Tripoli in an abortive campaign against Hama in Syria. Even faithful old Humphrey of Toron was out of action, seriously ill.[149]

So young Baldwin IV the leper was on his own when Saladin suddenly crossed the frontier of Egypt in November 1177 with 25,000 men, ravaging the coastal plain and marching north and east toward Jerusalem, destroying everything in his path, decapitating all prisoners. With less than 600 knights, outnumbered more than forty to one, the little leper king left the great fortress of Ascalon to which he had rushed when he heard the news of the invasion, and marched in pursuit. Saladin could not believe his stricken, outmaneuvered and wholly inexperienced adversary would attempt so bold a stroke against the odds. He kept poor watch, and did not even know that Baldwin and his men had left Ascalon. On November 25 Baldwin caught up with Saladin's army in a gully near the castle of Montgisard and charged. His men swore they saw St. George himself, mounted on a white horse, leading the assault. The surprise was total, the rout complete. Most of Saladin's bodyguard of a thousand mamelukes fell around him; he barely made his escape thanks to their sacrifice. His army was lost; once again, Jerusalem was saved.[150]

But Saladin's realms now surrounded the Holy Land. The glorious victory

---

[146]Steven Runciman, *A History of the Crusades* (Cambridge, England, 1952), II, 412-414, 426-427.
    [147]*Ibid.*, II, 411, 414-415.
    [148]*Ibid.*, II, 415.
    [149]*Ibid.*, II, 415-416.
    [150]*Ibid.*, II, 416-417; Glubb, *Lost Centuries*, pp. 88-89, Aubé, *Baudoin IV*, pp. 156-157, 160-171.

at Montgisard gave respite to the Christians in Jerusalem for little more than a year. In April 1179 Saladin's nephew Faruk-Shah attacked Baldwin IV and his army in a narrow valley in the forest of Banyas; magnificent old Constable Humphrey of Toron gave his life to save his young master, but the victory went to Faruk-Shah. It was followed up two months later by a victory of Saladin over Baldwin on the Litani River in the north, in which the Grand Master of the Templars was captured.[151] By 1181 Baldwin—now hideously disfigured by his leprosy, his arms and legs beginning to decay, unable to walk, nearly blind—was persuaded by his mother and his sister Sibyl to appoint her new husband Guy de Lusignan regent.   The appointment was a disaster.   Guy was young, inexperienced, and selfish, trading mostly on his extraordinary good looks; his older brother was a lover of Queen Dowager Agnes de Courtenay, Baldwin IV's mother.   Most of the fighting feudal nobility of the kingdom of Jerusalem despised him. But he and his friends were in control; they arranged the election of another of Agnes' lovers, the handsome and dissolute Archbishop Heraclius of Caesarea, as Patriarch of Jerusalem.   Heraclius proceeded to excommunicate and exile William of Tyre, who had been the principal teacher of Baldwin the Leper, leaving him with no real friend close to him on whom he could rely.[152]

Baldwin, at twenty, was slowly dying. No knowledge that age possessed could stop or even slow the advance of his malady. For a brief glorious moment at Montgisard it had seemed that his soaring heroism could somehow surmount it, and enable him to lead his kingdom at least for a substantial time in spite of it. Now that hope was gone; his own mother and sister had betrayed him; his teacher had been driven out; his great and totally trustworthy defender, Constable Humphrey, was dead. In an agony of spirit that is almost beyond imagination, Baldwin the leper king walked his *via dolorosa* of the soul as he must often have walked the original *via dolorosa* in the streets of Jerusalem—while he could still walk. Around him were none to comfort and none to help, only intriguers seeking personal gain from his horrible illness.

The whole history of Christendom shows no more shameful spectacle. Were *these* crusaders, men and women to bear the Cross to Jerusalem? Would God leave Jerusalem in *their* hands? By comparison to them, Saladin was a pillar of justice. It is not surprising that in the end—after Baldwin's long agony had finally dragged to its tragic close four years later—it was Saladin who triumphed, as the faithless crusaders died screaming for water in the blazing July sun on the bone-dry brush-covered plateau under the baleful twin rock peaks men called the Horns of Hattin.[153]

---

[151]Runciman, *Crusades*, II, 419-420; Setton, *Crusades*, I, 572-573.

[152]Runciman, *Crusades*, II, 424-425; Setton, *Crusades*, I, 596-597; Glubb, *Lost Centuries*, p. 90; Baldwin, *Raymond III of Tripolis*, pp. 35-40.

[153]See Chapter Four, below.

4
Jerusalem Lost
(1181-1204)
(Popes Lucius III 1181-85, Urban III 1185-87, Gregory VIII 1187, Clement III 1187-91, Celestine III 1191-98, Innocent III 1198-1216)

> "Why do we tarry, of what are we afraid? Christ reigns! Christ conquers! Christ commands!"—Emperor Frederick Barbarossa on crusade, to his men facing the army of the Turks of Konya, May 1190[1]

Baldwin IV, the leper king of Jerusalem, could no longer move without assistance or even sign his name, but within the decaying shroud of his body his brilliant young mind and bold spirit remained firm and clear. By 1183, two years after his mother and sister had imposed his sister's husband Guy de Lusignan upon him as regent, he knew that Guy was incompetent as a leader and as a soldier, that Guy did not and never would have the trust of the great nobles and the knights on whose fighting prowess and sound leadership the defense of Christ's city depended. Because of this, when Saladin invaded the kingdom that fall the crusading army, though relatively large and well-equipped, had made no offensive move. The Muslim leader had departed virtually untouched.[2]

Therefore on November 20, advised by Count Raymond III of Tripoli, great-great-grandson of Raymond of Toulouse who had been primarily responsible for the victory of the First Crusade, and the bold brothers Baldwin and Balian of Ibelin, the leper king declared Guy deposed and took over the government again in his own name. He designated his sister Sibyl's six-year-old son Baldwin as his heir.[3] That very day Saladin laid siege to the crusader castle of Kerak far to the southeast, beyond the Dead Sea. Astonishingly, sick as he was, Baldwin IV took the field at once, leading his army in a litter to the relief of

---

[1]Kenneth M. Setton, ed., *A History of the Crusades*, Volume II, ed. Robert L. Wolff and Harry W. Hazard (Philadelphia, 1962), p. 113.

[2]Marshall W. Baldwin, *Raymond III of Tripolis and the Fall of Jerusalem (1140-1187)* (Princeton, 1936), pp. 52-53.

[3]*Ibid.*, pp. 53-55; Kenneth M. Setton, ed., *A History of the Crusades*, Volume I (Madison WI, 1969), p. 600; Robert L. Nicholson, *Joscelyn III and the Fall of the Crusader States* (Leiden, 1973), pp. 120-122.

Kerak, from which Saladin withdrew at his approach.[4] Baldwin instantly turned back across the Jordan and summoned Guy de Lusignan—whom he heard had repudiated his allegiance—to appear before him. Ensconced in the strongly fortified city of Ascalon, Guy refused to come, pleading illness (a plea which must have grated with bitter irony upon the dying king). Baldwin took his army to Ascalon; Guy refused to let him in. Baldwin had his litter carried to the city gate, raised the glove covering the ravaged stump of his right hand, and symbolically pounded on the gate, demanding admittance. But Guy had no shame, or his fear was greater than whatever shame he might have had. The gate remained closed.[5]

It seems that something broke then in this transcendent young hero who had endured more than most men could imagine enduring. He recognized anew that his mortal illness made it impossible for him to govern. At Christmastide 1183 he made his will: Raymond was now to be military commander and regent until the leper king's heir Baldwin V reached his majority; if the boy died before then, the Pope, the Holy Roman Emperor, and the Kings of France and England were to choose his successor. The barons present, and the Grand Masters of the Knights of the Temple and the Hospital, swore to abide by the provisions of the will. Baldwin V was crowned in the Church of the Holy Sepulcher. The next spring, as soon as it was safe to travel by sea, the two Grand Masters and the unworthy Patriarch Heraclius of Jerusalem set sail for the West to plead their desperate need for help—not only military assistance, but a king.[6]

The aged Pope Lucius III, who had succeeded Alexander III, was meeting with Emperor Frederick Barbarossa at Verona in northern Italy when the delegation arrived there in October. Pope and Emperor received the men from the Holy Land with fair words but no action. They pressed on to France, where cautious, tight-fisted King Philip II also gave them fair words but no action.[7] Their journey ended at Reading in England, where in January 1185 Patriarch Heraclius laid the banner of the kingdom and the keys to the Holy Sepulcher and the Tower of David at the feet of King Henry II, whose grandfather Fulk of Anjou had been King of Jerusalem, pleading with him to assume the crown of Baldwin the leper and save the city where Christ had walked.[8]

Henry II was only 51 years old, but he was prematurely aged, spiritually adrift, haunted by memories of Thomas Becket, psychologically shattered by

---

[4]Steven Runciman, *A History of the Crusades* (Cambridge, England, 1952), II, 440-441.

[5]Nicholson, *Fall of the Crusader States*, p. 122.

[6]Setton, *Crusades*, I, 601; Baldwin, *Raymond III*, pp. 57-61; Nicholson, *Fall of the Crusader States*, pp. 123-127.

[7]Horace K. Mann, *The Lives of the Popes of the Middle Ages*, Volume XI (London, 1925), pp. 241, 248-270; Nicholson, *Fall of the Crusader States*, p. 127.

[8]W. L. Warren, *Henry II* (Berkeley CA, 1973), p. 604.

the unforgiving enmity of his wife Eleanor of Aquitaine and the continuing violent hostility of his sons toward one another and toward him. His sons had been fighting furiously with one another all through the preceding year.[9] He had just released Eleanor after eleven years of imprisonment; but such love as her cold heart held was reserved for their son Richard rather than for him.[10] Never since that murder in the cathedral had Henry II of England found comfort, peace, or clear purpose. The offer from Jerusalem was an opportunity to redeem and transform his fate, to end an increasingly tortured life in a cloud of glory. Another who had challenged the Church as Henry II had done, Emperor Frederick Barbarossa, was soon to seize a similar opportunity.

But two months after he was offered the crown of Jerusalem, Henry turned it down. He must remain in his present kingdom, he said, to tend to its distracted affairs. At almost exactly the same moment, Baldwin IV died in Jerusalem.[11] He was just 24 years old. For fifteen years he had lived under sentence of the most horrible death his age knew; but he had kept the faith, and held the holy city, to the end.

In the Church of the Holy Sepulcher, to this day, hangs the sword of Godfrey of Bouillon, the man who stormed Jerusalem in the First Crusade. But there is no monument, and scarcely a memory, of Baldwin the leper king.

Count Raymond III of Tripoli proved not a man to match his great-great-grandfather. When little Baldwin V fell seriously ill the next year the seneschal of the kingdom, Joscelin of Courtenay, an ally of Guy de Lusignan, tricked Raymond into leaving Jerusalem before he died. Patriarch Heraclius crowned the dead boy's mother Sibyl, who in turn crowned her husband Guy de Lusignan. The leading noblemen present all violated their oaths to maintain the will of the leper king, except the Grand Master of the Knights of St. John of the Hospital, Roger des Moulins, who refused to surrender the key to the strongbox containing the royal insignia, instead throwing it out of the window. Threatened with attack by Guy and his henchmen, Raymond turned to Christendom's inexorable foe, and made a treaty with Saladin toward the end of 1186.[12]

Saladin was no enemy before whom to play such games. For years, working tirelessly to unite the often deeply divided Muslims of the Middle East, he had been building up to the point where he could take advantage of such an opportunity.[13] Now he was ready. At the beginning of the following spring he began gathering his forces, and King Guy belatedly decided he should make

[9]*Ibid.*, pp. 596-597.

[10]John Gillingham, *Richard the Lionheart* (New York, 1978), p. 102.

[11]Warren, *Henry II*, pp. 604-605; Nicholson, *Fall of the Crusader States*, p. 132.

[12]Setton, *Crusades*, I, 604-606; Baldwin, *Raymond III*, pp. 71-85; Nicholson, *Fall of the Crusader States*, pp. 133-146.

[13]Setton, *Crusades*, I, 563-584.

peace with Count Raymond. The peace was made, their forces united, and what may have been the largest army ever raised by the kingdom of Jerusalem took the field in Galilee in June. Virtually every knight in the country was in it. A fragment of the True Cross was borne with the army's standards, but Patriarch Heraclius was too cowardly to bring it himself; he sent the bishop of Acre to carry it.[14]

On June 27 Saladin crossed the Jordan and took Tiberias on the Sea of Galilee, but Raymond's wife held out in the citadel. She sent a message reporting her situation, and her sons and other hot-headed knights called for an immediate march to her rescue, but her husband Raymond pointed out that for the crusaders to leave their well-protected camp and march immediately across barren country in great heat would risk disaster. Saladin could raise other armies, but this army was all the kingdom of Jerusalem had—if it was lost, all was lost. All through the evening of July 2 the question was debated, and by midnight Raymond had prevailed; the army would remain, at least for the next day, in its camp. But in the small hours of the morning Grand Master Gerard of the Knights of the Temple, who had willingly broken his pledge to maintain the will of the leper king (by contrast to Grand Master Roger of the Knights of the Hospital who had refused to break it) came to the royal tent, told Guy that Raymond was a traitor (tragically, he had been, though apparently was so no longer), and by threatening Guy with a public denunciation for cowardice, secured his agreement for a march on Tiberias at dawn.[15]

So the only army of the kingdom fo Jerusalem set out on a road without water through the growing heat of a summer day in the hill country of Palestine. Saladin awaited them, sure now that Allah had delivered them into his hands. He was encamped in a pleasant meadow near the town of Hattin, where water was abundant. Above him, over a rocky, sandy waste, loomed the sinister twin peaks called the Horns of Hattin. As the day drew on, Saladin sent more and more men upward to harry the advancing crusaders, whose pace slowed as heat and thirst took their toll. Finally Grand Master Gerard told King Guy that the Templars could go no farther. Many of the nobles urged Guy to press on to try to reach the lake, but he refused. Grand Master Gerard was telling him what to do. Raymond was not asked for his advice. Hearing of the fatal decision, he cried: "Ah, Lord God, the war is over; we are dead men; the kingdom is finished!"[16]

They made camp around a dry well. All night the crusaders suffered

---

[14]Runciman, *Crusades*, II, 451-455; Baldwin, *Raymond III*, pp. 87, 100-104; Nicholson, *Fall of the Crusader States*, pp. 153-155.

[15]Runciman, *Crusades*, II, 455-456; Setton, *Crusades*, I, 610-612; Baldwin, *Raymond III*, 100, 108-114; Nicholson, *Fall of the Crusader States*, pp. 157-158.

[16]Runciman, *Crusades*, II, 457 for the quotation; Setton, *Crusades*, I, 611-612; Baldwin, *Raymond III*, pp. 114-119.

agonies of thirst. Beyond the campfires the enemy prowled, surrounding the entire Christian army so that "not a cat" could have slipped through them. At some of their outposts in view of the Christians, Saladin's men poured water disdainfully upon the ground. About dawn, when the Battle of the Horns of Hattin began, the Muslims lit fires in the dry brush, so that the smoke would add to the sufferings of the Christians.[17]

The situation of the crusaders was hopeless; and it is nothing less than astounding that many of them nevertheless fought almost all day under these appalling conditions. Late in the afternoon the last remaining knights launched charge after charge directly at Saladin; but his courage and that of his bodyguard was as great as theirs, and they found that human bodies could not do what they were asking of them. Almost all the Christian foot soldiers were slain; almost all the Christian knights not killed were captured, though Raymond and Balian of Ibelin escaped. Saladin personally struck off the head of Reynald of Châtillon, a baron whom (with some reason) he particularly disliked. He ordered every captured Knight of the Temple and Knight of the Hospital killed, except for Grand Master Gerard of the Temple who had made his victory possible.[18]

By the end of September Saladin, vigorously following up his victory, had occupied the whole of Palestine except for Jerusalem.[19] (Only to the north, in ancient Phoenicia, was the coastal city of Tyre held for Christendom by the opportune arrival from Constantinople of a vigorous French nobleman, Conrad of Montferrat, who immediately took command there.)[20] And Jerusalem was virtually defenseless. Balian of Ibelin, commanding there, had only two other knights with him, and fifty women and children for every man. Saladin encamped on the Mount of Olives, like the Roman legions of Titus who destroyed the holy city in the year 70. Balian and his scratch militia fought Saladin's best hand-to-hand in the breaches in the city's walls. But prolonged resistance was impossible; on October 2 Balian had to surrender, though he did obtain terms making it possible for most of the Christians in the city to save their lives. On October 9—a Friday, the Muslim holy day—Saladin completed the removal of all external signs of Christian worship in the city. Accompanied by thousands, he went in procession to the mosque of al-Aqsa on the Dome of the Rock, where Solomon's temple had stood, to give thanks to Allah for their triumph.[21]

---

[17]Setton, *Crusades*, I, 612; Baldwin, *Raymond III*, pp. 119-120.

[18]Runciman, *Crusades*, II, 458-460; Setton, *Crusades*, I, 612-614; Baldwin, *Raymond III*, pp. 120-132; Nicholson, *Fall of the Crusader States*, pp. 160-163.

[19]Runciman, *Crusades*, II, 460-463; Nicholson, *Fall of the Crusader States*, pp. 164, 168-170.

[20]Runciman, *Crusades*, II, 472; Baldwin, *Raymond III*, p. 137; Nicholson, *Fall of the Crusader States*, pp. 166-167, 176-177.

[21]Runciman, *Crusades*, II, 464-468; Setton, *Crusades*, I, 616-618; Nicholson, *Fall of*

Jerusalem was lost. It was not to be regained for Christendom for 730 years, until 1917, in a world so different from that of 1187 that no one then living could have begun to imagine it—a world in which, for many in the once-Christian West, Jerusalem did not matter much any more. And so, in this our twentieth century, it was soon passed on to people to whom it still did and does matter very much indeed: the Jews of Israel.

Yet the Crusades were far from finished with the loss of Jerusalem. The news of it inspired at the time, and for many years afterward, a tremendous resurgence of the crusading spirit. Considering all that the crusades had come to mean to the unity and confidence of Christendom, it is one of the great tragedies of the history of Christendom that none of the crusades which may be regarded as direct responses to the loss of Jerusalem—the Third, the aborted crusade of Emperor Henry VI, and the Fourth—reached its objective.

The aged Pope Lucius III died in November 1185 and was succeeded by Urban III, who had been Humbert Crivelli, Archbishop of Milan, a strong supporter and good friend of Thomas Becket. The new Pope's family had suffered in the wars of Emperor Frederick Barbarossa in Lombardy, where Milan had been the chief victim, and when Barbarossa's son and designated heir Henry married Princess Constance, heiress to Sicily, Urban tried to prohibit his coronation as king of Germany and Italy. (With Constance, if she inherited Sicily, Henry would be the titular ruler of all of Italy except the Papal state and Venice.) The coronation took place despite the Papal ban, and a series of hostile moves by Emperor and Pope ensued. Urban III was ready to excommunicate Frederick once again when he suddenly died October 20, 1187, just before news of the fall of Jerusalem arrived in the West.[22]

That news came literally on the morrow of Pope Urban's death; the cardinals had it before electing his successor. They chose Papal Chancellor Albert of Morra, who took the name of Gregory VIII. In less than two months he was dead; but during this very short pontificate, he issued a ringing call for a new crusade in letters sent all over Christendom, demanding peace among Christians and calling for fasting, sacrifice, and self-denial as indispensable preliminaries to launching it.[23] First of all the princes of Christendom to respond was Richard, heir apparent to England and Anjou since his older brother Henry died in 1183, though his father Henry II had never explicitly

---

the Crusader States, pp. 170-174.

[22]Mann, *Popes of the Middle Ages*, XI, 271, 289, 292-298; *The Cambridge Medieval History*, ed. J. R. Tanner, C. W. Previté-Orton, and Z. N. Brooke, Volume V (Cambridge, England, 1926), pp. 457-458; Marcel Pacaut, *Frederick Barbarossa* (New York, 1970), pp. 188-192; John J. Norwich, *The Kingdom in the Sun, 1130-1194* (New York, 1970), pp. 346-348.

[23]Mann, *Popes of the Middle Ages*, XI, 313-316, 336-338.

recognized him as heir to all his domains. In November Richard took the Cross at Tours. He was thirty years old, already famous as a battle commander, destined to write his name imperishably in Christendom's lore and legend as Richard the Lion-hearted.[24]

In addition to launching the Third Crusade, Gregory VIII during his brief span as Pope had strongly indicated his desire for peace with Emperor Frederick Barbarossa, in keeping with his calls for peace among the lords of Christendom. His successor as Pope, Paul Scolari, Bishop of Palestrina, who took the name of Clement III, continued calling for a crusade and for peace within Christendom, including peace between Pope and Emperor, with a vigor that belied his age and poor health (he had a bad heart, and surprised contemporaries by living and reigning as Pope more than three years).[25] As early as January 1188 Cardinal Henry of Albano, who had refused the Papacy at the time of the election of Gregory VIII in order to devote himself fully and solely to the new crusade, and Archbishop Joscius of Tyre, whose city was at that moment under siege by Saladin, preached the crusade so powerfully to Henry II of England and Philip II of France at Gisors that they agreed to make peace and take the Cross. But Henry had missed his chance for crusading glory when he refused the crown of Jerusalem three years earlier; it is doubtful that he really expected to go this time. However, he and Richard did agree just a few days later to levy an unprecedented tax in their realms to finance the crusade, which came to be known as the "Saladin tithe."[26]

From France Cardinal Henry went to Germany, where he preached the crusade once again at the imperial Diet at Mainz in March, later called the "Diet of Christ." There the Emperor stepped forward to take the Cross.[27]

As a young man of twenty Frederick Barbarossa had marched with Emperor Conrad III on the Second Crusade, though never passing beyond Byzantine territory. Now in his early sixties, but still strong and vigorous, he saw his leadership of this crusade to restore Christian dominion over Jerusalem as the climax of his life. It appears that he resolved to go almost as soon as he heard of Jerusalem's fall.[28] Frederick Barbarossa had done much damage to

---

[24]For Richard's life up to this point, see the excellent biography by John Gillingham, *Richard the Lionheart*, pp. 1-110. Gillingham's work is particularly valuable for its meticulous and devastating disproof of the myth that Richard was a homosexual. Not only is there no contemporary evidence of this, but no historian even suggested it as a possibility until 1948! Gillingham reviews all of the events and circumstances in Richard's life which have been adduced as evidence of his homosexuality and shows that they are nothing of the kind (*op. cit.*, pp. 107, 130, 161-162, 283, 298). For the date that Richard took the Cross, see Warren, *Henry II*, p. 607.
[25]Mann, *Popes of the Middle Ages*, XI, 334-336, 342-345, 354-355.
[26]*Ibid.*, XI, 356-357; Gillingham, *Richard the Lionheart*, pp. 110-113; Setton, *Crusades*, II, 47.
[27]Setton, *Crusades*, II, 89-90.
[28]*Ibid.*; Pacaut, *Frederick Barbarossa*, pp. 46, 198-199. Pacaut gives Barbarossa's age

Christendom, for which there was need to atone; but he had always maintained his personal faith, and was a great leader of men. We have no means of knowing how much he regretted of what he had done; but we may hope that Pope Gregory VIII had spoken for him on his first appeal for the crusade to recover Jerusalem when he said: "To those who with contrite heart and humbled spirit undertake the labor of this journey, and depart in sorrow for their sins and in the true faith, we promise full pardon for their offenses and eternal life."[29]

Frederick Barbarossa was now firmly in control of Germany, so there was nothing to delay his departure comparable to the continuing civil strife in England and France that for the moment prevented the departure of any crusaders from those countries—or, at least, could be cited as a reasonable excuse for not departing. Frederick called upon his oldest son and namesake to accompany him on the crusade, and left the administration of the empire in the hands of the able but ruthless Henry, his second son.[30] Frederick seems to have assumed from the beginning that he and his men would take the overland route through Asia Minor, despite its difficulties and dangers—the route which had brought the First Crusade to success and a substantial part of the Second (including most of the German contingent) to disaster. So he requested permission of the Eastern Emperor, Isaac II Angelus, for passage of his army through Byzantine dominions on the way to the Holy Land, and for the right to purchase food for his troops within them. Isaac said he agreed, and a Byzantine embassy sent to Nuremberg in December 1188 after some hesitation confirmed the agreement; but in fact Isaac was resolved to oppose the passage of the crusaders, and made contact with Saladin to concert plans "to delay and destroy the German army."[31]

About this "Byzantine treachery" there is no doubt; even the many modern Western historians sympathetic to Byzantium and hostile to the Crusades have to admit it. Not in justification but in partial explanation, it should be understood that the Byzantine empire in 1188 was as weak or weaker than it had ever been in all its long history, causing Isaac and his court to fear that once the Western Emperor and his mighty army saw and sensed that weakness, they would be unable to resist the temptation to take advantage of it.

The rapid Byzantine decline dated back to the military disaster Emperor Manuel Comnenus had suffered at the hands of the Turks at Myriocephalon in

---

as 61 or 62 at the time he took the Cross. At the time and since, his age on this occasion has sometimes been exaggerated for dramatic effect. Much evidence indicates that he still had a large measure of mental and physical vigor at this time.

[29]Setton, *Crusades*, II, 89.

[30]Pacaut, *Frederick Barbarossa*, p. 201.

[31]Charles M. Brand, *Byzantium Confronts the West, 1180-1204* (Cambridge MA, 1968), pp. 176-177; Setton, *Crusades*, II, 91-92.

1176.[32]   The imperial standing army was never really reconstituted after Myriocephalon; primary reliance was now placed on the feudal levies of the great landholders. They had been generally loyal to Manuel, an able, long-lived Emperor who had been popular despite some resentment of his pro-Western views; but when he died in 1180 leaving an 11-year-old son as heir, the absence of an effective regency allowed Manuel's cousin, the vigorous and fantastically cruel 62-year-old Andronicus Comnenus, to take over Constantinople in the spring of 1182. Andronicus had immediately let it be known that he would offer no protection to Westerners ("Latins," as the Byzantines called them) and a nightmarish massacre of thousands followed, in which the slaughterers spared neither women nor children, neither old nor sick, neither priest nor monk. Cardinal John, the Pope's representative, was beheaded and his head was dragged through the streets at the tail of a dog; children were cut out of their mother's wombs; bodies of dead Westerners were exhumed and abused; some 4,000 who escaped death were sold into slavery to the Turks.[33]

During his ensuing four-year reign Andronicus had visited similar atrocities on his own people, if not in such large numbers. He blinded those he considered his enemies, drowned them, burned them alive, and had women tied to battering rams. He strangled the boy emperor in his sleep and married his twelve-year-old wife.[34] In June 1185 he proposed an alliance with Saladin.[35] That September he was overthrown and tortured to death in the Hippodrome, but it came too late for the empire in the Balkans. The new Emperor, Isaac II, was unable to retain Byzantine authority in most of that area. Within a year, three Bulgarian brothers—Peter, Asen, and John—rebelled and gained control of the region between the Balkan Mountains and the Danube. By the spring of 1188—when Frederick Barbarossa was taking the Cross—Isaac had been forced to recognize an independent Bulgarian state in this area, while the Serbs under Stephen Nemanya had become virtually independent in their region north and northwest of classical Macedonia and had taken the important city of Nish on the direct route from Germany to Constantinople (now the route of the Orient Express), through which Frederick would pass.[36] When he reached it, the Serb and Bulgar leaders would undoubtedly ask him to join them against the Empire in Constantinople, which had given the West abundant provocation.

Frederick Barbarossa and his counsellors seem to have been almost

---

[32]See Chapter Three, above.

[33]Brand, *Byzantium Confronts the West*, pp. 14-43. Historians who wax eloquent and indignant—with considerable reason—about the sack of Constantinople by the Fourth Crusade in 1204 rarely if ever mention the massacre of the Westerners in Constantinople in 1182.

[34]*Ibid.*, pp. 49-53, 56-57.

[35]Nicholson, *Fall of the Crusader States*, pp. 152-153.

[36]Brand, *Byzantium Confronts the West*, pp. 70-73, 89-92; John V. A. Fine Jr., *The Late Medieval Balkans* (Ann Arbor MI, 1987), pp. 7-16.

completely unaware of this hornets' nest which they were about to penetrate. On May 11, 1189 they set out—perhaps 20,000 strong—from Regensburg on the Bavarian Danube, with the utmost enthusiasm and excellent planning, fully prepared to march all the way to Jerusalem and thrust aside any obstacle in their way. Envoys were sent ahead to Constantinople to make final arrangements for the army's passage and for the purchase of food for the troops. Emperor Isaac II had the envoys immediately jailed; at the same time Saladin's envoys in the imperial city remained free and unharmed.[37]

On July 24 the Holy Roman Emperor reached Nish after encountering Byzantine harassment at various points along the way, but he still believed the Eastern Emperor friendly. Stephen Nemanya and Tsar Peter of Bulgaria met Frederick there, offering him no less than 60,000 men for the crusade in return for alliance against Constantinople. He rejected the offer out of hand, declaring that his only goal was Jerusalem. By August 25 Frederick had learned of the imprisonment of his envoys; on that day he received an arrogant and accusing letter from Isaac, requesting him to provide hostages for his future good conduct and to guarantee the Byzantines half his conquests. At once he seized the nearest city, Philippopolis, winning an easy victory over a greatly outnumbered Byzantine force and making it his base for the next several months.[38]

In September, learning that additional ambassadors he had sent to Constantinople had also been seized, Frederick ordered his army to march on the imperial city, destroying everything in its path. Finally persuaded by his more rational advisors that his policy toward the crusaders was bringing on rather than avoiding everything he had feared, Emperor Isaac released the imprisoned ambassadors in October. They returned to Frederick at the end of the month with infuriating (and accurate) reports of the Byzantine alliance with Saladin, plans to destroy the crusading army as it crossed the Dardanelles, and the violent anti-Western attitude of Patriarch Dositheus of Constantinople, who had offered unconditional absolution to any Greek killing a Westerner.[39] Frederick passed on this information to his son Henry, whom he requested to assemble a fleet to aid the crusading army in Byzantine territory if necessary, and to ask the Pope's approval for a crusade against the Eastern Empire because of its treachery and dealings with the enemy.[40] No Papal approval was given and Frederick soon thought better of the idea; but the seed of the later diversion of the Fourth Crusade had been planted. Though a war against

[37]Setton, *Crusades*, II, 92-93, 98-99; Pacaut, *Frederick Barbarossa*, pp. 201-202; Brand, *Byzantium Confronts the West*, pp. 177-178.

[38]Setton, *Crusades*, II, 93-94, 99-102; Fine, *Late Medieval Balkans*, pp. 24-26; Brand, *Byzantium Confronts the West*, pp. 178-181; Pacaut, *Frederick Barbarossa*, pp. 203-204.

[39]Brand, *Byzantium Confronts the West*, pp. 182-183; Setton, *Crusades*, II, 102-104.

[40]Setton, *Crusades*, II, 94-97.

Christians was indubitably a perversion of the crusading ideal, Emperor Isaac's acts against the crusaders had clearly been acts of war.

On November 22 Frederick took Adrianople—the nearest large city to Constantinople—without resistance, just after Isaac had absurdly blustered that he had the crusaders trapped in Thrace. Isaac opened negotiations, but was still demanding hostages, which Frederick refused to give him. New Serb and Bulgar envoys came to the Holy Roman Emperor, doubtless pointing out how convincingly their warnings about Byzantine treachery had been borne out by events. Still Frederick would not divert the crusade, while insisting upon the free passage Isaac had originally guaranteed. Finally, in January 1190, it was Isaac who gave the hostages, released all remaining captives, renewed his original promises, and agreed to pay an indemnity. Frederick required Patriarch Dositheus to add his signature to the agreement.[41]

The whole proceeding reflected the highest credit on the Holy Roman Emperor and strikingly demonstrated the firmness of his crusading purpose. Everything that the Fourth Crusade later did to Christendom's discredit, Frederick Barbarossa refused to do, though he was directly provoked as the leaders of the Fourth Crusade never were. The extent of Byzantine provocation of the Third Crusade is obvious from the sequence of events. It would be a long time before anyone in the West would trust them again.

Ships from Pisa in Italy, obtained by Prince Henry, reached Gallipoli on the Dardanelles late in March. During Holy Week an immense troop ferrying operation went on, though the Emperor halted it all Easter day to celebrate the great feast of the Resurrection. On April 28 the crusading army entered Turkish territory, where old Seljuk Sultan Kilij Arslan II was resolved to resist with all his strength. He had reigned for 35 years, and could remember in his youth the Turkish victories over the armies of the Second Crusade in Asia Minor.[42]

The old Holy Roman Emperor—about the same age as his opponent—never faltered. Day after day, through a hot, dry, denuded countryside where little food or shelter was available, he and his men marched on as the men of the First Crusade had done. By May 13, the feast of Pentecost, they were beginning to eat their horses; but the next day they won a major victory. The Emperor was in the thick of the fight and was thrown from his horse. The Turks offered to let the crusaders pass if they would give them 300 pounds of gold and recognize their rule over Christian Armenia. Frederick Barbarossa answered them: "Rather than making a royal highway with gold and silver, with the help of Our Lord Jesus Christ, Whose knights we are, the road will be opened with iron!" On May 18 they came up to the fortified city of

---

[41]*Ibid.*, II, 105-109; Brand, *Byzantium Confronts the West*, pp. 183-187; Fine, *Late Medieval Balkans*, p. 25; Pacaut, *Frederick Barbarossa*, p. 204.
[42]Setton, *Crusades*, II, 109-111 and I, 520.

Konya, Kilij Arslan's capital, and had to fight another battle, before which Frederick called upon his troops with the words which stand at the head of this chapter. The Turks then drew off, and by May 30 the crusaders had reached the borders of Cilician Armenia, a Christian country.[43]

But the route through the Taurus Mountains into Cilicia was extraordinarily difficult, the heat was intense, and the army had to move quickly before their food gave out entirely. Frederick unwisely tried to find and follow a better alternative route; there was none. The army broke up into files and groups, straggling over rocky mountains and narrow twisting trails. Frederick, with the vanguard, made his way down into the defile of the Saleph (Calycadnus) River. There, on June 10, 1190, something very strange occurred. No two accounts we have of it agree or can be harmonized, perhaps because it happened so fast that no one really knew what had taken place. The Emperor was pressing on, into the brawling stream or along its rocky shores, perhaps looking for a ford. His horse may have slipped and thrown him. He may have tried to dismount at the wrong moment. It seems wildly unlikely, as one account maintains, that he decided to go for a swim (supposing one could swim in that mountain torrent). But suddenly he was in the water. He was probably not wearing full armor, but very likely was wearing chain mail. He sank to the bottom and drowned before he could be pulled out.[44]

The blow to the sorely tried army was overwhelming. The catastrophe was so sudden, so strange, so inexplicable, that men seemed to go mad. We hear of wild lamentations, mass departures, even of soldiers losing their faith and deserting to the Turks. Frederick's son and namesake was unable to rally the army and restore its morale. It broke up into three groups. Two embarked at Tarsus in Cilicia, one going by sea to Antioch and the other to Tripoli. The third marched overland to Antioch, where the greater part of the survivors gathered in the unhealthy summer and were devastated by plague.[45]

Frederick Barbarossa's army, which had come so far and done so well, was destroyed as a fighting force by what seemed a thunderbolt from heaven. Though for some reason its significance has been greatly underestimated by most historians, the accidental death of Frederick Barbarossa and the consequent breakup of his army, when they had almost reached their goal, eliminated the best chance for the success of the Third Crusade.

Meanwhile, back in France, Henry II had died in despair the previous year, betrayed in the end by all his sons—even John, the only one he still loved. Richard the Lion-hearted was king in his stead.[46] He was still resolved to go on

---

[43]*Ibid.*, II, 111-113.

[44]*Ibid.*, II, 114; Pacaut, *Frederick Barbarossa*, p. 205; *Cambridge Medieval History*, V, 412.

[45]Setton, *Crusades*, II, 114-115.

[46]Warren, *Henry II*, pp. 625-626; Gillingham, *Richard the Lionheart*, pp. 123-130.

crusade, but felt he could not go leaving behind his wily and relentless enemy, Philip II of France. He had little confidence in the ability of the devoted but weak Pope Clement III to compel Philip to observe any prohibitions against seizing the lands of a king absent on crusade. But in November 1189 Philip told Richard that he and his nobles had agreed to meet at Vézelay in France in the coming April to go on crusade. On July 4, 1190 the two monarchs finally met at Vézelay and agreed to leave together.[47] Is it only coincidence that this was almost exactly the moment when the news of Frederick Barbarossa's death would have arrived in Western Europe?

The English and French crusaders were proceeding by sea, departing from Marseilles in the south of France. In September, just a few days apart, both Richard and Philip arrived in troubled Sicily, whose King William II had planned to join the crusade but had died suddenly, relatively young and without issue, the previous year. William's illegitimate cousin Tancred had taken the Sicilian crown, with Pope Clement III's support, to keep it from going to Constance, the wife of Barbarossa's son Henry VI, which would unite most of Italy under German control. These were troubled waters to fish in, and Richard had a genuine family interest in Sicily's problems since his sister was William II's widow. There was rioting, followed by negotiations; by the time everyone was satisfied, the season of winter storms had arrived, making large-scale voyaging on the Mediterranean too hazardous to attempt.[48] These delays were particularly reprehensible because throughout the year 1190 a local Christian force had been besieging Muslim-held Acre, strong enough to maintain the siege but not strong enough to take the city. Frederick Barbarossa had intended to bring his crusading army from Cilicia through Syria straight to Acre to raise the siege; but only scattered reinforcements reached the besiegers during 1190.[49]

In March 1191 Pope Clement III died and was succeeded by Cardinal Hyacinth Bobo as Celestine III. The new Pope was 85 years old but still remarkably vigorous. He had been three times to Spain as Papal legate and profoundly appreciated the long Spanish struggle against the Muslims; he was a co-founder of their Order of Santiago. Celestine III was consecrated Pope on Easter Sunday, April 14, and the next day crowned Henry VI Holy Roman Emperor in succession to his father Frederick Barbarossa.[50] Though still deeply disturbed by the prospect of Henry ruling southern Italy as well as Germany and claiming northern Italy as well, the Pope wisely decided that for the sake of

[47]Setton, *Crusades*, II, 49, 57; Gillingham, *Richard the Lionheart*, pp. 137, 140-142.

[48]Gillingham, *Richard the Lionheart*, pp. 147-149, 152-156; Setton, *Crusades*, II, 58-60; Norwich, *Kingdom in the Sun*, pp. 365-367, 370-371.

[49]Setton, *Crusades*, II, 51-52, 115; Nicholson, *Fall of the Crusader States*, pp. 182-183, 185, 187, 191.

[50]Mann, *Popes in the Middle Ages*, XI, 384-399; *Cambridge Medieval History*, V, 464.

Christian unity and the crusade, he should not deny imperial coronation to the son of the man who had led his crusading army so splendidly until his untimely death.

A few days before the coronation of Henry VI, early in Holy Week, Richard the Lion-hearted had sailed at last from Sicily, ten days behind Philip. By April 20 Philip was in Acre, but Richard followed a circuitous route via Crete, Rhodes, and Cyprus. At the last-named island his fiancée from Navarra in Spain, Berengaria, caught up with him and they were hastily married. He conquered Cyprus in a lightning campaign and then sailed on to Acre where he finally arrived June 8, 1191. Once on the scene he was irresistible; the siege, which had lasted no less than 22 months, was over by July 12. Not only did Acre fall, but the besiegers secured, as the price of the lives of its defenders, the pledge of a ransom of 200,000 gold dinars, the release of 1,500 Christian prisoners, and the restoration of the portion of the True Cross captured on the field of the Horns of Hattin. Saladin had not negotiated the terms and was furious when he heard of them, but felt himself bound to abide by what his men in Acre had agreed to.[51]

Richard and Philip took advantage of the moment to try to settle the division among the feudal lords of the kingdom of Jerusalem (now reborn at Acre) by designating the ill-fated Guy de Lusignan king for the rest of his life, but his rival Conrad of Montferrat (who had held Tyre while Guy was a prisoner of Saladin) and his descendants as Guy's successor. Three days after this agreement was announced, on July 31, Philip II of France declared that he was returning home. He had always been a reluctant crusader, and could not begin to compete with Richard as general, born leader of men, and charismatic personality in this alien environment. Richard does not seem to have strongly opposed Philip's departure, which in any case he could probably not have prevented; but Richard's prestige was now so high, and his confidence in victory so great, that he did not fear it as much as he would have earlier. Back in France, Philip was widely criticized for abandoning the crusade.[52]

Richard was eager to be on the march, and furious when Saladin—for reasons which are disputed—did not deliver on schedule his Christian prisoners and the promised first installment of the ransom payment for the Muslims captured at Acre. On August 20 Richard brought out 3,000 Muslim prisoners and had them slaughtered in full view of Saladin's troops. While no just man can fully defend such an action, it should be remembered that Richard had no effective means to guard or hold the prisoners after his army departed, could not possibly bring them with him, and could not simply release them to fight against him again with nothing in return; also that Saladin himself, often praised

---

[51]Gillingham, *Richard the Lionheart*, pp. 163-168, 172-176; Setton, *Crusades*, II, 61-69; Nicholson, *Fall of the Crusader States*, pp. 191-193.
[52]Setton, *Crusades*, II, 70-71; Gillingham, *Richard the Lionheart*, pp. 178-181.

by Christian as well as Muslim historians for his justice, had slaughtered all the Knights of the Temple and the Hospital captured after the Battle of the Horns of Hattin, except for the Grand Masters. Two days later Richard led his army south toward Jaffa, from which he intended to march directly on Jerusalem.[53]

Saladin marched in parallel, harassing the crusading army and looking for a good opportunity to attack. He thought he had found one in the forest (a rarity in increasingly barren Palestine) through which the coast highway passed just north of the village of Arsuf. He gathered his men there and attacked. By Richard's firm order his knights waited under heavy pressure until the enemy was fully committed. Though they still charged a little prematurely, before Richard signalled, he adapted instantly to the situation, followed up the first charge, rallied and re-formed the knights to repel the ensuing Muslim counterattack, and won another resounding victory. Jaffa (whose walls had been destroyed by the Muslims) fell to him without a fight, Saladin evacuated Ascalon, and the whole coast of Palestine was in the hands of the crusaders. Richard let himself be persuaded to remain in Jaffa while its fortifications were rebuilt.[54]

Against an ordinary opponent the delay might not have mattered, but Saladin was as committed to defend Jerusalem as the crusaders were to take it. Though many of his men were disheartened, he was not. He informed Richard's ambassadors that under no circumstances would he consider or discuss yielding Jerusalem to them. Richard wasted six weeks of good fall campaigning weather in Jaffa; when he finally did move inland, he stopped to rebuild almost every battered or ruined castle he found along his way. When he reached Ramleh in mid-November the winter rains had begun, turning the only available road into a river of mud. Saladin then pulled his main army back, though leaving a garrison in Jerusalem; but he had not gone far away, and would return at once if Jerusalem were besieged. Still Richard moved slowly forward, until in early January 1192 he was within twelve miles of Jerusalem. The holy city was well fortified, the weather remained very bad, and supplies were meager. Most of Richard's advisors recommended that he retreat, perhaps to try again in a more clement season. But the Lionheart had the initiative and the aura of victory; the morale of Jerusalem's garrison was low; it seems very likely that it could have been taken. The first Raymond of Toulouse would have pressed on. So would Frederick Barbarossa. But Richard the Lionhearted did not. In the first of two critical decisions of his, the strangest and saddest in the history of the Crusades, he ordered retreat from Jerusalem at the very threshold of triumph.[55]

He returned to the coast at Ascalon, the greatest fortress in Palestine, and

---

[53]Setton, *Crusades*, II, 71-73; Gillingham, *Richard the Lionheart*, pp. 182-185.
[54]Setton, *Crusades*, II, 73-75; Gillingham, *Richard the Lionheart*, pp. 186-192.
[55]Setton, *Crusades*, II, 76-78; Gillingham, *Richard the Lionheart*, pp. 196-200.

spent the next four months supervising its rebuilding,[56] restoring order in chaotic Acre, and making a new settlement of the royal succession controversy for the kingdom of Jerusalem. Now understanding the unreliability and incompetence of Guy de Lusignan, Richard deftly removed him from the scene in April by declaring him deposed (for the third time) as king of Jerusalem and given Cyprus, which Richard had conquered on his way to Palestine, in exchange. The much abler Conrad of Montferrat was recognized as king of Jerusalem in Guy's place. Twelve days later, for reasons which remain obscure, Conrad was murdered by the Assassins, and replaced by Count Henry of Champagne.[57] But Richard was clearly now the dominant figure among the Christians in Palestine, and all factions rallied to his support when in June he announced a new march on Jerusalem. As he drew near to the holy city at the end of the month, Count Henry arrived with substantial reinforcements, and the Christians captured an enormous Muslim caravan near the Dead Sea.[58]

Saladin commanded in Jerusalem in person. His army was restive and fearful; Richard the Lion-hearted had become a legend among them as well as among his own men—the Muslim troops both admired and feared him. But they also admired and feared Saladin, and he would neither move nor yield. The wills of the two great leaders met like crossed swords. Saladin had stopped or polluted all the springs around dry Jerusalem, and his hard-riding horsemen repeatedly raided the difficult road from the coast through the hill country by which alone the army could be supplied.[59] While Saladin was relentlessly determined, Richard was uncharacteristically pessimistic; for some reason he had come to feel that this campaign could not succeed. We know that one day he came close enough to see his goal, probably at Montjoie, the hill famous in crusading tradition from which pilgrims approaching on the road from the west could first catch sight of Jerusalem; the later legend may be very close to truth which tells how Richard at Montjoie "flung up his shield to cover his eyes and, weeping, begged God that he might not have to look upon the city if he could not deliver it."[60]

---

[56]Gillingham, *Richard the Lionheart*, p. 200. Richard fancied himself a great castle-builder, and though he had undoubted skills in this area, in the end he seemed to develop something of a Maginot-line mentality about castles, as demonstrated by his near-obsession with the construction of the castle of Chateau-Gaillard in Normandy, which he claimed he could hold even if its walls were made of butter. Perhaps he could have, but after his death Chateau-Gaillard—though stone and not butter—was besieged and taken by the French in 1204 (Gillingham, *op. cit.*, pp. 262-265; Austin Lane Poole, *From Domesday book to Magna Carta, 1087-1216* [Oxford History of England], 2nd ed. (Oxford, 1955), pp. 375, 383-384).

[57]Setton, *Crusades*, I, 125-126, II, 80-82; Gillingham, *Richard the Lionheart*, pp. 201-207.

[58]Setton, *Crusades*, II, 82; Gillingham, *Richard the Lionheart*, pp. 209-211.

[59]Gillingham, *Richard the Lionheart*, p. 211.

[60]*Ibid.*, p. 210.

Had he already concluded that he could not deliver it? It seems that he had. Why? The reasons for such a conclusion do not seem compelling, though most historians have defended Richard's second decision to retreat from Jerusalem. No general wins wars who dwells primarily upon his own army's problems, forgetting that the enemy's problems may well be as great or greater than his own. Richard the Lion-hearted was a superb battle commander; he was not a great strategist. Furthermore, his mind may have been clouded by worries about what was happening at home; for on May 29 he had learned of a conspiracy against him by Philip II of France and Richard's devious brother John (the later infamous King John), his heir since Richard was still childless. On July 4 Richard turned back. He never saw Jerusalem again.[61] The Third Crusade had failed.

Returning to the coast, Richard barely saved Jaffa from Saladin's attack, then brilliantly repulsed him in the field in an action marked by all of his old courage and dash. He left the coast of Palestine firmly held, but everything inland in infidel hands. This division was confirmed by a three-year truce September 2, 1192, in which Saladin also pledged to permit Christian pilgrims free access to Jerusalem. But they would still find no external signs of Christian worship when they reached it.[62]

On the essential issue—the possession of Jerusalem—Saladin had triumphed. But he lived only six months to enjoy it, and immediately after his death March 4 most of his short-lived but powerful empire, whose unity had been essential to fielding an army that could take Jerusalem and hold it against the crusaders, broke up.[63] By then Richard was a prisoner in Germany. When he announced his second march on Jerusalem in June 1192 he had pledged, even in the face of the news of the conspiracy against him at home, that he would remain in Palestine until the following Easter to secure it. If he had only done so, kept his promise and persevered, he would have won, and Jerusalem would have been regained; for Saladin was dead before Easter.[64]

History is changed more by perseverance than by genius. Never has this been more clearly demonstrated than by the history of the Third Crusade.

Richard sailed from Acre October 9, 1192. A month later he was in Corfu off the western coast of Greece, where he would very likely have received the latest news of political and military developments in Western Europe from his ally King Tancred of Sicily. Philip II had stirred up rebellion in Aquitaine, and in the course of putting it down the seneschal of Aquitaine and Richard's father-in-law the king of Navarra had made war on Count Raymond V of Toulouse. This made it dangerous for Richard to land in southern France. The

---

[61]*Ibid.*, pp. 209, 211-212.
[62]*Ibid.*, pp. 212-216; Setton, *Crusades*, II, 83-85, 523-524.
[63]Setton, *Crusades*, II, 693-694.
[64]Gillingham, *Richard the Lionheart*, pp. 210, 215-216.

new Emperor Henry VI was hostile to Richard because Richard was supporting
Tancred in Sicily, who had denied the right of his wife Constance to the throne
of Sicily; and Henry was now in effective control of most of the Italian
peninsula. The nearest friendly port for Richard was Barcelona in Spain, but
Barcelona was a very long way from Corfu across a sea increasingly threatened
by the dangerous winter storms. So the Lionheart decided to make his way
overland in disguise to Bohemia or Moravia, whose dukes were allied with the
great German nobleman Henry the Lion of the Welf family, Richard's brother-
in-law and an enemy of Henry VI. But Richard and his companions, pretending
to be ordinary pilgrims returning from the Holy Land, did not take enough care
to conceal their wealth. They were discovered crossing Austria, arrested near
Vienna, and brought captive to Duke Leopold of Babenberg, an ally of Henry
VI. The Emperor ordered him at once to bring Richard to court.[65]

At any period of history the capture of a head of state is a very serious
matter, and Richard at this hour—despite his failure to take Jerusalem—was
the most famous and admired king in Christendom. His capture violated every
guarantee for the safety of the persons and property of those on crusade; Pope
Celestine III excommunicated Duke Leopold of Austria the moment he heard
the news. But the case of Henry VI was different; to excommunicate him would
be to renew once again the strife between Pope and Emperor that had rent
Christendom so often during the preceding century and a quarter and destroy
all possibility of accommodation between them over the future of Sicily, as well
as making it more likely that Henry would simply turn Richard over to Philip II
of France, who hated him and might have kept him in captivity for life. So the
Pope only warned Henry VI that he must release Richard soon or face
excommunication, while Richard's charismatic personality made such an
impression on the court and the Emperor that Henry pledged to seek peace
between him and Philip. However, he required homage from him as a vassal,
and an enormous ransom of 150,000 marks—three times the annual income of
the whole of England—payable two-thirds down and the other third later.[66]

Philip and Richard's faithless brother John tried to match this by offering
the Emperor 150,000 marks cash down for Richard, but pressure from the
German nobles—many of whom were embarrassed by holding captive so
famous a crusader—compelled Henry to honor his original agreement. Richard
was released at Mainz in February 1194, fourteen months after his capture.
The taxpayers of England were paying off his ransom for the rest of his reign.[67]

It was an ugly episode, revealing the disunity of Christendom and the
greed and selfishness of many of its leaders; yet surely no one would have dared

---

[65]*Ibid.*, pp. 216, 222-225.
[66]*Ibid.*, pp. 226-230, 233-234, 239; Mann, *Popes of the Middle Ages*, XI, 414-415.
[67]Gillingham, *Richard the Lionheart*, pp. 235-238; *Cambridge Medieval History*, V,
467; Lane Poole, *Domesday Book to Magna Carta*, pp. 365-366.

to arrest Richard the Lion-hearted returning from crusade, if he had captured Jerusalem.

There is reason to believe that Philip had designs on the English throne as well as the vast possessions of the English royal family (the Plantagenets, descended from William the Conqueror) in France. This seems the only plausible explanation for his decision to make Ingeborg, princess of Denmark, his second wife (his first had died in 1190, leaving him with only a single son). Denmark was of very minor significance in European politics at this time, but the Danish king had an old claim to the English throne going back to Canute the Great in the early eleventh century, which Philip may have intended to revive. His marriage to the 18-year-old princess was solemnized August 14, 1193, during Richard's captivity. Though Philip saw Ingeborg for the first time that day, contemporary witnesses agree that she was beautiful, though she spoke no French. The next morning Philip emerged from his chamber "pale and nervous" and announced that he would seek an immediate annulment of the marriage, for reasons never explained but which can only have been, in the words of Philip's latest biographer, "personal and sexual."[68]

The French bishops obediently granted the annulment in November without even according Ingeborg a hearing.[69] Abandoned in a foreign land whose language she did not speak and shut up in a convent, the young princess nevertheless knew where and how to appeal. She wrote in incorrect Latin to Pope Celestine III, a simple and profoundly moving document:

> I, then, taken from my father's home, brought into the realm of the Franks, and by the will of heaven, raised to the royal throne, through the wickedness of the enemy of the human race, envious of my happiness, have been thrown on the ground like a dry and useless branch, destitute of all comfort and advice. My spouse, Philip, king of the Franks, has left me, though he could find nothing to condemn in me, except what malice had forged on the anvil of lies.... In my wretchedness I fly to the seat of mercy, so that, having won your pity, should better fortune befall me, I would henceforth be your handmaid, ever ready to obey your commands.[70]

In May 1195 Pope Celestine III overruled the annulment of Philip's marriage to Ingeborg by the French bishops, demanded that the king take her back, and warned him that no other marriage of his would be recognized by the Church while Ingeborg lived. The king resisted furiously, and in 1196 bigamously married Agnes of Meran; but Pope Celestine III and his successor, the great Pope Innocent III, continued to insist on Ingeborg's rights. In January

---

[68]John W. Baldwin, *The Government of Philip Augustus* (Berkeley CA, 1986), pp. 82-83; Gillingham, *Richard the Lionheart*, p. 234; Régine Pernoud, *Blanche of Castile* (New York, 1975), p. 20.
[69]Baldwin, *Philip Augustus*, p. 83.
[70]Mann, *Popes of the Middle Ages*, XIII, 90-91.

1200 Pope Innocent placed the whole kingdom of France under an interdict to enforce them. Philip made a pretense of yielding, but his heart remained hardened; only thirteen years later did he finally take Ingeborg back and reign with her at his side. Once again, the Vicars of Christ had defended a royal marriage bond regardless of the political cost.[71]

On Good Friday 1195 Emperor Henry VI unexpectedly took the crusader's cross, declaring his intention to follow in his father's footsteps by leading an army to recover Jerusalem.[72] No one had expected this from him, for in his person Henry seemed the antithesis of his father and of Richard the Lion-hearted, the archetypical crusaders of their time.

> Instead of the fine figure, the attractive mien, the charm of manner which distinguish the personality of Frederick Barbarossa, we are confronted with a man, spare and gaunt, of an unprepossessing appearance, which thinly disguised the harsh, cruel, unrelenting qualities of his character. Instead of the fearless and skilful soldier, the very personification of all that was knightly in an age of knights, we see a man whose honor even among friends could not be trusted, whose cruelty would stop short at nothing when it suited his purpose; a man who cared not for the field of battle, and whose only active pursuit was falconry and the chase.[73]

This modern portrayal of Henry VI reflects those of his time; yet his decision on Good Friday 1195 shows that there was more in this man than met the eye, for he had nothing personally to gain and much to lose by becoming involved with crusading in any way at that point in his reign. He and Constance of Sicily had just had a son three months before, and Henry wanted desperately to replace the old tradition of an elective emperor in Germany with a guaranteed hereditary succession which would assure that baby Frederick would succeed him as emperor. He had only just taken over Sicily following the death of King Tancred, and been crowned in Palermo on Christmas day 1194. He is said to have had grand designs, but he was young and there was no need, and much risk, in trying to do so much at once.[74] But the loss of Jerusalem hung over Christendom like a gigantic shadow. We have no idea what his father meant to Henry, though it is clear that his father regarded him highly—he chose him as his successor over his first-born. Cold and hard Henry might be in his dealings with the world, but perhaps he remembered a brave old man pushing on into the infidel's country crying "Christ reigns! Christ conquers! Christ commands!" and dying so mysteriously in a Cilician gorge just as he seemed ready to emerge from his ordeal in triumph.

---

[71]*Ibid.*, XIII, 91-95; Baldwin, *Philip Augustus*, p. 84-87; Pernoud, *Blanche of Castile*, p. 91.
[72]*Cambridge Medieval History*, V, 473.
[73]*Ibid.*, V, 454.
[74]*Ibid.*, V, 470-474; Norwich, *Kingdom in the Sun*, pp. 385-386, 388-389.

Henry VI soon proved that his taking of the Cross was no mere gesture. In the summer of 1195 he joined the 89-year-old Pope Celestine III in formally proclaiming a new crusade, which was preached all over Germany. Though few responded to it elsewhere, a large army was raised in Germany. Henry scheduled its departure, with himself at its head, for Christmas day 1196. When that time came Henry decided he could not go immediately due to revolts in Sicily, but he continued to recruit, collect, and equip the crusading army, and gathered a fleet to transport it. On September 22, 1197 the bulk of the army arrived at Acre and went immediately into action, taking Beirut from the Muslims a month later. Then they marched inland, to besiege Toron halfway to the Sea of Galilee.[75]

But a strange fatality hung over the crusading efforts of German royalty in these closing years of the twelfth century. Within less than a week of the arrival in the Holy Land of the army he had raised to regain Jerusalem, Henry VI—only 32 years old—died suddenly of dysentery in Sicily. He died at peace with the Church: he was reconciled with his wife Constance, from whom he had been estranged; he committed his three-year-old son Frederick to the guardianship of the Pope; he offered to return the ransom he had received from Richard the Lion-hearted.[76] When the news of his death reached Toron the German crusading army raised the siege and returned home.[77] Three-year-old Frederick could perhaps succeed his father as king of Sicily, but there never had been, and could not be, a child Holy Roman Emperor. Once again death had taken the leader of a German crusade at a critical moment, leaving no one to take his place.

At the western edge of Christendom in Spain and Portugal, the crusading that came for the rest of Europe mostly in response to crises in the Holy Land had been a way of life for more than 450 years. But—as the Popes always recognized—the Hispanic effort was an integral part of the crusade in its broadest sense, the centuries-long struggle of Christendom against militant Islam. In the late twelfth century the Reconquest in Spain encountered the same evils of greed, selfishness and division that had beset the kingdom of Jerusalem in its last days, and the Third Crusade that failed. Their consequences brought the Muslims back from the south where the reconquering Christians had at long last driven them, into the very center of Spain. For the first time in nearly a century, people living north of Toledo and Madrid, even to the foothills of the Guadarramas, saw upon their roads and fields the burnooses and scimitars and the crescent-moon banners of their ancient enemy.

Alfonso VII, who died in 1157, had proclaimed himself emperor of Spain,

[75]Setton, *Crusades*, II, 118-121, 530; *Cambridge Medieval History*, V, 474, 479.

[76]Mann, *Popes of the Middle Ages*, XI, 424-427; *Cambridge Medieval History*, V, 479.

[77]Setton, *Crusades*, II, 530.

but his authority was only grudgingly and partially accepted outside his own kingdom of Castile and León, and when he died, with astonishing unwisdom, he had divided his own kingdom into its two original components, making a total of no less than five Christian kingdoms in the Iberian peninsula: from east to west Aragon (including Catalonia), Navarra, Castile, León, and Portugal. There was recurring hostility between Castile and León and Portugal from the time of Alfonso VII's death, but the long minority of Alfonso VIII of Castile, beginning in 1158, and his close relationship with his uncle, King Fernando II of León, prevented the development of serious division between their two countries while Fernando lived.[78] But in 1188 he died and was succeeded by his ambitious and for a long time irresponsible 17-year-old son Alfonso IX, who almost at once became a bitter rival of his namesake in Castile, with both seeking the favor of yet another namesake, Alfonso II of Aragon.[79]

It was traditional for a newly crowned monarch to call a meeting of the representative assembly of the realm, called a *cortes* in Spain (parliament in England). The *cortes* of León, called by Alfonso IX in 1188, is distinguished as the first national parliament in Europe to seat representatives of towns as well as of the feudal nobility.[80]

By 1194, after the Almohad caliph ruling Morocco and southern Spain had proclaimed a new holy war against the Christians, the strife between the two Alfonsos of Castile and León had become so dangerous to the cause of the Reconquest and even the preservation of existing Christian dominions from the Moors that the Papal legate in Spain, Cardinal Gregory, essentially dictated a ten-year peace treaty between the two realms at Tordehumos. It required the breakup of an attempted marriage by Alfonso IX to his first cousin Teresa of Portugal, a marriage which had never received a Papal dispensation and was undertaken primarily to gain a powerful ally against Castile; declared that in default of legitimate heirs to Alfonso IX, León would revert to Castile; and pledged that neither country would attack the other nor seek aid from the Moors.[81]

The next year Almohad Caliph Jacob crossed the Straits of Gibraltar with a large army and marched directly north through the famous Despeñaperros Pass. A Castilian reconnaissance column was annihilated; Alfonso IX of León hung back, and Alfonso VIII of Castile went into battle alone at Alarcos near present-day Ciudad Real on July 19, 1195. Greatly outnumbered, almost all the

---

[78]See Chapter Three, above.

[79]Joseph F. O'Callaghan, *A History of Medieval Spain* (Ithaca NY, 1975), pp. 241-242.

[80]*Ibid.*, p. 242.

[81]*Ibid.*, p. 243; Derek W. Lomax, *The Reconquest of Spain* (London, 1978), pp. 118-119; Julio González, *El reino de Castilla en la época de Alfonso VIII* (Madrid, 1960), I, 717-718, 834-835; Julio González, *Alfonso IX* (Madrid, 1944), I, 66-68.

Castilians warriors were routed or slaughtered; the king escaped to Toledo with only twenty knights. There he had a tense meeting with Alfonso IX, who demanded several castles from him and refused to give him any aid; nor did any of the other Hispanic monarchs offer him help. Caliph Jacob held a magnificent victory parade in Sevilla and in the fall signed a formal alliance with Alfonso IX, in flat violation of the Treaty of Tordehumos.[82]

Alfonso II of Aragon was horrified by this betrayal of their compatriot, and spent the last few months of his life—he died in April 1196—trying ineffectually to make peace. León and Navarra continued to take advantage of Castile's defeat; Alfonso IX actually urged the Moors to invade Castile and collaborated with them in the invasion. But Aragon, led by Alfonso II's widow and his teen-age son and successor Pedro II, was now committed to Castile's support; and so, with great emphasis, was the Pope. Celestine III, seemingly indefatigable despite being ninety years old this year, on March 29 commanded Alfonso IX of León and Sancho VII of Navarra, on pain of excommunication, to give up their alliance with the Moors and join a perpetual peace among all the Christian kings in Spain. Sancho evidently heeded the Pope, but Alfonso IX did not; in October Celestine excommunicated him, freed his subjects from their duty of allegiance to him in accordance with the doctrine of Pope St. Gregory VII in the eleventh century, and extended crusading indulgences to anyone who fought against him so long as he remained allied with the Moors.[83]

In the spring of 1197 Caliph Jacob's army rode north once again, meeting little effective resistance. They passed Toledo's impregnable crag in battle array, passed Madrid, and assaulted and took Talamanca north of Madrid, razing its walls, killing its men, and carrying off its women. Then they ravaged the whole region around Madrid before returning to Andalusia, with Alfonso IX still offering them aid. Only the Muslims' own internal troubles saved the bitterly divided Christians of Spain from further catastrophe; Caliph Jacob faced rebellion in Tunisia and consequently granted a five-year truce to Castile after the conclusion of his campaign of 1197.[84]

Having lost his grim ally, Alfonso IX had to come to terms. He agreed to a peace treaty with Castile to be sealed by marriage to Berenguela, the beautiful and devout daughter of Alfonso VIII who was his first cousin. No Papal dispensation was requested or obtained. Pope Celestine III, and Innocent III after him, refused to recognize the marriage as valid, but the

---

[82]Lomax, *Reconquest of Spain*, pp. 119-121; González, *Alfonso VIII*, I, 953-971; González, *Alfonso IX*, I, 73-76.

[83]O'Callaghan, *Medieval Spain*, p. 245; Lomax, *Reconquest of Spain*, pp. 120-121; González, *Alfonso VIII*, I, 720, 722, 834-840, 973-976; González, *Alfonso IX*, I, 76-78, 83-84.

[84]Lomax, *Reconquest of Spain*, pp. 121-122; González, *Alfonso VIII*, I, 977-979; González, *Alfonso IX*, I, 86-87.

couple did not separate until 1204, after bearing four children. One of them was a son, who eventually reunited Castile and León: King St. Fernando III. When at last the royal couple submitted and separated, Pope Innocent III granted them a full pardon and legitimized their children.[85]

On January 8, 1198 Pope Celestine III died, in his ninety-second year. For seven stormy years he had guided the Church wisely and effectively despite his extraordinary age, working tirelessly for peace in Christendom in a time of division, cooperating with Emperor Henry VI—whom he had many reasons to distrust—to keep the crusading cause alive despite the failure of the Third Crusade, checking the incipient disintegration of Christian Spain, helping to secure the release of Richard the Lion-hearted from captivity, defending the rights of Queen Ingeborg of France. He has been overshadowed in the history of the Papacy by his brilliant and energetic successor, Innocent III, one of the greatest of all the Popes; but Celestine III performed splendid services of his own to Christ and His Church. Few men have done so much beyond their eighty-fifth birthday.[86]

In striking contrast, the new Pope, Lothar Conti, was the youngest Pope in at least 150 years, only thirty-seven. He was renowned as a scholar, who had studied at length at the two most famous universities in Christendom, those of Paris and Bologna; he was a cardinal and a canon of St. Peter's, and had worked closely with Celestine III. Despite his youth, he received a large majority of the cardinals' votes on the first ballot, for he was universally respected and had never involved himself in clerical or political factions.[87]

The address the new Pope delivered at his consecration included a substantial statement on the relation between spiritual and temporal power. Innocent III carefully and clearly set forth the doctrine, originating with Pope Gelasius in the fifth century and greatly developed by Pope St. Gregory VII in the eleventh century, that spiritual power is superior to temporal power and the Pope possesses the fullness of it, but that temporal power is autonomous within its own realm, and the Pope intervenes in it only on critical occasions to act as mediator and moral judge.[88] In this as in so many of its doctrines, the Church walks a narrow middle path between the extremes of those who claim (or, more often, unreasonably believe they see) the exercise of direct ecclesiastical authority in the temporal sphere, and those (so common today) who demand an

---

[85]O'Callaghan, *Medieval Spain*, pp. 244-245; Lomax, *Reconquest of Spain*, pp. 121-122; González, *Alfonso VIII*, I, 722-728, 730-734, 842-844; González, *Alfonso IX*, I, 88-89, 91-97, 102, 116-117; P. Luis Fernández de Retana, *San Fernando III y su época* (Madrid, 1941), pp. 23, 28-29.

[86]It is very much worthy of note that out of 263 legitimate Popes, a significant proportion of whom reigned beyond their eightieth birthday, not one is ever recorded as having become senile.

[87]Mann, *Popes of the Middle Ages*, XII, 9-29.

[88]Helen Tillmann, *Pope Innocent III* (Amsterdam, 1980), pp. 21-27, 40.

absolute separation of spiritual and temporal, with the Church refraining from any moral judgments on temporal affairs except as an echo of those given by temporal authorities or secular commentators.

This particular emphasis in his consecration homily indicated that Innocent III intended to exercise his authority firmly and widely, as indeed he did throughout his 18-year pontificate. Its first year was particularly active. The new Pope vigorously took up the causes of making peace among the Christian kingdoms of Spain, defending the rights of Queen Ingeborg of France, and compelling Prince Andrew of Hungary to fulfill his crusading vows.[89]   He refused to renew the legatine commission of the Archbishop of Canterbury because he had interfered with the autonomy of the community of monks in that city.[90] He excommunicated King Sverre of Norway for interfering with the freedom of his bishops, and decreed that the Bishop of Uppsala in Sweden, despite his desire to become a metropolitan, must continue to be subject to the Archbishop of Lund in Scania, then ruled by Denmark.[91]   He confirmed four-year-old Frederick, the only heir of Emperor Henry VI, as king of Sicily, and made him his ward when his mother Constance died.[92]   He recognized Leo II the Great as king of Armenia and sent an archbishop to crown him. He agreed to establish a Catholic hierarchy in Serbia for the first time in response to a request from its King Vukan.[93]

Most importantly, on August 15, the Feast of the Assumption of the Blessed Virgin Mary into heaven, Pope Innocent III proclaimed a new crusade to recover Jerusalem, despatching the proclamation to all the archbishops in Christendom, sending Cardinal Soffredo to preach it in Italy and Cardinal Peter Capuano to preach it in France. He wrote to those deadly enemies, Kings Richard the Lion-hearted of England and Philip II of France, telling them to make a peace of at least five years' duration at once so as not to interfere with the crusade, and warning each that he would place his kingdom under interdict if he refused. He wrote to the current Byzantine Emperor, Alexius III Angelus, and to the Patriarch of Constantinople, calling on them to support the new crusade, declaring that their hostility to the Third Crusade had scandalized all Christendom, and urging them to end the religious schism dating from 1054. Then he commissioned a famous preacher, Fulk of Neuilly, to preach the crusade to the people of Christendom in general, and ordered all clergy to contribute a fortieth of their revenue during 1199 to the crusade—something

[89]O'Callaghan, *Medieval Spain*, p. 245; González, *Alfonso VIII*, I, 726, 842-844; Mann, *Popes of the Middle Ages*, XIII, 3, 93-94.
    [90]Tillmann, *Innocent III*, pp. 36-37.
    [91]Karen Larsen, *A History of Norway* (New York, 1948), p. 147; Mann, *Popes of the Middle Ages*, XIII, 196.
    [92]Mann, *Popes in the Middle Ages*, XII, 139; Tillmann, *Innocent III*, p. 107.
    [93]Mann, *Popes of the Middle Ages*, XIII, 27-29, 59.

never asked before.[94]

All this was done during the first year of Innocent III's pontificate, from January 1198 to January 1199.

The Third Crusade had failed primarily because of the death of Emperor Frederick Barbarossa and the hesitations of Richard the Lion-hearted before Jerusalem; the crusade proclaimed by Emperor Henry VI and Pope Celestine III had failed because of Henry's sudden and early death. If the Fourth Crusade were to avoid a like failure, it must have strong leadership. But none could be forthcoming this time from Germany, hopelessly split between the great rival families of Hohenstaufen and Welf. In the course of the year 1198 both Philip of Swabia, Henry VI's younger brother, and Otto IV, son of Henry the Lion of Bavaria and Saxony, had proclaimed themselves elected Emperor. The former was crowned at Mainz and the latter at Aachen. In view of the long history of Hohenstaufen hostility to the Papacy, Innocent III preferred Otto, and in January 1200 pronounced in his favor.[95] But neither Otto nor Philip could win general acceptance in Germany. With civil war threatening, neither dared leave on crusade, no matter what assurances for the safety of persons and property the Pope or the bishops might give. Such assurances had not been worth much in the case of Richard the Lion-hearted.

Since Philip II of France had already made very clear his lack of interest in serious crusading, this left only Richard as a prospective royal leader for the Fourth Crusade. Though no contemporary source specifically mentions him in this role, it must have been on everyone's mind, and very likely was a major part of the reason for Innocent III's vehement insistence after proclaiming the crusade that Richard and Philip make a durable peace treaty for at least five years. But whatever hopes were nourished for a new crusade by the Lionheart were soon frustrated by the same capricious fatality that had dogged the crusades ever since the fall of Jerusalem. To the never explained death of Frederick Barbarossa in the Saleph River and the sudden attack of dysentery that carried off his son at the age of 32 was now added yet another, bitterly ironic stroke of ill fortune.

On March 26, 1199 Richard was besieging the castle of the rebel Viscount of Limoges at Chalus-Chabrol. At twilight he rode out to review the progress of the siege. On the ramparts of the castle he saw the lone figure of a common soldier with a crossbow, whose only shield was a frying pan. Ever the soul of chivalry, the Lionheart lowered his own shield to clap his hands in applause for the man's courage. Unimpressed, the hard-headed commoner dropped his frying pan and fired an extraordinarily well-aimed shot. Before Richard could

---

[94]Setton, *Crusades*, II, 154-158; Donald Queller, *The Fourth Crusade; the Conquest of Constantinople* (Philadelphia, 1977), pp. 1-3; Brand, *Byzantium Confronts the West*, p. 225.

[95]Alfred Haverkamp, *Medieval Germany, 1056-1273* (New York, 1988), pp. 238-241.

bring his shield back into position the crossbow bolt drove deep into his left shoulder. It could not be pulled out, and the removal of the eight-inch metal barb by an unskilled surgeon left so much damaged tissue that gangrene set in. Two weeks later the legendary crusader was dead at 42.[96] He left no children. His successor was his faithless brother John, who had if possible even less interest in recovering Jerusalem than Philip II of France.

However, the lack of royal leadership for the new crusade by no means meant that it could not succeed. The same situation had existed at the launching of the First Crusade, when the Holy Roman Emperor and the kings of France and England were all in the bad graces of the Church and excluded from the enterprise, yet it triumphed. Now as then, great nobles were coming forward to join the crusade, particularly in France. In November 1199 Count Theobald of Champagne, Count Louis of Blois, Geoffrey of Villehardouin (the principal contemporary historian of the Fourth Crusade), and many other famous knights took the Cross at a tournament in Champagne. On Ash Wednesday of 1200 Count Baldwin of Flanders, his brother Henry, and other famous Flemish knights took the Cross at Bruges. In February 1201 six French envoys including Geoffrey of Villehardouin arrived in Venice to make arrangements for the transport of an expected immense crusading host from Venice to the Holy Land by sea.[97]

The noblemen leading the Fourth Crusade appear to have assumed, like most later historians, that the failure of Frederick Barbarossa's crusade proved an overland march to Palestine to be militarily impossible, though the First Crusade under Raymond of Toulouse and Bohemond the Italian Norman had accomplished that march successfully, and Barbarossa had won his way through all significant Turkish opposition before his own accidental death had turned triumph into disaster. In past crusades some soldiers had marched overland while others had gone to Palestine by ship, and different groups coming by sea had made separate arrangements with different maritime cities and shipowners, arriving by contingents rather than all together. But this crusade (its leaders hoped) would be better organized and more united.

Within a month of arriving in Venice, Geoffrey de Villehardouin and his five colleagues had reached a complete agreement with the extraordinary man who for eight years had been Doge (Duke) of the great maritime city of Venice, Enrico Dandolo. Doge Dandolo is one of the most striking figures of medieval history, though we do not know nearly as much about his life before he became Doge as we would wish, and nothing of his inner personal life. Universally respected in Venice, with a dominating personality and an iron will, a powerful and convincing orator, he was nevertheless handicapped to a degree most

---

[96]Gillingham, *Richard the Lionheart*, pp. 276-277.
[97]Setton, *Crusades*, II, 158-159, 162; Queller, *Fourth Crusade*, pp. 3-5, 9.

historians have found, in view of his achievements, so incredible that they have simply dismissed explicit contemporary testimony about his handicaps. There can be no justification for this. All sources agree that Dandolo was exceedingly old at the time of the Fourth Crusade—at least eighty-five, perhaps as much as ninety. And he was stone-blind, unable to see his hand in front of his face. The Chronicle of Novgorod—the relevant portion written by a Russian who accompanied the crusade with Dandolo—says that while on a diplomatic mission to Constantinople he had been blinded by the Byzantines, who regularly inflicted this disability by means of a burning glass. Thirty years earlier, in 1171, on the orders or at least with the tacit approval of the Byzantine government, thousands of Venetians in the Eastern empire had been killed, mutilated, or arrested and held for years in prison. Dandolo's blinding may well have happened then, though we do not know for sure. We do know that he was a Venetian ambassador to Constantinople at some point after 1171, and again in 1184. Some motivation as powerful as having been blinded by the Byzantines seems necessary to explain what Dandolo, at his enormously advanced age, did to Constantinople during the Fourth Crusade. His may have been one of history's grimmest stories of revenge.[98]

In Venice in Lent of 1201, Dandolo quickly proved himself so superior a negotiator to the six nobles who had come to him that they were like children in his hands. Almost before they knew what had happened, their signatures were on a document committing them and the crusade to paying for ships to transport from Venice to Palestine, with all their gear and provisions, 4,500 knights and their horses, 9,000 squires, and 20,000 foot soldiers—at least three times the number of men so far enrolled in the crusade. The cost payable to Venice for the armada to transport this hoped-for host was no less than 85,000 silver marks, literally a king's ransom (it was only slightly less than the ransom originally offered Emperor Henry VI for Richard the Lion-hearted). The agreement was unconditional; the money must be paid whether the men appeared or not. Venice would get half of any conquests the crusaders made. A secret clause specified that the army would actually go to Egypt, rather than to Jerusalem where the men were expecting to go.[99] This was because Egypt

---

[98]Queller, *Fourth Crusade*, pp. 9-10; Setton, *Crusades*, II, 153, 161-162 (including references to the Chronicle of Novgorod); Brand, *Byzantium Confronts the West*, p. 203. Villehardouin, a leader of the Fourth Crusade and its principal contemporary historian, explicitly attests to Dandolo's total blindness. The assertion by Brand (*loc. cit.*) that "contrary to legend this condition [Dandolo's blindness] was not a result of Byzantine cruelty" is in flat contradiction to the statement in the chronicle of Novgorod by a contemporary witness.

[99]Queller, *Fourth Crusade*, pp. 10-14, 163-164. The cost is often incorrectly stated as 94,000 marks—the Doge's original offer—but when the agreement was reduced to writing he had lowered it to 85,000. Queller regards Villehardouin as a competent negotiator, but it is obvious that Dandolo emerged from these dealings with an

was the center of Muslim power in the region of Palestine; but to go there first was folly, for the whole concept of the crusades was to enlist the enthusiasm of Christian knights and foot soldiers to regain the city where Jesus Christ had preached, died, and risen from the dead. The history of the First and Third Crusades had shown unmistakably that any diversion from Jerusalem as the objective played havoc with morale; indeed, that is why the plan to go to Egypt was kept secret. The time to challenge Islam in Egypt was after Jerusalem was taken, not before.

Pope Innocent III had as good or better a mind than Enrico Dandolo, and was much wiser in the ways of the world than Geoffrey de Villehardouin. While he reluctantly confirmed the agreement between the crusaders and Venice, he warned the Venetians that the army and armament for the crusade must not be used against Christian peoples, specifically those ruled by the King of Hungary with whom Venice had often been in conflict.[100]

Late in June 1201 the leading noblemen of the crusade offered the command of it to Boniface of Montferrat in Savoy, brother of Conrad of Montferrat who had saved Tyre after the Battle of the Horns of Hattin and had been briefly king of Jerusalem before being killed by the Assassins. Boniface was well regarded by the Pope, by imperial claimant Philip of Swabia in Germany (his cousin), and by King Philip II of France. Boniface accepted the command in August at Soissons in France; the Bishop of Soissons, crusade preacher Fulk of Neuilly, and two Cistercian abbots ceremonially fastened the cross upon his shoulder. In December Boniface attended the Christmas court of Philip of Swabia to try to enlist Germans for the crusade, for it was already becoming apparent that the expected numbers of crusaders were not materializing. Philip of Swabia was married to a Byzantine princess, Irene. He introduced Boniface and his companions, including Geoffrey of Villehardouin, to his Irene's brother Alexius, about eighteen years old, the son of former Emperor Isaac II who had been reigning when Frederick Barbarossa passed Constantinople in the Third Crusade, but had been dethroned and blinded by Alexius III Angelus in 1195. Prince Alexius had just escaped from Constantinople and was urging anyone who would listen to him to help him become Byzantine emperor, a position to which he insisted he was entitled, though in fact under the law of the Eastern empire he was not.[101]

---

agreement by which he could not lose.

[100]*Ibid.*, pp. 16-18. Queller presents an excellent refutation of the argument often made (e.g. Setton, *Crusades*, II, 163n) that Pope Innocent III's warning was only attributed to him later and unhistorically by the contemporary author of the book reviewing the first ten years of his pontificate. As Queller points out, a letter from Innocent to Dandolo in February 1204 makes specific reference to this warning.

[101]Queller, *Fourth Crusade*, pp. 19-32; Brand, *Byzantium Confronts the West*, pp. 275-276. The position of Eastern emperor remained theoretically elective by the army, as it had been in the original Roman empire; in practice this meant election by the

Alexius talked; Boniface and his companions listened and were interested. They were in no position then to make commitments; but when Boniface visited the Pope in March 1202, he hinted at the possibility that the crusaders might stop on their way at Constantinople to help Alexius gain what he regarded as his rightful inheritance. Innocent III, who had heard Alexius' appeal the month before and sent him packing, responded sharply in the negative. "The crusade must not attack Christians," he told its commander, "but should proceed as quickly as possible to the Holy Land."[102]

The spring passed. Crusaders were arriving in Venice, but not nearly in the numbers expected. By July it was clear that they could not fill even half the ships for which they had so rashly committed themselves to pay Doge Dandolo, nor could they raise the promised money from their limited numbers. They were 34,000 marks short of their promised 85,000.[103]

The Doge could simply have given them fewer ships and thereby lowered the price; he and his city would have lost little or nothing in the long run, since mercantile Venice could always use ships and make a profit from them. But he made no such offer, and if any suggestion for such action was made, he rejected it. He had other plans. Late in August he gave the crusaders his proposal. Across the Adriatic stood the Catholic port city of Zara, the most commodious gateway to the oak forests of Dalmatia where Venice obtained the wood for her shipbuilding. Zara had once been ruled by Venice, but had revolted in 1181, placing itself under the protection of the Catholic King of Hungary. Since then Zara had repulsed three different Venetian attempts to reconquer it, the last commanded by Doge Dandolo himself. If the crusaders would help him reconquer Zara, Dandolo told them, he would in appreciation give them their ships without requiring payment beforehand of the last 34,000 marks.[104]

It is hard to imagine a more cynically unprincipled deal, and the willingness of the majority of the leaders of the crusade to accept it cannot be palliated, as many historians have tried to do, by claiming they had no alternative other than giving up the crusade altogether. Venice had more ships than any other city or nation in Christendom, but there were still plenty of other ships available—many of them in Italy, where the crusaders were. For the 51,000 marks they had raised, they could have obtained a very considerable number of them. Dandolo had no way to compel the crusaders to pay him the money other than by withholding the ships. If any of the leaders of the crusade suggested this evident alternative, history has not recorded it. But Dandolo

---

principal nobles. Though the son of a reigning emperor might often succeed his father, he had no legal right to do so unless he was *porphyrogenitus*—born *after* his father became emperor. See Brand, *op. cit.*, pp. 228-229.

[102]Queller, *Fourth Crusade*, pp. 32-35.

[103]*Ibid.*, pp. 37-43; Setton, *Crusades*, II, 166-167.

[104]Queller, *Fourth Crusade*, pp. 50-52.

gave them little time to think of alternatives. Within a few days of privately making his ugly proposal, on September 8, the feast of the Nativity of the Blessed Virgin Mary, the Doge "took the Cross" in a magnificent ceremony in St. Mark's cathedral, with the not very humble declaration: "I see that no one knows how to govern and direct you as I do, who am your lord."[105]

Many of the crusaders and the abbots and priests accompanying them were deeply disturbed—as well they might be—when the agreement on Zara became known. The Papal legate, Cardinal Peter Capuano, and the commander, Boniface of Montferrat, both left to consult the Pope. But most of the objections at that point seem to have been made privately. In the absence of Boniface, Doge Dandolo took effective command of the crusade. Early in October a fleet of 62 war galleys and 140 transports carrying some 10,000 fighting men sailed from Venice, making a splendid spectacle, with Dandolo in the lead in a vermilion-painted galley.[106]

Pope Innocent III was appalled when he heard the news, and sent Abbot Peter of Locedio at once to Zara (since he could not reach the fleet at sea) with a letter forbidding the crusaders from attacking the city on pain of excommunication. Copies of his letter were in the hands of city leaders when the crusading fleet and army arrived November 11. The next day a Cistercian abbot, Guy of Vaux-de-Cernay, strode into the great red tent of the Doge bearing the letter, and in the name of the Pope forbade him to attack Zara. The Doge furiously demanded that the crusaders keep their promise to him, saying "that he would not give up his revenge upon Zara, excommunication or not." The Venetians were about to attack the lone, white-garbed abbot when one of the principal noblemen of the crusade, Simon de Montfort, came forward to protect him.[107]

But the lords on crusade had promised Dandolo to help him take Zara. In their feudal code a man's word was his bond; to break it was profoundly dishonorable. They did not realize, or would not accept, that such obligations cannot hold for a Catholic when the obligation assumed has been defined explicitly as evil by the Vicar of Christ. Except for Simon de Montfort and Lord Enguerrand of Bovès, all the other commanders submitted to Dandolo. Simon and Enguerrand sorrowfully lowered their lances and rode away.[108]

---

[105]*Ibid.*, p. 53.

[106]*Ibid.*, pp. 58-60.

[107]*Ibid.*, pp. 62-63; Setton, *Crusades*, II, 173-174; Mann, *Popes in the Middle Ages*, XII, 247-248. It is sometimes said or implied that Innocent III delayed his condemnation until it would be too late to have any effect. Nothing could be further from the truth. The delays in transmitting letters in the Middle Ages must always be remembered. By the time the Pope was reasonably sure of Dandolo's intentions the fleet had departed. But he made his point and delivered his judgment before the assault on Zara took place.

[108]Queller, *Fourth Crusade*, p. 64.

With the notable exception of these two lords and their followers, the men of the Fourth Crusade proceeded to the assault on Zara. They undermined its walls, ignoring the crucifixes the defenders had hung there as signs of their allegiance, and took and sacked the city on November 24. Even its churches were plundered and profaned.[109]

King Imre of Hungary, who had himself taken the Cross, made a solemn protest to the Pope against this immoral misuse of the crusade. Innocent III responded with a strong condemnation of the attack upon and pillage of Zara, demanding that it be returned at once to the King of Hungary and the spoils from its pillage handed back. He did not specifically excommunicate the crusaders, but made it clear they had committed grave sin. He did formally excommunicate the Venetians, who unlike the crusaders (many of whom promptly sought absolution) refused to admit they had done any wrong. But the notice of the excommunication of the Venetians was never delivered, since Cardinal Peter Capuano did not return to the army for two years, and Marquis Boniface refused to mention it.[110]

The winter storms on the Mediterranean made it impractical for the fleet to sail anywhere after the capture of Zara until the advent of spring 1203. During the winter Prince Alexius came to Zara and renewed his proposal that the crusaders should take him to Constantinople and install him as emperor there. If they did, he promised them 200,000 marks (which would pay all their costs, including the debt to Venice), 10,000 fighting men for the crusade, the maintenance of 500 knights in Palestine for life, and an end to the Greek schism with the whole Byzantine empire rejoining the Catholic Church. Alexius had no real reason to believe he could fulfill such promises, but was ready to say anything to attain his ambition. Simon de Montfort reminded the others that it had been Alexius' father who had tried to destroy the Third Crusade under Frederick Barbarossa as it passed through the Eastern empire, in repeated violation of his pledged word. The debate waxed hot and prolonged. Doge Dandolo demanded that they go to Constantinople. Boniface of Montferrat, Count Baldwin of Flanders, and most of the other leading noblemen supported Dandolo. Simon de Montfort and Enguerrand of Bovès had had enough. With several other great nobles, they left the crusade to make their own way to the Holy Land, laboriously marching north along the rugged Adriatic coast with support from the grateful King Imre of Hungary, then down the Italian peninsula until they could take other ships directly to the coast of Palestine. Most of the rest of the crusade could have done likewise, though Marquis Boniface kept arguing that the only way for it to reach its objective was to continue cooperating with the Venetians.[111]

---

[109]*Ibid.*, pp. 64-65.

[110]*Ibid.*, pp. 68-69, 77-81; Setton, *Crusades*, II, 175.

[111]Setton, *Crusades*, II, 174-175; Queller, *Fourth Crusade*, pp. 69-76.

At the beginning of April the twice diverted crusaders sailed from Zara in their Venetian ships; a week later the Venetians who stayed behind razed the conquered city. Coming to the outlet of the Adriatic into the Mediterranean, they landed on Byzantine territory at Corfu, where Prince Alexius proclaimed himself Emperor, only to be scorned by its people. The crusaders ravaged the island after their leaders overcame a last protest against these continuing attacks on Christians by solemnly promising, on their knees and in tears, that they would continue on to the Holy Land no later than September of that year. Knees and tears notwithstanding, the promise was broken. Constantinople, the Eastern imperial capital for nearly a thousand years, the richest city in the known world, but with its government and military forces far gone in decline, was now the actual objective of this misnamed crusade.[112]

On June 23 the Venetian fleet dropped anchor before the abbey of St. Stephen seven miles southwest of Constantinople. The Byzantine navy had become too weak to make even a demonstration against them. The vast 40-foot-thick walls on the land side of the peninsula where Constantinople stood were far too much for the crusaders to tackle with the limited siege equipment they had brought with them, but the thinner sea walls along the Bosporus and especially the fabled harbor inlet called the Golden Horn looked more promising, and with control of the sea were equally accessible. On July 1 came the first skirmish between Greek and Western knights; the Greeks broke and fled at first contact. On the 6th the Westerners took Galata Tower and loosed the chain guarding the Golden Horn; on the 17th they were ready for the decisive assault.[113]

The Venetians believed the weakest point was the sea wall on the Golden Horn next to Blachernai palace, beyond which the great peninsular wall began, and chose that as the site of their assault. The Venetian ships crossed the Horn with blind Doge Dandolo standing in the prow of his vermilion galley carrying the banner of St. Mark. His ship was the first to touch land under the walls. Scaling ladders, battering rams, and flying bridges from the largest ships to the towers on the walls were brought up. The defense was half-hearted and the attackers soon prevailed. A large section of the wall with more than 25 towers was taken and the gates were opened. Then news came that the French were in trouble on the section of the wall they were attacking. Dandolo ordered fires set in the nearest buildings and withdrew to support his allies. But the day was won. Emperor Alexius III panicked and fled the city with a thousand pounds of gold and the imperial jewels. Doge Dandolo could have given him no lessons in cupidity.[114]

---

[112]Setton, *Crusades*, II, 176-177; Queller, *Fourth Crusade*, pp. 81-84.

[113]Brand, *Byzantium Confronts the West*, pp. 235-239; Setton, *Crusades*, II, 177-179; Queller, *Fourth Crusade*, pp. 88-92, 96-102.

[114]Brand, *Byzantium Confronts the West*, pp. 239-241; Queller, *Fourth Crusade*, pp.

The crusading army was quickly moved out of the city to avoid giving additional offense to the strongly anti-Latin populace. On August 1 young Alexius was crowned co-Emperor with his blinded father and paid his allies 100,000 marks, half of what he had promised them, much of it obtained by melting down precious metal vessels from the churches of the city. He wrote the Pope saying that he fully recognized his authority (though he had defied his authority by diverting the crusade again to attack Christians). He persuaded the crusade leaders (apparently without much difficulty) to break their promise made on bended knee to go on to the Holy Land in September and instead stay on at Constantinople until March, though a few demanded and were given ships to take them to Palestine (Doge Dandolo could let a few ships go now that his first goal had been achieved).[115] For a few months the restive population of the great city sullenly accepted Alexius IV, but he could raise no more money from it. When by November it was obvious that he could make no further payment to the crusaders, they formally renounced him. Rejected by both sides, his authority crumbled rapidly, and his blind and increasingly unbalanced father was no help. On January 28, 1204 Alexius IV was seized and imprisoned by yet another Alexius, known as "Mourtzouphlos" (Shaggy-Browed), who soon proclaimed himself Emperor Alexius V and excluded the crusaders from the city.[116]

Meanwhile Pope Innocent III, after an initial misstep when briefly he let himself believe Alexius' foolish promise to bring about by executive fiat an immediate reunion of the Greek with the Catholic Church, because he so much wished to see this happen, wrote to the crusading leaders in Constantinople in February reproving them for disobedience and commanding them to proceed at once to the Holy Land.[117] At the same time he wrote to Alexius telling him to take concrete steps to fulfill his promise of reunion with Rome, and he wrote to Doge Dandolo reminding him of the magnitude of his disobedience and of what his crusading vows taken in St. Mark's ought to mean. But the letters had not arrived before the Fourth Crusade had ended in the final infamy which shall forever blacken its name.[118]

Once it was clear that the new and vehemently anti-Latin Emperor Alexius V "Mourtzouphlos" was in control of the city and had killed Alexius IV, the former ally of the crusaders, Doge Dandolo, Boniface of Montferrat, Count Baldwin of Flanders, Count Louis of Blois, and Count Hugh of St. Pol met to

---

102-108.

[115]Brand, *Byzantium Confronts the West*, pp. 229, 242, 245-246; Setton, *Crusades*, II, 179-181; Queller, *Fourth Crusade*, pp. 112-113, 116-117.

[116]Brand, *Byzantium Confronts the West*, pp. 246-251; Setton, *Crusades*, II, 181-182; Queller, *Fourth Crusade*, pp. 124-128, 130-133, 136-137.

[117]Mann, *Popes of the Middle Ages*, XII, 260-261; Brand, *Byzantium Confronts the West*, pp. 243-244.

[118]Setton, *Crusades*, II, 180.

settle Constantinople's fate. All pretense of installing a rightful ruler or respecting the autonomy of the Christian empire of the east was dropped. Open conquest was decided upon and publicly proclaimed as their goal, with an equal division of offices and booty to be made between the Venetians on the one hand and everyone else on the other. Enrico Dandolo would get both his money and his revenge.[119]

The decisive assault was made on April 12, 1204. Peter of Amiens, a giant of a man, led a French force which discovered a small bricked-up gate in the sea wall facing the Golden Horn near the Euergetes monastery and battered it open. Alexius V tried to lead a counter-charge, but his men would not follow him. Peter opened the nearest large gate and the attackers swarmed in.[120] The great imperial city, the legendary Miklagard, which not even the Muslims at the high tide of their victories had been able to take, which had not known the tramp of an enemy in arms upon its streets since it was built 874 years before, had fallen to men who had taken the Cross and vowed regain lost Jerusalem.

The sack that followed was one of the worst in all of history. It lasted three days. No man, woman or child was safe from the ravagers. Robbery and rape were almost universal, mindless destruction widespread. Westerners who had once lived in the city and been expelled from it, or had lost friends and relatives in the massacres of their people that the Byzantine government had tolerated in the past, killed indiscriminately, without mercy or restraint.[121] Horrible and utterly indefensible as the sack was, it should in justice be remembered that it was not totally unprovoked; more than once (as in the massacre of 1182) the Greeks of Constantinople had treated the Latins there as they were now being treated. But for this to have been done by crusaders—men actually wearing the Cross of Christ—was an ineffaceable disgrace.

Three years later Nicholas Mesarites remembered the "war-maddened swordsmen, breathing murder, iron-clad and spear-bearing, sword-bearers and lance-bearers, bowmen, horsemen, boasting dreadfully, baying like Cerberus and breathing like Charon, pillaging the holy places, trampling on divine things, running riot over holy things, casting down to the floor the holy images of Christ and His holy Mother and of the holy men who from eternity have been pleasing to the Lord God, uttering calumnies and profanities, and in addition tearing children from mothers and mothers from children, treating the virgin with wanton shame in holy chapels, viewing with fear neither the wrath of God nor

---

[119]*Ibid.*, II, 182-184; Brand, *Byzantium Confronts the West*, pp. 253-254; Queller, *Fourth Crusade*, pp. 138-139.

[120]Brand, *Byzantium Confronts the West*, p. 256; Queller, *Fourth Crusade*, pp. 145-146.

[121]Brand, *Byzantium Confronts the West*, pp. 259-261.

the vengeance of men."[122]

Perhaps, somewhere during those hellish days, blind old Enrico Dandolo was remembering the burning glass with which the Byzantines had taken his sight, and smiling.

On May 9 Count Baldwin of Flanders was elected Latin Emperor of Constantinople, and soon afterward the Venetian Tommaso Morosini, though only a subdeacon, was installed as patriarch. The schism of 1054 was proclaimed at an end. Pope Innocent III first heard of all this in a self-serving letter from Baldwin, to which he responded with gratification at the ecclesiastical reunion, relief that the war was over, and continuing hope that the crusade might finally reach the Holy Land.[123] Only gradually did the terrible truth become known to him, but by the following year he knew the worst. He wrote Boniface of Montferrat, commander of the crusade, denouncing him like a Hebrew prophet in words which still burn across eight centuries:

> You rashly violated the purity of your vows; and, turning your arms not against the Saracens but against Christians, you applied yourselves not to the recovery of Jerusalem, but to seize Constantinople, preferring earthly to heavenly riches. . . .
> These "soldiers of Christ" who should have turned their swords against the infidel have steeped them in Christian blood, sparing neither religion, nor age, nor sex. . . . They stripped the altars of silver, violated the sanctuaries, robbed icons and crosses and relics. . . . The Latins have given example only of perversity and works of darkness. No wonder the Greeks call them dogs![124]

The Greeks never forgot the sack of Constantinople in 1204; its memory, more than anything else, has prevented the healing of the Greek schism from that day to this, despite several major efforts at reunion. And Jerusalem remained lost.

The wounds in Christendom were deep and festering. Only a new and irresistible visitation of holiness could cure them and change disaster into glory. But Christ was already preparing the men to bring it. Their names were Francis and Dominic.

---

[122]*Ibid.*, p. 269.

[123]Setton, *Crusades*, II, 189-190, 195-196; Joseph Gill, *Byzantium and the Papacy 1198-1400* (New Brunswick NJ, 1979), pp. 26-29.

[124]Mann, *Popes of the Middle Ages*, XII, 266-267; Mary Purcell, *St. Anthony and His Times* (Dublin, 1960), p. 26. It is evident from Mann's summary of this letter to Boniface and another to Cardinal Peter Capuano that these two quotations belong together.

5
St. Francis and St. Dominic
(1204-1227)
(Popes Innocent III 1198-1216 and Honorius III 1216-27)

> In the time I spent at the Curia I saw much that I was entirely dissatisfied with; all was so taken up with worldly and temporal affairs of politics and law, that it was hardly possible to get in a word of spiritual affairs. There was one thing, however, which comforted me in these surroundings: many men and women, among them many rich and worldly, have for Christ's sake forsaken everything and fled from the world. They are called Friars Minor, and stand in high repute both with Pope and Cardinals. But they take no heed of temporal things, but work day in and day out with zeal and diligence to draw souls away from the vanities of the world, so that they will not fall to the ground, and to take them along with themselves. And with the favor of God they have already reaped a rich harvest. — letter of Canon Jacques de Vitry from Genoa, October 1216[1]

One of the greatest paradoxes of the spiritual condition of humanity—and an essential element in the mystery of the Cross—is that prosperity of any kind tends to draw men away from God. The poor keep the Faith when the rich apostatize. The dark ages are ages of faith, while progress brings doubt and even scorn toward the truth which is God's and the God Who is Truth. Martyrdom builds the Faith, oppression strengthens it, while to be "at ease in Zion" opens the gates to every kind of temptation. The graces of the Redemption which came from crucifixion flowed at their fullest during the persecutions of Diocletian, when the barbarians sacked Rome, when the Vikings scourged the coasts, when the Moors hammered Pelayo and his tiny band back to their last mountain from which they still proclaimed the salvation of Spain would come. Never in modern history did men so love the Mass as in Ireland during the eighteenth century when it was a capital offense to say it. These times, these persecutions produced saints innumerable. But it may well be that the greatest saints of all are those sent in times of progress and prosperity, to recall men from sloth and greed and moral corruption, and call them back to their duty as children of God. For in those ages it is easiest for a man to lose his soul, and hardest of all to be a saint.

---

[1]Jorgensen, Johannes, *Saint Francis of Assisi* (New York, 1912), p. 142-143.

The twelfth century had been a time of surging growth in the wealth, power, and prosperity of Christendom. Figurehead kings had become real monarchs, towns had become cities building magnificent Romanesque cathedrals, trade had brought Europe more and more of the riches of the Orient. Even the setbacks of the crusaders at the end of the twelfth century and the beginning of the thirteenth were, as we have seen, more due to the sloth and greed and moral corruption stemming from prosperity than from any prowess of the infidel. While St. Bernard of Clairvaux lived and preached, he had kept Christendom on a spiritually upward course despite all the growing temptations. But when the century changed he had been in Paradise for nearly half a century, and none approaching his stature had come to take his place. If history were predictable—which the will of God and the wills of men make impossible—there was every reason to believe that the thirteenth century would be a time of weakening or even dissolution for Christendom, just as the sixteenth and nineteenth centuries later were to seem to be, at their beginnings.

Christendom was substantially weakened—though never dissolved —during the early sixteenth and nineteenth centuries, because by then it was tragically divided. But at the beginning of the thirteenth century Christendom was still united, and the heresies then challenging it, though very dangerous in limited areas, were not a threat to its body as a whole. It could all be encompassed in a great spiritual renewal. That is what happened; and consequently this thirteenth century has ever since been viewed—and rightly—as the most Christian of all centuries, the summit of the glory of Christendom we have known on earth.

This magnificent spiritual achievement was the work of thousands of men and women, not least of some of the greatest of the Popes—notably Innocent III, Honorius III, Gregory IX, Innocent IV, and Blessed Gregory X. But above all it was the work of two men, by worldly standards of small account: Francisco Bernardone, the Little Poor Man of Assisi; and Domingo Guzmán, a rustic priest from Caleruega in the barren rocky hills of Aragon—St. Francis and St. Dominic. It was their message above all that strengthened the Faith in men's hearts even when the great crusading enthusiasm was fading, that kept Christians loving their clergy and bishops even while demanding their reform, that held the new intellectuals in the Church and brought forth St. Thomas Aquinas, that flowered in the Gothic cathedrals, that not only reminded men but convinced them anew that no life devoted solely or even primarily to material gain is worth living.

St. Francis and St. Dominic came from God and returned to Him, passing through the world like twin meteors, in an astonishingly brief span of time from the perspective of the historian. They became conscious of their mission at virtually the same moment, the spring of 1206;[2] Dominic had only fifteen years to work, Francis twenty. In those two decades they transformed Christendom, leaving their mark upon it forever. Nearly eight centuries afterward, their spiritual sons and daughters march on. Some went astray, but many always remained on course. Their work and their inspiration still live. We may well believe that even in the last and darkest hour of the history of our planet and the human race, Christians will yet remain who remember St. Francis and St. Dominic.

Though the historian has good reason to speak of them together, they were two very different men with two very different vocations. Their great, fundamental, evident similarity was their commitment to holy poverty, to mendicancy. Though embraced by a few heretics (such as the Waldensians, followers of Peter Waldo of Lyons in southern France, and the Humiliati of Lombardy in northern Italy)[3] no religious order accepted by the Church before the Franciscans and Dominicans had lived literally by begging. All religious orders owned substantial property—both land and buildings—and supported themselves primarily from it, though receiving some gifts as well. Although later—after considerable internal opposition to the change in the case of the Franciscans—the new orders did acquire some property, their primary support was always donations. The increase of available wealth made this possible, but it still required a tremendous leap of faith to rely primarily on gifts for sustenance. After the French Revolution, this became and has remained the means of financial support for most of the Church.

But finance, rightly understood, is always only a means to an end. The end for the Franciscans was the sanctification of the Christian people, primarily the poor, chiefly by example, secondarily but always significantly by preaching. The end for the Dominicans was to develop Catholic education and the training of men to preach and defend the Faith in public debate at every level. St. Francis shaped popular Christianity: his veneration of the crucifix[4] has indelibly marked the Catholic Church ever since; his glorification of Christmas survives not only throughout all divisions of Christianity but even in neo-pagan guise in today's secularized world.[5] St. Dominic created a school for the advocacy and defense of Christianity which enabled defenders of the Faith eventually to meet

---

[2]For the dating of St. Francis' conversion experiences, beginning with the words of Christ he heard from the crucifix in the little church of San Damiano, see Omer Englebert, *St. Francis of Assisi* (Chicago, 1965), pp. 370-372; for St. Dominic, the starting point was his decision to join in a preaching mission to the Catharist heretics of southern France conducted in complete apostolic poverty and mendicancy (M.-H. Vicarie, *St. Dominic and His Times* [New York, 1964], pp. 80-81, 88-91).
[3]Jonathan Sumption, *The Albigensian Crusade* (London, 1978), p. 38; Philip Hughes, *A History of the Church*, rev. ed. (New York, 1949), II, 336-338.
[4]Jorgensen, *St. Francis*, p. 42.
[5]Englebert, *St. Francis*, pp. 299-301.

and vanquish every opponent, at least intellectually, down through the centuries.

God's call came to St. Francis as he knelt in prayer in the tiny, tumbledown chapel of San Damiano near Assisi in north central Italy, and heard Christ speak to him from the crucifix: "Francis, go and repair my church which, as you see, is nearly falling down!" At first interpreting these words strictly literally, Francis began collecting contributions to rebuild the little chapel and undertook the work of reconstruction himself; he renounced all his worldly possessions, even his clothes, and lived as a beggar. Then he began collecting money to restore other churches, notably the chapel at Portiuncula near which he lived. Only gradually did he realize that the church which his Savior had called him to repair was not one or a few little chapels, but the whole Church. He was to rebuild it by following explicitly Christ's gospel command to go forth to preach the kingdom of Heaven, begging his way with no more than a single set of clothes, staying in each town with those who would receive him. He began this way of life early in 1208, and during that year eleven others joined him in practicing it.[6]

St. Francis' preaching was marked by love of Christ and the Church and his fellow-man, by Christian joy, by the cheerful embracing of complete poverty, by a profound respect for the clergy, above all by total fidelity to orthodox doctrine. This full combination had never been seen since the earliest days of the Church. Francis wrote out a brief Rule defining his way of life, with special emphasis on literal obedience to the gospel prescriptions for the travelling apostle, the ideal of poverty, earning food by labor where possible and otherwise by begging, but carrying no money, with their primarily apostolic work specified as preaching. His followers were to wear only a cord and hood with their single garment, and to be called the Friars Minor. Soon, probably in the spring of 1209, they set out for Rome to gain the approval of Pope Innocent III for their way of life and their Rule.[7]

The scenes that followed are deservedly famous: the mighty Pope Innocent III, maker of crusades, breaker of kings, scion of one of the noblest families of Italy, facing the Little Poor Man with his rags and bushy eyebrows and matted coal-black hair. One account, possibly legendary, has the Pope first ordering Francis to a pigsty, to which he went and from which he immediately returned, covered with dung, to renew his appeal. This seems unlikely, as untrue to Innocent III's character, though certainly not to that of Francis. But all accounts agree that the Pope and most of the cardinals, on first hearing of

---

[6]*Ibid.*, pp. 74-99.

[7]Astonishingly, the text of this first Franciscan Rule is lost, though to some extent it can be reconstructed from later Rules (John Moorman, *A History of the Franciscan Order* [Oxford, 1968], pp. 15-17); for the date of this first journey of St. Francis and his companions to Rome, see Englebert, *St. Francis*, pp. 377-382.

the Franciscan rule, concluded that it was beyond human capability, only to have Cardinal John of St. Paul (after a discussion with Francis) remind them that to call literal obedience to a command of Jesus Christ beyond human capability was "to blaspheme Christ, its Author." While deliberating on what to do, the Pope had a dream. The great Lateran basilica, nine hundred years old, which went back to Emperor Constantine, was leaning, swaying, ready to collapse while the Pope watched in paralyzed horror. Then a little man ran up, set his shoulder against it, and the building straightened and stood firm again. The little man was St. Francis.[8]

Pope Innocent III approved the first Franciscan rule and made Francis the leader of his brotherhood. The brethren took a vow of obedience to him, and he made one to the Pope. They were given the right to preach. Francis was ordained a deacon.[9]

> "Go, brethren," said the Pope, dismissing the twelve Penitents, "and may the Lord be with you! If it please Him to increase you, come and tell me about it. And I shall see then about granting you more numerous favors and entrusting you with a more important mission."[10]

St. Francis' vocation was thus intensely personal, an act of God's will and his own, stimulated by no outside circumstance beyond the general spiritual malaise of Christendom in an intensely and increasingly materialistic time. St. Dominic's vocation, on the other hand, was born in combat against an explicit enemy of the truth of Christ. Before finding his vocation, St. Francis, that gentle son of sunny Assisi, had once thought that he would be a soldier, a man of war; it required only a few months to show him how far such a life was from his character and mission, which was above all to be, in his own immortal words, a channel of Christ's peace.[11] But St. Dominic from the stony slopes of Aragon, heir to eighteen generations of the Spanish Reconquest, the longest crusade, was made for war, though for him it was a war of the spirit.

Nine hundred and ninety years before that spring when both St. Francis and St. Dominic found their vocations, a boy named Mani was born at the Parthian capital of Ctesiphon in Mesopotamia. He was brought up in the Gnostic religion of the Mandaeans, a strange blend of heretical Christianity and Zoroastrianism. After a visit to India, Mani added to this the world-denying doctrine of Buddhism and the Hindu concept of reincarnation. He taught that the whole visible and material world is the creation of the Devil, who (he said) has power equal to God. The spirit is from God, the body from the Devil, according to Mani. The Incarnation never happened; the Passion and the

---

[8]Englebert, *St. Francis*, pp. 107-114.
[9]*Ibid.*, p. 115.
[10]*Ibid.*
[11]Jorgensen, *St. Francis*, pp. 28-32.

Eucharist were illusions; life itself was an abomination from which all men should desire to be released. Mani was a great organizer, and his Manichaean "church" and its doctrines spread over much of Europe and Asia, where it mingled with other Gnostic streams, some flowing from disillusioned Jews cosmically embittered by the destruction of Jerusalem.[12]

By the thousandth year of the Christian era, Mani and the Gnostics seemed very long ago and far away. Only a few theologians and historians in the West (most of them, probably, careful students of St. Augustine who had once been a Manichaean) even remembered this perverse and destructive teaching. In the east the Muslim whirlwind had swept most of the Manichaeans and Gnostics away, except for a few remnants here and there; but in Armenia, periodically conquered but never entirely subjugated by the Muslims, separated from the Catholic Church when it embraced the Monophysite heresy, the doctrines of Mani were re-established among an active minority called the Paulicians. As the Byzantine empire recruited more and more Armenians for its army, the heresy of the Paulicians moved west with these soldiers into its domains. The patriarchs, priests and monks of Constantinople knew the heresy and were vigilant against it, especially during the centuries before their final break from Rome; but the new converts among the Slavs of the Balkans did not know what it was. About the middle of the tenth century Tsar Peter of Bulgaria wrote Patriarch Theophylact of Constantinople describing a new heresy being preached in his country by a priest named Bogomil, asking what he should do about it. Theophylact identified what Bogomil was preaching as an outgrowth of Paulicianism even more uncompromisingly dualist than the Paulicians had been—more like original Manichaeanism. Another Bulgarian priest named Cosmas studied the Bogomilist heresy and wrote a book against it first circulated in 972.[13]

Bogomilism went underground; but it survived, grew, and kept moving west. By the early twelfth century it had appeared in France. In June 1119 Pope Calixtus II presided at a council in Toulouse, the principal city of southern France, which had been the seat of the man who more than any other won the First Crusade, Count Raymond. The council of 1119 anathematized heretics in the Toulouse region who denied the sacramental character of the Eucharist, baptism, and marriage, and rejected the priesthood and hierarchy of the Church. Just seven years later Peter de Bruys, who rejected infant baptism, hated the Cross and churches, denied the Mass and the Eucharist, and held prayers for the dead to be valueless, was burned for heresy at St. Gilles near Toulouse. At first called "Petrobrusians" for him, the believers in his doctrines soon came to be known as "Cathars," from the Greek word for "pure." St.

---

[12]See Volume I, Chapter 18 of this history.
[13]Steven Runciman, *The Medieval Manichee* (Cambridge, England, 1955), pp. 67-69, 73-74, 87n; Sumption, *Albigensian Crusade*, p. 35.

Bernard of Clairvaux twice preached against the Cathars in the south of France and set them back, but their growth resumed after his death. By 1165 the Cathars were so numerous and so strongly supported by many of the nobles that they were preaching their heresy openly; the bishops dared take no action against them.[14]

In 1167 the Cathars held a public synod at St.-Félix-de-Caraman in southern France attended by many of their own bishops, some coming all the way from Italy. A Greek named Nicetas, who claimed to be the Bogomil bishop of Constantinople, took charge, preaching an uncompromising dualist doctrine which was essentially Manichaean. Most of the French Cathars adjusted the doctrine they preached to reflect that of Nicetas. Barthélemy, who had been trained in Greece by Nicetas' predecessor Niphon, formally condemned as a heretic in Constantinople, was made Cathar bishop of the southern French city of Albi. There he built up the Cathar community to become the strongest in the region, giving the heresy its other name of "Albigensian."[15]

This synod and the intervention of Nicetas fixed the Cathar creed in the form that became familiar to Catholic Christendom in the thirteenth century during which it was finally extinguished. They held the old Manichaean beliefs rigorously, totally rejecting the humanity of Christ and the goodness of marriage and especially child-bearing. Those who would not curb their sexual drives were encouraged to express them homosexually or even in bestiality rather than heterosexually, so that no children would result from them. The Cathar elite, known as the Perfect, received their only sacrament, the Consolamentum, which appears to have included an explicit renunciation of the Church and the Cross. The Perfect lived with extreme austerity, never touching animal food. They would give the Consolamentum to ordinary believers (who were allowed almost complete license in behavior) only on their deathbed, and occasionally took measures to assure that those who had received it did not recover from their illness. For the Perfect, suicide was the highest form of death, carried out according to a ceremony called the *endura*.[16]

During the last years of his pontificate Alexander III sent two Cistercian cardinals to southern France to try to reconvert or suppress the Cathars, but to virtually no avail. Cardinal Peter was booed in the streets and had to excommunicate the Viscount of Béziers for open hostility to him and his mission; Cardinal Henry tried rational argument, then church reform, and finally force, but his actions were not followed up despite being vigorously

---

[14]Runciman, *Medieval Manichee*, pp. 117-119, 123; Sumption, *Albigensian Crusade*, pp. 39, 46-47.

[15]Runciman, *Medieval Manichee*, pp. 72-73, 123-124; Sumption, *Albigensian Crusade*, pp. 49-50.

[16]Runciman, *Medieval Manichee*, pp. 149-159, 176-177; Sumption, *Albigensian Crusade*, p. 52.

supported by the greatest nobleman of the region, Count Raymond V of Toulouse, a direct descendant of the crusader. But Count Raymond V died in 1194, and his son Raymond VI was known to be at least sympathetic to the heresy; his wife Beatrice of Béziers was one of the Cathar "Perfect," living in one of their convents. The Viscount of Béziers, dying that same year, named Bertrand de Saissac, a leading Cathar, as guardian of his minor son. Three years later Bertrand forced the monastic community of Alet to elect a Cathar as their abbot in a chapter meeting held in the presence of the exhumed corpse of their previous abbot.[17]

When Innocent III became Pope, as befitted his vigorous nature, he immediately offered a new challenge to the Cathars. In 1199, the first full year of his pontificate, he sent a legate, Pietro Parenzi, to act against them in Orvieto, Italy; when the Cathars murdered and mutilated Parenzi, the reaction against them was so great as to destroy the heresy in Orvieto. To southern France, where the Cathars were most strongly established, he sent that same year the monk Rainier as legate with a group including the Cistercian Peter of Castelnau. In 1200 the great Pope demanded that King Imre of Hungary and Ban Kulin of Bosnia suppress the heresy in their domains, where it was called Bogomilism. Both acted promptly, decisively and apparently with full effect. But the task of crushing the heresy in southern France was much more formidable. In 1203 Rainier was relieved as legate and replaced by Peter of Castelnau and Ralph of Fontfroide, and the next year Arnold Amaury, abbot of Cîteaux, was sent as a third legate. Bishop Fulk of Toulouse welcomed them, but few others would, and Count Raymond VI was distinctly cool. In 1205 Esclarmonde, sister of Count Raymond-Roger of Foix, received the Consolamentum and became a Perfect in a ceremony attended by most of the nobility of the county of Foix. The Pope appealed to King Philip II of France to intervene, but he found excuses to stand aloof.[18]

This was the situation the young priest Domingo (Dominic) Guzmán found when travelling with his bishop, Diego of Osma, through southern France in the spring of 1206. Meeting in Montpellier in June with the Papal legates and the few who had been trying to help them, Bishop Diego pointed out that one of the reasons the Cathars were prevailing was the appearance of holiness the "Perfect" gave by their austere way of life, contrasted to the greed and ostentation of many of the local Catholic prelates and clergy and aided by the

---

[17]Runciman, *Medieval Manichee*, pp. 132-134; Sumption, *Albigensian Crusade*, pp. 54-57, 59, 64.

[18]Horace K. Mann, *The Lives of the Popes of the Middle Ages*, Volume XII, 2nd ed. (London, 1925), pp. 106-107 and Volume XIII, 2nd ed. (London, 1925), pp. 41-45; Runciman, *Medieval Manichee*, pp. 103-105, 132, 136; John V. A. Fine Jr., *The Late Medieval Balkans* (Ann Arbor MI, 1987), p. 47; Sumption, *Albigensian Crusade*, pp. 68-70; Vicaire, *St. Dominic*, pp. 83, 87.

grievous lack of preaching and teaching of orthodox doctrine. Preachers should go out into the country where the heretics were, Bishop Diego said, living in apostolic poverty, begging their bread, and preaching their faith. Young Dominic enthusiastically agreed, and the work began. In November, Pope Innocent III approved itinerant mendicant preaching in southern France.[19]

In July, at Servian near Béziers, the itinerant preachers of orthodoxy made a considerable impression. But at Béziers itself they met immovable resistance, and that fall Peter of Castelnau was advised to withdraw from the country "for fear of assasination" becauase "the heretics hated him above all others." He withdrew for six months, then returned. Dominic and his Bishop Diego continued to preach.[20]

The Catharist heresy appealed particularly to women, who had an unusually great influence on public affairs in this region, home of the troubadours and "courtly love." Dominic consequently emphasized the personal counselling of women, and drew enough of them back from Catharism—including some of the "Perfect"—to feel the need for a convent of such women under his personal guidance and protection. At the crossroads of Prouille he saw on three successive evenings a globe of fire from Heaven descend upon its little chapel. He took it as a sign that the convent should be established there, and founded it in the winter of 1207 with the approval of Bishop Fulk of Toulouse, in whose diocese Prouille was located. In April 1207 he and the legates met the Cathar bishop of Toulouse, Guilabert de Castries, in debate at Montréal. The four judges of the debate, all sympathetic to the Cathars, refused to give a verdict, but 150 in the audience were reconverted to the Catholic Faith. Many of them were women, and some asked to join the new Prouille community. Lord Bérenger of Narbonne gave the church of St. Martin of Limoux to the community, though it was two years before they were able to gain undisputed possession of it.[21]

Late in April 1207, just after Easter, Abbot Arnold Amaury arrived from Cîteaux with 30 Cistercian preachers to work thorughout the Cathar areas of southern France. Peter of Castelnau returned with him, formed a league for the suppression of heresy in more loyal Provence to the east, and invited Count Raymond VI of Toulouse to join it. When the Count refused he was excommunicated, charged with employing foreign mercenaries which the Church had forbidden, violating the truce declared by the Church for high feast days, pillaging monasteries, and fortifying churches.[22] Pope Innocent III

---

[19]Vicaire, *St. Dominic*, pp. 88-93; Sumption, *Albigensian Crusade*, pp. 70-71.

[20]Vicaire, *St. Dominic*, pp. 93-95; Sumption, *Albigensian Crusade*, p. 72; Kenneth M. Setton, ed., *A History of the Crusades*, Volume II, ed. Robert L. Wolff and Harry W. Hazard (Philadelphia, 1962), p. 283.

[21]Vicaire, *St. Dominic*, pp. 115-124; Sumption, *Albigensian Crusade*, pp. 72-73.

[22]Sumption, *Albigensian Crusade*, pp. 72-74; Mann, *Popes in the Middle Ages*, XII,

confirmed his excommunication with a solemn warning:

> Do not forget that life and death themselves are in God's hands. God may
> suddenly strike you down, and His anger deliver you to everlasting
> torment. Even if you are permitted to live, do not suppose that misfortune
> cannot reach you. You are not made of iron. You are weak and
> vulnerable, like other men. Fever, leprosy, paralysis, insanity, incurable
> disease may all attack you like any other of your kind.... Are you not
> ashamed of breaking the oath by which you swore to eradicate heresy from
> your dominions?[23]

At this point Pope Innocent III was heavily engaged on many fronts.
Imperial claimant Philip of Swabia, younger brother of Emperor Henry VI who
had died in 1197, was slowly but surely prevailing in his prolonged struggle with
the Pope's choice, Otto IV, son of Henry the Lion of the house of Welf. In
April 1207 Philip made trimphal entry into Cologne, while Otto fled to England
seeking financial help from its King John. By August Otto was back in
Germany and two Papal legates persuaded him to meet with Philip. Little was
accomplished at the meeting, but Philip was relieved of his excommmunication
after agreeing to submit to Papal authority.[24] In England, a dispute over the
election of a new Archbishop of Canterbury had escalated into a full-scale
confrontation with the mercurial and self-willed King John. In September 1205
the Canterbury cathedral chapter, not wishing to confirm the King's nominee,
John de Gray, as primate of England, had secretly elected Subprior Reginald.
Three months later, under pressure from the King, the chapter reversed itself
and proclaimed John de Gray. Pope Innocent declared both elections to be
invalid and himself chose Cardinal Stephen Langton of Lincolnshire, until
recently a distinguished teacher at the University of Paris, as Archbishop of
Canterbury. The monks of the cathedral chapter unanimously accepted
Langton, but King John was furious at being bypassed, and refused to permit his
installation at Canterbury.[25] In May 1207 the great Pope replied to the King of
England:

> We do not think it necessary to ask again for the king's consent after all
> these approaches; but swerving neither to the right hand nor to the left, we
> have resolved to follow the course appointed by the canonical decrees of
> the holy fathers, that no delay or difficulty should be allowed to thwart

223.

[23]Sumption, *Albigensian Crusade*, p. 74.

[24]Mann, *Popes in the Middle Ages*, XII, 190-191; Christopher R. Cheney, *Pope
Innocent III and England* (Stuttgart, 1976), p. 292.

[25]Austin Lane-Poole, *From Domesday Book to Magna Carta, 1087-1216* (Oxford
History of England), 2nd ed. (Oxford, 1955), pp. 443-445; W. L. Warren, *King John*
(Berkeley CA, 1961), pp. 161-163; Cheney, *Pope Innocent III and England*, pp. 148-
152; Mann, *Popes of the Middle Ages*, XIII, 124-126.

good arrangements, lest the Lord's flock should for a long time be without pastoral care.[26]

The Pope personally consecrated Stephen Langton Archbishop of Canterbury at Viterbo in Italy, where he was then residing. Mortally offended and unyielding, John expelled the monks of the Canterbury cathedral chapter and Langton's father from England. On August 27, 1207 the Pope excommunicated those who had carried out the King's orders of expulsion, and warned John that he would lay the whole of England under an interdict unless he accepted the new Archbishop. John replied that, "by God's teeth," if an interdict was proclaimed he would exile bishops and clergy obeying it, confiscate their property, and slit the eyes and noses of any Roman clergy who remained in England in defiance of his will.[27]

In the east, Innocent III still hoped to consummate the reunion of the schismatic Greek Orthodox Church with the Catholic Church despite the bitter and still very recent memories of the sack of Constantinople. He declared that the Greeks could retain their Byzantine rite and that their monasteries—particularly those on Mount Athos—should retain their status and rules at the time of the conquest. The Greeks almost universally defied him, but he still had hopes for Georgia in the Caucasus, whose monks at Athos had accepted his jurisdiction; and in October 1207 he wrote to all the clergy and laity in Russia, explaining the unity of the Church and urging Russia to return to that unity. He sent Cardinal Gregory as his legate to Kiev and asked the Ukrainians and Russians to heed him.[28]

But these controversies were no more than schisms and quarrels within the Church; the challenge in the south of France came from a heresy so far separated from true Christianity that it could hardly be called Christian at all. The peaceful methods of persuasion that the papal legates and St. Dominic had been using could win back significant numbers of souls, but the evil was too deeply entrenched to yield to such methods alone. The Faith was challenged at its roots in the heart of Christendom. It was time for a crusade. This very same Pope had scathingly denounced the diversion of the Fourth Crusade against Christians; but, in truth, the Cathars were no more Christian than the Muslims. Their power must be broken, or they could well break Christendom.

Pope Innocent appealed to Philip II and the great barons of northern France, but they were not yet interested in this cause. They had little awareness of conditions in the south, which they believed the Pope was exaggerating; their

---

[26]Cheney, *Pope Innocent III and England*, p. 152.

[27]*Ibid.*, pp. 152, 298-302; Warren, *King John*, pp. 164-165.

[28]Joseph Gill, *Byzantium and the Papacy 1198-1400* (New Brunswick NJ, 1979), pp. 34, 37-38; Fine, *Late Medieval Balkans*, p. 79; Mann, *Popes in the Middle Ages*, XIII, 55-57.

focus was on the struggle with England for control of Poitou, Brittany, and Normandy, which had gone on for two generations. Thye needed some dramatic proof of the magnitude of the Cathar danger before they would act.[29]

At the turn of the new year 1208 it came. Peter of Castelnau, who had been laboring in the inhospitable vineyard of southern France for eight years and had already been warned about his personal safety, responded to an invitation by Count Raymond VI of Toulouse to meet him at his residence at St. Gilles to arrange for the Count's reconciliation with the Church and the Pope. Arriving on January 13, Peter and his companion, the Bishop of Couserans, found Raymond essentially unrepentant, alternating between compromise and defiance. The day passed with no real progress toward reconciliation. Peter said there was no point in his staying on. Count Raymond flared up, demanding that he and the Bishop stay, declaring that if they left "there was no place on land or water where he would not be watching for them." They departed at nightfall, with a bodyguard supplied by the Abbot of St. Gilles. The next day, in Arles on the Rhone, a knight of Count Raymond's household charged the unarmed legate and struck him down with his lance.[30]

When the news of the murder of Peter of Castelnau reached Rome in February, Pope Innocent III buried his head in his hands, then went to pray at the high altar of St. Peter's which stood over the grave of the Prince of the Apostles. Within a few days Arnold Amaury and the bishops of Toulouse and Couserans arrived to give the Pope a detailed and circumstantial account of the tragedy, emphasizing the strong suspicion attaching to Raymond and his failure to make any effort to apprehend or punish the murderer.[31] On March 10 Innocent III renewed Raymond's excommunication, released his vassals from their oath of fidelity to him, and called for his overthrow by the faithful knights of France:[32]

> "Forward, soldiers of Christ! Forward, volunteers of the army of God! Go forth with the Church's cry of anguish ringing in your ears. Fill your souls with godly rage to avenge the insult done to the Lord!"[33]

On March 28 the Pope declared specifically that the war being launched against the heretics of southern France was a crusade, to which all the special crusading indulgences applied.[34] Just five days earlier the bishops of London,

---

[29]Walter L. Wakefield, *Heresy, Crusade and Inquisition in Southern France 1100-1250* (Berkeley Ca, 1974), p. 92; Sumption, *Albigensian Crusade*, p. 75.

[30]Sumption, *Albigensian Crusade*, pp. 75-76; Vicaire, *St. Dominic*, p. 135; Mann, *Popes in the Middle Ages*, XIII, 236-237.

[31]Sumption, *Albigensian Crusade*, p. 77.

[32]*Ibid.*; Setton, *Crusades*, II, 285-286.

[33]Sumption, *Albigensian Crusade*, p. 77.

[34]Setton, *Crusades*, II, 285.

Ely, and Worcester, acting as the Pope had ordered them to act in the face of King John's continuing refusal to recognize Stephen Langton as Archbishop of Canterbury, laid an interdict upon England, closing all its churches and withholding all its sacraments but baptism and anointing those in immediate danger of death. King John replied the next day by seizing the property of all clerics obeying the interdict.[35] For a Pope to take two such sweeping actions within a week—one against a king, the other against one of the most powerful barons of Christendom—was unprecedented; but Innocent III showed no sign of doubt that he and the faithful Catholics would prevail both in England and in southern France. In the end they did prevail, but only after years of bitter strife.

In Germany, at least, Pope Innocent III believed he had finally achieved peace, reconciling the rival claimants Philip of Swabia and Otto IV of the house of Welf. Philip's daughter was to marry the Pope's nephew, Otto was to marry another of Philip's daughters, and Philip was to be Holy Roman Emperor. Though the Pope had at first favored Otto because he was not of the Hohenstaufen family that had provided so many Emperors hostile to the Church, he had come to see that Philip had too much support to be pushed aside and that Otto was too headstrong and ambitious to be reliable. Whether the agreements made in this spring of 1208 by Philip and Otto would have been maintained no man can say, though it is unlikely; but in June Philip was murdered by Otto of Wittelsbach, Count of Bavaria, who was furious because the daughter Philip had now promised to the Pope's nephew had originally been promised to him. The Pope had to turn back to Otto IV of Welf; but Otto was not likely to forget that Innocent III, after supporting him, had abandoned him, or that he was still strongly supporting young Frederick II, a Hohenstaufen, as King of Sicily and southern Italy, lands traditionally desired by the Holy Roman Emperor.[36]

In addition, Philip II of France was still in deep trouble with the Church over his refusal to accept the Danish Princess Ingeborg as his wife. Pope Innocent III now had suspicious or bad relations with all the great temporal sovereigns of Christendom. But he would not yield to any of them where the Church's cause and rights were concerned.

The response among the knights of northern France to the news of the murder of Peter of Castelnau was strong enough to overcome Philip II's reluctance to allow them to serve in the new crusade, and to frighten Count Raymond VI to try to gain favor by enlisting in the crusade himself. He sought the favor of Philip II and Otto IV, but neither showed any interest in helping

---

[35]Cheney, *Pope Innocent III and England*, pp. 302, 308-309; Lane-Poole, *Domesday Book to Magna Carta*, pp. 445-448; Warren, *King John*, pp. 166-168.

[36]Helene Tillmann, *Pope Innocent III* (Amsterdam, 1980), pp. 134-137; Alfred Haverkamp, *Medieval Germany, 1056-1273* (New York, 1988), p. 242; David Abulafia, *Frederick II* (London, 1988), pp. 104-105.

him. Returning to Toulouse at the end of 1208, he went down on his knees before Abbot Arnold Amaury, now the chief Papal legate in southern France, asking forgiveness; but Arnold, doubting his sincerity, referred his case to the Pope. When Raymond's appeal was carried to Rome, the Pope appointed two more legates to hear it with Arnold, but privately instructed them to defer to Arnold and let the crusade go forward.[37]   The assassination of Peter of Castelnau had not been an isolated incident, but the culmination of decades of the genesis and growth in southern France of what amounted to a new religion, hating Christianity. Even another Canossa scene would not remove the danger unless and until the Cathars were convinced that the Church was resolved to eliminate their heresy once and for all.

But a man fervently and publicly proclaiming his repentance could not be totally rejected by the Church which Christ had told to forgive seventy times seven. In June the legates reconciled Count Raymond after he swore that he was innocent of the murder of Peter of Castelnau and would support the crusade—and after one of them administered "the discipline" of a light switch on his bare back as he approached the altar.[38]   William Porcelet, who had sheltered the murderer of Peter of Castelanu in his house, submitted to the crusading army, now concentrating at Lyons, and Count Raymond joined it. Raymond-Roger Trencavel, Viscount of Béziers, one of the hotbeds of Catharism, offered the next month to make submission also; but when presented with a list of more than 200 known heretics in the city, he refused to turn them over. The crusading army was now encamped before Béziers, whose militia made a large-scale and poorly conducted sortie before the city's defenses were ready. The infantry and even the camp followers with the crusading army were therefore able to penetrate Béziers in a counterattack after the sortie. These undisciplined men ran wild before the crusading knights could take charge, looting Béziers and killing many—but nowhere near the 20,000 later reported, a figure more than twice the entire population of the city.[39]

The military leaders of what was now called the "Albigensian Crusade," meeting in council immediately after the fall of Béziers, declared they would give no quarter to the people of any city resisting them in the future. But in fact they did not hold to this bloody decision, since Legate Arnold Amaury obtained

---

[37]Sumption, *Albigensian Crusade*, pp. 78-82; Vicaire, *St. Dominic*, p. 139.

[38]Sumption, *Albigensian Crusade*, pp. 83-84; Wakefield, *Heresy, Crusade and Inquisition in Southern France*, p. 97. Terms such as "scourging" and "flogging" to describe the physical chastisement of Count Raymond are exaggerated. Many religious in the Church in those times were accustomed frequently to give themselves "the discipline" in the manner that it was inflicted upon the Count.

[39]Sumption, *Albigensian Crusade*, pp. 88-89, 92-94; Setton, *Crusades*, II, 288-289; Mann, *Popes in the Middle Ages*, XIII, 244. There is no reliable evidence that Arnold Amaury ever said the terrible words later attributed to him on this occasion: "Kill them all—God will know His own!"

the surrender of the formidable walled city of Carcassonne after a strong resistance during the first two weeks of August by allowing its people to leave with their lives and their liberty (though not with their goods). Count Trencavel was, however, arrested in violation of a safe-conduct and formally deposed as Viscount of Béziers and lord of Carcassonne.[40]

When higher-ranking nobles on the crusade all refused the offer of the Viscount's lands for themselves, not wishing to undertake the responsibility of maintaining and defending them, Simon de Montfort was induced by Arnold Amaury to accept them. Simon will be recalled as the principled knight who had refused to attack the Christian cities of Zara and Constantinople when the Fourth Crusade was diverted for that nefarious purpose. His spiritual advisor and strong supporter in that action, the monk Peter of Vaux-de-Cernay, had accompanied him on this new crusade, and joined Arnold Amaury in urging him to accept the lands of the Viscount of Béziers. By doing so, Simon de Montfort became the effective leader of the Albigensian Crusade, and fought on as its leader for no less than nine years. Even many of his strongest critics, then and since, have recognized Simon de Montfort's profound and sincere faith and unwavering dedication to the crusading ideal, for which he ultimately gave his life. He could be harsh, even cruel; but he was steel-true.[41]

His first acts as leader of the crusade were nothing but praiseworthy. He wrote to the Pope asking his confirmation that Simon's new feudal domains in southern France were rightly gained, reporting on the progress of the crusade so far, and asking for more support.[42] He offered his daughter in marriage to the son of Count Raymond VI of Toulouse, in an attempt to cement Raymond's dubious support for the cause of the crusade. Repulsed from the almost impregnable hill-fortress of Cabaret, defended by a lifelong Cathar, Simon secured Fanjeaux (where the Catholics welcomed the crusaders as the Cathars fled, and where he probably first met St. Dominic), took over Castres without bloodshed, then secured the whole northern half of the county of Foix. The Count of Foix, whose sister Esclarmonde was a well-known Cathar "Perfect," submitted to Simon.[43]

By the end of 1209 the crusaders were solidly established at many key strong points in southern France; but others were still held by the Cathars, and the present and future loyalties of Toulouse, by far the region's largest city,

---

[40]Sumption, *Albigensian Crusade*, pp. 96-99. He died in prison, of dysentery, in November of that year (*ibid.*, p. 102).

[41]*Ibid.*, pp. 100-102; Setton, *Crusades*, II, 289-290; Wakefield, *Heresy, Crusade, and Inquisition in Southern France*, pp. 102-103.

[42]Sumption, *Albigensian Crusade*, pp. 104-105; Mann, *Popes in the Middle Ages*, XIII, 245-246. Pope Innocent III confirmed Simon's title in November 1209 (Sumption, *loc. cit.*).

[43]Sumption, *Albigensian Crusade*, pp. 102, 106-107, 129, 180; Vicaire, *St. Dominic*, p. 143.

which had been placed under interdict by Papal legate Arnold Amaury for refusing to deliver up its leading Cathars, remained uncertain. It did not help regarding Toulouse that Arnold Amaury, who had become an irreconcilable foe of its slippery Count Raymond, had renewed his excommunication, for no very good reason, effective November 1. In January 1210 the Pope lifted both the interdict on Toulouse and the excommunication of Count Raymond VI, but named a new legate, Thedisius, to investigate substantial evidence of unwillingness by both the Count and his city to take action against the Cathars.[44]

In that same fall of 1209 Emperor Otto IV, apparently at the pinnacle of success and fame, came to Rome for his imperial coronation. On the way he and his dazzling escort passed a small, tumbledown shed on the banks of a crooked little river, the Rio Torto. The shed was just a few minutes' walk from Portiuncula chapel, where the new Franciscan community worshipped, and the community now made their lodging in it. St. Francis shut himself in the shed with all his companions except one, whom he instructed to go out and remind the Emperor that all human and earthly glory is short-lived and that his in particular would not last long.[45] There is no record of a response from Otto and his party, but Francis' prophecy was very soon proved true. Crowned October 4, by January 18, 1210 Otto had been denounced by the Pope for invading and plundering the Papal states and Sicily. In March Innocent III publicly voiced his regret that he had crowned Otto IV Emperor. In November he excommunicated him and relieved his subjects from their oaths of allegiance.[46]

During the winter and early spring of 1210 the fortunes of the Albigensian Crusade were suddenly reversed, as the full strength of the Cathars was finally revealed. More and more of the castles in the back country held out against the crusaders or were retaken from them. The conflict grew bitter and savage. Giraud de Pépieux, a southern knight who had joined the crusaders, betrayed them, seizing one of the castles they had occupied, mutilating the two knights commanding, and driving them naked from the gates in the middle of the winter. The Count of Foix repudiated his capitulation and joined the resistance. Montréal was betrayed by the priest Simon had placed there. By March the crusaders had lost more than forty castles in the southland and retained only eight.[47]

Simon struck back with terror. Rebels at Montlaur were hanged. When Bram, which had been betrayed to the enemies of the crusade, was recaptured

---

[44]Sumption, *Albigensian Crusade*, pp. 106-109; Setton, *Crusades*, II, 291; Wakefield, *Heresy, Crusade and Inquisition in Southern France*, p. 104.

[45]Englebert, *St. Francis*, pp. 117, 125, 377-382; Jorgensen, *St. Francis*, pp. 72-73, 77.

[46]Daniel Waley, *The Papal State in the Thirteenth Century* (London, 1961), pp. 58-60; Tillmann, *Pope Innocent III*, pp. 141, 145; Mann, *Popes in the Middle Ages*, XII, 207-208.

[47]Sumption, *Albigensian Crusade*, pp. 110-111.

Simon blinded all the garrison except one, who led the victims to the Cathar stronghold of Cabaret. This act, recalling some of the worst moments in Byzantine history, was much harder to justify by the standards of the time than the burning of 140 unyielding Cathar "Perfects" taken at the Cathar stronghold of Minerve in July. By then Simon had re-established crusader military domination in the south, and with the aid of Bishop Fulk put down the opponents of the crusade in Toulouse, but the atrocities on both sides had scarred the conflict with irreconcilable hatred.[48]

Pope Innocent III wanted moderation and compromise, but his legates did not. Increasingly they encouraged or at least reflected the passions of the crusaders, rather than speaking truly for the Vicar of Christ whose flock includes all men living on earth while he is pontiff. Arnold Amaury and Thedisius conferred in June on how to prevent the reconciliation of Count Raymond VI of Toulouse with the Church that the Pope had ordered. They found a passage in their instructions declaring that the Count must obey them until finally reconciled. Despite the fact that the Pope had lifted his excommunication, they decided to interpret that clause as giving them authority to deny him reconciliation if he did not obey their instructions, as they promptly claimed he had not. They refused even to try him on the charges of murder and heresy that had been made against him, as the Pope had ordered them to do. When by January 1211 they had run out of means to delay or evade executing the Pope's orders, they issued a series of extraordinary preconditions for Count Raymond's reconciliation: that he discharge all his mercenary soldiers within 24 hours, withdraw all protection from heretics and Jews, demolish all his castles, require all his nobles to live in the country, accept sharp restrictions on his personal expenditures, and then enter a crusading order and go to the Holy Land. When he refused these harsh terms they excommunicated him again; when Toulouse supported him, they renewed the interdict upon that city. On Holy Saturday Bishop Fulk of Toulouse left Toulouse to join Simon de Montfort, with whom St. Dominic had also become close, baptizing his new daughter in February.[49]

Pope Innocent III was still facing total defiance from Holy Roman Emperor Otto IV and King John of England. He had published John's excommunication in France in November 1209, and Otto's in Germany in March 1211.[50] England had been under interdict for three full years, a length of time almost unprecedented for the continuous imposition of this most severe of all Church penalties; yet still John would not yield. As if all this were not

---

[48]*Ibid.*, pp. 111, 115-119.

[49]*Ibid.*, pp. 119-120, 126-128, 131; Setton, *Crusades*, II, 291-292; Vicaire, *St. Dominic*, pp. 141, 143-144, 149, 483.

[50]Cheney, *Pope Innocent III and England*, pp. 319-321; Warren, *King John*, p. 169; Mann, *Popes in the Middle Ages*, XII, 210; Tillmann, *Pope Innocent III*, pp. 146-147.

enough, along with the winter crisis of 1211 in southern France and the renewed excommunication of Count Raymond VI of Toulouse and the renewed interdict on his city, the Pope was receiving a stream of reports on the advance of an immense army of Moors upon Christian Spain from the Almohad empire of Morocco. The Almohad army departed from Marrakesh in February, crossed the Straits of Gibraltar in May, and in July laid siege to the key Christian castle of Salvatierra just north of the Pass of the Overthrow of the Infidel Dogs. The Pope ordered Archbishop Rodrigo de Rada of Toledo, the Archbishop of Santiago de Compostela, and several other bishops in the Iberian peninsula to proclaim the upcoming war against the Moors a crusade and to excommunicate any Spanish Christian attacking Castile, the Christian kingdom most committed to the war of the Reconquest, while this crusade was going on.[51] Under this enormous multiple pressure, the Pope's courage only flamed higher. He would not retreat or compromise. Emperor Otto must halt his aggression in central and southern Italy. King John must accept the archbishop the Pope had appointed. Catharism must be rooted out of southern France. The Moorish offensive in Spain must be stopped.

The many-headed crisis rose to a pitch of almost unendurable intensity as the year 1211 unfolded. In May, after a fiercely contested siege, Simon de Montfort took Lavaur, a Cathar stronghold whose commander Aiméry was brother to Giraude de Laurac, a famous "Perfect;" he executed Aiméry and eighty of his knights, and had Giraude stoned to death in a well. Count Raymond VI of Toulouse decided to abandon all efforts at reconciliation with the Church and the crusade and commit himself totally to the resistance. All priests left the city of Toulouse; Raymond took it over, and marched against Simon de Montfort with an army outnumbering Simon's ten to one. Simon outgeneralled him and he retreated to Toulouse, but in the fall almost the whole country revolted against the crusaders; Simon lost all the towns and forts he had gained that year except hard-won Lavaur.[52] Buoyed by a triumph in Wales over its remarkably able Prince Llewelyn the Great, King John spurned the Pope's conditions for a lifting of the interdict on England, conveyed by the legate Pandulf.[53] No serious challenge had yet been made to Otto IV in Germany despite the Pope's excommunication of him. And the Moroccan Moors took Salvatierra castle in September after a 51-day siege during which its walls were badly battered by the Almohad siege machines and many of the

---

[51]Julio González, *El reino de Castilla en la época de Alfonso VIII* (Madrid, 1960), I, 985-989; Julio González, *Alfonso IX* (Madrid, 1944), p. 141; Derek W. Lomax, *The Reconquest of Spain* (London, 1978), p. 123; Javier Gorosterratzu, *Don Rodrigo Jiménez de Rada, Gran Estadista, Escritor y Prelado* (Pamplona, 1925), pp. 70-72.
[52]Sumption, *Albigensian Crusade*, pp. 129-142; Setton, *Crusades*, II, 292-294.
[53]Cheney, *Pope Innocent III and England*, pp. 324-325; Warren, *King John*, pp. 172-173, 198; John E. Lloyd, *A History of Wales*, 3rd ed. (London, 1939), II, 635-636.

defenders were slain or died of hunger and thirst. The Castilian army, brought by King Alfonso VIII to the San Vicente Mountains nearby, lacked the strength to challenge the Muslims on the plains and raise the siege.[54]

But for nearly five hundred years the Christians of Spain had looked into this lion's mouth, and survived. As always, a crisis like this brought out everything that was best in them. Archbishop Rodrigo de Rada of Toledo compared Salvatierra and its heroic though defeated garrison to Christ Himself:

> That castle is the castle of salvation, and its loss is the gaining of glory. Our people weep for it, and burst the chains binding their arms. Their zeal inspires us all.[55]

Returning from his fruitless sojourn in the San Vicente Mountains, Alfonso VIII of Castile—supported by an emergency session of his *cortes*, or parliament—gave orders that all that fall and winter there was to be no construction of additional defenses for any Castilian city or fortress, only the making and distribution of offensive weapons. Between Easter and Pentecost the next spring the crusading army would assemble at Toledo, the ancient capital of Spain. He wrote to Philip II of France asking his help, and Archbishop de Rada left at once for France to preach the Spanish crusade there. (The French already had one crusade on their hands—that against the Cathars—but this did not prevent many knights from answering the new crusading call.) They would march to meet the infidel at the famous and long embattled gateway to Andalusia which the Moors still held, the Pass of the Overthrow of the Infidel Dogs. Alfonso VIII's grandfather had died in that Pass, and he too would lay his bones among its crags if necessary to strike a decisive blow against the enemy of half a millennium of relentless struggle. In November 1211 Alfonso VIII met Pedro II of Aragon and obtained his oath to join him at Toledo the coming Pentecost. Then the dauntless King of Castile rode south across the mountains with a small but hard-hitting force which took three Moorish castles before winter closed in.[56]

Yet even Alfonso VIII needed the Pope, as a shield against the treacherous internecine warfare that had so weakened Spain against the Moors for the past fifty years; and the Pope's thunderous warnings did at least deter the rapacious kings who took little or no active part of the struggle from stabbing Alfonso VIII in the back at the critical moment. On February 4, 1212 Innocent III wrote to Alfonso, assuring him of his fullest support, telling him that he had written to the archbishops and bishops of France to call for

---

[54]González, *Alfonso VIII*, I, 989-993; Lomax, *Reconquest of Spain*, p. 123.
[55]González, *Alfonso VIII*, I, 994.
[56]González, *Alfonso VIII*, I, 987, 995, 997-1002; Gorosterratzu, *de Rada*, pp. 74, 172-173.

crusaders to aid him, urging him to have full confidence in God and make no truce with the infidel until they were defeated in the great battle now impending. On April 5 the Pope issued a ringing call to all in Spain and France to support the crusade. Thousands responded; and though the kings of León and Navarra did not, they dared not strike against Castile while she carried the banner of Christendom.[57]

In three of the four great theaters of action—Spain, England, and Germany—the decisive turning point was reached in the year 1212. Only the outcome of the Albigensian Crusade remained in doubt. The extraordinary emotional intensity of that year for Christendom, with two entirely different crusades in progress and widely preached—along with the continuing needs of what remained of the Kingdom of Jerusalem for support in the east—was probably reponsible for the heartrending tragedy of the Children's Crusade which occurred that year, when wild, heedless enthusiasm carried off thousands of children convinced that God would personally lead them to the reconquest of the Holy Land by opening the sea before them, as He had done for Moses and his people in their flight from Egypt. Every responsible Christian leader, clerical and lay, was appalled by the Children's Crusade and tried to stop it, but the deluded children would listen to no one. Only gradually did their disillusionment come, and when it did they were hundreds of miles from homes to which most of them were never able to get back.[58]

If we may see Satan's hand in the carrying off of the children by the distorted dream of a crusade of their own, we may surely see God's hand in the founding, in Holy Week of that same year 1212, of that great Franciscan sisterhood, the Poor Clares, by one of St. Francis' most devoted followers, St. Clare of Assisi.[59]

Of the three victories won for Christendom that year, the first was the complete and magnificent triumph of the crusade in Spain. In what has been called—probably with some exaggeration, in view of how many strong competitors it has for the title—the most important battle of the entire 770-year War of the Reconquest, at Las Navas de Tolosa just south of the Pass of the Overthrow of the Infidel Dogs, a heavily outnumbered, mostly Spanish army routed the Almohad host. This signal defeat ended forever the danger of a new Muslim drive north of Andalusia and Granada to regain any of the dominion over the Christians which they had lost in the Reconquest up to that point.

---

[57]González, *Alfonso VIII*, I, 747-748, 998, 1002-1005, 1009; González, *Alfonso IX*, pp. 143-144; Gorosterratzu, *de Rada*, pp. 79-80; Lomax, *Reconquest of Spain*, pp. 124-125.

[58]Setton, *Crusades*, II, 325-342.

[59]Englebert, *St. Francis*, pp. 160-163, 382-384; Jorgensen, *St. Francis*, pp. 100-115; Moorman, *Franciscan Order*, pp. 32-34; Nesta de Robeck, St. Clare of Assisi (Milwaukee, 1951), pp. 34-37.

The victory at Las Navas de Tolosa was achieved almost entirely by the Spanish themselves; most of the French crusaders had left for home ten days before the battle, complaining of the heat and shortages of food. Blocked at the Pass by Moorish defensive positions, the Spanish Christians were led around those positions over a hidden mountain track by a ragged, unknown shepherd who, it was said, was never seen again afterward. At midnight July 16, 1212 the crusading army confessed, heard Mass and a sermon by Archbishop de Rada, received Communion, then took up their arms. The battle lasted most of the day, at such close range that it was fought mainly with lances, swords and maces rather than with arrows. After King Alfonso VIII had almost lost hope and was preparing for a heroic death on the field, the battle was won by a charge led by Archbishop de Rada, carrying beside the banners of Castile a picture of the Blessed Virgin Mary.[60]

In England that same summer, King John learned just before undertaking a new campaign against Wales that there was a widespread plot against him by his own noblemen, involving his assassination. Thus made suddenly and alarmingly aware of the weakness of his position, John informed Rome in November that he was now ready to accept Legate Pandulf's terms, which he had scornfully rejected the previous year.[61]

In Germany, after an imperial diet meeting at Nuremberg proclaimed young Frederick II of Sicily, son of former Hohenstaufen Emperor Henry VI, Emperor in place of the excommunicated Otto IV with the strong support of the Pope and the Church, Frederick rushed north with only a small personal escort. By a combination of sheer youthful audacity and charismatic personal appeal, he gained the support of several of the north Italian and south German cities despite having almost no military force in being. By November he was formally allied with Philip II of France against Otto IV and his relative, King John of England; in December he was proclaimed emperor by a diet in Frankfurt and crowned at Mainz by its archbishop.[62]

---

[60]González, *Alfonso VIII*, I, 1017-1045; Lomax, *Reconquest of Spain*, pp. 125-127; Joseph F. O'Callaghan, *A History of Medieval Spain* (Ithaca NY, 1975), p. 248; Gorosterratzu, *de Rada*, pp. 101-102. Though some historians state or imply that Pedro II of Aragon was primarily responsible for the victory at Las Navas de Tolosa, he actually remained with the rear guard (some accounts say the left wing) throughout the battle, which was primarily conducted by Alfonso VIII of Castile and won by the charge of the reserve from behind the center led by Archbishop Rodrigo de Rada. (It was a long-standing tradition in Spain—though definitely open to criticism—for bishops, who almost all came from noble families with centuries of experience in warfare, to command in person in battles against the infidel.)

[61]Lane-Poole, *Domesday Book to Magna Carta*, pp. 300, 455-456; Lloyd, *History of Wales*, p. 639; Cheney, *Pope Innocent III and England*, pp. 328-329.

[62]Mann, *Popes in the Middle Ages*, XII, 212-216; Tillmann, *Pope Innocent III*, p. 148-149; Ernst Kantorowicz, *Frederick II* (New York, 1931, 1957), pp. 56-63; Lane-Poole, *Domesday Book to Magan Carta*, p. 452.

Time was to show Frederick II to be a far more dangerous enemy of the Church than the much less able and imaginative Otto IV could ever have been; but neither the Pope nor anyone else could have reasonably suspected this in 1212.

Indeed, of the apparent victories of 1212 only the Battle of Las Navas de Tolosa was all that it seemed, truly decisive. For King John's promise to accept the Papal terms of 1211, which included full recognition of Stephen Langton as Archbishop of Canterbury, could not be relied upon until it was entirely fulfilled; John's whole reign and life was a trail of broken promises. Innocent III knew that, as did John's chief temporal enemies, Philip II of France and Prince Llewelyn of Wales. On February 27, 1213 the Pope demanded that John ratify the terms by June 1 and swear to abide by them.[63] He sent Legate Pandulf back, empowered to release John from excommmunication if he believed him sincere;[64] but at the same time he wrote to Langton recalling that John was the son of Henry II who had persecuted St. Thomas Becket of Canterbury, and went on to say:

> We, therefore, fired by zeal for ecclesiastical liberty, charge you by apostolic letter and strictly command you that, if the king should violate the peace which has been restored between him and the English Church, neither you nor any others should presume to anoint or crown any of his heirs to be king.[65]

During 1212 the Albigensian Crusade had settled into a bitter stalemate, with neither Simon de Montfort nor Count Raymond VI able to prevail. King Pedro II of neighboring Aragon, whose sister was married to Count Raymond VI and who had received feudal homage for some of his lands from Count Raymond-Roger of Foix, Count Bertrand of Comminges, and Viscount Gaston of Béarn—all men of evident Cathar sympathies—was urging the Pope to order Simon to stop attacking them at least until they were formally tried and convicted of heresy.[66] The Pope's legates in southern France had not found sufficient evidence proving heresy to undertake such trials, but Arnold Amaury felt morally certain that Count Raymond and the other three abovementioned noblemen were in fact heretics. All the legates were well aware that Simon's limited numbers and relative lack of local support would probably cause the crusade to fail if its leading opponents among the nobility were given any significant opportunity to recover.

Pedro II's presence at the critical battle of Las Navas de Tolosa and his

---

[63]Cheney, *Pope Innocent III and England*, pp. 330, 338-339; Lane-Poole, *Domesday Book to Magna Carta*, p. 436.

[64]Warren, *King John*, p. 202.

[65]*Ibid.*, p. 207.

[66]Setton, *Crusades*, II, 297-298.

reported plans for further action against the Moors in Spain had given him the status and prestige of a true crusader in the eyes of the Pope, while Simon de Montfort's harshness had deeply disturbed him. In January 1213 Innocent III suspended the Albigensian Crusade pending his formal decision on the guilt or innocence of Raymond VI. He reproached Simon for attacking Christians as well as heretics, called for a peace conference, and ordered Simon to desist from attacking territory held in fief from Pedro II until the peace conference had been held. At almost exactly the same time a council of bishops at Lavaur, dominated by Arnold Amaury, rejected the appeals from Pedro II that had been heard and heeded by the Pope, and declared that Raymond VI and the Count of Foix and Viscount Gaston of Béarn were enemies of the Church. Pedro responded by taking Toulouse under his personal protection, condemning Simon de Montfort and refusing to recognize him as holding any lands in fief from himself, and throwing Simon's ambassador into prison.[67]

Both Pedro and the legates sent ambassadors to Rome to plead their opposing cases. A prolonged debate ensued throughout the spring of 1213, finally won by the legates and bishops. On June 1 Pope Innocent III reversed himself, accused Pedro II of lying to him, forbade him to interfere with the Albigensian Crusade, and permitted it to be resumed against the Counts of Foix and Comminges and the Viscount of Béarn, though he did not yet allow Simon de Montfort to gain full title to their lands. But Pedro II of Aragon was now committed and would not turn aside; in August he crossed the Pyrenees with his army and joined the rebel counts, including Raymond, at Toulouse.[68]

Simon and Arnold Amaury had been hoping for a major new infusion of help from the north in the form of an army led by Crown Prince Louis of France, an ambitious young man who showed much more interest in such an enterprise than his cautious father Philip II. But Philip was very much concerned about England, and hoped to take advantage of King John's conflict with the Pope to secure that whole country for his son, who in the spring of 1213 announced a claim to the English throne. To make it more likely that he would receive the Pope's support against England, Philip II finally took his rejected Queen Ingeborg back, though he never actually lived with her as man and wife. During May a French invasion fleet of several hundred ships was assembled at Damme, the port of Bruges in Flanders. Committing himself to this undertaking, Prince Louis rejected the proposed march south to aid Simon, who was therefore left on his own against Pedro II of Aragon and the Cathars and

---

[67]*Ibid.*, II, 298-299; Sumption, *Albigensian Crusade*, pp. 157-160; Wakefield, *Heresy, Crusade and Inquisition in Southern France*, p. 108.

[68]Sumption, *Albigensian Crusade*, pp. 162-163; Mann, *Popes in the Middle Ages*, XIII, 253-255; Setton, *Crusades*, II, 300; Wakefield, *Heresy, Crusade and Inquisition in Southern France*, pp. 108-109.

their sympathizers led by Raymond of Toulouse.[69]

As it turned out there was no invasion of England, because the Count of Flanders allied with John and a combined English-Flemish fleet destroyed most of the invasion fleet at Damme May 30,[70] and because in that same eventful month John met Papal legate Pandulf near Dover with the astonishing offer to resign England to the Pope and receive it back from his as a fief, along with a pledge to pay a large money indemnity to the Pope and the full acceptance of Stephen Langton as Archbishop of Canterbury. Pandulf instantly accepted the offer, and from the moment he learned of it the Pope became a partisan of John.[71] It was the greatest mistake of Innocent III's pontificate for which he was directly responsible; he seemed to take John's action entirely at face value despite his very bad personal record, and by so doing soon alienated not only most of the English nobility and public, but his own archbishop whom he had so long insisted on installing at Canterbury.

Left entirely on his own by these developments, Simon de Montfort with only about 800 cavalry had to face a heavily reinforced enemy with more than 2,000 cavalry and more than 15,000 infantry marching upon him in southern France early in September 1213. Reaching the small fortified town of Muret about twelve miles south of Toulouse, held by Simon's men, the militia from Toulouse attacked. Simon routed them with a surprise counterattack and put his men into the town. Pedro II of Aragon brought the main army up and refused all negotiations. Simon heard Mass at midnight before the day of battle, September 13. He remained in prayer long after Mass. At dawn Bishop Fulk of Toulouse spoke to the soldiers, holding up a crucifix, promising remission of sins for all who fell as crusaders this day. Simon followed with a brief exhortation, pointing out that they could only make up for their lack of numbers by remaining constantly on the attack and giving the best possible support to one another. Pedro II had spent his night with a mistress, and could not even stand upright at his army's dawn Mass.[72]

Simon's eight hundred came out of Muret at full gallop and charged across a full mile of open plain in the valley of the Garonne while Pedro's army watched them come as though paralyzed. They struck and scattered his line "like dust before a gale." He and Simon were at the center of the action; Simon's stirrup strap broke and he lost control of his sword. But Simon de Montfort was a giant of a man, a mighty athlete as well as a great general,

---

[69]John W. Baldwin, *The Government of Philip Augustus* (Berkeley CA, 1986), pp. 209-210; Warren, *King John*, p. 203; Sumption, *Albigensian Crusade*, p. 160.

[70]Baldwin, *Government of Philip Augustus*, p. 211; Warren, *King John*, pp. 125, 204-205.

[71]Cheney, *Pope Innocent III and England*, pp. 332-335; Warren, *King John*, pp. 208-209; Mann, *Popes in the Middle Ages*, XIII, 137-139.

[72]Sumption, *Albigensian Crusade*, pp. 163-167; Setton, *Crusades*, II, 300-302.

whose brawn matched his brain. He drove off his enemies with his fists until he could regain his sword and his balance upon his horse. Pedro was in no such condition, particularly after his night of debauchery; he was overborne and unhorsed, crying fruitlessly from the ground "I am the King!" as the swinging swords and star-headed maces and iron-shod hooves took his life. The Battle of Muret lasted just twenty minutes.[73] Against odds of at least twenty to one,[74] Simon and his crusaders gained the victory. It was an ugly end for one of the victors of Las Navas de Tolosa, and a dishonoring of the cause for which the Spanish Reconquest had been fought for five hundred years.

Toulouse remained defiant toward Simon and pleaded for mercy from the Pope. In January 1214 Innocent III sent yet another legate—his sixth to southern France—Cardinal Peter of Benevento, to reconcile any there who were willing to submit and seemed in good faith. He declared Toulouse under Papal protection. Simon was directed to restore Pedro's six-year-old son James, now titular King of Aragon, to his homeland—where he was to become one of the greatest Spanish reconquerors. In April Cardinal Peter ended the interdict on Toulouse and reconciled Count Raymond and the Counts of Foix and Comminges, but Raymond had to agree to go into temporary exile while his property claims were considered by the Church.[75]

The Catharist heresy still survived, but Simon's victory had imperilled it as never before, while the Pope's forbearance for the time being discouraged further atrocities. In June 1214 St. Dominic, who remained very active preaching the Faith in the midst of this struggle—and remained personally close to Simon de Montfort—presided at the marriage of Simon's son Amaury and the daughter of Prince Louis of France.[76]

Two months later the Papal legate in Aragon called a meeting of Catalan and Aragonese bishops and noblemen to set up a regency for seven-year-old James, Pedro II's son, and he was given into the custody of the crusading order of Templars at the fortress of Monzón. That summer Alfonso VIII of Castile, the victor of Las Navas de Tolosa, gravely ill, set out on his last campaign, in the hallowed tradition of the Reconquest that a Christian king should die with his boots on, marching against the infidel. That is what his grandfather Alfonso "the Emperor" had done, and that is what Alfonso VIII did. All summer, with his erstwhile rival Alfonso IX of León by his side, he ranged southern Spain, laying unsuccessful siege to Baeza, supporting Alfonso IX in his capture of the fortress of Alcántara (which he gave to the crusading Order of Calatrava) but unable to prevent his repulse from Cáceres and Mérida in the harsh dry hills of

---

[73]Sumption, *Albigensian Crusade*, pp. 167-169.
[74]Setton, *Crusades*, II, 302.
[75]Sumption, *Albigensian Crusade*, pp. 171-172; Setton, *Crusades*, II, 304; Mann, *Popes in the Middle Ages*, XIII, 256.
[76]Vicaire, *St. Dominic*, p. 145.

Extremadura. During that summer Alfonso IX's eldest son Fernando (born of his first wife, Teresa of Portugal) died, making his new heir the son of his second marriage (with Berenguela of Castile), who was also named Fernando.[77]

On October 6, 1214 Alfonso VIII of Castile, aged 59, died on the road, on his way to meet the King of Portugal. His successor was his boy son Henry I, aged 11.[78] But three years later young Henry was struck in the head by a stone while playing a game and died of it. Since Alfonso VIII had left no other sons, Princess Berenguela was next in line for the throne. She promptly renounced it in favor of her son Fernando, already heir to León, so that in his person he would reunite the kingdoms of Castile and León when Alfonso IX of León died.[79] This Fernando, later canonized, was to be one of Spain's greatest heroes and victors of the Reconquest.

By October 1213 the reconciliation between King John of England and the Pope was complete, and all prospect of Papal cooperation with Philip II of France against him was gone.[80] (After extended arguments over the terms and obligations of John's restitution of property taken from the Church, the long interdict on the church in England, which had lasted more than six years, was at last brought to an end the following June.)[81] John immediately took advantage of his changed status to try to regain his lost domains in France. Despite the grumbling of his barons, he raised a substantial army and landed with it in Poitou in western France. John had made alliance with Otto IV, who still claimed to be Emperor despite his great reverses at the hands of Frederick II, and with Counts Ferrand of Flanders and Renaud of Boulogne. The army of Otto and the two counts in Flanders so threatened Philip II from the east that he was unable to act against John in the west. Therefore John made a triumphal march through Poitou, with very little opposition. He brought his old enemies the Lusignans to terms, and took Nantes at the mouth of the Loire in a surprise attack. But in the course of the campaign John became steadily less popular both with his own barons and those in the part of France he claimed. Near Angers at the beginning of July 1214 they suddenly deserted him, and he had to flee to La Rochelle on the coast.[82]

[77]O'Callaghan, *Medieval Spain*, p. 334; Lomax, *Reconquest of Spain*, pp. 130-131; González, *Alfonso VIII*, p. 751.

[78]Lomax, *Reconquest of Spain*, p. 131; González, *Alfonso VIII*, p. 752.

[79]O'Callaghan, *Medieval Spain*, p. 335; González, *Alfonso VIII*, p. 759; González, *Alfonso IX*, pp. 173-174, 177.

[80]Cheney, *Pope Innocent III and England*, pp. 349-350, 361; Warren *King John*, p. 203.

[81]Cheney, *Pope Innocent III and England*, pp. 349-354; Mann, *Popes in the Middle Ages*, XIII, 143-144.

[82]Lane-Poole, *Domesday Book to Magna Carta*, pp. 462-463, 465-467; Warren, *King John*, pp. 217-219, 221-222; Baldwin, *Government of Philip Augustus*, pp. 212-214; Cheney, *Pope Innocent III and England*, p. 361; J. C. Holt, *Magna Carta* (Cambridge, England, 1965), pp. 133-134.

Later that same month, on the 27th, the main French army met the armies of Otto IV, Flanders and Boulogne near the Flemish town of Bouvines. Unlike many medieval battles among Christians, Bouvines was a fight to the finish. Philip II of France, bearing the legendary Oriflamme, was pitted against the lackluster army of the discredited Emperor and the disorderly feudal host of the two counts. The lack of cohesion and good leadership on the part of the allies more than negated their slight advantage in numbers. Philip II, for once in his cold and calculating life, showed real heroism, while Otto fled ignominiously from the field. The French victory at Bouvines ended any realistic prospect for reviving the Anglo-Norman dominion in northern France, though the English claims and interventions in the west and southwest of France would long continue.[83]

King John had not been at Bouvines, but had been abandoned by most of his own men. He returned to England appearing almost as vulnerable as before his reconciliation with the Pope. In November a group of northern barons demanded that he restore their "ancient liberties," producing a charter of his great-grandfather Henry I far back in 1100 which they demanded that he confirm. He refused them, seeing their demand as simply a disguise for rebellion; but later that month he granted a charter to the church, guaranteeing freedom of election of bishops and abbots to all cathedral chapters and monasteries in England and Wales—the freedom he had denied in the election of the archbishop of Canterbury. In March 1215 Innocent III welcomed and praised this action of King John, and forbade the English barons under pain of excommunication to conspire or rebel against their king.[84]

Before hearing of this pronouncement by Innocent III, a group of about fifty English barons, mostly from the north of England, renewed their demand for a royal charter limiting the king's powers, which they insisted (with much reason) he had frequently abused to their detriment and to the detriment of the rights and liberties of all his subjects. When John again refused a charter, the barons who had demanded it declared war on him May 3. At about this time the Pope's praise for the king and prohibition on conspiracy or rebellion against him by the barons arrived, and John called upon Archbishop Langton to enforce it. But the great Archbishop, himself an Englishman and a victim of John's duplicity and tyranny, saw that the barons had a case, even if they had chosen the wrong moment and means to make it. He courageously suspended the operation of the Pope's decree on the ground of the lapse of time and numerous important events that had occurred since its issuance, and offered

---

[83]Baldwin, *Government of Philip Augustus*, pp. 214-219; Lane-Poole, *Domesday Book to Magna Carta*, pp. 467-468; Warren, *King John*, pp. 223-224.

[84]Warren, *King John*, pp. 226-231; Cheney, *Pope Innocent III and England*, pp. 168-169, 363-365, 370-371.

himself as arbiter between the barons and the king.[85]

On May 17 the barons seized London, and John decided he had no choice but to come to an agreement with them.[86] There followed in mid-June King John's famous meeting with the barons at the meadow of Runnymede near London. Archbishop Langton was present, acting as mediator and arbiter,[87] and very likely played a major role in crafting the agreement made there, whose core was the royal charter guaranteeing rights and liberties, known as Magna Carta.

Magna Carta protected all classes against arbitrary imprisonment and dispossession of their goods by the King's order. The seemingly irrepressible "debunking" tendency of many historians and historical writers, which feeds on the fame of an individual or event whether or not that fame is deserved, has brought much belittling of Magna Carta, often presented as a document that helped only the great barons. On the contrary, Magna Carta explicitly addressed itself to "all free men of our realm" (cap. 39). Its most significant guarantees were specifically stated to apply not only to the barons but to all those dependent on them (cap. 60) and to all free men including villeins, merchants, and yeomen (cap. 9).[88] In the words of J. C. Holt's magisterial and comprehensive study published in 1965, Magna Carta "acknowledged non-baronial interests far more than most of the continental concessions and it covered a wider range of such interests more thoroughly than any other similar grant."[89] The High Middle Ages, the time of the glory of Christendom, did not approve or recognize as morally permissible the absolute rule of a king or the unlimited privileges of a small group of noblemen. It fostered an organic society which no man could despoil at his pleasure. Magna Carta is one of its finest monuments.

This great achievement was nearly undone by the stubbornness of Pope Innocent III in defending the king he still thought of as a kind of prodigal son just returned to the fold. Although separated by four to six weeks of message delay from the fast-breaking events in England, unwilling to trust the judgment of the man whose installation as Archbishop of Canterbury he had unwaveringly demanded for six stormy years, Innocent III compounded the error of his earlier acceptance of John's surrender of England to him and giving it back as a feudal fief, by denouncing Magna Carta (which he saw as tainted by the sin of rebellion) and suspending Archbishop Langton.[90]

---

[85]Lane-Poole, *Domesday Book to Magna Carta*, pp. 469-470; Warren, *King John*, pp. 231-234; Cheney, *Pope Innocent III and England*, pp. 370, 372-375; Holt, *Magna Carta*, p. 187.

[86]Warren, *King John*, pp. 235-236.

[87]Holt, *Magna Carta*, p. 187.

[88]*Ibid.*, pp. 180-185.

[89]*Ibid.*, p. 183.

[90]Cheney, *Pope Innocent III and England*, pp. 380-387; Mann, *Popes in the Middle*

Thus encouraged, John renewed his war with the barons. They called on the French for aid, and Philip II, while holding cautiously aloof personally, let his son bring it, along with a claim to the throne of England. The foreign invasion gained John additional support; England was split down the middle. But the war abruptly ended when John died of a digestive ailment in October 1216, to be succeeded by his nine-year-old son Henry III.[91] Most of the country rallied to the appealing young king, helpless in his own person but with a formidable and eloquent defender and advocate in the regent, William Marshal, England's most famous knight; and by then Innocent III too was dead and his successor Honorius III and all but a few of the most bellicose barons wanted peace. One of its terms was the reissuance of Magna Carta in the name of the new king, with only a few nonessential changes. Solemnly reconfirmed in 1225 when King Henry III was ruling on his own, Magna Carta was laid down as a cornerstone of English law and liberty.[92]

Campaigning in the south of France in the spring of 1215, between his two military undertakings against England, Prince Louis of France joined in the Albigensian Crusade and helped Simon de Montfort secure Toulouse. Its orthodox Bishop Fulk was restored, and immediately installed St. Dominic and his campanions—now numbering six—to preach the true Faith there. But the Pope had rejected the request of 23 bishops meeting in council at Montpellier with Papal legate Cardinal Peter of Benevento, to award Toulouse immediately and unconditionally to Simon by dispossessing Raymond VI as Count. Innocent III was preparing an ecumenical council in Rome in November and wanted it to help decide the much-debated and enduring question of Raymond's dispossession. In October, as Bishop Fulk and St. Dominic arrived in Rome for the council, the Pope received them in audience and at their request confirmed the Dominican Order of Preachers and their convent of Dominican sisters at Prouille in the heart of Cathar country.[93]

On November 11 the Fourth Lateran Council convened—the summit of Innocent III's great pontificate, and his supreme achievement. Its sessions continued until the end of the month, and its decrees were published in December. Both St. Francis and St. Dominic were present, along with 412 archbishops and bishops and over 800 abbots or their representatives. No such

Ages, XIII, 148-150; Warren, *King John*, pp. 244-246; Holt, *Magna Carta*, pp. 265-266.

[91]Lane-Poole, *Domesday Book to Magna Carta*, pp. 479, 483-486; Warren, *King John*, pp. 248-249, 251-256; Baldwin, *Government of Philip Augustus*, pp. 332-333.

[92]Maurice Powicke, *The Thirteenth Century, 1216-1307*, 2nd ed. (Oxford History of England, Volume IV) (Oxford, 1962), pp. 1-8, 28-30; Holt, *Magna Carta*, pp. 271-272; Sidney Painter, *William Marshal, Knight-Errant, Baron, and Regent of England* (Baltimore, 1933), pp. 228-233.

[93]Vicaire, *St. Dominic*, pp. 110, 165-166, 170-172, 178-179, 191-195; Sumption, *Albigensian Crusade*, pp. 178; Setton, *Crusades*, II, 304-306.

magnificent assembly had been held in Christendom for centuries.[94]

The former Byzantine empire was well represented. Latin Patriarch Gervasius of Constantinople was there, along with the Patriarch of Jerusalem, the Maronite patriarch, the Jacobite Patriarch of Alexandria and a representative of its Melchite patriarch, and a representatives of the sick Patriarch of Antioch. But the Greek Orthodox schism was far from ended, despite the Council's provision for maintaining the Byzantine rite in all eastern churches which desired it and the naming of the patriarch of Constantinople the second after the Pope. Only one former Greek Orthodox bishop attended, Theodore of Negroponte (Euboea). Though the Westerners held Constantinople and had extended their control over the greater part of Greece, and the Greeks had given some genuine support to the current Latin emperor Henry, most Greeks remained firm in their adherence to their schismatic church. Following the death in 1206 of John Kamateros, the Greek patriarch in office at the time of the fall of Constantinople, the Greek church had split into two factions, each with an archbishop claiming to be the rightful patriarch of Constantinople, dependent on the two principal Byzantine successor states: that of Greek imperial pretender Theodore Lascaris at Nicaea in Asia Minor and that of Michael Dukas, ruler of Epirus. So far as the East was concerned, the council was ecumenical more in form than in substance. Its achievements were in the West.[95]

Pope Innocent III opened the Council with the words of Christ at the Last Supper, "I have desired to eat this pasch with you before I suffer," to which the Pope added, "before I die." (He was still only 54, but was to die before another year was out.) He called for a new crusade, and for a great reform of the Church. He quoted the vision of the prophet Ezekiel, of six men approaching Jerusalem with deadly weapons in their hands, while God called to another clad in linen to go through the holy city and mark with the sign of the Tau—a letter in the shape of a cross—all those who regretted the abominations done within it, and then sent the six to smite all who did not bear the Tau.[96] Then the great Pope turned from Holy Scripture to his own words, with blazing eyes flinging down the challenge to the spiritual stewards of Christendom:

> And who are the six men charged with the divine vengeance? They are you, fathers of the Council, who with all the arms at your disposal—excommuncication, depositions, suspension and interdict—shall smite without pity those unmarked with the atoning cross who persist in dishonoring the city of Christendom.[97]

---

[94]Mann, *Popes in the Middle Ages*, XIII, 291-293; Englebert, *St. Francis*, pp. 194, 198.
[95]Gill, *Byzantium and the Papacy*, pp. 34-36, 43-47.
[96]Mann, *Popes in the Middle Ages*, XIII, 293; Englebert, *St. Francis*, pp. 194-195.
[97]Englebert, *St. Francis*, p. 195.

St. Francis was moved to his soul by these words of the Vicar of Christ. For the rest of his life he made the letter Tau the emblem of his order, using it as a signature, placing it upon his door and his writings. During the council St. Dominic dreamed that the Blessed Virgin Mary was presenting him to Christ, accompanied by one other man whom he had never seen, but who shared his mission of converting the world. Meeting St. Francis, he recognized him as this man, and went up to him to say: "Let us be friends, and nothing on earth can prevail against us."[98]

A few days later the two great saints met again at the residence of Cardinal Ugolino dei Conti, a relative of the Pope who had been the chief ecclesiastical patron of St. Francis, and was devoted to him and to St. Clare. The Cardinal proposed that some of the friar priests who followed Francis and Dominic be made bishops, but both saints rejected this prospect unequivocally, as incompatible with the apostolic poverty they so strongly emphasized. Dominic proposed to Francis that their nascent orders be combined, and live under the same rule. We are not told that Francis refused him, but he certainly did not agree; he was too vividly aware of the uniqueness of the Franciscan vocation. Dominic knew that he stood in the presence of a holiness so great that he could never expect to see its like in his lifetime. He begged Francis to give him his cord, and when he did so, at once put it around his waist. When Francis had departed, Dominic said to those around him: "I tell you truthfully there is not a religious who would not profit by following in the footsteps of so holy a man."[99]

The council proceeded to condemn the false, anti-life religion of the Cathars, urged the establishment of schools of theology to better prepare priests to teach doctrinal truth to the faithful, commanded all Catholics to confess and receive Holy Communion at least once a year, and issued decrees to curb the wealth and ostentation of bishops and to renew and strengthen the discipline of clerical celibacy. It prohibited the formation of new religious orders, which were thought to be proliferating excessively, but recognized the Franciscans as already approved. The Dominicans had not yet been approved as an order, though their initial activities had been authorized.[100]

There was prolonged discussion over the issue of divesting Count Raymond VI of Toulouse of his lands and giving them to Simon de Montfort. Count Raymond found unexpected support from his old enemy Arnold Amaury, the former head of the Cistercian order and Papal legate in southern France, now Bishop of Narbonne, who had clashed with Simon over the control of lands in the Narbonne area. Raymond was present, but said little; Simon was

---

[98]*Ibid.*, pp. 196-199 (quotation on p. 199).
[99]*Ibid.*, pp. 199-201 (quotation on p. 201).
[100]*Ibid.*, pp. 195-196; Moorman, *Franciscan Order*, pp. 29-30; Cheney, *Pope Innocent III and England*, p. 407.

not present, but represented by his brother Guy and above all by Bishop Fulk of Toulouse, who was eloquent in his behalf:[101]

> How can you bring yourself to dispossess Simon de Montfort? He is a faithful servant of the Church, entirely devoted to your cause. He had put up with hardship and exhaustion, thrown himself into the battle against heretics and mercenaries.[102]

All the other bishops from the region, except Arnold Amaury, supported Fulk. Though both the Pope and the Council were reluctant, in the end they declared Raymond rightfully deprived of all his lands in Languedoc because of his "inability to govern his dominions in accordance with the Faith," and gave those lands to Simon de Montfort. Raymond was ordered to stay out of Languedoc, but was allowed to keep his lands in Provence, east of the Rhone River which divided Provence from Languedoc, where the Cathars had not attained significant strength.[103]

The following March Simon took formal possession of Toulouse, with many of the lesser lords of the region swearing fealty to him. He then went with Bishop Fulk to do homage to Philip II of France for the lands of Toulouse. But Raymond VI would not accept the verdict of the Pope and Council, nor would his son Raymond VII, now nineteen and so far as anyone could tell untainted by heresy or collaboration with heretics. Father and son laid siege to Beaucaire on the west bank of the Rhone and took it late in April. In June Simon arrived to besiege Beaucaire in his turn, but had to raise the siege when told that the two Raymonds were marching on Toulouse. He arrived in time to forestall them, levied a heavy indemnity upon the city, seized hundreds of its leading citizens as hostages, and destroyed most of its remaining defenses.[104]

In January 1217 Fulk resigned as Bishop of Toulouse, perhaps despairing of ever bringing peace to it.[105] In September of that year Raymond VI returned to Toulouse in Simon's absence, and was welcomed back. The hard work of thousands quickly rebuilt the essential fortifications of the city. Simon's troops still held the citadel, but Simon was unable to penetrate the city. A fiercely

---

[101]Sumption, *Albigensian Crusade*, pp. 179-180; Setton, *Crusades*, II, 306-307; Wakefield, *Heresy, Crusade and Inquisition in Southern France*, pp. 114-115.

[102]Sumption, *Albigensian Crusade*, p. 180.

[103]*Ibid.*, p. 181.

[104]*Ibid.*, pp. 181-189; Setton, *Crusades*, II, 308-311; Wakefield, *Heresy, Crusade and Inquisition in Southern France*, pp. 117-118; Baldwin, *Government of Philip Augustus*, p. 337. Though it has often been asserted or implied that Simon de Montfort violated terms of capitulation contracted with Bishop Fulk's personal guarantee, in fact we do not have the specific provisions of the capitulation, and Simon's punishments did not put anyone to death or deprive anyone permanently of his liberty. There is no reason to suppose that the terms of capitulation debarred him from taking the steps he took.

[105]Vicaire, *St. Dominic*, p. 275.

contested siege followed, with atrocities on both sides, continuing through the fall and on through the winter of 1218. The siege lines could not be drawn tight enough to keep reinforcements from reaching Toulouse, but Simon's crusaders were also reinforced from the north of France. In the spring a flood damaged some of the improvised defenses of Toulouse, and Simon began construction of "an enormous cat, under the protection of which ditches might be filled in and the walls approached and surmounted." But the besieged now had siege engines of their own. In June one of these, called a trebuchet, smashed the cat; a few days later a catapult flung a stone from the city walls which struck Simon squarely on the helmet and killed him instantly. His son Amaury failed in a last assault July 1, 1218. For the time being the resistance to the crusade, in which the heretics were much aided by nationalistic passions and the personal loyalty of most of the people of Toulouse (many of whom remained Catholics) to their ancient noble house, had triumphed.[106]

In midsummer 1216, always a time of high mortality even for those born and bred in Italy, the great Pope Innocent III fell suddenly ill of a fever at Perugia near Rome. Within a few days he had breathed his last, though he was only 56 years old. The Cardinals assembled at once. Just three days after Innocent's death they elected as Pope the elderly Cardinal Cencio Savelli, who had been *camerlengus* or first minister of Innocent III. Cardinal Savelli as Pope took the name Honorius III. He regarded his predecessor as an inspired leader of Christendom and a saint and sought to follow and imitate him in all his policies, though Honorius III, whose great desire was peace, was a much gentler and less strong-willed man than Innocent III. But in one respect at least Honorius III was a true militant throughout his eleven-year pontificate, surprisingly long in view of his age: he never ceased to press for a new crusade that would reverse the verdict of the Horns of Hattin and the failure of the Third Crusade and bring a new Christian triumph in the East. He had been in office only six months when he commissioned the ablest and devoted of his cardinals, Ugolino Conti—the relative of Innocent III and friend of St. Francis who was to be the successor of Honorius III as Pope—to preach in northern Italy a new crusade, known to historians as the Fifth.[107]

Along with reviving the crusade, Honorius III's principal accomplishment as Pope was to give his certification and full support to the new Dominican order and to preside over the difficult, often traumatic process of organizing the Franciscan order into a religious institution that could endure once its unique founder had passed from Earth to Heaven. For St. Francis of Assisi had a

---

[106]Sumption, *Albigensian Crusade*, pp. 191-199; Setton, *Crusades*, II, 311-314 (quotation on p. 314); Wakefield, *Heresy, Crusade and Inquisition in Southern France*, pp. 118-122.

[107]Mann, *Popes in the Middle Ages*, XIII, 300-302; XIV (London, 1925), pp. 4-21; Vicaire, *St. Dominic*, pp. 226, 326.

charism perhaps more intense than that given to any other man since the apostles; he and his first followers truly believed that they could live out their lives almost like angels—as indeed they could, so long as St. Francis was with them. But in all that it creates, most certainly including religious orders, the Church of Christ builds for centuries and millennia, knowing the weakness of its human members and the rarity of great saints. It was Cardinal Ugolino Conti, chief advisor of Pope Honorius III on all matters pertaining to the Franciscans, who during Honorius III's pontificate and his own pontificate that succeeded it, made it possible for the Franciscan order to be all that it has since been to the Church since those glorious days of the climax of Christendom. In 1220 he was specifically designated by Pope Honorius as "protector, governor, and corrector of the [Franciscan] brotherhood."[108] It was on his recommendation that Pope Honorius III in August 1218 authorized the establishment of convents of Poor Clares—followers of St. Clare of Assisi who were, in effect, women Franciscans also living in poverty and mendicancy—and he provided them with their first rule.[109]

Pope Honorius III gave full recognition to the Dominican order in December 1216, the prohibition on new religious orders just enacted by the Fourth Lateran Council with his approval being evaded by their accepting the Augustinian rule. But that theirs was in fact a new religious order, no one could seriously doubt. St. Dominic was formally appointed its head, and the Dominicans were given a universal preaching mission.[110] Though a mendicant order, like the Franciscans in their total dependence on gifts from others rather than on income from property they owned, their mission was much more intellectual than the Franciscan mission, devoted not only to preaching but to the study and teaching of theology and philosophy which are required as foundations of good preaching. The Dominican vocation became the primary Catholic intellectual apostolate of the High Middle Ages, unchallenged by any other order until the coming of the Jesuits in the sixteenth century. It is surely no accident that this was the order to which St. Thomas Aquinas belonged.

The Franciscan general or "chapter" meeting in May 1217 set up the first real organization of the order, with six provinces in Italy, two in France, and one each in Germany, Spain, and Palestine. St. Francis had long had a keen interest in the Holy Places in Palestine, whose care has been a major Franciscan apostolate; he had always wanted to make a pilgrimage to Jerusalem himself, and was to do so during the Fifth Crusade. One of Francis' earliest companions—and the only one gifted with strong management skills—was appointed Minister General in 1217, in effect and in authority the second man

---

[108]Moorman, *Franciscan Order*, pp. 46-48; Englebert, *St. Francis*, pp. 199-200, 247-248 (the quotation is from p. 247); Jorgensen, *St. Francis*, pp. 158-159.

[109]Jorgensen, *St. Francis*, pp. 159-160; de Robeck, *St. Clare*, pp. 56-57.

[110]Vicaire, *St. Dominic*, pp. 219-221, 226-232.

in the order after Francis himself. St. Francis said: "I have chosen him as mother." His name was Elias Bombarone, and he was to play a great and much controverted role in the history of the Franciscan order in St. Francis' later years and after his death.[111]

It was probably at just this time, at Pentecost at the beginning of the last year of the Albigensian Crusade under Simon de Montfort when the great popular resistance was roused against it that culminated in Simon's death, that St. Dominic concluded that the work of his friar preachers should no longer be exclusively or even primarily concentrated in southern France, that they must now undertake their broader, universal mission. In August the Dominicans met at Prouille, the convent St. Dominic had founded in the heart of Cathar territory, the last time they were all together in Southern France. So the universal mission of the Franciscan and Dominican orders was first actually put into effect in the same year.[112]

In that same May a fleet carrying men from the Rhineland and the Frisian Islands, primarily assembled by the inspiring preaching of the scholasticus Oliver, left Vlerdingen in the Netherlands to go to the Holy Land to undertake the Fifth Crusade. In July crusaders set out from central Europe, led by King Andrew of Hungary and Duke Leopold of Austria. Pope Honorius directed Andrew and Leopold to meet with the titular King of Jerusalem, John of Brienne, and the papal legate Cardinal Pelagius on the island of Cyprus in September, and urged crusaders from Italy to take ship for Cyprus.[113]

But no such meeting occurred on Cyprus—the first example of the woeful confusion of leadership that was to characterize the whole of the Fifth Crusade. The army led by King Andrew and Duke Leopold boarded ships at Split on the Dalmatian coast of the Adriatic Sea and made their way by contingents to Acre in Palestine, while the fleet carrying the Germans and Frisians stopped at Lisbon. The Germans responded to the appeal of Bishop Suger of Lisbon to stay long enough to help the Portuguese take the great Moorish fortress of Alcaçer do Sal, just as the men of the Second Crusade in 1147 had helped the Portuguese reconquer Lisbon itself. With their help the fortress was taken October 21, and the German crusaders then spent the winter in Lisbon. The Frisian crusaders rejected the stay in Portugal as a diversion from their mission and sailed on, but only as far as the Papal states in Italy, where they spent the winter. The central European crusaders left Acre in November and the following month assaulted a strong new Muslim fortress on Mount Tabor, the probable site of Christ's Transfiguration, but were repulsed. At the end of the

---

[111]Moorman, *Franciscan Order*, pp. 30-31, 62; Englebert, *St. Francis*, pp. 215-216.

[112]Vicaire, *St. Dominic*, pp. 233-235.

[113]Setton, *Crusades*, II, 387-388, 395; James M. Powell, *Anatomy of a Crusade 1213-1221* (Philadelphia, 1986), pp. 123-124; Joseph P. Donovan, *Pelagius and the Fifth Crusade* (Philadelphia, 1950), pp. 30-32.

year 500 crusaders, mostly Hungarian, were ambushed near Sidon, with many killed, following which King Andrew of Hungary returned home with little accomplished. The Templars settled down to build the enormous, impregnable Castle Pilgrim on the Athlit promontory just south of Haifa.[114]

In May 1218 the German crusaders who had fought in Portugal and the Frisian crusaders who had wintered in Rome finally arrived at Acre, where Duke Leopold and King John met with the scholasticus Oliver, the heads of the military orders, and the patriarch of Jerusalem. It was probably at this time that the decision was made to adopt the strategy of Richard the Lion-hearted in the latter phase of the Third Crusade and make Egypt the chief military objective, on the grounds that even if the crusaders took Jerusalem they could not hold it until the Muslim power in Egypt was curbed or conquered.[115]

Consequently in late May the crusaders sailed from Acre to Damietta two miles up the Nile on the right bank of its main branch flowing northeastward into the Mediterranean. They encamped on an island called Jizat Dimyat, easy to defend but across the Nile from Damietta, and designated King John of Jerusalem their leader. Assaults on Damietta began immediately. A great chain stretched across the Nile from Damietta prevented the crusaders from moving upstream until after many attempts they captured the west chain tower, on their side of the Nile, in late August. The news of their success is said to have caused the death of old Sultan al-Adil of Egypt; his son al-Kamil succeeded him there, and another son al-Muazzim succeeded in Damascus.[116]

In September Cardinal Pelagius arrived in Egypt. Pope Honorius III had given him full authority to lead the crusade, as Bishop Adhemar of Le Puy had been the papally designated leader of the First Crusade.[117] Muslim counterattacks on Damietta in October were beaten off with the aid of a large force of French crusaders just arrived. A plague struck the crusader camp with much mortality, but they persevered, and in February 1219 the discovery of a conspiracy against al-Kamil caused a temporary abandonment of the Muslim

---

[114]Setton, *Crusades*, II, 388-396; Powell, *Anatomy of a Crusade*, pp. 125-127, 130-133; Stephen Howarth, *The Knights Templar* (New York, 1982), pp. 193-196.

[115]Setton, *Crusades*, II, 396. Powell (*Anatomy of a Crusade*, pp. 137-138) argues that the decision to go to Egypt rather than Jerusalem had already been made; but when and by whom? The campaigning of the crusaders in northern Palestine—at Mount Tabor and elsewhere—and along the coast where the Templars built Castle Pilgrim gives no hint of any plan to attack Egypt at all, let alone concentrate all their forces there, until May 1218.

[116]Setton, *Crusades*, II, 397-402; Powell, *Anatomy of a Crusade*, pp. 138-145; Donovan, *Pelagius and the Fifth Crusade*, pp. 38-43.

[117]Setton, *Crusades*, II, 402; Donovan, *Pelagius and the Fifth Crusade*, pp. 44, 46-49. Donovan and Powell (*Anatomy of a Crusade*, pp. 144-145) argue cogently that Pelagius did not immediately assume command of the Crusade in September, but exerted his authority only gradually, particularly so far as military operations were concerned, in the course of that fall.

positions, enabling the crusaders at last to cross the Nile and place Damietta under close siege.[118]

The conspiracy and its consequences seem to have caused al-Kamil to lose his nerve. He ordered the destruction of the walls of Jerusalem, expecting that the crusaders would soon attack it and believing it could not be held against them. It was probably at this time (February or March 1219) that al-Kamil made for the first time an astonishing offer to the crusaders, later to be several times repeated: to give them back Jerusalem and all of its former kingdom except two fortresses in Moab in southern Palestine commanding the desert road to Egypt, and grant a thirty-year truce, in return for their evacuation of Egypt.[119]

The fact that such an offer would be made at all is amazing enough; the crusaders had secured only the barest, most precarious lodgment in one of the richest and most populous countries in the world, in which they were vastly outnumbered and which no Westerner had a serious prospect of conquering until Napoleon came to Egypt almost six hundred years later. Still more astonishing is the refusal of Cardinal Pelagius, supported by the Italians and the Masters of the Temple and the Hospital, to accept the offer. King John of Jerusalem and the knights from what remained of the crusader kingdoms naturally wanted to accept it, and the French followed King John, himself a Frenchman. But the majority of the leaders of the Fifth Crusade rejected Jerusalem, whose liberation was the fundamental purpose of the crusades, even when the Muslims offered to pay them to take it! The siege of Damietta continued.[120]

No explanation of this incredible folly really makes sense, though many have been suggested. The crusaders had had immense difficulty holding a relatively small amount of territory in Palestine and Syria, in whose cities few Muslims lived. Even in the very unlikely event that the crusaders could conquer Egypt, the possibility of holding it—a country at least three-quarters Muslim (over 90 per cent of its population is Muslim today)—was virtually nil. While Egypt in Muslim hands would always constitute a serious threat to a Christian Kingdom of Jerusalem, if there was no practicable way to remove that threat

---

[118]Setton, *Crusades*, II, 402-406, 409; Powell, *Anatomy of a Crusade*, p. 145-148, 151; Donovan, *Pelagius and the Fifth Crusade*, pp. 49-54.

[119]Among authorities consulted, only Van Cleve in Setton, *Crusades*, II, 409-410, mentions this offer at this time. But he gives convincing reasons for this dating of the first offer by the Muslims to give up Jerusalem, and Powell (*Anatomy of a Crusade*, p. 151), Runciman (*A History of the Crusades*, Volume III [Cambridge, England, 1966], p. 158), and Donovan (*Pelagius and the Fifth Crusade*, p. 55) agree with Van Cleve in Setton (*loc. cit.*) that it was in March 1219 that the dismantling of the walls of Jerusalem began—strong confirming evidence that by then the Muslims were expecting to have to give it up.

[120]Setton, *Crusades*, II, 409-410.

and the crusaders were resolved to have Jerusalem, there was no alternative to living with it. The two fortresses in the Moab desert which the Muslims insisted on retaining might well be used in attacks on Jerusalem, but could also be used simply to keep communications open between Egypt and the Muslim nations of Asia. The two fortresses were hardly more of a threat to Jerusalem than the great Muslim city of Damascus, never taken, not much farther away from the holy city to the northeast than the fortresses were to the south.

Above all, the whole concept and strategy of the Crusades was to focus the public enthusiasm of Christendom on regaining and holding the city where Christ had lived, preached, died, and risen from the tomb. A strong crusader kingdom in Jerusalem drew Muslim aggression away from other Christian countries and provided the means for counterattacking them whenever they might attempt such aggression. But no Christian kings or lords would or could maintain a Christian kingdom in the midst of Islam acting by themselves, nor could such a kingdom survive on its resources alone. It must have continuing support from European Christendom. That support could only be maintained if its primary objective continued to be maintaining Christian control of Jerusalem. Already the Christian people of Europe had seen the Third Crusade diverted from Jerusalem toward Egypt and the Fourth Crusade diverted destructively to Constantinople. Now the Fifth Crusade had gone to Egypt. It could be argued that this was simply good military strategy, to bring pressure on the enemy in his homeland. If so, then the strategy had worked. The Muslims had agreed to give up Jerusalem. But the Christians, offered Jerusalem, would not take it.

The first seed of the slow, sad, but eventually vast Christian disillusionment with the crusading ideal was sown when Richard the Lion-hearted turned back from Montjoie at the high point of the Third Crusade. It sprouted into full view when the majority of the crusaders did not follow Simon de Montfort in rejecting the diversion of the Fourth Crusade to Constantinople. The decision of Cardinal Pelagius—repeated several times, and eventually endorsed by Pope Honorius III—to reject Jerusalem in favor of "the flesh-pots of Egypt" meant in all likelihood that this great disillusionment would finally prevail.

There was much more of good in Christendom in this century of glory than the crusading ideal, and its climax was achieved without it. How much more might it have been—how much longer might it have lasted—if a crusading triumph had accompanied that climax?

The struggle for Damietta swayed back and forth all through that spring and summer of 1219. From March to May it was the Muslims who were attacking the crusader camp; in June and July it was the crusaders who were attacking the Muslims in the blazing heat of an Egyptian summer, but making little progress.[121] Late in August a small, raggedly clothed man with bushy black eyebrows arrived in their camp. Some thought him mad, but many were impressed by the fervor of his prayers and devotions. Crusaders from Italy passed the word that this was the extraordinary holy man from Umbria, who had embraced utter poverty for Christ's sake, whose fame had already spread over much of their land. It was indeed St. Francis of Assisi, and he had come to try to convert Sultan al-Kamil to Christianity.[122]

No man but St. Francis would even have dreamed of such a thing, for most Muslims in all ages have proved relentlessly impervious to conversion, and none more than their leaders. Cardinal Pelagius was horrified by St. Francis' intention to preach Christianity to al-Kamil, did all he could to discourage him from it, and then washed his hands of all responsibility for it.[123] On a pleasant day in September, the Little Poor Man of Assisi went forth on the strangest and most audacious of all his missions. He knew none of the enemy's language, so could only keep crying out: "Soldan! Soldan!" ("Sultan! Sultan!")[124]

> The Saint took Brother Illuminato with him and set out toward the enemy lines, singing, "Though I walk in the midst of the shadow of death, I will fear no evil, for Thou art with me." To comfort his less reassured companion, Francis showed him two ewes peacefully grazing in this perilous spot. "Courage, Brother!" he cried joyously. "Put your trust in Him who sends us forth like sheep in the midst of wolves."[125]

The Muslim soldiers on watch seized St. Francis and his companion, chained them, and brought them before al-Kamil. Interpreters were brought out, and Francis urged al-Kamil to become a Christian. Conversion from Islam to any other religion was a capital offense in every Muslim country down to the twentieth century, and proselytizing for this purpose carried the same penalty; five Franciscan friars were to suffer it in Morocco just five months later. But al-Kamil heard Francis out, responding warmly to him personally. He would not permit Francis to enter a furnace to prove the truth of his faith by ordeal. He offered Francis rich gifts, all of which he refused excpet a horn to summon people for his preaching. The Sultan said he could not change his religion without totally alienating his people; but as al-Kamil himself escorted him back to the crusader lines, he said to Francis: "Remember me in your prayers, and may God, by your intercession, reveal to me which belief is more pleasing to Him."[126]

---

[121]*Ibid.*, II, 411-413; Donovan, *Pelagius and the Fifth Crusade*, pp. 54-56, 59.
[122]Powell, *Anatomy of a Crusade*, pp. 158-159; Englebert, *St. Francis*, pp. 234-235.
[123]Donovan, *Pelagius and the Fifth Crusade*, p. 60; Englebert, *St. Francis*, p. 236.
[124]Englebert, *St. Francis*, p. 236.
[125]*Ibid.*
[126]*Ibid.*, pp. 236-240.

It may well be more than coincidence that it was in this very month of September that al-Kamil renewed his extraordinary offer to give back Jerusalem to the crusaders, except for the two fortresses in Moab, now adding to it a promise to rebuild the holy city's walls, restore pieces of the True Cross captured at the Battle of the Horns of Hattin, and return Christian prisoners. Leaders of the recently arrived Germans joined the previous supporters of accepting the offer, but nothing could move Cardinal Pelagius. Once again he rejected it, and the now increasingly pointless struggle in Egypt went on.[127]

Damietta fell to the crusaders in November, its defenders demoralized, exhausted, and diseased. Cardinal Pelagius and King John of Jerusalem quarrelled fiercely over who should control it. St. Francis departed, evidently concluding he could accomplish little more there. Later that month the crusaders took the city of Tanis east of Damietta, between Lake Manzaleh and the sea, while at approximately the same time al-Kamil's brother, who had gone to Palestine, took Caesarea on its coast from the crusaders. Emperor Frederick II had committed himself to fulfilling his crusading vow and coming to the aid of the Christian army in Egypt in the spring of 1220, and in October 1219 had persuaded many German lords and knights to promise to join him on crusade. The general expectation was that the army would wait for Frederick II before undertaking major new operations.[128]

In that November of 1219 St. Dominic had audience with Pope Honorius III at Viterbo, informing him of the rapid growth of his new order from only about 20 members at the beginning of 1217 to over one hundred in eight houses in northern and southern France, Italy, and Spain. The Pope was deeply impressed, and in December issued a new bull specially recommending the Dominicans which declared rooting out heresy, as they had striven to do in southern France where their order was founded, to be one of their chief missions. The Pope took St. Dominic with him to celebrate Christmas in St. Peter's. In February 1220 he gave him unprecedented personal authority over his order, in sharp contrast to the federal structure used by older orders.[129]

St. Francis' authority over the Franciscans was, by contrast, now under heavy challenge, though no one dared to say it in so many words. The order has

---

[127]Setton, *Crusades*, II, 414-415; Powell, *Anatomy of a Crusade*, pp. 159-161; Donovan, *Pelagius and the Fifth Crusade*, pp. 60-63. The precise chronology of these important events is unfortunately uncertain. Though most authorities agree that the visit of St. Francis to Sultan al-Kamil and his offer to return Jerusalem (which Van Cleve in Setton, *op. cit.*, regards as a renewal of a February offer, while Powell and Donovan regard it as being now made for the first time) both occurred in September, it is impossible to fix the dates closely enough to know which came first.

[128]Setton, *Crusades*, II, 418-420, 433-434; Powell, *Anatomy of a Crusade*, pp. 163-164, 175-176; Donovan, *Pelagius and the Fifth Crusade*, pp. 64-67; Englebert, *St. Francis*, p. 238.

[129]Vicaire, *St. Dominic*, pp. 278-279, 286-287, 289, 294.

grown very rapidly, and not all the new members could accept the extraordinary demands of the holy poverty which St. Francis enjoined upon all his followers. After St. Francis spent Holy Week of 1220 in the holy places of Palestine as a pilgrim, which he had longed all his life to do, one of his brothers of Portiuncula found him in Acre and told him that worldly friars were destroying the spirit of his order, and had obtained new ordinances authorizing Franciscan communities to own property. Deeply distressed, suffering from the eye disease ophthalmia contracted in Egypt, and not fully satisfied even by the Pope's formal appointment of Cardinal Ugolino Conti as protector and governor of the Franciscan brotherhood during the development of its organization, St. Francis resigned as head of the order in September 1220. But no one would, or ever could forget that he was its founder and chief inspiration, so long as he lived—or afterward.[130]

In April 1220 Emperor Frederick II secured the German lords' election of his son Henry as King of the Romans and consequently his successor, which he had insisted upon as necessary before departing on his promised crusade. On July 24 the Pope wrote to Cardinal Pelagius stating that the last great step that had to be taken before the Emperor departed on crusade was his imperial coronation, then expected to take place in September. The coronation did not actually happen until November 22. Before Pope Honorius III crowned him that day, Frederick II promised that he would never unite Sicily with the Empire. At his coronation ceremony he renewed his crusading vow and pledged to leave the following August.[131]

He soon proved that both promises were worthless, that no confidence could then or ever be placed in the word of Frederick II. At the Diet of Capua in December 1220, Frederick clamped an iron royal absolutism on southern Italy and Sicily: he declared he would control all succession to the estates of the nobility and all marriages of the children of his barons, and he annulled all city charters for self-government.[132] Sicily and southern Italy might be juridically separate from the Empire, but Frederick had more power there than he had in the Empire; now the Papal states were truly caught in the vise that Popes had long feared. And Frederick did not leave on crusade in August 1221, when the crusaders' need for him was greatest (though he did send a considerable number of German troops to Egypt, under the command of Duke Louis of Bavaria).[133]

After once again rejecting al-Kamil's final offer to give Jerusalem back to Christendom, blindly confirmed by Pope Honorius III, Cardinal Pelagius led the

---

[130]Englebert, *St. Francis*, pp. 240-248; Moorman, *Franciscan Order*, pp. 50-51.

[131]Abulafia, *Frederick II*, pp. 129-130, 136-138; Setton, *Crusades*, II, 434-435; Donovan, *Pelagius and the Fifth Crusade*, pp. 77-78.

[132]Kantorowicz, *Frederick II*, pp. 115-116, 119.

[133]Setton, *Crusades*, II, 435.

crusaders, against the better judgment of their commanders, in an ill-planned lunge toward Cairo in July, through the summer heat and the Nile flood. Understanding how the flood rose as the crusaders did not, the Muslims trapped them August 26 by moving ships through quickly filling canals. Caught at Baramun between Damietta and Cairo, with the Nile now at full flood and no help forthcoming from Emperor Frederick II, the crusaders irretrievably lost the opportunity to regain Jerusalem which had been presented to them for more than two full years. They were allowed to evacuate Baramun only at the price of leaving Egypt altogether and getting in return only their prisoners and fragments of the True Cross captured at the Horns of Hattin—nothing in Palestine.[134]

Little wonder that on November 19, 1221 Pope Honorius III reminded Frederick II that Christendom had awaited his departure for the Holy Land for no less than five years, and warned him that if he did not soon fulfill his crusading vow he would be excommunicated.[135] The warning was not forgotten, though during the remaining five and a half years of his pontificate Honorius III never found the resolution to implement it. In March 1223 Frederick promised to go on crusade in 1225, then discovered that public eagerness to join it was sadly lacking[136] (should anyone have been surprised?). In July 1225 he promised to go on crusade in 1227. He then promptly married the young daughter of King John of Jerusalem (variously called Isabel and Yolande), and brusquely declared that doughty warrior thereby deprived of his crown, which Frederick put on his own head along with his others, the crown imperial and the crown of Sicily.[137] But he was much better at putting on crowns than at keeping his promises. He then managed to persuade Pope Honorius III that it was the Lombard cities of northern Italy—understandably concerned that he intended to impose Sicilian-style autocracy on them—that were blocking the crusade, inducing the Pope to denounce those cities as almost his last official act before he died in March 1227.[138]

It was to be Honorius' successor, Cardinal Ugolino Conti, the great Pope Gregory IX, who would at last take Emperor Frederick's measure and call his

---

[134]*Ibid.*, II, 423-428; Donovan, *Pelagius and the Fifth Crusade*, pp. 83-93; Powell, *Anatomy of a Crusade*, pp. 185-191. In a letter to Emperor Frederick II on August 21, just before the final disaster in Egypt, Pope Honorius III sharply and justly reprimanded him for placing the crusading army in great danger by his tardiness (Donovan, *op. cit.*, p. 105), though Cardinal Pelagius had surely done as much to the same end by his foolhardiness.

[135]Mann, *Popes in the Middle Ages*, XIV, 71; Setton, *Cruasdes*, II, 438; Donovan, *Pelagius and the Fifth Crusade*, pp. 105-106.

[136]Mann, *Popes in the Middle Ages*, XIV, 32-33, 73; Abulafia, *Frederick II*, pp. 149-150; Setton, *Crusades*, II, 438-439; Powell, *Anatomy of a Crusade*, p. 197.

[137]Setton, *Crusades*, II, 440-444; Kantorowicz, *Frederick, II*, pp. 138-140.

[138]Mann, *Popes in the Middle Ages*, XIV, 79-82, 163-164; Setton, *Crusades*, II, 445; Abulafia, *Frederick II*, pp. 154-157, 160.

bluff.

The crusade against the infidel for the Holy Land had failed—the third successive crusade in the East to fail. Though at the time of the disaster in Egypt it appeared that the Albigensian Crusade had also failed, it unexpectedly gained victory in the last year of Honorius III's pontificate. Amaury de Montfort had proved wholly unable to maintain the Church's cause in arms in southern France, and in January 1224 left that region forever, taking his father's body with him. Two years later Amaury made over all his rights and claims in southern France to France's new king, Louis VIII, who had ruled since the death of Philip II in 1223. Louis had on several occasions proved himself more militant and more willing to take risks than his careful father, and he was especially urged to undertake the crusade by his wife Blanche of Castile, heir to so many generations of the longest crusade of all. The Cathar heretics, influential as they were, did not actually control the greater part of southern France, and the orthodox majority proved much more willing to submit to the direct authority of their king than to a mere northern nobleman, even with the Church behind him. The excommunication of the young Count Raymond VII of Toulouse was renewed (his father Raymond VI had died excommunicate in 1222) and a large crusading army marched south under Louis VIII in June 1226. After proving its capabilities by besieging and taking Avignon, one of the strongest cities in the region, this army faced no further significant opposition. Before his sudden, unexpected death in November 1226, Louis VIII's authority was accepted everywhere in southern France, even by Toulouse. His successor, though then still a boy, was that greatest and best of all French kings, St. Louis IX.[139]

During the last year the Fifth Crusade was in Egypt, strange rumors had swept the crusading army of a new and mighty nation from the distant East, beyond Islam, that was marching upon their enemy's frontiers and might be a hitherto unknown Christian power.[140] The legend of a great Christian kingdom in the East had an immense and understandable romantic appeal to Christendom—it was later to be one of the inspirations of the Age of Discovery—but little substance. It was magnified from misunderstood reports of the hidden Christian kingdom of Ethiopia in the mountains of the Horn of Africa and of the surviving Christian communities in central Asia that had been evangelized just before the appearance of Islam. And in this case it was dark and deadly deception. For those marching from the East upon the frontiers of Islam in 1220 and 1221 were the enemies of all civilized men.

The Mongols under their leader, Temujin called Genghis Khan,[141] came

---

[139]Sumption, *Albigensian Crusade*, pp. 208-211, 215, 217-222; Setton, *Crusades*, II, 316-319; Wakefield, *Heresy, Crusade and Inquisition in Southern France*, pp. 125-126.

[140]Powell, *Anatomy of a Crusade*, pp. 178-179.

[141]"Khan" simply means king. As for "Genghis," theories about its meaning are as

upon the civilized world like the nuclear bombs mankind was not to know until seven more centuries had passed. The best horsemen on earth, the Mongols were nomads. They spent all their lives wandering the great plains of central Asia, pasturing their herds, living chiefly on meat and milk. Cities and even permanent buildings of any kind were for them alien places, strange and threatening. Mongols felt freer and more comfortable if cities were eliminated. Far from being Christians (though a few Nestorian Christians lived among them, perhaps giving rise to the rumors) they were primitive shamanists, children of Tengri, the Eternal Blue Sky. What morality they had concerned only themselves, and to some extent the conditions under which they felt war to be justified. Once war was launched it was waged to the end, to ultimate destruction.[142]

By the year 1218 Genghis Khan and his Mongol horsemen had already conquered most of northern China and the region between China and the Syr Darya River in central Asia which had belonged to people known as the Kara-Khitai. In 1218 a caravan from Mongolia, entering the Muslim kingdom of Khwarizm whose frontier was the Syr Darya River, was seized and robbed and its merchants killed, including a Mongol ambassador, by order of the local governor. Muhammad II, king of Khwarizm, refused compensation to Genghis Khan, who declared war. That war was like nothing Islam had ever seen.[143]

During the winter of 1220, when civilized armies awaited a more clement season to fight, the Mongol horsemen swept like a hurricane out of the steppes with Genghis Khan personally in command. In February he took the large and ancient city of Bokhara; in March, Samarkand. A team of horsemen was detached to pursue Muhammad II wherever he might flee, until he died or they killed him. They chased him hundreds of miles, until, abandoned by all but a handful and almost mad with terror, he sailed into the Caspian Sea in a boat with Mongol arrows falling in his wake. A few days later he died of pleurisy on an island in that inland sea. In the following year the Great Khan's son Tului took the city of Merv in Khorasan and killed almost all its population; he and another son, Ogodai, took Gurganj, the old capital of Khwarizm, and flooded it from the Syr Darya River so that it could not be resettled; then Tului took the historic and beautiful Iranian city of Nishapur and destroyed it, killing every human being he found within, and even the cats and dogs. To secure these

---

variant as its spellings, and as little significant to our purposes. Since transliteration of East Asian names is beset with linguistic, orthographical and pronunciation problems, it is in this writer's opinion always best to use the most familiar form, if there is one. Surely "Genghis," which most educated people have seen or heard, is better than "Jenghiz," "Chingis," "Chinggis," or any of its other modern disguises, none of which can fully satisfy a genuine expert on Oriental languages.

[142]René Grousset, *The Empire of the Steppes* (New Brunswick NJ, 1970), pp. 86-87, 189-197, 217-226.
[143]*Ibid.*, pp. 226-238.

gigantic and terrible conquests, one of Genghis Khan's best generals, Subotai, rode westward the next year (1222) all the way across the Caucasus Mountains and the Kuban and Don and Ukrainian steppes to the Dniester River at the edge of eastern Europe. And so the Mongols began their invasion of Christendom.[144]

Georgia in the Caucasus was a Christian kingdom, already ravaged by the Mongols in 1221; the Cumans of the Kuban and Don steppes were still pagan, but allied with the nascent Christian states in Russia and Ukraine. A Christian prince, Mstislav the Daring of Galicia (which ran from Poland southeastward to the Dniester River which Subotai had reached) formed a coalition of Ukrainians, Russians, and Cumans to resist the dread invaders should they come again the following year, as they had told the Cumans they intended to do. Defeating a Mongol advance party on the Dnieper River, Mstislav and his allies became overconfident, pressing on along the north shore of the Sea of Azov to the Kalka River halfway from Crimea to the mouth of the Don. There Subotai met them with the main Mongol army.[145]

Our word "horde" comes from the Mongol *ordu*, their name for a tent city, also meaning "army";[146] but its modern connotation of vast numbers does not reflect the reality of Mongol military operations. The Mongols could not have supported gigantic armies thousands of miles from home, nor could such armies have moved with the astonishing speed "the devil's horsemen" showed. In fact the Mongols at the Kalka River were probably outnumbered three to one by Mstislav's coalition. But Genghis Khan and Subotai had trained their riders into a peerless cavalry which had been fighting for years in every sort of terrain and climate, from China to Europe. They rode rings around the clumsy attack of Mstislav of Galicia and cut his disorganized and undisciplined troops to pieces. Another Mstislav, surnamed Romanovich, Prince of Kiev—the most civilized realm in this region—bravely held the Christians' fortified camp to cover the retreat of the rest of the army that had survived. Unable to break into the fortified camp, Subotai offered to let Mstislav and his men leave it in peace and go home if they paid a ransom. When they agreed, the Mongols promptly seized them all. Mstislav of Kiev and two other princes were boarded up in a box; the Mongol chieftains sat upon it eating a festive dinner while their betrayed victims slowly suffocated inside.[147]

That summer Genghis Khan called Subotai and his men home to

---

[144]*Ibid.*, pp. 239-241; James Chambers, *The Devil's Horsemen; the Mongol Invasion of Europe* (New York, 1979), pp. 1, 11-16, 25.

[145]George Vernadsky, *Kievan Russia* (New Haven CT, 1948), pp. 227-228, 236-238; Chambers, *Devil's Horsemen*, pp. 19-20, 26-28.

[146]Grousset, *Empire of the Steppes*, p. 255.

[147]Grousset, *Empire of the Steppes*, pp. 245-246; Vernadsky, *Kievan Russia*, p. 238; Chambers, *Devil's Horsemen*, pp. 28-29.

Mongolia. A Russian chronicler wrote: "We do not know where these evil Tartars came from and whither they went; only God knows."[148] But they would return—to Russia's cost and the world's, through centuries to come.

On August 6, 1221 St. Dominic had died at Bologna, near the great university where many of the young friars he had brought into his order were studying Catholic truth to strengthen their spiritual and intellectual armament against the errors that led men away from God. The preceding May, at its second chapter meeting, the new order had established provinces in Spain, northern and southern France, Lombardy (northern Italy), and Rome. The establishment of the first Dominican community in England had been authorized. Dominican preachers were in demand everywhere they were known. They had the unqualified support of the Pope. Their future was unlimited.[149] Well might St. Dominic pray, in his last hours:

> Holy Father, as you know, I have persevered with all my heart in following your will. And I have guarded and preserved those whom you have given me. I recommend them to you. Preserve them and keep them.[150]

At the next general chapter, meeting in May 1222, Blessed Jordan of Saxony, the German Dominican who had been made Provincial of Lombardy at the first general chapter, was chosen the second Master General of the Friars Preachers, who from then until now would bear the name of St. Dominic.[151]

The Franciscan order had now grown immensely; legend tells of full five thousand members at the famous "Chapter of the Mats," probably in May 1222, and though this is probably an exaggeration influenced by the five thousand Christ fed by the miraculous multiplication of the loaves and the fishes, the expansion of St. Francis' original tiny group at the Portiuncula had obviously been enormous. To sustain so many entirely by daily begging was clearly impossible; but St. Francis could not at first bear to sacrifice what he regarded as a fundamental requirement of the unique way of Christian life he had shown to his friars, that they should "take nothing with them" in the words of the Gospel. That fall he drafted a rule for the order, in which this provision and others much objected to were still included; it was handed over to Brother Elias Bombarone, now official head of the order, and disappeared—probably destroyed because it was found unacceptable, very likely by Brother Elias himself. In 1223 St. Francis produced another draft, which he took to Cardinal

---

[148]Vernadsky, *Kievan Russia*, p. 239.

[149]Vicaire, *St. Dominic*, pp. 356-362, 372-375.

[150]*Ibid.*, p. 373.

[151]Marguerite Aron, *Saint Dominic's Successor; the Life of Bd. Jordan of Saxony* (St. Louis, 1955), pp. 82-83.

Ugolino Conti. After weeks or months of effort and reluctant compromise on Francis' part, it was finally brought to a form which Pope Honorius III could and did approve November 29. The reference to "taking nothing with them" had been eliminated.[152]

It was an extraordinarily difficult moment. It took a great saint to accept the fullness of Church authority on matters so close to his heart; but St. Francis (unlike some of his wayward followers in the future, the so-called "Spiritual Franciscans") never rebelled. He did, however, find ways uniquely his own to continue reminding his brothers of the obligations of poverty, such as going begging on Easter 1224 to one of his own friaries he thought too well endowed.[153] The Franciscan ideal endured, and Franciscan vocations continued to multiply. It was during these years that the preaching genius of the Franciscan St. Anthony of Padua (originally from Portugal) became well known throughout Italy and France,[154] culminating in his famous sermon at the council of Bourges in November 1225 when he suddenly turned to address its president, the distinguished Archbishop Simon de Sully: "You there, with the miter! To you I address myself... for certain misdeeds that lie heavy upon your conscience."[155]

In truth St. Francis of Assisi was never really called to organizations, even his own. He and his example were more than enough. In his last three years on earth he reached heights of spirituality perhaps never matched since the death of the beloved Apostle. On Christmas day 1223 he said Mass as part of a living creche at Grecchio, thereby in essence beginning the way serious Christians have celebrated Christmas ever since. During the spring of 1224 he preached repeatedly on reverence for the Holy Eucharist. In August of that year he retreated to the top of the mountain of La Verna, with Brother Leo his only companion—and he was kept at a considerable distance. There, he told Brother Leo, Christ Himself appeared to him; and there, on September 14, the feast of the Exaltation of the Holy Cross, he received the stigmata—the wounds of Christ in visible form.[156] He and a priest of our own century, Padre Pio (a Franciscan), remain the only men in the Church's history to have received visible stigmata (a somewhat larger number of women have received this most extraordinary grace and sign).

Though the bleeding wounds in his feet made it very difficult for him to walk, St. Francis appeared again preaching in Umbria during the winter of

---

[152]Moorman, *Franciscan Order*, pp. 54-57; Englebert, *St. Francis,* pp. 287-289, 292-295.

[153]Englebert, *St. Francis*, p. 302.

[154]Mary Purcell, *St. Anthony and His Times* (Dublin, 1960), pp. 75-110.

[155]*Ibid.*, p. 111.

[156]Englebert, *St. Francis*, pp. 299-301, 303-312; Jorgensen, *St. Francis*, pp. 215-217, 240-248; Moorman, *Franciscan Order*, pp. 59-61.

1225. That spring, confined in a hut under the care of St. Clare due to near blindness from the ophthalmia he had contracted in Egypt, he wrote his glorious "Canticle of the Sun." In June he reconciled the Bishop and Podestà of Assisi in a talk that included a reading of the Canticle with a stanza added on the blessings of peace.[157]

In the summer of 1226 St. Francis dictated his last testament—a testament of his faith, his faithfulness and his love. Any of its shining words could well be quoted, but we choose these, his magnificent hymn of loyalty to the Church:

> The Lord gave me, and gives me now, towards priests who live according to the law of the Holy Roman Church, so great a confidence, by reason of their priesthood, that even if they sought to persecute me, I would nonetheless return to them. And if I were to have as great a wisdom as Solomon possessed, and were to meet with poor priests of this world, I do not wish to preach without their consent in the parishes in which they dwell. And these and all others I desire to reverence, love and honor as my lords. And I do not wish to discover if they are sinners, because I behold in them the Son of God, and they are my lords. And for this reason I do this: because in this world I see nothing with my bodily eyes of Him who is the most high Son of God except His most holy Body and His most holy Blood, which they receive and which they alone minister to others.[158]

When his doctors told Francis that death was approaching, he welcomed it literally with open arms, and with song—a last stanza added to the Canticle of the Sun.

> Be praised, my Lord, for and by our Sister Bodily Death,
> From whom no living man can escape.
> Woe to those who die in mortal sin.
> Blessed are they whom she shall find in Your most holy will,
> For the second death shall not harm them.[159]

He died October 3, 1226, laid at his request upon a coarse cloth on the ground before the Portiuncula Chapel, sprinkled with dust and ashes, singing the One Hundred and Forty-first Psalm. The wound in the side of his body, observers tell us, glowed rosy red, and "the stigmata of his hands and feet stood out like black stones on white marble."[160]

No mortal man upon this earth—still less a mere historian—can guess the magnitude of the blessings St. Francis of Assisi brought to mankind by his

---

[157]Englebert, *St. Francis*, pp. 317-323, 389; Jorgensen, *St. Francis*. pp. 252-260; Moorman, *Franciscan Order*, pp. 75-76.
[158]Englebert, *St. Francis*, p. 334.
[159]*Ibid.*, p. 338.
[160]*Ibid.*, pp. 343-344.

prayer and intercession during the twenty years when he knew and fulfilled his mission on earth. But we surely cannot go far wrong if we see many of those blessings in the glory of Christendom that flowered as never before or since in the fifty years that followed his death.

6
Destruction of the Tyrant Emperor
(1227-1254)
(Popes Gregory IX 1227-41, Celestine IV 1241, and Innocent IV 1243-54)

"With the help of God I will take my stand for the people, and boldly face the implacable pestilential Prince who stirs up the deadly blasts by which the world is wearied. It is absolutely fixed in my heart either to tear the evil roots of discord from the people of Christendom, or to destroy the cause of these evils, the tyranny of that malignant Prince, once Emperor [Frederick II], by which the whole world is falling to ruin, the orthodox faith overthrown, and the glory of ecclesiastical liberty uprooted."—Pope Innocent IV, August 30, 1248[1]

Of all the prelates and luminaries of the Church in his time, St. Francis of Assisi had been much the closest to Ugolino Conti, for 21 years Cardinal Bishop of Ostia, the grand-nephew of Pope Innocent III.[2] "A man of fine form and feature . . . of a clear understanding and of a retentive memory," Ugolino Conti was a distinguished canon lawyer and Scripture scholar. Sent to northern Italy by Pope Honorius III in 1217 to preach the Fifth Crusade, he met St. Francis on the way and became his fervent disciple. Throughout the remainder of St. Francis' life he and Ugolino Conti sang each other's praises. Finding in Ugolino "one who far outshone the rest [of the cardinals] in virtuous behavior and holiness of life," St. Francis (according to his best early biographer, Thomas of Celano) "submitted himself to him in all ways, and revered him with wondrous and respectful affection." St. Francis—who prophesied that Ugolino would one day be Pope—would greet him "with unheard-of blessings, and though he was a son in devout submission, yet at the Spirit's prompting he would sometimes confort him with fatherly intercourse." Thomas of Celano tells us that Ugolino "burned with exceeding love toward the holy man" and that "however disturbed

---

[1]Pope Innocent IV to Cardinal Stephen of Santa Maria in Trastevere, August 30, 1248, in Horace K. Mann, *The Lives of the Popes in the Middle Ages*, Volume XV (London, 1928), p. 108.

[2]The fact that Ugolino was a *grand*-nephew of Innocent III, the youngest Pope in recent history, who was only 56 when he died in 1216, is in itself sufficient to dispose of the absurd statement of Matthew of Paris that Ugolino was about 100 years old when he died, as Pope Gregory IX, in 1241. Ugolino was probably born about 1170 (*ibid.*, XIV, 170).

or vexed he might be, on seeing St. Francis and talking with him all mental clouds were dispersed, and serenity returned. ... He ministered to St. Francis as a servant to his lord ... would often kiss his hands." Cardinal Ugolino presented and recommended St. Francis to Pope Honorius III and assisted him in the drafting of the first formal Franciscan Rule. In full appreciation of his help and support, St. Francis begged the Pope to make Ugolino the special advisor of his new religious order. Ugolino would often go among the Franciscans dressed in their habit.[3]

Cardinal Ugolino was almost as close to St. Clare and her new religious order for women, the Poor Clares. He knew the power of her prayers, and beginning while he was still Cardinal Bishop of Ostia, wrote often to ask her for their help. Ugolino was also one of the three cardinals assigned by Pope Honorius III to support St. Dominic in his reform of congregations of religious women in Rome.[4]

Because his mission of preaching the Fifth Crusade in northern Italy had been so successful, and due to the great esteem in which he was universally held, Cardinal Ugolino was sent by Pope Honorius on a similar mission in 1221, when the crusaders were pinned down at Damietta in Egypt. The crusade he then preached was to be commanded by the recently crowned Emperor Frederick II and to regain Jerusalem at last. Once again the response was strong and enthusiastic. Promises of men and money for the crusade poured in. But Frederick II would not move, and the crusaders in Egypt had to return home.[5]

Ugolino Conti is not likely to have forgotten this first of many lessons he was to have in the unreliability and perfidy of Emperor Frederick II.

On March 19, 1227, the day after Pope Honorius III died—less than six months after St. Francis of Assisi—Ugolino Conti was elected Pope, by virtual acclamation. On Easter Sunday, April 11, he was crowned as Pope Gregory IX.[6] He is one of the greatest Popes in the history of the Church, though curiously neglected by posterity (particularly post-medieval posterity). By any standard, even that of the Church's enemies, his titanic grapple with Emperor Frederick II is one of the most dramatic stories of all time. Yet it seems to have embarrassed too many historians to be adequately told. Though over 6,000 documents survive from his pontificate, and though a good contemporary biography exists, no biography of Pope Gregory IX has been written in the

---

[3]*Ibid.*, XIV, 171, 177-186.
[4]*Ibid.*, XIV, 194-195, 200.
[5]*Ibid.*, XIV, 202-203; see Chapter Five, above.
[6]*Ibid.*, XIV, 204-205. As Mann points out, the fact that the election of Gregory IX occurred on the very next day after Honorius' death renders most unlikely the report of one chronicler that Cardinal Conrad, Bishop of Porto, was first chosen Pope but refused the office.

twentieth century; even the nineteenth century produced only biographies in Italian and German.[7]   By contrast there is a veritable twentieth-century literature on Frederick II.

The world-shaking conflict began in short order, for from the moment of his elevation to the Papal throne Gregory IX had the measure of his opponent.

> His long and varied experience as cardinal, extending over a period of 28 years, and his many diplomatic missions in the interests of the Holy See had enabled Gregory, as few other men of his time, accurately to appraise the aims and purposes of the [Hohen]Staufen Emperor.... He looked upon Frederick [II] as the champion of a form of Caesarism determined to restore to the Holy Roman Emperor and to the King of Sicily the full sovereign rights of the pre-Constantinian [non-Christian] emperors [of Rome].[8]

In his very first letter to Frederick as Pope, written March 23, 1227, Gregory IX warned him solemnly that he must fulfill his crusading vow, first taken no less than eleven years ago. Two years before, in the solemn Treaty of San Germano with Pope Honorius III, Frederick had promised on no account to leave on crusade later than August 15, 1227. If he did not keep that promise, Pope Gregory IX told him, the consequences would be devastating for Christendom. "Beware," the Pope said to Frederick II, "lest you place each of us in a position from which, even with the best will, we cannot easily extricate you."[9]

Frederick seemed to respond well, making extraordinarily generous offers of provisions and transportation to all crusaders, causing many more to rally to him.   Seven hundred knights came from Thuringia in Germany and from Austria, along with 250 mercenaries and 100 knights from his own household, thereby exceeding the thousand armed men he had personally pledged for the crusade during Honorius III's pontificate. The contingent from Thuringia was commanded by its Landgrave Louis, whose wife was St. Elizabeth of Hungary; she felt a premonition that he would never return.[10]

In August the crusaders assembled at the Italian port of Brindisi—a bad time of year especially in southern Italy, when malarial fevers flourished. Landgrave Louis was infected.   Nevertheless he and Frederick boarded their ship and departed with fifty other vessels September 8, already 24 days later than the latest date Frederick had promised to go. It soon became clear that Louis' illness was mortal. Frederick, claiming to have fallen ill as well, took his

---

[7]*Ibid.*, XIV, 165-168.

[8]Thomas C. Van Cleve, *The Emperor Frederick II of Hohenstaufen* (Oxford, 1972), pp. 190, 192.

[9]*Ibid.*, pp. 194, 161-162.

[10]*Ibid.*, pp. 194-195; Jeanne Ancelet-Hustache, *Gold Tried by Fire; St. Elizabeth of Hungary* (Chicago, 1963), pp. 132-133.

entire fleet into Otranto, the last port at the southern tip of the Italian peninsula facing the Adriatic Sea, to await his recovery. Louis of Thuringia died the day they landed.[11]

The death of the holy Landgrave cast a pall over the expedition, and caused many then and since to believe that Frederick's illness must have been genuine. But Pope Gregory IX, who knew Frederick and his record far more thoroughly than any modern historian can hope to do, did not believe him, seeing in his claim of illness merely another in a long train of excuses for not doing his duty. Be that as it may, Frederick recovered quickly and completely at the mineral baths of Pozzuoli near Naples; and his behavior may at least be significantly compared with that of King St. Ferdinand III of Castile, leading the unending Spanish crusade against the Moors, who never let even life-threatening illness stop him in his campaigns to reconquer Andalusia during these same years.[12] Tens of thousands of Frederick's men went on to Palestine on their own, where they milled about angry and leaderless during the fall, then gradually began trickling back to Europe.[13]

Therefore, on September 29, 1227, Pope Gregory IX excommunicated Emperor Frederick II for not leading what would have been the Sixth Crusade to Palestine as he had promised. On October 10 the Pope issued an encyclical explaining his excommunication. It reviewed the entire history of Frederick's life and dealings with the Church, his voluntary taking of the Cross in 1216 and his own suggestion that anyone failing to fulfill crusading vows should be excommunicated, the numerous postponements of his departure since then, his delay in procuring shipping for the crusaders and encouraging them to stay at an unhealthy port, and finally charged him with "preferring the pleasures of Pozzuoli . . . to the rigors of a crusading expedition."[14] Later that month, in a personal letter to Frederick, the Pope made clear that his objections to the Emperor extended beyond the immediate charge of failure to keep his crusading vow; he unequivocally condemned Frederick's personal direction of the Church in his kingdom of Sicily and southern Italy and his control of all ecclesiastical appointments there, saying "we can no longer tolerate these acts or with good conscience withhold our punishment."[15]

---

[11]Mann, *Popes in the Middle Ages*, XIV, 211-213; Van Cleve, *Frederick II*, p. 195; Ancelet-Hustache, *Gold Tried by Fire*, pp. 134-136; Kenneth M. Setton, ed., *A History of the Crusades*, Volume II, ed. Robert L. Wolff and Harry W. Hazard (Philadelphia, 1962), p. 446.

[12]For example, at the siege of Alcalá del Río in the spring of 1247, preliminary to the siege and reconquest of Sevilla (Julio González, *Las Conquistas de Fernando III en Andalucia* [Madrid, 1946], p. 106).

[13]Setton, *Crusades*, II, 448.

[14]*Ibid.*, II, 446-447 (for the quotation); Mann, *Popes in the Middle Ages*, XIV, 214-215; Van Cleve, *Frederick II*, pp. 196-199.

[15]Van Cleve, *Frederick II*, pp. 196-197.

Emperor Frederick II—a man of unquestionable mental brilliance, boundless ambition, and overweening pride—not only refused to yield, but lashed back with a furious counterattack against the Pope, calling his indictment "vicious and unworthy," intended only to "excite hatred against us." In letters to the kings of England and France he warned against alleged designs of the Pope and Church for temporal power, calling the clergy "insatiable leeches" and "ravenous wolves."[16]

Pope Gregory IX's answer was solemnly to re-proclaim the excommunication of Emperor Frederick II from St. Peter's on November 18.[17] No braver man has ever sat in the chair of the fisherman than Ugolino Conti. He would not be moved, then or ever, by threats and denunciations, by pressure and fear. Two of the most powerful personalities of their century, or of any century, had clashed head-on. In the end, the one who had a cause greater than himself would prevail, though he would not live to see it; the one whose cause was only himself would fail.

After his initial violent response, Frederick proceeded to behave as though his excommunciation had never happened. He held a Diet at Capua in southern Italy to impose new taxes for the crusade which he now promised for the following May, called a Diet of the whole Empire (Germany and northern Italy) to meet in March in Ravenna, and ordered priests in the lands he ruled (Germany and Italy) to carry on their clerical work regardless of the Pope's orders.[18]

But the Imperial Diet at Ravenna was not held in March. Instead, in that month the Pope renewed Frederick's excommunciation, imposed an interdict on any place where he might go, and threatened to proceed further against him "as a heretic and a despiser of the keys of the Church," using the mighty weapon forged by the Pope whose name he bore, St. Gregory VII,.by releasing his subjects from their duty of allegiance to him, along with depriving Frederick of his kingdom of Sicily and south Italy on the grounds that he held it as a fief from the Pope and had shown himself a disobedient vassal.[19]

Pope Gregory IX did not speak of Frederick II as a possible heretic without good reason. Though Frederick went through the motions of minimal Catholic practice, he did so very much in the manner of some modernist Catholics who often extravagantly admire this Emperor. He was sometimes accused of being a secret Muslim; but the Muslims themselves, even his friends among them, did not think that. They understood that Frederick II essentially believed in nothing but himself. In modern terms, he was an agnostic. Ibn al-Djusi, an Arab of Jerusalem, wrote of him when he appeared in that city in

[16]*Ibid.*, pp. 199-201.
[17]Mann, *Popes in the Middle Ages*, XIV, 215-216.
[18]*Ibid.*, XIV, 217-218; Setton, *Crusades*, II, 450.
[19]Mann, *Popes in the Middle Ages*, XIV, 221-222; Van Cleve, *Frederick II*, p. 204.

1229: "His conversation reveals that he does not believe in the Christian religion. When he spoke of it, it was to ridicule it."[20] Fakhr-ad-Din, ambassador of Sultan al-Kamil of Egypt, reported Frederick as saying to him in conversation about the claim of the Caliphs to a blood relationship with Muhammad:

> "That is excellent, far superior to the arrangement of those fools, the Christians. They choose as their spiritual head any fellow they will, without the smallest relationship to the Messiah, and they make him the Messiah's representative. That Pope there has no claim to such a position, whereas your Khalif is the descendant of Muhammad's uncle."[21]

On June 28, 1228 Frederick II sailed for Palestine from Brindisi, despite Pope Gregory IX having prohibited him from doing so until he was released from excommunication. Previous Popes had always carefully avoided having any crusade led by a king or lord not in good standing with the Church. A crusade was above all a religious expedition, though with a military character and purpose; and the Fourth Crusade had shown only too clearly that a crusade could be turned against Christians. But Frederick continued to defy Pope and Church. He arrived at Cyprus with his fleet and army just five days after Pope Gregory IX had presided at the solemn ceremony canonizing St. Francis of Assisi, and just ten days before Gregory proclaimed the oaths of allegiance of Frederick's subjects in the Kingdom of Sicily to be no longer binding.[22]

The "crusade" that followed was the strangest chapter in the baroque history of the crusading movement, which embodied so much of the best and the worst of medieval Christendom. Frederick II landed at Acre in Palestine September 7, 1228 and immediately opened negotiations with Sultan al-Kamil of Egypt about the disposition of Jerusalem and the Holy Land. When the negotiations made no immediate progress, he left Acre to march down the coast to Jaffa, following in the footsteps of Richard the Lion-Hearted (a man he resembled in few other ways), with the Knights of the Temple and the Hospital marching a day ahead of him so as not to associate with an excommunicated man. (They finally agreed to accept his orders as military commander, but only if they were issued "in the name of God and Christianity" rather than in his own name.)[23]

This show of force and resolution, and the immense pomp and panoply of power with which the Emperor surrounded himself (no Holy Roman Emperor

---

[20]Van Cleve, *Frederick II*, p. 225.

[21]Ernst Kantorowicz, *Frederick II* (New York, 1931, 1957), pp. 192-193.

[22]*Ibid.*, pp. 176-181; Van Cleve, *Frederick II*, pp. 206-207, 209; John Moorman, *A History of the Franciscan Order* (Oxford, 1968), p. 86.

[23]Setton, *Crusades*, II, 451-454; Van Cleve, *Frederick II*, pp. 214-219; Steven Runciman, *A History of the Crusades*, Volume III (Cambridge, England, 1966), p. 186.

before him had ever actually reached Palestine) impressed al-Kamil sufficiently so that he and Frederick agreed upon a treaty February 18, 1229. This extraordinary document, signed by two men neither of whom could be described as fervent in his faith, reflected Frederick's minimum demands, which he believed (wholly erroneously) would be seen as a crusading triumph in the West and consequently gain him release from excommunciation. By its terms, the Christians would be allowed to control Jerusalem for ten years, except for the enormous Temple platform built by Herod the Great on which the Muslim "Dome of the Rock" had been built by the revered Caliph Omar. In return, Frederick agreed not to support any Christian war against Muslims in that part of the world, and to do all he could to prevent any Christian military undertaking there. The most critical clause related to the fortification of Jerusalem. The treaty specified that the Christians, during their ten years' period of control, were to build "neither wall nor dwellings" there. However, al-Kamil gave Frederick *personal* permission to build defenses there, but the permission applied only to him. (Al-Kamil had undoubtedly divined that Frederick II actually had no personal interest in securing Jerusalem.) When the ten years had passed, the holy city would revert to the Muslims.[24]

No one liked this cynical compromise other than the two sovereigns who had drafted it. Patriarch Gerold of Jerusalem and the Knights of the Temple and the Hospital were bitterly opposed to it. On March 17 Frederick made his formal entry into Jerusalem through silent, empty streets. He went to the Church of the Holy Sepulcher to pray; but his chief religious advisor, Grand Master Hermann von Salza of the Teutonic Order, persuaded him not to challenge his excommunication directly by attending Sunday Mass there the next day. But he went there at another time, took the crown of Jerusalem from its empty altar, and in the absence of the Patriarch placed it on his own head. In his speech that followed he applied some of the royal messianic psalms to himself, but made no reference to the Church, except for ostentatiously announcing that he forgave the Pope for excommunicating him. He threatened to kill a priest who followed him afterward to the Dome of the Rock, and there said to the Muslims present (Frederick spoke fluent Arabic) "God has now sent you the pigs," using the vulgar Muslim word for Christians. He ordered the Muslim call to prayer to be resumed again in Jerusalem. Whatever his motives for these actions, he won no favor from most of the Muslims present.[25]

They were disquieted by his remarks against his own faith. They could

---

[24]Setton, *Crusades*, II, 455-457, 702; Runciman, *Crusades*, III, 187; Van Cleve, *Frederick II*, pp. 219-220.
[25]Runciman, *Crusades*, III, 188-190 ("God has now sent you the pigs," p. 190); Setton, *Crusades*, II, 457-458; Van Cleve, *Frederick II*, pp. 223-225; Mann, *Popes in the Middle Ages*, XIV, 228-231.

respect an honest Christian; but a Frank who disparaged Christianity and paid crude compliments to Islam roused their suspicions. It may be that they had heard the remark universally attributed to him that Moses, Christ, and Mahomet were all three impostors. In any case he seemed a man without religion.[26]

Pope Gregory IX had ordered an interdict levied upon any place where the excommunicated Emperor might be residing, and on the next day, March 19, Patriarch Gerold imposed it on Jerusalem. This meant that no more Masses could be said there until Frederick left the city. He departed that very day, saying he was concerned about the advance of the army of John de Brienne, the Papally recognized king of Jerusalem, in southern Italy. He remained in Acre until May 1, with resistance to him steadily rising. The Templars would no longer obey him, and before he left he destroyed all the arms he could find there, allegedly to prevent their use against the Muslims in violation of hte treaty, though perhaps equally to prevent their use against himself.[27]

He promptly took the field in southern Italy and drove out the army that had been supporting the rebels there who had followed the Papal recommendation to withdraw their support from their excommunicated sovereign. John de Brienne went home temporarily to his native France, while an army loyal to Frederick made substantial progress against his opponents in Lombardy (northern Italy). Under these circumstances, and strongly encouraged by several of his cardinals, the Pope opened negotiations with the Emperor, and on July 24, 1230 they signed the Treaty of San Germano. It provided that Frederick would pardon all who had supported the Church during his excommunication, return all Church property he had confiscated, withdraw his new taxes on the clergy, guarantee the independence and freedom from taxation of the Church in Sicily and southern Italy, and respect the frontiers of the Papal states.[28]

Frederick II had now fulfilled his crusading vow, however belatedly and inadequately, and the consequences of a lasting division of Christendom between adherents of the Pope and of the Emperor were too severe for Gregory IX to accept them yet, even though it is clear that he still did not trust Frederick II, and indeed would never trust him again. Frederick may have flattered himself that he had won; but it was only the first engagement in an immense conflict which was to end in his own destruction and that of all his house and line.

---

[26]Runciman, *Crusades*, III, 190.
[27]*Ibid.*, III, 190-192; Setton, *Crusades*, II, 458-460; Van Cleve, *Frederick II*, pp. 223-224, 226-228.
[28]Van Cleve, *Frederick II*, pp. 228-233; Mann, *Popes in the Middle Ages*, XIV, 242-243.

The scandal-giving enterprise of Frederick II was not, however, the only crusading undertaking of the first years of Gregory IX's pontificate. In southern France the Catharists, who rejected the Incarnation, were still strong, though no longer militarily dominant. Vigilance against their recovery of power had to be maintained and extended. Across the Pyrenees in Spain, the longest crusade went forward vigorously. Despite the splendid Christian victory at Las Navas de Tolosa in 1212, the infidel still held the whole of the great southern province of Andalusia, parts of Extremadura and of the Algarve in Portugal, and the southeastern Spanish provinces of Valencia and Murcia. An old king and two young kings were preparing to challenge them.

In 1229 a council at Toulouse required every person in Languedoc, the largest province in southern France, where the majority of the Cathars were to be found, to take an oath, renewable every second year, to remain a good Catholic and to denounce heretics, and provided for teams consisting of a priest and two laymen in each parish to search houses and outbuildings for Cathars. At the close of this council the Papal legate, Cardinal Romano Frangipani, heard confidential testimony from a former Cathar, William of Solier, who convinced him that to make public the names of witnesses against Cathars would endanger their lives. Out of these beginnings grew the first Inquisition in Catholic history, formally established by Pope Gregory IX in 1233 and directed by Dominicans because they were uniqiuely equipped for the task by their intellectual training, spiritual formation, and history (St. Dominic having found his vocation preaching for the Faith against the Cathars).[29]

The "black legend" of the Inquisition has been the most successful of all historical propaganda offensives against the Catholic Church; and the difficulty of responding to it persuasively is vastly increased by the almost complete inability of modern man to understand how any society could regard a man's religion as a matter of life and death. But in fact the heretic in Christendom was in every sense of the word a revolutionary, as dangerous to public order and personal safety as yesterday's Communist or today's terrorist. They brought fear, cruelty, bloodshed, and war wherever they appeared in sufficient numbers. The Cathars of southern France had become so strong that only a crusade eventually supported by the full power of the French king had overcome their armed power. Now they had gone underground and had to be rooted out lest they seize power there again.

Though persons accused by the Inquisition were not allowed to know the identity of their accusers in order to protect the witnesses from retaliation, each person arrested was instructed to make a list of his personal enemies and none

---

[29]Walter L. Wakefield, *Heresy, Crusade and Inquisition in Southern France 1100-1250* (Berkeley CA, 1974), pp. 134-136, 140; Jonathan Sumption, *The Albigensian Crusade* (London, 1978), pp. 229-230; Mann, *Popes in the Middle Ages*, XIV, 434-438; Régine Pernoud, *Blanche of Castile* (New York, 1975), pp. 193-194.

of their testimony was used against him. Though torture was used, contrary to legend it was infrequent and not lasting in its effects. Many of the accused were acquitted; many others were reconciled with the Church. In the fifty years (1227-1277) required finally to stamp out the Catharist heresy in southern France, there were no more than five thousand executions, a small proportion of the total executed for crime during this period.[30] Some Inquisitors—notably in Germany, where there were few Cathars and therefore more temptation for Inquisitors to go beyond their assigned duties—abused their power; they were promptly and firmly curbed by Pope Gregory IX.[31]

Count Raymond VII of Toulouse, though suspected throughout his life of Cathar sympathies, in fact seems to have given full and sincere support to the Church's efforts to restore peace and orthodoxy to his region after signing the Treaty of Paris in April 1229 that formally ended the Albigensian Crusade. He renewed his fealty to the French crown in the Treaty of Lorris in January 1243 after the murder of ten Inquisitors the previous year in which his half-brother was involved, and gave full support to the difficult military operation of reducing the last Cathar stronghold at Montségur, reputed to be impregnable. It was finally taken in March 1244. All the defenders were allowed to leave in peace except for those who insisted on publicly maintaining the Cathar religion; these, about 200 in number, were burned at the stake. A few Cathars escaped with treasure, secret documents and objects of their devotion, which were never seen again. The life-hating heresy was totally destroyed.[32]

In Spain the two young kings were Fernando III of Castile and James I of Aragon, while the old king was Fernando's 57-year old father, Alfonso IX of León. The marriage of Alfonso IX with Princess Berenguela, daughter of Alfonso VIII of Castile, had been disallowed by the Pope; Alfonso IX's father had been brother to Berenguela's grandfather.[33] But the four children of this marriage, including Fernando, were legitimized, and Fernando had succeeded to the throne of Castile in 1217 at the age of 19.[34] He was still much under the guidance of his mother, an extraordinary woman who played the same role in the life of this future saint that her sister Blanche played in the life of her son King St. Louis IX of France. In 1224 Fernando and his mother had agreed that the three-way division of the Morocco-based empire of the Muslim Almohads,

---

[30]Sumption, *Albigensian Crusade*, pp. 234-235.

[31]Van Cleve, *Frederick II*, pp. 367-369; Mann, *Popes in the Middle Ages*, XIV, 427-430.

[32]Pernoud, *Blanche of Castile*, pp. 142-144, 208-211; Margaret W. Labarge, *Saint Louis* (New York, 1968), pp. 44-46, 77, 79; Wakefield, *Heresy, Crusade and Inquisition in Southern France*, pp. 160-161, 169-173; Sumption, *Albigensian Crusade*, pp. 237-240.

[33]See Chapter Four, above.

[34]For a thorough review of the much-debated question of the date of birth of Fernando III of Castile, with the evidence that the correct date is 1198, see P. Luis Fernández de Retana, *San Fernando III y su época* (Madrid, 1941), pp. 17-23.

which had long ruled Spain, gave an opportunity for reconquest such as had not been seen for a century and a half; Fernando began campaigning immediately to take advantage of it. He won some striking victories during 1224 and 1225, but was unable to maintain most of them; regrettably he often killed his prisoners.[35]

Alfonso IX, King of León, had long fought more against rival Castile, which with his son Fernando as king could legitimately claim León when he died, than against the Moors. But in 1230, the last year of his life, the call of the ancient cause could no longer be denied. It was the noblest of all the traditions of Spain of the Reconquest that a true king ended his reign with a last march against the infidel conqueror. So his grandfather Alfonso VII and his cousin Alfonso VIII had done. So in February 1230, at the age of 58, Alfonso IX set out into the parched hills of Extremadura from recently reconquered Cáceres, marching on Mérida, a venerable city dating back to the Romans which had been held by the Moors for 518 years. Near the castle of Alange he fought and won a great battle with a defending force under Muhammad ibn Hud. Alfonso IX took Mérida as a result, then marched westward down the Guadiana River to the major city of Badajoz which he also took. The old king survived the actual campaign, but died shortly after it, on a pilgrimage to Santiago de Compostela to give thanks for his victory. By the end of the year, Fernando III had secured the complete and almost entirely peaceful reunion of Castile and León.[36]

Eastward, in the kingdom of Aragon and Catalonia, young James I had only attained his majority and begun to rule on his own in 1227,[37] at the age of nineteen. James, later called "the Conqueror," was a born leader of men, "a great warrior, brave, clever, experienced, a superb tactician and strategist, able to inspire his men and confident of the help of God,"[38] "a palm taller than other men . . . well built, with a ruddy face, straight nose, teeth as white as pearls, and golden hair."[39] On December 23, having assembled the Catalan *corts* (parliament) at Barcelona, he announced his intention to reconquer the Balearic Islands—three large islands well off the coast of Catalonia which, though originally Christian, had been Muslim-controlled for centuries. His leadership and charisma aroused a tremendous response; volunteers and

[35]Derek W. Lomax, *The Reconquest of Spain* (London, 1978), pp. 137-139; González, *Conquistas de Fernando III*, pp. 36-44; Fernández de Retana, *San Fernando III*, pp. 85-86, 97-98, 101-103, 107-110.
[36]Julio González, *Alfonso IX* (Madrid, 1944), pp. 206-210; Lomax, *Reconquest of Spain*, p. 142; Joseph F. O'Callaghan, *A History of Medieval Spain* (Ithaca NY, 1975), p. 340; Fernández de Retana, *San Fernando III*, pp. 131-135, 138-140.
[37]O'Callaghan, *History of Medieval Spain*, p. 335.
[38]Lomax, *Reconquest of Spain*, p. 142.
[39]F. Darwin Swift, *The Life and Times of James I the Conqueror* (Oxford, 1894), p. 34.

money came to him in abundance. Aragon approved as well; on Easter of 1229 James took the cross at Lérida, and on September 5 sailed for Majorca, largest of the Balearic Islands, with no less than 155 ships carrying 1,500 crusading knights and 15,000 foot soldiers. Met in battle at Santa Ponza within a week of his landing, he lost his best general in the fight, but broke the Moorish center with his personally led charges. Preparing for the final assault on Palma, the principal city on the island, the whole army took oath with James that no man would turn back after entering the city unless mortally wounded. On the last day of the year 1229 they stormed the city. During the following year they secured the whole of the island, and soon afterward the other Balearic Islands as well.[40]

Fired by this victory, three years later James undertook a still greater enterprise: the reconquest of the rich province of Valencia, which no Christian since the incomparable El Cid had been able to take and hold. In December 1232 Pope Gregory IX granted James a bull of crusade against Valencia, and its former Almohad governor made over to James his claim upon it, for whatever that might be worth among the Moors. In May 1233 James invaded Valencia with only 120 knights, but this tiny number included the Masters of the Temple and the Hospital, now unable to fight in Palestine because of the terms of the treaty the excommunicate Emperor had made four years before. They laid siege to the fortified city of Burriana on the coast near the border of Valencia and Catalonia, and took it in July. No more could be done that year with so small a force, and the following year James was distracted for a time from his crusading purpose by his betrothal to the beautiful Princess Violante of Hungary, whom he married in 1235 and passionately loved—favoring the three sons she bore him over his first-born Alfonso—until she died sixteen years later.[41]

In 1236 James tore himself from Violante's arms and, with renewed energy and invincible determination, pressed on to the reconquest of Valencia. He still had very few knights—only 130—but now had 2,000 foot soldiers to accompany them. With their help and labor he seized and fortified the height of Puig de Cebolla ("Onion Hill") just twelve miles north of Valencia. Using Onion Hill as a base, he besieged the city of Valencia by land and sea after defeating its army in the open field. During the winter he returned to Aragon, leaving a knight named Entenza in command of the garrison at Onion Hill. The

---

[40]Lomax, *Reconquest of Spain*, pp. 141-142; Swift, *James I the Conqueror*, pp. 34-36, 39, 41-43, 46-49, 52-54. The island of Minorca was taken by James' forces in 1232, Ibiza in 1235.

[41]O'Callaghan, *History of Medieval Spain*, p. 346; Swift, *James I the Conqueror*, pp. 56-61. There can be no doubt about James' extraordinary devotion to Violante and the children she bore him, which is manifested in all the arrangements he made for them as well as his constant concern to have her with him.

following spring Entenza with 50 knights and a thousand infantry beat off an Moorish attack by 600 horse and 40,000 foot. Rushing to the rescue of his garrison, James found when he arrived that they had already won. When Entenza suddenly died that December, James resolved once and for all to bring to full triumph the enterprise for which Entenza had given his life.[42]

Arriving at Onion Hill in January 1238, James knighted Entenza's ten-year-old son and swore not to return to Catalonia or Aragon until Valencia was taken. He scornfully rejected a Moorish offer of all of the province of Valencia north of the city, a large tribute, and a palace, declaring that he would "have both the hen and the chickens." He sent for Violante, who joined him at Onion Hill just after Easter. He brought up siege engines and a fleet, and obtained crusading knight volunteers from France and even from England, until his formerly small army had grown to 60,000. Leading his men against the walls of Valencia, James was severely wounded by an arrow in the face, but still refused to withdraw. Unable to match his invincible ardor, Valencia capitulated in September 1238. James allowed all Moors who wished to leave, to go with whatever they could carry, and rigorously protected them from robbery and violence as they departed. Reconquered Valencia became part of the Kingdom of Aragon.[43]

In 1233, the same year James I began the reconquest of Valencia, St. Fernando III of Castile made a similar commitment to the enduring reconquest of as much of the great southern province of Andalusia as he could secure. He had retained a foothold south of the Pass of the Overthrow of the Infidel Dogs as a result of his successful campaign of 1225, and the division among the Moors was worse than ever: the Almohad empire had essentially collapsed in Africa as well as Spain, leaving Muslim Andalusia divided between adherents of Muhammad ibn Hud, a soldier of fortune from Murcia, and those of Muhammad al-Ahmar "the Red," more politician than soldier, but a very good politician. Ibn Hud's fortunes rose and fell with the battles he fought; it was he whom Alfonso IX had defeated at the castle of Alange near Mérida, and in January 1233 Gonzalo Yáñez, Master of Santiago and an able and resolute commander, similarly prevented him from relieving Trujillo, the last major Moorish stronghold in Extremadura, which was reconquered that month. At the same time King San Fernando laid siege to the fortified town of Ubeda, the last remaining Moorish stronghold near the Pass of the Overthrow of the Infidel Dogs, and compelled it to capitulate in July. Showing a new respect for the humanity of his opponents, San Fernando—like James at Valencia—allowed Ubeda's defenders wishing to leave, to go with whatever they could carry.[44]

---

[42]Lomax, *Reconquest of Spain*, p. 148; Swift, *James I the Conqueror*, pp. 62-64.
[43]Lomax, *Reconquest of Spain*, p. 148; Swift, *James I the Conqueror*, pp. 64-69.
[44]Lomax, *Reconquest of Spain*, pp. 139-144; González, *Conquistas de Fernando III*, pp. 66-67; Fernández de Retana, *San Fernando III*, pp. 157-159.

During 1234 two of the great nobles of Castile—the former renegade Alvar Pérez de Castro, who had once fought for the Moors, and the Basque Lope Díaz de Haro—revolted when their feudally advantageous marriages were disallowed for consanguinity by the bishops of Castile. The suppression of this revolt—ended by a peace treaty with the two nobles arranged by Queen Mother Berenguela by which they gave up their purported wives but retained their liberty and estates—was followed by a new campaign in Andalusia after which Fernando accepted a large sum of money from Ibn Hud for a year's truce. This enabled him to turn his full strength against Muhammad the Red, aided by the additional income from Ibn Hud's tribute in procuring weapons and supplies. Ibn Hud had all he could do to hold Sevilla, the greatest city of Andalusia; Muhammad the Red was likewise hard pressed to hold what he had; Córdoba, for centuries the capital of Muslim Spain, controlled by neither, slipped into virtual anarchy. In January 1236 an independent band of Christians suddenly seized one of the two separately fortified sections of the city, and called on San Fernando for help.[45]

Reacting instantly, "like an eagle flying on its prey," Fernando dashed south from Salamanca, where he had been wintering, toward Córdoba, despite flooding rivers and mud-bound roads. All the great noble families of Castile and León united in support of this enterprise, for Córdoba loomed very large in the history and legend of the Reconquest.[46] It was to Córdoba that Pelayo was being taken as a prisoner ("Why must Death be there in ambush, as I come nigh to Córdoba," as García Lorca sang)[47] when he escaped to begin the Christian resistance to the infidel conquest of Spain that had now continued for more than five hundred years. It was to Córdoba that Almansur the Ever-Victorious had taken the sacred bells of Santiago de Compostela more than two hundred years before. In Córdoba stood the largest, most famous and most beautiful mosque in Muslim Spain, with its proverbial "forest of columns." Córdoba's political prominence was past, for it had not been the Moorish capital since the North African empires took power in Muslim Spain, but it was an unforgettable symbol.

On February 7, 1236 San Fernando laid siege to Córdoba. Ibn Hud brought up a relieving army, but having suffered two defeats in similar situations, beholding the size of the Spanish force that had so swiftly assembled and the strength of the walls of the half of Córdoba that the Christians had already been taken, he drew off without fighting. Reinforcements for the besiegers streamed in. Fernando made an alliance with Muhammad the Red, who hated the Cordobans because they had driven him out of their city.

---

[45]Lomax, *Reconquest of Spain*, pp. 138, 144-145; González, *Conquistas de Fernando III*, pp. 70-76; Fernández de Retana, *San Fernando III*, pp. 160-162, 196-197, 199-202.
[46]Lomax, *Reconquest of Spain*, p. 145.
[47]See Volume II of this history, p. 273.

Deprived of all aid from their co-religionists, the Cordobans had to capitulate on the usual terms: any who wished to leave could go with whatever they could carry, but the city would be turned over to the Christians. The capitulation was announced June 29; that day the Cross was raised atop the minaret of the great mosque, and San Fernando declared Christ the conqueror of Córdoba. The next day he made his triumphal entry, sat upon the throne of the old Muslim kings, declared the great mosque now a cathedral, and ordered the bells taken by Almansur from Santiago de Compostela to be returned at once to Spain's most revered shrine. On September 3 Pope Gregory IX issued a bull hailing San Fernando's greatest reconquest, and granting him substantial funds earmarked for crusading to pay some of the costs of his decisive campaign.[48]

After making his peace with the Pope in 1230, Emperor Frederick II concentrated for the next several years on establishing an unlimited despotism over the kingdom of Sicily and southern Italy, where he had grown up and which he ruled by inheritance from his long-dead mother, while allowing a large degree of local autonomy in Germany and the Lombard cities of northern Italy. Frederick was still a relatively young man at 36; if he were to live the normal span for a ruler in those days, he would have another 20 to 25 years to expand the totalitarianism in his native kingdom to all or most of the rest of the Empire.

In August 1231 Frederick issued the Constitutions of Melfi (*Liber Augustalis*), a codification of the old Norman laws of the Kingdom of Sicily combined with a large body of new laws decreed by Frederick. It was the first codification of law for a nation to have been done since the reign of the Roman Emperor Justinian, and it reflected a concept of absolute monarchy derived from pre-Christian Rome. Frederick II's admiring modern biographers testify unreservedly to the totalitarian and secular character of this law code,[49] which put Frederick almost in the place of God Himself:

> Roman law, never absent from a Hohenstaufen court, provided ample theoretical support for his [Frederick II's] absolutism; the Arabic states, intimately observed by him during his crusade, revealed to him the bureaucratic agencies through which the theory of absolutism could be applied in practice to an unlimited sovereignty. Just as he conceived of his temporal authority as ordained of God and independent of the restraints of the Pope, so he regarded his "Order of Justice" as resting, not upon a

---

[48]Lomax, *Reconquest of Spain*, pp. 145-146; González, *Conquistas de Fernando III*, pp. 77-80; Fernández de Retana, *San Fernando III*, pp. 204-212.

[49]This admiration of modern historians and biographers for Frederick II's claims of unlimited power is the most extreme example of the attitude also reflected in the leading modern biographies of Henry II of England and Emperor Frederick I Barbarossa, that centralized despotism—which surely most of these authors would reject in their own century—was preferable in the High Middle Ages to respect for the Pope's authority as moral judge of the actions of temporal government.

foundation of clerical and feudal officialdom, but upon a group of lay jurists schooled in ancient Roman administrative, legislative, and judicial processes. The Byzantine heritage of Sicily, with its pattern of sovereignty in which all the reins of government were joined and tightly held in the hands of a central hierarchy, served in part to create an atmosphere thoroughly congenial to the political ideals of Frederick II. . . .

After the promulgation of the *Liber Augustalis* in 1231, the trend toward secularization became more pronounced. While this trend was, in some measure, the most revolutionary feature of the Hohenstaufen era as a whole, its realization in the political sphere was so complete under Frederick II as to make of it the most striking characteristic of his reign. Indeed this political change is but a single manifestation of what has been aptly described as "a spiritual revolution of immeasurable importance which amounted in essence to a secularization of the whole of human life."[50]

In the Book of Laws he [Frederick II] unhesitatingly takes up his position to the philosophical query of the day: Did God create the world or did God only mould existing primeval matter? God fashioned existing matter, he says—that is, just like the Emperor. . . . It was a commonplace that the Creation (Adam in Paradise) and the Redemption (the birth of Christ) were the beginning and the middle of an epoch, to which the end should be like. This fulness of time had now come, under the sceptre of the Emperor of Justice, Frederick II, the expected Messianic ruler whom the Sibyls had foretold.[51]

Pope Gregory IX well knew what all of this meant. He warned Frederick against "promulgating new laws" which would make him a persecutor of the Church and a destroyer of the freedom of Christian people, and afterward condemned Archbishop Jacob of Capua for aiding in the drafting of the Constitutions of Melfi, which the Pope said "have renounced salvation and conjured up immeasurable ill."[52]

The Lombards in northern Italy sensed the coming danger. In October 1231 the Lombard League, triumphant against Frederick II's grandfather Barbarossa in the days of Pope Alexander III, re-formed and resolved to raise an army to fight him should he seek to impose his will upon them in contravention of Barbarossa's peace settlement for Lombardy agreed upon with Alexander III. Pope Gregory IX offered to arbitrate between Frederick and the Lombards, but the autocratic Emperor would consent to no arbitration—certainly not by the Pope who had once excommunicated him. He suppressed a rising in Sicily against his absolute rule, pushed his son Henry into rebellion against him in Germany, and then held Henry in prison until he committed suicide by riding his horse off a cliff while being transferred between

[50]Van Cleve, *Frederick II*, pp. 240, 257.
[51]Kantorowicz, *Frederick II*, pp. 250, 259.
[52]*Ibid.*, p. 261.

jails. In 1235, at a gorgeous Imperial Diet meeting at Mainz, Frederick II proclaimed "public peace" in German as well as Latin and promulgated a body of laws defining the jurisdiction of princes and bishops in Germany, specifying crimes and punishments, and creating an imperial Grand Justiciar. These seemed to be first steps toward introducing a Sicilian-type regime in Germany, though in fact Frederick never got that far because he could never overcome the Pope and the Lombards. At the Diet at Mainz Frederick declared his intention to invade Lombardy during the coming spring if the Lombards continued to defy him.[53]

Pope Gregory IX replied with new warnings in the winter of 1236. He reminded Frederick II that the liberties of the Lombard cities had been guaranteed by the Church for more than fifty years, and that if he went to war with them against the Pope's advice he would be violating those liberties which the Church had placed under her protection. The Pope also objected strongly to Frederick's taxation and control of the church in the Kingdom of Sicily, and to his maintenance of thousands of Muslims at public expense in the region of Lucera in southern Italy, from whom his personal bodyguard was drawn. As usual, Frederick paid no heed to the Pope's words; in August he descended into Italy with an army, took Verona and Cremona against strong Lombard resistance, and laid siege to Mantua. On November 1 Frederick took Vicenza after a 70-mile march and killed many of its leading citizens. Ferrara surrendered to him, but then he had to return to Germany to deal with an Austrian rebellion, before having reached his principal objective in Lombardy, the great metropolis of Milan.[54]

In May 1237 Pope Gregory IX's legates reported to him the horrible treatment of prisoners by the Emperor, including mutilation and reprisals against their wives and children, and his persistent lack of respect for sacred things. Frederick now demanded the complete dissolution of the Lombard League, and his spokesman to the Church, Grand Master Hermann von Salza of the Teutonic Knights, informed the Cardinals by letter in July that the war against the Lombards would continue until they were fully subjugated. In September Frederick returned to Mantua, his army reinforced not only by additional German contingents but by 10,000 Muslims from Lucera. He took Mantua in October, then pressed on toward Milan. On November 27 he defeated the whole army of the Lombard League at Cortenuova, taking the *carroccio* (a kind of carriage brought into the battlefield as the centerpiece of a city's army) of Milan to mark his triumph. He then demanded Milan's unconditional surrender. Its people heroically refused, calling on the Pope for

---

[53]Van Cleve, *Frederick II*, pp. 360-362, 378-379, 382-385; Kantorowicz, *Frederick II*, pp. 280, 376-377, 416-417; Mann, *Popes in the Middle Ages*, XIV, 251, 256-257, 260-261.
[54]Van Cleve, *Frederick II*, pp. 398-399; Kantorowicz, *Frederick II*, pp. 418, 430-432; Mann, *Popes in the Middle Ages*, XIV, 268-269, 272-273.

help. Frederick sent the captured *carroccio* to Rome to remind the Pope who was master of the battlefield.[55]

Seeking help outside Italy, Pope Gregory IX now appealed to the victorious James the Conqueror of Aragon, who promised to send him 2,000 knights after the reconquest of Valencia was completed (though in fact they never came). Frederick also secured international contingents for his army from England, France, Castile, Hungary, and even the Byzantine empire of Nicaea, to press the siege of Brescia in the summer of 1238. But a Spanish engineer named Calmandrinus was advising its defenders; the Spanish were experts in siege warfare, and Calmandrinus showed the Brescians how to destroy the siege engines being used against them. The siege stopped making progress, and Frederick II abandoned it after a brilliant sortie from the beleaguered city inflicted heavy losses on his army. Meanwhile the Pope had sent the capable and incorruptible Gregory of Montelongo as his legate to Lombardy, to inform Frederick II that unless he stopped the war and made "substantial satisfaction" to the Pope, he would be excommunicated again. In a public statement in October the Pope renewed his complaints against Frederick's oppression of clergy, churches, monasteries, and religious orders in Sicily, and his partiality toward Muslims.[56]

In reply Frederick wrote to the cardinals on March 10, 1239, denying Papal authority in the Church. Peter, Frederick said, had been "only spokesman and executor among the apostles," not their chief. Frederick declared the cardinals to be equally and personally responsible for the Pope's actions and their consequences. On Palm Sunday Pope Gregory IX excommunicated him for the second time, for claiming authority over the city of Rome and arousing it against the Pope; for imprisoning and slaying clergymen in Sicily and keeping 20 cathedrals and two monasteries there without bishops and abbots, respectively; for preventing a Papal legate from going to southern France to aid in the final suppression of the Catharist heresy; and for impeding the crusade that would be required again when the ten-year period of Christian control of Jerusalem that he had negotiated ended in August of this year. The Pope pronounced all oaths of fealty to Frederick II no longer binding, and called for his immediate removal from power.[57]

Frederick heard the news of his second excommunication at Easter. His response was total defiance. He ordered the removal of all Franciscans and Dominicans from Sicily and southern Italy, executed or exiled all priests in those

---

[55]Van Cleve, *Frederick II*, pp. 404-408, 411-413; Kantorowicz, *Frederick II*, pp. 435-438, 459-461; Mann, *Popes in the Middle Ages*, XIV, 274-275, 277-278.

[56]Van Cleve, *Frederick II*, pp. 414-417; Kantorowicz, *Frederick II*, pp. 463-465, 468; Mann, *Popes in the Middle Ages*, XIV, 283; Swift, *James I the Conqueror*, p. 67.

[57]Van Cleve, *Frederick II*, pp. 422-424, 428-429; Kantorowicz, *Frederick II*, pp. 471-473; Mann, *Popes in the Middle Ages*, XIV, 283-285.

regions who were reluctant to defy the Papal interdict by saying Mass, and appointed bishops there without the Pope's permission. On April 20 he circulated a letter to the kings and princes of Europe condemning the Pope's action against him in the most violent and apocalyptic terms, and demanding a general council.[58] He attacked Pope Gregory IX personally, calling him "an unfaithful man in your midst, a prophet of unwholesome mind, a priest who defiles the Church, who acts unjustly in a defiance of the law."[59]

This he said of Ugolino Conti, the friend and disciple and ardent champion of St. Francis of Assisi. And Pope Gregory IX replied:

> This King of the Pestilence has proclaimed that—to use his own words—all the world has been deceived by three deceivers, Jesus Christ, Moses and Muhammad, of whom two died in honor, but Christ upon the Cross. And further, he has proclaimed aloud (or rather he has lyingly declared) that all be fools who believe that God could be born of a Virgin, God Who is the Creator of Nature and of all beside.[60]

The battle was joined, on spiritual, political, and military fronts. The history of Christendom has seen none greater, for the very existence of Christendom was at stake. Christendom means the reign of Christ. Frederick II sought to rule all Christendom, by his sole fiat, with the Pope his obedient servant. And Frederick II did not appear to believe in Christ as king, or in anything or anyone but himself.

The Holy Roman Emperor was assaulting the Church from within; and from without, in this dark year 1239, the greatest external menace which civilization in Europe and Asia has ever faced was gathering on the eastern horizon. The Mongols, having conquered half China and all of central Asia, were riding westward, their deadly horse archers under the command of one of the greatest generals of all time, Subotai who never lost a battle. Their goal was no less than the conquest of all Europe, and of the whole civilized world.

The two mortal threats, from its own Emperor and from the alien horde, bore down upon Christendom like twin guided missiles from Hell during the summer and fall of 1239. In June Frederick II decreed the death penalty for anyone bringing any letter from the Pope into the kingdom of Sicily and south Italy. He announced that the same structure of totalitarian administration he had imposed upon that kingdom would now also be imposed throughout northern Italy and southeastern France, and sent his armies there to enforce its imposition. During the summer he hanged the son of the Doge of Venice who

---

[58]Van Cleve, *Frederick II*, pp. 429-430; Kantorowicz, *Frederick II*, pp. 473-474, 480-482, 496-498; Mann, *Popes in the Middle Ages*, XIV, 286-288.
[59]Van Cleve, *Frederick II*, p. 430.
[60]Kantorowicz, *Frederick II*, pp. 499-500.

fell into his hands and burned at the stake the daughter of the *podestà* (mayor) of Ravenna who had dared to resist him. Brother Elias, the former head of the Franciscans whom the order, with the Pope's tacit encouragement, had removed in May for his autocratic ways and luxurious life-style, went over to Frederick that summer, confident that neither of his shortcomings would disturb the Emperor; the Pope consequently excommunicated Brother Elias. The Pope's legate in Germany, Albert of Behaim, offered the imperial crown first to Duke Otto of Brunswick and then to King Abel of Denmark, but neither would accept it for fear of Frederick; nor would even King St. Louis IX of France, on the advice of his mother Blanche. By year's end Frederick was preparing for a full-scale invasion of the Papal states.[61]

Meanwhile the Mongol invasion force, under the tactical command of Subotai and the overall command of Genghis Khan's senior grandson Batu, had in 1238 taken and burned first Moscow and then the city of Vladimir, for nearly a century the capital of Russia, after a siege of only six days, killing all they found within including the family of the Grand Duke, who had taken refuge in the cathedral which the Mongols burned over their heads. A month later they had killed the Grand Duke in a battle on the Sita River near Yaroslavl.[62] The terror of the Mongol name now flew before them, and in 1239 the prince of the Cumans of south Russia asked King Bela IV of Hungary to permit his whole people, numbering over 100,000, to settle in Hungary if they promised to become Catholic. Bela agreed. The Mongols considered the Cumans their legitimate prey; they sent a letter warning Bela that because of his arrangement with him they now included him among their enemies.[63] In October they destroyed Chernigov, less than 100 miles north of Kiev, though its Prince Michael heroically maintained his resistance to them.[64]

Invading the Papal states in January 1240, Frederick II with his army soon reached his birthplace, Jesi. He hailed it in language which his opponents reasonably regarded as blasphemous, as:

> the place of our illustrious birth, where our divine mother brought us into the world, where our radiant cradle stood ... Thou, O Bethlehem, city of the March, art not least among the cities of our race, for out of thee the

[61]*Ibid.*, pp. 475-480, 482, 487, 490, 508-511; Van Cleve, *Frederick II*, pp. 433, 436-439, 441; Mann, *Popes in the Middle Ages*, XIV, 192-193, 292, 295-297; Moorman, *Franciscan Order*, pp. 101-102.

[62]George Vernadsky, *The Mongols and Russia*, Volume III of "A History of Russia" (New Haven CT, 1953), pp. 50-51; René Grousset, *The Empire of the Steppes* (New Brunswick NJ, 1970), p. 265; James Chambers, *The Devil's Horsemen; the Mongol Invasion of Europe* (New York, 1979), pp. 73-75.

[63]Denis Sinor, *History of Hungary* (New York, 1959), p. 68; Vernadsky, *Mongols and Russia*, p. 52; Chambers, *Devil's Horsemen*, pp. 77-78.

[64]Martin Dimnik, *Mikhail, Prince of Chernigov and Grand Prince of Kiev, 1224-1246* (Toronto, 1981), pp. 83-85, 166.

Leader is come, the prince of the Roman Empire, that he might rule thy people and protect thee and not suffer that thou be in future subject to a foreign hand [the Pope's].[65]

On February 22 Frederick was within sight of Rome. It was the feast of St. Peter's Chair. Pope Gregory IX emerged from his palace, the tiara on his head, to lead a procession of all ranks of the Roman clergy, wearing their vestments and bearing a fragment of the True Cross and the heads of the apostles St. Peter and St. Paul. Singing and praying, they marched through the streets to St. Peter's basilica, accompanied by a partly hostile crowd of laymen from the city, some actually carrying the imperial eagles of Frederick II. At the basilica the dauntless Pope turned to face them all. "I do not flee," Gregory IX declared in a firm, measured voice. "Here I await the mercy of the Lord." Then he took off his tiara and placed it over the relics of the two primary apostles. "Ye Holy Ones!" he cried. "Protect Rome when the Romans care for her no more!"[66]

This was defiance from beyond the world, defiance echoing in eternity; and the people knew it. It was as though they heard the trumpet of the Judgment. Those who carried eagles flung them into the dust; all knelt and made the sign of the Cross. With sobs and tears of remorse and passionate conviction they cried out their determination to defend the city of the Vicar of Christ to the death.[67]

Like Attila the Hun eight hundred years before, Frederick II with all his army was turned away from Rome by one white-haired old man with a staff. On March 16 the thirteenth-century master of propaganda could think of only this to say to explain his retreat: that Pope Gregory had "induced some boys and old women and a very few hired troops to assume the cross against us."[68]

If that were all the Pope had done, why had the mighty Emperor fled?

In June Frederick II offered to begin peace negotiations with the Pope, but Gregory IX would not hear of it; there would be no peace with this man while he still claimed to be Emperor and remained resolved upon the conquest of the Lombard cities, as Frederick uncompromisingly declared he still was. So in August 1240 Pope Gregory called a special council, which he called a "diet of Christendom," to judge the dispute between Frederick II and himself, to meet at Easter in 1241; he insisted it must include the bishops of the Lombard cities. Frederick's response was to declare flatly that he would "not allow the council to be summoned," that he would give no bishop a safe-conduct to attend it, and

---

[65]Kantorowicz, *Frederick II*, p. 512.

[66]*Ibid.*, p. 516; Van Cleve, *Frederick II*, pp. 444-445.

[67]Kantorowicz, *Frederick II*, p. 516; Van Cleve, *Frederick II*, p. 445; Mann, *Popes in the Middle Ages*, XIV, 300.

[68]Mann, *Popes in the Middle Ages*, XIV, 300n.

would arrest and imprison any who attempted to come.[69]

Meanwhile, during this summer of 1240, the Mongols were on the march again; they demanded the surrender of Kiev, the capital of Ukraine from which the conversion of all the Russian lands had begun 250 years before. Its current ruler, Prince Daniel of Galicia, refused their demand; but on December 6 the Mongols took Kiev by storm after fierce street fighting. So many desperate refeugees climbed to the roof of the Church of the Blessed Virgin Mary, as well as assembling inside, that it collapsed, killing everyone. Kiev was totally looted, even the tombs of its saints broken open, but its cathedral was spared, and some other buildings.[70]

The Mongols were now within striking distance of Hungary. They preferred to campaign in the winter, when the rivers and marshes were frozen and their astonishingly hardy men and horses could survive and function well while their civilized opponents were virtually immobilized.[71] General Subotai set the winter of 1241 as the time for the conquest of Hungary and the devastation of all Eastern Europe.[72]

Whether Subotai fully realized it or not, Christendom had virtually nothing with which to oppose the alien horde. The Emperor's armies were directed against the Pope; the Pope's armies were directed against the Emperor; the positions of the two men were utterly irreconcilable. A confused and apathetic crusade in Palestine, stimulated by the end of Frederick II's truce with the Muslims there and ineffectively led by Count Theobald of Champagne, had just ended in futility and bitterness in September 1240.[73] For all its glorious achievements from the consecration of Pope St. Leo IX to the death of St. Francis of Assisi, Christendom had not been so weak and divided in the face of a deadly enemy since the time of Pelayo in the eighth century.

But Christendom still had a great and valorous Pope, kings of France and of Castile who would later be honored as saints, brave knights who would fight to the finish for the Church and the Faith; and in Heaven, St. Francis and St. Dominic were surely praying for the Church so threatened in the world they had left.

On February 12, 1241 Pope Gregory IX formally proclaimed a crusade against Frederick II, entitling those taking part in it to all the indulgences granted to crusaders fighting in the Holy Land, and authorized vows of crusading in the Holy Land to be commuted by crusading against Frederick, or

---

[69]*Ibid.*, XIV, 301-303; Van Cleve, *Frederick II*, pp. 446-448; Kantorowicz, *Frederick II*, pp. 536-539.

[70]Vernadsky, *Mongols and Russia*, p. 52; Grousset, *Empire of the Steppes*, p. 265; Chambers, *Devil's Horsemen*, pp. 79-81; Dimnik, *Mikhail, Prince of Chernigov*, pp. 88-89.

[71]Vernadsky, *Mongols and Russia*, p. 50.

[72]Chambers, *Devil's Horsemen*, pp. 81-82.

[73]Setton, *Crusades*, II, 463-481.

redeemed for specified sums of money to be used against Frederick. Genoa, allied with the Pope, prepared a fleet to bring prelates to Rome for the Easter council the Pope had proclaimed; Frederick appointed a renegade Genoese Admiral of the Roman Empire with orders to stop the Genoese fleet.[74]

On February 13 the Mongols, swarming into Poland, took Sandomir and divided into three corps, one going north to attack Prussia, a second going west into Germany, and the third following the Vistula River south toward Cracow. The Hungarian army gathered at Budapest, but knew not in which direction to move. On March 12 the Mongols forced the Carpathian passes and descended into the Hungarian plain; on the 18th the Mongol detachment riding toward Cracow defeated the Polish army of King Boleslav V at Chmielnik. He fled to Moravia, while the Mongols, outstripping the news of their victory, appeared without warning before Cracow. Legend—which may well be true—tells how its trumpeter, atop the highest tower in the city, saw them coming and blew a frantic warning, cut off when a Mongol arrow pierced his throat. (A re-creation of that trumpeter's interrupted call is still heard every hour on the main square of Cracow.) The Mongols took and burned Cracow, then pressed on southward to join their compatriots in Hungary. On April 9 the westernmost Mongol army under the command of Baidar defeated 30,000 Germans, Poles, and Teutonic Knights at the Battle of Liegnitz, killing the Christian commander, Duke Henry of Liegnitz. But 50,000 Bohemians were only a day's march away, and Hungary remained the principal Mongol objective for this campaign; immediately after their victory, Baidar and his men rode away to join Subotai's main force in Hungary.[75]

The Hungarians had no chance; Subotai was one of the great generals of history, and they had never seen anything like the Mongol cavalry in battle. At the Sajo River April 11 the Mongols slew at least 60,000 Hungarians, and that many or more Hungarian civilians afterwards as they pursued their usual policy of making a city-less desert out of most countries they conquered. King Bela IV fled Hungary with a Mongol force behind him under orders to pursue him to his death; he escaped only by reaching an island in the Adriatic Sea, where they could not follow him for lack of boats or experience in them.[76] Frantic appeals for help from the conquered and threatened peoples came to both Emperor and Pope, but neither could send aid because of the exigencies of their struggle to the death with each other; but in July, as the first Mongol troops penetrated

---

[74]*Ibid.*, II, 352; Kantorowicz, *Frederick II*, pp. 542-546, 548; Mann, *Popes in the Middle Ages*, XIV, 308-309.

[75]Sinor, *History of Hungary*, pp. 70-72; Grousset, *Empire of the Steppes*, pp. 266, 277; Chambers, *Devil's Horsemen*, pp. 91-93, 97-101; Norman Davies, *God's Playground; a History of Poland* (New York, 1984), I, 87.

[76]Sinor, *History of Hungary*, pp. 72-73, 75; Grousset, *Empire of the Steppes*, pp. 266-267; Chambers, *Devil's Horsemen*, pp. 101-104, 111; John V. A. Fine Jr., *The Late Medieval Balkans* (Ann Arbor MI, 1987), p. 145.

Austria at Wiener Neustadt, the Pope did proclaim a crusade against them, at the very moment when Frederick II was laying waste the countryside around Rome.[77]

For during that same terrible spring of 1241 the conflict between Pope and Emperor had reached a climax almost as fierce as that created by Frederick's appearance before Rome in February 1240. More than a hundred prelates, including a substantial number of bishops and three cardinals, were captured when the Genoese fleet on which they were sailing to Rome was attacked and totally defeated by Frederick II's fleet, commanded by his illegitimate son Enzio, off the barren island of Montecristo. Twenty-two of the 27 ships were captured. On the vigorous demand of King St. Louis IX of France, Frederick soon released captured French bishops, but retained all the others, keeping them in close confinement in conditions of extreme harshness. The few bishops who escaped this disaster wrote the Pope urging him to hold firm and insisting that Frederick II never again be recognized as Emperor, for "under his rule the Church would never enjoy peace." But Cardinal John Colonna, who had long been wavering in his allegiance, left Rome in August to join the Emperor, and at approximately the same time Frederick seized a castle near Montefortino in Campania where several of the Pope's nephews and relatives had taken refuge, and hanged them all.[78]

Pope Gregory IX was an old man now, and had been under almost unendurable strain for the past two and a half years. Throughout medieval and early modern times August, with its enervating heat and rampant malaria, was the dying month in Rome; and it was in August 1241 that the great Pope who had been the good friend of St. Francis died. His imperial enemy rejoiced, thinking all his troubles were now over.[79]

But, until the end of the world, there will always be a Pope. Mortality never defeats the Vicar of Christ.

There can, however, be papal vacancies for a time. One of the worst of these, in all the Church's history, now ensued.

For the cardinals were profoundly divided and very much afraid. There were only fourteen of them—far too few. Two—James Pecoraria of Palestrina and Otto of St. Nicholas—were prisoners of Frederick and he would not let them go, apparently simply to remind the others of his despotic power, since Otto is said to have been ready to vote as the Emperor wished, though James

[77]Joseph Gill, *Byzantium and the Papacy, 1198-1400* (New Brunswick NJ, 1979), p. 186; Mann, *Popes in the Middle Ages*, XV, 182-183; Grousset, *Empire of the Steppes*, p. 267; Chambers, *Devil's Horsemen*, pp. 107-108; Kantorowicz, *Frederick II*, p. 553; Vernadsky, *Mongols and Russia*, pp. 56-57.

[78]Mann, *Popes in the Middle Ages*, XIV, 310-312, 316, 439-440; Van Cleve, *Frederick II*, pp. 450-451; Kantorowicz, *Frederick II*, pp. 548-550.

[79]Mann, *Popes in the Middle Ages*, XIV, 316, 440-441, 443-444; Kantorowicz, *Frederick II*, pp. 559-560.

would not. Two—Thomas and Peter of Capua—were away from Rome and showed no disposition to return for the conclave. The remaining ten were split six to four. The six were either Frederick's partisans or wanted peace at almost any price; the four—including two future Popes, Innocent IV and Alexander IV—stood as firm against Frederick as Gregory IX had done. Two-thirds were needed to elect a Pope, by the electoral procedure established by Pope Nicholas II's bull *In Nomine Domini* in 1059 and retained ever since. This time no two-thirds vote could be obtained, since none of the four constant cardinals would accept a nominee favorable to the Emperor, while none of the other six would accept anyone else.[80]

Unfortunately the struggle at the conclave was more than simply a continuation of the struggle between the dead Pope Gregory IX and Emperor Frederick II. A new potentate made his appearance: Senator Matteo Orsini of Rome. After the Roman people resolved to fight the Emperor under the inspiration of Pope Gregory IX in February 1240, Orsini had emerged as their leader, and his new authority had gone to his head. Like the Emperor, he now wanted a Pope subservient to him, and he wanted the new Pope chosen quickly. The longer the deadlock continued, the more precarious Orsini's position became, for the Pope's prestige was necessary to maintain the defense of Rome against the skillful and opportunistic Frederick.[81]

Therefore Orsini made the accommodations of the cardinals, both for living and for meeting, increasingly uncomfortable until they became actively dangerous to the health of these men, most of them advanced in years and some very infirm. In the end Orsini had them not only locked in, but bound hand and foot in a leaky room into which excrement dripped from the guards' latrine above it. He actually threatened to exhume Gregory IX's corpse and put it in the room with them. Eventually one of the cardinals, the Englishman Robert of Somercote, died; another, Sinibaldi Fieschi (the future Pope Innocent IV) appeared to be fatally stricken. But the two were on opposite sides, Robert being with the compromising majority. His death left the vote at five to four, and even if Fieschi died the majority for compromise would still be five to three, not yet two-thirds. And in the end Fieschi recovered.[82]

There are several conflicting stories about how the deadlock was broken; some or none of them may be true, but they cannot all be. The eventual choice was a dying man, his death clearly hastened by his ordeal bound in the locked chamber: Godfrey Castiglione of Santa Sabina, a Milanese who took the name of Celestine IV. He was one of the compromise faction, but the only significant official act of the seventeen days of his pontificate was to outlaw the power-mad

[80]Mann, *Popes in the Middle Ages*, XIV, 444-448; Van Cleve, *Frederick II*, pp. 456-457; Kantorowicz, *Frederick II*, pp. 574-576.

[81]Van Cleve, *Frederick II*, pp. 453, 456.

[82]*Ibid.*, p. 457; Mann, *Popes in the Middle Ages*, XIV, 448-449.

Senator Orsini. However, there was no one to enforce the outlawry; and as soon as Celestine IV died, six of the cardinals fled from Rome to Anagni. Orsini had imprisoned Cardinal John Colonna, while Sinibaldo Fieschi was still recovering from his near-fatal illness. The other cardinal remaining in Rome, Richard Annibaldi, was also an anti-imperialist. The already too small college of cardinals was therefore now split into no less than five groups: two prisoners of Frederick II, one prisoner of Senator Orsini, two remaining in Rome under Orsini's rule, six at Anagni, and the other two somewhere else outside Rome. No new conclave could possibly be held under such conditions, as the cardinals at Anagni vigorously pointed out, citing *In Nomine Domini* in favor of their position; and none was held for a year and a half.[83]

Frederick II appears to have been serenely confident through all this that his power position was so dominant that it must in the end be recognized by all reasonable churchmen, that Pope Gregory IX's unyielding opposition was unique to him. Frederick reminded the cardinals of his power by keeping captive the two cardinals he held—one for him and one against him—and by a march on Rome in July 1242. The next month he withdrew from Rome and released the imprisoned cardinal who favored him, Otto of St. Nicholas, but took no action to obtain the selection of any particular individual as Pope.[84]

On Christmas day 1241 the Mongols crossed the frozen Danube, taking Buda and besieging the Hungarian primatial city of Esztergom; at almost the same time they invaded Croatia and took Zagreb, while continuing the pursuit of the fugitive King Bela IV of Hungary. Though repelled from some strongly defended forts, they devastated lands in Austria as far as Vienna. During the winter of 1242 they seized the whole Dalmatian coast south to Cattaro.[85] But while they were doing so, news of the greatest importance came from far to the east via the extraordinary Mongol "pony express." Ogadai, the Great Khan, the third son of Genghis elected in 1227 to succeed him, had died in December—perhaps of alcoholism, perhaps by poison. The only other surviving son of Genghis Khan had died soon afterward, leaving Ogadai's widow Turakina—who knew little of the world beyond the steppes—regent pending the decision on a successor. By Mongol tradition that decision could only be made by a *kuriltai*, a council of all the Mongol leaders including the whole family and descendants of Genghis Khan.[86]

Batu, Genghis Khan's senior grandson, had deeply offended Ogadai and

[83]Mann, *Popes in the Middle Ages*, XIV, 449-450; XV, 5-6; Van Cleve, *Frederick II*, p. 458; Kantorowicz, *Frederick II*, pp. 576-577.

[84]Van Cleve, *Frederick II*, pp. 459-460; Kantorowicz, *Frederick II*, pp. 577-578; Mann, *Popes in the Middle Ages*, XV, 9-12.

[85]Sinor, *History of Hungary*, p. 75; Grousset, *Empire of the Steppes*, p. 267; Chambers, *Devil's Horsemen*, pp. 109-112.

[86]Grousset, *Empire of the Steppes*, pp. 268, 271; Vernadsky, *Mongols and Russia*, pp. 57-60; Chambers, *Devil's Horsemen*, p. 112.

Turakina's son Guyuk, whom he expected to intrigue against him; therefore he decided he must go back to Mongolia to protect his interests. He did not want the military campaigning in Eastern Europe to continue in his absence, so in the spring of 1242 he ordered a general withdrawal of the Mongols from Hungary, Croatia, and Poland. However, they retained their hold on Russia, where Batu was later recognized as head of what came to be called the Golden Horde of the Mongols ruling Russia and Ukraine.[87] Thus for Eastern Europe the Mongol threat vanished as quickly as it had come, leaving devastation in its wake, but devastation quickly restored to prosperity so long as the terrible invaders did not return. Europe (except for Russia and Ukraine—which history was to prove a very large exception) was spared a Mongol conquest, though Christendom had done almost nothing to prevent it. The many prayers begging for such a deliverance seem to have been heard.

The cardinals at Anagni had finally settled on a demand that Frederick II release the remaining cardinal he was keeping imprisoned, James of Palestrina, as their fundamental condition for electing a new Pope. As soon as Cardinal Romanus Bonaventura, Bishop of Porto, who was considered Frederick's chief opponent among the cardinals, died in May 1243, Frederick agreed to release Cardinal James. The next month Cardinal Sinibaldo Fieschi was unanimously elected Pope Innocent IV. Although the new Pope had been one of the firm hold-outs—even to the point of death—at the heavily pressured conclave in Rome in October 1241, Frederick had by now persuaded himself that Innocent would be favorable to him. He was soon disillusioned. The terms "Guelf" and "Ghibelline" had already come into use in Italy to identify, respectively, adherents of the Pope and the Emperor; in a moment of truth Frederick cried: "No Pope *can* be a Ghibelline!"[88]

The new Pope promptly sent an embassy consisting of an archbishop, a bishop, and an abbot to negotiate with Frederick II, and instructions to require as preconditions for peace that Frederick free all the bishops he still held who had been captured on the Genoese ships two years before, and agree to include the Lombard cities in any peace settlement. Frederick received the embassy hospitably but did not specifically agree to either precondition. Before a month had passed, Pope Innocent IV had demanded his prompt acceptance of the preconditions, declaring that otherwise he would withdraw the embassy. Before that happened, however, Frederick broke off the negotiations himself because Cardinal Rainer of Viterbo, though he had been one of the compromising party at the 1241 conclave, had induced his city to rise against Frederick. A garrison loyal to Frederick continued to hold the citadel of Viterbo for him. Frederick's

---

[87]Sinor, *History of Hungary*, pp. 75-76; Vernadsky, *Mongols and Russia*, pp. 57-58; Chambers, *Devil's Horsemen*, pp. 112-113; Grousset, *Empire of the Steppes*, p. 288.

[88]Van Cleve, *Frederick II*, pp. 460-462; Kantorowicz, *Frederick II*, pp. 578-582; Mann, *Popes in the Middle Ages*, XV, 12-14. Emphasis added.

army arrived before Viterbo in September, and Pope Innocent IV contributed 2,500 ounces of gold to help pay for its defense.[89]

The siege of Viterbo continued for two months, until Frederick had to raise it. An agreement was made between him and the defenders to allow the garrison in the citadel and supporters of Frederick in the city to depart freely with whatever they could carry. But Cardinal Rainer persuaded the people of the city to violate the safe-conduct, killing, wounding and robbing many of the imperial soldiers and other departing adherents of the Emperor. The Pope immediately condemned this gross breach of faith and demanded the release of those who had survived the attack and been thrown into prison, and the restoration of their property. But Cardinal Rainer was most reluctant to do this, and during the coming months in which Innocent IV's position in Italy steadily weakened, the Pope did not feel strong enough to compel him. Despite the implications and inferences freely and eagerly drawn by modern historians friendly to Frederick and hostile to the Papacy, there is no reason whatsoever to believe that Innocent IV had any part in this treachery or did not wish full recompense to be made for it.[90]

In Holy Week of 1244 it appeared for a moment that peace with Frederick II might be attained, at least temporarily, despite his continuing hostility. On Holy Thursday his envoys swore in the Lateran palace in the presence of the Pope that Frederick would at last release all the bishops captured in 1241 who were still in his hands, give up all the territory he had taken from the Church since his excommunication, forgive all offenses committed against him by those who remained loyal to the Church since his excommunication, and accord full respect and obedience to the Pope's authority in spiritual and religious matters. But no mention was made of the Lombards; Frederick still would not admit their rights of self-government, and the Pope would not accept his denial of it. Frederick also demanded that his excommunication be lifted immediately because of what his envoys had sworn to on Holy Thursday, while the Pope—quite reasonably, in view of Frederick's record—demanded that he first actually surrender the Church lands he had seized. So the agreement collapsed before the end of April. Probably neither

[89]Van Cleve, *Frederick II*, pp. 463-467; Kantorowicz, *Frederick II*, pp. 584-585; Mann, *Popes in the Middle Ages*, XV, 35-40.

[90]Van Cleve, *Frederick II*, pp. 467-469; Kantorowicz, *Frederick II*, pp. 586-587. Of the three major biographies of Frederick II written in this century, one (Kantorowicz's) is admiring almost to the point of idolatry; another (Van Cleve's) is likewise very friendly, if more restrained; the third (David Abulafia, *Frederick II, a Medieval Emperor* [London, 1988]) takes the astonishing position that this titanic figure, whom contemporaries called *Stupor Mundi* ("Wonder of the World") and whose struggle with the Church echoes down the ages, is not very important. All these authors are in varying degrees hostile to the Church. None can be depended upon for reporting the Church's view of the conflict.

Pope nor Emperor ever had much hope for it. Their dispute ran too deep to be readily papered over.[91]

In May 1244 Innocent IV created new cardinals. The total number of the College had fallen to seven; the new appointees totalled twelve. All but one were strong supporters of a firm policy toward Frederick II, of continuing to demand his full respect for the rights of the Church and of the Lombards.[92]

A meeting between the Pope and the Emperor was scheduled to take place June 7 in the city of Narni, to try again to negotiate a treaty along the lines of what had almost been agreed upon in March. But the Pope decided not to go to Narni, believing it might be a trap to capture him—as indeed it may have been, despite the scoffing of modern historians. Many reports show that Frederick was still livid with anger over the treachery of his foes at Viterbo, and might well have felt that this would justify a treacherous seizure of the Pope in retribution (if Frederick really felt he needed moral justification for anything he wished to do). Innocent IV sent to friendly Genoa for ships to transport him there. When he heard that they had arrived at Civita Vecchia, he went to Sutri where he celebrated the vigil Mass for the great feast of Saints Peter and Paul. Just before midnight he rode out of Sutri in disguise with only seven companions. He reached Civita Vecchia the following afternoon. That night he boarded the Genoese ships; they sailed for Genoa at dawn. Only four cardinals remained behind in Rome.[93]

The voyage was very stormy, the weather battering the Pope's flotilla for a full week. He became very ill, and after it was over he had to spend three months recovering at the Cistercian abbey of St. Andrew. For the time being he felt safe in Genoa; but he still wanted to put more distance between himself and his terrible adversary, and at last to hold the council that Pope Gregory IX had tried to convene to settle once and for all the long-drawn-out controversy with the Emperor. For its place of meeting he chose Lyons, nominally under imperial control but for all practical purposes a free city, on the border of France from which the Pope had every reason to believe that the holy French King Louis IX would provide protection against any move Frederick might make to threaten it. In mid-November 1244, despite continuing bad health, Pope Innocent IV crossed the Alps over the Mont Cenis Pass, accompanied by six of his most faithful cardinals, and took up residence at the fortified monastery of St. Just in Lyons December 2.[94]

Meanwhile there had been a new and shattering disaster in the Holy

---

[91]Van Cleve, *Frederick II*, pp. 474-476; Kantorowicz, *Frederick II*, pp. 587-588; Mann, *Popes in the Middle Ages*, XV, 41-46.

[92]Mann, *Popes in the Middle Ages*, XV, 46; Van Cleve, *Frederick II*, p. 476.

[93]Mann, *Popes in the Middle Ages*, XV, 47-51; Van Cleve, *Frederick II*, pp. 476-477; Kantorowicz, *Frederick II*, pp. 588-590.

[94]Mann, *Popes in the Middle Ages*, XV, 51-65; Van Cleve, *Frederick II*, pp. 477-479.

Land, where the cause of the Crusade had been almost unavoidably neglected in the face of the vast and more immediately threatening dangers of the struggle with Frederick II and the Mongol irruption. Except for its citadel, known as the Tower of David, little had ever been done to fortify Jerusalem since it came back into the possession of the Christians, who still held most of it even after the expiration of Frederick II's ten-year truce in 1239. In the spring of 1244 a three-way conflict broke out among the Middle Eastern Muslims. Sultan Aiyub of Egypt hired an army of 10,000 ferocious, veteran mercenaries from Khwarizm, the Muslim kingdom of Central Asia that had been the first land west of China conquered by Genghis Khan. This Khwarizmian legion, leaderless since the death of Prince Jalal-ad-Din of Khwarizm in 1231, which had been fighting almost continuously for thirteen years with no country and no home, had the best soldiers in the Middle East. In June 1244 they swept over Syria to Galilee, capturing and sacking Tiberias and Nablus. Early in July they arrived at Jerusalem. The Masters of the Knights of the Temple and the Hospital came and left, seeing that neither the means nor the men were available there to repel such assailants as the Khwarizmians. On July 11 they took the holy city; on August 23 the Tower of David surrendered to them. Of the approximately six thousand Christians—men, women, and children—then living in Jerusalem, only three hundred were able to escape to the coast. The Khwarizmians sacked Jerusalem, killed its remaining priests, and burned its churches including the Church of the Holy Sepulcher. It was the final fruit of Frederick II's policy of compromise and conciliation of the Muslims of the Middle East upon which modern historians lavish so much praise.[95]

The disaster of the Khwarizmian sack of Jerusalem was magnified and underscored when on October 17, 1244, at the Battle of Gaza, the Khwarizmians and Egyptians completely defeated the Christian army finally gathered on the coast of Palestine, killing five thousand including the Master of the Templars and the Archbishop of Tyre, and capturing the Master of the Hospitallers and Count Walter of Jaffa. In November Bishop Galeran of Beirut sailed to Europe to inform Christendom that a new crusade must be called and substantial forces sent to Palestine if even the remnants of the past crusader triumphs were to be preserved. Pope Innocent IV received his plea soon after arriving in Lyons, and responded at once by proclaiming a new crusade, sending Cardinal Otto (Eudes) of Tusculum, a Frenchman, to preach it in France, and others to preach it in England, western Germany, and Scandinavia. Young Louis IX of France, just thirty years old but recently recovered from an almost mortal illness, took the Cross at once, despite the vehement objections of his mother Blanche to whom he had always before deferred. He would lead the

---

[95]Setton, *Crusades*, II, 561-562; Runciman, *Crusades*, III, 223-224.

last great crusade to the Holy Land.[96]

In a sermon given in Lyons on the feast of St. John the Evangelist, December 27, 1244, Pope Innocent IV announced that the council he had proclaimed was to meet in that city on June 24 of the coming year. He called upon Frederick II to state his case before this council, in person or through a representative, but declared that Frederick's conduct precluded a formal written invitation to him. The council would discuss the relationship between the Papacy and the Holy Roman Empire along with the continuing schism of the Greeks, the disastrous situation in the Holy Land, and the Mongol menace.[97]

In January 1245 the Pope issued the encyclical formally summoning the bishops and abbots of the Church to the council at Lyons in June. On Holy Thursday he solemnly renewed Frederick's excommunication. By Easter he had received many pleas from German and Lombard bishops that the council formally proclaim the deposition of Frederick II as Emperor, a drastic step never before taken by a Church council nor maintained for long as a demand by any Pope even after the Hildebrandine reform.[98]

Also on Easter, the Franciscan friar John of Plano Carpini set out on one of the most extraordinary papal missions in the history of the Church, bearing a letter from Pope Innocent IV to the Great Khan of the Mongols, whoever he might be (in fact, no Great Khan had been chosen since Ogadai's death).[99] This fascinating document, one world speaking to another with which it had almost nothing in common—like a communication with beings from outer space—deserves quotation at some length:

> Since not only men but irrational animals and even the mechanical mundane elements are united by some kind of natural bond, after the example of the heavenly spirits whose hosts God, the Author of the Universe, has in a perpetual and peaceful order, we are compelled to

---

[96]Setton, *Crusades*, II, 489-491, 562-564; Runciman, *Crusades*, III, 226-227, 256; Mann, *Popes in the Middle Ages*, pp. 163-169; William C. Jordan, *Louis IX and the Challenge of the Crusade* (Princeton NJ, 1979), pp. 3-13; Pernoud, *Blanche of Castile*, pp. 231-236.

[97]Mann, *Popes in the Middle Ages*, XV, 66-67; Van Cleve, *Frederick II*, pp. 478-479. Mann's thoroughly documented account of these particular events, though much older, is much to be preferred to that of Van Cleve, who attempts to create the impression that Frederick II was never "formally summoned" to the council of Lyons because he was not sent a written invitation. This legalistic quibble is disposed of by Mann's fuller report on the sermon itself, explaining that Pope Innocent IV did not deem it fitting to send a written invitation to an excommunicated ruler to attend the council, yet still wanted to give him the opportunity to defend himself if he wished to take advantage of it.

[98]Mann, *Popes in the Middle Ages*, XV, 67-70.

[99]Vernadsky, *The Mongols and Russia*, pp. 62-63; Chambers, *Devil's Horsemen*, pp. 115-121.

wonder, not without reason, how you, as we have heard, have entered
many lands of Christians and of others, have wasted them with horrible
desolation, and still, with continued fury, cease not to extend further your
destroying hands, dissolving every natural tie, and sparing neither age nor
sex, but direct against all indifferently the fury of the sword.

We, therefore, after the example of the Prince of Peace, desiring all
mankind should live in peaceful unity and in the fear of God, warn, exhort,
and beseech you earnestly to desist henceforth wholly from such outrages,
and especially from the persecution of Christians. And since by so many
and such great offenses you have doubtless grievously provoked the wrath
of the Divine Majesty, we urge you to make satisfaction to God by suitable
penance. Moreover, be not so daring as to carry your rage further, because
the omnipotent God has hitherto permitted the nations to be laid prostrate
before your face by the power of your ravening sword; for He sometimes in
this world does not punish the proud for a season to the end, that after
they have failed to humble themselves, He may at length punish them in
this life, and even still more in the world to come.

And behold we send you our beloved brother John and his
companions, bearers of these presents, men conspicuous for religion and
honorable conduct, and endowed with a knowledge of the Sacred
Scripture, whom we hope you will kindly receive with divine reverence, and
honorably treat as if they were ourselves, placing confidence in what they
say from us, and specially treat with them on what relates to peace.[100]

Friar John's fantastic journey, the account of which has often been retold,
took him to Cracow by summer 1245, through the wintry Ukraine to devastated
Kiev in January 1246, across the Mongol frontier of the Dnieper River in
February, on to Batu's court at Sarai on the Volga River by Good Friday, then
along the excellent trans-Asiatic messenger routes of the Mongol empire to
Karakorum in the highlands of Mongolia, arriving July 22 in the very midst of
the long-awaited *kuriltai* at which Ogadai's stubborn widow Turakina at last had
her way and saw her eldest son Guyuk formally crowned Great Khan.[101] Guyuk
martyred the courageous Ukrainian Prince Michael of Chernigov when he
refused to bow before an idol of Genghis Khan; a few days later the son and
heir of the Grand Prince of Vladimir also died at Karakorum, allegedly
poisoned.[102] In November Guyuk finally received the Friar John, after having
read a translation of the Pope's letter, and gave him this chilling reply:

> The strength of God [when the Mongols spoke of God they usually
> meant Tengri, the Spirit of the Eternal Blue Sky], Guyuk Khan, the ruler
> of all men to the great Pope. You and all the Christian people who dwell
> in the West have sent by your messengers certain letters for the purpose of

---

[100]Mann, *Popes in the Middle Ages*, XV, 184-185. This letter is dated from Lyons on
March 13, 1245.

[101]Grousset, *Empire of the Steppes*, pp. 268-270; Chambers, *Devil's Horsemen*, pp.
116-125.

[102]Dimnik, *Prince Mikhail of Chernigov*, pp. 130-135.

making peace with us. . . . If you desire to have peace with us, you Pope, Emperors, all kings, all men powerful in cities, by no means delay to come to us for the purpose of concluding peace, and you will hear our answer and our will. The series of your letters contained [statements] that we ought to be baptized and to become Christians; we briefly reply that we do not understand why we ought to do so.

As to what is mentioned in your letters that you wonder at the slaughter of men, and chiefly of Christians, especially Hungarians, Poles, and Moravians, we answer shortly that this too we do not understand. Nevertheless, lest we should seem to pass over it in silence, we think proper to reply as follows: It is because they have not obeyed the precept of God and of Genghis Khan, and, holding bad counsel, have slain our messengers, wherefore God had ordered them to be destroyed, and delivered them into our hands. . . . We adore God, and in His strength will overwhelm the whole earth from the east to the west.[103]

After the Pope's solemn renewal of his excommunication on Holy Thursday 1245, Frederick II apparently fully realized for the first time that Innocent IV had become as committed as Gregory IX had been to the destruction of the tyrant emperor. Consequently in May Frederick sent the refugee Patriarch Albert of Antioch to offer Innocent IV full evacuation of the Papal State, unconditional acceptance of papal arbitration of the Lombard question, and a pledge to lead a real crusade to the Holy Land and not to return until the Pope gave him permission, if Innocent would recognize his young son Conrad as Holy Roman Emperor. But Frederick's record in crusading was definitely not one to inspire confidence in the veracity of his promises. The Pope replied that before he could be given absolution and have his son recognized as Emperor, Frederick must surrender all the lands and captives he had seized and make full compensation for all the damages he had inflicted, before the council met; then he must submit to its judgment. At this Frederick still balked, while the pamphlet warfare between his partisans and the Pope's escalated to new heights of invective, and Princess Gertrude of Austria, who had been promised to him as his fourth wife, refused to marry him because of reports (probably false) that he had murdered his three previous wives.[104]

On June 26, 1245, two days after the scheduled date, the Council of Lyons convened in preliminary session, attended by about 200 bishops and abbots from many countries, though none came from Hungary due to the Mongol depredations, and few from Germany or southern Italy and Sicily due to Frederick II's brutal threats against any who might dare attend. The Latin Emperor and Patriarch of Constantinople were present, though their power and authority were only a shadow of what they had been in the immediate

---

[103]Mann, *Popes in the Middle Ages*, XV, 193-194.
[104]Van Cleve, *Frederick II*, pp. 478-483; Kantorowicz, *Frederick II*, pp. 591-596, 612-613.

aftermath of the Fourth Crusade. Bishop Galeran of Beirut was present to report on the great peril and devastation of the Holy Land. Thaddeus of Sessa, representing Frederick II, declared that if absolved and brought back into the Church Frederick would, through his influence with John Vatatzes, the Byzantine Emperor at Nicaea, bring the Greeks back into full communion with the Church, fight the Mongols, undertake a crusade to Palestine at his own expense, and make full restitution to the Church of its possessions and losses. Pope Innocent IV replied grimly that he did not trust Frederick to keep any promise he might make.[105]

Two days later the council held its first regular session. The Pope spoke at length on what he called the five wounds of the Church, the first being the sins of the clergy and the spread of heresy, the second the new Muslim seizure and destruction of Jerusalem, the third the continuing schism of the Greeks, the fourth the destruction and conquests by the Mongols, and the fifth the persecution of the Church by Frederick II. Thaddeus of Sessa tried to apologize for Frederick and said he would ask him to come before the council in person; but the Pope had already asked that, in his sermon on December 27, 1244, and Frederick had not come.[106]

The second session of the council convened July 5. The sentiment of those present was overwhelmingly against Frederick. The Spanish bishops, fired by the recent triumphs over the Muslims in their country by Kings St. Ferdinand III of Castile and James I the Conqueror of Aragon, urged the Pope to act decisively against the Emperor and vowed to defend the Pope in any new combat with Frederick "with their goods and with their lives." The Pope then declared that in his opinion Frederick should be deposed, but agreed to a plea by Thaddeus of Sessa that before the council acted on his deposition, Frederick should be given a last chance to appear in person before it. The Emperor refused, declaring that the council was biased against him, and that he would not free the bishops he had taken on the high seas in 1241 and was still holding prisoner, because they were simply pirates. No one in Christendom believed this; Frederick himself could not have believed it.[107]

At the third session, meeting July 17, Thaddeus was reduced to arguing that Frederick had not been formally and legally summoned before the Council, and that he was right not to have come because of its hostility to him. But only twelve days earlier Thaddeus himself had agreed that Frederick should come. All the tyrant Emperor's defenses had collapsed; he stood condemned out of his own mouth. The time was clearly ripe to declare his formal deposition, and on this day Pope Innocent IV did so, reviewing the whole long history of his perfidious dealings with the Popes and the Church, the Muslims and the

---

[105]Mann, *Popes in the Middle Ages*, XV, 70-72; Van Cleve, *Frederick II*, pp. 484-486.
[106]Mann, *Popes in the Middle Ages*, XV, 72-75; Kantorowicz, *Frederick II*, p. 597.
[107]Mann, *Popes in the Middle Ages*, XV, 75-77.

Greeks. He absolved all from their allegiance to him, and forbade anyone to recognize Frederick II as Emperor or king under pain of excommunication. Germany was told to choose a successor to him.[108]

Frederick reacted with blazing fury, vowing war to the finish against Christendom. "I have been anvil long enough," he cried. "Now I shall play the hammer!"[109] He told King Henry III of England that he would fight on "even though the whole world should oppose him."[110] A last attempt by King St. Louis IX of France to reconcile the Pope and Frederick at a magnificent gathering at the famous monastery of Cluny on November 30 failed. Frederick would not come, and neither he nor the Pope would yield. Though it is said that Louis believed the Pope too intransigent, he was far too loyal a Catholic to think of challenging him on an issue of such magnitude on behalf of a man who had scorned, so many times and in so many ways, the Church Louis loved.[111]

Most twentieth century historians have also regarded Pope Innocent IV as too intransigent in this matter. But from the Catholic standpoint, especially in so profoundly Catholic a century, there could be no place for an agnostic Holy Roman Emperor—a man whose interest in the Church was unmistakably limited to the degree to which he could control it, who wanted unbounded power and would stop at nothing to get it. Frederick II had far more in common with Napoleon or even with Hitler than with any of his leading contemporaries. Both Napoleon and Hitler were also apostate Catholics. Both of them and their regimes were also condemned by the Church. Neither of them, at least while they retained power, genuinely sought reconciliation, any more than did Frederick II.[112]

For the five years that remained of his life Frederick II was an outlaw, facing an iron wall of rejection from most of Christendom. The Dominican and Franciscan orders in particular gave total support to the Pope against the excommunicated Emperor.[113] Gradually many of Frederick's most loyal adherents fell away, or became the victims of his increasingly devouring suspicion. Some of their alleged plots seem to have been imaginary; others

---

[108]*Ibid.*, XV, 78-80; Van Cleve, *Frederick II*, pp. 486-487; Kantorowicz, *Frederick II*, pp. 598-599.

[109]Kantorowicz, *Frederick II*, p. 599.

[110]Mann, *Popes in the Middle Ages*, XV, 83.

[111]*Ibid.*, XV, 87-89; Van Cleve, *Frederick II*, p. 489; Pernoud, *Blanche of Castile*, pp. 241-243; Labarge, *St. Louis*, pp. 88-89.

[112]For Napoleon's relations with the Church, see E. E. Y. Hales, *Revolution and Papacy* (Notre Dame IN, 1966); for Hitler's, see Anthony Rhodes, *The Vatican in the Age of the Dictators* (New York, 1973). Napoleon is said to have repented at the end of his life after six years of confinement on the island of St. Helena. The links between Frederick II and Hitler are apparent to any discerning reader of Kantorowicz's adulatory biography of Frederick II, published in Germany in 1931 just two years before Hitler came to power.

[113]Mann, *Popes in the Middle Ages*, XV, 87; Moorman, *Franciscan Order*, p. 112.

were real, but very possibly generated by fear that the furious Emperor would
strike them first.   When he captured such conspirators he blinded them,
mutilated them, or tortured them to death, often with their wives and
children.[114] Frederick's genius and immense energy kept his cause alive, but no
more.

Henry of Raspe, elected King of the Romans and imperial candidate in
Frederick's place, defeated Frederick's son Conrad in Germany in August 1246,
but died the following February.[115] Frederick loosed upon a mostly helpless
Italy his son-in-law Ezzelino di Romano, a man of cruelty so monstrous that it
remained for centuries the stuff of nightmarish legend. Except for the Lombard
cities close to Milan and the area immediately around Rome, no one was
effectively protected from the deposed Emperor's depredations.[116] In 1247
Innocent IV declared flatly that he would never make peace with Frederick nor
any of his sons—would never recognize them as rightful rulers in any part of
Christendom. When the snow began melting in the passes that year, Frederick
tried to lead an army across the Alps to attack the Pope in Lyons, but was
forced to turn back by the news that the important city of Parma in Lombardy
had been taken from him. In July he began a long siege of Parma, defended by
the veteran papal legate and commander Gregory of Montelongo, while revolts
against Frederick broke out all over the greater part of Italy that had remained
subject to him. In November 1247 Count William of Holland was crowned King
of the Romans at Aachen, and in February 1248 the Parmesans took
Frederick's besieging army by surprise while he was out hawking and utterly
defeated it, killing his faithful Thaddeus of Sessa and seizing all the royal
treasure, the royal seal, and Frederick's crown, which was picked up by a little
man called Short-step.[117]

Still Frederick II would not surrender; and it must be understood that

---

[114]The worst examples of these real or alleged plots and Frederick's ghastly
vengeance were the conspiracies of 1246 involving Orlando di Rossi, Pandulf of
Tuscany, and Tebaldo Francisco of Parma, and of early 1249 involving Peter della
Vigna. See Van Cleve, *Frederick II*, pp. 490-493, 520-523, and Kantorowicz, *Frederick
II*, pp. 632-636, 664-667. With reference to the former, which was unquestionably a
real conspiracy, Van Cleve (*op. cit.*, pp. 491-492) points out that evidence shows that
Pope Innocent IV was aware of the conspiracy and the plan of the conspirators to seize
power in southern Italy from Frederick, but does not prove the Pope's foreknowledge
that Frederick II was to be assassinated. It is, however, true as Van Cleve states, that
Pope Innocent IV did not then or later specifically condemn projected assassination of
the tyrant emperor. Van Cleve does not mention the Catholic doctrine of tyrannicide
which might well be applied in this case, given Frederick's character and the nature of
his rule.
[115]Mann, *Popes in the Middle Ages*, XV, 94, 97; Van Cleve, *Frederick II*, p. 495;
Kantorowicz, *Frederick II*, p. 637.
[116]Van Cleve, *Frederick II*, pp. 498-500.
[117]*Ibid.*, pp. 504, 507-512; Mann, *Popes in the Middle Ages*, XV, 96-104;
Kantorowicz, *Frederick II*, pp. 642-646, 648, 654-658.

though the Pope had vowed never again to recognize Frederick or any of his sons as emperors and kings, he would never have refused absolution to them personally as genuine penitents. But none of them ever offered themselves as such; and over the coming years and decades, first the father and then each of the sons fell like meteors from the night sky of their power.

In the summer of 1248 Pope Innocent IV ordered Cardinal Stephen to preach a crusade against Frederick in southern Italy, to excommunicate all clerics there who continued to adhere to him, and to proclaim an interdict over the entire Kingdom of Sicily so long as Frederick still ruled it.[118] "He thought he had but little if he had sway only over the things of this world," Pope Innocent IV said of him, "if the things of the spirit escaped his control."[119] The Pope confirmed the rights of Sicilian bishops, including canonical elections to the episcopate, and insisted on the sole jurisdiction of Church courts over the clergy[120]—the principle that St. Thomas Becket had died for in England eighty years before. In March 1249 Frederick accused the Pope of trying personally to assassinate him, and ordered his officials in Sicily to burn at the stake any Franciscan or Dominican found to be carrying papal letters or otherwise acting with the Pope against him.[121]

Still Frederick II fought on; as late as August 1250 his army in Lombardy won a major victory over embattled Parma. Louis IX was pressing the Pope hard for peace with Frederick in view of the urgent need of crusading in the Holy Land, but the iron-souled pontiff would not grant it; in the fall of 1250 he even asked King Henry III of England for sanctuary in Bordeaux (the capital of Aquitaine, which Henry controlled as the heir of his grandmother Eleanor of Aquitaine) in case Louis IX should not allow him to stay in Lyons. But Louis had no such intention; and on December 13, 1250 the tyrant emperor died.[122]

The cause of his death was a sudden attack of dysentery which struck him at Fiorentino Castle near Foggia in southern Italy. Some of his apologists spread the story that he repented before his death, amd put on a Cistercian habit. It was customary for great men brought to humility by approaching death to ask to be buried in religious habits. But the story of Frederick II's repentance gains no confirmation from his grave. When his tomb was opened in 1782, more than half a millennium after his death, no Cistercian habit was found within. Rather his bones were clad in rich red Arabic silk embroidered with Muslim designs, with one small incongrous cross upon his left shoulder.[123]

Frederick II left three sons: the legitimate Conrad and the illegitimate

---

[118]Van Cleve, *Frederick II*, p. 516.
[119]Mann, *Popes in the Middle Ages*, XV, 109.
[120]Van Cleve, *Frederick II*, pp. 517-518.
[121]Mann, *Popes in the Middle Ages*, XV, 110.
[122]Van Cleve, *Frederick II*, pp. 526-527.
[123]*Ibid.*, pp. 527-528.

Manfred and Enzio. All three, like their father, died tragic deaths in the pit he had dug for them: Conrad and Manfred leading armies against the Pope, Enzio languishing in prison from which none dared release him. After that there remained of the royal Hohenstaufen family with its vaulting ambition only the strange Kyffhaüser legend—the tale of the dead but perfectly preserved German royal giant in a cliff-top hideaway with his red beard growing through a wooden table, who would someday arise to lead Germany again. But the more kindly and more Catholic Germany which Frederick's defeat allowed to grow, transmuted the monarch of the Kyffhaüser legend from the tyrant to whom it had originally applied, to his grandfather and namesake Frederick Barbarossa who had died at peace with the Church of his fathers, leading a true crusade through the gorges of Cilicia near the home of St. Paul.[124]

The house of Hohenstaufen warred against the Pope instead of against the infidel, and lost all. But Christian Spain under King San Fernando III in 1248 regained the greatest prize of its infidel conquerors, the rich and populous city of Sevilla at the head of navigation on the Guadalquivir River, bringing the Reconquest back at last to the southern shore where the enemy had first landed more than five hundred years before.

In December 1245 San Fernando took personal command of the siege of Jaén, the rock-hewn town and frowning fortress which had long been the bastion of the Moorish defenses immediately south of the Pass of the Overthrow of the Infidel Dogs. At his side was the new Master of Santiago, the greatest of the Spanish military orders, Pelayo Pérez Correa, named for the hero who began the longest crusade, once a soldier of fortune who had commanded a free company in the East fighting for Latin Emperor Baldwin of Constantinople, now wearing the flowing white robe with the red cross that marked the Order of Saint James.[125]

Jaén was held by Muhammad "the Red" of Granada. San Fernando and Master Pelayo pressed him hard, all through that winter's cold and floods, and it was Red Muhammad's will that broke. He came to San Fernando and offered to surrender Jaén and become his vassal in peace and war, paying a tribute of 150,000 maravedis a year, if he were allowed to keep Granada, Málaga, Almeria and the surrounding region undisturbed. Jaén, which no Christian had ever taken, seemed worth it to San Fernando; he agreed, thereby creating the Muslim state of Granada which was to stand, the last remnant of Moorish Spain, for 250 years until reconquered at last by the great Queen Isabel. At the end of March 1246 San Fernando made his triumphal entry into Jaén, restoring the church there and establishing it as a royal city with a charter guaranteeing

---

[124]Kantorowicz, *Frederick II*, pp. 673-689; Peter Munz, *Frederick Barbarossa, a Study in Medieval Politics* (Ithaca NY, 1969), pp. 3-17.

[125]Fernández de Retana, *San Fernando III*, p. 275.

its rights of self-government, while most of its Moorish inhabitants departed with bitter lamentation.[126]

In June 1246 Sevilla rebelled against its governor sent by Abu Zakariyya of Tunis, who had succeeded the fading Almohads of Morocco in claiming jurisdiction over it. Earlier the Sevillan Moors had decisively rejected Muhammad the Red, so they had no outside defender left among their fellow Muslims. The bold Pelayo Pérez Correa saw the extraordinary opportunity and at once urged San Fernando to take advantage of it, despite the large population and strong defenses of Sevilla. In September the king moved on Sevilla with 300 Christian knights led by the Masters of Santiago and Calatrava, and 500 Moorish knights supplied by Muhammad the Red in accordance with the treaty of Jaén. Pelayo Pérez Correa urged an immediate assault on Sevilla itself, but more cautious counsellors persuaded San Fernando that he ought to take outlying towns and strong points first. This he proceeded to do, while calling up naval forces to blockade Sevilla's outlet to the sea.[127]

The naval aspect of this operation is in many ways the most fascinating. Castile, a power focussed inland, had never had a navy. Its few ships sailed from the Cantabrian ports on the Bay of Biscay in the far north, where the War of the Reconquest had begun. On this historic occasion San Fernando created the Castilian navy, destined in due time to become the most powerful on earth. He appointed Ramón Bonifaz of Burgos the first Admiral of Castile and set him to work building a war fleet in Castile's principal northern harbor of Santander and in the smaller nearby ports of Laredo and San Vicente de la Barquera. When completed, the fleet was to be sailed around Cape Finisterre and down the coast of Portugal to where the Guadalquivir River flowed into the Atlantic, and there take up station to prevent any help or supplies from reaching Sevilla by sea and the river.[128]

San Fernando's beloved mother Berenguela, who had always acted as his regent in Castile when he was campaigning in Andalusia, had died in November 1246; he named his brother Alfonso de Molina regent in her stead while he remained in Córdoba and Jaén throughout the winter. In April 1247 Pope Innocent IV authorized San Fernando to take one-third of the tithes of Castile for three years to help pay for the reconquest of Sevilla. During that spring, pressing steadily closer to Sevilla, the dauntless King of Castile fell seriously ill, but he soon rallied and besieged Alcalá del Rio until its 300 defending knights had to abandon the place and retreat to Sevilla itself. On July 13 the new

---

[126]*Ibid.*, pp. 276-279; González, *Conquistas de Fernando III*, pp. 94-97; Lomax, *Reconquest of Spain*, p. 150.
[127]Lomax, *Reconquest of Spain*, pp. 150-152; González, *Conquistas de Fernando III*, pp. 99-102; Fernández de Retana, *San Fernando III*, pp. 283-286.
[128]Lomax, *Reconquest of Spain*, p. 152; González, *Conquistas de Fernando III*, pp. 102-103; Fernández de Retana, *San Fernando III*, pp. 286-288.

Castilian navy arrived, consisting of 26 ships, with Admiral Bonifaz carrying an image of the Blessed Virgin Mary on the prow of his flagship. Greeted by San Fernando with the greatest joy, they went almost immediately into battle with thirty Moorish ships, defeating them in the river with the aid of a force of Castilian cavalry on the river bank.[129]

Sevilla was then closely beleaguered by land and sea. San Fernando had announced that he would not raise the siege so long as he lived, until the city fell—which, he declared, God had willed. In his camp he built three chapels as oratories, with an image of the Blessed Virgin Mary in each. The blockading ships lay at anchor in the river under the protection of the catapults of Pelayo Pérez Correa in his camp at Aznalfarache. The besiegers were steadily reinforced; the Sevillan suburb of Gelves was taken by assault, and the closer suburb of Triana was attacked. Ten thousand Moors sallied in counterattack in September. San Fernando rushed to a critical bridge over the Guadaira River and ordered two knights—Lorenzo Suárez and Garci Pérez de Vargas—and their men to hold it at all costs. They did not wait to be attacked, but led a tremendous counter-charge against the Moors advancing upon the bridge, inflicting 3,000 casualties and hurling them back into the city. San Fernando, who had watched their display of prowess, embraced them and praised their valor on their return from the victory. An attack that same month on the Castilian blockading fleet with fire rafts was repelled only with great difficulty; huge logs were put in place to block any such attempt in the future.[130]

The siege went on all through the next year. For many months both sides were unrelenting, with continuing attacks and counterattacks. But the defenders received no aid, while reinforcements from Castile continued to arrive—notably a large contingent under the great nobleman Diego López de Haro and another led by the Archbishop of Santiago de Compostela. On May 3, while San Fernando prayed in one of the Lady chapels, Admiral Bonifaz, on a rising tide and propelled by the full force of oars and sails, despite a tremendous bombardment from catapults and trebuchets in the Tower of Gold and other strong points in Sevilla, rammed the pontoon bridge connecting Sevilla and Triana with his two largest ships and broke it, causing an "explosion of joy" among the Christian soldiers, who were thereby able to tighten the siege still further. The fleet turned away a relief squadron from Tunis. The summer of 1248 was unusually hot even for southern Spain, always a cauldron in summer. The besiegers held on and kept up their enthusiasm, following the lead of their holy king. By contrast the morale of the defenders declined as starvation set in;

---

[129]Lomax, *Reconquest of Spain*, pp. 150-152, 157-158; González, *Conquistas de Fernando III*, pp. 102-107; Fernández de Retana, *San Fernando III*, pp. 281-282, 292, 296-300.
[130]Lomax, *Reconquest of Spain*, p. 152; González, *Conquistas de Fernando III*, pp. 107-112; Fernández de Retana, *San Fernando III*, pp. 302-306, 308-311.

seven Moorish cavalryman rode away rather than face in combat Garci Pérez de Vargas, the hero of the Guadaira bridge. In October the Moors of Sevilla opened negotiations with San Fernando. He told them he had no interest in their terms; he had his own, and they were all the Moors would get.[131]

"Toda la ciudad, libre y quita." "The whole of the city liberated, and you gone."[132]

The Moors agreed to leave within a month with whatever they could carry.[133] These became the standard surrender terms of victorious Spanish kings throughout the later centuries of the War of the Reconquest.

On November 23 Sevilla capitulated to the Christian army of Castile, after 537 years in the power of the infidel. Over 100,000 of its people went into exile to Granada, Jérez, Morocco or elsewhere in Africa.[134] "God helped us," the Spanish chronicler says. "O grand and noble city, so strong and well-populated and defended with such heroism and valor, only a saint could have taken and conquered you!"[135] Three days before Christmas San Fernando made his triumphal entry into the reconquered city. He and his wife and children escorted an image of Our Lady of the Kings conveyed in a carriage in the great procession. The splendid chief mosque of Sevilla, a triumph of Moorish architecture and art, was consecrated as a cathedral, and Mass was said there with the Blessed Virgin Mary's triumphal carriage as the altar. Sevilla was resettled almost entirely with Christians, making a complete break with its Muslim past.[136]

It was the greatest victory of the entire Reconquest between Covadonga and Queen Isabel's final conquest of Granada. On June 25, 1250 San Fernando gave formal and public thanks for it, in words full of the radiant and triumphant faith of Catholic Spain at the peak of its crusading history:

> Remember the great benefits, the great favors, the great gifts, the great honors, and the great successes that He Who is the origin and fountainhead of all good, has done and shown to all Christendom and especially to us of Castile and León, in our days and the time of Don Fernando King of Castile and León. . . .
>
> Understand and know how these benefits were manifested and accomplished, against Christians and against Moors, and not because of our merits, but out of His great goodness and mercy, and because of the merits and prayers of Holy Mary whom we all serve, and the aid she gave us with her blessed Son, and because of the merits of St. James, whose standard and insignia we bear, who always helps us to victory . . . and

[131]Lomax, *Reconquest of Spain*, pp. 152-154; González, *Conquistas de Fernando III*, pp. 112-118; Fernández de Retana, *San Fernando III*, pp. 312-323, 325-329.

[132]González, *Conquistas de Fernando III*, p. 118.

[133]*Ibid.*, pp. 118-119 (the terms of capitulation in full).

[134]Lomax, *Reconquest of Spain*, p. 154.

[135]Fernández de Retana, *San Fernando III*, pp. 335-336.

[136]*Ibid.*, pp. 339-341; Lomax, *Reconquest of Spain*, pp. 154-155.

through our efforts with the aid and counsel of Don Alfonso our first-born son, and Don Alfonso our brother, and our other sons, and with the aid and counsel of other nobles and our loyal vassals both Castilian and Leonese, we have conquered all Andalusia, in service to God and the expansion of Christendom, more fully and decisively than the conquest of any other king.[137]

The next year the reconquest of Portugal was completed when its Christian knights secured the last of the Algarve, its southernmost province.[138] The Moors in Spain still retained the kingdom of Granada, and also the territory around the Rock and Straits of Gibraltar, but the region around Cádiz directly south of Sevilla surrendered to San Fernando without fighting.[139] The victorious king planned to push on into Africa, beginning its reconquest from the Moors; but he was now past fifty, worn out from his mighty labors. In May 1252 he died in the lovely Alcázar (castle, or palace) of Sevilla, after making a general confession, putting on his finest clothing to be prepared to greet the Lord, blessing his family, and urging his son and heir Alfonso to maintain and if possible soon complete the Reconquest. The dying royal saint had a vision of Heaven, called for a blessed candle to be lighted, and at midnight departed from the earth.[140] The image of the Blessed Virgin Mary which he carried on his saddle-bow still graces the mighty Gothic cathedral of present-day Sevilla.

It remains to speak of the other king of those heroic days approaching the climax of Christendom who was a saint: Louis IX of France, San Fernando's first cousin; their mothers, Berenguela and Blanche, were sisters and had been regents of their two kingdoms. Extraordinarily devout, a dutiful son and a loving husband and father, St. Louis was by any reasonable standard the greatest king France ever had, whose life and holiness cast a luster on the French monarchy that endured to and even past its frightful revolution that launched the modern age's mightiest assault upon Christendom. Somewhat overshadowed in the politics at the time by the gigantic clash between Emperor Frederick II and the Popes, St. Louis (along with his mother Blanche, in the early years of his reign) nevertheless kept France peaceful and justly governed for more than forty years, though he was absent on crusade for more than eight of those years. The character of his rule in France is best summed up by the instructions he gave the special investigators he sent throughout the realm in January 1247:

"to set down in writing, and to examine in the manner we have prescribed, such complaints as may be brought against ourself or our ancestors, as

---

[137]Fernández de Retana, *San Fernando III*, pp. 406-407.
[138]Lomax, *Reconquest of Spain*, p. 144.
[139]González, *Conquistas de Fernando III*, pp. 121-122.
[140]Fernández de Retana, *San Fernando III*, pp. 405-412.

likewise allegations touching upon the injustices, extortions and all other faults of which our bailiffs, provosts, foresters, sergeants, and their assistants might have been guilty since our reign began."[141]

In 1244, on receipt of the news of the Khwarizmian sack of Jerusalem, King St. Louis had taken the Cross; but the competing pressures and requirements of the struggle against the tyrant emperor had greatly reduced the amount of support in men, money, weapons and supplies that would otherwise have undoubtedly been obtained for a crusade led by a monarch with so exalted a reputation. Nevertheless he did have Pope Innocent IV's active support; in October 1247 Innocent ordered his legate in France, Cardinal Eudes of Tusculum, to collect money for Louis IX's crusade before money for the Church or for aid to Constantinople, and to preach the crusade in Belgium and Lorraine as well as throughout France.[142] With this timely aid the crusade could become a reality; on August 25, 1248 St. Louis assembled his crusading host at the recently built port of Aigues-Mortes on the Mediterranean coast of France near the mouth of the Rhone River and, accompanied by his faithful and courageous Queen Margaret and his brothers Robert of Artois and Charles of Anjou, sailed for the East. Most of his army was French, but there was a substantial English contingent commanded by Earl William of Salisbury.[143]

The first destination of the crusading army was the island of Cyprus, where they remained until May 1249. During the prolonged strategic discussions on Cyprus, King St. Louis—a brave and constant but uninspired commander of very limited military experience—was persuaded, as several of his predecessors as crusade leaders had been, by cautious self-styled military "experts" that Egypt must be invaded and at least partly conquered before Jerusalem could be regained.[144] These "experts," refusing to learn from the failure of the Fifth Crusade, were condemned to repeat it. Louis' crusade turned out to be a virtual re-enactment of that tragically flawed and ultimately

---

[141]Pernoud, *Blanche of Castile*, p. 245.

[142]Mann, *Popes in the Middle Ages*, XV, 165, 168-169. Historians otherwise not usually marked by enthusiasm for crusades tend to become very much concerned with crusading imperatives in this case, since most Western historians of this century are very sympathetic with Frederick II and regard the determination of Popes Gregory IX and Innocent IV to destroy his power as so reprehensible that any stick will serve to beat them with.

[143]Setton, *Crusades*, II, 493; Runciman, *Crusades*, III, 257; Labarge, *St. Louis*, p. 109. Queen Margaret's faithfulness and courage were strikingly displayed later when her husband was captured in Egypt. There could hardly be a greater contrast with the selfish and dishonorable behavior of Queen Eleanor of Aquitaine when she accompanied her husband Louis VII on the Second Crusade (see Chapter Two, above).

[144]Setton, *Crusades*, II, 493-495, 614; Runciman, *Crusades*, III, 258, 261; Labarge, *St. Louis*, pp. 109-110, 112-113.

disastrous venture of thirty years before.[145]

Landing near Damietta on the eastern edge of the Nile delta, St. Louis and his crusaders took it easily—much more easily than the Fifth Crusade had taken it—but then he was persuaded to wait there throughout the summer of 1249 for reinforcements and to avoid the Nile flood. Mere passive waiting inside a strong enemy country is never good strategy; it is too easy for the defenders to bring up more reinforcements than attackers operating from distant bases can possibly provide. When in November St. Louis finally began an advance on Cairo, he was favored with what at first appeared to be an extraordinary stroke of good fortune: the sudden death of Ayyub, the long-time Sultan of Egypt. Pending the arrival of Ayyub's son Turan Shah, Fakhr ad-Din was put in command of the Egyptian army. Fakhr was not a brilliant commander, but he was competent, and knew how to take advantage of the unusual terrain of the Nile valley, with its many canals, wholly unfamiliar to the invaders.[146]

On February 8 a major battle was fought at Ansurah; Fakhr ad-Din died in the thundering charge of the Christian knights, but there the luck of the crusaders ran out. Into his place stepped Baybars, one of the great generals of history, who was to become the first man ever to defeat the Mongols on the battlefield. He counterattacked the crusading army while they were fording a canal, trapped them in a difficult position, and inflicted enormous casualties all the rest of the day while they stood at bay. For nearly two months St. Louis refused to retreat; but Egyptian boats on the Nile cut off his supplies, and in the end he had no choice. The new Sultan Turan Shah had now arrived, but Baybars was still present. On the second day of the retreat—April 6, 1250—he forced the crusaders into battle at Fanskur. After fighting fruitlessly all day, the exhausted army surrendered unconditionally on its own initiative, without St. Louis even knowing they had done so. Suddenly exposed, he was taken prisoner. The Muslims began cutting off the heads of three hundred of the captured crusaders every night.[147]

On April 10 the appalling news reached Queen Margaret in Damietta. The heroic and beautiful Savoyard princess, who had lived in the shadow of her formidable mother-in-law Blanche of Castile ever since she married Louis, rose to the occasion in a manner befitting that greatest queen in the history of Christendom, Isabel of Spain. She took command of the city, inspired the garrison to hold firm, and instantly ordered the payment of the colossal sum of 360,000 pounds to the Italian merchants in Damietta for all the food that they

---

[145]See Chapter Five, above.

[146]Setton, *Crusades*, II, 494-498, 711, 738-739; Runciman, *Crusades*, III, 262-265; Labarge, *St. Louis*, pp. 115-121.

[147]Setton, *Crusades*, II, 499-503; Runciman, *Crusades*, III, 266-281; Labarge, *St. Louis*, pp. 121-125.

had, so that they would not immediately flee with it. Three days later she bore a son, whom she named John Tristan ("John Sadness"); but she gave no other public sign of her sorrow. The Muslims, whose society had no place for women outside of harem, purdah, slavery or prostitution, were learning for the first time what a Christian heroine could do against them.[148]

The next month St. Louis negotiated his release, aided by the political turmoil resulting from Baybars' assassination of Turan Shah, which soon led to the establishment of the Mamluk kingdom of Egypt. St. Louis promised to evacuate the country and pay a ransom of 800,000 bezants, but firmly refused to pledge to renounce Christ if he did not fulfill his bargain. The Egyptians respected his fidelity and let him go anyway; but scarcely had he departed when they massacred all his wounded Christian prisoners.[149]

On May 13, 1250 St. Louis arrived at Acre in Palestine, where he was reunited with Margaret, and soon received a warm letter of appreciation from Pope Innocent IV, with condolence for his sufferings. On July 3 he announced that he would remain in Palestine for some time, but released his surviving brothers (Robert of Artois had been killed at the Battle of Fanskur) and all others who wished to leave, to go home. Most of the French knights did so, leaving only about 1,400 men (out of an original army ten times that number) with St. Louis.[150]

For the next four years he acted in effect as king of Jerusalem, though he was never able to assemble an army strong enough to attempt the liberation of the sacred city. He did win the release of all his surviving men who had been captured in Egypt. He made pilgrimages to Cana, Mount Tabor, and Nazareth. With unfailing courtesy, prudence, and good counsel he received ambassadors from most of the feuding Muslim rulers of the Middle East, and even from the Mongols and the Assassins. Everywhere he won golden opinions for his wisdom and goodness, but was unable to make any political or military progress. Late in 1252 his mother Blanche died, and in April 1253 the Muslim leader of Syria made peace with the Mamluk King Aybak of Egypt, eliminating any immediate prospect of St. Louis regaining Jerusalem by allying with one of these two Muslim powers against the other. On April 24, 1254, shortly after Easter, he left the Holy Land to return to his own kingdom, which he accomplished in July after a tumultuous voyage in which his ship was nearly wrecked on a sandbar off Cyprus, badly buffeted by winds, and then almost destroyed by fire. St. Louis credited his Queen Margaret's prayers and cool head with their deliverance

---

[148]Setton, *Crusades*, II, 502-503; Runciman, *Crusades*, III, 271-272; Labarge, *St. Louis*, p. 126.

[149]Setton, *Crusades*, II, 503-504, 712, 739-740; Runciman, *Crusades*, III, 272-274; Labarge, *St. Louis*, pp. 128-131.

[150]Setton, *Crusades*, II, 504-505; Runciman, *Crusades*, III, 274-275; Labarge, *St. Louis*, pp. 132-133.

from all these dangers.[151]

Among the Mongols, the corruption of sudden, overwhelming power and wealth had begun to undermine their empire in a manner that no civilized army on the battlefield had been able to accomplish. Guyuk Khan died of drink and debauchery after a reign of only two years; his widow, Oghul Qaimish, was deposed as regent on an accusation of witchcraft, sewed up in a sack, and drowned. Mangu, elected by *kuriltai* in 1251, is considered by some historians an able ruler, but was reported by St. Louis IX's special emissary to him, the Franciscan friar William of Rübruck, to have received him drunk.[152] Mangu's reply to St. Louis' letter urging him to become a Christian was not encouraging: "This is the commandment of Eternal Heaven. There is but one God in heaven, and on earth one sovereign: Genghis Khan, son of God."[153] But under Mangu, the vast Mongol empire was already beginning to break up, its Chinese extension ruled by Mangu's brother Kublai, its Middle Eastern extension ruled by Mangu's brother Hulagu, and its Russian province by Mangu's patron Batu. When Mangu died in 1259 these regions became effectively independent of the Great Khan. After Baybars defeated a Mongol army at Ain Jalut at the gates of Egypt in 1260 and the Mongol Khan of the Middle East became Muslim in 1282, Mongol aggression ceased to be a major threat to the civilized world west of China.[154]

For four years after the death of Frederick II his son Conrad IV maintained his imperial claim, though Pope Innocent IV never recognized it. Conrad, only 22 years old in 1250, was a mere shadow of his titan father. After leaving Lyons to return to Italy shortly after Easter 1251, Pope Innocent IV proclaimed Count William of Holland "King of the Romans" and therefore Emperor-designate, and tried to persuade Richard of Cornwall, brother of King Henry III of England, to accept the crown of Sicily and southern Italy. But Richard refused, having no desire for the war he would then have to fight against the still numerous Hohenstaufen partisans in the Kingdom of Sicily. Conrad IV took Naples in October 1253; Innocent IV was then able to persuade Henry III of England to accept the Sicilian crown for his young son Edmund. On Holy Thursday 1254 Innocent IV renewed Conrad's excommunication. The next month Conrad died, only 26 years old, on his way to Germany, possibly poisoned by his half-brother Manfred.[155]

---

[151]Mann, *Popes in the Middle Ages*, XV, 172; Labarge, *St. Louis*, pp. 135-143, 145; Pernoud, *Blanche of Castile*, pp. 286-288; Setton, *Crusades*, II, 506-508, 742-743; Runciman, *Crusades*, III, 276-277, 280.

[152]Grousset, *Empire of the Steppes*, pp. 272-276; Vernadsky, *Mongols and Russia*, p. 68; Runciman, *Crusades*, III, 296.

[153]Grousset, *Empire of the Steppes*, p. 281.

[154]*Ibid.*, pp. 285-286, 364-371.

[155]Mann, *Popes in the Middle Ages*, XV, 122, 126, 129, 132-138, 140-141; Pernoud, *Blanche of Castile*, p. 281; Setton, *Crusades*, II, 360.

Though he left an infant son, Conradin, and Manfred pressed his claims, such as they were (he being illegitimate), it was only southern Italy and Sicily that they could hope to control; the dream of an Emperor of Christendom who would humble the Pope was dead. When Pope Innocent IV died December 7, 1254[156] his great work was done: the shadow was lifted from Christendom, which could go on to reach its cultural climax and find—however long it might take—an Emperor who would be unshakably loyal to Christ's Church and to His Vicar.

---

[156]Mann, *Popes in the Middle Ages*, XV, 147-148.

7
The Climax of Christendom
(1254-1276)

(Popes Alexander IV 1254-61, Urban IV 1261-64, Clement IV 1265-68, Bd. Gregory X 1271-76)

"In the spirit of truth he prayed to the Supreme Teacher, using these words of the Psalmist: 'Save me, O Lord, for there is now no saint; truths are decayed from among the children of men.' With tears he begged for that understanding of divine things which had become so rare among men, and also for inspiration as to the theme he should choose for his inaugural lecture. Then he fell asleep and dreamed. He seemed to see an old man, white-haired and clothed in the Dominican habit, who came and said to him: 'Brother Thomas, why are you praying and weeping?' 'Because,' answered Thomas, 'they are making me take the degree of master, and I do not think I am fully competent. Moreover, I cannot think what theme to take for my inaugural lecture.' To this the old man replied: 'Do not fear; God will help you to bear the burden of being a master. And as for the lecture, take this text: 'Thou waterest the hills from thy upper rooms; the earth shall be filled with the fruit of thy works.'"—Bernard Gui, *Legenda Santo Thomae*, referring to St. Thomas Aquinas during a night in April 1256[1]

"Teachers [of sacred doctrine and Scripture] are comparable to mountains for three reasons: their elevation from the earth, their splendor in illumination, and their protective shelter against harm. Thus just as mountains are high above the earth, so teachers contemn earthly matters and aspire to heavenly things alone; mountains are the first to be illuminated by the rays of the sun, so teachers of Sacred Scripture are the first to receive mental splendor by participating in divine wisdom; and just as mountains protect the valleys, so teachers defend the faith against errors. Therefore teachers should be elevated in their lives so as to illumine the faithful by their preaching, enlighten students by their teaching, and defend the faith by their disputations against error."—from St. Thomas Aquinas' inaugural lecture as master at the University of Paris, April 1256[2]

---

[1]James A. Weisheipl, *Friar Thomas D'Aquino; His Life, Thought, and Work* (New York, 1974), p. 96.
[2]*Ibid.*, p. 93.

During the third quarter of the thirteenth century, from the death of the tyrant emperor Frederick II to the Council of Lyons under Blessed Pope Gregory X, Christendom reached its climax. These were the years when St. Thomas Aquinas taught at the University of Paris and in Dominican priories at Rome and the Papal residences of Orvieto and Viterbo; when the supreme achievements of Gothic cathedral architecture and art, at Chartres and Amiens, were dedicated; when Master Jean de Chelles began his work "to the glory of the Mother of God" on the south transept of the Cathedral of Notre Dame.[3] More than seven centuries have since passed, and the world has changed beyond the recognition or imagination of medieval man. But still the magnificently reasoning and ever-faithful mind of Thomas Aquinas, the soaring nave and the glorious stained glass and the almost living faces of the statues of Chartres cathedral, the shimmering beauty of the cathedral of Notre Dame de Paris that even the monsters who wielded the guillotine during the French Revolution feared to touch, awe their beholder whatever his religion, drawing admirers from the ends of the earth. This was Christendom at its summit. No other age has exceeded these its achievements; it may well be that no other age has matched them. Certainly no one since has ever made glass like the rainbow windows of Chartres and the great rose of Notre-Dame.

Such accomplishments transcend individual genius, however great. They arose from an overpowering spiritual, intellectual, and cultural commitment to the Christian Faith and the Catholic Church. The men and women who made and expressed this commitment—of all kinds, from philosophers and artists to Popes, kings, queens, priests, nuns, soldiers, and workmen—were still sinners. They did not live in some mythical golden age. The royal archers of St. Louis IX of France had to stand guard so that Thomas Aquinas could go to teach his classes and his students could go to hear him.[4] Jealousy and ambition never slept. Good men were cut down and evil men sometimes exalted. But underlying and overtopping this inevitable strife stood that Christian and Catholic commitment, like some gigantic marble pillar reaching down toward the center of the earth and up toward the zenith of the sky. It seemed unbreakable. For two hundred and fifty years it was.

Nine hundred years of Christianity and Christendom had gone into its construction. The marks of a hundred Popes and a thousand saints were on it, the fingerprints of Constantine and Charlemagne and San Fernando and St. Louis IX, most especially of Bernard of Clairvaux and Domingo called Dominic of Calaruega in the harsh brown hills of Aragon and Francis the little poor man of sunny green Assisi. The destruction of Empire Frederick II had confirmed

---

[3]Chartres cathedral was dedicated October 24, 1260, Amiens cathedral in 1269; de Chelles left his signature on the plinth of the south transept of Notre Dame February 12, 1258 (Wim Swaan, *The Gothic Cathedral* [London, 1969], pp. 89, 120, 134).
[4]Weisheipl, *Thomas D'Aquino*, pp. 86-87.

the irresistible strength of that thirteenth-century Catholic unity. None of Frederick's would-be successors and heirs dared echo his scoffing agnosticism; they insisted that they were good Catholics too. Many of them were. After all, even Dante, the poet of climactic Christendom, called himself a Ghibelline.

It was the special calling of the man whom God had given what may well have been the ablest mind in the history of Christendom to cast this heaven-storming commitment into an intellectual synthesis that should stand for the ages against all that hostile or misguided minds might do to break it. This was the life-work of the "Common Doctor of the Church," Saint Thomas Aquinas.

Thomas Aquinas came from a family of the lesser nobility of the kingdom of Sicily and southern Italy. His grandfather Ronald held the castle of Roccasecca upon a spur of the Cairo Mountains just north of Capua in the direction of St. Benedict's famous and ancient abbey of Monte Cassino. Thomas' family had originally been loyal to Frederick II. Thomas had two older brothers. The elder, Aimo, accompanied Frederick on his curious "crusade," was captured and held for ransom on Cyprus, and was then released through the intercession of Pope Gregory IX in 1233. When Gregory IX issued his second excommunication of Frederick in 1239, Aimo d'Aquino stood by the Pope. Thomas' other brother, Rinaldo, was a page at the imperial court in 1240 and upheld Frederick's cause until 1245, when the Council of Lyons declared him deposed. Then Rinaldo offered his services to the Papal cause and armies. The following year he was charged with involvement in a conspiracy to assassinate Frederick, and was executed. The d'Aquino family always regarded Rinaldo as a martyr.[5]

Thomas, the youngest son who was directed toward the Church from boyhood, took no part in politics, during the reign of Frederick II or at any time afterward.[6] But in his treatise *De regno*, written for the king of Cyprus about 1265, Thomas declared unequivocally:

> To him [the Pope] all kings of the Christian people are to be subject as to our Lord Jesus Christ Himself. For those to whom pertains the care of intermediate ends should be subject to him to whom pertains the care of the ultimate end, and be directed by his rule. . . . In the new law there is a higher priesthood by which men are guided to heavenly good. Consequently, in the law of Christ, kings must be subject to priests.[7]

Elsewhere in the same treatise, Thomas Aquinas makes it clear that he did not mean that the Pope should be the temporal ruler of all Christendom. Kings rule, he explained, in accordance with the natural law, by which the

---

[5]*Ibid.*, pp. 4-8.
[6]*Ibid.*, p. 8.
[7]Thomas Aquinas, *De regno* I, 14, Sections 110-111, cited by Weisheipl, *Thomas D'Aquino*, p. 193.

common good requires rulers. Grace perfects nature but does not destroy it. Therefore the presence and authority of the Pope does not override or eliminate the rightful natural authority of kings; but the Pope remains the ultimate source of moral judgment upon kings and emperors, the court of final appeal.[8]

In 1244, after four years of study in arts and philosophy at the *studium* or university at Naples, Thomas Aquinas had become a Dominican at the age of nineteen, without the prior knowledge of his family. About a month later, though travelling in the company of the Dominican master general, John of Wildeshausen, Thomas was abducted by his brother Rinaldo, then still in the service of Emperor Frederick II, and taken to the second family castle: Montesangiovanni in the Papal states. Thomas—a large, powerfully built young man—vehemently resisted attempts to tear the Dominican habit from his back, and in a famous episode which probably occurred on the night of his capture or the following night, drove away with a firebrand a prostitute who had been sent to his room to seduce him from his vocation.[9]

Thomas was held prisoner for an entire year, never wavering in his determination to remain a Dominican. When, following the deposition of Frederick II by the Council of Lyons, Rinaldo d'Aquino gave his support to the cause of the Pope, Thomas was released and went to Paris and to Cologne, where he studied under St. Albert the Great (Albertus Magnus)[10] and immensely impressed that famous teacher, philosopher, and scientist, who was just then beginning his encyclopedic commentaries on Aristotle. Because of his characteristic reserve and long hours spent in prayer and contemplation, Thomas became known to his Dominican brethren at Cologne as "the dumb ox." St. Albert is reputed to have said: "We call him the Dumb Ox, but the bellowing of that ox will resound throughout the whole world."[11]

Assigned to the University of Paris in the fall of 1252 "to study, preach, and establish a priory," Thomas at once found himself in the midst of a heated controversy as to whether members of the mendicant orders—Dominicans and Franciscans—should teach there at all. They were deeply resented by many other members of the faculty. William of Saint-Amour, "regent master" at this

---

[8]Weisheipl, *Thomas D'Aquino*, p. 194.

[9]*Ibid.*, pp. 13-14, 26-33. Though there may have been some confusion about its circumstances and location, Weisheipl concludes firmly that "there is every reason to think that the prostitute episode is historical fact." (*op. cit.*, p. 31)

[10]For St. Albertus Magnus see especially Hieronymus Wilms, *Albert the Great, Saint and Doctor of the Church* (London, 1933).

[11]Weisheipl, *Thomas D'Aquino.*, pp. 33-45. For reasons he does not make clear, Weisheipl doubts the historicity of the "Dumb Ox" nickname and of St. Albert's comment quoted in the text, though both are specifically attested by William of Tocco, whom Weisheipl calls "the earliest and one of the most reliable sources" on the life of Thomas Aquinas (*op. cit.*, p. 5).

time—roughly corresponding to a modern Dean of the Faculty—was determined to drive them out. Responding to their pressure, Pope Innocent IV in November 1254 had rescinded all Dominican and Franciscan privileges of preaching and hearing confessions without authorization from the local bishop. But two weeks later Innocent IV died. His successor Rinaldo Conti, who took the name of Alexander IV, was a nephew of Pope Gregory IX and, like his uncle, a great admirer of the Franciscans; he had served as their cardinal protector for 27 years. One of his very first acts as Pope, on December 20, 1254, was to restore all the privileges of the Franciscans and Dominicans. In the sweeping bull *Quasi lignum vitae* April 14, 1255, Pope Alexander reconfirmed those privileges and specifically ordered the University of Paris to accept two Dominican masters as members of its faculty consortium.[12]

Meanwhile Thomas was writing the first of his seminal works, the treatise *De ente et essentia* ("Concerning Being and Essence"), small in size but a cornerstone of his thought. It set forth with limpid clarity the absolutely fundamental truth that the existence of every created being derives from God's existence and could have no being without God's existence.

> Everything such that its existence is other than its nature has existence from another. And because everything which exists by virtue of another is reduced to that which exists in virtue of itself, as to its first cause, it follows that there must be something which is the cause of the existence of all things, because it is very existence alone; otherwise the causes would proceed to infinity, since everything which is not existence alone would have a cause of its existence, as has been said. It is clear, therefore, that an intelligence is form and existence, and that it has its existence from the first being which is existence alone, and this is the first cause which is God.[13]

During the academic year 1255-56 William of St. Amour stepped up his attacks on the Dominicans and Franciscans, climaxed in March 1256 by a diatribe entitled *De periculis novissimorum temporum* ("On the Danger of the Times"), in which he declared that mendicancy should not be permitted for any religious since they could support themselves by manual labor, and that religious should not preach nor hear confessions, only bishops and the diocesan clergy. He even implied that the mendicants were forerunners of the coming of Antichrist. In vain did St. Bonaventure, the great Franciscan master, try to refute William's arguments by rational disputations; the controversy had gone beyond reason.[14] In April 1256 the new Dominican minister general, Humbert of Romans, wrote that when friars passed through the streets of Paris:

---

[12]*Ibid.*, pp. 53, 80-86; Horace K. Mann, *The Lives of the Popes in the Middle Ages*, Volume XVI (London, 1929), pp. 4-6.

[13]Thomas Aquinas, *Concerning Being and Essence (De Ente et Essentia)*, tr. & ed. George G. Leckie (New York, 1937), p. 25.

[14]Weisheipl, *Thomas D'Aquino*, pp. 86-89.

the air was full of the "tumult of shoutings, the barking of dogs, the roaring of bears, the hissing of serpents," and every sort of insulting exclamation. Filthy rushes and straw off the floors of the dwellings were poured upon the cowled head from above; mud, stones, and sometimes blows greeted him from below. Arrows had been shot against the [Dominican] priory, which had henceforth to be guarded day and night by royal troops.[15]

It was precisely at this moment, in this very month, that St. Thomas Aquinas was "incepted" as a master teacher of theology at the University of Paris, the occasion for his doubts and prayers and vision recorded at the head of this chapter, followed by his initial lecture also quoted there. Pope Alexander IV was already familiar with Thomas Aquinas. He had written to the Chancellor of the University of Paris in March specifically congratulating him for granting Thomas a license to teach, and in June remarked with anger and sorrow on those masters and students at the University who "have opposed those who desired to attend the lectures, disputations, and sermons of the friars, in particular those who wished to be present at the inception of our beloved son, Friar Thomas D'Aquino."[16]

The holy king of France, Louis IX, had become involved in the controversy by making an arbitration decision favorable to the friars. In June the infatuated William actually attacked the piety of the king, ridiculing him for refusing to wear elegant robes and "leaping from his bed to say matins in the middle of the night." Louis was a mild and charitable man, but with a core of steel; he was not going to put up with being criticized for his virtues by a man who called himself a Catholic teacher. Louis complained to the Pope, and sent him a copy of William's violent pamphlet "On the Danger of the Times." Alexander IV referred it to a commission of four cardinals. Thomas Aquinas was writing a refutation of it, but the Pope did not wait to read it. On October 5 he condemned *De periculis* and ordered it burned. Several of William's influential colleagues who had supported his position promptly announced their submission to the verdict of the Pope, and Louis ordered William of St. Amour to leave Paris and return to his native village, a merciful if humiliating sentence for the proud intellectual.[17]

Throughout his relatively short but brilliant career as a master teacher and writer on theology and philosophy, St. Thomas Aquinas was always to have the enthusiastic and unwavering support of the Popes and of King St. Louis IX of France.

No one, not even William of St. Amour, had seriously challenged the

---

[15]*Ibid.*, p. 93.
[16]*Ibid.*, pp. 87, 94.
[17]*Ibid.*, pp. 88, 112-113; Margaret W. Labarge, *Saint Louis* (Boston, 1968), pp. 163-164.

orthodoxy of the Dominicans; but the controversy over the strict or mitigated observance of the rule of St. Francis had deeply divided his order while Brother Elias was its head. Many of those who favored the strict observance had become admirers of the writings of Joachim of Fiore, who had died in 1202 but had prophesied the appearance of two mendicant orders and a coming "Age of the Holy Spirit" in which "there would be no need for authoritative institutions, since men would now live according to the Spirit of God."[18] The Franciscan minister general, John of Parma, was one of the admirers of Joachim and his writings. When Pope Alexander IV condemned Joachim's works in 1256, John of Parma had to go. He was succeeded in February 1257 by St. Bonaventure, who had the painful task of bringing his predecessor to trial for heresy. John was convicted and sentenced to life imprisonment. He accepted the sentence with perfect humility, and it was soon commuted to simple retirement. St. Bonaventure combined intellectual brilliance, mystical vision, humility, obedience, and awareness of the need for varied forms of spirituality in the order. In June 1260 a Franciscan general chapter meeting, held at Narbonne in southern France under his presidency, undertook the codification of all the statutes of the order; prescribed strict enforcement of uniformity of habits, fasts, and silence; and set the normal age for admission of novices at eighteen. Under St. Bonaventure's leadership the Franciscan order found its way again, for the most part reunited.[19]

The predecessor of John of Wildeshausen, Thomas Aquinas' original Dominican patron, as Dominican master general had been St. Raymond of Peñafort, a Catalan who had resigned his high office in 1240 to devote the rest of his life to a profoundly Spanish apostolate: the conversion of the Muslims and Jews then being brought in large numbers into the Christian kingdoms of Spain by the conquests of King St. Ferdinand III of Castile and King James I the Conqueror of Aragon. Raymond even hoped to extend his apostolate to the wholly Muslim regions of North Africa. Probably about the year 1258 St. Raymond asked Thomas Aquinas to write an exposition of Christian doctrine with particular reference to the errors of the Muslims and Jews, so that those drawn toward conversion would better understand the beliefs they must reject and those they must profess. The result was the *Summa contra gentiles*, one of Thomas Aquinas' two longest and most influential works.[20]

Thomas began work on the *Summa contra gentiles* during the academic year 1258-59, his third as a master at the University of Paris. When that year ended Thomas was placed on a committee set up by the Dominican order, along with his old master St. Albert the Great and three other past or present

---

[18]John Moorman, *A History of the Franciscan Order from its Origins to the Year 1517* (Oxford, 1968), pp. 114-115.

[19]*Ibid.*, pp. 114-116, 145-154; Weisheipl, *Thomas D'Aquino*, pp. 113-114.

[20]Weisheipl, *Thomas D'Aquino*, pp. 130-131.

masters at the University of Paris, to discuss what fields of study were most important for Dominican friars and how they should be taught. The committee emphasized the value of the study of philosophy. At that time Thomas was recalled from Paris and spent the next two years at his home priory at Naples and at Rome, completing the greater part of the *Summa contra gentiles*, though the entire massive work was not finished until 1264.[21]

What St. Thomas Aquinas was to theology and philosophy and the principles of learning at this climax of Christendom, so the Gothic cathedral at Chartres became for the art of Christendom when it was dedicated on October 24, 1260, during this same pontificate of Alexander IV, just a little over a year after Thomas Aquinas departed from the University of Paris.[22] The Gothic cathedrals were intended to express, to reveal, and to honor the Christian cosmos and world-view in stone and glass; to a very great extent they succeeded in doing so. The harmonious construction in accordance with geometric principle, the immense height of the ceiling, and the interior filled with light were all intended to symbolize and draw men's thoughts and ardent desire to Heaven and the Lord Who reigned there; they were also intended to depict, in action as it were, light and harmony as God's means of penetrating and governing the universe.[23]

The cathedral at Chartres had long been considered the prime center of devotion to the Blessed Virgin Mary in France. Its diocese was one of the France's largest and richest, a producer of fine textiles. The city of Chartres held four great fairs every year on the four great feasts of the Blessed Virgin: the Purification, the Annunciation, the Assumption, and the Nativity. The life of the small city of 10,000 revolved around Our Lady and her shrine in its cathedral. When much of the cathedral burned down in 1194, after initial despair the townspeople were inspired by Cardinal Melior of Pisa, who had happened to be in Chartres at the time of the fire, to undertake the building of a still greater cathedral to honor Our Lady even more highly. Donations came from all over France; almost the whole city worked on the building project for the better part of a century.[24]

Guilds and patrons commissioned the glorious stained glass windows, the most beautiful ever created: 176 of them, depicting the entire history of salvation. Their deep rich colors overwhelm all pale modern efforts at imitation, filling the cathedral with a rainbow glow when the sun shines through them. The trade symbols of the guilds which paid the cost of particular windows and engaged the artists to design them—a shoe, a sock, a loaf of bread—appear unobtrusively in some tiny lower panel, but no artist's name appears. It is an

[21]*Ibid.*, pp. 138-145.
[22]Swaan, *Gothic Cathedral*, p. 120.
[23]Otto von Simson, *The Gothic Cathedral* (New York, 1958), pp. 227-228.
[24]*Ibid.*, pp. 159-182.

extraordinary and highly significant fact that, for Chartres cathedral alone among the greatest masterpieces of architecture built in the West during the last two thousand years, the name of the master builder is unknown. He worked for the glory of God and wanted none left over for him.[25]

Outside Chartres cathedral, to the right and left of the portals and along the sides of the nave, stand its statues, of Old Testament prophets and kings, of Christian apostles and saints. They are masterpieces to match the cathedral itself, depicting the men who built Christendom and the kind of man most admired by the Christendom they built. They do not glorify the human body; every figure of a saint or hero wears a full-length robe. But the faces are splendidly vivid. The stone eyes seem to burn. They are wide open, gazing *outward*. There could be no greater contrast to the inward-gazing Buddhas of the Orient. The God these men and women depicted by the doors of Chartres cathedral are now beholding in the Beatific Vision is objectively *real*, and every one of their faces is looking straight at Him.[26]

A day spent at Chartres cathedral is worth a hundred books in making the climax of Christendom come alive.

The seven-year pontificate of Alexander IV (1254-61) saw a continuation, though on a lesser scale, of the struggle between the Popes and the German Hohenstaufen family which had held the imperial and Sicilian crowns, but according to Popes Gregory IX and Innocent IV had forfeited those crowns because of the faithlessness of Emperor Frederick II. Frederick II's only legitimate son Conrad, who died in 1254, had left an infant son, known as Conradin. He was taken to Germany for safekeeping, and played no role in the continuing Hohenstaufen struggle in Italy until he reached adolescence. One of Frederick II's illegitimate sons, Manfred, established himself as king of Sicily and southern Italy and claimed dominion over the rest of Italy, though he was never able to establish it. He refused to acknowledge the Pope as his feudal overlord in Sicily and southern Italy. Pope Alexander IV excommunicated him on Holy Thursday 1255 on the grounds that he was responsible for the murder of a nobleman named Borello who had quarrelled with him about a fief the previous year. In September 1255 the Pope disavowed a treaty with Manfred by Cardinal Octaviano, commander of the Papal army in Italy, which would have acknowledged Manfred's authority in Sicily and southern Italy in return for his release of prisoners and some teritory. Pope Alexander maintained his predecessor's recognition of William of Holland as Holy Roman Emperor,

---

[25]*Ibid.*, pp. 230-231; Étienne Houvet, *Chartres Cathedral*, revised by Malcolm Miller (Paris, 1968), pp. 81-122 (with a description of each window); personal observations by the author.

[26]Adolf Katzenellenbogen, *The Sculptural Programs of Chartres Cathedral* (Baltimore, 1959), especially the 79 illustrations following p. 151.

though William was not strongly supported either in Germany or in Italy.[27]

In January 1256 William of Holland was killed on campaign against the Frisians in the Netherlands—he was thrown from his horse in an ice-covered marsh, leaving him helpless before the enemy. He had been planning to go to Rome to receive the Holy Roman Emperor's crown from the Pope immediately after finishing this campaign.[28]

First in the field to try to secure the now vacant imperial office was Duke Richard of Cornwall, younger brother of the feckless King Henry III of England. Henry III, King John's son, a minor at the time of his father's death, had wasted the substance of his kingdom on fruitless wars in France and by an imprudent pledge to the Pope that he would raise a large sum of money to defray the expenses of the Pope's war against Manfred in return for title to the kingdom of Sicily and south Italy for his young son Edmund. Richard, cautious and prudent in contrast to his royal brother, had amassed a great fortune; he was probably the richest man in Europe not a crowned sovereign. He sent an ambassador to Rome to advance his cause, and became the candidate of the pro-Papal party (Guelfs), though the Pope himself did not wish Richard to be elected because this would unite Germany, southern Italy and Sicily in the hands of one royal family. The Hohenstaufen supporters (Ghibellines) who felt they could not win with Manfred supported King Alfonso X of Castile, grandson of Emperor Frederick II's uncle. In March 1256 the Ghibelline city of Pisa in Italy proclaimed Alfonso Emperor, though without authority to do anything of the kind. The Castilian king accepted, sending a plenipotentiary ambassador to Germany to negotiate for support for his imperial bid.[29]

During the course of the thirteenth century in Germany a consensus had developed that a small group of electors should choose the Holy Roman Emperor rather than the whole large body of princes, unmanageable when there was no incumbent Emperor to keep them in order. Eike of Repgau in his *Sachsenspiegel* had declared during the reign of Frederick II that this electoral college for the Empire did, or should include three Rhineland prelates who had trditionally played major roles in the German assemblies to elect a king and emperor: the Archbishops of Cologne, Mainz, and Trier; and also the three

[27]Mann, *Popes in the Middle Ages*, XIV, 146; XV, 16-24; *The Cambridge Medieval History*, ed. J. R. Tanner, C. W. Previté-Orton, and Z. N. Brooke, Volume VI: "History of the Papacy" (Cambridge, 1929), pp. 110-112, 177.

[28]*Cambridge Medieval History*, VI, 114; T. W. E. Roche, *The King of Almayne* (London, 1966), p. 131.

[29]Steven Runciman, *The Sicilian Vespers* (Cambridge, England, 1958), pp. 72-76; *Cambridge Medieval History*, VI, 116; N. Denholm-Young, *Richard of Cornwall* (New York, 1947), p. 86; Antonio Ballesteros Beretta, *Alfonso X el Sabio* (Barcelona, 1984), pp. 154-158, 166, 214. For background on Henry III's reign (not covered up to this point in the text) see Maurice Powicke, *The Thirteenth Century, 1216-1307* (Oxford History of England), 2nd ed. (Oxford, 1962), pp. 1-106.

traditionally primary dignitaries of the imperial household: the steward, the marshal, and the chamberlain, which offices were hereditary in the Counts Palatine of the Rhine, the Dukes of Saxony, and the Margraves of Brandenburg, respectively. The office of cupbearer, a fourth primary dignitary of the imperial household, was hereditary in the King of Bohemia. Eike had tried to exclude him on the grounds that he was not a German, but by 1256 he had nevertheless become accepted as the seventh imperial elector.[30]

After negotiations with these seven electors by the envoys of both imperial candidates, the result was deadlock. Archbishop Arnold of Trier declared for Alfonso X of Castile, gained control of access to the city of Frankfurt where the imperial election was scheduled to take place January 13, 1257 and obtained the proxy of the Margrave of Brandenburg. Together with the Duke of Saxony who came to Frankfurt supporting Archbishop Arnold and his candidate, this made three votes for Alfonso. Arnold refused to admit to Frankfurt the three electors committed to Richard of Cornwall—Archbishop Conrad of Cologne, Archbishop Gerhard of Mainz, and Count Palatine Ludwig of the Rhineland—who therefore cast their vote for Richard outside the walls. The holder of the deciding vote, King Ottokar of Bohemia, wanted the imperial office for himself, but had no prospect of obtaining a majority of the votes needed to secure it. By January 13 he had announced no choice. His ambassadors in Frankfurt, dealing with Archbishop Arnold, declared their support for Alfonso, though without presenting any clear evidence that King Ottokar had authorized them to do so. Nine days later Ottokar announced that his vote was actually cast for Richard of Cornwall; on April 1, however, Ottokar gave Archbishop Arnold of Trier his proxy to vote for Alfonso. Consequently Archbishop Arnold once again declared Alfonso elected.[31]

Since there were no clear precedents nor procedures to guide the imperial electoral college, it was possible under these circumstances for men to argue in good faith that either candidate had been validly elected, though the most reasonable interpretation of the result would appear to favor Richard, since Ottokar's ambassadors had no authority to cast his vote for Alfonso in Frankfurt January 13, Ottokar had actually voted for Richard on January 22, and he had no right to change his vote afterward and pretend the election had not already been made. For the moment the Pope, more concerned about southern Italy and Sicily—still ruled by Manfred, whom he was determined to displace—than Germany, would not support or crown either Richard or Alfonso. The "Great Interregnum" in the history of the Holy Roman Empire had begun.

This peculiar election meant that neither Richard nor Alfonso could really

---

[30]*Cambridge Medieval History*, VI, 110-116.
[31]*Ibid.*, VI, 116-119; Roche, *King of Almayne*, pp. 131-134; Denholm-Young, *Richard of Cornwall*, p. 89; Ballesteros Beretta, *Alfonso X*, pp. 182-183.

act as Holy Roman Emperor, especially in view of the fact that many Germans still had not accepted the Papal dispossession of the Hohenstaufens as a family, and therefore regarded the imperial title as rightly belonging to little Conradin. Alfonso X never went to Germany at any point during the nearly twenty years during which he maintained his imperial claim. Richard was crowned in the traditional ceremony at Aachen on Ascension Day, May 17, 1257, and made three sojourns of considerable length in Germany, but never went beyond the Rhineland nor gained a significant following as Emperor elsewhere.[32]

In August 1258 Manfred—still under the Papal ban—was formally crowned King of Sicily at a parliament in Palermo. In April 1259 Pope Alexander IV finally decided to accept Richard of Cornwall as Emperor, and invited him to Rome for coronation. The problem that had concerned Alexander earlier, of the Holy Roman Emperor and the King of Sicily being in the same family, had been obviated by the Pope's cancellation in December 1258 of the grant of the kingdom of Sicily to Prince Edmund of England, due to nonfulfillment of its financial terms by his father Henry III. But by this time Richard had already been called home to England to help his brother Henry III deal with a unique regime set up by the majority of the feudal nobility of England to govern the country in effect independently of the king and his family. Nothing like it had ever before been seen in Christian Europe.[33]

In March 1258 Henry III had received from Pope Alexander IV what amounted to an ultimatum: to keep the Sicilian crown for his little son Edmund, he must pay 10,000 marks immediately and pledge 30,000 more; he must make peace with France, to free his army to go to the kingdom of Sicily; and he must go there within a year with at least 2,000 knights, 500 crossbowmen and 6,000 foot. Only an undertaking of this magnitude could hope to expel the well-entrenched Manfred. Henry immediately called a parliament, which met the next month. England was impoverished and famine-stricken; most of its great feudal lords descended from the original Norman conquerors were vehemently hostile to the presence of French adventurers among them, many from Poitou and connected to its Lusignan family into which Henry III's mother, Isabelle of Angoulême, had married following the death of King John.[34] A group of eight of the principal barons of England joined in a formal

---

[32]Roche, *King of Almayne*, pp. 137-145, 171-174, 201-208.

[33]*Ibid.*, pp. 150-154; *Cambridge Medieval History*, VI, 121-122, 177; Denholm-Young, *Richard of Cornwall*, p. 100; Runciman, *Sicilian Vespers*, p. 78.

[34]R. F. Trehearne, *The Baronial Plan of Reform, 1258-1263*, rev. ed. (New York, 1971), pp. 64-66; Margaret W. Labarge, *Simon de Montfort* (Toronto, 1962), pp. 153-154; Powicke, *Thirteenth Century*, pp. 129-134. The feudal lords of England were at this time also French, both by ancestry and language, being descended from the Norman conquerors; but since the expulsion of King John and his armies from Normandy some fifty years before, they had increasingly come to regard native-born Frenchmen as foreigners.

league April 12, taking oath "to stand by and help each other, one and all, against all men, to do the right and take nothing that they could not take without doing wrong, saving their fealty to king and crown."[35]

Events were soon to show that "fealty to king and crown" had by this point become little more than nominal for these men. They were disgusted with the weak, inconstant, and increasingly incompetent rule of Henry III, and led by a man whose remarkable strength, constancy, and competence stook in the starkest contrast to Henry: Simon de Montfort, Earl of Leicester, youngest son of that Simon de Montfort who had refused to assault the Christians at Zara or at Constantinople on the Fourth Crusade, had been asked by Pope Innocent III to lead the Albigensian Crusade, and had died in battle during it.[36]

The extraordinary career of Simon de Montfort the younger had begun in 1230 when he persuaded Ranulf, Earl of Chester, to give him possession of the earldom of Leicester, which had been seized by King John in 1207 and then in 1215, at the request of Pope Innocent III, granted to Ranulf, who was a nephew of the elder Simon, to hold for his use. When Simon the crusader was slain, the earldom of Leicester had reverted by feudal law to King Henry III, who granted it in fee to the Earl of Chester. The elderly Ranulf was without male heirs, so he knew his vast estates would soon be divided among many; but there is no apparent reason why he wanted Simon to have one of the greatest of his holdings.[37] Perhaps he simply believed Simon to be the rightful heir (his older brother Amaury having renounced all his English claims in Simon's favor) since John's seizure had been unjust. Perhaps he just liked Simon. Many others did, then and later, though others detested him. Like his father, Simon tended to arouse a sharply polarized response—love or hate.

Since becoming Earl of Leicester, Simon had married Henry III's sister, the blonde, beautiful, highly intelligent and determined Eleanor, despite the opposition of many of his jealous fellow barons.[38] He had made a great reputation for himself as a military commander and had quarrelled harshly with Henry over his military governorship in the French province of Gascony, which the English still ruled. In that quarrel Simon gained the support of the majority of the barons, much to Henry's fury.[39] Though Simon is sometimes presented as no more than an unusually able ambitious feudal lord, in fact he had a profundity of religious commitment, an acuteness of intellectual interests, and a sense of moral duty all much higher than any of his peers. (In those ways again he resembled his illustrious father, whom he had never known.) Simon and Eleanor were very generous donors to the Franciscans and Dominicans, and

---

[35]Powicke, *Thirteenth Century*, p. 130.
[36]See Chapter Five, above.
[37]Labarge, *Simon de Montfort*, pp. 27-31.
[38]*Ibid.*, pp. 39-52.
[39]Powicke, *Thirteenth Century*, pp. 106-115.

were much influenced by their close friendship with Robert Grosseteste, the famous and holy Bishop of Lincoln, with whom they shared a keen concern for "the practical application of Christian principles to government."[40]

On April 30, 1258 Hugh Bigod, acting as spokesmen for the English barons including Simon de Montfort who had sworn their oath of mutual support some days earlier, formally presented their demands to King Henry: he must expel all aliens and agree to make fundamental reforms in the government, in return for which the confederated lords would try to persuade "the community of the realm" to meet a substantial part of the costs for the Sicilian venture if the Pope would relieve England of some of the financial responsibility for that venture to which Henry had unwisely committed the kingdom. Henry reluctantly agreed the next day, and set up a commission of 24 barons to carry out the reform, twelve to be nominated by him and twelve by the confederates.[41]

At this point Simon led a new group of envoys to France to secure a permanent peace treaty which would meet the Papal requirement of peace with France. They gave up England's historic claims to Normandy, Anjou, Touraine, Maine, and Poitou, deriving from the inheritance of Henry II in the preceding century from his French father Geoffrey of Anjou.[42] Parliament met again at Oxford in June and provided for the choice of a Council of Fifteen from the commission of 24 to develop a program of reform and administer the government during its implementation, reporting back to Parliament three times a year. This is why the reform came to be called "the Provisions of Oxford." Most of the members of Parliament swore to regard anyone opposing this reform program as an enemy.[43]

The Council of Fifteen was constituted immediately. Only three members were supporters of the King; the dominant figure was Simon de Montfort.[44] His leading role in these early stages of the baronial struggle with Henry III has sometimes been questioned by historians, but Henry himself had no doubt of it. Caught on the Thames by a thunderstorm in July and forced to take refuge in a riverside house belonging to the Bishop of Durham where Simon happened to be staying, Henry exclaimed to Simon as soon as he saw him:

> "The thunder and lightning I fear beyond measure, but, by the Head of God, I fear thee more than all the thunder and lightning in the world."[45]

---

[40]Labarge, *Simon de Montfort*, pp. 77, 79.

[41]Powicke, *Thirteenth Century*, pp. 130-131, 135; Trehearne, *Baronial Plan of Reform*, pp. 66-68.

[42]Labarge, *Simon de Montfort*, pp. 154-155; Labarge, *St. Louis*, pp. 192-193.

[43]Trehearne, *Baronial Plan of Reform*, pp. 72-74, 86; Powicke, *Thirteenth Century*, pp. 135-137, 140-141; Labarge, *Simon de Montfort*, pp. 172-173.

[44]Trehearne, *Baronial Plan of Reform*, pp. 75. 84.

[45]Labarge, *Simon de Montfort*, pp. 150, 174.

In July Simon brought the mayor and aldermen of the city of London into the reform confederacy, persuading them to put the city seal on a charter bearing the oath taken by the barons at Oxford and sealed by Henry III and Prince Edward. On August 4 Henry swore to accept the decisions of the Council of Fifteen on all matters concerning him and his realm, and ordered his people to obey the Council; that same day the Council launched a full-scale investigation of wrongs complained of throughout the country, appointing four knights for each of the 37 shires to arrange for hearing the complaints, to report back October 6.[46]

In September Pope Alexander IV—though distressed by the reformers' unceremonious removal of the "foreigner" Aymer de Valence, Bishop of Winchester—declared himself willing to wait for further evidence before taking any punitive action, while insisting that Aymer be accorded an opportunity to defend himself, and continuing to press for payment of the funds for Sicily. Henry III accepted the reformer Hugh Bigod as Justiciar and the honest John of Crakehall as Treasurer. During a ten-day period at the end of October the Council of Fifteen appointed 19 new sheriffs in 28 shires. The reformers had overwhelming support; when imperial claimant Richard of Cornwall returned to England in February 1259 in response to his brother's urgent summons, he was not allowed into the country until he took oath to support the baronial reform.[47]

In February 1259 the reform movement was greatly broadened when the Council of Fifteen led by Simon de Montfort accepted, after acrimonious debate, that the same legal principles must be observed in judging the disputes of barons with their tenants as in judging the disputes of barons with the King.[48] This demonstrates the depth and sincerity of this reform movement, proving that it did not serve the interests of the great barons alone.[49] The substantial opposition among the barons to broadening the reform shows that the scope and impact of this action was well understood; Simon's support for it shows what his principles were. Embodied in an ordinance, this critically important measure was published in March. The Earl of Gloucester, second most powerful of the barons, seems to have been among its opponents. At this time he initiated contacts with Henry's son Edward, later to bear evil fruit.[50]

In October 1259 the Provisions of Westminster, essentially a codificaiton

---

[46]Trehearne, *Baronial Plan of Reform*, pp. 80-81, 83, 85, 99-100, 108-111.

[47]*Ibid.*, pp. 106-107, 118-119, 121-122; Powicke, *Thirteenth Century*, p. 137; Roche, *King of Almayne*, pp. 153-154.

[48]Powicke, *Thirteenth Century*, p. 147; Trehearne, *Baronial Plan of Reform*, p. 139.

[49]Trehearne, *Baronial Plan of Reform*, pp. 177-178.

[50]*Ibid.*, pp. 137-141; Powicke, *Thirteenth Century*, pp. 147-148; Labarge, *Simon de Montfort*, p. 176.

of the baronial reform, were presented to Parliament as amendments and additions to Magna Carta. One of their chief goals was to secure fair judicial hearings for all freemen and to protect them from reprisals for bringing suit. Another goal was to supervise much more closely the administration of justice and the treasury. Within a year, shire courts were to begin electing four knights who in turn would choose the sheriff with the approval of the barons of the Exchequer, in contrast to the former procedure of appointment by the King alone, often on the recommendation of favorites. Circuit judges were designated to hear appeals from arbitrary actions or decision of sheriffs. The Provisions of Westminster were vigorously implemented within a month. On November 19 Justiciar Hugh Bigod met with the new sheriffs and four shire knights who were given authority to nominate sheriffs until the election procedures for the four prescribed by the Provisions should be in place. Circuit judges began hearing appeals cases under the Provisions of Westminster in January 1260.[51]

In November 1259 Henry III left for France for the formal signing of the treaty between France and England December 4. He was in no hurry to return; in January he wrote to Justiciar Hugh Bigod, regent in his absence, that he wished the first of the triennial parliaments for 1260, scheduled to meet in February, to be delayed. Suspecting that Henry was planning resistance to the reform, Simon called for Parliament to meet regardless of the King's wishes, but Bigod delayed hoping the King would soon return. In March Henry wrote to Bigod ordering him to bring an army to London by April 25, summoning eight earls and 99 barons and their feudal service, but not including Simon de Montfort. Bigod obeyed. On April 11 Henry wrote an open letter reviewing his reign and rights, declaring that the proposal to hold a Parliament without his consent showed that a state of rebellion existed, and that he would come with an army to restore order. Simon tried but failed to persuade the Council of Fifteen to oppose Henry's return, and on April 23 the King landed with 300 French knights and the Earl of Gloucester by his side.[52]

Richard of Cornwall mediated between the two sides, so that there was no immediate clash. Henry had to send most of the troops back to France; St. Louis sent one of his bishops to assist Simon when Henry attempted to put him on trial, and he was acquitted by Parliament after a committee of bishops and the Council of Fifteen refused to indict him.[53] But Henry's tactics had

---

[51]Trehearne, *Baronial Plan of Reform*, pp. 167-191; Powicke, *Thirteenth Century*, pp. 146-151.

[52]Trehearne, *Baronial Plan of Reform*, pp. 195, 213, 219-220, 222-223, 225-229, 231; Powicke, *Thirteenth Century*, pp. 126-127, 155-158; Labarge, *Simon de Montfort*, pp. 158, 160-161, 181-182, 184.

[53]Trehearne, *Baronial Plan of Reform*, pp. 233-234, 238-241; Powicke, *Thirteenth Century*, pp. 160-161; Labarge, *Simon de Montfort*, pp. 185, 187-188.

effectively divided the baronial reformers, in particular by setting the Earl of Gloucester and Simon the Earl of Leicester at loggerheads. In October the barons had let Henry replace Hugh Bigod as Justiciar and Henry of Wingham as Chancellor with more compromising men; honest Treasurer John of Crakehall had died and been replaced by a more malleable man. In March Henry judged that the barons had weakened sufficiently for him to be able to denounce the rule of the Council of Fifteen as conducted for the private advantage of the barons, not for the benefit of the kingdom, and wrote the Pope asking for absolution from his oath to maintain the Provisions of Oxford, which he denounced by name, demanding his full royal power back.[54]

Pope Alexander IV, who had been angered by the refusal of the barons in 1259 to obey his order to restore Aymer de Valence to the see of Winchester,[55] on April 14 did absolve Henry III from his oath to maintain the Provisions of Oxford, on the grounds that it was extorted from him by force "on pretext of reforming the realm."[56] On May 7 the Pope directed the Archbishop of Canterbury to excommunicate anyone refusing to accept Henry III's full authority as King.[57]

Eighteen days later Pope Alexander IV died at Viterbo.[58] His last actions regarding the situation in England cloud the memory of an otherwise admirable pontificate, for the baronial reform movement had been one of the most high-minded and truly Christian undertakings of the age, despite the inevitable admixture of personal greed and ambition. No Papal decree could cancel it completely, but only escalate the struggle over it, at least so long as Simon de Montfort was alive; and this is exactly what happened. On the other hand, Henry was an exceptionally pious king, and the Popes had regarded themselves as bearing a special responsibility to protect the King of England ever since King John's spectacular gesture of handing the whole kingdom over to the Pope and receiving it back as a fief. The political theory of the age had no place for a parliament acting against the will of a king to reform the government, and Henry had now made it very clear that the reform was against his will.[59]

---

[54]Trehearne, *Baronial Plan of Reform*, pp. 232, 244-245, 252; Powicke, *Thirteenth Century*, pp. 162-163; Labarge, *Simon de Montfort*, p. 189.

[55]He had issued a bull ordering this in January, though it had not been delivered until August. The Council of Fifteen refused to obey, writing its protest to the Pope. See Trehearne, *Baronial Plan of Reform*, pp. 143-144.

[56]Trehearne, *Baronial Plan of Reform*, p. 260.

[57]Powicke, *Thirteenth Century*, p. 165.

[58]Mann, *Popes in the Middle Ages*, XVI, 45.

[59]That Simon de Montfort had envisaged a new political theory for England, bearing at least some substantial resemblance to the modern English system of government, has been scornfully dismissed by many historians as impossible. Yet the record of his actions, and his suggestions on more than one occasion that Parliament should act without the King or even against him, without any attempt to support another royal claimant—which was almost always the form taken in that age by political movements

The small conclave that met in late May 1261 to elect Pope Alexander IV's successor soon deadlocked. There were only eight cardinals; this meant that, under the two-thirds requirement, six votes were required to elect a Pope. There is evidence that this large majority might have been obtained for the Dominican cardinal, Hugh of St. Cher, or for the Cistercian cardinal, John Tolet of England, but both men refused the pontifical office. With no other cardinal able to get six votes, the conclave had to look elsewhere, though they hesitated long before doing so. Eventually, on August 29, they unanimously elected James of Troyes (capital of the province of Champagne in France), a learned and able man whom Pope Innocent IV had made Bishop of Verdun and Pope Alexander IV had made Patriarch of Jerusalem. James took the Papal name of Urban IV.[60]

James had been appointed Patriarch of Jerusalem in 1255 but had not reached Acre until five years later. During his year in the ever-embattled Middle East he had tried to heal the endless, vicious and often petty disputes among Christian merchants in the Levant, particularly the most bitter rivals, the Genoese and the Venetians. He had also faced the difficult question of the proper policy toward the Mongols, once again on the warpath.[61]

Hulagu, younger brother of the new Great Khan Mangu, had surged into Iran during 1256 and taken and destroyed the eyrie of the dreaded Assassins at Alamut. In February 1258 Hulagu had taken Baghdad, killing the Abbasid Caliph—who, though now much limited in his political and military power, was still regarded by most orthodox Muslims as their religious leader. Hulagu's ferocious warriors had sacked Baghdad for forty days, killed 80,000 people, taken away immense treasure, and left the great Muslim city a barely surviving shadow, which took forty years to regain one-tenth of its former size. Though Christian optimists hoping to convert the Mongols and make crusaders out of them made much of the fact that the mother of Mangu and Hulagu was a Christian, her faith seemed to have made little impression on her sons, who resembled much more their grandfather Genghis Khan. In May 1258 Mangu, at the other end of Asia, had launched an all-out invasion of southern China, then ruled by the highly cultured Sung dynasty. In September 1259 Hulagu had invaded Syria and in the winter of 1260 his Mongols had overrun it, taking

---

against a king—suggest that this scoffing is over-hasty. Simon may not have formulated his doctrine in the manner of a St. Thomas Aquinas, but there is good reason to believe he had some visualization of a kind of government the world had never seen before. Certainly the reform he led in England was unique, unparalleled elsewhere in Europe, and laid the foundations for the special authority in Parliament that distinguished England from all other European countries during much of its subsequent history.

[60]Mann, *Popes in the Middle Ages*, XVI, 45, 140-144.

[61]Steven Runciman, *A History of the Crusades*, Volume III: "The Kingdom of Acre and the Later Crusades" (Cambridge, England, 1966), p. 285.

Aleppo and Damascus.[62]

But by then Mangu had died in China. As when Genghis Khan's son Ogadai died in 1241, the Mongol leaders had to return to their distant homeland to choose a successor. (Kublai and Arikbuka contested the succession and Kublai prevailed, but was never able to exercise power west of Mongolia.) When Patriarch James, the Pope-to-be, arrived in Palestine the Egyptians under Kutuz and Baybars were already marching on Syria in a furious counterattack against the weakened Mongol forces, commanded in Hulagu's absence by a Christian general, Kitbogha. Kitbogha was supported by the crusader king Bohemond VI of Antioch and the Christian King Hetoum I of Armenia, but opposed by the remnant of the crusader kingdom at Acre, whose leaders allowed the Egyptian army to cross its territory as it marched to confront the Mongols. The advice of the newly arrived Patriarch James would certainly have played a significant role in this decision and may well have been in favor of it, though we do not know for sure.[63]

On September 3, 1260 the Mongols had suffered their first decisive defeat since the initial appearance of Genghis Khan, at the Battle of Ain Jalut. It was mainly due to the superb military abilities of the Mamluk general Baybars of Egypt. But Baybars was as ruthless as the Mongols themselves. Within a month of his victory he had murdered his sovereign Kutuz and become Sultan of Egypt. Because Antioch and Armenia had helped the Mongols, Baybars concluded that the crusader kingdoms were likely to support Mongol invasions in the future and must be eliminated.[64] In fact there was no reason to expect that in the long run the Mongols would be any more friendly to the Christians than the Muslims had been, and by the end of the century most of those living in the Middle East had become Muslim themselves.

Newly elected Pope Urban IV drew at once the needed lesson from the difficulties of the conclave that had finally chosen him: there were too few cardinals. During the first year of his pontificate he appointed no less than fourteen new cardinals, including three future Popes. Half were Italians and half Frenchmen.[65]

Urban IV was widely acclaimed as a patron of learning. He was certainly a patron of St. Thomas Aquinas. Just ten days after his consecration as Pope the Dominican provincial chapter meeting at Orvieto, where he resided, assigned Thomas indefinitely to the priory at Orvieto, where he lived and

---

[62]*Ibid.*, III, 299-307; Kenneth M. Setton, ed. *A History of the Crusades*, Volume II: "The Later Crusades, 1189-1311," ed. Robert L. Wolff and Harry W. Hazard (Philadephia, 1962), pp. 571-572; Morris Rossabi, *Khubilai Khan; His Life and Times* (Berkeley CA, 1988), pp. 44-46.

[63]Runciman, *Crusades*, III, 306-307, 311-312; Setton, *Crusades*, II, 571-574, 744; Rossabi, *Khubilai Khan*, pp. 51-54.

[64]Runciman, *Crusades*, III, 315-317; Setton, *Crusades*, II, 745-746.

[65]Mann, *Popes in the Middle Ages*, XVI, 146-148.

worked during most of Urban's four-year pontificate.[66] In the dedication of his commentary on St. Matthew's Gospel to Pope Urban IV, Thomas spoke of the "studious zeal" which had led Urban to ask him to write this commentary:

> I submit it to be examined and corrected by the decision of your supreme authority. It is the joint fruit of your solicitude and of my obedience. Deign to accept it so that, just as the order to write it came from you, the final appreciation of its value may be pronounced by you, as rivers return to the source whence they have sprung.[67]

Urban IV also requested Thomas to write a book delineating and explaining the erroneous doctrines of the Greek church. Just a month before Urban was elected Pope, Michael Palaeologus, the Greek Emperor of Nicaea who claimed the Byzantine imperial crown, had been surprised to find a small army of his regaining Constantinople from the moribund Latin imperial regime. His army was admitted under (or over) the poorly guarded walls by sympathizers within the city while most of the small Latin garrison and the guarding Venetian fleet were away trying to take some islands in the Black Sea. Michael Palaeologus had no idea the reconquest would be so easy.[68] The Greek recovery of Constantinople and restoration of the Byzantine empire had made the question of religious reunion with the separated Greek church more urgent.

It appears to have been during this period that Thomas Aquinas began his extraordinary practice of writing several books at once. Even if he had occasionally done so earlier, he had to do it on a grand scale during the year 1263, when there is no doubt that he was simultaneously writing the *Summa contra gentiles*, his book against the errors of the Greeks (*Contra errores Graecorum*), and his commentary on St. Matthew's gospel.[69]

But for all his learning and experience, Urban IV was not a decisive Pope. His letters and actions regarding the restored Byzantine empire during the years 1262 and 1263 are redolent with indecision. On the one hand he longed to restore the unity of Christendom through a firm acknowledgment of Papal authority by the Byzantine Emperor, Michael Palaeologus; on the other hand he preferred to work with leaders he knew better, particularly the French prince Charles of Anjou whom he hoped to place on the throne of Sicily and south Italy, and whom everyone knew had great ambitions in Greece. Michael's first letter which reached the Pope, probably in June 1262, called for

---

[66]Weisheipl, *Thomas D'Aquino*, p. 147.

[67]Mann, *Popes in the Middle Ages*, XVI, 145.

[68]Donald M. Nicol, *The Last Centuries of Byzantium, 1261-1453* (New York, 1972), pp. 39-41, 45; Deno J. Geanakoplos, *Emperor Michael Palaeologus and the West* (Cambridge MA, 1959), pp. 92-113.

[69]Weisheipl, *Thomas D'Aquino.*, pp. 168-172.

reconciliation and peace with the West (with a promise that the Greeks would forgive the injuries they had suffered from the Latins—a pointed reminder that these injuries had not been forgotten) but said nothing specific about full religious submission to the Pope or the apparent doctrinal differences that had developed between the Greek and Latin churches. The Pope surely knew by this time that Emperor Michael had ordered his young colleague John Lascaris, the legitimate Emperor, blinded on Christmas day 1261, and that his own patriarch had excommunicated him for it. Such an act did not encourage trust in Michael Palaeologus.[70]

Pope Urban IV made no reply to Michael Palaeologus for nearly a year. In July 1262 he made an alliance with Baldwin II, the bedraggled ex-Latin Emperor of Constantinople; with the redoubtable Prince William de Villehardouin of Achaea; and with the wealthy Venetians against the "Greek schismatics" of the Byzantine empire. The Pope released William from the oath he had taken not to bear arms against the Byzantines as a condition of his release by Michael after two years in captivity following his humiliating capture under a pile of hay following the disastrous Battle of Pelagonia in 1259.[71] But having brought the alliance together, Pope Urban IV did not press it into action, and it was Michael who acted first. Early in 1263 he sent an army under his brother Constantine which attacked William's capital of Andravida, defended in William's absence by a dauntless knight named John Katavas, whom we are told (perhaps with some exaggeration) put to flight the attacking army of 15,000 with only 300 men.[72]

On July 18, 1263 Pope Urban IV finally sent what was, so far as we know, his first written communication to Michael Palaeologus. Michael had written him again in the spring, this time declaring specifically that he would accept the Pope's judgment in all disputes that might arise between him and the Latins. Urban expressed satisfaction with this, admitted that some Latins in Constantinople had been actuated by greed and had sinfully profaned Greek churches, and said that if Michael would end the schism the Pope would probably recognize him as Emperor in the East if he would stop the war against William in Greece. A few days later the Pope wrote to William telling him that he was sending several Franciscan friars "to lead to unity, if possible, Michael Palaeologus, who considers himself Emperor of the Greeks," and directing William to refrain from hostilities against Michael until his religious intentions became clear.[73]

---

[70]Nicol, *Last Centuries of Byzantium*, pp. 48, 52-53; Geanakoplos, *Michael Palaeologus*, pp. 145-147, 195-196; Joseph Gill, *Byzantium and the Papacy, 1198-1400* (New Brunswick NJ, 1979), p. 107; Mann, *Popes in the Middle Ages*, XVI, 392-393.
[71]Geanokoplos, *Michael Palaeologus*, pp. 62-73, 156.
[72]*Ibid.*, pp. 158-159; Setton, *Crusades*, II, 253-254.
[73]Geanokoplos, *Michael Palaeologus*, pp. 157, 165-166; Gill, *Byzantium and the*

This letter crossed with another from Michael, borne by Nicholas of Durazzo on the coast of Epirus (now Albania), Bishop of Cotrone, an official of the Papal Curia and bilingual in Greek and Latin, whom Michael had invited to Constantinople the previous year and who had much impressed him. Michael credited Nicholas with convincing him that the Pope was the divinely appointed head of the whole Church and that there was no significant difference in doctrine between the Greeks and Latins. Michael Palaeologus pledged, for himself and for his clergy and empire, full willingness to submit to Papal authority and end the schism.[74]

It sounded magnificent; but the Pope was still doubtful, especially when he received reports that the Byzantines were continuing to make war in William de Villehardouin's domains in the Peloponnese regardless of their Emperor's sentiments. Thomas Aquinas' treatise on the errors of the Greeks, completed about this time, could also well have caused Urban IV to doubt that there were in fact no significant theological differences between the schismatic Greek Church and the Catholic Church.[75] In the summer of 1264 Urban sent Bishop Nicholas back to Constantinople with an offer to convoke an ecumenical council to settle the issues dividing the Greek church from the Church of Rome.[76]

During the first six months of his pontificate Urban IV took no action on the still simmering dispute between Henry III of England and the nobles who had insisted on reform of the English government. Momentum was now on Henry's side. As soon as he had in hand Pope Alexander IV's bull absolving him from his oath to support the Provisions of Oxford and Westminster, Henry III replaced the Justiciar and the Chancellor (who had been selected only with the consent of the barons) by nominees of his own choosing. Soon afterward he also removed the sheriffs and custodians of castles chosen by the baronial Council of Fifteen, replacing them also with his own personal appointees. In September 1261 Simon de Montfort, the Earl of Gloucester, and the Bishop of Worcester summoned a parliament of three knights from each shire to meet at St. Albans, without any reference to the King; Henry ordered them to meet at Windsor instead. Confused and fearful, most of the knights did not assemble at either place.[77]

By October the King's agents had completely separated Simon and the Earl of Gloucester. Gloucester came to terms with Henry while Simon

---

Papacy, pp. 108-109.
[74]Gill, Byzantium and the Papacy, pp. 109-110.
[75]Weisheipl, Thomas D'Aquino, pp. 168-171.
[76]Geanokoplos, Michael Palaeologus, pp. 179-180.
[77]Trehearne, Baronial Plan of Reform, pp. 261, 263, 266-267, 271; Powicke, Thirteenth Century, p. 163; Labarge, Simon de Montfort, pp. 195-198.

departed in disgust for France, saying he "preferred to die without a country, than as a perjurer to desert the truth."[78]

Richard of Cornwall was accepted as arbiter between the King and the barons, while Henry sent off messengers to Pope Urban IV asking him to renew Alexander IV's bull absolving him from his oath to uphold the Provisions of Oxford. Urban did so on February 25, 1262, on the grounds that the oaths interfered with the King's liberty, and in May Richard as arbiter ruled that Henry could choose whomever he wished as sheriff, regardless of any previous agreements to the contrary. All the barons but Simon de Montfort, who was remaining in France, accepted Richard's decision. It appeared that the great reform movement was dead.[79]

But it was not dead; Simon de Montfort had lit a fire in England which was never to be put out, launching that country on the long road to creating the first true national parliamentary government since the Roman republic of Cicero's day. Simon would not be reconciled to the full restoration of Henry III's misused power; St. Louis IX had to report that he could find no way to peace between the two men. Increasingly apprehensive, in March 1263 Henry demanded oaths of loyalty from the barons, the counties, and all the citizens of London. In April Simon returned to England at the urging of many of the barons, met with the new young Earl of Gloucester (his father had suddenly died the preceding year at the age of only forty), and renewed with him and others the earlier oath to treat as enemies all opposing the Provisions of Oxford. In May the oath-takers issued a written demand to the King that he renew his commitment to the Provisions of Oxford. Henry refused. His refusal meant war. By early June fighting had begun, the barons had allied themselves with the redoubtable Prince Llewelyn of Wales (a long-time and successful foe of Henry III), and Simon roused the people of London, where the royal family had taken refuge in the Tower.[80]

In mid-July Queen Eleanor, wife of Henry III and mother of the able and increasingly influential Crown Prince Edward, attempted to escape from the Tower up the Thames River to join her son at Windsor. She was bombarded from London Bridge by a mob, first with eggs and then with rocks. Though Mayor Fitz Thomas of London, a strong supporter of Simon de Montfort, came promptly to her rescue, Prince Edward never forgave this insult to his mother. But for the time being Henry III, almost without military support, had no choice but to accept all the demands of Simon and his associates, the most important

---

[78]Labarge, *Simon de Montfort*, p. 198.

[79]*Ibid.*, pp. 198-199; Trehearne, *Baronial Plan of Reform*, pp. 277-279, 282; Powicke, *Thirteenth Century*, pp. 166-168; Mann, *Popes in the Middle Ages*, XVI, 186.

[80]Trehearne, *Baronial Plan of Reform*, pp. 297-303; Powicke, *Thirteenth Century*, pp. 174-175; Labarge, *Simon de Montfort*, pp. 204-205, 207-210; R. R. Davies, *Conquest, Coexistence, and Change; Wales 1064-1415* (Oxford, 1967), p. 333.

being the restoration of the agreements made at Oxford in 1258. Though the Council of Fifteen was supposed to be restored, in fact Simon de Montfort was now the leader of England. On July 22 he entered London and Henry III and Queen Eleanor retreated to Westminster; early in August Prince Edward surrendered Windsor castle to Simon.[81]

The restoration of the reform was solemnly confirmed by a Parliament called, however reluctantly, by Henry III in September 1263. Meeting again in October, Parliament refused to permit Henry to choose even the officers of his own household (since some of them were among the chief officers of the realm) or to pay for the cost of property of the king's supporters destroyed or damaged during the battles and raids of June and July. Tempers flared furiously on both sides. In the midst of this Prince Edward struck, coolly and decisively, regaining control of Windsor castle near London and using it to block the movement of supplies for London down the Thames. Henry III withdrew his recognition of Fitz Thomas as mayor of London, and in mid-November dismissed the Chancellor favored by the barons, Nicholas of Ely, and appointed the royalist John of Chishull in his place. A renewal of the war seemed imminent.[82]

Both Pope Urban IV and King St. Louis IX of France were resolved to prevent this if they could; both were convinced that Simon de Montfort and the barons had gone too far, particularly in prohibiting their king from choosing officials of his own household. Parliamentary government seemed to them a prescription for anarchy, for the destruction of civilized and Christian order. If Henry III had not been so politically inept, he could surely have worked out a compromise; but once he had been forced into an agreement with the barons all he ever did was to try to find ways to break it. Consequently the basic issue of royal versus parliamentary power kept recurring in its most stark form. Pope Urban IV was a good man, but of limited imagination and ability; St. Louis IX was a great man and a saint; but neither had a mind which could leap out of its own time and cultural conditioning. Simon de Montfort had a mind which could and did do just that.[83]

On November 22, 1263 Pope Urban IV sent Cardinal Guy Fulcodi to London as his legate to restore peace in England and to restore Henry III to the control of the government of England with the help of St. Louis IX. Cardinal Fulcodi was given authority to release Henry III from any and all of his oaths to the barons, to punish those who opposed him, to dissolve all leagues of nobles against the king, and if necessary to preach a crusade against the barons continuing to reject Henry's authority. Probably knowing or suspecting that he

---

[81]Trehearne, *Baronial Plan of Reform*, pp. 307-308, 310-311, 314-319; Powicke, *Thirteenth Century*, p. 176; Labarge, *Simon de Montfort*, pp. 212-214.
[82]Trehearne, *Baronial Plan of Reform*, pp. 321-324, 327, 330-331; Powicke, *Thirteenth Century*, p. 177; Labarge, *Simon de Montfort*, pp. 215-217.
[83]See Note 59, above.

carried such instructions, the barons refused to admit Cardinal Fulcodi to England—an act which sealed their fate. No one in thirteenth-century Western Europe could defy the Pope so openly and get away with it.[84]

Surprisingly (particularly after their refusal to admit the Papal legate into England) the barons agreed December 13 to the arbitration of their entire dispute with Henry III by St. Louis IX of France, whose fame for justice, wisdom, temperance and charity had long caused him to be greatly in demand as an arbiter. The issue in England had gone beyond arbitration, but the barons did not fully understand that; though they knew the Pope was hostile, they seem not to have realized that Louis IX also had turned against them. Simon de Montfort later argued that he had not intended the arbitration to apply to the whole quarrel, but only to its most recent developments; and in person he might have been able to persuade Louis to accept this interpretation of his jurisdiction, for Louis greatly respected him. But on his way through England to the Channel ports and France, Simon was thrown from his horse and suffered a badly broken leg; he was unable to walk or ride for months. The argument before Louis took place without him, and the decision Louis handed down on January 23, 1264 was a heavy blow to Simon and his cause. St. Louis ruled that Henry had the right to govern his kingdom and appoint his own officials, and that the Provisions of Oxford were null and void because condemned by the Pope. But he did declare that royal privileges and charters issued in England before the Provisions of Oxford (chiefly, Magna Carta) must be upheld, and that for the sake of concord in the kingdom Henry III should pardon the barons who had supported the Provisions of Oxford, for they were no ordinary rebels.[85]

Simon and the barons, along with the city of London, refused to give up their cause even in the face of Papal authority as exerted through Cardinal Fulcodi as legate and of the arbitration authority of Louis IX. Such a surrender was certainly a great deal to ask of them, but the consequences of defiance were fatal. They manifested themselves very soon, when the baronial army sacked Rochester on Good Friday 1264 and looted even the church of St. Andrew there, and savage anti-Jewish pogroms broke out in London. Simon, a great general, won in May what appeared to be a decisive victory at Lewes, capturing Henry III and his brother Richard of Cornwall (their sons Prince Edward and Henry "of Almain" gave themselves up as hostages in their place). Simon continued to bar the Papal legate from the country. Cardinal Fulcodi demanded admission, on pain of excommunication; when Simon still refused he

---

[84]Trehearne, *Baronial Plan of Reform*, pp. 338-339; Powicke, *Thirteenth Century*, p. 180; Labarge, *Simon de Montfort*, p. 223; Mann, *Popes in the Middle Ages*, XVI, 189-190, 220.
[85]Trehearne, *Baronial Plan of Reform*, pp. 333-334, 339-342; Powicke, *Thirteenth Century*, pp. 182-183; Labarge, *Simon de Montfort*, pp. 220-224; Labarge, *St. Louis*, pp. 199-201.

was excommunicated and London was laid under an interdict.[86]

On October 2, 1264 Pope Urban IV died at Perugia after a short illness. On October 21 Cardinal Fulcodi excommunicated the other chief opponents of Henry III in addition to Simon de Montfort, and ordered the excommunication proclaimed throughout France and England.   The bishops carrying the excommunication were seized on landing in England, and the decree was torn up and thrown into the sea.[87]

One of Urban IV's last acts as Pope was to issue the bull *Transiturus* instituting a new feast of the Body of Christ (Corpus Christi), whose celebration he made obligatory for the entire Church. A whole new office or liturgy was written for the feast; it was ready when *Transiturus* was issued August 11, 1264. It was avowed at a Dominican general chapter held at Vienne in 1322 that this liturgy was written by St. Thomas Aquinas, and the preponderance of evidence indicates that this attribution is correct. This Corpus Christi liturgy includes the magnificent sequence *Lauda Sion*, the vesper hymn *Pange lingua* (concluding with the *Tantum ergo*, sung during Benediction of the Blessed Sacrament), the matins hymn *Sacris solemnis* (concluding with *Panis angelicus*), and the lauds hymn *Verbum supernum prodiens* (concluding with another Benediction song, *O salutaris hostia*). Familiar for centuries to every Catholic, these glorious Latin hymns continue to be widely sung to this day.[88]

The Common Doctor of the Church did not write only for scholars; in the office of Corpus Christi he wrote for the simple Catholic worshipper all down the ages.

The conclave to elect a new Pope met at Perugia, where Urban IV had died, at the end of October 1264. Eighteen of the 21 cardinals were present, and they were almost evenly divided between supporters and opponents of the most politically significant undertaking of the previous pontificate, the invitation to Charles of Anjou, brother of St. Louis IX of France, to accept the crown of Sicily.[89]

As we have seen, the infamous Emperor Frederick II had been hereditary king of Sicily; he had grown up in Sicily's capital, Palermo. His legitimate son Conrad had claimed Sicily despite the insistence of Pope Innocent IV that the whole Hohenstaufen family had forfeited their rights in Sicily in view of the magnitude of Frederick II's challenge to the Church and to Christendom. When Conrad died, his infant son Conradin inherited his claim, but it was not

---

[86]Powicke, *Thirteenth Century*, pp. 184, 187-190, 195; Labarge, *Simon de Montfort*, pp. 230-231, 234-236, 240; Mann, *Popes in the Middle Ages*, XVI, 188, 192-194.
[87]Mann, *Popes in the Middle Ages*, XVI, 198-199, 204; Labarge, *Simon de Montfort*, p. 241.
[88]Weisheipl, *Thomas D'Aquino*, pp. 179-184.
[89]Runciman, *Sicilian Vespers*, p. 99.

then pressed because of his age; Frederick II's illegitimate son Manfred had taken over Sicily. Pope Alexander IV, seeking to displace Manfred, had unwisely turned to Henry III of England, who proved totally incapable of acting in any capacity in Sicily. Pope Urban IV had considered the possibility of peace with Manfred, and in November 1262 had offered to recognize Manfred as king of Sicily if he would readmit the many political exiles driven out during the long struggle of its Hohenstaufen rulers against the Popes and restore their lands, and pay a large indemnity to the Pope in view of the immense costs of the wars against the Hohenstaufens in Sicily. When Manfred refused these terms, his excommunication was renewed, and in the following spring Pope Urban IV opened negotiations with Charles.[90]

Charles of Anjou was strikingly different from his brother St. Louis IX, though they had one fundamental aspect in common. Louis was blond, slender, handsome, gentle of mien though firm and decisive in policy, known throughout Christendom for his kindness and charity—a crusader, but not a great general. Charles was tall, muscular, dark-complexioned, with a big nose and a thundercloud often on his brow, known for his harshness, feared for his occasional cruelty. He was a strong man, brave as a lion, steadfast and persevering. He said little, slept little, lost no time in diversions, living a chaste and tightly disciplined life. He was a mighty warrior, but no crusader; during his long and active career as a prince of Christendom he never set foot in the Holy Land. Few men loved Charles of Anjou; all men respected him, and many feared him. What he and Louis shared was the pearl of great price: a rocklike faith, the kind that would stand though the heavens fell.[91]

In June 1263 Pope Urban IV's envoy had offered Charles of Anjou the crown of Sicily and southern Italy (except for Benevento and its environs), on condition that he guarantee the freedom of the Church in his kingdom, that he make large payments for it to the Pope and offer him the homage of vassal to lord, that he swear it should never again be united with the Empire, and that the exiles and their property should be restored. Charles would be expected to attack Manfred as soon as possible; the campaign would be proclaimed a crusade, with support from the crusading tenth of the income of the Church in France for three successive years.[92]

But Charles had disturbed Pope Urban IV by accepting the office of Senator of Rome for life. Rome had become so turbulent in recent years that most of the time the Popes dared not live there; Urban IV spent most of his pontificate in Perugia. He did not want Charles involved in Roman politics—certainly not for life!—and some of his cardinals disliked this prospect

---

[90]*Ibid.*, pp. 84-85; Mann, *Popes in the Middle Ages*, XVI, 159-160.
[91]Mann, *Popes in the Middle Ages*, XVI, 232-234; Runciman, *Sicilian Vespers*, pp. 87-89.
[92]Mann, *Popes in the Middle Ages*, XVI, 163-165; Runciman, *Sicilian Vespers*, p. 85.

even more than he. Charles finally agreed to give up the office of Senator when he had gained control of the kingdom of Sicily and southern Italy, but by the time of Urban IV's death negotiations with Charles were still going on in France, and he was gaining much influence in Italian politics. As tended to happen so readily in Italy, parties formed for and against him, and their reflection among the cardinals deadlocked the conclave for electing the next Pope.[93]

After the deadlock had continued for four months, the cardinals chose two of their number to make the election alone. The pair chose Cardinal Fulcodi, the legate Pope Urban IV had sent to England who had been unable to get into the country and had excommunicated its current leaders, but had stayed in France in pursuance of his mission and so was not at the conclave.[94]

Cardinal Fulcodi took as his Papal name Clement IV, because he had been born on the feast of Pope St. Clement. He was a Frenchman from Provence, the son of a lawyer of distinguished career, who had died a Carthusian monk. He had served St. Louis IX as one of his most trusted counsellors, and was famed for his sense of justice. Of Pope Clement IV's high principles, devotion to duty, and humility there could be no doubt; they were all clearly manifested in a letter written to his nephew shortly after his election as Pope, in which he made it very clear that his relatives could expect no special favors from him.[95]

Clement IV's past experiences had placed him firmly in support of Charles of Anjou as king of Sicily and southern Italy, and of King Henry III of England against Simon de Montfort and his associates. His alignment in their favor did not change when he became Pope. Just four days after his consecration he confirmed the award of Sicily to Charles, subject to 35 conditions, essentially those already agreed on in 1263; on Holy Thursday 1265 he solemnly renewed his excommunications of Simon de Montfort and his chief associates among the barons of England, and in May he sent Cardinal Ottobuoni Fieschi as his successor as legate to England, authorizing him to support Henry III by every means, including preaching a crusade.[96]

Decisive action followed quickly from these Papal confirmations. On May 10 Charles set sail for Rome, where he was enthusiastically welcomed. Manfred responded with a magniloquent proclamation in which he declared himself "lord of the world" and said he would come to Rome to restore the Roman Empire and break the temporal power of the Pope. On June 28 four cardinals,

---

[93]Runciman, *Sicilian Vespers*, pp. 94-97, 99; Mann, *Popes in the Middle Ages*, XIV, 167-168, 174-176.
   [94]Mann, *Popes in the Middle Ages*, XVI, 220-222; Runciman, *Sicilian Vespers*, pp. 99-100.
   [95]Mann, *Popes in the Middle Ages*, XVI, 211-220.
   [96]*Ibid.*, XVI, 226-229, 311-312, 314; Runciman, *Sicilian Vespers*, p. 100.

specially accredited by Pope Clement IV, invested Charles with the kingdom of Sicily and declared him the leader of a crusade against Manfred. On July 10 Peter de Vico, formerly one of Manfred's leading generals, made his peace with the Church, renounced Manfred, swore allegiance to the Papal state, and took service under Charles; a few days later the former head of the Ghibellines in Rome did likewise. In early October Charles' army, 26,000 strong, marched from Lyons toward Italy, arriving in Milan the next month.[97]

Meanwhile in England, the young Earl of Gloucester abandoned Simon de Montfort as his father had done, and Prince Edward escaped from the custody of Simon's son Henry and joined Gloucester. Simon had to turn to Llewelyn of Wales for an army sufficient to fight these formidable foes, but Prince Edward's brilliant generalship along the Severn River led to a double victory, first over the army of Simon's son and namesake near Kenilworth, then against Simon himself at Evesham. Simon died fighting as his father had done. His body was shamefully mutilated and refused burial in consecrated ground because of his excommunication. Simon de Montfort was always personally devout, however mistaken his course of action during the last tragic year of his life. He combined personal integrity and political imagination and foresight to an extraordinary degree. He retained many admirers in England, then and since, and not without reason. Pope Clement IV never relented toward Simon; but he counselled Henry III and Prince Edward in a series of strongly worded letters against the vengeful attitude they displayed in victory.[98]

The victory of Charles of Anjou over Manfred was no less complete. Manfred did not dare challenge his grim, relentless opponent at the border of his kingdom, and retreated steadily from him. Charles pressed on until he caught up with Manfred near Benevento in late February 1266.[99] A message sent to his opponent just before the battle was typical of Charles; referring to the Muslim soldiers from the colony which Frederick II had established at Lucera in Italy, Charles said: "Go and tell the Sultan of Lucera that this day I will send him to Hell, or he shall send me to Heaven!"[100] The heavily armored German cavalry which Manfred had believed invincible were not so; three thousand of the 3,600 of them present were slain on the battlefield, for Charles gave no quarter even to the wounded, and Manfred died in their midst. Pope Clement IV—perhaps remembering what had been done to Simon de Montfort's body—ordered an honorable burial for Manfred, even though like Simon he had been excommunicated and was not allowed burial in consecrated

---

[97]Runciman, *Sicilian Vespers*, pp. 101-102, 104-105; Mann, *Popes in the Middle Ages*, XVI, 230-232, 238-239.

[98]Labarge, *Simon de Montfort*, pp. 250-257; Powicke, *Thirteenth Century*, pp. 200-203; Davies, *Wales*, p. 314; Mann, *Popes in the Middle Ages*, XVI, 314.

[99]Runciman, *Sicilian Vespers*, pp. 107-109.

[100]Mann, *Popes in the Middle Ages*, XIV, 251.

ground. The French prince was now the universally recognized King of Sicily and southern Italy.[101]

There was an epilogue to Charles' victory, the last chapter in the sad history of the fall of the Hohenstaufen dynasty. Frederick II's only grandson, Conrad IV's son known as Conradin, fourteen at the time of Manfred's defeat and death, was encouraged by ambitious German nobles and diehard Italian Ghibellines to try to regain control of his ancestral realm. Charles' blunt and overbearing nature and his foreign origin had angered many Italians in and out of his newly acquired kingdom; when Conradin left Germany in September 1267 with only four thousand cavalry he picked up substantial support in Italy. Clement IV excommunicated him in November for aggression against Sicily, a Papal vassal kingdom, and within two months two of the most important of his German commanders, Duke Louis of Bavaria and Count Rudolf of Habsburg, had left him and returned home, very likely because of the excommunication. But Conradin persevered, and continued to gain Italian support. In June 1268 his army defeated that of Charles at a bridge on the Arno River in Tuscany, and in July he made a triumphal entry into Rome. Nevertheless Pope Clement IV and Charles of Anjou stood fast, and on August 23 Charles, with brilliant generalship, totally defeated his young challenger at the Battle of Tagliacozzo. Conradin was captured near Rome and Charles, rejecting all pleas for clemency, executed him.[102]

In September 1265 the Dominican provincial chapter for Rome met at Anagni and decided to establish a new center for the study of theology, Scripture, and philosophy by young Dominicans at Santa Sabina on the Aventine hill in Rome. They designated St. Thomas Aquinas to found and direct it. He taught there through the next two academic years. His absorption in the needs, questions, and responses of his students—for it should always be remembered, as his inaugural lecture as master at the University of Paris quoted at the head of this chapter so clearly shows, that Thomas Aquinas was above all, first and foremost, a *teacher*—led Thomas to envisage and begin to put on paper his supreme work, the *Summa theologiae*, as a guide for students beginning advanced work in theology. It was at Santa Sabina that Thomas wrote, in Question 3 of the *Summa theologiae*, probably the best known of all his expositions, the arguments for the existence of God.[103]

He outlines the five arguments: from the existence of change, from the necessity of a First Cause, from the necessity of an Eternal Being as the source

---

[101]Runciman, *Sicilian Vespers*, pp. 109-112.

[102]*Ibid.*, pp. 120, 122-133; Mann, *Popes in the Middle Ages*, XVI, 261-266, 275, 279-280, 282-283, 289-293; Ferdinand Schevill, *Medieval and Renaissance Florence*, rev. ed. (New York, 1961), pp. 139-140.

[103]Weisheipl, *Thomas D'Aquino*, pp. 195-198, 217-230.

of all existence, from the existence of gradations requiring an Ultimate Perfection, and from the order of nature. They are powerful and sound; but most men respond poorly and inadequately to logical argument, and some hardly at all. Thomas Aquinas' whole intellectual life was lived amid logical argument, but he well knew this sad truth about his fellow men, a consequence of the exile from Eden. In the introduction to Question 3 he speaks past this habitual or willful blinding of the mind, to every age and especially to our own. We may hear the voice of the twentieth century even more than that of the thirteenth in the objections that set his stage. The answer as God gave it to Moses rings from Sinai to eternity, for in the last analysis there is no other, and it is the heart and soul of the teaching of the Common Doctor—of God in Whom alone existence and essence are one:

> It seems that there is no God. For if, of two mutually exclusive things, one were to exist without limit, the other would cease to exist. But by the word "God" is implied some limitless good. If God then existed, nobody would ever encounter evil. But evil is encountered in the world. God therefore does not exist.
>
> Morever, if a few causes fully account for some effect, one does not seek more. Now it seems that everything we observe in this world can be fully accounted for by other causes, without assuming a God. Thus natural effects are explained by natural causes, and contrived effects by human reasoning and will. There is therefore no need to suppose that a God exists.
>
> On the other hand, Scripture represents God as declaring: *I am who am.*[104]

At the Dominican general chapter meeting in Bologna in June 1267 it was decided once again to assign Thomas Aquinas to the priory at the Papal court, which Clement IV held at Viterbo, which he had made his residence—not far from Rome but far enough to be secure from its endless unrest. Thomas stayed in Viterbo a year and a half, living and working with the great translator of Aristotle, William of Moerbeke. This new impetus to his lifelong study of Aristotle led to his undertaking the twelve extraordinary commentaries on Aristotle's major books which he wrote *simultaneously* with the *Summa theologiae* during the next six years.[105]

A new outbreak of the anti-mendicant controversy at the University of Paris may have been an important cause of the sudden decision of the Dominican minister general, John of Vercelli, to send Thomas Aquinas back to Paris in November 1268. Travelling through Lombardy, Thomas delivered Sunday Advent sermons at Bologna and Milan, crossed an Alpine pass at

---

[104]Thomas Aquinas, *Summa Theologiae*, ed. Thomas Gilby (Garden City NY, 1969), I, 67 (Question 3).
[105]Weisheipl, *Thomas D'Aquino*, pp. 230-232, 280-285.

Christmastide, and arrived in Paris in mid-winter, to occupy once again one of the two Dominican chairs at the premier center of learning in Christendom.[106]

Thomas Aquinas' biographer gives us an unforgettable picture of the saint and genius at the peak of his career:

> When Thomas and his companions entered the Porte Saint-Jacques in the winter of 1268-69, the 44-year-old Thomas was, no doubt, cold and tired, but he was at the height of his physical stamina and intellectual vigor. He could not have imagined how productive the next four years would be or the price he would have to pay for his incredible output between 1269 and 1273. He was tall, well-built, somewhat large, and at that time beginning to grow bald, which was noticeable enough to be mentioned, despite his monastic tonsure. He had a large head and always held himself erect, "as men of upright character do." His complexion was healthy, like "ripe wheat." His body had a delicate balance and texture "that goes with a fine intelligence"; yet virile also, "robust and prompt to serve the will."[107]

All eyes were on him as he took his place in Paris once again, and he fulfilled all and more than anyone could have expected of him. During the next four years he completed the writing of most of the *Summa theologiae* as he had planned it, the commentaries on Aristotle, a magnificent series of lectures on the Gospel of John, detailed refutations of the critics of the mendicant orders, and a memorable attack on the young master Siger of Brabant, an admirer of the Muslim philosopher and Aristotelian commentator Averroes whose doctrine in effect denied the individuality and therefore the immortality of the soul.[108] The complexity of philosophical argument enabled Siger and his fellow "Latin Averroists" to wend their way into heresy almost without knowing it, leading their students over the precipice by an abstract, posturing intellectuality that became divorced from reality—the ancient trap of sophistry. The greatest mind in Christendom knew very well how this worked; and this man who was a teacher above all was shocked to his soul at seeing young minds perverted. If anyone wished to challenge his answer to Siger, the "Dumb Ox" bellowed, "let him not speak in corners, nor in the presence of boys who do not know how to judge about such difficult matters, but let him write against this treatise, if he has sufficient courage."[109]

On December 10, 1270 Archbishop Stephen Tempier of Paris condemned 13 propositions of Latin Averroism as heretical. Six years later Siger was called before the French Inquisition. He appealed to the Pope, and was killed in

---

[106]*Ibid.*, pp. 238-239.
[107]*Ibid.*, p. 241; quotations given by Weisheipl are from Gui's biography of St. Thomas Aquinas.
[108]*Ibid.*, pp. 242-243, 246-247, 266-268, 272-276.
[109]*Ibid.*, p. 279.

Viterbo, "stabbed by his almost demented assistant."[110]

It seemed Thomas Aquinas' mighty mind never rested. A famous story tells of the royal banquet held by St. Louis IX in Paris in 1269, at which the king insisted on seating Thomas beside him. (Perhaps he remembered how he had once sent his royal archers to protect Thomas and his students on their way to class.) Thomas was then writing a refutation of Manichaeanism, and his mind was on it to the exclusion of the king, to whom he did not address a word. Suddenly he struck the long wooden table with a massive fist and a roar of *"That* settles the Manichees!" He called for his secretary, who had not been invited to the royal gathering; St. Louis, never one to stand on offended dignity, hastened to summon his own secretary to take down Thomas' insight.[111]

By that year of 1269 Pope Clement IV was dead,[112] the conclave to elect his successor was again deadlocked between Guelf supporters and Ghibelline opponents of Charles of Anjou (now properly called Charles I of Sicily)[113]—a deadlock which was to last more than two years—and King St. Louis IX of France had decided to undertake a crusade which he fervently hoped would restore the tarnished crusading ideal and bring victory to a united Christendom at this historic moment of its climax. Pope Clement IV had given St. Louis' crusade his unqualified blessing before he died.[114]

There was certainly need for it. In March 1268 Sultan Baybars of Egypt had taken Jaffa in Palestine, killing most of the people of the city and destroying its castle. Marching north, a week after Easter he took the Templar castle at Beaufort near Sidon, enslaving all the men he captured. Then he laid siege to Antioch, defended by Constable Simon Mansel in the absence of Bohemond VI, who was at Tripoli. Mansel led a rash sortie and was captured, and on May 18 Baybars took, looted, and destroyed Antioch, seizing vast treasures and killing or enslaving all Christians he found there. This was the end of the 1500-year-old history of Antioch; the ancient city never recovered. The next year Baybars broke a truce with Hugh III, King of Cyprus and Jerusalem, and appeared before Acre with a substantial force. Though he was not then able to take Acre, Baybars' relentless hostility to the Christian presence in the Holy Land had been made very clear. He had the means and the resolution to bring an end to the crusader states if aid from Western Christendom did not prevent

---

[110]*Ibid.,* pp. 273-274, 276.

[111]*Ibid.,* p. 236.

[112]He died November 29, 1268 (Mann, *Popes in the Middle Ages*, XVI, 294).

[113]*Ibid.,* XVI, 334-337; Runciman, *Sicilian Vespers*, p. 136.

[114]Louis had taken the Cross March 25, 1267 (Labarge, *St. Louis*, pp. 228-229) and Pope Clement IV had sent many letters in support of his undertaking during 1268, the last year of his pontificate (Mann, *Popes in the Middle Ages*, XVI, 201). In December 1268 St. Louis concluded an agreement with Genoa to provide ships for the passage overseas of a crusading army he would command, and had appointed Florent of Varennes his admiral (Labarge, *op. cit.,* p. 233).

it.[115]

King James I the Conqueror of Aragon, now sixty years old but still very much the knight-errant, had also taken the Cross, with equal enthusiasm if not quite with the unyielding resolution of St. Louis IX. At Christmas 1268 he met with his son-in-law Alfonso X the Wise of Castile at the ancient Castilian capital of Toledo. Alfonso urged James not to trust in the help of the ferocious though still non-Muslim Mongols in the Middle East (as James was inclined to do), but offered him men and money for his crusade.[116]

Alfonso felt close to James at this time and grateful to him, because James had done much to save him from the consequences of a Moorish rising in the reconquered parts of Andalusia in 1264, carefully and secretly planned by Muhammad al-Ahmar "the Red" of Granada, the greatest Moorish lord remaining in the region, and aided by the Muslim Marinids of Morocco. The rebels had seized the important towns of Jérez de la Frontera, Arcos de la Frontera, and Medina Sidonia, but had failed to take the larger cities of Sevilla, Córdoba, and Jáen. While in the past Spanish kings had too often taken advantage of Moorish defeats of one of their rivals to advance their own parochial interests, James had committed himself at once to the full support of Alfonso in regaining the lost cities and territories, exerting himself at considerable political cost to obtain funds for this purpose from the *corts* of Catalonia, though the *cortes* of Aragon turned him down. Pope Clement IV had called for a crusade in Spain against the resurgent Moors. By August 1265 Alfonso had regained everything that he had lost in Andalusia, but Red Muhammad in Granada continued to prove himself untrustworthy and treacherous, and the rebels held out in the province of Murcia adjoining Granada, which had been tributary to Castile. James had brought his army into action in November, and by January 1266 conquered Murcia. With an unselfishness extraordinary in this or any age, James had unhesitatingly turned the whole province back to Alfonso. Pope Clement IV warmly thanked James in June 1266 for all that he had done.[117]

In May 1269 King St. Louis announced that his crusade would depart one year hence from Aigues-Mortes, then the sole Mediterranean port included in his kingdom. Prince Edward of England was eager to join him, and St. Louis advancd him 770,000 marks to enable him to bring an English army to the crusade by August 1270. In the same month James of Aragon made his final

---

[115]Setton, *Crusades*, II, 508, 577-578; Runciman, *Crusades*, III, 324-326, 331.

[116]F. Darwin Swift, *The Life and Times of James the Conqueror* (Oxford, 1894), pp. 116-117; Joseph F. O'Callaghan, *A History of Medieval Spain* (Ithaca NY, 1975), p. 370.

[117]O'Callaghan, *Medieval Spain*, pp. 365-367; Swift, *James the Conqueror*, pp. 107-115; Derek W. Lomax, *The Reconquest of Spain* (London, 1978), pp. 161-162; Ballesteros y Beretta, *Alfonso X*, pp. 366-376, 384-403; Mann, *Popes in the Middle Ages*, XVI, 300.

commitment, designating his son Pedro as regent for his realm in his absence. Louis' barons had objected strenuously to his departure, and James' daughter Violante, the wife of Alfonso X, begged and pleaded tearfully that her father give up the project. Crusading was no longer popular. This expedition of Saint Louis would be the last of the crusades in the heroic model of "God wills it!" of 1095.[118]

James' commitment soon showed itself as more bravado than reality. After setting out with much fanfare from Barcelona in September 1269 with more than thirty ships, two of his illegitimate sons, the Bishops of Barcelona and Huesca, and the Masters of the crusading Orders of the Temple and of the Hospital, virtually the entire flotilla turned back at the first bad weather and put in at Aigues-Mortes, where the Bishop of Maguelonne condemned James for not pressing on, and the citizens of Montpellier refused to aid him unless he would pledge to put to sea again for the Holy Land. Later, part of the fleet commanded by his illegitimate son Fernán Sanchez did reach the coast of Palestine, but James of Aragon never did.[119]

King St. Louis IX of France likewise designated regents to rule his kingdom in his absence, and made his will. His health was not good, and he moved slowly; but in March 1270 he took the storied oriflamme from its precious receptacle in the Church of St. Denis in Paris and received the insignia of pilgrimage from its Abbot Matthew. By Easter he was at Mâcon, moving south. He celebrated Pentecost at Saint Gilles, home of the relentless leader of the First Crusade, the man who bore the primary responsibility for its extraordinary success, Raymond of Toulouse. A few days later St. Louis reached Aigues-Mortes, where he waited nearly a month for the fleet he had engaged from Genoa. On June 25 he wrote a last letter to his regents, summarizing the Christian principles by which they should govern while he was gone. On July 1 he sailed from Aigues-Mortes, accompanied by two of his three surviving sons and some great French noblemen; but he had only 327 knights and about 10,000 men altogether. On July 11 he arrived at Cagliari in Sardinia, where his third son, along with Theobald of Navarre, John of Brittany, and the Count of Flanders and their contingents joined him. Many others had found excuses not to come. His brother Charles, now king of Sicily, was scheduled to arrive soon with large additional forces.[120]

On July 12, 1270—the very next day after his arrival in Cagliari—St. Louis IX announced that this crusade, like the Fifth Crusade and his own previous

---

[118]Labarge, *St. Louis*, pp. 228-230, 234; Swift, *James the Conqueror*, p. 188. See Volume II, Chapter 20 of this history for the First Crusade preached in 1095.

[119]O'Callaghan, *Medieval Spain*, pp. 370-371; Swift, *James the Conqueror*, p. 119; Setton, *Crusades*, II, 580; Runciman, *Crusades*, III, 330-331.

[120]Labarge, *St. Louis*, pp. 235-238; Setton, *Crusades*, II, 514-515; Runciman, *Sicilian Vespers*, pp. 159-160.

mighty crusading effort, would not go directly to the Holy Land, where the Christians still controlled most of the coast, and march on Montjoie and Jerusalem. The Fifth Crusade and St. Louis' earlier crusade had attacked Egypt, strongest of the Muslim powers in the Middle East, which claimed Jerusalem and most of the time since the Battle of the Horns of Hattin in 1187 had occupied it. But this crusade abandoned Jerusalem without even targeting Egypt. Louis declared its goal to be Tunisia, on the north coast of Africa opposite Sicily![121]

Historians have speculated ever since on the causes and background of the holy king's astonishing decision. Though contemporary sources imply that it was made at a council of war on the day following St. Louis' arrival at Cagliari, there is strong circumstantial evidence that it must have been made many months earlier, since Louis had laid in no supplies for his army at Cyprus or anywhere east of Sicily, as he had been careful to do on his first crusade.[122] If so, on that day when he took the oriflamme from St. Denis St. Louis would have known he was not going to carry it to Jerusalem—or at least, not for a long time, not until a much later phase in the campaign.

Why did he go to Tunis?

No one knows—neither historians today nor, by all indications, anyone then, other than Louis himself.

The decision was obviously very much to the advantage of King Charles of Sicily, for whom Tunisia was a potential enemy on his flank, particularly if he attacked the Byzantine empire upon which he clearly had designs—as had rulers of Sicily during much of the past two hundred years, going back to the Norman Robert Guiscard before the First Crusade.[123] But this does not explain, or at best only partly explains why St. Louis made this decision. His whole reign had demonstrated that he was not controlled by family interests and loyalties, though he respected his relatives and tried to help them where he justly and reasonably could. He clearly needed Charles' soldiers and ships to augment his relatively meager force, but it is hard to imagine even Charles telling St. Louis that he would supply them only if Louis would use them against Tunis. No one put that kind of pressure on a man whose probity, justice, and independence of judgment were universally recognized in every corner of Christendom. His moral ascendancy protected him from it.

Charles probably did advise his brother very strongly to attack Tunis first. It may be true, as has been argued, that Louis' understanding of Mediterranean geography was so limited that he thought Tunis nearer to Egypt than it is. But he must have known that a considerable distance intervened between the two; after all, he had personally journeyed to Egypt and to Palestine earlier and

---

[121]Labarge, *St. Louis*, p. 238.
[122]Setton, *Crusades*, II, 511-513.
[123]*Ibid.*, II, 513-514.

knew that it was necessary to sail much longer to reach them than to reach Tunis.

Individual human decisions can change history. There are almost always some reasons for those decisions that historians do not know and will never know. Sometimes there are no reasons for a great decision that historians know, however many speculations abound. This is one of them.

Whatever the actual reasons for this decision in the mind of St. Louis IX, surely they had some connection with, or were to some extent a reflection of his earlier decision to divert his larger and better equipped previous crusade to Egypt rather than leading it to Jerusalem, despite the warning conveyed by the disaster of the Fifth Crusade which had attempted the same strategy. It was an error St. Louis had made before, a diversionary path already trodden. Men like to think they learn from their mistakes. Some do. History—and common experience—tell us that all too often men do not learn from their mistakes, but simply repeat them.

When Richard the Lion-Hearted turned back from Montjoie on the Third Crusade without striking for Jerusalem, it was the beginning of the end for the crusades to the Holy Land. When St. Louis IX forsook the city where Christ died for Tunis, it *was* the end for the Holy Land crusades. There is no more tragic moment in the history of Christendom than this failure of vision, of hope, and of commitment by the Heaven-destined king of "the eldest daughter of the Church"—and it came at the historic moment of Christendom's climax. Even in his brightest hours fallen man is never far from disaster.

The consequences came only too swiftly. St. Louis and his men landed on the blistering sands of Tunisia near the ancient site of Carthage, whose people had thrown their children into the fiery belly of the demon Moloch in the days of ancient Rome. A torrid sun blazed from a metallic sky. St. Louis gave strict orders to his men to remain inactive in camp until his brother Charles should arrive with his reinforcements. Dysentery and typhoid fever ran through the camp. John Tristan, Louis' second son who had been born in Egypt at the crisis of his father's earlier crusade, sickened and died. The Papal legate sickened and died. In Acre in Palestine, Assassins hired by Sultan Baybars of Egypt killed Philip de Montfort, the most renowned knight in what remained of the crusader kingdom, and the crusaders were not there to take his place. A Byzantine embassy reached Louis in camp on August 24 and found him sick unto death, though lucid and able to express his hope for peace between them and the Latins.[124] The next day he received viaticum, offered a prayer ("Gracious good God, have mercy on this people who stay here and lead them [back] to their country, that they do not fall into the hands of their enemies and

---

[124]Labarge, *St. Louis*, pp. 241-242; Setton, *Crusades*, III, 516; Runciman, *Crusades*, III, 292, 333; Runciman, *Sicilian Vespers*, p. 160; Gill, *Byzantium and the Papacy*, p. 123.

are not constrained to deny Thy holy name"), and died as his lips, with terminal sadness, shaped the words "Jerusalem! Jerusalem!"[125]

Charles arrived to find his brother's body still warm. He promptly took charge, negotiating a peace with the Emir of Tunis which gave him a doubled tribute plus an indemnity from the Emir, provided for the release of all Christian captives in Tunisia, and included a promise that henceforth Christians might live, do business, and practice their faith in that country. Charles now clearly intended to lead at least the greater part of the crusading host against Constantinople; but Prince Edward of England, just arrived, would have none of it. Like the father of his late great enemy Simon de Montfort, Prince Edward sailed alone with his men to Palestine, where two years later he barely escaped death after being stabbed by an Assassin with a poisoned dagger. Charles' fleet was struck off the coast of Sicily by a mighty storm November 23 and almost completely destroyed. Thousands of crusaders were drowned, almost all the money of the expedition was lost, and the survivors could only go home. King Theobald II of Navarre, son-in-law of Louis IX, died December 5. As the survivors of the French crusading army marched north through Calabria their young Queen Isabel of Aragon, wife of Louis IX's heir Philip III, fell from her horse and died from her injuries after giving birth to a dead child.[126] In the words of Joseph Strayer:

> It was not an army but a great funeral procession which returned to France. The young king carried with him the remains of his father, his wife, his stillborn son, his brother, and his brother-in-law. It is not surprising that the next appeal for an overseas expedition drew little response from the French.[127]

In this overwhelming disaster the Crusades, as a war of united Christendom against Islam to regain the Holy Land and the Holy Places, came to an end. But the heroic memory remained, to inspire embattled Christians down through the years to the great age of apostasy in the twentieth century.

Meanwhile the conclave to elect a new Pope was dragging on endlessly, one of the longest in the entire history of the Church. No one could justify it; everyone condemned it. In June 1270, after it had already lasted a year and a half, the people of Viterbo where the cardinals were fruitlessly meeting tore the roof off the building they were using, hoping that exposure to the elements would hasten their decision. That August Archbishop Vincent of Tours came to address and reprove them, telling them bluntly that their immensely prolonged

---

[125]Labarge, *St. Louis*, pp. 242-243; Runciman, *Crusades*, III, 292.
[126]Labarge, *St. Louis*, pp. 243-244; Setton, *Crusades*, II, 516-518; Runciman, *Crusades*, III, 338; Runciman, *Sicilian Vespers*, pp. 161-162; *Cambridge Medieval History*, VI, 191.
[127]Setton, *Crusades*, II, 517.

delay and inability to agree was giving great and destructive scandal to the whole Church. The next March the new King Philip III of France and his uncle Charles of Anjou, King of Sicily, came to speak to the conclave with a similar message. None of it helped; still they could not agree.[128]

Finally, in September 1271 they had recourse to a six-man committee, consisting of three cardinals from each of the two opposed factions, which (some said at the suggestion of St. Bonaventure, the head of the Franciscan order) chose Theobald Visconti of Piacenza, Archdeacon of Liège, one of the fathers of the Council of Lyons, who after the Council had spent twenty years in study at the University of Paris and therefore undoubtedly knew Thomas Aquinas well. From Paris he had been sent to England to help make peace after the defeat and terrible death of Simon de Montfort. When King St. Louis IX took the Cross, so did Theobald Visconti. Immediately after the king's death Visconti went to Acre, where he committed himself heart and soul to the crusading cause despite the fact that it seemed to be lost. Its revival was the constant theme of his pontificate, but disillusionment with crusading after the Tunisian debacle was too general for even his best efforts to this end to be successful.[129]

He took one of the most splendid and honored Papal names, Gregory—he was the tenth to use it—and was at least as great a Pope as the last of that name, who had made made the apocalyptic challenge to the agnostic Emperor Frederick II. Consecrated March 27, 1272, Pope Gregory X decided just four days later to summon another council to meet May 1, 1274 to bring help to the Christians in the Holy Land and to achieve reunion with the separated Greek Church. A year later he designated Lyons as once again the city where the ecumenical council should meet.[130] Taking note also of the recent rise of anti-semitism among Christians, notably during the recent civil war in England, he issued "an encyclical to all Christians forbidding them to baptize Jews by force or to injure their persons, or to take away their money, or to disturb them during the celebration of their religious festivals."[131]

In October 1272 Pope Gregory X wrote Byzantine Emperor Michael VIII

---

[128]Mann, *Popes in the Middle Ages*, XVI, 337-339, 341; Runciman, *Sicilian Vespers*, p. 162. The visit of the two kings to Viterbo in March 1271 was the occasion of one of the most atrocious and infamous crimes of the Middle Ages, when Guy de Montfort, the profoundly embittered son of the slain and dismembered Simon de Montfort of England, murdered Henry, son of Richard of Cornwall, before the altar of St. Sylvester's Church in Viterbo while Mass was being said (Mann, *op cit.*, XVI, 342-343; Denholm-Young, *Richard of Cornwall*, pp. 150-151; Roche, *King of Almayne*, pp. 212-213; Labarge, *Simon de Montfort*, pp. 268-269).

[129]Mann, *Popes in the Middle Ages*, XVI, 349-354.

[130]*Ibid.*, XVI, 358, 361-362; Runciman, *Sicilian Vespers*, pp. 167-168; Gill, *Byzantium and the Papacy*, p. 123.

[131]Mann, *Popes in the Middle Ages*, XVI, 496.

Palaeologus urging him to send plenipotentiary negotiators for religious reunion to the forthcoming council, prepared to acknowledge Papal primacy in the Church and the profession of faith sent him five years before by Pope Clement IV, including an explicit assertion of the procession of the Holy Spirit from the Son as well as from the Father—the one major doctrinal difference between the two churches.   The Pope's letter was carried east by John Parastron, a Franciscan born in Constantinople who during the preceding summer had brought a letter from Michael to the new Pope assuring him of the Byzantine Emperor's continued interest in Church reunion.   An important Byzantine envoy, John Veccos, Chartophylax of the Church of the Holy Wisdom (Hagia Sophia) in Constantinople—the largest and most splendid church in Christendom—had already been sent to France in June 1270 during the Papal vacancy, just a month before Louis' departure on crusade.[132]

This vigorous and decisive Pope also took firm action in 1273 to bring an end to the long interregnum between Holy Roman Emperors.   Of the two imperial claimants, England's Richard of Cornwall had died in April 1272 (his brother Henry III died that November, with his able son Edward I succeeding him on the English throne),[133] while Alfonso X of Spain had never garnered significant support in Germany and had only a limited following in Italy.   Philip III of France urged his own candidacy,[134] but there had not been a French Holy Roman Emperor for nearly four hundred years, and Pope Gregory X was not prepared to give that much more power and authority to the strongest monarch in Christendom even though Philip III, like his father, was generally very supportive of the Papacy.   Furthermore, with Philip's uncle Charles ruling Sicily and southern Italy, making Philip Emperor would once again bring all of Italy as well as Germany under the rule of the same family, which Papal policy had long—and rightly—opposed.[135]

---

[132]*Ibid.*, XVI, 400-402, 405-406; Geanokoplos, *Michael Palaeologus*, pp. 201-203, 239-241; Gill, *Byzantium and the Papacy*, pp. 124-126, 226.

[133]Denholm-Young, *Richard of Cornwall*, pp. 152-153; Powicke, *Thirteenth Century*, p. 225.

[134]Runciman, *Sicilian Vespers*, pp. 172-173; Langlois, *Philip III*, pp. 65-66.

[135]Historians deliberately or temperamentally hypercritical of the Papacy constantly harp on this Papal policy, presenting it as petty, selfish, and unjust to imperial claimants. It is very hard to see any rational foundations for such criticism.   The Popes were temporal sovereigns of the Papal state.   If the Pope were not a temporal sovereign, he would have to be subject to another state or lord, a situation which the Catholic Church has always regarded as intolerable (our ingenious modern way of avoiding it has been the creation of the sovereign state of Vatican City).   A single power or family controlling all of Italy but the Papal state would inevitably be a grave danger to its existence and to the personal independence of the Pope.   Therefore it was very much in the best interests of Christendom—which required an independent Pope—as well as of the Pope himself and the Papal states to do everything possible to prevent this from happening.

By September 1273 Pope Gregory X had found a solution. With no noble family dominant in Germany following the long-drawn-out but complete fall of the Hohenstaufens, it was possible to appoint as Emperor one of the principal nobles who would be religiously and politically reliable without being so powerful as to threaten the rest of the German aristocracy or the Italian city-states. Six of the seven imperial electors (all but King Ottokar of Bohemia) were now prepared to support Rudolf of Habsburg, lord of parts of Switzerland and the Austrian Tirol, whose father had died on crusade in the Holy Land.[136] Rudolf was 55, "a man of known experience and known piety, with a tall, rather austere presence and a quiet, courteous manner."[137]

In October 1275 Rudolf pledged "not to interfere with the rights of the Roman Church, and to restore whatever had been taken from it by his predecessors."[138] Pope Gregory X, well satisfied with Rudolf's prudence and loyalty, repeatedly promised to crown him in Rome, though he died before it could be done.[139] As he fell into his last illness in December 1275, Pope Gregory X wrote Rudolf: "Whether we live or die, we may glory in your deeds in the presence of Him Whom we must serve in this world."[140]

Just so did almost all the Habsburgs serve the Church and the Catholic cause, from this time forward for more than six hundred years, during most of which they reigned as Holy Roman Emperors, the temporal leaders of Christendom.

By March 1272 Thomas Aquinas had completed the second part of the *Summa theologiae* (much longer than the first part), and began on the third, concerning the Incarnation, and then the Sacraments. His last disputation at the University of Paris was on the Incarnation. In the summer of 1272 he was recalled to the Roman province, where he was asked to establish a new study center (*studium generale*) at any location in the province he chose. He selected his home territory of Naples. Charles of Anjou, King of Sicily and Naples, pledged an ounce of gold to the Dominican priory in Naples for each month that Thomas Aquinas taught there.[141] When in Lent 1273 he delivered a series of 59 sermons on charity, the Commandments, the Apostles Creed, the Our

---

[136]Mann, *Popes in the Middle Ages*, XVI, 455-461; Runciman, *Sicilian Vespers*, pp. 173-174; Langlois, *Philip III*, p. 70.

[137]Runciman, *Sicilian Vespers*, p. 173. He had marched with Conradin as far as Verona, so was acceptable to the Ghibellines; but by conviction he was Guelf, declaring himself ready to disown even his own son should he defy the Pope's authority as head of the Church. Rudolf was elected Emperor October 1, crowned in Charlemagne's city of Aachen October 28, and confirmed as Emperor by the Council of Lyons in June 1274.

[138]Mann, *Popes in the Middle Ages*, XVI, 470.

[139]*Ibid.*, XVI, 466-470; Runciman, *Sicilian Vespers*, p. 174.

[140]Mann, *Popes in the Middle Ages*, XVI, 472.

[141]Weisheipl, *Thomas D'Aquino*, pp. 294-297, 299, 307, 313.

Father, and the Hail Mary, "almost the whole population of Naples went to hear his sermons every day."[142] Once again the Common Doctor was proving that his doctrine was not only for learned theologians.

At Passion Sunday that Lent he went into ecstasy while saying Mass and remained rapt for many minutes until aroused by one of his brethren.[143] During the spring and summer he was writing superbly on the Eucharist for the *Summa theologiae*. It is at this point in his life that his biographer William of Tocco records the testimony of Friar Dominic of Caserta, the sacristan at San Domenico priory in Naples where Thomas Aquinas was then living, of how he concealed himself to watch the saint at prayer and saw him lifted into the air, and Christ speaking to him from the crucifix on the wall of the chapel:

"Thomas, you have written well about me. What reward will you have?"

"Lord, nothing but yourself."[144]

On December 6, 1273, Thomas Aquinas was saying Mass for the feast of St. Nicholas in the chapel in Naples dedicated to him. Some profound experience—spiritual, mental, and physical—suddenly overwhelmed him. He did not collapse or show external signs of change; but he declared to his long-time secretary, Reginald of Piperno, that he could write no more. "All that I have written," he said, "seems like straw to me." In the ensuing days and weeks he repeated this many times. Nor could he teach; in fact, he spoke but little.[145]

When Pope Gregory X, apparently not knowing or understanding what had happened to Thomas, asked him to attend the ecumenical Council of Lyons convening May 7, 1274, bringing his *Contra errores Graecorum* for consultation during the impending reunion of the Byzantine Greek Church with the Catholic Church, Thomas obediently set out. On the way he struck his head heavily on a low-hanging branch across the road. He stopped at the castle of Maenza where his niece Francesca lived, becoming increasingly ill. As he felt death approaching, he asked to be taken to the Cistercian abbey of Fossanova six miles away. There he made a general confession, received viaticum, and spoke often of his firm belief in the Real Presence of Christ in the Eucharist.[146] To those assembled about his bed he said:

I have taught and written much on this most holy Body and the other sacraments, according to my faith in Christ and in the holy Roman Church, to whose judgment I submit all my teaching.[147]

On March 7, 1274 he died. He was only forty-nine years old, but his work

---

[142]*Ibid.*, p. 319.
[143]*Ibid.*, pp. 300-301.
[144]*Ibid.*, 315-316.
[145]*Ibid.*, pp. 320-322.
[146]*Ibid.*, pp. 323-326.
[147]*Ibid.*, p. 326.

was done.[148] Christendom had its champion upon the loftiest peaks of intellect. No greater mind has been seen among the children of men than the mind of Thomas Aquinas, and he laid all his genius at the Feet of Christ.

The Council of Lyons, which Thomas Aquinas was journeying to attend when he died, convened for its first session May 7, 1274 with about 500 bishops in attendance from all over Christendom, including a canon of Trondheim, Norway representing the bishop of Skalholt in Iceland. All the kings of Christendom had been invited, and most sent representatives; but only James the Conqueror of Aragon came in person, being received with the greatest honor and seated at the Pope's right hand. A Byzantine delegation had set out in March carrying a letter of acceptance of Papal primacy and affirmation of the faith of the Church of Rome by Emperor Michael Palaeologus, and others from Greek bishops, and also letters of submission to the Pope from the Serbs and Bulgarians. Patriarch Joseph of Constantinople had refused to sign such a letter, but he had agreed, if the union was consummated, either to accept it or to resign his office. At the opening session of the Council Pope Gregory X announced its three principal purposes to be help for the shrinking crusader dominions in the Holy Land, reunion with the Greek church, and the reformation of morals.[149]

There can be no doubt that Pope Gregory X was profoundly, personally committed to reunion with the Byzantine church. Many leading Franciscans shared his commitment—when St. Bonaventure had to step down as minister general of the Franciscans due to poor health on the eve of the Council, his place was taken by Jerome of Ascoli, then actually in Constantinople carrying on the Catholic negotiations for reunion with the Byzantine churchmen.[150] John Veccos of the great Hagia Sophia Church in Constantinople, sent earlier as a Byzantine envoy to St. Louis IX, had become sincerely convinced that the difference between the Latin and Greek churches in the verbal formulation of the doctrine of the procession of the Holy Spirit did not reflect any major theological divergence.[151] But unfortunately Michael Palaeologus' support for the reunion seems to have been no more than a maneuver to relieve military and political pressure from King Charles of Sicily, whose army and navy were then pressing him hard in Albania and Epirus and threatening all of Greece. Michael admitted this publicly at a synod in Constantinople in April, a month

---

[148]*Ibid.*, p. 327.

[149]Mann, *Popes in the Middle Ages*, XVI, 382-384, 412-413; Gill, *Byzantium and the Papacy*, pp. 130-133; Nicol, *Last Centuries of Byzantium*, p. 60; Geanakoplos, *Michael Palaeologus*, pp. 258-259; Swift, *James the Conqueror*, p. 127.

[150]Moorman, *Franciscan Order*, pp. 147, 151, 178.

[151]Gill, *Byzantium and the Papacy*, pp. 129, 152-160. The name of this important churchman is variously spelled Beccus, Beccos, Veccus, and Veccos, since "b" and "v" had become indistinguishable in Greek, as they are in Greek (and in Spanish) today. Since modern Greek usage usually prefers the "v" and the "os," this form is used here.

before the Council of Lyons convened, "reassuring" his bishops that he did not really mean to do what he appeared to be doing, that he did not expect any actual change in the Greek church to result from the prospective reunion. While it is theoretically possible that Emperor Michael was misleading the Greek bishops and did favor a genuine reunion, there is no solid evidence to show it, and much to indicate the contrary.[152]

But Pope Gregory X—like a good priest hearing a confession—took the Greek Emperor's solemn avowals of submission at face value when they were delivered by his personal representative, the Grand Logothete George Akropolites, who fortunately survived an Easter storm off the southern capes of Greece that sank several ships of the flotilla bearing the Greek delegation to Lyons. At a solemn Mass attended by these Byzantine representatives June 29, St. Bonaventure—who died just fifteen days later—preached, and the creed (including the disputed *filioque* clause affirming the procession of the Holy Spirit from the Father and the Son) was sung in both Latin and Greek, though it was noted that the Bishop of Nicaea refused to sing the *filioque*. Michael Palaeologus' letters were read at the fourth session of the Council July 6; Pope Gregory X welcomed them and said a *Te Deum*. He wrote a letter full of the warmest gratitude to Michael Palaeologus and ordered Charles of Sicily to stop his war against the Byzantine Empire, now officially Catholic.[153]

There was much discussion at the Council about how best to support the remaining crusader principalities in Palestine, and an embassy from the Mongols now ruling Iran came seeking alliance with the Christians against Sultan Baybars, but nothing concrete resulted from this; the memory of the disaster in Tunisia was too fresh.[154] At the closing session of the Council in August Pope Gregory X expressed himself as satisfied with new crusading plans and with the Greek reunion, though he said not enough had been done for reform; he urged bishops to give the needed example by reforming their own lives, and to insist on pastors residing in their parishes.[155]

Two other important actions regarding the Papacy were taken at this time. The Pope presented and the Council approved strict new regulations on conclaves in light of the prolonged deadlock of the last one: the cardinals were to meet within ten days of the Pope's death, no matter how many were still absent at that time. They were to be confined to the Papal palace during the conclave, with no access from the outside, no messages in or out, and food

---

[152]*Ibid.*, p. 128; Geanokoplos, *Michael Palaeologus*, pp. 264-266, 279.

[153]Mann, *Popes in the Middle Ages*, XVI, 412-419, 452-453; Gill, *Byzantium and the Papacy*, pp. 134-139, 141; Nicol, *Last Centuries of Byzantium*, pp. 60-61; Geanokoplos, *Michael Palaeologus*, pp. 258-263; Runciman, *Sicilian Vespers*, pp. 183-185.

[154]Mann, *Popes in the Middle Ages*, XVI, 384-386; Runciman, *Crusades*, III, 338-342; Gill, *Byzantium and the Papacy*, p. 135.

[155]Mann, *Popes in the Middle Ages*, XVI, 453-454.

passed in through a revolving drum, and to be reduced to bread, wine and water after eleven days had passed without an election. The cardinals were not to receive any revenue so long as the Holy See was vacant, nor do any other Church business. A number of these regulations have remained in effect ever since, but in earlier times they were often difficult to impossible to enforce, and conclave deadlocks still occurred. The other action was the formal cession by Philip III of France to the Pope of the territory around the city of Avignon, known as the Comtat Venaissin. Avignon was to become the seat of the Papacy when the French gained control of it thirty years later.[156]

At the beginning of 1275 reunion with the Catholic Church was officially proclaimed in Constantinople, with Archbishop Nicholas of Chalcedon saying Mass in Latin as well as in Greek and proclaiming Gregory X "supreme pontiff of the Apostolic Church and ecumenical Pope." But most of the clergy and people refused to acknowledge Papal supremacy, as did Patriarch Joseph of Constantinople, who was consequently removed from office. He was replaced in June by John Veccos, who had come to believe strongly in the reunion and worked hard for it despite the vehement opposition. Michael Palaeologus continued to have his political reasons for favoring the reunion, especially after suffering a defeat in Thessaly in the spring of 1275 by a prince of Epirus allied with Charles of Sicily. But his own sister bitterly fought the reunion; the Latin sack of Constantinople in 1204 was still within living memory and the Latin occupation of the ancient Byzantine capital very much so, since it had not ended until 1261. We cannot know whether it would have made a difference if Michael had been sincere in supporting the reunion, but it is doubtful; he was not a very popular ruler, and men remembered that he had blinded the legitimate heir to the imperial purple. The outcome of the struggle remained uncertain when Gregory X's pontificate ended, but its prospects in the Byzantine empire were never good.[157]

Indeed, the schism remains unhealed today after nearly a thousand years, and the Greeks were to resist it as fiercely in the last years of their empire when a Latin alliance was absolutely essential to their survival, as they did in the 1270's when their condition, though perilous, was not so critical.

The last year of Gregory X's nobly intentioned pontificate was darkened by news of yet another invasion of Spain by the Moors. Alfonso X of Castile had refused to give up his shaky claim to be Holy Roman Emperor despite the unequivocal endorsement of Rudolf by the Pope and the Council of Lyons, and was still supported in Genoa and some of the cities of Lombardy. In December 1274 he had left Spain to pursue his imperial dream; in May 1275 a Muslim army from Morocco landed at Tarifa near Gibraltar. Alfonso's eldest son and

---

[156]*Ibid.*, XVI, 386-387, 449-452.

[157]*Ibid.*, XVI, 422-423; Gill, *Byzantium and the Papacy*, pp. 163-164; Geanokoplos, *Michael Palaeologus*, pp. 273-274, 282-284; Setton, *Crusades*, II, 257.

heir, Fernando de la Cerda, died marching south to meet the invaders. Moroccan Sultan Abu Yusuf arrived at Tarifa in person in August, confirming his alliance with Muhammad II of Granada. The Castilian army, led by the nobleman Nuño González de Lara, was badly beaten at Écija September 7. Lara was slain on the field; the Moors occupied Algeciras and Gibraltar as well as Tarifa, and sent a substantial raiding force to the walls of Sevilla.[158]

Alfonso X had had ample notice by this time to return to Spain, but had not yet done so. Immediate responsibility for recovery from the disaster therefore devolved upon his second son Sancho, only seventeen years old, later to be known as "the Fierce." Sancho and his companions had not forgotten the ancient resilience of the Spanish warriors in the War of the Reconquest, the longest in history, nor the help that the old crusader, James of Aragon, had given Castile in the past. They appealed to him, and not in vain, though he had just had to face a rebellion of his own nobles. In November James sent a thousand cavalry and five thousand infantry to aid Prince Sancho, who at the same time brought up a fleet from Sevilla to cut Abu Yusuf's communications with Morocco, so that when Alfonso X finally returned in December after a most reprehensible absence of a full year, the Sultan was ready enough to sign a truce and return to Morocco.[159]

In the Christmas season of 1275 Gregory X fell ill; he died at Arezzo in Italy on January 10, 1276.[160] He was the last of the great and universally respected medieval Popes, a fitting pontiff to conclude the climax of Christendom. He had set lofty goals for himself and for Christendom and won admiration, love and trust for his firmness of purpose and his unblemished integrity. His upright perseverance might have prevailed in the end even over the selfishness of Charles of Sicily and Byzantine Emperor Michael Palaeologus. His selection of Rudolf of Habsburg as the first generally recognized Holy Roman Emperor after the downfall of the Hohenstaufens was to benefit Christendom, through his descendants, for more than seven hundred years. The Church Gregory X headed has since beatified him. His strength and goodness were to be sorely missed in the troubled years that followed.

---

[158]O'Callaghan, *Medieval Spain*, pp. 374-376; Lomax, *Reconquest of Spain*, p. 164; Ballesteros y Beretta, *Alfonso X*, pp. 745-755, 760-761; *Cambridge Medieval History*, VI, 193; Mann, *Popes in the Middle Ages*, pp. 461-462, 464-466.

[159]O'Callaghan, *Medieval Spain*, p. 376; Lomax, *Reconquest of Spain*, p. 164; Ballesteros y Beretta, *Alfonso X*, pp. 765-777; Swift, *James the Conqueror*, pp. 134-135, 138-139.

[160]Mann, *Popes in the Middle Ages*, XVI, 498.

8
The Nemesis of Power
(1276-1314)

(Popes Bd. Innocent V 1276; Adrian IV 1276; John XXI 1276-77; Nicholas III 1277-80; Martin IV 1281-85; Honorius IV 1285-87; Nicholas IV 1288-92; St. Peter Celestine V 1294; Boniface VIII 1294-1303; Bd. Benedict XI 1303-04; Clement V 1305-14)

> "Enter Alagna, lo the fleur-de-lis
> And in his vicar, Christ a captive led!
> I see him mocked a second time—again,
> The vinegar and gall produced I see;
> And Christ Himself 'twixt living robbers slain."
> —Dante, *Purgatorio*, canto XX, 1, 86-90

When Christ said to Peter in the Garden of Gethsemane, "all who take the sword shall perish by the sword,"[1] this is often interpreted as a pacifist declaration. But in fact Christ was not a pacifist, for nowhere did He ever condemn war as such, explicitly or implicitly; nor (when speaking to Roman centurions, for example) did He ever indicate that He regarded soldiering as an evil occupation. His words to Peter may more reasonably be seen as a warning against too much reliance on temporal power, which ultimately rests on force, on the sword. Christ accepted that power, when He spoke of rendering unto Caesar's what was his, and told Pilate that his authority to judge Him came ultimately from God. But it was a necessary evil, open to abuse, dangerous to the soul. He who relied on it primarily or entirely would die by it.

More than any other factor and cause, it was failure to heed these words of Christ to Peter in Gethsemane that brought Christendom down from the glorious height it had attained in the years of St. Thomas Aquinas and the completion of Chartres cathedral, to a cockpit of bitter struggle from which it emerged so weakened, in every Christian country but Spain, that its unity in the West was eventually destroyed. Not only did temporal power become an end in itself for the burgeoning nationalisms of Europe; even the Vicars of Christ became increasingly preoccupied with the exercise of temporal power in

---

[1]Matthew 26:52.

Christendom, until at last—and inevitably, given their policy—it was turned on them.

Two hundred years earlier the great Hildebrand, Pope St. Gregory VII, had firmly established the principle that the Pope had the right and duty to act as moral judge of kings and emperors. An act of the temporal sovereign which was clearly immoral, or clearly directed against the liberty of the Church, should be condemned by the Pope; a long record of such acts, of defiance of the Church and the moral law, justified the Pope in proclaiming that the ruler who had created that record no longer deserved the obedience of his Christian people.[2] But since the Pope (except within the Papal states) was not a temporal sovereign, such acts of judgment should be rare, and limited to the most flagrant offenses.

This caution was particularly needed because in this age (and for long afterward) the Pope was frequently drawn into temporal politics in another way, through the necessity of providing dispensations for royal marriages. Most of the royal families of Christendom were related to one another within the very broad range of prohibited degrees for marriage which the Church then enforced. Yet royal marriages were considered an essential component of most important international treaties. The Pope granted such dispensations when he concluded that the common good served by the treaty overrode the desirability of maintaining the normal marriage laws. This thrust him into the midst of almost every major diplomatic negotiation. The most prudent way to deal with this problem was undoubtedly that which the Church herself ultimately chose, in the nineteenth century: to narrow the prohibited degrees of relationship for marriage to very close ties such as uncle and niece, or first cousins. But no one seems to have thought of that in the thirteenth century, or for long afterward.

During the years covered by this chapter, beginning with the pontificate of Martin IV from 1281 to 1285, the Popes involved themselves by a series of increasingly imprudent decisions in major issues of both international relations (war and peace and diplomacy) and internal politics among the nations and smaller states of Christendom, whose spiritual component was at best arguable and at worst virtually nonexistent. They expanded their political intervention far beyond anything done, or probably envisaged by any of their predecessors. They did not hesitate to use the most powerful spiritual weapons at their disposal—excommunication and interdict—to punish disobedience to their political decisions.

Consequently they were accused, then and since, of seeking to exercise direct temporal power over Christendom. It must be emphasized that there is no probative evidence of this. We have no document or first-hand report in which a Pope specifies expanded temporal power (beyond the Papal states of

---

[2]See Volume II, Chapter 19 of this history.

Italy) as his goal. Rather the Popes were drawn into their excessive political and temporal involvement step by step, by arguments derived from particular cases and problems that seemed reasonable to them; and the further they got into the political thicket, the harder it was for them to get out of it. Finally, at least one and probably two Popes in effect perished by the sword, their successor became a virtual captive of the wielder of that sword, and the glory of Christendom went for a time into eclipse.

The great ones of the temporal order fared no better. Popes Boniface VIII and Benedict XI at least died as victims, at peace with God. Holy Roman Emperors Adolf and Albert died literally by the sword, by assassination; Emperor Henry VII, Philip IV of France and Edward I of England died friendless, alone, full of hate and yearning for revenge, estranged from most still living who had loved and served them. The nemesis of power stalked them, and in the end it struck them down.

It was an age when holiness lay hidden, symbolized by Peter Murrone, the hermit of the Abruzzi, who spent more than sixty years in a cave, was called forth from his cave to become Pope Celestine V, resigned in five months, spent the last year of his life in a prison cell about the same size as his cave, and was canonized ten years after his death.[3]

But it was also an age when heroes took arms against tyranny and betrayal and won against all odds, when a poor unknown knight named William Wallace came from nowhere to strike for the liberty of Scotland by destroying Edward I's mighty army at Stirling Bridge; when Robert the Bruce secured Scotland's liberty for three hundred years at the Battle of Bannockburn; when the Flemish burghers at Courtrai overmatched the proud armored horsemen of Philip IV for freedom's sake; when Alfonso Pérez de Guzmán "the Good," who had vowed to hold the vital stronghold of Tarifa against the Moors, hurled his sword over its battlements after his own "Christian" prince swore to kill his son if he did not surrender, held it, and saved it.

This period began with an extraordinary series of Papal fatalities. The conclave which assembled the specified ten days after the death of the great Pope Gregory X chose Peter of Tarentaise, the Cardinal Archbishop of Lyons, as his successor by unanimous vote on the first ballot. Peter was a Dominican, a famous theologian and professorial colleague of St. Thomas Aquinas, one of the leaders of the Council of Lyons. Pope Gregory X had much trusted and admired Peter, who was with him when he died. The new Pope took the name Innocent V.[4] But within five months he was speaking to the cardinals who had elected him, on his own deathbed:

---

[3]Horace K. Mann, *The Lives of the Popes in the Middle Ages*, Volume XVIII (London, 1931), pp. 247-341.
[4]*Ibid.*, XVII, 3-14.

From the example of his own career, [he] showed them the emptiness of
this life, and the need we have of fixing our thoughts on the next. God, he
said, had given him high birth, riches, learning, and exceptional beauty of
person. How little did they avail him now, he asked; and, baring his breast,
he showed his body, all wasted away like that of Lazarus just risen from the
grave.[5]

The next pontificate was even shorter. The new Pope was Ottobuoni
Fieschi, the Papal legate to England who brought peace and a considerable
measure of forgiveness after the bitter civil war between Henry III and Prince
Edward, and Simon de Montfort the younger and his followers. Cardinal
Fieschi was elected after an eight-day conclave during which the cardinals were
tightly confined by order of the French prince Charles, now King of Naples and
Sicily and also Senator of Rome. Fieschi took the name Hadrian V. But he was
in very poor health and died less than forty days after his election, without ever
having been consecrated.[6]

Both these Popes had been cardinals, and neither in their very short
pontificates had appointed any new cardinals, so the size of the College was
reduced to nine when the third conclave in the year 1276 assembled late in
August. Five of the nine were Italians and three were French. The other was
Portuguese: Peter Julian, a physician and the son of a physician, and also a
teacher of logic. Consciousness of nationality was already strong in the College
of Cardinals (it was to get much stronger) and the initial ballots showed Italians
and Frenchmen tending to vote only for persons of their own nationality. Six
votes were required to elect a Pope, and by September 15 all agreed to
compromise on Peter Julian, who took the name John XXI.[7]

Within a week of officially notifying Christendom of his election, Pope

[5]*Ibid.*, XVII, 21-22.
[6]*Ibid.*, XVII, 23-30. For Ottobuoni Fieschi and the struggle between the King and
Crown Prince of England and de Montfort, see Chapter Seven, above.
[7]Mann, *Popes in the Middle Ages*, XVII, 32-41. The numbering of Popes named
John is the result of a double error. In one of the darkest periods in the history of the
Papacy, the late tenth century, even contemporary historians and chroniclers became
confused as new popes appeared and disappeared every few months. Some of them
recorded a Pope John, son of Robert, following antipope Boniface VII in 985, calling
him John XV. But there was no such person; the actual successor of Boniface VII was
John, son of Leo, actually John XV but sometimes called John XVI. To compound the
confusion, the next man named John claiming to be Pope (997-998) was actually an
antipope, but he was included in the numbering of the legitimate Popes named John.
The Pope John who ruled from 1024 to 1032 usually referred to himself, and is usually
referred to as John XIX, but when Peter Julian became Pope, he or his staff apparently
accepted both the mythical John XV and the antipope John as legitimate, and
therefore skipped XX and went to XXI. It is the most confusing situation in the history
of Papal nomenclature. For a good summary of it, see *The Catholic Encyclopedia*
(1910), VIII, 427-430.

John XXI sent John of Vercelli, master of the Dominicans, and Jerome of Ascoli, a leading Franciscan later to become Pope Nicholas IV, on a peacemaking mission to France. In Castile Prince Fernando de la Cerda, the eldest son and heir of King Alfonso X, had suddenly died the year before. Fernando's widow was the sister of King Philip III of France and insisted that her two small sons by Fernando should become the heirs to the throne, but Alfonso's second son Sancho the Fierce was demanding that he should be the heir, and had much support. Philip III was threatening war on behalf of his nephews. Probably because of the persuasion of the two distinguished Papal legates, Philip did not attack Castile at that time.[8]

John XXI also sent an embassy to Constantinople, with instructions to press Byzantine Emperor Michael Palaeologus to complete the Church reunion with hints that otherwise the Pope might withdraw recognition of his imperial title.[9]

But this Pope wished to continue his academic pursuits along with all the activities required by his high position. Finding that the pressure of business and visitors made this very difficult, he added a new chamber to the Papal palace to serve as a secluded study. On May 14, 1277 its roof collapsed while the Pope was in it, and he died six days later from the injuries he had received from the falling timbers.[10] He had been Pope just eight months, and like his two predecessors had made no cardinal appointments.

The smallest conclave in the history of the College of Cardinals followed, with just seven cardinals present: four Italians and three Frenchmen. Five votes were required to elect a Pope. It was a situation made for deadlock, and deadlock followed, for six months. It appears to have been resolved only by the death of one of the French cardinals. This left four Italian and two French cardinals, giving the Italians the necessary two-thirds, and in November an Italian cardinal was elected: Giovanni Gaetano Orsini, a member of one of the leading families of Rome, who took the name Nicholas III and was consecrated and crowned the day after Christmas.[11]

---

[8]Mann, *Popes in the Middle Ages*, XVII, 46-47; Joseph F. O'Callaghan, *A History of Medieval Spain* (Ithaca NY, 1975), pp. 376-377; J. N. Hillgarth, *The Spanish Kingdoms, 1250-1516*, Volume I (Oxford, 1976), p. 310.

[9]Joseph Gill, *Byzantium and the Papacy, 1198-1400* (New Brunswick NJ, 1979), pp. 165-166.

[10]Mann, *Popes in the Middle Ages*, XVII, 54.

[11]*Ibid.*, XVII, 59-61, 70. Mann provides all the data needed for an explanation of what happened at the conclave of 1277, but does not draw full conclusions from it. Available evidence indicates that the four Italian cardinals were present throughout the conclave, along with two French cardinals. The French cardinal Simon de Brion (later Pope Martin IV) seems to have been absent throughout. The other French cardinal, Bernard of St. Martin, is known to have died some time during the year 1277, though the month is not known. If he were present when the conclave assembled (presumably in early June, since Pope John XXI died May 20), so long as he lived he would have

The pontificate of Nicholas III lasted less than three years, which was very unfortunate for the Church, for during that short time he proved himself a remarkably able, prudent, and far-sighted Pope—in striking contrast to most of his successors for the next 125 years. In March 1278 he appointed nine new cardinals, including two Franciscans (one of whom was Jerome of Ascoli, now the head of the order, and the future Pope Nicholas IV) and two Dominicans (one of whom was Robert Kilwardby, the Archbishop of Canterbury). Six of the nine were Italians, one French, one English, and one Portuguese. The appearance of Italian domination of the College was illusory, for the Italians were divided by family and local loyalties and in this enlarged College no longer formed a solid bloc, as the next conclave was to demonstrate.[12]

Holy Roman Emperor Rudolf, true to the oath he had taken to Pope Gregory X,[13] pledged unswerving loyalty to the new Pope and specifically promised to agree to the Pope's request that he make no war against King Charles of Naples and Sicily and that he relinquish all claim to, and withdraw all imperial garrisons from the Romagna, the region north of the Apennines and south of the Po which the Pope claimed as part of the Papal state, and also from Tuscany.[14] Nicholas III then firmly requested Charles of Naples to yield his offices of sole Senator of Rome and vicar of Tuscany, and proclaimed a new constitution for Rome, restoring all governmental offices in the city to Roman citizens and providing that the office of Senator should not in the future be held by any Emperor, king, or powerful noble, or relative of such, and not for more than one year without the special permission of the Pope.[15]

Having thus effectively dealt with the problem of maintaining good relations with both the Holy Roman Emperor and the kingdom of Naples and Sicily, which had brought so much grief to his predecessors, Pope Nicholas III turned to the more intractable situation in the East, where there was strong continuing opposition among the Greek clergy to the great church reunion wrought by Pope Gregory X and the Council of Lyons.[16] A realistic man, as befitted one who had risen to the cardinalate through the labyrinth of Italian ecclesial intrigue and city politics, Nicholas III was well aware that the primary reason Byzantine Emperor Michael Palaeologus had accepted the Church

---

denied the Italians a two-thirds majority, but by November when Orsini was elected, he would almost certainly have died, leaving the Italians with four of six votes.

[12]*Ibid.*, XVII, 78-79.

[13]See Chapter Seven, above.

[14]Mann, *Popes in the Middle Ages*, XVII, 105-106, 108-109; Steven Runciman, *The Sicilian Vespers* (Cambridge, England, 1958), pp. 203, 206; Daniel Waley, *The Papal State in the Thirteenth Century* (London, 1961), p. 195.

[15]Mann, *Popes in the Middle Ages*, XVII, 100-101, 203-204; Waley, *Papal State in the Thirteenth Century*, pp. 190-195; George Holmes, *Florence, Rome and the Origins of the Renaissance* (Oxford, 1986), p. 26.

[16]See Chapter Seven, above.

reunion was to avoid an invasion by Charles of Naples. He was also aware, however, that the new Patriarch of Constantinople, John Veccos, was genuinely convinced that the Catholic position on the much-disputed *filioque* clause in the creed was correct.[17] Therefore, in preparing letters and instructions for the special embassy to Constantinople headed by Bishop Bartholomew of Grosseto, selected in October 1278, Pope Nicholas III praised Emperor Michael and his son for supporting the reunion, urged the Greek bishops to sing the creed with the *filioque* at every Sunday Mass and to sign a confession of faith including it, but told the ambassadors not to insist on that point if they judged opposition too great. Open opponents of the Church reunion were to be excommunicated, but the Greek liturgy was to be allowed to remain in use, though the ambassadors were given authority to take out any part of it which they judged not in accord with the true faith. At the same time the Pope called for a negotiated peace between Emperor Michael and King Charles, which Michael greatly desired.[18]

Before the Papal embassy arrived in June 1279, Emperor Michael had removed John Veccos as Patriarch on a charge that he had been too favorable toward opponents of the Church reunion. That seems so improbable that Joseph Gill's theory that Michael removed him as a sop to those opponents would appear more tenable. Whatever Michael's reason, he quickly restored Veccos when the ambassadors came. However, he also held a secret meeting with his bishops in which he promised them he would not insist on any additions to the creed, but urged them not to make a direct challenge to the Pope. The bishops promptly responded with a lengthy disquisition on the Procession of the Holy Spirit full of subtle Greek theological terms almost untranslatable into Latin. The Papal ambassadors had to be content with verbal assurances that the bishops upheld the reunion. Pope Nicholas III accepted these assurances for the time being and continued to forbid Charles to attack the Byzantine empire.[19]

Nicholas III maintained his strong interest in the Franciscans and Dominicans. In January 1279 he appointed the Franciscan John Peckham as Archbishop of Canterbury to replace Cardinal Kilwardby. Peckham and his successor, Robert of Winchelsea, were the most outstanding Archbishops of Canterbury since Stephen Langton, remarkable for charity, energy, humility, fairness, and courage—the last being a virtue indispensable for anyone who had to deal closely and frequently with Edward I of England.[20] In August 1279

---

[17]Gill, *Byzantium and the Papacy*, pp. 152-160.

[18]*Ibid.*, pp. 172-175; Runciman, *Sicilian Vespers*, pp. 207-208; Deno J. Geanakoplos, *Emperor Michael Palaeologus and the West* (Cambridge MA, 1959), pp. 311-317; Mann, *Popes in the Middle Ages*, XVI, 430-433.

[19]Geanokoplos, *Michael Palaeologus*, pp. 317-320; Gill, *Byzantium and the Papacy*, pp. 175-176; Runciman, *Sicilian Vespers*, pp. 209-210; Mann, *Popes in the Middle Ages*, XVI, 436-437.

[20]For Peckham, see Maurice Powicke, *The Thirteenth Century*, 1216-1307 (Oxford

Nicholas III approved a revised Franciscan constitution establishing a stricter rule of poverty, closer to that of St. Francis, which the "spiritual Franciscans"—some of whom had now gone into outright rebellion against the Church—had been demanding. But it still allowed the Franciscan order to hold and use some property so long as the Pope, and not the order, was the legal owner of that property. Again Nicholas III had demonstrated his prudence and wisdom.[21]

The year 1280 was generally peaceful, except for the continuing tension between France and Castile over the issue of the right of the little de la Cerda princes to inherit the Castilian throne. The *cortes* of Castile had supported the strong-willed Prince Sancho the Fierce in his demand to be designated heir. The resulting internal divisions had forced Alfonso X of Castile to break off his siege of the port city of Algeciras near the Rock of Gibraltar, which was still in the hands of the Moors. Sancho scornfully rejected Alfonso's proposal to establish a small tributary kingdom in northern Andalusia for the de la Cerda princes. Despite a two-year truce between Castile and France, the Pope could see no way to plan for a new crusade until this quarrel was settled.[22] With this one significant exception, the condition of Christendom was very good when in Italy's killer month of August—the month of steamy, enervating heat—Pope Nicholas III, an apparently vigorous and healthy 64, collapsed and died of a stroke at Viterbo.[23]

Nicholas III was the leading member of the powerful Orsini family, and during his pontificate resentment against the Orsini in Rome and in the kingdom of Naples had grown virulent. As soon as the news of his death came to Rome there was a general uprising, led by the rival Annibaldi family, with widespread popular support and very likely encouraged by Charles of Naples, who had not been pleased with the Pope who forced him out of the office of Senator of Rome and would not let him launch his long-planned war against the enfeebled Byzantine empire. When the conclave of 13 cardinals assembled at Viterbo early in September, the Orsini and anti-Orsini factions were each strong enough to block the other.[24] The deadlock continued through January. At the end of that month King Charles moved a substantial contingent of his

History of England), 2nd ed. (Oxford, 1962), pp. 470-472. His name is alternatively spelled Pecham, but seems to have been pronounced "Peckham."

[21]*The Cambridge Medieval History*, ed. J. R. Tanner, C. W. Previté-Orton, and Z. N. Brooke, Volume VI: "Victory of the Papacy" (Cambridge, 1929), pp. 146-152. The bull is *Exiit qui seminat*.

[22]O'Callaghan, *Medieval Spain*, pp. 377, 379; Derek W. Lomax, *The Reconquest of Spain* (London, 1978), p. 164; Antonio Ballesteros y Beretta, *Alfonso X el Sabio* (Barcelona, 1984), pp. 895-903; Mann, *Popes in the Middle Ages*, XVII, 69; Powicke, *Thirteenth Century*, p. 243.

[23]Mann, *Popes in the Middle Ages*, XVII, 163.

[24]*Ibid.*, XVII, 171-173.

troops into Viterbo.[25] With this armed support behind them, on Candlemas day, February 2, 1281, with the ringing of all the bells in Viterbo as a signal, local militia led by Viscount Rainer Gatti and the new Podestà[26] Ricciardello stormed the Bishop's palace where the conclave was taking place. They seized two of the Orsini cardinals and imprisoned them, and held one—Matteo Rosso Orsini, leader of the Orsini group in the conclave—until a new Pope was elected. Since the Orsini had only five votes in the conclave, the removal of Matteo Rosso permitted the opponents of the Orsini to secure a two-thirds vote of eight to four. The anti-Orsini faction promptly elected the French Cardinal Simon de Brion, the only cardinal who had never come to the previous conclave, a good friend of Charles of Naples and an uncritical admirer of everything French. The new Pope took the name of Martin IV.[27]

Though the Orsini accepted his election with little recorded protest, it is worth remembering that it was legally invalid because under duress, as any election must be which is won by imprisoning one of the electors. A Pope illegally elected under duress may nevertheless become a valid Pope if his tenure of office is unchallenged.[28] By that standard, and that only, was Martin IV a valid Pope. He was exemplary in his personal life, but no Vicar of Christ in the whole history of the papacy has displayed poorer judgment or more flagrant nationalistic bias. The pontificate of Martin IV was a disaster for almost every issue and every potentate it touched, and set the Church on the course which led to the tragedy at Anagni and the removal of the Popes from the Eternal City which had been the last home of St. Peter, for three-quarters of a century.

The new Pope lost no time in abandoning Emperor Michael Palaeologus and Patriarch of Constantinople John Veccos. On July 3, 1281, just over four months into his pontificate, a treaty was signed by King Charles of Naples and Sicily; his son-in-law Philip of Courtenay, titular Latin Emperor of Constantinople (who had never set foot in the city); and the Republic of Venice, at the residence of Pope Martin IV in Orvieto, presumably in his presence and by all indications with his full approval. It provided for the reconquest of Constantinople from the Greeks. Venice was to be restored to

---

[25]Runciman, *Sicilian Vespers*, p. 211.

[26]A city office unique to Italy of the High Middle Ages and the Renaissance, which combined some of the functions of a mayor and of a chief of police, whose holder was hired from another city so that he would not be tied in with local families and factions, though he sometimes was nevertheless.

[27]Mann, *Popes in the Middle Ages*, XVII, 174-177. Part II of Volume XVII in Mann's great history of the medieval Popes, covering the pontificates of Martin IV and Honorius IV, was the only part Mann did not live to finish. It was completed by Johannes Hollnsteiner in Vienna in 1931.

[28]See the case of Pope Vigilius, discussed at length in Volume II, Chapter 6 of this history, and other cases in the tenth and early eleventh centuries, discussed in Volume II, *passim*.

all the rights and privileges it had held under the Latin Emperors of Constantinople. Charles would provide 8,000 cavalry, Venice forty galleys. The expedition would sail within two years.[29] The treaty included a declaration of the religious purpose of the expedition:

> ... the exaltation of the Orthodox [Catholic] faith and the reintegration of the Apostolic power, which through the loss of the Empire of Romania [Byzantine Empire] (removed from obedience by the now ancient schism), has experienced severe maiming in the mystic body of church unity ... [and also] for the recovery of the Empire of Romania, which is held by Palaeologus.[30]

In other words, Byzantine Emperor Michael Palaeologus was no longer to be regarded as a Catholic. Pope Martin IV made this explicit by excommunicating him in October, calling him a "supporter of the ancient Greek schismatics" and scornfully dismissing him as a man "called Emperor of the Greeks." The Pope laid an interdict on his realm and ordered him to hand it over to the Pope by the following May or be formally deposed and outlawed.[31]

We have seen how much evidence indicates that Emperor Michael's Catholic conversion was insincere; but he had powerful political reasons for maintaining it, and after all he had said and done would lose the trust of all if he abandoned it. We have also seen that all available evidence shows Patriarch Veccos' Catholic conversion to have been entirely genuine. The Patriarch was very learned and very persuasive; in time his arguments and his persistence would have had substantial influence, and very possibly would have prevailed. But Martin IV never seems to have considered any alternative but total condemnation of the Uniates as pretenders, and full authorization for the long-planned expedition of Charles of Naples and Sicily to conquer Constantinople. Charles, it will be remembered, was French, the brother of St. Louis IX.

From this total rejection and unmerited condemnation of men who (whatever their motives) had risked their fortunes and their lives for the Catholic Faith and the Church of Rome, flowed all the ensuing evils of Martin IV's pontificate, and many of the still worse disasters that came after it. No Pope has made a greater mistake. Of course it involved only political judgment and personal assessment of individuals, not doctrine on faith or morals.

Michael Palaeologus, Emperor of Constantinople, was not easily swept into the dustbin of history. He had, after all, restored an empire which had been wholly lost, something that almost never happens. He was a man of consummate ability and iron determination, who had maintained that feeble

---

[29]Geanakoplos, *Michael Palaeologus*, pp. 337-339; Runciman, *Sicilian Vespers*, pp. 214-215.
[30]Geanakoplos, *Michael Palaeologus*, p. 341.
[31]*Ibid.*, p. 342; Runciman, *Sicilian Vespers*, p. 215.

and resuscitated state against all odds for twenty years. Perhaps mercifully, we are spared an account of what he said and did when his personal ambassador to Rome, Bishop Theophanes of Nicaea, who with his colleague had been captured by Charles on his way to see the Pope, returned by sea from Italy to give him the news.[32] He did not even then denounce the Church reunion; as Martin IV should have foreseen, he was not in a position to do so. He seemed isolated and friendless. But it is a rare political leader who can be totally isolated, if he remembers the Arab proverb "the enemy of my enemy is my friend."

There is reason to believe, though the wording of the relevant documents is mostly vague and evasive and there is no clear proof, that Emperor Michael had for several years been in touch with King Peter III of Aragon,[33] the able son and successor of King James I the Conqueror who died in 1276 after one of the longest and most successful reigns in European history. Peter's wife Constance was the daughter of Manfred of Hohenstaufen, whom Charles had slain and replaced as king of Naples and Sicily. The Catalans who formed the greater part of the population of Peter III's kingdom were a seagoing people fully capable of challenging Charles' navy in its own element. Whatever contacts and promises may have been made before Pope Martin IV's excommunication of Emperor Michael, there is no doubt about what Michael did immediately after his excommunication. He sent a famous Genoese sailor named Benedetto Zaccaria to Peter III with a large sum of money.[34] In January 1282 Peter wrote to the Italian city of Pisa, requesting its aid against Charles and explaining what he and Michael planned to do:

> You know, of course, that the wicked and impious Charles intends shortly to attack the Emperor of Constantinople, united to me by a bond of recent friendship. I have decided in my heart of hearts to oppose the presumptuous daring of this king with firm disposition and with all my power. For I intend... to enter the Kingdom of Sicily and there to establish myself... with a large force of my men. And thus, while that king will believe fictitiously that he has conquered the Greeks, the Sicilians will find themselves irrevocably subject to my rule.[35]

In mid-March 1282 Charles' fleet assembled in the harbor of Messina in Sicily to make the initial landing of his troops in Greece and begin the great expedition to reconquer Constantinople. Easter fell that year on March 29.

---

[32]Geanakoplos, *Michael Palaeologus*, pp. 343-344.

[33]There is a difficulty with the name of this monarch. He wrote it in the Catalan form, Pere; Spanish historians write it as Pedro, a form he never used. In view of the complete unfamiliarity of almost all English readers with Catalan, it seems best to use the English "Peter" for him.

[34]Runciman, *Sicilian Vespers*, pp. 221-232.

[35]Geanakoplos, *Michael Palaeologus*, p. 348.

The next day, Easter Monday, thousands of Sicilians gathered on a green in front of the Church of the Holy Spirit just outside their capital of Palermo for a traditional Easter Monday festival. Some of Charles' French troops were there as well, behaving in their usual arrogant fashion, occasionally searching some of the Sicilians present and insulting their women. One of them was a sergeant named Drouet. He seized an attractive Sicilian woman and dragged her away from her husband and her friends. Her husband whipped out a dagger and plunged it into Drouet's heart. As though it were a signal, most of the Sicilians present fell upon the French. Not one of them survived.[36]

A dubious later tradition says that the vesper bells of the churches in Palermo began to ring at this moment, and to the sound of their tolling men rushed into the center of the city crying "death to the French!" This tradition gave the deceptively peaceful name of "Sicilian Vespers" to this bloody uprising. Be that as it may, the bells were no signal for the rising: Drouet's lust and the vengeful young husband's dagger were. A frightful massacre followed. No Frenchman or woman found in Palermo was spared. About two thousand were slain.[37]

This revolt was not unprovoked; French rule in Sicily had long been very oppressive.[38] But the stark savagery of the massacre sent a shudder of horror through Europe, and the Pope, personally a gentle man, was appalled. He demanded Sicily's unconditional surrender to the raging Charles, on pain of excommunication for every Sicilian refusing full submission, and at the same time he renewed his excommunication of Michael Palaeologus, whose involvement in the uprising he strongly suspected.[39]

In fact, the manner in which the rising occurred virtually rules out foreign instigation. There is no evidence that either Peter III of Aragon or Emperor Michael expected it then. Peter was preparing a naval expedition to the coast of Muslim North Africa at the time, which he undertook in early June.[40] But there is reason to believe that he intended to come to Sicily from Africa later in the year, and that the "Vespers" merely anticipated plans he had already set in motion.[41] Evidently he had his agents already in place, for in less than a month a Sicilian ambassador had set off westward to offer Peter the rule of their island, while another had set off eastward to make contact with Emperor Michael.[42]

After an initial repulse, Charles secured a fiercely contested beachhead

[36]Runciman, *Sicilian Vespers*, pp. 234-237.
[37]*Ibid.*, pp. 237-238.
[38]*Ibid.*, pp. 232-233.
[39]*Ibid.*, p. 243; Mann, *Popes in the Middle Ages*, XVII, 244-245.
[40]Runciman, *Sicilian Vespers*, p. 244; O'Callaghan, *Medieval Spain*, p. 386.
[41]Runciman, *Sicilian Vespers*, p. 234.
[42]*Ibid.*, pp. 241-242; Mann, *Popes in the Middle Ages*, XVII, 240.

on Sicily July 25 and laid siege to Messina, only to be hurled back in five successive major assaults on the city. On August 30 Peter III of Aragon arrived with his fleet and army, and was crowned King of Sicily in Palermo September 4. Charles was not strong enough to face the combined Aragonese and Sicilian forces and had to withdraw from the island at the end of September. Peter's Catalan navy proceeded to gain command of the sea by inflicting two stinging defeats on Charles' warships, enabling the Aragonese to land on the narrowest part of the Calabrian peninsula and cut off Charles' army south of them. Though Charles' son broke through with 600 knights to rescue him, there was no question that the haughty king of Naples had suffered a devastating defeat, and that his long-planned invasion of the Byzantine empire would have to be postponed indefinitely. Emperor Michael Palaeologus and the oppressed Sicilians had won.[43]

Michael Palaeologus barely outlived his victory, dying on December 11, excommunicated by the Catholic Church and excoriated by his own Greek church, which went so far as to refuse burial of his body in consecrated ground. But some kindly priest who put a soul's salvation above politics gave him viaticum, and he died at peace with Christ.[44] Joseph Gill believes that by the end, despite everything, he may truly have come to share in the fullness of the Catholic Faith.[45] He had saved his country, and the city of Constantine; mostly because of him, they remained free for 170 more years. And he had brought his relentless enemy Charles of Naples down to ruin, along with the Pope who had so unwisely taken his part. Michael Palaeologus was the last great history-maker of the ancient imperial capital on the Golden Horn.

That ensuing disaster in Sicily still need not have been. Charles, maintaining his rule of Naples where he was relatively popular, could have made his peace with Sicily, as even the execrated King John of England had eventually accepted *de facto* the loss of Normandy. Once it was clear that the change wrought by the Sicilian Vespers was probably permanent, Pope Martin IV, even more than Charles, should have accepted it. The Sicilians deeply desired and repeatedly requested peace with the Pope. They were even willing

---

[43]Runciman, *Sicilian Vespers*, pp. 245-255.

[44]Gill, *Byzantium and the Papacy*, p. 180; Donald M. Nicol, *The Last Centuries of Byzantium, 1261-1453* (New York, 1972), pp. 99-101.

[45]Gill, *Byzantium and the Papacy*, pp. 180-181. The Church reunion collapsed immediately upon Michael's death. His son and heir Andronicus rejected it. The relatively few Greek clergy who had supported it were degraded and punished. Patriarch John Veccos was dismissed, sent to a monastery, forced to renounce his priesthood, and ordered to say no prayers for Michael's soul. (One hopes, and strongly suspects, that he disobeyed this sacrilegious order in the isolation of his monk's cell.) Eventually he was put on trial for heresy, but defended himself so brilliantly that the full massed advocacy of the established Orthodox church could not overcome him. (Gill, *op. cit.*, pp. 182-184; Mann, *Popes in the Middle Ages*, XVII, 306-308) It is surprising that no one has promoted the cause of John Veccos for canonization.

to have him rule them, or give their island to another lord—so long as it was not Charles of Naples, or any of his line. But that condition the Pope unwaveringly refused to consider. He continued to demand their unconditional submission to their oppressor still seeking vengeance upon them.[46]

On November 18, 1282 Martin IV excommunicated Peter III of Aragon for accepting the crown of Sicily, blaming him for the March 30 revolt and massacre. At the same time he granted full crusading indulgences to all who died in battle against Peter to regain Sicily for Charles. On January 13, 1283 he went so far as to formally proclaim the war to regain Sicily from Peter of Aragon for Charles a crusade, and to authorize taking money from the proceeds of the unprecedented crusade tax levied by the Council of Lyons to help pay for it.[47]

In designating the war against Sicily a crusade, Pope Martin IV doomed all that remained of genuine crusading enthusiasm in Europe. The crusades had originally been regarded strictly and solely as a mobilization of Christendom against the infidel Muslim foe who held the Holy Places. After Jerusalem was lost, the concept of crusading was extended to apply to wars against heretics (the Albigensians), schismatics (the Byzantine Greeks), pagans (the Baltic peoples attacked by the Teutonic Knights), and an Emperor (Frederick II) and his family widely believed, with some reason, to be secret heretics or pagans. These extensions, often of dubious justification, weakened but did not totally discredit the crusading ideal. But not even Pope Martin IV could seriously contend—nor did he try to contend—that the Sicilians were heretics, schismatics, or pagans secret or open. It was obvious to all that they were practicing Catholics, however many sins they might have committed and however defiant toward the Pope they had been. They might deserve to have war waged against them; there could be no excuse for calling such a war a crusade. Everyone knew it. It is hard to imagine how Pope Martin IV could even have justified it to himself.

All the fulminations from Rome and Naples had not the slightest effect on the situation in Sicily, but Martin IV refused to be drawn off his fatal course. In March 1283 he declared Peter III deprived of his crown and proclaimed a crusade against him in Aragon. He ordered Edward I of England to break off his daughter's engagement to Aragon's Crown Prince Alfonso. He laid Aragon under an interdict. In August 1283 he offered the whole of Aragon to Charles of Valois, second son of Philip III of France, who promised to swear fealty to the Pope for it each year. In September he called upon the French clergy to grant tithes for three years for the campaign against Aragon. In January 1284 he ordered the Archbishop of Genoa to read in his cathedral an account of the

---

[46]Mann, *Popes in the Middle Ages*, XVII, 232-236.
[47]*Ibid.*, XVII, 249-250, 254, 334; Runciman, *Sicilian Vespers*, p. 265; Geanakoplos, *Michael Palaeologus*, pp. 347-348.

Pope's proceedings against Peter III of Aragon and to remind the Genoese, Peter's allies, that they must have no dealings with him on pain of excommunciation.[48]

But at that same moment, Rome rose against the Pope. Followers of the Orsini and opponents of Martin IV and Charles of Naples stormed the Capitol, slaughtered the French garrison, and ended Charles' power in the city. Martin IV had to withdraw his appointment of Charles as Senator of Rome for life.[49]

Toward Sicily and Aragon, nevertheless, he remained unbending. The Sicilians had found an admiral named Roger of Lauria, the greatest sea warrior of the Middle Ages, who was actually blockading Naples in the spring of 1284. On June 5 Roger destroyed Charles' navy in the Bay of Naples, capturing his eldest son, namesake and heir who was delivered to Peter in Aragon, and forcing Charles to withdraw from Calabria.[50] On January 7, 1285 Charles died, leaving his son Charles II a king in chains. The French were now almost ready for a full-scale invasion of Aragon, and in February Pope Martin IV was hectoring James, then independent king of the island of Majorca, to join them.[51]

On March 28, 1285, three days after Easter, Pope Martin IV died of a sudden fever.[52] He had re-created the Eastern schism; destroyed the crusading ideal; riven the body of Christendom by incessantly demanding war to the finish against two large Christian countries, Sicily and Aragon—wars that could not be won, whose prosecution was to hang like a millstone round the necks of the Popes for the next quarter-century; and made himself little more than an instrument of French foreign policy. In just four years in office Martin IV had done as much harm to Christendom as any Pope in two millennia.

During Pope Martin's pontificate a harrowing drama had been played out in Castile. Its King Alfonso X was pulled backward and forward by the struggle for his inheritance between his second son Sancho and his grandsons by his deceased eldest son Fernando de la Cerda. A furious quarrel between Alfonso and Sancho in September 1281 was followed by Sancho's open rebellion against his father. An extra-legal assembly convened at Valladolid in April 1282. Alfonso's wife Violante took her son Sancho's side against her husband, along with her two other sons. Good bishops protested in vain. The assembly was pressured and threatened. It voted to depose Alfonso X, an action it had neither power nor right to take. But Sancho was a proven battle captain and he

---

[48]Mann, *Popes in the Middle Ages*, XVII, 254-259, 262, 299; Runciman, *Sicilian Vespers*, pp. 265-266; O'Callaghan, *Medieval Spain*, p. 388; Powicke, *Thirteenth Century*, p. 257.

[49]Mann, *Popes in the Middle Ages*, XVII, 209-210.

[50]Runciman, *Sicilian Vespers*, pp. 270-271, 273-274; O'Callaghan, *Medieval Spain*, p. 390.

[51]Runciman, *Sicilian Vespers*, pp. 278-280; Mann, *Popes in the Middle Ages*, XVII, 264-265, 302; Hillgarth, *Spanish Kingdoms*, I, 256.

[52]Mann, *Popes in the Middle Ages*, XVII, 354.

had assiduously cultivated outside support before rebelling. Peter III of Aragon and King Dinis of Portugal backed him, and so did the military orders.[53]

Alfonso X appealed to the Pope; but the Sicilian Vespers had just happened, and Martin IV had no time for Castile's problems until the following year. In bitterness and desperation St. Fernando's son turned to the ancient enemy, and made alliance with Abu Yusuf of Morocco. When Abu Yusuf arrived in Spain with an army in August to support his new ally, Alfonso X pawned the crown of Castile to him for funds to maintain an army in Andalusia and Murcia in the south, the only regions where he still had support. Sancho's forces repelled him from Córdoba in September, but the next month Spain shuddered at the spectacle of Moors riding with the horsemen of the King of Castile up the old raiding track through the Pass of the Overthrow of the Infidel Dogs to the high plains on which stood the ancient Christian capital of Toledo. In November Alfonso X bitterly cursed his sons as "traitors to God and Us and Spain," and gave his kingdom to the little de la Cerda princes, who had no real prospect of ever gaining control of it, and to the ruling house of France if they should die without issue.[54]

In August of the following year, 1283, Pope Martin finally spoke out to condemn the rebellion of Alfonso X's sons against their father, but few paid attention. In November Alfonso issued his will, a stark and terrible document in which he reiterated his solemn curse upon his sons, disinheriting them forever in favor of the de la Cerda princes and the Kings of France.[55] Twice a traitor, this once great king who has gone down in history with the inappropriate nickname of "the Wise" was prepared to deliver his country either to the infidel or to the French rather than to the rebel sons he had come to hate so much. On April 4 he died, and Sancho became king of Castile. He was blessed with a loving and faithful wife, who as a widow became guardian and protector of Castile, one of the great women in Spanish history: Maria de Molina. But Sancho IV "the Fierce" never escaped the shadow of the betrayal and curse of his father. When he died of tuberculosis in 1295 at the age of only 36, he said it was God's judgment on him for breaking the Fourth Commandment.[56]

Fifteen cardinals met in conclave April 1, 1285, four days after the death

[53]O'Callaghan, *Medieval Spain*, pp. 376-377, 380; Hillgarth, *Spanish Kingdoms*, I, 310; Ballesteros y Beretta, *Alfonso X*, pp. 949, 966-970.
[54]Lomax, *Reconquest of Spain*, p. 164; O'Callaghan, *Medieval Spain*, pp. 380-381; Hillgarth, *Spanish Kingdoms*, I, 310-311; Ballesteros y Beretta, *Alfonso X*, pp. 987-998.
[55]Mann, *Popes in the Middle Ages*, XVII, 299, 301; Ballesteros y Beretta, *Alfonso X*, pp. 1000-1007.
[56]O'Callaghan, *Medieval Spain*, p. 381; Hillgarth, *Spanish Kingdoms*, I, 312-315; Mercedes Gaibrois de Ballesteros, *Historia del reinado de Sancho IV de Castilla*, (Madrid, 1922), II, 371-374. For Maria de Molina see Mercedes Gaibrois de Ballesteros, *Maria de Molina, tres veces reina* (Madrid, 1936, 1967).

of Pope Martin IV. Within twenty-four hours they had unanimously elected a new Pope: Giacomo Savelli, a Roman, 75 years old and severely crippled in both hands and feet, so that he was unable to walk or to raise his hands at Mass without the aid of a "mechanical contrivance." He took the name of Honorius IV.[57] He meant well and tried hard, but he was probably elected primarily because he was not expected to live long, and he did not. The chief event of his two-year pontificate was the long-awaited French invasion of Aragon, which was fiercely resisted. The city of Gerona held out three months; the valiant Peter III of Aragon suffered a mortal wound fighting hand-to-hand in its defense. Within a week of its fall King Philip III, seriously ill, ordered his army home. It met disaster in the Col de Panissars high in the Pyrenees; most of the French knights and foot soldiers were killed or scattered. Philip III came down the fatal rock slopes a dying man. On October 5 he succumbed, and his 17-year-old son Philip IV was king of France.[58]

Philip IV *le bel* (usually translated "the Fair") is, in the memorable phrase of Joseph Strayer, the greatest American authority on his reign, "a hard man to get to know."[59] Historians have argued for centuries over whether he was his own man or little more than a puppet manipulated by powerful and ambitious advisors. One of his enemies once compared him to an owl, "the handsomest of birds ... who can do nothing but stare at men."[60] Strayer is convinced that Philip IV held ultimate authority firmly in his hands, but carefully screened himself by a cold, almost disdainful reserve.[61] Of the few who may have felt that they knew Philip the Fair well, none have left us any close-up personal glimpses of him. His motivations are almost wholly enigmatic. But his actions—and the actions of the ministers whom he not only tolerated but vigorously supported—speak for him. Above all, they suggest that nothing really mattered to Philip IV of France but power. Defenders and critics alike often speak of his piety. He did give the appearance of piety. But few and far between are any known actions of his that reflect its substance.[62]

Following the death of Peter III of Aragon from his mortal wound suffered at the siege of Gerona, his elder son Alfonso III inherited Aragon and

---

[57]Mann, *Popes in the Middle Ages*, XVII, 358-360, 364.
[58]O'Callaghan, *Medieval Spain*, pp. 390-391; Hillgarth, *Spanish Kingdoms*, I, 258-259; Runciman, *Sicilian Vespers*, pp. 282-283, 286.
[59]Joseph R. Strayer, *The Reign of Philip the Fair* (Princeton, 1980), p. 3.
[60]*Ibid.*
[61]*Ibid.*, pp. 24, 32.
[62]Strayer says that what he calls "the religion of monarchy ... made a deeper impression on him [Philip IV] than Christianity," and that he "understood and practiced this religion rather better than he did Christianity." (*Reign of Philip the Fair*, p. 13). This very perceptive judgment is marred only by the phrase "religion of monarchy," which is no religion, just as monarchy *per se*, at least in Christendom, does not mean absolutism or totalitarianism. But to Philip IV, quite evidently, it did.

his younger son James was crowned King of Sicily at Palermo in February 1286. Pope Honorius IV does not seem to have seriously considered breaking with the disastrous Sicilian policy of his predecessor. He promptly excommunicated James, his mother, and the bishops who had participated in the coronation ceremony. Though he approved an armistice between France and Aragon, taking effect in August 1286, he refused to consider any peace settlement including Sicily which would leave it in Aragonese hands, even though this meant that Charles' namesake and heir as ruler of Naples and claimant to Sicily would have to remain in prison in Aragon.[63]

During 1286 Pope Honorius IV gave full recognition to the Carmelite order, founded earlier in the century by monks who had taken up residence on Mount Carmel on the coastal strip of Palestine that still remained in the hands of the descendants of the Crusaders. On Holy Thursday 1287 he died of a stroke. The conclave of 15 cardinals assembling at the Aventine palace in Rome that spring could not agree on a Pope. The deadlock went on into the hot, unhealthy summer, during which no less than six, possibly seven of the cardinals died—the greatest percentage of mortality in the history of any conclave. The survivors understandably fled the city, still without having elected a Pope.[64]

Despite past papal regulations, the conclave did not remain secluded during this very unpleasant summer. It was called on to perform two important duties during July that would normally have been the responsibility of the reigning Pope. The first was to consider a treaty between Alfonso III, the new King of Aragon, and the captive Charles II of Naples (mediated by Edward I of England) providing for Charles' liberation for 50,000 silver marks with his three eldest sons taking his place in prison as hostages, and Charles pledged to work for peace among France, Aragon and Sicily for three years, and if peace was not achieved, either to return to captivity in Aragon or give up Provence to Aragon. The College of Cardinals reluctantly accepted this Treaty of Oléron, but Philip IV of France vetoed it, as usual giving no reasons.[65]

The other public action taken by the College of Cardinals that summer was to greet an exotic visitor, Rabban Sauma, a Christian monk from the western borderlands of China and a friend of Mar Yahbhallaha, the Catholicos (head) of the Persian Church (called Nestorian, though there was only the faintest historical and doctrinal connection between it and that ancient heresy). Sauma had been sent as ambassador to Western Christendom by the Mongol Il-Khan Arghun of Persia. Arriving in Naples in June, he "who had come to

[63]O'Callaghan, *Medieval Spain*, p. 394; Hillgarth, *Spanish Kingdoms*, I, 259; Runciman, *Sicilian Vespers*, p. 287; Mann, *Popes in the Middle Ages*, XVII, 376-377, 417-418.
[64]Mann, *Popes in the Middle Ages*, XVII, 431, 449; XVIII, 5.
[65]Runciman, *Sicilian Vespers*, pp. 288-289; Powicke, *Thirteenth Century*, p. 259.

Europe thinking to find Christendom ready to unite against the Muslims of the East" was surprised to find himself a spectator of a naval battle in its Bay, where Aragon's great admiral Roger of Lauria won another overwhelming victory over the Neapolitan fleet. Coming to Rome, Sauma toured its churches and met with the cardinals, who could offer him little encouragement. In September he went on to France where Philip IV received him with great honor, showed him the exquisite shrine of the Sainte-Chapelle built by his grandfather St. Louis IX, and promised to lead an army to regain Jerusalem. All we know of Philip and his reign indicates that nothing was further from his mind than actually to undertake such a crusade. Sauma went on to England, where Edward I—who had actually been in the Holy Land—impressed him. More honest than Philip, he would make no promises. Sauma returned to Rome in December and told Cardinal John of Tusculum that he gravely doubted the West was serious about sending any more crusades to Palestine.[66] The death-blow Pope Martin IV had dealt to the crusading ideal was becoming evident.

The increasing frequency of long conclaves reflected the extent to which the papacy and the cardinalate were becoming politicized and a target for power-seekers. But even the most selfish cardinals could never entirely forget the loftiness of their function, nor escape the reproaches of conscience for failure to perform it consonant with the dignity of the Vicar of Christ they were electing. After nearly a year of scheming and paralysis, the surviving cardinals in February 1288 finally, suddenly agreed unanimously on their colleague who was quite clearly the most deserving of the office: Jerome of Ascoli, master-general of the Franciscans, with much experience as a legate and good contacts and high respect throughout Christendom. Jerome had been chosen to head the Franciscan order at the Council of Lyons following the death of St. Bonaventure there. He had travelled and negotiated in France and Castile. He possessed the true Franciscan spirit of humility. He was not a good administrator; but he had the breadth of mind and vision and the holiness of spirit to be a great Pope. He might have been, had he lived longer. He chose the name Nicholas IV.[67]

One of Pope Nicholas' very first acts was to receive the somewhat disillusioned Rabban Sauma and give him the papal blessing. Nicholas asked Sauma to say one of the Holy Week Masses in Rome, and gave him communion with his own hand (which certainly indicates that the Pope had no doubt of Sauma's orthodoxy despite his "Nestorian" label). Sauma pledged, for himself and in the name of his religious superior, Catholicos Mar Yahbhallaha, that his

[66]Steven Runciman, *A History of the Crusades*, Volume III (Cambridge, England, 1955), pp. 398-400; Runciman, *Sicilian Vespers*, p. 288; Mann, *Popes in the Middle Ages*, XVIII, 43-45.
[67]Mann, *Popes in the Middle Ages*, XVIII, 6-11.

church and people would conform fully to the faith and the doctrinal teaching of the Pope, once they knew and understood it. Nicholas wrote out a profession of faith for Sauma and the Catholicos, to whom he sent a letter urging him to instruct his people in accordance with it, and a letter to Il-Khan Arghun explaining the doctrine of the Incarnation and the nature of the Church and urging him to accept baptism. In 1290 Mar Yahbhallaha accepted the profession of faith the Pope had sent him two years before.[68]

Meanwhile Nicholas IV had sent another emissary on one of history's most extraordinary missions: the Franciscan John of Monte Corvino, directed to go via Persia to India and then to China to deliver the Pope's message to the Great Khan Kubilai, grandson of Genghis and ruler of almost all the Far East. Departing Italy in July 1289, John set sail from Persia to India in 1292, in a frail craft literally sewn together, just as Marco Polo on the far Asiatic shore was beginning his return from China to Venice. John reached Kubilai's capital of Cambaluc (near Peking) the following year; but Kubilai was already in declining health, and died in February 1294. He never adhered to any of the great religions, but he had shown a sincere interst in Christianity, and might have been converted; if he had been, it would have changed the whole history of the world. As it was, though John of Monte Corvino stayed on in Peking, the West's doorway to the Orient effectively closed with Kubilai's death, and most dismissed Marco Polo as a teller of tall tales when he described the splendid realm of the Great Khan—though, two centuries later, Christopher Columbus listened.[69]

Back in Europe, sadly Pope Nicholas IV still did not feel that he could break with Martin IV's policy on Sicily. On Holy Thursday 1288 he once again condemned James of Aragon for ruling it. However, in October 1288 a new treaty was made between Alfonso III of Aragon and Charles II of Naples very similar to the earlier Treaty of Oléron. This time Philip made no difficulty; he even withdrew his support for the de la Cerda princes in Castile. Philip had many interests and ambitions, but the always difficult and dangerous task of intervening in Spain was low on his list of priorities. In 1290 his accord with Castile was formalized in the Treaty of Bayonne.[70]

In Castile Sancho the Fierce cut down with his own sword his principal rival among the nobles, the Count of Haro, at Haro's hall in Alfaro, and would have likewise killed his own traitorous brother Juan if his wife Maria de Molina

[68]*Ibid.*, XVIII, 46-49; Runciman, *Crusades*, III, 400.

[69]Mann, *Popes in the Middle Ages*, XVIII, 52-53, 91-93; Christopher Dawson, ed., *The Mongol Mission* (New York, 1955), pp. xxxi-xxxiii; Morris Rossabi, *Khubilai Khan; His Life and Times* (Berkeley CA, 1988), pp. 131, 147-152, 227-228.

[70]Mann, *Popes in the Middle Ages*, XVIII, 143-146; Runciman, *Sicilian Vespers*, pp. 289-290; O'Callaghan, *Medieval Spain*, pp. 395-396; Gaibrois de Ballesteros, *Sancho IV*, I, 213-214; II, 45-51.

had not stayed his hand. But Haro had friends in Aragon, so that when Sancho persuaded Philip IV of France to give up his support of the de la Cerda princes, the Aragonese promptly took up their cause, so Sancho gained little. Sancho then allied with Dinis of Portugal, who had put his country on good terms with the Pope again after a long estrangement going back to the reign of his father Afonso III, and with Dinis' aid was able to prevent Aragon from gaining any military advantage in the war with Castile that followed.[71]

Charles II of Naples was released from captivity in Aragon November 3, 1288. Pope Nicholas IV insisted on his formal coronation as King of Sicily in May 1289, thereby forcing the somewhat reluctant, less aggressive son of Charles of Anjou to pursue the foredoomed attempt to reconquer Sicily. In September the Pope issued a bull annulling all treaties involving Aragon, England, and Naples, and absolving Edward I of England (the mediator) and Charles II of Naples from any oaths they had taken in negotiating these treaties. Nevertheless Charles insisted that, as a man of honor, he go to the Pyrenean frontier of Aragon to offer to return himself to custody because he had sworn to obtain peace with Aragon and had not been able to do so. No one appeared to take him into custody; some called these proceedings a sham. But Charles was continuing to seek peace with Aragon, and even the Pope finally agreed to support that quest when he realized that it might be possible to separate Aragon from Sicily. In February 1291 the Treaty of Tarascon was agreed among France, Aragon, Naples, and the Pope, by which France gave up its claim to Aragon, Alfonso III of Aragon withdrew all support from his brother James in Sicily and in turn was recognized as King of Aragon, and the Pope lifted all Church sanctions against Aragon.[72]

It removed half of the scandal of this unnecessary and ruinous conflict, as Aragon was restored to the unity of Christendom. The Franciscan Pope had at last chosen peace, so far as Aragon was concerned. But Sicily remained an apple of discord for many years more, though there was a changing of the guard in June 1291 when Alfonso III of Aragon, only in his late twenties, suddenly died without issue. His brother James left Sicily to become King of Aragon, but his younger brother Frederick now assumed the title of King of Sicily, continuing to defy the power of Naples and the anger of the Popes.[73]

So the false crusade continued against Sicily, though ended against Aragon; and most men no longer wanted to hear about crusades. A continuing stream of ambassadors from Il-Khan Arghun of Persia and one from King

---

[71]Gaibrois de Ballesteros, *Sancho IV*, I, 188-196, 218-219, 230-237; O'Callaghan, *Medieval Spain*, p. 396; Mann, *Popes in the Middle Ages*, XVIII, 226-227.

[72]Mann, *Popes in the Middle Ages*, XVIII, 147-150, 152-154, 156-157, 159-160; Runciman, *Sicilian Vespers*, pp. 290-292; O'Callaghan, *Medieval Spain*, p. 396.

[73]O'Callaghan, *Medieval Spain*, p. 396; Runciman, *Sicilian Vespers*, pp. 292-293; Gaibrois de Ballesteros, *Sancho IV*, II, 125.

Henry II of Cyprus, warning of an impending new offensive from Egypt against the Christians in Palestine, were greeted in Western Europe with honor and respect, but no commitments were made to them. In April 1289 Sultan Kalavun of Egypt took and destroyed Tripoli after the Venetian and Genoese ships fled its harbor, leaving most of the Christian inhabitants behind. In September 1290 Kalavun began his preparations to do the same to the greatest Christian stronghold left in the Levant: Acre. In November he marched. A week later he died, but his son and successor al-Ashraf Khalil had promised his dying father to continue the expedition at all costs, and kept his promise. On April 6, 1291 the Egyptian Arabs laid siege to Acre.[74]

Il-Khan Arghun had died in March; Holy Roman Emperor Rudolf lay dying in Frankfurt; Philip IV of France had no interest whatever in a crusade, and Edward I of England was in the process of attempting to conquer Scotland.[75] Acre had strong walls, but its population was only about 40,000 and this included less than a thousand knights, though there were about 14,000 foot soldiers. On May 4 Henry II of Cyprus arrived to help, but he had only about two thousand men and was unable to command effectively due to severe epilepsy. In any case he came too late. Eleven days later the Muslim host breached the walls; on May 18 they burst through the breach in an early morning fog, and after overcoming heroic resistance in the streets, took the city. The Master of the Templars was mortally wounded; the Master of the Hospital was severely wounded; the Patriarch was drowned after letting too many desperate refugees crowd into his small boat. When the day was done the Templars held one last fortified building at the southwest corner of the city overlooking the sea. Ten days later this building collapsed after Muslim mining in the final assault, killing defenders and attackers alike. The Muslim conquerors destroyed Acre. During the next three months the last remaining coastal fortresses held by Christians fell one by one, ending August 14 with the Templars' Castle Pilgrim, just south of Mount Carmel, on a lofty cliff overlooking the sea on three sides, a position once thought impregnable.[76]

The Crusades were over; the infidel had won. The fall of Acre marked the end of the first great heroic age of Christendom, which had begun with the taking of Jerusalem almost exactly two centuries before.

In August Pope Nicholas IV tried to stimulate one more crusading effort,

---

[74]Kenneth M. Setton, ed., *A History of the Crusades*, Volume II: "The Later Crusades, 1189-1311," ed. Robert L. Wolff and Harry W. Hazard (Philadelphia, 1962), pp. 592-593, 595, 753-754; Runciman, *Crusades*, III, 401-402, 406-408, 410-413; Mann, *Popes in the Middle Ages*, XVIII, 50-52.

[75]Mann, *Popes in the Middle Ages*, XVIII, 60; *The Cambridge Medieval History*, ed. J. R. Tanner, C. W. Previté-Orton, and Z. N. Brooke, Volume VII, "Decline of Empire and Papacy" (Cambridge, 1932), p. 84. For Edward I's struggle with Scotland, see below, this chapter.

[76]Setton, *Crusades*, II, 394-395, 595-598, 754; Runciman, *Crusades*, III, 413-422.

in a series of letters to the kings and princes and bishops of Christendom. He even proposed another general council, like that held by his predecessor Gregory X at Lyons, to inspire and organize the crusade. The response was tepid and spotty. Before Nicholas IV could do more than become aware of the lack of enthusiasm—before he could make another effort to arouse it—he fell ill on Palm Sunday 1292, and died on Good Friday.[77]

The high-minded Franciscan Pope had done his best; his pontificate had not been a success, but he himself had been trusted, because men knew that his Franciscan simplicity and humility were proof against the desire for power. But power had more and more become the primary object of leading members of the College of Cardinals. The Papacy had become a prize of power politics, the more dangerously because, given spiritual prestige by the great Popes from St. Gregory VII[78] to Bd. Gregory X[79] and unwisely broad material application by Martin IV and his successors, its power had become so very great.

On April 14, 1292 a conclave of just twelve cardinals assembled at Rome. Eight votes were required to elect a Pope. Two of Rome's greatest families, bitterly at odds with each other, each had three votes in the conclave: the Orsini, represented by Cardinals Matteo Rosso Orsini and Napoleon Orsini and their close ally Latinus Malabranca, Bishop of Ostia; the Colonna, represented by Cardinals Peter Colonna and James Colonna and their close ally John Boccamazza, Bishop of Tusculum. Two of the cardinals were French—Hugh of Alvernia and John Cholet—and would vote as the autocratic Philip IV directed them. The other four cardinals were Italian and less controlled by factions, but full of ambition for themselves: Gerard the White, Bishop of Sabina; Matthew Acquasparta; Peter Petrogresso; and Benedetto Gaetani, the future Pope Boniface VIII. The required eight votes could only be obtained by enlisting two of the three firm factions and two or three of the four independent votes behind the winner. This proved absolutely impossible.[80]

For three and a half months the fruitless meetings and politicking went on among and around the deadlocked cardinals in Rome, until the fierce heat and deadly fevers of August fell upon the Eternal City, and riots broke out over the senatorial elections. The French Cardinal Cholet died, leaving eleven cardinals but still eight votes required to elect a Pope. All the non-Roman cardinals then left the city until late in September.[81]

By April 1293, a full year after the death of Pope Nicholas IV, the conclave had made no progress whatever. Rome fell into virtual anarchy due to

---

[77]Mann, *Popes in the Middle Ages*, XVIII, 57-58, 213-215, 245.

[78]See Volume II, Chaper 19 of this history.

[79]See Chapter 7, above.

[80]Mann, *Popes in the Middle Ages*, XVIII, 254-257; T. S. R. Boase, *Pope Boniface VIII* (London, 1933), pp. 29-32.

[81]Boase, *Boniface VIII*, pp. 32-33.

the Orsini-Colonna rivalry. All the cardinals but the two Colonnas and Boccamazzi left Rome for Rieti, each segment denouncing the other by letter. There were just enough cardinals in Rieti to elect a Pope, but Benedetto Gaetani had now made it very clear he wanted the Papacy for himself, and the Orsini were by no means ready to support him. Gaetani angrily left Rieti, thereby depriving the seven cardinals remaining in Rieti of sufficient numbers to elect. In October the conclave reassembled at Perugia with all eleven living cardinals present, but the deadlock remained unbroken.[82]

In March 1294, the papal interregnum now having lasted almost two years with no sign of when it might end, Charles II of Naples visited the cardinals at Perugia, urging them to elect a Pope without further delay. Cardinal Gaetani replied, firmly telling Charles—who was a much less formidable figure than his domineering father—that the votes of the cardinals must be free and that he should put no pressure on them. Charles accepted the rebuke without protest and returned to his royal seat at Naples, but on the way visited a well-known aged hermit named Peter, who lived alone in a cave on Mount Murrone (for which he was surnamed) above the town of Sulmona. Peter had inspired the formation of a small religious order, called the Order of St. Damian. Following his visit with Peter Murrone, Charles II announced that the monastery Peter had personally founded would receive an annual revenue of ten ounces of gold.[83]

Charles may also have spoken to Peter Murrone about the scandal created by the failure of the cardinals to elect the Pope. Although the aged hermit had never before shown himself inclined to intervene in any way in the affairs of the world or of the Church in the world, some time that spring he wrote a letter to Cardinal Malabranca, Bishop of Ostia, warning the cardinals of the punishment of God if they did not promptly do their duty. At one of the interminable meetings of the conclave, on July 5, 1294 (they were now well into their third year of such meetings) Cardinal Malabranca read Peter's letter, described his holy life and miracles, and declared that he would vote for Peter Murrone as Pope. Five other cardinals agreed on the spot, and then—more reluctantly—the two Orsinis, associates of Malabranca, providing the required eight votes. Whether likewise swept off their feet or simply for appearance's sake, the Colonna faction now joined as well, making the hermit's election unanimous.[84]

It was by any measure the strangest election in Papal history, the desperate action of men who had bound themselves for more than two years in such a web of power-seeking calculation and ambition that they were helpless to act in any normal way, striking blindly for liberation in an unprecedented move

---

[82]*Ibid.*, p. 33; Mann, *Popes in the Middle Ages*, XVIII, 258-259.
[83]Mann, *Popes in the Middle Ages*, XVIII, 262-263; Boase, *Boniface VIII*, pp. 36-37.
[84]Mann, *Popes in the Middle Ages*, XVIII, 263-265; Boase, *Boniface VIII*, pp. 40-41.

which must have seemed a slashing of their self-inflicted bonds by a sword of spiritual fire. For Peter the hermit of Murrone was more than eighty years old, and had lived in one or another of his solitary mountain cells for nearly forty years with only one interruption, a two-year period as abbot of the monastery of Santa Maria in Faysulis.[85] His holiness was evident, his austeries extraordinary:

> He brought his body into subjection by hair shirts, knotted leather girdles, and even iron chains. When his exhausted frame could no longer stand or kneel he lay down on boards in a cramped position, with a stone or a block of wood for a pillow, and in the bitter winter on an exposed mountain, with coverings utterly insufficient to keep out the cold. At no time did he eat more than was barely enough to support life. Often the bread that he ate was so stale and hard that it had to be broken with a hammer, and during the four or six "Lents" which, quite apart from everyone, he kept every year, he often ate only twice a week, and then took nothing but bread and water.[86]

His time was spent in prayer, manual work, reading the Bible or other spiritual reading, and providing spiritual counsel and advice to those who made the arduous trip to his mountain cell to obtain it. His conversations with these visitors were always on spiritual matters.[87] He knew nothing of the ways and affairs of the world. Despite his holiness, he was totally unqualified to be Pope.

Nevertheless, on July 20, an extraordinary procession wended its way a thousand feet up the steep mountain trail to Peter's cell, led by Cardinal Peter Colonna (the only cardinal to essay the climb—the others sent bishops as their representatives) and Charles Martel of Hungary, son of Charles II of Naples and representing him, the elder Charles having the excuse for not making the climb of a leg lame since boyhood. The bishops, mostly no doubt in well-fed middle age and not in prime physical condition, struggled up the path as best they could. Behind them came a vast crowd of priests, nobles, and peasants, sweating profusely in the hot summer sun. At last the leaders reached the hermit's cave. They officially notified Peter Murrone of his election as Pope. He had already prayed long and hard about whether to accept, and had been advised by counsellors he trusted that his refusal of the Papacy would be a defiance of the will of God and would lead to schism. Peter Murrone prostrated himself on the ground before the notification party in a last appeal to Heaven; then he arose, and accepted the Papacy.[88]

Despite a plethora of conspiracy theories then and since, neither historical evidence nor human probability justifies us in seeing in this unforgettable scene anything more than what it shows when viewed straight on: men stalked by the

---

[85]Mann, *Popes of the Middle Ages*, XVIII, 265-266, 269, 275.
[86]*Ibid.*, XVIII, 270.
[87]*Ibid.*, XVIII, 271.
[88]*Ibid.*, XVIII, 280-284.

nemesis of power seeking to escape its shadow by electing a man as Pope whom all knew could never be touched by power lust; and an aged and unworldly saint accepting an office whose duties in the world nothing in his long life had enabled him to comprehend.

Peter Murrone the hermit was crowned Pope, at the Neapolitan city of Aquila rather than in St. Peter's, on August 29, 1294, taking the name of Celestine V, since there could be only one Pope Peter. He was entirely in the hands of Charles II of Naples and his ministers, who became his only guides in dealing with the complexities of world affairs.   Charles II, it will be remembered, was French, a nephew of St. Louis IX; at his suggestion the new Pope doubled the size of the College of Cardinals, appointing no less than seven Frenchmen and five Neapolitans to the College. Peter Celestine took up his residence in Naples; he never set foot in Rome while he was Pope.[89]

But he soon realized his incapacity, and the harm it could do Christendom. Devoid of political ambition, relentless in judging himself, Pope Celestine V had decided by December that he must resign. He listened to none of the attempts, sincere or orchestrated by Charles II, to dissuade him. Canon lawyers were divided, for their knowledge of the six previous Papal resignations was very limited, and the last had occurred some two hundred and fifty years before. But enough of them said he could do it to be convincing. On December 13 Pope St. Peter Celestine V laid down the tiara. It has been the last Papal resignation, as it was the noblest.[90]

Peter Celestine may not have been worldly wise regarding international relations and clerical appointments, but the circumstances of his own election had showed him how great was the danger of a deadlocked conclave. During his brief pontificate he had re-enacted the strict legislation on the conduct of conclaves first imposed by Bd. Pope Gregory X twenty years and eight pontificates before. Each cardinal, for the duration of the conclave, was allowed only a ten-foot-square cell and a single servant.[91] But even without these deprivations, no one wanted a repeat of the two-and-a-half-year paralysis that had gripped the previous conclave. On an early ballot (one source says the first, another the third), the day before Christmas, the cardinals elected Benedetto Gaetani, probably about sixty years old, with only one or two dissenting votes. The two Colonna cardinals voted for him along with Matteo Rosso Orsini (Napoleone Orsini was absent). The new Pope took the name of Boniface VIII.[92]

---

[89]*Ibid.*, XVIII, 288-290, 294-296; Boase, *Boniface VIII*, pp. 43, 48.

[90]Mann, *Popes in the Middle Ages*, XVIII, 317, 319-323; Boase, *Boniface VIII*, p. 50.

[91]Mann, *Popes in the Middle Ages*, XVIII, 297-298; Volume XIX (London, 1932), p. 47; Boase, *Boniface VIII*, p. 48.

[92]Mann, *Popes in the Middle Ages*, XIX, 48-49; Boase, *Boniface VIII*, pp. 50-51. Boniface's age is given in most twentieth century biographical references (e.g. *The

It appears that Peter Celestine had particularly recommended Cardinal Gaetani for Pope:[93] a man not bound to any faction in the College of Cardinals, yet on good terms with all; of unusual administrative ability and impressive looks and presence (he was tall, with "a full oval face with lineaments noble, severe, and dignified, with slightly prominent ears, head nearly bald, broad brow, full cheeks, and firm massive jaw");[94] he had been nearly forty years a canon lawyer and thirteen years a cardinal in the service of three Popes.[95] Boniface VIII had almost all the qualities of practicality, experience and worldly wisdom that Peter Celestine V had lacked; he was devoted to the Church and a champion of the Papacy; he even had a touch of heroism, but it was not heroic virtue, because he lacked charity.

He demonstrated this immediately in the first year of his pontificate, by refusing to allow his holy predecessor to return to his cell on Mount Murrone, then arresting him when he tried to escape to Greece and imprisoning him in a castle, where he died a year later. Neither the fact that Peter welcomed his cell as very like his cave, nor the fact that some (with absolutely no encouragement from him) were claiming foolishly and unhistorically that Popes could not resign and therefore Peter was still Pope, could fully justify the action of Boniface VIII.[96] Considering the character of Peter Murrone, it was too obviously uncharitable. We need look no further than St. Paul's unforgettable thirteenth chapter of his First Letter to the Corinthians to understand why—though it could well be argued, as we shall see, that Boniface VIII was a papal martyr—no one has ever introduced a cause for his canonization. Only charity and holiness could turn aside the nemesis of power.

The resigned Pope Peter Celestine had urged the new Pope to revoke his own acts, only re-enacting those of which he approved, since Peter knew that in his innocence he had given many favors, gifts and revenues to unworthy recipients. Boniface VIII decreed that revocation only three days after his election as Pope. On January 23, 1295 he was consecrated in St. Peter's, beginning one of the most important pontificates in the Church's history, strikingly successful during its first six years, but a catastrophic failure at the end.[97]

Catholic Encyclopedia and *The New Catholic Encyclopedia*, and biographical dictionaries) as sixty or slightly less, presuming a birth date of about 1235. Nineteenth-century sources (and Mann, *op. cit.*, XIX, 5-6) repeat the tradition that Boniface VIII was in his late seventies when elected, which would seem incompatible both with his reported appearance at the time and the tremendous energy which marks his whole pontificate.

[93]Mann, *Popes in the Middle Ages*, XVIII, 325-326.
[94]*Ibid.*, XIX, 13.
[95]*Ibid.*, XIX, 6-11.
[96]*Ibid.*, XVIII, 328-331, 333-335; Boase, *Boniface VIII*, pp. 72-73.
[97]Mann, *Popes in the MIddle Ages*, XIX, 50-51, 54-58; Boase, *Boniface VIII*, pp. 57-

During the long papal interregnum and the brief and unique pontificate of
St. Peter Celestine V, Alfonso Pérez de Guzmán, called *el bueno* ("the Good"),
had written a new chapter of imperishable glory in the resplendent history of
the Christian reconquest of Spain. The Moors of Morocco still held both shores
of the Straits of Gibraltar, based on the triple strongholds of the Rock itself,
Algeciras across the bay from the Rock, and Tarifa just west of the
southernmost cape of Spain which marks the narrowest point of the Straits.
The kingdom of Granada to the northeast was still Muslim-ruled, but refused to
accept Morocco as overlord; both Castile and Morocco sought its alliance. In
the spring of 1292 the tainted King Sancho the Fierce of Castile and his devoted
wife Maria de Molina planned a great campaign to reconquer Tarifa "to the
service of God and the honor of all Christendom." The Spanish crusading
military orders of Santiago and Alcántara rallied their men, and the Christian
army set out late in June, with Queen Maria supporting it logistically from
Sevilla just as the great Queen Isabel was later to do during the final campaigns
leading up to the conquest of Granada. Much fighting followed, during which
Sancho received some support from Granada, whose ruler Muhammad II
hoped to obtain Tarifa for himself. Tarifa surrendered in October. Sancho
firmly refused to relinquish it to anyone, and appointed Guzmán to command
its garrison.[98]

Muhammad II of Granada now made alliance with Morocco in an attempt
jointly to recover Tarifa from Castile, weakened by a rebellion of Sancho's
brother Juan against him. Defeated, Prince Juan joined the Moors as his father
Alfonso X had done during the crisis at the end of his reign. The united Moors
besieged Tarifa. But James II of Aragon kept faith with the ancient cause by
sending 15 ships from his strong navy to aid his Christian brethren of Castile.
Learning of this and believing that they must consequently take Tarifa at once
or not at all, in August 1294 the besiegers adopted the vicious proposal of
renegade Prince Juan that they demand that Guzmán surrender Tarifa as the
price for the life of his son who was Prince Juan's prisoner. The demand was
made. Guzmán's answer was to hurl a sword over the ramparts at the enemy.
Tarifa held out, the relieving fleet from Aragon arrived, and the besiegers
withdrew, but not before they had killed Guzmán's son, just as they had

---

60.
[98]Lomax, *Reconquest of Spain*, p. 165; O'Callaghan, *Medieval Spain*, p. 397; Gaibrois
de Ballesteros, *Sancho IV*, II, 175, 177-184. Gaibrois de Ballesteros argues convincingly
in a lengthy footnote (*op. cit.*, II, 194-195) that the expedition against Tarifa was a
purely Castilian enterprise in no way dependent on Granadan aid. Lomax and
O'Callaghan accept Muhammad II's assertion that Sancho had promised him the city,
and he may have believed that such a promise was made; but as early as March 1292
Sancho had stated unequivocally in a letter to the Bishop of Badajoz that he would
never turn Tarifa over to the Moors (*op. cit.*, II, 194), and it seems most unlikely that in
fact he would ever have done so.

threatened. After Sancho's death the next year led to near-chaos and collapse of authority in Castile, Guzmán refused an order from its Regent to surrender Tarifa to the Moors. He was loyal to the Reconquest to the end, and Tarifa remained in Christian hands.[99]

The total fidelity to duty of Alfonso Pérez de Guzmán the Good became a legend in Spain; and 642 years later his deed was re-enacted, in extraordinarily similar circumstances, by a man who must have heard the tale of Guzmán the Good retold many a time. In the terrible summer of 1936, surrounded by an atheist army more alien than even the Moors had been, Colonel José Moscardó, commander of the garrison of the Alcázar (castle, or citadel) of Toledo, was ordered by his assailants to surrender as the price of the life of his son Luís, whom they held captive. They called Moscardó on the telephone and put Luís on the line, who confirmed their intention. "Then, my son," Moscardó said, "commend your soul to God, cry 'Long Live Spain!' and die like a hero, for the Alcázar will *never* surrender!" And the Alcázar of Toledo held out, and Luís Moscardó was slain.[100]

So does the Christian past enlace the present—especially in Spain.

The first major task undertaken by Pope Boniface VIII was to attempt the resolution of the long-standing Sicilian problem. His approach to it during the year 1295 shows the new pontiff at his best: an able and ingenious negotiator who always kept his primary goals in view. His primary goals were to end the conflict in Sicily and the conflict between France and Aragon about Sicily, and to restore Papal authority there, which had theoretically been re-established under Charles I of Naples (originally Prince Charles of Anjou in France) when he overthrew Manfred, the illegitimate son of Frederick II—though in fact Charles had governed and oppressed Sicily with little reference to the Pope. Boniface VIII's negotiations resulted in the Treaty of Anagni in June 1295, which provided for Aragon to renounce its claim to Sicily and return it to the Pope, in return for Sardinia and Corsica. James II of Aragon was to liberate the sons of Charles II of Naples whom he held hostage and to marry Charles' daughter Blanche, while Frederick of Sicily was to marry Catherine of Courtenay, heiress to the last Latin Emperor of Constantinople. Aragon was to abandon its claims on Sicily and France its claims on Aragon.[101]

As far as France and Aragon were concerned, the treaty was a success; but Catherine of Courtenay rejected marriage to Frederick and he in turn refused to submit to the Pope, continued to war against Naples, and had himself

[99]Gaibrois de Ballesteros, *Sancho IV*, II, 205, 209, 258-259, 291, 305-306, 326-327, 335-338; Lomax, *Reconquest of Spain*, p. 165; O'Callaghan, *Medieval Spain*, pp. 397, 401; Hillgarth, *Spanish Kingdoms*, I, 313.
[100]Hugh Thomas, *The Spanish Civil War* (New York, 1961), pp. 203-204.
[101]Mann, *Popes in the Middle Ages*, XIX, 68-73; Boase, *Boniface VIII*, pp. 70-72; Runciman, *Sicilian Vespers*, pp. 294-295.

crowned king of Sicily. The new Pope had narrowed the area of conflict but had not eliminated it. His firm commitment to uphold what he regarded as necessary Papal authority over Sicily barred any compromise with Frederick's defiance. So the struggle for Sicily continued, with no end in sight.[102]

The accord Boniface VIII obtained by these negotiations with Charles II of Naples and James II of Aragon, which these two sovereigns loyally upheld throughout his pontificate, proved to be his one real success at peacemaking, even though Frederick continued to maintain himself in Sicily. Toward the three great powers in Christendom—the Holy Roman Empire, France, and England, France being the strongest—Boniface placed himself, from early in his pontificate, in an adversary position. This was by no means entirely his fault. Philip IV of France and Edward I of England were obtaining from the Church in their countries a substantial part of the financial support for their war against each other and over Scotland, a French ally which Edward sought to conquer. In September 1294, while St. Peter Celestine was Pope, Edward had demanded and collected from the Church in England an unprecedented one-half of all its revenues for that year, declaring that any cleric who resisted would be deprived of the King's protection. In France, beginning that year, the tenths of clerical revenue past Popes had demanded for crusades—both those aimed ultimately at recovering Jerusalem and the "political crusades" in Europe proclaimed by the Pope, such as the war to regain Sicily—were now levied by Philip IV for himself, without seeking Papal approval. Germany was divided between the supporters of Adolf of Nassau, who had been elected Emperor after Rudolf's death, and supporters of Rudolf's son Albert of Habsburg; the Pope seemed hostile to both sides.[103]

Heavy, strictly enforced taxation of the Church without papal consent was an obvious and major threat to the Church's independence, and Edward's demand for half of all annual clerical revenues in England showed how great the threat could be.[104] On February 24, 1296 Pope Boniface VIII took firm

---

[102]Mann, *Popes in the Middle Ages*, XIX, 75, 78-81, 85-87; Boase, *Boniface VIII*, pp. 165-167; Runciman, *Sicilian Vespers*, p. 295.

[103]Powicke, *Thirteenth Century*, p. 672; Strayer, *Philip the Fair*, pp. 250-251; Mary M. Curley, *The Conflict between Pope Boniface VIII and King Philip IV the Fair* (Washington, 1927), p. 86; Mann, *Popes in the Middle Ages*, XIX, 117, 272.

[104]There is a tendency for historians of this period to concentrate almost exclusively on the struggle between Philip IV of France and Pope Boniface VIII over control of the French Church and its revenues, because France was the greatest power in Christendom and eventually "captured" the Papacy as a result of this conflict, but in fact Edward I was at this point equally defiant and equally threatening. Historians (e.g. Strayer, *Philip the Fair*, pp. 248-251) attempting to justify Philip IV's policies toward the Church by arguing that the French Church willingly cooperated with him because his financial demands were no more than previous Popes had made (one-tenth of annual revenues), almost all overlook Edward I's staggering financial demand on the English Church in 1294.

action against this danger in one of his most famous bulls, *Clericis laicos*, which prohibited clerics from paying, and government officials from receiving any money taxed from Church possessions without the consent of the Pope.[105] But though this action was clearly justified and much needed, the Pope's language was not. This was to be a recurring problem throughout Boniface VIII's pontificate and a major cause of its ultimate disaster. With rare exceptions, harsh and angry language is not a luxury the Vicar of Christ can afford in dealing with leaders in Christendom who, however reprehensible their acts, hold millions of the faithful under their control—especially when it leads to indefensible exaggeration. In this bull the unduly harsh language appeared in the very first sentence:

> Antiquity teaches us, and the experiences of the present time make clear that the laity are hostile to the clergy; inasmuch as, not content within their own bounds, they aim at what is forbidden them.[106]

Let two of the greatest and most orthodox Church historians of all time, Karl-Joseph Hefele and Henri Leclercq, in their monumental *History of the Councils*, answer:

> Sad indeed would it be for the Church if this mortal enmity were a normal condition rather than an exception, but happily this supposition is contrary to historical truth. Even if we abstract the first centuries of the Christian Church, we may well say that the majority of the faithful have a real sympathy for the clergy. This general accusation of Boniface seems little in keeping with the dignity and prudence of the Holy See, and can only be explained as one of the caprices which reappear frequently in Boniface VIII who, it must be said, was lacking in moderation.[107]

By assuming that he would have little or no lay support in restricting taxation of the Church, Pope Boniface VIII assured that he got little of it, though one sovereign, James II of Aragon, did eventually support *Clericis laicos*.[108] The French Church pleaded with the Pope to modify his position, which he eventually did by granting Philip IV the right to tax the Church in France in whatever Philip might deem an emergency situation.[109] But the English Church held firm for the Pope for more than a year, led by the heroic

---

[105]Boase, *Boniface VIII*, pp. 136-138; Curley, *Conflict between Boniface VIII and Philip IV*, pp. 73-76.

[106]Mann, *Popes in the Middle Ages*, XIX, 239.

[107]Hefele-Leclercq, *Histoire des Conciles*, VI, 359, cited in Curley, *Conflict between Pope Boniface VIII and Philip IV*, p. 76.

[108]Mann, *Popes in the Middle Ages*, XIX, 242.

[109]*Ibid.*, XIX, 246-247, 304-309; Strayer, *Philip the Fair*, pp. 253-254; Boase, *Boniface VIII*, pp. 147-148, 152; Curley, *Conflict between Pope Boniface VIII and Philip IV*, pp. 82-83.

Archbishop of Canterbury Robert of Winchelsea, who reminded the English clergy in January 1297, in convocation at St. Paul's in London, that "we have two lords over us, the King and the Pope; and though we owe obedience to both, we owe greater obedience to the spiritual than to the temporal."[110] The whole issue turned out to be essentially a test of strength, after which Church and state made accommodations that Pope Boniface VIII tacitly or explicitly accepted. Neither side prevailed, but each now saw the other as an adversary.

Pope Boniface VIII in *Clericis laicos* had certainly been imprudent in his language and may have been unnecessarily confrontational, but in Philip IV of France and Edward I of England he faced two monarchs who were evidently aspiring to more power than was good for Christian kings in a united Christendom. Philip was surrounding himself by men typified by William of Nogaret, appointed royal commissioner in the fall of 1295, whose grandfather had been burned as a heretic by the Inquisition at Carcassonne during the time of the Albigensian Crusade, and whose contemporary Yves de Loudéac called him "a body without a soul, who cares nothing about anyone's rights but only wants to increase the wealth of the King of France."[111] Edward had long been embarked on a career of shameless imperialism; he had crushed the freedom of Wales in a great war against its King Llewelyn the Last in 1282 and 1283 and put down a major Welsh uprising in 1295, and after the death of the child Queen of Scotland (Margaret, the "Maid of Norway") in 1290, had declared himself overlord of Scotland whose next king must swear fealty to him.[112] In December 1295 he declared war on the Scots and at first appeared to carry all before him, but in September 1297 a popular uprising led by a previously unknown knight named William Wallace destroyed an English army at Stirling Bridge. From that point on Edward was resolved to conquer Scotland at almost any cost.[113] If not as dangerous to Christendom as Emperor Frederick II had been—for both Philip and Edward were personally good practicing Catholics—their developing absolutism needed to be curbed, just as the developing absolutism of Frederick Barbarossa and Henry II of England in the preceding century had needed to be curbed,[114] for the Catholic Church can never accept a truly totalitarian state. Pope Boniface VIII was ready to act, at

---

[110]Mann, *Popes in the Middle Ages*, XIX, 244; Boase, *Boniface VIII*, pp. 142-144; Curley, *Conflict between Pope Boniface VIII and Philip IV*, pp. 76-77; Powicke, *Thirteenth Century*, pp. 665-666, 675-676.

[111]Georges Digard, *Philippe le Bel et le Saint-Siège de 1285 à 1304* (Paris, 1936), II, 29; Franklin J. Pegues, *The Lawyers of the Last Capetians* (Princeton, 1962), p. 99.

[112]John E. Morris, *The Welsh Wars of Edward I* (New York, 1901, 1969); Powicke, *Thirteenth Century*, pp. 601, 604; G. W. S. Barrow, *Robert Bruce and the Community of the Realm of Scotland* (Berkeley CA, 1965), pp. 42, 47.

[113]Barrow, *Robert Bruce*, pp. 99-100, 103-110, 117-126, 139-140; Powicke, *Thirteenth Century*, pp. 613-616, 686.

[114]See Chapter Three, above.

least against Philip IV, the nearer and stronger of the two—and with a heavy hand.

Before he could make any further move, however—indeed, while he was still involved in the later phases of the struggle over *Clericis laicos*—a new attack on the Pope arose unexpectedly out of the tangled family politics of Rome. Boniface VIII's Gaetani family, based in the small city of Anagni about forty miles east of Rome, had never had much influence in Rome, though Boniface was trying to build it up. The two greatest families in Rome, each with two members in the College of Cardinals, were the Orsini and the Colonna. The Colonna resented Boniface's efforts to improve the fortunes of his family, and were listening to the dissident Franciscans who called themselves "Spirituals" and claimed that Pope St. Peter Celestine V had not resigned, or could not resign, and was therefore still Pope when Boniface VIII took the tiara, rendering his election invalid. Having voted for Boniface in the December 1294 conclave, the Colonna were not in a good logical position to make this argument, but logic was never a strong point of the "Spiritual Franciscans." Early in May Stephen Colonna, a nephew of the two Colonna cardinals, seized a convoy from Anagni bearing 200,000 florins to purchase castles for the Gaetani family. Boniface VIII immediately summoned Cardinals Peter and James Colonna before him to demand that the captured treasure be returned, that Stephen Colonna and the three great Colonna castles south and east of Rome (near Anagni) be handed over to him, and that the cardinals declare that they still regarded Boniface VIII as Pope. The Colonna cardinals defied the summons and the "Spiritual Franciscans" put out a manifesto declaring that Boniface VIII was not a legitimate Pope and calling for an ecumenical council to settle the issue. Boniface thereupon excommunicated the Colonna cardinals, depriving them of all ecclesiastical revenues, and declared Stephen and other sons of John Colonna involved in the seizure of the treasure excommunicated to the fourth generation.[115]

Once again it was an action all too typical of those qualities of Boniface VIII which brought him and the Papacy and all Christendom to so much grief. No reasonable and just man could doubt that he was right to punish the two Colonna cardinals and Stephen Colonna heavily for what they had done. But it was, so far as we know, the first time in history that unborn children were excommunicated. Surely he did not need—nor was it right—to go that far.

The Colonnas responded with a statement of even greater violence, calling Boniface VIII a "savage tyrant" and the murderer of ex-Pope Peter Celestine. The Pope promptly applied the punishment of Cardinals James and Peter Colonna to several other members of the family including another James

---

[115]Waley, *Papal State in the Thirteenth Century*, p. 243; Boase, *Boniface VIII*, pp. 164, 170-172; Mann, *Popes in the Middle Ages*, XIX, 210-212; Curley, *Conflict between Pope Boniface VIII and Philip IV*, pp. 56-59.

Colonna known as "Sciarra" (the Quarrelsome), and declared that anyone assisting any of the excommunicated Colonnas in any way would himself be excommunicated and any city harboring any of them would be placed under interdict. The Pope obtained support from most of the cardinals; all but two of the 17 current members of the College other than the two Colonnas signed a statement declaring that Pope Peter Celestine V had resigned freely, that the election of Boniface VIII was valid and that the Colonna cardinals had voted for him and always until this time recognized him as Pope; the cardinals described the Colonnas as "madmen." Military operations began against them, which (in another example of excess) Boniface VIII actually designated crusades; their castles near Rome were taken one by one; in September 1298 they were forced to submit, but a bitter hatred for the Pope burned in the family, particularly in the heart of "Sciarra."[116]

Nevertheless the Pope's victory in this sudden and vicious engagement seemed to free him to attend to the larger concerns of Christendom that he had had to postpone while fighting the Colonnas. In January 1299 he wrote Philip IV telling him that he was abusing the privileges which had been granted to him and was diverting Church goods to his own use, or allowing his officials to do so.[117] Later in the year he learned that many of the Colonnas had taken refuge in France, where Philip had received them honorably.[118] In September 1298 he firmly refused to approve the excommunicated Albert of Habsburg as Holy Roman Emperor, calling him a traitor to his predecessor Adolf of Nassau (whom he had challenged and killed in battle in July), and a despoiler and destroyer of churches.[119]

In June the Pope challenged Edward I of England directly by endorsing the independence of Scotland in the bull *Scimus fili*. After conferring with William Lamberton, Archbishop of St. Andrews and primate of Scotland, Boniface VIII declared that the church in Scotland was under the Pope like any other national church, rather than under English ecclesiastical authority, and ordered Edward to make amends for imprisoning the Bishops of Glasgow and Sodor. Boniface consecrated a new Scottish bishop, David Murray, whose nephew Andrew had been mortally wounded at the Battle of Stirling Bridge.[120] He sent a letter to Edward I further confirming his recognition of Scottish independence and urging the English monarch, "for the love of Mount Zion

---

[116]Mann, *Popes in the Middle Ages*, XIX, 213-216, 218, 220-221; Boase, *Boniface VIII*, pp. 172-174, 176-178, 181; Curley, *Conflict between Pope Boniface VIII and Philip IV*, pp. 55, 59-61.

[117]Mann, *Popes in the Middle Ages*, XIX, 312; Strayer, *Philip the Fair*, p. 24.

[118]Mann, *Popes in the Middle Ages*, XIX, 222-223, 317; Boase, *Boniface VIII*, p. 183.

[119]Mann, *Popes in the Middle Ages*, XIX, 120-121, 123; Boase, *Boniface VIII*, pp. 217-218; *Cambridge Medieval History*, VII, 87-88.

[120]Mann, *Popes in the Middle Ages*, XIX, 250-251; Boase, *Boniface VIII*, pp. 209-210; Barrow, *Robert Bruce*, pp. 134-135, 163-164; Powicke, *Thirteenth Century*, p. 693.

and Jerusalem," to give up his attempt to conquer Scotland (he was evidently recalling the long-standing hope that Edward I, who had been a crusading leader as a prince in the time of St. Louis IX, would one day lead another crusade to the Holy Land).[121] Presented more than a year later with this papal letter, Edward made the following reply, which showed how much power-seeking had become central to his life and ambition: "By God's blood, I will not keep my peace for Mount Zion nor silence for Jerusalem, but while there is breath in my nostrils I will defend my right, which all the world knows, with all my power."[122] He meant every word of it; but the Scots, though badly beaten at Falkirk in 1298,[123] still would not submit.

The year 1300 marked the turn of a century, and for the first time a Pope took this occasion to proclaim a "Jubilee year," with special indulgences for pilgrims to Rome. Consequently pilgrims came in enormous numbers, which was undoubtedly a great gratification for Pope Boniface VIII and encouragement that papal leadership of Christendom was still fully recognized by the people, though he had little actual contact with the pilgrims since he spent the spring and summer (from April to October), when most of them were in Rome, at his home town of Anagni.[124]

During 1301 Boniface VIII, still hoping that King Edward I might be induced to lead a crusade to the Holy Land, provided him with the money which had been collected in England for the next crusade there, absolved him from punishment for his illegal taxation of the Church, and declared himself impressed by his specious arguments that he was the rightful overlord of Scotland.[125] The Pope maintained his uncompromising rejection of Emperor Albert of Habsburg, now threatening him with the ultimate penalty, which Pope St. Gregory VII had first levied against Emperor Henry V: if Albert did not send representatives to Rome within six months to justify to the Pope how he had taken power in Germany, Boniface would release all his subjects from their oaths of obedience, thereby encouraging widespread revolt against him.[126]

With Philip IV, the most powerful sovereign in Christendom, Boniface in 1301 kept a low profile until Philip challenged him with the sudden arrest of Bernard de Saisset, Bishop of Pamiers in Languedoc and a Papal legate, whom Philip especially disliked because he had once compared him to an owl. Bishop Saisset's correspondence with the Pope and cardinals was seized, his goods

---

[121]Mann, *Popes in the Middle Ages*, XIX, 252-253; Boase, *Boniface VIII*, pp. 210-211; Powicke, *Thirteenth Century*, p. 693.
[122]Ronald M. Scott, *Robert the Bruce, King of Scots* (New York, 1989), p. 57.
[123]For the Battle of Falkirk see Barrow, *Robert Bruce*, pp. 141-147.
[124]Mann, *Popes in the Middle Ages*, XIX, 175-183; Boase, *Boniface VIII*, pp. 231-237.
[125]Mann, *Popes in the Middle Ages*, XIX, 254-260, 297-298; Boase, *Boniface VIII*, p. 311; Powicke, *Thirteenth Century*, pp. 705-706; Barrow, *Robert Bruce*, pp. 163, 166.
[126]*Cambridge Medieval History*, VII, 89; Mann, *Popes in the Middle Ages*, XIX, 125-126; Curley, *Conflict between Pope Boniface VIII and Philip IV*, pp. 86-87.

were confiscated, and he was charged with speaking and prophesying against the King, a crime in every medieval state. Bishop Saisset's appeal to the Pope was ignored, and William of Nogaret drew up charges against him, many based on no evidence at all.[127]

Though Bishop Saisset had evidently been indiscreet and some of the charges against him were probably true, the Pope could not ignore a challenge of this magnitude. He responded in November 1301 with a demand that Philip IV release Bishop Saisset at once and return his confiscated estates, threatening the King with excommunication if he did not do so. He followed this a day later with the bull *Ausculta fili* ("Listen, son!") suspending the exemptions from *Clericis laicos'* restrictions on financial levies on the Church which he had previously granted to Philip, and condemning Philip for misgovernment and disrespect for the Church and its bishops.[128]   The introductory sentence of *Ausculta fili* again displayed Boniface VIII's unfortunate tendency to word his directives and offer his counsel in very provocative fashion: "Listen, son, to the words of thy father and to the teachings of thy master who, on this earth, holds the place of Him Who is the sole Master and Lord."[129] The doctrine was sound, but for the Pope to refer to himself as the king's "master" was not the most tactful way to state it. Boniface VIII followed this with another bull, *Salvator mundi*, in December, explicitly revoking the exemptions from *Clericis laicos* which he had given to Philip IV and forbidding the payment of any Church revenues to Philip without specific Papal authorization.[130]

Ausculta fili was received at the French court in February 1302 and was promptly burned.[131] Pierre Flotte, Philip's chief minister, then forged a Papal bull (*Scire te volumus*) which explicitly claimed temporal authority for the Pope in France, denied the King the income even of vacant sees and benefices, and condemned as heretics all who disagreed. In April Philip called the first known meeting of the Estates-General (the French parliament, not to be confused with the special courts known as *parlements*) at which the forged bull was presented as the document Boniface VIII had actually sent to Philip. The king declared that all who opposed him in this matter and supported the Pope would be treated as his personal enemies. The papal emissary who had brought *Ausculta fili* to Paris was expelled from France along with Bishop Saisset, and Bishop

[127]Mann, *Popes in the Middle Ages*, XIX, 324-328; Boase, *Boniface VIII*, pp. 298-300; Strayer, *Philip the Fair*, pp. 262, 265-266; Curley, *Conflict between Pope Boniface VIII and Philip IV*, pp. 90-94.

[128]Strayer, *Philip the Fair*, pp. 267-268; Boase, *Boniface VIII*, pp. 301-303, 310-311; Mann, *Popes in the Middle Ages*, XIX, 319-323; Curley, *Conflict between Pope Boniface VIII and Philip IV*, pp. 94-96.

[129]Mann, *Popes in the Middle Ages*, XIX, 321.

[130]Boase, *Boniface VIII*, p. 301.

[131]*Ibid.*, p. 304. Strayer, *Philip the Fair*, p. 270, doubts that the bull was burned, but Digard, *Philippe le bel*, II, 95n-96n, provides solid evidence that it was.

Peter de Mornay of Auxerre was sent to Rome bearing letters from the Estates-General condemning the Pope's action.[132]

The gauntlet had been thrown down, and Pope Boniface VIII did not hesitate to pick it up. He received Bishop Peter de Mornay in consistory with his cardinals, all of whom gave him full support. Cardinal Acquasparta opened the meeting with a lengthy explanation of the distinction among spiritual authority, temporal authority, and the Pope's right and duty to act as the moral judge of kings. Boniface denounced the forgery of the bull *Scire te volumus*, saying that of course he had never claimed and would never claim temporal authority over France, and reproving the French bishops for appearing to believe that he had; but, he went on, "our predecessors have deposed three kings of France; and, we say it with sorrow, we are ready to depose one like a groom."[133] Whether the Pope could, strictly speaking, depose a king was debatable, for absolving a king's subjects from their duty of allegiance and obedience was not quite that; but did he really need to add "like a groom"?

That spring the people of Flanders had risen against Philip IV's autocratic rule much as the people of Palermo had risen against Charles I of Naples in the "Sicilian Vespers," and in July 1302 the Flemish army defeated the French at the Battle of Courtrai. Pierre Flotte and Count Robert of Artois, who had done much to stir up the conflict between Philip IV and the Pope, were killed in the battle. There was briefly some hope that their elimination might reduce the tension between king and Pope; but the appointment of the able and utterly unscrupulous William of Nogaret as "first lawyer of the realm" suggested otherwise.[134] Boniface VIII, perhaps hoping for support from Edward I of England, abandoned the cause of the Scots in August, rebuking the patriotic Scots bishops as "sowers of discord" and urging them to accept Edward's authority.[135] But he saw no grounds for compromise with Philip IV, and on November 18, 1302 issued the bull *Unam sanctam* proclaiming, in the strongest terms in papal history, the superiority of the Pope's authority over all other authority, and his right and duty to be the moral judge of kings. It did not specifically claim the exercise of universal temporal authority for the Pope, but its language was open to the interpretation that it made such a claim. The imprudence of its language has caused trouble for the Church from its own time

---

[132]Mann, *Popes in the Middle Ages*, XIX, 331-334, 337-340; Boase, *Boniface VIII*, pp. 305-307; Curley, *Conflict between Pope Boniface VIII and Philip IV*, pp. 99-105; Strayer, *Philip the Fair*, pp. 271-272.

[133]Mann, *Popes in the Middle Ages*, XIX, 340-345 (quotation on p. 343); Boase, *Boniface VIII*, pp. 308-311; Curley, *Conflict between Pope Boniface VIII and Philip IV*, pp. 105-111.

[134]Strayer, *Philip the Fair*, pp. 333-335; Boase, *Boniface VIII*, pp. 312, 316-317; Curley, *Conflict between Pope Boniface VIII and Philip IV*, p. 112; Pegues, *Lawyers of the Last Capetians*, p. 46.

[135]Boase, *Boniface VIII*, pp. 327-328; Powicke, *Thirteenth Century*, pp. 709-710.

right down to the present.

> Spiritual power surpasses in dignity and in nobility any temporal
> power whatever, as spiritual things surpass the temporal. This we see very
> clearly also by the payment, benediction, and consecration of the tithes, by
> the acceptance of power itself and by the government even of things. For
> with truth as our witness, it belongs to spiritual power to establish the
> terrestrial power and to pass judgment if it has not been good....
> Therefore if the terrestrial power err, it will be judged by the spiritual
> power; if a minor spiritual power err, it will be judged by a superior
> spiritual power; but if the highest power of all err, it can be judged only by
> God, and not by man, according to the testimony of the Apostle: "The
> spiritual man judges all things and he himself is judged by no man." (1 Cor
> 2:15) ... We declare, we proclaim, we define that it is absolutely necessary
> for salvation that every human creature be subject to the Roman
> Pontiff.[136]

The great problem with this document comes in the last sentence, the last
and worst example of Pope Boniface VIII's tendency to overstate. The rest of it
is a clear, forthright, and effective exposition of the Hildebrandine doctrine of
the place of the Pope in Christendom. But the last sentence sounds like a claim
of universal sovereignty, temporal as well as spiritual, and also—though this was
not an issue at the time, more than two hundred years before the appearance of
Protestantism—a solemn declaration that only practicing Catholics can be
saved. In fact Pope Boniface VIII, as we have seen, had explicitly repudiated
any claim to be a temporal ruler outside the Papal state in this very year 1302,
and there is nothing whatever to indicate that he was even thinking of the
doctrinally separate question of the salvation of persons who are not practicing
Catholics. Rather he was addressing those in almost universally Catholic
western, central, and northern Europe[137] who might willfully refuse obedience
to the Pope despite fully understanding the nature of the office he held and his
supreme authority in the spiritual realm.

Boniface VIII did not intend to stop with an abstract disquisition on papal
authority. In December 1302 he sent Cardinal John Lemoine to present a 12-
point ultimatum to Philip IV, which required him to permit French bishops to
go to Rome at any time for meetings; to recognize the Pope's supreme
authority in bestowing ecclesiastical benefices and his right to send legates to
any country without obtaining anyone's permission; not to take away any goods
and rights from the Church in France without papal permission; to prove his

---

[136]Pope Boniface VIII, *Unam sanctam*, as cited by Curley, *Conflict between Pope
Boniface VIII and Philip IV*, pp. 115-116.
[137]The entire population in these regions was Catholic except for a relatively small
number of Jews. In the Byzantine empire and Russia there were many practicing
Christians who did not acknowledge papal authority, but Boniface VIII had nothing to
say about their spiritual status in this document or any others he issued.

innocence of burning the bull *Ausculta fili* or accept a penance for it; to return the city of Lyons to the political control of its bishop; and to make restitution for having twice debased the currency. If the king of France did not respond satisfactorily to these demands, the Pope told Philip IV he would "proceed against him spiritually and temporally."[138]

Cardinal Lemoine arrived in Paris early in February 1303 and delivered his message. Before the month was over William of Nogaret had developed a plan to seize the Pope by a surprise attack on him in Italy, try to force him to resign, and if he would not, bring him to Lyons where he would be tried by a rebel council in order to depose him as a heretic and simoniac. On March 7 royal patent letters were given to William and his companions Thierry d'Hirson and Jacques de Jasseines to treat with anyone, noble or common, clerical or lay, for the purpose of seizing the Pope and bringing him forcibly to France. Though the plan to seize the Pope was obviously kept secret, the charges against him were not; William of Nogaret presented them to an assembly of French bishops and nobles called by Philip IV to meet with him at the Louvre March 12. Boniface VIII, he said, was a "false prophet ... a master of lies, calling himself Good-doer [Boniface] whereas he is Evil-doer [Maleficus] ... though he is not a true president, still, as though he were, he now calls himself the lord, the judge, the master of all men." Nogaret made the absurd claim that Peter Celestine V, dead and buried for seven years, was still alive and still the true Pope; he called Boniface VIII a manifest heretic and self-confessed simoniac, and urged Philip IV to draw his sword against him and to call a general council to condemn and depose him and elect a better Pope.[139]

William of Nogaret had no evidence, no justification, and no precedent as a layman to make any of these wildly malicious charges; indeed, one would almost need to come down to the Nazi and Communist propaganda of the twentieth century to find so many lies and so little truth in a major public pronouncement of a high officer in a Western government. But he had the French King's favor, and we hear of no objections in France to his proceedings.

On April 13 Pope Boniface VIII wrote to Cardinal Lemoine in France that he was wholly dissatisfied with Philip's vague and evasive responses to his letters, and that Philip had clearly merited excommunication. In a prophetic moment, the Pope told the Cardinal that he was prepared to suffer martyrdom in this cause of maintaining the rightful authority of the Vicar of Christ. Seeking support from the temporal authority which had been set up primarily to defend the Pope, Boniface finally recognized Albert of Habsburg as

---

[138]Curley, *Conflict between Pope Boniface VIII and Philip IV*, pp. 127-129; Mann, *Popes in the Middle Ages*, XIX, 352-353; Boase, *Boniface VIII*, pp. 325-326.

[139]Mann, *Popes in the Middle Ages*, XIX, 335-336, 352-353; Boase, *Boniface VIII*, pp. 325-327; Curley, *Conflict between Pope Boniface VIII and Philip IV*, pp. 132-135; Digard, *Philippe le bel*, II, 145, 154-157; Strayer, *Philip the Fair*, p. 275.

Emperor, promised to crown him in Rome, and received in turn from Albert an oath of "fealty and obedience" which strongly suggests that he was more his father's son than the Pope had previously believed.[140]

In May peace was made between France and England, with Philip totally abandoning his ally Scotland, leaving him free to pursue his struggle against the Pope without distractions or outside threats. In June Philip publicly called for an ecumenical council, and had a huge crowd assemble at the Louvre to hear Nogaret's accusations translated from Latin into French, while a Dominican called on the people of the French capital to aid the King, whom he praised as a great defender of the Faith.[141]

By the beginning of summer Nogaret and his small group of conspirators were ensconced in the castle of Staggia near Siena in Italy. Charles II of Naples, a man of honor, refused to have anything to do with Nogaret's conspiracy despite his French blood; neither could the conspirators find any significant support in Rome. But Sciarra Colonna joined them with enthusiasm, and Rinaldo da Supino, captain of the city of Ferentino near Anagni, agreed to help if he were well paid, but only on condition that Nogaret lead the attack on the Pope carrying the French royal standard, which Nogaret reluctantly agreed to do. Meanwhile, in mid-August, the Pope scornfully dismissed the charges of heresy against him; deprived the teachers at the University of Paris, the most famous in Christendom, of their faculties to teach and confer degrees, saying Philip had corrupted them; and began the drafting of a new bull reiterating his right and authority to act as the moral judge of kings and stating that Philip IV's sins against the Church justified his excommunication and the freeing of his subjects from their oaths and duties of allegiance to him—though he stopped short of actually decreeing Philip's excommunication and of releasing his subjects from their obligation of obedience to him.[142]

September came, and William of Nogaret learned that the Pope planned to publish his new bull against Philip IV on the feast of the Nativity of Our Lady, Sunday September 8. Nogaret decided to prevent its publication by seizing the Pope on the 7th. On the evening of Friday the 6th he gathered the formidable force of 300 horse and 1,000 foot at Ferentino, the stronghold of Rainald of Supino. Sciarra Colonna supplied and commanded the greater part of the cavalry; he was accompanied by Peter Colonna, the former cardinal, his

---

[140]Mann, *Popes in the Middle Ages*, XIX, 127-130, 354-355; Boase, *Boniface VIII*, pp. 326, 328-330; Curley, *Conflict between Pope Boniface VIII and Philip IV*, pp. 129-131; *Cambridge Medieval History*, VII, 90.

[141]Boase, *Boniface VIII*, pp. 327, 335; Curley, *Conflict between Pope Boniface VIII and Philip IV*, pp. 140-141; Powicke, *Thirteenth Century*, pp. 653-654; Barrow, *Robert Bruce*, pp. 179-180.

[142]Jean Favier, *Philippe le bel* (Paris, 1978), pp. 370-371, 378, 383; Curley, *Conflict between Pope Boniface VIII and Philip IV*, pp. 144-148, 156; Mann, *Popes in the Middle Ages*, XIX, 368-370; Boase, *Boniface VIII*, pp. 336-337.

son Stephen, and various other Italian noblemen with grievances against the Pope or members of his family. The entire party was Italian except for William of Nogaret and two companions, but they led it carrying the French flag, as Rainald of Supino had specified. Through the night they picked their way along a remote hill path, undetected. At five o'clock in the morning they arrived at the walls of Anagni, where a gate was opened for them by a traitor.[143]

Pope Boniface VIII is close to seventy and has been in poor health. He has never been involved directly in any kind of combat. At dawn the alarm sounds in the usually peaceful streets of Anagni, now filling fast with armed strangers. The people gather in the central square. They elect a captain to organize their defense: Adenulf Conti. But his brother Nicholas is one of the leaders of the attacking force, and Adenulf makes no resistance. Seven cardinals are in the city. Three flee at once; the Dominican Nicholas Boccasini and Peter of Spain rush to the Pope's side; Napoleon Orsini and Richard of Siena remain unmolested, perhaps in league with the attackers. A truce is called until mid-afternoon, during which Boniface is told to reinstate the Colonna, hand over all his treasure to three senior cardinals, resign, and deliver himself up to the attackers as their prisoner. He refuses.[144]

The truce expires at three o'clock in the afternoon and an assault on the papal palace in Anagni begins at once. The palace is on the crest of the hill on which the town is built. The Pope's nephew, Marquis Peter Gaetani, directs the defenses. At first they seem to hold. Then the attackers storm the cathedral adjacent to the palace, set fire to its doors, plunder it, kill a visiting archbishop inside, and from it gain access to the palace. Peter Caetani capitulates.[145] At six o'clock the attackers break through the windows and doors of the street side of the palace, shouting: "Long Live the King of France and the Colonna! Death to the Pope!" Boniface, wearing his papal robes, takes in his hands a crucifix containing wood from the True Cross and orders: "Open the doors and my chamber; I wish to suffer martyrdom for the Church of God." He lies down upon a couch with the crucifix on his breast. The attackers storm into the room. He looks up at them and says: "Come forward, strike my head, I wish to suffer martyrdom, I wish to die for the Faith of Christ. . . . Here is my neck; here is my head."[146]

Sciarra Colonna wanted to kill him at once, but others restrained him. Boniface VIII was probably manhandled; Cardinal Boccasini, his successor as

---

[143]Favier, *Philippe le bel*, pp. 382-383; Digard, *Philippe le bel*, II, 178-180; Boase, *Boniface VIII*, pp. 344-345; Curley, *Conflict of Pope Boniface VIII with Philip IV*, pp. 148-149.

[144]Boase, *Boniface VIII*, p. 346; Curley, *Conflict between Pope Boniface VIII and Philip IV*, pp. 149-150; Favier, *Philippe le Bel*, p. 388.

[145]Boase, *Boniface VIII*, p. 346; Curley, *Conflict between Pope Boniface VIII and Philip IV*, pp. 150-151; Favier, *Philippe le Bel*, p. 388.

[146]Digard, *Philippe le bel*, II, 182.

Pope, who was in the palace at the time, says he was, though others deny it. One chronicle reports that Sciarra Colonna struck him in the face with a mailed fist. It is clear that for a few minutes his life hung in the balance. However, William of Nogaret did not want the Pope murdered; he rushed to the Pope's chamber just a few minutes after Sciarra arrived there, to be greeted by Boniface VIII with a magnificent flash of spirit: "What do you here, son of a Patarine [Catharist heretic]?"[147] Nogaret replied with a lash of his tongue:

> I wish to conserve the life of the Church against the violence of your enemies by presenting you to a general council which I request you to convoke; if you refuse to do so, it will be convened in spite of you. It is a question of heresy and you should be judged willingly or unwillingly.... I arrest you in virtue of the rule of public law, for the defense of the Faith, and the interest of our holy mother the Church, not to insult you nor anyone else. Sorry Pope that you are! Consider the goodness of your lord, the King of France, who guards and protects your kingdom against your enemies.[148]

Boniface VIII made no recorded response to this incredible farrago, beyond reiterating his refusal to resign and his desire for martyrdom. Ornaments were torn from his body and his palace was thoroughly plundered.[149]

All the next day, Sunday the feast of the Nativity of Our Lady, William of Nogaret debated with Sciarra Colonna and grappled with the insoluble problem always confronting those who capture a Pope: now that you have him, what do you do with him? Sciarra was still for killing him; Nogaret wanted to bring him to France, but was beginning to realize (one wonders why he had not thought of this before) just how difficult it would be: not all of his Italian force, perhaps very little of it, would escort him the whole way, and he had no naval support. In Anagni the initial shock and confusion from all the betrayals had given way to horror: Christendom would forever condemn a city that allowed the Pope to be murdered in its midst. At three o'clock in the morning of Monday September 9 the townspeople attacked the palace, crying "Long live the Pope, death to the foreigner!" There was only feeble resistance from the now thoroughly disorganized captors of the Pope. Sciarra Colonna leaped on his horse and galloped out of the city. Rainald of Supino and Adenulf Conti were captured. William of Nogaret was wounded and lost his French standard, which was dragged in the mud; but he could still walk, and slipped out through the crowd unrecognized until he could find a horse and ride away. Cardinal Richard of Siena fled in servants' clothes. Boniface VIII came into the central square to

---

[147]Boase, *Boniface VIII*, p. 348; Mann, *Popes in the Middle Ages*, XIX, 379-380.
[148]Curley, *Conflict between Pope Boniface VIII and Philip IV*, pp. 151-152.
[149]*Ibid.*, p. 153; Boase, *Boniface VIII*, p. 348.

absolve and thank the people, declaring that he forgave everyone who had injured him. Cardinal Matthew Rosso Orsini then arrived with 400 horsemen, who a week later escorted the Pope to Rome where Charles II of Naples sent 10,000 men to guard him.[150]

But the shock had been too great. On October 12, just over a month after the attack, Pope Boniface VIII died in the small hours of the morning, peacefully, after professing his faith and confessing his sins. The conclave to elect his successor convened nine days later. William of Nogaret had the staggering presumption to attend it as a representative of Philip IV. Cardinal Nicholas Boccasini was chosen Pope the following day and took the name of Benedict XI. On November 6 he issued an encyclical on the events at Anagni, describing the perpetrators of the seizure of the Pope as "sons of inquity, the first-born of Satan, children of perdition" and demanding restoration on pain of excommunication of all the papal property plundered in the palace and cathedral; but he took no specific action against the persons known to have taken part in the attack, and began removing some of the disabilities on Philip IV and on the Colonnas.[151]

Historians long believed that this vicious assault on Pope Boniface VIII, which clearly led to his death even if he was not seriously abused physically during it, sent a shock wave of horror around Christendom—as indeed it should have done. But in fact, except for a few unusually perceptive observers like Dante, quoted on the attack on Boniface VIII at the head of this chapter, there seem to have been few instances of such reaction. Boniface had not been popular, and the deep reverence for the Vicar of Christ that had characterized Christendom for 250 years was fading in the power struggles of the end of the thirteenth century. Surprisingly little notice was taken of the violence at Anagni, weakening the new Pope's hand as he prepared to deal with it.[152]

Pope Benedict XI seems to have decided that he was not strong enough to discipline Philip IV directly, but that he could and must still punish the leaders of the attack. On Holy Thursday 1304 he absolved Philip IV from excommunication, though he had shown no signs of repentance, and in the bull *Quanta ros* issued April 2 he absolved Philip of all censures pronounced against him.[153] But in May, after again condemning the attack on Boniface VIII, he

---

[150]Boase, *Boniface VIII*, pp. 348-350; Curley, *Conflict between Pope Boniface VIII and Philip IV*, pp. 153-157; Mann, *Popes in the Middle Ages*, XIX, 380-384, 386, 439; Digard, *Philippe le Bel*, II, 183.

[151]Mann, *Popes in the Middle Ages*, XIX, 386-387, 423, 437, 441-443 (quotation on p. 441); Boase, *Boniface VIII*, pp. 350-351, 355, 357; Curley, *Conflict between Pope Boniface VIII and Philip IV*, pp. 157-160, 162.

[152]Teofilo Ruiz, "Reaction to Anagni," *Catholic Historical Review*, LXV (1979), 385-401.

[153]Mann, *Popes in the Middle Ages*, XIX, 445-446; Curley, *Conflict between Pope Boniface VIII and Philip IV*, p. 162.

anathematized all who had been concerned in it; and in June he denounced the leaders of the assault by name, excommunicating them and ordering them before him for judgment during the octave of the feast of Saints Peter and Paul.[154] The bull *Flagitiosum scelus* which contains this denunciation reads like the cry of a Hebrew prophet:

> These crimes were committed publicly and under our very eyes ... crimes of *lèse-majesté*, of rebellion, of sacrilege, of felony, of theft, of rapine, the mere thought of which excites horror. Who would be so cruel as not to shed tears, so spiteful as not to be moved to compassion? What judge would be so negligent as not to be eager to proceed, or so merciful and clement as not to become severe? Security has been violated, immunity offended. One's own country has not been a protection; the domestic fireside has not been a refuge; a sovereign pontiff has been outraged; and with her spouse made a prisoner, the Church herself has been made a captive. Where, henceforth, find a safe place? What sanctuary will be respected, after the violation of that of the Roman pontiff? O inexplicable crime! O unfortunate Anagni! My the rain and the dew fall on you no more, but descending on other mountains, pass to the side of thee; because the hero has fallen, that which was invested with strength has been overcome under your eyes and you could have prevented it.[155]

The last day of the octave of the feasts of Saint Peter and Paul fell on July 7 in the year 1304. None of the leaders of the attack on Pope Boniface VIII had appeared in Rome. The next day Pope Benedict XI would pronounce his judgment upon them. But he never did so. Though he had apparently been in good health and was only in his early sixties, on July 7 he suddenly died, allegedly of dysentery. It was a death so spectacularly convenient for William of Nogaret, Sciarra Colonna, and Rainald of Supino—all men who had made it exceedingly clear that they would stop at nothing to gain their ends—that it is reasonable to have a strong suspicion of murder, though there is no proof and most historians have shied away from calling Pope Benedict XI's death other than natural.[156]

The conclave assembling at Perugia in July 1304 to elect the next Pope was split almost evenly between supporters of Boniface VIII (mostly cardinals he had appointed) and opponents, and consequently was soon entirely deadlocked. William of Nogaret, with his matchless arrogance, continued to demand an ecumenical council to review his charges against Boniface VIII, to

---

[154]Mann, *Popes in the Middle Ages*, XIX, 449-450, 452-453; Guy Mollat, *The Popes at Avignon* (New York, 1963), p. 246.

[155]Curley, *Conflict between Pope Boniface VIII and Philip IV*, p. 166.

[156]Boase, *Boniface VIII*, p. 357; Mann, *Popes in the Middle Ages*, XIX, 478; Curley, *Conflict between Pope Boniface VIII and Philip IV*, pp. 167-168. Curley does think that Pope Benedict XI was murdered.

which he had now added sacrilege, usury, homicide, and sodomy to his original counts of heresy and simony. He now denied that he had arrested Boniface or taken him prisoner, but only stopped him from doing further evil. In Perugia, the French embassy was now openly pushing the election as Pope of the French Bishop Bertrand de Got of Bordeaux, though he was not a cardinal. Since Bordeaux was in Aquitaine, the part of France still ruled by England, Bishop Bertrand was not under Philip IV's direct political control. It could therefore be argued that Bertrand would not necessarily be Philip's puppet; and in June 1305 three of the originally pro-Boniface cardinals joined the nine opposed to him to create a bare two-thirds majority, 12 of 18, to elect Bertrand. He took the name of Clement V.[157]

Though most of the cardinals pleaded with Clement V to come quickly to Rome, seeking to conciliate Philip IV he agreed to be crowned in Lyons in the French king's presence. The coronation took place November 14, 1305. During it a wall crumbled and collapsed under the weight of spectators just as the procession of high dignitaries was passing, killing Duke John of Brittany and severely injuring Philip IV's brother Charles of Valois. The new Pope was thrown from his horse, possibly receiving internal injuries, and the great ruby which Boniface VIII had placed in the pinnacle of the papal tiara in 1299 fell off and was lost or stolen.[158]

It was a grim omen. Contrary to what many later believed by historical hindsight, it does not appear that the new Pope had decided from the first not to go to Rome; but it is apparent that he was resolved not to cross the mighty and ruthless Philip IV, whom he may well have suspected of ultimate responsibility for the death of his last two predecessors. On February 1, 1306 he annulled both *Clericis laicos* and *Unam sanctam*, further specifying that the latter was not directed at the King of France, his kingdom, or his subjects. But Philip was inexorable. In May 1307, meeting with Pope Clement V at Poitiers, he renewed his demand for a canonical trial of Pope Boniface VIII as a heretic, with a further demand, if he was found guilty, to remove his name from the catalogue of the Popes, exhume his body and burn it, and scatter his ashes to the four winds. No such demand had been made in the history of the Christendom since the ghastly "Synod of the Corpse" in 897, when the body of Pope Formosus was dug up and put on trial. Furthermore, it appears that it was at this time that Philip first presented to Clement what he claimed was evidence that the famous crusading order of the Templars was involved in

---

[157]Georges Lizerand, *Clément V et Philippe le bel* (Paris, 1911), pp. 17-23; Strayer, *Philip the Fair*, pp. 281-282; Curley, *Conflict between Pope Boniface VIII and Philip IV*, pp. 168-171; Boase, *Boniface VIII*, p. 358; Holmes, *Florence, Rome, Renaissance*, pp. 183-184.

[158]Mollat, *Popes at Avignon*, pp. xvi, 67; Boase, *Boniface VIII*, pp. 243, 358-359; Curley, *Conflict between Pope Boniface VIII and Philip IV*, pp. 174-175.

occult and obscene practices, idolatry, and satanism and therefore should be suppressed. A short time afterward Jacques de Molay, grand master of the Templars, arrived in Poitiers and Pope Clement V informed him of Philip IV's accusations against him and his order.[159]

In September 1307 Philip IV issued secret orders to all his seneschals, bailiffs, deputies and other law enforcement officers throughout France, with instructions that they not be opened until the night of October 12. At dawn on the 13th, following these orders, almost all the Templars in France were arrested and their property confiscated. On the following day William of Nogaret, now Chancellor of France, called leading faculty members of the University of Paris to meet with him in a chapter room of Notre Dame cathedral to hear his charges against the Templars: that they had denied Christ and spat on crucifixes, worshipped an idol in the shape of a human head, omitted the words of consecration at Mass, and practiced sodomy. The fact that the Templars had a rule of secrecy regarding their rites and practices as an order made it easier for people to believe these fantastic accusations, which so resembled the fast-multiplying charges William of Nogaret had brought against the Pope he treacherously attacked and whose death his actions hastened.[160]

On October 19 interrogation of 138 Templar prisoners in Paris began in the cellar of their own former dwelling, supervised by Chief Inquisitor William Imbert. Within a week Grand Master de Molay and four other Templars had confessed to denying Christ and spitting on a crucifix. Pope Clement V protested vigorously and publicly on the 27th, declaring that as the Templars were a religious order, the Pope and not the King of France should decide when and who among them should be prosecuted, and by what means. After clearly implying that torture had been used to obtain the confessions, Pope Clement declared: "In this hasty action all men see, and not without reasonable cause, an insulting scorn of us and of the Roman Church."[161] But by the next month, now fully aware of Philip's relentless determination to destroy the Templars, Pope Clement's nerve failed him; he sent bulls to the King authorizing the general arrest of all Templars in France and calling for similar action in other European countries. Of the 140 Templars arrested October 12, all but four had confessed by November 24 to sacrilege and blasphemy, about three-quarters to obscenity, and about one-quarter to inciting others to sodomy.[162]

---

[159]Mollat, *Popes at Avignon*, p. 247; Curley, *Conflict between Pope Boniface VIII and Philip IV*, pp. 126, 178; Stephen Howarth, *The Knights Templar* (New York, 1982), pp. 270-272.

[160]Lizerand, *Clement V et Philippe le bel*, pp. 90-93; Mollat, *Popes at Avignon*, p. 233; Strayer, *Philip the Fair*, pp. 236, 286; Howarth, *Knights Templar*, pp. 272, 274, 277-279.

[161]Mollat, *Popes at Avignon*, p. 234; Lizerand, *Clement V et Philippe le bel*, pp. 99-100; Howarth, *Knights Templar*, p. 284.

[162]Lizerand, *Clement V et Philippe le bel*, pp. 96-98, 100-102; Mollat, *Popes at Avignon*, p. 234-235; Howarth, *Knights Templar*, p. 284.

Joseph Stalin and his secret police chiefs were to re-enact the whole repulsive spectacle in the Soviet purge trials 630 years later. A careful analysis of the charges against the Templars, demonstrating their inherent improbability, the absence of supporting evidence, and the mass of contradictions in the coerced confessions, renders it virtually certain that the Templars were as innocent as Stalin's purge victims of the crimes, plots and horrors imputed to them.[163]

In February 1308 de Molay and most of the other Templars who had confessed under torture repudiated their confessions in the presence of representatives of the Pope, and Pope Clement made another effort to take charge of the investigation and gain custody of the accused men, but predictably William of Nogaret and Philip IV fiercely opposed any restraint. When Clement continued to resist them, in July Philip renewed his demand that he convoke an ecumenical council in France, and exhume and burn the bones of Pope Boniface VIII along with condemning the Templars. He now added the highly significant demand that the Pope maintain his residence in France, not going to Italy.[164]

Pope Clement V was not a strong or a resolute man, and there is good reason to believe that he was very frightened of Philip IV (as indeed he had cause to be). He seems to have had very little of the divinely inspired courage that had sustained other Popes in situations equally, or even more difficult and dangerous. Clement V should not have accepted any of the four demands of Philip IV—to convoke a council in France, to condemn the Templars, to stay in France rather than going to Rome, and to convict the dead Pope Boniface VIII of heresy and strike his name from the list of the Popes. But it was only the last demand that he *could* not accept, since no Pope can teach heresy or be removed, alive or dead, from the catalogue of the Popes. And it was only the last demand that he did not accept.

On August 12, 1308, Pope Clement V announced to his cardinals that he would transfer the Papal court and residence indefinitely to Avignon, in a region of France called the Comtat-Venaissin which St. Louis IX had granted to the Papacy as a possession; that he would hold an ecumenical council at Vienne near Lyons, now effectively a part of France, in November 1310; and that he would agree to reopening the proceedings against Pope Boniface VIII in February 1309. He actually took up residence in Avignon in March 1309, but worked with considerable success to delay the commencement of the proceedings against Boniface VIII. In September 1309, in the bull *Laetamur in te*, he stated his personal conviction that Boniface VIII was not guilty of heresy. In December Philip sent three emissaries to Clement at Avignon—one of them

---

[163]Mollat, *Popes at Avignon*, pp. 242-245.
[164]*Ibid.*, pp. 235-236, 247; Lizerand, *Clement V et Philippe le bel*, pp. 104, 108-121, 126, 129; Howarth, *Knights Templar*, pp. 285-288.

William of Nogaret—all demanding that he speed up the process against the dead Pope. It finally began in March 1310, more than a year after it was originally scheduled, and the Pope continued his delaying tactics, postponing one of its hearings because he said he had a nosebleed, another because he had a stomach ache. William of Nogaret was the prosecutor; Pope Clement did not dare remove him from the case, though the late Pope's defenders vigorously demanded it, but he did personally refuse him Easter Communion, since he was still excommunicated for the crime at Anagni.[165]

On May 12, 1310 a French provincial Church council sentenced 54 accused Templars to execution for heresy by burning at the stake, despite the fact that all had withdrawn their earlier confessions before a papal commission, and now protested their innocence to the last.[166] It was clear that Philip IV and his ministers were determined to retain effective control of the disposition of the Templar prisoners. The reasons for their determination to destroy the Templars have never been fully clear; though they obtained some of the order's property and funds, much of it eventually went to the other crusading order, the Knights of the Hospital, which was clearly not involved in the prosecution.[167] It was probably simply an exercise in state terrorism, to impose the absolutist regime of Philip IV more firmly upon France. The astonishingly vicious prosecution of the Templars was essentially the work of the same man who had planned and carried out the assault on Pope Boniface VIII:

> The relentless pursuit of the Templars shows the same tactics as those employed against Boniface VIII and Guichard de Troyes: a war of propaganda, the summoning of the Estates, speeches to the common people, violence, charges of heresy and grotesque accusations of dealings with succubi and incubi. The whole course of the trial reveals the undisguised hand of Nogaret. . . .
> It is impossible to know for certain whether Nogaret inspired the king's policy, or was simply carrying out the orders of Philip the Fair. In any case, the king and his minister together contrived the suppression of the Templars. To achieve their ends, they exerted overbearing pressure on a pope poor in health and weak and conciliatory in character. They blackmailed Clement V by constantly threatening him with the resumption of the trial of Boniface VIII. In this way they succeeded in overcoming the pontiff's distaste for the task, and forced him to make the most regrettable concessions.[168]

---

[165]Mollat, *Popes at Avignon*, pp. xvii, 247-248; Lizerand, *Clement V et Philippe le bel*, pp. 130-132, 180-182, 184-185, 195, 215-216; Curley, *Conflict between Pope Boniface VIII and Philip IV*, pp. 179-184.

[166]Mollat, *Popes at Avignon*, p. 238; Lizerand, *Clement V et Philippe le bel*, pp. 146-147; Howarth, *Knights Templar*, pp. 298-299.

[167]Strayer, *Philip the Fair*, p. 288 argues that Philip did not expect this outcome, but rather to be able to arrange for the Templar wealth to go to a new religious order controlled by his family.

[168]Mollat, *Popes at Avignon*, pp. 245-246.

Meanwhile there had been a change of Emperors. Albert of Habsburg was assassinated in May 1308 by Duke John of Swabia and three companions on a forest path. Six months later the Count of Luxemburg, vigorous and in the prime of life, was elected Emperor Henry VII by six of the seven electoral votes. Henry obtained the cooperation of Frederick of Austria, Albert's son, despite the fact that he had been passed over in the election. Pope Clement V confirmed Henry's election in June 1309 and announced that he would crown him in St. Peter's in February 1312. The new Emperor sent messengers to the major Italian cities announcing his election and his intention to come soon to Italy to establish peace and his authority there. In September 1310 the Pope formally declared that Henry VII was worthy of the imperial crown and that Italians should support and obey him as their temporal lord.[169] Dante hailed his advent:

> This is he whom Peter, the vicar of God, exhorts us to honor, and whom Clement, the present successor of Peter, illumines with the light of the apostolic benediction; that where the spiritual ray suffices not, there the splendor of the lesser luminary may lend its light.[170]

Henry VII entered Italy in late October, and early in November the Pope announced an alliance between him and the Angevin royal family of Naples, which hopefully would heal at last the destructive division between Guelf and Ghibelline in Italy. By this time Philip IV was distinctly uneasy with Pope Clement's strong support of the vigorous new Emperor. If Henry were able to establish himself as ruler of northern Italy and allied with the king of Naples in southern Italy, this would create a strong counterweight to France as the greatest power in Christendom. Clement V would no longer be effectively controlled by the pressures Philip could bring to bear against him. He signalized this in January 1311 by sharply criticizing Philip for pillaging the property of the Templars, seizing Lyons, and challenging the rights of the Emperor, warning him not to follow the course of his ancestor and namesake Philip II Augustus at the beginning of the thirteenth century.[171]

This impressive and dramatic advent of a new Emperor intervening actively in Italy may well be the reason that at this point Philip IV abated some of his pressure on Pope Clement V and showed a willingness to settle the

---

[169]*Cambridge Medieval History*, VII, 91-93, 97; Mollat, *Popes at Avignon*, p. 190; William M. Bowsky, *Henry VII in Italy; the Conflict of Empire and City-Satte, 1310-1313* (Lincoln NE, 1960), pp. 19-22, 48; Holmes, *Florence, Rome, Renaissance*, pp. 190-191.

[170]Holmes, *Florence, Rome, Renaissance*, p. 191.

[171]Bowsky, *Henry VII in Italy*, pp. 23-25, 55; *Cambridge Medieval History*, VII, 98; Mollat, *Popes at Avignon*, pp. 190-191, 248; Strayer, *Philip the Fair*, pp. 366-367; Lizerand, *Clement V et Philippe le bel*, pp. 216-217.

disputes growing out of the assault on Pope Boniface VIII at Anagni.   In February 1311 Philip wrote to the Pope agreeing to let him decide on the disposition of the proceedings against Boniface VIII.   In other words, he was no longer insisting on his condemnation, removal from the catalogue of Popes, and the exhumation and desecration of his body.   But Philip coupled this with a renewed demand for the prompt conclusion of the proceedings against the Templars and their total condemnation.   Pope Clement V made no further attempt to save the Templars, and just after Easter 1311 formally declared the innocence of Philip IV and all other Frenchmen except William of Nogaret of the crime at Anagni.   Even Sciarra Colonna was absolved.   Nogaret was released from excommunication on condition that he make several pious pilgrimages and go to the Holy Land on the next crusade (there was no next crusade, and Nogaret never made the pilgrimages).   In effect, the Pope had dropped all action against the leaders of the attack on Pope Boniface VIII in return for Philip's willingness to leave his body and his memory in peace.[172]

It was not a satisfactory or heroic conclusion to the affair, but at least the integrity of the papacy had been upheld.   The council convening at Vienne in October 1311 continued the proceedings against the Templars, with Philip IV threatening to demand resumption of the trial of Boniface VIII if the accused Templars were allowed to make a formal defense before the council.   On March 20, 1312 Philip arrived at Vienne with an army; two days later the conciliar high commission reviewing the case against the Templars reversed itself in a secret meeting and voted by a four-fifths majority in favor of suppressing the order.   The Pope agreed, though he declared that the suppression was a "precaution" rather than an outright condemnation (much like the reason given centuries later by Pope Clement XIV for suppressing the Jesuits).   The inclusion of the archepiscopal territory of Lyons into France was tacitly approved by the Council; this and the suppression of the Templars under pressure were its only significant actions.   In March 1314 Templar Grand Master de Molay and the Templar Grand Preceptor of Normandy Geoffrey de Charnay were burned at the stake, proclaiming their innocence to the end.   A legend tells that as the flames rose around him, de Molay summoned the two men chiefly responsible for his death, Pope Clement V and King Philip IV, to the tribunal of God Himself before the year was out.   Whatever the truth of the legend, in fact both men did die that year, along with William of Nogaret.[173]

[172]Mollat, *Popes at Avignon*, pp. 248-249; Boase, *Boniface VIII*, pp. 243, 363-364; Curley, *Conflict between Pope Boniface VIII and Philip IV*, pp. 191-194; Lizerand, *Clement V et Philippe le bel*, pp. 222, 224-225; Strayer, *Philip the Fair*, pp. 294-295; Bowsky, *Henry VII in Italy*, p. 121.

[173]Mollat, *Popes at Avignon*, pp. 240-242, 249; Curley, *Conflict between Pope Boniface VIII and Philip IV*, p. 195; Lizerand, *Clement V et Philippe le bel*, pp. 234, 239-240, 245-247, 251-252, 310-311, 313, 320-321; Howarth, *Knights Templar*, pp. 13-18, 302-305, 307-308.

Philip IV left a grim memory during his last year. He condemned the wives of two of his three sons for adultery, imprisoning his daughters-in-law for the rest of their lives while mutilating and burning to death their lovers, thereby helping to assure the end of his own dynasty by lack of heirs. To say, as Joseph Strayer does, that "his behavior indicates a lack of affection between father and sons" is surely an understatement.[174] Philip IV died as he had lived, closed within himself, bitter, hating, relentless, and above all cold—cold as the mountains of the moon. The damage he had done would live with France and the Church for generations.

Emperor Henry VII had already died prematurely in August 1313, of malaria, so often fatal to Germans in Italy, while leading an army against Naples. The alliance with Naples had disintegrated along with all of Henry's grandiose dreams for Italy. The division between Guelf and Ghibelline had proved unbridgeable and the independently minded Italian cities ungovernable. Pope Clement V had withdrawn most of his support—whether because of pressure from Philip IV or Henry's manifest troubles in Italy we cannot say—and the one time Henry VII reached Rome the city was split by ferocious street fighting so that he could not get to St. Peter's, but had to settle for being crowned in St. John Lateran by his supporters in the College of Cardinals, since the Pope had refused to come. Emperor Henry VII was another victim of the nemesis of power.[175]

In this time of the twilight of the mighty, two beacons stood out on the darkening horizon. One was far north in Scotland, where a sparse but heroic population fought magnificently for their freedom against the worst Edward I of England could bring against them. Robert Bruce was their leader, grandson of one of the original contenders for the Scottish throne after the death of the Maid of Norway. In 1306 Edward had destroyed Bruce's army by a surprise attack at Methven near Perth, captured and imprisoned his wife, hanged and beheaded his brother Nigel, and captured his two sisters and hung them in iron cages from the walls of castles. Early in the following year two more of his brothers were captured and hanged, drawn, and quartered. Hiding in a cave in Galloway, near despair, Bruce watched a spider swinging back and forth at the end of a long strand of silk, again and again trying to reach the far rock wall to attach its web, learning a lesson in perseverance from the tiny creature which inspired him to continue his struggle. Wandering, sometimes alone, pursued by bloodhounds, Bruce was nevertheless able to gather a ragged but resolute army around him and hold out until the terrible old king died in camp in July 1307. His son and successor Edward II, fortunately for Scotland, was not much like him. After years of warfare Bruce won a famous and decisive victory over

---

[174]Strayer, *Philip the Fair*, p. 19; Pegues, *Lawyers of the Last Capetians*, p. 58.
[175]Bowsky, *Henry VII in Italy*, pp. 98-204.

Edward II at the Battle of Bannockburn in 1314 that assured Scotland's independence for the next three hundred years.[176]

The other beacon was lit by a poet, not a warrior: Dante Alighieri of Florence. Expelled from his beloved city in 1302, condemned *in absentia* to death by burning and an exile for the rest of his life, profoundly disappointed by the failure of Emperor Henry VII in Italy, Dante—guided by his shining vision of Beatrice, whom he had loved so much and who had died so young—did not succumb to bitterness, but rose to a summit of beauty and glory rarely matched and never exceeded in Western literature, in the *Divine Comedy* which he began to write probably in 1307, completing the "Inferno" and beginning the "Purgatorio" by 1314.[177] In addition to its extraordinary literary merits, the *Divine Comedy* depicts the world-view of the High Middle Ages with unmatched thoroughness and clarity.[178] That world-view is shaped above all by the thought of St. Thomas Aquinas. In his book *De Monarchia*, written during Emperor Henry VII's ill-fated sojourn in Italy from 1311 to 1313, Dante sums up that world-view with a serenity all the more striking when contrasted with the destructive tumult around him, its Christian essence forever immune to the nemesis of power:

> Ineffable providence has set two ends for man to strive towards: the beatitude of this life, which consists in the operation of his own virtue and is figured in the earthly paradise, and the beatitude of eternal life, which consists in the enjoyment of the vision of God, to which man's own virtue cannot ascend unless assisted by divine light, which is to be understood by the heavenly paradise.... We come to the first by the teaching of philosophy, if we follow it by exercising the moral and intellectual virtues; to the second by spiritual teaching, which transcends human reason, if we follow it by exercising the theological virtues of faith, hope and charity.[179]

---

[176]Barrow, *Robert Bruce*, pp. 216, 228-231, 240-242, 245, 290-332; Scott, *Robert Bruce*, pp. 81-82, 86-87, 90, 93-102.

[177]Holmes, *Florence, Rome, Renaissance*, pp. 233-249.

[178]See C. S. Lewis, *The Discarded Image* (Cambridge, England, 1967).

[179]*De monarchia* III, 15, cited in Holmes, *Florence, Rome, Renaissance*, pp. 249-250.

9
Popes Away From Rome
(1314-1347)

(Popes John XXIII 1316-34; Benedict XII 1334-42; Clement VI 1342-52)

"St. Peter's godchild, Avignon, who saw the saint's bark ride at anchor in her haven and who bears his keys at her battlemented girdle..." — Alphonse Daudet[1]

The move of the Popes to Avignon in France, where they maintained their residence for the seventy-two years from the consecration of Clement V to the return of Gregory XI to Rome, was a grave error of judgment, though not the unmitigated evil excoriated by Petrarch in his furious passages calling Avignon a "hell upon earth."[2] For the Pope belongs in Rome, as every visitor to St. Peter's knows. There lie the bones of the prince of the Apostles; there was the seat of the ancient empire won for Christ under the sign of the cross in the sky that was given to Constantine. Wherever the Pope may go, wandering or fleeing or driven, he remains the Bishop of Rome—and never was Rome more shamefully neglected than during these seventy-two years when ancient buildings were quarried for their stone and famous churches gaped open so that cattle ambled through in the very naves of St. Peter's and the Church of St. John Lateran.[3] In the tumults of the years we have been chronicling, many Popes had been unable to maintain a continuous residence in Rome; but none remained far away for long. The definitive transfer of their seat to Avignon by an unbroken series of French Popes, with only an occasional vague mention of the possibility of returning to Rome, not only aroused profound resentment in Italy but called into question the Pope's impartiality as the spiritual leader of Christendom in every country whose interests clashed with those of France—most notably England as the Hundred Years War began its long and bloody course.

Most of the Avignon Popes were not, however, in fact excessively deferential to the kings of France. Even Clement V, weak and often overborne by Philip the Fair, was not his creature and resisted him to the best of his

---

[1]Cited in Guy Mollat, *The Popes at Avignon* (New York, 1963), p. 279.
[2]Ludwig von Pastor, *History of the Popes*, Volume I (London, 1923), p. 64.
[3]*Ibid.*, I, 69.

limited ability. Clement V's successors John XXII and Benedict XII were no man's puppets, as even a cursory review of their character, public statements and policy makes very clear. Of all the Avignon Popes, only Clement VI comes close to fitting the scenario (mostly drawn by angry Italians) of the Avignon Popes as lackeys of Paris. But their official residence exposed even the best of the Avignon Popes to the constant suspicion of such subservience, accentuated by the splendor in which they lived and what Ludwig von Pastor calls the "deplorable worldliness" of a backwater provincial town suddenly become a new Rome, the destination of a steady flow of rich ambassadors and rich gifts from all over Christendom.[4]

The problem was accentuated by the fact that, throughout the years the Popes were in Avignon, return to Rome was not an easy option even when it might be sincerely desired. The bitter hostility of most Italians to the French Popes would indubitably place them in serious physical danger if they came to live in Rome, or indeed anywhere in Italy; and Italy, still the prey of the endless strife of Ghibelline and Guelf superimposed on its division into many quarrelling city-states, was in serious disorder with several substantial wars usually going on at any given time, both among cities and within them. A long-range undertaking was required to pacify Rome and its immediate surroundings, begin the restoration of the city, and create good will toward the Pope. Return to Rome had to become a fixed papal policy with a high priority. For the first fifty years of the Avignon papacy there was no such policy.

Partly due to this displacement of the papacy, but also for other reasons, Christendom in the first half of the fourteenth century was in a condition of malaise. There were no great saints, and no temporal leaders with broad vision. The ablest was Edward III of England, a splendid knight and remarkable strategist, but he rarely if ever looked beyond the interests of his own crown and kingdom. The four kings of France who succeeded Philip the Fair lacked both ability and vision. The dream of a great crusade, long a sustaining and uniting enthusiasm of Christendom, was dying. The Holy Roman Emperor was again at war with the Pope. Only in Spain did crusading sparks still fly up into flame; after two long royal minorities during which Castile was preserved from anarchy or disintegration only by the moral prestige of the widow of Sancho the Fierce, the strong and serene Maria de Molina, her grandson Alfonso XI the Avenger resumed the Reconquest and made notable advances in it.[5] The summer of the year 1315 was marked by exceptionally heavy rainfall; almost constant rains saturated the ground and the absence of sun greatly inhibited the growth of crops, leading to severe famine whose effects, particularly in northern Europe,

---

[4]*Ibid.*, I, 59-67.

[5]There is no biography, or adequate coverage of this remarkable woman in English. Even in Spanish it is thin. See Mercedes Gaibrois de Ballesteros, *Maria de Molina, tres veces reina* (Madrid, 1936, 1967).

lasted for several years.[6]

Under these circumstances, the history of the first half of the fourteenth century has a rather formless character. Despite the handicap of their Avignon residence, the Popes were able to maintain and even increase the centralization of the government of the Church; but Pope John XXII, approaching his ninetieth year, took one of the most imprudent actions in the history of the papacy by bringing a heresy up for discussion with the statement that he thought it true, but was not sure. Later he recanted it on his deathbed. The only great causes were the Reconquest in southern Spain led by Alfonso XI and the attempts to achieve and to resist Edward III's personal and national ambitions in Scotland and in France, which while dramatic had at this time no great significance for Christendom as a whole. In the east Catholic Poland was growing in unity and strength, but the Byzantine empire was steadily weakening and that strange and dangerous people, the Ottoman Turks, soon to build an empire, made their first appearance on the historical stage. Through these disparate developments we shall make our way.

Pope Clement V died two weeks after Easter in 1314. The conclave to elect his successor assembled at Carpentras in the Venaissin just a few miles from Avignon early in May. From the beginning it was apparent that the cardinals were so badly split that no candidate could gain a majority, let alone two-thirds. First there was a party of ten cardinals from Gascony, which had been Pope Clement V's home territory and was ruled by the English King Edward II but under feudal homage to the King of France; these cardinals had been appointed by Clement V and wished to elect one of his two nephews Pope. A second party consisting of all the seven remaining Italian cardinals and three French cardinals supported Cardinal Guillaume de Mandagout of Languedoc in southern France; a third consisting of six French cardinals unconnected with Gascony remained uncommitted. When the deadlock had continued into July, Gascon gangs appeared in Carpentras and attacked the houses where the Italian cardinals were staying, killing some Italians, setting fire to parts of the little town and looting others. The Italian cardinals consequently fled from Carpentras, refused to return, and declared they would not recognize any Pope chosen in an election in which they did not take part.[7]

The Gascon and Italian cardinals continued to defy one another throughout the remainder of 1314 and the whole of 1315, unable even to agree on a place to reconvene the conclave. Finally in March 1316, under a solemn promise that there would be no more violence and that they would not be forcibly confined, the cardinals agreed to meet again at Lyons under the protection of Prince Philip of Poitiers, the brother of King Louis X of France.

---

[6]May McKisack, *The Fourteenth Century, 1307-1399* (Oxford History of England) (Oxford, 1959), pp. 49-50.
[7]Mollat, *Popes at Avignon*, pp. xviii, 9-11.

Just as the cardinals were at long last about to resume their conclave in June Louis X, the colorless eldest son of Philip the Fair, suddenly died at a relatively young age. He had a daughter who was still a little girl, but no sons; however, his widow was pregnant. If she bore a son who lived, he would be the undoubted successor; if not, or if she bore a daughter, Prince Philip might succeed since France had never had a royal minority or a reigning queen since Hugh Capet founded the ruling dynasty more than three hundred years before. Philip wanted very much to be king, but he also wanted to influence and if possible control the election of the Pope. Since he could not be in both Paris and Lyons at the same time, he broke his promise and shut up the cardinals in the Dominican convent at Lyons on June 28 hoping that would pressure them into making a decision. It seems that it did.[8]

All through July various candidates were proposed but failed to gain the necessary two-thirds majority. Finally the Italian cardinals split between adherents of the ubiquitous Colonna and Orsini. The Gascons and Napoleon Orsini then gave their support to Jacques Duèse, who had held a multitude of offices both secular and religious including Bishop of Avignon and chancellor of the kingdom of Naples. He was favored by Prince Philip and appeared sickly at 72 and unlikely to live long, so the cardinals believed they would have another choice soon. (In fact he was extraordinarily vigorous and lived to be ninety.) On August 7 the remaining opposition to him collapsed and he was elected unanimously, taking the name of John XXII. Despite the unanimous vote, many cardinals—including some Gascons—remained dissatisfied with him, which suggests that Prince Philip may have brought more pressure to bear on the conclave than was recorded. There were even reported plots to poison the new Pope. But if Prince Philip wanted a subservient Pope, he miscalculated. Pope John XXII was a decisive (though sometimes very imprudent) and courageous man, very much alive to the importance of the full independence of the head of the Church, and also a highly efficient administrator.[9]

Consecrated at Lyons September 5, the new Pope immediately had to confront two contenders for Holy Roman Emperor. Following the sudden death of Emperor Henry VII of Luxemburg in Italy in 1313, the seven-man college of imperial electors had split five to two in October 1314 in favor of Duke Louis of Bavaria over Frederick of Habsburg, Duke of Austria, son and heir of Emperor Albert and grandson of the loyal Catholic Emperor Rudolf. Louis had been crowned Emperor Louis IV at Aachen, at the traditional place and with the traditional ceremony; but Frederick defiantly had himself crowned by the Archbishop of Cologne (the traditional crowner of Emperors) at Bonn. At that time the papal office was vacant; when John XXII became Pope, he

---

[8]*Ibid.*, p. 11; E. Perroy, *The Hundred Years War* (London, 1951), pp. 69-72.
[9]Mollat, *Popes at Avignon*, pp. 11-15.

clearly preferred Frederick, whose family history demonstrated consistent support for Pope and Church. But the greater part of Germany accepted the choice of the majority of the electors, and John XXII's only action at this time was mildly to urge the two claimants to settle their differences peacefully.[10]

However, in the following year John XXII issued a decretal claiming the right to govern Italy during a vacancy of the imperial office, maintaining that a vacancy now existed because he had not yet confirmed either Louis or Frederick as Emperor. In view of the recent history of the papacy and the conclave to elect John XXII, when so much hostility to Italians had been shown, Italians were especially unlikely to look with favor on such a claim, but the Pope firmly pressed it. He further proclaimed that those who had been appointed to office in Italy by the late Emperor Henry VII must now be confirmed by him. In December 1317 he began canonical proceedings against Matteo Visconti of Milan, probably the most powerful individual in Italy north of the kingdom of Naples, for continuing to use the title of imperial vicar. Visconti had led a campaign of Ghibellines against Guelfs in the spring despite the pleas of two papal legates in northern Italy that he keep the peace. He dropped the title of imperial vicar but kept his power and his aggressive policy. The Pope excommunicated him as a usurper.[11]

Meanwhile in France the widow of King Louis X had borne a son, who was King John I for five days, and then died. Prince Philip pushed aside the claims of Louis's little daughter Joan and on January 9, 1317 was crowned King Philip V. The next month he had an assembly of nobles in Paris officially proclaim that "a woman cannot succeed to the kingdom of France." This was to have more significance in the near future than anyone imagined at the time.[12]

In Great Britain the English under the ineffective King Edward II remained unable to reverse the verdict of the Battle of Bannockburn. The Scots harassed England's northern counties and in 1315 sent an army to Ireland under Edward Bruce, brother of their King Robert Bruce, who won several victories and cut a swath of destruction across northern Ireland. In May 1316 Edward Bruce was crowned King of Ireland at Dundalk.[13] The Irish had deep and long-lasting grievances against the English invaders; in 1317 Donnell O'Neill, supporting Edward Bruce, voiced those grievances in a remarkable petition to Pope John XXII calling his attention to the blatant English

[10]*Ibid.*, pp. 79, 206; *The Cambridge Medieval History*, ed. J. R. Tanner, Ch. Previté-Orton and Z. N. Brooke, Volume VII (1932), p. 114.

[11]Mollat, *Popes at Avignon*, pp. 78, 80-81; Dorothy Muir, *A History of Milan under the Visconti* (London, 1924), pp. 14-16.

[12]Perroy, *Hundred Years War*, pp. 72-73.

[13]*A New History of Ireland*, Volume II: "Medieval Ireland, 1169-1534," ed. Art Cosgrove (Oxford, 1987), pp. 282-287; G. W. S. Barrow, *Robert Bruce and the Community of the Realm of Scotland* (Berkeley CA, 1965), p. 339; McKisack, *Fourteenth Century*, p. 43.

discrimination against the Irish, and the contempt for Irish customs and for the
rights of the Irish church displayed by the English government, in violation of
Pope Adrian IV's bill *Laudabiliter* which Henry II had used to justify his initial
invasion and which the English continued to cite:

> Because of these wrongs and of numberless others which it is beyond
> the power of the human mind to readily understand and also on account of
> the kings of England and their officials and the perennial treachery of the
> English of the middle nation who were bound by decree of the papal curia
> to rule our nation with justice and moderation and have made its
> destruction their wicked objective, and in order to throw off the cruel and
> intolerable yoke of their slavery and to recover our native liberty which for
> a time through them we had lost, we are forced to wage war to the death
> against them.[14]

The Pope turned O'Neill's letter over to Edward II and asked him to look
into the charges, and it does seem there was some easing of English oppression
in Ireland as the century went on. But as ever the Irish were unable to unite,
and the devastation wrought by Edward Bruce turned many Irishmen against
him. In October 1318 he died in battle near the place where he was crowned.[15]

The Scots had a stronger sense of national unity and outstanding
leadership in their King Robert Bruce. At Arbroath in April 1320 the
noblemen of Scotland declared to the Pope their loyalty to Robert Bruce and
their determination never to accept English rule. Pope John XXII replied to
them promptly though evasively in August. In October 1322, at Byland in
Yorkshire, Robert Bruce won another striking victory, routing an English army
with a howling charge by his Highlanders down a Yorkshire moorland ridge;
King Edward II barely escaped capture and the Scots seized all his personal
belongings, equipment, and treasure. A thirteen-year truce between England
and Scotland was signed the next spring. Though Edward II still refused to
recognize Scottish independence, he promised not to hinder the Scots from
obtaining absolution from the Pope and the lifting of the excommunication of
Robert Bruce and the interdict placed on their country as rebels against their
so-called rightful overlord, the King of England. Edward II broke his promise,
but the next year Pope John XXII began addressing Robert Bruce as king of
Scotland for the first time. However, it was five more years before the Pope
finally relented and lifted all ecclesiastical penalties against Scotland and its
king and people.[16]

Pope John XXII displayed a much more sympathetic interest and a

[14]*New History of Ireland*, II, 349-350.

[15]*Ibid.*, II, 292-294, 301-302; McKisack, *Fourteenth Century*, p. 44.

[16]Barrow, *Robert Bruce*, pp. 345-346, 353-355, 424-429; Irene M. Davis, *The Black
Douglas* (Boston, 1974), p. 151; McKisack, *Fourteenth Century*, p. 75; Mollat, *Popes at
Avignon*, p. 262.

keener sense of justice in his strong and continuing concern for the development and rights of the Catholic kingdom of Poland, long cursed like Ireland by disunity and strife. In the evocative image of Norman Davies, "for the past two centuries the struggle of trying to reunite the Piast principalities [of Poland] resembled a game of primitive pin-ball, where each player sought to roll half a dozen marbles into their numbered sockets whilst his adversaries, as they barged and rocked the table, tried to do the same."[17] Persevering through a welter of civil wars and assassinations in which he was beaten again and again and exiled for several years, a prince named Wladyslaw Lokietek had finally secured Cracow in 1306. Though hard hit by a rebellion in Gdansk (Danzig) and Pomerania two years later, in which the rebels requested and received help from the so-called crusading order of the Teutonic Knights (here fighting against fellow Catholics) and overwhelmed troops loyal to him, Lokietek had gained recognition as "Duke of all Greater Poland" by 1315. Since the assassination of King Vaclav III in 1306 Poland had not had a king. Wladyslaw sent ambassadors to Avignon who in 1319 obtained secret letters from Pope John XXII consenting to his coronation (he did not wish to make his position public yet because of predictable opposition from the Teutonic Knights and their strong supporter, the famous knight-errant King John of Bohemia). He also appointed three Polish bishops to judge whether the Teutonic Knights had a right to control Pomerania, who two years later ordered the Knights to return Pomerania to Poland and pay Poland an indemnity of 30,000 marks. On January 20, 1320 Lokietek was crowned King of Poland at Cracow's hallowed Wawel cathedral.[18]

These years also saw the emergence of the core of a new European nation with the formation of the Swiss Confederation following a surprising victory by the Swiss mountaineers of the three Forest Cantons over the army of Duke Leopold of Austria (brother of imperial claimant Frederick) at Morgarten in November 1315. Leopold recognized their independence three years later.[19]

At the beginning of 1322 Pope John XXII laid Milan under an interdict after a final excommunication of its lord Matteo Visconti as a heretic because of his uncompromising defiance of the Pope; he was also charged with sorcery. Crusading indulgences were granted to those who took up arms against him, and imperial claimant Frederick of Austria appeared in Italy with two thousand troops. Under this kind of pressure the leading citizens of Milan agreed that Matteo Visconti must go; he was compelled to abdicate in favor of his son Galeazzo. The papal legate Cardinal de Poujet secured Parma and Piacenza in Lombardy and the next February opened a campaign against the Lombard

---

[17]Norman Davies, *God's Playground; a History of Poland* (New York, 1984), I, 93.

[18]*Ibid.*, I, 94-95; Paul W. Knoll, *The Rise of the Polish Monarchy* (Chicago, 1972), pp. 14-40, 43-44.

[19]*Cambridge Medieval History*, VII, 115, 191.

Ghibellines, soon laying siege to Milan.   Meanwhile, in September 1322, imperial claimant Louis and his close ally John of Bohemia defeated and captured Frederick of Austria in a battle at Mühldorf in Austria. Many of Frederick's supporters came over to Louis at this point, but Pope John XXII set his face against him. He made up his mind to reject him as Emperor, despite the objections of many of his cardinals, and in October of the following year demanded that Louis give up his imperial claim and annul all his acts as Emperor, while informing his subjects that they should withdraw obedience to Louis if he did not step down.[20]

It remains unclear why Pope John XXII took this momentous step. Certainly Louis of Bavaria had given far less provocation than earlier imperial challengers of the papacy such as Henry IV, Henry V, Frederick Barbarossa and Frederick II. Indeed, it is not easy to see how he had given any provocation at all. By all indications he had won election fairly with a majority of the votes. His allies in Italy, the Ghibellines, were strongly hostile to the Pope; but the Pope was no longer in Italy, so they presented no direct threat to him. Despite all the attempts of imperial propagandists to deny it, papal recognition was indeed required to become a lawful Holy Roman Emperor; why else had so many Emperors, including all those most hostile to the papacy, sought coronation in Rome?   But why did John XXII so stubbornly withhold recognition and confirmation from Louis of Bavaria?

The most likely explanation is the continuing strife in Italy, which seemed to have no end—the searing division of Guelf and Ghibelline which cut like a red-hot knife through almost every Italian city. The Italians might not like John XXII, but he wanted peace among them, and he did consider seriously at various points in his pontificate the possibility of returning to Rome. He may simply have concluded that there would never be peace in Italy until Pope and Emperor were in full harmony; and Louis of Bavaria had shown little interest in acting in concert with the Pope in Italy.

Be that as it may, it is evident that Louis himself had little or no idea why he had been rejected. He was a rather stolid man, no natural rebel; he was even willing to consider abdication if it could be done without humiliation, but he would not submit unconditionally to the papal demand.[21] Casting about for

---

[20]Mollat, *Popes at Avignon*, pp. 87, 91-95; Muir, *Visconti*, pp. 17-23, 25-26; *Cambridge Medieval History*, VII, 115-119. The final requirement in this declaration by Pope John XXII went well beyond the original formulation by Pope St. Gregory VII of the doctrine of the Pope as moral judge of kings and emperors, who could dispense his subjects from their allegiance to such rulers judged unfit, but not require them to revolt. Presumably Pope John XXII justified this by his position that Louis was no Emperor at all since the Pope refused to recognize him as such.

[21]In January 1326 Louis declared that he was willing to abdicate as Emperor in favor of Frederick of Habsburg (whom he had released from prison the previous year), if Frederick would confirm Louis' son in possession of Brandenburg and give him general

intellectual support and a voice more articulate than his own, he hit upon a unique mind—a man out of his time, a precursor and portent of things to come: the brilliant and iconoclastic Marsilio of Padua, an Italian physician and political theorist.[22]

Marsilio's *Defensor pacis* was nothing less than a rejection of all the independent and God-given authority of the Catholic Church as an institution. Instead of recognizing the spiritual order as higher than the temporal, as every writer of Christendom since Constantine had taken for granted however they might see the interaction of the two orders, Marsilio placed the spiritual order lower. Christ, he said, had not established a Church nor granted any authority to the Pope. Whatever authority the Pope possessed was held only by grant from the temporal order, specifically by legislative bodies selected by vote. An ecumenical council was superior to the Pope, and should be composed not only of clergy but of laymen elected by the people. Scripture was the only religious authority and the council should decide how it was to be interpreted when major differences arose. An ecumenical council could only be called by the state; the Pope and all the clergy were subject to the state. The Pope could only have whatever authority the state and a council chose to give him. They could appoint, suspend, or depose him. The property of the Church should not be exempt from taxation. The state should control its ultimate disposition.[23]

Such a doctrine leads straight to the Protestant revolt, and straight through it to the French Revolution. Christendom's deadliest internal enemy had shown its face. All that Marsilio advocated sooner or later came to pass. Even Emperor Frederick II had not gone this far. It was the first appearance of the world-view that was to destroy the medieval synthesis, and ultimately (in the late twentieth century) to destroy Christendom itself as a public order.

There is no reason to believe that Louis of Bavaria grasped any substantial part of the true nature of what Marsilio was recommending. He saw only that it was a way of upholding his right to be Emperor and his authority in Germany, and a condemnation of the Pope who was denying him both. (Marsilio called Pope John XXII "the great dragon and old serpent").[24] In similar fashion Louis suddenly became the champion of the "Spiritual Franciscans," who insisted that the possession of property by the Church or clergy was contrary to the command of Christ, and rejected the authority of the Pope when he denied it. Pope John XXII, who had brought great wealth to

---

support; Pope John XXII would not accept even this arrangement, but continued to demand Louis' unconditional submission and abdication (*Cambridge Medieval History*, VII, 121-122).

[22]Mollat, *Popes at Avignon*, pp. 96-97; Ferdinand Schevill, *Medieval and Renaissance Florence* (New York, 1961), I, 206.

[23]Von Pastor, *History of the Popes*, I, 76-81; Mollat, *Popes at Avignon*, pp. 96-97; Schevill, *Florence*, I, 206.

[24]Von Pastor, *History of the Popes*, I, 76.

Avignon and lived luxuriously there though he does not seem to have been personally avaricious,[25] gave particular offense to the "Spiritual Franciscans" who in turn gave particular offense to him. He had condemned them and their practices in two bulls in 1317 and another in 1323.[26] In his Appeal of Sachsenhausen issued in May 1324, Louis of Bavaria took their side, accusing John XXII of a fixed determination to destroy "perfect poverty," along with denying the necessity of papal recognition of the Holy Roman Emperor, calling the Pope an oppressor in Italy and even a heretic, and demanding a council.[27]

But neither hard words nor soft would move Pope John XXII from the position he had taken. On July 4, 1324 he declared Louis was not and would never be Emperor, and that he would be deprived of Bavaria and all his other fiefs if he did not give up his imperial claims by October 1. For more than two years Louis sought a compromise. Frederick of Austria was amenable, but the Pope was not. Once convinced of this, in 1327 Louis appeared with Marsilio of Padua at an assembly of Ghibellines in Trent on the northern border of Italy. He declared Pope John XXII unworthy of his office and withdrew recognition of him as Pope. He swore to lead an army into Italy and to Rome. The Pope responded immediately, ordering Louis to leave Italy within two months and appear at Avignon on October 1 for sentence, depriving him of his imperial fiefs, condemning him as a public supporter of heretics, and excommunicating Marsilio of Padua along with a number of Louis' other closest associates.[28]

In May 1327 the angry imperial claimant came to Milan where he received the storied old Iron Crown of Lombardy. The next January the Pope proclaimed a crusade against him (there were still traces of the crusading ideal left, enough to captivate a king of France in the next decade, but such proclamations did not improve their chances of survival). That same month Louis arrived in Rome and was crowned in St. Peter's. Marsilio of Padua was in attendance. None other than old "Sciarra" Colonna, who had done his best to take the life of Pope Boniface VIII, placed the imperial diadem on Louis' head. We may see the hands of Marsilio and Sciarra in Louis' next and wildest statement a few days later, declaring Pope John XXII "deposed by Christ" and deprived of clerical orders by *Louis'* authority. An antipope was set up, the "Spiritual Franciscan" friar Pietro Rainalducci of Corbara, who took the name "Nicholas V." Marsilio was put in charge of Rome, where he persecuted the clergy who refused to cooperate with Louis and with him, and fed the prior of the Augustinians at San Trifone to the lions in the Capitol, just as the persecuting emperors of Rome had done. But in August, the traditional dying month for Germans in Rome, they all left the city, while the antipope amused

[25]Mollat, *Popes at Avignon*, p. 14.
[26]*Ibid.*, p. 16.
[27]*Ibid.*, p. 26; *Cambridge Medieval History*, III, 120-121.
[28]Mollat, *Popes at Avignon*, pp. 97-98; *Cambridge Medieval History*, VII, 119, 123.

himself by condemning a dummy of Pope John XXII as a heretic, depriving it of its insignia of office and "turning it over to the secular arm."[29]

In the year 1328 the Franciscan philosopher William of Ockham, whose nominalist doctrine that the attributes and actions of God were impenetrable to human reason, therefore in effect denying the whole science of theology which St. Thomas Aquinas had devoted his life to advancing, escaped from Avignon where he had been imprisoned for heresy because of his doctrine. After going first to Italy, by 1330 he had made his way to Emperor Louis' court at Münich. Evidently he found its intellectual atmosphere pleasing, for he remained there for the rest of his life, some twenty years.[30]

Meanwhile there had been unsettling political changes in both England and France. Edward II, an essentially incompetent ruler, had virtually turned his government over to a father and son both named Hugh Despenser. The Despensers' accumulation of lands for themselves and their virtually complete control of access to the king increasingly angered the rest of the nobility. In August 1321 the barons marched on London and forced Edward to banish both Despensers from the kingdom, an action hitherto taken only against foreign-born noblemen. But neither Despenser actually left English-ruled territory; the elder went to Bordeaux in Gascony, part of the hereditary domain in France of the English monarchs whose title derived from that of Eleanor of Aquitaine, while the younger found refuge in one of the English Channel ports where he was protected by some of the King's men. In December Edward revoked the decree for their exile; in March 1322 he proclaimed the leading nobleman in the country, the Earl of Lancaster, and his chief adherents rebels and traitors for negotiating with the Scots. Taken by surprise, Lancaster was captured after a battle, convicted under martial law with no opportunity to defend himself, and executed. So were 62 other noblemen; the vindictive Edward (or Despenser) also imprisoned many of their wives and children and even several of their mothers. The nation sullenly accepted this outcome for the time being, but resentment against the bumbling but vicious king was now too deep to be eradicated.[31]

In the same year as Edward II's executions, King Philip V of France died as unexpectedly as had his brother. Like his brother, he left no sons. Though he had five daughters instead of his brother's one, it was now accepted in France that women could not inherit the throne. Therefore Philip's brother Charles took the throne without protest as King Charles IV. He too had no sons, but he was young and could still beget them. No one imagined that all

[29]Mollat, *Popes at Avignon*, pp. 206, 208-210, 212-213, 216-217; *Cambridge Medieval History*, VII, 123-124.

[30]McKisack, *Fourteenth Century*, p. 509.

[31]Natalie Fryde, *The Tyranny and Fall of Edward II, 1321-1326* (Cambridge, England, 1979), pp. 27-64; McKisack, *Fourteenth Century*, pp. 61-70.

three of the sons of Philip the Fair would die young without male heirs—though just that happened.[32]

The following year Charles IV summoned Edward II to do homage for the province of Gascony.[33] This curious arrangement had a long history. When William the Conqueror, Duke of Normandy, took over England in 1066, he became king in that country while still duke in France. As Duke of Normandy he owed feudal homage to the King of France; as King of England he owed no homage to anyone. A hundred and fifty years later England's King John of ill fame lost Normandy, but maintained a claim in southwestern France (Gascony, part of the ancient Roman province of Aquitaine) derived from his mother, Eleanor of Aquitaine. The later peace treaty between France and England arranged by St. Louis IX provided for the surrender of English claims to Normandy but the retention of their rule in Gascony. However, for that rule—like William and his immediate successors in Normandy—they were still expected to swear fealty to the King of France. Only the King of England among all European kings did homage to another king for part of his royal domain. Neither he nor the Kings of France were comfortable with this strange situation. The King of France wanted to bring Gascony under his direct rule, while the King of England wished to avoid the humiliating ceremony of homage.

In February 1324 Charles IV formally condemned and outlawed the English seneschal in Gascony, Sir Ralph Basset, and an aggressive Gascon nobleman, Raymond-Berard of Montpezat, for seizing a village near Montpezat which the French claimed as theirs. When the English would give Charles IV no satisfaction in this matter he declared Gascony confiscated in July and sent an army there which razed the castle of Montpezat to the ground. Edward II sent his wife Isabelle, Charles IV's sister, to remonstrate with him, and Pope John XXII intervened urging peace. Charles accepted a six months' truce and declared himself willing to restore most of Gascony to England if Edward II did proper homage for it. At first Edward agreed, but then he balked, apparently at the urging of the Despensers who did not wish to accompany him to France but also did not wish him to go out of their direct contact. Charles was persuaded to accept Edward II's son, Crown Prince Edward, to make the homage in his father's place, which the young Prince did in September.[34]

Queen Isabelle of England had long been deeply resentful of her fickle and incompetent royal husband, who had snubbed her for his favorite Piers Gaveston (with whom he appears to have had a homosexual relationship) immediately after their marriage, and allowed the Despensers to confiscate her estates because of alleged doubts about her loyalty in the event of a French

---

[32]Perroy, *Hundred Years War*, p. 73.

[33]McKisack, *Fourteenth Century*, p. 108.

[34]Jonathan Sumption, *The Hundred Years War; Trial by Battle* (Philadelphia, 1990), pp. 91-92, 95-96, 98, 100; Fryde, *Fall of Edward II*, pp. 146-149.

invasion.[35] Once in France with her son and out of the clutches of the Despensers, she showed no desire to return to England, telling her brother the King of France "that her marriage had been broken and that she must live as a widow until the Despensers had been removed from power."[36] Though scandalizing her brother and many others by openly cohabiting with the dashing Roger Mortimer, a lord of the Welsh marches and associate of the rebel Duke of Lancaster who had become only the second man to escape successfully from the Tower of London, she quickly became the repository of the hopes of many in England who hated the Despensers and despised Edward II.[37]

Turned out of France by her embarrassed brother, Isabelle went to Hainault in the Low Countries whose Count William II gave her 700 troops in return for the betrothal of Prince Edward to his daughter Philippa. With this small force and some English adventurers led by Mortimer and Edward II's brother the Duke of Kent, she landed on the coast of Essex in September 1326. Edward II ignominiously fled and the people of London rose in Isabelle's favor, brutally murdering Bishop Stapledon of Essex, the Royal Treasurer and former guardian of Prince Edward. The Archbishop of Canterbury barely escaped. Edward and Hugh Despenser Jr. were tracked down and captured at Neath Abbey on the Welsh border. Tried, condemned and executed in a single day, Despenser was hanged on a gallows fifty feet high, then drawn and quartered. Under enormous pressure from a delegation sent by Parliament and led by the very political Bishop Adam Orleton of Hereford, pitiful King Edward II "with tears and sighs" agreed in January 1327 to abdicate in favor of his fourteen-year-old son, who thus became King Edward III.[38]

The ex-king was shut away in prison and in September was said to have died, probably by murder.[39] An extraordinary document found centuries later hidden in the binding of a cartulary of the diocese of Maguelonne in France and preserved in the departmental archives of Hérault suggests that he may have escaped or been let go, to wander disconsolately to Avignon and finally to a hermitage in Italy where he died several years later. Be that as it may, Edward II was probably the most complete failure of any king in English history—which still does not justify his deposition, done without any legal or constitutional warrant.[40]

---

[35]McKisack, *Fourteenth Century*, pp. 2-10; Sumption, *Hundred Years War*, pp. 97-98.
[36]McKisack, *Fourteenth Century*, p. 82.
[37]Michael Packe, *King Edward III*, ed. L. C. B. Seaman (London, 1983), pp. 18-19, 25; McKisack, *Fourteenth Century*, pp. 82-83; Fryde, *Fall of Edward II*, pp. 160-161, 173; Sumption, *Hundred Years War*, p. 101.
[38]Fryde, *Fall of Edward II*, pp. 185-189, 191-194, 196-199; McKisack, *Fourteenth Century*, pp. 83-91; Roy Martin Haines, *The Church and Politics in Fourteenth-Century England; the Career of Adam Orleton* (Cambridge, 1978), pp. 161-177.
[39]McKisack, *Fourteenth Century*, pp. 94-95; Fryde, *Fall of Edward II*, pp. 202-206.
[40]Fryde, *Fall of Edward II*, pp. 200-206.

Edward III was made of different stuff. Fourteen years old—too young to rule—when his father was overthrown, even then he asserted himself by refusing to accept the crown until his father had consented to it.[41] His mother and Roger Mortimer set up a regency with the aid of the new Duke of Lancaster and made a peace with Scotland (the Treaty of Edinburgh) which explicitly recognized Scottish independence.[42] When the third successive King of France died without male issue—Charles IV in February 1328—Isabelle made no immediate claim to the throne either in her own name or in her son's, though she was now the only surviving child of Philip the Fair, thereby allowing the crown of France to pass to Count Philip of Valois, the nearest relative to Charles IV in the all-male line of descent.[43] Philip now claimed (falsely) that French law neither permitted a woman to rule nor the royal title to pass through a woman; only later, after much searching of ancient records, did French jurists locate the long-forgotten tradition that such had been the law of the Salian Franks before their conversion to Christianity eight hundred years in the past.[44] Later events strongly suggest that the young Edward III deeply resented these failures to claim what he regarded as his rights to rule Scotland and France, since he spent much of his reign trying to establish his claimed rights in both countries.

Compelled by his French mother and her paramour to go to France to do homage to King Philip VI for Gascony in June 1329, Edward III cut a very different figure from his father. Michael Packe describes this scene, the introduction upon the European stage of the man who would strike down France as the leading power of Europe in the Hundred Years War:

> The figure that swept up the aisle at Amiens on 6 June was very different from that presaged by memories of his inept father, or by the cringing letters prepared for his seal by Mortimer's clerks; and from the reedy boy who not long ago had been seen following about Paris in the shadow of his peremptory mother. His fair hair gleamed on the shoulders of his long crimson robe, powdered with leopards of gold, falling gracefully over his straight limbs. He had the crown on his head, his sword by his side, and spurs of gold on his heels. Jewels flashed fire from him in the pale sparkle of the candles.[45]

---

[41]Packe, *Edward III*, p. 31.

[42]Barrow, *Robert Bruce*, pp. 362-368; McKisack, *Fourteenth Century*, pp. 98-99.

[43]Perroy, *Hundred Years War*, pp. 74-76, 80; Sumption, *Hundred Years War*, pp. 103, 106-107. Isabelle did finally send her favorite bishop, Adam Orleton, to Paris May 16, 1328 to press her claim to the French succession, but it was much too late; Philip of Valois was crowned King Philip VI thirteen days later, with Orleton probably arriving barely in time for the ceremony (Packe, *Edward III*, p. 42, rightly calls this move "no more than a formal gesture").

[44]Sumption, *Hundred Years War*, pp. 103-106.

[45]Packe, *Edward III*, p. 43.

He performed homage by stepping up to Philip on his throne, bowing to him, and placing his hands between the French king's hands. But he refused the fullness of submission known as liege homage, by neither taking off his crown and sword and spurs, nor kneeling before Philip V, nor kissing him on the mouth.[46] In September 1329 William Montagu, sent by the regency government of England on a mission to Pope John XXII at Avignon, was secretly entrusted by the young king (the two were close friends) with the mission of informing the Pope that Edward was unable to act freely as King of England and giving him a code phrase which would identify any letter personally written to him by Edward III, as distinct from letters sent by order of Isabelle and Mortimer and written by their clerks.[47] Only when Edward III's wife Philippa of Hainault was five months pregnant did Isabelle consent to Philippa's coronation as Queen in February 1330; the next month Isabelle and Mortimer arranged the judicial murder of King Edward's uncle Edmund, Earl of Kent.[48]

Still only sixteen, in October 1330 Edward III struck. William Montagu led him and about 25 companions through a secret passage to Mortimer's chamber, where they killed two knights guarding his door and took him prisoner. Isabelle rushed into the room begging her son to "have pity on gentle Mortimer;" but Edward III did not regard Mortimer as "gentle" and had no pity on him. He hanged him at Tyburn in November 1330. But Edward III continued to respect his mother, giving her a handsome allowance and full freedom though removing her from all contact with public affairs. She died in the habit of the Poor Clares many years later.[49]

Edward III of England was now king indeed, and ready to take the long warpath.

The man who above all others had humbled his father, the great Robert the Bruce, King of Scots and victor at Bannockburn, died in June 1329. On his deathbed he called to his side his dearest friend and most glorious comrade-in-arms, James "the Black" Douglas, famous throughout Europe as one of the premier warriors of Christendom. Bruce told Douglas that due to the constant danger in which his homeland and realm had been placed by the refusal of the English to recognize or accept Scots independence until the previous year, when illness was already overtaking him, he had never been able to fulfill his life's dream of going on crusade. But he still wanted to go. And so he made the Black Douglas swear that when Bruce was dead he would take his heart from his body and carry it into battle against the infidel, and then to the Holy

---

[46]*Ibid.*, p. 44.

[47]Sumption, *Hundred Years War*, p. 114.

[48]*Ibid.*, p. 113; Packe, *Edward III*, pp. 44-46; McKisack, *Fourteenth Century*, p. 100.

[49]McKisack, *Thirteenth Century*, pp. 101-102; Sumption, *Hundred Years War*, pp. 115-116; Packe, *Edward III*, pp. 51-52.

Sepulcher in Jerusalem. Douglas faithfully promised.[50]

Three months later a safe conduct was issued to Douglas in the name of Edward III of England to carry Robert Bruce's heart across English land or through English waters on the way to the Holy Land. A letter was even granted commending Douglas to Alfonso XI of Castile, England's ally. Alfonso had been recognized as full ruler of Castile in August 1325 at the age of fourteen, even younger than Edward III had been when he secured his freedom. With the aid of the nobles and the bishops of the *cortes* Alfonso XI had begun restoring law and order in Castile in the fall of 1325; by 1327 he had launched his first attack on the Moors in their kingdom of Granada. He was then the only king in Christendom fighting the Muslim infidel. The Black Douglas would bring his beloved master's heart to Alfonso's aid.[51]

In March 1330 Douglas arrived at Sevilla to a warm welcome by Alfonso and other foreign knights assembling there to help the Spanish Christians against the infidel. In July the Castilian army, with 500 Portuguese knights and the foreign volunteers including Douglas, marched on the strongly fortified Moorish town of Teba de Ardales and besieged it. A large army came out of Granada to relieve Teba. The Moorish commander, Osmin, divided his more numerous army. Alfonso XI took the greater part of his army to pursue Osmin while leaving a lesser force under Pero Ferrández de Castro, including the foreign knights and the Black Douglas carrying Bruce's heart around his neck in a silver casket, to defend the crossing of the Guada Teba River. As was his way, Douglas did not wait for the enemy to come to him; he counterattacked and penetrated deep into their ranks. But then he saw the Scots knight William Sinclair of Roslin cut off and surrounded. Douglas rushed to his rescue carrying Bruce's heart, shouting his famed war-cry "A Douglas! A Douglas! I follow or die!"[52]

He died, of five wounds any one of which would have been mortal. But the Moors were defeated. The man from the far-off land of lochs and heather had come to the rocky yellowed plains of Andalusia in Spain and given his life there for Christendom and for the Reconquest, faithful unto death to his commission from King Robert Bruce. Teba de Ardales was taken and the infidel fell back.[53]

---

[50]Barrow, *Robert Bruce*, pp. 444-445; Davis, *Black Douglas*, pp. 152-154.

[51]Davis, *Black Douglas*, pp. 155-156; Joseph F. O'Callaghan, *A History of Medieval Spain* (Ithaca NY, 1975), p. 309; Juan Beneyto Pérez, *El cardenal Albornoz; Canciller de Castilla y Caudillo de Italia* (Madrid, 1950), pp. 45, 47; Antonio Ballesteros Beretta, "El agitado año de 1325 y un escrito desconocido de Don Juan Manuel," *Boletín de la Real Academia de la Historia*, Vol. CXXIV (1949), pp. 30-32.

[52]Davis, *Black Douglas*, pp. 161-164.

[53]Davis, *Black Douglas*, p. 164. Contrary to a myth which first appears in writing more than a hundred years later, Douglas did not throw Bruce's heart into the midst of the enemy and charge after it. He fought throughout with the casket containing it

The controversy over the Beatific Vision launched by Pope John XXII in a series of five extraordinary sermons at Avignon beginning November 1, 1331, is unique in the history of the Church. At the time of, and since the proclamation by the First Vatican Council in 1870 that the Pope is infallible when speaking *ex cathedra* on faith and morals, there has been much speculation about whether and under what circumstances a Pope might hold an erroneous theological opinion without teaching it so as to be binding on the whole Church; but the Beatific Vision controversy involving Pope John XXII is the only actual example of this kind. It has also sometimes been noted as a remarkable phenomenon that despite the large number of aged Popes in the history of the Church, none has become senile. But a touch of senility may help to explain the astonishing imprudence of John XXII in this particular matter; for this controversy spanned his 88th, 89th, and 90th years.

The Beatific Vision is the ultimate bliss of which the human soul is capable, the actual beholding of the Triune God Himself. It cannot happen on earth, except in the person of Christ (and some of His statements suggest that a part of the Beatific Vision, at least from time to time, was withheld even from Him while He was still on earth).[54] The Church has always believed that the Blessed Virgin Mary and all canonized saints enjoy the Beatific Vision. Mary has the Beatific Vision in its fullness because of her Assumption body and soul into Heaven; but for the saints, their appreciation of It will be enhanced after the resurrection of the body when they behold God with their physical senses rather than only from the soul through infused knowledge. The great problem arises from the concept of blessed souls "waiting" in eternity for the time of the Last Judgment and the bodily resurrection. Time-bound mortals can only visualize their condition thus, but in truth one cannot "wait" in eternity. The mystery here partakes of that which prevents us from fully understanding how divine foreknowledge and freedom of the human will can coexist.

Pope John XXII argued that only the complete human being—soul and body reunited, after the resurrection—can truly see God. Consequently, he said, the Beatific Vision—for all but Christ and His mother—must await the general resurrection. He went further, attempting to visualize the unimaginable: the souls of the blessed dead, he suggested, see the human Christ, but not His full divinity. (The Pope's critics—and he had many—did not hesitate to call this a revival of the Nestorian heresy, which separated too widely Christ's divine nature from His human nature.) These views, proclaimed suddenly and without warning in November 1331, were directly contrary to the

---

around his neck (*ibid.*, pp. 166-168).

[54]For example, His statement that the date of the end of the world is not even known to the Son, but only to the Father (Matthew 24:36) and His cry from the Cross: "My God, my God, why hast thou forsaken me" (Matthew 27:46).

position Pope John XXII had taken earlier on the same subject in his bull of canonization of the Franciscan Archbishop of Toulouse, Louis of Anjou, in 1317 and his correspondence with the Armenian Church in 1321 and with the Patriarch of Jerusalem in 1326. In 1332, early in the increasingly impassioned discussion that followed his initial sermon on the Beatific Vision, John XXII explained that his sermons were not intended to define doctrine but simply to begin discussion on a difficult theological issue. He was acting as no more than a private theologian.[55]

But a Pope can never really be only a "private theologian." While he may speak on theological issues without intending to bind the faithful, his unique post and duties and responsibilities make it inevitable that any pronouncement by him on such issues will have enormous impact. He cannot avoid seeming to teach whenever he speaks on theology. For a Pope to propose a doctrine, actually or apparently contrary to that held by most of the Church, when he is not sure of its truth, is imprudent in the highest degree. No Pope has ever gone so far in such imprudence as John XXII in the Beatific Vision controversy.

On January 3, 1333 the opposition to John XXII's teaching on the Beatific Vision, up to this point mostly private or anonymous, came into clear public view in the Pope's own city when it was denounced from the pulpit of the Dominican church of Avignon by the English Dominican Thomas Waleys. He was promptly imprisoned by the Inquisition on the Pope's request. Although John XXII claimed in a letter to Philip VI of France the next month that he had not orderd Waleys' imprisonment because of the sermon, he did include that sermon in a list of documents he wished a special commission of theologians to investigate, along with statements on the Beatific Vision by Cardinal Jacques Fournier and Durandus de St. Pourçain, Bishop of Meaux, which the Pope had requested but was dissatisfied with because they did not endorse his position. When this commission (or at least several members of it) also did not agree with the Pope's view of thie issue, he called for formal university disputations on it, notably by the theologians of the University of Paris, heirs of St. Thomas Aquinas.[56]

Clearly the Pope was not imposing his erroneous view, nor teaching it *ex cathedra*. But by continuing to press the issue he was putting himself and the Church in a most peculiar position—indeed, almost inviting the Church to repudiate him on a subject where he had supreme and infallible authority but was refusing to exercise it, evidently because he had genuine doubts about the truth of his propositions. But if he doubted them, why in the world did he keep proposing them?

---

[55]Guy Mollat, *The Popes at Avignon* (New York, 1963), p. 22; Katherine Walsh, *A Fourteenth-Century Scholar and Primate; Richard FitzRalph in Oxford, Avignon and Armagh* (Oxford, 1981), pp. 89-90, 101.

[56]Walsh, *FitzRalph*, pp. 91, 94.

History gives us no answer to that question; but a Catholic historian can well remind us that this would not have been the first time Satan had tempted a Pope, right up to the brink of a disaster which God will not allow to happen. Were Popes Liberius, Vigilius, and Honorius praying for John XXII in this his hour of testing?

When the Franciscan general, Guiral Ot, gave qualified support to the Pope's view of the Beatific Vision, theologians at the University of Paris vehemently protested, and an assembly of bishops and professors of theology meeting at the castle of Vincennes December 19, 1333 roundly declared that all the blessed dead enjoy the Beatific Vision.[57] A year later, on his deathbed at ninety, facing the Judgment, Pope John XXII retracted his error:

> We confess and believe that souls separated from their bodies and fully purged from guilt are above, in the kingdom of heaven, in paradise and with Jesus Christ, in the company of the angels, and that according to the universal law, they see God and the divine essence face to face and clearly, so far as the state and condition of a separated soul permits.[58]

The conclave assembled promptly at the papal palace at Avignon and on December 20, 1334 unanimously elected Cardinal Jacques Fournier, who had early indicated his disapproval of John XXII's teaching on the Beatific Vision, Pope Benedict XII.[59] He began his pontificate with glowing praise for the Dominicans, whose theologians had taken the lead in rejecting the erroneous view of the Beatific Vision, and sharp criticism of the Franciscans for "heretical tendencies, revolutionary spirit, contempt for the official Church and relaxation of discipline."[60] In January 1335, in the doctrinal constitution *Benedictus Deus*, he laid the matter to rest: the souls of the blessed dead do now "see the divine essence by intuitive vision and even face to face."[61]

Papal infallibility had once again been preserved—and once again, as with Popes Liberius, Vigilius, and Honorius, by a very narrow margin.

In the east, the resurgence of the apparently moribund Byzantine Empire under the vigorous and brilliant leadership of Michael Palaeologus soon proved a spent force after his death. By the end of the thirteenth century its days of greatness before the Fourth Crusade had slipped below the horizon of living memory. Michael Palaeologus had regained and held Constantinople and a substantial portion of the old empire, but during the forty long years of the uninspired reign of his son Andronicus II its essential continuing weaknesses

---

[57]Mollat, *Popes at Avignon*, pp. 22-23.
[58]*Ibid.*, p. 23.
[59]*Ibid.*, pp. 26-28.
[60]*Ibid.*, p. 31.
[61]*Ibid.*, p. 28.

became apparent. Public spirit had faded to a shadow; most of the empire's people would not fight, requiring the constant use of mercenaries; the taxation base was almost gone, with most of the fertile land locked up in a few large estates whose owners were often too strong to be forced to pay; and most of the commerce was in the hands of Italian aliens. Young, energetic and ambitious Slavic peoples in the Balkans pressed on the empire's northern borders; Greece was full of revolt, even to anarchy in some areas; and in the east, a flotsam of new peoples who had flowed west in the wake of the Mongols were settling down in nearby Asia Minor, past the longitude of Constantinople and the Bosporus. Most of them were Turks from central Asia; many do not seem even to have accepted Islam until they made their home in western Asia Minor. But then they did, and were filled with the zeal of recent converts. Among them was a small body of approximately 400 fighting men with their wives and children, given unity only by their common loyalty to a chief named Osman, son of Ertoghrul, and therefore called Osmanlis or Ottomans.[62]

During the last decade of the thirteenth century Osman and his men began winning battles and capturing castles, though still confined to a small area around the upper reaches of the Kara Su River. Their numbers grew tenfold, from 400 to 4,000. They repeatedly raided Byzantine territory, defeating a Byzantine army of about 2,000 near the ancient Greek city of Nicomedia in 1302. Gradually, over the ensuing years, they closed in on Nicomedia and the nearby, equally ancient Greek metropolis of Nicaea. Both cities were defended by immense walls, impregnable to the Osmanlis who still relied entirely on swords, arrows and their splendid horses. But in 1326, as Osman lay dying, his son Orkhan brought him news that the smaller but important Greek city of Brusa had been taken by his people. It was a foretaste of things to come, the beginning of the Ottoman empire.[63]

A long and ugly struggle for the succession in Constantinople between Emperor Andronicus II and his grandson and namesake Andronicus III finally ended in 1328—two years after the Osmanlis took Brusa—with the expulsion of the elder Andronicus. But the new Emperor was pleasure-loving and ineffective as a leader, and in June 1329, just a little more than a year into his reign, the Osmanli Turks badly defeated his army at the Battle of Pelekanon, driving him in ignominious flight, wounded and bleeding, from the field. This led in less than two years to the fall of Nicaea to the Osmanlis, in March 1331. The city where the epochal council had been held that marked the emergence of the Church as the leading institution in Western civilization, had now fallen

---

[62]Donald M. Nicol, *The Last Centuries of Byzantium, 1261-1453* (New York, 1972), pp. 114-156; Herbert A. Gibbons, *The Foundations of the Ottoman Empire* (London, 1916), pp. 13-29.

[63]Gibbons, *Foundations of the Ottoman Empire*, pp. 28-34, 46-48; Nicol, *Last Centuries of Byzantium*, pp. 153-154.

to Muslims. The Osmanlis allowed all Christians who wished to leave the city to go freely. For all its splendid Christian history, and the fact that it had been the capital of the Byzantine Empire during the 57 years that Constantinople was in the hands of the Latins, Nicaea's remaining Christian inhabitants soon began to give up their faith *en masse,* despite the anguished protests of the Patriarch of Constantinople in two burning letters to them in 1339 and 1340.[64]

The whole of western Asia Minor was in upheaval. Many of its people had been uprooted; many ancient cities had been abandoned. The conquering Muslims had seized all valuable property belonging to Christians and held them subservient. Only by conversion to Islam, or by pretending it, did these people have a chance to preserve their property and often their livelihood. Many were not strong enough to resist the temptation, or salved their consciences by regarding their conformity to Islam as only external and temporary. But the Ottoman dominion was to last for nearly six hundred years, and the loss of faith soon became permanent. The abandonment of native Christianity in Asia Minor was not to end until it was totally eliminated—one of the grimmest events in history for the Christian, especially when he remembers that these were the lands evangelized by St. Paul.[65]

Six years later it was Nicomedia's turn. Feeble efforts by Andronicus III to form a league with Italian cities, France, and the Knights of St. John at Rhodes against the Turks in general proved mostly fruitless, though League forces did win a naval victory in the Gulf of Adramyttium, and in August 1333 Andronicus agreed to pay an annual tribute to the Osmanlis. The city that had once been the imperial capital of the Eastern Roman Empire went the way of Nicaea. It became, and has remained a Turkish town.[66]

Andronicus III died quite young in 1341, leaving a nine-year-old son. Civil war soon broke out between John Cantacuzene, an able general acting as regent, and the boy's mother teamed with the ambitious minister Alexios Apokaukos. The conflict devastated the already weakened Byzantine Empire. John Cantacuzene finally emerged victorious after Apokaukos decided to inspect a prison and was brained with a block of wood when he entered an exercise yard filled with men he had confined there. But by that time John Cantacuzene could not stop the Serb chieftain Stephen Dushan from proclaiming himself an Emperor, nor avoid marrying his daughter to Orkhan the Osmanli, fervent Muslim though he was. In the same spring of 1346 when these two evident manifestations of Byzantine decline took place, the eastern

---

[64]Nicol, *Last Centuries of Byzantium,* pp. 168-169, 174-176; Gibbons, *Foundations of the Ottoman Empire,* pp. 59-63, 76-81.

[65]Joseph Gill, *Byzantium and the Papacy, 1198-1400* (New Brunswick NJ, 1979), p. 223.

[66]Nicol, *Last Centuries of Byzantium,* pp. 175, 178; Gibbons, *Foundations of the Ottoman Empire,* pp. 63-64; Gill, *Byzantium and the Papacy,* pp. 195-196.

end of the Church of Hagia Sophia, the Holy Wisdom, the greatest church in Christendom, collapsed. To many it seemed an omen.[67]

Eastward from the Oder River in Germany all the way to the Ural Mountains which mark the beginning of Asia stretches the greatest plain in Europe, level or gently rolling, often almost featureless, wholly without natural boundaries between the Carpathian Mountains and the Baltic Sea, and between the Black and Caspian Seas and the Caucasus Mountains, and the Arctic Ocean. This absence of natural frontiers, leaving the people in these lands open to invasion from all sides, made the attainment of stable national governments in this region exceedingly difficult.

The Mongols still ruled most of the territory now comprising European Russia and Ukraine, recruiting soldiers for their army and collecting taxes throughout it. Along with their own periodic ruthless intervention, they played off one prince against another with striking skill, enhancing the natural tendency toward division created by the land.[68] The Russian and Ukrainian people were Christian, but the combination of their historic ties with the Greek church in Constantinople and the disruptions following the Mongol conquests had now cut them off completely from Rome and even from the memory of connection with Rome. For them, the Latin West was distant and alien.

Immediately west of Russia proper, with Novgorod its outlier, in Belarus and along and behind the Baltic coast, the dominant people were the Lithuanians, still fiercely pagan—the last major pagan people left in Europe. Lithuania's retention of paganism was due partly to religious conservatism, but more to the ravages of the so-called "crusading" order of the Teutonic Knights, who had found the lack of Christian Faith among the inhabitants of the Baltic coast from Prussia to Estonia a useful justification for seizing their land. Having seized it, they pressed on inland against the Lithuanians in almost incessant wars, which the terrain with its lack of natural obstacles favored, especially for cavalry. But the Lithuanians were not simply a persected people; they were a warlike, conquering force in their own right, who, if the Teutonic Knights had not been there, would undoubtedly have seized the Baltic region for themselves.[69]

Between Lithuania and Germany dwelt the Poles. As we have seen, Pope John XXII looked with favor on the newly crowned King of Poland, Vladislav

[67]Nicol, *Last Centuries of Byzantium*, pp. 191-192, 194-199, 206-207, 211-212; John V. A. Fine Jr., *The Late Medieval Balkans* (Ann Arbor MI, 1987), pp. 305, 309; Gill, *Byzantium and the Papacy*, p. 202.

[68]George Vernadsky, *The Mongols and Russia* (Volume III of *A History of Russia*) (New Haven CT, 1953), pp. 214-232.

[69]Eric Christiansen, *The Northern Crusades; the Baltic and the Catholic Frontier, 1100-1525* (Minneapolis MN, 1980), pp. 132-153.

Lokietek, probably the more because of his long-standing quarrel with the claimant to the Holy Roman Empire whom he refused to recognize, Louis of Bavaria. In June 1325, in the first of a series of letters to Poland, Pope John XXII granted special indulgences to Poland for fighting "against schismatics, Tatars, pagans and other confused nations of unbelievers."[70] In 1327, writing to Prince Boleslav-George II of Ruthenia just southeast of Poland, he urged the Prince to undertake and the Polish King to assist in the re-evangelization of separated Ruthenia to bring it back into the Catholic fold.[71] The strong links between Catholic Poland and the Pope were being forged and Poland's evangelizing mission defined.

In October 1325 Polish Crown Prince Casimir (later to be called the Great) sealed an alliance between Poland and Lithuania directed primarily against the Teutonic Knights (who also coveted Polish territory, regardless of the Poles' Catholicity) by marrying the vivacious Lithuanian Princess Aldona, who became a Catholic and took the name Anna. The marriage proved unusually close and devoted, the union of the young couple becoming the first stone in a bridge that would eventually make of these two peoples one great Catholic kingdom.[72]

In 1329 the alliance against the Teutonic Knights was extended to include Riga in Latvia, but the Knights besieged and took Riga and, in alliance with King John of Bohemia, invaded both Lithuania and Poland. In Lithuania John and these misnamed crusaders "converted" several thousand of the pagan people to Christianity by force. The war continued until a truce was made in October 1330.[73]

In March 1333 King Vladislav Lokietek of Poland died, shortly after making a good confession and confirming his son Casimir as his successor. Casimir was enthusiastically accepted by the nobility and clergy, and formally crowned with his Lithuanian Queen Anna by the Archbishop of Gniezno. Casimir promptly announced the extension of the truce with the Teutonic Knights, though by the next year the Bishop of Cracow was urging renewed war against the land-hungry order which made no distinction between Christian and pagan in its military aggressions. The formal truce with the Teutonic Knights expired in 1335, but a new one was signed by Casimir and Margrave Charles of Moravia, son of King John of Bohemia and the future Holy Roman Emperor Charles IV; the two young men, both prudent and loyally Catholic, developed "a friendship which endured despite dynastic disputes and misunderstandings of

---

[70]Paul W. Knoll, *The Rise of the Polish Monarchy; Piast Poland in East Central Europe, 1320-1370* (Chicago, 1972), p. 45.
[71]*Ibid.*, pp. 123-124.
[72]*Ibid.*, p. 47.
[73]*Ibid.*, pp. 51, 55; Christensen, *Northern Crusades*, p. 154.

state."[74]

At the Congress of Wyszegrad in Hungary before the end of the year, an agreement was made among Casimir, John of Bohemia, and Charles Robert of Hungary to collaborate against the Teutonic Knights and to settle past disputes among their countries over land and money. In January 1336 Casimir asked Pope John XXII to confirm the Wyszegrad settlements and to remove his enemy Bishop Jan Grot of Cracow.[75]

Pope John XXII had just died (Casimir had written him before he had the news), and the new Pope Benedict XII was reluctant at first to act in a situation with which he was generally unfamiliar. But his legate in Poland, Galhard, sang Casimir's praises, and by September 1337 Benedict XII wrote to the Polish King "complimenting him on the steadfastness of his faith and ... urging him to continue firm in his devotion to the Church."[76] The following April the Pope wrote to Bishop Grot sharply criticizing him for anathematizing Casimir and Queen Anna on insufficient evidence and refusing to admit them into his church. The next month the Pope launched a canonical suit against the Teutonic Knights to determine if they had illegally taken territory from Poland and should consequently be required to return it and pay an indemnity; in November the legate Galhard published the charges and asked all who might have evidence regarding them to come forward. The trial began in February 1339; 126 witnesses were heard. The court handed down its decision in September, in favor of Poland; but the Knights ignored it.[77]

In May 1339 Anna, the beloved Lithuanian wife of Casimir III of Poland, suddenly died, leaving the King with no male heir. He devolved the succession upon his friend and brother-in-law Charles Robert of Hungary, or one of Charles Robert's sons, his nephews. That year the Mongols began a new menacing advance, crushing the principality of Tver in Russia and threatening Smolensk, Ruthenia, Poland, and Hungary. Prince Boleslav-George II of Ruthenia, whose conversion to the Catholic Church Casimir had been trying to encourage, was assassinated by his own noblemen who feared he was about to convert. On Easter Sunday 1340 Casimir set out for Ruthenia with Polish and Hungarian troops. He took Lvov, its principal city, and razed its citadel, bringing many of its Catholics back to Poland with him for protection. In August Pope Benedict XII called for a crusade against the Mongols, who were believed to be encouraging the Russian Orthodox against the Catholics, to help Casimir. There was little response; the crusading ideal had become too much tarnished. In the fall the Mongols struck Poland, devastating the region around Sandomir and besieging Lublin; but Casimir prevented them from crossing the

---

[74]Knoll, *Rise of the Polish Monarchy*, pp. 62, 66-68, 71, 73 (quotation on p. 73).
[75]*Ibid.*, pp. 75-81, 88.
[76]*Ibid.*, p. 94.
[77]*Ibid.*, pp. 71, 84, 100-107.

Vistula—the fabled horsemen of the steppes were not the irresistible warriors they had once been.[78]

Still they remained dangerous, and in the face of their new aggression Pope Benedict XII now urged quick and final settlement of the long-standing dispute between Poland and the Teutonic Knights. The result was the Treaty of Kalisz in July 1343 by which Casimir recognized the Knights' claim to Pomerania and Chelmno while the Knights agreed to the return of Kujavia and Dobrzyn to Poland. Casimir pledged to work to persuade Hungary not to act against the Knights and not to give aid and advice to pagan enemies of the Knights (obviously meaning the Lithuanians). The Polish clergy declared they had received satisfactory indemnification from the Knights, and the treaty was formally ratified in the presence of the Archbishop of Gniezno, the primate of Poland. New Pope Clement VI, in a bull issued in December 1343, granted Casimir a tenth of all ecclesiastical income from the archdiocese of Gniezno plus the papal tenth in Poland for two years, to help him against the Mongols, Lithuanians and Ruthenians. Believing they had isolated the Lithuanians by this treaty, the Knights led by John of Bohemia and his son Charles attacked them in the winter of 1344-45, but were halted by a fierce Lithuanian counterattack which nearly captured Prince Charles.[79]

Warfare remained endemic in this distracted region, with Catholics, Russian Orthodox, pagan Mongols and pagan Lithuanians all set against one another. Catholic leadership in the region demanded the emergence of Poland as its principal power, the conversion of Lithuania to the Catholic Faith, and an end to the depredations of the Teutonic Knights whom no one in the region really regarded as "crusaders" any longer. All these were the continuing objectives of Casimir III the Great, and were to be achieved by his grand-niece Jadwiga a quarter of a century later.

At the opposite end of Christendom, in Spain, King Alfonso XI "the Avenger" and Afonso IV of Portugal beat back a major new Muslim assault after the Moroccans had defeated the Castilian fleet in the Straits of Gibraltar in the spring of 1340 and landed a large army on the Andalusian shore to join with the army of the Moorish kingdom of Granada. Outnumbered four to one, the Castilian and Portuguese armies met the infidel at the Rio Salado near the besieged port of Tarifa on October 30, 1340. Following a great fighting sermon by Archbishop (later Cardinal) Gil Albornoz of Toledo, primate of Spain, and general confession and communion, the Christian knights rode into battle under the papal banner, carrying a relic of the True Cross. Aided by a sally from the Christian garrison of Tarifa, they won a decisive victory. The Moroccan

---

[78]*Ibid.*, pp. 98-99, 110, 125-126, 128-130, 132-133; John L. I. Fennell, *The Emergence of Moscow, 1304-1359* (Berkeley CA, 1968), pp. 165-170, 173-174.
[79]Knoll, *Rise of the Polish Monarchy*, pp. 108, 118-119, 135, 183-185.

survivors hurried back to Africa. It was the last time a substantial army from Morocco landed on Spanish soil. The era in the enormously long war of the Reconquest that began with the coming of the Almoravids and their African drums, under Yusuf ibn-Tashfin 250 years before, halted only by the magnificent stand of El Cid at Valencia, had ended at last. Spain's internal dissensions would enable the last Moorish kingdom—Granada—to last longer than anyone in Alfonso the Avenger's time thought possible; but the victory at Rio Salado ultimately sealed its fate.[80]

Two years later Alfonso XI, aided by crusaders from Catalonia, Genoa, France, and England, laid siege to the great Moorish fortress of Algeciras on a broad bay within sight of the Rock of Gibraltar. Pope Clement VI gave moral and material support. The siege was firmly maintained, continuing for no less than two full years, until the city surrendered to Alfonso "the Avenger" on March 26, 1344 and a ten years' truce was granted to Granada on payment of twice its earlier tribute.[81]

On October 2, 1332 Philip VI of France had announced to an assembly of his nobles gathered in St. Louis' glorious Sainte-Chapelle that he intended to lead a new crusade for the liberation of Jerusalem. A year later he formally took the cross in a brilliant ceremony at the gates of the abbey of St. Germain in Paris. No one outside France paid much attention, and even in France the continuing disputes with England and the desire to save Scotland from the military prowess of Edward III's armies made the actual launching of a new crusade seem unlikely. But Philip seems to have genuinely desired to go on crusade and to have been willing to make real sacrifices to this end. Therefore it came as a shock to him when the realistic and hard-spoken Pope Benedict XII curtly informed him in the week after Easter 1336 that poor recruitment and political troubles within Christendom (of which the situation in Scotland was the worst) had made the crusade impossible. For several months Philip VI still hoped that the Pope would change his mind. At length convinced that he would not, Philip—now in no compromising mood—turned all his energies to the dispute with England. He took the money he had collected for the crusade to finance a war against England, and demanded of Edward III the extradition of his former close advisor and now bitter enemy Robert, who claimed to be Count of Artois. When Edward would not send Robert to Philip VI and to death, the French King declared war on England in May 1337. The "Hundred Years War" had begun.[82]

---

[80]Derek W. Lomax, *The Reconquest of Spain* (London, 1978), pp. 166-167; O'Callaghan, *Medieval Spain*, pp. 412-413; J. N. Hillgarth, *The Spanish Kingdoms, 1250-1516* (Oxford, 1976), I, 341-342.

[81]Lomax, *Reconquest of Spain*, p. 167; Hillgarth, *Spanish Kingdoms*, I, 343-344.

[82]Sumption, *Hundred Years War*, pp. 132-137, 155-156, 166, 170-174.

Ever since the Norman conquest of England there had been three great powers in Europe: the German and Italian domains of the Holy Roman Emperor; France; and England. England and the Empire were natural allies, because there was always strife between the Empire and France along the Alsatian and Belgian borders which have been fought over for more than a thousand years, and there had been almost as much strife over the English feudal possessions in France, while England and the Empire rarely came into conflict. Louis of Bavaria still claimed to be Emperor; Pope Benedict XII was maintaining Pope John XXII's policy of not recognizing him as Emperor and excommunicating him because he would not abdicate. In the winter of 1337 Louis had offered to acknowledge that he had sinfully defied John XXII, give up his title of Emperor, revoke all his imperial acts, promise never to visit Rome without the Pope's permission, and to found churches and monasteries and make pilgrimages in reparation. But he still would not give up his title of "King of the Germans," and every Holy Roman Emperor since Otto the Great had also been King of the Germans; so Pope Benedict XII rejected his recantation as insufficient and the struggle between Pope and Emperor went on.[83] Edward III sought Louis' support in the war against France and got it, by the Treaty of Valenciennes in August; this pushed Benedict XII willy-nilly into political alliance with France. When he sent two cardinal legates to London in December to try to mediate an end to the war and they warned Edward of the sin involved in dealing with an excommunicate whose royal claims had been disallowed by the Pope, they were publicly heckled in the Painted Chamber at Westminster by the Archbishop of Canterbury himself, the formidable John Stratford.[84]

Meanwhile Edward III was pondering the fundamental question of whether to claim the throne of France through his mother, challenging the assumption of French jurists that not only could a woman not rule France, but also that she could not transmit the royal title through her son. This assumption was in fact groundless; no precedents for such an assertion existed before Philip VI took the French crown, neither in France nor in any other monarchy in Europe. But no French king would ever voluntarily give up his title of King of France, and French patriotism would assuredly support any King of France against any claim to the French throne by an English king. To insist upon such a claim would commit England to constant war against France—for twenty years, fifty, a hundred or even more. Yet Edward was now resolved no longer to do homage to the French King for Gascony and Guyenne in the southwest, and under feudal law he had no right to refuse it. He could only escape the

---

[83]*Cambridge Medieval History*, VII, 128-129.
[84]Sumption, *Hundred Years War*, pp. 211, 217-218. For Stratford's tumultuous career see Roy M. Haines, *Archbishop John Stratford; Political Revolutionary and Champion of the Liberties of the English Church* (Toronto, 1986).

dilemma if he himself were King of France.

For the moment Edward III compromised by giving his ambassador Bishop Henry Burghersh of Lincoln in October 1337 several alternative sets of instructions to use at his discretion, one of which rather naively authorized him to negotiate with Philip VI or his representatives "upon the question of the right to the kingdom of France and whether it ought to belong to him or to us" and others simply claiming the title of King of France for Edward III. Bishop Burghersh did not in fact go to France at this time because a temporary truce was arranged, so Edward's claim to the throne of France was not publicly enunciated; but his various instructions remained in England's diplomatic files.[85]

The next year the war actually began. In July Edward III sailed for Flanders; in August the Diet of the Empire defied the Pope and maintained support of the imperial claims of Louis of Bavaria, and Philip VI took the legendary Oriflamme from the abbey of St. Denis. Pope Benedict XII urged Edward to abandon his alliance with Louis, but by the time the Pope's letter arrived Edward had already met Louis at Coblenz on the Rhine and been appointed "imperial vicar west of the Rhine," despite his refusal to kiss Louis' foot. Money ran out that fall before Edward and the Belgian lieges of the Emperor could mount an actual invasion of France; but in 1339 they got to Cambrai and besieged it. When the French army approached, the English took a strong position with their deadly Welsh longbows at La Capelle, but Philip (despite much criticism from his hot-headed knights) refused to attack.[86] He thereby saved his army, because longbowmen in a prepared position could pick off charging knights like clay pigeons, though the archers with their unwieldy bows were almost impossible to maneuver on a battlefield. Even full plate armor was insufficient protection, because the knights' horses could not be so armored. If they were to attack—as knightly conventions favored—rather than maneuver, they must do so on foot.

In January 1340 Edward III obtained the full alliance of Flanders in his war against France and for the first time publicly proclaimed himself King of France at Ghent. His title was promptly recognized by the Flemings who had owed allegiance to the King of France, despite their many rebellions, and now could make a better case for their behavior in feudal law. But the Flemings were merchants before they were soldiers; Edward III—whose abilities as a financier, in contrast to his abilities as a soldier, were almost nil—was deeply in debt to them, and in February 1340 he actually had to leave his wife Philippa of the Belgian province of Hainault and one of his sons as hostages in Ghent for

[85]Sumption, *Hundred Years War*, pp. 294-295.
[86]*Ibid.*, pp. 239-240, 243-244, 255, 279, 281-282, 286-289; *Cambridge Medieval History*, VII, 130-131; McKisack, *Fourteenth Century*, pp. 122, 161; Packe, *Edward III*, p. 83.

the repayment of his debts. The next month there was another hostage, for in March Philippa gave birth to another son. He was named John, to be known throughout his long and stormy life as "John of Gaunt," from the late middle English pronunciation of the city which had under these strange circumstances become his birthplace.[87]

In April 1340 Pope Benedict XII laid Flanders under an interdict for rebellion against its liege lord, thereby making it very clear that he did not regard Edward's claim to the French throne as worth a moment's serious consideration, though the English would inevitably see partiality in this action by a French Pope. Parliament accepted Edward III's claim that same month, after extracting many domestic concessions including guaranteeing the Church against royal encroachment, especially during episcopal vacancies; even then, Parliament declared Englishmen must never be subjected to the French crown.[88]

In June 1340 the English secured a major victory, the destruction of the French fleet, accompanied by many Italian naval mercenary captains and sailors, at Sluys on the Flemish coast. Edward's captains caught the enemy in harbor and sailed in with the wind and tide behind them and the sun in the faces of their foes, shooting them down with their longbows in a deadly and irresistible hail. With this success to point to, Edward could sign a truce and quietly extend it for months and years while recouping his shattered financial position.[89]

The king tried to blame Archbishop Stratford for many of his financial losses, declaring that he should be held personally liable for much of the debt; in reply the Archbishop, in Canterbury cathedral on the feast day of St. Thomas Becket (December 29, 1340), tolled the bells, extinguished the candles, and in a ringing sermon blamed himself for too much preoccupation with secular affairs and for oppressing the clergy of England through excessive financial levies, promised amends in the future, and pronounced excommunication in advance on all outside the royal family "who should violate Magna Charta, the peace of the land, or the liberties of the Church."[90]

The angry King summoned Archbishop Stratford to London; he refused to go, declaring his life and liberty in danger, even after receiving a royal safe-conduct. Edward brought charges against him, and in an open letter to the Bishop of London called him "a mouse in the bag, a fire in the bosom, a serpent

[87]Sumption, *Hundred Years War*, pp. 291-305; McKisack, *Fourteenth Century*, p. 162; Perroy, *Hundred Years War*, p. 105.

[88]Sumption, *Hundred Years War*, pp. 303, 305-306; McKisack, *Fourteenth Century*, pp. 162-163.

[89]Sumption, *Hundred Years War*, pp. 325-329, 338, 358-360; McKisack, *Fourteenth Century*, pp. 128-130; Packe, *Edward III*, pp. 93-95.

[90]McKisack, *Fourteenth Century*, pp. 169-170.

in the lap, a broken reed."[91]   This oddly mixed invective did not shake the
Archbishop, who replied with a long review of his devoted service to Edward III
and to his father and grandfather before him and a circular letter sent to all the
English bishops defending himself against the King's charges. Edward appealed
to Pope Benedict XII against him, and to Parliament as well; the Pope did not
respond, and Parliament upheld Stratford.   In October 1341 Edward gave up
the struggle and was reconciled with the Archbishop. St. Thomas Becket, victim
of that unforgettable murder in the cathedral, had won again.[92]

Pope Benedict XII died April 25, 1342. Pierre Roger, who had been one
of the principal ministers of Philip VI of France during the preceding decade,
was unanimously elected Pope Clement VI on May 7 and consecrated at
Avignon May 19. Prince John of France, Duke of Normandy and heir to the
throne, held the reins of the new Pope's horse on that occasion and sat at his
right hand at dinner.[93]

Under this new French Pope, negotiations for a permanent settlement of
the conflict were undertaken at Avignon, but Edward III would now not yield
on his claim to be King of France and the envoys of Philip VI were
understandably not authorized even to discuss that issue. Edward remained
defiant even after an uprising in Ghent and the murder of Edward's chief
supporter there, Jacob van Artevelde, in July 1345 greatly reduced the
likelihood of effective Flemish support for a new campaign in France. But the
English were now ready to give massive support again to their much admired,
dashingly heroic if financially improvident monarch, and in July 1346 Edward
landed in Normandy (very near "Utah Beach" of the great amphibious "D-day"
invasion almost exactly six hundred years later) with a hard-bitten veteran
force.[94] Pope Clement VI made a secret loan of 372,000 florins to help equip
the French army—an act of reckless imprudence constituting one of the few but
highly significant documented instances of blatant partiality toward France by
the Avignon Popes.[95]

It availed nothing. Edward had caught Philip by surprise; the French King
had most of his army fighting under his son John in distant Gascony. Philip took
the Oriflamme as the English were already marching on Paris, sent a desperate
call to his son to rush to his assistance (he was much too far away to get there in
time), was brilliantly outmaneuvered by the fast-moving English army, saw a
suburb of Paris go up in flames and Seine bridges destroyed behind him, chased
furiously after the retreating English, and finally found them in a prepared

---

[91]*Ibid.*, p. 170; Packe, *Edward III*, pp. 101-102 (quotation on p. 102).
[92]McKisack, *Fourteenth Century*, pp. 171, 174-178; Packe, *Edward III*, pp. 102-103.
[93]Mollat, *Popes at Avignon*, pp. 35, 37; Sumption, *Hundred Years War*, pp. 395-396.
[94]Sumption, *Hundred Years War*, pp. 438-439, 461-462, 489-491, 500-501; Perroy,
Hundred Years War, pp. 116-118; Packe, *Edward III*, pp. 142-143.
[95]Sumption, *Hundred Years War*, p. 484.

position on a hillside at Crécy near the mouth of the Somme, with a thick forest behind them. Philip's wiser commanders begged him not to attack; the English longbowmen were waiting, shooting downhill, with cover impenetrable to cavalry right behind them—an ideal position for them. But other officers, their ardor overwhelming their judgment, cried to strike, and the many frustrations of his reign seemed to boil up in his mind and overwhelm Philip as well. He ordered a general assault, which the now blind King John of Bohemia insisted on joining. It was a total, almost farcical disaster. The longbowmen picked off the French knights like ducks in a shooting gallery as their horses labored up the hill in front of them; blind King John and the pro-French Count Louis of Flanders were slain; Philip was unhorsed and wounded, got up and remounted, was unhorsed and wounded again, and his squire only saved the Oriflamme by ripping it from its shaft, wrapping it about his body under his coat, and riding like mad for safety. The French lost 1,542 knights, the English forty.[96]

Crécy was not one of the decisive battles of history, often as it has been called that, because Edward III of England was in no position to conquer, occupy, and rule France; he had not the resources.[97] Its only lasting concrete result—important, though not decisive—was the capture of the Channel port of Calais, its resettlement by English, and its permanent annexation (for more than two hundred years) to the English crown, which took place the next year.[98] But Crécy did ensure a long-drawn-out struggle between an England seeking more victories in France and a France seeking revenge for its humiliation. And French Popes in Avignon would never be accepted by the English as mediators to bring that struggle to an end.

On Holy Thursday of this same year 1346, the traditional day for grand excommunications, Pope Clement VI issued a bull reviewing the whole long history of disobedience and defiance by imperial claimant Louis of Bavaria and pronouncing once and for all against his claims. Nine days later Charles of Moravia, whose blind father John was soon to die tragically and needlessly in the Battle of Crécy, took oath at Avignon that if elected Emperor he would annul all proceedings against Rome, Florence and Naples undertaken by Emperor Henry VII at the beginning of the century; revoke all the acts of Louis of Bavaria; respect the Church's domains and rights in Italy and never enter any of its territory without the Pope's permission; and remove all bishops not sanctioned by the Pope. It brought Charles into the same position regarding the Holy See that Rudolf of Habsburg had been when he became Holy Roman

---

[96]Sumption, *Hundred Years War*, pp. 499-500, 503, 513-532; Perroy, *Hundred Years War*, pp. 119-120; McKisack, *Fourteenth Century*, pp. 134-135; Packe, *Edward III*, pp. 158-161.

[97]Sumption, *Hundred Years War*, pp. 532-534.

[98]*Ibid.*, pp. 537-538, 568, 576-582; Perroy, *Hundred Years War*, pp. 119-120; McKisack, *Fourteenth Century*, pp. 136-137.

Emperor in 1273. Pope Clement VI gave him full support, and on July 11 he was unanimously elected Emperor. Louis did not yield to him, but in October 1347 Louis died and all opposition to Charles collapsed. He would begin a new era in papal relations with the Holy Roman Empire, renewing the loyal, mutually helpful relationship which Rudolf had established and the long struggle against Louis had suspended.[99]

This was a most promising development; but the chasm which had opened up between France and England showed how dangerous for Christendom was the continued residence of the Popes away from Rome, in the midst of the territory of the greatest political and military power in Europe, especially with all of them French and likely to remain all French indefinitely into the future, since the College of Cardinals had been two-thirds French for a generation. Spiritually Christendom was stagnant; not a single major saint had emerged during the first half of the fourteenth century. Economically it was declining. The climate in northern Europe had become colder and wetter; the famine of 1316 had been followed by epidemic diseases in livestock, raising prices, lowering the standard of living, and restricting markets for the hand-made goods of the time. General public health was poorer, resistance to disease was weak, and nothing whatever was known about how infectious diseases were transmitted.[100]

From the days of Genghis Khan who had died 120 years before, men had ranged freely and widely for the first time from Asia to Europe and from Europe to Asia. People, animals and bacteria never before brought into contact had been mingling. At the end of the thirteenth century Mongol armies had reached Yunnan on the steamy jungle border region of China, Burma, Thailand and Vietnam, home of the opium poppy. In that lush and deadly environment, the bacillus which causes bubonic plague was endemic. By the 1330's this terrible disease, carried by fleas upon rats who then jump to human hosts, which incubates for six days and then kills more than half its victims, was spreading rapidly through the teeming millions in China. In colder climates the bacillus often becomes pneumonic plague, which spreads from person to person like the common cold, but kills an appalling 95 per cent of those who contract it.[101]

By 1339 the great plague had crossed central Asia to Samarkand; by 1346 it was in Crimea and the Caucasus. Mongols besieging Genoese in the trading city of Caffa on the Crimea contracted it and passed it on to the besieged; when they fled to Sicily they brought the bacillus with them, nearly depopulating the

---

[99]Mollat, *Popes at Avignon*, p. 226; *Cambridge Medieval History*, VII, 134-135; Bede Jarrett, *The Emperor Charles IV* (London, 1935), pp. 105-107, 110-111.
[100]Robert S. Gottfried, *The Black Death; Natural and Human Disaster in Medieval Europe* (New York, 1983), pp. 16-32.
[101]*Ibid.*, pp. 7-8, 33-36.

city of Messina in October 1347. A new scourge had fallen upon Christendom—a scourge from which there was no escape.[102]

---

[102]*Ibid.*, pp. 36-43.

10
Shadow and Lightning
(1347-1378)

(Popes Clement VI 1342-52, Innocent VI 1352-62, Bd. Urban V 1362-70, Gregory XI 1370-78)

"Most holy and blessed Father in Christ sweet Jesus: your poor unworthy little daughter Catherine comforts you in His Precious Blood, with desire to see you free from any servile fear.... I tell you on behalf of Christ crucified, most sweet and holy Father, not to fear for any reason whatsoever. Come in security; trust you in Christ sweet Jesus; for, doing what you ought, God will be above you, and there will be no one who shall be against you. Up, Father, like a man! For I tell you that you have no need to fear. You ought to come; come, then. Come gently, without any fear. And if any at home wish to hinder you, say to them bravely, as Christ said when St. Peter, through tenderness, wished to draw Him back from going to His passion; Christ turned to him, saying 'Get thee behind Me, Satan; thou art an offense to Me, seeking the things which are of men, and not those which are of God. Wilt thou not that I fulfill the will of my Father?' Do you likewise, sweetest Father, following Him as His vicar, deliberating and deciding by yourself, and saying to those who would hinder you, 'If my life should be spent a thousand times, I wish to fulfill the will of my Father.'"—St. Catherine of Siena to Pope Gregory XI, Summer 1376[1]

When the great plague that later came to be called the Black Death[2] struck Europe in the fall of 1347, the consequences of the decline in morality and the prestige of the Church that had become evident during the pontificate of Boniface VIII had bitten deep into the sinews of Christendom. Though there was not yet any great new heresy to challenge the Faith, the sense of unity and common purpose growing out of an almost universally shared belief and world-view, which had so strikingly characterized Christendom in the time of St. Thomas Aquinas and the building of the Gothic cathedrals, was much

---

[1] Vida D. Scudder, ed. *St. Catherine of Siena as Seen in Her Letters* (London, 1911), p. 166; for the time of writing of this letter, see Johannes Jorgensen, *Saint Catherine of Siena* (London, 1938), pp. 232-233.

[2] It was not so called at the time, only being given this name some 200 years later (Philip Ziegler, *The Black Death* [New York, 1969], pp. 17-18).

enfeebled. To some extent new national loyalties took its place, but were far
too limited ever to match it. The cumulative effect of the forty-one years of
papal residence at Avignon and the evidence of partiality for the French by the
series of French Popes there—most evident in the incumbent Pope Clement
VI[3]—had reduced respect for the papal office to the lowest level since the great
Hildebrandine reform of the eleventh century. Even the Franciscans were
widely believed to be living in luxury; though the charges against them were
evidently exaggerated and often fomented by "Spiritual Franciscans" who had
openly rejected papal authority, there had to be sufficient basis to make them
so credible.[4]

The two principal kingdoms in Christendom, France and England, were
locked in a bitter conflict with each other, the Hundred Years War. Italy was a
welter of small states often violently hostile to one another. There was a
potential for serious conflict—soon to be realized—among the four Christian
kingdoms in the Iberian peninsula: Castile (the largest and strongest), Aragon,
Navarra, and Portugal, though at the moment Alfonso XI of Castile was still
focussed on the long crusade of the Reconquest from the Moors. The
developing Christian peoples of Eastern Europe were split between the
Catholic Church and the Eastern Orthodox. The new Holy Roman Emperor,
Charles IV, was a profoundly believing Catholic, thoroughly loyal to the Pope
(even the Popes in Avignon) and a man of peace, the most moral and charitable
ruler of his time; but he made little attempt to exert influence beyond Germany
and his native Bohemia.[5] The hammer of the great plague—the worst in
history, comparable in its impact to a nuclear war today—fell upon a society
already debilitated, almost as lacking in spiritual as in medical resources to
meet the fearsome challenge.

Yet Christendom survived. In most places the normal pattern of life
endured through even the worst ravages of the pandemic, despite evil
consequences that we shall review. Modern doomsayers to the contrary
notwithstanding, the human race is extraordinarily resilient in recovering from
disasters like this. Eventually—though not without periodic recurrences of
severe mortality—the plague declined as the bodies of the people of Europe
developed better means to fight the killer bacteria known to science as *Yersinia
pestis*.[6] And the spiritual darkness gave way to tongues of fire in the decade of

---

[3]Pope Clement VI had secretly loaned French King Philip VI 372,000 florins to help
equip the French army (see Chapter Nine, above).
[4]Katherine Walsh, *A Fourteenth-Century Scholar and Primate; Richard FitzRalph in
Oxford, Avignon and Armagh* (Oxford, 1981), pp. 407-408.
[5]See Bede Jarrett, *The Emperor Charles IV* (London, 1935), *passim*, for Charles'
character and policy—particularly valuable in view of the remarkable amount of hostile,
thoughtless or patently prejudiced criticism he has received from anti-Catholic or
antipapal historians.
[6]Robert S. Gottfried, *The Black Death; Natural and Human Disaster in Medieval*

the 1370's when one of the most vivid and glorious saints in the Church's history, Catherine of Siena, appeared on the scene scattering lightning.

The great plague, as we have seen, was brought to Sicily from southern Russia in October 1347 and from there spread with appalling rapidity and mortality throughout almost all of Europe.[7] By the end of December it had appeared in the port cities of Genoa, Pisa and Venice and in Constantinople, and in February 1348 it reached the busy southern French port of Marseilles.[8] Because of crowded and unsanitary conditions in the cities, the mortality was always greater there than in the country. The primitive medicine of that age knew no cure or treatment for the disease, which once the first symptom of its more common bubonic form appeared—a large black boil—often killed within 48 hours. Usually at least one-third of the population of the afflicted city died—often more. Since almost half of those who contracted bubonic plague survived (in contrast to pneumonic plague where the mortality rate was 95 per cent) this meant that the majority of the population almost everywhere had it. Its extraordinary contagion was its most terrible feature: when one member of a family or a confined religious community caught it, very soon most of the other family or community members would suffer it as well.[9]

In the prosperous Italian city of Siena more than half the population died in the spring and summer of 1348.[10] The chronicler Agnolo di Tura unforgettably describes those ghastly days:

> The mortality in Siena began in May. It was a cruel and horrible thing; and I do not know where to begin to tell of the cruelty and the pitiless ways. And it is impossible for the human tongue to recount the awful truth. Indeed, one who did not see such horror can be called blessed. And the victims died almost immediately. They would swell beneath the armpits and in their groins, and fall over while talking. Father abandoned child, wife husband, one brother another; for this illness seemed to strike through breath and sight. And so they died. And none could be found to bury the dead for money or friendship. Members of a household brought their dead to a ditch as best they could, without priest, without divine offices. Nor did the death bell sound. And in many places in Siena great pits were dug and piled deep with the multitude of dead. And they died by the hundreds, both day and night, and all were thrown in those ditches and covered with earth. And as soon as those ditches were filled, more were

---

Europe (New York, 1983), pp. 6-9.

   [7]For unknown reasons, Bohemia, much of Poland, part of Belgium, and the Pyrenees Mountains mostly escaped the Black Death. All the rest of Europe was devastated by it (Ziegler, *Black Death*, p. 116).

   [8]Gottfried, *Black Death*, pp. 37-38, 42-43, 48; Ziegler, *Black Death*, pp. 63-64.

   [9]Gottfried, *Black Death*, pp. 1, 8, 55, 109-117; Ziegler, *Black Death*, pp. 18-24, 227-231.

   [10]Ziegler, *Black Death*, pp. 58-59.

dug. And I, Agnolo di Tura, called the Fat, buried my five children with my own hands.[11]

The only hope of escape was to flee before exposure to the contagion; all doctors advised this course for those able to take it. When Avignon was stricken in March 1348, Pope Clement VI, on the advice of his physician Guy de Chauliac (one of the few truly scientific observers of the nature of the great plague, who distinguished between its bubonic and pneumonic forms), "retreated to his chamber, saw nobody, and spent all day and night sheltering between two enormous fires." In June he left the city to take refuge in his castle at Valence. The mortality in Avignon exceeded 50 per cent; 400 people died every day, and from March 14 to April 27 11,000 plague victims were buried there in a cemetery bought by the Pope. One-third of the college of cardinals died, and Petrarch's beloved Laura. The total mortality in Avignon was 62,000; seven thousand houses were shut up because all their former inhabitants were dead or gone.[12]

From his retreat at Valence the Pope kept himself well informed on the progress and consequences of the pestilence as it swept all the great port cities of the Mediterranean, surged northward through France and Bavaria, and leaped the English Channel at the end of June.[13] Clement VI was not a great nor heroic nor politically prudent Pope, but in this gigantic crisis he had the mind of Christ. He grasped the spiritual as well as the physical impact of the disaster, which he had witnessed so close at hand in Avignon. He saw how it generated despair and brought some to the edge of madness, and spoke out against the worst effects of these destructive emotions: the mass killing of Jews, irrationally blamed for the plague; and the burgeoning movement of Flagellants, whipping themselves through the streets of stricken cities, proclaiming that the great plague signalized the end of the world and calling all to absolution from their sins which the Flagellants—mostly laymen—claimed power and authority to grant.[14]

On July 4, 1348 the Pope warned that anyone molesting Jews on account of the plague would be excommunicated; on September 26, after returning to

---

[11]Gottfried, *Black Death*, p. 45.

[12]*Ibid.*, pp. 50, 133; Ziegler, *Black Death*, pp. 19, 50, 65, 67; Guy Mollat, *The Popes at Avignon* (New York, 1963), p. 40.

[13]Ziegler, *Black Death*, pp. 65, 79-80, 84, 114, 121; Gottfried, *Black Death*, pp. 50, 54-55; Joseph F. O'Callaghan, *A History of Medieval Spain* (Ithaca NY, 1975), p. 417. King Pedro IV of Aragon lost his wife and his youngest daughter to the plague in 1348 (Ziegler, *op. cit.*, p. 114), and Princess Joan of England, on her way to marry Prince Pedro of Castile (later known, after becoming king, as "the Cruel"), died of it in Bordeaux in August (Ziegler, *op. cit.*, p. 80; Richard Barber, *Edward, Prince of Wales and Aquitaine* [New York, 1978], pp. 82-83).

[14]Ziegler, *Black Death*, pp. 90-95, 102, 107.

Avignon from Valence despite the continuing danger, he reiterated this warning and welcomed to Avignon Jews fleeing from pogroms elsewhere.[15] He privately condemned the Flagellants soon after observing one of their processions in Avignon in May. After hesitating for some time because of opposition by some of the cardinals to their formal condemnation, he issued a bull in October 1349 declaring that "beneath an appearance of piety, [the Flagellants] set their hands to cruel and impious works, shedding the blood of Jews, whom Christian piety accept and sustain." He condemned them for creating unauthorized religious associations and acting in contempt of the Church, and ordered their pilgrimages and processions stopped.[16]

In the fall of 1348 the plague was raging in Paris, with 800 people dying every day and a third of the inhabitants eventually wiped out.[17] It had now reached northern Germany, and in Greece cleared the way for the conquest of Epirus and Thessaly by Stephen Dushan of Serbia when Byzantine governor John Angelos died of plague.[18] In London it switched from the bubonic to the even deadlier pneumonic form, killing 30,000 during the winter of 1349; later that year pneumonic plague devastated Norwich, then the second largest city in England, which never recovered its position in the country and did not regain its 1348 population for 250 years. Ralph of Shrewsbury, Bishop of Bath and Wells, sent a letter to the priests in his diocese commanding them either to go to those dying of the plague and hear their confessions, or to explain to them that in this unparalleled emergency they might make confession to one another in the absence of a priest; more than half the priests in his diocese perished in 1349. Newly appointed Archbishop of Canterbury John Offord died that May before he could be consecrated; his successor, the famous scholar Thomas Bradwardine, died likewise in August.[19] In the spring of 1349 the plague arrived in Ireland, where Franciscan friar John Clyn of Kilkenny wrote:

> I, as if among the dead, waiting till death do come, have put into writing truthfully what I have heard and verified [about the coming of the plague]. And that the writing may not perish with the scribe and the work fail with the laborer, I add parchment to continue it, if by chance anyone may be left in the future, and any child of Adam may escape this pestilence and continue the work thus commenced. . . . [continued in another hand] Here it seems that the author died.[20]

---

[15]*Ibid.*, p. 67; Mollat, *Popes at Avignon*, p. 41.

[16]Ziegler, *Black Death*, p. 95; Gottfried, *Black Death*, p. 73 (for the quotation); Mollat, *Popes at Avignon*, p. 41.

[17]Gottfried, *Black Death*, pp. 55-56.

[18]Ziegler, *Black Death*, p. 84; Donald M. Nicol, *The Last Centuries of Byzantium, 1261-1453* (New York, 1972), p. 226.

[19]Ziegler, *Black Death*, pp. 124-126, 128, 156-159, 170.

[20]Gottfried, *Black Death*, p. 67. Similarly, in 1348, the Florentine historian Matteo Villani, after a vivid description of the nature and rapid spread of the great pestilence,

Perhaps none of the many stories from these nightmare years so memorably captures the quality of their horror as that of the London ship with a cargo of wool which arrived in the harbor of Bergen in Norway in May 1349, when the great plague had not yet reached Scandinavia. The ship entered the harbor, but it did not tie up at any dock nor come ashore on any beach. It was drifting. City authorities ordered it boarded. The boarders found every man aboard the ship dead, and brought the deadly bacteria ashore in their own bodies. By the end of 1350 King Magnus II of Sweden would say: "God for the sins of men has struck the world with this great punishment of sudden death. By it most of our countrymen are dead." It was only a slight exaggeration; the death percentage seems to have been higher in the Scandinavian countries than in any others, with a majority of all their people perishing.[21]

In March 1350 the plague claimed its most illustrious victim: the King of Castile, Alfonso XI "the Avenger," in camp before the Rock of Gibraltar, the great Muslim fortress on the site of their first landing in Spain 639 years before. He had defied the danger of a camp in such times to be with his soldiers, struggling to take the next step in their immemorial task of liberating their land from the infidel. The black boils ravaged his body like that of any common soldier; he died on Good Friday, when his Lord too had suffered. The terrified army raised the siege, and Alfonso was succeeded by his 16-year-old son Pedro, who was to bring misery and disaster to his country which would divert it from the completion of the Reconquest for nearly a century and a half.[22]

In 1351 Pope Clement VI reported that, according to his investigators, 23,840,000 people had died of the plague in Catholic Europe—about 31 per cent of the total population. In 1353 the plague reached the most remote city in Europe, Moscow, where it killed Grand Duke Symeon and Archbishop Theognost. After that, its first visitation was over; but it would return in 1361 to attack those whom it had missed in its first coming, killing an estimated 20 per cent of the population in England and Normandy, and in Florence and other Italian cities. It came again in 1369, killing 10 to 15 per cent, and then periodically every four to twelve years until the end of the fourteenth century and on through the fifteenth, with each attack averaging 10 per cent mortality, though not so widespread as the first plague of 1347-50.[23]

All this Christendom survived—and survived without apparent major

---

wrote in his chronicle: "Many lands and cities were made desolate. And the plague lasted till —. . . ." He intended to fill in the blank when the plague ended; but before that happened, he himself was dead of it (*ibid.*, p. 53).

[21]*Ibid.*, pp. 57-58.

[22]O'Callaghan, *Medieval Spain*, p. 414; Derek W. Lomax, *The Reconquest of Spain* (London, 1978), p. 168; Ziegler, *Black Death*, p. 114.

[23]Gottfried, *Black Death*, pp. 77, 129-133; Georege Vernadsky, *The Mongols and Russia* (Volume III of *A History of Russia*) (New Haven CT, 1953), pp. 205-207.

political, social, cultural, or religious change. There were significant economic changes, though these have often been exaggerated. Self-evidently, the enormous mortality of the first coming of the plague produced a great shortage of laborers, and recovery of their pre-plague numbers was long delayed because of the recurrences of the pestilence. This affected the country more than the city, because in any case there was a fairly steady flow of population from country to city, and seems to have led to decline and change in the manorial system in western and central Europe, so that many more farm laborers worked for wages or were able to acquire their own land rather than being tied as in the past to the manors under the complete control of the nobility. But this process had already begun with the prosperity and urbanization of the thirteenth century, and was no more than accelerated by the effects of the Black Death. Similarly, social and political instability clearly increased after the plague, but its sources were already apparent in the conditions in Christendom before it struck. The plague fed the instability but did not create it.[24]

More significant was the decline in numbers and quality of clergy and religious, who suffered a higher mortality than the laity in the plague, often approaching or exceeding 50 per cent. The best of the clergy, who continued to try to serve their dying fellow Christians despite the danger of contagion, were most often plague victims. They could not be quickly replaced, and attempts to speed the process resulted in a sharp decline in the quality of priests. The episcopacy was affected as well; in 1348 alone, 25 archbishops and 207 bishops died, most of them undoubtedly plague victims. The Church ceased to supply the majority of government officials. The universities, which the Church sponsored and staffed, were hard hit; of the 30 universities in Europe when the plague struck, only ten remained by 1400. It has been claimed that the disaster weakened faith because people could not understand how God could have allowed such a calamity to happen. But this seems to be mostly an argument of skeptical or agnostic modern historians who think Christian people of the fourteenth century must have reacted that way because that is how the historians themselves would have reacted had they lived then; there is little concrete evidence of this kind of modern fashionable disillusionment after the plague, and much evidence of a passionate piety that endured and was actually strengthened by the increased awareness of human contingency aroused by the prevalence of pestilential death. There were many other causes of the weakening of the Church during this period—notably the "Avignon captivity" of the papacy before the Black Death and the Great Western Schism that followed it—but the loss of quality in the priesthood resulting directly from the

---

[24]Gottfried, *Black Death*, pp. 134-145; Ziegler, *Black Death*, pp. 232-251. Ziegler's discussion in particular emphasizes the arguments against making the Black Death primarily responsible for these changes.

plague was clearly one of them.[25]

All in all, the impact upon Christendom of the greatest medical disaster in history was a good deal less than might have been expected. The endurance and capacity for recovery even of a weakened Christendom under such a blow is striking testimony to how deeply its foundations had been laid in the great days of the thirteenth century in particular. Not so quickly and easily would the glorious edifice of Christendom be destroyed. The Black Death, like the Muslims and the Vikings and the Mongols, was an external assault upon Christendom. Ever since the conversion of Constantine, external assaults have always been less dangerous to Christendom than betrayal from within.

On December 3, 1352 a tremendous thunderstorm struck Rome, abandoned for nearly half a century by the Vicars of Christ who until the end of time will be bishops there. A lightning bolt struck St. Peter's and melted some of its bells. In the city, the Swedish princess Birgitta (Bridget), who had come there for the jubilee year of 1350 and remained in residence, living a holy life and receiving private revelations, believed that it had been revealed to her that Pope Clement VI, whom she had condemned for worldliness, was dying. He did in fact die three days later at Avignon.[26]

Ten days later a conclave of 25 cardinals assembled under relatively pleasant conditions, Clement VI having lifted the tighter restrictions of the past. The name of the holy general of the Carthusians, Jean Birel, was proposed to them as Pope. The Avignon cardinals were not—as they and their successors were amply to demonstrate during the remainder of the fourteenth century—men who wanted to be very close to holiness. They concluded that Birel was too lacking in worldly experience to be Pope (though any head of a substantial religious order is hardly lacking in worldly experience).[27]

On December 17, before proceeding to elect one of their own number as the next Pope, the cardinals jointly swore that in the future their number should be no more than 20 (they did not specify which five of them would be removed); that new cardinals should be chosen only with the consent of two-thirds of the existing cardinals; that no cardinal should be deposed or imprisoned by the Pope without the unanimous approval of the rest of the College, nor excommunicated without the approval of two-thirds of the College; that the Pope might not grant lands, towns or castles or appoint or dismiss officers of the

---

[25]Gottfried, *Black Death*, pp. 145-155; Ziegler, *Black Death*, pp. 259-279. Ziegler's hostility to Christianity is evident in his cited pages, but he does present substantial evidence showing that the faith of many was maintained and strengthened despite the impact of the plague.

[26]Johannes Jorgensen, *Saint Bridget of Sweden* (London, 1954), II, 16-17, 75-78; Mollat, *Popes at Avignon*, p. 42.

[27]Mollat, *Popes at Avignon*, p. 44.

papal state without approval of two-thirds of the College; that they must approve the levying of tenths or subsidies from kings and princes; and that the Pope was to give half his revenue to the College.[28]

No opposition to this barefaced power grab is reported; but one may hope and expect that one of the College's newest members, Gil Albornoz, primate of Castile, one of the best servants of the papacy in all its history, at least suffered some prodding from his conscience about it.

On December 18 the cardinals elected their colleague Stephen Aubert, who had been bishop of Noyon and Clermont and a professor of law at the University of Toulouse, as Pope Innocent VI. He was seventy years old, in relatively poor health and considered weak and vacillating.[29]

He soon showed himself to be not nearly so weak and vacillating as they thought—or else, like so many of his predecessors, he changed once seated in the chair of the fisherman. On June 30, 1353 he appointed Cardinal Albornoz his legate and vicar in the Papal state in Italy, with the evident purpose of reconquering and pacifying it for him so that he might be able to return there. In the Reconquest tradition of Spanish bishops, Cardinal Albornoz had much military experience. He had fought at the Battle of the Rio Salado, saving the life of Alfonso XI there; he had helped rally the Spanish Christians before Tarifa in 1340 and taken part in the sieges of Algeciras in 1342 and of Gibraltar in 1349-50, the latter tragically ended with the death of Alfonso XI in camp from plague. Albornoz had left Spain almost immediately after the succession of Alfonso's young son Pedro, whose character he knew and whose dark destiny he may have foreseen.[30] Seven days later Innocent VI rejected the oath he had taken at the conclave, citing the Decretals of Popes Gregory X and Clement V, who had forbidden the cardinals to deal with any other business except the election of a Pope when the papal office was vacant. No Pope can bargain away the powers of the office that Christ gave Peter, or be bound by a prior promise to give them up. The cardinals grudgingly accepted Innocent VI's assertion of papal authority.[31]

Losing no time, in the tradition of campaigners of the Reconquest, Cardinal Albornoz left for Rome in August. He started with only a small force, but picked up 500 cavalry in long pro-papal Florence, 100 more in Siena and 200 more in Perugia. At Orvieto in the Papal state he encountered a sample of Italy's predatory and ruthless warlords in Giovanni di Vico, who at first tried to

---

[28]*Ibid.*, pp. 44-45.

[29]*Ibid.*, p. 45.

[30]*Ibid.*, p. 126; Juan Beneyto Pérez, *El cardenal Albornoz; canciller de Castilla y caudillo de Italia* (Madrid, 1950), pp. 174, 186-188; Luis Suárez Fernández and Juan Reglá Campistol, *Historia de España* (ed. Ramón Menéndez Pidal), Volume XIV: "España Cristiana: crisis de la Reconquista; luchas civiles" (Madrid, 1987), p. 10.

[31]Mollat, *Popes at Avignon*, p. 46.

deceive him and then defied him. Neither deception nor defiance could divert the veteran of Rio Salado, Tarifa, Algeciras and Gibraltar from his purpose; he tells us that he prayed for help, and his "sorrow turned to joy." Troops rallied to the papal banner from surrounding towns weary of anarchy and the depredations of di Vico and his kind. On June 5, 1354 di Vico submitted, recognizing the Pope's authority over Orvieto and Viterbo.[32]

Rome was now ruled by the half-mad Cola di Rienzo, who dreamed of restoring the ancient Roman Republic, and enforced his authority by beheading those he believed to be conspiring against him on the feast of the beheading of St. John the Baptist. The disillusioned Romans overthrew and killed di Rienzo in October 1354, opening the way for Albornoz, who immediately established a peaceful and orderly government in Rome. In 1355 he proceeded to pacify the Duchy of Spoleto, adjoining the Papal state, and secured Rimini after capturing its warlord, Galeotto Malatesta. Like most of his kind, Malatesta was for sale, and Albornoz bought him to use against Francesco Ordelaffi, warlord of Cesena and Forli. By such methods he had gradually regained control in the name of the Pope of the greater part, though not all, of the Papal state when he was unexpectedly superseded as legate and vicar there by Pope Innocent VI in 1357.[33]

Meanwhile Emperor Charles IV had come to Rome to be crowned. It was the most unpretentious imperial coming to the papal city in the history of the Holy Roman Empire, for Charles—both humble and realistic, with the clearest understanding of the true nature of the Holy Roman Empire in generations—sought no direct rule in Italy. He was content with an expression of willingness by those he found in power to accept the designation of "imperial vicar." Even the proud and turbulent Visconti of Milan were willing to do that, and with their consent Charles IV receives the ancient (and now only ceremonially significant) Iron Crown of Lombardy at Milan on the day of Epiphany in January 1355. From Milan Charles proceeded to Pisa, where Cardinal Pierre Bertrand de Colombiers, who was to crown him Emperor, said a high requiem Mass for Charles' grandfather, Holy Roman Emperor Henry VII of Luxemburg.[34]

On Holy Thursday Charles arrived in Rome, where he pledged in writing (delivered to Cardinal de Colombiers) to ratify all grants of Henry VII, except any which might be contrary to the rights of the Pope; to repudiate everything done by Louis of Bavaria during the period he claimed to be Emperor; neither to claim nor occupy territory in the Papal state nor in the kingdom of Sicily; to

---

[32]*Ibid.*, pp. 130-132; Beneyto Pérez, *Albornoz*, pp. 192, 194-197.

[33]Mollat, *Popes at Avignon*, pp. 133, 135, 137, 153-154; Beneyto Pérez, *Albornoz*, p. 212; Jorgensen, *St. Bridget of Sweden*, II, 101-102, 110-112.

[34]Jarrett, *Charles IV*, pp. 150-151; Mollat, *Popes at Avignon*, p. 134; Dorothy Muir, *A History of Milan under the Visconti* (London, 1924), p. 54.

require his vicars in northern Italy to support the Pope; and to leave Rome the day after his coronation. All these undertakings he kept, except for requiring all his "vicars" in northern Italy to support the Pope, which in view of the condition of Italy was beyond his power. He was crowned on Easter and left as promised the following day. On his way back he met with Cardinal Albornoz at Montepulciano; the Pope's vicar had not attended the coronation, for reasons which are unclear, but Charles IV left the meeting on the best of terms with the great fighting Spanish churchman. By July Charles was back in Germany. He only returned to Italy once during the 23 years which remained of his long imperial reign.[35]

In November Charles IV convened a great Diet of the Empire at Nuremberg. These Diets were periodic congresses at which the variegated German states and the kingdom of Bohemia were represented by their rulers and leading noblemen and churchmen. They were roughly equivalent to a parliament for Germany, and their approval was effectively—though not legally—necessary for the issuance and enforcement of imperial decrees. The number of potentates present made the Diets occasions of great pomp and ceremony, for the patchwork quilt of medieval Germany included well over a hundred legally sovereign states. To this heterogeneous gathering Charles presented a carefully prepared plan to regularize imperial elections in order to reduce strife over them, which had become endemic. It came to be called the Golden Bull. In keeping with his policy of governing cooperatively rather than in an authoritarian manner, Charles specifically declared that the Diet must ratify this decree. After two months of detailed consideration, it did so.[36]

The Golden Bull confirmed the traditional seven electors and established precedence among them, significantly with the three bishop electors first: the Archbishop of Mainz, traditionally the Chancellor of Germany who convoked the imperial electoral college; the Archbishop of Trier, traditionally Chancellor of Italy (though this office had now lost most of its meaning); the Archbishop of Cologne, who had the privilege of crowning the Emperor as King of the Romans at Aachen; the King of Bohemia, traditionally the imperial cup-bearer; the Count Palatine of the Rhine, traditionally Seneschal of the Empire and bearer of the orb of state, who was imperial vicar in the Rhineland, Swabia and Franconia; the Duke of Saxony, traditionally Marshal of the Empire, who carried the Emperor's sword; and the Margrave of Brandenburg, traditionally imperial chamberlain who carried the Emperor's scepter.[37]

The Golden Bull specified that when an imperial election was proclaimed by the Archbishop of Mainz, all electors must attend or send a deputy with a

---

[35]Jarrett, *Charles IV*, pp. 151-153, 170; Mollat, *Popes at Avignon*, p. 134; Beneyto Pérez, *Albornoz*, pp. 208-210.
[36]Jarrett, *Charles IV*, pp. 170-172.
[37]*Ibid.*, pp. 175-176.

proxy, or lose their vote; that they could not bring a bodyguard of more than 200 horsemen; that they could not pledge or sell their vote ahead of time; and that if they had made no election in thirty days they would be confined on bread and water until they made a choice. The Pope's claim that he must confirm the imperial election was not mentioned, but not precluded; Pope Innocent VI made no objction. Votes were tied to the offices of the electors and could not be transferred by them. The lay electoral principalities were declared indivisible, to be inherited only by primogeniture. It was specifically provided that the crown of Bohemia, as a non-German independent kingdom, could not be reassigned by the Emperor and that the King of Bohemia would be elected by the Bohemian Estates, though the Emperor's approval was necessary for the person chosen. (Elsewhere the Emperor could reassign a principality when the direct line of its rulers died out.)[38]

The Golden Bull was universally accepted as a fundamental law of Germany and remained in effect without essential change until its provisions played a central role in the opening drama of the Thirty Years War in 1618. It reflected Charles' deep commitment to limited government and ethnic and cultural diversity within the overarching unity of Christendom:

> Since the glory of the Holy Roman Empire consists in the variety of customs, ways of life, and language of the various nations that go to make it up, it must have laws and a method of government that take all this variety into consideration.[39]

The war between England and France, following the Battle of Crécy and the English capture of Calais, had for the most part ceased during the time of the Black Death. In April 1354 negotiators from the two nations meeting at Guînes agreed on preliminary terms of peace, by which Edward III of England would drop his claim to be King of France in return for the abandonment of all French claims to Aquitaine and also the surrender of the territories that had once owed allegiance to Henry II and the Angevins: Poitou, Touraine, Anjou, Maine, and Normandy. This meant giving up essentially half of France to England. Pope Innocent VI approved the treaty, but the French government—now under John II, known as the "Good Fellow," son of Philip VI who had died in 1350—refused in December to ratify it. In June 1355 the truce between the two powers expired and the war resumed.[40]

This time the leadership of the veteran English army with their formidable longbowmen was assumed not by King Edward III, but by his son Edward,

---

[38]*Ibid.*, pp. 176-180; *The Cambridge Medieval History*, ed. J. R. Tanner, C. W. Previté-Orton, and Z. N. Brooke, Volume VII (Cambridge, 1932), 143-146, 163-164.

[39]Jarrett, *Charles IV*, p. 179.

[40]Édouard Perroy, *The Hundred Years War* (London, 1951), pp. 125, 129; Michael Packe, *King Edward III*, ed. L. C. B. Seaman (London, 1983), pp. 211, 213.

known as the Black Prince. In October and November 1355 he swept across southern France from the Atlantic to the Mediterranean, bypassing strongly held fortified positions but ravaging the countryside and taking and burning Montgisard, Castelnaudary, and the towns (though not the citadels) of Carcassonne and Narbonne. There was no major battle; the Black Prince returned to his base at Bordeaux virtually untouched.[41]

John II and the humiliated French, after driving the Duke of Lancaster (who had landed in Normandy) back to the Cotentin peninsula in the far north, came south to challenge the English. The armies met at Poitiers on September 19, 1356, with the English greatly outnumbered. Most of the French knights were now wearing plate armor, impervious to arrows, but a horse could not be covered with plate armor, and the English longbowmen methodically picked off the French knights' chargers. However, on the advice of Sir William Douglas of Scotland, the majority of the French army advanced on foot, and the English were hard pressed by their numbers before overwhelming the foot soldiers with cavalry charges (since the French had no longbows). At one point some of the English commanders thought they were lost, but the Black Prince cried: "While I am alive it is blasphemy to say we are beaten," and to his best commander, Sir John Chandos: "John, get forward—you shall not see me turn my back this day!" It was the most splendid victory of Edward the Black Prince, a great general; when the day was done the King of France was his prisoner, along with some two thousand other knights.[42]

France was plunged into instant crisis by the loss of its king and the enormous ransom demanded for him. The Crown Prince or Dauphin Charles,[43] just 19 years old and timid, found himself with an army almost totally discredited by two shattering defeats in a decade by greatly inferior forces, and an Estates-General, convened in Paris and dominated by the revolutionary Stephen Marcel, demanding rule by a council appointed by the Estates which Charles must obey. The Dauphin's namesake Charles "the Bad" of Navarre was advancing his own claim to be king, as the son of Louis X's daughter who had been passed over for the succession in 1317 without clear justification in French law or precedent for doing so. In March 1347 Dauphin Charles yielded to the Estates, signing their *Grande Ordonnance* requiring representatives of the

---

[41]Barber, *Edward, Prince of Wales and Aquitaine*, pp. 117-127.

[42]*Ibid.*, pp. 132, 138-147; Perroy, *Hundred Years War*, pp. 130-131; Packe, *Edward III*, pp. 217-222.

[43]Charles was the first Crown Prince of France to bear the title "Dauphin," which the ruler of the province of Dauphiné in the foothills of the Alps in southeastern France, Humbert II, had sold to him for 200,000 florins in 1349, in lieu of the King of France whose diplomats negotiated the deal since Charles was then only twelve. Henceforth all heirs to the French throne bore the title Dauphin (Eugene L. Cox, *The Green Count of Savoy; Amadeus VI and Transalpine Savoy in the Fourteenth Century* [Princeton, 1967], pp. 74-75).

Estates to sit on the royal council and supervise the administration of the kingdom, along with purging unpopular nobles. He gained a two-year truce with the English in that same month; but the immediate effect even of this was destructive, since in the anarchic state of the kingdom the demobilized soldiers formed mercenary bands which preyed on the countryside.[44]

In September 1357 there was a peace conference in London, attended by representatives of Edward III of England, the captive John II of France, Dauphin Charles, and the Pope. By January the negotiators had accepted the First Treaty of London, setting four million gold écus as the ransom for King John and providing for the full cession of the entire southwestern quarter of France to England. (Meanwhile Scots King David II, also a captive of the English since 1346, had been ransomed for 100,000 marks—an enormous sum for the impoverished northern kingdom.) In February the Paris mob stormed the Dauphin's residence and killed the Marshals of Champagne and Normandy in his own chamber, spattering him with their blood. The next month Charles (more fortunate or more resolute than his later successor Louis XVI at the time of the French Revolution) escaped from the riotous city, put his family in the fortress of Medaux for safekeeping, called his own Estates, and raised an army.[45]

In May 1358 the spreading anarchy had its most terrible result: the outbreak of a peasant revolt around Beauvais, quickly spreading to other parts of France. The peasants were driven to desperation by the ravages of the demobilized troops and were conscious in their own way of the vacuum of authority at the top. They slaughtered any members of the aristocracy they could get their hands on, regardless of age or sex. Revolutionary leader Marcel supported the rebels, but the Dauphin fought them after saving his family from them, now aided by Charles "the Bad" of Navarre who trapped and killed their leader, Guillaume Cale called Jacques Bonhomme. The Paris mob turned on Marcel and killed him, and on August 2 Dauphin Charles regained control of his capital.[46]

Under these tumultuous circumstances it is not surprising that the first installment of the ransom of King John II was not paid on schedule in November. Edward III of England promptly declared the Treaty of London void and went back to war. A second Treaty of London, signed in March 1359, would have surrendered the northwestern quarter of France along with the

---

[44]Packe, *Edward III*, pp. 222-223, 228; Perroy, *Hundred Years War*, pp. 133-134; Mollat, *Popes at Avignon*, p. 49.

[45]Perroy, *Hundred Years War*, pp. 134-135, 137; Packe, *Edward III*, pp. 223-224, 227; Mollat, *Popes at Avignon*, p. 50; Ronald Nicholson, *Scotland: the Later Middle Ages* (Edinburgh, 1974), p. 163.

[46]Perroy, *Hundred Years War*, pp. 135-136; Packe, *Edward III*, pp. 224-226; Gottfried, *Black Death*, pp. 98-101.

southwestern quarter to England in return for Edward's abandonment of his claim to be king of all France, but Dauphin Charles and the Estates-General stoutly rejected it. At the end of the year Edward III appeared before Reims to besiege it, intending to be crowned King of France there in the traditional manner of French kings; but the leaders and people of Reims would have none of it, and Edward realized that despite all his military victories he did not really have the strength to subdue and keep in subjection a country so much larger and more populous than his own. Therefore in May 1360 he signed the Peace of Brétigny, confirmed in October, by which Edward was to receive southwestern France (Aquitaine), but not Normandy and Anjou, to which he formally gave up his claim along with his claim to the throne of France. The ransom for the hapless John II was reduced by 25 per cent and he was set free October 25, though he had to leave three of his sons as hostages for fulfillment of the terms of the treaty, and soon afterward to sell his eleven-year-old daughter Isabelle to the vicious Gian Galeazzo Visconti of Milan for 600,000 gold florins to help pay the ransom.[47]

The agony of France had been primarily caused by English aggression, but the parallel agony of Castile during the pontificate of Innocent VI was primarily caused by the extraordinary vices of its King Pedro, called the Cruel. Succeeding his crusading father Alfonso XI, who had died of the Black Death before Gibraltar, at the age of only sixteen, Pedro was at first dominated by his mother Maria and a coalition of nobles led by Juan Alfonso de Alburquerque. Queen Mother Maria had a long-standing and bitter grievance, because for most of their married life Alfonso XI had abandoned her for a mistress named Leonor de Guzmán, who had borne him four sons; Pedro was his only legitimate child. Early in 1351 Maria and Alburquerque arranged to have Leonor killed. Neither his father's nor his mother's example was lost on Pedro.[48]

In the spring of 1352 Pedro fell violently in love with a girl named Maria de Padilla, from a prominent Castilian family. The next spring they had their first child, Beatriz. Negotiations were already well advanced for a French marriage for Pedro, and in 1353, under heavy pressure from Alburquerque and even from some members of Maria de Padilla's family, Pedro married Blanche of Bourbon. Three days after the wedding he abandoned her and returned to Maria de Padilla; nine months later, after persuading two Castilian bishops to annul his marriage to Blanche, he married Juana de Castro, sister of his most loyal supporter among the nobility, Fernando de Castro of Galicia. A month

---

[47]Perroy, *Hundred Years War*, pp. 137-140; Packe, *Edward III*, pp. 234-235, 238-239, 245-247; Barber, *Edward, Prince of Wales and Aquitaine*, pp. 158-163, 167-169; Desmond Seward, *The Hundred Years War* (New York, 1978), p. 100.

[48]O'Callaghan, *Medieval Spain*, p. 419; J. N. Hillgarth, *The Spanish Kingdoms, 1250-1516* (Oxford, 1976), I, 375-376; Menéndez Pidal, *Historia de España*, XIV, 12-13.

later he left Juana and returned to Maria de Padilla. Understandably appalled by these proceedings, Pope Innocent VI in May 1354 overruled the annulment of Pedro's marriage to Blanche, directed him to return to her, and encouraged the Castilian nobles to support Blanche and pressure Pedro. Blanche sought sanctuary in the cathedral of Toledo and was protected by its Archbishop. Pedro declared Toledo in rebellion and civil war broke out.[49]

At first the war went against him, and he became a virtual prisoner in the city of Toro; then early in 1355 he escaped, whereupon the Pope's legate in Castile excommunicated him and laid an interdict on any city supporting him. But he was the legitimate king; he was young, vigorous and active; many of the people rallied to him, and in May he took Toledo, captured and closely confined Blanche, and executed 22 city councillors for rebellion. Pope Innocent VI offered to lift his excommunication if he would take Blanche back, but Pedro scornfully refused. As soon as he had triumphed over his enemies in the nobility, he went to war with neighboring Aragon. The papal excommunication was renewed in 1357. Encouraged by Aragon, Pedro's half-brothers, the sons of Leonor de Guzmán, began to challenge him, along with some more distant relatives. His near-pathological cruelty now began to emerge; he had his half-brother Fadrique assassinated in Sevilla and then ostentatiously ate dinner in the house where the bloody corpse lay, and the next month he had his cousin and rival Juan hammered to death with maces in Bilbao, afterward throwing his body from a balcony to a crowd in the street.[50]

Leadership of the resistance in Castile was now assumed by the youngest son of Alfonso XI and Leonor, Henry, Count of Trastámara, who invaded Castile in September 1359 and won a victory at Araviana. But the following April Pedro defeated him at the First Battle of Nájera and almost captured him in that town. In May 1361 Pedro briefly made peace with Aragon; immediately afterward his Queen Blanche disappeared and was never seen again, and in July Maria de Padilla died, though she was only 28. Pedro went before the *cortes* of Castile to claim that he had been betrothed to Maria de Padilla before his marriage to Blanche (betrothal was a complete impediment to marriage in the church law of that time) and that he had secretly married her during the brief interval between Blanche's death and hers. The *cortes* accepted this unlikely story—Pedro's fearsome reputation undoubtedly discouraged any awkward questioning of it—and his four children by Maria de Padilla (three daughters

---

[49]Menéndez Pidal, *Historia de España*, XIV, 19-26; O'Callaghan, *Medieval Spain*, pp. 420, 423.
[50]Menéndez Pidal, *Historia de España*, XIV, 27-28, 30-34, 36, 47, 54, 57, 59; O'Callaghan, *Medieval Spain*, pp. 422, 424; Mollat, *Popes at Avignon*, p. 275; P. E. Russell, *The English Intervention in Spain and Portugal in the Time of Edward III and Richard II* (Oxford, 1955), pp. 14, 55.

and a son) were legitimized.[51]

In April 1362 Pedro murdered the rival king of Moorish Granada with his own hands, and in June invaded Aragon and made a treaty of alliance with England as a counterweight to French support for his enemies Pedro IV of Aragon and Henry of Trastámara. Edward the Black Prince, now governing Aquitaine, was eager for new military glory and found satisfaction in upholding a legitimate king against a bastard challenger regardless of the king's moral character. Facing the best general in Europe, Henry of Trastámara sought to balance the odds by hiring mercenaries.[52]

Ferocious bands of these mercenaries, now introduced to Spain, had been ravaging France and Italy for five years, at one point severely threatening Pope Innocent VI in Avignon, adding greatly to the suffering from the wars being almost constantly fought among the official rulers and noblemen of those three lands. Scandinavia was likewise stricken by a war between Denmark and Sweden, in which the Danes ravaged the prosperous Swedish island of Gotland.[53] Repeated attempts by Pope Innocent VI and his legates to make peace had been almost entirely fruitless everywhere. He had vacillated in his support of Cardinal Albornoz in the Papal state by removing him as legate and vicar there in 1357, though restoring him in 1358, whereupon he secured Bologna, the largest city in the papal state which had remained outside papal rule.[54] But in 1361 the tyrant Bernabò Visconti of Milan had hurled an incredible defiance at the Vicar of Christ: when his legates came to Milan to read the Pope's decree of excommunication of Bernabò, the tyrant forced them literally to eat it, and when the Archbishop protested, Bernabò screamed at him "that here in his own land he was Pope, emperor and God himself, for here God could do nothing without [his] permission."[55] The great historic Lateran church and palace burned down that same year. In Rome, St. Bridget of Sweden was hurling condemnation upon the Pope's head for his use of the Inquisition against the "Spiritual Franciscans."[56] And Innocent VI had made no move to return to Rome despite the remarkable success of Cardinal Albornoz in re-establishing the dominion and security of the papal state.

The access of unexpected strength which had come to Innocent VI the year after his election as Pope by a College of Cardinals sworn to restrict papal

---

[51]Menéndez Pidal, *Historia de España*, XIV, 69, 73, 76; O'Callaghan, *Medieval Spain*, pp. 422-423; Russell, *English Intervention in Spain*, pp. 1-2, 25-26, 173.

[52]Menéndez Pidal, *Historia de España*, XIV, 76, 78, 80; Russell, *English Intervention in Spain*, pp. 3-4, 27; Barber, *Edward, Prince of Wales and Aquitaine*, pp. 175, 186.

[53]Mollat, *Popes at Avignon*, p. 50; Franklin D. Scott, *Sweden: the Nation's History* (Minneapolis, 1977), pp. 74-75.

[54]Mollat, *Popes at Avignon*, pp. 137-142; Beneyto Pérez, *Albornoz*, pp. 213-217, 221-222.

[55]Sigrid Undset, *Catherine of Siena* (New York, 1954), p. 137.

[56]Jorgensen, *St. Catherine of Siena*, p. 159; Mollat, *Popes at Avignon*, p. 46.

power had left him. He seems to have felt himself a failure. "Overcome with grief, depressed by the turn of events, and worn out in spirit," Pope Innocent VI died September 12, 1362, "asking that his remains should be buried in the Charterhouse at Villeneuve that he had founded in 1356 and where, amid all the upheavals of his life, he had enjoyed in the course of his reign a few hours of peace and quiet."[57]

The conclave of mostly French cardinals assembled in Avignon. Casting an immediate vote without prior consultation, everyone was astonished to find that they had elected Hugh Roger, brother of the late Pope, by 15 votes out of 20. But Hugh declined to serve, and when no cardinal could obtain the necessary two-thirds vote, the College chose a man both experienced and holy: Guillaume de Grimoard, Abbot of St. Victor of Marseilles, who had been a teacher of canon law and papal legate to Naples. He took the name Urban V.[58]

Six months later, on Good Friday 1363, the new Pope proclaimed a new crusade at the urging of King Peter de Lusignan of Cyprus and John II of France, who was hoping to retrieve his reputation from the disaster at Poitiers and his long captivity. Lip service was given to recovery of the Holy Land and an attack on Egypt was also planned, but one objective of this crusade at least in the Pope's mind appears to have been to check the advance of the Ottoman Turks, now present in force in northern Greece—Thrace and Macedonia. Waldemar IV of Denmark also took the cross, though he was still embroiled in his war with Sweden and the newly formed Hanseatic League of Baltic cities, and never went. Neither did John II, who died in April 1364 in England, where he had returned to captivity when one of his sons who had been confined as a hostage escaped. This left Peter alone, with a very limited force, able to do no more than conduct a raid on Alexandria in Egypt in October 1365.[59]

The Turkish advance could not be ignored; Pope Urban was convinced that he must try again to stop them. The Ottoman Turks were emerging not only as a threat to the dying Byzantine empire, but to all of Christendom. Byzantine Co-Emperor John Cantacuzene had employed them in northern Greece in such numbers that they had become very familiar with the territory and ambitious to plunder and even to conquer it for themselves. His appeals to his own people to show more public and fighting spirit had been unavailing; in 1348 the Genoese had destroyed most of the Greek ships in the famous Byzantine harbor of the Golden Horn, and Serb imperial challenger Stephen Dushan had conquered Thessaly and Mount Athos, the heart of Greek

[57]Mollat, *Popes at Avignon*, p. 51.

[58]*Ibid.*, p. 52.

[59]Joseph Gill, *Byzantium and the Papacy, 1198-1400* (New Brunswick NJ, 1979), p. 212; Kenneth M. Setton, ed., *A History of the Crusades*, Volume III, ed. Harry W. Hazard (Madison WI, 1975), p. 73; Packe, *Edward III*, pp. 256-258; Nicol, *Last Centuries of Byzantium*, pp. 274-275; Scott, *Sweden*, p. 76.

Orthodox monasticism. The sailors and soldiers manning a new Byzantine fleet built, equipped and sent out against the Genoese in March 1349 had fallen into ludicrous panic when the first strong wind blew, leaping into the sea, some of them in full armor. John Cantacuzene had brought in the Turks again to fight for him against his co-Emperor John V Palaeologus, and the strife had continued until John Cantacuzene was forced to abdicate in 1354, though as the monk Joasaph he continued periodically to advise the failing Byzantine government. Earlier in 1354 an earthquake had levelled the walls of Gallipoli, the key fortress at the narrowest point of the Hellespont; the Turks had at once taken, occupied and held it, giving them unrestricted entry to Europe. By 1359 they had first appeared under the walls of Constantinople; by 1363 they had taken Philippopolis, a major city in northern Thrace.[60]

In 1365 Pope Urban V gave some encouragement to Byzantine Emperor John V Palaeologus, who had been unable to interest Pope Innocent VI in his problems even though expressing in a series of remarkable letters his intention to become a Catholic. Holy Roman Emperor Charles IV had met with the Pope in Avignon in the spring of 1365 to encourage him to send a crusade specifically against the Ottoman Turks. Early in 1366 the Pope wrote again to the Byzantine Emperor promising a new effort to help him, to be led by King Louis of Hungary, Peter de Lusignan of Cyprus and the Emperor's own cousin, Amadeus the "Green Count" of Savoy. Perhaps fearing, in view of the failure of the crusade proclaimed in 1363, that the promise would remain empty, the Byzantine Emperor travelled in person to Hungary to prod King Louis to act. The full extent of Byzantine weakness was revealed when the Bulgarians refused to allow the Emperor to cross their territory to return home, leaving him stranded in Hungary until a campaign in Bulgaria by the "Green Count" later in the year brought about his release. Neither Louis nor Peter did anything to help, and the campaign in Bulgaria to free the Emperor left Amadeus VI, one of the few princes in Europe still devoted to the crusading ideal, with no money remaining to engage the Turks. He had succeeded in reclaiming Gallipoli from them, but control of Gallipoli was no longer necessary for them to get into Europe, so widespread had their incursions become. In 1369 they took Adrianople, the principal city in Thrace other than Constantinople itself.[61]

All hope of unity among the South Slavic lands had collapsed with the death of the great Serb leader Stephen Dushan, who had styled himself

---

[60]Nicol, *Last Centuries of Byzantium*, pp. 226-232, 245, 249-256, 273; John V. A. Fine Jr., *The Late Medieval Balkans* (Ann Arbor MI, 1987), pp. 307, 320, 378.

[61]Gill, *Byzantium and the Papacy*, pp. 208-214; Nicol, *Last Centuries of Byzantium*, pp. 275-277, 285; Fine, *Late Medieval Balkans*, pp. 367-368, 378; Cox, *Green Count of Savoy*, pp. 211-239; E. A. Gibbons, *The Foundation of the Ottoman Empire* (London, 1916), pp. 112, 114; Mollat, *Popes at Avignon*, p. 156.

Emperor, in December 1355.[62] There remained no major obstacle to Turkish expansion in the Balkans or in Greece. Only the West could stop it, and so far—except for the "Green Count"—no one had really tried.

To the north and east two new Christian powers were developing, one Catholic and one Eastern Orthodox. Catholic Poland under King Casimir the Great continued very faithful to the Church and strongly supported by all the Popes of this period. The Lithuanians immediately east of Poland were still pagan, though periodically considering conversion; the Popes repeatedly aided King Casimir against them with substantial grants of money.[63] The power of the Mongol "Golden Horde" in Russia was weakened by the murder of several of their rulers in quick succession beginning in 1357, allowing the rise of Orthodox Moscow under its young, aggressive ruler Dmitri Donskoy and his wise counsellor Archbishop Alexis, the first native Russian (as distinct from Greeks) to hold that position. Moscow's citadel, the Kremlin, was rebuilt in stone in 1367 and withstood a massive attack by the pagan Lithuanians late in the following year.[64]

The situation in Spain was little changed during the first years of Urban V's pontificate. The war between Castile and Aragon continued, waged savagely by Pedro of Castile, who ordered Aragonese prisoners' hands cut off, and at least once ordered that no Aragonese prisoners be taken alive.[65] The war became increasingly involved with the continuing hostility between France and England as implementation of the terms of the Peace of Brétigny—notably the formal renunciation by the French King, now Charles V, and Edward III of England of their claims to Aquitaine and the whole of France, respectively—was delayed again and again.[66] In December 1364 Charles V of France offered to make a military alliance with Pedro IV of Aragon and Henry of Trastámara, the illegitimate claimant to the Castilian throne. Secret negotiations continued until September 1365, when Pedro IV reported to the *corts* of Catalonia that he, Charles and Pope Urban V had each offered 100,000 gold florins to support Henry of Trastámara. When delegates in the *corts* objected to bringing the mercenaries who would be receiving this money into Spain, they were curtly told that the mercenaries were coming anyway, and

---

[62]Fine, *Late Medieval Balkans*, pp. 335-337. As Fine explains, though it was later believed he had actually been on the march to attack Constantinople when he died, this is unproved and modern research suggests that it is unlikely.

[63]Paul W. Knoll, *The Rise of the Polish Monarchy* (Chicago, 1972), pp. 161-162, 210, 229.

[64]Vernadsky, *Mongols and Russia*, pp. 208, 226, 245-246, 252-253; John Meyendorff, *Byzantium and the Rise of Russia* (Cambridge, England, 1981), pp. 185-186, 188-190.

[65]Menéndez Pidal, *Historia de España*, XIV, 82-83; Russell, *English Intervention in Spain*, p. 33.

[66]Perroy, *Hundred Years War*, p. 142; Barber, *Edward, Prince of Wales and Aquitaine*, p. 175.

would simply ravage Catalonia or take service with King Pedro of Castile if not paid. The alliance was implemented, the *corts* reluctantly agreed to pay the 100,000 florins, and before the end of the year an army of French and English mercenaries under France's best commander, Bertrand du Guesclin, entered Spain.[67]

Pedro of Castile was not popular; only in the far northwestern province of Galicia was he solidly and almost universally supported. In any case he did not have and could not raise an army even close to matching du Guesclin's. The invaders carried all before them. On Palm Sunday 1366 Henry was formally crowned King of Castile at Burgos. By July Pedro had left his last refuge in Galicia for Bayonne in Gascony where he appealed to Edward the Black Prince under the terms of the alliance of 1362. Edward agreed at once, despite the warnings of his beloved wife Joan "the fair maid of Kent" whom he had married less than five years before.[68]

By February 1367, in the dead of winter, the Black Prince crossed the fabled Pass of Roncesvalles with his veteran English knights and archers. Arriving in Castile, he wrote to Henry calling him a usurper; Henry responded tellingly by pointing out that King Pedro had murdered at least ten of his relatives along with many others, was guilty of rape, and had been excommunicated and was an enemy of the Church. Unheeding, the Black Prince pressed on; at the Second Battle of Nájera in April, he destroyed the Franco-Castilian army. The English longbowmen, never before seen in Spain, were as deadly as at Crécy and Poitiers (they "shot thicker than rain falls in winter," wrote the Spanish historian Péro Lopez de Ayala, who was there) and Prince Edward as brilliant in his generalship. Du Guesclin, Marshal of France d'Audrehem, Henry of Trastámara's brother Sancho, the Master of Calatrava, the Master of Santiago, and many others fell into his hands as prisoners. But the most important quarry was missing; Henry of Trastámara got away.[69]

No one emerged with much credit from these terrible years in Castile, but Henry of Trastámara had more than his share of a quality burned into Spanish souls by the long crusade: perseverance. He seems never to have thought of

---

[67]Russell, *English Intervention in Spain*, pp. 33-37, 40; Barber, *Edward, Prince of Wales and Aquitaine*, p. 188.

[68]Russell, *English Intervention in Spain*, pp. 49, 55, 57-58, 62-68; Barber, *Edward, Prince of Wales and Aquitaine*, pp. 188-191; Henry D. Sedgwick, *The Life of Edward the Black Prince* (Indianapolis, 1932), p. 221. Prince Edward's letter of April 5 telling Joan of his great victory at Nájera movingly begins "my dearest and truest sweetheart and beloved companion." He would have been better advised to listen to her, for in the end his Spanish venture was a complete failure, and it appears that it was in Spain that he acquired the chronic dysentery that was to kill him before he could succeed to the throne of his father.

[69]Russell, *English Intervention in Spain*, pp. 83-85, 94-105; O'Callaghan, *Medieval Spain*, p. 425; Hillgarth, *Spanish Kingdoms*, I, 381.

abandoning his cause, even after this crushing defeat and narrow escape. When Pedro IV of Aragon made an agreement with Prince Edward to give no more support of any kind to Henry, the Castilian royal claimant, now in France, wrote him saying he hoped he would change his mind, but would carry on without him if necessary. He still had 3,000 soldiers and the backing of the King of France and the powerful Duke of Anjou in the south of France. Henry hardly knew Prince Edward and certainly did not like him, but he knew Pedro of Castile only too well and may have foreseen that two men so antithetical in character would not long cooperate effectively. For the Black Prince, though profligate with money and sometimes harsh in manner, was a man of honor, famous for his devotion to the chivalric code, while Pedro was nothing of the kind. The two men soon drew apart, the more quickly because of Pedro's complete inability to fulfill his lavish promises of paying the whole cost (naturally very great) of Prince Edward's massive expedition in his behalf. By November of the very year of Edward's triumph at Nájera, he, Pedro IV of Aragon, and Charles II of Navarra delivered an ultimatum to Pedro to pay, or else they would switch their support to Henry. Meanwhile Henry had returned to Castile; when he crossed the border from Aragon he made a cross in the sand, kissed it, and vowed never to leave his country again—a vow he kept.[70]

Pedro of course could not pay, but for all his cruelty he was still the legitimate king of Castile and consequently many Castilians were still willing to fight for him. The civil war raged on through 1368. Meanwhile in France Charles V, unwilling to give up his claim to Aquitaine, prepared to resume the Hundred Years War, which broke out again in June 1369. There could be no more thought of committing the limited English forces to war in Castile on either side. But the French, with larger forces available and du Guesclin burning to avenge his humiliation at Nájera, could still help Henry. In December 1368 Charles V sent du Guesclin back to Castile with the blunt instruction "to finish off Pedro with the least possible delay."[71]

Henry had been besieging almost impregnable Toledo for nearly a year when Pedro brought up a largely Moorish army—he had always had a marked partiality for Moors and Jews, as compared to his Christian subjects—from Sevilla to try to relieve it. At du Guesclin's urging, Henry did not wait for his rival to come to Toledo, but marched south to meet him in the dead-flat plain of La Mancha. They met on March 14, 1369 for their last battle, at Montiel just north of the Sierra Morena, the Dark Mountains. Pedro was overwhelmed, and had to take refuge in the unprepared and poorly defended castle of Montiel,

[70]Russell, *English Intervention in Spain*, pp. 115-116, 119, 127-128, 130-131, 134-137; Barber, *Edward, Prince of Wales and Aquitaine*, pp. 207-208.
[71]Russell, *English Intervention in Spain*, pp. 138-140, 145-146; Barber, *Edward, Prince of Wales and Aquitaine*, pp. 219-221; Packe, *Edward III*, pp. 274-275; Perroy, *Hundred Years War*, p. 161.

which could hold out only a few days. He surrendered to du Guesclin and offered him a large sum to set him free; du Guesclin told Henry, who promised to match it if the French commander would bring King Pedro to him.[72] Du Guesclin brought him. In one of the most terrible scenes in Spanish history, the two deadly enemies faced each other across a small room. It had been so many years since they had met that they did not recognize each other; Henry had to ask if the man facing him was indeed King Pedro. "I am he," said Pedro the Cruel, at least no coward at the end. Henry sprang on him and daggered him in the face. The two men fell to the floor in a death grapple. But Pedro was unarmed; Henry stabbed him again and again until he lay still.[73]

In this dark and bloody moment was established the Trastámara dynasty of Castile, which was to bring Spain and Christendom to heights undreamed of in 1369; for Henry of Trastámara was the great-great-grandfather of Queen Isabel, savior of her country, final victor of the Reconquest, reformer of the Church, and patron of the discovery of America.

During the first three years of his pontificate Urban V gave no sign of an intention to return to Rome. He gave very little support to Cardinal Albornoz, dismissing him as papal representative in northern Italy in order to make a humiliating treaty with the Visconti in Milan in February 1364 by which the Pope promised to pay them 500,000 gold florins to give up their ill-gotten gains in the papal states, including the city of Bologna. The Visconti, who knew their enemy, had insisted on Albornoz's dismissal as part of their price, and did not relax their pressure until Albornoz was also specifically deprived of his commission as legate in the papal state. Urban V, not wanting to lose his services entirely, sent him as legate to Naples, now ruled by the wayward Queen Joanna whom he found almost impossible to deal with.[74]

But at least in Rome Albornoz's great work endured. The Eternal City was at peace at last, governed by a non-Roman Senator; and the peace had endured a full decade, since the fall of Cola di Rienzo in 1354. The war with the Visconti was ended, however dishonorably; there was no military obstacle nor serious danger to threaten the Pope's return to Rome. The French cardinals were bitterly opposed, but Emperor Charles IV strongly favored it; in June 1365 he even offered to escort the Pope personally to Rome. The Pope declined, but three months later signaled that he was at least seriously considering a return

[72]Russell, *English Intervention in Spain*, pp. 147-148; O'Callaghan, *Medieval Spain*, p. 426.
[73]O'Callaghan, *Medieval Spain*, p. 426.
[74]Mollat, *Popes at Avignon*, pp. 144-146. Joanna, beautiful and wanton, became Queen of Naples at 17 in 1343 and quickly went through three husbands. No one could control or reform her, though many tried, including both St. Bridget of Sweden and St. Catherine of Siena. See Jorgensen, *St. Bridget of Sweden*, pp. 119-124, 189, 234-237, and Jorgensen, *St. Catherine of Siena*, pp. 365-367.

when he ordered major and costly repairs to the Vatican palace to make it habitable again.[75]

By June 1366 he had made up his mind. He officially informed the cardinals, the Emperor, the King of France, Bernabò Visconti, and the Romans that he had irrevocably decided to return to Rome. The Italians hailed the decision; the French condemned it. But Urban V remained unshaken in his resolution. On April 30, 1367 he left Avignon. At Marseilles on May 6 the cardinals made a last attempt to stop him, some going so far as to threaten not to accompany him to Rome. In response he made young Guillaume d'Aigrefeuille, age 28, a cardinal and told the others he would create still more new cardinals if they deserted him. On May 19 Urban sailed from Marseilles with a large fleet, and on June 3 he landed on the beach before the town of Corneto in the papal state.[76]

Johannes Jorgensen paints the dramatic scene:

> Driven by a brisk north wind the papal fleet speedily approaches Corneto. The ship with sails of silk, carrying Urban, can soon be distinguished. A short while yet and the first galleys glide past the bridge head, but without coming alongside. With lowered sails and backing the oars with all their might they bring to and form a path of honor for the Pope's ship. Up in Corneto all the bells begin to ring. Along the shore men stand shoulder to shoulder and in towards the coast head can be seen by head. The first row of spectators is pressed so far forward that the waves run over their feet.
>
> And so galley after galley glides past and swerves aside. Four men come carrying the baldacchino of gold-embroidered brocade under which the Pope is to walk. For now the Pope's ship is coming alongside—a galley with three rows of oars. A gangway is put out from the high poop, and a silken carpet is spread over it. Then the Pope's retinue begin to go ashore—the French noble guard, the officials of the papal court, the French cardinals, easily distinguished by their surly and discontented looks (five of them had stayed behind in Avignon).... And then, at last, comes the Pope, *il nostro dolce Cristo in terra* as Caterina of Siena was to say later, the pious little Benedictine Guillaume Grimoard de Grisac, who wears his common black habit beneath the gold and silk of the papal robe.[77]

The Pope spent the summer in Viterbo, at last making his entry into Rome October 16, in a splendid procession of thousands to St. Peter's. By then the Pope and the Church had already suffered a great loss: Cardinal Albornoz, who had greeted the Pope whose coming he had done so much to make possible, as he stepped off his ship at Corneto, was dead in Rome's dying month of August.[78]

[75]Mollat, *Popes at Avignon*, pp. 154-157.

[76]*Ibid.*, pp. 57-58, 157-158.

[77]Jorgensen, *St. Bridget of Sweden*, II, 202-203.

[78]*Ibid.*, II, 205-206; Mollat, *Popes at Avignon*, pp. 146, 158; Beneyto Pérez, *Albornoz*,

The Pope had never sufficiently appreciated Albornoz; and even in Italy, he continued to show partiality for French churchmen. The Italians were shocked and angry when in September 1368, more than a year after his return to Italy, he appointed eight new cardinals of whom six were French, one English, and only one an Italian and a Roman. The next month Emperor Charles IV, making his second visit to Italy, entered Rome with the Pope, holding his mule according to the ancient custom for Emperors going back to Charlemagne. But much of Italy was still dangerously turbulent. In January 1369 there was a riot in Siena from which the Emperor barely escaped with his life; he returned at once to Germany and never came back to Italy. This alarming event very likely increased the Pope's own fears and nostalgia for Avignon. The renewal of the Hundred Years War also distressed him. In October 1369 he announced in Viterbo that he planned to leave Rome soon, giving as his reason that he wanted to try to end the war between France and England and needed to be closer to it to do so.[79]

He had one brilliant moment in Rome just before this sad announcement. In September 1369 Byzantine Emperor John V Palaeologus arrived for the solemn ceremony of his reception into the Catholic Church. He made his profession of faith, renounced his errors, and accepted the Pope's primacy. But John V's prestige at home was low and the opposition to church reunion was still very strong in Constantinople. As John V himself realized, he had little hope of bringing his church and people with him back into communion with Rome, at least without an ecumenical council to settle their differences. And Pope Urban V explicitly refused to call a council for this purpose; he never gave his reasons.[80]

The Pope did not hurry his departure; he did not sail for France until September 1370. In May he rejected a moving appeal from the people of Rome to stay, responding only—and coldly—that "the Holy Spirit brought me to this region; now He takes me to other regions for the honor of the Church."[81] One night during the oppressive heat of a Roman August, St. Bridget of Sweden believed that she received a message from the Blessed Virgin Mary about Pope Urban V and his departure from Rome:

> I will speak to you of the Pope whose name is Urbanus. To him the Holy Spirit gave the counsel that he should come to Rome to work justice and strengthen the Christian faith and renew the Holy Church. As a mother

---

pp. 252-253.
[79]Mollat, *Popes at Avignon*, pp. 58, 159-160; Jarrett, *Charles IV*, p. 155; Jorgensen, *St. Bridget of Sweden*, II, 211; Jorgensen, *St. Catherine of Siena*, p. 89; Undset, *Catherine of Siena*, p. 86.
[80]Gill, *Byzantium and the Papacy*, pp. 219-221; Nicol, *Last Centuries of Byzantium*, pp. 281-282; Mollat, *Popes at Avignon*, p. 58.
[81]Mollat, *Popes at Avignon*, p. 160.

leads her child whither she will, by showing him her breasts, so I led him to Rome by my prayers. But what does he do now? Now he turns his back on me and not his face and would leave me. And a false and evil spirit would entice him to do this. For it wearies him to do his duty, and he is longing for ease and confort. He is longing for his own country, and his carnally minded friends urge him to depart, for they think more of his temporal welfare and conform more to his will than to the will of God and to what serves the glory of God and the everlasting good of the Pope. . . . If he should succeed in getting back to his own country he will be struck such a blow that his teeth will shake in his mouth. His sight will be darkened and all his limbs will tremble. . . . The friends of God will no longer include him in their prayers, and he will be called to account to God for what he did and what he did not do.[82]

Men remembered St. Bridget's prophecy when Pope Urban V, returning to Avignon in September 1370, was stricken with a mortal illness in November and died six days before Christmas. Yet he remained the first Pope at Avignon who had returned to Rome, despite weakening at the end. The ultimate verdict of the Church was that his life as a whole had demonstrated heroic sanctity; in 1870 he was beatified.[83]

The conclave to elect his successor was short and harmonious. It met ten days after Urban V's death; the following morning Cardinal Pierre Roger de Beaufort, a brilliant and upright canon lawyer only 42 years old, noted for modesty and piety though of a weak physical constitution, was unanimously elected as Pope Gregory XI.[84] Within a few days of his consecration St. Bridget was writing him that the Mother of God had said to her:

If Pope Gregory will come to Rome and will return to Italy to stay there and like a good shepherd will take upon himself the cause of the Church, then like a good Mother . . . I will give him joyful warmth at my breast, which is the love of God, and fill him with the milk of piety and prayer. And I will pray to my Son for him, that He will send His Holy Spirit to Gregory and pour it into the depths of his heart. . . . For it is the will of God that he shall humbly bring back the Chair of Peter to Rome. And that he may not let himself be mocked or deceived by anyone I foretell him this: If he does not obey, he shall be made to feel the rod of justice, his days shall be shortened, and he shall be called to judgment.[85]

St. Bridget followed up with a still more peremptory letter in March when she learned that the new Pope was hesitating, with his Avignon counsellors strongly advising against his going to Rome.[86] The return of Pope Urban V to

---

[82]Jorgensen, *St. Bridget of Sweden*, II, 221.
[83]Mollat, *Popes at Avignon*, p. 58.
[84]*Ibid.*, p. 59.
[85]Jorgensen, *St. Bridget of Sweden*, II, 224.
[86]*Ibid.*, II, 226.

Avignon and the renewed influence of the Pope's French counsellors and cardinals had accentuated the hostility to papal authority which had been growing elsewhere in Europe, and particularly in England now at war again with France. The English Parliament in 1371 passed a bill requiring that only laymen, not clerics, hold the highest offices in the state; Edward III signed and enforced it, dismissing his Chancellor and Treasurer who were bishops. In 1372 King Edward prohibited English bishops from making any payments to Rome. In 1373 Prince Edward browbeat the Archbishop of Canterbury at a council which considered and rejected the request of Pope Gregory XI for a crusade tax, despite the striking victory of the Turks over the Serbs in the Battle of the Marica River in 1371, followed immediately by their conquest of Macedonia, rendering Serbia tributary, and pushing northward through Serbia to Bosnia and Dalmatia.[87]

In October 1372 the monasteries of Cologne in Germany agreed to refuse payment of the papal tithe on their revenues, declaring:

> In consequence of the exactions with which the Papal Court burdens the clergy, the Apostolic See has fallen into such contempt that the Catholic Faith in these parts seems to be seriously imperilled. The laity speak slightingly of the Church, because, departing from the customs of former days, she hardly ever sends forth preachers or reformers, but rather ostentatious men, cunning, selfish, and greedy.[88]

In May 1372 Pope Gregory XI announced at a meeting of his cardinals that he intended to return "very shortly" to Rome, and St. Catherine of Siena was later to reveal that he had taken a private vow before his election that he would go to Rome if he became Pope.[89] But he was irresolute, yielding to pressure from the cardinals to stay in Avignon, while the condition of the Church and Christendom worsened. The Hundred Years War went on, with no end in sight. The English Prince John of Gaunt had now laid claim to Castile, by virtue of his marriage to the elder surviving daughter and heir of Pedro the Cruel, and in the latter half of 1373 he was marching an army across France to try to reach it, though his force arrived at Bordeaux so weakened that he could not go on to invade Castile.[90] What was left of the Byzantine Empire had become tributary to the Ottoman Turks; when the son of Emperor John V and the son of Ottoman Sultan Murad rebelled jointly against their fathers and were

---

[87]Mollat, *Popes at Avignon*, p. 163; Packe, *Edward III*, pp. 288-289; Barber, *Edward, Prince of Wales and Aquitaine*, p. 230; Nicol, *Last Centuries of Byzantium*, p. 286; Fine, *Late Medieval Balkans*, pp. 379-380; Gibbons, *Ottoman Empire*, pp. 146-147.

[88]Ludwig von Pastor, *The History of the Popes from the Close of the Middle Ages*, Volume I (London, 1923), p. 91.

[89]Mollat, *Popes at Avignon*, p. 162; Undset, *Catherine of Siena*, p. 186.

[90]Russell, *English Intervention in Spain*, pp. 168-169, 175, 187, 192-193, 204, 207, 216-217; Packe, *Edward III*, pp. 280, 283.

defeated and captured, Murad gouged out his son's eyes with his own hands and killed him, then demanded that John blind his son and his five-year-old grandson. Not daring to defy his savage overlord, John felt he could do no more than provide for his son and grandson to be only temporarily blinded. His envoy later conveyed his apology to the Pope for having felt constrained so to act (Emperor John V, it will be remembered, was now a Catholic).[91]

Early in 1373 Gregory XI received a last terrible warning, in the name of the Blessed Virgin Mary, from St. Bridget, who died that July:[92]

> I will be merciful and warn you yet once more, and advise you on what is for the salvation of your soul—namely this: You must go to Rome as quickly as you can, yet I leave it to you to choose the time. But the sooner you come the more will the virtues and gifts of the Holy Spirit inflame your soul—therefore come and do not delay. And do not come with the usual worldly splendor, but come in humility and love. And when you have come, cleanse away all the vices of the Roman Curia. Pay no heed to your worldly-minded friends, do not fear, show yourself a man and begin to renew my Church which I have bought with My blood, so that it may be born again and return to its former state.... But this you shall know of a surety, that if you do not obey My will, judgment will be passed upon you as upon a prelate who is degraded and deprived of his ecclesiastical vestments. Everything that has formerly been peace and honor to you shall then be damnation and shame. And every devil in hell shall have a piece of your soul and fill it with everlasting damnation.[93]

The place of St. Bridget in urging the Pope to return permanently to Rome was quickly taken by the burning soul of St. Catherine of Siena.

The twenty-fifth child of a wool dyer of Siena, this wielder of lightning bolts unsurpassed in the whole history of the Church was at the time of St. Bridget's death not yet 27 years old. A mystic who had locutions from Christ Himself and received from Him invisible stigmata which became visible after her death,[94] she nevertheless did not speak private revelations like St. Bridget; her words were her own, and unique to her. She called the Pope "our sweet Christ on earth"; she also called him "Daddy."[95] The torrent of passionate,

---

[91]Nicol, *Last Centuries of Byzantium*, pp. 287-288; Gill, *Byzantium and the Papacy*, p. 225; Gibbons, *Ottoman Empire*, pp. 149-151. The Pope replied to him understandingly, with condolence rather than condemnation.

[92]Jorgensen, *St. Bridget of Sweden*, II, 300-302.

[93]*Ibid.*, II, 283-284.

[94]Undset, *Catherine of Siena*, pp. 95-102, 160-161; Jorgensen, *St. Catherine of Siena*, pp. 194-196.

[95]As Vida Scudder, editor of *St. Catherine of Siena as Seen in Her Letters*, points out (p. 124), her pet name for the Pope, "Babbo" in Italian, "could be translated only by Daddy" (Undset, *Catherine of Siena*, p. 170, concurs)—but, Scudder says (in 1911), that "would sound so strange in English ears that it seems best to let the Italian stand." In a less restrictive age we may let "Daddy" stand; in any case, it could hardly have sounded less startling in Italian than in English. Nobody before or since Catherine of Siena ever

divinely inspired conviction and love, utter humility, vivid clarity, fearless correction, clarion warning, and innocent, almost girlish enthusiasm in the letters of St. Catherine of Siena must be read in full or quoted at length to be believed; no saint since John the Evangelist ever wrote more powerfully. Across more than six centuries her letters burst like rockets and sear like branding irons. What must have been their effect at the time on their recipients?

Her way of life and her appearance were as extraordinary as her letters. A Dominican tertiary, she was never a member of that or any other religious order.[96] Though spending many hours in solitary prayer, she was almost as much in the company of her friends and spiritual disciples—a company whose holy joy was marked by all who saw them.[97] She suffered strange and painful illnesses with delight that she might experience them in union with her Lord on the Cross or in recompense for sins.[98] Along with everything else she was doing, she was very active in corporal works of mercy, as when she spent weeks treating victims of a recurrence of the Black Death in Siena in 1374, not only absolutely confident that she would not catch the plague, but also curing any of her co-workers who seemed about to come down with it.[99] All who knew Catherine and recorded their knowledge—notably her confessor, Blessed Raymond of Capua—remark on her unfailing, almost explosive happiness, whatever happened to her.[100] She had long narrow brilliant eyes and a firm mouth which smiled with an unforgettable sweetness.[101] For years she could eat nothing but the Blessed Sacrament, though she prayed that she might be enabled to consume at least a little food as others did, to avoid drawing so much attention to herself.[102] But God evidently did not intend St. Catherine of Siena to be able to avoid drawing attention to herself, because He was manifested through her so clearly. She passed through the cities and countryside of Italy, and on one memorable occasion to Avignon, like a comet from Heaven, saving

---

called a Pope "Babbo."

[96]Undset, *Catherine of Siena*, pp. 38-40; Jorgensen, *St. Catherine of Siena*, pp. 178-179.

[97]Jorgensen, *St. Catherine of Siena*, pp. 127-128, 132-133; Undset, *Catherine of Siena*, pp. 59-60, 128-131.

[98]Jorgensen, *St. Catherine of Siena*, pp. 99, 101, 133; Undset, *Catherine of Siena*, pp. 57-58.

[99]Jorgensen, *St. Catherine of Siena*, pp. 181-183; Undset, *Catherine of Siena*, pp. 69-72, 147-151.

[100]Jorgensen, *St. Catherine of Siena*, pp. 94, 96, 143; Undset, *Catherine of Siena*, pp. 44, 129, 189.

[101]Jorgensen, *St. Catherine of Siena*, pp. 139, 335. See the contemporary fresco, drawn from life by her disciple Andrea di Vanni, in the Cappella delle Volte in the Church of St. Dominic in Siena, appearing as the frontispiece in Jorgensen, *op. cit.*

[102]Jorgensen, *St. Catherine of Siena*, pp. 117-118; Undset, *Catherine of Siena*, pp. 95-96.

souls and changing history. In person, she was irresistible; the only way to avoid being overcome by her was to stay away from her entirely. It was St. Catherine of Siena, above all, who brought the Pope back from Avignon to Rome to stay.

Let us introduce her with the beginning of the letter she wrote in the summer of 1373—the summer St. Bridget of Sweden died—to Gérard du Puy, Abbot of Marmoutier, one of the Pope's legates in Italy:

> With great joy I have received your letter, and it comforted me to see that you think of so mean and miserable a creature. Your three questions I will answer thus: I think it would be well if our dear Christ on earth [the Pope] would set himself free from two things which cause the misery of the Bride of Christ. The first is his too great love and care for his relations. There must be an end of this abuse at once and everywhere. The other is his exaggerated gentleness, which is the result of his lenience. This is the cause of corruption among those members of the Church who are never admonished with severity. Our Lord hates above all things three abominable sins: covetousness, unchastity and pride. These prevail in the Bride of Christ, that is to say in the prelates who seek nothing but riches, pleasure and fame. They see the demons from Hell stealing the souls which have been put into their keeping, and are completely unmoved, for they are wolves who do business with divine grace. Strict justice is needed to punish them. In this case exaggerated mercy is in fact the worst cruelty. It is necessary for justice to go hand in hand with mercy to put a stop to such evil.[103]

The love, the humility, the passion, the clear precision, the prophetic judgment are all there, and all Catherine—as in so many of her letters.

As she came upon the Italian scene, some of the Machiavellis of that day actually thought at first that they could use and manipulate her to their own advantage. The excommunicated Bernabò Visconti of Milan wrote asking her mediation in his quarrel with the Pope. Catherine, who yielded to none as a critic of the Pope, but was always totally loyal and obedient to him, flashed back:

> Foolish is he who departs from the Vicar of Christ Crucified, who has the keys of the blood, or who goes against him. . . . Therefore I beseech you no longer to set yourself up against your superior. Give not ear to what the Devil whispers to you, that it is your duty to speak against the bad shepherds of the Church. Do not believe the Devil, do not seek to pass judgment, where it is not for you to judge. It pleases not Our Savior.[104]

By the summer of 1375 Pope Gregory XI, despite his now three-year-old public promise to return to Rome, had taken no serious steps to do so, and was

---

[103]Jorgensen, *St. Catherine of Siena*, p. 169; Undset, *Catherine of Siena*, p. 141 (quotations from the same letter combined).
[104]Jorgensen, *St. Catherine of Siena*, pp. 174-175.

falling back on his predecessor's argument that he must be in Avignon to facilitate the peace negotiations seeking to bring an end to the current phase of the Hundred Years War (in which the French had forced the English back to their primary bases of Calais across the Straits of Dover, Brest in Brittany, and Bordeaux and Bayonne in Gascony). Though he still said he planned to leave for Rome the next spring, St. Catherine—and many others—were not at all sure he meant it.[105] In September Catherine wrote the first of her astonishing letters to the Vicar of Christ, taking as her theme the name he had assumed as Pope and the papal saint who had first borne it, Gregory the Great at the dawn of the Middle Ages:

> I will, then, that you be so true and good a shepherd that if you had a hundred thousand lives you would be ready to give them all for the honor of God and the salvation of His creatures. O Daddy mine, sweet Christ on earth, follow that sweet Gregory! For all will be possible to you as to him; for he was not of other flesh than you; and that God is now Who was then; we lack nothing save virtue, and hunger for the salvation of souls. . . .
>
> If up to this time we have not stood very firm, I wish and pray in truth that the moment of time which remains be dealt with manfully, following Christ, Whose vicar you are, like a strong man. And fear not, Father, for anything that may result from those tempestuous winds that are now beating against you, those decaying members which have rebelled against you. Fear not, for divine aid is near. . . .
>
> Remain in the sweet and holy grace of God. I ask you humbly for your blessing. Pardon my presumption, that I presume to write to you. Sweet Jesus, Jesus love.[106]

The Italians assumed the worst from the Pope's latest hesitation. Florence, long rigorously Guelf (pro-papal) in the Italian wars, now began stirring up rebellion in the papal states, exploiting the anger of the people there against French officials perceived as hostile or condescending. In December 1375 Perugia drove out the papal vicar Gérard du Puy (to whom St. Catherine had written earlier) and the people of Viterbo stormed the citadel held by a papal garrison in their city and razed it to the ground. The vicious circle of lack of trust of the Italians by the Pope and of the Pope by the Italians took another turn when in that same month the Pope created nine new cardinals: seven French, just one Italian, and the other Spanish—the strongly pro-French and elementally stubborn Pedro de Luna, later the Antipope who was to keep the Great Western Schism alive for a full generation.[107]

---

[105]Mollat, *Popes at Avignon*, p. 163; Perroy, *Hundred Years War*, p. 167; Packe, *Edward III*, p. 284.

[106]St. Catherine of Siena to Pope Gregory XI, *Letters* ed. Scudder, pp. 120-121, 123.

[107]Mollat, *Popes at Avignon*, pp. 165-166; Undset, *Catherine of Siena*, p. 174; Alec Glasfurd, *The Antipope (Peter de Luna, 1342-1423); a Study in Obstinacy* (London, 1965), pp. 15-24.

Disregarding St. Catherine's counsel to show mercy and a willingness to compromise with Florence, in March 1376 Pope Gregory XI demanded that the city surrender to him the members of its governing council, known as the "Eight of War." When his demand was refused, he excommunicated the Eight and placed the city under interdict. As this terrible verdict was pronounced, the Florentine ambassador in Avignon raised his eyes to the crucifix hanging over the Pope's throne and cried: "Look down on me, God of my salvation, and help me; do not forsake me, for my father and my mother have forsaken me."[108]

St. Catherine wrote to the Eight offering to mediate between them and the Pope, and to the Pope urging him more passionately than ever to return quickly to Rome, a veritable trumpet call:

> Let not your holy desire fail on account of any scandal or rebellion of cities which you might see or hear; nay, let the flame of holy desire be more kindled to wish to do swiftly. Do not delay, then, your coming. Do not believe the Devil, who perceives his own loss, and so exerts himself to rob you of your possessions in order that you may lose your love and charity and your coming be hindered. I tell you, Father in Christ Jesus, come swiftly like a gentle lamb. Respond to the Holy Spirit Who calls you. I tell you, Come; come; come; do not wait for time, since time does not wait for you.[109]

By June 1376 a army of ten thousand bloody-minded mercenaries sent by the Pope and commanded by the proud Cardinal Robert of Geneva—himself a future Antipope—was ravaging the papal state in a manner that Cardinal Albornoz would never have permitted, filling up the wells of Italian wrath. But Pope Gregory XI still would not come, had not even set a firm date for his departure from Avignon.[110] In England Edward the Black Prince died after a long illness and his old father Edward III was slipping into senility; the heir to the throne was now Prince Richard, a boy of nine, and Charles V of France was pressing his advantage, refusing to make peace.[111] Christendom seemed to be disintegrating. It was time for the twenty-fifth child of the wool dyer of Siena to take charge. St. Catherine of Siena had already set out for Avignon, and on June 18 she arrived.[112]

She spoke neither French nor Latin, no language but her native Tuscan dialect; her confessor, Raymond of Capua, had to interpret for her. It did not

---

[108]St. Catherine of Siena to Pope Gregory XI, March 1376, in *Letters* ed. Scudder, pp. 127-128; Mollat, *Popes at Avignon*, p. 166; Jorgensen, *St. Catherine of Siena*, pp. 217-218; Undset, *Catherine of Siena*, pp. 176, 179 (for the quotation).

[109]St. Catherine of Siena to Pope Gregory XI, *Letters* ed. Scudder, p. 132.

[110]Mollat, *Popes at Avignon*, p. 168.

[111]Barber, *Edward, Prince of Wales and Aquitaine*, pp. 233-236; Packe, *Edward III*, pp. 286, 291-292; Perroy, *Hundred Years War*, p. 168.

[112]Jorgensen, *St. Catherine of Siena*, pp. 224-225.

matter. Neither the Pope nor the worldly cardinals had ever seen or imagined a phenomenon like her. She reminded Gregory XI of his secret vow to return to Rome if he should be elected Pope. She warned him of the vices and corruption of many of the priests and bishops and their families who lived in Avignon. "How have you," Gregory asked in amazement, "who have been here such a short time, got such knowledge of all that goes on here?" "To the glory of Almighty God I am bound to say," Catherine responded, "that I smelt the stink of the sins which flourish in the papal court while I was still at home in my own town more sharply than those who have practiced them, and do practice them, every day here." The Pope's family watched her receiving Holy Communion in ecstasy; his sister was much edified, but his nephew's wife stabbed Catherine in the foot with a large needle to see if she could truly feel nothing while in ecstasy, so that she was unable to stand for days afterward. Three distinguished Inquisitors were sent to interview Catherine; they began by calling her a "wretched little female" (which is no more than what Catherine habitually called herself), and ended by singing her praises and telling a doctor of theology who was present: "Let her answer for herself; she does it much better than you." Even Pedro de Luna was charmed, and almost won over; he dropped his opposition to the Pope's return to Rome. Catherine made a more lasting impression on Archbishop Bartolomeo Prignano, who was to be the next Pope.[113]

When Gregory XI still hesitated to return to Rome, Catherine wrote him the letter that stands at the head of this chapter. Then he borrowed 90,000 florins for the expenses of the journey,[114] and she wrote to a friend in Florence: "Behold that now he [the Pope] is coming to his bride, that is to hold the seat of St. Peter and St. Paul. Do you run to him at once, with true humility of heart and amendment of your sins, following the holy principle with which you began. So doing you shall have peace, spiritual and bodily."[115]

She found time that summer also to write to Charles V of France, urging him to make peace with the English and go on crusade—and warning him of the consequences of failure to do so:

> I tell you [said the wool-dyer's daughter to the king], on behalf of Christ crucified, to delay no longer to make this peace. Make peace, and direct all your warfare to the infidels. Help to encourage and uplift the standard of the most holy Cross, which God shall demand from you and others at the point of death—demanding also from you account for such ignorance and negligence as has been committed and is committed every day. Sleep no

---

[113]*Ibid.*, pp. 227-232; Undset, *Catherine of Siena*, pp. 182-186; Glasfurd, *Antipope*, pp. 30-37.

[114]Mollat, *Popes at Avignon*, p. 171.

[115]St. Catherine of Siena to Buonaccorso di Lapo, midsummer 1376, *Letters* ed. Scudder. p. 178.

more, for love of Christ crucified, and for your own profit, during the little
time that remains to us: for time is short, and you are to die, and know not
when.[116]

In September, as the Pope was on the verge of setting out, he received a
letter probably from the Franciscan Pedro of Aragon, considered a great
spiritual authority, warning that he would die if he went to Rome.[117] Once
more the Pope wavered; once more Catherine strengthened him:

> I beg of you, on behalf of Christ crucified, that you be not a timorous child,
> but manly. Open your mouth, and swallow down the bitter for the sweet.
> It would not befit Your Holiness to abandon the milk for the bitterness. I
> hope by the infinite and inestimable goodness of God that if you choose
> He will show favor both to us and to you; and that you will be a firm and
> stable man, unmoved by any wind or illusion of the Devil, or counsel of
> devil incarnate, but following the will of God and your good desire, and the
> counsel of the servants of Jesus Christ crucified.... Pardon me, Father,
> my over-presumptuous speech. Humbly I ask you to pardon me and give
> me your benediction. Remain in the holy and sweet grace of God.... I
> beg you, sweet Father, to grant me audience when it shall please Your
> Holiness, for I would find myself in your presence before I depart.[118]

On the morning of September 13 the Pope set out for the city of Peter.
Everyone seemed to realize that this time the Pope, if he got to Rome, would
not come back to Avignon. Cardinals pled with him in tears to stay; his sisters
raged; his mother fainted; his aged father threw himself down on the threshold
of the great door of the papal palace to block his way. But St. Catherine was
watching; he could not flinch. Pope Gregory XI stepped over the prostrate
body of his father and into the waiting ship on the Rhone River.[119]

The struggle was not quite over yet. On October 18 the Pope reached
Genoa after his fleet was battered by a severe storm off Monaco. In Genoa
they heard that Rome was in revolt and that the Florentines had won victories
over the papal troops. The majority of the cardinals still wanted to return to
Avignon, and took a formal vote to do so. But Catherine was in the city, and
the Pope knew it. He went to see her in disguise, dressed as a simple priest.
They talked far into the night.[120] No one knows what they said; but tradition
has preserved a prayer which Catherine was believed to have offered, there in

---

[116]St. Catherine of Siena to Charles V of France, midsummer 1376, *Letters* ed.
Scudder, pp. 170-171.
[117]Jorgensen, *St. Catherine of Siena*, p. 236.
[118]St. Catherine of Siena to Pope Gregory XI, September 1376, in *Letters* ed.
Scudder, p. 185.
[119]Glasfurd, *Antipope*, pp. 37-38; Mollat, *Popes at Avignon*, p. 62; Jorgensen, *St.
Catherine of Siena*, p. 237.
[120]Mollat, *Popes at Avignon*, p. 63; Jorgensen, *St. Catherine of Siena*, pp. 245-246.

Genoa, to hold the Pope on his course:

> If the Pope's delay offend thee, Eternal Love, then punish it on my body, which I offer and sacrifice to thee, that thou mayest torment it and destroy it as seems good to thee.... Cause thy Vicar therefore, O Eternal Mercy, to become a devourer of souls, burning with holy zeal for Thy glory and serving Thee alone.[121]

Ten days later Pope Gregory XI boarded ship again and faced out into the stormy Mediterranean. He sailed from Genoa to Leghorn, and from Leghorn to Corneto, the final journey taking three weeks amid high winds and lashing seas. On January 17, 1377 he entered Rome at last, welcomed by enthusiastic processions forming near the Church of St. Paul Outside the Walls where the Apostle to the Gentiles lay buried. St. Catherine was already back in Siena, making her accustomed rounds from her cell to the cathedral and to the hospital.[122] Not for her the trappings of victory. She knew that the "Avignon captivity" of the Papacy was over. She had won—though she would have said, and rightly, that Christ had won.

But the wars in Italy went on, exacerbated by the cruelties of Cardinal Robert of Geneva, who in February 1377 massacred 4,000 people at Cesena which he had taken in the course of the war against Florence. The famous English mercenary John Hawkwood, who had been fighting for the Pope, shifted to fight for his enemies.[123] Peace negotiations between England and France to end the Hundred Years War finally and decisively failed. Old King Edward III of England died in June, succeeded by his grandson under a regency dominated by John of Gaunt, who favored the heretic John Wyclif whose defiance of a morally compromised papacy was sweeping the country.[124] St. Catherine had brought back Pope Gregory XI to Rome; but she could not make him strong enough to reunite Christendom. Clear-sighted as ever, she knew it. She even suggested that he resign. Her last letter to him tolls a judgment:

> Alas, alas, sweetest Daddy mine, pardon my presumption in what I have said to you and am saying; I am constrained by the Sweet Primal Truth to say it. His will, Father, is this, and thus demands of you: that you execute justice on the abundance of many iniquities committed by those who are fed and pastured in the garden of Holy Church, declaring that brutes should not be fed with the food of men. Since He has given you authority and you have assumed it, you should use your virtue and power;

---

[121]Jorgensen, *St. Catherine of Siena*, p. 246.

[122]*Ibid.*, pp. 246, 249-250; Mollat, *Popes at Avignon*, p. 63; Glasfurd, *Antipope*, pp. 45-47.

[123]Mollat, *Popes at Avignon*, pp. 171-172.

[124]Packe, *Edward III*, pp. 296-300; May McKisack, *The Fourteenth Century, 1307-1399* (Oxford History of England) (Oxford, 1959), pp. 396-397. For a full discussion of Wyclif, his heresies, and his movement of "Lollards," see Chapter Eleven, below.

and if you are not willing to use it, it would be better for you to resign what you have assumed; more honor to God and health to your soul would it be....

If you want justice, you can execute it. You can have peace, withdrawing from the perverse pomps and delights of the world, preserving only the honor of God and the due of Holy Church. Authority also you have to give peace to those who ask you for it. Then, since you are not poor but rich—you who bear in your hand the keys of Heaven, to whom you open it is open, and to whom you shut it is shut—if you do not do this, you would be rebuked by God. I beg you most gently on behalf of Christ crucified to be obedient to the will of God, for I know that you want and desire no other thing than to do His will, that this sharp rebuke fall not upon you: "Cursed be thou, for the time and the strength entrusted to thee thou has not used."[125]

It does not appear that Pope Gregory XI would see Catherine again after receiving this letter. On the night of March 26-27, 1378 he died in Rome. On his deathbed, he implied that Catherine had led him astray by "infatuated visions."[126] In fact, she had led him home.

---

[125]St. Catherine of Siena to Pope Gregory XI, fall 1377, *Letters* ed. Scudder, pp. 234-235.
    [126]Jorgensen, *St. Catherine of Siena*, pp. 278-283; Glasfurd, *Antipope*, p. 47; Mollat, *Popes in Avignon*, p. 63.

11
The Great Western Schism
(1378-1410)

(Popes Urban VI 1378-89, Boniface IX 1389-1404, Innocent VII 1404-06,
Gregory XII 1406-15)
(Antipopes Robert of Geneva 1378-94, Pedro de Luna 1394-1423, Peter
Philargis 1408-10)

You clearly know the truth, that Pope Urban VI is truly Pope, the highest
pontiff, chosen in orderly election, not influenced by fear, truly rather by
divine inspiration than by your human industry. And so you announced it
to us, which was the truth. Now you have turned your backs, like poor
mean knights; your shadow has made you afraid. You have divided
yourselves from the truth which strengthens us, and drawn close to
falsehood, which weakens soul and body, depriving you of temporal and
spiritual grace. What made you do this? The poison of self-love, which has
infected the world. That is what has made you pillars lighter than
straw—flowers which shed no perfume, but stench that makes the whole
world reek!... This is not the kind of blindness that springs from
ignorance. It has not happened to you because people have reported one
thing to you while another is so. No, for you know what the truth is; it was
you who announced it to us, and not we to you. Oh, how mad you are! For
you told us the truth, and you want yourselves to taste a lie! Now you want
to corrupt this truth, and make us see the opposite, saying that you chose
Pope Urban from fear, which is not so; but anyone who says it—speaking
to you without reverence, because you have deprived yourselves of
reverence—lies up to his eyes.... You could not endure, not only an
actual correction indeed, but even a harsh word of reproof made you lift up
rebellious heads. This is the reason why you changed.... Return, return,
and wait not for the rod of justice, since we cannot escape the hands of
God! We are in His hands either by justice or by mercy; better it is for us
to recognize our faults and to abide in the hands of mercy, than to remain
in fault and in the hands of justice. For our faults do not pass unpunished,
especially those that are wrought against Holy Church.—St. Catherine of
Siena to Cardinals Orsini of Rome, Corsini of Florence, and Bursano of
Milan, October 1378[1]

In all her volcanic life the glorious St. Catherine of Siena wrote nothing

---

[1]Vida D. Scudder, ed., *Saint Catherine of Siena as Seen in Her Letters* (London
1911), pp. 278-279, 281-283.

that strikes home like this letter. It transfixes the heart of the Great Schism of the West with a flaming sword. And its every declaration, even its every passionate outcry, is fully substantiated by the facts of history. The great French scholar Noel Valois, in the first of four large volumes on the Great Schism of the West written at the turn of the century,[2] as he followed the complex and tumultuous events of the conclave of the cardinals which elected Pope Urban VI in April 1378 and the anti-conclave which set up an antipope against him, assembled the historical facts for us, page by page, step by step, from the original sources. The most noted papal historian of the twentieth century writing in English, Walter Ullmann, does little more than footnote Valois.[3] St. Catherine spoke true.

Inspired by her and by her memory (for she died, just 33 years old—the traditional age of her Savior at His crucifixion—in 1380) most of Italy held out for the true Pope through all the bitter and confusing years that followed the rending split of 1378. But France—the greatest power in Europe, where the Popes had lived in preference to Rome for three-quarters of a century—was aligned most of the time with the antipopes. In the centuries that have followed, while anti-Catholic historians have been satisfied to use the Great Schism as a stick to beat the Church with, those not so prejudiced have mostly sought—as, increasingly with the passage of time, men living during the Schism sought—to find some way of avoiding the awful choice between two (and later three) powerfully supported contenders for the highest office in Christendom.

Yet there was in truth no way to escape that choice then, and there is no way now. One of these contenders was truly the Pope; the others were antipopes. The Church can have no more than one Pope at a time. Christ did not entrust the leadership and the future of His Church to a committee, still less to a council of hundreds or thousands. One searches the Gospels in vain for any mention of a Church council called by Christ. Many in the years of the Great Schism may have honestly tried to make the right choice of Pope and yet made the wrong one. But there was a right choice to be made. St. Catherine of Siena knew that best of all. She was there, observing all that happened. She made her choice: Pope Urban VI. And she was right.

Let us review the evidence.

Pope Gregory XI, the last of the French Popes at Avignon, died on March 27, 1378.[4] In the evening of April 7 sixteen of the 22 cardinals gathered in the Vatican palace for the conclave.[5] Eleven of them were French,[6] four were

---

[2]Noel Valois, *La France et le grand schisme d'Occident*, Volume I (Paris, 1896).
[3]Walter Ullmann, *The Origins of the Great Schism* (London, 1948), pp. 1-101.
[4]Guy Mollat, *The Popes at Avignon* (New York, 1963), p. 63.
[5]Ullmann, *Origins of the Great Schism*, pp. 16-17.
[6](1) Jean de Cros, Cardinal-bishop of Palestrina, called Cardinal of Limoges; (2) Guillaume d'Aigrefeuille, Cardinal-priest of St. Stephen; (3) Bertrand de Lagery,

Italian,[7] and one was Spanish: Pedro de Luna, who was to outlive them all, dying at 81 in the castle of Peñíscola off the coast of Aragon, maintaining the Great Schism until his last hour.[8] Every one of these men marched into the center of the history of the Church that April evening in 1378, and all but one—the Roman Cardinal Tebaldeschi—came out of that year a traitor to the Pope and to the Church.

The numerically dominant French contingent was sharply divided between the followers of Jean le Cros, the Cardinal of Limoges, and of Cardinal Robert of Geneva, who tended to favor Archbishop Prignano of Bari. The Roman people wanted an Italian Pope, preferably a Roman, fearing that any French Pope would be strongly tempted to go back to Avignon, as Pope Urban V had done. They were shouting their demand for a Roman or at least an Italian Pope as the cardinals entered the Vatican, though all observers agree that the crowd called out no name—only the new Pope's nationality seemed to concern them. Few outside the conclave itself seem to have even thought of Prignano, who was much better known to the cardinals with whom he had worked closely, than to the general Italian public.[9]

Roman city officials who had come into the palace with the not yet enclosed cardinals urged them to respond positively to the public demand for an Italian Pope, but the cardinals refused to make any promises. By nine o'clock in the evening the cardinals were confined, though not hermetically sealed in. At about midnight a city official was heard shouting through a window that the cardinals must elect an Italian, and the people outside—fortified by alcohol and energized by dancing—kept up their chants all night, clearly audible through most of the palace. There was to be no voting

---

Cardinal-priest of Santa Cecilia, called Cardinal of Glandève; (4) Hugh de Montelais, Cardinal-priest of the Four Crowned Saints, called Cardinal of Brittany; (5) Count Robert of Geneva, Cardinal-priest of the Twelve Apostles, called Cardinal of Geneva; (6) Guy de Malesset, Cardinal-priest of the Holy Cross, called Cardinal of Poitiers; (7) Pierre de Sortenac, Cardinal-priest of San Lorenzo, called Cardinal of Viviers; (8) Gérard du Puy, Cardinal-priest of San Clemente, called Cardinal of Marmoutier; (9) Pierre Flandrin, Cardinal-deacon of St. Eustace; (10) Guillaume Noellet, Cardinal-deacon of San Angelo; (11) Pierre de Vergne, Cardinal-deacon of Santa Maria in Via Lata (Ullman, *Origins of the Great Schism*, pp. 9-10).

[7] (1) Pietro Corsini, Cardinal-bishop of Porto, called Cardinal of Florence; (2) Pietro Tebaldeschi, Cardinal-priest of Santa Sabina, called Cardinal of St. Peter (a Roman); (3) Simon de Brossano, Cardinal-priest of Sts. John and Paul, called Cardinal of Milan; (4) Jacopo Orsini, Cardinal-deacon of San Giorgio in Velabro (another Roman) (Ullmann, *Origins of the Great Schism*, p. 9).

[8] See Alec Glasfurd, *The Antipope, Pedro de Luna (1342-1423); a Study in Obstinacy* (London, 1965).

[9] Valois, *France et le grand schisme*, I, 26-36; Charles-Joseph Hefele and Henri Leclercq, *Histoire des Conciles*, Volume VI, Part 2 (Paris, 1915), pp. 978-988; L. Salembier, *The Great Schism of the West* (New York, 1907), pp. 34-36; John H. Smith, *The Great Schism* (New York, 1970), p. 136.

until morning, but canvassing proceeded among the electors.   Cardinals
d'Aigrefeuille and Malesset asked Tebaldeschi, the senior Italian cardinal, if he
would accept Prignano. He replied that he assuredly would.[10]

After Mass in the morning someone in Rome began ringing the
tocsin—church bells sounded rapidly as an alarm—and the Bishop of
Marseilles, who had the difficult task of guarding the conclave, told the
cardinals there was real danger of violence and even killing if they did not elect
an Italian. But still, no name of any cardinal or bishop was included in the
demand, only nationality. The cardinals debated the threat. They could have
gone to the famous and formidable fortress of Castel Sant' Angelo close by,
which was strongly guarded by a man they trusted. They did not do so. The
Roman Cardinal Orsini was sent outside to try to quiet the crowd, without much
success. By now it was nine o'clock in the morning. The cardinals assembled in
the chapel and prepared to vote.[11]   Cardinal Pedro de Luna nominated
Prignano. "Since God has not given us to be of one mind as to the choice of
one of the members of the sacred college," he said, "I think we should elect
someone from outside. I do not see anyone as worthy as the Archbishop of
Bari. He is a saintly man, known to us all, a man of ripe age and fitting
attainments. I propose him freely and spontaneously."[12]

It was immediately evident that a substantial majority already favored
Prignano. No one opposed him, but Cardinal Orsini did propose delaying the
election and pretending that they had elected a Roman Pope, to appease the
crowd. The others rejected his proposal, and called for the ballot. All voted for
Prignano except Orsini, who abstained. Several cardinals specifically declared
their choice to be free and that Prignano should "be undeniably Pope."[13]

Orsini then went outside to try to announce the results. In an age long
before microphones, without even a convenient raised platform to speak from,
nobody could hear him; most probably assumed that he had come again to try
to quiet them, and so shouted louder than ever. "You Roman pigs, get away
from here!" he finally snapped in disgust, and went back inside the palace.[14]

Archbishop Prignano and six other bishops summoned by Orsini made
their way with some difficulty and danger to the Vatican, but did not join the
cardinals, who were still officially confined. By the dinner hour much of the
vocal tumult had finally died down (even the most leather-lunged Roman must

---

[10]Valois, *France et le grand schisme*, I, 36-39; Ullmann, *Origins of the Great Schism*,
pp. 16-17, 33-34; Smith, *Great Schism*, p. 7.
     [11]Valois, *France et le grand schisme*, I, 39-43; Ullmann, *Origins of the Great Schism*,
p. 17; Salembier, *Great Schism*, p. 37.
     [12]Salembier, *Great Schism*, p. 38.
     [13]Valois, *France et le grand schisme*, I, 43-47; Ullmann, *Origins of the Great Schism*,
p. 35.
     [14]Valois, *France et le grand schisme*, I, 47; Ullmann, *Origins of the Great Schism*, p.
36.

have felt a need to rest his voice after 24 hours of shouting) and the cardinals enjoyed a leisurely dinner. Most of them went to the chapel after dinner. In the chapel, Cardinal Tebaldeschi suddenly proposed taking advantage of this period of quiet by confirming the election of Archbishop Prignano under less immediately threatening conditions (perhaps it had already occurred to him that someone might challenge the validity of the election on grounds of duress). All of the 13 present in the chapel but Cardinal Noellet agreed to do this, and all (including Noellet) again voted for Prignano except for the abstaining Orsini, though the three lingering in the dining room never got to vote in this unusual confirmation ballot.[15]

By now rumors had begun to run through the crowd that a Pope had been elected, but no one knew his identity or nationality. Cardinal Orsini tried again to announce the election, and this time some tried to listen, but others were still making too much noise for anyone to hear clearly. Prignano was Archbishop of Bari in southern Italy, and Orsini began screaming "Bari! Bari!" at the top of his lungs. Most heard only the first syllable; by a malign coincidence, there was a French relative of the late Pope Gregory XI named Jean de Bar who was highly unpopular in Rome, and many thought Orsini was saying "Bar! Bar!" In a fury the mob now began throwing stones at the windows of the palace and attacking the doors with picks and axes. There was no effective defending force; the crowd stormed in. The terrified cardinals begged Tebaldeschi, the Roman senior cardinal known to everyone, to pose as Pope to satisfy the mob. Tebaldeschi firmly refused, but the desperate cardinals and their aides, taking advantage of the physical weakness of his years (he was past eighty), pushed him onto the papal throne (one of his nephews literally knocking him down into the seat), dropped a papal cope over his shoulders, and put a papal miter on his head, with Tebaldeschi crying out over and over that he was not the Pope, that Prignano was Pope. The crowd called for a pontifical blessing; Tebaldeschi refused it, saying again that he was not the Pope. Meanwhile the cardinals fled, six of the French cardinals going to Castel Sant'Angelo, while Prignano locked himself up in a small out-of-the-way room. Finally those in the crowd nearest to Tebaldeschi began to listen to him, and passed the word. They had an Italian Pope, but it was not Tebaldeschi.[16]

It might have helped to have written a sign, but there is no indication that anyone thought of that in the wild vortex of confusion and fear, and in any case undoubtedly the majority in the mob could not read.

The Spanish Cardinal de Luna, from the land of the Reconquest where men did not panic easily, seems to have kept his wits and his courage about him all during that wild day of April 8. That night he calmly wrote a letter to several

---

[15]Valois, *France et le grand schisme*, I, 48-51.

[16]*Ibid.*, I, 51-55; Ullmann, *Origins of the Great Schism*, pp. 18-21, 36-38, 40-41; Smith, *Great Schism*, pp. 138-139; Salembier, *Great Schism*, pp. 39-41.

bishops in Spain: "We have elected a real Pope. The Romans may tear me limb from limb before they get me to go back on today's election."[17]

The history of the Church and the world might have been very different if Pedro de Luna had kept that promise he made in writing on the day of the conclave in April 1378.

By the next day, the 9th, word of Prignano's election had spread through the city; there was complete calm and general satisfaction. The Pope-elect formally asked the cardinals if they had elected him freely and canonically. They confirmed in writing that they had, and asked him if he accepted their election. He said that he did, and would take the name Urban VI, which was then announced to the people.[18]

Two days later was Palm Sunday. Pope Urban VI was enthroned at St. Peter's in the presence of twelve cardinals and a large crowd. All the cardinals present asked him (as was customary with a new Pope) for absolution from their sins. He absolved them, blessed the palms, and distributed them to the Church dignitaries and the people in St. Peter's.[19] The French Cardinal Pierre de Vergne wrote to the Bishiop of Reti and Macerata that day: "Throughout my whole life I have not experienced such joy as I have today, because we have completed this business so peacefully."[20] Also on that day Fernando Pérez of Tarazona, a member of Cardinal de Luna's household staff, wrote to a friend in Avignon describing all these events in terms almost identical with the official report of them later published by Urban VI.[21] Three days later, on April 14, Cardinal Robert of Geneva, who before the end of the year was to be Antipope, wrote to Holy Roman Emperor Charles IV:

> I would inform you that the ten days after the death [of Pope Gregory XI] required by canon law having passed, my lords the other cardinals and I were shut up in conclave and the name of the Archbishop of Bari, as he then was (but now the Supreme Pontiff), a man of the nation of the Neapolitans, having been suggested to us ... the cardinals and I unanimously gave our votes to him on the eighth day of this month, in solemn conclave, one night's delay having passed, because the Romans would not consent to any more time being spent in the said conclave.[22]

On Holy Saturday, which fell on April 17 that year, all sixteen cardinals who had elected Pope Urban VI formally presented him with the Fisherman's ring and the pallium and received Easter communion from his hands. On

---

[17]Salembier, *Great Schism*, p. 45.

[18]*Ibid.*, pp. 41-42; Valois, *France et le grand schisme*, I, 56-62; Ullmann, *Origins of the Great Schism*, pp. 22-23, 38.

[19]Ullmann, *Origins of the Great Schism*, p. 23.

[20]*Ibid.*, p. 31.

[21]*Ibid.*, p. 30.

[22]Smith, *Great Schism*, pp. 8-9.

Easter Sunday he was consecrated.[23] On Easter Monday the sixteen cardinals
wrote to the six who had not come to the conclave, but remained stubbornly in
Avignon:

> We have given our votes for Bartolomeo, the Archbishop of Bari,
> who is conspicuous for his great merits and whose manifold virtues make
> him a shining example; we have in full agreement elevated him to the
> summit of apostolic excellency and have announced our choice to the
> multitude of Christians. On the 9th April the elect assumed the name of
> Urban VI and on Easter Sunday he was crowned at St. Peter's, solemnly
> and magnificently, in the presence of a huge and joyful crowd. We have
> firm hope and confidence in our Pope and believe that under his guidance
> the orthodox faith will be strengthened and that the state of the universal
> Church will begin to blossom again. May our Savior grant that he may
> serve for a very long time.[24]

And this was why St. Catherine of Siena had every right to say to these
men, when within six months they announced that the election of Pope Urban
VI was invalid because under duress and that they could therefore proceed to
elect another Pope: "You know what the truth is; it was you who announced it
to us, and not we to you. . . . Now you want to corrupt this truth, and make us
see the opposite, saying that you chose Pope Urban from fear, which is not so;
but anyone who says it—speaking to you without reverence, because you have
deprived yourselves of reverence—lies up to his eyes."[25]

The cardinals immediately began seeking their accustomed favors from
the new Pope, but got few. Urban VI, who appears to have been a retiring, self-
effacing man before his elevation to the pontificate, displayed at once a burning
zeal for reform—particularly to eliminate the bribery and simony which had
become all too common in the papal court—coupled with a shocking lack of
prudence and tact. He called Cardinal Orsini a "half-wit;" directed that no
cardinal should eat more than one course per meal; physically attacked the
Cardinal of Limoges at a private meeting, waving his stick as though to beat
him; denounced Cardinal Robert of Geneva for sowing discord and war; and
warned that he might soon begin excommunicating cardinals for simony, on his
own authority and without canonical process.[26] Cardinal Robert, young (36)
and vehement, weighed in with a warning of his own: "Unlike your
predecessors, Holy Father, you do not treat the cardinals with that honor which
you owe to them. You are diminishing our authority, but verily I tell you that

---

[23]Ullmann, *Origins of the Great Schism*, p. 24; Salembier, *Great Schism*, p. 44.
    [24]Ullmann, *Origins of the Great Schism*, p. 29. The six cardinals who had stayed in
Avignon wrote tendering their unqualified homage to Pope Urban VI on June 24
(Valois, *France et le grand schisme*, I, 65-66).
    [25]Scudder, ed., *St. Catherine of Siena as Seen in Her Letters*, p. 279.
    [26]Ludwig von Pastor, *History of the Popes*, Volume I (London, 1923), pp. 123-124;
Ullmann, *Origins of the Great Schism*, pp. 45-48; Smith, *Great Schism*, pp. 140-141.

we will do our best to diminish yours."[27] The next few months were to show that Cardinal Robert meant exactly what he said.

St. Catherine was in Florence attempting to make peace between that city and the Pope, who had been Gregory XI when she left Siena in December, and was now Urban VI. On the night of June 22, just as the cardinals' hostility and resistance to the new Pope was beginning to coalesce, there was an outburst of rioting against the pro-papal Guelfs in Florence, with looting and burning of the houses of Guelf leaders, and killings in the streets. Armed men burst into the garden where she was praying, shouting: "Where is the damned woman? Where is Catherine?" She came forward at once and knelt before their leader. We may imagine her long narrow eyes glowing in the reflected red light of the burning buildings and a smile of anticipated triumph on her lips, for we know from her own testimony soon afterward that she was filled by joy at the prospect of martyrdom. The leader sheathed his sword and urged her to go away. "Here I am," she said to him. "Where do you want me to go? I have always longed to suffer for God and His Church. So if you have been appointed to kill me, do not hesitate to do so. Only you must leave my friends untouched." The leader left everybody untouched; he turned on his heel and fled.[28] As Catherine soon wrote to her confessor, Raymond of Capua:

> The desire I had that God would show His providence and destroy the power of the demons that they might not do so much harm as they were ready to do, was fulfilled; but my desire to give my life for the Truth and the sweet Bride of Christ was not fulfilled. The Eternal Bridegroom played a great joke on me . . . It seemed that the hands of him who wanted to kill me were bound. My words, "I am she. Take me, and let this family be," were a sword that pierced straight through his heart. . . . I never experienced in myself such mysteries, with so great joy! There was the sweetness of truth in it, the gladness of a clean and pure conscience; there was the fragrance of the sweet providence of God; there was the savor of the times of new martyrs, foretold as you know by the Eternal Truth. Tongue would not suffice to tell how great the good is that my soul feels.[29]

By the day of this extraordinary episode, all the French cardinals who had attended the conclave in Rome which elected Urban VI Pope had arrived, in several different groups, at Anagni of evil memory. The new Pope, suspecting nothing, had given them permission to go there for the summer. In mid-July, while writing a letter to Urban assuring him of their loyalty, they agreed among themselves that the April election had been invalid due to duress by the surrounding mob and that, using this as a reason, they would withdraw recognition from Urban. On July 20 they wrote to the Italian cardinals who had

---

[27]Ullmann, *Origins of the Great Schism*, p. 48.
[28]Sigrid Undset, *Catherine of Siena* (New York, 1954), pp. 209-214.
[29]St. Catherine of Siena to Bd. Raymond of Capua, *Letters* ed. Scudder, p. 258.

been at the conclave calling upon them to come to Anagni within five days and announcing that they now regarded the Holy See as vacant. All came at once but Tebaldeschi, who was too ill to travel.[30]

Catherine had already sent her first letter to the new Pope early that month:

> Most holy Father, God has placed you as a shepherd over all His sheep who belong to the whole Christian religion; He has placed you as the minister of the Blood of Christ crucified, whose Vicar you are; and He placed you in a time in which wickedness abounds more among your inferiors than it has done for a long time, both in the body of Holy Church and in the universal body of the Christian religion. Therefore it is extremely necessary for you to be established in perfect charity, wearing the pearl of justice.[31]

A few days later she wrote to him again, urging him to be patient in listening to those who wished to serve and help him; undoubtedly she had already heard reports of his often vehement and abusive ill temper, and very probably had heard by then of the cardinals' plans.[32] It seems that the canonist Baldus, professor at the University of Bologna and "the most famous jurist of the day," had heard of them, for that July he published a treatise recommending an ecumenical council to deal with the dispute about the election of Pope Urban VI, but stating roundly that he was the true Pope, validly elected, and that "there were no grounds on which the cardinals could repudiate a Pope once they had elected him, and none on which the Church as a whole could depose him, except persistent and open heresy."[33] By August Catherine unquestionably knew what was going on, and wrote to Cardinal de Luna, whom she had met at Avignon and who had admired her, urging him to stand fast for the true Pope. She sensed the enduring, persevering strength in the able and redoubtable Spaniard, and how he was now being tempted to forsake the loyalty to the Vicar of Christ he had so proudly proclaimed immediately after the conclave. In a torrent of her matchless eloquence she called upon the best that was in Pedro de Luna:

> I will, dearest Father, that you shall be a column that cannot be shaken by any persecution. . . . But if you have not put off the love of self, there is no doubt that you will be weak, and weakness will make you fail. . . . I have

---

[30]Valois, *France et le grand schisme*, I, 74-75; Ullman, *Origins of the Great Schism*, pp. 52, 54, 57; Glasfurd, *Antipope*, p. 79; Salembier, *Great Schism*, pp. 54-55.

[31]St. Catherine of Siena to Pope Urban VI, early July 1378, *Letters* ed. Scudder, p. 244.

[32]St. Catherine of Siena to Pope Urban VI, mid-July 1378, Letters ed. Scudder, pp. 261-263.

[33]Smith, *Great Schism*, pp. 141-142; Ullmann, *Origins of the Great Schism*, pp. 143-146.

heard that discord has arisen down there between Christ on earth and his
disciples.... For the sake of the blood of Christ I beg you never to stray
from virtue and from him who is set over you ... Be a man and a pillar
which never gives way![34]

But she was too late. By August 9, almost certainly before he received her
letter, Pedro de Luna had made his decision, after all the other cardinals
present at Anagni had made theirs. They declared the election of Urban VI as
Pope invalid because made under threat of death, a threat which they
alleged—despite all the evidence, both verbal and documentary, to the
contrary—had continued up to and even after his consecration.   They
summoned him to Anagni to face their judgment. De Luna said he felt himself
constrained to believe their explanation of why they had voted as they did in the
April conclave. He did not say whether his own vote was likewise to be
explained.[35] His confessor, the Prior of Santa Sabina, who had accompanied de
Luna to Anagni, was appalled, and condemned him in the strongest terms:

> Do not imagine that the things you told me earlier in Rome were just
> words written on water. If all of you here, now that you have come to this
> place, were to tell me the exact opposite of what you said before, I would
> not pay it any more attention than I would to that cat there playing with
> the flies on the wall.... How can you go back on what you said
> earlier—on what you said then, speaking so calmly, to me, to your faithful
> friend, to your beloved son, to your fellow-countryman?[36]

From his deathbed in Rome, aged Cardinal Tebaldeschi—who had stood
in the midst of the swirling mob on the day of the April papal election shouting
to them in his cracking voice that he was not the elected Pope and so could not
give them the pontifical blessing they demanded—alone held true, affirming the
legitimacy of Urban VI. On September 7 the lion-hearted old man passed to
the Judgment, and there were no faithful cardinals left.[37]

Thirteen days later, at Anagni, the eleven French cardinals who had been
at the April conclave—and Pedro de Luna—elected Cardinal Robert of
Geneva Antipope. The three surviving Italian cardinals all abstained, but
accepted Robert when he was enthroned and consecrated later that same day,
taking the name "Clement VII."[38] It was these three Italian cardinals—Orsini

---

[34]Johannes Jorgensen, *Saint Catherine of Siena* (London, 1938), pp. 324-325;
Glasfurd, *Antipope*, p. 79.

[35]Von Pastor, *History of the Popes*, I, 127; Ullmann, *Origins of the Great Schism*, pp.
54-55, 59; Smith, *Great Schism*, pp. 10, 137; Salembier, *Great Schism*, p. 57; Glasfurd,
Antipope, pp. 82-83.

[36]Glasfurd, *Antipope*, p. 83.

[37]Salembier, *Great Schism*, p. 58; Ullmann, *Origins of the Great Schism*, p. 62.

[38]Von Pastor, *History of the Popes*, I, 127; Ullmann, *Origins of the Great Schism*, pp.
55, 63; Salembier, *Great Schism*, pp. 59-60. As has been the previous practice regarding

of Rome, Corsini of Florence, and Brossano of Milan—whom St. Catherine of Siena excoriated in her letter quoted at the head of this chapter, written the next month presumably very soon after she received the news of what they had done. Antipope Robert was young, vigorous, good-looking, and brutal—chiefly known as the war leader whose mercenary troops had ravaged the papal state before Pope Gregory XI's arrival from Avignon and massacred 4,000 helpless people, mostly civilians, at Cesena early in the previous year.[39]

The choice of Antipope Robert was in effect an attempted restoration of the Avignon papacy, under more obvious and direct French domination than that papacy had been when the Popes, though living in Avignon rather than in Rome, were at least not schismatic. King Charles V of France, when he heard the news, cried out: "I am now Pope!" Holy Roman Emperor Charles IV, on the contrary, declared that he had no doubts that Urban VI was the true Pope. When he died November 29, he urged his son and successor Wenceslas (Wenzel) to remain always faithful to Pope Urban VI, and he did so. England fully endorsed Urban, the more readily because of its continuing war with France. On November 29, the same day that Emperor Charles died, Urban VI excommunicated the Antipope and three of his cardinals and proclaimed the struggle against him a crusade. He had already dismissed the entire College of Cardinals at the end of September, a week after their election of the Antipope, and replaced them with a new College of 28 cardinals all appointed on the same day. Antipope Robert appointed nine pretender cardinals to extend his base of support, sending many of them out through Europe for this purpose.[40]

St. Catherine of Siena was now in Rome, called there by Pope Urban VI to help him in his hour of trial.[41] She found confusion and faint hearts all around, even in places where they might least have been expected. The Pope had suggested that she and St. Catherine of Sweden, St. Bridget's daughter, go

---

antipopes in this history, Antipope Robert will be called herein only by the name which he bore as a cardinal. As the evidence presented in this chapter makes clear, Cardinal Robert was not entitled to a papal name; even dissident historians who suggest that he might have been (few if any would now assert that he surely was) can only create confusion by applying to him the same name and number later borne by a legitimate and very important Pope, who led the Church at the time of Henry VIII's English schism (1527-34). Although almost all historians, despite these cogent arguments, persist in using "Clement VII" for Cardinal Robert from this point until his death in 1394, and in calling his supporters "Clementists," this designation for this man will not be used again in this history.

[39]See Chapter Ten, above.

[40]Von Pastor, *History of the Popes*, I, 134; Smith, *Great Schism*, pp. 13, 148; Ullmann, *Origins of the Great Schism*, pp. 89, 93, 104-105; Bede Jarrett, *The Emperor Charles IV* (London, 1935), pp. 234-235; Hefele-Leclercq, *Histoire des Conciles*, VI-2, 1085, 1092.

[41]She arrived November 28, just over two months after his cardinals went into full rebellion with the choice of Antipope Robert (Jorgensen, *St. Catherine of Siena*, p. 330).

to Naples to try to win the wayward Queen Joanna over to the true Pope's cause, since both she and St. Bridget had corresponded at length with Joanna. St. Catherine of Siena was ready to go at once, but St. Catherine of Sweden demurred, remembering the disgusting scene in Naples when Joanna had once tried to seduce her brother in the presence of her mother and herself; Raymond of Capua, confessor to St. Catherine of Siena, also did not think such an embassy should be risked. On this occasion a saint and a *beatus* felt the sting of St. Catherine of Siena's words as much as any sinner: "If Agnes, Margarita, Caterina and the other holy virgins had been so timid, they would never have won the martyr's crown. Have not all good virgins a Spouse mighty enough to defend and preserve them?"[42]

But they did not go, and perhaps it was as well, because the harassed and seething Pope needed Catherine's presence more than anyone else, to keep him from giving way entirely to his anger. She knew that to a degree he had brought this disaster on himself as on the Church through his own harshness, imprudence, and lack of charity—qualities he was to demonstrate still more destructively when she was no longer at his side. At Christmas she sent him a box of candied oranges with a recipe for preparing them, and a letter explaining how the bitterness was drawn out of the orange by boiling water, leaving only a sweet taste. In this letter she told him how much she desired to free him "from the bitter agony which rages in your soul. May the cause of this agony disappear so that you know nothing but the sweet pain which makes the soul strong and passionate. It is the pain which springs from the love of God—I mean the sorrow and pain caused by our own faults."[43]

By April 1379 Antipope Robert had brought up an army to besiege Rome, but the Romans took Castel Sant'Angelo late that month, and the famous English soldier of fortune John Hawkwood joined with Alberico da Barbiano, leader of the mercenary Company of St. George in the service of Pope Urban, to raise the siege. The Antipope's army was then defeated in the Alban Hills; he fled to Naples and from there to France, taking up his residence in Avignon June 20. Pope Urban VI declared Queen Joanna of Naples, who had rejected him, deprived of her kingdom, and in July Charles of Durazzo entered Naples to take it from her.[44] (Two months earlier Catherine of Siena had warned Joanna: "Do not await the time which you are not sure of having! Do not choose that my eyes should have to shed rivers of tears over your wretched soul and body—a soul which I hold as my own! If I consider that soul, I see that it is dead, because separated from its body; it persecutes, not Pope Urban VI, but our truth and faith. . . . He wearies himself in vain who will guard

---

[42]*Ibid.*, p. 331.
[43]Undset, *Catherine of Siena*, p. 250.
[44]Ullmann, *Origins of the Great Schism*, pp. 94-95; Smith, *Great Schism*, pp. 12-13, 144; Salembier, *Great Schism*, p. 71; Jorgensen, *St. Catherine of Siena*, pp. 353, 361.

the city with force and with great zeal, if God guard it not. And can you say that you have God with you? We cannot say it, for you have put Him against you for putting yourself against truth.")[45] King Louis of Hungary and Poland declared for Urban. Even in Aragon, home of Pedro de Luna, its cautious King Peter IV would not take a stand on the schism, nor would Juan I of Castile, son and successor of Henry II of Trastámara. The only nation supporting the Antipope so far was France, though Duke Leopold III of Austria proclaimed him in 1380.[46]

Canonists and theologians at this stage generally supported Urban VI. The Augustinian Johannis de Braculis at the University of Prague published a detailed argument that Urban VI was the true Pope, never specifically demanded by the shouting mob during the conclave. Baldus reiterated and enlarged his arguments for Urban which he had first published at the moment the schism was being hatched, in July 1378.[47] Even John Wyclif of England, in his treatise *De ecclesia* which expressed a predestinarianism as rigid as Calvin's (he said that the Pope was not necessarily head of the Church since he might not be of the elect), opposed the veneration of the saints (except for the Blessed Virgin Mary), and condemned indulgences and prayers for the dead, referred to Urban as "a man of the gospel, a humble servant of Christ, well fitted to carry out the necessary reforms within the Church" and called Antipope Robert "Vicar of Lucifer."[48] The University of Paris remained doubtful of the Antipope it had reluctantly endorsed at the French King's bidding; Henry of Langenstein and Conrad of Gelnhausen, German theologians teaching here, refused to commit themselves on who was the true Pope and called for an ecumenical council to settle the question.[49]

That and other evasions of the real issue—who *was* the true Pope?—were to become very popular; but in the presence of death evasions are often abandoned. King Charles V of France died in September 1380, affirming in his last hours his firm belief that Antipope Robert was truly the Pope, insisting that no temporal considerations had influenced his decision to support him, and calling like Henry of Langenstein and Conrad of Gelnhausen for an ecumenical council to decide the sundering issue authoritatively.[50] The French monarch

---

[45]St. Catherine of Siena to Queen Joanna of Naples, May 1379, *Letters* ed. Scudder, pp. 320-321.

[46]Oscar Halecki, *Jadwiga of Anjou and the Rise of East Central Europe*, ed. Thaddeus V. Gromada (Boulder CO, 1991), pp. 69-70; P. E. Russell, *The English Intervention in Spain and Portugal in the Time of Edward III and Richard II* (Oxford, 1955), pp. 286-287; Glasfurd, *Antipope*, p. 94; Valois, *France et le grand schisme*, I, 286-288.

[47]Swanson, *Great Schism*, pp. 29-30; Smith, *Great Schism*, pp. 141-142.

[48]Ullmann, *Origins of the Great Schism*, pp. 134-135; Herbert B. Workman, *John Wyclif; a Study of the English Medieval Church* (Oxford, 1926), II, 7-20.

[49]Swanson, *Great Schism*, pp. 40, 59-61; Smith, *Great Schism*, pp. 12, 145-147.

[50]Valois, *France et le grand schisme*, I, 326-329; Salembier, *Great Schism*, p. 100.

was very possibly sincere, but he knew of the April 1378 conclave in Rome mostly from the French cardinals. In August 1379 the relatively young Cardinal Orsini, who had been at both the April conclave and at Anagni, died. He had abstained at the conclave, abstained again at Anagni, but accepted Antipope Robert. Now, facing the Judgment (and perhaps remembering Catherine of Siena's letter to him and Corsini and Brossano) he found his courage at last, and declared Urban VI the true Pope. Few paid any attention to him and to his dying statement.[51]

On Sexagesima Sunday, January 29, 1380, St. Catherine of Siena went to St. Peter's to offer a long and passionate prayer for Pope Urban VI at the grave of the Fisherman. Johannes Jorgensen unforgettably describes the scene:

> She kneels there, a little, thin, white-robed figure; the two great black eyes are burning, the deadly pale face is luminous, the delicate lips of the slightly protruding mouth move softly in prayer, like leaves quivering in a slight puff of wind. The tiny folded hands are like the motionless flame of a candle upon the altar; her whole figure is white and luminous and aflame like a blessed candle. Her women friends are kneeling by her side; they are praying too, but always watching anxiously over their beloved spiritual mother, *la dolce venerabile Mamma*. Suddenly they see her collapse, as if crushed beneath a burden that is too heavy, see her sink into herself like a building tumbling into ruins. They try to raise her up, but it is almost impossible, she has become like one palsied, for Jesus has laid *la Navicella* upon her slight, weak girl's shoulders, laid upon them the whole ship of the Church with all the sins that it has on board.[52]

The next day she rallied enough to write her last letter to Pope Urban:

> Dearest and sweetest father in Christ sweet Jesus: I Catherine, your poor unworthy daughter, write to you with great desire to see a prudence and sweet light of truth in you . . . I pray the inestimable charity of God that He clothe your soul in this; for it seems to me that light and prudence are very necessary indeed to us, and especially to Your Holiness and to anyone else who might be in your place, most chiefly in these current times.[53]

Then came her last message to him and to the defiant ex-cardinals, through her confessor Blessed Raymond of Capua in February when she could

---

Earlier that year Conrad, in his *Epistola concordiae* on ending the schism by means of an ecumenical council, had become the first writer openly to assert that such a council could be called without the consent of the true Pope, whoever he might be (R. N. Swanson, *Universities, Academics and the Great Schism* [Cambridge, England, 1979], pp. 62-63).

[51]Ullmann, *Origins of the Great Schism*, p. 63n.

[52]Jorgensen, *St. Catherine of Siena*, p. 371.

[53]St. Catherine of Siena to Pope Urban VI, Jan. 30, 1380, *Letters* ed. Scudder, p. 334.

no longer write:

> Say to My Vicar that he must try to make his nature milder and that he must be willing to grant peace to all who are willing to be reconciled to him. Say to the cardinals, the pillars of the Holy Church, that if they really wish to compensate for all that has been laid waste, they must unite and stand together, so that they form a cope to cover their father's faults.[54]

On Easter 1380 she staggered from her bed to the altar in the chapel in her home and received Communion there; this day, March 25, was her thirty-third birthday. Her disciple Stefano Maconi said it seemed to him that he could count every bone and every nerve in her body as she lay upon her bed. Paralysis came in April; she made a fervent and profoundly humble last confession and then prayed almost constantly, saying at the end: "Thou, Lord, callest me, and I am coming to Thee. I come, not by my merits, but through Thy mercy alone, for which I beseech Thee by virtue of Thy blood!" She had prayed often that God would bring her to Himself soon; after she had borne the heaviest crosses, He answered her prayer. St. Catherine of Siena died at noon on April 29, 1380; her blessed body has never yet known corruption.[55]

No saint has more greatly deserved the yearned-for reward she now received; but on this Earth she was irreplaceable. The great Western schism was established; its leaders were becoming steadily more stubborn and widely supported; and no end was in sight.

Outside Germany, where Holy Roman Emperor Wenceslas continued to favor the Roman Popes for thirty years but soon showed himself to be an incompetent alcoholic, and divided Italy which remained mostly on the side of an Italian Pope, England was much the most important national supporter of Urban VI. England's active intervention in Spanish affairs now that her greatest nobleman, John of Gaunt, had a claim on the throne of Castile through his wife, daughter of Pedro the Cruel, assured that her weight would be thrown on Urban's side in Spain against the French influence, strong in both Aragon and Castile. But England's King Richard II was just fourteen years old, inevitably dominated at such an age by his ambitious uncles, most of whom were very unpopular. Their unpopularity and the royal minority both contributed to an unprecedented explosion in England in June 1381: the peasants' revolt, triggered by vigorous enforcement of an oppressive poll tax, led by the revolutionary Wat (Walter) Tyler and the renegade rhyming preacher John Ball ("when Adam delved and Eve span, who then was the

---

[54]Undset, *Catherine of Siena*, p. 271.
[55]Jorgensen, *St. Catherine of Siena*, pp. 389-394; Joan Carroll Cruz, *The Incorruptibles* (Rockford, IL, 1977), pp. 120-122.

gentleman?").[56]

This revolt (called "the hurling time") came upon England like a summer thunderstorm in June 1381 and passed away almost as quickly. Thousands of armed peasants stormed London. The gates of the Tower were opened to them; they found Simon of Sudbury, Archbishop of Canterbury, at prayer in the Tower's chapel, seized him, dragged him out, and cut off his head, the inexpert axe-wielder requiring eight gruesome strokes to accomplish it. Royal Treasurer Robert Hales, Marshal John Imworth, and the Franciscan William Appleton died with Sudbury; John of Gaunt escaped only because he was on a mission to Scotland, and his son Henry Bolingbroke only because he was expertly concealed by a loyal retainer.[57]

But the aura of the Lord's anointed surrounded young Richard; with magnificent courage he rode with a retinue of 200 into a mob of at least 10,000 at Smithfield, and when Tyler spat at his feet, confronted him with demands to seize all lands of the Church in England and abolish all dioceses but one, and then called for a flagon of beer, Richard ordered his arrest. Tyler resisted, and one of the King's attendants ran him through with his sword. As some in the crowd prepared to attack him and his party, Richard cried: "Sirs, will you shoot your king? I am your captain, follow me!" Many did; by that evening an army of 7,000 had joined him and the revolt was suppressed, with notably little bloodshed afterward.[58]

Yet the outbreak was a warning that England was neither united nor firmly governed, and the special hostility to the Church it had revealed was not confined to peasants. Its principal source was at the University of Oxford, where John Wyclif had published a thousand-page treatise five years before calling for the confiscation of Church property and declaring that the Pope could err and was not necessary for the government of the Church. In 1377 Pope Gregory XI had condemned 19 propositions attributed to Wyclif, and directed the University of Oxford to investigate to see if he had said these things and if so, to put him on trial for heresy. Wyclif had responded by calling the Pope "an abiding heretic," and no further action was taken against him. On May 15, 1382 one of Wyclif's disciples, Nicholas Hereford, preaching at St. Frideswide's Church in Oxford, declared that Archbishop of Canterbury Simon

---

[56]Charles Oman, *The Great Revolt of 1381* (Oxford, 1906, 1969), pp. 29-52; Harold F. Hutchison, *The Hollow Crown; a Life of Richard II* (New York, 1961), pp. 56-63; May McKisack, *The Fourteenth Century, 1307-1399* (Oxford History of England) (Oxford, 1959), pp. 408-409.

[57]Oman, *Great Revolt of 1381*, pp. 55-72; Hutchison, *Hollow Crown*, pp. 63-70; McKisack, *Fourteenth Century*, pp. 409-412.

[58]Oman, *Great Revolt of 1381*, pp. 73-79, 82-88; Hutchison, *Hollow Crown*, pp. 71-77; McKisack, *Fourteenth Century*, pp. 412-419. Ball was executed July 17 by hanging, drawing and quartering, apparently unrepentant (Workman, *Wyclif*, II, 236-237).

of Sudbury had been "justly slain" by the rebel peasants.[59]

Just two days after Hereford's sermon a synod convened in London, consisting of seven bishops, 14 canon lawyers, and 22 theologians, most of them Franciscans or Dominicans. Urged on by the new Archbishop of Canterbury, William Courtenay—a long-time critic of Wyclif—the synod found that Wyclif had advocated ten formally heretical propositions: that transubstantiation does not occur in the Mass; that a bishop or priest in mortal sin may not ordain, consecrate or baptize validly (the ancient Donatist heresy); that oral confession of sins is unnecessary; that the Gospel does not show that Christ ordained the Mass; that on some occasions God must obey the Devil; that it is contrary to Scripture for the clergy to have temporal possessions; that a sinful Pope has no authority; that there would be no Pope after Urban VI. The synod did not call for Wyclif's trial (Archbishop Courtenay had promised John of Gaunt, who had been Wyclif's patron but was now shocked by his heresies, that he would not be physically harmed) but demanded his immediate removal from Oxford. Archbishop Courtenay promptly ordered the synod's condemnation to be read in St. Paul's and directed Oxford Chancellor Robert Rigg to remove Wyclif from Oxford as the synod had directed.[60]

Chancellor Rigg and most of the faculty resisted strongly, in striking proof that claims of total "academic freedom" are not exclusively a modern invention, but can be an expression of intellectual pride in any era. But in Archbishop Courtenay, the Oxford scholars determined to enforce no law but their own met their match. Courtenay may well have been remembering those eight axe-strokes to his predecessor's neck as he contended with them. He sought out and supported the minority of the faculty willing to apply the decree against Wyclif, and ordered Rigg to publish the synod's decree "clearly, plainly, and without equivocation or sophistry, in both English and Latin." Rigg said he did not dare do this "for fear of death." Courtenay responded: "Then is the University a patron of heresies, if she does not permit Catholic truths to be published," and summoned Rigg before the Privy Council, which confirmed the order to publish the synodal decree at Oxford and soon afterward ordered Wyclif and any who persisted in following him to be dismissed from the University.[61]

---

[59]Workman, *Wyclif*, I, 261-266, 293-295, 306-307; II, 252-253; McKisack, *Fourteenth Century*, pp. 511-512; Ullmann, *Origins of the Great Schism*, pp. 130-131; Joseph Dahmus, *William Courtenay, Archbishop of Canterbury 1381-1396* (University Park PA, 1966), pp. 44-49, 53.

[60]Workman, *Wyclif*, II, 253-268, 272; Dahmus, *Courtenay*, pp. 78-84; McKisack, *Fourteenth Century*, pp. 514-515. For the Donatist heresy, see Volume I, Chapter 20 of this history.

[61]Workman, *Wyclif*, II, 269, 273-284, 286; Dahmus, *Courtenay*, pp. 84-97, 99-101; McKisack, *Fourteenth Century*, pp. 517-518. The quotations are from Dahmus, *op. cit.*, pp. 90 and 91.

Before the end of the year Courtenay's victory was complete: Wyclif had left Oxford with all hopes gone of reaching the higher levels of English society and government with his challenge to the Church, and most of his leading supporters at Oxford had made their submission. Two years later Wyclif died of a stroke.[62] He was to have a major posthumous impact in far-off Bohemia, where scholars at the University of Prague very similar to those at the University of Oxford picked up his doctrines after academic exchanges resulting from Richard II's marriage in 1382 to Princess Anne of Bohemia, and passed them to the great pre-Protestant rebel John Hus.[63] In England the "Lollards" who followed Wyclif never became much more than a handful of dissenting country preachers whose limited popularity mostly resulted from their use of the first English translation of the Bible, a project Wyclif had inspired but had little if any time to work on, which was completed some years after his death.[64]

Despite his initial support for Wyclif, John of Gaunt was personally orthodox; young Richard II was strongly orthodox; both strictly upheld legitimacy in office and would have been naturally inclined in any case to support Pope Urban VI. Even regardless of the merits of his case, more than forty years of war between England and France assured that few in England would look with favor on a French Antipope living in Avignon over an Italian Pope living in Rome. Richard II, his uncles, and Parliament gave full strong support to a "crusade" (so proclaimed by Pope Urban VI) against Flanders, whose Count Louis supported Pope Urban VI but which had largely been taken over by French armies whose leaders proclaimed Antipope Robert. The leader of the "crusade" was Bishop Henry Despenser of Norwich, grandson of Hugh who had ended his life on a 50-foot gibbet at the overthrow of Edward II; he was not militarily competent and the venture failed completely.[65]

Pope Urban VI also declared John of Gaunt a crusade leader in his attempt to enforce his wife's claim to the crown of Castile, after that country endorsed the Antipope in May 1381. Castile was at war with Portugal, and the English offered aid to Portugal, in the form of an expedition led by John of Gaunt's brother Edmund, which was just as ineffective as Bishop Despenser's "crusade" in Flanders. Castile and Portugal made peace in August 1382, sealed by a commitment that young Princess Beatriz, heiress to Portugal, should marry

---

[62]Dahmus, *Courtenay*, pp. 101-105; Workman, *Wyclif*, II, 294, 316.

[63]Hutchison, *Hollow Crown*, pp. 86-88; McKisack, *Fourteenth Century*, p. 427; Matthew Spinka, *John Hus* (Princeton, 1968), pp. 53, 59, 62-65. See Chapter Twelve, below.

[64]Workman, *Wyclif*, II, 160-165, 325-404; McKisack, *Fourteenth Century*, pp. 522-524.

[65]Ullmann, *Origins of the Great Schism*, pp. 114-119; McKisack, *Fourteenth Century*, pp. 429-433; J. J. N. Palmer, *England, France and Christendom, 1377-99* (London, 1972), pp. 45, 47, 49; Richard Vaughan, *Philip the Bold; the Formation of the Burgundian State* (London, 1962), pp. 28-31.

the young Castilian Prince Fernando. But then Juan I of Castile demanded that she marry him instead, and when she did, claimed Portugal for Castile just as John of Gaunt was claiming Castile thorugh his wife, and invaded Portugal to try to annex it.[66]

The Portuguese resisted valiantly, led by John of Aviz, an illegitimate son of former King Pedro of Portugal and head of their nation's crusading military order, established during their Reconquest, which had been completed in the 1260's. A young Portuguese general, Nun'Alvares Pereira, displayed strategic and tactical brilliance. The English sent about a thousand men to help, including some of the deadly longbowmen. In April 1385 the Portuguese *cortes* elected John of Aviz king, after proclaiming the nation's loyalty to Pope Urban VI. On August 14, 1385, aided by the English, Pereira defeated a substantially larger Castilian army in the decisive Battle of Aljubarrota, securing Portugal's independence—which was to have great consequences for Christendom and for the whole world a generation later in the time of Prince Henry "the Navigator."[67]

The next year the Treaty of Windsor established a perpetual alliance between England and Portugal—which remains in being to this day, now subsumed under the North Atlantic Treaty, the oldest alliance in Europe—and John of Gaunt brought 7,000 English to Galicia to try to seize Castile in his wife's name with the aid of the Portuguese. The attempt failed—Castile was as firmly opposed to English rule as Portugal was to Castilian rule—and in July 1388 John of Gaunt surrendered his claim in return for a large sum of money by the terms of the Treaty of Bayonne. But the Anglo-Portuguese alliance stood, now sealed by the marriage of John of Gaunt's eldest daughter, the beautiful, blonde, devout Philippa, to the new King of Portugal (now dispensed from his vow of celibacy because of his royal status). They were to be the parents of Prince Henry the Navigator and the great-grandparents of Isabel the Catholic of Spain.[68]

John of Gaunt's absence in Spain on this unsuccessful venture left a power vacuum in England which his youngest brother Thomas of Woodstock and other great nobles were quick to fill by moving against Richard II. The young

---

[66]Russell, *English Intervention in Spain*, pp. 292, 312-313, 318-321, 337-340, 352-354; Glasfurd, *Antipope*, pp. 99-100; Joseph F. O'Callaghan, *A History of Medieval Spain* (Ithaca NY, 1975), pp. 528-531.

[67]Russell, *English Intervention in Spain*, pp. 360-362, 365-366, 371-376, 384-397; O'Callaghan, *Medieval Spain*, pp. 531-533; Swanson, *Great Schism*, p. 33. Prince Henry of Portugal was the world's first great promoter of overseas exploration, but he never actually commanded an expedition in person, so his title "the Navigator"—though almost universally used—is something of a misnomer. See Chapters Twelve and Thirteen, below.

[68]Russell, *English Intervention in Spain*, pp. 414, 417-418, 429, 431, 449-451, 477-481, 505-508, 514.

King of England, 19 in the year Gaunt departed, had never trusted his uncles or the great nobles, and had surrounded himself with men owing nothing to them. Richard II had already clashed furiously with his uncles in 1384, when for a time he believed false reports that John of Gaunt was trying to kill him, and told the prestigious Earl of Arundel to go to the Devil. There were reports that Richard was involved in a plot to kill Gaunt later that year or early in 1385, though this seems unlikely. Gaunt was in fact the only man then able to hold England together; just three months after he left for Spain in July 1386, Parliament demanded that Richard II dismiss his Chancellor, Michael de la Pole, Earl of Suffolk. Richard haughtily replied that he would not grant their request to remove a scullion from his kitchen. Thomas of Woodstock reminded him of the fate of Edward II and warned that the same could be visited upon him. Richard had to dismiss de la Pole and accept rule for a year by a 14-member commission of the nobility, followed by the calling of a new Parliament. He tried to raise an army to fight for him, but it was defeated at Radcot Bridge in December 1387. He had to call the Parliament, and it met as scheduled February 3, 1388.[69]

Most English Parliaments in those times were given descriptive nicknames; this one was deservedly called the "Merciless Parliament." Five great nobles called the "Lords Appellant," led by the King's youngest uncle Thomas of Woodstock, appeared arm-in-arm at the first session to charge all of the King's chief ministers with treason for taking advantage of the King's youth to get control of the government (this being precisely the goal of the Lords Appellant) and for provoking civil war against themselves. Though the chief judges of the realm declared this appeal against the ministerial choices of a monarch fully of age to rule (21) to be illegal by every standard of law known to them, Parliament declared its own jurisdiction to try the ministers on the charges brought by the Lords Appellant, outside the courts. Thus was impeachment invented. Chancellor de la Pole; the Duke of Ireland, Robert de Vere; the Chief Justice of the King's Bench, Robert Tresilian; and the Mayor of London, Nicholas Bembre, were all tried without even being present, found guilty, condemned to death, and executed as soon as they were caught, as all were within a few months.[70]

Next to be impeached were several lesser officials including Sir Simon Burley, who had been the King's teacher as a boy and was greatly loved by both the King and Queen. All these were quickly executed, despite Queen Anne's tearful plea to Thomas of Woodstock on her knees for Burley's life, and the horrified criticism of several leading nobles including John of Gaunt's son Henry Bolingbroke, the future King Henry IV, who was one of the Lords

---

[69]McKisack, *Fourteenth Century*, pp. 434, 436, 443-446, 452-454; Hutchison, *Hollow Crown*, pp. 91-94, 96-97, 104-107, 113; Dahmus, *Courtenay*, pp. 173-174.

[70]McKisack, *Fourteenth Century*, pp. 454-458; Hutchison, *Hollow Crown*, pp. 116-119; Anthony Steel, *Richard II* (Cambridge, England, 1962), pp. 147-157.

Appellant. Parliament then renewed its members' oaths of allegiance to Richard II and declared that its actions should not be a precedent for the future, but that it would be high treason ever to attempt to reverse them.[71] These grimly ironic gestures could not disguise what had been done. Nearly all those the King had selected to conduct his government had been killed for their loyalty to him. He never forgot; and his bitter though understandable desire for revenge ultimately destroyed him as well as the men who had aroused it.

One striking positive achievement marked the otherwise disastrous pontificate of Urban VI, for which he deserves credit for discrimination and good judgment notably lacking in other aspects of his work as Pope: the conversion of the Lithuanians, the last major pagan people left in Europe. But the primary credit for this last of the great evangelizations on that continent goes to Poland's national heroine: young Queen Jadwiga. In a time when two Hispanic princesses—Catalina, Princess of Castile, the silent wife of John of Gaunt, and Beatriz, Princess of Portugal, the silent wife of King Juan I—allowed themselves to be used solely as instruments of their husbands' ambitions, Jadwiga (who became Queen of Poland at 12, just the age of Beatriz when she became Queen of Portugal) brought her husband and all his people into the Catholic Church and, by joining them to Poland, made it the greatest Catholic nation of the east.

Jadwiga was the youngest of three daughters of King Louis of Hungary and Poland; he had no sons. Louis was a descendant of Charles of Anjou, brother of St. Louis IX of France, who had secured southern Italy and Sicily for the Church from Manfred, son of the heretic Emperor Frederick II. King of Hungary as son of the Angevin Charles Robert who had succeeded to the crown of St. Stephen when the native Arpad dynasty became extinct in 1301, Louis had gained Poland when its king, his friend and ally Casimir III, died without male issue in 1370, having designated Louis as his successor in that situation. In addition Louis had designs on his ancestral domain of Naples and Sicily, now ruled by the scandalous Queen Joanna. He negotiated brilliant marriages for all three of his daughters, well under marriageable age though all three of them were in the 1370's: Catherine, the eldest, was to marry Duke Louis of Orléans, second son of King Charles V of France, and inherit Poland; Mary, the second, was to marry Sigismund of Luxemburg, second son of Holy Roman Emperor Charles IV, and inherit Hungary; Jadwiga, the youngest, was to marry Duke William of Austria, the Habsburg scion, with her inheritance initially undetermined.[72]

---

[71]McKisack, *Fourteenth Century*, pp. 458-459; Hutchison, *Hollow Crown*, pp. 120-121; Steel, *Richard II*, pp. 159-161.

[72]Halecki, *Jadwiga*, pp. 19-59; Paul W. Knoll, *The Rise of the Polish Monarchy* (Chicago, 1972), pp. 197, 200, 235-236; Denis Sinor, *History of Hungary* (New York,

But, as often happened in that age of high mortality, these marital plans were disrupted by death: Catherine died in 1378 at the age of eight. Louis now assigned Mary to Poland and Jadwiga to Hungary, but when he died in September 1382, the arrangement came apart. Many Poles did not trust Mary's prospective husband Sigismund because of his German background; they had been fighting the Teutonic Knights in the north of their country too long, and Sigismund and his father and grandfather had been closely tied to the Knights. The Poles demanded Jadwiga as their Queen instead. Her prospective husband William of Austria was also German, but less powerful than Sigismund; and they might be able to find a way to prevent the marriage. So King Louis' arrangements were reversed, and Jadwiga was crowned Queen of Poland at Cracow in October 1384 at the age of ten, while Mary became Queen of Hungary.[73]

Under Church law Jadwiga must be twelve before she could marry. From her earliest memories she had expected to marry William of Austria, whom she knew well, having stayed with his family in Vienna from her fourth to her sixth year. She had seen little of her father King Louis, who was always on the road, but she had been profoundly affected by the fervent faith of her grandmother, sister of Polish King Casimir III the Great, and by the similarly strong faith of her Croatian mother, Elizabeth Kotromanich. Devout in spirit, resolute in heart, brilliant in mind, tall and strong in body even as a girl, Jadwiga was already unusually mature for her age even before her coronation, and the challenge and danger facing her from the moment of her coronation matured her still more. She was determined to be her own mistress; but she must have a husband's help. She wanted and intended that husband to be William, as her father had provided for.[74]

But many Polish nobles did not want any German king; and when King Jagiello of Lithuania offered in January 1385 to receive Catholic baptism and bring his whole pagan people into the Church if Jadwiga would take him as her husband, the majority of the nobles favored acceptance of his offer. But Jadwiga's mother Elizabeth Kotromanich in Hungary continued to favor William of Austria, as naturally did Jadwiga herself—the fierce 35-year-old pagan chieftain could hardly have been as attractive to her as an adolescent close to her own age who had been her childhood playmate. In August 1385

1959), pp. 83-98.
[73]Halecki, *Jadwiga*, pp. 69-76, 97-109. Just before Jadwiga's coronation, Duke Ladislas of Opole—then her strong supporter, later a traitorous opponent—had brought a much venerated picture of a dark, thin-faced Blessed Virgin Mary, slashed by three cuts allegedly from a Mongol sword, to the monastery of Czestochowa which the Duke had founded in 1382 on behalf of King Louis, Jadwiga's father. It became the centerpiece of what was later Poland's holiest shrine to the Blessed Virgin Mary (*ibid.*, p. 115).
[74]*Ibid.*, pp. 77-96.

young William arrived in Cracow. He was not allowed inside Wawel castle, where Jadwiga resided, but they met on several occasions at the Franciscan monastery at the foot of Wawel hill. A secret marriage was arranged by Duke Ladislas of Opole, the donor of the monastery of Czestochowa where the venerated picture of the Blessed Virgin Mary had been installed, now Poland's greatest national religious treasure. Since William and Jadwiga had already been married by proxy as children, no further Church permission was required, though a priest must be present at the final ceremony.[75]

On August 14 Jagiello confirmed his January offer in writing; on the 22nd a group of Polish knights found out about the plans to secretly solemnize and immediately consummate the marriage of William and Jadwiga, and locked Jadwiga in her chamber. The first response of the fiery and precocious eleven-year-old Queen was to call for an axe to chop the door down. Finally persuaded by her treasurer Demetrius of Goraj to give further thought and prayer to the great decision facing her, Jadwiga prayed for long hours in the Wawel cathedral before a crucifix still preserved there. In prayer she gradually came to see how much more than her own personal desires was involved in this decision: the conversion of a mighty monarch and his whole people, the liberation of thousands of Polish prisoners he held, a great and peaceful extension of Polish territory into lands whose people had long been (many unknowingly) in schism by their membership in eastern Orthodox churches, who could now be led to the Church Christ founded. In the end she chose the greater good; ever since, millions of Catholics in Poland and Lithuania and on the borderlands of Russia have blessed her for it. No girl of eleven ever changed history so much.[76]

At Christmastide in 1385 she sent Jagiello her acceptance of his offer of marriage and conversion, and wrote William "explaining that she was giving him up because she wanted to serve the propagation of the Christian faith." She also sent a personal envoy to Pope Urban VI to explain the situation to him. On February 12, 1386 Jagiello made solemn entry into Cracow; the following day Jadwiga met him for the first time. Two days later he was baptized in the Wawel cathedral. On February 18 Jadwiga solemnly avowed that her marriage with William of Austria had never been consummated, leaving her canonically free to marry Jagiello; the marriage ceremony followed immediately, and he and his young bride became King and Queen of a united Poland and Lithuania. Archbishop Maffiolo Lampugnano of Ragusa, Pope Urban VI's legate, approved all these arrangements, and reported back to the Pope in July that he found Jagiello "a true confessor and propagator of the Faith" and that he had made a formal act of submission to Urban VI. In March 1388 Pope Urban recognized the marriage of Jagiello and Jadwiga, and

---

[75]*Ibid.*, pp. 115, 121-124, 127-132.
[76]*Ibid.*, pp. 134-145.

continued to give them his full support and approval up to his death the following year.[77]

In an age when so many promises were broken and so much fealty ignored—by the cardinals of 1378, by the nobles of England, by the King of Castile—Jagiello, with the holy and beautiful Jadwiga at his side, kept every one of his promises. In February 1387, on the anniversary of his baptism, he endowed a Catholic diocese and cathedral at the Lithuanian capital of Vilnius, and soon afterward a parish structure was set up for the whole of Lithuania. The conversion of its people proceeded rapidly and was virtually complete when Jagiello died an octogenarian in 1434. Jadwiga worked tirelessly to keep Poles and Lithuanians working closely and harmoniously together, and to make and maintain peace with the Teutonic Knights, the ancient enemies of both her people and her husband's. When she died tragically in childbirth in 1399, only 25 years old, all Christendom mourned her. Her last will and testament urged her husband now to marry Anne of Cilli, granddaughter of King Casimir the Great of Poland, to maintain the union with Lithuania; and he did. The age of the prospective re-conversion of Russia might well open a cause for Jadwiga's canonization.[78]

The year and a half following Jadwiga's marriage to Jagiello was a time of horror for her sister and her mother. In December 1385 Charles III of Naples was crowned King of Hungary and Croatia after election by the Hungarian Parliament, deposing Mary. Two months later he was murdered, allegedy by agents of Queen-mother Elizabeth Kotromanich. The Horvats, a noble family of Croatia which had supported Charles, arrested Elizabeth and Mary on the road in the fall of 1386. Sigismund at once marched to her rescue. As his troops approached, in January 1387, the Horvats strangled Elizabeth before her daughter's eyes, calling it an execution for murder. This ghastly crime turned public opinion in Hungary in favor of the previously unpopular Sigismund; he was crowned King of Hungary in March, liberated Mary in June, and drove the Horvats into the mountain fastnesses of Bosnia. Thus, in the best chivalric fashion, did this doughty Catholic champion—one of the most underrated and misunderstood Catholic leaders in the whole history of Christendom, who did much to end the Great Schism, and unflinchingly fought the Hussite heresy in his homeland of Bohemia—emerge upon the stage of late medieval history.[79]

---

[77]*Ibid.*, pp. 147-153, 158-159, 170, 182-183.

[78]*Ibid.*, pp. 161, 213-255, 257, 264-265, 282-285.

[79]*Ibid.*, pp. 145-150, 157, 164, 167; Valois, *France et le grand schisme*, II, 118; Smith, *Great Schism*, p. 152; John V. A. Fine Jr., *The Late Medieval Balkans* (Ann Arbor MI, 1987), p. 397. The most astonishing bibliographical non-discovery in all of the writer's research for the history of Christendom is that in five hundred years no English, French, or Spanish historian has taken the trouble to write a scholarly biography of this extraordinarily important, history-making Emperor. Even in German, his native language, no such biography has been written for 150 years, since Joseph von

King Charles V of France, who died in 1380 in early middle age, left two sons too young to rule for many years (Charles and Louis, both with destinies darker than anyone could have imagined in the days of their gleeful and flamboyant youth) and three younger brothers, all able men and strong personalities who left their mark on history: Louis, Duke of Anjou; John, Duke of Berri; and Philip called the Bold, Duke of Burgundy. All three were convinced partisans of Antipope Robert, as their eldest brother Charles V had been. Louis, the senior member of that generation of his family when Charles V died, bore the famous title that had been held by Charles, the brother of King St. Louis IX, who had taken and held the kingdom of Naples—southern Italy and Sicily—for the Pope in the middle of the preceding century. He was appalled to learn of the victory of Charles III of Durazzo in Naples under Pope Urban VI's banner, and that Queen Joanna of Naples had surrendered to Charles in August 1381 and was closely confined in the castle of l'Oeuf. He resolved to lead an expedition to rescue Joanna and secure to her the kingdom of Naples, hoping that it might also be possible to drive Pope Urban VI from Rome in the same campaign. He persuaded Amadeus VI, the famous "Green Count" of Savoy, to join him, despite the uncomfortable insistence of this long-time genuine crusader from the Alps that the ultimate objective of the campaign ought to be the liberation of Jerusalem.[80]

But there was a major obstacle: the splendid city-republic of Florence, now delivered from the revolutionaries that had almost torn her apart and had even dared threaten the life of St. Catherine of Siena, and restored to her long-standing Guelf tradition as a loyal supporter of the true Pope. St. Catherine's Siena was a Tuscan city like Florence, and her winged words still seemed to dance in the Tuscan air. Florence would fight the minions of the Antipope with everything she had. Louis of Anjou, marching from France on May 31, 1382, therefore decided to give Tuscany a wide berth, though it meant forsaking the direct route to Rome. He went all the way to the coast of the Adriatic near Ravenna, there deciding to march straight south to the kingdom of Naples. Meanwhile Charles III of Naples had moved captive Queen Joanna to the castle tower at Mora and there had her strangled in her bed.[81]

Joanna was not loved, and had scorned St. Catherine's warning that she was bringing herself into the midst of such horrors by her own will; the manner

---

Aschbach's four-volume *Geschichte Kaiser Sigmunds* (1838-45). The only modern studies of Sigismund are in Hungarian.

[80]Eugene L. Cox, *The Green Count of Savoy; Amadeus VI and Transalpine Savoy in the Fourteenth Century* (Princeton, 1967), pp. 324, 327-330; Vaughan, *Philip the Bold*, p. 40.

[81]Ferdinand Schevill, *Medieval and Renaissance Florence* (New York, 1936, 1961), pp. 283-284, 336-339; Cox, *Green Count of Savoy*, pp. 333-335; Glasfurd, *Antipope*, pp. 103-104; Hefele-Leclercq, *Histoire des Conciles*, VI-2, 1105.

of her death does not seem to have aroused the kind of reaction that came in Hungary when Queen Mother Elizabeth met the same kind of death after being accused of murdering Joanna's murderer, Charles III. But it was evilly done. Pope Urban VI voiced no objection; indeed, that spring his legate Cardinal Sangro had gone to the kingdom of Naples and ordered the Archbishop of Salerno burned at the stake for having cooperated with the Antipope, again without objection from Urban VI.[82] A tide of combined fear and anger was rising in the Pope as the Duke of Anjou's army marched through Italy—all that St. Catherine had warned him against: "the bitter anger which rages in your soul"; "say to My Vicar that he must try to make his nature milder and that he must be willing to grant peace to all who are willing to be reconciled to him."[83] He was rejecting mildness and reconciliation, giving way to the bitter anger. He had cause—much more cause than hypercritical, mocking anti-Catholic historians are willing to admit. No Pope has ever been betrayed as Urban VI was betrayed, by every single one of his cardinals except magnificent old Tebaldeschi, and he at death's door. Christ had but one Judas; Urban VI had fifteen. Yet mercy is not to be measured in numbers; Christ said forgive seventy times seven, a figure for infinity. Pope Urban VI was forgetting how to forgive.

By October Duke Louis of Anjou had established a fortified camp near Naples, from which Charles III could not immediately dislodge him; but John Hawkwood, the Englishman who had long been the most famed and skillful mercenary captain in Italy and preferred the service of Florence which fought for the Pope, had arrived to strengthen the garrison of Naples and Anjou did not dare attack Charles there. Duke Louis went into winter quarters, without an adequate supply of food for his men. Then the plague struck—the Black Death still periodically recurred in situations favorable to its renewed spread—and on March 1, 1383 it took his best general, the only one really competent to cross swords with Hawkwood: Amadeus "the Green Count" of Savoy. The antipapal French expedition to Italy had been defeated. The next year Duke Louis of Anjou died in Bari, to be succeeded by his adolescent son Louis II.[84]

Before Pope Urban VI crowned Charles III king of Naples on June 2, 1381, he had extracted from him a promise to hand over Capua, Caserta, Aversa, Nocera, and Amalfi—all rich, substantial cities—to the Pope's nephew once he had gained possession of them. But Charles III had not done it, and he did not turn them over even now that the danger from the Duke of Anjou was virtually gone. Pope Urban therefore left Rome and came to Aversa in October 1383 to claim it personally for his nephew. Watched and followed by

---

[82]Glasfurd, *Antipope*, p. 104.
[83]See Notes 43 and 54, above.
[84]Cox, *Green Count of Savoy*, pp. 335-337; Hefele-Leclercq, *Histoire des Conciles*, VI-2, 1106; Valois, *France et le grand schisme*, II, 83-84.

armed Neapolitans wherever he went, the Pope began to feel himself almost a prisoner as he entered Naples and was lodged under heavy guard at the Castello Nuovo, as the tale spread throughout the city that his nephew had raped a nun at the convent of St. Savior. (The story may not have been true, but was widely believed.) Under these threatening circumstances the stubborn Pope stayed on in the southern kingdom.[85]

In June 1384 he moved to Nocera, another of the cities Charles III had promised to turn over to his nephew, but had not. The majority of his College of Cardinals (28 appointed at the time of the schism, six more just before he went south) were with him, but increasingly frightened. They begged him to allow them to leave Nocera. He refused. They fled; he ordered them back. Soon afterward he learned that six of them had consulted the canonist Bartolino of Piacenza on whether they could lawfully remove the Pope from office. For that there was only one precedent, the action at Anagni in 1378 against this same Pope Urban VI. Bartolino, who must have relied on that precedent, told them they could.[86]

Not only did Pope Urban now turn on the six (five Italians and one Englishman) with the ferocity of a cornered tiger, putting them all to the torture; he also leaped to the conclusion (unsupported by any evidence, though with a certain degree of abstract plausibility) that Charles III must be involved in what had happened. Urban therefore excommunicated Charles and his posterity to the fourth generation and laid Naples—where up to this time he had enjoyed, as everywhere in Italy, substantial support—under an interdict. Charles, a man of pride and violence, reacted decisively and at once. He sent an army to Nocera to take the Pope, dead or alive.[87]

From February to July 1385 the Pope was besieged in Nocera. His courage was unshakable but his judgment continued to be abominable. Three or four times every day he appeared on Nocera's battlements with bell, book, and candle, repeating his excommunication of Charles III, his wife, his children, and every soul in the besieging army. Nothing could have brought the spiritual weapon of excommunciation—already long overused by most of the Popes—into greater disrepute. It was one of the darkest hours in the history of the papacy.[88]

Eventually Urban was rescued by a relieving army commanded by the Count of Nola—whose loyalty to so misguided a pontiff in such a situation is

---

[85]Von Pastor, *History of the Popes*, I, 136; Hefele-Leclercq, *Histoire des Conciles*, VI-2, 1107-1108.

[86]Hefele-Leclercq, *Histoire des Conciles*, VI-2, 1107-1110. The six were: Gentile de Sangro of Naples; Barthélemy de Cucurno, Cardinal of Genoa; Louis Donato, Cardinal of Venice; Jean, Cardinal of Santa Sabina; Marin, Cardinal of Taranto; and Adam Easton, Cardinal of England.

[87]*Ibid.*

[88]*Ibid.*, VI-2, 1110-1111; Valois, *France et le grand schisme*, II, 114-115.

beyond praise—and taken to Salerno on the coast. (His legate Sangro had ordered its archbishop burned at the stake three years before, but was now loaded with chains as one of the six new cardinal-traitors.) In September he arrived at Genoa by sea, with his cardinal prisoners. Soon afterward he released the English Cardinal Easton on the plea of his faithful supporter Richard II of England. By the end of the year the other five cardinal prisoners had disappeared. It was generally believed the Pope had ordered them thrown into the sea.[89]

It is not surprising, though hardly commendable, that at this point two of his other cardinals changed hats and joined Antipope Robert.[90]

For the next three years Pope Urban VI remained relatively quiescent. But he was still obsessed by the kingdom of Naples and all that had happened there. In August 1388 he gathered an army to lead in a new invasion of that kingdom, now ruled by Charles' young son Ladislas after his father was murdered in Hungary. Pope Urban VI now lacked the physical health as well as the prudent judgment to lead an army; he fell from his horse and his army broke up. He went back to Rome, which he had avoided ever since his return from the disastrous campaign of 1385, and died there a year later, in October 1389. The fourteen cardinals who had stood by him despite everything were resolved above all to heal the breach with Naples. They elected its Cardinal Pietro Tomacelli—young, strong, kindly, popular, prudent, and of irreproachable morals—Pope Boniface IX. He promptly attained full reconciliation with Ladislas of Naples, showing how easily it could have been done earlier, and confirmed a large number of ecclesiastical appointments proposed for Lithuania and Poland by Jagiello and Jadwiga.[91]

Antipope Robert was as militant as ever, and the son and namesake of Duke Louis of Anjou was now old enough to take the Italian warpath. In 1390 he sailed for Naples. Though some cities supported him, he could not obtain control without the support of a new expedition overland from France. It never materialized, in substantial part because the French could not induce the ambitious yet cautious Duke Gian Galeazzo Visconti of Milan to support them. Personally, the Duke of Milan told them, he accepted the legitimacy of Antipope Robert; but most Italians, including most of his Milanese, did not, and he could not afford to go so much against them.[92]

The soul of St. Catherine of Siena had left the Earth ten years before, but

---

[89]Hefele-Leclercq, *Histoire des Conciles*, VI-2, 1111-1112; Valois, *France et le grand schisme*, II, 115-117.

[90]Hefele-Leclercq, *Histoire des Conciles*, VI-2, 1112.

[91]*Ibid.*, VI-2, 1113, 1121-1122; Von Pastor, *History of the Popes*, I, 137, 164;Valois, *France et le grand schisme*, II, 145; Halecki, *Jadwiga*, p. 184.

[92]Palmer, *England, France, and Christendom*, p. 193; E. R. Chamberlin, *The Count of Virtue; Giangaleazzo Visconti, Duke of Milan* (New York, 1965), p. 151; Hefele-Leclercq, *Histoire des Conciles*, VI-2, 1126-1127.

the leashed lightning of her soft quick words still flashed across the heavens; her people yet kept faith in the true Pope.

There was increasing talk of a council to settle the schism; but in March 1391 Pope Boniface IX reminded the ecclesiastical speculators that no ecumenical council could be held unless called by the Pope and would have no authority which he did not give it; and he said he had no plans to call a council. Perhaps his judgment in refusing a council was poor; but only he had the authority to make that judgment.[93]

With the "way of a council" for ending the schism thus foreclosed, just three ways of ending it remained without one side admitting its error: military action, binding arbitration, or mutual resignation of both claimaints.

Military action still had its advocates, most of whom now embraced the new concept of a "kingdom of Adria" ruled by Duke Louis of Anjou which would incorporate the Adriatic coast of Italy north of the kingdom of Naples, including most of the papal state, and would adhere to Antipope Robert.[94] But Italy had too many states already; adding one more, even if it could be done, was not likely in actuality to give anyone preponderance.

The "way of cession"—resignation—was endorsed in strong terms by Jean Gerson, Chancellor of the University of Paris, in December 1392,[95] but could never prevail unless both Pope and Antipope could be persuaded to resign, which neither showed the slightest inclination to do. If mutual resignation and binding arbitration were rejected, the moral imperative for the serious Catholic became to decide, for himself and for his country insofar as he was able, who was in truth the rightful Pope, and adhere to him. The evidence proving that Urban VI had been the rightful Pope and Boniface IX consequently his rightful successor was not easy for everyone to obtain, but not really difficult for those in authority. The documents of the cardinals of 1378 avowing full adherence to the Pope days and weeks after the alleged duress ended, and the arguments of St. Catherine of Siena, were available and irrefutable.[96] But few now thought the schism could be resolved that way. Both sides—especially France—had invested too much in their previous commitment to one or the other papal contender. The supporters of the Antipope gave no sign of possessing the moral courage to admit that they had simply been wrong. Christendom was in a trap.

Antipope Robert was more a military man than a churchman, and he

---

[93]Smith, *Great Schism*, p. 161; Hefele-Leclercq, *Histoire des Conciles*, VI-2, 1123.

[94]Chamberlin, *Count of Virtue*, pp. 152-154.

[95]Howard Kaminsky, *Simon de Cramaud and the Great Schism* (New Brunswick NJ, 1983), p. 55.

[96]In May 1379 Holy Roman Emperor Wenceslas had written to Richard II of England declaring that he was keeping in his archives "for eternal memory" the letters of the cardinals written after the election of Pope Urban VI expressing satisfaction with his election and fealty to him (Ullman, *Origins of the Great Schism*, p. 94).

remained committed to a military solution. He embraced the will-o'-the-wisp of the "kingdom of Adria" with enthusiasm. But few others did. Pressures for his resignation grew in France, upon which any hope of his ultimate victory absolutely depended. The University of Paris took the lead in challenging him, and increasingly the leaders of the realm listened. Young King Charles VI, declared of age to rule at the end of 1388, went horrifyingly insane on a campaign to Brittany in 1392, killing five men in a manic frenzy, and continued for the rest of his long life to slip periodically into madness and then, weeks or months later, to recover his sanity. His lucid intervals were inevitably shadowed by fear of the next outbreak, so he was incapable of following through on any consistent policy. Consequently France was actually ruled by his surviving uncles, the Dukes of Berry and Burgundy, and his brother Louis, Duke of Orléans. The Duke of Berry, the senior of the three, who had been the most favorable to the Antipope, was more and more demanding an end to the schism by mutual resignation.[97]

Finally one of the Antipope's strong supporters, Pierre d'Ailly, along with Chancellor Gerson and Nicholas Clemanges, the French titular patriarch of Alexandria, presented a statement to the King and the government which threw down the gauntlet:

> If one or both of the rivals should obstinately refuse to enter upon one of these three ways [a council, binding arbitration, or mutual resignation], and offer no suitable alternative, we deem that he should be judged a pertinacious schismatic and consequently a heretic, no pastor of Christ's flock but rather its disperser and tyrant. His orders should henceforth not be obeyed, and he should not be allowed to retain any administration of government or the use of the Church's patrimony. He himself should be driven out of Jesus Christ's sheepfold as a savage wolf rather than a sheep or a shepherd, the harshest punishments for schismatics should be inflicted upon him, and his portion should not be in the land of the living.[98]

It is said that soon after reading and pondering this extraordinary declaration, ending in a not very veiled assertion that a Pope who refused to resign ought to be hunted down as an outlaw and killed without mercy, Antipope Robert dropped dead of a stroke. He died September 16, 1394. The moment they received the news, the Dukes of Berry and Burgundy, through the mentally weakened King Charles VI, called on the cardinals in Avignon to delay their conclave so that a plan for reunion might be developed. By now the

---

[97]Kaminsky, *Cramaud and the Great Schism*, pp. 32-33, 50-51, 53, 56-57; Chamberlin, *Count of Virtue*, p. 154; Palmer, *England, France, and Christendom*, pp. 195, 199-200; R. C. Famiglietti, *Royal Intrigue; Crisis at the Court of Charles VI, 1392-1420* (New York, 1986), pp. 2-4, 16-21; Hefele-Leclercq, *Histoire des Conciles*, VI-2, 1139.

[98]Kaminsky, *Cramaud and the Great Schism*, pp. 58-59.

Avignon cardinals included only two of those who had made the schism; but one of them, disregarding the plea for delay and reconciliation, promptly had himself elected Antipope (calling himself "Benedict XIII") September 28: Pedro de Luna.[99] Ever since he helped begin the schism in the summer of 1378 by betraying the special confidence which both Pope Urban VI and St. Catherine of Siena had placed in him, Pedro de Luna had bent all the resources of a brilliant mind and an eloquent tongue and pen to the unfailing service of his cause—a man tough as the rocky hills of his native Spain, balky as a camel, long-lived as an elephant, "a study in obstinacy"[100] who would maintain his false pretensions against all pressure and all odds for the twenty-nine interminable years that remained to him to afflict the Church and Christendom.

Christendom still remained a unity, despite the Great Schism; the growing vigor of the efforts to heal it, especially in France, showed that. The course which suggests itself to the modern liberal mind—simply allowing the division to remain, with two Popes—was never advocated, or by all indications imagined, by anyone. And if there might have been any weakening of the bonds of union, it was quickly offset by the countervailing pressure toward resurrecting the glorious though fading ideal of the crusade to meet a grave new military danger in Europe itself.

Crusading to regain Jerusalem and the Holy Places, however hallowed in tradition and fervently believed in by a few men such as the Green Count of Savoy and the publicist Philip de Mézières, was no longer a practical possibility. But now the ancient enemy was bringing the war again into Christian territory, and on a grand scale. The incursions of the Ottoman Turks into Eastern Europe, which had actually made the once-mighty Byzantine Empire into a tributary state during the 1360's,[101] were escalating with alarming rapidity.

In June 1389, in a fierce and bloody battle near Kosovo in southern Serbia, the Ottomans inflicted devastating losses on the combined Serb-Bosnian army which fought them there. The Serbs assassinated Ottoman Sultan Murad I just before the battle began, but he was succeeded on the field by his son Bayazid, called "the Lightning," who won the battle. Prince Lazar of Serbia was slain in combat. Ottoman losses, also heavy, were much more easily replenished. The next year, when a new Ottoman army marched on Serbia, Lazar's widow Milicha, whose minor son was now the ruling prince, offered her submission in his name, having not enough troops left to fight. The Serbs accepted Ottoman rule, and with it tax and military service liability and the right

---

[99]*Ibid.*, pp. 47-48, 111-113, 116; Glasfurd, *Antipope*, pp. 124-126; Smith, *Great Schism*, p. 154; Salembier, *Great Schism*, pp. 136-137. De Luna persuaded the anti-conclave at Avignon not even to read the letter from King Charles VI of France.

[100]The subtitle of Alec Glasfurd's biography of Peter de Luna.

[101]See Chapter Ten, above.

of free passage for Turkish armies through Serbia. Milicha made personal obeisance to Bayazid, and sent her sister Olivera to his harem. The last independent Serb leader, Vuk Brankovich, fought on until 1392, but then he too made his submission.[102]

The road to Hungary was now open to the Turks. Hungary's King Sigismund—who had secured his position there with great difficulty, as we have seen—promptly set to work reviving the crusade in Europe: not to regain Jerusalem, but to save Christendom. Determined to set an example rather than just proclaiming and preaching the crusade, Sigismund was marching south to fight the Turks himself in June 1392, just as Vuk Brankovich was giving way, when Jadwiga of Poland came to Hungary to ask her sister Mary how she and her kingdom could help.[103] The next year the Ottoman Turks totally subjugated Bulgaria. In the winter of 1394 Ottoman Sultan Bayazid summoned all Christian rulers under Turkish overlordship to the north Greek city of Serres where he was holding court. Virtually all of them came, including Byzantine Emperor Manuel II Palaeologus. Bayazid first threatened them, then announced they were all to be executed, then that he had decided to spare their lives. Most of them came back from Serres terrified, with a sense of utter helplessness. In June 1394 Bayazid laid siege to Constantinople, determined this time to take it and make it the capital of his new empire. On the third of that same month, Pope Boniface IX proclaimed a crusade in Eastern Europe against the Ottoman Turks.[104]

Both English and French leaders had been discussing the possibility of a crusade against the Turks since 1393, when a small force from both nations had been sent to help Sigismund. The crusade proved to be a cause transcending the Schism. Its main support (other than from Sigismund of Hungary) came from France, particularly from Duke Philip of Burgundy. The ever-changing situation in France with the periodic insanity of the King, and Philip's long-drawn-out and difficult attempt to create a kingdom for himself and his descendants in the Low Countries, caused him to decide not to lead the crusade himself; but he entrusted its leadership to his son John, known as the Fearless.

---

[102]Fine, *Late Medieval Balkans*, pp. 408-414; Donald M. Nicol, *The Last Centuries of Byzantium, 1261-1453* (New York, 1972), pp. 300-301; John W. Barker, *Manuel II Palaeologus (1391-1425); a Study in Late Byzantine Statesmanship* (New Brunswick NJ, 1969), pp. 66-67.

[103]Halecki, *Jadwiga*, pp. 195-196. One of the few scholarly studies of Sigismund, G. Beckmann, *Der Kampf Kaiser Sigismund gegen dei werdende Weltmacht der Osmana 1392-1437* (Gotha, 1902), maintains that crusading against the Ottoman Turks was the most important policy of his whole long reign in the eyes of King and later Emperor Sigismund.

[104]Fine, *Late Medieval Balkans*, pp. 412-413; Nicol, *Last Centuries of Byzantium*, pp. 314-316; Barker, *Manuel II Palaeologus*, pp. 116-119, 123, 481; Palmer, *England, France, and Christendom*, p. 202; Aziz S. Atiya, *The Crusade of Nicopolis* (London, 1934), pp. 33-34.

In February 1396 Sigismund of Hungary concluded a formal alliance with Byzantine Emperor Manuel II Palaeologus, now the committed enemy of the Ottoman Turks, and Ottoman Sultan Bayazid declared war on him. In March a 28-year truce in the Hundred Years War between England and France was at last signed, after years of inconclusive negotiations. Both kings, Richard II and Charles VI respectively, at once announced that they would encourage their fighting men to join the crusade now that they were no longer needed against each other.[105]

By May 1396 the crusaders were marching east along the Danube, joined in Bavaria by a considerable number of German volunteers. By late July they were at Sigismund's Hungarian capital of Buda; in August they entered Ottoman-ruled territory in Bulgaria, ravaging as they went. Bayazid brought up his Turkish army from the siege of Constantinople. He was a far more experienced commander than young John of Burgundy, only 25, who had never before led a large army in battle. On September 10 the crusaders laid siege to Nicopolis on the Bulgarian south shore of the Danube, with a strong Turkish garrison on an almost impregnable site. Refusing to heed reports of the approach of Bayazid's army, the crusading host was essentially unprepared when it struck. No English longbowmen were in that host, which consisted mostly of ill-disciplined cavalry. Bayazid successfully concealed his 40,000 excellent cavalry and planted sharp-pointed stakes to keep the Christian mounted knights off his infantry; they had to dismount to attack them, and as they struggled through the stakes on foot in their armor in intense summer heat, Bayazid launched his massive cavalry force against them. They defended themselves bravely but hopelessly; four of the principal French leaders were slain on the field and John of Burgundy was captured. Sigismund barely escaped on a Venetian ship down the Danube.[106]

The Christian disaster was complete, the Ottoman Turks triumphant. For more than five hundred years, in consequence, Greece and the Balkans belonged to them. Their conquest, at least up to the borders of Hungary which Sigismund still strongly held, would have been completed almost immediately, including the reduction of long impregnable Constantinople, had it not been for the sudden appearance of the mighty Asiatic conqueror Timur (often called Tamerlane), who in forty bloody and savage years of conquest had extended his rule from Turkish Central Asia to the heart of India, the borders of China, the

---

[105]Palmer, *England, France, and Christendom*, pp. 172-174, 199-203, 205; Vaughan, *Philip the Bold*, pp. 62-63; Atiya, *Crusade of Nicopolis*, p. 56; Barker, *Manuel II Palaeologus*, p. 131; McKisack, *Fourteenth Century*, p. 475; Hutchison, *Richard II*, pp. 161-163.
[106]Atiya, *Crusade of Nicopolis*, pp. 53-56, 63-68, 86-97; Vaughan, *Philip the Bold*, pp. 69-71; Palmer, *England, France, and Christendom*, pp. 203-205; Nicol, *Last Centuries of Byzantium*, pp. 318-319.

Volga River in Russia, the Syrian shore of the Mediterranean, and finally to
Asia Minor, where his sledgehammer blow fell upon Bayazid and his hitherto
invincible army at the Battle of Ankara July 28, 1402 and destroyed them.
Bayazid was captured and died in captivity; his empire was split up among his
rival sons.[107]
    Christendom had no military force capable of stopping Timur, but most
fortunately he now turned in the other direction, indeed to the other end of the
world, to undertake the conquest of China. But he was already 66 years old
when he won the Battle of Ankara, and he set out across the steppes of central
Asia toward China in the middle of the winter of 1405. Even the hardy Mongol
nomads under Timur's command had never known such cold. Men's breath
froze on their beards; ears and noses were lost to frostbite; snow clouds surged
endlessly across leaden skies. At Otrar on the Syr Darya River Timur stopped
to rest, seeking to warm himself with enormous fires and gallons of heated wine.
His digestive tract became inflamed; he could not eat; fever racked him until, in
the words of a Muslim chronicler who hated him, "the hand of death gave him
the cup to drink . . . and drew forth his soul like a spit from a soaked fleece."[108]
    Unwittingly Timur had spared the Byzantine empire for half a century;
the sons of Bayazid proved able to hold their father's conquests, but not to gain
much more, during that time. But it was only a reprieve; before the power of
the Ottoman infidel the city of Constantine was ultimately doomed.

    When the anti-college of cardinals met at Avignon soon after Antipope
Robert's death, every member present swore to "pursue to the extent of his
ability all useful and apt ways for the utility and union of the Church, without
tricks or excuses or delays . . . even if elected Pope; these ways extend even to
his having to abdicate if that should seem advisable to a majority of the present
or future cardinals."[109] De Luna had perforce taken this oath himself, with
what mental reservation no man knows. The next month he sent two envoys to
Paris to explain that he had accepted election to avoid breaking the Petrine
succession, since allowing a new Pope to be elected by "pseudo-cardinals"
would mean that "the world would be set in permanent error," and offering to
accept any way of union proposed by Paris "as far as he can do so with God and
a clear conscience."[110] To King Charles VI he wrote directly, personally and
with less equivocation:

---

[107]Nicol, *Last Centuries of Byzantium*, pp. 319-320, 328; Barker, *Manuel II
Palaeologus*, pp. 139-145, 216-217; Fine, *Late Medieval Balkans*, pp. 499-500; Hilda
Hookham, *Tamburlaine the Conqueror* (London, 1962), pp. 248-252 and *passim*.
[108]Hookham, *Tamburlaine*, pp. 298-303 (quotation on p. 303).
[109]Kaminsky, *Cramaud and the Great Schism*, p. 113.
[110]*Ibid.*, p. 115.

I give you notice of my promotion and at the same time I assure you of my fixed and sincere desire of bringing the schism to an end. I have made use of your good counsels, and of those of the princes your uncles, that to you may belong all the glory of having rendered this great service to the Church. To arrive at my object, I shall employ all reasonable and possible means; but I beg you to despatch an important embassy to Avignon at once. I will accept without any tergiversation everything proposed by it. I would rather end my days in the desert or the cloister than contribute in any way to prolong a state of disorder so prejudicial to everyone.[111]

In St. Catherine of Siena's evocative words, he "lied up to his eyes." Within a year Antipope de Luna had broken every promise so solemnly made in this letter.

In February 1395 a special assembly of prelates and jurists of the French Church, later known as the First Council of Paris, meeting at St. Louis IX's glorious Sainte-Chapelle, voted 87-22 to call for resignations by both papal claimants, with de Luna required to give unconditional assent to this program and leave to the French court and bishops the negotiations to obtain the concurrent resignation of Pope Boniface IX. The only significant opposition was offered by Cardinal Pierre d'Ailly, who preferred binding arbitration of the schism, with both Popes agreeing in advance to accept the verdict of the arbiters.[112]

To give the strongest possible endorsement to this program for ending the schism drawn up by the Church assembly in Paris, the three actual leaders of the French government (in view of the King's mental illness), his uncles the Dukes of Berry and Burgundy and his brother Louis, Duke of Orléans, went to Avignon in June 1395 to convey it in person to de Luna. Their first demand was that he read aloud before them the oath he had taken before his election at Avignon that, if elected Pope, he would resign the office for the sake of Church union if the majority of cardinals agreed. Here was the "important embassy to Avignon" de Luna had asked for in his letter of the previous October to King Charles VI, in which he pledged to "accept without any tergiversation everything proposed by it."[113]

Tergiversation began immediately. Exasperated by de Luna's delaying tactics, the Dukes called a meeting of his college of cardinals without his presence. Under their pressure the college decided to work for the resignation of both Popes, with only Martin de Salva, Cardinal of Navarra and a close friend of de Luna, dissenting. Now the explicit condition of his conclave oath

---

[111]Salembier, *Great Schism*, pp. 143-144.
[112]Kaminsky, *Cramaud and the Great Schism*, pp. 120-138; Smith, *Great Schism*, pp. 158-159; Glasfurd, *Antipope*, pp. 138-139.
[113]Glasfurd, *Antipope*, pp. 139-142; Kaminsky, *Cramaud and the Great Schism*, pp. 140-141; see Note 111, above.

was met. De Luna's Spanish temper flared, and in speaking to a royal counsellor named William he took the stand he was never thenceforth to relinquish: "I will never accept that way of cession [resignation] so long as I live, not even if I were to see the coals blazing and the fire ready. I would let myself be burnt rather than accept it!"[114]

The deadlock was now complete. De Luna would not, would never yield. Mutual concurrent resignation of the two papal claimants was not going to happen. France could withdraw obedience from de Luna, and many were proposing that this be done; but to whom should it then offer obedience? Far as the French government had gone in trying to heal the schism, it would not depart so far from its original position as to offer obedience to the true Pope. They were caught in a cleft stick, and the Antipope knew it. He intended to hold them there until they surrendered to him, and eventually that is what they did.

In their embarrassment and anger, the French theologians dealing with the issue began to take positions contrary to the immemorial traditions and teaching of the Church, which in time became the full-fledged heresy of conciliarism. In his treatise entitled *On Subtraction of Obedience*, published in 1397, Archbishop Simon de Cramaud declared that "even a true and undoubted Pope is not to be obeyed but rather resisted if he does anything that notoriously scandalizes the Church or works to the peril and subversion of souls."[115] Cramaud did not explain who was to judge whether a Pope's actions fell into those categories (later that judgmental role was assigned to a council). He went on to say, in the same treatise: "Today it is more clear that both [papal claimants] are schismatics than has ever been clear about one of them ... this is undoubtedly clearer to the universal church than which of them is the true Pope and which the intruder."[116] The illogic was breathtaking: while one claimant must be a schismatic, both could not possibly be. There was now no workable alternative to deciding which was the true Pope and which was the schismatic, and a man with the prestige and connections of Archbishop Cramaud could easily have obtained the evidence proving that Urban VI had been validly elected; but he would not.[117]

By 1397 de Luna's Spanish countrymen in Castile and Aragon had dropped all attempts to persuade him to resign and restored full obedience to him as Pope.[118] In October of that year the French government drafted a letter

---

[114]Glasfurd, *Antipope*, pp. 142-145 (quotation on p. 145); Kaminsky, *Cramaud and the Great Schism*, pp. 141-142.

[115]Kaminsky, *Cramaud and the Great Schism*, p. 181.

[116]*Ibid.*, p. 185.

[117]See Note 96, above.

[118]Kaminsky, *Cramaud and the Great Schism*, p. 169; Ramón Menéndez Pidal, ed., *Historia de España*, Volume XIV: "España Cristiana: crisis de la Reconquista; luchas civiles," by Luis Suáre Fernández and Juan Reglá Campistol (Madrid, 1987), pp. 580-

declaring that because of de Luna's refusal to resign they would no longer accept his ecclesiastical appointments, but the letter was not sent until January 1398 and was never effectively enforced. A meeting was held at Reims in March 1398 between Holy Roman Emperor Wenceslas and King Charles VI of France to try to find a way to end the schism, but the proceedings were "interrupted by the periodic drunkenness of Wenzel [Wenceslas] and cut short by a recurrence of Charles VI's insanity." In April Cardinal d'Ailly led another embassy to Avignon to ask de Luna to resign; he replied that he had become convinced that for him to resign would be a mortal sin.[119]

The Third Council of Paris in July 1398 voted 140-68 to withdraw obedience from de Luna, and a royal ordinance to that effect was published in Paris August 1 and proclaimed in Avignon September 1. Eighteen of de Luna's 23 anti-cardinals left him; only four Spanish cardinals and one Italian maintained their allegiance to him. The eighteen cardinals hired Marshal Godfrey de Boucicaut to besiege the heavily defended papal palace in Avignon. In his element now—for his family had been mighty warriors in Spain for generations, and his grand-nephew Alvaro de Luna was to be the sword and shield of Juan II, father of Queen Isabel, for many years—Pedro de Luna resisted mightily, leading the defense against attackers attempting to penetrate the palace through a large drain-pipe and routing them by ladles of burning pitch. By April 1399, after seven months' fruitless struggle, the besiegers were willing to accept a cease-fire on de Luna's mere assurance that he would "think again" about resigning. Confined to the papal palace (Marshal Boucicaut's troops had captured the city of Avignon in the first few days, and continued to hold it), he "thought again"—and maintained his claim.[120]

Secure in his intransigence, de Luna now settled down to wait his critics out. He knew that divisions among the three Dukes who really ruled France were deepening and would make it increasingly difficult for them to cooperate against him. In December 1401 he scornfully rejected an ecumenical council proposed by most of the French cardinals and bishops; he rightly saw this as a retreat from the previous French demand for his unconditional resignation, and anticipated further retreats. In April 1402 Duke Louis of Orléans, the King's brother, presented a legal memorial from the University of Toulouse in support of de Luna, as a counterweight to the many statements from the University of Paris calling for his resignation. In January 1403 de Luna felt strong enough to excommunicate the cardinals who had withdrawn obedience from him. In March, still spry at 61, he made a spectacular escape from Avignon through an

---

581.
[119]Kaminsky, *Cramaud and the Great Schism*, p. 211; Vaughan, *Philip the Bold*, p. 54 (for the quotation); Glasfurd, *Antipope*, pp. 155-156; Smith, *Great Schism*, p. 160.
[120]Kaminsky, *Cramaud and the Great Schism*, pp. 224-226, 232-232, 247-248; Glasfurd, *Antipope*, pp. 161-170, 175-178; Smith, *Great Schism*, pp. 161-162.

unguarded postern gate, was immediately offered sanctuary and a large bodyguard in Provence, and wrote cheerfully to Charles VI announcing his new freedom. Almost at once the opposition collapsed; the French court and church restored obedience to de Luna on the sole conditions that he would continue to "consider resignation," not punish any who had withdrawn obedience from him, and hold a council of his obedience within a year.[121]

In 1404 Pope Boniface IX fell ill. De Luna sent ambassadors to him—the first direct communication he had had with his rival since becoming Antipope—proposing with matchless arrogance that the two of them should prohibit their cardinals from electing a successor to whichever died first. (De Luna continued to be in excellent health.) Pope Boniface's mind was very clear and he totally rejected this self-serving proposal before dying October 1 in Rome. Before proceeding with their conclave, his cardinals contacted the French envoys to tell them they would not not do so if de Luna now gave up his claim, presaging a reunification of the Church. The envoys knew by bitter experience there was no hope of that; de Luna would never give up his claim, they told the cardinals in Rome. They proceeded to elect another Neapolitan, Cosmo Migliorato, aged 68, who took the name Innocent VII.[122]

The age and indecisiveness of the new Pope exposed him to many perils, and to excessive influence by his relatives. Riots against his nephew's harsh exercise of his powers forced Innocent VII to flee Rome for Viterbo in July 1405; de Luna asked for a French army to take Rome, and if he had had it Rome could almost certainly have been taken. But France had come to a crisis of its own that summer, which precluded sending any troops to Rome. John of Burgundy, the defeated commander of the crusade of Nicopolis, had succeeded his father Philip as Duke of Burgundy the previous year, and he marched on Paris August 16. The Queen escaped but the heir to the throne, Dauphin Louis, a young boy, was seized and brought back to Paris. Duke Louis of Orléans challenged Duke John. In October they patched up a peace, but hatred endured between them.[123]

In the summer of 1406 Pope Innocent VII returned to Rome from Viterbo when the repentant Romans invited him back, but arrived in poor health and died of a stroke in November. Thirteen cardinals met for the conclave, all taking oath that, if elected, they would work above all for the

---

[121]Kaminsky, *Cramaud and the Great Schism*, pp. 253-266; Smith, *Great Schism*, pp. 162-163; Glasfurd, *Antipope*, pp. 186-193; Vaughan, *Philip the Bold*, p. 56; Famiglietti, *Royal Intrigue*, pp. 25, 34.

[122]Kaminsky, *Cramaud and the Great Schism*, pp. 259-260, 270; Glasfurd, *Antipope*, pp. 198-199; Smith, *Great Schism*, p. 163; Salembier, *Great Schism*, pp. 198-199.

[123]Smith, *Great Schism*, p. 164; Glasfurd, *Antipope*, pp. 204-205; Kaminsky, *Cramaud and the Great Schism*, pp. 260-262; Famiglietti, *Royal Intrigue*, pp. 46-51; Richard Vaughan, *John the Fearless; the Growth of Burgundian Power* (New York, 1966), pp. 33-35.

reunion of the Church, resigning if necessary to bring about that reunion, and creating no new cardinals. On November 30 they elected Cardinal Angelo Correr, a Venetian of austere and holy life, aged 69, who took the name Gregory XII. During the conclave the Fourth Council of Paris was once again debating withdrawal of obedience from Antipope de Luna, but since this had already been tried and failed, clerical opinion in France was inclining more and more toward a council, called even if neither papal claimant approved. The University of Paris called for both withdrawal of obedience and a council, and as an institution renounced obedience to de Luna that December.[124]

On December 12, 1406, thirteen days after his election as Pope, Gregory XII wrote to the stubborn Antipope. Since the Schism began, this letter was the first document in the exchange of the papal rivals to express the genuine spirit of Christian charity. Pope Gregory pleaded with de Luna to work with him for the sake of the Church. He was ready, Pope Gregory said, like the woman before Solomon, "to surrender his own child, the Church, rather than see it torn in two." They must meet, he said—"I will hurry to the place of reunion, by sea, in a fishing boat if necessary, or by land, with a pilgrim's staff in my hand."[125]

Tragically he later failed to keep this promise. The history of the Great Western Schism is a trail of broken promises. But it was a pontificate well begun, and even better ended. It was fitting that the Pope who could thus offer to sacrifice himself at the beginning of his pontificate should have found, nine years later, the way out of the trap in which the Church was caught, which none before him in thirty-seven years had been able to find.

Meanwhile in England, Richard II had been darkly and silently awaiting his opportunity for revenge on the Lords Appellant of the Merciless Parliament. Only once had he let his brooding hatred show, and that only under the greatest provocation: when his beloved young wife, Anne of Bohemia, died in 1394 at 28, still childless, and the Earl of Arundel, one of the Lords Appellant, failed to pay his respects to her body lying in state at St. Paul's and then was late for her funeral, Richard accosted him after the funeral and clubbed him to the ground with a stick. Three years later Richard obtained the election of a speaker of the House of Commons who would cooperate with him; secured the good will of his uncle John of Gaunt by inducing Parliament to legitimize his children born in adultery with Katherine Swynford, whom Gaunt had subsequently married when his Castilian wife, daughter of Pedro the Cruel, had died; and had Gloucester, Arundel, and the Earl of Warwick arrested and impeached just as they had arrested and impeached their victims before the

---

[124]Smith, *Great Schism*, pp. 165-166; Kaminsky, *Cramaud and the Great Schism*, pp. 264-267; Salembier, *Great Schism*, pp. 208-210, 218-220; Hefele-Leclercq, *Histoire des Conciles*, VI-2, 1304-1305; Glasfurd, *Antipope*, pp. 208-209.

[125]Smith, *Great Schism*, p. 165.

Merciless Parliament. When Gloucester begged for mercy, Richard replied that he should have the mercy he had shown to his teacher Simon Burley when the late Queen Anne begged him, on her knees and in tears, for Burley's life.[126]

Gloucester was found dead in his jail cell, presumably murdered; Arundel was executed, and his brother the Archbishop of Canterbury ordered into perpetual exile; Warwick was imprisoned. Henry Bolingbroke, John of Gaunt's son and a fourth Appellant, was exiled for ten years, reduced to six on his father's plea. A Parliament at Shrewsbury in January 1398 officially annulled all acts and judgments of the Merciless Parliament. Heavy financial penalties were levied on the 17 counties which had most strongly supported the Lords Appellant. In February 1399 John of Gaunt died; the next month Richard II, working through a Parliamentary committee, extended his son's banishment to life and disinherited him—and John of Gaunt had been by a wide margin the largest landowner in England.[127]

History offers few more striking examples of the futility of revenge, no matter how justified it may seem. The disinherited Henry Bolingbroke turned almost at once on Richard II, already unpopular for his extravagance and inconstancy (except in obtaining revenge), who, anticipating no such defiance, had left England for an extended stay in Ireland to try to reduce that individualistic and turbulent country to better order. Henry landed in Yorkshire in July 1399 with just 300 men and raised the standard of rebellion; thousands soon flocked to his banners. Richard rushed back from Ireland to Wales, with many of his lords deserting him, and found most of the Welsh unwilling to fight for a cause not their own. Trying to negotiate, he was seized, brought to Flint Castle as Henry Bolingbroke's prisoner, and treated "with shameful indignity." An attempt by a few loyal Welshmen and Cheshiremen to rescue him failed, and he was taken to London and immured in the Tower.[128]

Richard, possibly in a state of psychological collapse, was prevailed on in September to abdicate, and "placing the crown of the kingdom upon the ground he resigned his right to God."[129] By no stretch of legal imagination did Henry have a right to that crown, though he proceeded immediately to take it. His father, John of Gaunt, was the fourth son of King Edward III; Richard II had been the only descendant of Edward III's eldest son Edward "the Black Prince," and Edward III's second son William had died young without issue, but Edward III's third son Lionel, Duke of Clarence, had a daughter Philippa who

---

[126]Hutchison, *Hollow Crown*, pp. 143-145, 171-175, 178-179; McKisack, *Fourteenth Century*, pp. 470, 477-479.
[127]Hutchison, *Hollow Crown*, pp. 179-185, 188-192, 195-198, 205-208; McKisack, *Fourteenth Century*, pp. 480-485, 487-490.
[128]Hutchison, *Hollow Crown*, pp. 209, 215-216, 220-222; McKisack, *Fourteenth Century*, pp. 488-489, 491-494; E. F. Jacob, *The Fifteenth Century, 1399-1485* (Oxford History of England) (Oxford, 1961), pp. 1-4.
[129]Jacob, *Fifteenth Century*, p. 14.

married Edmund de Mortimer, third Earl of March. Their son Roger de Mortimer, fourth Earl of March, had been named by Parliament in 1385 heir presumptive to the throne, and had been killed at the Battle of Kells in Ireland in 1398. His son Edmund, fifth Earl of March, thereupon became heir presumptive at the age of seven. Since Richard II had no children, Edmund was by law the rightful heir.[130]

But he was only a child, and the party of the Lords Appellant, now once again in the saddle, wanted no part of him; he was brushed aside. Henry Bolingbroke was crowned as Henry IV, a usurper; Parliament's actions against the Lords Appellant were annulled, with Thomas Arundel brought back from exile and restored as Archbishop of Canterbury and his nephew Thomas given the estates of his executed father the Earl of Arundel. Ex-king Richard II was announced dead in February, his body displayed to the people with only his face visible for recognition; centuries later, however, his bones were medically examined and found without marks of violence. Apparently he died of starvation, whether by his captors or by his own will.[131]

Henry IV's lack of a true royal title was well known, and the cause of repeated uprisings against him in England and a major rebellion in Wales, led by the last great Welsh national leader, whom Shakespeare made famous: Owen Glendower. The memory of Welsh independence still lived, though dimly, for it had been crushed 115 years before by Edward I; the descendants of Llewelyn the Great's famous Seneschal Ednyved Fechan fought beside Glendower during his ten years of military challenge to the English which began in 1400 and had become really formidable by 1402. In that year, following a Welsh victory at the Battle of Pilleth, Glendower captured Edmund Mortimer, uncle of the rightful heir to the throne of England, his namesake. Soon Mortimer had joined Glendower, marrying his daughter. The French, impressed by Glendower's victories and hoping to weaken England, made alliance with him in 1404. Lady Despenser, sister of the Duke of York and guardian of young Edmund Mortimer, attempted to go to Wales with her son in February 1405, but was arrested and brought back. Later that month Glendower, Edmund Mortimer the uncle of the rightful heir, and the Earl of Northumberland made an agreement at Bangor by which Northumberland would rule the north of England, Mortimer the south, and Glendower Wales.[132]

It was Glendower's high point; but Henry IV responded to the threat with energy, crushing the incipient revolt in northern England before it was really underway and driving the Earl of Northumberland into Scotland, and repelling

---

[130]*Ibid.*, p. 15; Hutchison, *Hollow Crown*, p. 204.
[131]Hutchison, *Hollow Crown*, pp. 231, 233-237; Jacob, *Fifteenth Century*, pp. 19-21.
[132]Jacob, *Fifteenth Century*, pp. 37-39, 42, 56-57; John E. Lloyd, *Owen Glendower* (Oxford, 1931), pp. 29-31, 35-37, 43-44, 50-52, 58-59, 85-86, 93-95; J. L. Kirby, *Henry IV* (London, 1970), pp. 134, 185-186.

a Welsh attack on Usk with Glendower's brother killed and his eldest son captured (he was imprisoned in the Tower of London for the rest of his life). The French did send 3,000 men to Glendower's aid, but they were unable to sustain themselves in the rugged and unfamiliar countryside and all left within a year. In 1406 the Earl of Northumberland escaped from Scotland and joined Glendower, but the young and able Crown Prince Henry of England was put in command of the English forces in Wales that year and began winning a long series of victories. Northumberland left Wales on a fruitless mission to France, which as we have seen had its own serious problems in that period, culminating in the assassination of Duke Louis of Orléans by Duke John of Burgundy in November 1407. Over the next three years the vastly superior military and economic strength of England prevailed over Wales. In January 1409 Glendower lost his last stronghold of Harlech Castle; during the English siege of it his son-in-law Edmund Mortimer died and his wife (Glendower's daughter) and Glendower's own wife were captured and sent to London as prisoners. By 1410 organized Welsh resistance had ended. But Owen Glendower was never caught; he fades from history into legend, and his ultimate fate is unknown.[133]

In Castile the failure of the attempt to conquer Portugal in 1385 had been followed five years later by the sudden death of its King Juan I, of a fall from his horse apparently caused by a heart attack or stroke, at the young age of 32. His son and heir, Henry III, was only eleven; the ensuing three-year regency was full of disorder, with massacres of Jews in many cities in 1391 causing large numbers of them to convert to Christianity during the remainder of the decade—some sincerely, but many out of fear or ambition. According to the law of Castile, Henry III was declared of age in 1393 at fourteen. He was in poor health, but had a strong will and was highly intelligent and mature for his age; by the end of 1395 he had the country well in hand. In 1402 he sponsored an extraordinary expedition by two Norman French seamen, Jean de Bethencourt and Gadifer de la Salle, to the Canary Islands off the coast of Africa. They claimed four of the islands for him and settled one (Lanzarote). By 1404 he was ready to resume the great war of the Reconquest, the longest crusade, which civil strife in Spain had in effect suspended since Henry III's great-grandfather Alfonso XI had died of the Black Death besieging Gibraltar in 1350.[134]

He made little progress at first, and a two-year truce was signed with the Muslim kingdom of Granada in October 1406. Henry vowed to lead the next

[133]Jacob, *Fifteenth Century*, pp. 58-61, 63-66; Lloyd, *Glendower*, pp. 96-98, 101-102, 106-107, 126, 128-129, 136-138; Kirby, *Henry IV*, pp. 181, 185-187, 217-218, 220-221, 233-234; Vaughan, *John the Fearless*, pp. 45-47.

[134]O'Callaghan, *Medieval Spain*, pp. 536-538, 606-607; Menéndez Pidal, *Historia de España* XIV, 303, 311, 315, 325, 340, 374; see Chapter Nine, above, for Alfonso XI before Gibraltar.

campaign in person. Then suddenly he died of one of his many ailments, on Christmas day 1406, leaving as his successor his 22-month-old son Juan, who was to be the father of the great Queen Isabel. Henry III's brother Fernando was immediately accepted as regent, and he was as committed to the renewal of the Reconquest as his brother had been. In October 1407 Fernando took the important border fortress of Zahara from the Moors of Granada after an impressive bombardment with primitive artillery. The Castilian nobles of the south had not really taken war against the Moors seriously for two generations; Fernando had great difficulty holding them to the task, and consequently was not able at this time to advance beyond Zahara. After another truce to gather his strength and improve discipline, in the spring of 1410 Fernando brought 2,500 knights and 10,000 infantry to besiege Antequera, one of the principal strongholds of the Moorish kingdom. He decisively defeated an army sent to relieve Antequera. The Moors in the city fought on all summer, refusing to consider surrender; in September Fernando stormed it with scaling ladders. It was the first great victory for the Reconquest since Alfonso XI took Algeciras 64 years before.[135]

In that same year of 1410, an unexpected crisis descended upon the kingdom of Aragon in eastern Spain. Its King Martin the Humane died without issue, following the death of his son and namesake in Sardinia the year before, without legitimate issue. Martin had been a strong supporter of his countryman, Antipope de Luna, in the Great Schism, and Castile had long supported de Luna also. With France so reluctant to obey him, de Luna depended heavily on Aragon and Castile. Of the seven claimants to the throne that the dying Martin would leave vacant, the best qualified personally was unquestionably Prince Regent Fernando of Castile, whose mother was King Martin's sister. His designation as King of Aragon would effectively unite both countries under a strong ruler favorable to the Antipope. It seems that de Luna pressed King Martin hard to name Fernando his successor, but Martin had a fondness for his seven-year-old grandson, the illegitimate son of Prince Martin. Torn between his love for the boy and the pressure of the masterful Antipope, King Martin took refuge in silence; he died without naming an heir, and civil war immediately threatened.[136]

On April 21, 1407 Antipope de Luna, meeting at Marseilles with envoys of Pope Gregory XII, agreed that he and Gregory should meet some time during

---

[135]O'Callaghan, *Medieval Spain*, p. 541; Derek W. Lomax, *The Reconquest of Spain* (London, 1978), p. 168; I. I. Macdonald, *Don Fernando de Antequera* (Oxford, 1948), pp. 63-80; Menéndez Pidal, *Historia de España*, XIV, 375; see Chapter Nine, above, for the reconquest of Algeciras.

[136]Macdonald, *Fernando de Antequera*, pp. 133-145; Menéndez Pidal, *Historia de España*, XIV, 598-603.

the following October at Savona on the Mediterranean coast near Genoa, in Italy about fifty miles east of the French border. Simon de Cramaud, titular Patriarch of Alexandria and effective head of the French clergy, who had long been involved in negotiations with de Luna about the Schism, now headed a delegation which visited both de Luna and Pope Gregory, urging them to be sure to meet as they were pledged to do, and to agree to mutual resignation of their papal claims at their meeting. De Luna refused to make any promises, and Pope Gregory XII was now wavering in the face of vehement objections to his resignation by his relatives, King Ladislas of Naples, and the people of Rome. He began to equivocate: first he refused to travel by land, and said he had no ships to come by sea; when ships were offered to him, he said he had changed his mind and would now travel only by land. Then he said he would not come as far as Savona, but would come to Pisa, and set out from Rome to the north. He took a week to reach Viterbo, spent two weeks there, and then travelled north to Siena in September. De Luna arrived in Savona that same month, but Pope Gregory would not move from Siena.[137]

"I will hurry to the place of reunion, by sea, in a fishing boat if necessary, or by land, with a pilgrim's staff in my hand,"[138] he had said, less than a year before. But now he would not do it.

During January 1408 the Pope and the Antipope sidled closer to each other, de Luna moving to Portovenere in Liguria east of Genoa, and Pope Gregory XII to Lucca in northern Tuscany. There they were still forty miles apart, and each was still in a jurisdiction supporting his claims (Genoa having been under French control since 1394, and St. Catherine of Siena's Tuscany being still staunch in support of the Roman Pope). Further than this they would not go. On Easter the French court, through Charles VI, delivered an ultimatum to de Luna: he must resign by Ascension day or France would withdraw obedience from him once again. He responded with a threat to excommunicate the King. He had already planned a new attempt at a military solution to the schism, assembling an Aragonese fleet—with the eager cooperation of King Martin—to attack and take Rome. But the fleet was scattered by a storm, and as soon as the threat became known, at the end of April, Ladislas of Naples occupied Rome with a substantial army.[139]

Gregory XII, faced with this example of his adversary's perfidy, took refuge in indignation. Sounding all too much like his adversary, he announced

---

[137]Kaminsky, *Cramaud and the Great Schism*, pp. 273-276; Glasfurd, *Antipope*, pp. 211-216, 219-220; Salembier, *Great Schism*, pp. 221-223, 225-226; Hefele-Leclercq, *Histoire des Conciles*, VI-2, 1321.

[138]See Note 125, above.

[139]Kaminsky, *Cramaud and the Great Schism*, p. 277; Glasfurd, *Antipope*, pp. 321-325; Smith, *Great Schism*, pp. 167-169; Hefele-Leclercq, *Histoire des Conciles*, VI-2, 1336.

that he would never resign—indeed, he ordered that resignation never again be mentioned in his presence. He convened the cardinals at Lucca in May in a palace full of armed men, declared himself no longer bound by his earlier promise not to create new cardinals, and appointed four who were known to be vehemently anti-French and opposed to the Pope's resignation. Seven cardinals now left him (some departing from Lucca in disguise) and publicly called on him to reconsider his decision and to summon an ecumenical council. He condemned them the next month for having acted in defiance of his authority.[140]

De Luna had now excommunicated the King of France, thereby burning his bridges in France; the French government issued an order for his arrest and that of his chief clerical supporter in France, Cardinal d'Ailly. After a last viciously disrespectful letter to Pope Gregory on June 15 ("you, man, if you have a spark of decency in you . . . make up your mind for God's and pity's sake to do your duty"), he took the Aragonese fleet King Martin had sent him and sailed for his native land. The absolute intransigence of both claimants and the shameless breaking of their promises had angered most of Christendom, wearied and scandalized by the now thirty-year-old schism. Henry IV of England withdrew his kingdom's obedience from Gregory XII. On June 29 six of the cardinals who had left Pope Gregory and six who had left de Luna met in the northwestern Italian port city of Livorno and issued a call for an ecumenical council to meet at Pisa March 25, 1409, to compel both claimants to resign (though how they would compel them they did not say), form a new college of cardinals from all the existing cardinals of both obediences who would cooperate with it, and choose a new Pope. The Italian cardinals at Livorno issued a special call to all Pope Gregory's Italian supporters to withdraw their obedience from him.[141]

Five cardinals stood by the beleaguered Pope, as did Florence and Siena. They provided him with a strong bodyguard. Other cardinals who had not been at Livorno now published their reasons for rejecting his authority and supporting the proposed council. Then, in September, Pope Gregory created ten new cardinals, none from Florence or Siena. Those cities, which had so long remembered St. Catherine and kept faithful to her memory, now forgot her, abandoned the Pope, and endorsed the Council of Pisa.[142]

---

[140]Kaminsky, *Cramaud the Great Schism*, pp. 278-279; Glasfurd, *Antipope*, pp. 225-226; Smith, *Great Schism*, p. 169; Hefele-Leclercq, *Histoire des Conciles*, VI-2, 1340-1343.
[141]Kaminsky, *Cramaud and the Great Schism*, pp. 279-280; Glasfurd, *Antipope*, pp. 226-227 (quotation on p. 227); Smith, *Great Schism*, p. 170; Salembier, *Great Schism*, pp. 229-231; Hefele-Leclercq, *Histoire des Conciles*, VI-2, 1360-1364, 1367, 1370.
[142]Kaminsky, *Cramaud and the Great Schism*, p. 279; Smith, *Great Schism*, pp. 170-171; Salembier, *Great Schism*, p. 233; Hefele-Leclercq, *Histoire des Conciles*, VI-2, 1361.

It cannot be denied that they had provocation. But St. Catherine's words were for them as well as for the cardinals of 1380:

> Say to the cardinals, the pillars of the Holy Church, that if they really wish to compensate for all that has been laid waste, they must unite and stand together, so that they form a cope to cover their father's faults.[143]

The essential, inescapable fact was that by the whole history, tradition, and canon law of the Church, an ecumenical council could not be held without papal approval. Not only had neither papal claimant given his approval to the Council of Pisa, both had already called councils of their own: Gregory's to meet somewhere in the papal state at Pentecost in 1409, de Luna's at Perpignan in Roussillon in November 1408. The canonist John of Imola of Padua, writing in the fall of 1408, reminded his colleagues of this essential point even while favoring the Council at Pisa. He declared his conviction that Gregory XII was the true Pope and urged him to legitimize the council and then resign. But there seemed no prospect of that. In January 1409, when none of the cardinals who had rejected his authority had responded to his offer to renew their obedience to him without penalty for what they had done, he denounced them all as "apostates, schismatics, calumniators, perjurers [and] conspirators" and excommunicated them all.[144]

Pope Gregory XII now took refuge with Carlo Malatesta, prince of Rimini, a medium-sized city at the middle of Italy's Adriatic coast. Malatesta was a rare figure in that or any age, loyal to the end, scornful of intrigue and self-interest, knowing his duty and doing it without question or hesitation. Sure that Gregory was the true Pope, he knew that therefore he must defend him, and he did. When even Florence and Siena had abandoned the rightful Pope, Carlo Malatesta stood fast. St. Catherine would have been proud of him.[145]

Gregory's only other supporters were the kingdom of Naples and Bohemia and large parts of Germany, where the alcoholic Emperor Wenceslas had been overthrown in 1400 and declared replaced by Count Rupert of Bavaria, though he was never recognized as Emperor, since Wenceslas, despite

---

[143]See Note 54, above.

[144]Smith, *Great Schism*, pp. 170-171; Swanson, *Great Schism*, pp. 161-162 (for Imola of Padua); Glasfurd, *Antipope*, pp. 233-235; Hefele-Leclercq, *Histoire des Conciles*, VI-2, 1361, 1371-1372, 1390 (for the quotation). De Luna's council met at Perpignan as scheduled, attended by approximately 300 including seven cardinals, three patriarchs, eight archbishops, 33 bishops, 83 abbots, four heads of religious orders, and representatives of four universities, but most of the delegates were from Scotland, Savoy, Lorraine, Castile and Aragon, though a few came from France. Most were unquestioning supporters of de Luna, who presided at every session, talking interminably, and at one point threatening with perpetual imprisonment a cardinal whom he suspected of intending to suggest his resignation.

[145]Salembier, *Great Schism*, p. 241.

his personal weaknesses, remained faithful to Pope Gregory, and continued ruling Bohemia. German sentiment still generally favored the rightful Pope, and on this issue Rupert agreed with his enemy.[146]

Through the fall of 1408 and the winter of 1409 debate continued to rage among the theologians and canonists. Most of them, in varying degrees of desperation, now favored the council regardless of who the true Pope might be or how it was to be authorized. The famous French prelates Gerson, Cramaud and d'Ailly all now proclaimed the ultimate authority of a council to act without papal authorization in a crisis, without saying who was to define when such a crisis existed or how authority could be differently derived in a crisis than in less critical times.[147] It became—in a manner with which discerning scholars in a later age are very familiar—a badge of academic respectability to be conciliarist. The last warning voice before the Council of Pisa against this highly dangerous trend was that of a scholar at the German University of Heidelberg; either because of his own modesty or the hostility of his colleagues, not even his name has come down to us. But he spoke, clear as a bell, for tradition and truth:

> One must submit unconditionally to the Pope, however wicked he may be. Gregory XII is the true Pope. Hence it is unlawful to deny obedience to him, and one cannot damage him in any way, no matter what good may be the purpose of it. The cardinals' withdrawal of obedience, made without any semblance of due form, is invalid. The arguments made in support of this action carry no weight. It is impossible to say [as many theologians now were saying] that Gregory has committed a heresy by being involved in the schism.... The Pope will have to give account to God for the vows he made to bring unity to the Church; no mere human being has any right to judge him in respect of them, nor has an assembly of bishops, and still less one of the cardinals.... They are trying to force the hand of the Holy Ghost![148]

That was exactly what these prelates and theologians were doing. But no man forces the hand of the Holy Spirit. When the council met at Pisa, He was far away.[149]

---

[146]*Ibid.*, p. 279; Smith, *Great Schism*, pp. 170-171; Kaminsky, *Cramaud and the Great Schism*, p. 247; Hefele-Leclercq, *Histoire des Conciles*, VI-2, 1245-1246.

[147]Swanson, *Great Schism*, p. 167; John B. Morrall, *Gerson and the Great Schism* (Manchester, England, 1960), pp. 77-81; Smith, *Great Schism*, pp. 172-173.

[148]Smith, *Great Schism*, p. 173.

[149]See von Pastor, *History of the Popes*, I, 178-190, for a clear and thorough explanation of why this council was in no way legitimate by Catholic standards. It was, von Pastor says, "from the outset an act of open revolt against the Pope. That such an essentially revolutionary assembly should decree itself competent to re-establish order, and was able to command so much consideration, was only rendered possible by the eclipse of the Catholic doctrine regarding the primacy of St. Peter and the monarchical constitution of the Church, occasioned by the Schism." (*op. cit.*, p. 178).

In the eyes of the world the Council of Pisa was indeed a glittering assembly, attended by 24 cardinals (fourteen formerly adhering to Pope Gregory XII, ten to de Luna including Guy Malesset, the only survivor of the 1378 conclave that began the schism except for de Luna), four patriarchs, 80 bishops, 89 abbots, 41 priors, the heads of four religious orders, and representatives of virtually every university, crowned head, and great noble house in Catholic Europe. Peter Philargis, the Greek-born, widely respected Cardinal Archbishop of Milan, who had been of Pope Gregory's obedience, gave the opening address, condemning both papal claimants, who were formally summoned at the doors of the church where the council was meeting, and formally declared contumacious when they did not respond, nor any representative for them.[150]

On April 10 Carlo Malatesta of Rimini arrived at Pisa. The cardinals and other leaders promptly descended on him, urging that he deliver Pope Gregory XII up to them. They were asking the wrong man to betray his Holy Father. Malatesta replied that the cardinals should not persecute Christ in his representative on earth. "The essential point," he reminded them, "is the peace of the Church, and the Pope will do everything he can to secure it. Let the cardinals take care: if they continue their present line of action they will have three Popes instead of one." Pressed by Cardinal Philargis on why Pope Gregory XII would not resign, with Philargis suggesting it was because he loved power, Malatesta responded that Philargis evidently loved power too, since everyone knew he wanted to be Pope.[151]

The ambassadors of imperial claimant Rupert arrived in Pisa from Germany bearing 24 well-reasoned objections to the holding and authority of the Council, but finding few in a mood for discussing or even listening to them, they tacked them to the door of the cathedral and departed. On April 24, at its sixth session, the Council adopted a 37-point memorandum on the history of the schism, on the basis of which it declared the two papal claimants "notorious schismatics and heretics" from whom all obedience should be withdrawn; their own authority now paramount; and the cardinals present constituted as a college to elect a new Pope. There was some reluctance to formally condemn Gregory XII and de Luna as heretics (since this could only be based on the absurd argument that a schism too long continued somehow metamorphosed into a heresy by implicitly denying the unity of the Church) but eventually the Council confirmed its position that both were guilty of both heresy and schism.[152]

---

[150]Smith, *Great Schism*, pp. 173-174; Salembier, *Great Schism*, pp. 244-246; Glasfurd, *Antipope*, pp. 236-237; Hefele-Leclercq, *Histoire des Conciles*, VII-1, 3-11.

[151]Salembier, *Great Schism*, p. 249 (for the quotation); Hefele-Leclercq, *Histoire des Conciles*, VII-1, 12, 18-21.

[152]Salembier, *Great Schism*, pp. 248, 251-253; Hefele-Leclercq, *Histoire des Conciles*,

On June 14 the sensational news filled Pisa that Antipope de Luna—as so often with Spaniards, right or wrong, no one could question his courage—had arrived in person, accompanied and guarded by King Martin of Aragon. The Chancellor of Aragon obtained permission to address the council to urge that de Luna be heard. His plea was referred to committee; the representatives of the Antipope were insulted in the streets, and the entire party left Pisa secretly within a day or two.[153]

On June 26 the council's college of 24 cardinals unanimously elected Peter Philargis Pope. He called himself "Alexander V." A 70-year-old Franciscan, he had supported the Roman Popes from the beginning of the schism until this council, but had also served the cold-hearted and power-hungry Duke Gian Galeazzo Visconti of Milan, who privately favored de Luna, as archbishop of his city. On July 1 Philargis took over the presidency of the council, intoning "Come, Holy Spirit" and preaching on the text "there shall be one flock and one shepherd."[154]

But there was not one flock and one shepherd. Now there were three.

New Antipope Philargis had the support of England, most of France, the Low Countries, Bohemia (ex-Emperor Wenceslas had finally adhered to him, and so with great reluctance did Archbishop Zbynek of Prague, formerly one of Gregory XII's great champions), Poland under Jagiello (who must have been sadly bewildered by all these divisions in the church into which the saintly Jadwiga had led him), his own Milan, Venice, and Florence. De Luna retained the support of his own Aragon, Castile, parts of southern France, and Scotland (which had come to his support as France's ally when France supported him, and remained stubbornly on the opposite side from England). Gregory XII was the weakest of the three, retaining the loyalty only of Naples, western Germany, some north Italian cities, and steel-true Carlo Malatesta of Rimini.[155]

Pope Gregory XII's thinly attended council of his obedience at Cividale declared in its final session in September 1409 that Church unity could be regained only if all three claimants would withdraw and two-thirds of the cardinals of all three existing colleges would vote for a new Pope. Failing this, a new council was recommended.[156] This action, overlooked by most historians,

---

VII-1, 12-18, 22-28, 44-48; Kaminsky, *Cramaud and the Great Schism*, pp. 282-283.

[153]Salembier, *Great Schism*, pp. 253-254; Hefele-Leclercq, *Histoire des Conciles*, VII-1, 51-53.

[154]Smith, *Great Schism*, p. 176; Salembier, *Great Schism*, pp. 255-257; Kaminsky, *Cramaud and the Great Schism*, p. 284; Hefele-Leclercq, *Histoire des Conciles*, VII-1, 54-58. In keeping with the practice of this history regarding Antipopes, Philargis will be referred to hereinafter only by his own name, not the papal designation "Alexander V" he assumed without proper authority.

[155]Kaminsky, *Cramaud and the Great Schism*, pp. 284-285; Matthew Spinka, *John Hus* (Princeton, 1968), pp. 96, 106.

[156]Hefele-Leclercq, *Histoire des Conciles*, VII-1, 63-64.

is very significant because the Pope made no effort to change or reject his council's action. He must have been already beginning to regret his own obstinacy which, joined with de Luna's, had helped bring this new tripartite division of the Church and Christendom. He who had lately forbidden any mention of resignation in his presence was now ready to consider it again, and even a new council. In five years he would have a new opportunity.

The day after his council adjourned, Pope Gregory XII had to flee in disguise from Cividale, under threat by Venice which now acknowledged Antipope Philargis. He took ship to Gaeta in the kingdom of Naples, that refuge of so many fugitive Popes since the days when Robert Guiscard protected St. Gregory VII. Cardinal Archbishop Balthazar Cossa of Bologna, in alliance with Louis II of Anjou and the Florentines, now occupied Rome and most of the papal state. Cossa, a very ambitious and domineering personality who was already expecting to be the successor of the septuagenarian Philargis, encouraged him to leave Rome and to go Bologna in January 1410, leaving Cossa a free hand in the Pope's city. On May 3 Philargis suddenly died in Bologna. Unrepentant, on his deathbed he reconfirmed all the decrees of the Council of Pisa.[157]

On May 17 Cossa was unanimously elected his successor, and took the title—deeply ironic to the Catholic living at the end of the twentieth century—of "John XXIII."[158] Let the great papal historian Ludwig von Pastor tell us the kind of man Antipope Cossa was:

> Of all the miserable consequences of the disastrous Synod of Pisa, this election was the worst. John XXIII was not, indeed, the moral monster his enemies afterward endeavored to represent him, but he was utterly worldly-minded and completely engrossed by temporal interests, an astute politican and courtier, not scrupulously conscientious, and more of a soldier than a Churchman.[159]

The Great Western Schism had become a triangle of distorted loyalties, with the true Pope the weakest of the contenders, and most of his supporters (with the notable exception of Carlo Malatesta) actuated by no higher motives than those of their opponents. The Catholic Church seemed to be suffering the fate that would overtake later Protestantism: repeated, irrepressible subdivision. Still Catholic by doctrine, the Church no longer displayed its great distinguishing mark of unity. Worst of all, no rescue from this disaster seemed possible. Every way to reunion had been blocked, not only for years but for

---

[157]*Ibid.*, VII-1, 71, 73-76; Smith, *Great Schism*, p. 178; Salembier, *Great Schism*, pp. 258, 265. See Volume II, Chapter 19 of this history.
[158]Smith, *Great Schism*, pp. 178-179; Hefele-Leclercq, *Histoire des Conciles*, VII-1, 77-80.
[159]von Pastor, *History of the Popes*, I, 191.

decades. Stubborn pride and boundless ambition rode high. Both qualities unquestionably characterized Antipopes Cossa and de Luna. Even Pope Gregory XII had showed more of both qualities than anyone had expected at his election, and especially after the first letter he had written as Pope to his rival. From where, and how, could rescue come?

No one could tell. But it would come. In an age littered with the broken promises of this conflict that rent the Mystical Body of Christ, Christ's promise to Peter stood. On that rock He had built His Church, and the gates of Hell should not prevail against it.

12
Reunion
(1410-1434)

(Popes Gregory XII 1406-1415, Martin V 1417-1431, Eugenius IV 1431-1447)
(Antipopes Pedro de Luna 1394-1422, Baldassare Cossa 1410-1415, Gil Muñoz
1423-1429)

On Thursday, July 4 [1415], a happy and a famous day indeed, the Council
[of Constance] held a session, the King [Emperor Sigismund] being present
in his imperial insignia, as before, that is, in a crimson dalmatic with a
crimson silk cape over it, without a cope, and with the imperial crown,
scepter and orb. At that session Charles Malatesta abdicated with great
solemnity from the papacy on behalf of Angelo Corrario, called Gregory
XII.... First was read a bull of the said Gregory conferring on his
delegates power to sanction the council. Next was read a bull addressed to
Charles alone, conferring the same and even fuller power.... When these
had been read, Charles rose and explained the terms of the bulls, saying
that since by force of the second bull he had fuller power than the Cardinal
of Ragusa, including the power of appointing a substitute, therefore he
appointed the Cardinal of Ragusa as his substitute for the time being. The
Cardinal of Ragusa then rose and delivered a noble harangue on the text,
"Who is he and we will praise him? For in his lifetime he has done
marvellous things," applying the words to his lord. Then, by authority of
his lord Gregory, he convoked and sanctioned the Council and all the acts
it should thereafter perform... Then the Council, through the mouth of
the Archbishop of Milan, who stood high in the pulpit along with the four
prelates from the four nations, accepted the said convocation and sanction
as contained in the memorandum just read.... But note that this
acceptance was compulsory because without it Charles refused to carry out
the abdication. It seemed better to the Council to make some concession
in return for the great gain than to lose the advantage of Gregory's
abdication.—Diary of the Council of Constance by Cardinal Guillaume
Fillastre, July 4, 1415[1]

The action by Pope Gregory XII thus described, though without full
understanding, by Cardinal Fillastre at Constance, saved the Church, the
papacy and Christendom. It ensured that the apostolic succession and

---

[1]John H. Mundy and Kennerly M. Woody, eds. *The Council of Constance; the
Unification of the Church* (New York, 1961), pp. 253-254.

ecclesiastical authority of the Popes from the Apostle Peter remained unbroken. We know so little of the later pontificate of Gregory XII, when he was abandoned by almost all Christendom, that we have no idea whence (in human terms) the thought came to link his resignation with a demand that the Council accept convocation, sanction and approval from the man who was in fact the true Pope, though the overwhelming majority of delegates to the Council (including Cardinal Fillastre) did not believe it. In the absence of such data, it is reasonable to conclude that the idea came from Gregory XII himself, by the inspiration of the Holy Spirit Whom the Council of Pisa had presumed to command. The strategy seems too spectacularly brilliant, from a pontiff who up to this point had shown no sign of spectacular brilliance, to have come from him alone. For without papal authority, the Council of Constance and anyone it chose as pretender Pope could only have suffered the fate of the Council of Pisa and its choice, Antipope Philargis and his successor Cossa. Few would have accepted the authority of a pontiff so chosen when it was no longer to their advantage to do so. But by its acceptance of authority from the true Pope to govern the Church in the interim before the selection of the next Pope, and to provide for the manner of that selection, the Council was invested with divine authority and would choose a true Pope; and the Holy Spirit dwelt with it. Consequently the Council of Constance succeeded in ending the Great Schism and restoring the papacy.[2]

But because so very few delegates to the Council understood how they had been blessed by what Pope Gregory XII had done, a visible temporal leader was necessary to protect, assist and guide them as they carried out their designated task. That leader was Holy Roman Emperor Sigismund, thereby fulfilling the highest duties of the magnificent and venerable office of temporal head of Christendom and protector of the papacy. Though by the time of the Council of Constance Sigismund had withdrawn his previous support for Gregory XII, he knew that his duty was to help the Council clear away the claimants of the Great Schism and then fairly elect a new Pope. He discharged that duty superbly.

Sigismund was elected Emperor in January 1411 following the deposition of his brother Wenceslas as Emperor (though not as king of Bohemia) in 1400 and the death of the succeeding Emperor Rupert in 1410. Wenceslas abandoned his imperial claims in favor of his brother, and Sigismund secured the votes of five of the seven imperial electors. The other two, the Archbishops of Mainz and Cologne, demanded that Sigismund renounce Pope Gregory XII, whose cause he and his father and brother had always supported, in return for their support. Sigismund wanted unanimous electoral endorsement, and in

---

[2]The significance of Pope Gregory XII's resignation and its terms, and their acceptance by the Council of Constance, is well though briefly explained by Ludwig von Pastor, *History of the Popes*, Volume I (London, 1923), pp. 200-201.

view of the widespread abandonment of Gregory XII by many of those who had previously obeyed him (notably in Italy and in England) Sigismund's own confidence in Gregory's legitimacy may have been sincerely shaken. No true Pope in the Church's history had so little support as Gregory XII following the Council of Pisa. Sigismund met the archbishops' condition, renounced Gregory XII, and was unanimously confirmed as Emperor in Frankfurt July 21, 1411.[3]

The only major sovereign now supporting the true Pope was the dissolute King Ladislas of Naples, and it was much more from fear of him than of Gregory XII that Antipope Cossa proclaimed a crusade against the true Pope and Naples in September 1411. Though in much of Christendom the response was tepid—Cossa's total worldliness was becoming more and more evident—enough accrued to him in Italy to enable him to defeat the not very pugnacious or well led Neapolitan army, driving it out of Rome. In June 1412 Ladislas made peace with Cossa, giving up the papal states and agreeing to renounce obedience to Gregory XII in return for recognition as King of Naples. Pope Gregory, who had gone to the kingdom of Naples, had to leave by sea for Rimini, where the ever-faithful Carlo Malatesta held firm for him. A poorly attended council held in Rome in February 1413 accomplished little more than a condemnation of the heresies of John Wyclif. But when Cossa rejected Ladislas' 125-year-old claim to Sicily, the Neapolitan prince came storming back, taking Rome and stabling his horses in St. Peter's. Cossa fled to Bologna after Florence refused to admit him.[4]

A beaten fugitive, Cossa now put himself under the protection of Emperor Sigismund. But the Emperor, well aware of the steadily growing threat of the Ottoman Turks in Eastern Europe and of his special responsibility both as Emperor and as King of Hungary to resist them, wanted the united support of Christendom in a new crusade, and knew that there was no hope of such union unless the Great Schism was ended. It was now quite clear to a man of Sigismund's political perspicacity that Baldassare Cossa was not and was unlikely ever to become the man to end it. Therefore Sigismund threw his full support behind a new ecumenical council that would not simply seek to end the Schism on its own dubious authority, but would obtain with his aid the resignation of all three papal claimants and the election of a new Pope to reunite Christendom. Cossa agreed to the council almost at once. Just a few days after their first meeting, on October 30, 1413, Sigismund announced that

---

[3]George C. Powers, *Nationalism at the Council of Constance* (Washington, 1927), p. 26; Charles-Joseph Hefele and Henri Leclercq, *Histoire des Conciles*, Volume VII, Part 1 (Paris, 1916), p. 86; Howard Kaminsky, *Simon de Cramaud and the Great Schism* (New Brunswick NJ, 1983), p. 285.

[4]Powers, *Council of Constance*, pp. 30-33; Matthew Spinka, *John Hus* (Princeton, 1968), pp. 132-133, 178; Joseph Gill, *Eugenius IV, Pope of Christian Union* (Westminster MD, 1961), p. 24; Noel Valois, *France et le grand schisme d'occident*, Volume IV (Paris, 1902), pp. 130-131.

an ecumenical council would be held at the imperial city of Constance, on the shore of Lake Boden between Switzerland and Germany, on All Saints day, November 1, 1414, and that he and Cossa would attend and the other two papal claimants would be invited. Cossa confirmed this in an apostolic brief the following day.[5]

In September 1414 Cossa left Bologna to begin making his way to Constance, via Venice and the passes of the Tyrol. Travel through the Alps in the first snows of fall was slow, and the route he had chosen required him to cross the towering massif of the Arlberg, where his carriage overturned in the snow and ice and pinned him for a time beneath it. When finally, toward the end of October, he reached the heights overlooking Lake Boden, with the little city of Constance nestled along its shore under the mountain slope, the place seemed to him like a trap. "That's how they catch foxes!" the nervous Antipope said as he gazed upon it. But when he entered, accompanied by nine of his cardinals, many bishops and a total entourage of 600, under a golden canopy behind nine white horses (eight carried his baggage, and one the Blessed Sacrament), he was "received with every mark of respect and loyalty."[6]

That was not to last long.

Cossa was one of the first to arrive at Constance; there were not nearly enough prelates present yet to begin the Council. On the appointed day for its opening, November 1, nothing more happened than Florence's able Cardinal Francisco Zabarella reading the bull convoking the Council in the cathedral of Constance.[7]

Two days later a Czech priest named John Hus, bearing a safe-conduct from Emperor Sigismund, appeared in the conciliar city. The knight leading Hus' small escort, John of Chlum, went to Cossa the day after their arrival to ask his protection for Hus as well, which Cossa promised to maintain "even if he had murdered my own brother."[8]

Hus' appearance at Constance had a long history. For twelve years he had inveighed against corruption in the Church, with increasing vigor and asperity, in Bethlehem Chapel in Prague, endowed and built to provide a center for preaching in the Czech vernacular. Corruption had indeed become widespread in the Church particularly during the Great Schism, when Popes and Antipopes were so involved in struggle with one another that they had little time and means to govern the Church properly. In Hus' native Bohemia the

---

[5]Powers, *Council of Constance*, pp. 30-33; John P. McGowan, *Pierre d'Ailly and the Council of Constance* (Washington, 1936), pp. 24-25; Mundy and Woody, eds., *Council of Constance*, pp. 70-75.

[6]Powers, *Council of Constance*, pp. 38-39 (quotation on 39); McGowan, *d'Ailly and the Council of Constance*, p. 28; Spinka, *Hus*, pp. 231-232.

[7]Powers, *Council of Constance*, pp. 39-40.

[8]*Ibid.*, pp. 41-42; Spinka, *Hus*, pp. 230, 232.

struggle had become acute when in 1409, following the Council of Pisa, King Wenceslas abandoned Pope Gregory XII and accepted Philargis, the conciliar Antipope. The loyal and courageous Archbishop Zbynek of Prague for a time defied the king, refusing to abandon the legitimate pontiff. It was not a situation favorable to maintenance of papal authority. Hus began challenging it as a matter of doctrine, and recommending the teachings of John Wyclif who had been condemned for heresy, even after Archbishop Zbynek burned Wyclif's books. When Hus refused to appear for examination before Cardinal Odo Colonna (the future Pope Martin V), Colonna excommunicated him in February 1411. Wenceslas supported Hus, demanding that the excommunication be annulled. Zbynek refused to obey the King, condemning him for supporting priests "who openly carried on and preached errors and blasphemies against Holy Church," and fled to Sigismund for protection, but died (perhaps by foul play) before he could reach him.[9]

Hus continued to defy the excommunication, appealing "to God and Christ" against Cossa, the man those who had condemned him considered to be the Pope. In August 1412 Cossa had ordered the Bethlehem Chapel destroyed, but the people of Prague would not permit it. At a general synod of the Czech clergy in February 1413 Hus defended himself vigorously, declaring that no ordained priest could be prohibited from preaching; loyal Catholics at the synod, led by Stanislav of Znojmo and Stephen Palech, upheld the supreme authority of the Pope and declared that he must be obeyed in all things "save the absolute prohibition of good and prescription of evil." But Hus would have none of this; in April 1413 he declared explicitly, in a letter to Christian of Prachatice, that "I acknowledge that the Pope is the vicar of Christ in the Roman Church, but do not hold it as an article of faith."[10] Soon afterward he published his major treatise on the Church, *De ecclesia*, in which he stated that the Church was built on personal faith as demonstrated by St. Peter's confession rather than upon the Popes as his successors, that the Pope has no universal jurisdiction over the Church, and that all necessary truths of Christianity are found in Scripture. Warned by colleagues at the University of Prague that this was heresy, he replied that he would not accept their counsel, "even if I should stand before the fire prepared for me."[11]

Before that fire he was soon to stand.

The position which Hus had taken contained most of the essential

---

[9]Spinka, *Hus*, pp. 39, 106, 109-113, 119-120, 124-129 (quotation on 128); Howard Kaminsky, *Simon de Cramaud and the Great Schism*, pp. 284-285; Howard Kaminsky, *A History of the Hussite Revolution* (Berkeley CA, 1967), pp. 74, 84.

[10]Spinka, *Hus*, pp. 162-163, 167-177 (quotation on 176); Kaminsky, *Hussite Revolution*, pp. 92-95.

[11]Spinka, *Hus*, pp. 177-178, 183-189 (quotation on 178); Kaminsky, *Hussite Revolution*, pp. 95-96.

elements of the Protestant revolt which was to come almost exactly a century later. There can be no question of Hus' passionate sincerity, however mistaken. He accepted Emperor Sigismund's offer of a safe-conduct to attend the Council of Constance in order "to profess publicly the faith I hold," though he was warned by his legal advisor, John of Jesenice, that he would probably be condemned there, and "that a condemned heretic could not be shielded before ecclesiastical authorities even by a royal safe-conduct." New Archbishop Conrad of Prague, perhaps bowing to public pressure, certified Hus' orthodoxy in writing and urged Sigismund to make sure he had a fair hearing. But on November 28, 1414 Hus was arrested, on charges brought by Stephen Palech, who had been a Catholic spokesman at the synod of February 1413, that he had denied transubstantiation in the Eucharist, declared that the Church should not possess property, and maintained that a priest cannot be forbidden to preach by any Church authority. Hus insisted that he had not denied the Real Presence in the Eucharist; he did not deny the other charges. On December 6, questioned by a three-man panel of ecclesiastical judges on his views on Wyclif's 45 condemned propositions, he said that twelve of them might have a correct sense. He was then thrown into a cell in a Dominican monastery on an island in Lake Constance, to await trial by the Council as a heretic.[12]

Delegates to the Council arrived slowly but steadily during November and December 1414. Eventually the number who had come for the Council was overwhelming: five patriarchs, 29 cardinals, 33 archbishops, more than 500 bishops, about 100 abbots, more than 300 doctors of theology and canon law,

---

[12]Spinka, *Hus*, pp. 220-230, 234-236 (quotations on 223 and 224, respectively); Powers, *Council of Constance*, pp. 41-42; Kaminsky, *Hussite Revolution*, p. 138. The precise provisions of the safe-conduct became and have remained a major historical issue after Hus was burned at the stake in Constance. In addition to the general limitation on its applicability noted by Hus' own lawyer, the issue is complicated by the fact that Sigismund's initial offers of the safe-conduct were either oral, or left no written document that has survived. Lord Henry Lefl of Sazany, a chief minister of King Wenceslas, said Sigismund agreed to grant Hus a safe-conduct "assuring safe passage to and from the Council no matter what the decision of that august body might be" (Spinka, *Hus*, p. 222), but when Hus accepted the offer, he made no explicit reference to free return from the Council, and the document finally delivered to him, two days after he arrived at Constance, said nothing about his return (*ibid.*, pp. 230-231). But if it did not apply to his return from Constance, why deliver it after he had arrived there? Hus' knight escort, John of Chlum, certainly believed that Hus' imprisonment violated the safe-conduct, affixing proclamations on the door of the cathedral of Constance December 15, 1414 stating just that, and at that time Sigismund demanded Hus' release, to no avail; he was told that the Council would suspend all its work if they were not allowed to proceed against Hus (*ibid.*, pp. 236-237). It is likely that Sigismund intended the safe-conduct to apply to a two-way journey from Prague to Constance and back, but that when the Council condemned Hus to death, he concluded that their jurisdiction in a Church matter could not be challenged without destroying the Council and thereby continuing the Great Schism indefinitely.

and some 18,000 other clerics, along with many high-ranking laymen and their numerous escorts. In all perhaps as many as 100,000 people, about a third of them mounted, came to the little lakeside city. Even the horses ridden in by this horde of guests far outnumbered the permanent population of Constance. It is very hard to imagine how everyone was accommodated.[13]

Only one regular session of the Council was held during November and December,[14] but much planning and jockeying for political position went on then. It soon became apparent that the majority of the Italian prelates and clerics present supported Cossa, but that few from outside Italy did. French Cardinal Pierre d'Ailly made his position clear at the outset, in a speech delivered December 2 attacking Cossa for excessive ambition, dishonesty and corruption, and demanding sweeping reform of the Church. Five days later, in a meeting of cardinals and archbishops at the bishop's palace in Constance, Cardinal d'Ailly called for the Council to elect a new Pope, a committee of 12 of its members who were not cardinals collaborating with the cardinals in the election. Except among the Italians, his proposal was favorably received. He emphasized the independence of the Council of Constance from the Council of Pisa and from Cossa, pointing out correctly that it had in fact been convoked as much by Emperor Sigismund as by Cossa.[15]

At two hours after midnight on Christmas day the Emperor himself arrived in Constance. On Christmas morning, seated upon a throne prepared for him in the cathedral, he attended Mass celebrated by Cossa. Reporting to the Council December 29, Sigismund said that he had persuaded both of the other papal claimants to send representatives to the Council; in fact, representatives of Pope Gregory XII had already arrived. Speaking at a solemn reception for the Emperor, Cardinal d'Ailly declared that the Council must end the Schism and reform the Church, both together, and that the Council had power equal to that of the Pope. In making that last claim, Cardinal d'Ailly was not so far from the position of John Hus as he presumably thought he was.[16]

The second plenary session of the Council was not held until March 2, 1415. It could have been held in February, but most of that month was spent in working out a unique new voting system for the Council. Cardinal d'Ailly had already called for granting votes to the doctors of theology and of canon or civil law present, as well as to bishops and abbots, as had been done at the Council of Pisa, and went further to grant votes to temporal princes and their

---

[13]McGowan, d'Ailly and the Council of Constance, pp. 26-27.
[14]On November 16. See Powers, Council of Constance, pp. 43-44, and Cardinal Fillastre's diary, in Mundy and Woody, eds., Council of Constance, pp. 204-206.
[15]McGowan, d'Ailly and the Council of Constance, pp. 31-39; Valois, Le grand schisme, IV, 263-265; Powers, Council of Constance, pp. 47-48, 50-51.
[16]McGowan, d'Ailly and the Council of Constance, pp. 39-42; Powers, Council of Constance, pp. 55-56; Valois, Le grand schisme, IV, 265.

ambassadors "since the peace of Europe was at stake." His proposal had been accepted. But voting by so many in a single group would be difficult and unwieldy, and the majority of voters were still favorable to Cossa. More distant nations, particularly England, were very underrepresented for their Catholic population and the power wielded by their rulers; England had only 20 out of nearly a thousand votes. So on February 6 a meeting of the German and English delegations proposed that all matters coming before the Council be voted on by "nations," four in number: Germany (with Hungary and Poland), England (with Scotland, Ireland, and Scandinavia), Italy (with Crete and Cyprus), and France. Each nation would have one vote; each would nominate a committee of delegates to discuss proposals for the Council, the committee would report its conclusions to the full nation, and the four nations would then meet in general session for final action, with majority vote prevailing. Thus England and Germany acting together could block any action by the Council, while Italy alone could be outvoted. Emperor Sigismund gave strong support to this plan, particularly since his influence was currently dominant in the German and English delegations (though he was unsuccessful in adding his own Hungary as a fifth nation, which would have given him even greater influence). The French delegation accepted the vote by nations the following day, leaving the Italians with no choice but to accept it or see the council break up.[17]

This political coup—a defeat of the first magnitude for Antipope Cossa—was decisive in shaping the course of the Council of Constance. On February 16 the German, English and French nations publicly demanded the resignation of all three papal claimants, and were joined by a considerable number of Italians. An unknown person, thought to be Italian, sent to leaders of the four nations a detailed list of crimes of which Cossa had been accused, calling for an inquiry into them by the Council. In a series of meetings at the end of February the German, English and French nations discussed undertaking just such an inquiry, covering Cossa's whole history as a cleric. The Antipope evidently feared such an inquiry, for on March 1 he made a formal statement of his firm intention to resign his claims to the papacy if Pedro de Luna and Gregory XII did likewise. His statement was presented to the Council at its second formal session the following day; a *Te Deum* was sung, and Emperor Sigismund theatrically threw himself down before Cossa and kissed his foot.[18]

Sigismund now declared his intention to go to Aragon to negotiate with Pedro de Luna (whom it seems he had never met, nor fully gauged his capacity

---

[17]Powers, *Council of Constance*, pp. 53-54, 58-65; McGowan, *d'Ailly and the Council of Constance*, pp. 45-49.
[18]Powers, *Council of Constance*, pp. 65-67; McGowan, *d'Ailly and the Council of Constance*, pp. 49-50; Cardinal Fillastre's diary, in Mundy and Woody, eds., *Council of Constance*, pp. 217-219.

for obstinacy) for his resignation, and wanted to be designated by Cossa as his "procurator" (deputy with authority to proclaim final resignation in his name); but Cossa, knowing now that Sigismund was determined to eliminate him as papal claimant, balked. Reports spread that Cossa was planning to leave Constance, hoping this would de-legitimize the Council in the eyes of many outside it who still regarded him as a valid Pope. Sigismund closed the city's gates. The Council, meeting again on March 15, demanded that Cossa appoint the Emperor as his procurator, stay in the city, and not try to dissolve the Council until full unity was restored to the Church. Responding defiantly the following day, Cossa refused to designate Sigismund procurator and proposed that the Council be moved to Nice in southern France, where he promised he would finally resign. The Council replied that it and the Emperor must agree to any change of site, and Sigismund made it clear that he would insist on a city in imperial territory, like Constance.[19]

The disagreements between the Emperor and the Antipope had now become a test of wills; and Cossa's broke so suddenly and completely as to suggest the real possibility of grave doubt in his own mind about the validity of his title. On March 20 the Council and the Emperor presented Cossa with their firm rejection of his position of the 16th. That evening Cossa fled Constance, riding on a small dark horse (in contrast to the nine white horses behind which he had entered the city in October), huddled in a large gray cloak wrapped round and round him to hide most of his face and body, accompanied only by a squire, a crossbowman and a priest. He spent the night at an obscure rectory, and the next morning went by boat to Schaffhausen. He had been promised protection by the ambitious Duke Frederick of Austria, an enemy of Emperor Sigismund, who left a tournament, rode through a graveyard, and caught up with the fleeing Antipope at Schaffhausen. Awakened in the morning with the startling news of Cossa's flight, Sigismund moved quickly and effectively to maintain order in the city, forbid anyone else from leaving, and with the Council's approval denounce Duke Frederick and order his arrest. From Schaffhausen Cossa called for his cardinals to follow him; some did, defying Sigismund's order, but most of them refused.[20]

On March 26 the Council held its third formal session, with Cardinal d'Ailly presiding. Resolutions were passed affirming the Council's legitimacy and declaring that it could not be dissolved nor transferred elsewhere until the Schism was ended and the Church reformed.[21] The claim was hollow; never

[19]Powers, *Council of Constance*, pp. 68-69; McGowan, *d'Ailly and the Council of Constance*, pp. 52-54; Valois, *Le grand schisme*, IV, 279-280, 284; Cardinal Fillastre's diary, in Mundy and Woody, eds., *Council of Constance*, p. 219.

[20]Valois, *Le grand schisme*, IV, 284-285; Powers, *Council of Constance*, pp. 70-74; McGowan, *d'Ailly and the Council of Constance*, pp. 56-57.

[21]Cardinal Fillastre's diary, in Mundy and Woody, eds., *Council of Constance*, pp.

since the Council of Nicaea had an ecumenical council been called by anyone other than a Pope[22] until the Council of Pisa, which was hardly an encouraging precedent. With the papal claimant who had called the Council of Constance now in flight, its legitimacy rested only on its own self-serving claims and the patronage of Emperor Sigismund, which however well-intended had no canonical authority. The Council of Constance could only acquire legitimacy from Gregory XII, who was in fact the true Pope, whatever people thought; but that was soon to come.

Conscious of these problems at least to some degree, on Good Friday (March 29, 1415) the Council drafted the essential provisions of what was later to become the famous and highly dangerous decree *Sacrosancta* which, along with denouncing the flight of Cossa, declared that the Council held authority directly from God and that the Pope as well as all the faithful must obey it in matters of faith, the Schism and reform of the Church.[23] On the same day, in a storm of freezing rain, Cossa left Schaffhausen apparently with some vague thought of reaching French territory, where he hoped to receive more favorable treatment because of the long history of hostilities between France and Germany. None of his cardinals would accompany him, not even his nephew.[24] From the hamlet of Laufenberg he sent a pathetic letter to the Council:

> We were driven by the fear that can beset even the constant man to leave the city of Constance and come to the town of Schaffhausen, in the diocese of Constance, believing that there we could accomplish everything that would promote the peace and union of the Holy Church of God, which from day to day we more earnestly desire. But through the agency of the enemy of the human race such difficulties obstructed us there that on Friday of Holy Week, after celebrating Mass, we were compelled to leave in the height of a violent storm because of these fears, in order that we might find a place and a time both plainly suitable and secure for the general Council, where and when it might be safe to come.[25]

Meeting April 17, the Council passed a resolution guaranteeing Cossa's personal safety, ordering him to appoint procurators for his abdication, and summoning him to return to Constance or at least remain within imperial

---

223-225; McGowan, *d'Ailly and the Council of Constance*, pp. 58-59.

[22]And Nicaea probably was as well, though we have no explicit historical evidence of the fact; see Volume II, Chapter One of this history.

[23]Powers, *Council of Constance*, p. 77; McGowan, *d'Ailly at the Council of Constance*, pp. 60-61. For the precise wording of this fundamental point in the decree *Sacrosancta*, as approved by the Council of Constance in final form April 6, 1415, see Cardinal Fillastre's diary, in Mundy and Woody, eds., *Council of Constance*, p. 229. This decree is also known as *Haec sancta*.

[24]Cardinal Fillastre's diary, in Mundy and Woody, eds., *Council of Constance*, p. 226.

[25]Chronicle of Ulrich Richental, in Mundy and Woody, eds., *Council of Constance*, p. 119.

territory on pain of immediate formal prosecution. A committee was sent to bring Cossa these decrees. They chased him for days, finally catching up with him at an inn at the village of Breisach am Rhein, where the innkeeper tried to shield him by insisting that he did not know where he was. Finally located, Cossa saw the committee the next day, then stole out of the inn at first light the following morning, on foot and alone except for a single servant. He tried to cross the Rhine by a bridge there, turned back when he discovered that it was guarded, then hid in a barn where a cavalry escort sent by Duke Frederick of Austria found him. But Cossa trusted no one now. Perhaps hearing of an order sent out by Emperor Sigismund for his immediate arrest, Cossa shed his clerical garb for a layman's jacket, found another small dark horse, and cantered away "leaving everything behind him" while his cardinals followed "in haste and wild disorder" through the night "though with no pursuers"—back to Breisach. Why Cossa went back there defies rational explanation; he must have been almost out of his mind with fear. Duke Frederick's escort caught up with him, the committee from the Council caught up with him, and they spent most of the night of April 27 arguing with him and with each other over whether and with whom he should return to Constance.[26]

On May 2 the Council formally indicted Cossa for "heresy, promotion of the present schism, simony, maladministration, and notorious waste of the property and rights of the Roman Church and of other churches, and other grave offenses, and as flagrantly involved in the same, to the scandal of the Universal Church; as incorrigible also in his own acts and deeds, life and character."[27] On May 14 they declared him suspended from the papacy for having administered it "disgracefully, dishonorably, and scandalously, particularly as regarded the making of provisions for churches, monasteries, priories, dignities, dispensations, and the like. All such functions he had exercised, as he did most things, in sordid ways, in return for money in vast quantities, appointing to each benefice whoever offered him most ... Almost everything he owned was for sale."[28] A few days later he was brought back to the vicinity of Constance and flung into the tower prison of Gottlieben castle, where he surrendered his papal seal and the fisherman's ring, with tears, to representatives of the Council. In another room of that same castle tower lay John Hus, chained to the wall.[29]

The Council's final verdict was given at its twelfth session May 29, finding

---

[26]Cardinal Fillastre's diary, in Mundy and Woody, ed., *Council of Constance*, pp. 231-237; Valois, *Le grand schisme*, IV, 304-305.

[27]Cardinal Fillastre's diary, in Mundy and Woody, eds., *Council of Constance*, p. 238. There is no evidence that Cossa was ever guilty of heresy. This charge was the result of the confusion and misunderstanding created by the repeated attempts of clerics seeking to end the Great Schism to define, against all reason, long-continued schism as heresy.

[28]*Ibid.*, p. 244.

[29]*Ibid.*, p. 496; Spinka, *Hus*, pp. 246, 253-255.

Cossa guilty of 54 of the 72 charges on which he was indicted, and declaring that "by his detestable and dishonorable life and character he has notoriously scandalized the Church of God and the Christian people, both before his elevation to the papacy and since." He accepted the verdict without protest, was put into the custody of Duke Louis of Bavaria, and kept in prison for the next three years.[30]

The Council of Pisa and its creatures had not, after all, successfully manipulated the Holy Spirit.

Having disposed of the leading Antipope, the Council of Constance now proceeded to the trial of John Hus. Responding to numerous charges of heresy brought against him, he either denied that he had spoken or written words attributed to him, or insisted that his words had been misinterpreted. The quality of his defense is exemplified by modern historian Howard Kaminsky:

> Accused of having preached that the Pope was Antichrist, Hus responded that he had not said it—all he had said was that a Pope who sold benefices, who was arrogant, greedy, and otherwise contrary to Christ in way of life, was Antichrist. Accused of having preached that the Curia was the synagogue of Satan, Hus responded that he had not said it as a fact, but that he had heard it said by those returning from Rome.[31]

Exasperated by such evasions, Cardinals d'Ailly and Zabarella and others among Hus' judges declared that whether or not he admitted professing the heresies attributed to him, he ought to be willing to "abjure" them publicly and swear never to preach them, but rather their opposite. Hus replied that to "abjure" a doctrine implied that one had once believed and taught that doctrine. The judges said "abjure" implied no such thing; Hus stubbornly insisted that it did. Cardinal Zabarella told him that he would be given "a sufficiently qualified formula of those articles" and then "ought to abjure them"; Emperor Sigismund told him the same; but he continued to refuse. The thirteenth formal session of the Council, meeting June 15, found Hus guilty of heresy in 30 of the 39 articles selected from his writings, and ordered him to repudiate these errors. At the same time the Council condemned as heresy the doctrine known as "utraquism," which Hus had endorsed just before coming to Constance, that the Church had no right to prevent the laity of the Latin rite from receiving Communion in both kinds, the Body and the Blood of Christ, as was done in the Byzantine rite and had been the practice of the early Church. Hus declared in response that the Council had condemned "as error the act of

---

[30]Cardinal Fillastre's diary, Mundy and Woody, eds., *Council of Constance*, pp. 246-247 (for the quotation); Powers, *Council of Constance*, p. 90; Valois, *Le grand schisme*, IV, 315-318.
[31]Kaminsky, *Hussite Revolution*, pp. 39-40.

Christ along with the acts of His apostles and other saints."[32]

Because utraquism—insisting on the chalice for the laity at Mass—became and remained a major issue in Bohemia for the next two hundred years and the principal proclaimed cause for a series of savage wars for the next fifty years, a brief explanation of the Catholic and Hussite views on it is in order. To the Hussites the withholding of the chalice from the laity became a symbol of a corrupt and overbearing church arrogantly denying essential spiritual benefits to everyone but the privileged clergy, in contravention of apostolic practice. Later they went so far as to proclaim reception of the Blood of Christ in the chalice essential to salvation, apparently unconcerned that such a doctrine condemned to Hell all the faithful since the reception of the chalice by the laity had been discontinued about four hundred years before, including St. Francis, St. Dominic, St. Louis IX, and St. Catherine of Siena. The Catholic Church, on the other hand, rested its case on the full authority of the Pope as head of the Church to prescribe the forms of the Mass and the manner of reception of Communion, and the doctrine that Christ is really and fully present in both His Eucharistic Body and Blood, so that no spiritual benefit is lost by communicating in one species only. To deny that, as Hus and his followers had done, was the heresy condemned at Constance. Simply to ask for Communion in both kinds for the laity was not heresy, since it had been given by the apostles (though not by Christ at the Last Supper, since the Church has always regarded the apostles who alone received it there as clergy) and was still given to the laity in the churches of the Byzantine rite; but the Church had the authority to grant this or to refuse it, and continued to refuse it to the Czechs for many years.

On July 1 Hus declared that "fearing to offend God and to fall into perjury, [I] am not willing to recant any or all of the articles produced against me in the testimonies of false witnesses" and that while he would repudiate any "false sense" in which articles drawn from his books might be taken, he would not "recant" any of them. On the 5th Cardinal Zabarella went to him, asking him to recant condemned statements which he admitted to be in his books and in testimony he had not denied, while for statements which he denied having said, it would suffice "to swear that he did not hold them and to promise that he would believe concerning them what the Church teaches." Hus rejected this reasonable and merciful offer out of hand. The next day he was brought before the full Council at its fifteenth session, with Cardinal John Brogli of Ostia presiding and Emperor Sigismund seated on his throne. The charges against Hus were read; he was not allowed to comment on them further, but did remind Sigismund of his safe-conduct, and it is said the Emperor blushed. The Council declared Hus a contumacious heretic and follower of John Wyclif, and turned

---

[32]Spinka, *Hus*, pp. 256-257, 260-275, 282 (quotation on 282); Powers, *Council of Constance*, p. 88.

him over to Duke Louis of Bavaria as representing "the secular arm." Duke
Louis made a last effort, in the same manner as Cardinal Zabarella, to induce
him to recant. Still he would not. He was burned at sunset, and his ashes
thrown into the Rhine.[33]

The burning of Hus has often been fiercely condemned by non-Catholic
writers, and by not a few Catholics as well. But it is hard to see how, under the
laws of the time, it could have been avoided in view of Hus' absolute refusal to
take advantage of the repeated opportunities given him, especially by Cardinal
Zabarella and Duke Louis of Bavaria, to save his life. He was not asked to
admit saying anything he claimed he did not say. Yet his safe-conduct might still
have been honored, as a later Emperor, the great Charles V, was to honor the
safe-conduct he gave to Martin Luther when he came to Worms for their
dramatic confrontation in 1521.[34] The violation of the safe-conduct is the one
aspect of the proceedings against Hus at Constance that was contrary to the
law, practice, and sense of honor of the time, as Sigismund's response to Hus'
reference to it on the day of his execution clearly shows.

Meanwhile, on July 4 came the extraordinary and deeply significant action
recorded by Cardinal Fillastre in the quotation at the head of this chapter, when
the Council accepted convocation and authorization of all its future acts from
the designated representatives of the true Pope, Gregory XII, whose
resignation was declared immediately after the Council's acceptance. This act,
and this alone, gave the Council of Constance canonical legitimacy. On the
same day the Council approved decrees uniting the two colleges of cardinals
which had upheld Gregory XII and Cossa and confirming in office the few
bishops who had continued to obey Gregory XII. Significantly, the Council also
reserved to itself that day "the right of determining the time, place and mode of
the election of the new Pope." Gregory XII's approval in advance of the future
acts of the Council legitimized whomever they should elect as the true Pope,
preserving the Petrine succession.[35]

No Holy Roman Emperor since Charlemagne had so vivid an awareness
of the full responsibilities of his exalted office as Sigismund. Leaving Constance
on July 21 for direct negotiations with Pedro de Luna, the only remaining papal
claimant who had not given up his claim, he stopped in France on the way to try
to make peace between France and England, whose Hundred Years War had
reached a new crisis in this same eventful year 1415.[36] Sigismund had no

---

[33]Spinka, *Hus*, pp. 284-290 (quotations on 284-285); Powers, *Council of Constance*,
pp. 88-90.
[34]See Volume IV, Chapter One of this history.
[35]See Note 1, above; Powers, *Council of Constance*, pp. 86-87 (quotation on 87);
McGowan, *d'Ailly and the Council of Constance*, pp. 67-68; Valois, *Le grand schisme*,
IV, 313.
[36]Powers, *Council of Constance*, pp. 92-93; McGowan, *d'Ailly and the Council of
Constance*, p. 68.

immediate personal or political interest in this conflict; it had been many years since a Holy Roman Emperor had concerned himself seriously with these two countries, which had been outside the Emperor's sphere of normal political involvement for five centuries. But Sigismund's goal was the reunion and peace of all Christendom, and a renewal of crusading against the advancing Turks in Eastern Europe.

Unfortunately he had chosen the most difficult possible moment for intervention, when civil strife in France—resulting largely from the periodic insanity of King Charles VI—had weakened her to a level of debility never seen since Henry II of England and his sons ruled half the country two hundred years before, and England—led by young, resolute, hard-hitting King Henry V, who had renewed the claim of his dynasty to the throne of France—had an army of invasion ready at Dover to cross the Channel. The rivalry between Duke Louis of Orléans, brother of the King of France, and his uncle Duke John "the Fearless" of Burgundy had culminated in John's murder of Louis in 1407. Louis' son Charles, in a bitter quest for vengeance, had created a faction called the "Armagnacs" who gained control of the tragically incapable king and his teen-age sons. Ousted from Paris by a popular uprising fomented by John in 1413, the Armagnacs struck back in 1414, driving John from Paris in his turn and through the King declaring full-scale war on him. John promptly allied himself with the English. In February 1415 Charles VI offered a treaty to John, but it exempted no less than 500 persons from its amnesty for rebellion, so John would not accept it until the English had actually landed in Normandy in August, and even then gave no help to the French army put into the field in September to fight the English.[37]

Coming to France in August, the month of the English landing, Sigismund had no chance of a serious hearing by any of the parties involved, and he did not get it. The war continued. On September 22 the English took the Norman port of Harfleur after a month's siege, then set out October 8 on a 200-mile march to Calais, the French Channel port they had held since the aftermath of the Battle of Crécy 67 years before. On their way the Armagnac French army (the Burgundians being absent) came up to challenge them October 25 near the village of Agincourt. The French outnumbered the English at least four to one, but they were disorganized, disunited and essentially leaderless, while the English army had been shaped into a superb fighting instrument by the inspiring presence and great military ability of their young king. Knowing the prowess of the English archers, the French knights left their vulnerable horses behind and

---

[37]R. C. Famiglietti, *Royal Intrigue; Crisis at the Court of Charles VI, 1392-1420* (New York, 1986), pp. 63, 70, 88, 93, 95-96, 116-118, 131, 144-145, 150, 157-158, 163, 175; Richard Vaughan, *John the Fearless; the Growth of Burgundian Power* (New York, 1966), pp. 45-47, 73-74, 82, 84-85, 87-90, 99-102, 204, 208; Alfred H. Burne, *The Agincourt War* (Fair Lawn NJ, 1956), pp. 40-41.

marched in their ponderous plate armor into a narrow muddy passage between two forests. The mobile English archers descended on them with massive clubs and literally beat them to death, for a man in plate armor who has slipped and fallen in mud and is being hammered with a club cannot get up. The slaughter was enormous: the Constable of France, the Admiral of France, two brothers of the Duke of Burgundy, the Duke of Alençon, 90 counts, over 1,500 knights, and over 4,000 other soldiers were slain at almost no cost to the English, while Duke Charles of Orléans and the Duke of Bourbon were captured. Agincourt was one of the most overwhelming battle victories in all of history, leaving the whole of France open to English conquest.[38]

Meanwhile Emperor Sigismund had gone on to the kingdom of Aragon, arriving at Perpignan just north of the Pyrenees September 19. He was counting on the support of the King of Aragon, that Prince Fernando of Castile who had won the great victory over the Moors at Antequera in 1410, and two years later had been elected to the vacant throne of Aragon to which he had a strong claim through his mother. In the three years of his reign Fernando had maintained Aragon's traditional support for Antipope de Luna—himself an Aragonese—but without any great enthusiasm. King Fernando wanted to see the Schism ended and the Church reunited, and before Sigismund arrived he had told de Luna he ought to go to Constance and resign. St. Vincent Ferrer, the great Spanish preacher and evangelist who had unwaveringly supported de Luna ever since he was elected by Robert of Geneva's college of pretender cardinals in 1394, joined in the recommendation. De Luna, obstinate as ever, refused to leave Aragon. Now Fernando was seriously ill with a kidney ailment which was soon to take his life. But he had insisted on coming to Perpignan anyway, to support Sigismund in putting pressure on de Luna to clear the way to the undisputed election of a new Pope which the resignations of Cossa and Gregory XII had opened.[39]

De Luna was not yet flatly denying that he would resign under any circumstances. But his response to Fernando and Sigismund in September was only too revealing of his invincible obstinacy and arrogance. He declared that since he was the last surviving cardinal from the College appointed before the Schism, if he were not to continue as Pope he alone should elect the new Pope, or at least have a veto on whoever else might be elected. A special commission of three bishops reported to Fernando, after studying the abdications of Cossa

---

[38]E. F. Jacob, *The Fifteenth Century, 1399-1485* (Oxford History of England) (Oxford, 1961), pp. 150-157; Burne, *Agincourt War*, pp. 46-47, 49-54, 76-94; Christopher Hibbert, *Agincourt* (Philadelphia, 1964), pp. 106-129.

[39]Joseph F. O'Callaghan, *A History of Medieval Spain* (Ithaca NY, 1975), pp. 544-545; I. I. Macdonald, *Don Fernando de Antequera* (Oxford, 1948), pp. 158-160, 203-204, 219-222; Alan Ryder, *Alfonso the Magnanimous, King of Aragon, Naples and Sicily, 1396-1458* (Oxford, 1990), pp. 31, 35-37, 39-40; Alec Glasfurd, *The Antipope (Peter de Luna, 1342-1423); a Study in Obstinacy* (London, 1965), pp. 249-250.

and Gregory XII, that de Luna ought to be compelled to follow their example, and Fernando called on him to do just that. Probably only trying to gain time, de Luna offered to resign if the Council would move to any of seven cities he named in France, but Emperor Sigismund told him that only the Council could move itself, and they had firmly resolved against doing so. At a meeting with Fernando and Sigismund in St. Matthew's Church in Perpignan October 29, de Luna reiterated his demand to be the sole elector of a new Pope, leading to an explosion of temper as Emperor Sigismund walked out in a fury, saying he would leave Perpignan immediately.[40]

Fernando persuaded him to stay a little longer, but could do nothing with the stubborn Antipope, and after a week Sigismund left without notice for the north. Fernando sent messengers after him, promising to withdraw his obedience from de Luna if he continued to refuse to resign. Sigismund stopped at Narbonne in southern France, de Luna remained unyielding, and Fernando called a council which recommended that de Luna be summoned three times to resign and if he did not, all the realms supporting him in the region—Aragon, Castile, Navarra, and the counties of Foix and Armagnac in southern France—should withdraw their obedience, which would leave de Luna with only the support of Scotland in all Christendom. St. Vincent Ferrer in a thundering sermon told de Luna he must yield, and if he did not, no Christian should obey him any longer. The first summons was delivered to de Luna at Perpignan November 10; the second reached him at the little port of Collioure, where he was about to embark for the impregnable sea-girt fortress of Peñíscola to hold out there to the end. He sent this reply to Fernando: "My greetings to His Majesty. Tell him I can do nothing more. He will do as he pleases. And be good enough to add these words: You have driven me, who made you what you are, into the wilderness." The last summons reached him at Peñíscola—which he now compared to Noah's ark—December 1.[41]

On December 13 the kings of Aragon, Castile and Navarra declared to Emperor Sigismund at Narbonne their withdrawal of obedience from de Luna and acceptance of the Council of Constance, on the conditions (which Sigismund had been empowered by the Council to grant) that Spain become a fifth "nation" at the Council and that de Luna's past ecclesiastical appointments in the areas of his obedience would be honored. The good news arrived at Constance December 29; and though a need was still felt to go through a formal

---

[40]Valois, *Le grand schisme*, IV, 341-345; Ramón Menéndez Pidal, ed., *Historia de España*, Volume XV: "Los Trastámaras de Castilla y Aragon en el Siglo XV," by Luis Suárez Fernández, Angel Canellas López and Jaime Vicens Vives, 4th ed. (Madrid, 1986), p. 58; Ryder, *Alfonso the Magnanimous*, p. 40; Macdonald, *Fernando de Antequera*, pp. 226-227.

[41]Ryder, *Alfonso the Magnanimous*, pp. 40-41 (quotation on 41); Macdonald, *Fernando de Antequera*, pp. 226-228; Valois, *Le grand schisme*, IV, 345-346, 349; Henri Ghéon, *St. Vincent Ferrer* (New York, 1939), pp. 140-143.

process of deposing de Luna which was not completed until July 1417, he was now for all intents and purposes a papal claimant without an obedience (and one whose claim had never, in fact, had any just standing).[42]

The Great Schism was over. The man primarily responsible for the process that brought it to an end was Emperor Sigismund, for which—whatever his other mistakes—he deserves the eternal gratitude of Christendom. Pope Gregory XII's resignation on the condition that the Council of Constance accept convocation and authorization from him was indispensable to this triumph as to the preservation of the Church, but the presence and generally right guidance of the Council in its critical early months were the achievements above all of Sigismund.

As if these world-shaking events—the organization of the Council of Constance and its authorization by Pope Gregory XII, the elimination of the pretensions of Antipope Cossa, the removal of the obedience of Pedro de Luna even in his home country, the English invasion of a distracted France and smashing military victory at Agincourt—were not enough for this one year 1415, there remains one last event in that year to describe, with consequences both natural and supernatural, spanning the whole of the nearly six hundred years from then until now, and extending on far into the future. This was the event that, through its effect on one of the leaders who took part in it, ultimately opened the whole world to the Gospel of Christ and ended the isolation of Christendom in Europe imposed for 750 years by militant Islam: the conquest of the port city of Ceuta on the African shore of the Straits of Gibraltar by the hitherto rather insignificant little Christian kingdom of Portugal.

The most remote and poorest of the Hispanic kingdoms, which had barely preserved its existence with English help in the war against Castile in the late fourteenth century, whose reconquest from the Moors had ended with the liberation of the Algarve in 1260, Portugal seemed at first glance to have little to distinguish it, though a geographer might well be struck by the fact that it was the only European kingdom south of Norway which fronted exclusively on the Atlantic Ocean. Most of its population lived on or close to the seacoast, facing west or south upon the great unknown sea. But the geographical horizons of the age were narrow; the Norse voyages to America in the Viking age had never been followed up and had been almost completely forgotten even by the people who had made them, and those who had travelled eastward through the Mongol domains to China just 150 years before had also been largely forgotten or disbelieved. No such travel was possible now that the rulers of central Asia had

---

[42]Powers, *Council of Constance*, pp. 94, 121-123; McGowan, *d'Ailly and the Council of Constance*, p. 84; Valois, *Le grand schisme*, IV, 346-348, 350-351; Ryder, *Alfonso the Magnanimous*, pp. 41-42; Menéndez Pidal, *Historia de España*, XV, 59; Chronicle of Ulrich Richental, in Mundy and Woody, eds., *Council of Constance*, p. 138.

become all Muslim. Islam had always been unfriendly to Christian travellers. The able Portuguese seamen had nothing to draw them far from their colorful, richly scented coast. There was nothing automatic or foreordained that would make them pioneers of Christian Europe's Age of Discovery.

Like so many of the great events of history, this was the work of individuals who made it happen, above all two of the giants in all the human story: Prince Henry "the Navigator" and Christopher Columbus. Columbus is the more famous but Prince Henry was the greater man, because he came first and showed the way. Reaching the fabled Orient by sea was his project; he designed the ships with which Columbus discovered America; Columbus sailed the great western ocean for more than a decade of the formative years of his professional life as a seaman in the service of Portugal. And 1415 was the year when Prince Henry first appeared on the stage of history; when he and his three brothers, with the rather reluctant approval of their father King John I of Portugal, accomplished the conquest of Ceuta, the first place in Muslim North Africa ever to be reconquered and held for Christendom since the whirlwind of Islam had first swept over it at the end of the seventh century.[43]

Portugal had been peaceful and prosperous for thirty years under the rule of John and his English wife Philippa and their unusually close family. Despite the country's poverty, so long a period of flourishing had provided the means for a major military enterprise. There was no realistic possibility of the conquest of the whole of Morocco, a much larger, richer and more populous country than Portugal, where no Christian inhabitants remained; Ceuta itself could only be held because of its extraordinarily defensible position on a long and easily fortified peninsula and the existence of a Portuguese fleet that could command the surrounding sea. But the quick and brilliant success against the ancient enemy, the scourge of God, fired the imagination of the young Portuguese princes and particularly Henry, 21 years old. Almost any other young prince or nobleman of his age would have dreamed only of further military triumphs. But Henry's mind was of extraordinary power, the kind of mind that leaps horizons. Henry saw the struggle against Islam in truly geopolitical terms. The resources of all Christendom had never been sufficient to defeat Islam. But what if it could be outflanked? What if there were more Christians beyond the Muslim domains who could be found and summoned as allies? How far did the Muslim domains actually extend?

No one in Christendom knew. The age had no maps beyond the coasts of

---

[43]Bailey W. Diffie and George D. Winius, *Foundations of the Portuguese Empire, 1415-1580* (Minneapolis MN, 1977), pp. 46-55; Elaine Sanceau, *Henry the Navigator* (New York, 1969), pp. 27-79. Occasional Christian attacks had been made upon the coasts of Muslim North Africa, from Egypt to Tunisia, during and after the period of the Crusades, but none had led to permanent Christian retention of any territory there. King St. Louis IX of France had died besieging Tunis (see Chapter Seven, above).

Europe and the Mediterranean. The Canary Islands had been discovered in the Atlantic, and there were rumors of more islands there. But for Africa, the great continent to the south, knowledge ended with the enormous Sahara Desert beyond its settled northern fringe. The land trails across the Sahara, from Algeria to the Niger River, were controlled entirely by the Moors; no Christian had ever travelled them.[44] But the coast was unknown. For where the cultivable land of Morocco faded into desert in the south, the barren waterless coast faced a shallow sea into which the wind swept the dunes until the ocean seemed to boil. In the midst of this terrifying desolation, under the fierce tropical sun, a grim rock-bound hook of land clawed far out into the steaming sea: Cape Bojador. The sailors said no life could exist beyond Cape Bojador.

Prince Henry did not believe it. God had given the world to man in the Garden of Eden. There was no place in His world that could not some day be reached by men of courage with the necessary material means. Furthermore, there was documentary evidence available of the rounding of Africa, though we do not know when or even if Prince Henry discovered it: an account in classical sources of a three-year voyage around Africa from Egypt back to Egypt, by Phoenician seamen in service of the Pharaoh.[45]

We know neither the details nor the date when Henry conceived his project which was to change the history of the whole world forever; documentation for this critical period in Portuguese history is lamentably scant. Most of whatever records may have existed were probably destroyed in the devastating Lisbon earthquake of 1755. But we do have the priceless contemporary "Chronicle of the Discovery and Conquest of Guinea" by Gomes Eanes de Zurara, preserved in Paris. Zurara knew Prince Henry intimately and worked for him for many years. He tells us that Henry began sending expeditions directed to round Cape Bojador in the year 1422, though it required 12 years and 15 expeditions before one finally attained the goal Henry had set for them.[46] At about the time these expeditions began, Portuguese mariners,

---

[44]The repeated suggestion of historians governed by the economic interpretation of history, that the capture of Ceuta was motivated primarily by a desire for more trade with the Moors and more access to these trans-Sahara trade routes, is decisively refuted not only by the extensive and reiterated Portuguese laws against most trade with the Moors (not to be minimized by citing the arrival of Moorish produce in Portugal via Italians as middlemen, which had nothing to do with Ceuta) but also by the proven fact that Ceuta, once established as a Portuguese outpost, engaged in almost no trade with the Moors and consequently was an economic liability to the Portuguese government throughout the fifteenth century (Diffie and Winius, *Foundations of the Portuguese Empire*, pp. 46-49, 55).
[45]Sanceau, *Henry the Navigator*, pp. 85-87.
[46]Diffie and Winius, *Foundations of the Portuguese Empire*, p. 68. In their invaluable study of Portuguese overseas expansion, Diffie and Winius also take note of the oft-described voyages of the Chinese admiral Cheng Ho, a eunuch in the imperial service, with large fleets of immense ships, in the Indian Ocean during the years 1405 to

with Prince Henry's encouragement and aid, discovered and settled the previously uninhabited Atlantic island of Madeira, the first habitable but unpeopled land found by Christian Europeans since the Viking voyages to Iceland and Greenland in the ninth and tenth centuries.[47] Zurara describes the elements of Prince Henry's grand exploring enterprise, as he first envisioned it before the dreaded cape had been passed:

> Since in former chapters we have set forth the Lord Prince [Henry] as the chief actor in these things, giving as clear an understanding of him as we could, it is meet that in this present chapter we should know his purpose in doing them. . . . After the taking of Ceuta he always kept ships well armed against the infidel, both for war, and because he had also a wish to know the land that lay beyond the isles of Canary and that Cape called Bojador, for up to his time, neither by writings, nor by the memory of man, was known with any certainty the nature of the land beyond that Cape. . . . Since it seemed to him that if he or some other lord did not endeavor to gain that knowledge, no mariners or merchants would ever dare attempt it (for it is clear that none of them ever trouble themselves to sail to a place where there is not a sure and certain hope of profit), and seeing also that no other prince took any pains in this matter, he sent out his own ships . . . and this was the first reason of his action.
>
> The second reason was that if there chanced to be in those lands some population of Christians, or some havens into which it would be possible to sail without peril, many kinds of merchandise might be brought to this realm, which would find a ready market . . . and also the products of this realm might be taken there, which traffic would bring great profit to our countrymen.
>
> The third reason was that, as it was said that the power of the Moors in that land of Africa was very much greater than was commonly supposed . . . and because every wise man is obliged by natural prudence to wish for a knowledge of the power of his enemy; therefore the said Lord Prince exerted himself to cause this to be fully discovered, and to make it known determinately how far the power of those infidels extended.
>
> The fourth reason was because during the 31 years that he had warred against the Moors, he had never found a Christian king, nor a lord outside this land, who for the love of Our Lord Jesus Christ would aid him in the said war. Therefore he sought to know if there were in those parts any Christian princes, in whom the charity and the love of Christ was so ingrained that they would aid him against those enemies of the faith.
>
> The fifth reason was his great desire to make increase in the faith of Our Lord Jesus Christ and to bring to him all the souls that should be

---

1433—almost the same years that Prince Henry was developing his project and sending ships toward Cape Bojador. But, as they trenchantly point out, these Chinese voyages "cannot be called exploring expeditions inasmuch as the seas from the East African shore to China were known to the numerous traders of those days, including the Muslim merchants." (*ibid.*, pp. 66-67). The accounts of the seven Chinese voyages to the Indian Ocean by Cheng Ho nowhere indicate that any of them went further east than Mogadishu in Somalia. They reached no coast not already occupied and well known by civilized men.

[47]*Ibid.*, pp. 57-58; Sanceau, *Henry the Navigator*, pp. 89-103.

saved . . . whom the said Lord Prince by his travail and spending would fain
bring into the true path. For he perceived that no better offering could be
made unto the Lord than this . . . For I that wrote this history saw so many
men and women of those parts turned to the holy faith, that even if the
Prince had been a heathen, their prayers would have been enough to have
obtained his salvation. And not only did I see the first captives, but their
children and grandchildren as true Christians.[48]

The Council of Constance marked time during 1416. Emperor Sigismund,
delayed by more futile attempts to negotiate peace between England and
France (Henry V was now determined to conquer the whole of France and in
no mood to accept any lesser concession), did not return until January 1417;
without either him or a Pope, there was no effective leadership to move the
Council forward.[49] Nevertheless Cardinal d'Ailly presented a treatise to the
Council in October which asserted that it had "the plenitude of power" rather
than the Pope, and could not err though the Pope could. To show the greater
power of the Council, d'Ailly recalled the Council of Pisa which "had
condemned and deposed two Popes, one of whom must have been
legitimate."[50] Clearly he had not yet grasped the significance of the acceptance
of convocation and authorization by the Council of Constance from the true
Pope whom the Council of Pisa had claimed to depose. So thick was the cloud
of confusion with which the Great Schism had enveloped even the best
Christian minds that it required decades for this truth to dawn. It did not
become fully understood until the nineteenth century, obvious though it should
have been to canonists at the time.

Once Sigismund had returned to the Council, it was clear that it should
proceed as soon as possible to the election of a new Pope. But the election was
delayed for months by arguments over the electoral procedure and whether a
general reform of the Church in "head and members" should be launched
before or after the election. These disagreements pitted the reunited College

---

[48]Gomes Eanes de Azurara [Zurara], "The Chronicle of the Discovery and
Conquest of Guinea," *Hakluyt Society Publications* No. 95 (London, 1896), pp. 27-29.
The obsolete translation "Infant" for *Infante* in the quoted translation, based on the
chance resemblance of the unrelated English word, is here replaced by the true
rendering "Prince." It should be emphasized that Zurara's explanation of Prince
Henry's motives in launching his exploring expeditions is the only contemporary
explanation we have, from one well placed to know it by his own observation and
conversations with Prince Henry; no modern historian is in a position to gainsay it.
Zurara's explanation indicates that the specific goal of reaching India by sailing around
Africa had not yet taken shape in Henry's mind when these voyages began. It did
however develop well before his death, as will be demonstrated in Chapter Thirteen,
below.
[49]Jacob, *Fifteenth Century*, pp. 163-168; Powers, *Council of Constance*, p. 106.
[50]Powers, *Council of Constance*, p. 100.

of Cardinals—consisting of all the living cardinals who had gathered at Pisa, and others subsequently appointed by Antipopes Philargis and Cossa, as well as the few who had remained loyal to Pope Gregory XII and a few who had come over from Pedro de Luna before the Council—against Emperor Sigismund, the cardinals demanding election of a Pope first and Sigismund demanding that reform begin immediately, with the election to follow. The "nations" were evenly divided, the Italian and French supporting the cardinals, the Germans and English supporting the Emperor, while the new Spanish "nation" split, with Castile and Navarra supporting the cardinals and Aragon and Portugal supporting the Emperor. Sigismund also demanded power to veto any proposed Pope, but the cardinals refused to give it to him.[51]

Both sides realized a new Pope must be elected soon, and at Constance, or the Schism might reappear. Following the death of Bishop Hallam of Salisbury, their spiritual leader, the English delegation changed its position on this issue to support the cardinals, and Sigismund promptly gave way, agreeing to pass decisions on reform to the new Pope and to give up his veto demand. On October 9, 1417, at its 39th formal session, the Council approved the decree *Frequens*, which repeated the claims of the decree *Sacrosancta*, passed in 1415, that the Council was superior to the Pope, and scheduled ecumenical councils to meet five years after the Council of Constance adjourned, then seven years after that, then every ten years thereafter, whether the Pope wished these councils to meet or not. Most of the cardinals supported *Frequens*, so they can hardly be regarded as papalists at this time, despite their strong desire to elect a Pope.[52]

There was still substantial disagreement on the election procedure, but the opportune arrival and vigorous intervention as a mediator of Bishop Henry of Winchester, uncle of the victorious King Henry V of England who had become quite close to Emperor Sigismund, produced a workable arrangement by the end of October. For the first—and only—time in the Church's history there would be two papal electoral colleges, the cardinals and a second group consisting of six delegates selected by each of the five "nations" at the Council. The new Pope must be approved by two-thirds of both colleges. The decree embodying this procedure, approved by the Council October 30, also included a detailed pledge by the Council for general reform, including limitation of the number of appeals to the curia and the number, quality and nation of future cardinals, along with measures against simony, excessive dispensation from holy

---

[51]*Ibid.*, pp. 129-131; McGowan, *d'Ailly and the Council of Constance*, pp. 86-87; Menéndez Pidal, *Historia de España*, XV, 62-63; Cardinal Fillastre's diary, in Mundy and Woody, eds., *Council of Constance*, pp. 395-397.

[52]Cardinal Fillastre's diary, in Mundy and Woody, eds., *Council of Constance*, pp. 401-404, 407-412; Powers, *Council of Constance*, pp. 131-132, 135-137; McGowan, *d'Ailly and the Council of Constance*, p. 88; Valois, *Le grand schisme*, IV, 391.

orders, plurality of benefices, and objectionable practices in the granting of indulgences.[53]

During this month of reconciliation and achievement of common purpose at the Council of Constace, Pope Gregory XII died near Ancona in Italy, still in the domain of his faithful Carlo Malatesta. His last words were: "I knew nothing of the world, and the world knew nothing of me."[54]

On November 8 the double conclave began, with Emperor Sigismund guaranteeing its privacy and safety: the market hall of Constance was reserved for their deliberations; a fence "as high as a tall spear" was built around it to keep all unauthorized persons out; Sigismund prohibited any noise near the fence and warned all boats on the lake not to approach within a crossbow shot. There would be no repetition of the disgraceful scenes in Rome at the fateful conclave of April 1378 that began the Great Schism. As each elector entered the market hall, limited to a single servant accompanying him, Sigismund spoke to him personally, "entreating him to perform his task with the aid of the Holy Spirit and to start no dissension." After the conclave began, Sigismund and all the rest of the Council marched to the high fence and knelt down in the street before it to pray for its success.[55]

Inside, the French electors wanted Cardinal d'Ailly, the man who had said repeatedly that henceforth in the Church the Council should be superior to the Pope; but the electors of the other "nations" stood firm against him. On the first ballot, the one man receiving votes from all the "nations" and from the cardinals as well was Cardinal Odo Colonna of Rome. On later ballots Colonna's vote total grew in all the groups of electors, until on the 11th he attained the required two-thirds of the cardinals and of the representatives of the "nations," was declared elected, and took the papal name Martin V. Appointed cardinal by Pope Innocent VII, he had deserted his successor Gregory XII in favor of the Council of Pisa and was one of those who had at first followed Antipope Cossa in his flight, but then decided with the Council that he must be rejected. Of a friendly and outgoing disposition, personally temperate and prudent, he seemed well fitted to bind up the deep wounds inflicted on the Church by the Schism, and in many ways he was; but he was widely and correctly suspected of being little interested in reform.[56]

---

[53]Powers, *Council of Constance*, pp. 138-139, 142-145; McGowan, *d'Ailly and the Council of Constance*, pp. 88-90; Cardinal Fillastre's diary, in Mundy and Woody, eds., *Council of Constance*, pp. 412-413.

[54]L. Salembier, *The Great Schism of the West* (New York, 1907), p. 349.

[55]Chronicle of Ulrich Richental and diary of Cardinal Fillastre, in Mundy and Woody, eds., *Council of Constance*, pp. 161-166, 422-426 (quotation from Richental); Powers, *Council of Constance*, pp. 145-146; McGowan, *d'Ailly and the Council of Constance*, p. 90.

[56]Cardinal Fillastre's diary, in Mundy and Woody, eds., *Council of Constance*, pp. 427-428; Powers, *Council of Constance*, pp. 146-147, 162; McGowan, *d'Ailly and the*

On November 21 the end of the Great Schism was gloriously celebrated with the consecration of Pope Martin V by the Cardinal Bishop of Ostia, the traditional consecrator of Popes. The ceremony began with the ringing of all the bells in Constance for a full hour soon after midnight, and culminated in the consecration itself at 7:30 in the morning, with Emperor Sigismund and personal representatives of most of the kings or princes of Europe present, and the new Pope then going out to bless the immense crowd, swelled by the tens of thousands of retainers of the churchmen and lay lords attending the Council.[57]

The next month the new Pope appointed a commission of cardinals and representatives of the "nations" at the Council to undertake the much-needed reform of the Church, but the mutual suspicion and friction between the cardinals and the deputies hampered its progress. Antipope de Luna—not surprisingly in view of his history—refused obedience to the new Pope, but his three remaining cardinals left him to tender it. In January 1418 Martin V formally recognized Sigismund as Holy Roman Emperor (though this was not equivalent to papal coronation of the Emperor, which by tradition could only be done at Rome). At the end of that month Martin V made his first formal statement on reform since becoming Pope, promising to reduce the number of cardinals and select them from all parts of Christendom and to excommunicate simoniacs, curb abuses connected with indulgences, require recipients of benefices to reside in them, and to make thirty years the minimum age for holding a priory or church. But he declared that he could not surrender papal privilege regarding appointment to benefices, though he promised to consult the cardinals on appointments and to limit the number of reserved benefices "to those acknowledged by law." Most significantly, he rejected any measures to grant authority to ecumenical councils, the College of Cardinals, or any other group to control or depose the Pope.[58]

The long-drawn-out Council finally came to an end in April 1418, soon after arguing vigorously over the Pope's refusal to confirm the Council's earlier condemnation of a Dominican named John Falkenberg with ties to the Teutonic Knights, who had allegedly called King Jagiello of Poland and Lithuania an idolater who should be killed. It does not appear that by this action the Pope was declaring Falkenberg innocent of this heinous charge, only that he had not had the opportunity adequately to investigate it, and did not want the Council usurping his role as administrative head of the Church. He also refused to consider an appeal against his decision to the next Council,

---

Council of Constance, pp. 90-91; Valois, *Le grand schisme*, IV, 404; von Pastor, *History of the Popes*, I, 208-209.
  [57]Chronicle of Ulrich Richental, in Mundy and Woody, *Council of Constance*, pp. 168-172; Powers, *Council of Constance*, p. 148.
  [58]Powers, *Council of Constance*, pp. 149-152, 154-156; Ryder, *Alfonso the Magnanimous*, p. 59.

supposed to be called in five years in accordance with the decree *Frequens*.[59]

As he prepared his decree dissolving the Council, Pope Martin V faced an extraordinarily difficult and delicate decision: how much, and to what extent, to confirm its actions. Under canon law and the unbroken tradition of the Church, no action even of an ecumenical council is authoritative for the universal Church without the approval of the Pope. Clearly Pope Martin V did not and could not approve the decrees *Sacrosancta* and *Frequens*, the former denying the supreme leadership of the Church which Christ had given to Peter and his successors, the latter usurping his essential prerogative of deciding when to summon councils. But for Martin V openly to strike down these decrees, which had been overwhelmingly approved, could well resurrect the schism in a different and even more virulent form, Council against Pope. Pope Martin V had to find a way to do the seemingly impossible: neither endorse nor disapprove them while still making the necessary statement about the status of the Council's actions.

No Pope could have been better fitted to such a task. Martin V had been Odo Colonna, a member of an ancient Roman family which had served the Church, for better or for worse, for centuries.[60] He could therefore draw, not only on his personal experience—service to the Church since the desperate pontificate of Urban VI, from which he may well have learned the necessity of exceptional prudence in high Church office—but on that of his family, in devising a verbal formula that would transcend the apparently unavoidable contradiction he faced. The phraseology he found was masterful. He confirmed the work of the Council, "all that here has been done, touching matters of faith, in a conciliar fashion, but not otherwise or after any other fashion."[61] Unpacked, this meant that he confirmed everything the Council had decreed regarding doctrine and heresy, and everything else it had done in its proper role as a council, that is, not against the necessary authority of the Pope; but that he did not confirm anything it had done which was not proper for a council, that is, which did challenge the necessary authority of the Pope. Neither the Pope nor the Council wanted to say or ask what this convoluted formula precisely meant, though its meaning can hardly have been unclear to any well-educated canonist. Obviously it would not lay the question to rest, but enabled the struggle over the rival authority of Pope and Council to be deferred for years, while the papacy was regaining the strength drained from it by the

---

[59]Powers, *Council of Constance*, pp. 163-166.

[60]There had been Colonnas in the College of Cardinals throughout most of the thirteenth and fourteenth centuries. The family had been bitterly opposed to Pope Boniface VIII and had conspired with King Philip IV of France to overthrow him; one of them, "Sciarra" Colonna, had almost killed him (see Chapter Eight, above).

[61]Gill, *Eugenius IV*, p. 38. The Latin for the most critical words ("conciliar" and "not otherwise or after any other fashion" is *conciliariter . . . non aliter nec alio modo.*

Great Schism.

Pope Martin V left Constance in May 1418, resolved to take up residence in Rome, but he did not regard it as safe to do for some time. He went first to Mantua, then to Florence; at Mantua Antipope Cossa, just released from prison, came to him and made formal submission, and was appointed Cardinal Bishop of Tusculum. He died the following year. The Pope remained at Florence for a year and a half. Ladislas of Naples had died before the Council of Constance met, probably by foul play; having no issue, he was succeeded by his middle-aged, also childless sister Joanna II, who bore more than a little resemblance to her wayward namesake whom St. Bridget of Sweden and St. Catherine of Siena had failed to redeem. But at this point she was being cooperative, agreeing to support the new Pope in regaining control of the papal state in return for recognition of her queenship during her lifetime, with Louis III of Anjou to be her heir. Finally, in a deal with *condottiere* Braccio di Montone finalized in July 1420, Pope Martin V temporarily recognized Braccio's rule of four cities in the papal state in return for possession of Bologna, the largest city in the papal state outside Rome.[62]

This cleared the way for the Pope's return to Rome September 28. He found the city at peace but in a ruined condition, with most of its classical buildings which had survived the Avignon residence of the Popes now destroyed, many churches roofless, many houses fallen, the streets blocked by rubble and infested with robbers, and wolves prowling the Vatican Gardens and digging up the dead from cemeteries. Martin V began at once the work of restoration, which symbolized the restoration of the unity and the true constitution of the Church to which his pontificate was dedicated.[63]

A wave of anger had surged through Bohemia on receipt of the news of the execution of John Hus, the condemnation of Communion in both kinds, and the appointment by the Council in late August 1415 of the widely disliked Bishop John "the Iron" Zhelezny[64] of Litomysl in Moravia as special legate in Bohemia with full powers from the Council to excommunicate, lay interdicts, and suspend or remove holders of office in the Church there. Fifty-eight nobles of Bohemia and Moravia protested the execution of Hus, declaring that anyone claiming Hus was a heretic "speaks lies as a treacherous enemy of our kingdom and our nation, being himself a malicious heretic, and even a son of the Devil."

---

[62]Von Pastor, *History of the Popes*, I, 211-214; Powers, *Council of Constance*, p. 166; Salembier, *Great Schism*, pp. 274, 376; Valois, *Le grand schisme*, IV, 251; Ryder, *Alfonso the Magnanimous*, pp. 78-79. For the first Joanna, see Chapters Ten and Eleven, above.

[63]Von Pastor, *History of the Popes*, I, 214-216; Salembier, *Great Schism*, p. 376.

[64]To facilitate proper pronunciation for those unfamiliar with Czech and to avoid the use of difficult diacritical marks, the Czech c and z when rendered under an inverted circumflex are herein transcribed as "ch" and "zh."

A Hussite League of nobles was formed in September 1415 to oppose the Church and issued a manifesto signed by 452 noblemen, while only 14 initially dared to support the Catholic counter-league formed in response. The University of Prague endorsed Hus and his defenders. Archbishop Conrad of Prague laid an interdict on the city for harboring condemned Hussites, but only a few obeyed it, and the Hussites simply took over most of the churches of the city which the Archbishop had ordered closed.[65]

The execution of Hus had added so great a grievance to the widespread protest against Church corruption which had long been developing in Bohemia, that most were not prepared to wait to see what a reunited Church might do. They went over to revolution. The savage words of Nicholas of Dresden in Bohemia, in a pamphlet published in October 1415, set the tone for their uprising:

> Now, alas, the secular rulers of Christendom are occupied with their own dissensions, weighed down by greed, blinded by sensual indulgence, hemmed in by other vices—they do not pay attention to the great corruption of the church of Christ, but rather protect, promote and even foster priests who are simoniac, heretic and greedy, hateful to God and useless to prince and people.... O Lord, will I live to see that blessed hour when the Whore of Revelations will be stripped bare and her flesh consumed by the fire of tribulation?[66]

It might have been Calvin, Knox, or Oliver Cromwell speaking. The great and terrible cleaving that was to sunder most of Christian Europe in the sixteenth century came to Bohemia in the fifteenth century. But Bohemia was a small country, though its people were to prove themselves mighty warriors. It was cut off from the heartlands of Europe by its language, which few but fellow Slavs understood; and the only Slavs with whom the Bohemian Czechs were in direct contact were the Poles, for whom the memory of Queen Jadwiga was too fresh and the convert's devotion of King Jagiello too strong to permit them to be drawn into the revolutionary firestorm. So the searing religious conflict remained confined to Bohemia and adjacent Moravia; their neighbors saw the Hussites only as raiders, not as evangelists. This limits the importance of this struggle for a history of Christendom, but it cannot be overlooked—it was too clarion a warning of the vast religious wars to come, a warning that was not heeded; and it has a vivid intrinsic drama of its own, though we are hampered in seeing it from the Catholic viewpoint by the obvious and flagrant bias in favor of the Hussites in almost all sources available on it (with the possible exception of

---

[65]Kaminsky, *Hussite Revolution*, pp. 143-145, 147, 159-161; Frederick G. Heymann, *John Zizka and the Hussite Revolution* (Princeton, 1955), p. 58 (for the quotation).
[66]Kaminsky, *Hussite Revolution*, p. 208.

the Hungarian).[67]
Hussites clearly knew what they were against; but what were they for? Jakoubek of Stribro, a master at the University of Prague widely considered to have inherited Hus' theological mantle, tried to formulate it in various writings in 1416: most fundamental, communion in both kinds for the laity (how strange to find this doctrine, especially in light of its Catholic history, practice and thought, the foundation of a militant heresy), with all who did not accept it condemned as heretics; rejection of the Church hierarchy, leaving a kind of congregational structure of religious authority dominated by charismatic preachers; condemnation of possession of wealth and property by the Church; downgrading of devotion to images; permission to say Mass frequently or even regularly outside of Church buildings; Mass in the vernacular.[68] Some Hussites accepted all of these doctrines and more, others only some of them; insistence on Communion in both kinds for the laity was the one positive doctrine that united them all.

In October 1416 Bishop John "the Iron" of Litomysl, legate of the Council for Bohemia and Moravia, published after a long delay the Council's formal condemnation of reception of Communion in both kinds by the laity.[69] There was, it is necessary to reiterate, no theological objection to this practice; insofar as it was heretical, it was so only in those who insisted that such Communion was essential to salvation or that anyone who refused to give or receive it was himself a heretic. But both sides had already become prisoners of symbolism on this issue. The chalice for the laity had become a symbol for religious revolution, and the Church for years refused to yield in the face of fiercely defiant challenge to its right to prescribe who might receive the chalice, and under what conditions.

By 1417 differences were already emerging among the Hussites—the inevitable result, throughout all the history of the Church, of rejecting the authority of the Pope and the hierarchy. With no common source of religious authority, human nature does not permit any considerable group of men to agree entirely for long on religious issues. Divisions appeared within the University of Prague, and between University masters and the popular preachers, who tended to be more radical on such questions as the value of intercession of the saints and prayers for the dead, the existence of purgatory, the desirability of honoring images and relics of the saints, and giving Communion in both kinds to babies and small children (if such Communion was essential to salvation, as many Hussites insisted, then they could and did

---

[67]The writer does not read any Eastern European language. Available translated Czech sources do not indicate any substantial Catholic historical literature on this period in Czech—nor any other language.
[68]Kaminsky, Hussite Revolution, pp. 184-198.
[69]Ibid., pp. 224, 240.

logically conclude that it must be administered even to those too young to understand it).[70]

But for the moment these divisions would still disappear when the Hussites faced a challenge from outside their community. In March 1417 the archdiocese of Prague, which had refused to ordain any Hussite priests since the publication of the decree against utraquism, began action to deprive existing Hussite priests of their parishes; the then Hussite Lord Chenek of Wartenberg arrested auxiliary Bishop Hermann of Prague and forced him to ordain several of the most radical Hussites as priests, probably including John Chapek, author of the wholly unauthorized vernacular Czech Mass. Archbishop Conrad at once condemned these forced ordinations, removed Bishop Hermann, and declared the ordinations null and void. In January Archbishop Conrad had refused to allow the University of Prague to grant degrees until further notice. The University consequently closed ranks more tightly with the Hussites and imprisoned one of its own professors, Peter of Unichov, a strong critic of utraquism. They tortured him and threatened him with death until he recanted his views in the main hall of the University, and issued a statement declaring John Hus free from error. Hearing of all this, in the summer of 1417 the Council of Constance suspended the University of Prague from all functions.[71]

Well might Emperor Sigismund write to the clergy of Bohemia, in September 1417:

> The divine services are profaned, and the obedient clergy are compelled to profane them; those who have been excommunicated and interdicted are tolerated and protected in contempt of the keys of the Church; rectors of parish churches and other beneficed clergy are disgracefully expelled from their benefices by the power and ferocity of laymen. Indeed some of these clergymen have been hurt and are imprisoned by laymen; they are cruelly tortured and payments are forced out of them. Horrible to say, moreover, Catholic preachers and also certain masters preaching and teaching the Catholic faith are forced by tortures, torments, and Neronic persecutions to abjure the Catholic faith that they have preached and taught.[72]

On February 22, 1418 Pope Martin V issued the bull *Inter cunctas* formally condemning the heresies of John Wyclif and John Hus and the doctrine of utraquism held in Bohemia. In its last sessions, the Council of Constance and new Pope Martin V demanded strong and immediate action to crush the Hussite revolution—action that Sigismund's brother Wenceslas, the King of Bohemia, was most reluctant to take, believing that the majority of Czechs would vigorously oppose any such attempt. Though Wenceslas himself

---

[70]*Ibid.*, pp. 171-179, 230-235.
[71]*Ibid.*, pp. 238-240, 242-243, 246.
[72]*Ibid.*, p. 245.

had no Hussite leanings so far as is known, his wife Sophia clearly did; in February 1419 she was cited by the new papal legate in Bohemia, Bishop Ferdinand of Lucena, to appear before him to answer for expelling and persecuting Catholic pastors, introducing and favoring Hussite priests, and allowing her officials to do likewise. Meanwhile in December 1418 Sigismund published an open letter urging his brother to act at once to crush the heresy, and threatening him with all spiritual and military Church sanctions if he continued inactive.[73]

Both sides were rushing toward a maximal confrontation. In 1419 and 1420 the Hussites were going far beyond utraquism. On Easter thousands of them received Communion in the open on a little mountain near Bechnye castle in southern Bohemia, which they called Tabor. They rejected the Catholic Church openly, condemning all its traditional rites and ceremonies, including the use of holy water and oils, consecrated chalices, priestly vestments, all feast days except Sunday, all fasts, auricular confession, prayers to the saints, and devotion to holy images. The Church Fathers were largely rejected, purgatory was denied, prayers for the dead were held useless, and missals were destroyed. Many of these "Taborites" became convinced that the Second Coming of Christ would occur in 1420. On July 30, 1419, following a violent sermon by the priest John Zhelivsky, quoting numerous Scriptural passages about killing and overthrow, thousands of Hussites massed in the streets of Prague, seized the Church of St. Stephen, then stormed the town hall and threw 13 councillors and other officials out of the windows, killing them. The long ineffective and alcoholic Wenceslas, facing that most terrifying challenge to a ruler—all-out revolution by an armed and murderous mob of thousands—sent a desperate message to his brother Sigismund to come and help him, then collapsed and died of a stroke.[74]

The rampaging, victorious Hussites began seizing monasteries all over Bohemia, at first merely burning their buildings, later burning the monks they found within as well. Churches were assaulted and damaged or destroyed. Emperor Sigismund, brother and thence heir of the childless Wenceslas, sent a message to Prague early in October 1419 demanding that the destruction of churches and monasteries cease and the expelled monks and nuns be restored, and that unauthorized congregations break up, but expressing a willingness to

---

[73]*Ibid.*, pp. 266-267; Powers, *Council of Constance*, p. 156.

[74]Kaminsky, *Hussite Revolution*, pp. 278-283, 287, 290-291, 295-296, 338-349; Heymann, *John Zizka*, pp. 61-62, 66-67. This seems to have been the first instance of that curious method of murder which became a dark national tradition in Bohemia: defenestration. Another defenestration of Prague launched the Thirty Years' War in 1618 (though on that occasion the defenestrated ones survived by landing on a pile of manure) and yet another (this one fatal) seems to have been performed on Czech Foreign Minister Jan Masaryk by the Communists when they seized control of Czechoslovakia in 1948. See Volumes IV and VII of this history.

tolerate both Catholic and utraquist communion for the time being. The new city officials of Prague agreed to stop the destruction of images, churches and monasteries if utraquist communion were permitted. At Christmas their representatives went to meet the Emperor in Brno, capital of Moravia, where they knelt in personal homage to him, asked his forgiveness for the rebellion in Prague, and promised to dismantle their fortifications and protect Catholics returning to the city.[75]

Many of the most influential Hussites in Prague, including most of the masters at the University of Prague and Jakoubek of Stribro in particular, had recoiled from the demon of revolution they had conjured up, and in the opening months of 1420 showed themselves willing to carry out the agreement they had made with Sigismund.[76] While this did not mean that they were ready to return to the Catholic Church, a concession on Communion in both kinds—purely a prudential policy decision, which the Church could easily have made—might have brought many of them soon to do so. The Taborites feared or even expected this. But the Church was unwilling to make this concession for thirteen years. First there had to be a trial by battle.

Whatever the magistrates and University masters of Prague might have done, left to themselves, the Taborites had put far from them any thought of submission or compromise. Since the world had not ended at the beginning of 1420 as many of them had predicted, they prepared to fight to the finish in the world they had. On Ash Wednesday they seized the fortified town of Sezimovo Ustí when its defenders were sleeping off a Mardi Gras debauch, and quickly built up its fortifications and those of an abandoned castle on a nearby hill until the complex became for them a new Tabor, where thousands of them moved to create a new city.[77]

On March 1 Pope Martin V proclaimed a crusade against the Hussites, at Emperor Sigismund's request. Sigismund had the proclamation read out in the main square of Breslau, capital of Silesia, where he was then staying, burned a local Hussite named John Krasa at the stake, and declared that any Hussite caught in Bohemia would meet the same terrible death. In immediate response, the Hussites of Prague united with the Taborites to form a Hussite Union with an army, and issued a manifesto including what later became known as the Four Articles, cornerstones of Hussite doctrine: (1) administration of Communion in both kinds to the laity; (2) "that the Word of God be freely, publicly and truthfully preached by those whose concern it is to preach"; (3) that all "civil dominion" be taken away from the clergy; (4) that the faithful

---

[75]Kaminsky, *Hussite Revolution*, pp. 298, 304-306, 308, 314-315; Heymann, *John Zizka*, pp. 69, 81, 84-85, 105-107.
    [76]Kaminsky, *Hussite Revolution*, pp. 314, 317-320, 323-327, 362-363; Heymann, *John Zizka*, p. 107.
    [77]Kaminsky, *Hussite Revolution*, pp. 334-336; Heymann, *John Zizka*, pp. 87-88, 90.

should repress all public sins.[78]

It is not clear why Sigismund did not then make a greater effort to split the more conservative Prague Hussites from the Taborites, but he tended to be an impulsive man and had apparently come to the conclusion (not then altogether unwarranted) that as a group they were impossible to deal with. But his decision marked the beginning of a war to the death, a war of no quarter, since each side regarded the other as resolved on its own total elimination. A new Hussite manifesto issued in Prague in April 1420 renounced all obedience to Emperor Sigismund as a "great and cruel enemy of the Bohemian realm and nationality" because he had launched a crusade against its people, violated his safe-conduct for John Hus, and burned John Krasa in Breslau. At almost the same time, a Taborite army commanded by John "Zhizhka" captured the castle of Sedlec, residence of Lord Ulrich of Ustí, killed Ulrich with all his retainers, and told a group of six other prisoners that if any one of them was prepared to decapitate the other five, his life would be spared and he would be taken into their army. (One volunteered to do exactly that, and did it.) When, entering Bohemia in May, Sigismund demanded the unconditional surrender of Prague, the city leaders not surprisingly refused; and they called on John "Zhizhka" for help.[79]

And so, in this dark spring of 1420 in the fair land of Bohemia, there comes into history like a thunderstorm this grim and terrible figure, unique in the history of warfare, for all the striking resemblances he bears to Oliver Cromwell two hundred years later. Like many men of his time, he had no surname; in his youth he called himself John of Trocnov, for the village where his family held a small freehold, and where he was born. He lost an eye in a fight as a boy, and for the rest of his life wore a patch over it; hence he was nicknamed "zhizhka," which in Czech means "one-eyed." After he became famous as a Hussite general, he signed himself John of the Chalice. But to his men and to the world he was simply One-Eyed John, and so he will be called here.[80]

Though he remains little known outside his native Czech republic, One-Eyed John was one of the greatest generals in all of history. The evidence of his military genius might well seem fabulous were it not so well attested historically. He was confronted at the outset of the Hussite wars with the apparently insoluble problem of how to fight well-armed and armored knightly cavalry with armies which included only very small contingents of horse and archers, the majority of his soldiers being peasants who had nothing to bring with them to

---

[78]Kaminsky, *Hussite Revolution*, pp. 335-336, 364, 368-369 (quotations on 368-369); Heymann, *John Zizka*, pp. 110-112; von Pastor, *History of the Popes*, I, 278.

[79]Heymann, *John Zizka*, pp. 101-103, 114-115, 119-123; Kaminsky, *Hussite Revolution*, pp. 370-371.

[80]Heymann, *John Zizka*, pp. 16-23, 219.

battle but clubs and threshing flails. But many peasants had available one means of transportation other than their own feet: wooden carts. One-Eyed John made their wooden carts into war wagons, protected by the addition of heavy boards and carrying the primitive artillery of his time. Gunpowder had been in use since the middle of the previous century, but the guns were so heavy and unwieldy that no one had yet thought of using them for anything but battering walled cities and castles from fixed positions. One-Eyed John invented field artillery. The wagons brought the guns into action offensively, or withdrew defensively into a circle almost impossible for even heavy cavalry to penetrate. In a mechanized age, "drawing the wagons into a circle" has become a joke. But in a pre-mechanized age, it worked. One-Eyed John invented it as a battle tactic. It never failed him. He never lost a battle.[81]

As a commander and a combatant, he was relentless and he was pitiless. Like all great generals, his objective was always not simply to defeat, but to destroy the enemy army; and more than once he accomplished just that. Like all great generals, he never rested, but was always on the move. The war in which he fought was a war to the death, and he never forgot it. The ghastly scene at Sedlec castle was typical for him. He killed his prisoners, unless he thought he could exchange them for some of his men, or hold them for a high ransom. Captured priests and monks he burned alive, since that was the penalty he saw their kind as having inflicted on Hus and his followers. But be this much said for One-Eyed John: there is no record that he ever harmed a woman or a child, and his standing orders were that all of them, in every captured city and town and castle, were to be spared.[82]

Square-built, square-jawed, massive, tireless, with an iron constitution, One-Eyed John was almost sixty years old when he marched to the aid of threatened Prague in the spring of 1420. Sigismund's men held the two great castles of Prague, Hradcany and Vysherad, but the Hussites held the main part of the city, fortified separately from the castles, and John occupied and fortified the strategic heights of Vitkov Ridge. After repulsing a major assault by the imperial crusading army July 14, he counterattacked from the top of the hill down the slope with irresistible enthusiasm and determination, winning the first of his many great victories. But the Catholic lords of Bohemia—now in considerable numbers, horrified by the excesses of the Taborites—defiantly crowned Sigismund King of Bohemia in St. Vitus cathedral on Hradcany Hill. The struggle would continue.[83]

The hatred deepened. Nicholas of Pelhrimov, whom the Hussites now recognized as their sole bishop, condemned the Blessed Virgin Mary, because

---

[81]*Ibid.*, pp. 97-101.
[82]*Ibid.*, pp. 102, 181, 448-449.
[83]*Ibid.*, pp. 18-22 (for John's age); illustration facing p. 146 (for his appearance); pp. 135-141 (for the Battle of Vitkov Ridge); pp. 142-144 (for Sigismund's coronation).

devotion to her made people think they would not be damned, even if they ought to be. Divisions among the Hussites soon reached the point where One-Eyed John was sent out to burn members of their dissident sects as he burned Catholic priests and religious. Some of Sigismund's commanders slaughtered 700 Taborite prisoners in northern Bohemia in March 1421, half of them by burning; Taborites retaliated by killing 1,400 Catholics at Chomutov in the northwest. When Jaromer in northern Bohemia fell to the Hussites, 24 priests were captured, and were offered their lives if they affirmed the Hussite Four Articles. No less than 21 of them refused, and died at the stake as martyrs. Neither Sigismund nor John was present for these atrocities, but if they had been they might not have shrunk from them. In June 1421 a joint diet of Bohemia and Moravia at Cháslav formally declared independence from Emperor Sigismund and affirmed the Four Articles of the Hussites as the national religion, with both Taborites and the more conservatived Utraquists equally accepted; One-Eyed John was one of the signatories. Archbishop Conrad of Prague betrayed his faith and joined the Hussites. Emperor Sigismund declared in response that these men were revolutionaries who had roused "the whole of Christendom . . . against this kingdom."[84]

The diet at Cháslav finished its work June 7. One-Eyed John, ever on the move, hurried across Bohemia to lay siege to the strong castle of Rabí in the southwest. As he scouted its walls, searching for a weak place, an archer upon the battlements took careful aim at the stocky figure of the great general. The arrow struck him in the right eye—the only one he had. And One-Eyed John was blind.[85]

Medieval soldiers did not often recover from arrows in the eye, even when they had two. Harold, last of the Saxon kings, died from an arrow in the eye at the Battle of Hastings. But One-Eyed John, though deathly ill for two months, recovered.[86]

It would seem incredible, were it not repeatedly and explicitly attested by several independent Czech sources for the period; but One-Eyed John, despite being totally blind, resumed command of his army after that two-month convalescence, and continued to win victories—the only blind general in recorded history.[87] Sent to the northwestern border of Bohemia adjacent to the German state of Meissen, where a German army had just won a major victory over a Hussite army led by the priest-politician John Zhelivsky of Prague, One-Eyed John scattered the Germans simply by the terror of his name; there was no battle. In October the same thing happened again, Germans besieging

---

[84]Heymann, *John Zizka*, pp. 206-207, 213, 216-217, 224-237; Kaminsky, *Hussite Revolution*, pp. 451-452, 493.
[85]Heymann, *John Zizka*, pp. 254-255.
[86]*Ibid.*, p. 255.
[87]*Ibid.*, pp. 255-258.

Zhatec when he advanced toward them in so great a hurry to escape that a devastating fire broke out in their camp and tents and the garrison sallied to inflict some 2,000 casualties before John even arrived. In November, with only 2,000 men, forced to retreat from the area of Pilsen in western Bohemia by large enemy forces, John circled his war wagons on Vladar hill, and after holding fast for three days and two nights, counterattacked in the middle of the third night, doing so much damage that Sigismund's forces were unable to pursue. And in December, surrounded by Sigismund's main force near the important city of Kutna Hora, John broke out successfully with his wagons rolling and artillery firing between midnight and dawn.[88]

So One-Eyed John won two battles by assaults launched in the darkest hours of the night—tactics well suiting a blind general. And in January 1422 he went on to drive Sigismund's army out of Bohemia entirely, into Moravia, storming the fortified town of Nemecky Brod near the frontier and mercilessly sacking it, though as usual sparing the women and children.[89]

But Emperor Sigismund, though indubitably outclassed in the field by his great opponent, matched him in perseverance and energy. Within six months he was planning a new crusade against Bohemia, with the active encouragement of Pope Martin V's legate, Cardinal Branda. He could hope to benefit from increasing dissension among the Hussites, who by 1422 had divided into no less than three factions: the more conservative Utraquists of Prague, now supported by a prince brought in from Poland, Sigismund Korybut; the radically revolutionary Taborites, mainly concentrated in southern Bohemia; and the "Orebites" of northern Bohemia led by the priest Ambrose of Hradec, whose theological position lay somewhere between the first two. One-Eyed John, a long-time friend of Ambrose, was drawn to the Orebites and broke with the Taborites. In April 1423 Utraquists and Taborites went to war against each other, though a truce was soon made while they held an elaborate debate on the issue of ritual and vestments. By August an Utraquist army from Prague felt strong enough to attack One-Eyed John himself. They met at a place called Strachov Dor. Hussite armies habitually carried an "ark" into battle containing consecrated Hosts; on this occasion both armies had arks. One-Eyed John was so furious that anyone would carry an ark into battle against him that he had the priest-bearer of the Utraquist ark brought before him after he had won the inevitable victory; in a nightmarish scene, the blind general (presumably after having the terrified priest immobilized) swung his iron-spiked battle club and bashed out his brains.[90]

Meanwhile, in March 1423, Duke Witold of Lithuania, Jagiello's brother,

---

[88]*Ibid.*, pp. 252-253, 274-275, 284-285, 290-294.
[89]*Ibid.*, pp. 299-303.
[90]*Ibid.*, pp. 343-346, 354-355, 364-365, 367-371, 389-390; Kaminsky, *Hussite Revolution*, p. 466.

had ordered Prince Sigismund Korybut, a relative, out of Bohemia, declaring that he would "stand with the Roman Church, with King Sigismund, with the other Catholic princes and with the whole of Christendom, and will help them in the fight against the Bohemians." King Jagiello made essentially the same declaration a year later, removing all hope for outside help for the Bohemian Hussites. One-Eyed John fought his last great battle in June 1424 at Maleshov east of Prague against the Prague Hussite army, placing his war wagons on a flat-topped hill and then filling some of them with stones and rolling them down the hill, followed by an artillery barrage and a charge. It was a tactical masterpiece by a general who could not see. Catholics and Hussites in Bohemia then made a six months' truce, while One-Eyed John led an army of 20,000 to conquer Moravia, his first major offensive operation outside Bohemia. At the border he suddenly fell ill and died on October 11. His men, convinced there could never be another commander like him, remained an independent military force calling itself the Orphans.[91]

During the ensuing seven years, until negotiations for a comprehensive religious settlement at last began at the Council of Basel in 1431, the pattern of the Hussite wars continued: sharp internal conflicts among the Prague Utraquists, the Taborites, and the Orphans allied with the Orebites, but with most of the three coming together whenever a new crusade was launched against Bohemia. The Taborites developed an effective military leader in the priest Prokop, called "the Shaven," though he would never be another One-Eyed John. The Taborites and Orphans made deeper penetrations into the territories from which the crusades were organized: Austria, Hungary, Silesia, Lusatia, and central Germany.[92] Periodic negotiations with Emperor Sigismund always wrecked on the rock of the continuing Hussite refusal to accept the authority of the Catholic Church, either Pope or Council.[93] New crusades would then be launched, but again and again they failed.

The last of them, conducted in 1431, was the most humiliating. Ceremonially launched by Cardinal Cesarini, already designated leader of the new Council of Basel, who solemnly invested Elector Frederick of Saxony with banner and sword in the Church of St. Sebald in Nuremberg June 29, the crusading army was large in numbers but low in morale and poorly led. Wandering in the forests on the eastern slope of the mountains ringing Bohemia early in August, it became even more disorganized. Near the town of Domazlice a quarrel broke out between Cesarini and Elector Frederick, whom the Cardinal finally accused of treason to Sigismund. In the midst of this the

---

[91]Heymann, *John Zizka*, pp. 359-360, 410-415, 419-420, 434-440; Kaminsky, *Hussite Revolution*, pp. 477-478.

[92]F. M. Bartos, *The Hussite Revolution, 1424-1437* (New York, 1986), pp. 27, 34-35, 50-52, 57; Heymann, *John Zizka*, p. 460.

[93]For example, at Bratislava in April 1429 (Bartos, *Hussite Revolution*, pp. 41-44).

Taborites under Prokop the Shaven attacked, with war wagons rumbling, singing the Hussite battle hymn "Ye Warriors of God." Routed by the singing and the rumbling alone, the German army fled without a fight.[94] One-Eyed John was seven years dead and probably few of the Germans at Domazlice had ever met him in combat, but the rumble of his wagons had become the stuff of legend, and those who commanded them fought by his battle plan. One-Eyed John was still winning victories beyond the grave.

The Hussites could not be overcome by military force. Christendom had not regained enough health from the near-disaster of the Great Schism to mount a successful crusade, nor did the methods many of the Catholic leaders had used in Bohemia deserve a victory. Shrewd diplomacy, taking advantage of the Hussite divisions, and greater flexibility were needed. The Church could always grant Communion in both kinds to Bohemia at any time. The time had come at least to put it on the bargaining table.

As if these second and third decades of the fourteenth century had not already brought achievement and peril and drama enough, they were also the setting for a deathless story unique in the annals of Christendom: the brief but ever-glorious career of St. Joan of Arc—or, as she always called herself, Jeanne *la Pucelle*, Joan the Maid.[95]

St. Joan's mission began in 1428; her supreme triumph was gained in 1429; she was martyred in 1431. To grasp the political and military situation in France from the devastating defeat at Agincourt in 1415 until those years is essential in understanding what she was called upon to do, and what she achieved. Henry V of England, determined to rule all France as he claimed the right to do, kept up the military pressure after Agincourt. In January 1419 he took the large city of Rouen, capital of Normandy. On September 10 of that year Duke John "the Fearless" of Burgundy, called to a conference with Dauphin (Crown Prince) Charles at the bridge of Montereau near the confluence of the Seine and Yonne Rivers, was murdered there with the knowledge, if not the actual participation of the Dauphin. John's grief-stricken 23-year-old son Philip inherited the dukedom of Burgundy, now including a continuous strip of land from modern Belgium to the heart of France, with an

---

[94]Bartos, *Hussite Revolution*, pp. 66-70; Heymann, *John Zizka*, p. 464; Gerald Christianson, *Cesarini: the Conciliar Cardinal; the Basel Years, 1431-1438* (St. Ottilien, 1979), pp. 23-24.

[95]Her father was called Jacques d'Arc, perhaps due to a family connection with the village of Arc-en-Barrois in that region. She never used the "d'Arc" for herself, and it was never used to designate her until 1576. The word *pucelle*, now obsolete in French, derived form the Latin *puella* ("little girl"), had almost precisely the sense of the English "maid" in the nineteenth century—a young woman, often meaning a servant girl, but also with a connotation of virginity. See Frances Gies, *Joan of Arc; the Legend and the Reality* (New York, 1981) pp. 9-10.

angry determination to avenge his father. The shrewd Henry V moved immediately to take advantage of this; his envoys told Duke Philip that he intended to force the Dauphin aside, marry mad King Charles VI's daughter Catherine, and have himself proclaimed heir to the mad king and regent until he should die. If Philip agreed to this, Henry promised to punish the murderers of his father; if he did not, Henry would make war upon him to the finish. He gave Philip two weeks to decide. Philip accepted his terms.[96]

Early in March 1420 the English won another major victory at Fresnay-le-Vicomte near Le Mans, killing 3,000 French and capturing their commander, Marshal Rieux. In May of that year the pathetic Charles VI agreed in the Treaty of Troyes to everything Henry V demanded, consenting to his marriage to his daughter Catherine, recognizing him as his heir and regent to bring into being a perpetual union of England and France, with Dauphin Charles to get nothing at all. Henry married Catherine in June. In December the Estates-General met in Paris and ratified the treaty, following which Henry V of England sat beside Charles VI of France as a joint royal court which pronounced Dauphin Charles an accessory in the murder of Duke John of Burgundy and condemned him to death *in absentia* for it. In January 1421 Charles VI formally disinherited this last survivor of his sons. In December a son was born to Henry V and Catherine, named for his father; as Henry VI of England and Henry II of France, he would reign over both countries. Though about a third of France—the central region and Languedoc in the south—remained loyal to the Dauphin, the English were far better led and now had a strong juridical claim to rule France as well as preponderant military power.[97]

In August 1422 Henry V suddenly died at the age of only 35. On his deathbed he named the older of his two brothers, John, Duke of Bedford, regent for the baby king, the youngest person ever to come to the throne of England, and Cardinal Henry Beaufort, Bishop of Winchester, tutor for the boy. Both were strong and able men, and under Bedford there was every reason to believe that France would still be secured. The English army was the best in Europe at the time, excepting only One-Eyed John's Czechs; Bedford was a commander of dogged determination and had under him two generals of real ability, the Earl of Salisbury and Lord John Talbot. Though the loss of their famous and highly capable king was a major blow, the English retained the

[96]Richard Vaughan, *Philip the Good; the Apogee of Burgundy* (London, 1970), pp. 2-3; Vaughan, *John the Fearless*, pp. 274-286; M. G. A. Vale, *Charles VII* [of France] (Berkeley CA, 1974), pp. 28-31; Famiglietti, *Royal Intrigue*, pp. 191-192, 194; Jacob, *Fifteenth Century*, pp. 176, 181-183; Burne, *Agincourt War*, p. 133.

[97]Jacob, *Fifteenth Century*, pp. 184-188; Harold Hutchison, *King Henry V* (New York, 1967), pp. 189, 193-194, 208; Burne, *Agincourt War*, pp. 145-146; Famiglietti, *Royal Intrigue*, pp. 196-197; Vale, *Charles VII*, p. 31; Vaughan, *Philip the Good*, pp. 5-6.

advantages he had given them and under Bedford's leadership were not likely to lose them. Furthermore, just a few months later the tormented Charles VI of France died, leaving baby Henry his designated heir.[98]

The English proceeded quickly to demonstrate their military superiority by winning new victories at Cravant in July 1423 and at Verneuil in August 1424. The French lost 2,500 more soldiers at Cravant, so weakening their army that only a large force of Scots who had come to help them enabled them to fight another major battle as soon as the following year. Verneuil was an even greater disaster; the French lost 1,500 more and almost the entire Scots contingent of 6,000 was cut down, including Archibald, Earl of Douglas, grandson of the great Sir James "the Black" Douglas, the beloved and ever-faithful comrade of Robert the Bruce. After Verneuil there was no French army in the field until Joan the Maid appeared, and Charles VII, though by heredity the rightful king of France, timid and fearful, doubting his own paternity, remained uncrowned, a spectacle of weakness and irresolution.[99] Against all odds, and primarily as a result of the long and tragic reign of the mad King Charles VI, it appeared very likely that the smaller but more aggressive country of England would absorb the larger but beaten France, creating a united nation which by its size and power would unquestionably dominate Europe for decades or even centuries to come.

It was at this point that Joan the Maid appeared upon the historical scene, and saved France.

In the summer of 1425, in the garden of her father Jacques, one of the most prosperous of the small farmers of the village of Domremy in Lorraine, thirteen-year-old Joan heard a voice and saw a brilliant light. As she later testified at her trial, she knew immediately that the voice and the light were "sent by God" and that the beautiful clear voice was that of an angel. Later she identified him as St. Michael. At first he spoke only of the need to follow God's law, to seek and practice goodness and attend church regularly. Again and again he appeared to her, eventually coming daily or even more frequently, and she saw him with "the eyes of my body," though not clearly perceiving his bodily form (to be expected when viewing a purely spiritual being). Soon St. Michael began to speak of a mission God was giving her, to "go to France"—the center of the kingdom, which was in great misery.[100] He told her that two of the most

---

[98]Ralph A. Griffiths, *The Reign of King Henry VI* (Berkeley CA, 1981), pp. 11-19; Jacob, *Fifteenth Century*, p. 201; Hutchison, *Henry V*, pp. 212-214; Vale, *Charles VII*, pp. 32-33. Though Griffiths says "the famous king could not have died at a less opportune moment" (*op. cit.*, p. 18) his own data show how smoothly the transition of power proceeded in France and how strong the English position was there even after the death of Henry V.
[99]Vale, *Charles VII*, pp. 32-42; Burne, *Agincourt War*, pp. 185-193, 198-215; Jacob, *Fifteenth Century*, pp. 242-244.
[100]Gies, *Joan of Arc*, pp. 9-10, 23-24; Victoria Sackville-West, *Saint Joan of Arc*

venerated women saints of the Middle Ages, Margaret and Catherine, would soon appear to her also, and they did. She would embrace all of them around the legs, which she could touch and feel. She wanted to be with them always.[101]

Over the next three years, the instructions to Joan from the Archangel Michael and the saints became more and more specific. She must go to Charles VII and see him crowned as King of France. She must inspire his soldiers to fight better, even lead them into battle. No one else would do it, or could; God had chosen her—chosen, as so often in His dealings with mankind, the weak to shame the strong. Specifically, she must go to the King's representative in the nearest large town, Vaucouleurs: the knight Robert de Baudricourt. In May 1428 she went. Baudricourt heard her request to be sent officially to the King with incredulity and scoffing, and said her father should box her ears.[102]

Her voices told her she must try again; not only was this mission God-sent and necessary, however improbable it might seem, but it must be completed by the following year. In January 1429 she went back to Vaucouleurs, and

---

(New York, 1938), pp. 56-61. The relative prosperity of Jacques d'Arc is indicated by the fact that he possessed one of the few stone houses in the village of Domremy, which still stands there. Most of the details of Joan's visions come from Joan herself, in detailed testimony at her trial for heresy in 1431 of which a complete transcript has been preserved; sharp cross-questioning by churchmen with lifetimes of experience in ecclesiastical trials and claims of mystical phenomena never shook her testimony (Gies, *op. cit.*, pp. 2-3). Most modern historians writing of Joan find it psychologically or professionally impossible to affirm a belief in the objective reality of her visions and voices, including both her best biographers, cited above. But they are firm and well-reasoned in rejecting all alternative explanations of the visions and voices (Gies, *op. cit.*, pp. 27-28; Sackville-West, *op. cit.*, pp. 343-356), and Sackville-West has a fascinating passage in which she admits that, as between "the scientific and the religious" explanations, "I have been painfully torn myself. There are moments when I am not at all sure that the religious line of approach may not, in the end, prove right" (*op. cit.*, p. 345). The fashionable and fanciful psychological and physiological explanations bear almost no resemblance to the real Joan, whom we know so well from the voluminous records of her trial.

[101]Sackville-West, *Joan of Arc*, pp. 59-60. By what Joan's biographer Frances Gies is pleased to call a "reverberating irony," (*Joan of Arc*, p. 139) Saints Margaret and Catherine were removed from the Church calendar after the Second Vatican Council because Catholic historians have determined that no reliable information about their lives and deeds has survived. But this does not mean that they never existed. Their known cults date back to the eighth century, and must have been based on some earlier tradition believed to be valid. Hundreds of martyrs whose historical existence is generally accepted were remembered, often with few if any historically reliable details about their martyrdom, from the terrible persecution launched by the Roman Emperor Diocletian in 304. The cult of St. Margaret first appeared at Antioch and that of St. Catherine at Alexandria, which had been the two largest cities in the eastern Roman empire. It is reasonable to presume an authentic tradition of the martyrs in these two cities, though all its details have perished. See *Butler's Lives of the Saints*, edited, revised and supplemented by Herbert Thurston and Donald Attwater (Westminster MD, 1956), III, 152-153 and IV, 420-421.

[102]Gies, *Joan of Arc*, pp. 30-32; Sackville-West, *Joan of Arc*, pp. 63-74.

Baudricourt turned her down again. One of Baudricourt's knights, Jean de Metz, asked her what she thought she was doing. She answered him:

> I have come here to the royal chamber to speak to Robert de Baudricourt, so that he may take me or have me taken to the king; but he does not care about me or my words. Nonetheless, before mid-Lent, I must go to the king, even if I have to walk my feet off to my knees. No one [else] in the world ... can restore the kingdom of France, nor will [the king] have any help, except from me, although I would rather stay with my poor mother, for this is not my station in life. But I must go, and I must do this, because my Lord wants me to do it.[103]

Her absolute sincerity convinced Jean de Metz, and he told her he was willing to escort her to the king. But neither of them could go without Baudricourt's permission. The parish priest at Vaucouleurs, who knew Joan, vouched for her goodness and piety. For the first time she told Baudricourt about her voices, and he was sufficiently impressed to send a messenger to Charles VII's court at Chinon in the Loire region, asking if he might send Joan to them. Someone there agreed that she might come. On February 12, returning from a visit to the Duke of Lorraine at Nancy, whom she greatly impressed, Joan told Baudricourt that the French had suffered a severe defeat at the hands of the English that day. When news was brought several days later that the English had indeed prevailed at the Battle of Rouvray on February 12, bringing a large supply train to support their siege of the strategically placed city of Orléans on the Loire almost at the geographical center of France, Baudricourt was convinced. He sent her to Chinon with his blessing and an escort led by Jean de Metz. For greater safety on the journey she donned men's clothes, which she was henceforth to wear until her death.[104]

On March 9 Joan arrived at Chinon castle. Charles VII decided to receive her incognito, but she knew his true identity at once, and held a private conference with him in which she convinced him immediately and completely of her supernatural powers by telling him a secret known only to him and to God, probably specific elements of a prayer that he had offered that God would assure him of his own legitimacy (which he and others doubted because of his father's madness and his mother's reputed promiscuity); that he alone rather than his whole country should be punished if the troubles which had come upon France were due in any way to his sins; and that God would forgive the French people if it was their sins which had angered Him. As Victoria Sackville-West

---

[103]Gies, *Joan of Arc*, p. 34.
[104]*Ibid.*, pp. 34-36; Sackville-West, *Joan of Arc*, pp. 94-98, 105-106; Burne, *Agincourt War*, pp. 234-236. Gies states that the report of Joan of Arc's clairvoyance regarding the Battle of Rouvray is "almost surely apocryphal" (*Joan of Arc*, p. 36n) but gives no reasons. Sackville-West, far from an uncritical biographer of Joan, accepts it in the pages above cited.

points out in her detailed and very rational analysis of this oft-discussed "secret," Charles could have seen nothing supernatural in a mere assurance by Joan of his legitimacy, but most certainly would have seen it in her knowledge of specific details of a private prayer.[105]

With the favor of her king supporting her, Joan the Maid could now unfurl her banners. On March 22, 1429 she sent this letter to the Duke of Bedford:

> Jesus, Mary. King of England, and you duke of Bedford, calling yourself regent of France; William de la Pole, Earl of Suffolk; John Lord Talbot, and you, Thomas Lord Scales, calling yourselves lieutenants of the said Bedford . . . deliver the keys of all the good towns you have taken and violated in France to the Maid who has been sent by God the King of Heaven. . . . Go away, for God's sake, back to your own country; otherwise await news of the Maid, who will soon visit you to your great detriment . . . I have been sent by God, the King of Heaven, to drive you, body for body, out of all France . . . If you will not believe the news sent you by God and the Maid, wherever we find you we will strike you.[106]

It was not so much the language of this letter that was unique, extraordinary though it was; fanatics and madmen and madwomen have written such letters throughout history. What was unique about this letter from Joan the Maid was that she not only meant every word of it but carried out every word of it. All that she said she would do, she did. All that she warned would happen, did happen. Joan the Maid in 1429 turned the tide of the Hundred Years War in France, and in 25 years the English had been entirely driven out—except for Calais, and they lost that a hundred years later.

Not everyone among supporters of Charles VII yet believed in Joan; there were questions and doubts, including doubts about the source of her revelations. She was examined by a commission of churchmen at Poitiers, including two bishops, the confessors of the king and queen, and several famous masters of the Universities of Paris and Orléans. They pronounced her "to be of irreproachable life, a good Christian, possessed of the virtues of humility, virginity, honesty and simplicity." Charles VII also consulted the famous theologian Jean Gerson, who had been a leader at the Council of Constance, and performed a last service for his Church and his country (he was to die later that year, aged 66) by describing Joan as "good, divinely inspired, and worthy of leading the king's armies" and pointing out that the Biblical prohibition on wearing clothing of the opposite sex (which Joan's critics were already using against her) "did not forbid women to wear men's clothing for military purposes," citing Esther and Judith. The Bishop of Embrun pointed out that God might well have chosen a peasant girl to save France in order to "humble

---

[105]Sackville-West, *Joan of Arc*, pp. 114-127.
[106]*Ibid.*, p. 141; Gies, *Joan of Arc*, p. 57 (for the last two sentences).

the proud" who had been unable to do so.[107]

On April 27, now with the Church's approval as well as her king's, Joan the Maid set out to make good her warning to the Duke of Bedford and the English invaders, with an army of about 4,000 commanded by the young Duke of Alençon, who had become her ardent admirer and advocate. Her leadership endowed that army at once wtih a unique character: oaths were no longer heard, the usual camp followers were dismissed, and the army marched chanting psalms. The English had besieged Orléans since the preceding October, but were not strong enough to invest the city completely. Joan entered the city at eight o'clock in the evening of April 29, riding a white horse, in full armor with her famous battle standard in her hand, representing Jesus holding the world in his hand, with an angel kneeling on each side of Him, and the words JHESUS MARIA and a scattering of fleurs-de-lis. She was hailed rapturously by the people of the besieged city.[108]

Her reinforced army was in the city by May 4, as word came that a strong English force commanded by Sir John Fastolf, the victor of Rouvray in February, was on the march for Orléans. Joan, napping, was roused from sleep by her voices telling her to go at once into battle. Not sure at first whether they meant that she should march against Fastolf or attack the besiegers' forts near the city, she opted for the latter, sprang on her white horse, galloped through the streets with such verve that the horse's shoes struck sparks from the pavement, and led the soldiers in a charge against English-held Fort St. Loup that nothing could stop. They stormed it almost without pausing for breath, killing three-quarters of the garrison. Joan mourned the English dead, remembering that they had died on the vigil of the Ascension, and reminded her soldiers to confess and give thanks to God for their victory, and to touch nothing in the church of St. Loup within the fortress.[109]

She refused to fight on Ascension Thursday, but on Friday the 6th she and her men carried the English fort of Augustins across the river, and the next day attacked the strongest English position of all, Tourelles fort also across the river. This could not be carried by a single charge, but required no less than 13

---

[107]Gies, *Joan of Arc*, pp. 53-57 (second and third quotations); Vale, *Charles VII*, pp. 55-56 (first quotation). Vale points out that the attribution of the written defense of Joan to Gerson has been questioned, but there is contemporary evidence for it, and despite Vale it is really no evidence against it to point to earlier writings by Gerson warning of the errors of "'strange women' claiming to predict the future and perform wonders." The Church always has more charlatans, hysterics and hallucinators than genuine recipients of messages from God, His mother and His saints. But Joan the Maid had already established her *bona fides*. By their fruits you shall know them.

[108]Gies, *Joan of Arc*, pp. 59-61, 72-74; Sackville-West, *Joan of Arc*, pp. 158-160, 165-166, 177; Burne, *Agincourt War*, pp. 237-239.

[109]Gies, *Joan of Arc*, pp. 74-75; Sackville-West, *Joan of Arc*, pp. 177-183; Burne, *Agincourt War*, pp. 239-240.

hours of fighting, during which Joan was wounded. She pulled out the arrow with her own hand—this 17-year-old peasant girl who had never seen a battle until two days before—and when Dunois, the commander of the assault, prepared to sound the retreat, overrode him and led a final charge standard in hand. (Joan always fought simply by carrying her standard; her short sword was only for self-defense—she would not use it to cut down English soldiers.) The English panicked, knights plunging into the river in full armor. Tourelles fort was taken and burned and all the bells of Orléans rang out, with priests and people singing *Te Deum laudamus*. The next day all the English around Orléans withdrew, and on May 10 Joan rode into Tours, standard in hand, to greet her king and urge him to go at once for his coronation to Reims, the traditional place for the crowning of the kings of France.[110]

Now it was Sir John Fastolf's turn. An effective veteran campaigner, grossly libelled if in fact Shakespeare took him as the model of Falstaff, he favored caution in the face of the inexplicable; but Lord John Talbot outranked him and on June 17 ordered Fastolf's reinforcing army to keep on marching to relieve the castle of Beaugency, down the Loire from Orléans, which had been held by the English and attacked by the French. Learning the next day that Beaugency castle had already fallen, the English began to retreat, but too late. Joan the Maid was upon them near the village of Patay, shouting to her men: "You have spurs, use them!" She faced some of the best soldiers and two of the best commanders the English had, veterans of fourteen years of war; it did not matter. The battle was over in a few minutes. Two thousand English were killed, 200 captured; Lord Talbot and Lord Scales were captured, Fastolf barely escaped. It was the only battle Joan the Maid ever fought in the open field, and as quick and complete as a military victory can be. Afterwards Joan took a mortally wounded English soldier on her knees and persuaded him to confess his sins before he died. It is moments like this that show Joan the Maid as not only a saint for France, but for Christendom.[111]

And this brings us to the threshold of mystery, for the question must now be asked even though we cannot answer it, either from history or by faith: Why were God and His heavenly messengers so much on the side of France in this conflict? Why did they send Joan the Maid to save France? No matter how often His aid is asked, He rarely takes sides openly in warfare among Catholics, provided they are serious Catholics; and for all their personal and collective sins, the French and English in 1429 were both serious Catholic peoples. In all the history of sainthood there is no one else like Joan the Maid, not only as a

---

[110]Gies, *Joan of Arc*, pp. 59, 75-82; Sackville-West, *Joan of Arc*, pp. 183-196, 199-201; Burne, *Agincourt War*, pp. 240-246, 265-267; Jacob, *Fifteenth Century*, pp. 246-247.
[111]Gies, *Joan of Arc*, pp. 95, 97-100; Sackville-West, *Joan of Arc*, pp. 207-213; Burne, *Agincourt War*, pp. 252-260, 267-269; A. J. Pollard, *John Talbot and the War in France, 1427-1453* (London, 1983), pp. 16-17.

military commander, but as a recipient of a divine calling to bring victory to one
side in a war between Catholics. The only explanation this writer can guess
at—admittedly highly speculative—is that if France had become a mere
appanage of England, as appeared so likely in 1429, it would probably have
been drawn after England in rejecting the Catholic faith in the Protestant revolt
during the following century, and that this might have ended in the destruction
of the Church in the course of that revolt. It is a fascinating and very significant
historical fact that none of the succession of political and military forces most
inimical to Christendom from the sixteenth to the twentieth centuries has been
able to control more than one of the three great nations on the western fringe
of Europe: Great Britain, France and Spain. The Protestant revolt took
Britain, but not France or Spain. The French Revolution took France, but not
Britain or Spain. Communism and its allies in the 1930's briefly took Spain, but
not Britain or France. Nazi Germany took France, but not Britain or Spain.
The real importance of the preservation of French independence in 1429 may
have been prospective, to prevent a threat that would only materialize in the
future, and fulfill Christ's promise to Peter that His Church would stand until
the end of the world.

As for Joan herself, she was always more than simply a French patriot, as
is shown not only by her care and concern for the English dead and wounded,
but by her frequent invocation of the ideal of the crusade as the only rightful
employment of arms by the Christian except in self-defense. At one memorable
moment in her brief career she revealed her own desire to be a crusader.
Having heard of the destruction of churches, holy images and monasteries by
the Hussites in Bohemia, she dictated a letter to them, with a holy anger and a
fiery enthusiasm that is all Joan:

> I would have long since visited you with my avenging arm if I were
> not occupied with the English war. But if I do not soon learn that you have
> amended your ways and returned to the bosom of the Church, perhaps I
> will leave the English and turn against you to exterminate this frightful
> superstition with the sword and end either your heresy or your lives. If you
> return to the light, if you enter the bosom of the Catholic faith, send me
> your ambassadors. But if you persist in your resistance . . . expect to see
> me, with the strongest human and divine power, to pay you in your own
> coin.[112]

It was not to be; Saint Joan crosses history's sky from horizon to horizon

---

[112]Gies, *Joan of Arc*, p. 135; Bartos, *Hussite Revolution*, p. 58. Gies and Sackville-
West (*Joan of Arc*, p. 250) make a great point of the fact that Joan did not dictate this
letter since it is written in Latin. Obviously it had to be written in Latin, since it was
directed to Czechs who did not speak French. But there is no reason whatever to
believe that Joan did not dictate the letter in French, which was then translated into
Latin. It sounds exactly like her.

with the speed of a meteor, and she was never to leave her own country. But of this we may be absolutely certain: that a crusading army led by Joan the Maid, descending the forested hills of Bohemia toward its ruined monasteries and the ashes of its martyrs, would never have fled before the rumbling of the war wagons of One-Eyed John.

Even after the great victory of Patay, it took Saint Joan ten days of pleading, sometimes with tears, before the still timid Charles VII at last consented to set out for Reims to be crowned. The city opened its gates to him, or more likely to Joan; on Sunday, July 17, 1429 she stood beside him, standard in hand, as he took the ancient oath "to uphold the faith of his ancestors, to defend the Church, and to adhere to the justice of his forefathers in ruling the kingdom which God had entrusted to him" and was anointed with the holy chrism of St. Remi.[113] Kneeling before him and embracing his legs, weeping but now with joy, Joan said: "Gentle king, now is executed the pleasure of God, Who wanted the siege of Orléans to be raised, and Who has brought you to this city of Reims to receive your holy consecration, showing you that you are the true king, and that the kingdom of France belongs to you."[114] Immediately afterward Joan wrote Duke Philip of Burgundy calling for him and Charles VII to make "a good firm peace, which will last a long time" and to "forgive each other, with a good heart, wholly, as faithful Christians should, and if you want to make war, go and fight the Saracens."[115]

The final step in the victorious campaign to which Joan felt God calling her had always been, in her mind, the capture of Paris and the enthronement of the duly crowned King Charles VII there. But this was not to be just yet. The assault on Paris made by Dunois and other supporters of Joan on September 8, with wholly inadeqeuate forces and only minimal support from the King, was a failure. Joan took a crossbow shot in the leg and was "left lying in the open till dark." Charles ordered her not to attempt another attack; and, being far from sure that she would obey such orders, had the bridge across the Seine which the Duke of Alençon intended for her to use in the next attack destroyed. Then Charles returned to the Loire region, ordering Joan to accompany him. Sadly and reluctantly, she did. For the next six months she engaged in only the most minor military actions.[116]

---

[113]Gies, *Joan of Arc*, pp. 103-106, 109-111 (quotation on 111); Sackville-West, *Joan of Arc*, pp. 213-216, 220-223.
[114]Gies, *Joan of Arc*, p. 112.
[115]*Ibid.*, pp. 113-114.
[116]*Ibid.*, pp. 123-127, 131-134; Sackville-West, *Joan of Arc*, pp. 233-236, 241-243, 252; Burne, *Agincourt War*, p. 263. Joan's action of leaving her armor before an image of Our Lady in St. Denis cathedral just before departing from the Paris area at the King's order has often been a seen as a kind of renunciation of active military leadership, but this was certainly not her intent; she soon acquired new armor, and fought in several more battles before her capture in May 1430. Gies is undoubtedly

But, despite these reverses, that Joan the Maid had turned the tide of the war could not be doubted. Testimonies from her enemies suffice to show it. First, the Burgundian chronicler Jean Wavrin de Forestal:

> By the renown of Joan the Maid the courage of the English was much altered and weakened. They saw, it seemed to them, the wheel of fortune turn harshly against them, for they had already lost several towns and fortresses which had returned to the obedience of the king of France, principally by the enterprises of the Maid, some by force, others by treaty; they saw their men struck down, and found them no longer of such firm purpose and prudence as they had once been; thus they all were, so it seemed, eager to retreat.[117]

Then the words of the man in the best position to know just what the impact of Joan the Maid on his previously victorious army had been—the Duke of Bedford, regent in France and commander-in-chief of the English army:

> There fell by the hand of God, as it seems, a great stroke upon your people that was assembled there [at Orléans] in great number, caused in great part of lack of sad belief and unlawful doubt that they had of a disciple and limb of the Fiend, called the *Pucelle*, that used false enchantments and sorcery, which stroke and discomfiture not only lessened in great part the number of your people there, but as well withdrew the courage from the remnant in marvellous wise.[118]

In April 1430 Joan's voices told her that some time during the next two months she would be capured. To her horrified protests they replied only that it must be and she must endure it. Their prediction was fulfilled on May 24, Ascension Thursday, almost exactly one year after she had raised the siege of Orléans. Having come to Compiègne to help defend it against the Burgundians, she rode out from the town to lead a sally against the besiegers, who were quickly reinforced. Her troops broke, she waited too long to retreat, and when she did the frightened garrison had closed the gates and raised the drawbridge, leaving her cut off. An archer in the service of the Bastard of Wendonne pulled her off her horse, and she was a prisoner.[119]

In November the Burgundians sold her to the English for 10,000 *livres tournois*, and the English put her prosecution in the hands of Pierre Cauchon, fugitive Bishop of Beauvais, who had cooperated with them and had consequently been expelled from his see when the French regained control of it

---

correct in explaining that leaving one's armor in a church after a serious wound was a custom of soldiers who could afford it (Gies, *op. cit.*, p. 127).

[117]Gies, *Joan of Arc*, p. 100.

[118]Sackville-West, *Joan of Arc*, p. 197.

[119]*Ibid.*, pp. 252-253, 258-261; Gies, *Joan of Arc*, pp. 137-142; Burne, *Agincourt War*, pp. 264-265.

following Joan's great victories in 1429. Bishop Cauchon therefore had a score to settle with Joan, and he believed in being well prepared. In January 1431 he assembled an enormous staff, consisting of a cardinal, six bishops, 32 doctors of theology, 16 bachelors of theology, seven doctors of medicine, and 103 other associates, all to interrogate and produce the indictment of Joan. She was not allowed a single counsel. One 19-year-old illiterate peasant girl faced the massed brainpower of no less than 56 ecclesiastical magnates and intellectuals (counting Cauchon with his staff), with the most painful of all deaths her portion if she failed. Indeed, God had chosen the weak to shame the strong.[120]

The interrogation that followed is a drama that has fascinated nearly all who have read it for six hundred years. Against the pulverizing 56-1 odds any ordinary man or woman, however experienced or well educated, would have crumbled almost immediately. Joan held out for three full months, through fifteen formal interrogation sessions and numerous browbeatings in her cell, often by Bishop Cauchon personally. She was refused permission to pray in the chapel, or to make sacramental confession.[121] When she did finally break, it was for only five days; then she recovered and went to her martyrdom. The story of her persecution by Bishop Cauchon is retold at length, and deservedly, in all the multitudinous biographies of Saint Joan; there is neither need nor space to retell it here. A few highlights must suffice: Joan to the Bishop, at the third interrogation session: "You say that you are my judge; beware of what you do, for truly I have been sent by God, and you are placing yourself in great danger";[122] Joan later in that same session, asked if she thought she was in a state of grace, though excommunicated: "If I am not, may God put me there; if I am, may God keep me there";[123] Joan, asked by Cauchon if she were willing to submit to the judgment of the Church, replying that if she could be shown to have said anything against the faith, she would retract it, but would not deny her voices; asked if she would submit to the Pope, she replied: "Take me there and I will answer him"; asked if she would submit to the Council of Basel, she replied that she would, whereupon Cauchon bellowed: "Be silent, in the name of the devil!" and then told the stenographer to write none of that exchange down; later, facing the stake: "All the works which I have said and done should be submitted to Rome to our lord the supreme pontiff, to whom, after God, I refer myself. And as for my words and deeds, I did them on behalf of God."[124] When at last she broke, she was handed an act of abjuration to sign, which she could not read; she signed it anyway, was sentenced to perpetual imprisonment, and repented of her weakness in five days, to the undisguised satisfaction of

---

[120]Sackville-West, *Joan of Arc*, pp. 272-274, 288-289.
[121]Gies, *Joan of Arc*, pp. 161-165.
[122]*Ibid.*, p. 165.
[123]*Ibid.*, p. 166.
[124]*Ibid.*, pp. 184-186, 202-203, 213 (for quotation).

Cauchon, who cried out on hearing it: *"Capta est!"* ("We've got her!")[125]

On May 30, 1431, Joan the Maid was burned at the stake in the main square of Rouen. The treacherous Nicholas Loiseleur, who throughout the interrogations had pretended to be her friend while seeking damaging information against her for Cauchon in their private conversations, tried in tears to crawl into the execution cart to beg her pardon, but the English guards pushed him away. Cauchon, after some hesitation, allowed her to receive viaticum; Joan looked him in the eye and said: "Bishop, I die through you." For half an hour, before the stake, Joan prayed, asking the forgiveness of and for all present. As the fires were lit she asked for a cross; a nameless English soldier made one from two bits of wood and handed it to her. With a last cry of "Jesus!" she died in the flames. John Tressart, secretary to the King of England, fled saying: "We are lost; we have burned a saint!"[126]

Twenty-five years later, on July 7, 1456, in a France entirely liberated from the English invader (except for Calais), in the cathedral of that same city of Rouen, its Bishop Jean Jouvenel des Ursins proclaimed the official verdict of a commission appointed by Pope Calixtus III in response to a petition from Joan's mother, to re-examine the proceedings of Bishop Cauchon, now dead:

> We say, pronounce, decree and declare the said trial and sentence to be contaminated with fraud, calumny, wickedness, contradictions, and manifest errors of fact and law, and together with the abjuration, the execution, and all their consequences, to have been and to be null, without value or effect... We proclaim that Joan... did not contract any taint of infamy, and that she shall be and is washed clean.[127]

The terms of the decree *Frequens* passed by the Council of Constance before Pope Martin V had been elected required a new council to be convened five years after the adjournment of the Council of Constance, then seven years after the adjournment of the next council, then every ten years thenceforth. Pope Martin's very carefully qualified endorsement of the Council's decrees did not confirm any action placing the Council's authority above the Pope's, which *Frequens* as well as *Sacrosancta* specifically stated. But Pope Martin, a pontiff of great discretion, thought it better to follow the schedule for holding councils set forth in *Frequens*, to which many believed he had agreed, though undoubtedly he feared another council and the likelihood that it would again claim authority superior to the Pope, this time when there was an incumbent Pope from whom to withhold it.

So he was undoubtedly greatly relieved when the new council, duly

---

[125]*Ibid.*, pp. 213-218.
[126]*Ibid.*, pp. 219-224; Sackville-West, *Joan of Arc*, pp. 338-342.
[127]Gies, *Joan of Arc*, p. 236.

convened at Pavia in April 1423, was so poorly attended that no one could reasonably regard it as ecumenical. In June he moved it to Siena because of an outbreak of plague, and in March 1424 he dissolved it, despite vigorous objections from Guillem Armengol, Catalan delegate to the council in the service of Alfonso V of Aragon. Alfonso had been reverting to the long-time hostility of Aragon toward Italian Popes, so vigorously encouraged by the Aragonese Pedro de Luna during the Great Schism, as his interest grew in laying claim to the kingdom of Naples, where the Popes had always favored the French house of Anjou over that of Aragon. De Luna had died at last in November 1422, past eighty, intransigent as ever, appointing cardinals on his deathbed to maintain his claims and elect a new antipope, which they did in June 1423, choosing Gil Sanchez Muñoz for the purpose. Though hardly anyone else in Christendom paid any attention to Sanchez Muñoz—the Count of Armagnac in France was his only significant supporter outside the kingdom of Aragon—Alfonso found him useful to play off against Pope Martin, though he never actually proclaimed the antipope except for a few brief weeks in the spring of 1426. Sanchez Muñoz finally gave up his futile claims in 1429.[128]

By the terms of the decree *Frequens*, the next council was due to convene seven years after the adjournment of the previous one, whose few delegates had met first at Pavia and then at Siena. That would mean March 1431. On February 1, 1431 Pope Martin V called for a new council to meet at Basel in Switzerland to reform the Church, establish peace, and seek the return of those who had ceased to practice the Faith. The able Cardinal Giuliano Cesarini, young and vigorous at 41, was appointed president of the new council, to speak there in the Pope's name. Cardinal Cesarini had served Pope Martin well in Germany, England and Venice, though he had had no more success than anyone else in launching crusades against Bohemia in the time of One-Eyed John. Then, on February 20, Pope Martin V suddenly dropped dead of a stroke.[129]

His successor, duly chosen by the fourteen cardinals in office with a minimum of controversy—though they did demand that the new Pope pledge to hold the council immediately, reform the Church, and give the College of Cardinals veto power over actions regarding the cardinals—was Cardinal Gabriel Condulmaro, a tall, handsome, imposing man, but of simple life and known for his humility. He took the name Eugenius IV and was consecrated March 12. He issued the agreement the cardinals had demanded as a bull, but declared that he reserved all decisions about the council to himself. For the moment, no decisions were needed; by April, only one bishop, two abbots, and three representatives of the University of Paris had arrived at Basel for the

---

[128]Von Pastor, *History of the Popes*, I, 239-240, 274-275, 277; Valois, *Le grand schisme*, IV, 450-454; Ryder, *Alfonso the Magnanimous*, pp. 109, 134-135, 137-139, 163.
[129]Von Pastor, *History of the Popes*, I, 280-281; Christianson, *Cesarini*, pp. 10-17.

council, and Cardinal Cesarini was off on the Bohemian border attempting to organize the "crusade" that ended in the wild flight before the rumbling of the Hussite war wagons. In August 1431 the new Pope suffered a severe stroke, which endangered his life and left his right side paralyzed for several months, though in the end he completely recovered and enjoyed one of the longer pontificates in the history of the papacy, sixteen years.[130]

Cardinal Cesarini arrived to preside over the council at Basel September 9. With the Pope prostrate, there was no one at first to prescribe Cesarini's policy or control his actions. His mind full of his recent experiences in Bohemia, he decided reasonably enough that the highest priority should go to a serious attempt at reconciliation with the Hussites. They were formally invited to come to the Council to present their position, under safe-conduct.[131]

However, attendance at Basel was still very sparse, and in his physical condition Pope Eugenius IV was probably even less eager than he otherwise would have been for the Council to be held at that time. On November 12 he drafted a bull proroguing the council at Basel and transferring to Bologna, to reopen there in 18 months. Apparently doubtful about this course of action, he held up proclamation of the bull until he heard of the Council's invitation to the Hussites, of which he strongly disapproved. Then, on December 18, he issued the bull publicly, and sent it to Cardinal Cesarini in Basel with a cover letter directing him "in view of holy obedience" to leave Basel and try to start another crusade against the Hussites.[132]

News of the bull ran ahead of it; most members of the Council refused to attend the session at which young Dr. John Ceparelli read the Pope's dissolution order. Those who were present, led by Cardinal Cesarini, protested vigorously, defending the decision to invite the Hussites, emphasizing the danger of schism if the Council rejected the order, and reminding the Pope of *Frequens*, which he had never endorsed. On January 23, 1432 Cesarini wrote arrogantly to the Pope warning him of "the terrible tribunal of the One God" which would judge his actions. On February 8, probably knowing that the Council was about to defy the Pope explicitly and not yet willing to go into schism himself, Cesarini resigned the presidency of the Council. On the 15th the Council re-enacted the decree *Sacrosancta*, asserting its supremacy over the Pope, and declared that the Pope did not have the power to transfer or adjourn it or to prevent anyone from attending it. By Easter the Council had grown to 83 high-ranking members (bishops, abbots, and representatives of princes and

---

[130]Von Pastor, *History of the Popes*, I, 284-285; Gill, *Eugenius IV*, pp. 36-40, 42; Christianson, *Cesarini*, pp. 19-20, 28.

[131]Gill, *Eugenius IV*, p. 40; Christianson, *Cesarini*, pp. 27, 29; Bartos, *Hussite Revolution*, p. 71.

[132]Gill, *Eugenius IV*, p. 43; Christianson, *Cesarini*, pp. 31-33; von Pastor, *History of the Popes*, I, 287.

universities) and on April 29 it summoned the Pope and his cardinals to appear before it within three months or face formal prosecution, in the manner that the Council of Constance had proceeded against Antipope de Luna. On June 5 Cesarini wrote to the Pope upholding the doctrine of conciliar supremacy in the Church and stating that an ecumenical council had the power to try, judge and depose a Pope for heresy or for giving scandal through schism and failure to reform the Church.[133]

Meanwhile delegates from the Council had met Hussite delegates at the Bohemian border town of Cheb and agreed that in the prospective discussion of their religious differences at Basel the Hussite Four Articles should be judged by the practice of Christ, the apostles and the primitive Church "together with the councils and doctors truly founded on this practice"—an ingenious compromise formula. There was enough desire for peace on both sides now so that the Hussites accepted the conciliar safe-conduct for their delegates without the giving of hostages, despite their vivid memories of what had happened to their founder at the last council.[134]

The Council and the Pope now temporarily stepped back from the brink of confrontation. The Pope, though holding out for a meeting site somewhere in the papal state, said that the Council might advance the date of its reconvening there, and dropped his opposition to any discussion with the Hussites. When the original three months' deadline for the Pope's appearance before the Council passed, the Council extended it for three months more. On January 18, 1433 the Pope declared that the Council might reconvene in Germany if it had the protection of a friendly lay ruler. Meanwhile the Hussite delegation had arrived and the Council's disputation with them began. It continued at overwhelming length, with individual presentations lasting for days; the Taborites and some of the Catholics denounced the opposing side very harshly, but the new Hussite leader in Prague, John Rokycana, proved more moderate, and Cardinal Cesarini sought diligently for areas of agreement. The incipient schism of Council and Pope certainly did not help the Catholic cause; Hussite spokesman Ulrich of Znojmo responded trenchantly to an argument that his people should submit to the authority of the Pope by reminding the Council on March 2 of its own unwillingness to do that.[135]

But in dealing with the Hussites, reason and prudence gradually began to prevail as the year 1433 unfolded. In March, canon lawyer and future Cardinal Nicholas of Cusa successfully urged the Council to offer the Hussites permission to take Communion in both kinds if they would rejoin the Church, correctly

---

[133]Von Pastor, *History of the Popes*, I, 288-289; Christianson, *Cesarini*, pp. 33-51, 54, 56-63; Gill, *Eugenius IV*, pp. 44-45.

[134]Bartos, *Hussite Revolution*, pp. 79-82; Christianson, *Cesarini*, p. 56.

[135]Christianson, *Cesarini*, pp. 64-67, 75-85, 93-94; Bartos, *Hussite Revolution*, pp. 88-95.

pointing out that while they saw this as a matter of faith, in fact it was not, so the Church could afford to concede it to them, while the rest of the Four Articles involved differences on reform and behavior, not doctrine. The Council sent a delegation to Prague to present Nicholas' proposal to the Bohemian diet. After weeks of debate they neither accepted nor rejected it, instead making counter-proposals and sending a new delegation to Basel to deliver them.[136]

At a meeting with his cardinals in February, Pope Eugenius IV showed them the draft of a new bull allowing the Council to continue to sit in Basel, if it would accept a new president. (The Pope no longer fully trusted Cesarini—and with reason.) Receiving the final version of this bull in June, the Council refused to accept it because it implied that their past decisions might not be confirmed and that the Pope still held supreme authority over them. This swung both parties back toward confrontation, with the Council threatening in May to depose the Pope within two months if he did not come to terms with them. The Council of Basel was now a fairly large body (though not nearly as large as the Council of Constance had been), including seven cardinals, two patriarchs, 42 bishops, 30 abbots, and 311 doctors of theology. But the Pope would not yield to their demands, and on July 29, 1433 he formally annulled all decrees of the Council "contrary to the Holy See" (obviously including *Sacrosancta*).[137]

Emperor Sigismund now moved back into the picture. Sixty-five years old, his thick red beard broadly streaked with gray, his normally jovial mien tempered by his decades of struggle with church and state, bewildered by Antipope Cossa, frustrated by Antipope de Luna, hammered by One-Eyed John, having lost more crusades than any other ruler in the history of Christendom,[138] the pertinacious Emperor remained unsinkable. It is easy to criticize Sigismund for his many mistakes and his military ineptitude, and most historians have done so almost to the extent of scorn; but despite his mistakes, no one who held his office but Charlemagne and Charles V ever contributed more to Christendom than Emperor Sigismund. He had been more responsible than any other man operating strictly in the world for the success of the Council of Constance in ending the Great Schism (Pope Gregory XII's even more essential contribution was on a higher plane, mostly invisible at the time). Now he intended to save Christendom from being torn asunder by the Council of Basel—and, for the moment, he did.

In August he persuaded Pope Eugenius IV to prepare two drafts, not one,

---

[136]Christianson, *Cesarini*, pp. 88-90; Bartos, *Hussite Revolution*, pp. 97, 99-100, 102-103.

[137]Christianson, *Cesarini*, pp. 94, 96-97, 101; Gill, *Eugenius IV*, pp. 49-50.

[138]There had been at least five against the Hussites, though it is sometimes difficult to demarcate them, and also the disastrous Crusade of Nicopolis against the Turks in 1396, in which Sigismund had played a leading role (see Chapter Eleven, above).

of his next bull (*Dudum sacrum*) regarding the Council, the first demanding that it recognize the new papal legates as presidents and withdraw all actions taken against the Holy See, the other omitting both demands while not yielding to the Council's pretensions. From the Council, Sigismund demanded yet another extension of the oft-extended deadline for the Pope to appear before it, which the Pope was obviously not going to do so long as the Council did not recognize his authority. (Late in September Eugenius IV wrote to the Doge of Venice: "We shall have renounced the apostolic office, and life itself, before being the cause of the papal office and the Apostolic See being subordinated to the council against all canons.") The Council would grant only thirty more days, with the specific proviso that there would be no more extensions. On October 11 the aging Emperor, having crossed the rugged valley trails and mountain saddles of the Austrian Tyrol by forced marches, and Lake Constance by boat, arrived at Basel on the day this final extension expired. He assembled the Council in the cathedral and addressed them, his voice still strong and commanding, demanding that they hear the final version of *Dudum sacrum* and an explanation of it (copies of both the earlier versions had been leaked, along with a spurious bull called *Deus novit*, so there was total confusion about what the Pope had said and meant) and announcing in no uncertain terms that he would never allow another schism; he had seen too many.[139]

Following a bitter debate between the Pope's spokesman Archbishop Zabarella of Spalato and Cesarini, who had now gone over entirely to the conciliar position, Emperor Sigismund spoke to the Council again. He was still telling some of his old jokes (which fell rather flat), but he was very much in earnest. He meant what he had said. They must allow another deferment of the deadline. They must swear to it. Reluctantly Cesarini did, though only for himself and other higher prelates, not for the full Council.[140]

The old Emperor prevailed. On November 7 another 90-day extension of the deadline was granted by the Council. In December, in a new version of the bill *Dudum sacrum*, Pope Eugenius IV restored recognition to the Council of Basel, withdrew his decree dissolving it, and authorized it to deal with heresy, war and peace, and reform, but without specifically confirming any of its acts, notably its reiteration of the heretical decree *Sacrosancta*. At almost the same moment, on November 30, the Council's delegates in Prague made a compact for settlement with the Hussites, to which astonishingly even the spokesmen for the Taborites and "Orphans" agreed, approving Communion in both kinds for those now practicing it, but with priests requested to teach that Christ is fully present under either species; preaching to be done without impairing the authority of the Church; Church endowments to be permitted; and public sins

---

[139]Christianson, *Cesarini*, pp. 100-103 (quotation on 101), 110 (Sigismund's voice); Gill, *Eugenius IV*, pp. 50, 53-54.

[140]Christianson, *Cesarini*, pp. 104-111 (for the jokes, see 111).

to be punished, but only by legitimate authority. It was a Catholic victory against all odds; and for maintaining an apparently hopeless cause through so long a series of humiliating defeats, Catholic Czechs and Christendom could again thank Holy Roman Emperor Sigismund.[141]

In Bohemia it soon became apparent that by no means all of the Hussites were actually prepared to accept the agreement of November 30, 1433. The Bohemian Diet in January 1434 demanded that the whole country be required to accept the chalice, including Catholic areas. But the more conservative Utraquists of Prague were solidly in support of the original agreement, and allied with Czech Catholics against the objectors. The two sides marshalled yet again for war, with the Catholics and Utraquists having the larger army. On May 30 they decisively defeated the radical Hussites at the Battle of Lipany, laying down a heavy, smoky artillery barrage so limiting visibility that the Taborites and Orphans left their wagon circle too soon, thinking their enemy had retired when he had not. (Blind John, who needed no visibility, would not have made that mistake.) Prokop the Shaven was killed, along with thousands of the veteran fanatic warriors. No longer would they dominate Bohemia.[142]

On June 4, 1434 Pope Eugenius IV was driven from Rome when the hostile Colonna family (to which his predecessor Pope had belonged) and Milanese mercenaries gained control of the city. He fled in a boat on the Tiber, disguised as a Benedictine monk, but the disguise was ineffective. His boat was bombarded by rocks thrown from the shore (the Tiber is not a wide river), from which he protected himself by lying in the bottom covered by a shield. A few boats took to the river to threaten him, and one moved up to a blocking position, only to pull away when the Pope's boat captain rushed forward as though to ram him. (Who was that boat captain? History does not tell us.) The Pope got away safely to Florence, where he was warmly received by large crowds. Perhaps emboldened by this indication of his weakness in Rome, the

---

[141]Christianson, *Cesarini*, p. 111; von Pastor, *History of the Popes*, I, 292; Gill, *Eugenius IV*, pp. 57-58; Bartos, *Hussite Revolution*, p. 110; Otakar Odlozilik, *The Hussite King: Bohemia in European Affairs, 1440-1471* (New Brunswick NJ, 1965), p. 6. Christianson, despite giving a vivid depiction of Emperor Sigismund's dramatic intervention, credits Cardinal Cesarini with this striking settlement. Though initially Cesarini had tried to be conciliatory, during the course of 1432 and 1433 he had clearly placed himself on the Council's side, and Pope Eugenius IV had made evident his complete loss of confidence in him by demanding his replacement as president of the council. During the final near-total break in the summer and early fall of 1433 Cesarini had repeatedly insisted on conciliar supremacy in the Church (Christianson, *op. cit.*, pp. 104-109), which the Pope would not and could never admit. The record shows that Cesarini did nothing to avert the threatening irrevocable split. Emperor Sigismund did.
[142]Christianson, *Cesarini*, pp. 119-121; Bartos, *Hussite Revolution*, pp. 111, 117-118; Heymann, *John Zizka*, pp. 468-469; Odlozilik, *Hussite King*, pp. 8-9.

Council of Basel renewed the decree *Sacrosancta* again at the end of the month.[143]

As these disturbing events showed, by 1434 Christendom was far from fully recovered from the immense damage the Great Schism had done; but it was on the road to recovery, and in the end the schismatics at Basel would not prevail.[144] The Church had been reunited by the agency of the Council of Constance, but more specifically and personally by the fidelity of Emperor Sigismund and the self-abnegation and brilliant initiative of Pope Gregory XII at Constance. It had experienced the first great heresy in Christendom for two hundred years, the forerunner of Protestantism, but was finding a way toward peace and reunion even with the Hussites. It had seen the triumph and the martyrdom of Saint Joan the Maid. At the end of this tumultuous and splendid period of twenty-four years, full of some of the most thrilling dramas in all history, at some time during 1434, a lonely ship was making its way southward under the blazing tropical sun along a low ochre coast where whirlwinds of sand curtained the sky and to be wrecked ashore meant certain death from thirst. Of its captain Gil Eanes, a squire of Prince Henry the Navigator, we know only of his life until then that in the previous year he had been sent out by Prince Henry to round Cape Bojador, but like so many before him, had lost heart and failed to do it. Now Prince Henry had sent him back to try again: "Go forth, then, and . . . make your voyage straightway, inasmuch as with the grace of God you cannot but gain from this journey honor and profit."[145] Let Gomes Eanes de Azurara (perhaps a relative? we do not know) tell the story, brief but imperishable, symbol and inspiration to all whose life and achievement are blocked by the loom of a fearsome obstacle that would bar them from the land of their dreams:

> [Gil Eanes] resolved not to return to the presence of his lord without assured tidings of that for which he was sent. And as he purposed, so he performed—for in that voyage he doubled the Cape, despising all danger, and found the lands beyond quite contrary to what he, like others, had expected. And although the matter was a small one in itself, yet on account of its daring it was reckoned great—for if the first man who reached the Cape had passed it, there would not have been so much praise and thanks bestowed on him; but even as the danger of the affair put all

---

[143]Von Pastor, *History of the Popes*, I, 294-295; Gill, *Eugenius IV*, pp. 62, 65; Christianson, *Cesarini*, p. 123.

[144]See Chapter Thirteen, below.

[145]Eanes de Zurara, "Chronicle of the Discovery and Conquest of Guinea," *Hakluyt Society Publications* No. 95, p. 33. For other especially good accounts of this epochal voyage see Diffie and Winius, *Foundations of the Portuguese Empire*, pp. 68-69; Sanceau, *Henry the Navigator*, pp. 112-114; Ian Cameron, *Lodestone and Evening Star* (New York, 1966), pp. 110-112.

others into greater fear, so the accomplishing of it brought greater honor to this man. . . . He related to the Prince how the whole matter had gone, telling him how he had ordered a boat to be put out and had gone in to the shore without finding either people or signs of habitation. And since, my lord, said Gil Eanes, I thought that I ought to bring some token of the land since I was on it, I gathered these herbs which I here present to Your Grace, which we in this country call Roses of Saint Mary.[146]

Captain Eanes had rounded the dread promontory and landed in its lee upon the howling desert, finding there the tiny starlike green plants with the lovely name. There was life—and hope—beyond Cape Bojador. The Age of Discovery, which would open up the whole world to Christendom, was underway.

---

[146]Eanes de Zurara, "Chronicle of the Discovery and Conquest of Guinea," *Hakluyt Society Publications* No. 95, pp. 33-34.

13
Renaissance
(1434-1464)

(Popes Eugenius IV 1431-1447, Nicholas V 1447-1455, Calixtus III 1455-1458, Pius II 1458-1464))
(Antipope Amadeus of Savoy 1440-1449)

"We are therefore obliged to imitate St. Augustine, and retract our errors. We exhort you, then, to give no credit to those earlier writings which oppose the supremacy of the Roman See, or contain anything not admitted by the Roman Church. Recommend and counsel all, especially to honor the throne on which our Lord has placed His Vicar, and do not believe that the Providence of God, which rules all things and neglects none of His creatures, has abandoned the Church Militant alone to a state of anarchy. The order given by God to His Church requires that the lower should be led by the higher, and that all, in the last resort, be subject to the one Supreme Prince and Ruler who is placed over all. To St. Peter alone did the Savior give the plenitude of power: he and his lawful successors are the only possessors of the Primacy. If you find in the Dialogues, or in our letters, or in our other works—for in our youth we wrote a great deal—anything in opposition to this teaching, reject and despise it. Follow that which we now say; believe the old man rather than the youth; do not esteem the layman more highly than the Pope; cast away Aeneas, hold fast to Pius."—Bull of Retractation, Pope Pius II to the University of Cologne, April 26, 1463[1]

The middle years of the fifteenth century have long been seen as preeminently the time of transition between the medieval and the modern age. The work of cultural and intellectual historians has established that there is at least some truth in that view of this period, though the concepts "medieval" and "modern" are sufficiently vague to allow a great deal of confusion and misinterpretation, and the distinction and transition are not nearly so clear in political and religious history as in cultural history, if indeed they exist there at all.

The historian of Christendom should be particularly aware of the bias inherent in the use of the term and concept "medieval" pejoratively, as

---

[1]Ludwig von Pastor, *The History of the Popes from the Close of the Middle Ages*, Volume III (London, 1894), p. 284.

something from which men needed to be liberated. The High Middle Ages had been the glory of Christendom. What remained of their spirit was still glorious. The "Renaissance" in the sense of a greater appreciation of Greek and Roman intellectual and artistic achievements was an outgrowth of the culture of the High Middle Ages, as is shown clearly by St. Thomas Aquinas' emphasis on Aristotle and the fact that Petrarch—usually considered the founder of the Italian Renaissance—was a near-contemporary of Dante, brightest of all medieval literary lights. Prince Henry the Navigator, founder of the Age of Discovery, was in every way a son of high medieval Christendom as he was a son of the Reconquest of the Iberian peninsula which spanned almost the entire Middle Ages.

There were, undoubtedly, new and disturbing elements intermingled with the old in the middle of the fifteenth century. Irreverence and selfishness—always lamentably common in human affairs—were less reproved and therefore more openly displayed. A corrosive cynicism was increasingly manifest in public policy. The new classical learning was often—though by no means always—combined with a scorn for theological learning and religious literature. Many able minds were breaking bonds of discipline, both those which were unnecessarily constricting and those which had kept Christian thought on Christian paths. It was a time of danger and of opportunity.

The Church had been gravely weakened by the Great Western Schism, and these were the years of her recovery from that debility—an aspect of the time rarely mentioned by twentieth century historians. Indeed, the term "renaissance," usually applied only to the classical literary and artistic revival among intellectuals, could equally well be applied to the papacy of the mid-fifteenth century—not in the sense of patronage of the humanist intellectuals, but in the rebirth of its own power and prestige. Not for more than eight hundred years—not since Pope Vigilius in the sixth century—had the papacy been so threatened as by the Great Western Schism and its consequences; but by the pontificate of Pius II (1458-64) its recovery from those consequences was essentially complete. As for the moral laxity usually associated with the term "Renaissance Papacy," it did not emerge for another twenty years, and then only in and under two Popes—Innocent VIII and Alexander VI—though the damage they did and allowed was very great.[2] The insufficiency of reform in the Church following the restoration of the papacy was regrettable, but as yet far from catastrophic. A time in which the city often, and to a large extent rightly seen as the cultural leader of Christendom—Florence—enjoyed a canonized saint as bishop for thirteen years can hardly have been fundamentally corrupt.[3]

---

[2]See Chapters Fourteen and Fifteen, below.
[3]St. Antoninus, Bishop of Florence from 1446 to 1459, and before his episcopate, in 1436, founder of the convent of San Marco, which during his episcopate gained one of the finest Renaissance libraries and the best of the paintings of Fra Angelico. See

No political events of this period mark in any special way a change from medieval to modern—certainly not the one most often cited, the fall of Constantinople to the Muslim Turks, an event indeed of great significance, but far more medieval than modern. The long grapple with Islam had been one of the great shaping constants of medieval experience. If one specific event, dateable precisely or within a narrow range, may be selected as the point of separation, it should clearly be the invention of printing, one of the few most towering landmarks in the world's technological history. It was probably in the year 1448 that the first printed documents appeared, produced in Mainz by Johann Henne Gänsfleisch zur Laden zu Gutenberg, who borrowed 150 gulden on October 17 of that year from a relative apparently to finance his press, the first to use movable type. The first printed documents were a calendar for the year 1448 and a poem on the Last Judgment. By 1453, in partnership with a wealthy investor named Johann Fust, Gutenberg began printing his renowned Bible, the first complete printed book, which was ready for sale in 1455.[4]

The explosion of knowledge and literacy which this epochal invention made possible, especially coming as it did in a period when intellectual writing from classical to current was particularly admired and carefully studied, changed the cultural and intellectual environment of Western man and the transmission of ideas within Christendom fundamentaly and irrevocably. It ended the age when clergy and religious were almost the sole possessors of written knowledge. The good this did is obvious, the evil apparently less so. Modern propaganda, that most effective of all weapons of the totalitarian state, became possible for the first time. Error could overwhelm truth by sheer volume of words on paper. But, as with all such technological change, there was no turning back. Until the coming of television five hundred years later, the printed word ruled over the visual image, and any man with access to Gutenberg's invention could, if his words were telling enough, become for good or ill a power in the land.

Such were the currents of the age. As always, we must remember that the generalizations of later historians often do not report or reflect the attitudes of the time. That is why, even when useful, they are best used sparingly. The concepts "medieval" and "modern" had not yet been invented, so no one in 1450 could think of himself or his time as on a threshold between the two. The real issues and controversies were far less abstract. At the everyday political

---

Butler's Lives of the Saints, edited, revised and supplemented by Herbert Thurston and Donald Attwater (Westminster MD, 1956), II, 263-265, and Ferdinand Schevill, *The Medici* (New York, 1949), pp. 87, 99-100. Unfortunately there is no full biography of St. Antoninus in English, though there is a good biography in French by Raoul Morçay (Paris, 1914).

[4]*Catholic Encyclopedia* (1910), VII, 90; *Encyclopedia Britannica*, 11th edition (1910), XII, 740.

level, they revolved about persons, power and money. On the grander geopolitical scale, they encompassed the resurgence of France against England, Aragon's push into southern Italy, and above all the grim advance of the Ottoman Turks from Asia into Europe. In a class by itself was Prince Henry the Navigator's venture down the long, long African coast, pressing on into the unknown, rolling back horizons, opening up the world. And, as ever, the most cosmic issues and controversies revolved about the Church. Neither the Council of Constance, the restoration of the papacy, nor the staunch common sense of old Emperor Sigismund had yet decided whether councils or Popes were ultimately to govern Christ's Church. In the last analysis, did authority lie with Peter's successor or a clerical assembly? And was there only that stark choice, or could a compromise be made, some sort of sharing of authority at the top?

No more critical issue has ever faced the Church. Christ had given Peter the keys to the kingdom of Heaven. Was that only a figure of speech? Were Peter and his successors answerable to some clerical legislative body for how they used, or even whether they held the keys? Could that legislative body rightfully defy Peter's successor? Could it rightfully remove Peter's successor?

Before we begin relating the historical facts of how this great controversy developed, beyond the point to which we have already followed it, some much earlier history needs to be quickly recalled. While Christ was on Earth, no Christian could doubt that He and He alone had been head of the Church. His commission to the Apostle Peter in the Gospel of Matthew gives no hint of any group or other person whose authority impinged on Peter's. The Book of Acts contains no report or suggestion of any authoritative collective action by the apostles and disciples except for the Apostolic Council of Jerusalem in the year 49 or 50, called to decide whether gentile converts to Christianity should be required to follow the Jewish Law. The Apostles were divided and Peter pronounced the decision: with three minor exceptions, gentile converts should not have to follow the old Law. The next ecumenical council was not held for nearly three hundred years, at Nicaea in 325, where the Pope's personal representative, Bishop Hosius of Córdoba, presided. Though we have no specific information about the ratification of the decisions of the Council of Nicaea by the incumbent Pope Silvester I, there is every reason to believe that he did approve them, and Hosius certainly did; his signature appears first on the council decrees. All later councils generally recognized as ecumenical until the Great Western Schism were called by Popes, and only those conciliar decrees approved by Popes were universally accepted. None of the attempts to depose Popes or support antipopes, before the Great Western Schism, involved councils.[5]

---

[5]See Volumes I and II of this history.

By any reasonable standard of historical judgment, the idea of councils holding supreme authority in the Church—first tentatively advanced by some academic controversialists during the Great Western Schism, then specifically proclaimed by the Council of Pisa and in the decrees *Sacrosancta* and *Frequens* by the Council of Constance—was a complete innovation. It had no grounding in history or tradition. No earlier councils had acted and legislated independently of the Pope. None had elected a Pope, or claimed the right to do so.

It cannot, therefore, be rationally maintained that conciliar government of the Church can be found anywhere in its original constitution or in its first fourteen hundred years of operation among men. Its establishment would have been a fundamental remaking of the entire institution. In the change-obsessed twentieth century this may not seem to be a fatal objection, but every serious Catholic must recognize its force. A Church founded by Christ which is to last until the end of the world cannot reconstitute its essential structure and remain the Church He founded.

All Christian religious bodies which have broken away from that traditional structure—that is, all non-Catholic churches—have found the problem of ecclesiastical government insoluble. Where episcopal hierarchies have remained, they have been effectively without a head, except sometimes in a particular political or ethnic subdivision. Where only a legislative body—a sort of local council—exists, as in the Presbyterian, Baptist, and other Protestant churches, that body is essentially run by political techniques and dissenters always have the option, which they have frequently exercised, of leaving that sect and forming another. The last resort is a *de facto* if not *de jure* congregationalism, in which each congregation governs itself, hiring and firing its minister, choosing its own doctrines or letting the hired minister do it. Ecumenical authority is lost.

The historian writing from the Catholic perspective will not be surprised to see so essential a part of the forthcoming gigantic struggle for Christendom—the Protestant denial of the authority of the Pope—foreshadowed in this struggle within the Church over papal authority challenged by a council. Christ's Church militant mans the first ditch as well as the last. She meets each new foe before its full nature is revealed, as she survives it when its career of destruction is done.

The Council at Basel, held back from schism by the stubborn papal loyalty of old Emperor Sigismund and finally sanctioned as a council by Pope Eugenius IV at the end of the year 1433,[6] in June 1435 decreed the abolition of "annates," a practice whereby the first year's income from a diocese or other benefice granted by or with the approval of the Pope was paid to Rome.

---

[6]See Chapter Twelve, above.

Income from annates was an essential part of the financing of the papal establishment. Two months later the Council ordered all papal collectors to send all the moneys they collected to Basel for use as the Council should direct, including even the annates coming due whose receipt by the Pope they had just prohibited. They also ordered a judicial inquiry into the conduct of the papal legates to the Council who had vigorously protested the abolition of the annates. Pope Eugenius IV responded in October that he could not accept the abolition of the annates unless he was provided with an alternative source of income to make up for what would be lost. The Council fired back that annates were a great evil and must be abolished whether the Pope liked it or not, while Cardinal Cesarini, the president of the Council who had been the Pope's original representative there, wrote urging Eugenius to imitate earlier Popes who had "observed the canons of general councils." He did not mention the Popes who had disapproved conciliar decrees. When in December the Pope refused the *pallium*, symbol of high episcopal office, to the Archbishop of Rouen in France who had refused to pay annates, the Council of Basel purported to give the Archbishop of Lyons authority to confer the *pallium* on the Archbishop of Rouen. The Council was therefore arrogating to itself both the Pope's financial authority to collect clerical dues and his appointive authority to designate bishops.[7]

The Council made its intention to limit the Pope's appointive power explicit in March when, along with prescribing an oath of office for the Pope, it decreed that bishops-elect were henceforth to be confirmed by their metropolitan archbishops rather than by the Pope, and that the Pope might not deny confirmation to archbishops-elect without the consent of the College of Cardinals, and then only to hold a new election, not to make the appointment himself.[8] In May 1436 Cardinal Nicholas Albergati and Archbishop Giovanni Berardi of Taranto, who had been designated by Pope Eugenius as presidents for the Council but had not been allowed by the Council to serve in that capacity, left Basel after having to listen to "a long and bitter tirade" against the Pope in one of the Council sessions. When the Pope sent Cardinal Albergati to Basel he had described him as "an angel of peace," but no peace had been found.[9] After the cardinal and the archbishop reported back to Eugenius IV, he issued a long memorandum to the Catholic princes of Europe, laying down the fundamental principles at stake in his quarrel with the Council, which never

---

[7]Gerald Christianson, *Cesarini, the Conciliar Cardinal: the Basel Years, 1431-1438* (St. Ottilien, 1979), pp. 138-139, 144; Joseph Gill, *The Council of Florence* (Cambridge, England, 1959), pp. 61-63; Joachim W. Stieber, *Pope Eugenius IV, the Council of Basel, and the Secular and Ecclesiastical Authorities in the Empire* (Leiden, 1978), p. 25.

[8]Stieber, *Council of Basel*, pp. 26, 29, 31.

[9]*Ibid.*, pp. 26-27; Christianson, *Cesarini*, p. 161; Gill, *Council of Florence*, p. 68; Joseph Gill, *Eugenius IV, Pope of Christian Union* (Westminster MD, 1961), p. 80.

changed through the eleven years of struggle with it that filled all the remainder of his pontificate:

> It was an indictment of the council, which was accused of denying that the Pope was head of the Church or St. Peter head of the Apostles, thereby changing the age-old constitution established by Christ and making instead two heads, a situation which could result only in schism; it had become the refuge of ecclesiastical malcontents and rebels; it had turned itself into a vast tribunal completely absorbed in petty trials, instead of attending to the serious business of reform for which in six years it had done almost nothing; it had abolished the annates, proclaimed an indulgence, created legates *a latere*, all in spite of the Pope...; it had made simple clerics the equal of prelates in voting, so that the bishops had abandoned Basel in disgust, for of the one hundred and fifty mitres there when the council was confirmed in December 1433, barely twenty-five remained in 1436, and only one cardinal; the taxes the council forbade the Pope, it collected itself...; a Pope could not, declared Eugenius, abdicate the office he held in favor of any council or approve blindfold all its decisions; the princes should understand that and should help him to preserve the ancient customs and form of the Church.[10]

It is important to remember Pope Eugenius' point about the curious character of voting membership in the Council of Basel. It appears that almost any cleric, professor or lawyer able to get there could vote. In all councils held before the Great Western Schism, only bishops and abbots had voted. At Pisa the extraordinary precedent was created of granting votes to other clerics approved by the council, particularly doctors of theology and law. The Council of Constance, at the insistence of Emperor Sigismund, had voted by nations. The Council of Basel had "one man, one vote," but there was no evident reason other than physical presence why many of the clerics present had a vote. In a critical vote of April 14, 1436 only 20 bishops and 13 abbots were included in more than 500 casting ballots.[11]

The issue that made the break between the Council of Basel and the Pope irrevocable was, at first sight, an odd one to have had such shattering effect: the question of relocating the Council to meet the desires and needs of delegates from the Greek Orthodox Church in the Byzantine empire who were now once again prepared, in the face of alarming Turkish advances, to seriously consider rejoining the Catholic Church. The Emperor and the Patriarch of Constantinople were prepared to come to the Council in person. Patriarch Joseph was a frail octogenarian; lengthy overland travel would be exceedingly

---

[10]Gill, *Eugenius IV*, pp. 85-86. Stieber, *Council of Basel*, pp. 27-33, summarizes this memorandum in even greater detail. Stieber's history of the Council is the most comprehensive available in English, and though he appears to write as a Protestant and is harshly critical of Gill, in fact the two men agree on almost every essential point of fact, though very divergent in interpretation of the facts.

[11]Gill, *Council of Florence*, pp. 68, 70n.

difficult for him, and crossing the Alpine passes to northern Switzerland out of the question. Failing in their original efforts to have the council held in Constantinople, the Greeks indicated they would accept an Italian city.[12] They had always insisted that Church reunion must be achieved through a council, as had almost been accomplished at the Council of Lyons in 1274.[13]

In November 1436 Cardinal Cesarini proposed that the Greeks be offered four Italian cities (Florence, Parma, Pavia and Udine) to any of which the Council would move to accommodate them if they refused to come to Basel or Avignon, an alternative site which did in a sense have access to the sea up the navigable Rhone River, though it was much farther from Constantinople than Italy. Cesarini did his best to muster support for such an offer. But on December 5 the Council rejected his proposal, requiring that the Greeks come to Basel, Savoy (also inland and Alpine) or Avignon. The vote of rejection was 355 to 242. The majority included three cardinals, two patriarchs, two archbishops, 16 bishops, and 28 abbots; the other 304 negative votes came from lower level clerics and professors.[14]

Of the three choices now offered by the Council of Basel to the Greeks, only Avignon was in any way feasible; but the Greeks definitely did not want to go there, and memories of the papal residence and French domination of the Church from Avignon in the preceding century did not make it an auspicious meeting place. Even the Council had required that Avignon put up a deposit of 70,000 ducats to guarantee its financial capability to host the Council. In the absence of this deposit Cardinal Cesarini, still acting as president of the Council, refused to confirm the decree moving it to Avignon. But in February 1437 the Council overrode him, relying on verbal promises that the money was on the way. It finally arrived in April, but with only part of the sum in gold as it was all supposed to be, the rest being in securities of uncertain value.[15]

By this point Cardinal Cesarini's determination to resist a clearly illegitimate majority in the Council of Basel[16] had hardened, and on April 23 he led most of the minority which had voted for moving the Council to Italy if the Greeks wished it, to outright defiance of the majority. On May 24 the two

---

[12]*Ibid.*, p. 60; Gill, *Eugenius IV*, pp. 76-78, 80; Christianson, *Cesarini*, pp. 154-155.
[13]See Chapter Seven, above.
[14]Christianson, *Cesarini*, pp. 164-165; Gill, *Eugenius IV*, pp. 89-90; Gill, *Council of Florence*, p. 70n; Stieber, *Council of Basel*, p. 35. Stieber's vigorous refutation (*op. cit.*, p. 28n) of the claim by some Catholic writers that the Council was packed with local clergy from Basel for this critical vote is beside the point. The Council was already packed by the large majority of voting clerics who were not bishops or abbots and who gained votes merely by being there, regardless of whether they came from Basel or elsewhere.
[15]Christianson, *Cesarini*, pp. 165-167; Gill, *Council of Florence*, pp. 71-72.
[16]Because of its lack of any reasonable basis for credentialling voting delegates and its repeated defiance of the Pope.

Greek envoys who had been at Basel met the Pope at Bologna and declared their rejection of Basel, Savoy and Avignon as sites for the reunion council. Six days later Eugenius IV issued the bull *Salvatoris et Dei nostri* accepting an Italian site for the Council. After this he refused to deal officially with the majority at Basel, though contacting some of its members individually. On June 13 he announced in a letter to Emperor Sigismund and the kings of France, England and Portugal that the relocated Council would meet at Ferrara in Italy.[17]

The Council's response was a virtual re-run of its actions four years before.[18] At the end of July it approved 25 charges against the Pope, for "notorious misconduct in office, especially his refusal to observe the council's reform decrees," to which it demanded his reply within sixty days. Emperor Sigismund was very busy again fighting the Taborite Hussites, besieging a castle they had presumptuously named Zion, but on September 13 he called on the Council to extend the 60-day deadline for the Pope's reply. But now the Council would not listen to the aged Emperor, and he could not this time hurry to Basel to impose his will by his personal presence; he was nearly seventy years old and in very poor health.[19]

Nor was the Pope any longer ready to compromise as he had done in 1433. On September 18, by the bull *Doctoris gentium*, he formally ordered the Council to move to Ferrara immediately, and condemned its hostility to him and to the majority of the cardinals. He declared that the Pope is the final judge of the validity of ecumenical councils and must approve all their decisions before they take effect. He did, however, give carefully qualified approval to the settlement which the Council of Basel had made with the Hussites, declaring the compacts the Council had made with them, by which Communion in both kinds was allowed in Bohemia, "neither expressly confirmed nor bluntly rejected," and allowing the Council to continue these negotiations for another month—its only approved activity henceforth.[20]

Now the battle lines were clearly drawn, and in October 1437 the Council of Basel went openly into schism, formally citing Pope Eugenius IV for contempt of the Council (though it did agree to suspend further legal proceedings against him for two months, in response to Emperor Sigismund's request), declaring the bull *Doctoris gentium* null and void, and insisting on the

---

[17]Gill, *Council of Florence*, p. 78; Gill, *Eugenius IV*, p. 91; Christianson, *Cesarini*, p. 171; Stieber, *Council of Basel*, p. 37.
[18]See Chapter Twelve, above.
[19]Christianson, *Cesarini*, p. 172; Stieber, *Council of Basel*, p. 46 (for the quotation); F. M. Bartos, *The Hussite Revolution, 1424-1437* (New York, 1986), pp. 145-146.
[20]Von Pastor, *History of the Popes*, I, 312-313; Gill, *Council of Florence*, pp. 91-92; Stieber, *Council of Basel*, pp. 38-39; Otakar Odlozilik, *The Hussite King; Bohemia in European Affairs, 1440-1471* (New Brunswick NJ, 1965), p. 16.

superior authority of councils over the Pope.[21] Emperor Sigismund was now a
dying man, and a courageous attempt in November by the electors of the Holy
Roman Empire to take his place by proposing a compromise whereby the
Council would suspend its proceedings against the Pope in return for his
suspension of the Council at Ferrara, coupled with a request that the Council
return to Sigismund's system of voting by nations, fell on deaf ears.[22] On
November 11 the old Emperor left Prague on a stretcher to join his daughter
and her husband Albert of Austria, his heirs. On December 9 he died with
them at his side.[23] At least one historian who had been unimpressed by
Sigismund's performance during his reign became suddenly conscious at this
point of how great was the loss to Christendom by his death:

> The death of the Emperor Sigismund on 9 December 1437 removed from
> the scene one of the few political figures who might have been able to heal
> the open break between the Council of Basel and Eugenius.   The
> Emperor's death freed the Pope and the Council from their promises to
> accept Sigismund's mediation.[24]

On the day that the news of Emperor Sigismund's death arrived at Basel,
December 27, in the Christmas season, Cardinal Cesarini addressed the Council
there for the last time, stressing the Christmas message of peace, reminding
them that reform could never be achieved by schism, and declaring firmly that
the Holy Spirit had departed from the Council. On January 8, 1438 the new
papally approved council officially opened at Ferrara. The group then present
there was quite small—five archbishops, 21 bishops, 11 abbots, two generals of
orders, and two Dominican theologicans—but not much smaller than clerics of
comparable rank at the now schismatic Council of Basel. On the 10th the
Council at Ferrara excommunicated all still at Basel, and declared all its acts
after September 18, 1437 null and void. On January 24 the Council at Basel
declared Pope Eugenius IV suspended form office and liable to deposition if he
did not submit to them within two months.[25]
    Obviously conscious of the disastrous effects of the refusal of the Council

---

[21]Stieber, *Council of Basel*, pp. 46-48; Gill, *Eugenius IV*, p. 102; Christianson,
Cesarini, p. 173. In a public statement explaining its position on the superior authority
of councils, issued October 19, the Council could only cite as Scriptural authority the
passage of Matthew (18:20) that "where two or three are gathered in my name, there
am I in the midst of them." It is hard to imagine a more ludicrous argument. If every
gathering of two or three Christians could be deemed a council with authority superior
to the Pope, then indeed ecclesiastical anarchy was established.
[22]Stieber, *Council of Basel*, pp. 133-135.
[23]Bartos, *Hussite Revolution*, p. 147.
[24]Stieber, *Council of Basel*, p. 39.
[25]*Ibid.*, pp. 43, 49-50; Christianson, *Cesarini*, pp. 177-179; Gill, *Council of Florence*,
p. 95; Von Pastor, *History of the Popes*, I, 315, 328; Stieber, *Council of Basel*, pp. 43, 49-
50.

of Basel to prescribe conditions for voting membership, the Council at Ferrara established a membership list in February and recognized three "estates" in the Council, the first consisting of cardinals, archbishops and bishops, the second of abbots and high officials of religious orders, the third of doctors of theology, professors, and canon lawyers. Two-thirds of each estate were required to vote in favor of any decree adopted by the Council. Early in March Emperor John VIII Palaeologus of Constantinople arrived with Patriarch Joseph and a number of Greek bishops, including the particularly able Bessarion of Nicaea. On March 21 Cardinal Cesarini arrived from Basel and prostrated himself before Pope Eugenius IV to ask his pardon for the times when he had cooperated with the Council of Basel against the Pope's will and direction. Eugenius generously accepted his apology.[26]

In that same month a new Holy Roman Emperor was elected: Albert Habsburg of Austria, husband of Emperor Sigismund's daughter and heir. While the imperial electors were assembled at Frankfurt, delegations from the Pope and the Council of Basel both addressed them. Unwilling to make a decision between Pope and Council at this time, they took refuge in a "protestation of neutrality" and said they would make no canonical appeals to either the Pope or the Council for the next six months, meeting again after that if the breach had not been healed. With a new schism, the role of the Emperor and the electors had become very important in dealing with it, but they were not yet prepared to act. One who was prepared to act was Duke Stephen of Bavaria, who wrote to the Council of Basel April 30 withdrawing all safe-conducts for its members in view of the Pope's condemnation of it.[27]

In August a Russian delegation arrived at Ferrara, led by Archbishop Isidore of Kiev, creating a considerable sensation—very few Russians had been seen in the West since the Eastern schism of 1054. The Council had already begun its extensive discussions of the theological issues which separated, or appeared to separate the Eastern Orthodox Church and the Catholic Church. The only really significant theological difference concerned the question of whether the Holy Spirit proceeded from the Father alone, or from the Father and the Son. It was not so much the question itself that concerned the Greeks as the fact that the word *filioque* ("and the Son") had been added to the creed in the West without agreement by the Greeks. This was why they had always insisted on a council to settle this question. The theological debates—in which the Latins, by the Greeks' own admission, demonstrated markedly superior skill in argument—went on for months. During these debates, in January 1439, the Council was moved from Ferrara to Florence, partly for greater security, since the city of Milan near Ferrara was hostile, and partly for financial reasons, since

[26]Gill, *Council of Florence*, pp. 97, 104-106; Christianson, *Cesarini*, p. 181.
[27]Stieber, *Council of Basel*, pp. 136-139, 141; Gill, *Eugenius IV*, p. 113; Gill, *Council of Florence*, p. 131.

the Florentine government under the very wealthy Cosimo de Medici offered free accommodations for everybody and a subsidy of 1,500 ducats per month.[28]

Meanwhile a very important action had been taken by the Church in France. Charles VII (sometimes called "the Well-Served," in memory of Joan the Maid) had generally supported the Council of Basel, but drew back from its suspension of the Pope. He saw an opportunity in the new schism to declare the effective administrative independence of the Church in France from the Pope, which had been a goal of French policy from the time of King Philip the Fair—except when the Pope was French. On July 7, 1438 a document called the Pragmatic Sanction was proclaimed at Bourges, one of the favorite residences of Charles VII. It sharply restricted Papal governance of the Church in France (giving the King correspondingly more authority over it) and adopted some of the decrees of the Council of Basel that the Pope had not approved, relating to financial levies by the Church and the conferring of benefices. The Pragmatic Sanction also explicitly endorsed conciliar supremacy over the Pope. It was widely but not universally supported in France; the Estates of Languedoc, the southern province which was one of the largest in France, condemned it and urged the French King to assert the Pope's authority in France and reproached him for actions helping to maintain the conciliar schism.[29]

Late in April 1439 the theologians in the Greek delegation to the Council of Florence voted 24-12 to accept the essentials of the Catholic position on the procession of the Holy Spirit. On May 27 Pope Eugenius IV gave a major address to the Council calling for union and promising aid of all kinds if it was achieved; the Greeks were reportedly much moved. On June 1 Archbishop Isidore of Kiev obtained a specific commitment from the Pope to support a permanent guard of 300 soldiers and two ships in Constantinople if reunion was attained, and more in an emergency, while calling for a new crusade against the Turks. Patriarch Joseph declared his acceptance of the Catholic creed June 3, and in the end only four Greek delegates dissented from it.[30] A week later the aged Patriarch died, leaving this statement as his testament:

> Since I am come to the end of my life and shall soon have to pay the debt common to all, by God's grace I write openly and sign my profession for my children. Everything, therefore, that the Catholic and Apostolic Church of Our Lord Jesus Christ of the elder Rome understands and teaches I too understand, and I declare myself as submitting in common on these points; further the most blessed father of fathers and supreme pontiff

[28]Gill, *Council of Florence*, pp. 141-146, 174-178; Gill, *Eugenius IV*, pp. 112-113, 116.
[29]Gill, *Eugenius IV*, p. 112; Stieber, *Council of Basel*, pp. 70-71; Gill, *Council of Florence*, pp. 314-315.
[30]Gill, *Council of Florence*, pp. 247-251, 253-254, 257-266.

and vicar of Our Lord Jesus Christ, the Pope of elder Rome, I confess for the security of all.[31]

The Greek delegates, following this last appeal of their Patriarch, agreed June 25 to accept the unconditional primacy of the Pope, and on July 6 the reunion of the Latin and Greek churches was formally and publicly proclaimed in Florence, with the full support of Byzantine Emperor John VIII. Bishop Bessarion of Nicaea and Archbishop Isidore of Kiev were made cardinals at the end of the year, and gave long and outstanding service to the Church, particularly in central and eastern Europe.[32]

That reunion with the separated Greeks had been proclaimed before, by the Council of Lyons in 1274,[33] but was not maintained, and that the same was to happen to this reunion though for very different reasons, should not be allowed to dim the luster of this achievement. A schism nearly four hundred years old is immensely difficult to heal. Prejudices and hatreds built up between rival churches through so long a period are almost indestructible. Probably only the imminence and magnitude of the Turkish danger brought the Byzantines to the council in Ferrara and Florence. But once they had come there, all the evidence (and there is much) indicates that they were genuinely and honestly persuaded of the correctness of the Catholic position. Patriarch Joseph, facing the Judgment, spoke for them all. It was well done; and if the crusade that followed upon the reunion had been successful, there would have been good reason to hope that this reunion between churches no longer divided by any doctrinal issue and sharing valid sacraments would have been at last secured.

It was probably not just coincidence that on the same day reunion with the separated Eastern Orthodox Church and its acceptance of full obedience to the Pope was proclaimed in Florence, the Council of Basel proclaimed the Pope deposed. The Council of Basel did not wish the Pope to benefit from the triumph at Florence. What he had gained in the east they proposed to take away from him in the west.

On May 16, 1439, after the delegations from Aragon, Castile and Milan had withdrawn in protest against the Council's course, the one remaining

---

[31]*Ibid.*, pp. 267-268 (quotation on 267); Donald M. Nicol, *The Last Centuries of Byzantium, 1261-1453* (New York, 1972), p. 376. Though the authenticity of Patriarch Joseph's testament has been challenged, both Gill and Nicol, leading authorities on this subject and period, accept it. The most common argument against its authenticity is its date of the 9th rather than the 10th when Patriarch Joseph died; but since we do not know exactly what time of day he died, nor whether he wrote this just a few moments before his death rather than, perhaps, after being stricken the night before, either date could be correct.
[32]Gill, *Council of Florence*, pp. 283-284, 293-296; Gill, *Eugenius IV*, p. 130; Von Pastor, *History of the Popes*, I, 320.
[33]See Chapter Seven, above.

cardinal present, Louis Aleman of France, distributed relics of saints collected
from the churches in Basel on the empty seats of the departed delegates, and
led the Council in a formal vote that the Pope may not dissolve, prorogue or
transfer an ecumenical council without its consent, and that denying that
proposition was heresy. Only 19 bishops remained in Basel to vote for this
measure, all from France, Germany or the kingdom of Naples in southern Italy.
On June 13 the Council declared that "for the future peace of Christendom it
had to be made manifest that the Pope was subject to correction by a general
council and that, unlike a prince in secular society, he should not dominate the
church." The final form of indictment of the Pope was presented by Thomas
Livingston, Abbot of Dundrennan in Scotland, and Archdeacon William Huyn
of Metz, both of whom openly expressed doubts about its "legal style and
soundness." On June 25, the day that final agreement was reached in Florence
on reunion with the Greeks, the Council of Basel declared Pope Eugenius IV
deposed for disobeying its claimed authority. About 300 members voted for the
deposition, but they included only seven consecrated bishops, together with
about 30 bishops-elect, some of whom undoubtedly saw little prospect of being
confirmed by Pope Eugenius IV so long as he remained in office.[34]

In September 1439 Pope Eugenius, in the bull *Moyses vir Dei*, set out a
tightly reasoned case against the entire conciliarist heresy as it had now
developed, and the arguments it attempted to draw from recent church history.
He referred back to the consistent teaching of the Church since the commission
to St. Peter, by which each Pope had "full power of feeding, ruling and
governing the Universal Church [which] was delivered by Our Lord Jesus
Christ, as is contained in the acts of the ecumenical councils and in the sacred
canons." He pointed to the small size and lack of prestige of the remnant at
Basel which claimed authority to govern the full Church. For the first time he
addressed explicitly the decree *Sacrosancta* (or *Haec sancta*) of the Council of
Constance, the real fountainhead of the doctrine of conciliar supremacy due to
the particular prestige of this council which had ended the Great Western
Schism. This decree, he pointed out, was issued when Cossa was in the process
of being deprived of the papal authority he claimed, while the schism still
existed and the papal office was effectively vacant.[35] The argument as stated
had merit, but it is astonishing to find even this highly intelligent Pope, generally
so effective a controversialist, unable or unwilling to see or say that the Church
had been virtually leaderless at this point in the history of the Council of
Constance primarily because the authority of the true Pope, Gregory XII, had
been almost universally rejected.

───────────────
[34]Stieber, *Council of Basel*, pp. 51, 54-56, 179-180, 182-183 (first quotation on 182,
second on 51); Gill, *Eugenius IV*, pp. 137-138; Gill, *Council of Florence*, pp. 310-311.
[35]Gill, *Eugenius IV*, pp. 138-141 (quotation on 139); Gill, *Council of Florence*, pp.
312-313; Stieber, *Council of Basel*, pp. 43-44.

Only one step remained after the pretended papal deposition, and the Council of Basel quickly proceeded to take it: the election of an Antipope, the last in the history of the Church. On November 5, 1439 it chose Duke Amadeus VIII of Savoy, a widower with four sons who had ostentatiously "retired from the world" to a rather busy hermitage in the country from which he was generally believed to be still in fact governing his duchy. Amadeus chose the papal name Felix V.[36]

Just a few days before, on October 27, had occurred the shockingly sudden death of Holy Roman Emperor Albert II, just 42 years old. He left no sons, but his wife was pregnant, and four months later she gave birth to a son, who was named Ladislas and usually known as Ladislas Postumus. However, there was no tradition of minorities in the elective office of Holy Roman Emperor, though a tradition of succession of adults in the same family did exist there. On February 2, 1440 the imperial electors chose another Habsburg, Frederick, Duke of Styria, a cousin of the late Albert II. Five of the seven electors were present and all five voted for Frederick.[37]

Historians have for the most part mocked and scorned Holy Roman Emperor Frederick III even more than Emperor Sigismund. Only 24 at his election, he was not a great or inspiring leader, and he lacked the impressive perseverance and buoyancy that characterized Sigismund. He was easily distracted and somewhat timid. But he was not a bad ruler or emperor, and throughout his life he remained—as was characteristic of most of the Habsburg family, then and later—a loyal Catholic. His steady support for Pope Eugenius IV did more than any other single factor outside the Pope's own resolution to bring him final victory over the schism of Basel. Frederick III first demonstrated his constancy in the second year of his reign, when in June 1441, after receiving an appeal from a papal envoy, he rejected the proposal for a new council to judge between the Council of Basel and the Pope which had been presented at the recent imperial Diet of Mainz by the Emperor's own representative, Thomas Ebendorfer. Ceremonially crowned at Charlemagne's capital of Aachen a year later, Frederick III rejected a proposed marriage alliance with the eldest daughter of the Antipope and appointed the papalist Kaspar Schlick his Chancellor.[38]

As mentioned earlier, almost all the remaining support for the schismatic Council of Basel came from France, Germany, and the kingdom of Naples in

---

[36]Von Pastor, *History of the Popes*, I, 328-329; Gill, *Eugenius IV*, p. 145. Though most historians refer to Duke Amadeus as "Felix" after he made his claim to be Pope, in keeping with previous practice for antipopes, this history will continue to use his ducal name Amadeus.

[37]Stieber, *Council of Basel*, pp. 121, 203-206; Bartos, *Hussite Revolution*, p. 153; Odlozilik, *Hussite King*, p. 25.

[38]Stieber, *Council of Basel*, pp. 209, 232-234, 239, 246, 260-261.

southern Italy. The delegates from Aragon, Castile and Milan had withdrawn in
protest before the final steps were taken to the attempted deposition of the
Pope, and England had firmly rejected this action and the proclamation of an
Antipope that followed.[39] In 1443, after Alfonso V of Aragon had secured firm
control of the kingdom of Naples the preceding year, Pope Eugenius IV
prudently recognized and accepted his new dominion, whereupon the
Archbishop of Palermo and another prelate from the southern kingdom
withdrew from the Council with the recommendation that it disband while it
could still do so with dignity.[40] But the clerics who had committed themselves to
the Council of Basel as a higher authority than the Pope had made an
enormous investment of pride in their defiance, and their future if the conciliar
claims were rejected was problematical at best. They fought on. But gradually
their ranks dwindled. The decisive loss, as was soon to become clear, was the
brilliant young Sienese priest and Renaissance scholar Aeneas Sylvius
Piccolomini, who had supported the Council from its inception until March
1445, when he came back to Rome and made his public submission to Pope
Eugenius IV:

> *Aeneas Sylvius*: "Many are the things that, while I was at Basel, I
> spoke and wrote and did against you. I deny nothing. And yet it was my
> intention less to hurt you than to defend God's church. For when I
> persecuted you I thought I was obeying God. I erred ... I stayed three
> years with the Emperor. There I listened to more and yet more disputes
> between the Basilians and your legates, until no doubt was left me but that
> the truth resides with you.... Now I stand before you, and because I
> sinned in my ignorance I implore you to forgive me."
> *Pope Eugenius IV*: "We, forgetful hereafter of past offenses, shall
> love you dearly while you walk aright."[41]

Aeneas Sylvius Piccolomini had set his foot upon the path that would end
in his living martyrdom, seeking as Pope Pius II, in a swamp of apathy and
broken promises, to mount a crusade to regain Constantinople from the infidel.

By the fall of 1445 Imperial Chancellor Kaspar Schlick was involved in
negotiations with Cardinal Juan de Carvajal for closer cooperation between his
master Frederick III and the Pope. In February 1446 the Pope promised
Frederick III imperial coronation in Rome, the supreme accolade for every
Holy Roman Emperor; and Frederick, who from time to time during the past
five years had wavered in his allegiance while never abandoning it, now

---

[39]Gill, *Council of Florence*, pp. 319-320.
[40]Alan Ryder, *Alfonso the Magnanimous; King of Aragon, Naples and Sicily, 1396-
1458* (Oxford, 1990), pp. 244-248, 250-251, 255-256; von Pastor, *History of the Popes*, I,
331-332; Gill, *Eugenius IV*, p. 150; Stieber, *Council of Basel*, pp. 196, 255-256.
[41]R. J. Mitchell, *The Laurels and the Tiara; Pope Pius II* (New York, 1963), pp. 87-
88.

declared firmly and permanently for Eugenius IV. There were still many difficulties to be surmounted and details to be worked out before the schism was ended. Aeneas Sylvius Piccolomini was at the Emperor's side throughout these critical months. He advised him to reject the demand of the imperial electors March 21 that the Pope accept the declarations of the supremacy of councils in the Church. At an assembly of bishops and princes of Germany at Frankfurt in September 1446, Aeneas persuaded two of the electors, the Archbishop of Mainz and the Margrave of Brandenburg (through his representative) to support the Pope, breaking the common front among the electors in support of the Council's pretensions of superior authority.[42]

Charles VII of France soon began to back down as well, proposing in November 1446 to recognize Pope Eugenius IV, "honorably retire" Antipope Amadeus, cancel the censures by both Pope and Council, and hold a new council when "peace had been restored."[43]

A proposal for final settlement of the schism, known as the Concordat of Frankfurt, was presented to the Pope in February 1447, shortly after he fell seriously ill. (Eugenius IV had now reached the age of 64, and had been Pope for sixteen tumultuous and exhausting years.) It was soon evident that his illness was mortal. But his mind remained not only clear, but shrewd and supple to the end. He accepted changes in procedure and practice in the German Church, which it called reforms and which the Council of Basel had endorsed, only temporarily, until a legate could examine them more closely. He accepted judicial decisions and granting of benefices by the schismatic German church since 1438, in return for avowal of obedience to the Pope by the representatives of all the great ecclesiastical and secular magnates of Germany. On the critical issue of conciliar supremacy, which most of the German leaders were still expecting him to acknowledge, he said only that he "venerated and embraced in the manner of his predecessors the decree *Frequens* and other decrees of the Council of Constance and of other general councils as well as their power, authority, and eminence." There was no mention of the Council of Basel, the decree *Sacrosancta*, or of conciliar supremacy in his statement, though the form of the concordat drafted at Frankfurt had spoken of conciliar "pre-eminence." Pope Eugenius IV gently dropped the "pre," thereby changing the whole meaning of the statement. His reference to endorsing conciliar decrees "in the manner of his predecessors" clearly harked back to Pope Martin V's very carefully qualified endorsement of the decrees of the Council of Constance.[44]

[42]Stieber, *Council of Basel*, pp. 274, 277-283, 285-286, 288-293; von Pastor, *History of the Popes*, I, 338-340, 346-347; Gill, *Eugenius IV*, pp. 162-163; Gill, *Council of Florence*, pp. 339, 341.
[43]Gill, *Council of Florence*, p. 340.
[44]*Ibid.*, p. 342; Stieber, *Council of Basel*, pp. 298-301 (quotation on 298); von Pastor,

Less than three weeks later the great "Pope of Christian union"[45] was dead, his task—one of the most difficult given to any Pope—accomplished. The schism was effectively dead. In August 1447 Emperor Frederick III commanded everyone in the Holy Roman Empire to recognize Eugenius IV's successor, Nicholas V, as true Pope, and nearly all the prelates and princes obeyed. In February 1448 the Concordat of Vienna confirmed the Pope's authority to approve or reject all bishops-elect and in special cases to appoint anyone he chose to the episcopal office, and reinstated annates, whose deprivation by the Council of Basel had begun the schismatic movement. In April 1449 Antipope Amadeus surrendered his claims and the Council (now moved to Lausanne) went through a charade of electing Nicholas V Pope and then dissolved itself, after a last unheeded plea for another council at Lyons in two years. The victory was complete; papal authority was not only undiminished, but actually strengthened by having survived so formidable a challenge.[46]

Pope Eugenius IV had promised at the Council of Florence his best efforts to arouse a crusade to help the Byzantine empire, now reunited with the Catholic Church. The troubles with the Council of Basel and resistance to the reunion in the East delayed the fulfillment of his promise, but he never forgot or abandoned it. Early in 1442 he proclaimed a crusading tithe and volunteered a fifth of the papal income for the crusade, and sent Cardinal Cesarini, now restored to his complete confidence, eastward to coordinate the preparations. At the beginning of 1443 he repeated the tithe levy and the gift of a fifth of the papal income. A crusading fleet was formed in May, and the following month a crusading army of nearly 40,000 set out from Buda in Hungary, crossing the Danube into Turkish territory early in September. The principal commander was John Hunyadi of Hungary, the greatest Christian general of his time; there were also young king Wladyslaw III of Poland (19), old King George Brankovich of Serbia (nearly 80), and the Count of Wallachia (present Rumania), the dread Vlad Dracul the Impaler, origin of the Dracula legend. None of this oddly assorted group had much trust in any of the others, but Cardinal Cesarini worked hard and successfully to maintain their cooperation, and they were united in passionate resentment of the infidel invader and determination to strike heavy blows against him, which they did.[47]

During the fall they took the important cities of Nish and Sofia in Turkish-

History of the Popes, I, 349-350; Gill, *Eugenius IV*, pp. 163-165.

[45]The subtitle of Gill's excellent biography of Pope Eugenius IV.

[46]Ludwig von Pastor, *The History of the Popes from the Close of the Middle Ages*, Volume II (St. Louis, 1949), pp. 36-37, 46; Stieber, *Council of Basel*, pp. 308-309, 312-313, 327-328.

[47]Von Pastor, *History of the Popes*, I, 325-326; Stieber, *Council of Basel*, p. 200; Gill, *Council of Florence*, pp. 328-339; Joseph Held, *Hunyadi; Legend and Reality* (New York, 1985), pp. 95-96.

occupied Serbia and Bulgaria, respectively. Turned aside from Thrace near the European Turkish capital of Adrianople by a battle in December, the army under Hunyadi's command then defeated the Turks in January 1444 near Mount Kunovica, capturing some of their officers and pursuing them for a long distance. In February the rigors of winter finally forced them to return to base. In April young King Wladyslaw III of Poland solemnly swore before the Hungarian Diet at Buda to continue the crusade; but when approached by an envoy of Ottoman Sultan Murad II that same month with a request to begin negotiations for a truce, he sent an emissary to hear them, along with another from Hunyadi and two from George Brankovich. Wladyslaw's and Hunyadi's emissaries were men of little rank and standing; Wladyslaw's was not even Polish, but an obscure Serb named Stojka Gisdanich, and Hunyadi's is identified only by the one otherwise unknown name of Vitislaus. These shadowy individuals signed a ten years' truce at Adrianople with the Ottoman Sultan, but contemporary evidence cleary shows that the truce had to be ratified by the Christian sovereigns involved before taking effect.[48]

The Italian humanist Cyriacus of Ancona, who had chanced to be in Adrianople during these negotiations, hurried on to Constantinople after they were over and from there wrote Hunyadi urging him to reject the truce because he had learned that the bulk of the Turkish army was going to Asia Minor, creating an excellent opportunity for the Christians to strike in their absence. Byzantine Emperor John VIII wrote to the same effect to Wladyslaw III. Cardinal Cesarini, when he heard of the proposed truce, strongly opposed it. George Brankovich of Serbia did ratify the truce and withdraw his troops from the crusading army, but there is no good contemporary evidence that either Hunyadi or Wladyslaw ever ratified it. Some later reports said they did, and many historians still accept those reports despite the trenchant arguments against their validity set forth by Polish historian Oscar Halecki in his book on the Crusade of Varna. The chronological evidence alone is decisive. On July 24 Wladyslaw III wrote the King of Bosnia that he was "setting out to destroy the Turks." On or about August 1 he arrived in Szeged, Hungary where he was later thought by some to have accepted the truce. But on August 4 he announced in Szeged that he was continuing the crusade. If he ratified the truce (and no contemporary document says that he did) then the ratification was in effect for so brief a time that the Turks could not even have heard of it before it was revoked.[49]

---

[48]Held, *Hunyadi*, pp. 96-98; John V. A. Fine Jr., *The Late Medieval Balkans* (Ann Arbor MI, 1987), pp. 548-549; von Pastor, *History of the Popes*, I, 326-327; Gill, *Council of Florence*, pp. 330-331; Oscar Halecki, *The Crusade of Varna* (New York, 1943), pp. 16-23.
[49]Halecki, *Crusade of Varna*, pp. 24-29, 36, 38-39, 44-46; Fine, *Late Medieval Balkans*, p. 549; Held, *Hunyadi*, pp. 103-105; Stieber, *Council of Basel*, pp. 200-202;

The issue is important because many historians, usually those with strong moral objections to crusading, have expatiated at length and vehemently on the perfidy of the Christians in breaking this imagined oath, and stated or implied that this brought disaster to the crusade by infuriating the Turks and embarrassing the crusaders.[50] The "crusade of Varna" was morally justified by any reasonable interpretation of the right of self-defense in the face of invasion, and there would have been no reason for Wladyslaw III and Hunyadi, whose countries were not immediately threatened by the invasion as was Serbia, to have ratified the treaty of Adrianople.

The main Turkish army did march to Asia Minor in July 1444, and the crusading army promptly advanced to the Black Sea coast of Turkish-ruled Bulgaria. Informed of this, the Ottoman ruler moved back quickly into Europe, brushing aside feeble opposition offered to his passage of the Bosporus by a small and inadequately supplied crusading fleet. Expected Byzantine and Albanian reinforcements were not able to reach the crusading army in time. On November 10 Sultan Murad II met the crusading army at Varna on the Black Sea with odds of three to one in his favor (they would have been substantially less had George Brankovich and his Serbs remained in the campaign). Nevertheless Hunyadi fought the first part of the battle magnificently from a strong defensive position, inflicting such losses on the Turks that only the steadiness of the janissaries held their army together and kept up the courage of the Sultan. But then 20-year-old Wladyslaw III let the impetuosity of youth get the better of him, and came charging with 500 horsemen into the center of the janissaries in an attempt to slay the Sultan. The king's horse went down and a janissary cut off his head and held it up on his lance for all to see. The Polish troops panicked and carried the Hungarians away in the rout. Hunyadi escaped but Cardinal Cesarini was killed, and the last of the medieval crusades ended in a bloody twilight that meant the end for thousand-year-old Constantinople. Nothing was left but honor for the ghost of the second Rome.[51]

In each of the next two years after Gil Eanes' epoch-making passage around Cape Bojador, ships of Prince Henry the Navigator pushed southward

---

Gill, *Council of Florence*, pp. 331-332.

[50]Fine, *Late Medieval Balkans*, p. 549, uses *ad hominem* argumentation in a particularly objectionable form when he notes that most of the scholars who have denied that Wladyslaw ratified the treaty have been Poles whose "motive seems to have been to make the Polish king look better by denying that he broke his oath." One might reply that the motive of anti-crusade historians in declaring that an oath was broken "seems to have been" to make the crusaders look bad; but asserting motives of alleged bias is far less convincing than arguing on the chronological facts and the documentary evidence.

[51]Held, *Hunyadi*, pp. 108-112; Halecki, *Crusade of Varna*, pp. 29-30, 63-64; Nicol, *Last Centuries of Byzantium*, pp. 380-381; Gill, *Council of Florence*, pp. 331-333.

along the incredibly desolate Sahara desert coast. In 1435 Eanes and Afonso Baldaia found footprints of men and camels in the sands; in 1436, at the misnamed Rio d'Ouro ("River of Gold"—which is not a river and has no gold) they saw a few men at a distance, but could not make any contact with them.[52] The Rio d'Ouro is a shallow bay of considerable length, the first such formation the Portuguese had seen on the African coast beyond Cape Bojador, so they hopefully assumed it was a river, somehow connected with the legendary gold-bearing Niger. Then in 1437, a Portuguese military enterprise against the Moors of Morocco which came terribly to grief diverted all attention, even—or especially—that of Prince Henry, from his great mission of exploration and discovery.

The goal of the Portuguese attack was to capture and hold Tangier, the one other good port and substantial city in the northern extremity of Morocco fronting the Straits of Gibraltar besides Ceuta, which the Portuguese had captured twenty-two years before and firmly held ever since. The great King John I of Portugal had died in 1433; his son Duarte, elder brother of Prince Henry the Navigator, now wore the crown. Duarte had never forgotten the glory of the expedition against Ceuta, and now that he was king his great ambition was to repeat it against Tangier. But Duarte, though a good and just ruler of high moral character, was no general; he does not seem to have grasped the difference between defending Ceuta on its long narrow peninsula and defending Tangier with nothing but open land behind it. His brother Pedro warned him of the danger, but he would not listen. His Aragonese queen Leonor favored the expedition, but she knew even less of generalship than Duarte. Henry advocated it outspokenly, which is hardest of all to understand, since one would expect Henry above all to understand the importance of geography. But Henry was a crusader as much as he was an explorer, and at the moment his explorations down the parched and uninhabited Sahara coast were advancing nothing but geographical knowledge. He wanted more action against the immemorial foe.[53]

The result was disaster, militarily and personally for the Portuguese royal family. Ten thousand Portuguese landed before Tangier under the command of Henry and his youngest brother Fernando, and laid siege to the city. The resolute Moorish garrison commander, Sala ben Sala, held out strongly, and soon a large relieving army arrived. Caught between two fires, the Portuguese were surrounded. They were only allowed to depart after signing a treaty pledging to return Ceuta (an entirely Portuguese town ever since its capture in

---

[52]Bailey W. Diffie and George D. Winius, *Foundations of the Portuguese Empire, 1415-1580* (Minneapolis MN, 1977), p. 69; Elaine Sanceau, *Henry the Navigator* (New York, 1947), pp. 114-115; Edgar Prestage, *The Portuguese Pioneers* (London, 1933), pp. 57-58.
[53]Sanceau, *Henry the Navigator*, pp. 127-137.

1415) to the Moors and not to attack any part of Morocco again for a hundred years, and delivering Prince Fernando as a hostage for the fulfillment of these terms. Even then, a substantial number of the Moors disagreed with the terms and harassed the retreating Portuguese, killing many. This could reasonably be taken as rendering the treaty no longer binding, and King Duarte decided he should not hand Ceuta back to the Moors. But nothing could help Prince Fernando, who wasted away for six years in a foul dungeon at Fez and died there in chains in 1443, faithful to the end, a heroic and beloved legend to his countrymen, "the constant prince."[54]

The sons of King John I and the holy English Queen Philippa had always been exceptionally close; King Duarte was devastated by this tragedy. He died, probably partly from its effects, in 1438 at the age of only 47, to be succeeded by his six-year-old son Afonso. Duarte's brother Pedro and Afonso's mother Leonor disputed the regency. Henry, a far stronger spirit than Duarte, returned to his mission of discovery, bearing a heavy cross. But it was not until three years after the Tangier disaster, in 1440, that ships began sailing once again down the unexplored coast of Africa.[55]

Meanwhile, in 1439 Prince Pedro, as regent of the kingdom, granted Henry the Navigator the right to colonize the seven islands of the mid-Atlantic Azores chain which had been discovered some time during the preceding ten to fifteen years, a remarkable achievement in navigation since the nearest of them was 745 miles from the Portuguese mainland and no voyage had yet been made into the open ocean so far from any known coast.[56]

In 1441 a Portuguese expedition of two ships captured ten natives on the shore of the bay called Rio d'Ouro, one of them a chieftain named Adahu who had travelled widely in the Sahara and could speak Arabic. One of the ships brought him immediately back to Portugal to give Prince Henry information about the country through readily available Arabic interpreters. The other ship pressed on to the south. Her captain was Nuno Tristao, a knight of Prince Henry's household, with orders—repeated to bold captains again and again during the twenty years that remained of Henry the Navigator's life—to sail to the farthest point reached by their predecessors, and then press on farther still.[57]

Nuno Tristao's ship was a caravel—a new design introduced by Prince Henry, built primarily for the purpose of oceanic exploration. Caravels were

[54]*Ibid.*, pp. 139-160, 174-178; Prestage, *Portuguese Pioneers*, pp. 59-61; Diffie and Winius, *Foundations of the Portuguese Empire*, pp. 71-72.
[55]Sanceau, *Henry the Navigator*, pp. 161-174, 179-180; Diffie and Winius, *Foundations of the Portuguese Empire*, pp. 72-73, 77.
[56]Diffie and Winius, *Foundations of the Portuguese Empire*, pp. 60-62; Sanceau, *Henry the Navigator*, pp. 109-112.
[57]Sanceau, *Henry the Navigator*, pp. 181-185; Diffie and Winius, *Foundations of the Portuguese Empire*, p. 77.

remarkably seaworthy, with big triangular "lateen" sails that moved them fast before the wind and could even go against the wind, a rare and difficult feat for sailing ships in those days. Caravels were of shallow draft and therefore less likely than other oceangoing ships to run aground. They were small and handy, manageable by a crew of only twenty, or less in an emergency—very important in long voyages for which most of the food and water for the crew had to be carried from the home port.[58] When Christopher Columbus set out across the Atlantic in 1492, he had two caravels, *Pinta* and *Niña*, and one larger ship, *Santa Maria*. Only the two caravels came back, through the stormiest winter the North Atlantic had seen in decades.

In his caravel, Nuno Tristao sailed down the stark barren coast south of Rio d'Ouro for a hundred almost featureless miles until he reached its next striking geographic feature, a long narrow cape he named Branco (White), because there was upon it "no sign of grass nor of any vegetation whatsoever,"[59] nothing but white sand, and no trace of humanity.

But Prince Henry remained undaunted, and he had probably learned from the captured chief Adahu that there were habitable areas inland despite the utter desolation of the coast, and more people to the southward. No further advance was made during 1442, but in 1443 Nuno Tristao sailed again under orders to go to White Cape and press on beyond. He reached Arguim Bay, fifty miles south of Cape Branco. The bay held an island on which human habitation was possible, and Nuno Tristao encountered there about 25 dugouts of the most primitive type, which the natives rowed with their legs. He captured 29 of them and sent them back to Portugal.[60]

The initial justification of these captures had been the refusal of the natives to communicate in any way with the explorers; Henry was determined to get information about these new lands. But at Rio d'Ouro in 1442 the Muslim chiefs had ransomed their captives taken the previous year with black slaves from further south, who were then brought to Portugal and sold. Nuno Tristao's 29 captives of 1443 were treated in the same manner, even though they had not previously been slaves. Suddenly the desolate coast was yielding a source of profit, and for several years after 1443 many of the Portuguese ships sailing to the newly discovered African coast went primarily in search of slaves.[61]

There is no record that anyone in Portugal challenged the morality of

---

[58]Sanceau, *Henry the Navigator*, pp. 180-181; Diffie and Winius, *Foundations of the Portuguese Empire*, p. 77.

[59]Prestage, *Portuguese Pioneers*, p. 99.

[60]Diffie and Winius, *Foundations of the Portuguese Empire*, p. 79; Gomes Eanes de Zurara, "The Chronicle of the Discovery and Conquest of Guinea," *Hakluyt Society Publications* No. 95 (London, 1896), p. 59.

[61]Diffie and Winius, *Foundations of the Portuguese Empire*, pp. 78-81; Sanceau, *Henry the Navigator*, pp. 187-189.

enslaving the Africans. Southern Europe had no experience in dealing with uncivilized peoples, and had been familiarized with slavery (though only a few slaves were held there) by its widespread use among the Muslims. After the heartrending scenes of their capture and separation from one another on arriving in Portugal, the men and women from Africa were usually well treated, and many were freed. All but the committed Muslims among them accepted Christianity and many practiced it. A considerable number married Portuguese; this Catholic people has always been noted for relative rarity of racial prejudice based on color alone. But all this is at best palliation of the evil, for evil it indubitably remained; and Henry the Navigator, for all his virtues, watched it done before his eyes, as families of the black prisoners were separated in the port city of Lagos in 1444.[62] Cultural relativism cannot excuse him; Spain's great and holy Queen Isabel, his own grand-niece, struck off the chains of enslaved Indians when Columbus brought them to her ports before the end of the century, saying: "Who authorized my admiral to treat my subjects in this manner?"[63]

In October 1443 a decree of his brother Pedro, regent for the boy-king Afonso V, granted Henry the Navigator sole right to send ships south of Cape Bojador, with one-fifth of all profits obtained from Africa to come to him. The decree also gave him title to the rocky promontory of Sagres, at the very southwestern tip of Portugal, surrounded on three sides by the open Atlantic, pointing in the direction of his explorations, near the harbor of Lagos from which his African expeditions sailed and to which they returned. Henry made Sagres his residence. Maps of his discoveries were prepared there, and there are persistent stories of research and development of navigational and shipbuilding techniques at Sagres, though they cannot be confirmed by contemporary documentation. A school of navigation, at least, probably was conducted there.[64]

In 1444 a record number of Portuguese ships sailed south along the African coast. The majority came for slaves, but the black men were already fighting back effectively; they killed a famous Portuguese captain named Gonçalo de Sintra with six of his companions on a slaving raid. Some of these slave-catchers reached and raided the island of Tidra fifty miles south of Arguim island, whose inhabitants had now fled into the interior. Nuno Tristao made his third African voyage in 1444 and once again went farther than any of his predecessors, though unfortunately we do not know just how far. After him came Dinis Dias, sailing in a single caravel purely for exploration rather than to

---

[62]Diffie and Winius, *Foundations of the Portuguese Empire*, pp. 80-82; Sanceau, *Henry the Navigator*, pp. 188-191.
[63]See Chapter Fifteen, below.
[64]Diffie and Winius, *Foundations of the Portuguese Empire*, pp. 78, 80; Prestage, *Portuguese Pioneers*, p. 164; Sanceau, *Henry the Navigator*, pp. 107-108, 185.

seize and transport slaves, vowing "to do more with it [the caravel] than any had done before." He did just that. In the most important voyage since Gil Eanes rounded Cape Bojador, Dinis Dias passed beyond the vast desert. Two hundred and fifty miles south of Tidra Island he reached the mouth of the Senegal River, described by the voyager Cadamosto a few years later as a mile wide at its mouth and deep, with two entrances, and the tide flowing more than sixty miles upriver, surrounded by a large population in a green and fertile land. Nor did Dinis Dias stop there. He sailed on another hundred miles, to the great forested cape terminating in twin hills that is the westernmost point of the African continent. He named it Cape Verde for the glowing green of its color, in such striking contrast to the desert coast between Cape Bojador and the Senegal. This new land was called Guinea—or by some name which sounded like that to Portuguese ears—by its people.[65]

Most of the Portuguese voyages to Africa in 1445 were primarily for the purpose of collecting slaves, but one caravel, commanded by Alvaro Fernandes and owned by his uncle Joao Gonçalves Zarco of the island of Madeira, rounded Cape Verde and sailed south to what Fernandes named Cape of the Masts because of its tall palm trees whose bushy tops had been torn off by some mighty storm. This cape cannot now be precisely located. The next year Fernandes returned and sailed even farther, but again we do not know how far, because the chronicler Eanes de Zurara's reports of distance traversed by the exploring ships are inconsistent and usually much exaggerated, and he gives no other clue. It is likely that Fernandes reached the Gambia, the broad river that becomes a 27-mile-wide estuary where it enters the sea, about a hundred miles south of Cape Verde. He may well have passed the Gambia and gone even further south.[66]

Somewhere in this region of jungle rivers, in 1445 or 1446, the bold explorer Nuno Tristao met his doom. His caravel carried 22 men and five boys. Sailing up a narrowing stream, he put the men into two small boats. Suddenly they were showered with arrows from twelve native canoes. The arrows were tipped with a deadly poison, not previously encountered by the Portuguese. Every man was wounded. Weakening and pain-wracked, they rowed back to their ship. Four died before they could reach it. When they had struggled into the caravel they no longer had the strength to raise the anchor. They cut the cable and put to sea. Soon every man was helpless from the poison; Nuno Tristao and all but two of the other men died, and those two took weeks to

---

[65]Diffie and Winius, *Foundations of the Portuguese Empire*, pp. 80-83; Prestage, *Portuguese Pioneers*, pp. 69-78, 101-102, 115; Sanceau, *Henry the Navigator*, pp. 192-199.
[66]Diffie and Winius, *Foundations of the Portuguese Empire*, pp. 83, 86-87; Prestage, *Portuguese Pioneers*, pp. 86, 88; Sanceau, *Henry the Navigator*, pp. 201-203, 208. Even the best sources are singularly unhelpful on the geography of the voyages beyond Cape Verde in 1445 and 1446.

recover. The caravel was left in the hands of the five teen-aged boys, none of whom had ever handled a ship. They prayed fervently for help. One of them, Aires Tinoco, had been brought up in Henry the Navigator's household and taught there to read and write. He had not been taught seamanship and navigation, but was a keen observer and had picked up some essential knowledge of both on the outward voyage. Probably the two surviving seamen were able to help him by verbal instructions. The little caravel was so well designed that the five boys could actually sail her with no other help, and Aires Tinoco knew that his course should be north to Cape Verde and then north-northeast to Portugal. He dared not risk shipwreck by staying close to land, for shipwreck meant certain death for all aboard; and there was not yet any permanent Portuguese outpost on the Atlantic coast of Africa. After two months in the open sea the boys reached Portugal, to be greeted with high honor by Prince Henry, coupled with regret for his brave captain Nuno Tristao. History cheats us by telling us nothing more of the life and career of Aires Tinoco.[67]

Such was the price paid and the heroism shown in the epochal advance down the African coast. The slave raiding darkened the great enterprise but did not eclipse it. Prince Henry the Navigator insisted, year after year, on sailing farther . . . ever farther. The fame of his discoveries and his undertaking was spreading through Christendom—for whose glory it was intended. Foreign seamen began coming to share in it. Perhaps fortunately, no one—not even Prince Henry—knew or could really imagine how immensely long was the course still before them. In the twelve years since Gil Eanes rounded Cape Bojador they had come a thousand miles. But to go all the way around Africa and reach India, they had nine thousand miles more to sail.

It required the resurgent French twenty-two years after the martyrdom of St. Joan the Maid to attain final victory over the invading English in the Hundred Years War, but there was never much doubt about the outcome once the peasant girl from Domremy had done her work. The two decisive developments after Joan's execution were the Peace of Arras between Charles VII of France and Duke Philip of Burgundy in 1435 and the French capture of Paris the following year. Burgundian troops, by their presence or absence, had been essential to the English victories; none appeared to help their French liege lord at Agincourt, and Burgundians had captured Saint Joan. An able administrator, Duke Richard of York, and an excellent field general, Lord John Talbot, made no difference in the result; the Duke of York after several years gave up France and went to Ireland, and Talbot, whom Joan the Maid had

[67]Gomes Eanes de Zurara, "Chronicle of the Discovery and Conquest of Guinea," *Hakluyt Society Publications* No. 95, pp. 252-257; Sanceau, *Henry the Navigator*, pp. 206-208.

beaten at Patay, finally lost his life in the last battle of the war, at Castillon in Gascony, by which the most tenaciously English-held of the provinces of France was finally restored to its ancient allegiance.[68]

The step by step fighting retreat across Normandy, original seat of their conquering kings, was very painful for the English, particularly since it was now obvious that Henry VI, whose twentieth birthday fell in 1441, was wholly unfit to rule a nation: timid and irresolute to the last degree, shy and pliable, a man born to be the tool of other men—or women. His wife Marguerite, daughter of Duke René of Anjou in France, soon became the real ruler after their marriage in 1445, and was certainly not inclined to press for more aggressive military action in France even if it had been possible. England looked for scapegoats. In July 1450, three months after the final defeat of the last English field army in Normandy, an adventurer calling himself "Jack Cade" seized London for four days, re-enacting the Wat Tyler revolt of seventy years before and killing the Lord Treasurer. In 1453, after the ultimate disaster at Castillon in Gascony, Henry VI went quietly insane. Characteristically, he did not rave and hew about with his sword like his grandfather Charles VI of France in his fits of madness, but fell into a catatonic stupor in which he neither spoke nor heard. His wife Marguerite was pregnant; two months after the onset of his malady she gave birth to a son, whom she named Edward. A council met to provide for the government of the realm during the king's incapacity; Queen Marguerite claimed the regency, but in March 1454 the council awarded it to the Duke of York.[69]

Following the death of Pope Eugenius IV a few days after signing the Concordat of Frankfurt that effectively brought the schism of Basel to an end, a conclave of eighteen cardinals assembled in Rome. The majority were Italian again, and all but two had been appointed by Eugenius during his long pontificate. The ancient rivalry between the Colonna and Orsini families flared again after the first ballot, in which Cardinal Prospero Colonna received ten votes, just two short of the required two-thirds majority. When Prospero Colonna failed to gain that majority, Cardinal Tommaso Parentucelli, noted for

---

[68]E. F. Jacob, *The Fifteenth Century, 1399-1485* (Oxford History of England) (Oxford, 1961), pp. 262-263, 465, 505-506; Richard Vaughan, *Philip the Good; the Apogee of Burgundy* (London, 1970), pp. 84, 99-101, 113; M. G. A. Vale, *Charles VII* [of France] (Berkeley CA, 1974), p. 59; Alfred H. Burne, *The Agincourt War* (Fair Lawn NJ, 1956), pp. 278, 283-284, 288-289, 294-302, 332-342; P. A. Johnson, *Duke Richard of York, 1411-1460* (Oxford, 1988), pp. 28-50, 68-77; A. J. Pollard, *John Talbot and the War in France, 1427-1453* (London, 1983), pp. 1-5, 26-67, 131-139.

[69]Ralph A. Griffiths, *The Reign of Henry VI; the Exercise of Royal Authority, 1422-1461* (Berkeley CA, 1981), pp. 248-261, 274-290, 610-649, 715-726; Jacobs, *Fifteenth Century*, pp. 491, 503, 508-509; Burne, *Agincourt War*, pp. 314-324; Johnson, *Duke Richard of York*, pp. 122, 128-134.

his interest in and support of the cultural Renaissance, was elected on the third ballot with twelve votes. He took the name of Nicholas V.[70]

The new Pope moved quickly to reassure Holy Roman Emperor Frederick III and Alfonso V of Aragon and Naples that he would maintain the agreements Pope Eugenius IV had made with them, and during the course of 1447 saw with gratification those agreements fully carried out, with the German princes and bishops and even (reluctantly) the universities restoring their allegiance to the Pope, along with Charles VII of France.[71] In 1450 Nicholas V used the mid-century jubilee year, with pilgrims coming to Rome from all over Europe, as an occasion for celebrating of the reunion of the Church. The additional income from the pilgrims was used to restore Church buildings in Rome and to greatly enlarge the Vatican library. On May 24, at the height of the pilgrimage season, the great popular preacher Bernardine of Siena, who had died just six years before, was canonized in St. Peter's. Already his example of preaching was being strikingly followed by the Franciscan friar John of Capistrano, a leader in the stricter Observant branch of the Franciscans who had separated from the Conventuals in 1446 with the permission of Pope Eugenius IV.[72]

As Cardinal Parentucelli, Pope Nicholas V had been well known as a patron of Renaissance art and humanistic studies, and as Pope he was in a unique position to extend that patronage and through it greatly to facilitate their development. He brought the exquisite religious painter Fra Angelico from Florence to Rome and established the Vatican library as a major institution possessing 807 Latin manuscripts at his death, a very large collection for that time.[73] He also encouraged the bringing of classical Greek manuscripts from Constantinople to Italy, and many were secured just in time before the fall of Constantinople in 1453.

The collection of manuscripts for the Vatican library highlighted one of the great scholarly passions of the age: finding ancient manuscripts, especially those believed lost, which would illuminate the knowledge and culture of the classical ages of Greece and Rome. Though many important classical works, such as the philosophical books of Plato and Aristotle, had long been known in Christendom and available in many copies, in the thousand years since the fall of the Western Roman Empire the losses had been very great. Since every manuscript had to be laboriously copied by hand, and manuscripts often did not

---

[70]Von Pastor, *History of the Popes*, II, 6-7, 10-13, 21-25.

[71]*Ibid.*, II, 30-31, 37-39; Stieber, *Council of Basel*, pp. 84, 303, 308-321, 324-325.

[72]Von Pastor, *History of the Popes*, II, 76-77, 80-82, 102-104; Gill, *Eugenius IV*, p. 108; John Hofer, *St. John Capistran, Reformer* (St. Louis, 1943), pp. 136-154 and *passim*; Iris Origo, *The World of San Bernardino* (New York, 1962).

[73]Von Pastor, *History of the Popes*, I, 186-189; II, 212-213, 335-336; Christopher Hibbert, *The House of Medici: its Rise and Fall* (New York, 1974), p. 94.

receive the care and protection needed to survive for centuries even if written on relatively durable materials such as parchment, many important works survived only in a few copies or even a single copy, and in fragments.

Italian Renaissance scholars—especially Poggio Bracciolini, a long-time papal secretary—pursued these rare manuscripts with diligence and enthusiasm, finding many which had been thought irretrievably lost, copying them repeatedly, and later in the fifteenth century taking advantage of Gutenberg's invention to begin printing the most important of them. One notable manuscript discovery during Nicholas V's pontificate was three shorter works of the great second century Roman historian Tacitus: *Germanica*, *Agricola*, and the *Dialogue*. The first six books of his *Annals* appeared in 1508, preserved in a single manuscript; no other copy has ever been found. There were untiring efforts, not only in Italy but throughout Europe, to locate the "lost decades of Livy." This Roman historian, writing in the reign of Caesar Augustus at the beginning of the Christian era, produced the longest history composed during classical times, in 146 books, usually kept in sets of ten ("decades"). Only the first, third and fourth decades of Livy were known in the mid-fifteenth century. Despite the diligent searching, most of Livy remained a casualty of the pre-printing age; the task of copying so many books had been so formidable that not enough had been copied to preserve most of them through the Middle Ages. Only five more complete books of Livy were ever found—the first half of the fifth decade. They were located in the German abbey of Lorsch, and not until 1527. The book-hunting scholars were much more successful with Cicero, hundreds of whose letters and orations were found.[74]

These discoveries were of great significance in preserving and enhancing the intellectual heritage of the West, for all humanity is deprived by the total loss of a great book, and it is a loss that can never be made good. Not all our modern archeological excavations and scientific techniques for restoring ancient manuscripts have come close to matching the volume and value of the manuscripts discovered and preserved by the Italian scholars of the fifteenth century, with the particular encouragement of Pope Nicholas V.

The first six years of the pontificate of Nicholas V were thus full of satisfaction and heady optimism, for the Pope himself and for Christendom. But such conditions never last long in a fallen world. In February 1451 Murad II, Sultan of the Ottoman Turks, died suddenly of a stroke at the age of 47, leaving his 19-year-old son Muhammad (Mehmet in its Turkish form) II as his successor. Murad II had been a cautious campaigner, though he had added substantially to the Ottoman domain in eastern Europe; his vigorous, brilliant, cold and cruel son aimed from the first at total victory and supremacy. His first

---

[74]Leo Deuel, *Testaments of Time; the Search for Lost Manuscripts and Records* (New York, 1965), pp. 29-51.

step was characteristic. He was only the son of a slave-girl in Murad II's harem; his father's principal wife had a baby son, and Muhammad had him drowned in his bath. He then officially proclaimed himself Sultan at Adrianople. The next year, with a deliberate resolve and careful preparation belying his mere twenty years, Muhammad II undertook the enterprise that his fellow Muslims had attempted so many times in their long history without success: the conquest of Constantinople.[75]

He began by building a strong fortress at the narrowest point of the Bosporus, to cut Constantinople off from the Black Sea. The work was completed in just four months. Meanwhile in June he beheaded the last envoys from the new Byzantine Emperor Constantine XI (brother of John VIII who had been at the Council of Florence and died without issue four years before) and declared war.[76]

The day after the fortress on the Bosporus was completed, Muhammad II personally reconnoitred the far-famed walls and defenses of Constantinople. The imperial city was built on a broad peninsula, created by the Sea of Marmara on the south, the Bosporus on the east, and the inlet called the Golden Horn on the north. The land approach from the west was blocked by a gigantic double wall, largest in the medieval Christian world, faced by a moat and breastwork, the outer wall 25 feet high and 10 feet thick, the inner wall 40 feet high and 20 feet thick, with 60-foot octagonal watchtowers at frequent intervals. The original wall had been built almost exactly a thousand years before and had been kept in excellent repair. None of the many sieges of the great city had ever breached it. The narrow Golden Horn was barred at its entrance by a huge chain. The waterfront on the north, east and south of the city was protected by walls, much smaller than the great wall on the land side but sufficient against all but overwhelming numerical odds and the best shiphandling. The Turks were not known as seamen, and although Muhammad II had built a fleet large enough to command the sea approaches to Constantinople with the aid of his new fortress, he never intended to make his major attack against the city from the sea. He proposed to break through the giant land wall by the use of gunpowder.[77]

Muhammad II inherited a collection of powerful artillery from his father's wars, but knew he needed more and bigger to attack the world's most famous

---

[75]Lord Kinross, *The Ottoman Centuries; the Rise and Fall of the Turkish Empire* (New York, 1977), pp. 87-90, 95, 98; Nicol, *Last Centuries of Byzantium*, pp. 392-393, 395-397; Steven Runciman, *The Fall of Constantinople, 1453* (Cambridge, England, 1965), pp. 55-59.

[76]Runciman, *Fall of Constantinople*, pp. 65-66; von Pastor, *History of the Popes*, II, 253.

[77]Runciman, *Fall of Constantinople*, pp. 73-77, 87-92; von Pastor, *History of the Popes*, II, 254. The immense ruined land wall of Constantinople can still awe the visitor today even after five hundred years of abandonment.

fortress. In the summer of 1452 a Hungarian engineer named Urban came to Constantinople and offered his services to the enemy of Christendom. Muhammad II had him brought into his personal presence. Urban told him he could cast a cannon "that would blast the wall of Babylon itself." Muhammad paid him well and told him to proceed. Three months later Urban delivered his cannon; Muhammad immediately sent him back to build one twice as large. It was completed in January 1453 and bears comparison with the heavy ordnance of the twentieth century, though it fired solid shot since the shell had not yet been invented. It was 27 feet long and eight inches across the muzzle and hurled a colossal ball weighing 1,200 pounds a full mile. Sixty oxen and 700 men were required to move it. No stone wall man ever made or imagined could stand against this thundering titan. The age of walled cities had ended.[78]

Constantinople had almost nothing left to defend itself but its walls. At the end of March 1453, with a Turkish army of at least 80,000 approaching, Constantine XI directed his secretary Phrantzes to make a census of all the men in the city, including monks, capable of bearing arms. Phrantzes carried out his assignment thoroughly and meticulously. The total number of Greeks able to bear arms, he reported, was only 4,983. There were also about 2,000 foreigners, including 700 well-armed soldiers who had arrived at the end of January under a famous Genoese commander named Giovanni Giustiniani. There was supposed to be a Venetian fleet with 800 soldiers coming to the assistance of Constantinople, but it did not set out until after the siege began in April, and never arrived. Numerically, therefore, the odds in favor of the Turks were more than eleven to one; and the wall's prospects against Urban's monster cannon were precisely zero.[79]

Without massive reinforcements there was no hope for the ancient city of Constantine. To Christendom's eternal shame no reinforcements ever came, except for three ships from the Pope;[80] nor were more than a trickle sent. The few Latins aware in advance of the Ottoman threat minimized it. After all, the Muslims had failed so often before to take Constantinople.

On April 6 Muhammad II made his formal demand for the surrender of Constantinople. It was firmly refused. On April 11 the bombardment began, concentrating on the weakest point in the land wall, where a small but vigorous stream called the Lycus flowed under it. Urban's cannon could be fired only seven times a day, so long did it take to load the enormous ball and the huge

[78]Runciman, *Fall of Constantinople*, pp. 77-78.
[79]*Ibid.*, pp. 81-85.
[80]*Ibid.*, pp. 100-104. Thanks to the extraordinary naval skills of their Genoese captains and crews, these three ships broke through the Turkish naval blockade and entered the Golden Horn April 20, after the siege and the bombardment of Constantinople had already begun. Muhammad II was so furious that he ordered his chief admiral beheaded, and though he was finally persuaded to let him live, he had him publicly whipped and dismissed from his service forever.

quantities of gunpowder needed to fire it; but each 1,200-pound shock upon the wall did great damage, which was spread by other, smaller but faster-firing guns. On April 21 a tower fell at the Lycus span and the first breach opened in the outer wall, but it was repaired. The next day about 70 Turkish ships were drawn overland from the Bosporus to the Golden Horn and launched in the inlet above the chain boom, but the boom was held and kept the two parts of the Turkish fleet separated. The Turks tried mining, but a Scottish military engineer named John Grant supervised the digging of successful countermines. On May 18 the Turks brought up a huge wheeled wooden tower to try to protect their men filling in the moat before the outer wall, but the defenders succeeded in blowing it up.[81]

On May 26 the Ottoman chief minister Halil Pasha urged Muhammad II to abandon the siege, fearing that a large Venetian fleet would soon come to the rescue of Constantinople (as it could and should have); but Zaganos Pasha, a general who had been second minister under Murad II, declared correctly that the Western powers were too divided among themselves to cooperate in any such enterprise, and asked his sovereign what Alexander the Great—much admired by the Muslims, who had entered their folklore as "Iskander"—would have done. Muhammad talked with his troops, especially the redoubtable janissaries, and most of them called for an immediate assault.[82]

On May 27, a Sunday, Urban's cannon was brought up to hammer the weakened outer wall in the Lycus valley at point-blank range, and blasted a large breach in it. Muhammad II told his soldiers that the grand assault would come soon, and that they would have three days to sack the city without hindrance if they took it. The next day, Monday, the guns fell silent as the besiegers prepared for the assault. Muhammad II rode the whole length of the walls, haranguing his men and conferring with his officers, assuring them that he would lead the attack on the breach in person. Constantine XI had icons and relics from Constantinople's churches brought out and carried round the walls and through the city in procession, with Greeks and Latins singing the *Kyrie Eleison* together. He spoke to his soldiers, saying that a man should always be ready to die for his faith, or his country, or his sovereign, or his home, and that when the assault came on the morrow they would be fighting to the death for all four. The Church of the Holy Wisdom, Hagia Sophia, erected originally by Emperor Justinian nine hundred years before, the largest church in Christendom (for the modern St. Peter's was not yet built), was filled with worshippers, the bitter disputes over the reunion of Florence forgotten. Cardinal Isidore of Kiev was there, and all Greek bishops in the city. Constantine XI received his last holy communion at the altar, then rode away to

---

[81]*Ibid.*, pp. 94-98, 104-106, 112, 118-120; Nicol, *Last Centuries of Byzantium*, pp. 402-405; von Pastor, *History of the Popes*, II, 264-265.

[82]Runciman, *Fall of Constantinople*, pp. 124-126.

say farewell to his family.[83]

The grand assault on Constantinople began at one-thirty in the morning of Tuesday, May 29, 1453, supported by Urban's giant cannon erupting out of the night through fire and smoke. At five o'clock in the morning one of its 1,200-pound balls shattered the makeshift defenses that had been erected behind the breach. But Emperor Constantine was there, sword in hand, to lead his men in driving the Turkish attackers back. Then Muhammad II led the janissaries forward. In the early light of dawn they grappled for an hour in the breach, fighting hand-to-hand with the Christian defenders. At this critical moment two events disastrous for the Christians occurred. A small group of about fifty Turks found a postern gate near the breach called the Kerkoporta that had not been adequately secured after an earlier sortie, opened it, ran through, climbed the nearest tower, and unfurled from its top the dreaded blood-red Turkish banner with its silver crescent and star. And Giovanni Giustiniani, the Genoese commander, was mortally wounded by a small cannon-ball and had himself immediately carried away from the wall, through the city, and out to one of the Genoese ships in the Golden Horn. Seeing their leader carried off, most of his men broke and fled; seeing the Turkish flag on the tower near the Kerkoporta, many of the Greek defenders did the same.[84]

The penetration of the Kerkoporta gate had occurred a few minutes before Giustiniani fell, and Emperor Constantine had ridden to it immediately to try to repel the small penetrating force. But not enough of his frightened soldiers would follow him, and more Turks, with their Sultan outside bellowing "The city is ours!" were swarming through the little gate. Constantine rode back to find panic developing at the breach as well. He had just three men with him: his friend the roving Spaniard Francisco de Toledo, whose forebears had been fighting the followers of Muhammad the prophet for seven hundred years; his cousin Theophilus; and a soldier named John Dalmata. The Emperor wore, as he had worn throughout the battle, his cloak of imperial purple, the last visible symbolic link of his empire with ancient Rome, for the Emperor's cloak had always been dyed royal purple since Caesar Augustus nearly 1,500 years ago. He saw, with a clear and steady vision, that the battle was lost, and the siege, and the city, and the empire—a whole world slipping into darkness and the deep. Few rulers have ever faced so cosmic a disaster. A Constantine, son of Helena, had built this city more than a thousand years ago; another Constantine, son of another Helena, had now lost it forever.[85]

Constantine XI, last of the Roman Emperors, tore the purple cloak from his back and raised his sword to catch the morning sun upon its blade. With

[83]*Ibid.*, pp. 126-132; Nicol, *Last Centuries of Byzantium*, pp. 406-407.
[84]Runciman, *Fall of Constantinople*, pp. 133-138; Nicol, *Last Centuries of Byzantium*, pp. 407-409; von Pastor, *History of the Popes*, II, 266.
[85]Runciman, *Fall of Constantinople*, pp. 138-139.

Francisco de Toledo, Theophilus and John Dalmata at his side, he plunged into
the melee at the breach, to die fighting as a common soldier against the
triumphant infidel. Turbans and scimitars overshadowed him. He vanished
from sight. He was never seen again. His body was never found.[86]

At Hagia Sophia morning Mass had just been completed on the high altar,
and the Blessed Sacrament reserved again in the tabernacle. Refugees began
streaming into the church. A few of the Italians among the defenders could still
get away to their ships, but for the people of the city there was no escape. By
the hundreds, then by the thousands, they came to Hagia Sophia to suffer or to
die with the crucified Christ. The vast church filled wall to wall.[87]

Then came the conquerors. They herded the wailing mass of humanity
outside, and opened a slave market to dispose of them. They tore down the
great crucifix and carried it through the streets with a janissary's cap on its
thorn-pierced head, shouting: "Behold the God of the Christians!" Sultan
Muhammad II, entering the city, rode directly to Hagia Sophia and proclaimed
it a mosque. The sack of Constantinople went on for the three days he had
promised to his men. Four thousand Christians were killed. More than 50,000
others, virtually the entire surviving population, were seized, and all but the few
who could pay large ransoms were enslaved.[88]

There are no altars in mosques. Everything Christian in Hagia Sophia was
torn away or covered with whitewash; every decoration was stripped as a prize
of war. But the altar was left standing. It had been the center of the largest
church in Christendom; every day for nine hundred years Mass had been said
upon it. Not once, never again, for five hundred and forty years as of this
writing, has the Body and Blood of God come down to the high altar of Hagia
Sophia. It still stands there today, a great bare slab. And in Istanbul (as the
Turks renamed Constantinople) today, hardly a Christian remains who can
trace his lineage back to the time of Constantine XI.[89]

Upon Earth we have no abiding city. Christ promised that His Church
should never be banished from the Earth; He did not say that there is any spot
on Earth's surface where the Church is guaranteed to remain.

The dreadful news arrived in Rome July 8.[90]   The shock was
overwhelming. No one had expected so enormous and complete a disaster.
The gentle, scholarly Pope struggled to face and accept his new, inevitable role

---

[86]*Ibid.*, pp. 139-140; Nicol, *Last Centuries of Byzantium*, p. 409.

[87]Runciman, *Fall of Constantinople*, p. 147; Nicol, *Last Centuries of Byzantium*, pp. 409-410.

[88]Runciman, *Fall of Constantinople*, pp. 147-151; Nicol, *Last Centuries of Byzantium*, pp. 410-412; von Pastor, *History of the Popes*, II, 267-268.

[89]From personal observation of Hagia Sophia by the author in 1971.

[90]Von Pastor, *History of the Popes*, II, 272; Ryder, *Alfonso the Magnanimous*, p. 289.

as crusade leader. For even a cynical and widely corrupted Christendom, snared by its own self-interests, could not wholly overlook its duty in the presence of such a catastrophe. They must try to reverse the verdict of history, knowing that Jesus Christ is Lord of history. And were even Christendom's best to falter and the Church's elect tempted to look away, there was one voice which would never cease to cry out during the nineteen years of life that remained to him: Cardinal Bessarion, Bishop of Nicaea, born in Trebizond, one of the two remnants of the Byzantine empire which the Turks had not yet overrun,[91] educated in Constantinople where he had lived for twenty-three years, all of whose people were in the lion's mouth or the lion's belly. Cardinal Bessarion waited for nothing and nobody. Five days after the news arrived he was writing passionately to Doge Francisco Foscari or Venice calling upon him to defend and restore Christendom in the east, as he had so conspicuously failed to do during the siege of Constantinople. Doge Foscari replied promising war against the Turks.[92]

But promises were cheap, and crusading was costly and risky. For most of Europe in this age of slow transportation and communication Constantinople seemed far away, and there was a strong residue of the centuries-old prejudice against the schismatic Greeks that had been harshly reciprocated by the Byzantine prejudice against the Latins dating back to the Christian sack of Constantinople in 1204. Not even the report of Cardinal Isidore of Kiev, who had made a fantastic escape from Constantinople,[93] on the horrors of the sack and the strong possibility that the victorious Turks might be about to invade Italy, could shake the Italian cities from their apathy. Pope Nicholas V's formal call for a crusade the next year, to be financed by a tithe on all Christendom, received little more than lip service. England's king was catatonic, Alfonso V of Aragon and Naples was bedridden with an ulcer on his leg, Charles VII of France apparently never thought what Joan the Maid would have done in this situation, and Holy Roman Emperor Frederick III did not even take the trouble to attend the imperial Diet at Regensburg called to support the crusade. The only specific response from outside the Pope's own entourage was that of Duke Philip of Burgundy, who loved grand gestures. On February 17, 1454, at a traditional gathering at Lille (where wine flowed freely) called the Feast of the

---

[91]The other was the Morea (Peloponnesus) in southern Greece, which the Turks overran in 1460 and 1461. They conquered Trebizond, a rather thinly populated littoral strip along the southern shore of the Black Sea in northeastern Asia Minor, without a fight in 1461. See Runciman, *Fall of Constantinople*, pp. 172, 174-176; Nicol, *Last Centuries of Byzantium*, pp. 422-423, 432; Fine, *Late Medieval Balkans*, p. 568.
[92]Von Pastor, *History of the Popes*, II, 279.
[93]He had given a beggar his clothes and the beggar had been taken for him, arrested and killed. Isidore was then seized and put into the slave market unrecognized, but a Greek merchant from the lands already ruled by the Turks recognized him, bought him, and then set him free. See Runciman, *Fall of Constantinople*, p. 150.

Pheasant, Philip took oath "to God my creator and to the most glorious Virgin his mother and to the ladies and . . . on the pheasant" to undertake the crusade. A pheasant seemed a curious emblem to set against the master of the cannon that fired 1,200-pound shot.[94]

Only in Hungary did the nobility and the people fully grasp the magnitude of the danger, for Hungary then extended south to the Sava River and to Belgrade, and this area would clearly be the next target for the Ottoman conquerors after they had disposed of the last remnants of Serbia. In January 1454 the Hungarian Diet gave John Hunyadi full powers as commanding general for a year and called on every estate to supply its full quota of men for military service, along with arming their peasants and even training some of them as cavalry. No exceptions were granted to anyone, and heavy fines were levied on those who failed to support the crusade. But Hungary could not stand alone against a victorious empire. Pope Nicholas V knew his duty, but it seemed that few others not immediately threatened knew theirs. Under the stress of repeated appeal and repeated disappointment he collapsed physically. In March 1454, attacked by severe gout, he took to his bed and rarely rose from it again. Almost exactly a year later, he died.[95]

The conclave assembled on Good Friday, April 4, 1455, with 15 of 20 cardinals present—seven Italians, four Spaniards, two French and the two Greeks, Bessarion and Isidore. After the current political consequences of the endless Colonna-Orsini feud had been sorted out, the majority looked to Bessarion, an inspirational figure in a dark hour. It would have been a splendid choice and might have changed the course of history, though the failure of the splendid effort and sacrifice of the future Pope Pius II to launch the crusade suggests not. But French Cardinal Alain was able to rouse enough of the old prejudice against Greeks to prevent Bessarion from obtaining the required ten votes. With no consensus, the conclave turned, like many before it, to an old man not expected to live long: the Spaniard Alfonso Borja, 76 years old, a long-time minister of Alfonso V of Aragon and Naples who had nevertheless refused to act as his ambassador to the Council of Basel because of that council's rejection of the authority of Pope Eugenius IV.[96]

That fact alone should have suggested to the conclave that the pontificate of Alfonso Borja (whose name with its harsh Spanish "j" the Italians softened to Borgia, and who took Calixtus III as his papal name) would be more than a death watch. It was indeed more than that. For, like Francisco de Toledo at the breach when Constantinople fell, Alfonso Borja was a man of the

---

[94]Von Pastor, *History of the Popes*, II, 275-278, 287-288, 300-302; Ryder, *Alfonso the Magnanimous*, p. 288; Vaughan, *Philip the Good*, pp. 297-302 (quotation on 297). For England see Note 69, above.
[95]Von Pastor, *History of the Popes*, II, 278, 311-313, 394; Held, *Hunyadi*, pp. 148-150.
[96]Von Pastor, *History of the Popes*, II, 319-328.

Reconquest. He understood the Turkish threat almost as well as Cardinal Bessarion; the consequences of Muslim conquest were seared into his soul by his people's seven hundred and forty years of struggle against it. At his papal consecration he too took an oath, which had nothing to say of pheasants:

> I, Pope Calixtus III, promise and vow to the Holy Trinity, Father, Son and Holy Spirit, to the Ever-Virgin Mother of God, to the Holy Apostles Peter and Paul, and to all the heavenly host, that I will do everything in my power, even if need be with the sacrifice of my life, aided by the counsel of my worthy brethren, to reconquer Constantinople, which in punishment for the sin of man has been taken and ruined by Mahomet II, the son of the devil and the enemy of our Crucified Redeemer.
>
> Further, I vow to deliver the Christians languishing in slavery, to exalt the true Faith, and to extirpate the diabolical sect of the reprobate and faithless Mahomet in the East. For there the light of faith is almost completely extinguished. If I forget thee, O Jerusalem, let my right hand be forgotten. Let my tongue cleave to my jaws, if I do not remember thee. If I make not Jerusalem the beginning of my joy, God and His holy Gospel help me. Amen.[97]

In September the preaching of the crusade began, with Pope Calixtus III sending cardinals for that purpose to France, Germany and Poland. The Pope's countryman Alfonso V of Aragon and Naples took the cross November 1 and agreed to supply 15 galleys for the crusading fleet. Afonso V of Portugal, now ruling in his own right, pledged 12,000 men for a year. St. John Capistrano, the fiery Observant Franciscan preacher, raised men for the crusade throughout Hungary and Transylvania, reaching past the aristocracy to the common people.[98]

They moved quickly for the age, but except for St. John Capistrano, they were still not in time. Muhammad II the Conqueror was a man before whom any delay could be deadly. On April 7, 1456 the news reached Hungary that he was on the march for Belgrade with a force of almost the same size that had taken Constantinople—about 80,000 men and 300 cannon. Sixteen-year-old King Ladislas Postumus of Hungary fled in a panic to Vienna, and many of the once boastful Hungarian nobles abandoned Belgrade for their home estates. Hunyadi's field army and the garrison of Belgrade held firm, perhaps 16,000 in all; and St. John Capistran brought at least 8,000 crusaders with him, though many of them were poorly armed and little trained. The odds in favor of the Turks were therefore between three and four to one. On June 29, the feast of St. Peter and Paul, Pope Calixtus III called on all archbishops, bishops, and abbots in Christendom for prayer, fasting and penance for deliverance from the

---

[97]*Ibid.*, II, 346.
[98]*Ibid.*, II, 349-350, 359-360; Ryder, *Alfonso the Magnanimous*, p. 413; Prestage, *Portuguese Pioneers*, p. 152; Hofer, *St. John Capistran*, pp. 341-350.

Turks, who three days later had fully invested the city of Belgrade.[99]

July 4 was a Sunday. St. John Capistran said Mass in Belgrade castle, and instructed the many priests present not to participate in any way in the battle, except by their prayers and assistance to the wounded. The odds shook even the redoubtable Hunyadi, who proposed retreat if it were possible; Capistran replied that he and his crusaders would never leave Belgrade, but would go down fighting to the last man like Constantine XI if Hunyadi abandoned them. There was no doubt of the total loyalty to the great preacher of the crusaders he had raised; if he would stay they would stay, and John Hunyadi would not be outdone by them in courage. Instead of retreating he advanced, with 200 boats on July 14 to win a naval battle on the Danube while St. John Capistran stood on the shore praying and holding up a crucifix which Pope Calixtus III had sent him. This victory enabled the resupply of the garrison and the city.[100]

Belgrade could not now be starved out; it must be taken, if at all, by assault. Its walls had been shattered by the overpowering Turkish cannon; Hunyadi did not see how they could be defended, and he was right. Again he proposed retreat; again St. John Capistran interposed his absolute veto. The grand assault began in the evening of July 21 and by midnight the Turks had broken into the city at several points. But that was not, as at Constantinople, the end of the battle—only its beginning. All through the night and into the following day Hunyadi and Capistran commanded from a high tower, Hunyadi directing his troops, Capistran holding up the papal crucifix. The Christians would not yield; they contested every street, almost every building. The Turkish artillery could not help the attackers now; the gunners could not see inside the city, where they were as likely to hit their own men as the Christians. As the sun rose it became apparent that the Christians were prevailing. Some of the Turks were retreating back through the breaches; great numbers lay dead or wounded in the bloody streets. Turkish attempts to send reinforcements into the city were met by masses of flaming brushwood flung into the breaches.[101]

By noon the city was virtually clear and the Turks were fought out, but Hunyadi and Capistran were not done. In early afternoon they counter-attacked, streaming across the wrecked walls and into the fields beyond at a measured pace, with the 71-year-old Franciscan in their midst, still holding up his crucifix. Hunyadi seized some of the Turkish guns and turned them on their makers. An arrow found its mark in the Sultan's body; though the wound was not serious, it underscored his defeat, and in the evening he was in full retreat, abandoning his camp and the city. For the moment at least, the infidel advance

---

[99]Held, *Hunyadi,* pp. 155-160, 164-167; von Pastor, *History of the Popes,* II, 390-393, 400-401; Hofer, *St. John Capistran,* pp. 348-350, 353-355.
[100]Hofer, *St. John Capistran,* pp. 355-361; Held, *Hunyadi,* p. 161.
[101]Held, *Hunyadi,* pp. 161-162; von Pastor, *History of the Popes,* II, 396-397; Hofer, *St. John Capistran,* pp. 367-369.

had been halted. Pope Calixtus III called it "the happiest event of my life."[102]

In the full heat of summer the thousands of unburied corpses in and around Belgrade rotted and bred disease, and the consequent plague carried off both the victors, Hunyadi after only a few days, the lean and whipcord-tough Capistran only after three months of struggle.[103] In the long sweep of history the victory of Belgrade was of only marginal significance for Christendom, but it did hold up the final Turkish triumph in the Balkans for a generation—along with the remarkable fight waged by the ex-Muslim and reconverted Christian "Skanderbeg" (George Castriota) in Albania, whom Pope Calixtus III in December 1456 named "Captain-General for the Turkish war," and who maintained a successful resistance until his death in 1468.[104] But the triumph at Belgrade shows what might have been done by a united Christendom and a great martial Pope at the siege of Constantinople.

There is a gap in our record of the Portuguese exploration of the African coast between 1448, when the unique "Chronicle of the Discovery and Conquest of Guinea" by Gomes Eanes de Zurara comes to an end, and the beginning of the personal narrative of his African voyages by Alvise de Cadamosto of Venice, who first arrived in Portugal and saw Prince Henry the Navigator in 1454. In January 1455 Pope Nicholas V issued the bull *Romanus pontifex* granting Prince Henry authority over all Christian voyages and exploration in and around Africa as far as the dwelling place of "the Indians who are said to worship the name of Christ." A follow-up bull *Inter caetera* issued by Pope Calixtus III March 13, 1456 gave the Portuguese Order of Christ, of which Prince Henry was governor, "ecclesiastical and ordinary jurisdiction in the islands, villages, harbors, lands and places, acquired or to be acquired from Capes Bojador and Nam [Nun] as far as and through all Guinea, and past that southern shore all the way to the Indies."[105]

---

[102]Von Pastor, *History of the Popes*, II, 397-398, 402 (for the quotation); Held, *Hunyadi*, pp. 162-163; Hofer, *St. John Capistran*, pp. 370-371.

[103]Von Pastor, *History of the Popes*, II, 406; Held, *Hunyadi*, p. 163; Hofer, *St. John Capistran*, pp. 378-380.

[104]Von Pastor, *History of the Popes*, II, 433-435; Fine, *Late Medieval Balkans*, pp. 556, 595-598. Albanian resistance continued for the rest of the century under Skanderbeg's son John, but without dependable Western support their cause was hopeless, as many Albanians themselves recognized by migrating to Italy during the decade following Skanderbeg's death (Fine, *op. cit.*, pp. 601-602).

[105]Diffie and Winius, *Foundations of the Portuguese Empire*, pp. 65-66, 90, 94-97; Prestage, *Portuguese Pioneers*, p. 165 (first quotation); John W. Blake, *West Africa; Quest for God and Gold, 1454-1478*, 2nd ed. (London, 1977), pp. 22-23 (second quotation). The dating of these two bulls has caused confusion because of the failure of some historians to take note of the practice at this time of beginning the new year on March 25 in dating papal documents, causing these two bulls to be dated a year earlier than their correct date according to the modern calendar. See the excellent clarifying

The interpretation of the language used in these bulls is of critical importance in determining what Prince Henry the Navigator—who undoubtedly requested and possibly drafted them—saw as the goal of his great exploring enterprise toward the end of his life. No earlier document specifies India as his objective; these seem to do so, though it has been argued that Ethiopia (often confused with India in the vague visualizations of lands beyond the Muslim barrier which Christians had in that age) was meant. Ethiopia was Christian, and on the other side of Africa. But though the term "India" was sometimes used to mean Ethiopia, that land was rarely if ever referred to as "the Indies"—the name Columbus gave to the islands of the Americas; and though he always thought them part of Asia, he certainly never thought them part of Ethiopia. Zurara in his chronicle speaks of Indians and Ethiopians separately. At the very least it would seem reasonable to assume that, though the term "India" might be extended to include Ethiopia, it nevertheless still included the actual India, where there were also many Christians, who traced their history back to the Apostle Thomas. And there is no doubt that the Christians of either India or Ethiopia, or both, were among the major objectives of Prince Henry's explorations. So there is good reason to conclude that at least by this point Henry the Navigator did intend for his ships to go around Africa all the way to India.

In June 1455 Cadamosto and his associate Antoniotto Usodimare of Genoa sailed as far as the Gambia, where Diogo Gomes followed them in 1456. Gomes sailed far upstream on the broad estuary and river, reaching the city of Kantor and meeting there the black chief Nomimansa who requested baptism. Gomes had no priest with him, and though a layman is entitled to baptize, Gomes apparently did not feel capable of judging the religious purity of Nomimansa's intentions. He said he would ask Prince Henry to send a priest; we have no record of whether he did.[106]

In 1456 Cadamosto made a second voyage, on which he discovered the Cape Verde Islands about 300 miles west of Cape Verde in the Atlantic, returned to the Gambia, and then sailed south 150 miles to the Bijagos archipelago off the coast of what was later to be called Portuguese Guinea and today, Guinea-Bissau. After that, for lack of records, the curtain falls until the beginning of 1460, when Pedro de Sintra with two caravels reached Sierra Leone, which he named "Lion Mountain" either for a fancied resemblance to the shape of a crouching lion, or for the thunder that roared over it. Sierra Leone is 250 miles southeast of the Bijagos archipelago and it is unlikely, though possible, that Pedro de Sintra covered that much coast as new

---

note on this point in Diffie and Winius, *op. cit.*, p. 94.
[106]Diffie and Winius, *Foundations of the Portuguese Empire*, pp. 101, 106; Prestage, *Portuguese Pioneers*, pp. 114-115, 130-140; Sanceau, *Henry the Navigator*, pp. 266-268, 272-280.

exploration. Unrecorded voyages in 1457, 1458 or 1459 are likely to have opened up part of it. Prince Henry's instructions to each voyager continued to be to go as much farther along the African coast, beyond the last point explored, as he possibly could—though not all obeyed those orders.[107]

Prince Henry the Navigator died at Sagres November 13, 1460 at the age of 66, having lived all his life as a lay celibate, wearing a hair shirt and carrying a fragment of the True Cross, and was buried in the Portuguese royal shrine at Batalha Abbey. Few men who ever lived have influenced history more.[108] When he was born, ocean seafaring hardly existed in Europe; even the Norsemen had lost most of their skill and could barely sail to Iceland, while Greenland and American Vinland beyond had faded into mist. Christendom was geographically entrapped by the Muslims, cut off in a small corner of the globe, unable to reach the rest of humanity. When he died, the bolder mariners of his country had been exploring for forty years, and were drawing kindred spirits from all over Europe. The goal of rounding Africa had been set, and approved by two Popes. Long as the sea-road was, there was no doubt that eventually it would be traversed, and the impetus of that achievement would drive explorations elsewhere, including that of Columbus across the Atlantic.

It has recently become fashionable to decry the expansion of the West to the Orient and Africa and the New World, and to assert or imply that it would have been better if these regions and peoples had never encountered the West. The conflicts, misunderstandings, and bloody wars which arose out of this encounter, and especially the immense evil of black slavery to Europeans, seem at first sight to support this view. So devout a Catholic as Prince Henry the Navigator should assuredly have recoiled from the horrors of slavery when he saw them displayed before his eyes when the first human cargo from Africa was discharged at Lagos in 1444. But the human story since Eden is always laced with evil, which good must unceasingly fight. The Christian faith provided the spiritual resources to fight and in substantial part to defeat the evils that arose from Christendom's contacts with new cultures during the Age of Discovery. Slavery was eventually abolished in Christendom; there is not the slightest indication that, outside of Christendom and without the Christian example, its abolition would ever have been thought of anywhere else. Strip away the romantic veneer from the Orient, from Africa before Prince Henry, from America before Columbus, and an abyss of tyranny and horror opens that looks more like Gehenna than Eden. It is not considered polite to mention these things today, but in justice they must be spoken of: the million victims of the

---

[107]Diffie and Winius, *Foundations of the Portuguese Empire*, pp. 103-105, 110-111; Prestage, *Portuguese Pioneers*, pp. 122-124, 128-130; Sanceau, *Henry the Navigator*, pp. 280-281.
[108]Prestage, *Portuguese Pioneers*, pp. 154-161; Sanceau, *Henry the Navigator*, pp. 298-304.

Thug strangler cult and the millions of innocent widows burned on their husbands' funeral pyres in India—the most painful of all deaths; the mutilated parade of the court eunuchs and the bound-footed women in China; the vicious female circumcision practiced in much of black Africa; the 80,000 human sacrifices at fifteen seconds per man during the dedication of the temple of Huitzilopochtli in Mexico City in 1487 and the island populations literally devoured by the Caribs in the New World sea that still bears their name.[109] These vast and ancient evils Christendom would destroy, and for their destruction the Church of Christ has the right to ask thanks, not condemnation, from the people she delivered from them.

In England the tragic King Henry VI recovered his sanity—more or less—at the end of 1454, but was even less capable than he had been before of controlling the fractious barons, or his strong-willed wife Marguerite. In May 1455 Richard, Duke of York, who had been regent during the king's insanity, gained physical control of him after a battle in which York's principal rival, the Duke of Somerset, was killed. But the Queen remained influential, and bitterly opposed to York. Gradually she prised the helpless monarch out of York's control, formed her own faction of the nobility, and forced York out of England to Ireland in October 1459. Meeting the next month, what many called a "Parliament of Devils" at Coventry, consisting almost entirely of enemies of York, attainted him, his son and the Earls of Salisbury and Warwick who were his chief supporters. England was split between supporters of King Henry VI as managed by Queen Marguerite—the Lancastrians—and supporters of the Duke of York, the Yorkists, whose emblems were, respectively, a red and a white rose (hence "wars of the roses").[110]

There was a genuine issue of title to the throne between them. Puzzling and petty as questions of royal title seem to a post-monarchical generation, rightful royal title was then the basis of legitimate government. Though questionable royal titles might not be widely challenged under a good and effective government, they were sure to be when government was incompetent. The victories of Henry V had cast their luster before and after him, quieting objectors for many years; but the fact was that his father Henry IV of Lancaster, son of John of Gaunt, was a usurper who had seized the throne of England illegally from Richard II.[111] By strict hereditary succession, the next in line for the throne after the childless Richard II was his uncle Lionel, his father's oldest brother, who had died in 1368 and whose grandson Roger died in 1398, before

---

[109]See Volumes IV and VI of this history.

[110]Jacobs, *Fifteenth Century*, pp. 503, 511-513, 516; Griffiths, *Henry VI*, pp. 744-746, 757, 822-825; Johnson, *Duke Richard of York*, pp. 156-158, 172-173, 177, 191-192; John Gillingham, *The Wars of the Roses* (London, 1981), pp. 100, 104-105.

[111]See Chapter Eleven, above.

Richard's overthrow. But Roger left a young son and daughter. The son died without issue. The daughter, Anne—in fact the rightful queen, though she never claimed the throne—married Richard, Earl of Cambridge, second son of Richard II's *third* uncle Edmund, whose older son died childless. Richard, Duke of York in 1459, was the oldest son of Richard Earl of Cambridge and Anne the great-granddaughter and only heir of Prince Lionel, thus combining in his person two royal lines of descent, the line through his mother being clearly superior by primogeniture to the title of Henry VI, great-grandson of John of Gaunt.[112]

Henry VI, left to himself, would probably have been happy enough to abdicate, and Queen Marguerite—who was hardly in a pleasant position, with a half-mad and always futile husband, dwelling in a foreign land surrounded by enemies—might have been bought off, were it not for the presence of her baby son and only child Edward, whose rights she was naturally determined to defend to the end. Whether little Prince Edward had paramount right to the throne was the legal issue; the actual outcome of the dispute over his title depended on how many noblemen adhered to one cause as compared to the other and how well they were led. There is no immediate Catholic significance in all of this, though the story of the Wars of the Roses is a much more compelling human drama than most students of it have realized;[113] but the outcome of the 25-year struggle was to be of very great significance, because it brought the Tudor dynasty to the English throne, and it was the Tudors who took and kept England out of the Catholic Church in the next century.

In a battle at Northampton in July 1460 the Yorkists, led by the Earl of Warwick and supported by the city of London, defeated the Lancastrians and once again seized possession of the king. In September the Duke of York returned from Ireland and the next month he claimed the crown. Parliament was not quite ready yet to give it to him. They prepared a compromise whereby Henry VI would continue as king for the rest of his life but accept York as his heir, disinheriting his son Edward. Since Edward's rights were the real issue, the Lancastrians could not be satisfied with this arrangement, and Queen Marguerite would never accept it. In December the tables were turned at the Battle of Wakefield. The Duke of York was killed, along with his second son Edmund and the Earl of Salisbury, one of his two principal supporters among the nobility. But his oldest son, confusingly also named Edward, a very capable

---

[112]See the excellent genealogical table in Charles Ross, *Edward IV* (Berkeley CA, 1974), p. 4. The genealogical table of York and Lancaster in the widely used and generally accurate *Encyclopedia of World History* edited by William L. Langer contains two major errors which make it impossible to understand York's claim by studying it.

[113]As the outstanding (and remarkably historically accurate) historical novelist Sharon Kay Penman has demonstrated in her impressive *The Sunne in Splendour* (New York, 1982).

leader and commander despite his youth (he was only 18), immediately stepped into his father's place, winning a major victory at Mortimer's Cross in February 1461. Two weeks later in another part of England, Queen Margaret's army defeated the Earl of Warwick, but Edward of York reached London first and rallied its people, who on March 4 acclaimed him King Edward IV. At Towton on Palm Sunday 1461 Edward won a long, bloody, hard-fought and decisive battle over the Lancastrians and apparently secured his power permanently. Queen Marguerite fled to Scotland, taking Henry VI and little Prince Edward with her.[114]

But Queen Marguerite was dangerous so long as she lived, and Edward IV not as secure as he thought in the heady wake of his victory at Towton. The disintegration of government and society in England had gone on too long, the after-taste of defeat in France was too bitter, and the examples of successful rebellion had been too many for the restoration of real peace and good order in the land without a long period of further struggle. The conflict was to continue, with periodic remissions, for twenty-four years after the Battle of Towton until, through a series of events demonstrating anew that truth is stranger than fiction and involving the most impenetrable historical mystery in the annals of England, it brought down the ancient and renowned house of Plantagenet after fourteen generations in power and placed the grandson of a Welsh clerk on the throne of William the Conqueror.[115]

King Alfonso V of Aragon, Naples and Sicily died in June 1458, without legitimate issue. Honoring the terms of his father's will, he provided for the succession in Aragon to pass to his brother Juan, while reserving Naples and Sicily for his illegitimate son Ferrante. Old Pope Calixtus III, his countryman and former minister, knew the potential of endless trouble for the papacy in the rule of the southern part of Italy by a powerful non-Italian king, and declared he would not recognize Ferrante. But Calixtus III outlived his former master only six weeks, passing away in the hot and sultry August which had always been Rome's dying time, at the age of 79. The outspoken, committed and militant old man had been an inspiration to the best spirits in a Christendom still reeling from the shock of the fall of Constantinople. But there had not been enough open to inspiration; the victory of John Hunyadi and St. John Capistran at Belgrade in 1456 had not been followed up. And in an earlier act of family partiality in 1456, Calixtus III had stored up coals of fire for the Church in the future; he had made his young and licentious nephew Rodrigo Borgia a

---

[114]Jacobs, *Fifteenth Century*, pp. 518-526; Griffiths, *Henry VI*, pp. 855, 859-863, 867-871; Johnson, *Duke Richard of York*, pp. 206, 210, 213-219, 223; Gillingham, *Wars of the Roses*, pp. 110-114, 116-121, 124-136; Ross, *Edward IV*, pp. 31-32, 34, 36-38.
[115]See Chapter Fourteen, below.

Cardinal at the age of only 25.[116]

The conclave met on August 16 with 18 cardinals present—eight Italians, five Spaniards, two "very influential" Frenchmen, one Portuguese, and the two Greeks, Bessarion and Isidore. The highly respected Cardinal Capranica had almost unanimous support as the next Pope when Calixtus III died, but he died unexpectedly two days before the conclave assembled. The first ballot showed no clear leader. Then the French Cardinal d'Estouteville made a vigorous effort to gain the necessary votes, and came within one. But the able and well-liked Aeneas Sylvius Piccolomini, who had come so far since his days as a supporter of the schismatic Council of Basel, never gave up and eventually swung the College in his favor. In the first ballot on the second day of voting he had nine votes to six for d'Estouteville, and one by one three other cardinals gave him their votes, beginning with the astute Rodrigo Borgia who probably hoped thereby to curry favor from Piccolomini as Pope (if so, he totally misjudged his man). Piccolomini was proclaimed Pope Pius II at the age of 52, with great rejoicing in Rome. He was known as a good and charitable and persevering man, friend to all but impossible to manipulate, an outstanding diplomat and a brilliant writer; however, few if any saw him as a crusader. But the crusade to regain Constantinople became his primary goal as Pope, though unattained.[117]

Less than two months into his pontificate, on October 12, 1458, in a lengthy speech to the cardinals, bishops and prelates, and ambassadors in Rome, Pope Pius II reviewed the defeats inflicted upon the Christians by the Turks and showed how the Turks aimed at the destruction of all Christendom. He declared an immediate counterattack was necessary, and called a congress at Mantua in Italy for the following June to plan it. Soon afterward, reversing his predecessor's policy, he recognized Ferrante as king of Naples, as his contribution to a policy of peace within Christendom to facilitate a united effort in the crusade.[118]

But the Congress of Mantua proved a bitter disappointment to Pope Pius II. When it opened on schedule not a single Christian prince was present in person, nor had any sent a representative with plenipotentiary powers—those they had sent were little more than observers. Pius wrote immediately to Holy Roman Emperor Frederick III strongly urging him to come: he was the temporal head of Christendom, the natural leader of a crusading army; he was needed above all. But Frederick, involved in a dispute with the Duke of Bavaria and seeking to secure for himself the crown of Hungary, did not

---

[116]Von Pastor, *History of the Popes*, II, 427, 448-451, 468-473, 479; Ryder, *Alfonso the Magnanimous*, pp. 428-430.
[117]Von Pastor, *History of the Popes*, III, 3-20; Mitchell, *Laurels and Tiara*, pp. 110-116.
[118]Von Pastor, *History of the Popes*, III, 23-24, 26.

respond.[119]

In August one major delegation finally arrived at Mantua, the large and brilliantly accoutred embassy of Duke Philip of Burgundy. It might well be said that all their promises and posturing bore a faint odor of spoiled pheasant, but by this time Pius II was so eager for support from any official quarter that he took the Burgundians at face value. The Italian city-states would not break away from their parochial concerns; Florence would only offer help secretly, and Venice not even that. In October envoys from the Duke of Savoy and Duke Albert of Austria (brother and foe of Emperor Frederick) arrived, but were no help; the Austrian envoys openly insulted the Pope. Matters became even worse when in November Duke Sigmund of Tyrol arrived with the vehemently anti-papal propagandist Gregor Heimburg in his train. Heimburg had played a leading part in supporting the schismatic Council of Basel and had not changed his views. When French envoys came later in November they made sure that the Pope understood that their master, Charles VII, had no intention whatever of revoking the Pragmatic Sanction of Bourges which had removed the whole church in France from the Pope's administrative and governing authority, and spokesmen for Duke René of Anjou who accompanied them attacked the Pope for endorsing the claims of Ferrante to Naples in preference to the Angevin claim.[120]

In the end, all that Pope Pius II could extract from this discouraging meeting was a German promise to raise 10,000 horse and 32,000 foot to fight the Turks, with no clear indication of which states were going to provide how many men, nor of who would lead them. He tried to make the best of it, appointing Emperor Frederick III their commander-in-chief with the power to select another commander if he did not feel able to serve, and calling for a tithe from all the clergy and a thirtieth from the laity to finance a three-year campaign. Further planning of the crusade was supposed to be done at the imperial Diet scheduled for Nuremberg in March 1460, but the only leading prince present there was Albert Achilles of Brandenburg, and Cardinal Bessarion's exhortation on the need for peace among the Christian princes in order to concert efforts for the crusade fell on deaf ears. The situation was even worse at the next imperial Diet, at Vienna in October 1460. New Archbishop Diether of Mainz was strongly hostile to the Pope and succeeded in blocking any action to implement the crusade, to the near despair of Cardinal

---

[119]*Ibid.*, III, 59-61, 65-67, 158. The legitimate king of Hungary, Emperor Sigismund's grandson Ladislas Postumus, had died with suspicious suddenness in Bohemia in November 1457 at the age of seventeen, without issue. John Hunyadi's son Matthias Corvinus Hunyadi was favored in Hungary to take the vacant throne, even though he was not of royal blood. See *ibid.*, II, 441 and Frederick G. Heymann, *George of Bohemia, King of Heretics* (Princeton, 1965), pp. 145-157.

[120]Von Pastor, *History of the Popes*, III, 69, 71-72, 84-90, 185; Mitchell, *Laurels and Tiara*, pp. 143-144.

Bessarion, who fell into furious, well-justified but wholly ineffective denunciation of the German princes and bishops for their inaction, and asked the Pope to recall him.[121] Pius II replied:

> God's honor and the honor of the Apostolic See require that we should be steadfast in hope, using every means by which the minds of men may be led to better counsels. If others withdraw from the work, it does not become us to folow their example. Perseverance in good leads to good even those who are ill disposed, and hearts that are now depraved may not be so always. The conversion of men is wrought by a hidden power, and the way of salvation often opens where no one expects it.[122]

That theme of extraordinary perseverance, "steadfast in hope," runs throughout the noble pontificate of Pius II. In the fall of 1461 he demonstrated it in a new and unique way in a long letter to Sultan Muhammad II urging him to convert to Christianity. But the resistance of Muslims to conversion remains a dark mystery of grace. Where even St. Francis of Assisi failed to convert the Sultan of Egypt in person, Pope Pius II could hardly convert the Sultan of Turkey by letter.[123]

Though his primary concern was always to implement his vision of a great crusade against the Ottoman Turks, Pius II had many other problems to contend with during his six-year pontificate. He ruled the Church with a firm hand, and in view of the lack of support for his greatest enterprise he was remarkably successful in his lesser undertakings. When the rebellious Archbishop Diether of Mainz proposed at the Diet of Nuremberg in February 1461 that another council meet without papal authorization, in August he declared Diether removed from his see and replaced by his arch-rival Adolf of Nassau, who had the strong support of the redoubtable Albert Achilles of Brandenburg. Diether eventually had to bow, though with bitter resentment, to the Pope's decree. When Charles VII of France died in July 1461 and was succeeded by his son Louis XI, who had hated his father, Pius II took shrewd advantage of this hostility to persuade Louis to revoke the Pragmatic Sanction of Bourges, three months after his coronation. And when the devious Hussite king of Bohemia, George Podebrady, broke his coronation oath by refusing to restore Catholic practice in that country, Pius II in March 1462 declared the "compact" with the Hussites of a generation before no longer valid, a temporary measure whose time had passed. It had never been intended, he said, to permanently authorize a different way of receiving Communion than the Latin rite provided, but simply to ease a transition back to liturgical unity with the rest of Latin Christendom. King George had promised to facilitate and

---

[121]Von Pastor, *History of the Popes*, III, 95-99, 160-161, 168-170.
[122]*Ibid.*, III, 170.
[123]*Ibid.*, III, 256-257. See Chapter Five, above.

ultimately to lead that return; he had not done so.[124]

Fantino de Valle, the Dalmatian doctor of canon law who for three years had been King George's ambassador in Rome, was sent to Prague by the Pope to obtain obedience to his order. When the king refused to obey, Fantino taxed him publicly in August 1462 with breaking his coronation oath and his personal promises to Fantino to reunite Bohemia with the universal practice of the Latin rite in the Catholic Church, and resigned his office of ambassador. The enraged King George almost killed Fantino on the spot, and the next day threw him into prison.[125]

Since Fantino was now a papal representative as well as a former Bohemian ambassador, King George eventually felt constrained to free him; and in December 1462 the Pope reluctantly acceded to an appeal by Emperor Frederick III to suspend proceedings against George because he needed George's alliance and protection against his hostile brother Albert of Austria. But in the last days of his pontificate Pius II took the final step, on June 16, 1464 declaring King George Podebrady a perjured and relapsed heretic and summoning him to Rome to answer the charges against him.[126]

In March 1462 Pope Pius II came to an epochal decision. Convinced after four years of fruitless efforts that no Christian prince would step forward to take the lead in the projected crusade against the Ottoman Turks, he decided to take the lead himself—despite his failing health and total lack of military experience—in the hope of shaming the other princes into cooperating. He first announced his decision privately to six cardinals, who approved it. Late in August 1463, at long last, Venice publicly proclaimed the crusade and levied a tithe to finance it. Matthias Corvinus Hunyadi of Hungary and Skanderbeg of Albania promised help, but the other Italian cities still held back, alleging fear of Venetian aggression.[127] On September 23 the Pope proclaimed his purpose

---

[124]*Ibid.*, III, 138-139, 192-193, 203-207, 224-230; Paul M. Kendall, *Louis XI, the Universal Spider* (New York, 1971), p. 117; Heymann, *George of Bohemia*, pp. 262-264, 266-272, 275-277. When George was crowned King of Bohemia in May 1458 he had to be consecrated by two Hungarian bishops, there having been no Bohemian bishops since the Hussite revolt forty years before. They insisted that he swear "fidelity and obedience to the Roman Catholic Church, her head, Pope Calixtus III, and his lawful successors" and promise to "lead back the people who are my subjects" to the "observation, obedience, conformity and union with the true Catholic and orthodox faith" and to "restore among them the ritual and cult of the Holy Roman Church." He swore to all of it, but in secret, though in the presence of eight witnesses. See von Pastor, *op. cit.*, II, 443 for the first quotation; Heymann, *op. cit.*, p. 170 for the other three.

[125]Von Pastor, *History of the Popes*, III, 232-236; Odlozilik, *Hussite King*, pp. 137-140; Heymann, *George of Bohemia*, pp. 283-287.

[126]Von Pastor, *History of the Popes*, III, 236-237, 239; Odlozilik, *Hussite King*, pp. 143, 159; Heymann, *George of Bohemia*, pp. 329-336, 381-382.

[127]Von Pastor, *History of the Popes*, III, 311, 319-324; Mitchell, *Laurels and Tiara*, p. 229; Heymann, *George of Bohemia*, p. 320.

in a magnificent address to the full College of Cardinals:

> Our cry, Go forth! has resounded in vain. Perhaps if the word is, Come with me! it will have more effect. That is why we have determined to proceed in person against the Turks, and by word and deed to stir up all Christian princes to follow our example. It may be that, seeing their teacher and father, the Bishop of Rome, the Vicar of Christ, a weak and sickly old man, going to the war, they will be ashamed to stay at home. Should this effort also fail, we know of no other means to try. We are well aware that at our age we are going to meet an almost certain death. But let us leave all to God, His holy will be done! Nevertheless, we are too weak to fight sword in hand, and this is not the priest's office. But we will imitate Moses, who prayed upon a height while the people of Israel were doing battle with the Amalekites. On the prow of a ship, or on the summit of a mountain, we will beseech our Lord, whose Holy Body will ever be with us, to grant us deliverance and victory.[128]

On October 22, 1463 Pope Pius II issued "the last bull calling for a crusade against the Turks," promising a plenary indulgence to all who served in arms for at least six months or gave a substantial financial contribution, and reviewing Turkish atrocities, their inveterate hostility to Christianity, and their determination to conquer Europe. This portion of the bull was pierced by an extraordinary cry of anguish: "O stony-hearted and thankless Christians, who can hear of all these things, and yet not wish to die for Him Who died for you!"[129]

The last betrayal came, not altogether surprisingly, from Duke Philip of Burgundy, the man who swore on pheasants. In March 1464 he announced that, at the command of his liege lord Louis XI of France, he had deferred his participation in the crusade for a year, though he might still supply 3,000 men for the current year. (He did not supply them.) Louis had turned against the Pope in 1462 when he would not endorse the French Angevin claim to Naples, and in 1463 had restored many of the provisions of the Pragmatic Sanction of Bourges "to defend ourselves against the aggressions of Rome, and for the restoration of the ancient Gallican liberties." But the proud Burgundian ruler only recognized Louis XI as his "liege lord" when it suited him; he had defied Louis' father on numerous occasions. It seems Philip was quite relieved to have this excuse to renege on his crusading promise, and it is even possible that he asked Louis for it.[130]

On Holy Thursday 1464 Pope Pius II repeated that the crusade would go forward, whoever came or did not come, and he threatened all kings and princes who hindered the crusade (obviously thinking of Louis XI) with

---

[128]Von Pastor, *History of the Popes*, III, 326.

[129]*Ibid.*, III, 331-332.

[130]*Ibid.*, III, 141-150, 152-153, 156 (for the quotation), 345; Mitchell, *Laurels and Tiara*, pp. 176-178.

excommunication. On June 18 he took the cross at the Vatican and departed from Rome. On July 19 he reached Ancona, where the crusading fleet and army were to assemble. Only six galleys were there, and most of the crusading soldiers were lower-class Spanish or French, of good heart but ill-equipped or not equipped at all. There was almost no money or weapons for them, and soon they began to scatter. Finally, on August 12, a handful of Venetian galleys appeared. Doge Cristoforo Moro, who had promised to accompany them, was not aboard. Pope Pius II was dying. His crusade against the Turks was not even a failure; it had never happened at all.[131]

But the Vicar of Christ never despairs, for he always remembers the divine promise that the gates of Hell shall not prevail against the Church. On August 14 Pope Pius II gathered his cardinals around him. He had already been anointed; the morrow would be his last day on Earth. He remained "steadfast in hope." He said to them:

> My hour is drawing near. God calls me. I die in the Catholic Faith in which I have lived. Up to this day I have taken care of the sheep committed to me, and have shrunk from no danger or toil. You must now complete what I have begun but am not able to finish. Labor therefore in God's work, and do not cease to care for the cause of the Christian Faith, for this is your vocation in the Church. Be mindful of your duty, be mindful of your Redeemer, who sees all, and rewards every one according to his deserts.[132]

The fall of Constantinople and the inability to launch a crusade to regain it showed that much of the old unity of purpose in Christendom had been lost, and much of its innocence and moral enthusiasm. Yet still Christendom was full of vigor and new life, as the Renaissance and the African voyages and discoveries of the mariners of Prince Henry the Navigator bore witness. The astonishing career of Pius II manifested both the new versatility and vigor, and the old fidelity. The scholar had become a crusader; the schismatic had become, very likely, a saint.

Across the Mediterranean Sea in Spain, as Pope Pius II lay dying at Ancona watching for the crusading fleet that never came, a thirteen-year-old girl dwelt in an apartment in the royal palace in Madrid. Her father, who had been King Juan II of Castile and almost as pathetic a puppet ruler as Henry VI of England, was dead. Her mother was insane. Her half-brother, now King Henry IV of Castile, was severely neurotic, a psychological cripple. The intrigues of uncontrolled, avaricious noblemen, who would stop at nothing including murder to satisfy their greed, swirled around her. She was even more

---

[131]Von Pastor, *History of the Popes*, III, 346, 353-354, 357-360, 367-369; Mitchell, *Laurels and Tiara*, pp. 234-235.
[132]Von Pastor, *History of the Popes*, III, 369.

alone than the abandoned Pope at Ancona. He at least had his faithful cardinals. She had no one but a younger brother dependent on her, a dear friend named Beatriz her own age, and a teacher of exemplary goodness and integrity, Gonzalo Chacón. She was one day to be known as "the Catholic Queen," to change the world almost as much as Prince Henry the Navigator changed it, and to revive the Church and Christendom as he had never tried to do and as even Pope Pius II had been unable to do. Her name was Isabel.[133]

---

[133]Warren H. Carroll, *Isabel of Spain, the Catholic Queen* (Front Royal VA, 1991), pp. 17-26. The form in which her name is usually given, "Isabella," is not Spanish but Italian, and became standard because of the predominance of Italians in historical writing in her time. The Spanish form is preferable.

14
The Rise of Isabel the Catholic
(1464-1492)

(Popes Paul II 1464-1471, Sixtus IV 1471-1484, Innocent VIII 1484-1492)

Thou, Lord, in Whose hands is the rule of kingdoms, Who hast put me by Thy Providence into royal estate, I beg humbly to hear now the prayer of Thy servant, and show forth the truth, and manifest Thy will with Thy marvellous works; so that if I am not in the right, I may not sin through ignorance, and if I am in the right, that Thou mayest give me wisdom and strength so that with the aid of Thine arm I may be able to carry on and to prevail, and bring peace to these realms, which until now have suffered so much evil and destruction.—public prayer of Queen Isabel of Castile on the eve of war between Castile and Portugal, April 1475[1]

Pope Pius II had been a man of the Renaissance, but also a Vicar of Christ who literally gave his life attempting to inspire Christendom to a true crusade against its implacable enemy, the Ottoman Turks. He had been willing to humble the personal and intellectual pride which was the dark side of the brilliance of the Renaissance ("cast away Aeneas, hold fast to Pius"). Of his self-sacrificing courage there could be no doubt; in his sanctity, though never confirmed by canonization, there is good reason to believe. But that even such a leader could not draw significant support for his greatest cause showed how the glory of Christendom had faded by his time; for a full century he did not have a successor to match him, until the coming of his namesake St. Pius V. When the eyes of that frail but indomitable figure, watching for the crusading ships that never came, closed at last at Ancona, an age began in which, for the first time since the great Hildebrandine reform of the eleventh century, Popes of a united Church became more followers than leaders, manipulated by history rather than making it.[2]

The first of them was Paul II, who had been Cardinal Pietro Barbo of Venice, chosen with unusual speed on August 30, 1464 by a single ballot. The

---

[1]Fernando del Pulgar, *Crónica de los Reyes Católicos*, ed. Juan de Mata Carriazo (Madrid, 1943), I, 101 (chapter XXXI).
[2]See Volume II of this history. As has been shown in Chapters Nine and Ten, above, the Popes at Avignon exercised stronger leadership in the Church than they have often been credited with.

THE GLORY OF CHRISTENDOM

initial count gave him eleven votes to nine for French Cardinal d'Estouteville and seven for fellow Italian Cardinal Scarampo, but before the vote was formally announced, enough cardinals voting for d'Estouteville and Scarampo had changed their votes to give Barbo the required two-thirds. He was 48, strikingly handsome, known for his love of luxurious display, not remarkable for holiness though genial and benevolent, with few intellectual interests and no clear policy goals, who left but a faint mark upon history and the Church. In this he was typical of many of his immediate successors.[3]

Despite the ugly reputation of the "Renaissance Papacy," the fourteen Popes between Pius II and St. Pius V were not evil men, with the exception of Alexander VI, the Borgia Pope; some of them were notably good and a few of them genuinely holy. But by and large (except for Pius IV, Pope during the final session of the Council of Trent) they provided little real leadership for the Church and Christendom. Whatever their personal character, their policies were generally neither heroic nor successful. During this century, from 1464 to 1566, the Church and Christendom were cloven, sundered as far into the future as can be seen or imagined. The Popes neither prevented this from happening nor were primarily responsible for saving the remnant, though once they understood the magnitude of the danger (which they were very slow to realize) they did their best to resist it, and made some positive contributions. Christendom was saved, in its time of greatest danger since the Muslim irruption in the century after Muhammad, primarily by a laywoman, a layman and a religious: Queen Isabel of Castile; her grandson, Holy Roman Emperor Charles V, who was also King of Spain; and St. Ignatius of Loyola, a Basque from northern Spain, the founder of the Jesuits. Isabel came first, preparing the way and building the base for the other two.

It may be strongly argued that Isabel of Castile was the greatest woman ruler in history, by secular standards or religious. Under the rule of her pathetic half-brother Henry IV, Castile had descended into virtual anarchy—the laughingstock, the whipped dog of Europe. In thirty years Isabel made it, united with her husband Fernando's Aragon as the Kingdom of Spain, the greatest power in the world. She accomplished this by no harsh and domineering rule, but by bringing justice and peace, integrity and incorruptibility, responsibility and honor with her wherever she went, sealed by the love she bore her people and the love they bore her. By her marriage to Fernando of Aragon, and the love that sealed that marriage and the unity and harmony in action which she and he consistently maintained, they made reality of what hitherto had been no more than a dream of unity. Together, with Isabel providing the primary impetus, they completed the 770-year war to reconquer

---

[3]Ludwig von Pastor, *The History of the Popes from the Close of the Middle Ages*, Volume IV (St. Louis, 1914), pp. 11-16.

Spain from the Muslims by the conquest of Granada. Immediately afterward, Isabel sent Christopher Columbus to open up a new world. She struck down slavery in the Canary Islands and in America. She demanded and obtained the appointment of a holy and ascetic Franciscan, Ximénes de Cisneros, as primate of Spain so that he might reform the Church in Spain from top to bottom. With her unfailing support, he did exactly that. Consequently there was never any support in Spain for the revolt against the Church that swept almost all the rest of Europe during the first half of the sixteenth century. Spain became the bastion from which Isabel's grandson Emperor Charles V saved all that was left of Catholic Christendom.[4]

The holiness of Isabel's personal life matched and exceeded the magnitude of her temporal accomplishments. She lived a life of prayer, loving God with all her heart and mind and soul, keeping the Commandments, forgiving her enemies, protecting the poor and the oppressed. She honored her father and her mother, though they had left her alone and unprotected among designing, predatory men. She was always a dutiful wife and a loving mother. No breath of scandal ever touched her personal life, though she lived at court in Renaissance Europe, where scandal was rampant, expected, assumed, when even Popes had illegitimate children. She was humble, prudent, persevering despite great personal suffering from the tragedies that later befell her children.[5]

Her life and reign transformed history. Before her Spain, despite the drama of its immensely long reconquest, had exercised only a minor influence on Christendom as a whole. After her Spain was the leading power in Europe for nearly 150 years—rock-solid in faith, indestructible in strength, the last flowering of the glory of medieval Christendom upon the dawn of the modern age. Without her this could not have happened. She raised up the banners of the crusade that had fallen at Ancona when she was thirteen years old. She sent Columbus to bring the cross to half the world.

That is why, from the Catholic perspective upon history, the focus of attention in the forty years from 1464 to 1504 must be primarily upon Isabel "the Catholic" of Spain.[6]

In 1465 the great nobles of anarchic Castile had reached a pitch of power from which they were confident they could depose the hapless, neurotic, pacifistic and sexually impotent King Henry IV from his throne and replace him

---

[4]More details about these achievements appear below, in this chapter and in Chapter 15, and at much greater length in the writer's *Isabel of Spain: the Catholic Queen* (Front Royal VA, 1991).

[5]*Ibid.*

[6]On December 19, 1496, by Papal bull, Isabel and Fernando were formally designated *los reyes católicos*, "the Catholic sovereigns," by which title they have ever since been known in Spain (Vicente Rodriguez Valencia, *Isabel la Católica en la Opinion de Españoles y Extranjeros*, Volume I [Valladolid, 1970], p. 48).

with Isabel's eleven-year-old brother Alfonso, a minor wholly under their control. They held a mocking ceremony of deposition on a platform at Avila, with a crowned wooden dummy standing in for Henry. Archbishop Carrillo of Toledo, the primate of Spain, took off its crown and the dummy was kicked off the platform to shouts of "Down, queer!" But this went too far; the people of Castile rose against such treatment of an anointed king, however incompetent, and the rebels had to negotiate with him. Their leader, the Marqués of Villena, a master plotter and betrayer, who in a proverb of the time "never speaks ill or does well," in March 1466 offered peace to Henry at the price of the marriage of his half-sister Isabel to Pedro Girón, Villena's brother. Girón was 43 years old, master of the once-crusading order of Calatrava, by canon law a monk vowed to chastity, whose lechery and multitude of bastards were the talk of Spain, a swaggering bully as different from the devout 14-year-old girl as two human beings could be. Asked for a dispensation to permit Girón to marry Isabel, Pope Paul II granted it without hesitation or investigation of the circumstances. When Isabel was told her fate, she was completely trapped. Her king and her Pope had decided against her; no human appeal remained. Girón would arrive to marry her in less than a month. The marriage would rape her virtue, destroy her innocence, and erase her from history.[7]

Isabel went straight to God, on her knees in prayer for a full day and night—over and over, simple, straightforward, direct as Isabel always was. There were just two ways out, which could be opened only by His hand. "Either let him die, or let me die. . . . Either let him die, or let me die."[8]

From Jaén Girón rode northward with his men to take Isabel. He rode into the Sierra Morena, the Dark Mountains; he rode through the most famous defile in Spanish history, gate of reconquerors, home of heroes: Despeñaperros, the Pass of the Overthrow of the Infidel Dogs; he rode across the dead-flat plain of La Mancha to the Sierra de la Virgén, the Mountains of the Blessed Virgin Mary, to stop for the night at the little town of Villarrubia de los Ojos, Villarrubia of the Eyes. And there his men noticed that Pedro Girón was swaying in his saddle. They helped him down from his horse. Fever was flaring through his body. His throat burned and filled with alien matter. He called for water, but he could not drink. The next day he grew worse; the next, worse still. Choking, strangling, cursing God with his last breath because He had not let him live to claim his virgin bride, on the third day Pedro Girón died.[9]

---

[7]Townsend Miller, *Henry IV of Castile* (Philadelphia, 1972), pp. 171-183, 187-189; Carroll, *Isabel of Spain*, pp. 20-21, 27-30.

[8]Mosén Diego de Valera, *Memorial de diversas hazañas; Crónica de Enrique IV*, ed. Juan de Mata Carriazo (Madrid, 1941), p. 118; Alonso de Palencia, *Crónica de Enrique IV*, Volume I (Biblioteca de Autores Españoles, Vol. 257, Madrid, 1973), pp. 203-204 (Decade 1, Book 9, Chapter 1). Indirect quotation in the original changed to direct in the translation.

[9]Valera, *Hazañas*, p. 119; Palencia, *Crónica de Enrique IV*, I, 204 (Decade 1, Book 9,

For Jesus Christ is King of Kings, and the earth is the Lord's, and prayers to Him are heard—as Isabel the Catholic had always known, and would never forget. The rebellion continued sporadically for the next two years, until Prince Alfonso suddenly died in July 1468 after a supper of trout. Villena and Carrillo turned to Isabel, expecting to carry on the rebellion in her name while she still took orders from them. But Isabel, 16, was now old enough and strong enough to act on her own, even though she had no one to help or protect her. (Her father, King Juan II of Castile, had died when she was three, and her mother had been insane for much of the time since then.) She would never demand what was not hers by right.[10]

> So long as King Henry may live I shall not take over the government, nor call myself Queen, but will make every effort to the end that King Henry, while he lives, may govern this realm better than he has done.[11]

> Henry is my brother, the King of Castile and León, and I should not please God if I were to commit so grave an act of disrespect [as you propose].[12]

Villena, who had never wanted Henry completely overthrown because he was so well able to control him, quickly adapted himself to the new situation by proposing that Henry recognize Isabel as his successor. This required repudiating his wife and her daughter Juana, who was widely and probably correctly believed not to be Henry's. She was now seven months pregnant with another child after having been completely separated from him for a year, and he wanted nothing more to do with her. The Treaty of Toros de Guisando in September 1468 declared Isabel Henry's successor. At her insistence the treaty provided that she should not be required to marry without her consent, though Henry had to consent as well.[13]

The ink was scarcely dry on the official record of the solemn pledges of

---

Chapter 1); Diego Enríquez del Castillo, "Crónica del Rey don Enrique IV," *Crónicas de los Reyes de Castilla*, ed. Cayetano Rosell, Biblioteca de Autores Españoles, Volume 70 (Madrid, 1878), p. 154 (Chapter 85).

[10]Miller, *Henry IV of Castile*, pp. 222-224, 228-229; Isabel del Val, *Isabel la Católica, Princesa* (Valladolid, 1974), pp. 63-67; Luis Suárez Fernández, "En Torno del Pacto de los Toros de Guisando," *Hispania* XXIII (1963), 345-365; Carroll, *Isabel of Spain*, pp. 34-35.

[11]Valera, *Hazañas*, p. 139. Indirect quotation in the original changed to direct in the translation.

[12]"Libre de las dones," by an anonymous Franciscan, a chaplain to Adrian of Utrecht, reprinted in Rodríguez Valencia, *Isabel la Católica*, I, 314.

[13]Miller, *Henry IV of Castile*, pp. 229-238; del Val, *Isabel la Católica*, pp. 68-91; Baltasar Cuartero y Huerta, *El Pacto de los Toros de Guisando y la Venta del Mismo Nombre* (Madrid, 1952); Carroll, *Isabel of Spain*, pp. 36-39.

Toros de Guisando, sworn upon Bible and crucifix, when the grandees were plotting again how to twist and break them to their own advantage. Villena arranged Isabel's marriage to King Afonso V of Portugal, 43; when she protested this violation of the treaty, she was told she would be locked up in a castle if she did not consent.[14]

"God is my refuge," she replied. "I call upon Him to keep me free from so great a shame and to guard me from such cruel injury."[15] Reasonably and justly concluding that this violation of the compact of Toros de Guisando freed her from the reciprocal obligation to obtain Henry IV's consent for her marriage, she made confidential contact with an envoy of King Juan II of Aragon to indicate her willingness to marry his son Fernando (Ferdinand), who was almost her own age. Juan II was fully a match for Villena; he could and did provide at last the protection which Isabel had so long needed.[16]

The next year was filled with long-range maneuvers and hairbreadth escapes, culminating in Prince Fernando's journey in October 1469, disguised as a mule-driver, from Aragon through hostile territory to Castile and Isabel. Archbishop Carrillo married them at Valladolid on October 19, and the greatest royal partnership in history was launched.[17] The union of Aragon and Castile, along with their subsequent conquest of the Muslim kingdom of Granada, created Spain; the manner in which they ruled it, inspired and guided by Isabel and enriched by the discoveries of Columbus, created the greatest power in the world; and the reform of the Church, which Isabel provided for and insisted upon, accomplished at last, within Spain, the work that had consistently failed elsewhere since the Avignon papacy and the Great Western Schism showed how necessary it had become.

A princess alone, with none but God to aid her, Isabel had begun the shaping of her destiny which in a quarter of a century was to make her the lay leader of Christendom. By constant vigilance and the love of her people for her (which she fully reciprocated), she preserved herself and her new husband from the bitter hostility of the barons she had outwitted, during the five years that remained of her half-brother's life and reign.[18] Let us see her, at this moment

---

[14]Ramón Menéndez Pidal, director, *Historia de España*, Volume XV: "Los Trastámaras de Castilla y Aragon en el Siglo XV," by Luis Suaréz Fernandéz, Angel Canellas López, and Jaime Vicens Vives (Madrid, 1986), p. 289; Carroll, *Isabel of Spain*, pp. 41-42.

[15]Palencia, *Crónica de Enrique IV*, I, 270 (Decade 2, Book 1, Chapter 7). Indirect quotation in the original changed to direct in the translation.

[16]Menéndez Pidal, *Historia de España*, XV, 290; Miller, *Henry IV of Castile*, pp. 96-97, 227, 241; Carroll, *Isabel of Spain*, pp. 39, 43-46.

[17]Miller, *Henry IV of Castile*, pp. 251-253; del Val, *Isabel la Católica*, pp. 151-152, 176-198; Menéndez Pidal, *Historia de España*, XV, 291-292, 295-296; P. Tarsicio de Azcona, *Isabel la Católica* (Madrid, 1964), pp. 145-146; Carroll, *Isabel of Spain*, pp. 47-59.

[18]Carroll, *Isabel of Spain*, pp. 59-72.

of triumphant beginning, as she is sketched by the anonymous contemporary chronicler of these years of her life, a portrait clearly drawn from life by one who loved her:

> The Princess had blue-green eyes with long eyelashes, full of sparkle along with great frankness and dignity. High arching eyebrows much enhanced the beauty of her eyes and countenance. Her nose was of a size and shape that made her face more beautiful. Her mouth was small and red, her teeth small and white. Her laughter was quiet and controlled; rarely was she seen to laugh in the customary manner of youth, but with restraint and moderation. In this and in all things the character and honor of womanly virtue shone in her face. She was regarded with such respect that no great prince who dealt with her had the audacity to be in the least discourteous to her. From her childhood she was brought up by her mother in honesty and virginal purity, so that never did her worst enemy find any reason or suggestion to stain her reputation.
> Her face colored readily under its white skin, and was of royal mien. Her hair was very long and golden-red, and she would often run her hands through it, to arrange it so as better to display the configuration of her face. Her throat was high, full and rounded, as women prefer it to be; her hands were exquisitely graceful; all her body and her person were as lovely as a woman's could be. She was moderately tall. In person and countenance no one in her time touched her perfection, refinement and purity. Her aspect as she moved, and the beauty of her face, were luminous.[19]

Elsewhere in Western Europe during these years when Isabel was Princess of Castile with the right of succession, a three-cornered contest was in progress among France, England, and Burgundy—the last once a duchy ruled by a branch of the reigning French Valois dynasty, which had expanded well beyond historic French territory by absorbing most of the Low Countries to become a virtual kingdom in its own right and an inveterate rival to France, whose devious King Louis XI never stopped seeking to regain control of it. France and Burgundy each sought to use England against their rival, aided by the cleavage in that country between the dispossessed Lancastrians and the reigning Yorkists.

Louis XI drew the ambitious English "kingmaker" Richard Neville, Earl of Warwick, into his nets, taking advantage of his bitter resentment over his sovereign's secret marriage to Elizabeth Woodville, to use him against King Edward IV of England whose sister Margaret married Duke Charles of Burgundy. In the fall of 1470 a French-supported rising by Warwick expelled Edward IV from England. He took refuge in the Low Countries under Duke Charles' protection, and with Burgundian help returned to England and regained his throne, defeating and killing Warwick at the Battle of Barnet in

---

[19]*Crónica incompleta de los Reyes Catolicos (1469-1476), según un manuscrito anónimo de la epoca*, ed. Julio Puyol (Madrid, 1934), pp. 88-89.

April 1471 and shortly afterward defeating Marguerite of Anjou, wife of the incompetent deposed King Henry VI, at the Battle of Tewkesbury.[20] But Duke Charles' initial success went to his head. His ambition became inordinate, and with too limited resources he sought to seize Alsace and penetrate Switzerland and the Rhineland. Holy Roman Emperor Frederick III denounced him in August 1474, the Swiss defeated him at Héricourt in November, the French defeated him in June 1475, and his ally Edward IV of England betrayed him and made peace with the French in August. The Swiss proved themselves the best infantry in Europe as they devastatingly defeated Charles' armies again at Grandson and Murten in March and June 1476. Joan of Arc's province of Lorraine, which Charles had roughly annexed, then rose against him, and at the Battle of Nancy in January 1477 the Burgundians were routed and Charles was killed. His work and his kingdom endured, but shorn of its French extension; under his only child and heiress Mary, it was confined to the Low Countries (now known as Belgium and the Netherlands) and linked with the fortunes of the imperial Habsburgs by Mary's marriage to the heir to the Holy Roman Empire, Archduke Maximilian, in August 1477.[21]

Neither in these events nor in those of Spain did Pope Paul II have significant influence. He was not even a major player in the affairs of turbulent Italy. The one area where he tried to wield a strong arm was Bohemia under its King George Podebrady, who continued to defy the Church on the issue of Hussite communion. In the first year of his pontificate Paul II reiterated his predecessor's condemnation of George and demanded his removal. In May 1466 he called upon the Catholic kings of Eastern Europe to assist in expelling George. The ambitious young King of Hungary, Matthias Corvinus, son of the great John Hunyadi, gained the support of a rebel league of Catholic Czech nobles and made the attempt. But the Czechs were still stout fighters, and memories of One-Eyed John endured. Though taking over some parts of Moravia near Hungary, Matthias could make no more than brief penetrations into populous and well-defended Bohemia.[22]

However, George had no hereditary title to the Bohemian throne, and though able to maintain himself as its king until his death in 1471, he could not gain sufficient support there to pass on the royal title to his children. The widely respected and long-lived Hussite leader John Rokycana died just a

---

[20]Paul M. Kendall, *Warwick the Kingmaker* (New York, 1957), pp. 193-369; Paul M. Kendall, *Louis XI, the Universal Spider* (New York, 1971), pp. 196-243; E. F. Jacob, *The Fifteenth Century, 1399-1485* [The Oxford History of England] (Oxford, 1961), pp. 550-570; Charles Ross, *Edward IV* (Berkeley CA, 1974), pp. 104-177; Richard Vaughan, *Charles the Bold; the Last Valois Duke of Burgundy* (London, 1973), pp. 41-83.
[21]Vaughan, *Charles the Bold*, pp. 261-432; Kendall, *Louis XI*, p. 319.
[22]Frederick G. Heymann, *George of Bohemia, King of Heretics* (Princeton, 1965), pp. 384-546; Otakar Odlozilik, *The Hussite King; Bohemia in European Affairs, 1440-1471* (New Brunswick, NJ, 1965), pp. 168-248.

month before King George, and in August 1471 Prince Vladislav, son of Casimir IV of Poland, was crowned King of Bohemia in Prague by three Polish bishops who distributed Communion at the ceremony in the Catholic manner (without the chalice). But in the end the stern policy of Popes Pius II and Paul II against the Hussites failed. Fourteen years later King Vladislav felt obliged to accept the Accord of Kutna Hora, which put the Compacts of 1433 back into effect, with Hussites and Catholics each to control their own churches, each side enjoined from attacking the other, and neither permitted to try to convert adherents of the other. The Pope at that time, the weak Innocent VIII, made no objection to this agreement which actually prohibited Catholic evangelization. So the long struggle ended with Czechs distributed among three churches: Catholic, Utraquist Hussite (recognized by the Accord of Kutna Hora, schismatic but for the most part not heretical), and the Moravian Brethren who maintained the radically anti-Catholic element in Hussite history and theology.[23]

On July 26, 1471 Pope Paul II died suddenly of a stroke at the age of only 54. The conclave to elect a new Pope assembled August 6 with eighteen cardinals present. The completeness of the restoration of the Roman and Italian papacy was evident in its composition: fifteen of the cardinals were Italian and a sixteenth, Rodrigo Borgia, was a Spaniard who had lived almost all his adult life in Italy. French Cardinal d'Estouteville and Greek Cardinal Bessarion were the other cardinals at the conclave. On August 9 Cardinal Francisco della Rovere, aged 57, was elected Pope Sixtus IV, with Cardinals Orsini, Gonzaga and Borgia mainly responsible for his elevation.[24]

The new Pope was a learned and holy Franciscan, distinguished both for his writing and his preaching, who had risen to the leadership of his order in 1464 and had made a serious attempt to reform it during the three years he served in that office, before Paul II made him a Cardinal in 1467. As Cardinal he maintained a simple Franciscan life-style and carried on his scholarly work just as he had done before, rejecting the ostentation which was becoming more and more typical of Cardinals during these years. He sought to revive Pius II's project of a crusade against the Turks, sending out four Cardinals as legates to preach it, but had no more success than Pius. The aged Cardinal Bessarion, watching his life-work for union of the Eastern and Western churches crumble into dust, died on this mission, in November 1472. In this same month Zoe Palaeologus, niece of the heroic last Byzantine Emperor Constantine XI and ward of the Pope, whom Bessarion had offered to Ivan III of Moscow as a Greek Catholic wife, married Ivan; but she would not allow the papal legate

---

[23]Heymann, *George of Bohemia*, pp. 584-585; Odlozilik, *Hussite King*, pp. 228-230, 261-262, 268, 271-272.
[24]Von Pastor, *History of the Popes*, IV, 190, 199-204.

who accompanied her to Moscow to be identified as such, and by conforming entirely to the Russian Orthodox ritual effectively abandoned her Catholic ties.[25]

Of Sixtus IV's good intentions there could be no doubt, and from the first he sensed a kindred spirit in Isabel; one of his earliest acts as Pope was to regularize her marriage to Fernando, which had been solemnized under a forged dispensation (almost certainly without her knowledge). He admired her and worked closely with her during the first ten years of her reign.[26] But his pontificate was shadowed by the terrible mistake he made almost at its beginning, in December 1471, when he appointed two of his nephews Cardinals. One, Giuliano della Rovere, the future Pope Julius II, though only 28, was extraordinarily intelligent and capable, and though too worldly, had a genuine love for the Church; his was a defensible appointment. But the other, Piero Riario, was only 25, and though cultivated, popular and generous, was full of avarice, ambition and pride. The harm he did to the Church was great.[27]

Sixtus IV made Piero Riario Archbishop of Florence (until recently the seat of St. Antoninus), patriarch in exile of Constantinople, and bishop of four other dioceses, with a colossal annual revenue amounting to millions of dollars in today's money. In the evocative and in this case only too true phrase of the anti-Catholic German papal historian Gregorovius, Riario was "transformed in one night from a mendicant friar into a Croesus, plunged into the maddest excesses." His fantastic costumes and banquets were the talk and scandal of Rome: his clothes were covered with gold and the gowns of his openly flaunted mistress with pearls; courses at his dinners (a particularly notorious dinner had 44 of them including a whole bear and ten baked ships) were announced by a lavishly dressed man on horseback, and the meals concluded with a lascivious Moorish dance. That Piero Riario had originally been a Franciscan vowed to poverty made the scandal still worse. Sixtus IV would not curb him, and no one else could. In just three years the Last Judge called Piero Riario before His own tribunal at the age of only 28, his body wrecked by his excesses. He repented with apparent sincerity on his deathbed, but the evil he had done lived after him—not only in the damage he had done to the reputation of the Church, but in his brother Girolamo, heir to his vast fortune, a totally unprincipled schemer whose position as advisor and confidant of the Pope gave still more scandal only somewhat mitigated by the fact that Girolamo was at least not a cardinal or a bishop.[28]

[25]*Ibid.*, IV, 204-210, 217-221, 229-230; George Vernadsky, *Russia at the Dawn of the Modern Age* (New Haven CT, 1959), pp. 18-21.
[26]Del Val, *Isabel la católica*, pp. 195-198; Menéndez Pidal, *Historia de España*, XV, 306; Carroll, *Isabel of Spain*, pp. 58-59, 62-63.
[27]Von Pastor, *History of the Popes*, IV, 232, 235-238.
[28]*Ibid.*, IV, 238-254, quotation on p. 238; Ernst Breisach, *Caterina Sforza, a*

With the help of his uncle the Pope, Girolamo Riario purchased the strategically placed town of Imola in the Romagna, which Lorenzo "the Magnificent," one of the two young Medici brothers now ruling Florence, coveted for his Tuscan state. Lorenzo in turn supported a rebellion in one of the towns of the Papal State. When Piero Riario died, Lorenzo demanded the appointment of his brother-in-law Rinaldo Orsini to the archbishopric of Florence. The Pope had intended to appoint Francesco Salviati to that office, and though he reluctantly yielded to Lorenzo's demand, he insisted on appointing Salviati to the nearby and also vacant archbishopric of Pisa. The city of Pisa had long since been incorporated into the Florentine state, and the Popes had a working agreement with Florence that no episcopal appointments would be made in its territory without the consent of its government. In this case the consent of Florence was neither asked nor given. Consequently Lorenzo refused Archbishop Salviati admission into Tuscany. For three years, in growing anger, Salviati was kept waiting in Rome, unable to take possession of his archdiocese.[29]

At the end of 1476 Galeazzo Maria Sforza, dictator of Milan, was assassinated by three young men on his way to Mass. Galeazzo Maria had been Lorenzo's ally, and the much discussed crime may well have suggested to Lorenzo's enemies that he might be disposed of in the same manner. Early in 1478 Girolamo Riario, Archbishop-designate Salviati, and Francesco de Pazzi, the Florentine manager of the Pazzi bank in Rome, began developing a plot to kill Lorenzo and his brother Giuliano. Pazzi came from an ancient Florentine family whose fame and fortune had been virtually eclipsed by the politically successful and immensely wealthy Medicis. He was popularly regarded as the prime mover in the plot, which has consequently gone down in history as "the Pazzi conspiracy." The three conspirators sought to engage the services of a mercenary captain in the service of the Pope named Gian Battista da Montesecco, but he would not accept their offer unless the Pope approved.[30]

Girolamo Riario and Archbishop Salviati consequently went to Sixtus IV. The discussion that followed has often been quoted, because it appears in dramatic dialogue form in a later confession extracted from Montesecco under torture. Historians who instantly dismiss all confessions obtained by the Spanish Inquisition under torture or threat of torture have nevertheless not hesitated to accept Montesecco's confession under torture, implicating the Pope in the assassination plot, as complete, literal truth. The dialogue Montesecco reports has Sixtus IV agreeing that there is great need for a change of government in Florence in view of Lorenzo's hostility to the Pope, but

Renaissance Virago (Chicago, 1967), pp. 23-25.
[29]Von Pastor, *History of the Popes*, IV, 292-299; Christopher Hibbert, *The House of Medici: its Rise and Fall* (New York, 1980), pp. 128-130.
[30]Hibbert, *House of Medici*, pp. 131-132.

repeatedly insisting that the change of government must involve no deliberate killing. But the Pope is said to have agreed to let the plot go forward even after being told that it might involve the death of Lorenzo.[31]

Montesecco never had a trial; no defense attorney ever took his testimony. Four days after his torture and confession he was beheaded in the courtyard of the Bargello in Florence.[32] Though his confession may be taken to indicate that there was some discussion with the Pope on a violent overthrow of the government in Florence, and that the Pope repudiated assassination as a part of that overthrow (since this is mentioned no less than three times) it cannot reasonably upheld as literally accurate as to the Pope's exact words and implications.

The conspirators at first planned to invite Lorenzo to Rome and murder him there. When he cautiously refused to come to Rome, they planned to assassinate him and his brother Giuliano at a reception for Raffaele Riario, the Pope's grand-nephew and a student at the University of Pisa whom he had just made a Cardinal despite the fact that he was only 17. But Giuliano did not come due to an injury to his leg, so the plotters now decided to kill both brothers at Mass in Florence's splendid cathedral, at the moment when the bell rang for the consecration of the Host. Adding such sacrilege to murder was too much for Montesecco; a believing Catholic for all his sins, he refused to kill on the signal that Christ had come to the altar. Riario, Salviati and Pazzi found two priests to take his place who bitterly hated Lorenzo and were undisturbed by the sacrilege, but inexpert in the use of daggers.[33]

Though by this time the plot had been revealed to many, no information about it reached the Medici. On April 26 Giuliano was horribly hacked to death at the moment of consecration at Mass in the Cathedral of Florence, his life's blood pouring from nineteen wounds in full view of the petrified young Cardinal Raffaele Riario. But the inexperienced priest assassins only gave Lorenzo a slight wound in the neck. Using his cloak as a shield and swinging his sword, the athletic young Medici jumped over the altar rail, ran into the sanctuary and closed its heavy bronze doors just in time.[34]

As word of the atrocity—committed in the full view of hundreds and in the hearing of thousands—spread through the city, there was an overwhelming reaction in favor of Lorenzo. Archbishop Salviati's attempt to take over the government in the Pope's name was spurned. Almost all the principal

---

[31]*Ibid.*, pp. 132-133; Ferdinand Schevill, *Medieval and Renaissance Florence* (New York, 1961), pp. 383-384; Von Pastor, *History of the Popes*, IV, 303-307. Even Von Pastor calls Montesecco's statement "thoroughly credible," without making reference to the fact that he was tortured before giving it.

[32]Hibbert, *House of Medici*, pp. 141-142.

[33]*Ibid.*, pp. 134-136; Von Pastor, *History of the Popes*, IV, 307-309.

[34]Hibbert, *House of Medici*, pp. 136-139; Von Pastor, *History of the Popes*, IV, 309-310.

conspirators in Florence were quickly seized and slain. Archbishop Salviati and Francesco de Pazzi were summarily hanged from a transom and their bodies thrown to a furious crowd to be torn to pieces. Lorenzo saved the life of young Cardinal Raffaele Riario, correctly believing that he was not involved in the conspiracy, but held him in prison for several weeks. But Girolamo Riario, who had prudently stayed away from the scene of the crime he had played a leading part in planning, retained his position in Rome and Imola and the trust and confidence of Pope Sixtus, giving immense scandal even to those convinced that the Pope himself had never approved the intended assassination. And Sixtus, while condemning the assassination and the sacrilege, nevertheless excommunicated Lorenzo and placed Florence under interdict for its treatment of Archbishop Salviati and imprisonment of the young Cardinal.[35]

War followed between Florence and the Pope, continuing until the shocking Turkish attack on Italy itself in 1480 recalled both the Pope and Lorenzo to the importance of the unity of Christendom.[36] But that unity was steadily weakening, the gains which had been made by the reunion following the Great Schism being frittered away. Love and respect for the Pope—the cornerstone of the Church—were fading. It is always difficult for limited and fallible human beings to separate the office from the man, to understand and remember that no individual's weaknesses or even sins can stain a seat made by God Himself. The Great Schism had revealed the danger in a different form, when so many of the Church's best had lost sight of the importance of knowing and proclaiming who the true Pope was. Then he had been seen as just one of several equally probable claimants to the office. Now he was beginning to be seen more as another Renaissance prince than as head of the Church Christ founded.

A little more than three years before the Pazzi conspiracy exploded into bloodshed and horror in the cathedral of Florence, Isabel at 23 had succeeded to the throne of Castile upon the death of her half-brother Henry IV. She had strong support among the common people and arranged a quick though impressive coronation the day following Henry's death. Fernando came immediately to her side and within a few weeks they had begun to practice their uniquely fused coregency by which every official action was taken in both their names and every official document bore both their names. But Isabel's right to the Castilian throne was almost immediately challenged by King Afonso V of Portugal in the name of Juana, the daughter and namesake of Henry's estranged queen whom he had repudiated at the Treaty of Toros de Guisando,

---

[35]Von Pastor, *History of the Popes*, IV, 310-318, 348-349; Hibbert, *House of Medici*, pp. 138-142, 147-149.

[36]Von Pastor, *History of the Popes*, IV, 320-330. See below for the Turkish attack on Otranto, Italy in 1480 and its consequences.

but endorsed again later under pressure from Villena. Though Juana's paternity was widely doubted, the possibility could not be excluded that Henry was her father, and Afonso proclaimed his intention to marry her, though she was thirteen to his fifty and his niece, and he did not yet have a papal dispensation. A substantial part of the predatory, lawless Castilian nobility—seventy years of weak or puppet government had made many of them little more than robber barons—supported the foreign challenge. It was in this difficult and dangerous situation that Isabel offered, again and again before her people, the prayer that stands at the head of this chapter—that God would help her if she was in the right, but tell her if she was in the wrong.[37]

She went in person to try to persuade Archbishop Carrillo, the primate of Castile who had married her and Fernando, not to desert her cause; but he had committed himself to the challengers and would not speak to her. On May 10, 1475 a well-equipped Portuguese army crossed the border, led by King Afonso V in person. Isabel, crowned less than five months before, had no army at all; she and Fernando were still in the process of raising one. She fired off condemnations of the rebel Castilian nobles by letter to the principal cities of her kingdom; she rode to Toledo to gather troops, then to Avila, across the arid, rocky high plains of Castile. She was pregnant with her second child, and on the way to Avila she suffered a miscarriage. The baby had been a son.[38]

Despite this heavy personal blow, Isabel soon brought thousands to join the army assembled under the command of Fernando in early July to attack the invaders at the city of Toro which they had seized, near the Portuguese border. But before the slow-moving and untrained troops could be brought to Toro, the invaders had taken two more cities. Fernando hesitated, the army ran short of supplies, and soon it returned to its base with nothing accomplished.[39] With firmly controlled passion Isabel told its commanders:

> One must first give battle to be able to proclaim victory; he who begins nothing, finishes nothing. Where will we go and what will we attempt that is good, when with so many people and so many resources we bring forth so cold a triumph? ... Those who do not recognize opportunity when it comes, find misfortune when they do not look for it.[40]

---

[37]William H. Prescott, *The Reign of Ferdinand and Isabella the Catholic* (Philadelphia, 1893), I, 235-236; Ramón Menéndez Pidal, director, *Historia de España*, Volume XVII: "España de los Reyes Católicos," by Luis Suárez Fernández and Manuel Fernández Alvarez (Madrid, 1969), Part 1, pp. 98, 114; Carroll, *Isabel of Spain*, pp. 72-78.
[38]Eloy Benito Ruano, *Toledo en el siglo XV; vida política* (Madrid, 1961), pp. 288-292; Carroll, *Isabel of Spain*, pp. 80-84.
[39]Menéndez Pidal, *Historia de España*, XVII (1), 132-134; Carroll, *Isabel of Spain*, pp. 84-87.
[40]Puyol, ed. *Crónica incompleta*, p. 240.

Inspired by her confidence and zeal, in September her commanders challenged and halted an attempted Portuguese advance across the high plains of Castile to Burgos, whose citadel was held by rebels. The turning point was the magnificent all-day fight of Isabel's champion, the Count of Benavente, with 150 men against odds of forty to one in the little town of Baltanás. After that the invaders turned back, awaiting reinforcements. Prince John of Portugal arrived with a new army in February 1476, but the combined Portuguese and Castilian rebel army was decisively defeated by Fernando at the Battle of Toro on March 1, effectively ending the war. Queen Isabel had rallied from defeat as her people had rallied to her.[41]

She set to work immediately restoring order in her long-ravaged realm. During the spring and summer of 1476 she established throughout much of the country a volunteer police force on a permanent basis called the *Santa Hermandad* ("Holy Brotherhood"), financed by local nobles, to suppress and punish violent crime. It was strikingly and almost immediately successful. But even as the Holy Brotherhoods were being formed, in mid-summer of 1476, there was a revolt in Segovia where Isabel's best friend Beatriz and her husband Andrés de Cabrera had been staying with Princess Isabel, the Queen's only child. The revolt occurred when the Cabreras were away, and Cabrera's father was unable to stop it. The rebels confined the six-year-old princess and her attendants to one beleaguered tower in the castle.[42]

Isabel got the news in Tordesillas, 65 miles away. The historian Palencia (who was present) tells us that not a muscle moved in her face when she received the appalling report. But she sprang instantly into action. Within an hour she was on her horse and riding southward with only two companions: Cardinal Mendoza, her chief supporter among the clergy, and the Count of Benavente, the hero of Baltanás. Across the high plains they galloped, unprotected, unescorted, their straining horses casting ever-longer shadows in the reddening light: the 25-year-old Queen like some legendary Valkyrie, burnished in the sunset glow; the dark, almost swarthy Cardinal, no longer a young man, striving manfully to keep up; and the peerless warrior count who had held Baltanás for the Queen an entire day against odds of forty to one. They alone could tame Segovia and save the princess; they needed no one else.[43]

They stopped briefly at Olmedo, about a third of the way to Segovia, and

---

[41]Menéndez Pidal, *Historia de España*, XVII (1), 141-147; Carroll, *Isabel of Spain*, pp. 88-97.

[42]Menéndez Pidal, *Historia de España*, XVII (1), 232-245; Rafael Fuertes Arias, *Alfonso de Quintanilla, Contador Mayor de los Reyes Católicos* (Oviedo, 1909), I, 117-119, 131-132; Carroll, *Isabel of Spain*, pp. 97-100.

[43]Palencia, *Crónica de Enrique IV*, II, 305-306 (Decade 3, Book 7, Chapter 3); Carroll, *Isabel of Spain*, p. 101.

then pressed on all through the night. As the morning advanced, they caught their first glimpse of the castle of Segovia gleaming in lofty splendor atop its gigantic rock far across the rolling, rising foothills of the Guadarrama Mountains. At noon they drew rein at the gates of the city. A delegation of rebels met her, prepared to negotiate.[44] Isabel sat tall in her saddle, and her clear voice rang:

> Tell those cavaliers and citizens of Segovia that I am Queen of Castile, and this city is mine, for the king my father left it to me; and to enter what is mine no laws nor conditions may be laid down for me. I shall enter the city by whatever gate I choose; I shall enter with the Count of Benavente, and all others whom I need for my service. Say to them also that they should all come to me, and obey my orders, like loyal subjects, and stop making tumults and scandals in my city, lest they suffer harm in their persons and in their property.[45]

The rebels fell silent, abashed; Isabel and the Cardinal and the Count rode through the nearest gate. They had to traverse the whole length of the city to reach the castle. Throngs of belligerent people fell back respectfully to make way as they appeared. No one dared shut the lone gate of the castle in the Queen's face, though the place is almost overwhelming in its impregnability even today: a single small bridge crossing a moat so deep that it might better be called a gorge, to the one door opening in a towering turret-crowned wall of stone. Inside, Isabel assured herself of her daughter's safety, then returned to the gate, where an enormous crowd was shouting its hostility and demands. The Cardinal and the Count urged Isabel to bar the gate. But she knew better. These were her people, whom she loved and who loved her; they would not fight her. The evildoers among them could not stand against her face to face. With a serene and magnificent confidence, she ordered the lone gate opened and the entire crowd invited in. She promised them an investigation of their complaints, and justice. They cheered her to the echo. The rebel leader fled for his life. After her investigation revealed that Cabrera had done nothing wrong, she reinstated him and the people accepted it. It was the most striking single demonstration in her reign of how Queen Isabel ruled.[46]

The next year she went south to Sevilla, the great city of Andalusia, which had been without effective royal government during almost all living memory, full of faction, strife and corruption, in which everything and everyone had a price. On July 25, the feast of the Apostle St. James the Greater, patron of Spain, Isabel set up her judgment seat, draped with cloth of gold, in the once

---

[44]Carroll, *Isabel of Spain*, pp. 101-102.
[45]Fernando del Pulgar, *Crónica de los Reyes Católicos*, ed. Juan de Mata Carriazo (Madrid, 1943), I, 270 (Chapter 78).
[46]Carroll, *Isabel of Spain*, pp. 102-103.

Moorish palace with its slim red pillars, half-dome arches and an orange ceiling carved like a cloud. Each litigant was brought to face her personally. Often she delivered summary judgment on the spot. More difficult cases were referred to one of her councillors or jurists with orders to investigate further and report back to her. Bribes, however disguised, were scornfully rejected. Isabel spared no one whom she considered guilty. No less than four thousand malefactors fled the city rather than face her. The Marqués of Cádiz, one of the principal noblemen of the region, who like so many others there had scorned the law, came in person to beg her forgiveness and offer his services—which she graciously accepted, and were to prove of inestimable value to Spain during the forthcoming reconquest of Granada.   When Fernando arrived in mid-September, the essential work was done. It was then that they conceived their only living son, Juan, born in June 1478.[47]

On October 3, 1477, in a festive mood, Isabel and Fernando boarded a galley for a fifty-mile trip down the Guadalquivir River from Sevilla to San Lucár de Barrameda at its mouth. Before the galley stopped at San Lucár, Isabel suggested that they sail out into the open Atlantic, rolling to the far horizon at the mouth of the river.[48] For the first time, Isabel's attention had been drawn to the vast western ocean, which guarded one of the supreme mysteries of the ages, on which the best remembered of all her subjects was to find his destiny and change the world. The Portuguese had ventured hundreds of miles out upon it, but no once since the Norsemen five hundred years before and far to the north had ever crossed it.

Prince Henry the Navigator had established so firmly the tradition of pushing steadily onward along the unexplored coast of Africa that this progress had continued steadily during the fifteen years after his death. No history or detailed reports of these voyages of discovery have survived, and many of them are completely unknown. Their progress comes into historical light when in 1469 King Afonso V granted the wealthy merchant Fernao Gomes a five-year trade monopoly in Africa in return for an annual advance of 100 leagues along its coast. His first expedition to fulfill this agreement, commanded by Joao de Santarem and Pedro de Escolar and sent out the following year, reached Cape Three Points on the Gold Coast (now Ghana) and found gold there. But since Cape Three Points is no less than seven hundred miles beyond Sierra Leone which the last voyage of exploration dispatched by Prince Henry had reached, it seems likely that there were several unknown expeditions during the intervening decade. In 1472 another expedition reached the site of the present Lagos, Nigeria, four hundred miles beyond Cape Three Points. In 1473 Fernao Po sailed all the way to the Cameroons, where the coast of Africa, after running

---

[47]*Ibid.*, pp. 113-116, 122.
[48]*Ibid.*, p. 116; Menéndez Pidal, *Historia de España*, XVII (1), 226, 276-278.

almost a thousand miles nearly due east, makes a right-angle bend to the southward—undoubtedly a great disappointment to this bold captain, who also on this voyage discovered the large island off the Cameroons coast which still bears his name. The equator lies just over 200 miles south of Fernao Po Island; Ruy de Sequeira crossed it in November 1474, a month before Isabel's coronation.[49]

After that, it seems that his war against Castile so preoccupied King Afonso V of Portugal that he lost interest in African exploration, for we hear no more of it during the remainder of his reign. Only after his death in 1481 was it resumed by his able son and successor John II.

Up to this time, Spain's only Atlantic venture had been the conquest and settlement of four of the Canary Islands, an archipelago off the Moroccan coast northwest of Cape Bojador. These islands had native inhabitants. In June 1472 Pope Sixtus IV had issued a bull calling for their conversion to Christianity, along with the blacks of Guinea which Portugal was exploring.[50] Isabel took that missionary responsibility very seriously indeed. On September 28, 1477, in Sevilla, just five days before their trip down the Guadalquivir and view of the ocean that led to the Canary Islands and beyond, Isabel and Fernando issued this uncompromising condemnation of oppression and enslavement of these natives at the hands of their subjects:

> We have heard that some persons have brought some natives of the Canary Islands and, by the will of the lord of those islands and other persons, have sold them and divided them out among themselves as slaves, though some are Christians, and others on the way to converting to our Holy Catholic Faith. This is a great disservice to God and to us and is detrimental to our Holy Catholic Faith, and it would be a great burden on our consciences to consent to it, because it would lead to no one wishing to convert to the Holy Faith.[51]

The language and emphasis strongly suggest Isabel's personal authorship of this decree. It went on to prescribe severe fines and confiscation of goods for anyone found guilty of enslaving the natives of the Canary Islands, particularly those who had become Christians or whose conversion was likely. Isabel would maintain this special emphasis and concern throughout her reign, extending the same protection to the natives of America.

Isabel climaxed her restoration of law and order and good government in

---

[49]Bailey W. Diffie and George D. Winius, *Foundations of the Portuguese Empire, 1415-1580* (Minneapolis MN, 1977), pp. 146-147; Edgar Prestage, *The Portuguese Pioneers* (London, 1933), pp. 57-58; John W. Blake, *West Africa; Quest for God and Gold, 1454-1478*, 2nd ed. (London, 1977), pp. 26-27.

[50]Antonio Rumeu de Armas, *La política indigenista de Isabel la Católica* (Valladolid, 1969), pp. 39-40, 151-157.

[51]*Ibid.*, p. 164.

Castile by summoning its parliament, the *cortes*, to meet at Toledo during the first five months of 1480. The most critical problem then facing the realm was an acute shortage of public funds resulting from the alienation of the greater part of the royal lands during the chaotic reign of Isabel's predecessor, Henry IV. This had caused a drastic reduction of income for the ruler and necessitated the return of the lands or heavy new taxes. Isabel required all the noblemen of Castile who had obtained lands from the crown during the reign of Henry IV to provide a written statement of what (if anything) they had done to earn them. A commission headed by Isabel's confessor, Fray Hernando de Talavera, then reviewed the statements and decided which of the properties should be returned to the crown as never having been in any genuine sense earned.[52]

Talavera's findings showed that most of the noblemen ought to give back at least a quarter or a third of their lands. Isabel called on them to do so. Astonishingly, not one refused. Few monarchs, however powerful, of any time and country could have brought about so massive a land reform without vocal and violent opposition and at least a major threat of civil war. But in just five years of reigning, Isabel's prestige and moral authority had risen so high that nothing of the kind occurred. Almost everyone involved actually seemed to take pride in at long last behaving like statesmen. Isabel insisted that two-thirds of the first year's new income be used to compensate those who had suffered with particular severity from the war with Portugal and internal disorder—notably the widows and orphans of those who had died in defense of the kingdom or in the plunder, rapine and mayhem that had scourged the land until Isabel's Holy Brotherhood put it down.[53]

The two months following the close of the *cortes* of Toledo in May 1480 were a time of high drama in the eastern Mediterranean. The empire of the Ottoman Turks, having digested and absorbed its far-flung conquests in Greece, the Balkans, and around the Black Sea, was ready for new aggression. Its obvious initial target was the large island of Rhodes within sight of the Turkish coast, held by the celibate crusading order of the Knights of St. John of the Hospital, founded 350 years before in Jerusalem soon after the First Crusade. On May 23 an immense Ottoman host, said to number 70,000, arrived at Rhodes with as much of the artillery that had broken the walls of Constantinople 27 years before as could be conveyed by ship. Grand Master Pierre d'Aubusson had only about 600 of his Knights to provide the core of the defense, and only minimal support from about 1,500 mercenaries and local

<hr>

[52]Menéndez Pidal, *Historia de España*, XVII (1), 357-365; Carroll, *Isabel of Spain*, pp. 129-131.

[53]Menéndez Pidal, *Historia de España*, XVII (1), 365-372; Carroll, *Isabel of Spain*, pp. 131-132.

militia.[54] In a message to all the other Knights of his order throughout Europe, he flung down the gage of battle:

> We resist with all our power and energy and with courage sustained by our faith in the Mercy of God who never abandons them whose hope is in Him and who fight for the Catholic Faith.... We will continue to confront the enemy while we await the aid of our brethren. Above all we are sustained by our loyalty to the Holy Religion.... What is more sacred than the defense of the Faith? What is happier than to fight for Christ? What is nobler than to redeem the promises which we made when we put on the habit of our order?[55]

A key to the defenses of Rhodes was the Tower of St. Nicholas, with 24-foot-thick walls. After days of bombardment the gigantic Turkish cannon that had smashed their way into Constantinople had reduced the tower to a ruin. Nevertheless the knights repelled every assault on it, and d'Aubusson scornfully dismissed all Turkish offers to negotiate so long as their army stood on Rhodian soil. In July the Turks transferred their bombardment to the south wall of the city of Rhodes, which they likewise laid in ruins. On the 27th they raised the black flag, which meant that if their attack was successful, every man taken in arms in the city would be killed, every woman and child sold into slavery, and every Knight impaled upon a stake. Turkish attackers reached the top of the wall. D'Aubusson and a dozen Knights blocked the way along the top, planting the standards of the Holy Cross, Our Lady, and St. John the Baptist, fighting chest to chest, halting the whole enemy army in its tracks. Many of the knights later said they saw at that moment in the sky "a refulgent cross of gold, by the side of which stood a beautiful woman clothed in garments of dazzling white, a lance in her hand and a buckler on her arm, accompanied by a man dressed in goatskins and followed by a band of heavenly warriors armed with flaming swords." The Turks fell back at the very moment d'Aubusson took a spear through his breastplate into his lung, a wound considered invariably fatal before the advent of modern medicine. Yet he survived, to live to be eighty and to govern his order for 23 more years. The Turks were utterly defeated (against odds of 35 to 1) and correspondingly humiliated.[56]

They sought revenge by a wholly unexpected assault on the city of Otranto at the southern tip of Italy in August, storming it and capturing 22,000 people. Twelve thousand were killed, many after refusing offers to spare their lives by converting to Islam; the rest were sold into slavery. The Turks killed every cleric in the city and sawed the Archbishop of Otranto in two. Isabel reacted at once, sending a Castilian fleet to Italy the moment she heard the news. A year

---

[54]Eric Brockman, *The Two Sieges of Rhodes, 1480-1522* (London, 1969), pp. 64-67.
[55]*Ibid.*, pp. 71-72.
[56]*Ibid.*, pp. 67-90 (quotation on p. 88).

later, after a siege and the death of their Sultan, the Turkish garrison remaining in Otranto surrendered; but the whole episode was a flare-lit warning that the Turks could now descend upon any city on the shores of the Mediterranean and do the same again.[57]

On September 26, 1480, approximately six weeks after the Turks stormed Otranto and inflicted their multitudinous horrors upon its people, Queen Isabel established an Inquisition in Castile, as Pope Sixtus IV had authorized her to do two years before whenever she thought it necessary. By February 1481 the Inquisition was in action, handing down its first six convictions which resulted in the infliction of the death penalty.[58]

The Spanish Inquisition was established to deal with the special problem created in Spain by the very large numbers of its citizens known as *conversos*. These were people who had converted from Islam or Judaism to Christianity, either recently in person or as a result of the conversion of their forebears within three or four generations. Many of these conversions were genuine, or had become so with the passage of time and generations. But many others had been stimulated by ambition and greed—only Christians were allowed to hold high public office, and obviously only they could hold positions in the Church, which were very influential—or by fear, particularly when there was large-scale mob violence against non-Christians. And once an individual was baptized, he was not permitted to return to Judaism or Islam.[59]

There is convincing, indeed overwhelming evidence, which even the most critical modern historians have acknowledged, that tens of thousands of false *conversos*, who did not believe in the Christianity they professed, continued to live secretly by the teachings and rites of their or their forebears' former religion. Many had risen high in Christian society, even in the Church; some were priests who mocked the Mass as they said it. While most of the reports of *conversos* engaging in Satanic rites and crucifying children were probably false, it would be rash to say that all of them were; for the worst passions in human nature feed on the kind of situation in which the false *conversos* found themselves.[60]

Every false *converso* in Spain was a potential traitor—a man capable of,

---

[57]Von Pastor, *History of the Popes*, IV, 333-343; Carroll, *Isabel of Spain*, pp. 137-138.
[58]Townsend Miller, *The Castles and the Crown; Spain 1451-1555* (New York, 1963), pp. 110-114; Henry Charles Lea, *A History of the Inquisition of Spain* (New York, 1906), I, 148-160; Bernardino Llorca, *La Inquisición en España* (Barcelona, 1936), pp. 73-74; Menéndez Pidal, *Historia de España*, XVII (2), 211-214; Carroll, *Isabel of Spain*, pp. 139-140.
[59]Edward Peters, *Inquisition* (New York, 1988), pp. 77-83.
[60]Lea, *Inquisition*, I, 145-147; Henry Kamen, *Inquisition and Society in Spain* (Bloomington IN, 1985), p. 28; William Thomas Walsh, *Isabella of Spain, the Last Crusader* (New York, 1930), pp. 195-203; Menéndez Pidal, *Historia de España*, XVII (2), 210-212; Carroll, *Isabel of Spain*, p. 138.

and very possibly inclined to opening the gates of its coastal cities to the likes of the Turkish mass killers of Otranto. And by the same token, every true *converso*—men such as Fray Hernando de Talavera, Isabel's saintly confessor; Alonso de Burgos, her choice as reforming Bishop of Cuenca; and Andrés de Cabrera, husband of her dearest friend[61]—was open to suspicion of infidelity and treason, their reputation and careers forever in jeopardy of a false accusation to this effect. The danger was greatest in the south, particularly in Sevilla, the most populous city in Spain, not reconquered until 1250, where at least half the population had been non-Christian. Particularly after the horror of Otranto, this danger simply could not be ignored.

The Inquisition is the centerpiece of the "black legend" of Spanish history. The torture it occasionally inflicted (though not as regular practice) and the burning at the stake which the government ordered for those the Inquisition had convicted twice, cannot be defended—though they were by no means evils unique to the Inquisition or to Spain. But the historian has a duty to put the Inquisition in perspective, rarely though this may be done. It did not engage in mass murder. The contemporary historian Pulgar estimates the total number of those burned to death because of its findings during Isabel's reign as no more than 2,000, an average of about 100 a year. Some 15,000 were found guilty of false profession of Christianity, but were reconciled with the Church in the public ceremony known as the *auto-de-fe*, meaning "act of faith"—that is, public confession of their error and reconciliation with the faith they had rejected. Because on that same occasion the few deemed irreconcilable were burned, the term *auto-de-fe* has come to mean, for those who know no Spanish, "burning at the stake," but the number reconciled was always much larger than the number burned. And a large majority of all those questioned by the Inquisition were completely cleared—including St. Ignatius of Loyola and St. Teresa of Avila and all so-called witches whose cases were brought before the Inquisition in the next century. For them, the Inquisition was a shield against calumny.[62]

The Inquisition had no jurisdiction over practicing Jews and Muslims, only over professed Christians who were in fact still Jews or Muslims, though concealing it. After its initial abuses were eliminated following the appointment of Tomás de Torquemada as Inquisitor-General for Castile in 1483, the inquisitorial tribunals were generally very fair; many preferred to have their cases heard by them rather than in other courts. Those questioned by the

Inquisition were not allowed to face their accusers because of the danger of blood feuds and revenge-seeking if their identity were known. But no one could be confined even briefly without the prior testimony of three witnesses against him, and anyone brought before the Inquisition as a suspect was asked first of all to make a list of all his personal enemies, whose testimony against him, if made, was immediately thrown out. No anonymous testimony was permitted. The accused had a defense attorney, often two, although they were assigned by the Inquisition.[63]

The Inquisition was a Church court because by Catholic belief only the Church has the right and authority to decide whether a man is or is not a Christian; therefore it did not execute the death penalty on its own authority, because the Church condemns no man to death. The Inquisition turned those it found most guilty over to the state (the "secular arm") for the punishment its law reserved for heretics and traitors. These two crimes were then regarded similarly, though heresy was deemed even worse, as treason against God. Every government in Europe in the fifteenth century punished both treason and heresy by a very painful death. Then and long afterward, the punishment for treason in England was hanging, drawing and quartering. In this ghastly procedure, the traitor was hanged, but cut down before he was dead; his intestines were drawn out, and he was cut into four pieces, all while still alive. Let us by all means condemn such punishments, but not attribute them to some imaginary unique evil of Spain.

The modern world regards heresy as not a crime, but a joke. But the vast slaughters of men, women and children by the two worst totalitarian regimes of the twentieth century were carried out by men who bitterly hated Christianity and never hesitated to say so. Hitler was an apostate Catholic, Stalin an apostate Orthodox seminarian. Between them, they took at least thirty million lives, beside which the grand total of executions by referral from the Spanish Inquisition over its entire 300-year history is hardly measurable by comparison. They would not have been free to gain power in a time which would have taken them at their word and knew the cost and consequences of their hatred of Christianity, which many of those condemned by the Inquisition also nourished. Tomás de Torquemada would have known how to deal—and to deal early—with Hitler and Stalin.

Isabel saw the Inquisition as necessary to preserve the national security and to promote the spiritual and social unity of Spain. In deeply Catholic Spain, people who pretended to be Catholic but were not could never be trusted. Such deceivers must be exposed, then reconciled if possible, or forced to leave if they could not be reconciled. If stubborn and beyond reclamation in their hostility,

---

[63]Llorca, *Inquisición*, pp. 106-107, 171-176, 196-199, 203-205; Lea, *Inquisition*, I, 45; Walsh, *Characters of the Inquisition*, pp. 162-169; Menéndez Pidal, *Historia de España*, XVII (2), 232-235; Carroll, *Isabel of Spain*, pp. 140-141.

as a second conviction by the Inquisition would indicate, she believed they had to be executed. She regarded this as her duty, an essential part of the administration of justice to which she had devoted most of her energies and unyielding resolve since victory in the war of the succession in Castile permitted her to concentrate upon it. Justice was also the shield of the innocent. Those falsely accused of hidden heresy, of not being genuine Christians, deserved and would receive full vindication from a court uniquely competent to determine whether such accusations were true, whose judgments were accepted as definitive by the great majority of the nation.

These considerations were Isabel's justification for establishing the Inquisition in Spain. The initiative for its establishment and the determination for its retention were hers. Her admirers must face it, while the critics of the Spanish Inquisition must try to explain how a woman so good, so honest and so just could have brought such an institution into being and maintained it if it were in fact as evil as is commonly thought. And the Spanish Inquisition succeeded; it accomplished the task Isabel had set for it. Religious peace was preserved in Spain while religious wars savaged the rest of Europe. Whenever there was a dispute involving accusations of heresy or occult practices, the Inquisition was available to settle it and did settle it before it became a threat to the Church or to the country.

This is not to justify burnings at the stake, or torture. The Church and Isabel permitted both; they should not have. But these were common evils of the age, against which almost no one even protested. And there is evidence that torture was very rarely used by the Inquisition during Torquemada's years as Inquisitor-General (1483-1498). Far from the ogre of legend, Torquemada was a just and devout man and a careful administrator, who took his responsibilities to the accused as well as to the accusers very seriously, and seems to have been the architect of most of the procedures that kept the inquisitorial tribunals fair and almost universally respected. He was one of Isabel's best appointments.[64]

On December 26, 1481 the ancient war of the reconquest in Spain flared anew with the seizure of the Spanish frontier fortress of Zahara in a surprise attack by the Muslims of the kingdom of Granada in the middle of a stormy night. Thus fiercely and directly challenged, Isabel responded with a total commitment to bring an end at last to the 759-year-old conflict, the longest war in the history of the world, by completing the reconquest by taking the whole kingdom of Granada. The Marqués de Cádiz, who had so generously and dramatically offered her his services and his loyalty when she came to Sevilla to establish order and justice there four years before, now in effect took command

---

of the war against Granada. In a daring move at the end of February 1482, he brought five thousand men through a wild mountain tangle to surprise and take the Moorish town of Alhama just 25 miles from Granada itself, and held it against all the Moors could send against him. Fernando came himself to its relief in April, while Isabel helped finance and supply the army from the old Moorish capital of Córdoba. But Fernando suffered a major repulse at the great Moorish fortress of Loja in July, which made it obvious that the reconquest of Granada was going to require a lengthy struggle.[65]

The Moors inflicted an even more damaging defeat on the Christians during an ill-advised Christian raid through the mountain fastness called the Ajarquia in the western part of the kingdom of Granada in March 1483. Almost every noble family in Andalusia named one of its own among the dead in this ambush, over 800 in all, while nearly 1,500 Christian soldiers fell into the hands of the infidels, about 400 of them noblemen. But Isabel was unshaken.[66]

> I know all about what happened with the Moors, which has greatly distressed me. But this is nothing new in war. In such matters we are in the hands of Our Lord. We may not and ought not to do otherwise than give thanks to Him for everything. Truly, since this was done in service to Our Lord and for the exaltation of our Holy Faith, that is consolation for whatever death or loss may result from it.[67]

Her constancy was soon justified; the tide of war turned as Boabdil, now ruling the Moorish kingdom of Granada, was captured in an attack on the Castilian town of Lucena in April. His father Abul Hassan, whom he had displaced, resumed the government of Granada. In September Isabel and Fernando released Boabdil with the promise to support him against his father in return for his promise to become their vassal and not to fight against them. In the following month the Marqués of Cádiz recaptured Zahara.[68]

Early in 1484 Fernando declared his intention to campaign against France rather than Granada, but Isabel insisted on the greater importance of completing the age-old conflict with the infidel, and Fernando eventually agreed with her. From the end of May 1484 through the whole of the year 1485 Isabel and Fernando remained in southern Spain, conducting both fall and spring campaigns. French artillery experts were called in to speed the construction of the giant cannon known as lombards, similar to those with which the Ottoman Turks had battered down the walls of Constantinople in 1453.

---

[65]Carroll, *Isabel of Spain*, pp. 144-151.

[66]*Ibid.*, pp. 151-154; Menéndez Pidal, *Historia de España*, XVII (1), 489-493.

[67]Isabel to the Council of Sevilla, April 6, 1483, in *El Tumbo de los Reyes Católicos del Concejo de Sevilla*, ed. Juan de Mata Carriazo, Volume III (Sevilla, 1969), p. 319.

[68]Agustín G. de Amezúa de Mayo, *La batalla de Lucena y el verdadero retrato de Boabdil* (Madrid, 1915); Menéndez Pidal, *Historia de España*, XVII (1), 509-515, 536; Carroll, *Isabel of Spain*, pp. 155-157.

They proved irresistible once brought to the scene of action. It was not easy to transport these monsters over the primitive roads of southern Spain, but it was done under Isabel's constant prodding. While Fernando commanded in the field, she kept the army supplied and the artillery moving, discharging this duty as if she had been doing it all her life. One Moorish stronghold after another was overborne by the Castilian cannon, climaxed by the taking of heavily defended Ronda, the principal stronghold in the western part of the kingdom of Granada, after ten days of bombardment in May 1485. On June 2 the feast of Corpus Christi was celebrated in Ronda for the first time in more than seven centuries, followed by a great fiesta with music and song. Isabel and Fernando ordered the walls of Ronda rebuilt, with some lombard balls fired during the siege to be placed on top of them as mementoes of the great victory.[69]

But they were not satisfied to stop with Ronda. Isabel in particular continued to aim at total victory, the redemption at last of all the soil of Spain from the grip of the ancient invader, the inveterate foe of Christendom.

Meanwhile in England from 1483 to 1485 a drama was unfolding that has enthralled students of English history ever since, creating a controversy among historians which is now over three hundred years old and shows no signs of abating, but instead has intensified in the last forty years: Was Richard III, who took the crown of England in 1483, a usurper and a tyrant who murdered his nephews, or a true and just king innocent of that crime? Along with its intrinsic interest and demonstration of the importance of the personal factor in history, the reign of Richard III has enduring significance in that it brought a completely new and very different dynasty to the throne of England, whose second generation was to breach the millennial English tradition of loyalty to the Catholic Church and whose third generation was to destroy that tradition forever—the worst single loss the Catholic Church has suffered in its entire history. Certainly from the perspective of eternity, sometimes vaguely even from human perspective, coming events cast their shadows before, as we have already seen with St. Joan of Arc. Whatever the truth about Richard III, by hindsight we may certainly say that it was not in any way to the advantage of the Church Christ founded that the Tudor dynasty should occupy the English throne.

As the year 1483 opened, no one in England could have expected the fantastic upheavals that year would bring to her. Except for a desultory war with Scotland, the country was at peace. Its 40-year-old king, the brave and victorious Edward IV, was universally popular. He had two sons, Edward aged thirteen and Richard aged nine, to inherit his crown. Edward's Queen, the

---

[69]Miguel Angel Ladero Quesada, *Castilla y la conquista del reino de Granada* (Valladolid, 1967), pp. 117-125; Menéndez Pidal, *Historia de España*, XVII (1), 557, 564-566; Carroll, *Isabel of Spain*, pp. 158-166.

beautiful but cold Elizabeth Woodville, was unpopular and her large extended family even more so, but Edward himself was so well-liked that little of the feeling against his queen and her family reflected upon him. Edward IV had been known as "the handsomest prince in Christendom" but too much good eating had made him very fat; his standard of sexual morality was notoriously low; but he had lost none of his charm and few held these faults against him. Throughout his stormy career, which had included two major defeats and one exile from England along with the many triumphs of his 22-year reign, his brother Richard had stood unswervingly at his side; indeed, Richard—made Duke of Gloucester by Edward IV as soon as he was old enough to lead armies in battle—had adopted as his motto "Loyalty binds me."[70]

But by Holy Week of 1483 it was suddenly clear that Edward IV was paying a higher price for his physical excesses than anyone had suspected. Though until then he had almost always been in excellent health, he fell seriously ill. His malady—never accurately diagnosed—progressed with shocking speed. By April 7 it was clear to him and to his court that he was dying. He called his wife's principal relatives, his close friend Will Hastings, and his other ministers together around his bed, urging them to love one another and to work together in the future. But he knew them too well to trust them fully to do that. He summoned his brother Richard, who was at Middleham castle in Yorkshire, preparing to lead a new campaign against Scotland—too far away to arrive before the King died. In a codicil to his will Edward IV designated Richard Protector of England until young Edward V should reach his majority. There was no explicit tradition in England as to what age constituted adulthood for a king. The three royal minorities since the Norman conquest had each been handled differently, with the young kings gaining authority in a series of stages, and not exercising it fully until they were in their twenties, if then. Edward IV knew these unpleasant histories; surely he would have wished to spare his son from repeating them, and chose Richard as the man most likely to accomplish this.[71]

---

[70]Cf. Ross, *Edward IV*, and the first chapters of the two major biographies of Richard III, both demonstrating solid scholarship but written from totally opposed viewpoints: Paul M. Kendall, *Richard III* (New York, 1955), pp. 27-177 (very favorable to Richard), and Charles Ross, *Richard III* (Berkeley CA, 1981), pp. 3-59 (very critical of Richard). Curiously, most historical writings about Richard III persist in giving his motto in the old French which by this point in English history was almost entirely confined to law and heraldry: *"loyauté me lie."* This has far less impact than when translated, and the motto is critical to a full understanding of Richard III. Is this usage perhaps a touch of the widespread anti-Ricardian prejudice among historians?

[71]Jacob, *Fifteenth Century*, pp. 589, 607-608; Ross, *Edward IV*, pp. 414-416; Kendall, *Richard III*, pp. 189-190. The three minorities were those of Henry III, who was nine years old when King John died in 1216 and did not gain full power until he was 25; Richard II, who was ten years old when King Edward III died in 1377 and did not gain full power until he was 22; and Henry VI, who was nine months old when King Henry V

Edward IV died on April 9. A few days later his son was proclaimed King Edward V at Ludlow castle in Wales. On April 24 the new young king left Ludlow with an escort of 2,000 men provided by the Woodvilles; it was only with great difficulty that Hastings, at that time opposed to the Woodvilles, persuaded the royal council to limit the escort to that number. Hastings wrote Richard warning him that the Woodvilles planned to refuse him recognition as Protector, declare Edward V king with full powers, and kill Hastings if they could. Richard believed it, and it was plausible; control of a minor king almost always meant control of the government, and for years there had been no love lost between Richard and his sister-in-law's kin. Nevertheless he made a point of administering an oath of loyalty to Edward V to the magistrates of York and the men-at-arms accompanying him to London. At Northampton, the day before he was to join the King's party, he was met by Henry Stafford, the 29-year-old Duke of Buckingham, a direct descendant of King Edward III of England through his youngest son Thomas of Woodstock. The young Duke had been compelled to marry the Dowager Queen's sister, but he hated her family. He immediately attached himself to Richard, and told him the Woodvilles would never accept him as Protector. At dawn April 30 Richard arrested Earl Rivers (Anthony Woodville), the young king's half-brother Richard Grey, and his treasurer Thomas Vaughan, a Woodville appointee. Thereby he gained control of the young king. The Dowager Queen went into sanctuary at Westminster as soon as she heard the news, while Hastings supported Richard.[72]

Early in May the royal council formally proclaimed Richard Protector of England. He immediately required the lords of the council and the mayor and aldermen of London to take an oath of loyalty to Edward V, as he had previously done at York. If he was then planning to usurp the throne, it seems unlikely—though not impossible—that he would have made such a point of requiring these oaths of loyalty to a boy king he was about to remove. There was little opposition to his action against the Woodvilles because of their unpopularity. The council set June 24 as the date for Edward V's coronation. Though one of the principal authorities on Richard III has suggested that Richard was only intended to be Protector for six weeks, until the coronation, this begs the question of who was supposed to rule afterward, since it was obvious that 13-year-old Edward V was not yet old enough to do so. The only

---

died in 1422 and never really reigned. Though Giles St. Aubyn, *The Year of Three Kings, 1483* (New York, 1983), p. 78, says that only the unreliable later writer Rous specifically states that Edward named Richard Protector, the contemporary Italian witness Dominic Mancini and the later historian Polydore Virgil—who, like Rous, was hostile to Richard—also report it (Kendall, *Richard III*, p. 193).

[72]Jacob, *Fifteenth Century*, pp. 589, 611, 613; Ross, *Edward IV*, p. 416; Ross, *Richard III*, pp. 65-73; Kendall, *Richard III*, pp. 181-182, 193-202, 206; St. Aubyn, *Year of Three Kings*, pp. 82-84, 91, 95-101.

possible choices were Richard or the Woodvilles. Since the leading Woodvilles were under arrest when Richard was declared Protector by the council, it seems evident that Richard was expected and intended to govern until Edward V was capable of reigning in his own right; and this is confirmed by the fact that Bishop Russell of Lincoln, the new Chancellor selected by Richard, began work in May on a speech to be given to the Parliament that had been summoned for the day after the coronation, explaining why a protectorate was needed until the King matured.[73]

So far the course of events, though fast-moving and dramatic, had been straightforward and understandable; everything that had happened fit the record and character of the principal participants. There was no reason to believe that Richard would not be true to his brother's memory and charge as he had always been true to him during his life and reign. Everyone in England was aware of the inordinate ambition of the Woodvilles; historians writing five hundred years later cannot credibly portray them as innocent victims (as some have nevertheless done), whether or not they were specifically plotting to keep Edward V and Richard apart or to kill Hastings. But Richard had moved effectively and decisively against them, and seemed to have secured his position as Protector and to be preparing in good faith for the coronation of the young king. On June 5 all appeared to be well; Richard's wife Anne joined him in London, and more than 50 letters went out from the office of Chancellor Russell summoning noblemen to the coronation, whose date had been moved up two days so as to fall on a Sunday, June 22.[74]

But five days later, on the 10th, we find Richard writing to his faithful city of York asking for military aid against the Woodvilles, who "daily do intend to murder and utterly destroy us and our cousin the Duke of Buckingham," and the next day Richard called upon several noblemen to come to his assistance at once with armed men. Something new, unexpected and alarming had obviously happened between the 5th and the 10th. Richard's critics say that what had happened was simply his own decision to usurp the throne from his young nephew; his defenders say that he had discovered the conspiracy which he signally punished on the 13th by the summary execution of Hastings, his former friend, without trial, on a charge of treason concerted with Bishop John Morton of Ely and the Woodvilles, possibly due to Hastings' jealousy of the ascendant influence of the Duke of Buckingham with Richard—and possibly also a startling report that Edward IV's children were not legitimate.[75]

---

[73]Ross, *Richard III*, pp. 74-76; Kendall, *Richard III*, pp. 218-219, 224; St. Aubyn, *Year of Three Kings*, pp. 104-105, 110-111.

[74]Kendall, *Richard III*, pp. 237-239; St. Aubyn, *Year of Three Kings*, p. 110.

[75]Jacob, *Fifteenth Century*, pp. 618-619; Ross, *Edward III*, pp. 81-86 (quotation on 81); Kendall, *Richard III*, pp. 245-250; St. Aubyn, *Year of Three Kings*, pp. 119-120, 122-131.

By the middle of the following week (the 16th or the 17th) Richard had decided to postpone the coronation and the meeting of Parliament.[76] On the 22nd, evidently with his knowledge and support, Friar Ralph Shaw, brother of the mayor of London, shook the nation with a sermon declaring that all of Edward IV's children were illegitimate because Edward had been betrothed to another woman, Lady Eleanor Butler, when he secretly married Elizabeth Woodville in 1464, making his brother Richard the rightful king in the absence of legitimate issue of Edward.[77]

Not enough evidence survives to surely determine whether this allegation was true, but there is considerable reason to think that it was. The information came from Bishop Robert Stillington of Bath and Wells, who said he had himself conveyed Edward IV's marriage promise to Eleanor Butler. It was formally accepted by Parliament in 1484, without any indications of coercion by Richard III. It was repeated as common knowledge by the Spanish ambassador to England in 1533. When Henry Tudor came to the throne of England and married Edward IV's eldest daughter to strengthen his very weak claim to that throne, he went to great trouble to suppress and destroy all records of Bishop Stillington's report and its acceptance by Parliament, which he would not have done had it not been widely believed. There is no question that betrothal to one woman invalidated marriage to another under Church law at that time, so long as the betrothal was in effect. While only a Church court could decide a specific case of this kind, all that would have to be proved before it was the fact of the betrothal; if it existed, marriage to another woman was *ipso facto* invalid. Eleanor Butler had died in 1468 and could not testify on the issue herself. After her death Edward IV could have legitimized his marriage by another ceremony and his children by act of Parliament; but he had never done either, apparently believing the whole matter could be kept secret. Richard had been known as a man of high moral principle and a devout Catholic. His conscience would not have permitted him to keep silent about such a fact if it were true, or he believed it true, however much he might have wished to save his brother's reputation. That proclaiming it served his personal interest so well will always cast some doubt on the reality of the betrothal; but Richard's record up to this point makes it harder to imagine him inventing so despicable a betrayal of his brother's memory, if it were false, than accepting that he genuinely discovered a truth which happened also to make him King.[78]

On June 26, just four days after Edward V was to have been crowned, his

---

[76]Kendall, *Richard III*, p. 556.

[77]*Ibid.*, pp. 262-264; Jacob, *Fifteenth Century*, p. 620.

[78]For a diametrically opposed presentation of the arguments for and against the existence of Edward IV's prior betrothal to Lady Eleanor Butler when he married Elizabeth Woodville, see Kendall, *Richard III*, pp. 257-262, 553-556 (for), and Ross, *Richard III*, pp. 88-92 (against).

uncle took the royal oath as Richard III, with the consent of the members of what would have been Edward V's first Parliament. There was no significant opposition, though the amazing speed with which events had unfolded in the preceding sixteen days perhaps gave it no time to form. A formal coronation ceremony for Richard III was held July 6. Richard knew that the country was uneasy and confused, and almost certainly for that reason he very soon undertook an extensive tour of England to show himself to the people as King, departing from London July 22, exactly one month from the day Friar Shaw had announced the illegitimacy of Edward IV's children.[79] His two sons had been sent to the Tower of London, where for a time, in the words of the Italian observer Mancini, who left London about the same time as Richard III, they were seen "shouting and playing in the garden by the Tower," but then "day by day began to be seen more rarely behind the bars and windows" until they were seen no more.[80]

The "two little princes in the Tower" were never seen again by anyone. Their disappearance is the most impenetrable mystery in English history. Ever since Richard III died fighting for his crown at Bosworth Field in 1485, the dominant viewpoint among historians and in English tradition is that he had them killed. But no one knows when or how.[81] If Richard did kill them, he must have done it very quickly indeed, between July 6 and 22, since Mancini's statement strongly implies that they were alive for a significant length of time after going to the Tower, and Richard is most unlikely to have had so perilous a murder done in his absence, when he could not supervise its execution and provide any necessary cover-up. It must be stressed that we have no evidence of any strong movement or sentiment on behalf of the young princes *before* they disappeared (Mancini refers only to having seen "men burst forth into tears and lamentation when mention was made of him [Edward V] after his removal from men's sight").[82] Is it reasonable that Richard III would have killed them so

---

[79]Jacob, *Fifteenth Century*, pp. 620-622; Ross, *Richard III*, p. 93; Kendall, *Richard III*, pp. 261-266, 272-276, 301.

[80]Jacob, *Fifteenth Century*, p. 624; late middle English put in modern English. It will be the practice in the remainder of this volume and in Volume IV of this history to modernize spelling, punctuation, and occasionally sentence structure to put late middle and Elizabethan English into the modern form. Use of the original distracts attention from meaning to accidents for today's reader.

[81]The story told in Thomas More's history of Richard III about the alleged confession of James Tyrrell in 1502, though apparently very circumstantial, has now been rejected by almost all historians, even those most hostile to Richard (Jacob, *Fifteenth Century*, p. 624; St. Aubyn, *Year of Three Kings*, pp. 178-179). The alleged discovery of the bones of the princes in 1674 has yielded no genuine clues to the mystery, and their identification—though widely believed by historians—is very dubious. See Ross, *Richard III*, pp. 233-234; Kendall, *Richard III*, pp. 481-482; A. J. Pollard, *Richard III and the Princes in the Tower* (New York, 1991), pp. 124-127.

[82]Kendall, *Richard III*, p. 466.

quickly? If he intended to do away with them, he had no need to hurry; the more time which intervened between his supplanting his nephews and their disappearance, the less likely people were to react strongly to it, unless there were a movement in their favor. But until their disappearance, there was none.

Before Richard could return to London, rebellion had broken out against him—not in the name of the young princes, though their disappearance was already being charged to Richard by his enemies, but in the name of Henry Tudor and the Duke of Buckingham, who both had a claim to the throne, though only if Richard were eliminated and the princes were truly illegitimate or dead.[83]

Henry's claim was one of the oddest in the whole history of monarchy. His grandfather Owen Tudor had been a low-level courtier (though he claimed nobility in Wales—claims which most Englishmen did not recognize) with a golden tongue, who had charmed Henry V's widowed queen Catherine of Valois and fathered two sons upon her without benefit of marriage. The elder, Edmund, legitimized by act of Parliament during the reign of Henry VI, married Margaret Beaufort, who was a great-granddaughter of the famous Prince John of Gaunt, fourth son of Edward III, by his liaison with Catherine Swynford—which was also without benefit of marriage. John of Gaunt's children by Catherine Swynford were also later legitimized by Parliament, but with the proviso (added by King Henry IV only on his own authority) that their legitimization was not to provide the basis for a claim to the throne. Henry Tudor was the only child of Edmund Tudor and Margaret Beaufort. His father's descent could give no support for his royal claim, and his claim through his mother bore the stain of initial illegitimacy and was cast into doubt by Henry IV's proviso.[84]

The Duke of Buckingham, on the other hand, had a direct hereditary link with the youngest son of Edward III, Thomas of Woodstock, with no touch of the bar sinister.[85] Buckingham was much more a prime mover of the rebellion than Henry, being actually on the scene in England while Henry was in France. Richard had trusted Buckingham completely and had made him Constable of England,[86] but the young Duke did not hesitate to betray him. Though Buckingham did not claim the throne at this time, but chose instead to support Henry, it is hard to believe that, given his genealogy and his character, he was not biding his time until he could remove and supplant Henry after, with his indispensable help, Henry removed and supplanted Richard III. By murdering the princes Buckingham could throw the odium for their disappearance upon

[83]*Ibid.*, pp. 311, 313, 316-325, 483-484; Jacob, *Fifteenth Century*, p. 625; Ross, *Richard III*, pp. 114-116.
[84]St. Aubyn, *Year of Three Kings*, pp. 188-189; Ross, *Richard III*, p. 115n.
[85]St. Aubyn, *Year of Three Kings*, p. 92.
[86]On July 13, 1483 (Kendall, *Richard III*, p. 300).

Richard, create a basis for challenging Richard's own right to rule, and remove a potential threat if he should later gain the throne. As Constable of England, Buckingham could as easily have entered the Tower of London and done what he wished there, as Richard himself. There is reason to believe that Buckingham did not leave London with Richard on July 22, but remained there without him for several days. If he killed the princes there, or abducted them and then killed them elsewhere, it probably happened then.[87]

The case against the Duke of Buckingham as the murderer of the princes is at least as plausible as the case against Richard, even when the character of the two men is disregarded. When their character is added to the equation the case against Buckingham becomes much stronger. The manner in which he gained great favor with Richard and then betrayed him, all in less than six months, reveals a man with no moral restraints on his ambition. Richard's record, at least up to the execution of Hastings—and in many respects even after that—displays a much higher moral standard.

Buckingham's rebellion failed ignominiously. Henry Tudor, approaching the coast and learning of its failure, sailed away without landing. Buckingham was captured. From the moment of his capture at the end of October 1483 to his execution about a week later, he begged and pleaded for permission to speak with Richard, if only for a few moments. Richard refused to see him. Buckingham may have hoped to gain his life in return for information about the fate of the two princes that he alone could provide.[88]

For the next year and a half Richard, by almost universal report, provided excellent and just government for England. Compelled reluctantly to admit this, his critics say that he only ruled well because he was trying to gain the favor of the people which he had largely lost because of the widespread belief that he had killed the princes. But the exercise of power by evil men in history does not suggest that they commonly seek popularity by doing good, but on the contrary are further corrupted by holding power. Richard's just government is a further argument for a character that would have recoiled from the betrayal of the

---

[87]While the later Tudor historians Vergil and More say that Buckingham did accompany Richard III as far as Gloucester, the contemporary Croyland Chronicle makes no mention of it, and the Register of Magdalen College, Oxford does not list the Duke of Buckingham as among those attending Richard during his visit to Oxford July 24-25, the third and fourth days after he left London (Kendall, *Richard III*, p. 559). Ross (*Richard III*, p. 148n) dismisses this evidence on the sole ground that it supports Kendall's thesis that the Duke of Buckingham murdered the princes—a purely *ad hominem* argument. Elsewhere Ross argues against Kendall's thesis by stating that Buckingham would not have "ventured to act independently on such a vital issue" because, except for St. Thomas a Becket and during rebellions, political murders were not done in England without the approval of the King (*op. cit.*, pp. 102-103). Since Buckingham was in the process of launching a rebellion, Ross' argument is self-refuting.
[88]Kendall, *Richard III*, pp. 324-330; Jacob, *Fifteenth Century*, pp. 626-627.

memory of his beloved brother and the murder of his young nephews.[89]

Richard and his wife Anne had just one child, a son whom they had named Edward. He died suddenly in 1484; Anne herself died—probably of tuberculosis—early in the following year. There is much evidence that Richard had a profound love for Anne, which makes the reports that almost immediately after her death he wanted to marry his niece Elizabeth, eldest daughter of Edward IV and Elizabeth Woodville, even more implausible than they would otherwise be, though they were widely believed at the time. These two intense personal tragedies and the suffering Richard must have undergone if he were innocent of the murder of his nephews, and yet had given Buckingham the powers and office which enabled him to kill them, may help explain the apparent fatalism with which Richard approached the decisive battle with Henry Tudor, who landed in Wales with a relatively small army of 2,500 men (mostly French) on August 7, 1485, and marched from there into central England. Richard did not muster all the forces he might reasonably have brought to the field. The north of England was still loyal to him, but in the south many held back, having heard so many whispers that their king was responsible for the disappearance and probable death of the boy princes in the Tower. When battle was joined near Bosworth on Redmore Plain, Richard—though known as an excellent military tactician—simply charged Henry personally, accompanied by no more than a hundred men. He had almost reached Henry when the treacherous Sir William Stanley, commanding several thousand men supposedly supporting Richard, turned on him and rescued Henry. Crying "Treason!" over and over, Richard went down fighting, sword swinging, his crown upon his head. Despite Shakespeare, he never offered his kingdom for a horse. His crown fell off as he died and was later found under a hawthorn bush. Henry married Edward's daughter Elizabeth to strengthen the royal claim for their children, and reigned as Henry VII.[90]

That many Englishmen did not regard Henry Tudor's claim to the English throne as valid is indicated by the astonishing history of the pretenders Lambert Simnel, who claimed to be the son of Edward IV's executed brother the Duke of Clarence, and Perkin Warbeck, who clamed to be the younger of the two princes who had disappeared from the Tower. No credible evidence was ever presented in support of the claims of these two imposters, but many followed them and even gave their lives for them in battles against the Tudor king. His rule was not notably oppressive, though he had little to make men love him; such persistence in rebellion in the absence of great oppression suggests a genuine commitment to the memory of the last Plantagenets and a widespread awareness that Henry Tudor had no right to the throne. But in the absence of a

---

[89]Ross, *Richard III*, pp. 170-190; Kendall, *Richard III*, pp. 370-391.
[90]Kendall, *Richard III*, pp. 125-132, 349, 365, 392-396, 409-444; Ross, *Richard III*, pp. 201, 213-225.

genuine Plantagenet claimant and aided by the popularity of his Plantagenet queen, Henry Tudor finally prevailed.[91]

Historians are left with the mystery of the two vanished princes and the choice of whether to see Richard III, corrupted by ambition, usurping the throne of England, killing them, and consequently suffering his just deserts by being overthrown and slain by Henry Tudor, or to see him as the innocent victim of as searing a cumulative tragedy as may be found in all the annals of the kings of Christendom. The mystery will never be conclusively resolved. Each student weighing the evidence can only make his own best judgment. The writer of this history judges that Richard III was innocent.

On August 12, 1484 Pope Sixtus IV died at the age of seventy. His irresponsible nepotism had reaped a harvest of hatred and strife in Italy, but for the rest of Christendom he had been a good Pope, particularly notable for his strong support of Queen Isabel in Castile. The bloody shadow of Girolamo Riario overhung the upcoming conclave. He brought an army to Rome by forced marches as soon as he heard of his uncle's death, and his wife Caterina Sforza seized Rome's great fortress, Castel Sant'Angelo. The Colonna raised an army to oppose Riario, and Cardinals Giuliano della Rovere and Rodrigo Borgia also brought substantial forces into the city. The streets of Rome were full of armed men; artillery was brought in as well, and the bridges over the Tiber were closed. Holding a conclave in these conditions was impossible. Everyone feared the outbreak of full-scale civil war at any moment.[92]

The generally trusted Cardinal Marco Barbo, nephew of former Pope Paul II, now took charge. Girolamo Riario, frightened by the size of the forces arrayed against him, was induced by a payment of 8,000 ducats to give up Castel Sant'Angelo and return to his lands in the northern part of the papal state, and consequently the Colonna agreed to remove their army from Rome. On August 26 a conclave of 25 cardinals, the largest number at such a meeting in many years, went into session. Twenty-one of them were Italian, two Spanish, one Portuguese, and only one French. Most of them were worldly-minded and had been appointed by Sixtus IV for political or personal reasons rather than for merit.[93]

It was quite clear that the best candidate was Marco Barbo, who received about half the votes on the first ballot, but he never had a serious prospect of election because he was a Venetian, and wealthy Venice had aroused much envy and fear in Italy. Rodrigo Borgia did all he could to promote his own

[91]J. D. Mackie, *The Earlier Tudors, 1485-1558* [The Oxford History of England] (Oxford, 1952), pp. 59-80, 117-147.
[92]Ludwig von Pastor, *The History of the Popes from the Close of the Middle Ages*, Volume V (St. Louis, 1914), pp. 229-232.
[93]*Ibid.*, V, 232-233.

candidacy, but his personal and political immorality was so well known and he was so little trusted that even his remarkable cleverness, personal charm and open purse were not yet sufficient to gain him the office he coveted. Borgia's principal rival was Giuliano della Rovere, the ablest of Sixtus IV's nephews. Unable to gain sufficient votes for himself to be elected Pope, he threw his support to Cardinal Giovanni Battista Cibò, a Genoese with two illegitimate children who had however lived morally since being consecrated bishop in 1469. Cibò was kindly and popular but weak and easily led by others. On August 29 he was elected Pope and took the name of Innocent VIII.[94]

During much of his pontificate Innocent was crippled by illness, saddled by financial and military obligations he could not meet, and at his wits' end on how to make his way through the turbulent political seas of Renaissance Italy. He followed any advice he could get that sounded good to him at the time, regardless of how it matched his previous policy. He especially feared the power of Ferrante, the illegitimate son of Alfonso V of Aragon who ruled the kingdom of Naples, and appealed both to Emperor Frederick III and to Venice to help him against Naples. Frederick was on the point of retirement and not interested, Venice was kept away by an attack by King Matthias Corvinus of Hungary in scandalous alliance with the Turks, and in May 1486 the Neapolitans severely defeated the papal army at Montorio. In September 1489 the increasingly desperate Pope fruitlessly declared Ferrante deposed; four months later he signed a treaty with him; but nothing seemed to work, and hostilities continued. By July 1490 Innocent was talking of resigning the papacy because of his inability to cope with Ferrante.[95]

To an increasingly immoral, avaricious and disunited Christendom Pope Innocent VIII offered little more than a spectacle of futility. In spiritual guidance he did no better. In the first year of his pontificate he issued a very unfortunate bull directed primarily to Germany with the sensational title *Malleus maleficarum* ("Hammer of Witches"). It included no dogmatic pronouncements on witchcraft, which was already widely believed in, condemned, and prosecuted in Germany, but his extensive review of alleged incidents of spells, incantations, curses, and sexual relations with devils could well have had and probably did have an unhealthy effect, and his exhortation to German inquisitors to prosecute such matters more vigorously probably made it less likely that they would apply the common-sense criteria to judging

---

[94]*Ibid.*, V, 233-242.
[95]*Ibid.*, V, 255, 259-261, 277-280; Menéndez Pidal, *Historia de España*, XVII (2), 99-100. In February 1486 Emperor Frederick III, past seventy, effectively retired, turning over exercise of the imperial powers to his son Maximilian, who was also the guardian of his young son Philip, heir to the Netherlands. Four years later Matthias Corvinus died without issue and was succeeded as King of Hungary by Ladislas of Bohemia. His dual kingdom was recognized by Maximilian in 1491.

allegations of this kind that characterized the Spanish Inquisition. Contrary to the impression of many non-Catholics, the Church in its official documents rarely dwells on the supernatural powers of the Devil and how they are exercised. Though it is part of the deposit of faith that such powers exist, the Church has not generally considered it prudent to advertise them. To this policy the ill-advised bull *Malleus maleficarum* is the most striking exception in the Church's history.[96]

Innocent VIII, though not personally an evil man, was a failure as Pope, and his failure opened the way to the disastrous pontificate of Rodrigo Borgia that was to follow after Innocent died in 1492.[97]

The weaknesses of Pope Innocent VIII reflected those of Christendom in his time. The Renaissance had given the men of Europe much greater confidence in their ability to open up new frontiers of material and intellectual knowledge and power, but less inducement to show moral responsibility in how they did it. Italy, leader of the Renaissance, was giving the worst examples of irresponsibility. The void left by a weak and confused Pope could in no way be filled by the scheming Henry VII who had treacherously seized the throne of England from Richard III; nor by the dull-witted shambling teen-aged boy Charles VIII who had followed Louis XI "the spider king" to the throne of France; nor by Archduke Maximilian, heir to the Holy Roman Empire now exercising his father's authority there (such as it was), full of fantastic plans of aggrandizement which he could never realize. But Spain and Portugal had rulers ready to take the moral as well as the material leadership of Christendom, and to open up the rest of the world to Christendom as they did so.

When King Afonso V of Portugal, who had wasted the last years of his reign trying to seize Isabel's Castile, died in 1481 and was succeeded by his far superior son John II, the great enterprise of Prince Henry the Navigator was instantly resumed with full royal backing. The old Portuguese fort and base at Arguim Island, originally constructed by Prince Henry, was renewed and rebuilt, and a thousand miles further along the African coast a new and larger fort and base was set up where Joao de Santarem and Pedro de Escolar had found gold in 1470. Guarded by 500 soldiers and constructed by a hundred skilled workmen, the new outpost—Christendom's furthest—was located near the present city of Cape Coast in Ghana and named St. George of the Mine. Among those who sailed with the expedition of Diogo de Azambuja to build St. George of the Mine was a very capable thirty-year-old red-haired seaman who had sailed for Portugal for five years, but came originally from Genoa where he had been baptized Cristoforo Colombo—in Latin form, Christopher Columbus.

---

[96]Von Pastor, *History of the Popes*, V, 347-350.
[97]See Chapter Fifteen, below.

Before he joined this expedition, Columbus had already been in correspondence with the famous Florentine scholar Paolo Toscanelli, who told Columbus he believed there was a shorter route to the Indies than the route around Africa the Portuguese were opening up, west across the Atlantic to Japan and China which had been described in the thirteenth century by the Venetian traveller Marco Polo, though his account had been widely dismissed as imaginary.[98]

In the spring of 1482 one of Portugal's finest captains, Diogo Cao, was sent out to make a great new advance along the African coast. Stopping at St. George of the Mine for resupply, he sailed on around the right-angle bend in the African coast and south from Fernao Po's island to Cape Catarina (now Cape Lopez) in Gabon, the bold promontory just south of the equator that had been the farthest point reached by Ruy de Sequeira on the last Portuguese voyage of exploration in 1474. Four hundred and fifty miles further Cao sailed, past jungle-covered, almost uninhabited shores, until he came to the mouth of an enormous river which carried fresh water more than fifty miles out to sea. The natives called this river Zaire; the Portuguese later renamed it the Congo, for the black king who reigned there. Cao made his way up the river a short distance against the strong current, raised a stone pillar at its mouth, and sailed on—another 550 miles down the coast of what is now Angola, to a cape he named for the Blessed Virgin Mary, at about 13 degrees South Latitude, near the southern boundary of the present Benguela province. Cao raised a second stone pillar there and returned to Lisbon at the end of March 1484, bringing some of the natives of the Congo to learn Portuguese language and culture in the homeland. King John II, greatly impressed, knighted Cao—with the best of reason. His extraordinary voyage was much the longest in the entire history of the Portuguese exploration of the African coast thus far, extending the known coast nearly a thousand miles further south.[99]

Three years later Diogo Cao sailed south again, in a second voyage as remarkable as his first, but even more poorly reported. He apparently sailed straight to Cape Santa Maria, with a stop at the mouth of the Congo to return the natives he had taken to Portugal three years before, and perhaps another

---

[98]Diffie and Winius, *Foundations of the Portuguese Empire*, p. 154; Prestage, *Portuguese Pioneers*, pp. 199-204; Samuel Eliot Morison, *Admiral of the Ocean Sea* (Boston, 1942), pp. 33-35, 63-65. Toscanelli's letter to Columbus is not dated, but encloses an earlier letter dated in 1474. Since Toscanelli died in May 1482, almost certainly before Columbus returned from distant St. George of the Mine, it was probably written earlier, most likely in 1480 or 1481.

[99]Diffie and Winius, *Foundations of the Portuguese Empire*, pp. 154-156; Prestage, *Portuguese Pioneers*, pp. 206-207. Some of the Portuguese sources suggest that Cao made a second voyage the following year in which he first explored the coast of Angola, but Diffie and Winius conclude that he accomplished all this on the 1482 voyage and that he did not return to southern Africa again until 1485.

stop at St. George of the Mine—already a journey of almost four thousand miles. Then he proceeded on southward no less than seven hundred miles farther—and this was no ordinary seven hundred miles. South of Cape Santa Maria the coast grows increasingly dry. For four hundred miles beyond the Cunene River that now marks the boundary between Angola and Namibia there is no water at all. Long known as the Skeleton Coast, the edge of the Namib Desert, it is one of the most desolate and terrifying shorelines in the world, matching in every respect the coast around Cape Bojador which Prince Henry the Navigator had worked for fifteen years to persuade his captains to pass. Like that coast it is almost harborless, an invitation to a shipwreck that means certain death from thirst. The one harbor, surrounded by a small habitable area, is Walvis Bay. There Diogo Cao arrived some time during 1486, and there he set up his last pillar. There remains only a stark concluding notice in a map drawn by the cartographer Martellus in 1489: *hic moritur*, which may, but not certainly, mean "here he died." It probably does mean that, because we hear no more of Diogo Cao, and no authentic grave site for him is known in Portugal. But his ship returned. It may have carried the famous later globe-maker Martin Behaim.[100]

Columbus seems to have remained in Portugal for the greater part of the time between his return from St. George of the Mine in 1482 and the end of 1485. During these years he developed a detailed argument in explanation and support of his plan of reaching the Orient by voyaging west across the Atlantic, which he intended to present and did eventually present to King John II in an attempt to gain his sponsorship for the voyage. In all probability Columbus was encouraged by the success of Diogo Cao, a man of the people like himself rather than an aristocrat, who achieved so splendidly by his own efforts; he may even have met Cao personally during the interval between his two great African voyages. Columbus was convinced that God Himself had designated him to surpass the ancient barrier of the western ocean, as the Roman philosopher Seneca had prophesied in his *Medea* at the beginning of the Christian era:

> An age will come after many years when the [western] Ocean will loose the chains of things, and a huge land lie revealed; when Tiphys will disclose new worlds and Thule [Iceland] no more be the ultimate.[101]

But Columbus could not convince the Portuguese experts called by John II to review his project, for the simple and sound reason that his data and arguments were deeply flawed in both fact and logic. In estimating the length of his proposed voyage, he had applied every premise and calculation so as to reduce it and make it seem more practicable. Though (contrary to legend)

---

[100]Diffie and Winius, *Foundations of the Portuguese Empire*, pp. 156-159.
[101]Quoted in Morison, *Admiral of the Ocean Sea*, p. 54.

every educated man then knew the world is round, no one was sure just how large it is, nor did the writings of Marco Polo provide specific data on how far east China and Japan extended. But Columbus stretched the Orient as far east as the most inflated estimates of its geographical size could possibly carry him, and then adopted the smallest estimate of the length of a degree ever made to cut down the width of the ocean remaining between that inflated estimate and the western coast of Europe. By an extraordinary coincidence, his highly inaccurate calculations eventually led him to conclude that Japan lay almost exactly where the Caribbean islands, outliers of the American continents when sailing west from the Canary Islands, are in fact located. The actual distance from the Canary Islands to Japan is more than four times Columbus' estimate. No caravel or other ship of the time could have traversed it before the entire crew died of thirst or starvation. The Portuguese geographers and navigators, the best in the world, knew Columbus' estimate could not be accurate. Consequently, some time during 1485 they dismissed him.[102]

Columbus' belief in his enterprise remained unshaken; he went immediately to Spain to present it to Isabel and Fernando. On January 20, 1486, at the request of Fray Antonio Marchena, head of the Franciscan monastery at La Rábida in Palos on the south coast of Spain and a noted astronomer and cosmographer, Isabel and Fernando received Columbus in audience.[103]

Columbus and Isabel were of exactly the same age, and very similar in appearance and character, though he lacked her calmness and unfailing good judgment in dealing with people. Both had strikingly fair skin and blue eyes. Columbus' hair had originally been close to the red-gold color of Isabel's, but had been bleached almost white by sun and sea. Both were tall, strong in their bodily constitution, brilliant in their minds, highly articulate, of commanding presence and with striking personal attractions. Far more significant than any of this, both were profound, devoutly believing Catholics. Of this epochal meeting we have only Andrés Bernáldez's brief and vague account, written many years later on we know not what authority:

> And so Colón came to the court of King Fernando and Queen Isabel, and told them what he had imagined, to which they did not give much credit, and he talked with them and told them that what he said was true, and showed them his world map, arousing in them a desire to know those lands [of which he spoke].[104]

---

[102]*Ibid.*, pp. 64-73.

[103]Paolo Taviani, *Christopher Columbus; the Grand Design* (London, 1985), pp. 169-172; Juan Manzano Manzano, *Cristóbal Colon; siete años decisivos de su vida, 1485-1492* (Madrid, 1964), pp. 55-60.

[104]Andrés Bernáldez, *Memorias del reinado de los Reyes Católicos*, ed. Manuel Gomez-Moreno and Juan de Mata Carriazo (Madrid, 1962), p. 270 (chapter 118).

But subsequent history makes it clear that a spark was struck between Queen Isabel and Columbus on that cold January day in 1486, kindling a fire which the Queen never allowed to go out. She knew virtually nothing of navigation and seamanship; she could not herself judge Columbus' claims and his project. In the midst of the final struggle to attain the age-old goal of reconquering all Spain from the infidel, she had little time and no money to spend on an enterprise to open up a new route to Asia over the unknown western ocean. What impressed her was the man, for she was a superlative judge of men. This was a man like none she had met before, a man with a vision and a mission, overmastering, overwhelming, with an absolute confidence that he could triumph over all odds if only given the opportunity to begin. Isabel knew and well understood that sense of mission and confidence; all her life she had had it herself, and had achieved her goals against odds as great in her own world as any this poetic mariner would encounter in his uncharted seas. She believed in him; she never forgot him; in the end she gave him what he asked, and he discovered a new world for her and for Christendom.

In that year 1486 the Spanish crusaders took Loja, the great dark fortress against its long rock ridge which had defied so many Christian assaults. Fernando led in the field; Isabel kept the army supplied, supervised bringing up the siege artillery, and unfailingly saw to the care of its wounded. At the beginning of June the giant stone and marble and iron missiles from the lombards hammered down the walls of Loja, and the city surrendered on the usual terms: the Moors could stay and become subjects of Queen Isabel, or leave with whatever property they could take with them.[105]

The next year Fernando and Isabel laid siege to Málaga, the second city of the Moorish kingdom of Granada. It was fiercely contested for three months, from May to August. During the siege a Muslim fanatic attempted to assassinate Isabel and Fernando when they were in the besieging camp together. However, the assassin did not know them by sight, and mistook Isabel's friend Beatriz and a Portuguese nobleman who was playing cards with her, for the King and Queen. The nobleman suffered a near-mortal wound, but Beatriz dodged the scimitar, called for help, and the assassin was seized and executed. The siege went on until the defenders could fight no more. Fernando, probably in view of the assassination attempt, imposed exceptionally harsh surrender terms: all those captured in Málaga had to pay at least a small ransom, and those who could not or would not were enslaved.[106]

In the month that Málaga fell, August 1487, John II of Portugal sent one of his best captains, Bartolomeu Dias, along the coast of Africa to pass Diogo

---

[105]Menéndez Pidal, *Historia de España*, XVII (1), 648-650; Carroll, *Isabel of Spain*, pp. 172-173.
[106]Carroll, *Isabel of Spain*, pp. 179-184.

Cao's pillar at Walvis Bay and sail on to the south. On December 8 Dias passed Walvis Bay. In January 1488, after many days battling a furious storm beyond the sight of land, he came back north to find the coastline trending a little north of east. He had rounded the southern cape of Africa without knowing it; he sighted it only on his return voyage, after his men had forced him to turn back in March at the coast of Natal in South Africa, and named it the Cape of Good Hope. He returned to Lisbon with his glorious news in December 1488. Columbus' brother Bartholomew was there when he arrived, and actually had an opportunity to examine Dias' navigation chart.[107]

But now, on the very threshold of success for the tremendous 70-year-old enterprise of Prince Henry the Navigator, there was a pause. On the Sunday after Easter in 1490, just a few weeks after Isabel and Fernando had once more been successful against the Moors in the long and gruelling siege of Baza, their daughter Isabel, their eldest child, was betrothed to John II's only son, Crown Prince Afonso of Portugal. The marriage was splendidly celebrated in Portugal in November, and quickly proved to be a very happy one. Just eight months later tragedy struck. Prince Afonso died of a fall from his horse, and both his young widow and his loving father were left inconsolable. John II never really recovered from the shock. He lived and reigned only three more years, and never again showed interest in opening the sea route to India.[108]

Isabel and Fernando began the climactic siege of Granada in April 1491 with 80,000 men. It took all the rest of the year. Though their camp burned, the Moors fought desperately, and the tragic news of their daughter's bereavement weighed heavily upon their hearts, they never wavered in its prosecution. On November 25 Boabdil, king of Granada, agreed to surrender the city in January. On the 2nd of that month the Cross, the royal standard, and the pennant of St. James the patron of Christian Spain rose over the Alhambra, commanding the city the infidel had held for 770 years. The bodies of Isabel and Fernando still lie, as they had directed, in the Royal Chapel at Granada, with those standards in the adjoining room.[109]

Isabel had already promised Columbus that the moment Granada had

---

[107]Diffie and Winius, *Foundations of the Portuguese Empire*, pp. 160-162. As Diffie points out, the oft-told tale of Dias naming the long-sought cape the Cape of Storms, and John II changing its name to Good Hope, derives from the Portuguese historian Joao de Barros writing sixty years later, and is contradicted by the contemporary Duarte Pacheco Pereira, who actually sailed with Dias and declares that the name Good Hope was his.
[108]Elaine Sanceau, *The Perfect Prince* [John II of Portugal] (Barcelos, Portugal, 1959), pp. 317-320, 325-333, 337-343, 353-355, 381-382; Carroll, *Isabel of Spain*, pp. 189-195.
[109]Menéndez Pidal, *Historia de España*, XVII (1), 803-804, 810-813, 820-821, 840-843; Maria del Carmen Pescador del Hoyo, "Cómo fué de verdad la toma de Granada," *Al-Andalus* XX (1955), 283-344; Carroll, *Isabel of Spain*, pp. 198-202.

been reconquered, she would make a decision about sponsoring his project. She had summoned him to Granada and sent him travelling expenses to come there from the La Rábida monastery where he had continued to live. Probably in the Christmas season of 1491 he arrived, weary and travel-stained, at the now stone-built Spanish besieging camp which they had named Santa Fe (Holy Faith).[110]

The reconquest of Spain had been accomplished, and the opening up of America and of the Orient to Christendom was about to begin.

---

[110]Taviani, *Columbus*, pp. 193-194; Manzano, *Cristóbal Colón*, pp. 232-240, 248-249.

15
New Worlds
(1492-1504)

(Popes Alexander VI 1492-1503, Pius III 1503, Julius II 1503-1513)

"An age will come after many years when the Ocean will loose the chains of things, and a huge land lie revealed; when Tiphys will disclose new worlds and Thule [Iceland] no longer be the ultimate."—Seneca, *Medea*

"This prophecy was fulfilled by my father... the Admiral in the year 1492."—marginal notation by Fernando Columbus in his edition of Seneca's tragedies[1]

The opening up of the whole world to Christian Europe, so long prevented by the barrier of lands and seas controlled by Christendom's ancient enemy Islam, so long portended by the magnificent enterprise of Prince Henry the Navigator, is an event of towering and unique significance in history. Its inevitable consequence, gradually realized in the ensuing decades and centuries, was the creation of a civilization girdling the planet—a civilization initially shaped by Christendom. That the final stages of this process coexisted with the beginning of the great apostasy from Christendom in the twentieth century does not mean that there is any real historical relationship between the two developments, for the Westernization of the world had begun long before the apostasy, and nothing could stop it. Any clear-eyed observer of the world at the end of the second Christian millennium, able to see past self-conscious archaizing and fruitless attempts to revive dead Oriental and African cultural traditions, must be aware that there are now only two viable cultures in the world: the Western (however corrupted from its Christian origins) and the Muslim. This has been the result of Christendom's breakthrough accomplished by Christopher Columbus in 1492 and by Vasco da Gama in 1497. It was a breakthrough achieved by intention and design and not by accident, by the most Catholic and in many ways the most "medieval" of the nations of Europe in that decade: Spain and Portugal. It was a blazing double star to complete the

---

[1]Samuel Eliot Morison, *Admiral of the Ocean Sea; a Life of Christopher Columbus* (Boston, 1942), p. 50.

constellation of the glory of Christendom, just twenty-five and twenty years before its unity was sundered—massively and so far ahead into the future as any man can see or imagine—by the Protestant revolt.

By no means all the results of that breakthrough were glorious. It brought Christians into contact with utterly alien civilizations, extraordinarily difficult for the discoverers to understand and deal with. Many of the differences were morally neutral, merely customary; a few contrasted the alien societies favorably with the Christian West; more reflected evils abominable to God and man which the missionaries and warriors of Christendom would destroy. In the early contacts, and often for long afterwards while the alien cultures survived, great crimes were committed by both sides—some deliberately, some accidentally. These crimes should not and cannot be ignored or passed over. But in the long run, the consequences of the impact of the Christian West upon the world were good—at least until the West largely ceased to be Christian. No honest and reflective Oriental or African really wishes for a return to the society, economy, government and way of life of his people before the West made contact with them, or anything that could reasonably be expected to have developed from those cultures on their own. For the most part, non-Western societies—even when highly civilized, as in China and India and Japan—respected few if any rights of the individual person and offered no political freedom. They confined economic enterprise within narrow limits. Their religions aroused fear of angry spirits or offered spiritual escape from an evil world, but provided little moral guidance and no hope for perfecting souls or improving the world in which they dwelt.

The late twentieth century is not a time when it is easy for the Christian believer or the Christian historian to take pride in how Christendom opened up the world outside Europe, beginning with Columbus and da Gama. The sins of the Christian captains and colonists are now trumpeted from the housetops by those whose political and cultural agenda this serves, and the serious Christian must often deplore the contemporary impact of Western culture upon underdeveloped nations in an age of apostasy. It will be our purpose here and subsequently to survey the blessings as well as the evils which Christians brought to the new worlds they opened up, and to restore to a proper place of honor the brilliant achievements of the missionaries and the dispensers of justice in the far lands, now mostly ignored or unknown.

Immediately after the fall of Granada, Queen Isabel presented the enterprise of Columbus to her royal council with her recommendation now for its approval, along with that of Cardinal Mendoza, the primate of Spain. But the council objected to Columbus' insistence that he be made "Admiral of the Ocean Sea," with full ownership of all lands he discovered, and the title to pass on to his descendants. At first Isabel and Fernando deferred to the council's objections and rejected Columbus' proposal. But influential figures at court joined in supporting Columbus against this patently narrow-minded concern of the council, and Luis de Santángel, keeper of the Queen's privy purse, offered to lend a substantial part of the comparatively small cost of the proposed expedition. Official approval was finally given just as Columbus was preparing to leave Spain for France to present his enterprise to its king.[2]

The human consequences of the last-minute decision of Isabel and Fernando to support Columbus are so great as to be far beyond calculation. Even in the strictly material sense, they are awesome. It has been calculated that for every *maravedí* the Spanish Court, aided by Santángel's loan, invested in Columbus' expedition, during the next hundred years they received back, in gold and silver alone, a profit of 1,733,000.[3]

Isabel's final decision to sponsor Columbus—in which she was belatedly but fully supported by Fernando—was based not on geographic knowledge (of which they had little, and Columbus less than he thought) or any economic calculation. By such standards the decision was evidently wrong. But in human terms it was overwhelmingly right. For Columbus was a man born and driven to discover a new world, and such a discovery was bound to bring transcendent glory, power and wealth to whatever nation made it. In fact it made Isabel's Spain the world's greatest power for a century and a half, and the savior of Catholic Europe. Isabel, and the others who believed in Columbus, could see in him a history-maker, a man capable of opening up material and spiritual opportunites never known before. It was the man to whom they ultimately gave their blessing, far more than to his project. Because it had so often happened to her, Isabel above all understood how and why it is that fortune favors the brave.

Columbus sailed from the little port of Palos in southwestern Spain, which had supplied two of his three ships and most of their crews, on August 3, 1492, the dawn following the fiesta of Our Lady of Angels, patroness of the Franciscan monastery of La Rábida near the town, whose friars had long supported him and his undertaking. He steered for the Canary Islands, still only partly occupied by the Spanish who had sovereignty over them. There he repaired a broken rudder on *Pinta* and re-rigged *Niña*, the little caravel of Prince Henry the Navigator's design which was the most seaworthy of his ships. On September 6, shortly before noon, his three ships hoisted sail at their anchorage off the island of Gomera and set course due west into the unknown.[4]

The weather was almost perfect—"like April in Andalusia," Columbus

---

[2]*Ibid.*, pp. 100-104; Paolo Taviani, *Christopher Columbus; the Grand Design* (London, 1985), pp. 199-201, 494, 497-500; Juan Manzano Manzano, *Cristóbal Colón; siete años decisivos de su vida, 1485-1492 (Madrid, 1964), pp. 256-260, 263-277; Warren H. Carroll, Isabel of Spain; the Catholic Queen (Front Royal VA, 1991), pp. 203-204.*
[3]Taviani, *Columbus*, p. 500.
[4]Morison, *Admiral of the Ocean Sea*, pp. 158-165; Carroll, *Isabel of Spain*, pp. 214-216.

says, "smooth as the river of Sevilla."[5]   For ten days the trade winds blew
steadily from the northeast, ideal sailing. After September 18 the winds became
variable; the little fleet had entered the "Sargasso Sea," where a pelagic weed
often seems to fill the ocean, though actually offering no obstacle to a ship's
passage. Columbus' men became restive as they sailed farther and farther from
their home shores, without any indication of how they could return against the
prevailing winds. Columbus knew that further north the prevailing winds blew
from the west, and planned to go north to catch the westerlies on the voyage
home. But he never explained this to his men, nor told them his real objective;
he had told them only that he wanted to look for undiscovered islands in the
Atlantic. He insisted that he would find land soon. His men were not so sure.[6]
       By October 9 they had come more than three thousand miles in just over a
month, the longest voyage out of sight of land in recorded history up to then.
His other two captains, the Pinzón brothers, now also wanted Columbus to turn
back, but he persuaded them to follow him for three days more. On October 11
signs of nearby land were picked up from the sea—floating plants which were
not seaweed, and a carved stick. The wind was blowing almost a gale and the
following sea was heavy.[7] At the daily vespers prayer, Columbus tells us, "a
special thanksgiving was offered to God for giving us renewed hope through the
many signs of land He has provided."[8] The sun set, but Columbus kept up all
the sail his ships would carry, while doubling the lookouts. Through the
whistling dark, at ten o'clock in the evening, Columbus says: "I thought I saw a
light to the west. It looked like a little wax candle bobbing up and down. . . . It
was such an uncertain thing that I did not feel it was adequate proof of land."[9]
The wind continued to blow hard; the white sails strained against their halyards,
the dark hulls swooped over the waves. Let Admiral Samuel Eliot Morison, one
of America's greatest historians, describe that climactic moment as only he can:

> His ships rush on, pitching, rolling, and throwing spray, white foam at
> their bows and wakes reflecting the moon. *Pinta* is perhaps half a mile in
> the lead, *Santa Maria* on her port quarter, *Niña* on the other side. Now
> one, now another forges ahead. With the fourth glass of the night watch,
> the last sands are running out of an era that began with the dawn of
> history. Not since the birth of Christ has there been a night so full of
> meaning for the human race.
>   At 2:00 a.m. 12 October, Rodrigo de Triana, lookout on *Pinta*, sees

---

[5]*The Log of Christopher Columbus*, ed. Robert H. Fuson (Camden ME, 1987), pp.
63-64.
[6]Morison, *Admiral of the Ocean Sea*, pp. 197-214; Carroll, *Isabel of Spain*, pp. 219-
220.
[7]Morison, *Admiral of the Ocean Sea*, pp. 220-223; Carroll, *Isabel of Spain*, pp. 220-
221.
[8]*Log of Columbus*, ed. Fuson, October 11, 1492, p. 73.
[9]*Ibid.*, pp. 73-74.

something like a white cliff shining in the moonlight and sings out *"Tierra!*
Tierra!" "Land! Land!"[10]

The landfall was in the Bahama Islands, according to the latest analysis
probably the island now called Samaná Cay.[11] The natives Columbus found
there, whom he called "Indians" in the conviction that he had reached his
Asiatic goal (a conviction he seems never to have abandoned), were peaceful
and primitive. They were friendly, though the then unbreakable language
barrier made communication of any kind very difficult. But Columbus did
manage to learn from them that there was more land to the southward. Sailing
in that direction, he reached Cuba before the end of October, and in early
December Hispaniola (the big island now divided between Haiti and the
Dominican Republic). The fabled riches of the Orient were nowhere to be
seen, but some gold was found on Hispaniola. Exploring its coast, running risks
every day and hour in a sea never before navigated by a sailing ship, Columbus
and his men became exhausted. On Christmas Eve, with a very young sailor at
the wheel and everyone else asleep, the *Santa Maria* ran aground and was lost.[12]

There was not enough room in the two remaining small caravels for most
of the flagship's men, who therefore had to remain behind and await the coming
of another expedition. On January 16 *Pinta* and *Niña* left Hispaniola.
Columbus led them northeast, found the westerlies February 1, and began
sailing homeward.[13] But this was winter in the North Atlantic, which no seaman
since the Vikings of Leif Ericsson's time had experienced. One of its typical
howling storms struck Columbus' ships and separated them. On the wild gray
morning of February 13, Columbus says in his famous Log, "the wind became
stronger and the crossing waves more terrible; I carried only a low mainsail, so
that the ship might escape some of the waves breaking over her and not sink."[14]
For six hours the ordeal continued with no sign of relief. Columbus called his
men together and they vowed a pilgrimage to the great shrine of Our Lady of

[10]Samuel Eliot Morison, *The European Discovery of America; the Southern Voyages*
(New York, 1974), p. 62.

[11]Joseph Judge, "The Island of Landfall," and Luis Marden, "Tracking Columbus
Across the Atlantic," *National Geographic*, November 1986, pp. 566-599; Carroll, *Isabel
of Spain*, p. 222.

[12]Morison, *Admiral of the Ocean Sea*, pp. 254-263, 291-302; Carroll, *Isabel of Spain*,
pp. 222-224, 228-231.

[13]Morison, *Admiral of the Ocean Sea*, pp. 302-306, 316-318; Carroll, *Isabel of Spain*,
pp. 232-233. Both Paolo Taviani and Robert H. Fuson, major recent Columbus
authorities, are convinced (unlike Morison) that Columbus understood the pattern of
prevailing westerly winds in the Atlantic and the latitude where they could be reached
(Taviani, *Columbus*, pp. 127-164, 383-388, 393-427; *Log of Columbus*, ed. Fuson, p. 22).
The fact that on his return voyage from the Caribbean Columbus followed precisely the
correct course to pick up the westerlies is hard to accept as mere coincidence.

[14]*Log of Columbus*, ed. Fuson, February 14, 1493, p. 184.

Guadalupe in Spain if they were spared, with a representative chosen by lot to make it; Columbus was chosen. This shrine in central Spain was a favorite of Isabel and Fernando; they had spent a full two weeks there in June 1492. Columbus fulfilled the vow after his return. When the Blessed Virgin Mary first appeared in the New World, to the Indian convert Juan Diego in Mexico in 1531, she named herself to him as Our Lady of Guadalupe.[15]

After sunset on the 14th the skies began to clear, though the seas were still high. The next morning one of the Azores Islands was sighted. Columbus sent men ashore for food and water, and compelled their release by the Portuguese authorities after they were briefly imprisoned. Columbus was now back in waters he knew well from the years he had lived in Portugal and sailed from it, but his ordeal was not yet over. This winter of 1493 was one of the worst of the century. On March 2 another mighty storm overtook *Niña* and stripped every sail she was carrying off her masts. All through the day of March 3 she hurtled eastward under bare poles before a roaring northwest wind. Columbus' superb dead reckoning, and signs visible even in the tempest, warned him that he was approaching land. Just after sunset "the waves came from two directions, and the wind appeared to raise the ship in the air, with the water from the sky and the lightning in every direction." But the wind was tearing at the clouds as well as the waters, so that occasionally the full moon shone through. Between the moon and the lightning, at seven o'clock land was sighted dead ahead, high enough to mean cliffs. A rockbound lee shore in a near-hurricane for a ship driven before the wind means certain death if its course cannot be changed.[16]

There is no more dramatic moment in all of maritime history. They had one sail left. Columbus and his men must get it up the mast without its being shredded as the others had been, and wear ship at a right angle to take the gale abeam. They must do it quickly, for the cliffs were close ahead. They must do it in the dark, except for the bursts of unearthly brilliance from the cloud-wracked moon and the lightning bolts. The slightest error in turning into the monster waves rolling up from behind would swamp the ship and sink it like a stone. They could not do it in trough or on crest, but only on the upward roll, when there was moonlight or lightning to show them their opportunity. The tall Admiral, his once red hair bleached white by sun and strain, stood with feet braced, waiting for his moment. So far as he knew, his ship and men and they alone bore the secret of the greatest geographical discovery of all time. Their

---

[15]*Ibid.*, p. 185; Antonio Rumeu de Armas, *Itinerario de los Reyes Católicos, 1474-1516* (Madrid, 1974), pp. 194-195; Carroll, *Isabel of Spain*, pp. 233-234; Warren H. Carroll, *Our Lady of Guadalupe and the Conquest of Darkness* (Front Royal VA, 1983), pp. 104-105.
[16]Morison, *Admiral of the Ocean Sea*, pp. 329-338; *Log of Columbus*, ed. Fuson, March 4, 1493, p. 192 (for the quotation); Carroll, *Isabel of Spain*, pp. 234-235.

lives and its fate depended on what would happen in the next few minutes.[17]

Niña made the turn flawlessly and squared away on her new course. "God protected us until daylight," Columbus says, "but it was with infinite labor and fright."[18] The Admiral of the Ocean Sea, the discoverer of America, had not let storm and death cheat him of his victory.

Within weeks the news of what he had done was all over Europe; everyone who heard it seemed to realize its immense importance. John II of Portugal, in whose kingdom Columbus had so nearly been wrecked on his return, cried: "Why did I let slip an enterprise of such great importance?" Isabel and Fernando loaded Columbus with praise and honors, stood as godparents at the baptism of six Indians he had brought with him, and at once began preparing a much larger second expedition across the Atlantic which he would lead.[19]

On July 25, 1492, just before Columbus departed on his epoch-making voyage, Pope Innocent VIII had died in Rome. The conclave to elect his successor began August 6. The cardinals were divided into two parties of nine each, one led by Giuliano della Rovere (of the powerful family of former Pope Sixtus IV, who had exercised a very strong influence over Innocent VIII) and the other by Ascanio Sforza of Milan, uncle of its young duke. Four cardinals were not attached to either party, but even if they voted together with one of them, they would still not constitute the necessary two-thirds majority of 15. Consequently three ballots were held without result, making it clear that neither party leader had any real hope for election. Other names were put forward, but none could break the deadlock. An unusual procedure was followed in these ballots whereby each cardinal was allowed to name three candidates in order of preference, though only the first named was considered as receiving his vote. In the ballots cast by Ascanio Sforza's party the name of Rodrigo Borgia frequently appeared, though usually as a second or third choice.[20]

---

[17]Morison, *Admiral of the Ocean Sea*, pp. 338-339; Carroll, *Isabel of Spain*, p. 235.

[18]*Log of Columbus*, ed. Fuson, March 4, 1493, p. 192.

[19]Morison, *Admiral of the Ocean Sea*, pp. 346, 354-360, 375-385; Carroll, *Isabel of Spain*, pp. 236-238.

[20]Michael Mallett, *The Borgias; the Rise and Fall of a Renaissance Dynasty* (New York, 1969), pp. 112-116; Ludwig von Pastor, *The History of the Popes from the Close of the Middle Ages*, Volume V (St. Louis, 1914), pp. 320, 379-381. Von Pastor's famous account of this conclave, in which he declares the election of Rodrigo Borgia as Pope to have been clearly simoniacal, requires major revision in light of later discoveries of the actual ballots by the cardinals with their three choices. As Mallett points out, though Borgia made many promises to his supporters of offices and benefits if he became Pope, the cardinals appear to have been more influenced in their voting by political considerations than by prospects of personal financial gain, believing—with some reason—that Rodrigo Borgia was the cleverest and most effective political operator among the papal candidates.

Rodrigo Borgia had been Vice-Chancellor to all the Popes since his uncle Alfonso, Pope Calixtus III, in 1456—thirty-five years. The Vice-Chancellor held authority second only to the Pope in the administration of the Church and the papal state. He was responsible for the daily operations of papal government. Rodrigo Borgia had proved a very able administrator, but one who had no hesitation in using his position for his personal economic advantage. He held five wealthy dioceses—one in Italy, one in Portugal, and three in his native Spain; two wealthy Italian abbeys, and three strategic fortresses controlling the northern approaches to Rome. He had been a candidate for Pope in 1484, but the envoy of Florence reported that he "has the reputation of being so false and proud that there is no danger of his being elected." That reputation was not diminished during the eight years of Innocent VIII's pontificate which followed. However, Rodrigo was personally charming and adroit, and a very shrewd politican; and the scandals of his personal life were less damaging to him as a papal candidate than they would have been at any other period in the history of Christendom.[21]

The dark side of the splendid artistic flowering and the scholarly and intellectual achievements of the Italian Renaissance was the moral license accompanying them. It was undoubtedly stimulated by the excessive admiration bestowed on pagan literature, including that which was explicitly erotic, pornographic and obscene. With only a few exceptions, the wealthiest and most powerful families of Renaissance Italy were deeply stained by vice. Illegitimate children were accepted almost as readily as the fruits of a Church-recognized marriage; the majority of the rulers of the Italian states in the late fifteenth century were illegitimate. Giampaolo Baglione of Perugia even lived publicly in incest with his sister. Vicious cruelty and political assassinations among the state leaders were common. Though only a very few rejected Christianity openly, its moral teachings were widely ignored, and shame seemed impossible to arouse.[22]

Immorality was almost as widespread among the clergy as among the laity in Italy, encouraged by the growing practice of appointing very young men—sometimes even children—as bishops and abbots, part of a pattern by which rich and powerful families controlled dioceses and abbeys for generations. But even in this degenerate moral climate, it was unusual for bishops to maintain open liaisons with women and have illegitimate children into middle age, and many refrained from them entirely after their consecration. But Rodrigo Borgia had seven illegitimate children as a Cardinal.

---

[21]Mallett, *Borgias*, pp. 85-87, 98 (for the quotation), 114-115.

[22]Von Pastor, *History of the Popes*, V, 113-124. Even in the late twentieth century, another age of moral decline and license, fathering illegitimate children still carries a significant moral stigma for a major public figure, and a devastating stigma for a priest or minister.

They were born to two different women, with their baptisms recorded, the first when he was 31 and the seventh when he was 51. He publicly and repeatedly acknowledged all seven of them as his own, and there is some reason to believe that an eighth child of his was born while he was Pope, though this is not certain. All attempts to rehabilitate Rodrigo Borgia—and there have been several—must founder in the face of this appalling scandal, unmatched in the whole 2000-year history of the papacy. The lush and lurid Borgia legend, mushrooming down the years, is certainly not all true; many of its stories (such as the incest of Rodrigo Borgia's daughter Lucrezia with her brother and/or her father) are historically unsupported and unworthy of belief. But the seven children fathered by Rodrigo Borgia while a Cardinal are indubitable historical fact.[23]

An hour before dawn on August 11, 1492—just a week and a day after Columbus had set sail from Palos—Rodrigo Borgia was elected Pope on the conclave's fourth ballot and took the name Alexander VI. Instead of signifying his acceptance of the election by the traditional *"Volo!"* the new Pope, belying his sixty-one years, gave vent to joyful cries of "I am Pope! I am Pope!" Young Cardinal Giovanni de Medici, one day to be Pope Leo X in a dark hour for Christendom, turned to the Cardinal standing beside him and said: "Flee! We are in the clutches of the wolf!"[24]

Queen Isabel of Spain had known her countryman Rodrigo Borgia for twenty years. He had intervened to help her during the troubled and dangerous last years of the reign of her half-brother Henry IV. He had always shown her respect. He wrote twice to her about the time of his consecration—formally announcing his elevation to the pontificate and declaring his intention to appoint his son Caesar to succeed him as Archbishop of Valencia, while praising Isabel as a "zealous defender of the Holy See."[25] But such flattery could not deceive Isabel; she saw the new Pope for what he really was. She had

---

[23]Mallett, *Borgias*, pp. 101-107, 181-182, 294-295; von Pastor, *History of the Popes*, V, 399-402. The five-volume apologia for Rodrigo Borgia by Peter de Roo, *Materials for a History of Alexander VI, his Relatives and his Times* (Bruges, 1924), though extensively researched and occasionally a useful corrective to exaggerations of the Borgia legend, is essentially vitiated as a reliable source by the author's persistent refusal to admit that Pedro Luis (1462-88), Isabella (1467-1541), Girolama (1469-83), Cesare (1475-1507), Juan (1476-97), Lucrezia (1480-1519), and Jofrè (1482-1518) were in fact Rodrigo Borgia's children, as he always acknowledged. The eighth child, Giovanni, was born in 1498, and though Mallett says his papal paternity "has been usually accepted" (*op. cit.*, p. 181), de Roo presents strong arguments that a papal bull asserting that paternity is a forgery (*op. cit.*, V, 244-258).
[24]Mallett, *Borgias*, pp. 118-120 (second quotation on p. 120); E. R. Chamberlin, *The Fall of the House of Borgia* (New York, 1974), p. 49 (for the first quotation).
[25]Pope Alexander VI to Queen Isabel, August 24 and 26, 1492 (Rome), in Luis Suárez Fernández, *Política internacional de Isabel la Católica*, Volume III (Valladolid, 1969), pp. 299-303.

grown up in the shadow of Archbishop Carrillo of Toledo, a man very similar to Rodrigo Borgia in both immorality and greed. After years of struggle she had beaten Carrillo, terminating his influence in her kingdom. But she could not do anything like that with a man, however unworthy, who had become the successor of St. Peter, the Vicar of Christ.

Isabel was appalled to her very soul. Her warnings rang like alarm bells in the night. In the most prophetic moments of her life, she foresaw much of the train of disasters heralded by this man's accession to the leadership of Christ's Church on Earth. Writing to the Count of Tendilla September 23 from Zaragoza, where she and Fernando were then holding court, the Italian humanist Peter Martyr de Anglería (who had left Italy to come to Spain because of the corruption of his homeland) spoke of the distress he had seen on the faces of Isabel and Fernando as they contemplated the election of this Pope, of their shame at his boasting about his "sons in sacrilege," of their fear that the hour of "pillaging of the tiara of St. Peter" would soon come.[26] In a letter written just four days later to Cardinal Ascanio Sforza, who had given his support to Borgia's election, Peter Martyr's rolling, florid Renaissance Latin suddenly gives way to a blunt directness that sounds so much like Isabel that we can almost hear her telling the Cardinal of Milan what she really thought of what he had helped to do:

> You must understand, most illustrious prince, that the death of Pope Innocent and the pontificate falling upon Alexander has aroused the utmost disgust in my king and queen, whose subject he was. They regard his ambition, lewdness, and grave weakness for his sons as pushing the Christian religion toward ruin. And you are not free from censure for having contributed to his election, it is said, with many votes.[27]

At his first consistory (meeting with the College of Cardinals) as Pope, Alexander announced a number of ecclesiastical appointments including that of his nephew Juan Borgia-Lanzol as Cardinal and his son Caesar (so miscast as a clergyman that he later resigned as Cardinal) as Archbishop of Valencia as well as Bishop of Pamplona. As though anticipating the strife and wars that were to fill his pontificate, Alexander soon engaged a Florentine architect and a large contingent of workmen to rebuild the old mausoleum of Hadrian known as Castel Sant' Angelo (Castle of the Holy Angel) into the most impregnable urban fortress in Europe, proof against even to the new cannon because of its round construction and the impossibility of clearing an adequate field of fire near it. Storage space was provided for three years' supply of food, enough to outlast any siege. As soon as the rebuilt fort was ready, Alexander made it his

---

[26]*Documentos inéditos para la Historia de España*, published by the Duke of Alba et al, Volume IX (Madrid, 1955), p. 216.
[27]*Ibid.*, IX, 218.

residence, also constructing a covered walkway from the Vatican palace nearby, along which he could flee unseen to Castel Sant' Angelo if attacked.[28]

From the beginning of his pontificate Pope Alexander's continued liaison with the beautiful 19-year-old Giulia Farnese, who was openly his mistress, produced endless prurient gossip. Giulia's husband, Orsino Orsini, was not always inclined to yield her to him. According to a reliable contemporary, in October 1494 Alexander wrote angrily to Giulia saying: "We have heard that you have again refused to return to us without Orsino's consent. . . . We herewith ordain, under pain of excommunication and eternal damnation, that you shall not go to [him at] Bassanello."[29]

In September 1493 the Pope appointed twelve new cardinals. Bernardino Lopez de Carvajal of Spain was known as a reformer, and some of the other choices were unexceptionable, but several gave great scandal—most of all the appointment of his son Caesar. Since canon law prohibited anyone of illegitimate birth from serving as Cardinal, a papal commission headed by Alexander VI's ally Ascanio Sforza blandly declared Caesar to be the son of the second husband of the Pope's former mistress Vanozza, an elderly lawyer who had died shortly after Caesar was born; but simultaneously Alexander drew up a secret bull disclaiming responsibility for the commission's verdict and specifically declaring Caesar to be in fact his son. Such shameless duplicity needs no comment; and though the secret bull did not become known for some time, almost no one believed the commission because Rodrigo Borgia had so long and so often in the past made it clear that Caesar was his son. Alexander VI's Cardinal appointees of 1493 also included John Morton of England, now Archbishop of Canterbury, the devious intriguer who had done so much to help destroy Richard III; Ippolito d'Este, the 15-year-old son of the Duke of Ferrara, later to become a byword for immorality and cruelty; and Alessandro Farnese, brother of the Pope's mistress Giulia. Called "the petticoat cardinal," despite all appearances Alessandro Farnese proved an excellent appointment and much later became the worthy Pope Paul III (1534-1549). Cardinal Giuliano della Rovere, who had been Rodrigo Borgia's chief opponent at the conclave, was particularly outraged by these appointments, and soon afterward began plotting with France to overthrow Alexander VI.[30]

[28]Mallett, *Borgias*, pp. 121-122; Von Pastor, *History of the Popes*, V, 398; Chamberlin, *Fall of the House of Borgia*, pp. 82-86.

[29]Chamberlin, *Fall of the House of Borgia*, p. 52. Orsini's letter is not extant, but is quoted in the history of his own time by Sigismondo de Conti, described by historian Michael Mallett as "an important contemporary account by a curia official with . . . a sympathy for papal aims" (*Borgias*, p. 325). Even Peter de Roo, maximum apologist for Pope Alexander VI, says of Sigismondo de Conti that he is "an ideal witness of nearly all the events which he relates, and his history deserves as much credibility as any other written about that time" (*Alexander VI*, V, 314).

[30]Mallett, *Borgias*, pp. 131-132; Von Pastor, *History of the Popes*, V, 416-419;

Queen Isabel was also deeply distressed, particularly by the appointment of Caesar Borgia. On November 5 Francisco des Prats, papal nuncio, reported that in conversation with him she had strongly urged the Pope to change his way of life and not to give so much favor to his sons.[31]

Meanwhile Columbus' second expedition had departed for America September 25, a proud fleet of 17 ships carrying 1,500 men. The Admiral of the Ocean Sea set a more southerly course than on his first voyage, and made landfall on Dominica Island in the West Indies November 3. Sailing north along the Antillean chain, Columbus passed Puerto Rico and arrived at Hispaniola before the end of the month, only to find that all the men he had left behind after the wreck of the *Santa Maria* had been killed by the Indians (after having given, it later appeared, much provocation). Despite this evil omen, Columbus had been directed to found a permanent Spanish colony on Hispaniola, and did so January 2, 1494 at a site on the north coast of the island which he named Isabela. Four days later, on the feast of Epiphany as part of the dedication of the site for the colony's church, Fray Buil, the chief priest accompanying the expedition, said the first Mass in America. Twelve of the 17 ships then returned to Spain, arriving in March with gold from Hispaniola, American spices, 26 Indians sent to learn Spanish so they could act as interpreters, and a report from Columbus with a request to send two caravels loaded with food and medicine.[32]

Isabel and Fernando replied to Columbus with great approval on April 13 and send him three caravels, one more than he had requested. Commanded by his brother Bartholomew, they arrived at Isabela June 21. Bartholomew found that his brother had left the colony two months before, and already serious trouble was brewing.[33]

Christopher Columbus was the greatest mariner of his age, probably of any age—a visionary genius, whose personality and career sum up all that is

---

Chamberlin, *Fall of the House of Borgia*, pp. 95-96, 129.

[31]Francisco des Prats to Pope Alexander VI, November 5, 1493, in Vicente Rodríguez Valencia, *Isabel la Católica en la opinión de españoles y extranjeros, siglos XV al XX*, Volume I (Valladolid, 1970), pp. 45-47; Ramón Menéndez Pidal, director, *Historia de España*, Volume XVII, "España de los Reyes Católicos, 1474-1516," by Luis Suárez Fernández, Juan de Mata Carriazo and Manuel Fernández Alvarez (Madrid, 1969), Part II, p. 354. This important letter provides indisputably contemporary testimony of Isabel's attitude toward Pope Alexander VI early in his pontificate. It has been alleged (*e.g.* de Roo, *Pope Alexander VI*, V, 326-328) that Peter Martyr's letters, cited above to show Isabel's reaction to Alexander VI's election, were rewritten or interpolated later, though there is no proof that they were substantially changed from their original form.

[32]Morison, *European Discovery of America: Southern Voyages*, pp. 100-101; Morison, *Admiral of the Ocean Sea*, pp. 401-436; Carroll, *Isabel of Spain*, pp. 240, 248.

[33]Morison, *Admiral of the Ocean Sea*, pp. 436, 481-483; Carroll, *Isabel of Spain*, p. 249.

denoted and connoted by the word "explorer." But he had none of the particular talents required for administration, or for leading men anywhere but at sea. Though his pride prevented him from ever admitting that, his first love was always exploration. Give a choice between governing on land and sailing away across new horizons, Columbus always chose to sail away. That is what he did in April 1494. After establishing a fort in the gold country and sending the greater part of its garrison out under the command of Pedro Margarit with vague orders to look for gold and "live off the country," Columbus set off to explore the south coast of Cuba. He followed it almost to its end, stopping just fifty miles short of proving Cuba an island; for the rest of his life he believed it to be a peninsula of Asia. His return journey, beating against the trade winds, required more than three months. During Columbus' prolonged absence Margarit ran wild on Hispaniola, robbing, ravaging and raping the Indians, then seized the three caravels Isabel and Fernando had sent and sailed back to Spain in them—accompanied by Fray Buil, who in his brief stay on Hispaniola had not converted a single Indian.[34]

Knowing nothing of all this, but disturbed by the long period of time that had elapsed since they heard from their Admiral, Isabel and Fernando wrote him in August urging him to come home as soon as possible, and sending him a copy of the Treaty of Tordesillas between Spain and Portugal which had been signed June 7. This supplemented and modified a bull of Pope Alexander VI (*Inter caetera*) issued in 1493 which had drawn a line of demarcation 100 leagues west of the Azores between transoceanic lands to be discovered and developed by the Spanish and by the Portuguese. The Spanish were to have exclusive rights to everything west of that line, the Portuguese to everything east. (No one had yet thought of extending the line around the globe.) The Treaty of Tordesillas moved the Pope's demarcation line from 100 to 370 leagues west of the Azores, which meant that Newfoundland and Brazil (not yet discovered, or at least not yet known to have been discovered) lay on the Portuguese side of the line.[35]

On January 25, 1494 King Ferrante of Naples, illegitimate son of Alfonso V of Aragon, died. The French claim to the kingdom of Naples, going back to

---

[34]Morison, *Admiral of the Ocean Sea*, pp. 437-479, 483-484; Carroll, *Isabel of Spain*, pp. 249-250.

[35]Morison, *Admiral of the Ocean Sea*, pp. 373-374, 485; Elaine Sanceau, *The Perfect Prince; a Biography of the King Dom Joao II* (Barcelos, Portugal, 1959), pp. 370-380; Carroll, *Isabel of Spain*, pp. 250-251. No reason for moving the original demarcation line, or for the odd figure of 370 leagues, is given in any document that has come down to us. If it was coincidence that Brazil with all its riches lay on the Portuguese side of the new line, it was certainly a very fortunate coincidence for Portugal. There are unconfirmed reports that both Newfoundland and Portugal had been reached earlier by Portuguese mariners.

the mighty conflict of the Popes against Emperor Frederick II and his sons in the thirteenth century, had passed from the defunct Angevin house to the kings of France. Charles VIII was now king—young (24), small, misshapen, of limited intelligence but very romantic, thrilled with the idea of leading an invasion of Italy to reach Naples and enforce his claim to it. His advisors almost universally counselled against so risky and grandiose an undertaking, and a chastened Charles seemed ready to abandon it when Cardinal Giuliano della Rovere arrived, hoping to use the French to overthrow Pope Alexander VI. The Cardinal was an overwhelming personality, vehement and explosive, highly intelligent and relentless in getting his way. He told the King and anyone else who would listen that the Italians were not accustomed to real warfare; what they called war was little more than a charade of mercenaries who were rarely killed or even wounded, for all their maneuvering and bluster. They could not stand against the disciplined, veteran French army equipped with cannon of the latest and most mobile design, which shot round cast iron balls instead of the old roughly worked stone. No one at the French court was a match for Cardinal della Rovere. Under the lash of his personality and tongue the enterprise was launched. On September 3, 1494 Charles VIII crossed the Alps into Savoy with an army of 50,000 men and much artillery, supported by a strong fleet.[36]

The Pope immediately made two "anguished appeals for help" to Spain—indeed, he really had nowhere else to turn. The Italian states, as Cardinal della Rovere had predicted, were virtually helpless in the face of the powerful and genuinely warlike invader; Turin, Pavia, and Piacenza opened their gates to the French without a fight. Emperor Maximilian—his strength scattered in far-flung and often chimerical ventures throughout much of Europe—had no capability to intervene significantly in Italy on short notice. England was far away and its penurious King Henry VII unconcerned. In his desperation the Pope even tried to get money from the Sultan of the Ottoman Turks, on the grounds that if the French conquered Rome they would get possession of the Sultan's fugitive brother Jem who was living there.[37]

In response to the Pope's requests, on October 6 Fernando made his first formal offer of military aid to him, and sent a fleet to Sicily. Meanwhile the splendidly bannered and equipped French army, unblooded except for a brief

---

[36]Von Pastor, *History of the Popes*, pp. 423-427, 431-432; Louis Batiffol, *The Century of the Renaissance* (part of *The National History of France*) (New York, 1916), pp. 8, 10-14; Chamberlin, *Fall of the House of Borgia*, pp. 129-130; Ferdinand Schevill, *Medieval and Renaissance Florence*, rev. ed. (New York, 1961), p. 436; Menéndez Pidal, *Historia de España*, XVII (2), 356-360. For the character and personality of Cardinal Giuliano della Rovere, later Pope Julius II, see Ludwig von Pastor, *The History of the Popes from the Close of the Middle Ages*, Volume VI (St. Louis, 1898), pp. 212-216.

[37]Von Pastor, *History of the Popes*, V, 428-430, 434-435; Menéndez Pidal, *Historia de España*, XVII (2), 362; Carroll, *Isabel of Spain*, pp. 246-247.

and farcical encounter with a few Neapolitans near Genoa, had secured all of northern Italy and were marching on Florence. In that beautiful, highly cultured, ostentatiously wealthy but unwarlike city an extraordinary figure had appeared like a latter-day Elijah: Girolamo Savonarola, a Dominican friar. He preached the rising wrath of God against his sinful city—where, indeed, the vice of the Renaissance intellectuals and of many holders of high church office had profoundly undermined both public and private morality, as the writings of the Florentine Niccolò Machiavelli (then 25) were soon to testify. Savonarola blamed the Medici for the political corruption in Florence and Pope Alexander VI for the religious corruption. At this point he had not yet publicly defied the Pope, but he had defied the Medici, and he and his followers were prevailing. Savonarola welcomed Charles VIII and his French army as God's host sent to cleanse Florence of its sins. This made Piero de Medici, weak son of Lorenzo the Magnificent who had died two years before, even less able than he would otherwise have been to offer any serious resistance to the invaders. On November 9 he was overthrown and Savonarola came to Pisa to welcome the French; on the 17th Charles VIII entered Florence with his army.[38]

On Christmas day 1494 Pope Alexander VI reluctantly concluded that he lacked the military means to defend Rome against the French. On December 31 Charles VIII made triumphal entry into the city of St. Peter, with great pageantry and pomp, and several Cardinals headed by Giuliano della Rovere riding in his van. On January 7, 1495 the Pope, with his Cardinal son Caesar and his Cardinal nephew Juan Borgia-Lanzol, fled by the tunnel he had built to the fortress of Castel Sant' Angelo. Charles VIII brought up his potent artillery, but did not quite dare open fire on the Pope, who in turn had no way to get out of the castle. The deadlock produced an agreement on January 15 providing that Caesar Borgia would go with the French to Naples, effectively a hostage; that the fugitive Turkish prince Jem would be turned over to the French; that those who had supported France against the Pope would be given amnesty; but that Rome would be turned back to the Pope, who would keep all the papal state, while Charles would profess religious obedience to him and guarantee his personal liberty and safety.[39]

Charles made his submission four days later, and before the end of

---

[38]Von Pastor, *History of the Popes*, V, 188-212, 437-439; Menéndez Pidal, *Historia de España*, XVII (2), 363; Schevill, *Florence*, pp. 436-438; Christopher Hibbert, *The House of Medici; its Rise and Fall* (New York, 1980), pp. 186-190; Carroll, *Isabel of Spain*, p. 251. Savonarola hailed Charles VIII in these extravagant terms: "At last, O King, thou hast come. Thou hast come as the minister of God, the minister of justice.... We hope that by thee Jehovah will abase the pride of the proud, will exalt the humility of the humble, will crush vice, exalt virtue, make straight all that is crooked, renew the old and reform all that is deformed" (Hibbert, *op. cit.*, p. 188).

[39]Von Pastor, *History of the Popes*, V, 448-460; Menéndez Pidal, *Historia de España*, XVII (2), 368; Carroll, *Isabel of Spain*, p. 253.

January the resourceful Caesar Borgia had escaped his lax French guards. A month later the French lost their other trophy from the settlement when Turkish Prince Jem died of overeating. Charles pushed on southward, making triumphal entry into Naples February 22. But the French were now in a very dangerous situation strategically, for both the Pope and Fernando of Spain had made it very clear that they would never accept French rule of Naples. A Spanish army was preparing to go to Italy under the command of Gonzalo de Córdoba, who had fought brilliantly in the Granadan war and was highly esteemed by Queen Isabel, and the Spanish were bringing up a fleet fully equal to that of the French. Alexander VI greatly strengthened his position by forming a Holy League (proclaimed Palm Sunday, April 12) with Emperor Maximilian, Spain, and the north Italian states of Venice and Milan against the French invaders. This left Charles VIII with no choice but to retreat immediately to avoid being trapped in southern Italy. To salve his dignity he had himself crowned King of Naples in an empty ceremony, then went north May 20 with half his army, leaving the rest to try to hold the kingdom of Naples. Just six days later Gonzalo de Córdoba and his army landed at the foot of Italy determined to drive them out.[40]

Charles' retreat was very different from his advance; those who had hailed him when he came spurned him as he left. The Pope would not even see him as he passed through Rome. Savonarola met him near Siena, but only to berate him for not having reformed the Church as the honest but naive friar had genuinely believed Charles intended to do. The French had to fight a major battle at Fornovo near Parma July 6 in which the Italians, Germans, and Bohemians, though weakly commanded and poorly trained, gave the French a stiff fight and seized most of their baggage train, with the plunder of Italy and Charles' own helmet, sword, and royal seal. In October Charles VIII and his officials finally succeeded, after much behind-the-scenes negotiation, pressure, and bribery, in breaking Milan away from the Holy League so that the French army might pass peacefully out of Italy and back to France. By then Gonzalo de Córdoba had already totally defeated the remaining French in the kingdom of Naples in a campaign which began the creation of the personal legend of the man who came to be called "the great captain." This campaign also proved the mettle of his troops, displaying for the first time on the European stage what remained a pre-eminent fact in the history of Europe for the next century and a half: that Spanish infantry and cavalry, their military tradition formed by the reign of Isabel and the splendid reconquest of Granada, were man for man the best soldiers in Christendom.[41]

[40]Von Pastor, *History of the Popes*, V, 459-460, 462-468; Menéndez Pidal, *Historia de España*, XVII (2), 367, 374, 385-386, 388, 390-391; Carroll, *Isabel of Spain*, pp. 252, 254-255.
[41]Von Pastor, *History of the Popes*, V, 470-474; William H. Prescott, *History of the*

While Isabel was providing the commander for, and supporting the great military enterprise undertaken by her husband to defend Pope Alexander VI in Italy—despite her vivid awareness of his moral shortcomings—she was moving on her own to deal with the problem of which this Pope had become a personal symbol: the corruption of the Church in most of Christendom. The Church in Spain was somewhat better than the Church in Italy, but many of the same ecclesiastical evils were present in both countries. Isabel had been given ugly lessons in them by the late Archbishop Carrillo of Toledo; she had even had to watch, without public protest, while her husband installed his six-year-old illegitimate son (conceived shortly before their marriage) as Archbishop of Zaragoza, the capital of his nation of Aragon. She had established the Inquisition to root out enemies hidden inside the Church, and the Inquisition had done that with considerable success; but those hidden enemies were only a part, and not the greatest part of the problem in the Church in Spain.

As ever, the Church's heaviest cross was not anti-Christians but bad Christians. Isabel knew how often men and women without a real religious vocation were shunted into monasteries and convents, to get them out of the way or even as a special kind of preferment; she knew that many genuine vocations were lost in the kind of religious communities created by these practices. In Cardinal Mendoza, who had occupied the primatial see of Spain since Carrillo's death in 1482, she had an old friend whom she could trust; but he was one of Spain's wealthiest men, essentially a political rather than a religious figure, not hostile to Church reform, but not one to push it. And Pope Alexander VI (not surprisingly in view of his character and history) had shown no interest in reform whatsoever.

Isabel decided to launch Church reform in Spain on her own. Reigning monarchs in the fifteenth century had much more authority over the Church in their countries than Catholics of the past two centuries would expect any government to have; the Protestant and French revolutions were still in the future, and though there had been many clashes between royal and papal authority, at least since Emperor Frederick II they were always in the context of a shared Catholic commitment. The Church might resist a king or queen, but could never ignore them. A king or queen might resist the Church, but could never ignore it. Major changes required the cooperation of both Church and monarch. Most reforms had been the work of monks, supported by bishops and the Pope; but a queen could launch one as well. And that is what Isabel did.

As early as March 1493 Pope Alexander VI (undoubtedly on Isabel's request) had authorized Isabel and Fernando to nominate Visitors to reform

Reign of Ferdinand and Isabella the Catholic (Philadelphia, 1872), II, 279-294; Mary Purcell, *The Great Captain, Gonzalo Fernández de Córdoba* (London, 1962), pp. 106-111; Menéndez Pidal, *Historia de España*, XVII (2), 382, 392-393, 398, 405; Carroll, *Isabel of Spain*, pp. 253, 255, 260-261.

convents. A series of letters in December 1493 launched the reform. Some were signed by Isabel alone, others by both her and Fernando, but all evidently spoke with her voice. Here is a sample:

> The reformation of the nuns must be carried out in the service of God and well done, so we have begun it, for this is a great service for Our Lord, and we will not relax our efforts until it is brought to completion. To this end we command you to heed us and pursue this task with great diligence and write us often about how it is going.[42]

"We will not relax our efforts until it is brought to completion"—this was the theme of Isabel the Catholic's whole life: of securing her succession in Castile, restoring justice, conquering Granada, discovering America.

By the spring of 1494 Isabel had begun the reform of Benedictine and Franciscan monasteries and convents, with specific authorization from Pope Alexander VI to do so. In October of that year Cardinal Mendoza fell ill, and on January 11, 1495 he died. The man Isabel wanted to take his place as primate of Spain and to achieve the full reform of the Church as only a great bishop could, was the Franciscan ascetic Francisco Ximénes de Cisneros, who had already become her confessor and whom she had recently designated chief Visitor and reformer of all Franciscan communites in Castile.[43]

With her superb judgment of men, Isabel knew that Cisneros, in his humility and love of contemplative solitude, would strongly resist the appointment she intended to press upon him; for the primate of Spain was as much a worldly office as a religious one. Archbishops of Toledo had stood beside the Kings of Castile on many a bloody battlefield of the Reconquest; they had often been virtual prime ministers, and made or broken kings. A new thrust and emphasis could be given to the office, but by no means all of its worldly aspects could simply be rejected or ignored. When he joined the Franciscan order Cisneros had intended to leave the world, to be a man of the Church alone. He did not want to come back to the world. It was not enough to appeal to his sense of duty; he could always reply that others were as well or better qualified than he. He must, ultimately, be ordered; and only the Pope had authority to do that. That the reigning Pope was a public sinner did not disturb either Isabel or Cisneros in the slightest regarding his authority as head of the Church. Cisneros would obey him without question regarding a Church

---

[42]Isabel and Fernando to Bishop Juan Daza, December 11, 1493 (Zaragoza), in José Garcia Oro, *La Reforma de los Religiosos Españoles en tiempo de los Reyes Católicos* (Valladolid, 1969), pp. 150-151.

[43]Letter of Isabel and Fernando, April 18, 1494, in García Oro, *La Reforma de los Religiosos Españoles*, p. 453; Isabel and Fernando to Cisneros, July 20, 1494 (Segovia), *ibid.*, pp. 457-458; brief of Pope Alexander VI, June 18, 1494, in Luis Suárez Fernández, ed., *Politica internacioinal de Isabel la Católica*, Volume IV (Valladolid, 1971), pp. 205-206; Carroll, *Isabel of Spain*, pp. 243-244.

apopintment. Obedience to proper ecclesiastical authority was one of his monastic vows.[44]

Within three weeks of Cardinal Mendoza's death Isabel wrote to Pope Alexander VI telling him that she was resolved to have Cisneros, and no one else, as Archbishop of Toledo and primate of Spain. Her letter would have arrived in Rome during February 1495—during the very days of Charles VIII's triumphal march on Naples, while the Pope was staying in Castel Sant' Angelo with the Spanish ambassador only a month after literally looking into the mouths of French cannon. With the French was Cardinal Giuliano della Rovere, constantly seeking a means to remove Alexander as Pope. He was utterly dependent on Spanish support. At no time in his life and pontificate would Alexander VI have moved so fast to grant any ecclesiastical request from the King or the Queen of Spain. On February 22, just 41 days after Cardinal Mendoza's death, he sent to Spain his official brief designating Cisneros Archbishop of Toledo.[45]

The scene of Cisneros' reception of that letter is deservedly famous in Spanish history. It probably occurred on the first Sunday in Lent. Cisneros was preparing to leave to spend Lent at an isolated retreat. Isabel invited him to *comida* (the Spanish early afternoon meal) before his departure. During or just after the meal she told him that she had letters for him from Rome. One was from the Pope, addressed to Francisco Ximénes, Archbishop-elect of Toledo. Cisneros took one look at this superscription and dropped it on the ground. The Queen picked it up. For all her enormous respect for Cisneros and the habitual gravity of her presence, we may well imagine the hint of a smile on her lovely face as she did so. "Reverend Father," she asked, "may I open it?" Cisneros responded that he was Her Highness' servant and would do whatever she commanded; but he could not bear to hear the letter read, knowing now what it contained. "My lady," he said in much distress, "this is not for me." And he fled. We are told she was "not offended"; no doubt she had expected exactly this reaction.[46]

---

[44]Carroll, *Isabel of Spain*, p. 257.

[45]*Ibid.*; brief of Pope Alexander VI, February 21, 1495 (Rome), in Suárez Fernández, *Política internacional de Isabel*, IV, 303-340.

[46]Luis Fernández de Retano, *Cisneros y su siglo* (Madrid, 1929), I, 158; Juan de Vallejo, *Memorial de la vida de fray Francisco Jiménez de Cisneros*, ed. A. de la Torre (Madrid, 1913), p. 12; Carroll, *Isabel of Spain*, pp. 257-258. Luis Suárez Fernández, in *Historia de España* ed. Menéndez Pidal, XVII (2), 273, casts doubt on the reality of Cisneros' resistance to the appointment on the grounds that later correspondence from Pope Alexander VI to and about Cisneros makes no mention of such resistance. But the Pope would not necessarily have been immediately notified of Cisneros' resistance, and in any case would have continued to communicate with him officially as the Archbishop-elect, unless and until the appointment was revoked, which assuredly Alexander had no intention of doing. The Pope's eventual command to Cisneros to accept the appointment may have been sent orally rather than in writing, or may simply

After Cisneros had completed his Lenten retreat, Isabel sent Fernando's uncle and the president of her council to persuade him to accept the primatial appointment. They met him on the road, accompanied only by his little donkey Benitillo, and made their appeal by the roadside. Cisneros kept insisting that he lacked the sanctity, knowledge, judgment, and eloquence for so lofty a position (they might have replied that it had been a long time since its occupants were noted for sanctity). And he did not accept it until he had received a direct command from Pope ordering him, under holy obedience, to do so. Even then, at first he refused to change his manner of life. He continued to wear his old friar's habit, which he had sewed and mended himself; he would ride no mount but plodding little Benitillo; he refused a bed and slept on a board. Ordered by the Pope to meet public expectations of splendor in an archbishop, he began wearing his archepiscopal robes in public, but always with his friar's habit and a hair shirt underneath; he had a magnificent bed installed, but never slept in it, keeping his board underneath and pulling it out when he was ready for the little sleep he took.[47]

The prophet Jeremiah has been called "God's iron." The phrase fits equally well Archbishop Francisco Ximénes de Cisneros, Queen Isabel's choice for primate of Spain. This was the man who carried on and brought to fulfillment the reform of the Church in Spain, purifying it so thoroughly that for more than three hundred years neither Protestant nor secularist—critics and enemies of the Catholic Church who gain their credit and their base from scandals inside the Church—could establish even a foothold in Spain.[48]

The establishment of the Holy League against France, by bringing Emperor Maximilian and the reigning monarchs of Spain formally into alliance, speeded the negotiations, begun in late 1493, for a double Habsburg marriage for two of Fernando's and Isabel's children. Juan, their only son, was to marry Princess Margaret, only daughter of Emperor Maximilian; Juana, their second daughter, was to marry Archduke Philip, Maximilian's son and heir. By July 1496 all treaties, ratifications, and other necessary advance arrangements had been made, leaving only the actual transportation of the two brides to their new countries—Spain for Margaret, Flanders for Juana. Queen Isabel in particular had all the traditional understanding and respect of the medieval and early modern Catholic for the office of Holy Roman Emperor. It was a glittering seal on her magnificent achievements as Queen of Spain to be able to look forward

---

have been lost, as were many important documents in that age.
[47]Fernández de Retana, *Cisneros*, I, 159-160, 178-180; Reginald Merton, *Cardinal Ximenes and the Making of Spain* (London, 1934), pp. 65-66; Menéndez Pidal, *Historia de España*, XVII (2), 274; Carroll, *Isabel of Spain*, pp. 258-260. In this case we have the letter from Pope Alexander VI to Cisneros commanding him to make more use of the trappings of his office (dated December 15, 1495, text in Fernández de Retana, *Cisneros*, I, 179).
[48]Carroll, *Isabel of Spain*, p. 260.

to the day when her grandson would be Emperor (as indeed he was, in Charles V). Even wholly secular historians recognize that these two Spanish-Habsburg marriages in 1496 and 1497 created a lasting bond which remained a central political fact in Europe until the line of Philip and Juana finally died out in the year 1700. That bond was the creation of Isabel and Fernando.[49]

Along with the two Habsburg marriages, Isabel and Fernando had for some time been negotiating marriages for their other daughters with the King of Portugal and the Crown Prince of England (entitled Prince of Wales). King Manuel of Portugal wanted the widowed Princess Isabel for his wife. King Henry VII of England very much wanted Isabel's youngest daughter Catherine for his son Arthur. These four marriages, taken together, would bring Spain to a level of influence in Europe which no royal dynasty had enjoyed since the fall of the Roman empire.[50]

The first of these marriages to be solemnized was that of Archduke Philip and Juana, on October 18, 1496 in the Flemish city of Lille. At first all seemed well with them, with no hint of the tragedies to come.[51] Prince Juan and Princess Margaret were married March 19, 1497, Palm Sunday, at the ancient Castilian capital of Burgos. Archbishop Cisneros presided, and we may well believe that even his gaunt hawklike countenance found a smile that day for the vivacious, delightful Princess Margaret and her Prince, the heir to Spain. Admiral Christopher Columbus, at last returned from America after many troubles there, was guest of honor. No one could remember such rich, joyous, and magnificent celebrations ever before in Spain.[52]

For six months Juan and Margaret lived an idyll, deeply in love and deeply loved by all Spain. During the summer Margaret announced that she was pregnant. Their future and their country's seemed secure. On September 30 King Manuel of Portugal and Princess Isabel were married at Valencia de Alcántara near the Portuguese border. Then, almost at that very moment, Prince Juan fell suddenly ill with a raging, rising fever the doctors could not

---

[49]*Ibid.*, pp. 268-269; Menéndez Pidal, *Historia de España*, XVII (2), 426-427.

[50]Carroll, *Isabel of Spain*, p. 269.

[51]Menéndez Pidal, *Historia de España*, XVII (2), 429; Townsend Miller, *The Castles and the Crown; Spain 1451-1555* (New York, 1963), pp. 182-185 (though Miller's dates are incorrect).

[52]Menéndez Pidal, *Historia de España*, XVII (2), 431-432; Morison, *European Discovery of America: the Southern Voyages*, p. 161; Carroll, *Isabel of Spain*, p. 275. Before returning to Spain in *Niña* in June 1496, Columbus had engaged in all-out war with the Indians of Hispaniola and enslaved 1,500 captives (Morison, *Admiral of the Ocean Sea*, pp. 484-501). Isabel had refused to allow the sale of some 200 of them sent to Spain in 1495 (letter of Isabel and Fernando, April 16, 1495, in Antonio Rumeu de Armas, *La Política Indigenista de Isabel la Católica* [Valladolid, 1969], p. 315). On his return the following year Columbus brought 30 Indians with him as free men, and had them baptized at the shrine of Our Lady of Guadalupe (Morison, *Admiral of the Ocean Sea*, p. 507).

control. On October 4 he was dead, and the whole court put on sackcloth.[53]
They entombed him in the church of the monastery of Santo Tomás in
Avila, where his remains rest to this day. Let Townsend Miller, in his poetic
prose, describe it:

> Even the foreigner cannot escape a tremor of emotion as he walks
> down the dusty road to the Convent of Santo Tomás . . . and stands beside
> the tomb that enshrined the hopes, the whole future, of Spain. White,
> heavy, still, cruelly alone in the icy transept with the small figure lost in
> tons of marble—surely it is one of the world's saddest monuments.[54]

Isabel was ill in bed at Valencia de Alcántara. Fernando had ridden a
hundred miles to Salamanca to reach his son just before his death. Returning to
his wife, he could not bear to tell her the shattering news. No chronicler reports
how or when or by whom the truth finally came to her. But the contemporary
historian Andrés Bernáldez tells us what that truth was for her: a "dagger of
grief that transfixed the soul of the Queen and lady Isabel."[55]

And this was only the beginning of her maternal tragedies. Juan's and
Margaret's unborn child miscarried. This made Princess Isabel, now Queen of
Portugal, heir to Spain. She and King Manuel had then just conceived a child.
Young Isabel became convinced she would die in childbirth. She did, in August
1498. The baby lived; it was a son, christened Miguel, now the heir to both
Spain and Portugal. But Prince Miguel was weak and sickly, and many doubted
that he would live long. And just a few days after her daughter's death, Isabel
received an alarming report from a priest she had sent to Flanders to observe
the condition of her daughter Juana: that Juana was sullen and withdrawn,
unwilling to communicate with her parents and unwilling to confess her sins.[56]

Contention and strife continued in Italy even after the Spanish military
triumph was completed by Gonzalo de Córdoba in 1496. Savonarola was
preaching with increasing violence in Florence, now claiming the gift of
prophecy and defying a summons to Rome by Pope Alexander VI and then
(after four months of compliance) an order from the Pope to stop preaching.
On May 12, 1497 Alexander excommunicated Savonarola. Meanwhile he also
excommunicated the powerful Orsini family for having actively supported
France in its recent invasion of Italy, and war broke out between the Pope and
the Orsini. Alexander designated his son Juan, Duke of Gandia in Spain, as

---

[53]Carroll, *Isabel of Spain*, pp. 276-278.
[54]Miller, *Castles and the Crown*, p. 175.
[55]Andrés Bernáldez, *Memorias del reinado de los Reyes Católicos*, ed. Manuel
Gómez-Moreno and Juan de Mata Carriazo (Madrid, 1962), p. 380; Carroll, *Isabel of
Spain*, p. 278.
[56]Carroll, *Isabel of Spain*, pp. 281-287; Miller, *Castles and the Crown*, pp. 192-193;
Tomás de Matienzo to Isabel, August 16, 1498 (Brussels), in Suárez Fernández, *Política
Internacional de Isabel la Católica*, V, 287-288.

commander of the papal army to go against the Orsini. Duke Juan had virtually no military experience or aptitude for command, and was soon defeated and wounded by the Orsini in the Battle of Soriano in January 1497.[57]

On the night of June 14, 1497 Duke Juan disappeared returning from a party attended by his brother Caesar, who had dined that night with their mother Vanozza. Two days later Duke Juan's murdered body, which had been tortured with a sword but still bore valuable jewels in its dress and a purse full of gold pieces on its belt, was fished out of the Tiber. The murderer was never identified, but more and more suspicion fixed on Caesar as his dark passions and insatiable ambition became better known. He may well have seen the recall of his elder brother from Spain to command the papal army as threatening his own position and prospects, since he was known at least by September to be planning to renounce his Cardinal's hat and launch a political and military career. But no one knows for sure.[58]

Whatever the truth about the murder of Duke Juan Borgia and whatever suspicions Pope Alexander VI may have had, the immediate effect upon him was a passionate grief and (all too briefly) a profound repentance for the evil that he had done. On June 19 he went before the Cardinals in consistory to declare that the murder of his son was a punishment for his sins, and declared a new and vehement commitment to the reform of the Church. He appointed a commission of six cardinals to begin the reform and even wrote Fernando that he was thinking of resigning as Pope. But it soon came to nothing. A reform bull was drafted, but never published; most of the cardinals had little interest in reform and Alexander's own commitment faded as the first devastating effects of the shock wore off. Caesar now emerged as the most powerful man in Rome next to the Pope, a position underscored when he resigned as Cardinal in August 1498, declaring that since he was in fact the son of Pope Alexander VI and therefore illegitimate, he was disqualified to be cardinal or priest. He had been cultivating France's new King Louis XII (Charles VIII had died from hitting his head on a beam in one of his palaces) and was able immediately to assume the position of Duke of Valentinois in France with a large income, going to France hoping to secure its support for large-scale military operations in Italy which he would lead.[59]

Meanwhile the only real reform in the Church was being carried out by Archbishop Cisneros in Spain. The reform of the diocesan clergy of Castile was

---

[57]Von Pastor, *History of the Popes*, V, 490; VI, 5-6, 8-13, 19-21; Mallett, *Borgias*, pp. 144-146, 148.

[58]Von Pastor, *History of the Popes*, V, 493-500, 503-511; Mallett, *Borgias*, pp. 153-157; Chamberlin, *Fall of the House of Borgia*, pp. 147-157.

[59]Von Pastor, *History of the Popes*, V, 500-502, 512-519; Mallett, *Borgias*, pp. 157-159; Chamberlin, *Fall of the House of Borgia*, pp. 151-152; William T. Walsh, *Isabella of Spain, the Last Crusader* (New York, 1930), p. 440.

finalized under his direction at the Synod of Talavera in October 1498. It provided a virtual blueprint for the reforms finally adopted and made binding on the universal Church by the epochal Council of Trent 65 years later. Priests were to say Mass every Sunday morning without fail (an obligation that many, probably a majority, had long neglected). Children were to be regularly instructed in the faith every Sunday. The Blessed Sacrament was to be reserved in all major chuches and given due reverence; all entering the Church were required to kneel to It after blessing themselves with holy water. Priests were to reside in their parishes or in whatever other place they might be duly assigned. Priests who had been keeping concubines must send them away or face canonical penalties which could include arrest and imprisonment. Parishes must maintain baptismal records and complete registers of all parishioners, with an indication of who had not confessed and communicated at Easter. Immediately following the promulgation of these "constitutions of Talavera," Cisneros set to work personally to prepare the now requried catechism for children.[60]

On March 1, 1498 Savonarola publicly condemned Pope Alexander VI for his immoral life and declared he would no longer obey him. A few days later he called for a council to depose the Pope, then preached a sermon on the right of resistance to "unlawful" authority. The Dominican friar, for all his passionate sincerity and his well-justified denunciation of the immorality of Renaissance Italy, was now in rebellion against the Pope's authority and therefore in schism. Florence, still orthodox in belief for all its perversions, knew it. Savonarola's support quickly ebbed. A Dark Age ordeal by fire which one of his friar supporters offered to undergo for Savonarola was cancelled when the friar insisted on carrying a consecrated Host into the flames. The next day Savonarola was arrested in the library of the monastery of San Marco, where so many of Fra Angelico's paintings hung. He was tried, shamefully tortured, condemned for heresy (of which he was certainly not guilty, though clearly disobedient and schismatic), and burned at the stake May 23.[61]

Savonarola's memory endured. His ringing denunciations of the evil-living Pope and the vices of the age was remembered, while his own prideful disobedience, false prophecies, and irresponsible political agitation were mostly forgotten.

In the summer of 1497 began the voyage which opened up a second new world for Europe: Vasco da Gama's immense journey around Africa to India which at long last fulfilled the dream of Prince Henry the Navigator. In that

---

[60]Vallejo, *Cisneros*, pp. 22-23; Fernández de Retana, *Cisneros*, I, 272-279; Carroll, *Isabel of Spain*, p. 288.
[61]Von Pastor, *History of the Popes*, V, 28, 34-35, 43-46, 50-51; Schevill, *Florence*, pp. 452-454; Hibbert, *Medici*, pp. 198-200.

same year Giovanni Caboto (John Cabot), a Venetian sailing for England, rediscovered the island of Newfoundland just off the continent of North America, which had been found and partly explored by the Norsemen five hundred years before, and possibly again by Portuguese fishermen come to catch its swarming cod.

Da Gama's voyage was much the more important of these two, and though not as spectacular as Columbus' discovery, had comparable consequences for the future of humanity. The new world to the east was slightly known to Europe while the New World to the west had been utterly unknown. But for nine hundred years since the time of Muhammad there had been no way for European Christians to get to the Orient, save by arduous overland travel possible only during the single century of the Mongol empire before its rulers converted to Islam. Prince Henry's goals and strategy were triumphantly vindicated by da Gama, who brought the West in full power to an Orient that had known no more of the West than Europe had known of the Orient. Little Portugal became for a few years the richest kingdom in Christendom. Her captains so far from home performed prodigies of seamanship and valor, though too often stained with cruelty. The missionaries who followed—though not for a generation after da Gama—found before them the greatest evangelizing opportunity since St. Paul, though even more difficult than the task he had faced; and the end of their story is not yet.

Compared to Columbus, we know little about Vasco da Gama—almost nothing personally, and only one contemporary account of his voyage by a participant has survived.[62] There is nothing like Columbus' Log. The historian of Portugal constantly struggles with lack of documentation. The hot climate of India rots paper records; the great Lisbon earthquake is said to have destroyed the once better preserved archives of Portugal, though some whisper of a "policy of secrecy" that caused many records never to be made at all. Whatever the explanation, they are amazingly few for so stupendous an enterprise as Prince Henry's plan and its fulfillment.

So da Gama emerges, suddenly, unheralded, full-blown out of oblivion, to take command of history's second most important voyage. He was no visionary genius, like Columbus. He was a strong broad-shouldered silent man, heavily bearded, with deep-set dark eyes. Though about 35 years old, he had no wife and no children. He had a brother whom he loved, and a young captain who was his friend. King Manuel had decided at a conference in Montemor in December 1495, two months after the death of King John II, that the enterprise of reaching India which he had abandoned (apparently in grief for the death of

---

[62]Vincent Jones says: "It is astounding that almost nothing is known about Portugal's most famous conquistador before he was given this great command. Later, when his name had become a legend in the land, many stories were told. . . . But all is uncertain." (*Sail the Indian Sea* [London, 1978], p. 13).

his only son) after Bartholomew Dias reached the Cape of Good Hope in 1488, should be resumed. Vasco da Gama had been chosen to resume it and to finish it. On a little beach at the village of Restello on the banks of the Tagus near Lisbon, hard by a chapel built by Prince Henry the Navigator for departing seamen, the King's secretary unfurled the banner of the Order of Christ and handed it to da Gama with his orders: to find and follow the rest of the way to India, to trade there for spices, to contact the legendary Prester John. Neither he nor those who sent him had any better information about India than Columbus had about China, where he sought a "Grand Khan" where there had been none for 124 years.[63]

Between Vasco da Gama and his objective stretched ten thousand miles of ocean. His predecessors voyaging down the African coast had required eighty years to explore the first six thousand miles. For the other four he was on his own. The total journey was more than three times as long as that of Columbus.

He had two ships of a new type, an enlargement of the caravel while maintaining much of its characteristic form and sailing qualities, designed by Bartholomew Dias, the discoverer of the Cape of Good Hope. As later developed it was called a carrack. Both these ships were named for archangels: Gabriel and Raphael. Vasco da Gama commanded in *San Gabriel*, his brother Paulo in *San Raphael.* His young friend Nicolau Coelho commanded a regular caravel, the *Berrio*. Sailing with them were a caravel commanded by Dias which was going to Guinea, and a supply ship which would accompany them until its supplies were used up and it would be abandoned or destroyed. The supply ship made it possible to carry supplies for all the men for no less than three and a half years.[64]

Da Gama sailed on July 8. The winds were fair. After a week they passed Spain's Canary Islands, and heard the thundering surf on once dreaded Cape Bojador as they passed it by night. Fog and storm off Rio d'Ouro divided the fleet on July 17; they rejoined at the next rendezvous point designated in case of separation, the Cape Verde Islands, where they took on meat, water and firewood, and repaired damage from the storm. There Dias left them to go to the Portuguese colony of Mina on the Gold Coast, founded by John II in 1481 at the beginning of his reign, and visited by Columbus. Da Gama squared away for the open South Atlantic, following almost exactly modern directions for the fastest sailing voyage from West to South Africa: not along the coast but south and a little west across the equator until the southern westerlies begin to blow

---

[63]*Ibid.*, pp. 11-13; Bailey W. Diffie and George D. Winius, *Foundations of the Portuguese Empire, 1415-1580* (Minneapolis MN, 1977), pp. 177-178, 196-197. The rule of the Mongols in China—"Khan" was a Mongol title—had ended in 1368 with the establishment of the Ming dynasty in Peking.
[64]Jones, *Sail the Indian Sea*, pp. 27-31.

and carry the ship to the Cape of Good Hope. How da Gama came to follow this correct course we do not know; the answer is locked in the mystery of those missing Portuguese documents. History tells us of no one who sailed those waters before, and da Gama was out of sight of land for 84 days (compared to Columbus' 33 on his first Atlantic crossing).[65]

On November 22 da Gama rounded the Cape of Good Hope to a triumphal blare of trumpets from the flagship. Three days later he stopped ashore at what Dias had called the Bay of the Cowboys, but da Gama renamed the Bay of San Braz. There da Gama unloaded the supplies that remained in the storeship, distributed her crew among the other three ships, and burned her, while collecting wood and water. The primitive Hottentot natives were at first friendly, and the Portuguese marvelled at their unique clicking language; later the Portuguese became suspicious of them and drove them off with gunpowder explosions, though no shot was fired. Soon after they had resumed their journey a storm struck, and some of the frightened seamen began to plead and then demand to be taken home. A pilot supported them; da Gama put him in chains and threw his instruments overboard. Without them, he told the men, they could never get home.[66] He would go forward:

> God alone is master and pilot to guide and deliver us. Commend yourselves to Him and beg mercy. Let no one speak to me of putting back. Know for certain that if I find not what I have come to seek, to Portugal I do not return.[67]

On December 16 they passed Cape Padrone, Dias' furthest east, where they found his pillar still standing. Now they were in totally unknown territory, never before seen by a European, or probably any other civilized man. Held up by the surging Agulhas current, they made only slow progress along the coast of Natal, named by da Gama because they spent Christmas there. Going out to sea to find a way around the current, the ships ran short of water, but after 36 days at sea they came in to the coast of Mozambique and anchored near the mouth of a river. The black people there were friendly and there was no conflict with them during the expedition's five-day stay. As they sailed north back into the tropics, the coast became increasingly jungled. At some point near the mouth of the mighty Zambezi River, da Gama's interpreter at last

---

[65]*Ibid.*, pp. 32-34, 46-47; Diffie and Winius, *Foundations of the Portuguese Empire*, pp. 178-179.

[66]Jones, *Sail the Indian Sea*, pp. 50-54; Diffie and Winius, *Foundations of the Portuguese Empire*, p. 180. Not all sources report this mutiny, and Diffie and Winius consequently omit it from their history as unproved. But it is hard to believe it would have been invented by contemporaries or those writing within living memory of da Gama.

[67]Jones, *Sail the Indian Sea*, p. 54, quoting G. Correa's account of Vasco da Gama.

found someone who could speak a little broken Arabic. They had reached the outer fringe of Muslim penetration in East Africa—in touch with civilization again, but with the ancient enemy.[68]

They had to stop there for a month for the men to recover from scurvy—that dread diet deficiency disease of long-distance mariners which could strike only on a voyage as long as da Gama's, whose simple cure (the juices of lemons and limes) was not to be found for 250 years. As they sailed north, into Muslim areas, they were at first taken for Muslims themselves, but when they were identified as Christians they were attacked. This happened to them at Mombasa in Kenya which they reached early in April. But their reception at the next major port, Melindi, where they arrived on the 15th, Easter Sunday, was much friendlier, apparently simply because of the good character of the ruler. They asked him for a pilot to India, and he sent them Ahmad ibn Majid, one of the most famous navigators of the Indian Ocean. Ibn Majid seemed unconcerned that the Portuguese were Christians, and agreed to guide them to India for a fee. They sailed on April 24, picking up the first breezes of the spring monsoon, which gathered strength and began to make its characteristic thunderstorms as they approached the Malabar coast of India, where on May 22 Ibn Majid brought them in to the roadstead of Calicut.[69]

Da Gama sent a *converso* who could speak some Arabic ashore. Walking up the beach, he was astounded to be greeted in excellent Spanish by a Moor from Tunis: "May the devil take you! What brought you here?"[70]

This striking encounter and not very friendly greeting dramatizes at the very outset of the direct Portuguese contact with India an essential fact which must never be overlooked in studying and evaluating the enormously impressive but not always inspiring history of the Portuguese in India: that nearly everywhere they went they met Muslims, of greater or less power and influence, but ubiquitous. To fully achieve Prince Henry's goal of outflanking Islam by finding a coastline of civilized men untouched by it, they would have to go much farther, all the way to China and Japan. By 1498 Muslims had been penetrating India, both forcibly and peacefully, for five hundred years. They dominated the greater part of it. They did not fully control the Malabar coast politically, but the rulers of its small states usually could not afford to offend them. The Portuguese were always in the presence of the enemy as well as an unfamiliar culture. For many Muslims, the coasts of the Indian Ocean were home. But the

---

[68]Jones, *Sail the Indian Sea*, pp. 54-57; Diffie and Winius, *Foundations of the Portuguese Empire*, p. 180.

[69]Jones, *Sail the Indian Sea*, pp. 57-73; K. G. Jayne, *Vasco da Gama and His Successors, 1460-1580* (London, 1910), pp. 47-52.

[70]Diffie and Winius, *Foundations of the Portuguese Empire*, p. 181; Jones, *Sail the Indian Sea*, pp. 73-74. Despite his unfriendly greeting, this Moor, called Monçaide, soon took service with the Portuguese, helping them greatly, and was brought back by da Gama to Portugal.

Portugese were ten thousand miles from home. Any serious misstep meant death. They could be struck at any time. Except out to sea, and to established strongholds on the coast so long as they could hold out, they had nowhere to flee. As it was, only half of the men who left Portugal for the Indian Ocean ever returned. Without their superlative courage and irrepressible ardor, most of them would not have come back. All this does not justify their too frequent atrocities, but at lest makes them more understandable. The Portuguese in India could trust no one but themselves (and not always themselves—they had their renegades), and they expected—with some reason—no one else to trust them.

For Vasco da Gama, this looming danger was compounded by his total ignorance of those aspects of the society he had entered which were not Muslim. It does not appear that he or anyone in Portugal had ever heard of Hinduism. Throughout da Gama's initial stay on the Malabar coast he and all his people assumed the Hindus there were somewhat heretodox Christians, and repeatedly addressed them as such. Neither the Hindu ruler of Calicut, who bore the exotic title of Zamorin, nor any of his people with whom the Portuguese had contact ever corrected them, though they must have known who Christians were; there were substantial communities of Christians on the Malabar coast, descendants of Indians evangelized by St. Thomas the Apostle, though none in Calicut. Seeing the many statues venerated by the Hindus, the Portuguese assumed they were intended to represent saints and the Blessed Virgin Mary, though statues with four and five arms and long protruding teeth aroused some doubt (kneeling in what the Portuguese thought a "church" and beholding such statues, seaman John de Sá murmured to da Gama: "If these be devils, I worship the true God!").[71]

Though a Hindu, protected by warriors of the high Hindu caste of Nairs to which he himself belonged, the Zamorin was under strong Muslim influence. Calicut was world-famous for its trade; even with their very limited knowledge of India, the Portuguese had heard of it before da Gama sailed. Almost all Calicut's trade was carried in Muslim ships and handled by Muslim merchants. The Muslims knew from the beginning who the Portuguese were and shrewdly divined their purpose of taking control of the Indian trade for themselves by the new seaway. They made every effort to persuade the Zamorin to imprison or kill the newcomers and destroy their ships.[72]

For the three months of da Gama's stay in Calicut the Zamorin wavered between following the advice of his Muslim customers and maintaining his

---

[71]Jones, *Sail the Indian Sea*, pp. 76-81; Jayne, *da Gama and his Successors*, pp. 54-55. For the Thomas Christians and their apostolic origin, see Volume I, Chapter 17 of this history.
[72]Jones, *Sail the Indian Sea*, pp. 85-90; Jayne, *da Gama and his Successors*, pp. 53-54.

policy that Calicut was a free port and trading center open to all. He was impressed by the two flattering letters from King Manuel which da Gama presented and had read to him by interpreters (the letters intended for Prester John) and by da Gama's account of the immensely long way he had come and the (much exaggerated) great wealth of the King of Portugal. He was not impressed by da Gama's trade goods, which were fit only for primitive tribes on the African coast—the only non-Westerners with whom the Portuguese had dealt until now.[73]

After da Gama came to the Zamorin in person May 28, he was detained four days under guard by 200 Nairs with naked swords, a tense confrontation during which he showed no sign of the fear which the honest Portuguese chroniclers admit he and all his men felt, but remained calm, confident and decisive. Told to order his ships closer to the shore, he replied that any such order would be their signal to sail for Portugal. If the Zamorin wanted him to stay, he would stay; but the man with whom he was dealing was only the chief minister, called the Catual, and da Gama eventually suborned him by ordering more trade goods sent ashore, to which the Catual (presumably hoping they would be more valuable than those displayed by the Portuguese earlier) would have first access. The Zamorin repudiated the detention and there was a period of friendly contact and trade limited by the low value of the Portuguese trade goods, which ended in mid-August when da Gama's lieutenant ashore, Diogo Dias, was arrested with several other Portuguese. Da Gama promptly seized 25 hostages including six Nairs and used them to bargain successfully for the release of Dias and his men.[74]

It now being very clear that the Zamorin was not trustworthy, and enough spices and other valuables having been accumulated to prove that the riches of India had not been exaggerated, da Gama resolved to depart to bring news to Portugal of the opening of the sea road to the Indies. But first he went north, perhaps for further exploration before returning home, or to seek favorable winds for which the season was too early at Calicut. Reaching a group of six offshore islands called the Angedivas about three hundred miles north of Calicut, he prepared his ships there for the long journey back to Portugal, while maintaining vigilance against the Indians who came to trade, watch, and in some cases to spy. Believing that Indian ships were being readied to attack him, da Gama left the islands after twelve days, on October 5, 1498.[75]

It was too early for the northeast monsoon, which when blowing carries ships as easily and quickly across the Arabian Sea from India to Africa as does

---

[73]Jones, *Sail the Indian Sea*, pp. 83-84, 88-92; Diffie and Winius, *Foundations of the Portuguese Empire*, p. 182.
[74]Jones, *Sail the Indian Sea*, pp. 92-100.
[75]*Ibid.*, pp. 100-104; Diffie and Winius, *Foundations of the Portuguese Empire*, pp. 183-184.

the northwest monsoon in spring in the opposite direction, which they had encountered at exactly the right time on the last leg of their voyage to India. Becalmed for days, then battered by tempests and sudden squalls, often with the wind foul, da Gama's ships were out of sight of land for no less than 87 days, the crews again stricken with scurvy, with water strictly rationed in a very hot climate. Finally came a fair wind for Melindi, where they arrived January 7, 1499, at their last extremity. Revived by its fresh fruits and the hospitality of its remarkably kind and tolerant ruler, they could proceed, though now with only two ships since they no longer had men enough for three.[76]

They skirted most of Mozambique, averaging 56 miles a day, and rounded the Cape of Good Hope March 20, shivering in the winds of the southern fall which seemed very cold to men who had been living in the tropics. The winds held fair on most of the long diagonal across the South Atlantic from the Cape to the bulge of Africa, though as they were approaching the Cape Verde Islands a severe storm separated the two remaining ships. Nicolau Coelho's caravel *Berrio* made straight for Lisbon, arriving July 10 with the first news that India had been attained. Da Gama in *San Gabriel* went to the Azores Islands, to bring his brother who was dying of tuberculosis to a Christian land for a Christian burial. Paulo da Gama died on the island of Terceira the day after his arrival; da Gama buried him, then returned to Portugal in September, where King Manuel and his court rejoiced and gave da Gama high honor. Manuel sent an account of the voyage to Portuguese Cardinal Jorge da Costa in Rome, directing him to ask the Pope "for a fresh expression of satisfaction with reference to a matter of such novelty and great and recent merit."[77]

Columbus had sailed in quest of the Indies, and found America; Vasco da Gama had sailed in quest of India, and reached it.

The other great voyage begun in that same year 1497—and, because it was much shorter than da Gama's, completed in that year—was John Cabot's to North America. Not much is known about Cabot; the man who could have told us a great deal about him, his son Sebastian, traded all his life on his father's fame but never had much to say of him personally. Somehow John Cabot gained the ear of the parsimonious King Henry VII of England, who wished to reap some benefit for his country from Columbus' discovery without spending much money for it. He provided Cabot with just one small ship, the *Mathew*, manned by a crew of only eighteen. No fewer men could possibly have sailed across even the comparatively short span of the North Atlantic. Cabot was a good seaman; he did not risk his tiny ship in the stormy season, but sailed from Bristol at the best possible time, the end of May. Even so he encountered one

---

[76]Jones, *Sail the Indian Sea*, pp. 104-106; Diffie and Winius, *Foundations of the Portuguese Empire*, p. 184.

[77]Jones, *Sail the Indian Sea*, pp. 106-109, 117 (for the quotation); Diffie and Winius, *Foundations of the Portuguese Empire*, p. 185.

gale, but *Mathew* weathered it and at dawn June 24 he sighted land: Cape Degrat on Quirpon Island, just off the Newfoundland coast and only a few miles from L'Anse aux Meadows where Leif Ericsson had landed and Thorvald Ericsson and Thorfinn Karlsefni had established their short-lived Norse colonies at the beginning of the eleventh century. Cabot took possession of the "new-found land" for the King of England.[78]

For a month Cabot explored the rugged Newfoundland coast, then made a quick passage back before the westerlies, sighting England just sixteen days after leaving Newfoundland. Henry VII rewarded him, and was sufficiently impressed to give him six ships for a second expedition, with a commission to go past Newfoundland and on to Japan, and to set up a trading post there. By May 1498 five ships were ready and Cabot sailed. One ship carried Fray Buil who had so abruptly left Columbus in Hispaniola after saying the first Mass in the New World. A few days later the ship bearing Fray Buil put into an Irish port in distress. Cabot sailed on with the other four.[79]

They were never seen again. Every ship and every man disappeared without a trace. No hint of their fate has ever been found.[80] The English court lost all interest in overseas exploration for more than half a century. The loss of John Cabot and all his men, and its consequences for English exploration, further demonstrates the overwhelming importance of those dramatic moments when Columbus and da Gama defied disaster and death to bring their ships home against all odds. The disappearance of either of their expeditions, as Cabot's disappeared, would have changed the history of the world for many decades, perhaps in some ways forever.

In that same month of May 1498 when John Cabot sailed on his voyage from which no man returned, Christopher Columbus set out on his third voyage to the new world he had discovered (though he was still convinced that its lands were outliers of Asia). He followed a still more southerly course than on his second voyage, and after being becalmed for a full week in the torrid heat of equatorial waters, he reached the island of Trinidad and then the nearby mainland of South America. After sailing along what is now the coast of Venezuela for ten days, he concluded that this was indeed a new continent, an "other world," a "wonderful thing and will be so regarded by all men of learning." Since on earlier voyages both he and Cabot had reached only islands, Columbus was thus the first to reach the American mainland as well as the Americas as a whole.[81]

[78]Samuel Eliot Morison, *The European Discovery of America: the Northern Voyages* (New York, 1971), pp. 157-159, 166-180. See Volume II, Chapter 16 of this history for the Norse voyages to America.
[79]*Ibid.*, pp. 180-191.
[80]*Ibid.*, p. 191.
[81]Morison, *Admiral of the Ocean Sea*, pp. 513-517, 524-545; journal of Columbus for

On August 31 Columbus arrived at Hispaniola's new capital of Santo Domingo, which he had established just before leaving the island in 1496 after his prolonged second voyage. He was bitterly disappointed to find that his brother Bartholomew had been no better able than he to establish order among the Spaniards on the island, many of whom refused to accept the authority of a foreigner. Francisco Roldán, a power-seeking nobleman whom Columbus had unwisely appointed chief judicial officer for Hispaniola, was in full rebellion, holding the southwestern peninsula called Xaragua. His forces now outnumbered the loyal troops, and he was preparing an attack on the principal fortress of the Columbus regime, Concepción de la Vega in the lush central valley of the big island. Not strong enough to overcome Roldán, Columbus had to negotiate. Meanwhile he despatched letters to Isabel and Fernando October 18, which sounded vague and confused. He asked for more men and ships to suppress the rebellion, but at the same time talked of colonizing the new lands he had discovered in South America. He asked without apology for the full legalization of a slave trade in Indians, though Isabel had repeatedly made it clear she would never permit that.[82]

These letters from Columbus created a bad impression which was supplemented by other critical reports from Hispaniola, and convinced Isabel that Columbus should not continue as sole governor of the lands he had discovered, despite her agreement with him before his first voyage that he should hold that authority. He had proved lacking in both the personal qualities and the special talents of a good administrator. Isabel liked and admired Columbus and fully realized how great a service he had rendered her and Spain, but she must have been disappointed by the very small spiritual return in Indian conversions thus far, and by Columbus' persistent attempts to enslave those whose souls he claimed to have gone there to save. She decided to send a judge who would also have power to hear and settle disputes and grievances including those against the Admiral himself, who thereby lost his original full authority over the colony. The man appointed in May 1499 to exercise these powers was Francisco de Bobadilla, a nobleman of fine lineage and reputation, which tragically he was not to honor when he found himself far from home and law.[83]

Bobadilla did not leave to take up his duties in Hispaniola for more than a year. During that year Columbus felt he had to mollify the rebels by granting each Spanish settler a substantial tract of cultivated land with a number of Indians to till it, solely for their own personal support and enrichment. This was

his third voyage, in Samuel Eliot Morison, ed., *Journals and Other Documents on the Life and Voyages of Christopher Columbus* (New York, 1963), pp. 276, 280 (for the two quotations, respectively).

[82]Morison, *Admiral of the Ocean Sea*, pp. 561-567; Carroll, *Isabel of Spain*, p. 292.

[83]Morison, *Admiral of the Ocean Sea*, pp. 569-570; Carroll, *Isabel of Spain*, pp. 292-293.

the infamous *repartimiento* or *encomienda* system, which Bartolomeo de Las Casas, the "apostle to the Indians," spent his life fighting, and which Isabel's mighty and just grandson Charles V was to struggle desperately and with only limited success to eliminate. If not quite slavery, the *repartimiento* was certainly serfdom, imposed upon a people who had no custom or tradition of regular hard work on the land and would often die quickly if forced to do it.[84]

When Bobadilla finally arrived in Hispaniola he seized full power at once, countermanded all Columbus' standing orders, and ordered his arrest. When Bobadilla arrived, Columbus was in the La Vega valley in the northern part of the island. Never having been shown Bobadilla's commission, he could not at first believe that his great patroness Queen Isabel had given someone else authority over him. So at first Columbus attempted to overrule Bobadilla's decrees appointing officials, remitting financial obligations for twenty years, and granting permits for gathering gold to many whom Columbus knew would steal from the Crown's share. Bobadilla soon caught Columbus and put him in chains. He seized his property, including papers and household goods as well as gold; most of it was never seen again. Bobadilla never spoke to Columbus nor sent him any message. Early in October 1500 the great discoverer was sent back to Spain in a caravel, still in chains. The caravel's captain offered to remove his shackles, but Columbus proudly refused. The Queen's deputy had put them on; only by her direct order should they now be taken off.[85]

On board the caravel Columbus wrote a letter to Juana de Torres, a friend of Isabel who had been governess of two of her children. She passed the letter on to Isabel, who ordered Columbus' chains removed immediately. All his rights and privileges were temporarily restored, at least on paper. But investigations continued, and by the summer of 1501 Isabel and her advisors had concluded that both Columbus and Bobadilla were in the wrong. Bobadilla was summarily removed as governor, to be replaced by Nicholas de Ovando, who was given strongly worded orders to protect the Indians from robbery, rape, and other abuses they had suffered. Bobadilla was ordered to restore to Columbus all of his personal wealth and possessions he had taken from him. Columbus was to remain entitled to an eighth of the profits from all Spanish trade with Hispaniola. But he was not restored as governor, and was directed not to return to Hispaniola.[86]

Early in 1502 Ovando departed from Sevilla for Hispaniola with 30 ships carrying 2,500 men. In Sevilla for the occasion, Isabel explained to Columbus

---

[84]Morison, *Admiral of the Ocean Sea*, pp. 567-568, 570; Carroll, *Isabel of Spain*, p. 293.

[85]Morison, *Admiral of the Ocean Sea*, pp. 570-572; Carroll, *Isabel of Spain*, pp. 309-310.

[86]Morison, *Admiral of the Ocean Sea*, pp. 576-580; Carroll, *Isabel of Spain*, pp. 310-311.

face-to-face why she had deprived him of the governorship, but also told him how highly she still regarded him as an explorer, and authorized his fourth and last voyage. He set out in May with four ships and and largely inexperienced crews. Disobeying the royal order not to go to Hispaniola, Columbus sailed to Santo Domingo where he found 28 of Ovando's 30 ships preparing to sail home with ex-Governor Bobadilla, a large number of Spaniards who had come to Hispaniola to get rich, and their ill-gotten gains: a considerable quantity of gold including the largest nugget ever found on the island, worth 3,600 pesos and known (with a bit of exaggeration) as the "golden table." Ovando would not allow Columbus into the harbor, since the Queen had not authorized him to come there. Columbus cast his mariner's eye skyward and saw that a hurricane was making up. He had sailed more than enough in the Caribbean during the last ten years to know how dangerous West Indian hurricanes are. He sent a message to Ovando warning the fleet not to set out until the hurricane had passed, and asking shelter for his four ships from it. The warning was scornfully dismissed and his request to enter the harbor was again denied.[87]

The hurricane struck. Every ship but one of the 28 in the returning flotilla from Hispaniola went to the bottom of the sea, along with the "golden table," Francisco de Bobadilla, and most of the greedy gold-hunters who had robbed and raped the Indians. Off the thundering coast as darkness fell, Columbus anchored his flagship *Capitana* so well that her anchors held throughout the storm. His other three ships were torn loose; but on *Santiago* the admiral's brother took command from her terrified captain, pointed her seaward into the howling night, and survived. Three days later all four ships rendezvoused at a little harbor known only to Columbus. Not a man had been lost. Perhaps some on board reflected that in such a storm it was better to sail with the Admiral of the Ocean Sea than with a golden table.[88]

On July 14 Columbus' proud survivors sailed from Hispaniola. They raised the Central American mainland at Honduras, and beat southward along the coasts of what are now Honduras, Nicaragua, and Costa Rica, Columbus hoping to find a strait by which he could reach civilized Asia, still his goal. All during the fall and on into the winter he explored the coasts of Panama, where the American continent is in fact at its narrowest—though it does not appear Columbus knew that—in the hope of finding the strait. He carried on until Easter 1503, when his ships were so riddled by the holes made by the teredo or shipworm (previously unknown to European mariners) that he had to sail back toward Hispaniola. He was unable to reach it, beaching his last two ships on Jamaica in a sinking condition in June. He was abandoned there for a full year, and got back to Spain only a few days before Queen Isabel's death in November

---

[87]Morison, *Admiral of the Ocean Sea*, pp. 580-590; Carroll, *Isabel of Spain*, p. 322.
[88]Morison, *Admiral of the Ocean Sea*, pp. 591-592; Carroll, *Isabel of Spain*, pp. 322-323.

1504.[89]

On September 4, 1504, just two months before Columbus' return, a journeyman publicist, sometime seaman, and very amateurish Italian navigator named Amerigo Vespucci wrote a mendacious letter, later published, in which he claimed to have sailed on the first voyage to discover a continental mainland in the Indies. What Vespucci had actually done was to sail with a murderous pirate named Alonso de Ojeda who followed Columbus' track to the Venezuelan coast in 1499, the year after Columbus discovered it, looking for pearls; and to sail again two years later with the Portuguese captain Gonçalo Coelho to collect logwood on the coast of Brazil, discovered (or revealed) by Pedro Alvarez Cabral on the second Portuguese voyage to India in 1500. By predating his voyage with Ojeda to 1497 and writing a vivid though largely imaginary account of it, and making himself its hero, Vespucci convinced enough European scholars and writers of the truth of his claims to have the new continent named for him rather than for its actual discoverer, Columbus.[90]

The second expedition from Portugal to India sailed in March 1500 from Restello, where King Manuel was now building a church dedicated to the Blessed Virgin Mary at Bethlehem (Belém in Portuguese, the site now marked by a famous tower washed by the waters of the Tagus) in thanksgiving for the success of da Gama's voyage. It included 13 ships—seven carracks and six caravels—and was commanded by a nobleman in high favor at court, Pedro Alvarez Cabral. Vasco da Gama had been appointed Admiral of the Seas of India (rather similar to Columbus' title "Admiral of the Ocean Sea") with the right to take command of any expedition to India at his own option. For whatever reason—and the silent da Gama gave history no clue to his reason—he did not exercise that option in 1500. Cabral seems to have had little if any experience at sea, but he had Bartholomew Dias under his command and followed da Gama's sailing directions for going south and a little west from the Cape Verde Islands for a long distance before turning east toward the Cape of Good Hope.[91]

Nevertheless, Cabral's lack of sailing experience may have contributed to the course error—if such it was—that brought him so far west on his way south of the Cape Verde Islands that on April 22 he made landfall in Brazil, at 1,800-foot Monte Pascoal somewhat south of Brazil's easternmost extension. King John II's insistence, when negotiating the Treaty of Tordesillas, on placing a

---

[89]Morison, *Admiral of the Ocean Sea*, pp. 592-658; Carroll, *Isabel of Spain*, pp. 323, 347-348.
[90]Morison, *European Discovery of America: Southern Voyages*, pp. 276-297; Carroll, *Isabel of Spain*, p. 348.
[91]Jones, *Sail the Indian Sea*, pp. 110-112; Diffie and Winius, *Foundations of the Portuguese Empire*, pp. 187-189; Morison, *European Discovery of America: Southern Voyages*, pp. 219-222.

revised demarcation line with Spain at 370 rather than 100 leagues west of the Azores suggests prior knowledge of land somewhere between those two lines, and Vincent Jones states categorically that "for many years the Portuguese had known well that there was land on the west of the South Atlantic." But this does not necessarily mean that Cabral, whose expedition to India had enormous importance in its own right, would also have been delegated by secret instructions to go to Brazil so as to publicly proclaim its existence. It is more likely, as Samuel Eliot Morison and Bailey W. Diffie believe, that he was in fact carried much farther west than he intended.[92]

However he got there, Cabral stayed very briefly in Brazil, only ten days, just long enough to find a good harbor and make an initial contact with the local Indians. One of the expedition's priests said Mass on the one Sunday they spent ashore. Cabral sent a ship back to Portugal to announce the discovery (another ship had disappeared earlier), and sailed on for India with the remaining eleven, swinging well to the south. In these colder and more stormy waters a sudden tempest struck his fleet, sinking four ships and damaging most of the others. One of the ships sunk was that of Bartholomew Dias, who went down with it.[93]

With the men shocked and disoriented and the ships difficult to handle because of the damage, the fleet became separated, rounding the Cape of Good Hope and going a long distance up the eastern coast of Africa before six of them were rejoined.[94] The Portuguese were welcomed at Melindi as before; Cabral sent his able lieutenant Ayres Correa ashore to present its ruler with a richly deserved gift from King Manuel. On September 13 they reached Calicut and reopened relations with the Zamorin; this time they had impressively rich presents for him. Trading began, under the overall direction of Ayres Correa, but it was hampered by mutual incomprehension between the Hindus and Portuguese and harassment by Muslim merchants. In three months only two of Cabral's six ships were loaded with spices. Muslim hostility escalated, and on December 16 Muslims led an attack by three thousand man on the Portuguese compound. The Portuguese there numbered about eighty; despite a valiant

---

[92]Jones, *Sail the Indian Sea*, p. 112; Morison, *European Discovery of America: Southern Voyages*, pp. 222-223; Diffie and Winius, *Foundations of the Portuguese Empire*, p. 189-193.
[93]Jones, *Sail the Indian Sea*, pp. 112-113; Morison, *European Discovery of America: Southern Voyages*, p. 228.
[94]Jones, *Sail the Indian Sea*, p. 113. The seventh ship, commanded by Diogo Dias who had sailed with da Gama on his epochal voyage and given him outstanding service in Calicut, was driven far to the east, discovered the great island of Madagascar, reached the inhospitable desert shores of the Horn of Africa north of Mogadishu, and turned back there to Portugal. She reached the Cape Verde Islands months later with most of her crew dead of scurvy. Diogo Dias was one of thirteen survivors picked up by Cabral on his voyage home.

resistance they were overwhelmed by numbers. Only 36, many badly wounded, were able to reach their boats and get away to the ships. The others mostly died fighting, including Ayres Correa; some escaped and were hidden by friendly local residents. A Muslim historian declares the Zamorin gave orders for the attack.[95]

Cabral reacted fiercely and indiscriminately; he seized the first ten boats he could find and killed some six hundred men captured aboard them, roasting some of them alive. Then he sailed down the coast to Cochin, the next major port to the southward, whose ruler was hostile to the Zamorin of Calicut and welcomed the Portuguese. In three weeks they had loaded 400 barrels of cinnamon on the other four ships. At Cochin the Portuguese finally met two real Indian Christians (the Cabral expedition had come to realize that the Hindus definitely were not Christians). They came from Cranganore, where the Apostle Thomas had landed in 52 A.D., and were named Mathias and Joseph. Mathias died soon afterward, but Joseph accompanied the fleet back to Portugal. On Cabral's return in July 1501, his spices proved to be worth many times the cost of the entire expedition.[96]

King Manuel and his council lost no time in sending out a third expedition; indeed, henceforth Portugal sent at least one fleet to India every year. This was again commanded by Vasco da Gama; Cabral is heard of no more. This time da Gama had 15 ships, ten well-armed carracks with the specific mission to punish the Zamorin of Calicut for the killing of Ayres Correa and the other Portuguese at the compound in his city, and five caravels commanded by da Gama's uncle Vicente Sodre which were to raid Muslim commerce in the Indian Ocean. Five more ships under da Gama's nephew Estevao were to follow him after three months and meet him in the Arabian Sea. King Manuel attended a solemn Mass in Lisbon cathedral on January 30, 1502, and after Mass gave a speech praising da Gama's ability, character and achievements, received his oath of loyalty, and gave him a ring from his own finger and the royal standard. On February 10 the indomitable Portuguese admiral set out on his second 20,000-mile voyage to the Orient and back.[97]

He made good time; after all, he had sailed the long, long route before. He arrived in the Angediva Islands by mid-August, sent a letter to the Zamorin telling him that he intended to avenge further the killing and robbery of the Portuguese of the Cabral expedition, and proceeded to do so almost immediately in an appalling manner. He intercepted a large ship returning from a pilgrimage to Mecca, carrying more than 400 men, women and children.

---

[95]*Ibid.*, pp. 114-115; R. S. Whiteway, *The Rise of Portuguese Power in India, 1497-1550* (Patna, India, 1979), pp. 84-87.

[96]Whiteway, *Portuguese Power in India*, p. 86; Jones, *Sail the Indian Sea*, pp. 115-116.

[97]Jones, *Sail the Indian Sea*, pp. 107-108.

He stopped the ship, took all the valuables its passengers were carrying, and set it afire. But the passengers, though mostly unarmed, fought back when they saw that the foreigners intended to kill them all. They put out the fires and battled for their lives with hand-made weapons for four full days. At one point they even took a Portuguese caravel, and da Gama had to bring up most of his fleet to overcome a resistance so heroic that Thomé Lopes, who took part in the fight and seems to have had no regrets for it, could not refrain from praising their valor. Of all those aboard only twenty children were spared, to be taken back to Portugal and raised as Christians. One wonders what they were told about the fate of their parents.[98]

After that, and inevitably, it was war to the finish between the Portuguese and the ruler and people of Calicut. Da Gama was victorious so long as his full fleet was there to overpower the city with its irresistible bombardment, and the king of Cochin, Trimumpate whom the Portuguese called Trimumpara, remained their loyal ally. The Thomas Christians of Cranganore offered their allegiance and support. The ruler of Cananor, another major port on the Malabar coast north of Cochin, also offered his alliance. It was from Cananor that da Gama left to return to Portugal at the end of February 1503, knowing now that this was the best month for the northeast monsoon. Once again he made good time for the immense journey, arriving in Lisbon just over six months later, at the end of September, carrying fifteen times as many spices as Cabral had brought, at enormous profit to the court and the merchants of Portugal. But once he had gone, the Zamorin of Calicut attacked Cochin with his full strength, conquered the city, and burned most of it down, taking away the "sacred stone" on which its king was crowned.[99]

Even before da Gama returned the Portuguese sent three small squadrons of additional ships to the Indian Ocean, the first to depart—early in April 1503—being commanded by a man whose fame was later to ring from the banks of the Nile to the shores of the South China Sea: Afonso de Albuquerque. Arriving in Cochin in September, he drove out the army of the Zamorin of Calicut and restored Trimumpara to his throne. Albuquerque's cousin Francisco, leading a second squadron, joined Afonso there with Nicolau Coelho, who had commanded the caravel *Berrio* on da Gama's first voyage. Duarte Pacheco Pereira, who had sailed with Bartholomew Dias and commanded one of the ships in Afonso de Albuquerque's squadron, remained behind with ninety men and some small vessels to help defend Cochin. On the long journey back to Portugal both Francisco de Albuquerque and Nicolau Coelho disappeared, never to be seen again, but Afonso completed the voyage safely; while Duarte Pacheco Pareira with his ninety Portuguese and 8,000

---

[98]*Ibid.*, pp. 121-123; Whiteway, *Portuguese Power in India*, pp. 90-92.
[99]Jones, *Sail the Indian Sea*, pp. 128-137; Whiteway, *Portuguese Power in India*, pp. 92-96.

native soldiers held Cochin against an army of 60,000 from Calicut in an epic six-month siege from January to June 1504 that earned him the title of the "Lusitanian Achilles."[100]

While these mighty deeds were being done in the new worlds opened up east and west at this climax of the Age of Discovery, the last years of the pontificate of Alexander VI were further shadowed by the dark notoriety of his son Caesar, now lord of the papal state. In November 1499 Caesar entered long rebellious Romagna, that state's northern extension, with a largely French army (it will be recalled that upon resigning as Cardinal he had been made a French Duke) and quickly seized two cities there ruled by Caterina Sforza, a beautiful if ferocious woman whom he captured and raped. In February 1500 he made a triumphal entry into Rome to be welcomed by his father the Pope, and immediately took over as the real governor of the papal state. In July Duke Alfonso of Naples, husband of Caesar's sister Lucrezia, was attacked and badly wounded by five masked men in St. Peter's Square. He was brought bleeding and helpless into the Vatican palace, where Pope Alexander ordered him constantly guarded by sixteen men, and Lucrezia watched over him day and night; but Alexander also said "if Caesar had indeed attacked Alfonso, then Alfonso must have brought it on himself." Alfonso at least was convinced that Caesar had indeed attacked him, for when he saw him walking in the garden outside the window of his sick-room he fired a crossbow bolt at him, but missed. Shortly afterward Alfonso was strangled in his bed by Michael Corella, one of Caesar's chief lieutenants, after Lucrezia had been lured out of the room. The Venetian ambassador in Rome ended his report on the murder with the words: "The Pope loves, and has great fear of, his son the duke." There is reason to believe that from this point, at least in many respects, Caesar dominated his aging father.[101]

Keeping up with the latest developments in military technology, before the end of 1500 Caesar Borgia's army was notably well equipped with the latest-model cannon and with the first individually portable firearms used in war: arquebuses. It was ready to cooperate with the French when in June 1501 they marched south through Italy again intending to seize the northern half of the kingdom of Naples, which Louis XII of France and Fernando of Spain had agreed to partition by the Treaty of Granada in 1500. In July Caesar's army took Capua in the Neapolitan kingdom and horribly sacked it, killing 6,000 of its

---

[100]Whiteway, *Portuguese Power in India*, pp. 96-101; Elaine Sanceau, *Indies Adventure; the Amazing Career of Afonso de Albuquerque* (London, 1936), pp. 8-9, 13-16.

[101]Mallett, *Borgias*, pp. 169-172, 174, 176-177; Chamberlin, *Fall of the House of Borgia*, pp. 186-199, 219-224 (quotation on 224); von Pastor, *History of the Popes*, VI, 76-78; Ernst Breisach, *Caterina Sforza; a Renaissance Virago* (Chicago, 1967), pp. 210-211, 217-218, 221-223, 229-232.

inhabitants, including many women; a French chronicler records that thirty of the most beautiful women were sent to Rome as captives. Two days later Pope Alexander VI left Rome for a tour of his new estates gained from the Colonna and put Lucrezia in charge of the Vatican in his absence, with authority to open all his mail, which "astonished and shocked contemporaries"—in that age not easily shocked. Further shock was created when at a party given by Caesar Borgia on Halloween of 1501 some fifty prostitutes "danced naked with the servants, competed to pick chestnuts off the floor, and were then competed for themselves by the men present" in the presence of Pope Alexander VI and Lucrezia, according to papal master of ceremonies Burchard and three somewhat later writers well within living memory of the event.[102]

There is no reason to believe that Pope Alexander VI, for all the sins of his personal life, suggested or favored such a performance, which was in all probability Caesar's idea. But the Pope did not stop it, nor are we told that he even left when it began. Perhaps he genuinely feared to cross his terrible son who seemed to scorn all moral law.

In June 1502 the strangled corpse of Astorre Manfredi, the former lord of Faenza in the Romagna whom Caesar had captured the preceding year and had held prisoner in the Castel Sant' Angelo ever since, was found floating in the Tiber. That Caesar ordered Manfredi strangled is almost certain; he had done no less with Duke Alfonso in 1500, and was to do likewise with two of his enemies captured at Sinigaglia on the last day of 1502. Later in July, in one of the lightning military moves for which he was famous, Caesar swept into the duchy of Urbino and conquered it almost without firing a shot. It was soon after this that Niccolò Machiavelli of Florence joined him, becoming his great admirer and making him the generally recognized model for "the prince" in his famous and evil book on politics so entitled. In July the alliance of France and Spain to conquer and divide Naples disintegrated and these two countries went to war with each other again. Gonzalo de Córdoba was still in command for the Spanish, and after much careful maneuvering he triumphed at the Battle of Cerignola in April 1503. This battle, fought in the twilight, is the first in history won primarily by infantry gunfire, with the arquebus; the long invincible squares of Swiss pikemen were broken up by this fire. By July Gonzalo had secured Naples and had laid Gaeta, north of it, under siege.[103]

Now it was August, the dying month in Rome for so many centuries, and

[102]Von Pastor, *History of the Popes*, VI, 83-84, 103-104; Mallett, *Borgias*, pp. 180, 231 (first and second quotations, respectively); Chamberlin, *Fall of the House of Borgia*, pp. 241-244; Batiffol, *Century of the Renaissance*, p. 29; Menéndez Pidal, *Historia de España*, XVII (2), 532-533, 544, 547-549.

[103]Mallett, *Borgias*, pp. 187, 193-195, 204, 208; Chamberlin, *Fall of the House of Borgia*, pp. 282-284, 286-287; von Pastor, *History of the Popes*, VI, 120, 123-124; Breisach, *Caterina Sforza*, p. 243; Menéndez Pidal, *Historia de España*, XVII (2), 558, 591-593, 596-597.

on the 12th both Pope Alexander and his son Caesar fell suddenly ill with the high fever of malaria. Six days later the 72-year-old Pope was dead, just after anointing, confession and viaticum. The Vatican fell into chaos; the papal guards attacked the priests keeping watch over the late Pope's body, while the staff of the helpless and desperately ill Caesar seized the keys of the papal treasury and brought to his sickbed 100,000 ducats in gold coin together with a large quantity of gold plate and jewels.[104]

The Borgia Pope was gone. So great was the scandal he had given to the Church that the wildest legends attached themselves to his dishonored name; scarlet as were his sins, the legends raised them to incredibility and thereby stimulated in reaction, particularly in the nineteenth and early twentieth centuries, a number of attempts to rehabilitate him. Recent research has largely cleared him of the charge of simony at his election as Pope, but the disgrace of his personal life stands. The Catholic historian can do no better than quote the magisterial verdict of one of the greatest of his kind, Ludwig von Pastor:

> Thus he who should have been the guardian of his time, saving all that could be saved, contributed more than any other man to steep the Church in corruption. His life of unrestrained sensuality was in direct contradiction with the precepts of Him whose representative on earth he was; and to this he gave himself up to the very end of his days. But it is noteworthy that in matters purely concerning the Church, Alexander never did anything that justly deserves blame; even his bitterest enemies are unable to formulate any accusation against him in this respect. Her doctrines were maintained in all their purity. It seemed as though his reign were meant by Providence to demonstrate the truth that though men may hurt the Church they cannot harm her. . . .
>
> Just as the intrinsic worth of a jewel is not lessened by an inferior setting, so the sins of a priest cannot essentially affect his power of offering sacrifice or administering sacraments or transmitting doctrine. The personal holiness of the priest is, of course, of the highest importance for the lives of the faithful, inasmuch as he constitutes a living example for them to follow, and compels the respect and esteem of those who are outside. Still the goodness or badness of the temporary minister can exercise no substantial influence on the being, the divine character, or the holiness of the Church; on the word of revelation; on the graces and spiritual powers with which she is endowed. Thus even the supreme high priest can in no way diminish the value of that heavenly treasure which he controls and dispenses, but only as a steward. The gold remains gold in impure as in pure hands.[105]

Prostrated by his illness, though he was beginning slowly to recover,

---

[104]Von Pastor, *History of the Popes*, VI, 132-134; Mallett, *Borgias*, pp. 242-243; Chamberlin, *Fall of the House of Borgia*, pp. 292-293, 298.
[105]Von Pastor, *History of the Popes*, VI, 140-141.

Caesar Borgia had to agree to the demands of the Cardinals that he and his army leave Rome during the conclave, for he was widely suspected of intending to influence it by force or threat. He offered Louis XII of France his support for a French candidate for the papacy in return for protection and guarantees of his position in the Romagna. But the French had no significant candidate for the papacy, and 22 of the 37 Cardinals were Italian. Giuliano della Rovere received a plurality on the first ballot, but could not secure a majority; so Francesco Piccolomini, nephew of Pope Pius II, was chosen and took the name Pius III. He was in very poor health and not expected to live long under the strain of the highest office in the Church, nor did he. Elected September 22, 1503 and consecrated October 8, he was dead on October 18.[106] During this very brief pontificate Pius III urged reform and a council,[107] and had this to say of Caesar Borgia:

> I don't wish the Duke any harm, because it is the duty of the Pope to have love for all. But he will come to a bad end by God's judgment; that I can see.[108]

Many others had come to the same conclusion. On October 15, forsaken by most of his soldiers, Caesar tried to flee from Rome, but was stopped by the Orsini and took refuge in Castel Sant' Angelo. His only remaining support came from the Spanish cardinals. After Pope Pius III died three days later, the conclave quickly elected Giuliano della Rovere Pope as Julius II. Della Rovere obtained this easy election by gaining the votes of the Spanish cardinals by promising to confirm Caesar as papal captain-general and restore his dukedom of Romagna. But the new Pope had despised the Borgias for most of his life, and he was no sooner installed than he let it be known that he had never intended to guarantee more than Caesar's personal safety and movable property. When Caesar refused to give him the passwords allowing the papal troops to enter the strongholds in the Romagna, Pope Julius placed him under arrest, and also arrested his henchman Michael Corella, the strangler, so that he "might be questioned about the deaths of many persons." Protesting and weeping, Caesar was dragged into the very room where Corella had strangled Duke Alfonso, and the Duke had fired his crossbow at Caesar in the garden. His days as "the prince" were over.[109]

---

[106]*Ibid.*, VI, 187-189, 192-194, 196-199, 203-207; Mallett, *Borgias*, pp. 245-247; Chamberlin, *Fall of the House of Borgia*, pp. 299-300.

[107]Menéndez Pidal, *Historia de España*, XVII (2), 201.

[108]Chamberlin, *Fall of the House of Borgia*, p. 300.

[109]*Ibid.*, pp. 300-303, 306-308 (quotation on 307); Von Pastor, *History of the Popes*, VI, 205, 210, 239. In January 1504 Caesar bartered all his castles in the kingdom of Naples for his freedom (von Pastor, *op cit.*, VI, 241). Pope Julius set him free, but he was soon arrested by Gonzalo de Córdoba on orders of Isabel and Fernando (*ibid.*, VI,

The last years of the fifteenth century and the first of the sixteenth marked the appearance of Muscovite Russia as a major power in Europe. Though still only a grand duchy rather than a kingdom, by 1494 Grand Duke Ivan III, called the Great—a tall thin man with haughty features whose very appearance, it was said, could cause women to faint—was claiming to be "by the grace of God sovereign of all Russia." Early in his reign, which began in 1462, he had completely subjugated the once free and wealthy city of Novgorod on the old Dvina-Dnieper trade route from the Baltic to the Black Sea. In 1476 he had refused tribute to the remnants of the Mongol Golden Horde, and in the summer of 1491 broke their military power forever. He used firearms to defeat the Tartars of Kazan at the Battle of the Ugra River in 1480, and seven years later gained full control of Kazan. Married (as we have seen) to Zoe (whom the Muscovites called Sophia), niece of the heroic last Byzantine Emperor Constantine XI, Ivan III saw himself as the champion of Eastern Orthodox everywhere and the enemy of the Roman Catholic Church—a role later to be described by Abbot Filofei of Pskov as that of the "third Rome." In 1489 he completed the Church of the Annunciation in the Kremlin to help symbolize that role. While hardly to be compared with Hagia Sophia or St. Peter's, it was a very striking church for a still quite poor and primitive country. Two years later he marked Russia's diplomatic coming of age by a treaty with Holy Roman Emperor Maximilian.[110]

The treaty of 1494 in which Ivan claimed sovereignty over all Russia was made with Catholic Lithuania, an adversary of Muscovy ever since the Mongols ceased to be able to keep the peace in north Russia. In this document Lithuania under its Grand Duke Alexander, brother of King John Albert of Poland who had succeeded Jagiello's second son Casimir IV in 1492, formally recognized the incorporation of Novgorod into the Grand Duchy of Moscow in return for Moscow's recognition of Lithuanian rule over Smolensk. The peace was to be sealed by the marriage of Ivan's daughter Elena (Helen) to Grand Duke Alexander, on the condition that she be allowed to maintain and practice

---

243), who did not share the Spanish cardinals' friendliness toward him. On May 2, 1504 they wrote to their ambassador in Naples regarding Caesar: "We hold the man in deep abhorrence for the gravity of his crimes, and we have no desire whatever that a man of such repute sould be considered as in our service, even though he came to us laden with fortresses, men and money." (Chamberlin, *op. cit.*, p. 310) In August he was sent a prisoner to Spain, where he made a spectacular escape from a castle two years later, then was killed in March 1507 when he charged a French army almost alone near Pamplona (*ibid.*, pp. 317-318, 323-326).

[110]J. L. I. Fennell, *Ivan the Great of Moscow* (London, 1961), pp. 54-55, 72, 81-82, 95-96, 104-105, 126-127, 152-153, 354; George Vernadsky, *Russia at the Dawn of the Modern Age* (New Haven CT, 1959), pp. 15, 59, 75, 82, 169. For Ivan's marriage to Zoe see Chapter Fourteen, above. Abbot Filofei propounded the theory of Moscow as the third Rome in a letter to Duke Vasili III, son and successor of Ivan III, in 1510.

her Russian Orthodox faith.   The marriage took place a year later in the
Lithuanian capital of Vilnius.   Elena was very beautiful, and it is said that
Alexander fell in love with her at first sight.   The marriage was held in the
Catholic cathedral, but Orthodox elements were added to the ritual for the
occasion.[111]

For several years the peace treaty held and relations between Russia and
Lithuania seemed good.   Duke Alexander even refrained from helping his
brother the King of Poland against Ivan's ally Duke Stephen of Moldavia in
1497, at Ivan's request.   But Ivan's passionate anti-Catholicism was aroused by
Alexander's appointment in May 1498 of Bishop Joseph Bolgarinovich of
Smolensk as Archbishop of Kiev, since Joseph was known to favor the union
between the Catholic and Eastern Orthodox churches established by the
Council of Florence and supported by former Cardinal Archbishop Isidore of
Kiev.   (Joseph Bolgarinovich did in fact make formal submission to the Pope in
August 1500.)   In May 1500 Ivan declared war on Lithuania, giving as his
primary reason that Grand Duke Alexander and the Lithuanian bishops were
pressuring his daughter Elena to become a Catholic in contravention of the
treaty of 1494, though Alexander vigorously denied he had done anything of the
sort.[112]

The war began immediately in the summer of 1500 with a three-pronged
Russian attack which secured substantial territories (mostly in the upper basin
of the Desna River) which Lithuania had long controlled, though the majority
of their inhabitants were ethnic Russians.   Russian armies badly defeated the
Lithuanians after a long and bloody battle at the Vidrosha River about fifty
miles east of Smolensk, capturing the Lithuanian commander, though Lithuania
continued to hold Smolensk itself.[113]   In June 1501 King John Albert of Poland
suddenly died and his brother Alexander was elected to succeed him, though
required to make humiliating concessions including making the Lithuanian
monarchy elective like Poland's and giving up much of his executive authority to
a senate of nobles.[114]   Under these difficult circumstances Duke Alexander
suffered another major defeat at the hands of the Russians at Mstislavl near the
site of the Battle of the Vidrosha River the previous year.   This time the
Lithuanian losses were even greater, with as many as 7,000 killed.   At about the
same time another large Russian army further north overwhelmed the Teutonic
Knights at the fortress of Helmed in Estonia, annihilating and occupying much

---

[111]Fennell, *Ivan the Great*, pp. 152-154. 157-158; Vernadsky, *Russia at the Dawn*, pp.
86-89; Pawel Jasienica, *Jagellonian Poland* (Miami FL, 1978), pp. 245-252, 261.

[112]Oscar Halecki, *From Florence to Brest (1439-1596)* (New York, 1968), pp. 111-
112, 114-115; Vernadsky, *Russia at the Dawn*, pp. 93-94; Fennell, *Ivan the Great*, p. 220;
Jasienica, *Jagellonian Poland*, pp. 253-254.

[113]Fennell, *Ivan the Great*, pp. 220-223; Vernadsky, *Russia at the Dawn*, p. 95;
Jasienica, *Jagellonian Poland*, p. 258.

[114]Jasienica, *Jagellonian Poland*, pp. 259-260.

of Estonia and Latvia in consequence.[115]

The next year the Lithuanians checked the Russians by a firm defense of Smolensk, and early in 1503 Duke Alexander began actively seeking peace. But Ivan firmly refused to make peace, declaring his unyielding purpose to bring all ethnic Russians under his rule and never to give up any of the territories he had just conquered from Lithuania.[116] Many of the nobles of the border region, profiting from the war, were eager to continue it. Ivan continued to insist that his daughter was being pressured and persecuted to force her to become a Catholic, prompting a measured and impressive reply from Elena herself. Her husband, she said, had always been kind and tolerant. "He allows me to maintain my faith according to the Greek custom," she explained, "to go from one holy church to another, and to have at my court priests, deacons and choristers."[117] She then bravely reproved her mighty father with a moving protest:

> My subjects saw me as a messenger of peace, but I brought them only blood, fire and tears, as though I had been sent to Lithuania only to spy out its weaknesses. And those shifty princes, like Cains dripping with blood up to their necks, who had betrayed Moscow before and are now betraying Lithuania—do they merit your trust, Father?[118]

Since the terms of a peace treaty could not be agreed on, in April Russia and Lithuania concluded a six years' truce, with the Russians to hold the territories they had conquered for at least that long. The Russian ambassadors to Lithuania were ordered to obtain King Alexander's signature on a pledge not only to allow Elena to remain in the Orthodox Church, but not to permit her to convert to Catholicism even if she wanted to. The pledge is not further mentioned in the records; though the chief English authority on these events thinks Alexander made it (because Ivan made no recorded protest of his failure to do so), the relationship between Alexander and Elena, of which we have considerable evidence featuring her own letter quoted above, makes this very unlikely.[119]

When Ivan III died in 1505 at the age of 66 he had set Russia firmly on the path it would follow until the reign of Peter the Great, to be revived under Communist rule in the twentieth century: deep hostility to the West and especially to Catholic Christendom. In the trenchant words of J. L. I. Fennell:

> Militarily glorious and economically sound though his reign may

---

[115]Fennell, *Ivan the Great*, pp. 238-239, 242.

[116]*Ibid.*, pp. 250-251, 262-263.

[117]*Ibid.*, pp. 264-265.

[118]Jasienica, *Jagellonian Poland*, p. 261.

[119]Fennell, *Ivan the Great*, pp. 269-273, 280-281.

have been, it was also a period of cultural depression and spiritual barrenness. Freedom was stamped out within the Russian lands. By his bigoted anti-Catholicism Ivan brought down the curtain between Russia and the West. For the sake of territorial aggrandizement he deprived his country of the fruits of Western learning and civilization.[120]

This brief but volcanic age of the supreme geographical discoveries of all time, so full of both brilliance and atrocity, whose Pope was a public sinner and in which a Niccolò Machiavelli could win literary and intellectual fame for scorning all morality in public life, had been given one great soul to stand out like a glowing beacon against the stormy skies: Queen Isabel of Spain. At the summit of her glory from 1492 to 1497, then plunged deep into personal tragedy, she bore yet heavier crosses into the last years of her reign. Her little grandson Miguel, who would have united Spain and Portugal and half the world which Spain and Portugal were coming to rule, died in her arms in the summer of 1500.[121] That made her second daughter Juana her heir—and Juana was going mad. Insanity is terrible enough in the poorest, most insignificant family; but the Habsburgs of the Holy Roman Empire (of which Juana's husband the Archduke Philip was scion) and the Trastámaras of Castile (thanks to Isabel's towering achievements) were the two first families of Christendom. Across them now the shadow of unreason fell like a curse from Hell.

Juana loved Philip passionately; but it was a disordered passion expressing itself much more in violent jealousy than in tenderness. Philip was a cold man of dull wit and little sympathy for others, captivated by his own good looks. He philandered constantly and regarded Juana with increasing and obvious distaste. He cared nothing for her feelings or for her. His rejection made her condition steadily worse. Outside of its regular production of children (five while Queen Isabel lived) the marriage was a complete failure. But though Philip frequently threatened to lock up his wife and on a few occasions did so for short periods, he could not long confine the future Queen of Spain, through whom only he could fulfill his ambition to reign over the world's leading power as well as his small though wealthy native Netherlands and the Austria he would inherit from his imperial father. And because Juana was by law her heir, and perhaps could give at least the apperance of reigning after her mother was dead, Isabel had to try to prepare her people for the foreign presence that Philip would bring by ruling in her name.[122]

She tried her best; but under all the circumstances the task was impossible. Philip came to Spain with Juana early in 1502; he disliked the

---

[120]*Ibid.*, p. 354.

[121]Peter Martyr de Anglería to Cardinal de Carvajal, July 29, 1500 (Granada), *Documentos inéditos para la Historia de España*, IX, 411.

[122]Carroll, *Isabel of Spain*, pp. 305-309.

country intensely and almost everyone in Spain disliked him. Nevertheless the *cortes* (parliament) of Castile and of Aragon swore fealty to them as the rightful heirs to the realm. The *cortes* of Aragon, which had traditionally followed France in rejecting women rulers, made many difficulties, and their assent was not secured until late October. Philip immediately began insisting on returning home. Juana wanted desperately to go with him, but she was pregnant again; the renewed conflict in Italy between Spain and France meant that she might be seized and held as a hostage if she crossed France, and the winter weather made travel by sea dangerous. Isabel did not feel she could let her go. Both Isabel and Juana made great efforts to persuade Philip to stay longer, but he would not listen, and departed from Spain December 19.[123]

After he had gone Juana turned on her mother, whom she had long resented, much as Isabel loved her. All during the ensuing year of 1503 her hostility and her desperation grew. In November she heard of a partial truce in Italy, and received a letter from Philip asking her to rejoin him. Ablaze with passion and hope, Juana—who was staying at the castle of La Mota in the high plains of Castile—announced that she would leave at once to cross France to Flanders, where Philip was.[124]

Isabel could not let her go so quickly. A truce was not nearly as reliable as a peace; it could be broken at any time. Juana could be caught in France and imprisoned. At the very least, she must be properly accompanied and guarded by a substantial, well-equipped escort.[125]

But Juana was waiting for no one. She would listen to no arguments, no alternative plans, no appeals for delay; she was going *now*, and there was nothing more to be said about it. On Isabel's orders, Bishop Fonseca of Córdoba, whom she had sent to La Mota castle to try to make Juana see reason, closed the castle gates in her face when he knew that he had failed.[126]

What followed was the stuff of nightmare. Juana raged; she screamed; she howled. She gripped and tried to shake the iron bars and the cold stone of the battlements of the fortress. Hour after hour, her face distorted and her knuckles white, she clung to them. Afternoon passed, and twilight. Night fell on the high plains of Castile, which in November become quite cold. Still Juana would not move. Her skin blanched, her body shivered, but she did not seem to notice. Her attendants, the Bishop, and priests came to her, begging her at least to take shelter. She would not. The long, hellish night passed—how

[123]*Ibid.*, pp. 317-319, 321, 323-326; Menéndez Pidal, *Historia de España*, XVII (2), 566, 577, 580-581, 585; Antonio Rodríguez Villa, *La Reina Doña Juana la loca* (Madrid, 1892), pp. 68-71.

[124]Menéndez Pidal, *Historia de España*, XVII (2), 601, 606, 628-629; Carroll, *Isabel of Spain*, pp. 327-333.

[125]Carroll, *Isabel of Spain*, p. 333.

[126]*Ibid.*, p. 334; Isabel to Gutierre Gómez de Fuensalida (estimated date January 1504), *Correspondencia de Gómez de Fuensalida* (Madrid, 1907), p. 197.

slowly, only those who were there could truly understand. When the sun rose at last over the far serrated horizon, Juana was still gripping the wall. The next night they were finally able to persuade her to leave the open wall and go to a kind of lean-to the castle guard had set up against the wall, where they kept a fire going to boil water and do a little rough cooking. There she could find some warmth and shelter, but would still remain in contact with the wall she refused to leave.[127]

Isabel, no longer well, knowing that her daughter hated her, had hesitated to come to La Mota; but now she must. She sent a messenger ahead to tell Juana she was coming. Juana replied that she wanted nothing to do with her. Late in the afternoon of November 28 Isabel arrived at the castle gate. The drawbridge dropped. The portcullis opened. Through the gate, toward the guard's dirty kitchen, came the Queen of Castile, Aragon, Sicily, and the Indies, the most powerful woman and most successful ruler on the face of the earth in her time. She walked slowly now; her once strong athletic legs were swollen with the beginnings of the dropsy that was so greatly to afflict her in the coming year. Her beautiful red-gold hair now streaked with gray, her large blue-green eyes dimmed with tears, she entered the squat structure. Surely she was offering a prayer with every step she took. Her daughter looked up at her from where she crouched clinging to the stones of the wall, as she had clung for six full days and nights, and loosed upon her mother a torrent of obscene vituperation. "She spoke such words to me," Isabel said later in the saddest letter she ever wrote, to Juana's husband who had spurned her, "as no daughter should say to a mother, which I would never have endured if I had not seen the condition she was in."[128]

Yet once more, she endured. And when Juana's mad fury was for the moment spent, Isabel the Catholic drew upon the deepest wells of strength in her own being, and in the Precious Blood of her Lord Who died upon a cross, and spoke to Juana as a mother to a child, a desperately sick child who even in delirium still knows her mother's voice. Her mother was calling her in, out of the cold and the dark. Juana got to her feet, stepped away from the wall, and went with her mother to her room.

---

[127]Isabel to Gómez de Fuensalida (estimated date January 1504), *Correspondencia de Fuensalida*, p. 197; Peter Martyr de Anglería to Cardinal of Santa Cruz, March 10, 1504 (Alcalá de Henares), *Documentos inéditos para la Historia de España*, X, 47-48; Carroll, *Isabel of Spain*, pp. 334-335.

[128]Isabel to Gómez de Fuensalida (estimated date January 1504), *Correspondencia de Fuensalida*, pp. 195-196; Peter Martyr de Anglería to Cardinal of Santa Cruz, March 10, 1504 (Alcalá de Henares), *Documentos inéditos para la Historia de España*, X, 47-48; Rumeu de Armas, *Itinerario de los Reyes Católicos*, pp. 299-300; Carroll, *Isabel of Spain*, p. 335. Isabel's letter to Philip is not extant, but is extensively summarized and paraphrased in her letter to Fuensalida, probably written in January 1504.

"*Yo vine y la metí,*" Isabel said, in her letter to Philip. "I came and put her in."[129]

The dreadful scene was over; but now there could be no reasonable doubt that Juana was insane. For several years her insanity would remain periodic, and no historian at this distance in time can always be sure when during these years she was insane and when she was not,[130] but it was clear that she could never provide stable government for Spain. Nor could Philip, for quite different reasons. Isabel and Fernando must skip a whole generation, and look to Juana's and Philip's first-born son Charles, their heir, for the rescue of Spain. But Charles was just four years old.[131]

Isabel, only 52, lived but one year more after the harrowing scene at the La Mota castle wall. During that year Juana suffered several attacks of outright insanity in Flanders. The report of the last of these came to Isabel on her deathbed. There can be little doubt that this dreadful tragedy hastened her death.[132]

But she did her duty to the end, and her magnificent last will and testament ("being infirm in body with the illness God has chosen to send me, but free and sound in mind, believing and confessing firmly all that the Holy Catholic Church of Rome holds, believes, confesses and teaches ... in which Faith and for which Faith I am prepared to die ... I ordain this my last will and testament")[133] provided as best she could for the many unpleasant consequences that were likely to follow her death. Juana was still to be her heir, but was prohibited from granting governmental and ecclesiastical offices in Spain to foreigners. If she "does not wish to, or is unable to exercise authority in the governance of these kingdoms," Isabel declared, her husband Fernando should act as regent until Prince Charles reached his majority. Isabel signed her will October 12, 1504, but she lived six more weeks, and on November 23 added a last codicil, which concluded with a charge upon Fernando, Juana and Philip to make a special effort to protect the natives of the newly discovered lands across the Atlantic from harm inflicted upon them by the Spanish, and to bring the Indians to the Christian and Catholic Faith by actively supporting

[129]Isabel to Gómez de Fuensalida (estimated date January 1504), *Correspondencia de Fuensalida,* p. 197; Carroll, *Isabel of Spain,* p. 335.

[130]Unfortunately many have tried to make such determinations, and some to deny that Juana could rightly be described as insane at this time and for several years afterward. But periodic insanity is actually more common than permanent insanity, and Juana's behavior in November 1503 renders untenable any and all theories that her insanity was (at least for some time) faked by others or that she was somehow driven into insanity later by her father and her son. It is impossible realistically to imagine any sane person doing what Juana did during those six days at the La Mota castle gate (Carroll, *Isabel of Spain,* p. 336n).

[131]Carroll, *Isabel of Spain,* p. 336.

[132]*Ibid.,* pp. 339-340, 344-345.

[133]Isabel the Catholic, *Testamento y codicilo* (Madrid, 1956), pp. 13-16.

missionary work among them.[134]

When this last codicil was drafted and ready, Isabel was just able to scratch the famous, oft-made signature, *Yo la Reina* ("I the Queen") at the end of it. The tremulous, spidery, barely legible letters reveal the extremity of her physical weakness.[135] But her mind and spirit were still strong, steady and luminous as they moved through her last few days and nights upon earth toward the golden door at the end of the trail for one who knew and had served her Lord and Savior so well, and loved Him with all her heart.

Isabel the Catholic died in a simple building overlooking the main plaza of Medina del Campo, a little after the noon Angelus hour, November 26, 1504, with her beloved husband Fernando and her lifelong friend Beatriz de Bobadilla at her bedside. She died at peace with God and man, aware that there were great stresses and dangers ahead, but knowing she had done her duty as best she could. She had done it far better than her humility would ever permit her to know on this earth.[136]

That day Fernando wrote:

Today, upon this date, it has pleased Our Lord to bring to Himself the most serene Queen Lady Isabel, my most dear and most beloved wife. Although her death is for me a greater hardship than any that could have come to me in my life—part of this grief which pierces my heart is for what I have lost in losing her; and part for what all these kingdoms have lost—yet since she died as holy and as Catholic as she lived, we may hope that Our Lord took her into glory, to a better and more lasting kingdom than what she had here.[137]

Peter Martyr de Anglería, the good Italian humanist who had come to Isabel's Spain to escape the turmoil and corruptions of Renaissance Italy, wrote:

My right hand droops for sorrow.... We cannot fail to mourn,

[134]*Ibid.*, pp. 17-18, 22-41, 64-68; Carroll, *Isabel of Spain*, pp. 344-346.
[135]Prescott, *Reign of Ferdinand and Isabella*, III, 182.
[136]Carroll, *Isabel of Spain*, p. 346. Much has been made in recent years of Isabel's decree of March 1492 expelling all Jews from Castile as showing that she was not always good and just. None but God is always good and just. This was the one definitely unjust act in Isabel's thirty-year reign; though some of her Jewish subjects had been proved to be, or could reasonably be expected to be traitors, and some had been proved by the Inquisition to have enticed *conversos* to betray and blaspheme the Christian faith, the edict of expulsion covered all without exception, the innocent majority along with the guilty minority. Those exiled were not otherwise harshly treated; they were given four months to wind up their affairs and take all they wished with them except precious metal, and their persons were under royal protection throughout that time. Yet the expulsion was still unjust. See my *Isabel of Spain*, pp. 207-210.
[137]Fernando to the Constable of Castile, November 26, 1504 (Medina del Campo), in Rodríguez Valencia, *Isabel en la Opinión*, I, 7.

beginning with ourselves, continuing with all the inhabitants of these kingdoms, and ending with all Christendom, the loss of this mirror of virtue, refuge of the good, scourge of the evils that through so many years assaulted Spain. Those, like us, who knew her spirit, her words, and her actions, must rejoice. We may be sure that her soul, called to the highest heaven, transformed to the new order of celestial spirits, sits in close proximity to the Most High.[138]

On November 7 Christopher Columbus had finally returned from his last voyage, a mere passenger on a slow ship, arriving at Sanlúcar at the mouth of the Guadalquivir River, from which he made his way upriver to Sevilla. His letters to the dying queen went unanswered. Crippled by arthritis and gout, he was unable to set out on the long overland journey to Medina del Campo far to the north. The news of Isabel's death, when it came to him, meant the end of his career; for he had no other real friend at court. He was to die himself, almost forgotten by the old world to which he had given a new, before two years were out.[139]

But he thought first, not of himself, but of her. On December 3 he wrote to his son Diego about her. If Isabel knew what was being said of her in these first days after she left Earth, of all the tributes after her husband's it might have been these words from Christopher Columbus that would have pleased her most.[140]

The most important thing is to commend lovingly and with much devotion the soul of the Queen our lady, to God. Her life was always Catholic and holy, and prompt in all things in His holy service. Because of this we should believe that she is in holy glory, and beyond the cares of this harsh and weary world.[141]

[138]Peter Martyr de Anglería to the Archbishop of Granada, *Documentos inéditos para la historia de España*, X, 90-91.
[139]Morison, *Admiral of the Ocean Sea*, pp. 658-671; Carroll, *Isabel of Spain*, p. 348.
[140]Carroll, *Isabel of Spain*, p. 348.
[141]Christopher Columbus to his son Diego, December 3, 1504 (Sevilla), in Rodríguez Valencia, *Isabel en la Opinión*, I, 254.

16

Renaissance Fulfilled, Reform Forgotten

(1504-1517)

(Popes Julius II 1503-1513, Leo X 1513-1521)

"Although in his youth he [Pope Julius II] had lived very much as the other prelates of that day did, and was by no means scrupulous, he devoted himself to the exaltation and welfare of the Church with a whole-heartedness and courage which were very rare in the age in which he was born.... In all his ways and aims, as well as in his stormy and fervent character, he was the exact contrary of the Borgia."—Francesco Guicciardini, contemporary historian of Italy (1483-1540)[1]

"God has given us the papacy; let us enjoy it!"—Pope Leo X to his brother Giuliano, March 1513[2]

In these last few years before Christendom broke asunder, its glory flamed up in a blaze of beauty even as it was being overshadowed by a cloud of shame. For the ten-year pontificate of Julius II included the composition of three of the supreme works of art of all times and all cultures, and the design and beginning of construction of the greatest and most splendid religious building in the world. In that brief decade the construction of today's St. Peter's in Rome was undertaken; Michelangelo's painting of the ceiling of the Sistine chapel was begun and completed; Raphael's painting of the walls of the Vatican chambers was begun and completed; and Leonardo da Vinci's "Mona Lisa" ("La Gioconda") was finished.

The world has seen nothing to match them since. For all the perversions of the Renaissance into strutting pride and anti-Christian humanism, for all its pervasive and often repulsive immorality, its impetus had been Christian and these its greatest works were profoundly Christian. No one has ever questioned

---

[1]Ludwig von Pastor, *The History of the Popes from the Close of the Middle Ages*, Volume VI (St. Louis, 1898), p. 217.
[2]Christopher Hibbert, *The House of Medici; its Rise and Fall* (New York, 1980), p. 218.

that St. Peter's and the ceiling of the Sistine chapel represent in their every aspect the Christian and Catholic view of the cosmos. There is little if any basis for the attempts that have been made to read prefigurations of the modern world-view into Raphael's paintings in the Vatican chambers. The special emphasis on the Mass, and particularly the depiction of the Eucharistic miracle of Bolsena of 1263, show the falsity of this interpretation.[3] In the memorable words of Ludwig von Pastor:

> The whole fabric of the enchanted realm of Raphael's Vatican pictures rests upon one simple but far-reaching thought. It is that of the greatness and triumph of the Church; her greatness in her wisdom, and her center, the papacy; her triumph in the wonderful ways in which God continues to guard and protect the successor of him to whom the promise was given: "Thou art Peter and on this rock I will build my Church, and the gates of Hell shall not prevail against it."
>
> It seems a remarkable providence of God that Julius II, the founder of the great Cathedral of the world, should have been led to charge the greatest of Christian painters with the task of illustrating the doctrine of the most Holy Sacrament, which was on the point of being so passionately controverted, and the unfailing divine protection, which ever preserves the Church and the Head, at the very moment when the most terrible storm which the papacy in its course of nearly two thousand years has ever had to encounter, was about to burst upon it.[4]

As for Leonardo da Vinci, the centrality of the Christian vision in his soul's love and mind's eye can scarcely be doubted after beholding his world-famous "The Last Supper," painted in the last years of the fifteenth century in Milan, now so impressively restored. "Mona Lisa" does not have an obviously Christian theme, but that it depicts a truly Christian woman with inner Christian joy, few who contemplate it with a knowledge of the artist's other work can doubt.

The fascination of these works has endured undimmed, perhaps even enhanced, into the age of apostasy in the twentieth Christian century, of which the distortion and ugliness of visual art is one of the most striking characteristics. Artists of this age do not wish to paint a Last Judgment, a Creation, a Blessed Virgin Mary. But can we doubt that they would wish to paint a Mona Lisa, if they could? But because they have deliberately cut themselves off from beauty, they cannot.

Pope Julius II decided some time in 1505 to build a new St. Peter's, and quickly approved the magnificent plan of the architect Bramante, to build by far the largest church in the world directly over the grave of St. Peter, even though it meant completely destroying the venerable basilica which then stood there,

---

[3]Von Pastor, *History of the Popes*, VI, 584-606.
[4]*Ibid.*, VI, 606-607.

originally built by Emperor Constantine. A mighty dome would soar over Peter's grave, originally no more than a poor hollow scratched out of the earth by persecuted Christians digging by night in a pagan cemetery. Four smaller domes would complete the church in the shape of a Greek cross. Bramante's plan was later considerably modified and scaled down. The St. Peter's it envisioned was considerably larger even than the colossal building now standing over the bones of the fisherman whom Christ chose to lead his Church.[5]

Pope Julius laid the cornerstone of the new St. Peter's on April 18, 1506, and followed its progress with the closest attention.[6] It was not entirely finished for more than 150 years, and many then and since have complained of its great cost. But man does not live by thought or even doctrine alone. For full appreciation of the glory he worships he must *see* it shown forth, as much as man's limited abilities permit. The Catholic Church has never been found only or primarily in books. It sanctifies and sacralizes places, adorned by the best that human hands and brains can produce in honor of the Creator and the Savior. The heart and center of Christendom could never, in the long run, settle for less than the greatest church in the world.

Pope Julius II commissioned Michelangelo to paint the ceiling of the Sistine chapel in March 1508, just after he had finished a large bronze statue of the Pope for the cathedral of Bologna (where it was later destroyed by Julius' enemies). Relations between the Pope and the temperamental artist had been stormy (they had a towering quarrel in 1506) and Michelangelo hesitated to accept the new assignment, believing himself to be more sculptor than painter. But the Pope insisted, and the volcanic Julius II was not easily gainsaid. Work began in June, under conditions of extraordinary difficulty: day after day he had to stand on high scaffolding, head thrown back, arms extended upward, with paint dripping on his upturned face. Michelangelo could find no one else able to do such work adequately. By January 1509 he had discharged all his assistants and was painting by himself.[7]

He completed the central vault in August 1510 and then proceeded to the interspaces and lunettes. Two years later the entire ceiling was finished and in October 1512 it was unveiled and instantly recognized as one of the supreme art masterpieces of all ages. The creation scene, in which the visible finger of God calls Adam into life, is magnificent beyond compare. The scene of the expulsion of Adam and Eve from Eden is almost equally superb. The colossal figures of the prophets are overpowering. The very recent cleaning of the

---

[5] *Ibid.*, VI, 461-468. See Volume I, Chapter 17 of this history for a discussion of the grave and bones of St. Peter under the high altar of the present St. Peter's.
[6] *Ibid.*, VI, 473-476.
[7] *Ibid.*, VI, 503-515; David Jeffery, "A Renaissance for Michelangelo," *National Geographic*, December 1989, pp. 697, 703. The common belief that Michelangelo lay on his back on the scaffolding to paint the Sistine Chapel ceiling is incorrect.

ceiling has revealed the paintings there to be more brilliantly done, with brighter colors, than many art critics had previously believed.[8]

These glorious works of architecture and art which Julius II sponsored and so much appreciated are one of the best proofs that he was not the primarily or exclusively worldly and militaristic Pope which he is widely thought to have been. He was indubitably a Renaissance man, with some of the vices along with many of the virtues that elastic concept connotes. He too had illegitimate children in his youth—three daughters. But when he became Pope he had put such immorality behind him for many years, and was sincerely concerned for the independence, safety and improvement of the Church. Though he did not give reform the attention it deserved, he never forgot it, but was led astray by his belief that the papal state, so gravely threatened by the political turmoil in Italy, should be more firmly secured first. He was never a Machiavellian, being characterized throughout his life and pontificate by a remarkable and refreshing frankness and honesty. He was very headstrong and often would not listen to good advice. But even many of his enemies in his own time, as well as many subsequent critics, admit that he was a great Pope.[9]

His first objective, as demonstrated by his treatment of Caesar Borgia in the first year of his pontificate, was to regain full military and political control of the papal state. The greatest immediate problem was the hostility of Bologna, the largest city in the Romagna, the northern extension of the papal state which was essential to its political and economic viability. In August 1506 Julius led an army in person to subdue the city. After excommunicating the rebel Duke of Bologna and placing the city under interdict October 11, he entered it in triumph a month later. He had needed and obtained an assurance of French neutrality before launching the campaign, and appointed three French cardinals in December as Louis XII's price for it. The next problem was Venice, whose great wealth had fed ambitions for a land empire as well as dominance on the eastern seas, leading to its recent conquest of substantial territories in northern Italy including Ravenna on the border of the papal state and Faenza and Rimini within that state. In March 1509 Pope Julius joined with Emperor Maximilian and Louis XII of France in the League of Cambrai against Venice. The armies of the League dealt Venice a heavy blow in the Battle of Agnadello in May, forcing her out of Faenza and Rimini, which were restored to the papal state. Early in 1510 the Pope lifted the excommunication and interdict from Venice, much to the anger of the King of France and the Emperor, who wanted to continue the war until Venice's land dominions were entirely eliminated.[10]

---

[8]Von Pastor, *History of the Popes*, VI, 517-533; Jeffery, "A Renaissance for Michelangelo," *National Geographic*, December 1989, pp. 688-713.

[9]Von Pastor, *History of the Popes*, VI, 214-219, 440, 443-454.

[10]*Ibid.*, VI, 266, 276-285, 300-303, 310-316, 319-320, 327; Pierre Batiffol, *The Century of the Renaissance* (The National History of France) (New York, 1916), pp. 33-

Meanwhile in Spain, upon Isabel's death Fernando at once proclaimed Juana Queen of Castile, with himself as governor of that realm in her absence, as Isabel's testament had provided. (He, of course, remained as lawful King of Aragon.) Many advised him not to proclaim Juana Queen, in view of all that was known or suspected about her mental condition; but he did it anyway. No plausible explanation for this action in terms of Machiavellian politics is possible; he can only have done it out of respect for Isabel's memory and the explicit language of her testament, and for the love he had borne her.[11]

Fernando's continued governorship of Castile was quickly challenged by those Castilian noblemen who wanted most to rid themselves of the strong hand of royal authority and return to the unrestricted license to plunder which their kind had possessed during the reign of another mentally disturbed monarch, Isabel's predecessor Henry IV. They objected to Fernando's calling of the *cortes* of Castile to meet within a few weeks of Isabel's death, and still more to his presenting reports of Juana's mental condition to it as a basis for a formal declaration by the *cortes* on her capacity to govern. Some of these noblemen began writing to Brussels, urging Philip to come to Spain at once with Juana to override Fernando's authority, and Philip responded favorably.[12]

Fernando sent an agent to obtain a letter from Juana designating him governor and administrator of Castile. She signed it, but it was intercepted and Fernando's agent was imprisoned in the Netherlands. Then someone (presumably Philip) had her sign a letter to her father saying that she was much improved in health and was resolved to remain with her husband. In April 1505 a treaty between Philip and Louis XII of France provided that Philip would support Louis' claims to both Milan and Naples in return for French support in securing his control of Castile.[13]

Striking back immediately, Fernando opened negotiations with the French court in May for his marriage to the French princess Germaine de Foix, with their children to inherit Naples. By the terms of a reservation in the oath sworn by the *cortes* of Aragon to Juana and Philip in October 1502, a son born to Fernando by a second marriage would displace Juana as heir to Aragon and

[11]Ramón Menéndez Pidal, ed., *Historia de España*, Volume XVII, "La España de los Reyes Católicos," by Luis Suárez Fernández and Manuel Fernández Alvarez, Part II (Madrid, 1983), pp. 649-650; Warren H. Carroll, *Isabel of Spain, the Catholic Queen* (Front Royal VA, 1991), pp. 349-350.

[12]Menéndez Pidal, *Historia de España*, XVII (2), 649-650, 653, 655; Roger B. Merriman, *The Rise of the Spanish Empire in the Old World and the New*, Volume II (New York, 1918), p. 627.

[13]Menéndez Pidal, *Historia de España*, XVII (2), 655, 657; William H. Prescott, *History of the Reign of Ferdinand and Isabella the Catholic* (Philadelphia, 1872), III, 216-219; Carroll, *Isabel of Spain*, p. 350. It is surprising to find no reasonably thorough coverage in English of Fernando's reign alone, after Isabel's death, since the very old though excellent dual biography by Prescott.

its Italian dominions. Castile, however, would remain in the hands of Juana and Philip, or their son Charles, after Fernando's death. The unification of Spain which Isabel and Fernando had brought about would be destroyed. In October 1505 Fernando married Germaine.[14]

No act in all of Fernando's life has been more sharply condemned—and with reason. There was an element of spite in it, of desperation. Galling though the prospect of Philip, selfish and greedy consort of his mad daughter, taking over his own Aragon must have been to Fernando, Isabel had built for the ages, not for a single generation; to cast away the unification of Castile and Aragon that he and she had achieved together was folly and betrayal. Fernando was a highly skilled negotiator and intriguer; but without Isabel, he lacked the long view and the moral sheet-anchor she had always given him.[15]

But now, at long last, when Isabel was beyond suffering and tragedy, the Grim Reaper appeared in her service. Probably because of Fernando's advancing age, he and Germaine conceived only once. The baby was born May 3, 1509—a son, named Juan. But he died before midnight on the same day that he was born. So Fernando's maneuver failed for lack of an heir, and Castile and Aragon remained united.[16]

The affront to Isabel's memory which most Castilians saw in Fernando's remarriage deprived him of most of his remaining support in Castile, forcing him to make an agreement with Philip's ambassadors in November 1505 that he and Philip and Juana would rule jointly. Because of the treaty sealed by Fernando's marriage to Germaine, Louis XII would not now allow Philip and Juana to cross French territory. So they sailed from the Netherlands in the dead of winter, almost died in a savage storm in the Bay of Biscay which drove them into English ports, and finally arrived at La Coruña in northwestern Castile in April 1506. Philip avoided Fernando as long as he could. When at last he had to meet him, he came protected by thousands of armed men. Fernando shrewdly came to the parley unarmed (in a famous exchange with the Count of Benavente, who appeared with a cuirass under his clothes, he felt the Count's bulging chest and said: "Why, how fat you have grown!"). He yielded rule of Castile to Philip in return for recognition of his oft-disputed title to Naples, the continued control of the Castilian military orders, and the revenue of the Indies. A secret clause declared Juana incapable of ruling. Scarcely were these negotiations completed when Fernando swore before three of his counsellors that the agreement was null and void because made under duress, that he had wished to liberate Juana and regain the rule of Castile. Nevertheless the agreement was confirmed publicly (except for the secret

---

[14]Menéndez Pidal, *Historia de España*, XVII (2), 658-660; Merriman, *Rise of the Spanish Empire*, II, 327-329; Carroll, *Isabel of Spain*, pp. 350-351.

[15]Carroll, *Isabel of Spain*, p. 351.

[16]*Ibid.*; Merriman, *Rise of the Spanish Empire*, II, 332.

clause) in the little village of Villafáfila.[17]

Soon afterward the *cortes* of Castile conducted a debate on whether Juana should be publicly adjudged incapable of ruling on account of mental illness. Admiral Fadrique, after a long interview with her, refused to support such a judgment; Archbishop Cisneros, on the basis of much more experience with her dark history (and perhaps of confidences from her late mother), favored it. In the end the *cortes* took no action on the excruciatingly painful question. But Juana was now caught in a vicious circle. Though she probably did not know of the secret clauses in the agreement of Villafáfila, the debate in the *cortes* had alarmed her. She was still rational most of the time—certainly rational enough to fear for her liberty and safety. She knew that insane people were usually locked up, and began to have an obsessive fear of castles in which she might be imprisoned, refusing to stay in them even for a night. This unbalanced her still more, while reports of it further damaged her reputation.[18]

During the summer of 1506 Philip gave lucrative gifts of land and castles and official appointments to his close associates, both Flemish and Spanish, and Castile spiralled back down toward the anarchy from which Isabel had rescued it as dispossessed nobles fought with the newcomers over these awards. In the midst of it all, in September, Philip was suddenly taken ill. Though he was only 28 years old and had always been remarkably healthy, within a week he was dead.[19]

Fernando had gone to Italy two weeks before to secure his hold on Naples. That is probably a sufficient alibi to save him from the charge of poisoning, since he would have been unlikely to leave the country if he knew Philip was about to die. But Philip's death was so sudden, so improbable, so completely unexpected, and so opportune for so many aggrieved people, that suspicion of its natural character has lingered ever since.[20]

Whatever the explanation of Philip's demise, its effect on Juana was catastrophic. She went immediately from a condition of occasional insanity to being out of touch with reality most of the time. Her psychosis was not yet total;

[17]Menéndez Pidal, *Historia de España*, XVII (2), 661-664, 667-668; Prescott, *Reign of Ferdinand and Isabella*, III, 227-242; Merriman, *Rise of the Spanish Empire*, II, 330-332; Garrett Mattingly, *Catherine of Aragon* (New York, 1941), pp. 78-81, 84-86; Carroll, *Isabel of Spain*, pp. 351-352.

[18]Prescott, *Reign of Ferdinand and Isabella*, III, 256-257; Carroll, *Isabel of Spain*, p. 352.

[19]Menéndez Pidal, *Historia de España*, XVII (2), 674-676, 678-679; Merriman, *Rise of the Spanish Empire*, II, 332-333; Prescott, *Reign of Ferdinand and Isabella*, III, 257-258; Carroll, *Isabel of Spain*, p. 352.

[20]Carroll, *Isabel of Spain*, p. 352. Analysis of the question is not helped by mindless repetition by many fine historians, even in the medically sophisticated twentieth century, of the old wives' tale that the cause of Philip's death was drinking too much cold water after vigorous exercise. If that were a cause of death, half the population of the United States would be dead because of it.

she had remissions and periods of partial rationality. But they were now exceptional. She refused to sign any document, vehemently rejected the company of all women, and would move about only at night. On All Saints day, November 1, 1506, she opened Philip's coffin, and the next month took it from its tomb and began carrying it about the countryside with her. She kept her husband's mouldering corpse with her for more than two years—one of the most macabre stories in the world's history—until at last, in February 1509, Fernando took it away from her and locked her up for the rest of her life in the frowning old castle at Tordesillas.[21]

Fernando did not return immediately from Italy on the news of Philip's death, but wisely entrusted Archbishop Cisneros with the extremely difficult task of restoring order amid the suspicions and recriminations that followed it. All men trusted Archbishop Cisneros (while all definitely did not trust Fernando). Despite widespread hunger, economic depression, and pestilence during 1507, Cisneros was successful; when Fernando finally came back to Spain that August, nearly a full year after Philip's death, almost all opposition to him had evaporated. Juana, who seems to have still had some feeling for her father, agreed immediately on his return to sign a surrender of all governmental authority in Castile to him, despite her refusal to sign almost any other document since Philip's death. Fernando took over as regent for his daughter in Castile, acting once again in effect as its king as well as king of Aragon, and continued to do so for the rest of his life. The rebellious nobles, now deprived of all legal cover and high-level support, quickly made their peace with him, and on his request Pope Julius II made Cisneros a Cardinal.[22]

This struggle over the succession in Spain from the end of 1504 through 1507 meant that the Spanish court and government had almost no time and energy to spare for planning and launching further exploration and colonization in America, which consequently came to a halt during these years. By contrast, during this period Portugal was building with amazing rapidity on the foundations of her new power in the Indian Ocean laid by Vasco da Gama. In March 1505 the largest Portuguese expedition to India so far, 20 ships (14 carracks and six caravels, with six more to follow in two months) carrying 1,500 men, sailed under the command of Francisco d'Almeida, who received from King Manuel the first appointment as viceroy in India—a three-year commission that authorized him to command and govern throughout the Indian Ocean region in the King's name. Almeida was a mighty warrior, 45 years old, the seventh son of the Count of Abrantes. He had fought in his early youth at the Battle of Toro in which Isabel and Fernando defeated the Portuguese

---

[21]Menéndez Pidal, *Historia de España*, XVII (2), 679-680, 695-696; Merriman, *Rise of the Spanish Empire*, II, 333; Carroll, *Isabel of Spain*, pp. 352-353.

[22]Menéndez Pidal, *Historia de España*, XVII (2), 680-683, 694-696; von Pastor, *History of the Popes*, VI, 291; Carroll, *Isabel of Spain*, p. 353.

challengers to Isabel's succession in Castile, then later with great distinction as a foreign volunteer in the reconquest of Granada. He was accompanied by his son Lorenzo, also famed for proficiency in arms and for his great physical strength.[23]

Viceroy Almeida's instructions were nothing if not sweeping: to capture and fortify Mombasa and Kilwa on the East African coast; to fortify the Angediva Islands off the Indian coast; to hold Cochin and try to annex it if its king should die; to negotiate peace with Calicut on the basis of full reparations for the killing of Cabral's men and the expulsion of all Muslims from the city, and to engage in total war against Calicut if these demands were refused; to send ships to Cambay in Gujerat and Ormuz on the Persian Gulf to seize all Muslim vessels in or near those ports and to persuade both cities to acknowledge Portuguese sovereignty, break off all trade with the Muslims, and pay tribute to Portugal; to build a fort near the Strait of Bab-el-Mandeb (connecting the Red Sea with the Indian Ocean) which could be used as a base for blockading that strait; to establish diplomatic relations with the inland Hindu empire of Vijayanagar, which carried on almost constant war against the Muslims; and then, as if this were not enough, during his second year in India Almeida was to take and fortify a stronghold in Ceylon (the great island just off the southern tip of India, now called Sri Lanka) and another stronghold in or near Malacca on the other side of the Indian Ocean in Malaya, while also exploring the coast of Burma. These instructions envisioned nothing less than a Portuguese Oriental empire based on naval control of the entire Indian Ocean—an undertaking which, when one compares on a globe the size of Portugal with the size of the ocean and region she proposed to dominate, borders on the fantastic.[24]

Yet the entire program was fulfilled and this empire achieved in just ten years, by Almeida and far more by his successor, the great Afonso de Albuquerque.

On his way to India, Viceroy Almeida took Mombasa and fortified Kilwa and the Angediva Islands as ordered, arriving in Cochin early in October 1505. Learning in February 1506 that the Zamorin of Calicut, with the help of the Muslims, was preparing a large fleet to attack him, with cannon supplied by two renegade Portuguese, Viceroy Almeida sent his son Lorenzo to attack first with only four ships against 200. But the Portuguese ships were so far superior and the Indian crews so untrained that Lorenzo d'Almeida destroyed the greater

---

[23]Vincent Jones, *Sail the Indian Sea* (London, 1978), p. 138; Bailey W. Diffie and George D. Winius, *Foundations of the Portuguese Empire* (Minneapolis MN, 1977), p. 227; R. S. Whiteway, *The Rise of Portuguese Power in India, 1497-1550* (Patna, India, 1979), p. 104.

[24]Jones, *Sail the Indian Sea*, pp. 138-139; Diffie and Winius, *Foundations of the Portuguese Empire*, pp. 227-229.

part of the Zamorin's fleet without the loss of a man. After that Lorenzo sailed for Ceylon, made contact with the King of Kotte there, and collected much cinnamon.[25]

In April 1506 the next annual fleet for India left from Portugal, commanded by the low-born but famous "sea dog" Tristan da Cunha, consisting of ten cargo ships and four warships, and carrying Afonso de Albuquerque with a commission from King Manuel to take over as the second Portuguese Viceroy in India when Almeida's three-year term expired in 1508. Da Cunha's flagship proved a poor sailer, delaying the fleet; it swung far southward, below the latitude of the Cape of Good Hope, all the way to the stark, windy, remote South Atlantic isle, at the northern limit for Antarctic icebergs, that has ever since borne da Cunha's name. The lashing storms of those latitudes scattered his fleet, which was not reassembled until December in Mozambique. They were now too late for the monsoon to India, so da Cunha directed an exploration of the large island of Madagascar, discovered by Diogo Dias during da Gama's second voyage. After landing on the island, exploring some of its coastline, and finding few spices or other valuables, da Cunha's ships sailed on to the Horn of Africa, where in April 1507 they took control of the inhospitable island of Socotra in the Gulf of Aden, seizing an Arab fort there and hoping to use it to block the entrance to the Red Sea as the royal instructions to Almeida had called for. They were astonished and delighted to find, hidden in Socotra's tangled ochre hills, Christian natives who said that, like the Christians of the Malabar coast, they had been evangelized centuries before by the Apostle Thomas.[26]

While Tristan da Cunha was ranging across unknown seas and shores, much trouble was brewing for the Portuguese in India. The whole Muslim world was aware by now of the threat they presented, and the chief Muslim power—Ottoman Turkey—had decided to take a hand. A fleet had been constructed in Istanbul to help the Muslims of the Indian Ocean against the Portuguese. Thirty ships with more than 3,000 men set out from what had been Constantinople. Because of the urgency of the situation in the Indian Ocean they sailed in winter, a dangerous sailing season in the Mediterranean, and encountered a severe storm as well as an attack by the crusading Knights of St. John at Rhodes, who had so heroically endured and repulsed the great Turkish assault of 1481. Consequently only twelve ships and 1,500 men (a substantially smaller force than Almeida had commanded when leaving Portugal, though the

---

[25]Diffie and Winius, *Foundations of the Portuguese Empire*, pp. 229-230, 232-233, 244-245; Whiteway, *Portuguese Power in India*, pp. 105, 108-109.

[26]Whiteway, *Portuguese Power in India*, pp. 112-115; Diffie and Winius, *Foundations of the Portuguese Empire*, p. 245; Elaine Sanceau, *Indies Adventure; the Amazing Career of Afonso de Albuquerque* (London, 1936), pp. 21, 25, 28-29. See Volume I, Chapter 17 of this history for the Apostle Thomas in Socotra.

Muslim warships were considerably larger, and heavily armed) remained when the fleet reached Egypt, where the ships were laboriously dragged across the isthmus of Suez. The reduced flotilla under Egyptian admiral Amir Hussein then set sail for India, arriving in September, its passage unobserved from Socotra, too far out from the Strait of Bab-el-Mandeb to bottle it up as King Manuel's instructions to Almeida had directed. And in India the King of Cananor had gone to war against the Portuguese, besieging a Portuguese garrison in the city; the newly constructed fort in the Angediva Islands had to be abandoned after an attack by a fleet from the nearby mainland port of Goa; and the friendly, stout-hearted King Trimumpara of Cochin had died and been succeeded by a much less friendly ruler who was preparing to assault the Portuguese there as well.[27]

Unaware of all this, Tristan da Cunha at Socotra divided his fleet in July, taking the greater part of it on to India while leaving Afonso de Albuquerque in Arab waters with six ships and 400 men and orders to try to gain control of the entrance to the Persian Gulf at Ormuz. With this very limited force Albuquerque exploded upon the coast of Oman. Bombarding and storming here, demanding and obtaining provisions peacefully there, he was soon receiving offers from the Omanis to become tributary to the King of Portugal if only the fearsome "Frank" would leave them alone. On September 25 Albuquerque arrived at Ormuz itself and at once demanded its submission. Its vizier Cogeatar brought up 60 large warships—odds of ten to one against the Portuguese—but the Portuguese artillery was far superior and the Muslim fleet was shattered. On the 28th Ormuz surrendered, agreeing to pay tribute to Portugal and allow a Portuguese fort to be built there. Afonso de Albuquerque was now lord of Oman, Muscat and Ormuz where hardly a Christian face had been seen for the past eight hundred years.[28]

On the Malabar coast of India, Tristan da Cunha arrived just in time to save the Portuguese at Cananor and Cochin. His ships and men raised the siege of Cananor on August 27 and prevented an attack on Cochin in September. The Zamorin of Calicut had now assembled another fleet, but Almeida and da Cunha easily destroyed it November 25. Having thus emphatically made his mark during just three months in India, da Cunha set out on his return voyage to Portugal in mid-December.[29]

It is not clear if Almeida had learned of the arrival of the Turkish-Egyptian fleet when da Cunha departed; if he had, it is surprising that he let

---

[27]Diffie and Winius, *Foundations of the Portuguese Empire*, pp. 231-233; Whiteway, *Portuguese Power in India*, pp. 111-112, 116.

[28]Sanceau, *Indies Adventure*, pp. 30-38, 44-51; Diffie and Winius, *Foundations of the Portuguese Empire*, pp. 237-238; Whiteway, *Portuguese Power in India*, pp. 115, 119-120.

[29]Whiteway, *Portuguese Power in India*, pp. 112, 115; Diffie and Winius, *Foundations of the Portuguese Empire*, p. 233.

him go. He may not have known of its existence until it struck a flotilla of light galleys commanded by his son Lorenzo in the harbor of Chaul, just south of Bombay, some time during the winter of 1508. Taken by surprise, young Lorenzo fought valiantly, but found his ship pinned against the pilings of the harbor by an incoming tide. Unlike the Indians they had been fighting, the Turks aboard this fleet knew artillery; their forebears had beaten down the storied walls of Constantinople. Lorenzo was obliterated by a cannon ball and his ship went down against the pilings.[30]

Lorenzo d'Almeida was his father's only son, his pride and joy. What tears the Viceroy may have shed in private we do not know, but his response to the news of his son's death became part of Portugal's Indian legend: "Who ate the young cock must now taste the old one!" Francisco d'Almeida had vowed himself to revenge.[31]

When Albuquerque, some of his captains in revolt against his fiercely driving spirit and his ships leaking so badly that fish swam into and out of their hulls, made his way from Ormuz to India late in 1508, expecting to take over as Viceroy now that Almeida's three-year term of office was up, he found Almeida unwilling to relinquish his authority until he had avenged his son. In December Almeida sailed with 18 ships and 1,200 men for the port of Diu on the broad peninsula of Kathiawar northwest of Bombay where the Turkish-Egyptian fleet was based. On February 2, 1509, with a strong wind behind him, Almeida struck Diu like a thunderbolt, surprising the Muslim fleet at anchor, ignoring the shore batteries, raking the Turks and Egyptians with point-blank broadsides, then boarding and storming. All the Portuguese seemed to pick up the fighting fury of their avenging commander; they lost about a hundred men, mostly in hand-to-hand combat, but cleared the decks of the enemy and dyed the harbor crimson with his blood. The Battle of Diu has been called one of the most decisive in history. It ended forever Muslim naval power in the Indian Ocean.[32]

Even after this tremendous victory Almeida was reluctant to relinquish his high command at the royal order. But most of the Portuguese in India supported Albuquerque as the duly designated Viceroy, and when the fleet of 1509 arrived in the fall bringing Fernando Countinho, Marshal of Portugal and a member of the royal household, Almeida finally agreed to go home. It is one of history's strangest ironies that this mighty warrior, landing near the Cape of

---

[30]Diffie and Winius, *Foundations of the Portuguese Empire*, pp. 236-237 (who dates the battle to January); Whiteway, *Portuguese Power in India*, pp. 117-118 (who dates it to March).

[31]Diffie and Winius, *Foundations of the Portuguese Empire*, p. 237.

[32]*Ibid.*, pp. 238-241; Whiteway, *Portuguese Power in India*, pp. 121-125; K. G. Jayne, *Vasco da Gama and His Successors, 1460-1580* (London, 1910), pp. 75-76; Sanceau, *Indies Adventure*, pp. 65-66, 69-70, 75-78, 82-83.

Good Hope on his way back to Portugal, was slain along with several of his men by the spears of primitive Hottentots shielded behind a herd of cattle, whom he had gone to chastise with such contempt for their fighting ability that he neither wore body armor nor brought any firearms.[33]

Ever since the invasion of 1494 the French military threat had been hanging over Italy. Prevented by the Spanish from making good their claims to the southern kingdom of Naples, the French were now concentrating on northern Italy, where they had a claim to Milan at least as strong legally as their claim to Naples, in a region much more open to their penetration. Louis XII of France bitterly resented Pope Julius II's separate peace with Venice in February 1510, because it was his intention to despoil Venice of all its land possessions. He already controlled Milan and Genoa and had very strong influence in Florence. The Pope sought help elsewhere, getting a good response only from the Swiss, who were themselves threatened by the growing power of the French and were famous fighters. The Bishop of Sion, Matthaeus Schinner, made Cardinal in 1508, emerged as the Swiss leader in the papal cause. In March 1510 the twelve cantons then making up Switzerland ratified a five-year alliance with the Pope for "the defense of the Church and of the Holy See," pledging not to ally themselves with any other power nor to supply any other power with troops without the Pope's permission. With this strong backing Julius prepared for war against France, urging his native city of Genoa to rise against their rule, and planning a Swiss attack on Milan.[34]

Julius II had good reason to insist on restoration and full control of the papal state and to oppose further extension of French power in Italy, but in launching aggressive war against the areas they already controlled he went beyond what the independence of the Church required, and provided substance for the reproaches directed against him then and ever since, for militarism and imperialism. Julius sincerely believed that the best interests of the Church required that the French be ousted from Italy, and it certainly would have been better and safer for the Church if they had been; but to try to drive them out by aggressive war, when they were still well outside the boundaries of the papal state, was hard to justify.

The French, aware at least in general of the Pope's plans and certainly of his encouragement of rebellion in Genoa, revived "Gallicanism"—the theory that the French church should be administratively independent of Rome, given legal form by the "Pragmatic Sanction"—and began to talk of a new ecumenical council which would pick up the role finally abandoned by the Council of

---

[33]Diffie and Winius, *Foundations of the Portuguese Empire*, p. 247; Jayne, *Vasco da Gama and His Successors*, p. 77; Whiteway, *Portuguese Power in India*, pp. 126-127; Sanceau, *Indies Adventure*, pp. 88-94.

[34]Von Pastor, *History of the Popes*, VI, 321-327.

Basel.[35] Louis XII fumed and blustered, one day speaking of leading an army to Rome to depose Pope Julius, another day hesitating and declaring he must have the support of Emperor Maximilian and the new young King of England, Henry VIII. In the late summer Julius intended the armies of his allies to march on the French and their allies in northern Italy, but all found excuses not to go, and the Pope fell seriously ill under the strain and frustration. Nevertheless in January 1511 he joined the camp of his army in the field, living in a convent kitchen and reviewing his troops in a snowstorm. The French countered by seizing Bologna late in May. Earlier that month most of the French bishops, supported by six cardinals and Emperor Maximilian, called for a new ecumenical council to meet at Pisa in defiance of the Pope.[36]

Pope Julius responded splendidly, calling a council himself to meet in Rome the following April, while condemning the schismatic council. In the Roman dying month of August his illness returned in a much more severe form. He was anointed and given viaticum, but his tremendous vitality was not yet exhausted; he amazed everyone by recovering almost completely. In October he formed the Holy League with Spain and Venice against the French in Italy and excommunicated four of the rebel cardinals. Arriving in Pisa with a company of archers to protect them, these cardinals found that the people of Pisa were strongly opposed to what they were doing. A few days later 16 French bishops, four French abbots and one Italian abbot had arrived, hardly an ecumenical assemblage. The pro-French government of Florence forced the reluctant Pisans to open their cathedral for the unathorized council; the people responded by rioting which so frightened the French bishops that they decided to move their council to Milan, where the French could protect them directly.[37] On November 17, 1511 King Henry VIII of England joined the Holy League with a statement condemning the "great sin of the king of France" who would "lacerate the seamless garment of Christ [and] . . . wantonly destroy the unity of the Church" by "the most pernicious schism."[38]

This was the same Henry VIII who twenty-three years later was to do himself precisely what he condemned the King of France for doing in this ringing statement of 1511.

And so Henry VIII strides upon the stage of history, almost as different as could be imagined from the terrifying figure of later years—the gimlet-eyed, shark-mouthed, hulking bullfrog of a man painted by Hans Holbein, who marked his lusts like firebrands on the monarchy and the church of England. The young Henry VIII was everything the middle-aged Henry VIII was not: kind, even in his own way gentle; joyful, and generous to a fault; open, honest

---

[35]*Ibid.*, VI, 329-330. See Chapter Thirteen, above.
[36]*Ibid.*, VI, 331-349, 352-355.
[37]*Ibid.*, VI, 364-374, 389-392.
[38]J. J. Scarisbrick, *Henry VIII* (Berkeley CA, 1968), pp. 28-29 (quotations on 29).

and loyal; tall and clean-limbed, a superb athlete, handsome as sunrise; devout, glorying in his orthodoxy, yearning to defend the Faith; profoundly and radiantly in love with the youngest daughter of Queen Isabel, Catherine "of Aragon." Catherine had left her mother and her homeland to marry Henry's elder brother, Arthur, Prince of Wales, in 1501; Arthur, young and delicate, had died six months after a marriage which was never consummated. Isabel and Fernando wanted Catherine to marry Arthur's younger brother Henry, but he was too young (just eleven) to marry her for several years, and his father Henry VII was doubtful. But Prince Henry grew up loving Catherine, who was sweetly beautiful yet with a deep underlying strength inherited or acquired from her mother, and she returned his love. Almost his first act after becoming king on the death of Henry VII in April 1509 was to marry her. She was then twenty-three to his seventeen.[39]

Let Catherine's eloquent biographer Garrett Mattingly describe the atmosphere of their first years as King and Queen of England:

> If the tireless, versatile young King was the center of all this bustling life in England, its center and focus for Henry was Catherine, the chief trophy of his new reign, the necessary audience for all his triumphs. He defied custom by wearing her favors in the lists, by inventing allegorical devices and high-sounding pseudonyms to proclaim his utter devotion to her, by accepting the meed of his prowess only at her hands. He was always seeking her out to show off a new present or a new musician, or to share with her the latest book from Italy or the latest budget of news from his ambassadors. "The Queen must hear this" or "This will please the Queen" were often on his lips. . . .
>
> At ease at the center of the court, Catherine fulfilled and complemented all the King's tastes. Her tranquil grace was the best foil to his exuberance, her effortless dignity the right touch in the center of his flamboyant effects. And she had a natural buoyance and high spirits of her own . . . She loved music and dancing as much as Henry did himself, and her skill in both was almost as notable as his. She was passionately fond of hawking, and—though she could not always keep pace with her husband's mad gallops—she rode fearlessly and well. She bore a merry part in all his prankish entertainments, and managed besides to draw about her a circle of the older families, links with the great past and her special friends, who gave the court a tone it might otherwise have lacked.
>
> She shared, too, tastes of her husband's into which few of his courtiers could enter. Like Henry she was an eager reader of devotional and theological books, and she had an equally meticulous piety. . . .
>
> In the first flush of his kingship he [Henry] found Catherine, and for a while it seemed the quest might end at its beginning. From the guarded eyes and careful tongues of his father's councillors, who met his every wish with bland agreement while they measured the strength of this young whelp they would have to manage, he turned to the quiet, wise, admiring

---

[39]Mattingly, *Catherine of Aragon*, pp. 19-22, 42-43, 47-49, 59-68, 117-127; Carroll, *Isabel of Spain*, pp. 315-316, 320, 328-329.

wife to whom he could pour out his whole heart. To confide in Catherine compromised neither his dignity nor his independence; her womanly dependence appealed to his boastful young strength, her inner strength complemented his secret weakness.[40]

It was a different kind of royal husband-and-wife team than that of Fernando and Isabel, but had the potential of changing history for the better as much as those two had changed it for the better—and Catherine was their daughter, by far the best and strongest of their five children. What might a Holy Roman Empire ruled by Isabel's grandson Charles V, and an England ruled by a faithful Henry VIII and Isabel's daughter Catherine, have done together for Christendom? It is one of the most alluring might-have-beens of history. Queen Catherine never changed. Emperor Charles kept the faith. But King Henry VIII betrayed it, and that glory was not to be.

Henry VIII was eager to assert the old English claim to the throne of France, especially now that he could fight the French in the cause of the Church; and Pope Julius actually prepared a bull stripping Louis XII of the kingship of France and bestowing it upon Henry, though he prudently noted that it should not be published until France was defeated, and it never was published. The able young French general Gaston de Foix defeated the combined Spanish and papal army in a battle fought near Ravenna on Easter Sunday 1512, though his death in the combat encouraged the losing side. Emperor Maximilian withdrew from the war, Genoa and Milan rose against the French, the Swiss took Pavia, and the French had to retreat across the Alps, to the great joy of the Pope. Meanwhile Julius' official ecumenical council, called the Fifth Lateran, convened in the Lateran basilica May 3, with 16 cardinals, 70 bishops, 12 patriarchs, and three generals of religious orders present, representing many countries of Christendom. On May 10 the Pope, addressing the council, declared its objectives to be the defeat of schism, the reform of the Church, and the launching of a crusade against the Turks.[41]

In August a congress held at Mantua declared Milan restored to the rule of the Sforzas and Florence to the rule of the Medici, awarding Lugano and Locarno to the Swiss (they remain to this day part of the Italian Swiss canton of Ticino) and Parma and Piacenza to the papal state. On November 29, in a major triumph of papal diplomacy, Emperor Maximilian switched sides, rejecting France and allying himself with the Pope, pledging to defend him against all attacks, repudiating the schismatic council, and acknowledging the Fifth Lateran Council, while in turn the Pope promised to support Maximilian against Venice in his demand for the north Italian cities of Verona and Vicenza.

---

[40]Mattingly, *Catherine of Aragon*, pp. 134-136.
[41]*Ibid.*, pp. 149-150; von Pastor, *History of the Popes*, VI, 399-403, 406-410, 414-418; Hibbert, *House of Medici*, pp. 412-413; Scarisbrick, *Henry VIII*, pp. 33-34.

Maximilian's envoy Matthaeus Lang was made a cardinal and much honored at the fourth session of the Fifth Lateran Council in December 1512. The Pope had won his military and political struggle; the French no longer exercised predominant influence in Italy. But the cost had been heavy, in every sense; aside from the glorious works of art he had commissioned, Julius II had given little more to the Church than this worldly victory. He had given the Fifth Lateran Council no real guidance toward reform, only in repudiating the French schism which had no support whatever outside France. Perhaps he was thinking of this dereliction when, upon receiving viaticum for the second time as illness gripped his 70-year-old body, he asked his cardinals for prayers "as he had been a great sinner and had not ruled the Church as he ought." The next day—February 21, 1513—he died.[42]

The arrival of Marshal of Portugal Fernando Coutinho in India led almost immediately (January 3, 1510) to a very ill-advised ground assault on the city of Calicut. The Portuguese had proved themselves invincible at sea, but on land and out of reach of their naval artillery, the numerical odds against them could easily become overwhelming. Fighting in the streets of Calicut, invisible to their ships, the Portuguese suffered a devastating defeat, their worst since entering the Indian Ocean. Marshal Coutinho was killed, along with 300 Portuguese soldiers; more than 400 were wounded, many seriously, including new Viceroy Afonso de Albuquerque who lost most of the use of his left arm for the rest of his life, along with sustaining a severe head wound. But his almost tireless, whipcord body—Albuquerque was rod-thin, hawk-faced with a long white beard, and extraordinarily energetic—quickly threw off the shock of the wounds. Within a few days he was on his feet, planning and outfitting a new fleet.[43]

Just a week after the dolorous battle in Calicut, Diogo Lopes de Sequeira came sailing back to India from the east with three ships. An independent commander outside the Viceroy's authority, he had been on a special mission to Malacca, the famous trading city fronting the strait connecting the Indian Ocean with the China Sea, gateway to yet more new worlds. King Manuel had made clear his special interest in Malacca and Sequeira was the first Portuguese captain to go there. He found Malacca under Muslim rule. Sequeira seems to have been that great rarity among Portuguese captains of his generation, a coward. When the Muslims roused Malacca's people to attack the Portuguese he fled, abandoning his men ashore, about sixty of whom were killed and more

---

[42]Von Pastor, *History of the Popes*, VI, 420-421, 425-429, 435-436 (quotation on 435).
[43]Diffie and Winius, *Foundations of the Portuguese Empire*, pp. 247-248, 250; Whiteway, *Portuguese Power in India*, pp. 129-131; Jayne, *Vasco da Gama and his Successors*, pp. 79-80, 100; Sanceau, *Indies Adventure*, pp. 95-102.

than thirty captured. A few were rescued when a young officer seized the only small boat available in the fleet and took it in to shore on his own initiative to save his dear friend Francisco Serrrano. The young officer's name was Fernando Magellan and he was to be the first man to sail around the world.[44]

On the way back to India, two of Sequeira's five ships were lost on the dangerous coast of Sumatra; again he abandoned the shipwrecked men, except for a few Magellan managed to save. Reaching India, Sequeira learned that Albuquerque had taken over as Viceroy. That paragon of valor was the last man Sequeira wanted to face in light of his record; he hastily directed the two remaining ships with him to go to Cochin, and squared away his own sails for Portugal. Magellan and Serrano remained in India.[45]

Considering the history and problems of Portuguese operations in India, Albuquerque had concluded that they must establish a truly secure base, not dependent on the vagaries of native kings and their successors. None of the offshore islands was suitable; they were too small and hard to defend. He decided on Goa for the main base. King Manuel had already ordered him to take that city, located in the middle of the west coast of India, midway between Calicut and Bombay. Lying between the mouths of two large rivers, Goa had an excellent harbor; it was on a fairly large island, separated from the mainland by a channel joining the two rivers, too shallow for ships but too deep to ford, full of crocodiles. It did much business in the finest Arabian horses. On March 1 Albuquerque (still less than two months after receiving his two serious wounds) descended upon Goa without warning and seized it, declaring his intention to make it a permanent part of the Kingdom of Portugal (as it remained for nearly 450 years). He promptly guaranteed the life and property of all the inhabitants and their full freedom to observe their religion and customs, except for that of burning their widows on funeral pyres (the first recorded action of Christendom in India against the ancient evil of *suttee*).[46]

Ismail Adil Shah, the Sultan of Bijapur whose realm had included Goa, attacked it with 50,000 men in mid-May, the driest and hottest time of the Indian year, when the channel between the rivers was fordable. His troops overran the island and the walls of Goa city proved impossible to hold against such numbers. Albuquerque embarked his men on his ships. He could not get them across the bar at the mouth of the river until the monsoon came, but the Indians had learned from bitter experience to stay away from Portuguese ships, and Albuquerque was able to wait until they could leave safely. Meanwhile he informed an envoy of Sultan Ismail that he would never make peace with him

---

[44]Diffie and Winius, *Foundations of the Portuguese Empire*, pp. 245-246; Whiteway, *Portuguese Power in India*, p. 132; Sanceau, *Indies Adventure*, p. 139.

[45]Whiteway, *Portuguese Power in India*, pp. 132-133.

[46]*Ibid.*, pp. 133-134; Diffie and Winius, *Foundations of the Portuguese Empire*, pp. 250-252; Sanceau, *Indies Adventure*, pp. 114-118.

until Goa was restored.[47]

In November 1510 Albuquerque returned with every ship and man he could assemble in Indian waters—28 ships and 1,700 men—and carried Goa in a magnificent assault against odds of at least four to one. During the storming Jeronymo, brother of assault commander Joao de Lima, fell mortally wounded. The commander stopped to help him. Jeronymo waved him away, saying: "You go your way, brother, and I go mine." Albuquerque saw the hand of Christendom's ancient enemy in all that had happened at Goa, and ordered every Muslim found in the city killed—an indefensible act.[48] But in condemning such acts, in fairness it must always be remembered that there were never more than a few thousand Portuguese in India against tens of millions of Muslims, so that the slightest sign of weakness could be fatal. Diogo Lopes de Sequeira and his men had learned that.

All that winter Albuquerque drove himself and his men to build the strongest possible fortifications for Goa, and organized it as a permanent colony, encouraging his men to marry Indian women and raise families (very few women were ever taken on the immensely long and dangerous 10,000-mile journey from Portugal to India).[49] Writing from India to a friend at the King's court back in Portugal soon after his second capture of Goa, Albuquerque said: "The King trusts you and takes your advice: bid him hold on to Goa until the Day of Judgment."[50]

By Easter Albuquerque had decided that the necessary foundations were laid in Goa and no longer required his personal attention, and set off with fifteen ships, three galleys, 800 Portuguese and 200 Indian troops for Malacca, knowing he could do a better job there than Sequeira had done. (The Muslims attacked Goa as soon as they heard he had gone; the garrison commander was killed, but the others fought on and held the city until the annual fleet from Portugal arrived in the summer to relieve it.) On July 1, 1511 Albuquerque arrived at Malacca and immediately demanded the return of the Portuguese prisoners taken from the Sequeira expedition two years before. Malacca's Sultan Muhammad defied him, but Albuquerque made enough shore contacts to learn that the Sultan was very unpopular and that the city's Chinese population (the first known contact of the Portuguese with Chinese) would not help him. Albuquerque assaulted a bridge that divided the city and was able to induce the governor of the half of the city on one side of the bridge, a Javanese

---

[47]Diffie and Winius, *Foundations of the Portuguese Empire*, pp. 252-253; Whiteway, *Portuguese Power in India*, pp. 134-136; Sanceau, *Indies Adventure*, pp. 124-133, 139.

[48]Diffie and Winius, *Foundations of the Portuguese Empire*, pp. 253-255; Whiteway, *Portuguese Power in India*, pp. 139-140; Jayne, *Vasco da Gama and His Successors*, pp. 84-85; Sanceau, *Indies Adventure*, pp. 147-150.

[49]Sanceau, *Indies Adventure*, pp. 153-161.

[50]Jayne, *Vasco da Gama and His Successors*, p. 104.

of Indian descent, to remain neutral. But the battle was still fierce; it continued for nine days, during which the Portuguese—in the manner of the first Western troops in India 1,800 years before under Alexander the Great—had to fight off an elephant charge with pikes.   At one point one of Albuquerque's best captains, Antonio d'Abreu, was struck by a missile that knocked out all his teeth and tore off part of his tongue. Albuquerque ordered him to go to the ships for medical treatment. Abreu proudly refused. He still had feet to walk on, hands to fight with, and half a tongue to give orders, he declared; he should stay where the fight was hottest.[51]

The plunder of Malacca was the richest the Portuguese had yet gained in the Indian regions, for Malacca traded with the whole of the Orient and was full of every kind of wealth.   Albuquerque built a fort there, received an ambassador from Java, sent one to Siam, and in November 1511 dispatched the heroic Antonio d'Abreu with three caravels and a Chinese junk to find the legendary Spice Islands (Moluccas) two thousand miles to the east, beyond Java and Borneo—the first Europeans to sail into Pacific waters. One of Abreu's caravels was commanded by Magellan's friend Francisco Serrano, though Magellan—who now commanded his own caravel—remained in Malacca.[52]

A storm struck Abreu's little fleet as they were passing between Java and Borneo. One of the three caravels was lost; another—the caravel commanded by Serrano—was separated from the flagship. Abreu went on with his ship and the junk past Celebes to Banda Island, one of the Moluccas but well south of the most famous Spice Islands, Ternate and Tidore; he was unable to sail north to them due to contrary winds. However, all the Moluccas had cloves and nutmegs; Abreu filled his ship with this exceedingly valuable cargo and sailed back to Malacca. Serrano, reaching the Moluccas separately, was wrecked and made his way to Mindanao Island in a small boat, thereby discovering the Philippines. Eventually he was able to get to Ternate, where he became its chieftain and by marrying the daughter of the king of Tidore acquired effective control over that island as well. For several years he sent periodic messages to Albuquerque, presumably by junk to Malacca and thence to Goa, asking to be named governor of the Spice Islands and sent reinforcements; but no answer came. Perhaps even Albuquerque did not feel competent to open up both the Indian and the Pacific Oceans at the same time; perhaps he simply did not get the messages, sent across four thousand miles by unreliable messengers. But

---

[51]Diffie and Winius, *Foundations of the Portuguese Empire*, pp. 255-259; Jayne, *Vasco da Gama and his Successors*, pp. 85-88; Whiteway, *Portuguese Power in India*, pp. 142-143; Sanceau, *Indies Adventure*, pp. 161-163, 168-170, 173-178, 194-196.

[52]Whiteway, *Portuguese Power in India*, pp. 143-144; Jayne, *Vasco da Gama and his Successors*, p. 108; Sanceau, *Indies Adventure*, pp. 181-185; William L. Schurz, *The Manila Galleon* (New York, 1939), p. 16; Charles M. Parr, *Ferdinand Magellan, Circumnavigator* (New York, 1964), p. 121.

there is reason to believe that Magellan sailed these waters during those years, very possibly reaching his friend on Ternate at least once, and concluding in the process that the Spice Islands were so far east that if the demarcation line laid down by the Treaty of Tordesillas between the Portuguese and Spanish spheres were extended around the world, the Spice Islands would lie on the Spanish side of it. (Since there was no method of accurately measuring longitude at that time, the location of the demarcation line in the Pacific could not then be established; in fact—contrary to Magellan's belief—it would have fallen well to the east of the Spice Islands.)[53]

In January 1512 Albuquerque departed from Malacca to return to India, leaving 300 men to garrison the fort he had built in Malacca and 200 more to patrol the coast with eight ships, all in somewhat better condition than the three he was taking back to India. He put most of the treasure from the plunder of Malacca in his flagship, *Frol de la Mar*, which had been in Indian waters for several years and was very leaky. In its semi-waterlogged condition it was driven ashore on the rocky coast of Sumatra by a storm. The unsinkable Albuquerque escaped on a raft, but all the treasure was lost.[54]

After a year spent in India, Albuquerque sailed for Arabia in February 1513 with 24 ships and 1,700 men to try to establish forts at Aden and Ormuz to block the narrow entrances to the Red Sea and the Persian Gulf. His assault on Aden, though made with splendid dash and heroism, failed for want of adequate scaling ladders. He brought his fleet into the Red Sea, where no Christian ship had sailed for centuries, but its desert shores created great problems for him; he found only one plentiful source of water, on Kamaran Island where there was almost no food and about 500 of his men died from dysentery, probably from a diet of shellfish in the terrible heat (the Red Sea is one of the hottest places on earth, with the temperature rising to over 140 degrees in the summer, and Albuquerque and his men were on the island in June). Even under these grim conditions Albuquerque's imagination and planning were as busy as ever; he wrote to King Manuel that with the aid of Ethiopia Portugal could gain control of the Red Sea despite all the difficulties, land on the Arabian coast, and burn Mecca or take and exchange it for Jerusalem. After one last try at Aden in July (where he learned that his presence in the Red Sea had created near panic in Cairo) Albuquerque returned to Goa with nothing to show for the 1513 expedition but intelligence.[55]

Back in India in October, he made peace at last with Calicut, whose new

[53]Parr, *Magellan*, pp. 123-127.

[54]Diffie and Winius, *Foundations of the Portuguese Empire*, p. 260; Whiteway, *Portuguese Power in India*, pp. 144-145; Sanceau, *Indies Adventure*, pp. 190-193.

[55]Diffie and Winius, *Foundations of the Portuguese Empire*, pp. 263-265; Jayne, *Vasco da Gama and his Successors*, pp. 91-93, 101; Whiteway, *Portuguese Power in India*, pp. 154-158; Sanceau, *Indies Adventure*, pp. 208, 210-222, 308.

Zamorin agreed to pay a yearly tribute, send an ambassador to Lisbon, and make full compensation for goods taken from the Portuguese in the past. Albuquerque also learned of plots against him by resentful subordinates, but did not know that sufficient calumny against him had reached King Manuel to cause him to designate a new Viceroy in the fall of 1514, who sailed with the annual fleet in 1515: Lopo Soares de Albergaria, a man whom Albuquerque had sent home years before as unfit to govern in India.[56]

Meanwhile, in March 1514, old Captain Tristan da Cunha led a spectacular Portuguese embassy to Rome to present to new Pope Leo X some of the wealth and wonders of the Orient—not only gold and jewelry, but also an exotic menagerie including a white elephant, a panther, and two leopards. It was remembered and talked about in Rome for years.[57]

Albuquerque knew King Manuel was unhappy with some aspects of his governorship, though he believed that his towering achievements—unmatched by any overseas governor in the whole history of Western colonization—would surely cause the king to retain him in office so long as he was still able to perform his duties. He worked to the maximum as he always had. At the end of 1514 he began preparing a new expedition to Arabian waters, this time to Ormuz. He led it out from India on Ash Wednesday 1515, 27 ships and 3,000 men, half Portuguese and half Indians, who were now being taken into Portuguese military service in increasing numbers, just as the British were later to do in India. He found a Persian named Rais Hamid controlling the government at Ormuz, but young King Saifuddin listened eagerly to Albuquerque's proposal that Rais Hamid be removed and himself enriched by dealing with the Portuguese. Rais Hamid was treacherously slain by Portuguese daggers at a parley, and Saifuddin accepted vassalage to King Manuel.[58]

Albuquerque then set to work with most of his men to build a great fort at Ormuz in the blinding summer heat. All through the summer he worked, and the terrible strain at last broke the thin hard 62-year-old body that had seemed indestructible. As his illness worsened, he had his sickbed placed at a window from which he could talk with his officers and watch the progress of the fort. Rumors of his supercession were now circulating, angering his loyal officers; on September 26 he made his captains and knights swear to obey anyone properly appointed by the king to take his place. On November 1 he made his will, and on the 8th left Ormuz apparently at the point of death. But he rallied a little at

---

[56]Sanceau, *Indies Adventure*, pp. 225-228, 248-252; Elaine Sanceau, *Reign of the Fortunate King* [Manuel] (Hamden CT, 1969), pp. 103-110.

[57]Von Pastor, *The History of the Popes from the Close of the Middle Ages*, Volume VII (St. Louis, 1950), 74-76.

[58]Diffie and Winius, *Foundations of the Portuguese Empire*, pp. 269-270; Jayne, *Vasco da Gama and his Successors*, pp. 93-96; Whiteway, *Portuguese Power in India*, pp. 161-164; Sanceau, *Indies Adventure*, pp. 256-257, 262, 274-280.

sea, and after learning definitely that Lopo Soares was the new Viceroy, wrote a last letter to King Manuel, begging his favor for his illegitimate son Braz, who had a black mother, and declaring: "I leave India with the principal heads fallen into your power; everything is settled except that it were well to lock the door of the Straits [of Bab el-Mandeb at the entrance to the Red Sea—which the Portuguese were never able to do]. So I have done what Your Highness charged me."[59]

Indeed he had—all of it, and more.

On December 15, 1515 the ship carrying Albuquerque approched Goa harbor. Someone came on board to tell him that the new Viceroy was appointing his enemies to official positions and preparing to seize his property. Albuquerque said that if the King were against him, he would take refuge in the Church, and prayed before a crucifix. He had himself propped against the door of his cabin to see Goa for the last time as evening fell. He died an hour before dawn the next day.[60]

Afonso de Albuquerque is not a man whom a Christian can fully take to his heart. There was too much blood on his hands. But no man before or since Albuquerque has secured one of the world's great oceans and all its shores almost single-handed. And though some of his means must be condemned, he knew the good he served and brought to India. The days of the immemorial evils of its ancient and perverted culture were numbered because Afonso de Albuquerque had come and conquered.

Across the world in America, the Spanish had a very different situation and organization from the Portuguese in the Indian Ocean. They did not yet have to deal with any civilized culture which could field armies against them. Instead of operating in an ocean most of whose shores and trading centers were already known, they were surrounded by the unknown and unexplored. No clear picture of American geography had yet emerged, though as Columbus had realized by the time of his fourth voyage, there was evidently a long land barrier confronting them which, though it might be pierced somewhere by a strait, could not be easily bypassed. Indeed, so prolonged was the American land mass from north to south, and so great would have been the value of a sea passage through it if found, however difficult to reach, that the search for such a passage continued for centuries. But the only sea passages to the north were perpetually blocked by ice, and there was nothing to the south but the Strait of Magellan, only a relatively short distance above the ultimate promontory of

---

[59]Jayne, *Vasco da Gama and his Successors*, pp. 96-97, 105 (quotation on 97); Whiteway, *Portuguese Power in India*, pp. 164-165; Sanceau, *Indies Adventure*, pp. 280-283, 290-292, 294-296.

[60]Jayne, *Vasco da Gama and his Successors*, p. 97; Whiteway, *Portuguese Power in India*, pp. 166, 181; Diffie and Winius, *Foundations of the Portuguese Empire*, p. 270; Sanceau, *Indies Adventure*, pp. 297-298.

Cape Horn. Valuable trade goods were to be found in coastal America despite the primitive culture of its native inhabitants, though not to be compared to the spices readily obtained on the coasts of India and Southeast Asia, but there was little surplus available in America for the daily necessities of life for civilized men, making the establishment of colonies very difficult, especially in view of the disdain for farming characteristic of most of the Spanish who came to the New World. Furthermore, there was no one overall authority for Spain in the New World like the Portuguese Viceroy in the Indian Ocean, to launch and protect colonizing enterprises; rather King Fernando's practice was to parcel out the coastlines, as they became known, among several different local commanders.

As mentioned earlier, there was almost no progress in American discovery and development during the three years of confusion and peril in Spain that followed Isabel's death and the succession of Juana. But by 1508 the situation in Spain had stabilized with Philip's death and Fernando's regency for his insane daughter, and expansion could resume. In that year Sebastian de Ocampo circumnavigated Cuba, establishing that it was an island, and Alonso de Ojeda and Diego de Nicuesa were appointed governors of the South American coast from Maracaibo in present-day Venezuela to Panama (then called Darien), with the Gulf of Uraba near the border between present-day Colombia and Panama as their dividing line, Ojeda having authority over the coast east of the center of that Gulf and Nicuesa over the coast west of it. Settlement of Cuba and on the eastern shore of the Gulf of Uraba began the following year. There were few problems in Cuba, where the natives were peaceful, but those on the eastern shore of the Gulf of Uraba fought back with poisoned arrows. In May 1510 Ojeda left the struggling colony there in charge of Francisco Pizarro, a strapping, courageous but almost illiterate soldier of fortune from Extremadura (later the blood-stained conqueror of Peru) and went to Santo Domingo for food and other supplies. He was wrecked on Cuba in a region not yet settled by Spaniards, and only returned to Hispaniola much later, "broken in health, spirit and fortune." Meanwhile Enciso, an associate of Ojeda, had sailed from Hispaniola for the Gulf of Uraba in a single ship, on which a young man named Vasco Núñez de Balboa stowed away in a barrel to escape his creditors. Balboa proved to be a natural leader. He soon took charge of the dispirited colony and in October moved it across the Gulf of Uraba to the other side, where there was fertile soil and the Indians did not use poisoned arrows. The Indians there were promptly defeated in battle and the town of La Antigua del Darien established, the first permanent Spanish colony on the American continent.[61]

---

[61]Merriman, *Rise of the Spanish Empire*, II, 213-214; Samuel Eliot Morison, *The European Discovery of America: the Southern Voyages* (New York, 1974), pp. 192-193, 201; Charles L. G. Anderson, *Life and Letters of Vasco Núñez de Balboa* (Westport CT, 1970), pp. 31, 33-38, 65-66.

Meanwhile Nicuesa had founded a colony at a bay called Nombre de Dios in Panama not far east of the present Atlantic terminus of the Panama Canal, but by December 1510 most of the 580 colonists there had died. The survivors were evacuated to La Antigua del Darien in July 1511. Balboa was now travelling widely among the Indians, trading with them for gold and obtaining information about a great sea not far to the south. In January 1512 the first ship sailed from Darien for Hispaniola with gold. It was wrecked on a reef off Jamaica; the sixteen survivors in a small boat were unable to reach that island, but drifted for many days before landing on Yucatán peninsula of Mexico, the first white men to see it. Seven died of thirst and exposure on the harrowing journey; four more were killed and eaten by cannibals on their arrival. The other five escaped, but three soon died in the jungle. One of the two who stayed alive was a friar named Jerónimo de Aguilar, who found a tribe of the local Maya people who accepted him. Living with them for the next seven years, he learned their language thoroughly. He was discovered by Hernán Cortes on his historic expedition which conquered Mexico, and working through an Aztec princess who knew the Mayan language, served as the interpreter without whom Cortes' astounding achievements in Mexico would almost certainly have been impossible.[62]

Receiving laudatory reports about Balboa's work in Darien, King Fernando appointed him acting governor. In January 1513 Balboa wrote a long letter to his sovereign explaining his plans to develop Darien and to lead an expedition to investigate the reports of a great sea to the south. At the begining of September Balboa set out on that expedition, aided in his journey by his reputation for fair and friendly treatment of the Indians, nearly 600 of whom he brought with him, along with about 200 Spanish. The distance was short though the terrain was rugged (no through highway has been constructed in it to this day). On September 25 he beheld the Pacific, the largest ocean on earth, "from a peak in Darien" to which the Indians had led him. In October he sailed out upon the new-found sea and found pearls on islands in the Gulf of Panama.[63]

In April 1514 a fleet of twenty ships carrying some 2,000 gold-hungry Spaniards sailed from Spain for Darien, their imaginations fired by wildly exaggerated tales of its riches and the beckoning "South Sea" beyond, commanded by a ruthless old soldier named Pedrarias Dávila. Among these 2,000 were Hernando de Soto, the later discoverer of the Mississippi River, and Bernal Diaz, the historian of Cortes' conquest of Mexico. Balboa welcomed Dávila but Dávila never trusted him. Before the end of the year Dávila had authorized enslavement of the Indians, totally without royal authority and against Balboa's advice; Balboa wrote two letters to King Fernando strongly

---

[62]Anderson, *Balboa*, pp. 44, 68, 77-83.
[63]*Ibid.*, pp. 73-74, 107-126, 156-162, 166, 179-181; Morison, *European Discovery of America: Southern Voyages*, pp. 202-203.

protesting this action and calling for a royal investigation.[64] Receiving such letters, Queen Isabel would have acted immediately; but Fernando, now in the last year of his life, delayed and was dead before he could act. Unlettered Francisco Pizarro learned from what he saw at Darien that royal authority could usually be safely flouted at the far end of the long line of communication from Spain to America.

The same year Balboa reached the Pacific on its American shore (by a fascinating coincidence, the very next year after Antonio d'Abreu and Francisco Serrano had reached it from the east, sailing from Malacca toward the Spice Islands) the Spanish captain Juan Ponce de Leon, who had come to America with Columbus' second voyage, sailed with three ships from Puerto Rico where he was governor, to explore to the north. (Despite the legend, his primary purpose was not to find the "Fountain of Youth," though rumors of such magical sites were not uncommon in a time and place where it seemed, with so many undiscovered and previously unimagined realms opening up, that anything might be possible.) He sailed through the Bahamas, finding many islands that Columbus had not discovered, reaching Florida at the beginning of April near present Daytona Beach. On the way he observed and described the Gulf Stream. He then sailed south along the east coast of Florida, past the Florida Keys, and up the west coast of Florida as far as Tampa Bay. From there he sailed diagonally across the Gulf of Mexico to Yucatán, returning to Puerto Rico in October after having greatly expanded Spain's geographical knowledge of the lands and seas north and west of Cuba.[65]

The conclave to elect the successor of the mighty Pope Julius II met in Rome March 9, 1513 with 25 of the 31 cardinals present, not counting those who had been dismissed for supporting the schism: 19 Italians, two Spaniards, a Frenchman, a German-Swiss, a Hungarian, and an Englishman. Pope Julius' strict provisions against simony in the conclave were closely observed. There was no clear front-runner when deliberations began. The "capitulation" which it had become usual for the Cardinals to sign at the beginning of a conclave committed them and the Church to reform, the continuation of the Fifth Lateran Council, and further efforts to mount a crusade against the Turks. The first ballot gave Spanish Cardinal Serra fourteen votes, but he had no chance of obtaining a two-thirds vote; the memory of the Borgias had left too much anti-Spanish feeling in Italy for that, and the majority of the Cardinals were Italian. In that ballot the Cardinal of Florence, Giovanni de Medici, received only one vote. But support for him grew rapidly, and despite considerable resistance by the older cardinals—Giovanni was only 38—he was elected on March 11 and

---

[64]Anderson, *Balboa*, pp. 244, 261-262, 277-283, 297, 300-302; Morison, *European Discovery of America: Southern Voyages*, pp. 203-204.
[65]Morison, *European Discovery of America: Southern Voyages*, pp. 503-507, 510-512.

took the name of Leo X.[66]

Giovanni de Medici was a son of Lorenzo the Magnificent. His resplendent father had designated him for the Church at the age of seven, and had prevailed on the compliant Pope Innocent VIII to make him a Cardinal at thirteen, though the appointment was not announced until he was seventeen, shortly before Innocent's death. He had received a fine Renaissance education and was intelligent, cultured, and genial. He seems to have been chaste, but was self-indulgent in his personal habits, immensely fat and consequently in poor health for his age. He had strongly opposed the Borgias and had travelled widely in Europe during the exile of the Medici from Florence. He had given loyal and valuable service to Pope Julius II. After the Battle of Ravenna, when the French defeated the papal army, he remained behind on the field comforting the wounded until the French captured him.[67] He was not an evil man—surely a far better man than Alexander VI. But he was not the Pope this age demanded, and showed no comprehension of its deeper needs. The infamous words that stand at the head of this chapter, as he celebrated his election as Vicar of Christ, are all the proof required of that.

As a Medici born and bred, Pope Leo X was at home (as much as anyone could be) in the swirl of political intrigue that was Renaissance Italy. He acquitted himself well there during the first three years of his pontificate. He kept the hard-won peace of Italy through 1513, and in December of that year, at the eighth session of the Fifth Lateran Council, Louis XII of France was formally reconciled with the Church after rejecting the schismatic council for which he had been primarily responsible, and accepting the Fifth Lateran as the only legitimate council. The Council also adopted some dogmatic decrees at this session, confuting heresies taught by some of the more extreme paganizing humanists who denied the immortality and individuality of the soul and asserted that the world was eternal rather than created. But virtually nothing was said about reform.[68]

To help protect Italy and the papacy against a revival of French aggression, Pope Leo X signed a secret agreement with Fernando in September 1514 by which both parties guaranteed the security of each other's Italian possessions during their lifetimes and pledged to make no agreement with France or any other state regarding the control of Milan and Genoa without the knowledge of the other. In March 1515 Leo offered France alliance on condition of waiver of the old French claim to the kingdom of Naples, now clearly unenforceable; but King Louis XII had died in January and his successor, the young and ambitious Francis I, refused to consider such a renunciation. He soon made it clear that he intended to return to Italy in arms,

[66]Von Pastor, *History of the Popes*, VII, 15-28.
[67]*Ibid.*, VII, 28-33.
[68]*Ibid.*, VII, 71-72, 155-156.

and in July 1515 the Holy League was revived against him.[69]

Intervening events had deprived the Pope, at least for the time being, of the support against France of Henry VIII of England, whose striking personality and obvious ability had made a great impression throughout Western Europe. In June 1513 Henry had taken personal command of a large and well-equipped English army crossing the Channel in pursuit of the now nearly two-century-old claim of English kings to be the rightful monarchs of France. He left Catherine behind as his regent with a tough old veteran general, the Earl of Surrey, to deal with France's ally Scotland if it should invade the north of England under its energetic and popular King James IV while Henry was away. Cooperating closely with Emperor Maximilian and armies from the Netherlands assembled by his daughter Margaret, once the widow of Prince Juan of Spain and now regent of the Netherlands for 13-year-old Charles (the eldest son of Philip and Juana), the English army took the French cities of Thérouanne and Tournai during the summer, driving the French in headlong retreat at the "Battle of the Spurs" in August and capturing the famous Chevalier Bayard. The expected attempt of the Scots to intervene ended in total disaster for them at Flodden September 9. Surrey destroyed their army, inflicting ten thousand casualties including knights from almost every noble family in Scotland, and leaving King James IV dead on the field.[70]

Catherine wrote to Henry VIII, as soon as she had news of the victory:

> You see I can keep my promise, to send for your banners [captured at the Battle of the Spurs] a king's coat.... With this I make an end, praying God to send you home shortly, for without [that] no joy can here be accomplished, and for the same I pray, and now go to Our Lady at Walsingham that I promised so long ago to see.[71]

Henry had gone to the shrine of the Blessed Virgin Mary at Walsingham to give thanks for their first-born son, born on New Year's Day in 1511, who had died 52 days later, to the great grief of both parents. Catherine was saying that when her beloved husband returned she would go to that shrine herself to pray for the birth of another son. Six months later she did conceive a son, but he died at birth in December 1514.[72]

But in August 1514 Henry had made peace with France, disillusioned by the failure of Fernando of Spain to support him effectively despite many

---

[69]*Ibid.*, VII, 103-104, 108, 111; Batiffol, *Century of the Renaissance*, p. 42.

[70]Scarisbrick, *Henry VIII*, pp. 35-38; Mattingly, *Catherine of Aragon*, pp. 155-157, 159; J. D. Mackie, *The Earlier Tudors, 1485-1558* (The Oxford History of England) (Oxford, 1952), pp. 279-283; Jane de Iongh, *Margaret of Austria, Regent of the Netherlands* (New York, 1953), pp. 180-182; R. L. Mackie, *King James IV of Scotland* (Westport CT, 1976), pp. 246-280 and *passim*.

[71]Mattingly, *Catherine of Aragon*, pp. 159-160.

[72]*Ibid.*, pp. 142-143, 169.

promises, sealing the treaty by the marriage of his 18-year-old sister Mary to the elderly French king, a mismatch which is alleged to have hastened Louis XII's death just a few months later. Henry held aloof from continental affairs during 1515, as Francis I marched into Italy at the head of more than 100,000 men and won the hard-fought Battle of Marignano in September, breaking the squares of Swiss pikemen with artillery fire and a series of magnificent charges led by Chevalier Bayard and the bold young king himself. Francis I made triumphal entry into Milan October 11, and two days later Pope Leo X had to accept the preliminary draft of a peace treaty providing for French control of that city and also of Parma and Piacenza, in return for a guarantee of the security of his native Florence and of the withdrawal by Francis I of the "Pragmatic Sanction" which Louis XII had renewed, separating the government of the French Church from the authority of the Pope. This preliminary treaty was confirmed at a meeting of the Pope and Francis I at Bologna in December.[73]

On January 22, 1516 the long and epochal life and reign of King Fernando of Aragon and Spain came to an end. On his deathbed he recognized his 15-year-old grandson Charles, whom he had never seen, as his successor in both Aragon and Castile, with Cardinal Cisneros to be regent for Castile until Charles should arrive.[74]

He was an awkward, unprepossesing boy, with a small thin body, a narrow face, an ugly underslung jaw, and hesitant speech. He spoke not a word of Spanish. Few saw great potential in him; many thought to take advantage of him. The worldly-minded paid no heed to the impact upon him of the characters of the two adults closest to him, who had become almost his foster father and mother: Adrian of Utrecht, later the holy Pope Adrian VI, the last non-Italian Pope before John Paul II; and his Aunt Margaret, so briefly the wife of Isabel's only son, and always highly regarded by Isabel. Born and baptized at Ghent, Charles had spent all his life in the Netherlands. There was no enthusiasm for him in any part of Spain—at best, a reluctant acceptance of his legal claims; at worst, a firm determination to oppose him and the foreign parasites he was expected to bring with him when he came. Without the unwavering support of 80-year-old Cardinal Cisneros he would have had little chance to prevail in Spain despite his unquestionable legal title to the throne. But the iron-souled primate Isabel had chosen, drawing on his last wells of strength, gave all he had left in him to the young prince, holding Spain together for the full year that intervened between Fernando's death and Charles' arrival, and during the first tumultuous weeks after his arrival. It was the last contribution, and one of the greatest, of Francisco Cardinal Ximénes de

---

[73]Scarisbrick, *Henry VIII*, pp. 53-55; Mattingly, *Catherine of Aragon*, pp. 166-168; Mackie, *Earlier Tudors*, p. 284; Batiffol, *Century of the Renaissance*, pp. 46-47; von Pastor, *History of the Popes*, pp. 100, 114-115, 119-120, 126-127, 135-140, 145-146.
[74]Merriman, *Rise of the Spanish Empire*, III, 6-7.

Cisneros to the Church as to the country he had loved and served so well.[75]

For Charles—though often traduced in his time and since, as by modern historians who tend to be hypercritical of him whatever their orientation—was to save Christendom in the shattering crisis now about to descend upon it.

It is March 16, 1517, and the twelfth and last session of the Fifth Lateran Council is underway in the presence of the Pope. High above the august assembly, utterly alone in the great pulpit so unfamiliar to a layman, Gianfrancesco Pico della Mirandola faces the leadership of the Church, arrayed in all their panoply of splendor and authority in the hallowed Church of St. John Lateran. Most laymen so placed would have been awed into almost inarticulate subservience. But the fire of the Spirit is upon Gianfrancesco, and the thundering voice of the prophets is his. You have heard a great deal during this long and fruitless council, we may imagine him saying, about the politics of Italy and Europe, the future of the papal state, the oft-discussed but little implemented crusade against the Turks who are swallowing up Eastern Europe. You have spoken of the laws of the Church, and you have defined and denounced heresy. But, as all Christendom knows, the Church is foul with corruption. You have done nothing about it, and this council will end with your having done nothing about it. An evil so pervasive, become so deeply rooted, can only be successfully fought by the heir across fifteen hundred years of Peter the fisherman, whom the great church now rising on the Vatican hill across the Tiber will honor forevermore. Look to your duty, Vicar of Christ!

Below the pulpit, Leo X's rubicund moon face has lost its normally jovial expression, and gone pale like wax. Was he remembering that he had said: "God has given us the Papacy; now let us enjoy it"? For Popes, too, come to judgment...

The speaker's words roll out like a great slow bell... like Amos before the king of Israel, or Jeremiah before the kings of Judah... no presumption, no rebellion, but a solemn reminder, that He Who sent down the Assyrian "like a wolf on the fold,"[76] and commissioned Nebuchadnezzar to destroy His own Temple,[77] and loosed the red Muslim whirlwind from the Arabian desert upon the feuding heresiarchs of the decadent Christian East and the cruel, small-minded kings and churchmen of later Visigothic Spain,[78] neither slumbers nor sleeps...

If Leo leaves crime any longer unpunished, if he refuses to heal the

---

[75]Karl Brandi, *The Emperor Charles V* (Atlantic Highlands NJ, 1965), pp. 45-48, 72-73; de Iongh, *Margaret of Austria*, pp. 168-170; Carroll, *Isabel of Spain*, p. 354.

[76]See Volume I, Chapter 5 of this history.

[77]See Volume I, Chapter 6 of this history.

[78]See Volume II, Chapter 8 of this history.

wounds, it is to be feared that God Himself will no longer apply a slow remedy, *but will cut off and destroy the diseased members with fire and sword.*[79]

Seven months later, a thick square-faced dark-browed figure, with vigorous stride rustling his black Augustinian monk's habit, steps defiantly up to the door of the parish church in the Saxon town of Wittenberg in the heart of Germany. In one hand he holds a paper and a nail, in the other a hammer. With sharp, fierce blows of the hammer upon the nail he affixes the paper to the door. It contains 95 theses which this monk, whose name is Martin Luther, proposes to defend against all comers—theses attacking the Church's doctrine of indulgences. His theses are defensible; many are later to be adopted in essence by the Church. But Luther's hammer is more important than his paper, for his purpose is to annihilate the Catholic Church root and branch, to condemn it as the work of Antichrist and substitute another church of his own making.[80]

The fire Luther kindled, the sword he wielded, would indeed destroy many diseased members of the Body of Christ, but at a terrible price that Christendom has been paying ever since.

The glory of united Christendom was over; its cleaving had begun.

---

[79]Von Pastor, *History of the Popes*, VII, 6. Emphasis added.
[80]This purpose was made clear in Luther's own pamphlet *The Babylonian Captivity of the Church*, published just three years later. See Volume IV, chapter 1 of this history, forthcoming.

Bibliography

1. GENERAL

The Cambridge Medieval History, ed. J. R. Tanner, C. W. Previté-Orton, and Z. N. Brooke (Cambridge, England, 1926)

Gottfried, Robert S. *The Black Death; Natural and Human Disaster in Medieval Europe* (New York, 1983). Probably the best scholarly study of this greatest of plagues.

Ziegler, Philip. *The Black Death* (New York, 1969)

2. THE POPES AND THE CHURCH

Aron, Marguerite. *Saint Dominic's Successor: the Life of Blessed Jordan of Saxony* (St. Louis, 1955)

Baldwin, Marshall W. *Alexander III and the Twelfth Century* (New York, 1968). Good summary of the pontificate by an exceptionally sound and well-balanced authority on the period.

Beneyto Pérez, Juan. *El cardenal Albornoz; Canciller de Castilla y Caudillo de Italia* (Madrid, 1950). The best, though disappointingly brief biography of this great bishop who regained control of the papal state, making it possible for the Popes to return from Avignon to Rome.

Bernard de Clairvaux, assembled by Commission d'histoire de l'ordre de Cîteaux (Paris, 1953). Extensive collection of essays on the life and work of St. Bernard.

Bernard of Clairvaux, St. *Letters*, tr. Bruno S. James (London, 1953)

Blumenthal, Uta-Renate. *The Early Councils of Pope Paschal II, 1100-1110* (Toronto, 1978)

Boase, T. S. R. *Pope Boniface VIII* (London, 1933). The best treatment of this outstanding and controversial Pope in English. Fair and thorough.

Butler's Lives of the Saints, edited, revised and supplemented by Herbert Thurston and Donald Attwater, 4 vols. (New York, 1956)

Catherine of Siena, St. *Saint Catherine of Siena as Seen in Her Letters*, ed. Vida D. Scudder (London, 1911). An old and incomplete but still indispensable collection of many of St. Catherine's finest letters.

Chamberlin, E. R. *The Fall of the House of Borgia* (New York, 1974). Quite well researched but sometimes exaggerated in its presentation of the evils of the Borgias, though not nearly as exaggerated as many 19th century works. Displays a consciousness of character and human reactions lacking in Mallett's study of the Borgias.

Cheney, Christopher R. *Pope Innocent III and England* (Stuttgart, 1976). Much the most thorough study of the subject in English, appreciative of the character and abilities of Pope Innocent III.

Christianson, Gerald. *Cesarini: the Conciliar Cardinal; the Basel Years, 1431-1438* (St. Ottilien, 1979). Excellent, very well documented and reasonably well written study of this leading figure at the Council of Basel.

Cruz, Joan Carroll. *The Incorruptibles* (Rockford IL, 1977)

Curley, Mary M. *The Conflict between Pope Boniface VIII and King Philip IV the Fair* (Washington, 1927). Well researched and well presented. Outspokenly Catholic viewpoint, but not uncritical.

Digard, Georges. *Philippe le bel et le Saint-Siège de 1285 à 1304*, 2 vols. (Paris, 1936). Covers relations between Philip IV and the Papacy during the first half of Philip's reign.

Englebert, Omer. *St. Francis of Assisi* (Chicago, 1965). The best scholarly Catholic biography of St. Francis.

Gill, Joseph. *The Council of Florence* (Cambridge, 1959). The definitive work on this Council.

————. *Eugenius IV, Pope of Christian Union* (Westminster MD, 1961). Well researched, well written and revealing study from a solidly Catholic viewpoint.

Gilson, Étienne. *Héloise and Abelard* (Ann Arbor, MI, 1960). Brief but very important study resolving or greatly contributing to the understanding of many of the most vexed questions about Abelard.

Glasfurd, Alec. *The Antipope, Pedro de Luna (1342-1423); a Study in Obstinacy* (London, 1965). The best available biography of Pedro de Luna, but not as comprehensive as might have been hoped, and often disfigured by a slapdash, mocking anti-Catholic tone.

Hefele, Charles-Joseph and Henri Leclercq. *Histoire des Conciles*, Volumes VI and VII (Paris, 1915-16). The monumental, definitive work on the councils of the Church and their background, particularly valuable for the period and councils of the Great Western Schism.

Houvet, Étienne. *Chartres Cathedral*, revised by Malcolm Miller (Paris, 1968)

Howarth, Stephen. *The Knights Templar* (New York, 1982)

Hughes, Philip. *A History of the Church*, rev. ed., 3 vols. (New York, 1949)

James, Bruno S. *Saint Bernard of Clairvaux* (New York, 1957). Fine short biography based on extensive familiarity with the original sources; strongly Catholic.

Jorgensen, Johannes. *Saint Bridget of Sweden*, 2 vols. (London, 1954). Much the most comprehensive treatment of St. Bridget in any language, written by a famous Scandinavian convert to Catholicism.

————. *Saint Catherine of Siena* (London, 1938). Outstanding presentation of Catherine's extraordinary life by a great Catholic biographer.

————. *Saint Francis of Assisi* (New York, 1912). Movingly written biography of St. Francis, but shows some signs of its age.

Kaminsky, Howard. *Simon de Cramaud and the Great Schism* (New Brunswick NJ, 1983). Though confined to the French response to the Great Western Schism before the Council of Pisa, it is exceedingly thorough and valuable for this aspect of the history of the Schism.

Katzenellenbogen, Adolf. *The Sculptural Programs of Chartres Cathedral* (Baltimore, 1959)

King, Archdale A. *Cîteaux and Her Elder Daughters* (London, 1954)

Kirkfleet, Cornelius. *History of St. Norbert* (St. Louis, 1916). Comprehensive but unfortunately uncritical.

Lackner, Bede K. *The Eleventh-Century Background of Cîteaux* (Washington, 1972)

Lewis, C. S. *The Discarded Image* (Cambridge, England, 1967). Imaginative and beautifully written evocation of the medieval world-view.

Lizerand, Georges. *Clément V et Philippe le bel* (Paris, 1911). The best history of the momentous struggle between this weak Pope and the powerful King Philip IV the Fair. Very thorough.

Mallett, Michael. *The Borgias; the Rise and Fall of a Renaissance Dynasty* (New York, 1969). The best relatively recent history of the Borgias; a valuable corrective to earlier exaggerations of the black legend of the Borgias and attempts in reaction to exonerate them completely.

Mann, Horace K. *The Lives of the Popes in the Middle Ages*, Volumes IX-XIX

(London, 1925-1932). Fundamental and indispensable to the Catholic understanding of the unfolding of medieval Church history.

McGowan, John P. *Pierre d'Ailly and the Council of Constance* (Washington, 1936). Thin and only occasionally useful.

Mitchell, R. J. *The Laurels and the Tiara; Pope Pius II* (New York, 1963)

Mollat, Guy. *The Popes at Avignon* (New York, 1963). Indispensable work of papal history, the most detailed available in English for this period, bridging much of the gap between Mann's and von Pastor's multi-volume papal histories.

Moorman, John. *A History of the Franciscan Order* (Oxford, 1968). Well-researched, thorough and impartial.

Morrall, John B. *Gerson and the Great Schism* (Manchester, England, 1960). Meager but occasionally useful.

Mundy, John H. and Kennerly M. Woody, eds. *The Council of Constance; the Unification of the Church* (New York, 1961). An invaluable publication of the principal contemporary narratives of this critically important council, unfortunately with few editorial notes to help the student not already very familiar with it.

Pastor, Ludwig von. *History of the Popes* (St. Louis, 1895-1935) 40 vols. One of the premier works of history of all time. It has been said—and rightly—that it will never be superseded. Von Pastor spent the better part of a lifetime researching it personally in the Vatican Library, beginning immediately after that Library was opened by Pope Leo XIII to scholars without restriction. The 40 volumes, covering the history of the Papacy from 1417 to 1799, were published in German from 1886 to 1933 and soon translated into English. For the Catholic historian in particular, they are a mine of essential information.

Pernoud, Régine. *Héloise and Abelard* (New York, 1973)

Powers, George C. *Nationalism at the Council of Constance* (Washington, 1927). The best available secondary history of this Council, yet still inadequate; there is great need for a thorough new history of the Council of Constance in English.

Robeck, Nesta de. *St. Clare of Assisi* (Milwaukee, 1951)

Roo, Peter de. *Materials for a History of Alexander VI, his Relatives and his Times*, 5 vols. (Bruges, 1924). Though providing some useful corrective material on the Borgia Pope, this prolonged and overblown apologia repeatedly sacrifices credibility by dismissing the solid as well as the improbable evidence against him, and portraying him as not only a maligned but actually a holy Pope, which he clearly was not.

Ruiz, Teofilo, "Reaction to Anagni," *Catholic Historical Review* LXV (1979), 385-401. Provides evidence that the seizure and near-slaying of Pope Boniface VIII did not arouse nearly as much negative reaction throughout Christendom as has generally been assumed.

Salembier, L. *The Great Schism of the West* (New York, 1907). Strongly Catholic and brings out many important points, but not always free from bias nor as thorough as other treatments of the subject.

Simson, Otto von. *The Gothic Cathedral* (New York, 1958)

Smith, John H. *The Great Schism* (New York, 1970). A workmanlike survey, somewhat abbreviated.

Stieber, Joachim W. *Pope Eugenius IV, the Council of Basel, and the Secular and Ecclesiastical Authorities in the Empire* (Leiden, 1978). Very thoroughly researched and comprehensively presented. Distinctly Protestant orientation, but Stieber is fair and his facts, if not all his interpretations, match well with those of Catholic historians.

Swaan, Wim. *The Gothic Cathedral* (London, 1969)

Swanson, R. N. *Universities, Academics and the Great Schism* (Cambridge, England, 1979)

Tillmann, Helene. *Pope Innocent III* (Amsterdam, 1980). Erudite but disjointed, poorly organized study yielding surprisingly little information of clear historical significance.

Ullmann, Walter. *The Origins of the Great Schism* (London, 1948). Much the best study of this subject in English, comprehensive and straightforward in its analysis. Mostly confined to the first year of the schism.

Undset, Sigrid. *Catherine of Siena* (New York, 1954). Excellent, thoughtful biography, unfortunately marred by lack of notes and bibliography.

Valois, Noel. *La France et le grand schisme d'Occident*, 4 vols. (Paris, 1896-1902). The monumental, virtually definitive review of the evidence of what actually happened during the Great Schism, from the disputed election of Urban VI in April 1378 to the end of the pontificate of Martin V in 1431, on which most subsequent histories largely build.

Vicaire, M.-H. *St. Dominic and His Times* (New York, 1964). Well-rounded product of many years of orthodox Catholic scholarship, this is the best biography of St. Dominic we are likely to get, though still with much less hard evidence about his life and achievements than we should like to have.

Waley, Daniel. *The Papal State in the Thirteenth Century* (London, 1961)

Walsh, Katherine. *A Fourteenth-Century Scholar and Primate; Richard FitzRalph in Oxford, Avignon and Armagh* (Oxford, 1981). In addition to his activities in England and Ireland, FitzRalph was much involved in two important ecclesiastical controversies of his day: whether the souls of the just dead enjoy the Beatific Vision before the resurrection of the body, and whether mendicant religious orders are justified.

Weisheipl, James A. *Friar Thomas d'Aquino; His Life, Thought, and Work* (New York, 1974). The best modern scholarly biography of St. Thomas Aquinas.

Williams, Watkin. *Saint Bernard of Clairvaux* (Manchester, 1935). The definitive biography of the great saint, the dominant figure of his age.

Wilms, Hieronymus. *Albert the Great, Saint and Doctor of the Church* (London, 1933)

3. CENTRAL EUROPE (GERMANY AND ITALY)

Abulafia, David. *Frederick II* (London, 1988). The latest biography of the enigmatic Emperor, oddly dedicated to the proposition that he was not as distinctive or important as most historians have believed.

Bowsky, William M. *Henry VII in Italy; the Conflict of Empire and City-State, 1310-1313* (Lincoln NE, 1960). Covers its brief period with great thoroughness and clarity.

Brandi, Karl. *The Emperor Charles V* (Atlantic Highlands NJ, 1965). The best biography available in English of this extraordinary man, and a very good one, though Charles V's greatness cries out for even fuller and better treatment.

Breisach, Ernst. *Caterina Sforza, a Renaissance Virago* (Chicago, 1967)

Butler, W. F. *The Lombard Communes; a History of the Republics of North Italy* (London, 1906; Westport CT, 1969). Old and somewhat sketchy, but still a useful synthesis.

Chamberlin, E. L. *The Count of Virtue; Giangaleazzo Visconti, Duke of Milan* (New York, 1965)

Cox, Eugene L. *The Green Count of Savoy; Amadeus VI and Transalpine Savoy in the Fourteenth Century* (Princeton, 1967). Excellent study of the greatest of the Counts of Savoy, a crusader.

Denholm-Young, N. *Richard of Cornwall* (New York, 1947). Good biography of the English imperial pretender of the mid-thirteenth century.

Deuel, Leo. *Testaments of Time; the Search for Lost Manuscripts and Records* (New York, 1965). Early chapters fascinatingly survey the Renaissance rediscoveries of historically significant manuscripts from classical times.

Greenaway, George W. *Arnold of Brescia* (Cambridge, England, 1931)

Haverkamp, Alfred. *Medieval Germany, 1056-1273* (New York, 1988). Brief but useful survey.

Hibbert, Christopher. *The House of Medici; its Rise and Fall* (New York, 1974). Reasonably comprehensive and quite well-written.

Holmes, George. *Florence, Rome, and the Origins of the Renaissance* (Oxford, 1986). Unusual and original blending of political, religious, and intellectual history, with particular emphasis on Dante and Giotto.

Jarrett, Bede. *The Emperor Charles IV* (London, 1935). An essay more than a detailed biography, this is a very important corrective from the Catholic viewpoint to the usual picture of this Emperor as a weak papal puppet.

Jeffery, David. "A Renaissance for Michelangelo," *National Geographic*, December 1989. Describes the restoration of the ceiling of the Sistine Chapel painted by Michelangelo and what has been learned from it about how the ceiling was painted.

Kantorowicz, Ernst. *Frederick II* (New York, 1931, 1957). Almost idolizes Frederick II; hostile to the Catholic Church.

Knapke, Paul J. *Frederick Barbarossa's Conflict with the Papacy* (Washington, 1939). Catholic interpretation.

Muir, Dorothy. *A History of Milan under the Visconti* (London, 1924). The only real history of Milan during this period available in English, but quite superficial and antipapal.

Munz, Peter. *Frederick Barbarossa; a Study in Medieval Politics* (Ithaca NY, 1969). The most extensive and well documented biography of Frederick Barbarossa available in English, but repeatedly hobbled by the author's extraordinary theories about alleged political schemes of Frederick which are nowhere mentioned in the original sources.

Norwich, John J. *The Kingdom in the Sun, 1130-1194* (New York, 1970). Vivid narrative style based on sound research, but somewhat anti-Catholic.

———. *The Other Conquest* (New York, 1967)

Origo, Iris. *The World of San Bernardino* (New York, 1962). Largely cultural survey of the work and times of the great preaching saint of Siena.

Pacaut, Marcel. *Frederick Barbarossa* (New York, 1970). Despite the high reputation of the author as an historian, disappointingly sketchy with a number of significant chronological inaccuracies.

Purcell, Mary. *St. Anthony and His Times* (Dublin, 1960)

Runciman, Steven. *The Sicilian Vespers* (Cambridge, England, 1958). An outstanding, seminal work in European history, very valuable despite the author's pervasive anti-Catholic bias.

Roche, T. W. E. *The King of Almayne* (London, 1966). Another good biography of the English imperial pretender of the mid-thirteenth century, Richard of Cornwall.

Ryder, Alan. *Alfonso the Magnanimous, King of Aragon, Naples and Sicily, 1396-1458* (Oxford, 1990). The first comprehensive scholarly biography of this peripatetic king, and an excellent one.

Schevill, Ferdinand. *The Medici* (New York, 1949)

———. *Medieval and Renaissance Florence*, rev. ed. (New York, 1961). Still the most thorough history of Florence, both cultural and political, but displays strong antipapal bias.

Van Cleve, Thomas C. *The Emperor Frederick II of Hohenstaufen* (Oxford, 1972). Much the best and most thorough biography of Frederick II, well balanced in assessing him though harshly and sometimes vehemently and unjustly critical of the Catholic Church.

4. FRANCE AND THE LOW COUNTRIES

Baldwin, John W. *The Government of Philip Augustus* (Berkeley CA, 1986). Good presentation of the political and military history of the reign of Philip II of France as well as surveying its governmental administration.

Batiffol, Louis. *The Century of the Renaissance* (Volume III of *The National History of France*) (New York, 1916)

Famiglietti, R. C. *Royal Intrigue; Crisis at the Court of Charles VI, 1392-1420* (New York, 1986). The only political history in English of the reign of France's mad king.

Favier, Jean. *Philippe le bel* (Paris, 1978). Detailed biography of Philip IV the Fair in French.

Gies, Frances. *Joan of Arc; the Legend and the Reality* (New York, 1981). The best recent biography of St. Joan among many—cautious, thorough, and respectful of the sources.

Iongh, Jane de. *Margaret of Austria, Regent of the Netherlands* (New York, 1953). The author draws an appealing picture of the life of Margaret as Regent and provides some insight into her policies, but does not fully convey her striking character and achievements.

Kendall, Paul M. *Louis XI, the Universal Spider* (New York, 1971). King Louis XI of France appears to bewilder modern historians almost as much as he bewildered his own time. Widely divergent new interpretations of him keep appearing. Kendall's analysis is sound and thoughtful, straightening out much of the confusion. A very valuable biography.

Labarge, Margaret W. *Saint Louis* (Boston, 1968). Barely adequate summary of the great king's reign, often superficial; does not really live up to its subject. Strangely enough, however, nothing as good on St. Louis is available in English, and nothing better even in French.

Palmer, J. J. N. *England, France and Christendom, 1377-99* (London, 1972). Despite the title, is confined mostly to the Hundred Years War and negotiations between England and France growing out of it.

Pegues, Franklin J. *The Lawyers of the Last Capetians* (Princeton, 1962). Mainly concerns the reign and activities of Philip IV the Fair and his corps of lawyers helping him try to build an absolutist state.

Pernoud, Régine. *Eleanor of Aquitaine* (New York, 1968). Beautifully written and full of striking insights; Catholic viewpoint.

Perroy, Édouard. *The Hundred Years War* (London, 1951). Long the best general treatment of this great conflict, though inadequately documented, it is now being superseded by Sumption's new history of that war. Still valuable for the periods not yet covered by Sumption.

Pollard, A. J. *John Talbot and the War in France, 1427-1453* (London, 1983). Biography of the best English general in the later stages of the Hundred Years War, who was nevertheless defeated by Joan of Arc and others.

Runciman, Steven. *The Medieval Manichee* (Cambridge, England, 1955). Outstanding treatment of the origins and character of the revival of Manichaeanism in the

Middle Ages in Bogomilism and Catharism, with particular emphasis on the Albigensian movement in southern France.

Sackville-West, Victoria. *Saint Joan of Arc* (New York, 1938). Thoroughly researched and written in an unusual, highly personal style, this biography is idiosyncratic but insightful.

Seward, Desmond. *The Hundred Years War* (New York, 1978). Fairly brief and somewhat superficial, though occasionally useful.

Strayer, Joseph R. *The Reign of Philip the Fair* (Princeton, 1980). Sums up the author's life-work as the leading authority on this important reign writing in English. Even-handed but lacks appreciation of the Catholic viewpoint.

Sumption, Jonathan. *The Albigensian Crusade* (London, 1978). Surprisingly, this is the only solid, dependable, and scholarly book-length history of the Albigensian Crusade written in English in the twentieth century. Generally but not obtrusively modern viewpoint—not particularly friendly to Catholics, but usually fair.

————. *The Hundred Years War; Trial by Battle* (Philadelphia, 1990). The first volume of a new, definitive history of the Hundred Years War, this covers the years from its origins to the English capture of Calais in 1347.

Vale, M. G. A. *Charles VII* (Berkeley CA, 1974). A major disappointment. Although highly regarded by professional historians, this volume does not provide any clear understanding of Charles' personality or the policies and goals that guided his reign, and gives only a limited and inadequate survey of its events.

Vaughan, Richard. *Charles the Bold; the Last Valois Duke of Burgundy* (London, 1973). Fourth and final volume in the monumental history of the Valois Dukes of Burgundy by an English historian, the best written and best presented of the four.

————. *John the Fearless; the Growth of Burgundian Power* (New York, 1966). Second volume of Vaughan's history of the rise of the Burgundian-Dutch state, brief because of John's relatively short and undistinguished reign.

————. *Philip the Bold; the Formation of the Burgundian State* (London, 1962). First volume of Vaughan's history, limited by the scant material available on the first of the Valois Dukes of Burgundy.

————. *Philip the Good; the Apogee of Burgundy* (London, 1970). Third volume of Vaughan's history of the rise of the Burgundian-Dutch state, very thorough but often pedestrian and unimaginative.

Wakefield, Walter L. *Heresy, Crusade and Inquisition in Southern France 1100-1250* (Berkeley CA, 1974). Ambitious in coverage, disappointingly superficial in actual treatment of its subject.

5. THE BRITISH ISLES

Barber, Richard. *Edward, Prince of Wales and Aquitaine* (New York, 1978). Good biography of Edward "the Black Prince."

Barlow, Frank. *Thomas Becket* (Berkeley Ca, 1986). Well researched and less hostile to Catholics than this author's other historical works.

Barrow, G. W. S. *Robert Bruce and the Community of the Realm of Scotland* (Berkeley CA, 1965). Outstandingly researched and written. Definitely the best source for the life and achievement of this great king of Scotland.

Burne, A. H. *The Agincourt War* (Fair Lawn NJ, 1956). A purely military history of the last forty years of the Hundred Years War, but a very good one, thoroughly researched by an English army officer.

Cosgrove, Art, ed. *Medieval Ireland, 1169-1534* (New History of Ireland, Volume II) (Oxford, 1987). Collective history, very useful and thorough.

Dahmus, Joseph. *William Courtenay, Archbishop of Canterbury 1381-1396* (University Park PA, 1966). A major, well-researched biography of the bishop who kept England in the Church in his time by suppressing Wyclif's heresies at the University of Oxford.

D'Alton, E. A. *History of Ireland from the Earliest Times to the Year 1547*, 6 vols. (Dublin, 1903). Of limited value partly due to its age, but occasionally useful.

Davies, R. R. *Conquest, Coexistence, and Change; Wales 1063-1415* (Oxford, 1987). A good modern synthesis, but does not add much to Lloyd's classic history of Wales.

Davis, Irene M. *The Black Douglas* (Boston, 1974). Best scholarly biography of Robert Bruce's most loyal and militarily effective companion in his wars for Scotland.

Davis, R. H. C. *King Stephen, 1135-1154* (Berkeley CA, 1967)

Denholm-Young, N. *Richard of Cornwall* (New York, 1947)

Fryde, Natalie. *The Tyranny and Fall of Edward II, 1321-1326* (Cambridge, England, 1979)

Gillingham, John. *Richard the Lionheart* (New York, 1978). Much the best biography of the famous English crusader king, thoroughly researched and well analyzed.

——. *The Wars of the Roses* (London, 1981). Probably the best general survey of the subject.

Griffiths, Ralph A. *The Reign of King Henry VI* (Berkeley CA, 1981). Immense and almost unreadable. A few significant facts are all but buried under an avalanche of undigested data.

Haines, Roy M. *Archbishop John Stratford: Political Revolutionary and Champion of the Liberties of the English Church* (Toronto, 1986). A comprehensive study of the Archbishop of Canterbury during the early part of the reign of Edward III, who was not a revolutionary, but a strong personality very influential in the affairs of his time.

——. *The Church and Politics in Fourteenth-Century England; the Career of Adam Orleton* (Cambridge, 1978). Thorough study of one of the leading opponents of King Edward II.

Hibbert, Christopher. *Agincourt* (Philadelphia, 1964). A rousing account of the battle.

Holt, J. C. *Magna Carta* (Cambridge, England, 1965). Comprehensive, well documented and well argued explanation of why Magna Carta was in truth the great landmark in the development of English law and government that earlier generations declared it to be, but that some twentieth century historians have ostentatiously denied.

Hutchison, Harold F. *Edward II* (New York, 1971). The only biography of this ill-fated English monarch.

——. *King Henry V* (New York, 1967). Clearly written, workmanlike biography, like all those by this author.

——. *The Hollow Crown; a Life of Richard II* (New York, 1961). The best biography of Richard II.

Jacob, E. F. *The Fifteenth Century, 1399-1485* (Oxford History of England) (Oxford, 1961). More political history than in the preceding volume of the Oxford series.

Johnson, P. A. *Duke Richard of York, 1411-1460* (Oxford, 1988). The only scholarly biography of the founder of the Yorkist branch of the Plantagenet dynasty, father of King Edward IV.

Kendall, Paul M. *Richard III* (New York, 1955). The book that did more to rehabilitate the reputation of Richard III than the work of any other historian. Strongly controverted, it continues to stand up well to hostile criticism, which tends to concentrate more on its free-wheeling style than its substance. Kendall's research matches or betters that of any of his critics.

————. *Warwick the Kingmaker* (New York, 1957). Classic biography of the great English nobleman of the age of the Wars of the Roses.

Kirby, J. L. *Henry IV* (London, 1970). Pedestrian and overladen with the government finance of the reign, this remains the only twentieth-century biography of this king, and is occasionally useful.

Knowles, David. *The Monastic Order in England* (Cambridge, England, 1950). A masterwork.

————. *Thomas Becket* (Stanford CA, 1970). Short study but with striking insights; strongly Catholic viewpoint.

Labarge, Margaret W. *Simon de Montfort* (Toronto, 1962). Solid, clearly written biography; much better than her biography of St. Louis.

Lane-Poole, Austin. *From Domesday Book to Magna Carta, 1087-1216* (Oxford History of England), 2nd ed. (Oxford, 1955). A particularly well done volume in this important series.

Lloyd, John E. *A History of Wales*, 3rd ed. (London, 1939). The classic history of Wales, still unsurpassed.

————. *Owen Glendower* (Oxford, 1931). Presents almost all of the relatively little that is known about this Welsh national hero, immortalized by Shakespeare.

Luddy, Ailbe J. *Life of St. Malachy* (Dublin, 1930). Unfortunately superficial. Catholic viewpoint but sometimes uncritical.

Mackie, J. D. *The Earlier Tudors, 1485-1558* (the Oxford History of England) (Oxford, 1952). One of the more disappointing of the uneven Oxford History volumes, somewhat thin in its facts and quick and superficial in some interpretations, though still a useful review of some of the most active and dramatic years in English history.

Mackie, R. L. *King James IV of Scotland* (Westport CT, 1976). The only scholarly biography of the Scots king who triumphed over feuding nobles in his kingdom but lost all at Flodden Field.

Mattingly, Garrett. *Catherine of Aragon* (New York, 1941). One of the finest, most evocative and fully realized biographies ever written by an American historian.

McKisack, May. *The Fourteenth Century, 1307-1399* (Oxford History of England) (Oxford, 1959). Institutional history emphasized at the expense of political history, especially for the reign of Edward III, with almost no coverage of the Hundred Years War.

Morris, John E. *The Welsh Wars of Edward I* (New York, 1901, 1969)

Nicholson, Ronald. *Scotland: the Later Middle Ages* (Edinburgh History of Scotland, Volume II) (Edinburgh, 1974). The only recent comprehensive treatment of its subject, long on administrative and economic analysis but short on narrative.

Oman, Charles. *The Great Revolt of 1381* (Oxford, 1906, 1969). Remains the standard work on Wat Tyler's rebellion.

Orpen, Goddard H. *Ireland under the Normans, 1169-1216*, 2 vols. (Oxford, 1911). Still definitive for its period.

Packe, Michael. *King Edward III*, ed. L. C. B. Seaman (London, 1983). The only recent scholarly biography of this great king. The author died in the midst of writing it and, despite the efforts of the editor, some evidences of its not having been completed remain.

Painter, Sidney. *William Marshal: Knight-Errant, Baron, and Regent of England* (Baltimore, 1933)

Pernoud, Régine. *Eleanor of Aquitaine* (New York, 1968). Beautifully written and full of striking insights; Catholic viewpoint.

Perroy, Édouard. *The Hundred Years War* (London, 1951). Long the best general treatment of this great conflict, though inadequately documented, it is now being superseded by Sumption's new history of that war. Still valuable for the periods not yet covered by Sumption.

Pollard, A. J. *Richard III and the Princes in the Tower* (New York, 1991). Impartial review of the latest evidence and speculation in the perennially interesting and not fully soluble case of Richard III and the disappearance of his two nephews from the Tower of London.

Powicke, Maurice. *The Thirteenth Century, 1216-1307* (Oxford History of England, Volume IV), 2nd ed. (Oxford, 1962). One of the best and most thorough of the Oxford histories, with ample political coverage.

Roche, T. W. E. *The King of Almayne* [Richard of Cornwall] (London, 1966)

Ross, Charles. *Edward IV* (Berkeley CA, 1974). An excellent, thorough biography of this remarkable king.

————. *Richard III* (Berkeley CA, 1981). Presents the opposite, conventional interpretation of Richard III to that of Paul M. Kendall and does it quite well, though in my opinion Kendall wins the debate.

St. Aubyn, Giles. *The Year of Three Kings, 1483* (New York, 1983). Well done popular history, though with some flaws due to spotty research. Distinctly hostile to Richard III.

Scarisbrick, J. J. *Henry VIII* (Berkeley CA, 1968)

Scott, Ronald M. *Robert the Bruce, King of Scots* (New York, 1989). An adequate biography but not comparable to Barrow's.

Sedgwick, Henry D. *The Life of Edward the Black Prince* (Indianapolis, 1932). Older biography, now largely superseded but occasionally useful.

Steel, Anthony. *Richard II* (Cambridge, England, 1962)

Sumption, Jonathan. *The Hundred Years War; Trial by Battle* (Philadelphia, 1990). The first volume of a new, definitive history of the Hundred Years War, covering the years from its origins to the English capture of Calais in 1347.

Trehearne, R. F. *The Baronial Plan of Reform, 1258-1263*, rev. ed. (New York, 1971). Comprehensive, profoundly researched, and brilliant; answers most of the enduring questions about the nature and purposes of the English political reform and the birth of the English Parliament associated with Simon de Montfort the younger.

Walsh, Katherine. *A Fourteenth-Century Scholar and Primate; Richard FitzRalph in Oxford, Avignon and Armagh* (Oxford, 1981)

Warren W. L. *Henry II* (Berkeley CA, 1973). Outstanding biography, indispensable for the period, but quite hostile to the Catholic Church and especially to St. Thomas Becket, who is treated less than fairly.

————. *King John* (Berkeley CA, 1971). Less thorough and polished than his biography of Henry II and equally biased, but still valuable.

Winston, Richard. *Thomas Becket* (New York, 1967). Definitely the best biography of Becket.

Workman, Herbert B. *John Wyclif; a Study of the English Medieval Church*, 2 vols. (Oxford, 1926). The most thorough study of Wyclif.

6. THE IBERIAN PENINSULA (SPAIN AND PORTUGAL)

Amezua de Mayo, Agustín G. de. *La batalla de Lucena y el verdadero retrato de Boabdil* (Madrid, 1915)

Ballesteros y Beretta, Antonio. *Alfonso X el Sabio* (Barcelona, 1984). Encyclopedic, definitive biography of Spain's most famous medieval king.

————. "El agitado año de 1325 y un escrito desconocido de Don Juan Manuel," *Boletín de la Real Academia de la Historia* CXXIV (1949), 9-58. One of the few scholarly treatments of any part of the reign of Alfonso XI of Castile, who has never received comprehensive scholarly treatment even in Spain.

Benito Ruano, Eloy. *Toledo en el siglo XV; vida política* (Madrid, 1961)

Biggs, Anselm G. *Diego Gelmírez, First Archbishop of Compostela* (Washington, 1949). Catholic viewpoint.

Carroll, Warren H. *Isabel of Spain, the Catholic Queen* (Front Royal VA, 1991)

Cuartero y Huerta, Baltasar. *El Pacto de los Toros de Guisando y la Venta del mismo Nombre* (Madrid, 1952). Excellent study of the pact that made Princess Isabel the heir to Castile.

Fernández de Retana, Luis. *Cisneros y su siglo*, 2 vols. (Madrid, 1929). Excellent biography of the great reforming primate of Spain.

Fletcher, R. A. *Saint James's Catapult; the Life and Times of Diego Gelmírez of Santiago de Compostela* (Oxford, 1984). Well researched, but non-Catholic and mocks its subject.

Fuertes Arias, Rafael. *Alfonso de Quintanilla, Contador Mayor de los Reyes Católicos* (Oviedo, 1909)

Gaibrois de Ballesteros, Mercedes. *Historia del reinado de Sancho IV de Castilla*, 3 vols. (Madrid, 1922). Very comprehensive, by far the best source for this reign.

————. *Maria de Molina, tres veces reina* (Madrid, 1936). The only scholarly biography of this great queen and later regent of Castile, but somewhat sketchy.

García Oro, José. *La Reforma de los Religiosos Españoles en tiempo de los Reyes Católicos* (Valladolid, 1969). Seminal, comprehensive, very important study of the reform of the Church in Spain begun by Queen Isabel and completed by Cardinal Cisneros.

Ghéon, Henri. *St. Vincent Ferrer* (New York, 1939). The only readily available biography of this saint, but lacks notes and a bibliography.

González, Julio. *Alfonso IX* (Madrid, 1944). The only scholarly biography of the King of León during the early thirteenth century.

————. *Regesta de Fernando II* (Madrid, 1943)

————. *El reino de Castilla en la época de Alfonso VIII*, 3 vols. (Madrid, 1960). Very comprehensive; indispensable for Spain during this reign.

Gorosterratzu, Javier. *Don Rodrigo Jiménez de Rada, Gran Estadista, Escritor y Prelado* (Pamplona, 1925). Comprehensive, well-researched biography of this great bishop, author of the first true history of Spain.

Hillgarth, J. N. *The Spanish Kingdoms, 1250-1516*, 2 vols. (Oxford, 1976). Poorly organized, spotty and sometimes confusing in its coverage; nevertheless includes a broad range of valuable data on late medieval Spain.

Isabel the Catholic, Queen. *Testamento y codicilo* (Madrid, 1956). The text of her magnificent last will and testament, with its final codicils.

Kamen, Henry. *Inquisition and Society in Spain* (Bloomington IN, 1985). Some useful data, but marked by much of the usual modern prejudice against the Spanish Inquisition.

Lacarra, José Maria. *Alfonso el Batallador* (Zaragoza, 1978). Brief but good; the only biography of this great king in any language.

Ladero Quesada, Miguel Angel. *Castilla y la conquista del reino de Granada* (Valladolid, 1967)

Lea, Henry Charles. *A History of the Inquisition of Spain*, 4 vols. (New York, 1906). Only the first part of the first volume applies to the years covered by this volume of my history, and despite Lea's reputation the material he found on the Spanish Inquisition in the time of Fernando and Isabel is very scanty.

Llorca, Bernardino. *La Inquisición en España* (Barcelona, 1936). This little known book is, in my view, the best available study of the early history of the Spanish Inquisition.

Lomax, Derek W. *The Reconquest of Spain* (London, 1978). An outstanding synthesis, remarkably comprehensive despite its relative brevity. The only history of this specific subject in English.

Macdonald, I. I. *Don Fernando de Antequera* (Oxford, 1948). Reads like a dissertation (which perhaps it was)—very erudite but often difficult to follow, with not all aspects of its important subject explored.

Menéndez Pidal, Ramón, director. *Historia de España.* Three volumes in this magnificent series which had been published by 1991 very thoroughly cover Spanish history during the period of this volume in my series, beginning in 1350: XIV, "España Cristiana: crisis de la Reconquista; luchas civiles," by Luis Suárez Fernández and Juan Reglá Campistol (Madrid, 1987); XV, "Los Trastámaras de Castilla y Aragon en el Siglo XV," by Luis Suárez Fernández, Angel Canellas López and Jaime Vicens Vives, 4th ed. (Madrid, 1986); XVII, "España de los Reyes Católicos," by Luis Suárez Fernández and Manuel Fernández Alvarez (Madrid, 1969).

Merriman, Roger B. *The Rise of the Spanish Empire in the Old World and the New,* Volume II (New York, 1918). Tries to cover too broad a subject in too little space, but occasionally useful.

Merton, Reginald. *Cardinal Ximenes and the Making of Spain* (London, 1934). The only biography of Cardinal Cisneros in English is disappointingly sketchy and superficial.

Miller, Townsend. *The Castles and the Crown; Spain 1451-1555* (New York, 1963). Brilliantly written history, but episodic and affected at critical points by a highly unrealistic view of the psychological condition of Isabel's daughter Juana, whose descent into insanity Miller unreasonably delays.

———. *Henry IV of Castile* (Philadelphia, 1972). A well researched and extraordinarily well written book, presenting an unforgettable picture of this tragic king and his times. Indispensable for his reign.

O'Callaghan, Joseph F. *A History of Medieval Spain* (Ithaca NY, 1975). Still the only general history of medieval Spain in English, unimaginative but thorough.

Peters, Edward. *Inquisition* (New York, 1988). A reasonably fair but somewhat superficial treatment of the subject.

Prescott, William H. *The Reign of Ferdinand and Isabella the Catholic,* 3 vols. (Philadelphia, 1872, 1893). Very old but classic and still useful biography, exceedingly well researched.

Purcell, Mary. *The Great Captain, Gonzalo Fernández de Córdoba* (London, 1962)

Recuero Astray, Manuel. *Alfonso VII, Emperador* (León, 1979). Limited in scope and coverage, but the only historical biography of this ruler.

Reilly, Bernard F. *The Kingdom of León-Castilla under King Alfonso VI, 1065-1109* (Princeton, 1988). Outstanding new history based on immense research.

———. *The Kingdom of León-Castilla under Queen Urraca, 1109-1126* (Princeton, 1982). Same high quality as his study of Alfonso VI.

Rodríguez Villa, Antonio. *La Reina Doña Juana la loca* (Madrid, 1892)

Rumeu de Armas, Antonio. *Itinerario de los Reyes Católicos* (Madrid, 1974)

———. *La política indigenista de Isabel la Católica* (Valladolid, 1969). Important collection of documents showing Isabel's great concern for the rights of indigenous peoples and determination that they should not be enslaved.

Russell, P. E. *The English Intervention in Spain and Portugal in the Time of Edward III and Richard II* (Oxford, 1955). More comprehensive in its coverage than any history of this period in Spanish.

Ryder, Alan. *Alfonso the Magnanimous, King of Aragon, Naples and Sicily, 1396-1458* (Oxford, 1990). The first comprehensive scholarly biography of this peripatetic king, and an excellent one.

Suberbiola Martínez, Jesús. *Real Patronato de Granada; el Arzobispo Talavera, la Iglesia y el Estado Moderno (1486-1516)* (Granada, 1982)

Sanceau, Elaine. *The Perfect Prince* (Barcelos, Portugal, 1959). The only good biography of King John II of Portugal available in English.

———. *Reign of the Fortunate King* (Hamden CT, 1969). The only good biography of King Manuel of Portugal available in English.

Swift, F. Darwin. *The Life and Times of James the Conqueror* (Oxford, 1894). This very old book, displaying considerable hostility toward its subject and his faith, nevertheless contains much more information on James I of Aragon than is obtainable anywhere else in English.

Tarsicio de Azcona, P. *Isabel la Católica* (Madrid, 1964). The best biography in Spanish of the great Catholic Queen.

Val, Isabel del. *Isabel la Católica, Princesa* (Valladolid, 1974). A thorough if unimaginative treatment, avoiding Queen Isabel's strong Catholic convictions.

Walsh, William T. *Characters of the Inquisition* (London, 1940). Particularly good on Torquemada.

———. *Isabella of Spain, the Last Crusader* (New York, 1930)

7. SCANDINAVIA AND THE BALTIC

Almedingen, Edith M. *The English Pope* [Adrian IV] (London, 1925). Despite its title, this book is concerned almost exclusively with the visit of Cardinal Nicholas Breakspear to Scandinavia before he became Pope Adrian IV. It contains substantial data on the Scandinavian Church at this period not readily available elsewhere.

Birch, J. H. S. *Denmark in History* (London, 1938)

Christiansen, Eric. *The Northern Crusades; the Baltic and the Catholic Frontier, 1100-1525* (Minneapolis MN, 1980). Contains more information about the Teutonic Knights than may be found in any other easily available source.

Jutikkala, Eino and Kauko Pirinen. *A History of Finland* (New York, 1988)

Larsen, Karen. *A History of Norway* (New York, 1948)

Scott, Franklin D. *Sweden: the Nation's History* (Minneapolis MN, 1977)

8. EASTERN EUROPE AND RUSSIA

Atiya, Aziz. *The Crusade of Nicopolis* (London, 1934). Written by an Egyptian historian quite impartially, this is the standard account of the great disaster which allowed the Ottoman Turks to gain control of much of Eastern Europe.

Bartos, F. M. *The Hussite Revolution, 1424-1437* (New York, 1986). Written to fill a gap in Hussite history between Kaminsky's and Heymann's studies of its early years and Heymann's and Odlozilik's biographies of King George Podebrady, this work by a Czech historian is barely adequate for the purpose, being disconnected and very difficult to follow, perhaps due to a poor translation.

Chambers, James. *The Devil's Horsemen; the Mongol Invasion of Europe* (New York, 1979)

Constable, Giles. "The Second Crusade as Seen by Contemporaries," *Traditio* IX

(1953)

Davies, Norman. *God's Playground; a History of Poland.* 2 vols. (New York, 1984). The best general history of Poland in English, though disappointingly skimpy for the whole medieval period and showing only limited understanding of the central role of the Catholic Church in Polish history.

Fennell, John L. I. *The Crisis of Medieval Russia, 1200-1304* (London, 1983). The fullest treatment of this century of Russian history available in English.

————. *The Emergence of Moscow, 1304-1359* (Berkeley CA, 1968). Again, the fullest treatment of this century of Russian history in English.

————. *Ivan the Great of Moscow* (London, 1961). Much the most comprehensive treatment of its subject available in English.

Fine, John V. A. Jr. *The Late Medieval Balkans* (Ann Arbor MI, 1987). The first complete political history of this region and period in English; balanced and very thorough.

Halecki, Oscar. *The Crusade of Varna* (New York, 1943). This study by a great Polish Catholic historian tried to correct a very widespread error of historians analyzing the Crusade of Varna in 1444, but was unsuccessful because not enough historians paid attention to Halecki's arguments. A very important book deserving reconsideration.

————. *From Florence to Brest (1439-1596)* (New York, 1968). Provides a Catholic review of the continuing attempt to reunite the Eastern Orthodox Christians with the Catholic Church in the 15th and 16th centuries.

————. *Jadwiga of Anjou and the Rise of East Central Europe*, ed. Thaddeus V. Gromada (Boulder CO, 1991). The Polish Catholic historian's last work, much the most extensive and best documented study of the great Catholic Queen Jadwiga in English.

Held, Joseph. *Hunyadi; Legend and Reality* (New York, 1985). Held's wooden prose cannot conceal the fact that Hunyadi's legend in truth comes very close to reality.

Heymann, Frederick G. *George of Bohemia, King of Heretics* (Princeton, 1965). Very thorough and well analyzed, if at points somewhat repetitive. Protestant viewpoint, strongly sympathetic to King George.

————. *John Zizka and the Hussite Revolution* (Princeton, 1955). Outstanding, brilliantly written and thoroughly researched history, but strongly pro-Hussite and anti-Catholic.

Hofer, John. *St. John Capistran, Reformer* (St. Louis, 1943). Comprehensively researched and written from a strongly Catholic viewpoint. Avoids some controversial issues involving this saint.

Jasienica, Pawel. *Jagellonian Poland* (Miami FL, 1978). Though unfortunately undocumented, this thorough survey by a very competent Polish historian is much the best available source in English on the Jagellonian period.

Kaminsky, Howard. *A History of the Hussite Revolution* (Berkeley CA, 1967). Mostly intellectual rather than political history of the first years of the Hussite movement after the death of Hus; valuable but disjointed.

Knoll, Paul W. *The Rise of the Polish Monarchy* (Chicago, 1972). Actually a biography of King Casimir III the Great, reigning in the fourteenth century. Scholarly, thorough and clearly written, opening a new world to students of history who do not read German or Polish, since there are no other works in English on this subject or period.

Kosztolynik, Zoltan J. *From Colomon the Learned to Bela III (1095-1196); Hungarian Domestic Policies and Their Impact upon Foreign Affairs* (New York, 1987). The only history of this specific period available in English. Suffers from poor organization and a poor translation.

Manteuffel, Tadeusz. *The Formation of the Polish State; the Period of Ducal Rule, 963-1194* (Detroit, 1982)

Meyendorff, John. *Byzantium and the Rise of Russia* (Cambridge, England, 1981). Mostly institutional and cultural history; some significant religious and political history.

Odlozilik, Otakar. *The Hussite King; Bohemia in European Affairs, 1440-1471* (New Brunswick NJ, 1965). Reviews Bohemian history during this period. Sometimes difficult to follow and chronologically unclear.

Runciman, Steven. *The Medieval Manichee* (Cambridge, England, 1955). Outstanding treatment of the origins and character of the revival of Manichaeanism in the Middle Ages in Bogomilism and Catharism.

Sinor, Denis. *History of Hungary* (New York, 1959). Covers the whole of Hungarian history, but often in disappointingly abbreviated fashion.

Spinka, Matthew. *John Hus* (Princeton, 1968). Comprehensive, well researched biography of this proto-Protestant leader, sympathetic to him and hostile to the Catholic Church.

Vernadsky, George. *Kievan Russia* (Volume II of his *A History of Russia*) (New Haven CT, 1948). First of a series of important volumes on early Russian history which remain the necessary starting points for research in this field, though written in a very pedestrian manner.

————. *The Mongols and Russia* (Volume III of his *A History of Russia*) (New Haven CT, 1953). A fine summary and review of the period when the Mongols dominated Russia—the 13th and 14th centuries.

————. *Russia at the Dawn of the Modern Age* (Volume IV of his *A History of Russia*) (New Haven CT, 1959). Continued high quality, though more detail on Russian political history during the long reign of Grand Duke Ivan III of Moscow is provided in the biography by J. L. I. Fennell.

9. THE BYZANTINE EMPIRE AND THE CRUSADES

Atiya, Aziz. *The Crusade of Nicopolis* (London, 1934). The only book exclusively devoted to this disastrous crusade.

Aubé, Pierre. *Baudouin IV de Jérusalem, le roi lépreux* (Paris, 1981). Dramatically written but adds almost nothing to other, better documented histories.

Baldwin, Marshall W. *Raymond III of Tripolis and the Fall of Jerusalem (1140-1187)* (Princeton, 1936). Penetrating review of the causes of the fall of the kingdom of Jerusalem.

Barker, John W. *Manuel II Palaeologus (1391-1425); a Study in Late Byzantine Statesmanship* (New Brunswick NJ, 1969). Outstanding, definitive biography of the last great Byzantine Emperor—a mine of information about him and his times.

Belloc, Hilaire. *The Crusades* (Milwaukee WI, 1937). Striking and often unique insights; unfortunately, like all this great Catholic author's historical works, undocumented.

Brockman, Eric. *The Two Sieges of Rhodes, 1480-1522* (London, 1969). Vivid and well researched account of the great Ottoman Turkish siege of Rhodes in 1481.

Donovan, Joseph P. *Pelagius and the Fifth Crusade* (Philadelphia, 1950). Generally thorough coverage of the facts but disappointingly superficial in its analysis of Cardinal Pelagius.

Geanakoplos, Deno J. *Emperor Michael Palaeologus and the West* (Cambridge MA, 1959). Outstanding, well-researched and well-written scholarly biography of the last great Byzantine Emperor who (for whatever motives) almost healed the Great Eastern Schism.

Gibbons, Herbert A. *The Foundations of the Ottoman Empire* (London, 1916). A pioneering and seminal work in its field, but marred by strong anti-Catholic and even anti-Christian bias.

Gill, Joseph. *Byzantium and the Papacy 1198-1400* (New Brunswick NJ, 1979). Excellent, thorough survey from a strongly Catholic viewpoint.

Glubb, John B. *The Lost Centuries; from the Muslim Empires to the Renaissance of Europe, 1145-1453* (London, 1967). The last volume of this author's outstanding, too much neglected history of Islam to the capture of Constantinople.

Hill, John L. and Laurita L. *Raymond IV, Count of Toulouse* (Syracuse NY, 1962). The only full historical biography of the most successful of the Crusaders.

Nicholson, Robert L. *Joscelyn III and the Fall of the Crusader States, 1134-1199* (Leiden, 1973)

Nicol, Donald M. *The Last Centuries of Byzantium, 1261-1453* (New York, 1972). Excellent, detailed and well-researched history of this sad period for the Byzantine empire.

Powell, James M. *Anatomy of a Crusade, 1213-1221* (Philadelphia, 1986). Preoccupied with economic and military organizational analysis, only limited coverage of the Fifth Crusade itself.

Riley-Smith, Jonathan. *The Knights of St. John in Jerusalem and Cyprus* (New York, 1967)

Runciman, Steven. *The Fall of Constantinople, 1453* (Cambridge, England, 1965). Well-researched, striking and memorable account of its dramatic subject.

———. *A History of the Crusades*, 3 vols. (Cambridge, England, 1952). Classic history of the Crusades, written in a fine narrative style, but marked by a strongly pro-Byzantine, anti-Catholic viewpoint.

Sandoli, Sabino de. *The Peaceful Liberation of the Holy Places in the XIV Century* (Studia Orientalia Christiania, Monographiae 3) (Cairo, 1990). A study of the little-known circumstances in which the Holy Places were opened to Christian pilgrimage and worship under Franciscan custody by the rulers of Egypt in the fourteenth century.

Setton, Kenneth M., ed. *A History of the Crusades*, 3 vols. (Madison WI, 1969). New collective history of the Crusades, well-balanced and thorough.

10. BEYOND CHRISTENDOM; THE GREAT DISCOVERIES

Anderson, Charles L. G. *Life and Letters of Vasco Núñez de Balboa* (Westport CT, 1970). An older history with a strongly Protestant, anti-Catholic viewpoint, this nevertheless provides much the most comprehensive study available not only of Balboa and his discovery of the Pacific Ocean, but also of the development of the first Spanish colonies in South America and Panama.

Blake, John W. *West Africa; the Quest for God and Gold, 1454-1478*, 2nd ed. (London, 1977). Adds some significant additional data on the Portuguese exploration and development of West Africa in the 15th century, to other histories of Portuguese exploration.

Columbus, Christopher. *The Log of Christopher Columbus*, ed. Robert H. Fuson (Camden ME, 1987). Columbus' Log is one of the very few most important original sources in all of history, and Fuson's editing enhances its usefulness to the student.

———. Journal of Columbus' third voyage, in Samuel Eliot Morison, ed., *Journals and*

Other Documents on the Life and Voyages of Christopher Columbus (New York, 1963)

Dawson, Christopher, ed. *The Mongol Mission* (New York, 1955). Original accounts of the first extraordinary Catholic missionary journeys across the Mongol empire to China, with introduction and commentary by this great Catholic historian.

Diffie, Bailey W. and George D. Winius. *Foundations of the Portuguese Empire, 1415-1580* (Minneapolis MN, 1977). Much the best general scholarly treatment of its very important subject, assembling most of the too often scanty historical evidence pertaining to the Portuguese voyages of discovery.

Grousset, René. *The Empire of the Steppes* (New Brunswick NJ, 1970). Classic and very valuable history of the Mongols.

Hookham, Hilda. *Tamburlaine the Conqueror* (London, 1962). The fullest scholarly account in English of the great conqueror (more usually called Tamerlane or Timur), but overloaded with verbose descriptions of Oriental produce and products.

Jayne, K. G. *Vasco da Gama and His Successors, 1460-1580* (London, 1910). Relatively brief coverage of its subject, but based on thorough research and adding some significant details to other accounts.

Jones, Vincent. *Sail the Indian Sea* (London, 1978). This little-known book does for Vasco da Gama much of what Samuel Eliot Morison does for Columbus in his world-famous biography.

Judge, Joseph, "The Island of Landfall," and Luis Marden, "Tracking Columbus Across the Atlantic," *National Geographic*, November 1986. Convincing new evidence placing Columbus' 1492 landfall in the Bahamas on Samaná Cay.

Kinross, Lord. *The Ottoman Centuries; the Rise and Fall of the Turkish Empire* (New York, 1977)

Manzano Manzano, Juan. *Cristóbal Colón; siete años decisivos de su vida, 1485-1492* (Madrid, 1964). Another monument of solid Columbus scholarship before the media hurricane against Columbus on the occasion of the 500th anniversary of his discovery. The most comprehensive treatment of the years of development of Columbus' project available anywhere.

Morison, Samuel Eliot. *Admiral of the Ocean Sea; a Life of Christopher Columbus* (Boston, 1942). The classic biography of the discoverer of America, which despite some errors recently demonstrated, is unlikely ever to be matched in its combination of historian's skill and sailor's vision.

————. *The European Discovery of America; the Northern Voyages* (New York, 1971). Includes the most comprehensive treatment available of the voyage of John Cabot as well as the earlier voyages of the Norsemen to America.

————. *The European Discovery of America; the Southern Voyages* (New York, 1974). Morison's last work of history, fully equal to all he had written previously.

Parr, Charles M. *Ferdinand Magellan, Circumnavigator* (New York, 1964)

Prestage, Edgar. *The Portuguese Pioneers* (London, 1933). Disappointingly thin, adds little to other books on this subject, though still occasionally worth consulting.

Rossabi, Morris. *Khubilai Khan; His Life and Times* (Berkeley CA, 1988). First modern scholarly biography of Kublai Khan, and a very good and reliable one.

Sanceau, Elaine. *Henry the Navigator* (New York, 1969). Like all of Sanceau's works (of which this is probably the best), well and movingly written, clear and thorough in its coverage of events, but inadequately documented and too dependent on the contemporary chronicles, insufficiently corrected by later research.

————. *Indies Adventure; the Amazing Career of Afonso de Albuquerque* (London, 1936). Effective and memorable retelling of one of the most thrilling sagas of Western penetration of new worlds.

Schurz, William L. *The Manila Galleon* (New York, 1939). Describes the opening up
    of the Philippines by the West.
Taviani, Paolo. *Christopher Columbus; the Grand Design* (London, 1985). A recent
    major addition to Columbus scholarship focussing on Columbus' project in the
    making and adding much to our knowledge of it.
Whiteway, R. S. *The Rise of Portuguese Power in India, 1497-1550* (Patna, India, 1979).
    The most thorough treatment of the early years of Portuguese colonization of
    India and how Portugal gained control of the Indian Ocean. Shows a remarkable
    balance of sympathy with both Portuguese and Indian viewpoints.
Zurara, Gomes Eanes de. "The Chronicle of the Discovery and Conquest of Guinea,"
    Hakluyt Society Publications No. 95 (London, 1896). The indispensable original
    source for the beginning of the Age of Discovery.

Tables of Popes, Emperors, and Kings, 1100-1517

POPES
(numbers are in succession from St. Peter; antipopes in parentheses)

158. Paschal II (Raineri of Bieda) 8/13/1099-1/21/1118
159. Gelasius II (Giovanni Coniulo of Gaeta) 1/24/1118-1/29/1119
    (Antipope Maurice Bourdon, "Gregory VIII," 3/8/1118-4/1121)
160. Calixtus II (Guy of Burgundy) 2/2/1119-12/13/1124
161. Honorius II (Lambert Scannabecchi of Bologna) 12/21/1124-2/13/1130
162. Innocent II (Gregory Papareschi of Rome) 2/14/1130-9/24/1143
    (Antipope Piero Pierleoni, "Anacletus II," 2/14/1130-1/25/1138)
    (Antipope Gregory Conti, "Victor IV", 1/25/1138-5/29/1138)
163. Celestine II (Guido di Castelli of Tuscany) 9/26/1143-3/8/1144
164. Lucius II (Gerard Caccianemici of Bologna) 3/12/1144-2/15/1145
165. Bd. Eugenius III (Bernard Paganelli of Pisa) 2/15/1145-7/8/1153
166. Anastasius IV (Corrardo della Suburra of Rome) 7/12/1153-12/3/1154
167. Adrian IV (Nicholas Breakspear of England) 12/4/1154-9/1/1159
168. Alexander III (Roland Bandinelli of Siena) 9/7/1159-8/30/1181
    (Antipope Ottaviano Conti, "Victor V," 10/4/1159-4/20/1164)
    (Antipope Guido da Crema, "Paschal III," 4/22/1164-9/1168)
    (Antipope Giovanni Unghieri, "Calixtus III," 9/1168-8/1178)
    (Antipope Lothario Conti, "Innocent III," 9/1179-1/1180)
169. Lucius III (Ubaldo Allucingoli of Lucca) 9/1/1181-11/25/1185
170. Urban III (Umberto Crivelli of Milan) 11/25/1185-10/20/1187
171. Gregory VIII (Alberto di Mora of Benevento) 10/21/1187-12/17/1187
172. Clement III (Paolo Scolari of Rome) 12/19/1187-3/20/1191
173. Celestine III (Giacinto Buboni of Rome) 3/30/1191-1/8/1198
174. Innocent III (Lothario Conti of Rome) 1/8/1198-7/16/1216
175. Honorius III (Cencio Savelli of Rome) 7/18/1216-3/18/1227
176. Gregory IX (Ugolino Conti of Ostia) 3/19/1227-8/21/1241
177. Celestine IV (Godfrey di Castiglione) 10/25/1241-11/10/1241
178. Innocent IV (Sinisbaldo Fieschi of Genoa) 6/25/1243-12/7/1254
179. Alexander IV (Rinaldo Conti of Rome) 12/12/1254-5/25/1261
180. Urban IV (Jacques Pantaleon of Troyes) 8/29/1261-10/2/1264
181. Clement IV (Guy Foulques of Languedoc) 2/5/1265-11/29/1268
182. Bd. Gregory X (Tebaldo Visconti of Piacenza) 9/1/1271-1/10/1276
183. Bd. Innocent V (Pierre de Tarentaise of Savoy) 1/21/1276-6/22/1276
184. Adrian V (Ottobuoni Fieschi of Genoa) 7/11/1276-8/18/1276
185. John XXI (Pedro Juliani Rebulo of Lisbon) 9/8/1276-5/20/1277
186. Nicholas III (Giovanni Gaetano Orsini of Rome) 11/25/1277-8/22/1280
187. Martin IV (Simon de Brion of France) 2/22/1281-3/28/1285
188. Honorius IV (Giacomo Savelli of Rome) 4/2/1285-4/3/1287
189. Nicholas IV (Girolamo Maschi of Ascoli) 2/15/1288-4/4/1292
190. St. Celestine V (Pietro Murrone of the Abruzzi) 7/5/1294-12/13/1294

191. Boniface VIII (Benedetto Gaetani of Anagni) 12/24/1294-10/12/1303
192. Bd. Benedict XI (Niccolò Boccasini of Venice) 10/22/1303-7/7/1304
193. Clement V (Bertrand de Got of Bordeaux) 6/5/1305-4/20/1314
194. John XXII (Jacques Duèse of Cahors) 8/9/1316-12/4/1334
    (Antipope Pietro Rainalluci, "Nicholas V," 1328-1330)
195. Benedict XII (Jacques Fournier of Foix) 12/20/1334-5/25/1342
196. Clement VI (Pierre Roger of Rouen) 5/7/1342-12/6/1352
197. Innocent VI (Étienne Aubert of Limousin) 12/18/1352-9/12/1362
198. Bd. Urban V (Guillaume de Grimoard of Grisac) 9/28/1362-12/19/1370
199. Gregory XI (Pierre Roger of Beaufort) 12/30/1370-3/27/1378
200. Urban VI (Bartolomeo Prignani of Bari) 4/8/1378-10/5/1389
    (Antipope Robert of Geneva, "Clement VII," 9/20/1378-9/16/1394)
201. Boniface IX (Pietro Tomacelli of Naples) 11/2/1389-10/1/1404
    (Antipope Pedro de Luna, "Benedict XIII," 9/28/1394-11/29/1422)
202. Innocent VII (Cosmo Megliorati of Bologna) 10/17/1404-11/6/1406
203. Gregory XII (Angelo Corrario of Venice) 11/30/1406-7/4/1415
204. Martin V (Odo Colonna of Rome) 11/11/1417-2/20/1431
    (Antipope Gil Sánchez Muñoz, "Clement VIII," 6/10/1423-7/26/1429)
    (Antipope Bernard Garnier, "Benedict XIV," 1429-1430)
    (Antipope Jean Carrier, "Benedict XV," 1430-1433)
205. Eugenius IV (Gabriel Condulmaro of Venice) 3/3/1431-2/23/1447
    (Antipope Duke Amadeus of Savoy, "Felix V," 11/5/1439-4/7/1449)
206. Nicholas V (Tommaso Parentucelli of Bologna) 3/6/1447-3/24/1455
207. Calixtus III (Alfonso Borgia of Valencia) 4/8/1455-8/6/1458
208. Pius II (Aeneas Sylvius Piccolomini of Siena) 8/19/1458-8/14/1464
209. Paul II (Pietro Barbo of Venice) 8/30/1464-7/26/1471
210. Sixtus IV (Francesco della Rovere of Savona) 8/10/1471-8/12/1484
211. Innocent VIII (Giovanni Battista Cibò of Genoa) 8/29/1484-7/25/1492
212. Alexander VI (Rodrigo Borgia of Valencia) 8/11/1492-8/18/1503
213. Pius III (Francesco de Piccolomini of Siena) 9/22/1503-10/18/1503
214. Julius II (Giuliano della Rovere of Savona) 11/1/1503-2/20/1513
215. Leo X (Giovanni de Medici of Florence) 3/11/1513-12/1/1521

EMPERORS

Holy Roman Emperors
Henry IV 1056-1105
Henry V 1105-1125
Lothair II 1125-1137
Conrad III 1138-1152
Frederick I Barbarossa 1152-1190
Henry VI 1190-1197
Philip of Swabia 1198-1208
Otto IV 1208-1211
  (claimed Empire 1198)
Frederick II 1211-1250
Conrad IV 1250-1254
William of Holland 1254-1256
Richard of Cornwall 1257-1272
Rudolf I of Habsburg 1273-1291
Adolf of Nassau 1292-1298
Albert I of Habsburg 1298-1308

Byzantine Emperors
Alexius I Comnenus 1081-1118
John II Comnenus 1118-1143
Manuel I Comnenus 1143-1180
Alexius II Comnenus 1180-1182
Andronicus I Comnenus 1182-1185
Isaac II Angelus 1185-1195
Alexius III Comnenus 1195-1203
Alexius IV Angelus 1203-1204
Alexius V Ducas 1204
Theodore I Lascaris 1206-1222
John III Dukas Vatatzes 1222-1254
Theodore II Lascaris 1254-1258
John IV Lascaris 1258-1261
Michael VIII Palaeologus 1261-1282
Andronicus II Palaeologus 1282-1328
Andronicus III Palaeologus 1325-1341

Henry VII of Luxembourg 1308-1313
Louis IV of Wittelsbach 1314-1346
Charles IV of Luxembourg 1346-1378
Wenceslas 1378-1400
Rupert 1400-1410
Sigismund 1410-1437
Albert II of Habsburg 1438-1439
Frederick III of Habsburg 1440-1493
Maximilian I of Habsburg 1493-1519

John V Palaeologus (1st reign) 1341-1347
John VI Cantacuzene 1347-1354
John V Palaeologus (2nd reign) 1354-1376
Andronicus IV Palaeologus 1376-1379
John V Palaeologus (3rd reign) 1379-1391
Manuel II Palaeologus 1391-1425
John VII Palaeologus 1425-1448
Constantine XI Palaeologus 1448-1453
(Ottoman Turkish conquest)

KINGS OF GREAT BRITAIN

England
Henry I 1100-1135
Stephen 1135-1154
Henry II 1154-1189
Richard I 1189-1199
John 1199-1216
Henry III 1216-1272
Edward I 1272-1307

Edward II 1307-1327
Edward III 1327-1377
Richard II 1377-1399
Henry IV 1399-1413
Henry V 1413-1422
Henry VI 1422-1461, 1470-1471
Edward IV 1461-1470, 1471-1483
Richard III 1483-1485
Henry VII 1485-1509
Henry VIII 1509-1547

Scotland
Edgar the Atheling 1097-1107
Alexander I 1107-1124
David I 1124-1153
Malcolm IV 1153-1165
William the Lion 1165-1214
Alexander II 1214-1249
Alexander III 1249-1286
Margaret "Maid of Norway" 1286-1290
John Balliol 1292-1296
(English rule 1296-1306)
Robert I the Bruce 1306-1329
David II 1329-1371
Robert II Stuart 1371-1390
Robert III 1390-1406
James I 1406-1437
James II 1437-1460
James III 1460-1488

James IV 1488-1513
James V 1513-1542

FRANCE AND THE LOW COUNTRIES

France
Philip I 1060-1108
Louis VI "the Fat" 1108-1137
Louis VII "the Young" 1137-1180
Philip II Augustus 1180-1223
Louis VIII 1223-1226
St. Louis IX 1226-1270
Philip III "the Bold" 1270-1285
Philip IV "the Fair" 1285-1314
Louis X "the Quarrelsome" 1314-1316
Philip V "the Tall" 1317-1321
Charles IV "the Fair" 1322-1328
Philip VI of Valois 1328-1350
John II "the Good Fellow" 1350-1364
Charles V "the Wise" 1364-1380
Charles VI "the Mad" 1380-1422

Burgundy/Netherlands

Philip II "the Bold" 1363-1404

John "the Fearless" 1404-1419

Charles VII "the Well Served" 1422-1461   Philip III "the Good" 1419-1467
Louis XI "the Spider" 1461-1483   Charles "the Bold" 1467-1477
Charles VIII 1483-1498   Marie 1477-1482
Louis XII 1498-1515   Philip IV "the Handsome" 1482-1506
Francis I 1515-1547   Charles V 1506-1529

ITALY

Naples   *Milan*
Roger II 1130-1154
William I 1154-1165
William II 1165-1189
Tancred 1189-1194
(rule by Holy Roman Empire 1194-1250)
Manfred 1250-1266   Martino della Torre 1257-1263
Charles I of Anjou 1266-1285   Filippo della Torre 1263-1265
                                           Napoleone della Torre 1265-1278
Charles II 1285-1309   Archbishop Otto Visconti 1278-1295
Robert "the Wise" 1309-1343   Matteo I Visconti 1295-1300, 1311-1322
                                           Galeazzo I Visconti 1322-1328
                                           Azzo Visconti 1328-1339
                                           Luchino Visconti 1339-1349
Joanna I 1343-1381   Archbishop Giovanni Visconti 1349-1354
                                           Bernabò & Galeazzo II 1355-1378
                                           Bernabò & Gian Galeazzo 1378-1385
Charles III of Durazzo 1381-1386   Gian Galeazzo alone 1385-1402
Louis II of Anjou 1387-1399
Ladislas 1399-1414   Giovanni Maria 1402-1412
Joanna II 1414-1435   Filippo Maria 1412-1447
Alfonso II of Aragon 1435-1458   (Ambrosian Republic 1447-1450)
Ferrante 1458-1494   Francesco Sforza 1450-1466
                                           Galeazzo Maria Sforza 1466-1476
                                           Gian Galeazzo Sforza 1476-1494
Alfonso II 1494-1500   Ludovico Sforza 1494-1500
Frederick 1500-1501   (French rule 1500-1512)
(Spanish rule from 1501)   Maximilian Sforza 1512-1515

SPAIN

Castile   *Aragon*
Alfonso VI 1072-1109   Pedro I 1094-1104
Queen Urraca 1109-1126   Alfonso I "the Battler" 1104-1134
Alfonso VII "the Emperor" 1126-1157   Ramiro II "the Monk" 1134-1137
Sancho III of Castile 1157-1158   Queen Petronilla 1137-1164
Fernando II of León 1157-1188   Alfonso II 1164-1196
Alfonso VIII of Castile 1158-1214   Pedro II 1196-1213
Alfonso IX of León 1188-1230   James I "the Conqueror" 1213-1276
Henry I of Castile 1214-1217
St. Fernando III of Castile 1217-1252
        (of León 1230-1252)
Alfonso X "the Wise" 1252-1284   Pedro III "the Great" 1276-1285
Sancho IV "the Fierce" 1284-1295   Alfonso III 1285-1291

Fernando IV 1295-1312
Alfonso XI "the Avenger" 1312-1350
Pedro I "the Cruel" 1350-1369
Henry II of Trastámara 1369-1379
Juan I 1379-1390
Henry III "the Ailing" 1390-1406
Juan II 1406-1454
Henry IV 1454-1474
Isabel "the Catholic" 1474-1504
Juana "the Mad" 1504-1509
    (Fernando of Aragon regent 1509-1516)

James II "the Just" 1295-1327
Alfonso IV "the Courteous" 1327-1336
Pedro IV "the Ceremonious" 1336-1387
Juan I 1387-1395
Martin I "the Humane" 1395-1410
Fernando I of Antequera 1412-1416
Alfonso V "the Magnificent" 1416-1458
Juan II 1458-1479
Fernando II "the Catholic" 1479-1516

PORTUGAL

Afonso I Henriques 1139-1185
Sancho I 1185-1211
Afonso II "the Fat" 1211-1223
Sancho II 1223-1247
Afonso III 1247-1279
Dinis 1279-1325
Afonso IV 1325-1357
Pedro I "the Cruel" 1357-1367
Fernando 1367-1383
John I of Aviz 1385-1433
Duarte 1433-1438
Afonso V "the African" 1438-1481
John II "the Perfect Prince" 1481-1495
Manuel I "the Fortunate" 1495-1521

POLAND AND HUNGARY

Poland
Vladislav I Hermann 1081-1102
Boleslav III "Wry-mouth" 1102-1138
Vladislav II 1138-1146
Boleslav IV 1146-1173
Mieszko III "the Old" 1173-1177
Casimir II "the Just" 1177-1194
(period of civil war 1195-1201)
Leszek II "the White" 1202-1227
Boleslav V "the Chaste" 1227-1279

Leszek III "the Black" 1279-1288
Henry of Breslau 1288-1290
Przemyslav II 1290-1296
Vladislav IV Lokietek 1296-1333

Casimir III "the Great" 1333-1370
Louis I of Hungary 1370-1382
Queen Jadwiga 1382-1399
Jagiello 1399-1434

Hungary
Coloman "the Learned" 1095-1114
Stephen II "Thunderbolt" 1114-1131
Bela II "the Blind" 1131-1141
Geza II 1141-1161
Stephen III 1161-1173
Bela III 1173-1196
Imre 1196-1204
Ladislas III 1204-1205
Andrew II 1205-1235
Bela IV 1235-1270
Stephen V 1270-1272
Ladislas IV 1272-1290

Andrew III 1290-1301
Prince Wenceslas of Bohemia 1301-1304
Prince Otto of Bavaria 1304-1308
Charles Robert of Anjou 1308-1342
Louis I "the Great" 1342-1382
Queen Maria 1382-1395
Emperor Sigismund 1395-1437

Vladislav III 1434-1444
Casimir IV 1446-1492

John Albert 1492-1501
Alexander 1501-1506
Sigismund I 1506-1548

Emperor Albert II 1437-1439
Vladislav III of Poland 1439-1444
Ladislas VI Postumus 1445-1457
Matthias Corvinus Hunyadi 1458-1490
Ladislas II of Bohemia 1490-1516

Louis II 1516-1526

THE MONGOLS AND RUSSIA

Mongol Great Khans
Genghis (Temujin) 1206-1227
Ogodai 1229-1241
Queen Turakina 1242-1246
Guyuk 1246-1248
Queen Oghul Khaimish 1248-1251
Mangu 1251-1259
Kublai 1260-1295

Khans of the Golden Horde (Russia)
Batu 1242-1255
Sartak 1255-1256
Ulagchi 1256-1258
Berke 1258-1266
Mangu-Temir 1266-1280
Tuda-Mangu 1280-1287
Tele-Buga 1287-1291
Tokhta 1291-1312   *Russia (Moscow)*
Uzbeg 1312-1341   Ivan I "Moneybags" 1332-1341
Tinibeg 1341-1342   Simeon 1341-1353
Yanibeg 1342-1357   Ivan II 1353-1359
Berdibeg 1357-1359
Kulpa 1359-1360   Dmitry III Donskoi 1359-1389
Nevruz 1360-1361
Mamai 1361-1381
Tokhtamysh 1381-1397   Vasili I 1389-1425
Timur-Kutlugh 1397-1400
Shadibeg 1400-1407
Bulat-Saltan 1407-1410
Timur-Khan 1410-1411
Jalal al-Din 1412-1419
Ulug Mahmed 1419-1445   Vasili II 1425-1462
Mahmudek 1445-1465   Ivan III "the Great" 1462-1505
Ahmad 1465-1481   Vasili III 1505-1533

OTTOMAN TURKISH EMPIRE (SULTANS)

Osman II 1281-1326
Orkhan 1326-1359
Murad I 1359-1389
Bayazid I "Lightning" 1389-1402
Muhammad I "the Restorer" and Sulayman I 1403-1411

Muhammad I "the Restorer" and Musa 1411-1413
Muhammad I "the Restorer" alone 1413-1421
Murad II 1421-1451
Muhammad II "the Conqueror" 1451-1481
Bayazid II 1481-1512
Selim I "the Grim" 1512-1520

Index

Note: Dates given after an individual's name are those during which he held the office mentioned, unless marked with b. and d. for born and died. All Popes are identified by their pontifical rather than by their original name. Identical names are listed with Popes first; then cardinals; then bishops alphabetically and chronologically by see; then abbots (and masters and generals of orders) alphabetically and chronologically by monastery or order; then emperors and empresses, then kings and queens, then other rulers alphabetically and chronologically by country, then others. Saints are alphabetized by their first names only. The victor in a cited battle is indicated by the first contender named.